Close Encounters

Fifth Edition

To our daughters—Gabrielle, Kristiana, Kirsten, Leila, and Rania
And to Peter's granddaughter—Elise
Our relationships with them bring us great joy.

Sara Miller McCune founded SAGE Publishing in 1965 to support the dissemination of usable knowledge and educate a global community. SAGE publishes more than 1000 journals and over 800 new books each year, spanning a wide range of subject areas. Our growing selection of library products includes archives, data, case studies and video. SAGE remains majority owned by our founder and after her lifetime will become owned by a charitable trust that secures the company's continued independence.

Los Angeles | London | New Delhi | Singapore | Washington DC | Melbourne

Close Encounters
Communication in Relationships

Fifth Edition

Laura K. Guerrero
Arizona State University

Peter A. Andersen
San Diego State University

Walid A. Afifi
University of California, Santa Barbara

Los Angeles | London | New Delhi
Singapore | Washington DC | Melbourne

FOR INFORMATION:

SAGE Publications, Inc.
2455 Teller Road
Thousand Oaks, California 91320
E-mail: order@sagepub.com

SAGE Publications Ltd.
1 Oliver's Yard
55 City Road
London, EC1Y 1SP
United Kingdom

SAGE Publications India Pvt. Ltd.
B 1/I 1 Mohan Cooperative Industrial Area
Mathura Road, New Delhi 110 044
India

SAGE Publications Asia-Pacific Pte. Ltd.
3 Church Street
#10–04 Samsung Hub
Singapore 049483

Printed in the United States of America

Library of Congress Cataloging-in-Publication Data

Names: Guerrero, Laura K., author. | Andersen, Peter A., author. | Afifi, Walid A., author.

Title: Close encounters : communication in relationships / Laura K. Guerrero, Arizona State University; Peter A. Andersen, San Diego State University; Walid A. Afifi, University of California at Santa Barbara.

Description: Fifth edition. | Thousand Oaks : SAGE Publications, Inc., 2017. | Includes bibliographical references and index.

Identifiers: LCCN 2016050544 | ISBN 9781506376721 (pbk. : alk. paper)

Subjects: LCSH: Interpersonal communication.

Classification: LCC BF637.C45 G83 2017 | DDC 153.6—dc23 LC record available at https://lccn.loc.gov/2016050544

Acquisitions Editor: Karen Omer
Development Editor: Anna Villarruel
Editorial Assistant: Sarah Dillard
eLearning Editor: Jennifer Jovin
Production Editor: Kelly DeRosa
Copy Editor: Alison Hope
Typesetter: Hurix Systems Pvt. Ltd.
Proofreader: Susan Schon
Indexer: Jeanne Busemeyer
Cover Designer: Candice Harman
Marketing Manager: Amy Lammers

This book is printed on acid-free paper.

SUSTAINABLE FORESTRY INITIATIVE

Certified Chain of Custody
Promoting Sustainable Forestry
www.sfiprogram.org
SFI-01268

SFI label applies to text stock

17 18 19 20 21 10 9 8 7 6 5 4 3 2 1

BRIEF CONTENTS

Preface xvii

Acknowledgments xxi

Chapter 1 • Conceptualizing Relational Communication 1

Chapter 2 • Communicating Identity 25

Chapter 3 • Drawing People Together 57

Chapter 4 • Making Sense of Our World 85

Chapter 5 • Changing Relationships 112

Chapter 6 • Revealing and Hiding Ourselves 139

Chapter 7 • Communicating Closeness 169

Chapter 8 • Making a Love Connection 197

Chapter 9 • Communicating Sexually 228

Chapter 10 • Staying Close 257

Chapter 11 • Coping With Conflict 287

Chapter 12 • Influencing Each Other 315

Chapter 13 • Hurting the Ones We Love 345

Chapter 14 • Healing the Hurt 378

Chapter 15 • Ending Relationships 407

Glossary 436

References 451

Author Index 492

Subject Index 507

About the Authors 527

DETAILED CONTENTS

Preface xvii

Acknowledgments xxi

Chapter 1. Conceptualizing Relational Communication: Definitions and Principles 1

The Field of Personal Relationships: A Brief History 2

Contributions of Interpersonal Communication Research 3

Contributions of Social Psychology 4

Roots in Other Disciplines 5

Relationships 6

General Types of Relationships 6

Need Fulfillment in Close Relationships 7

Relationship Categories 8

Characteristics Distinguishing Different Relationship Types 10

Principles of Interpersonal Communication 12

Verbal and Nonverbal Messages 12

Communication as Inevitable 15

Interpersonal Communication Goals 16

Effectiveness and Shared Meaning 17

Content Versus Relational Information 18

Symmetry in Communication 19

Principles of Relational Communication 19

Relationships Emerge Across Ongoing Interactions 20

Relationships Contextualize Messages 20

Communication Sends a Variety of Relational Messages 20

Relational Communication Is Dynamic 21

Relational Communication Follows Both Linear and Nonlinear Patterns 22

Summary and Application 23

Key Terms 24

Discussion Questions 24

Chapter 2. Communicating Identity: The Social Self 25

The Development of Personal Identity 26

Defining Identity 26

Human Nature and Identity 26

Communication and Identity 26
Cultural and Ethnic Identity 29
The Image: Creating an Identity 29
"Talkin' 'Bout Your Generation": Millennials and Generation
  Z-ers' Identity 30
Social Networking and Identity 33
Identity, Perception, and Self-Esteem 35
Expanding Identity 36

Principles of Identity Management 38
Identity and Hierarchical Structure 38
Identity and the Looking-Glass Self 38
Identity and the Interpretation of Feedback 39
Identity, Expectations, and Behavior 39
Identity and Self-Evaluation 39
Identity and Goal Achievement 40
Identity and Relationships 40

Communicating Identity to Others 41
General Issues in Self-Presentation 41
"Life Is a Stage": The Dramaturgical Perspective 44
Politeness Theory 46

Summary and Application 54
Key Terms 55
Discussion Questions 56

Chapter 3. Drawing People Together: Forces of Social Attraction 57

Attraction 58
Types of Attraction 58
Fatal Attraction 60

A Framework for Understanding Attraction 60

Personal Qualities 61
Perceptions of Reward Value 61
Expectations 62
Biological Aspects of Attraction 64
Demographic Characteristics 65
Personality 67

Other People's Qualities 68
Physical Attractiveness 68
Interpersonal Communication Skills 71
The "Hard-to-Get" Phenomenon 73

Qualities of the Pair 73
Similarity: "Birds of a Feather Flock Together" 74
Complementarity: Sometimes Opposites Attract 78

   Similarity and Complementarity in Initial Versus Committed Relationships 78

  Qualities of the Physical or Social Environment 79

   Physical Environment 79

   Proximity 80

   Social Environment 81

  Summary and Application 83

  Key Terms 84

  Discussion Questions 84

Chapter 4. Making Sense of Our World: Managing Uncertainty and Expectancy Violations 85

  Uncertainty 86

   Uncertainty Reduction Theory: Issues and Challenges 86

   The Motivation to Reduce Uncertainty 88

   The Relationship Between Communication and Uncertainty 90

   General Strategies for Reducing Uncertainty 93

   Secret Tests 96

   Predicted Outcome Value Theory 97

   The Theory of Motivated Information Management 98

   Relational Turbulence Theory 100

  Expectancy Violations 102

   Expectancy Violations Theory 102

   Types of Expectancy Violations in Close Relationships 104

   Expectancy Violations and Uncertainty in Specific Contexts 106

  Summary and Application 109

  Key Terms 110

  Discussion Questions 111

Chapter 5. Changing Relationships: Stages, Turning Points, and Dialectics 112

  Communication Skills 113

  Relationship Stages 116

   The "Coming Together" Stages 117

   The "Coming Apart" Stages 123

   The Ordering and Timing of Stages 126

  Turning Points 126

   Communication-Based Turning Points 127

   Activities and Special Occasions 128

   Events Related to Passion and Romance 128

   Events Related to Commitment and Exclusivity 128

   Changes in Families and Social Networks 129

   Proximity and Distance 129

   Crisis and Conflict 129

   Perceptual Changes 130

The Dialectical Perspective 130

    Relational Dialectics Theory 131

    Dialectical Tensions in Friendships 134

Summary and Application 135

Key Terms 137

Discussion Questions 137

Chapter 6. Revealing and Hiding Ourselves: Self-Disclosure and Privacy 139

Self-Disclosure 140

    Dimensions of Self-Disclosure 140

    Self-Disclosure and Liking 144

    Reciprocity of Self-Disclosure 145

    Risks Associated With Self-Disclosure 146

Privacy 149

    Privacy Ownership 149

    Privacy Control 150

    Privacy Turbulence 151

    Influences on Rules for Privacy Management 152

    Negotiating Privacy in Relationships: Challenges and Violations 153

Topic Avoidance and Secret Keeping 154

    Topics Commonly Avoided or Kept Secret 155

    Reasons for Topic Avoidance and Secret Keeping 156

    How People Engage in Topic Avoidance 158

    Topic Avoidance During Relationship Transitions 159

    Consequences of Topic Avoidance 159

    Consequences of Secret Keeping 160

    Consequences of Revealing Secrets 163

Summary and Application 166

Key Terms 167

Discussion Questions 168

Chapter 7. Communicating Closeness: Affection, Immediacy, and Social Support 169

Closeness in Relationships 170

    Physical Closeness 170

    Emotional Closeness 170

    Relational Closeness 170

    Communicating Closeness 170

Affectionate Communication 171

    Affection Exchange Theory 171

    Communicating Affection 174

Immediacy Behavior 176
    Verbal Immediacy 176
    Nonverbal Immediacy 177
Cognitive Valence Theory 179
    Behavior 179
    Perception 181
    Arousal 181
    Cognition 181
    Relational Outcomes 183
Supportive Communication 184
    The Dual Process Model of Supportive Communication 185
    Invisible Support 188
    Person-Centered Messages 190
    Nonverbal Immediacy 191
Sex Differences in the Experience and Expression of Closeness 192
    Perceptions of Closeness 192
    Communication of Closeness 193
    Preferences for Same-Sex Versus Cross-Sex Friendships 193
Summary and Application 194
Key Terms 195
Discussion Questions 196

Chapter 8. Making a Love Connection: Styles of Love and Attachment 197
What Is Love? 198
Love Versus Liking 198
    Love as a Triangle 198
    Finding Love and Falling in Love 201
Love Styles 203
    Lee's Love Styles 203
    Ways to Communicate Love 212
Attachment Theory 214
    The Propensity for Forming Attachments 214
    Internal Working Models and Attachment Styles 215
    Attachment Styles in Childhood 215
    Attachment Styles in Adulthood 217
    Attachment and Relational Satisfaction 220
    Stability and Change in Attachment Styles Across the Life Span 222
Summary and Application 225
Key Terms 226
Discussion Questions 227

Chapter 9. Communicating Sexually: The Closest Physical Encounter 228
Sex in Relationships 229
    Sex in Short-Term and Early Dating Relationships 229

    Sex in Long-Term Relationships 230
    Sex Differences 231
    Sex in Same-Sex Relationships 233

  Sexual Attitudes 235
    Developing Sexual Attitudes and Beliefs 237

  Communication About Sex 239
    Courtship and Flirtation 239
    Communication, Sexual Satisfaction, and Relational Satisfaction 243
    Sexual Scripts 245
    Pillow Talk 247

  Sexual Coercion and Harassment 248
    Sexual Coercion 248
    Sexual Harassment 250

  Communication and Safe Sex 251

  Summary and Application 254

  Key Terms 255

  Discussion Questions 256

Chapter 10. Staying Close: Maintaining Relationships 257

  Defining Relational Maintenance 258

  Behaviors Used to Maintain Relationships 259
    Prosocial Maintenance Behaviors 259
    Antisocial Maintenance Behavior 260
    Modality of Maintenance Behavior 261
    Strategic and Routine Maintenance Behaviors 265

  Maintenance Behavior in Romantic Relationships 265
    Changes in Maintenance Over the Course of Romantic Relationships 266
    Maintenance in Gay and Lesbian Relationships 266

  Maintenance Behavior in Same-Sex Friendships 267
    Talking Versus Doing 267
    Men and Women Are From the Same Planet 268

  Maintenance Behavior in Cross-Sex Friendships 268
    Challenges in Cross-Sex Friendships 268
    Coping With Romantic Intent 270
    Keeping Friendships Platonic 271

  Maintenance Challenges in Other Relationships 273
    Friends-With-Benefits Relationships 273
    Long-Distance Relationships 275
    Cohabiting Relationships 277

  Equity Theory 279
    Principles of Equity Theory 280
    Reducing Distress in Inequitable Relationships 283
    Combined Influence of Benefit-Cost Ratios and Equity 283

Summary and Application 284

Key Terms 285

Discussion Questions 286

Chapter 11. Coping With Conflict: When Relational Partners Disagree 287

Conflict in Relationships 288

Defining Conflict 288

Frequency of Conflict in Various Relationships 289

Effects of Conflict on Relationships 289

Conflict Styles 290

Competitive Fighting 291

Compromising 294

Collaborating 294

Indirect Fighting 295

Avoiding 296

Yielding 297

Patterns of Conflict Interaction 298

Negative Reciprocity 298

Demand-Withdraw 301

The Four Horsemen of the Apocalypse 302

Accommodation 305

Explanations for Conflict Patterns 306

Emotional Flooding 307

Attributions 308

Communication Skill Deficits 310

Summary and Application 312

Key Terms 313

Discussion Questions 314

Chapter 12. Influencing Each Other: Dominance and Power Plays in Relationships 315

Defining Power and Related Terms 316

Power Principles 317

Power as a Perception 317

Power as a Relational Concept 319

Power as Resource Based 319

Power as Having Less to Lose 321

Power as Enabling or Disabling 322

Power as a Prerogative 324

Interpersonal Influence Goals 325

Making Lifestyle Changes 325

Gaining Assistance 325

Sharing Activities 326

Initiating Sexual Activity 326

    Changing Political Attitudes 326
    Giving Health Advice 326
    Changing Relationships 327
  Verbal Power Ploys 327
    Verbal Influence Strategies 327
    Relational Control Moves: One-Ups and One-Downs 330
    Powerful and Powerless Speech 331
  Nonverbal Positions of Power 332
    Physical Appearance 333
    Spatial Behavior 333
    Eye Behavior 334
    Body Movements 334
    Touch 335
    The Voice 335
    Time 336
    Artifacts 336
  Power and Influence in Families 336
    Parent and Child Relationships 336
    Traditional Versus Egalitarian Marriages 339
  Summary and Application 342
  Key Terms 343
  Discussion Questions 343

Chapter 13. Hurting the Ones We Love: Relational Transgressions 345

  Hurt Feelings in Relationships 345
    Relational Transgressions 346
    Hurtful Messages 347
    Types of Hurtful Messages 348
    Responses to Hurtful Messages 348
  Deception 349
    Types of Deception 350
    Motives for Deception 350
    Deception Detection 353
    Effects of Deception on Relationships 354
  Infidelity 356
    Types of Infidelity 356
    Behavioral Cues to Infidelity 357
    Sex Differences in Reactions to Infidelity 358
  Jealousy 360
    Characteristics of Jealousy 360
    Experiencing Romantic Jealousy 361
    Communicative Responses to Jealousy 364
    Jealousy and Relational Satisfaction 365
    Sex Differences in Jealous Emotions and Communication 365

Unrequited Love 368

Obsessive Relational Intrusion 369

Reasons People Use Obsessive Relational Intrusion Behavior 370

Consequences of Obsessive Relational Intrusion Behavior 372

Relational Violence 372

Common Couple Violence 373

Intimate Terrorism 374

Summary and Application 375

Key Terms 376

Discussion Questions 376

Chapter 14. Healing the Hurt: Relationship Repair and Reconciliation 378

The Investment Model of Relationship-Maintaining Behavior 379

Commitment 380

Pro-Relationship Behaviors 382

The Model of Accommodation 384

Destructive Behaviors 384

Constructive Behaviors 385

Remedial Strategies 387

Apologies and Concessions 388

Appeasement 390

Explanations 391

Denials 391

Avoidance and Evasion 392

Relationship Talk 392

Forgiveness 392

What Forgiveness Means 392

Forgiving Communication 393

Conditions That Promote or Impede Forgiveness and Forgiving Communication 396

Relational Reconciliation 397

Reconciliation Strategies 397

Reintegration in the Social Network 400

On-Again Off-Again Relationships 400

Relational Redefinition 403

Summary and Application 404

Key Terms 405

Discussion Questions 406

Chapter 15. Ending Relationships: Disengagement and Termination 407

Why Relationships End 408

Infidelity and Interest in a Third Party 410

Incompatibility 411

Alcohol and Drugs 412

Growing Apart 412
Loss of Love 413
Equity Issues Related to Family Obligations 413

Communication as a Cause of Relational Breakup 415
Withdrawal 415
Negative Communication 416
Lack of Openness and Intimacy 416
Abusive Communication 417

The Disengagement Process 418
A Process Model of Relational Dissolution 418

Catastrophe Theory 420

Fifteen Ways to Leave Your Partner 421
Unilateral and Indirect Strategies 422
Unilateral and Direct Strategies 425
Bilateral and Indirect Strategy 428
Bilateral and Direct Strategies 428

Outcomes: The Results of Relationships Endings 429
Negative Outcomes of Relational Breakups 429
Healing After a Separation 432
Positive Outcomes of Relational Breakups 433

Summary and Application 433

Key Terms 434

Discussion Questions 435

Glossary 436

References 451

Author Index 492

Subject Index 507

About the Authors 527

PREFACE

We are pleased and privileged to release the fifth edition of *Close Encounters*. We wrote the first edition of this book in response to the increasing number of upper-division courses on relational communication and advanced interpersonal communication being taught at colleges and universities across the country. Since then, more courses in relational communication are being offered, and research on close relationships has continued to flourish. Indeed, it is challenging to update the content in this book because there is so much new research on relational communication published each year. Because of space limitations, we could not include everything we wanted to include. Nonetheless, we believe that this edition contains an appropriate mix of recent and classic research related to communication in relationships.

Our goal in writing *Close Encounters* continues to be to produce an informative yet readable textbook that will help students understand their relationships better and be more critical consumers of information about relationships. This book is research based. We strive to present concepts and theories in more depth than the average textbook on interpersonal communication while writing in an accessible style. For us, writing this textbook is a rewarding experience; it lets us reach beyond the pages of scholarly journals to share information with students who are eager to learn more about relationships.

APPROACH

The book takes a relational approach to the study of interpersonal communication by focusing on issues that are central to describing and understanding close relationships, particularly between romantic partners, friends, and family members. One of the most exciting trends in the field of personal relationships is the interdisciplinary nature of research and theory. Scholars from fields such as communication, family studies, psychology, and sociology, among other disciplines, have all made important contributions to scholarly knowledge about relationships. This book reflects the interdisciplinary nature of the field of personal relationships while focusing strongly on interpersonal communication.

ORGANIZATION

Close Encounters is organized loosely around the concept of relationship trajectories. However, we use the term *trajectory* loosely because all relationships are different, and no two follow exactly the same path. Nonetheless, from a developmental perspective it is helpful to think of how relationships progress from initial meetings toward farewells. It is also important to acknowledge, however, that there are different perspectives on how relationships change and develop over time. Thus, we include a chapter on relational stages, turning points, and dialectics to show students how these different perspectives complement one another. The organization of the book also reflects that various forms of communication, such as disclosure and conflict, can occur during any point in a relationship. For example, conflict can be studied in terms of a couple's first big fight, the mundane disagreements that people have on a fairly regular basis, the conflicts that enhance relational functioning, or the argument that ultimately marks the destruction of a relationship. Some topics are also related to one another in important ways that guided our organization of *Close Encounters*. For example, theorists taking a dialectical perspective have argued that both disclosure and privacy are important in relationships. Thus, we include information on "revealing ourselves" and "hiding ourselves" in the same chapter. Similarly, relational scholars have long recognized that conflict is not inherently good or bad; rather, it is how conflict is managed that determines positive or negative outcomes. Accordingly, the conflict management chapter now follows the relational maintenance chapter so that instructors can emphasize that both relational maintenance behaviors and constructive conflict management are key ingredients in happy relationships. The three chapters that focus on relational transgressions, relationship repair, and relational disengagement are packaged together at the end of the book to showcase how people deal with challenges in their relationships. Although these chapters may be considered to reflect the "dark side" of interpersonal communication, we believe that most topics covered in this book have a dark side and a bright side. For example, affection is generally seen as a positive behavior, but too much affection can be smothering; breakups are generally seen as negative actions, but ending a bad relationship can pave the way for a better one in the future. These are examples of the complexities highlighted throughout this book.

FEATURES IN THIS EDITION

For this edition we retained the features that have made *Close Encounters* successful. Each chapter starts with a scenario that features fictional characters dealing with communication issues, and each chapter ends with a section called "Summary and Application." These chapter endings tie back to the scenarios at the beginning of each chapter so that students can see how the information they learned can be applied to a specific situation. Throughout each chapter, we refer to the opening scenarios at various times to provide examples of how the concepts we discuss relate to real-life situations. With the exception of Chapter 1, all chapters include at least one Put Yourself to the Test box that enables students to find out how they rate on a particular concept. Our students have told us that they find these boxes very helpful in identifying their communication style as well as some of the characteristics of their relationships. Some instructors incorporate these self-tests into their course assignments. For example, students may complete some of these tests and then write self-reflection papers about their own communication style.

Each chapter includes an Around the World box, featuring ways that relational communication is similar and different across cultures or within intercultural versus intracultural couples. Every chapter also includes a Tech Talk box that highlights research showing how various aspects of communication using technology and new media, such as texting, Facebook, Snapchat, and Instagram, function within close relationships. Highlights boxes throughout provide definitions and details for key concepts discussed in the book. There is also a word list at the end of each chapter, as well as a glossary at the end of the book, to help students identify and define key concepts.

Content has been updated throughout this edition, with new material added on topics such as on-again off-again relationships, different types of friends with benefits and cohabiting relationships, pillow talk, and identity issues in generation Z. More research on new technologies, such as Facebook and Snapchat, as well as texting, was added throughout the book. In Chapter 5, for example, the discussion of relational stages includes the role that texting, Snapchat, and other new technologies play in developing, maintaining, and ending relationships. This edition of the book also includes updated versions of privacy management theory, the four horsemen of the apocalypse in conflict interaction, and relational goal pursuit theory. As was true in past editions, our goal is to present topics that are at the forefront of relational communication research and that are of high interest to students.

FEATURES

In addition to the features already discussed, *Close Encounters* is designed to appeal to students and professors alike based on the following features:

Current, interdisciplinary research: The research in *Close Encounters* reflects the interdisciplinary nature of the study of personal relationships and draws from across the social science disciplines while maintaining a focus on communication. This edition has been carefully updated to include recent cutting-edge research on interpersonal communication.

High-interest topics: Intriguing subjects, such as long-distance relationships, cross-sex friendships, friends with benefits, flirting, sexual interaction, on-again off-again relationships, cohabitation, and the dark side of relational communication are explored in depth.

Put Yourself to the Test boxes: These boxed exercises, found throughout the book, assess various aspects of students' own relationships and communication styles.

Around the World boxes: These boxes help students understand and appreciate that relational communication is partially determined by culture and that they should not assume that someone from another culture thinks or communicates the same as they do.

Tech Talk boxes: These boxes feature research that looks at how people use technology and new media (such as cell phones, social networking sites, the Internet, and blogs) to develop and manage relationships.

Highlights boxes: These boxes take a closer look at issues in relational research and challenge students to think critically about research and popular concepts.

Discussion Questions: These questions, found at the end of each chapter, can help students prepare for class or can be used as springboards for classroom discussion. Some instructors also have students write position papers in response to some of the discussion questions.

DIGITAL RESOURCES

edge.sagepub.com/guerrero5e
SAGE edge offers a robust online environment featuring an impressive array of free tools and resources for review, study, and further exploration, keeping both instructors and students on the cutting edge of teaching and learning.

SAGE edge for Students provides a personalized approach to help students accomplish their coursework goals in an easy-to-use learning environment.

- Mobile-friendly eFlashcards and quizzes strengthen understanding of key terms and concepts
- A complete online action plan includes tips and feedback on students' progress and allows them to personalize their learning experience
- Learning objectives reinforce the most important material
- Video and multimedia links encourage further exploration of certain topics, which appeal to students with different learning styles
- Full-text SAGE journal articles support and expand on the concepts presented in each chapter

SAGE edge for Instructors supports your teaching by making it easy to integrate quality content and create a rich learning environment for students. SAGE edge includes:

- Test banks that allow you to edit any question and/or insert your own personalized questions, helping you assess students' progress and understanding
- Sample course syllabi for semester and quarter courses that assist in structuring your course
- Editable, chapter-specific PowerPoint® slides that offer flexibility in creating multimedia presentations
- EXCLUSIVE! Access to carefully selected SAGE journal articles, which support and expand concepts presented in each chapter
- Video and multimedia links, which appeal to students with different learning styles
- Lecture notes that summarize key concepts by chapter to aid in preparing lectures

ACKNOWLEDGMENTS

Writing a textbook is an exciting challenge and a daunting task. As we worked on this edition of *Close Encounters,* our dens were cluttered with articles and our families had to listen to the click-click-click of our computer keyboards even more than usual. The support of our families and colleagues was critical in helping us complete this project, and we owe them our sincere gratitude. We are especially indebted to our partners—Vico, Janis, and Tammy—and our daughters—Gabrielle, Kristiana, Kirsten, Leila, and Rania—who provide social support as well as examples and feedback.

We would also like to thank the many people who helped during the writing and editing process. We are especially grateful to our editors, Karen Omer and Matthew Byrnie, and our editorial assistant, Sarah Dillard, who were supportive through all aspects of the publication process. We would also like to thank our copy editor, Alison Hope; production editor, Kelly DeRosa; and to acknowledge two other people who we consider to be part of the *Close Encounters* family—Holly Allen and Todd Armstrong. Holly was the editor for the first edition; a conversation between Laura and Holly back in 1998 started the *Close Encounters* ball rolling. Todd Armstrong stepped in to publish a second and third edition of the book for SAGE, and he was always enthusiastic and supportive regarding our work.

Many of our colleagues across the discipline also deserve a word of praise. We have received formal and informal feedback from many valued colleagues throughout the years, including (but not limited to) Katherine Adams, Jess Alberts, Guy Bachman, Jennifer Bevan, Dawn Braithwaite, San Bolkan, Brant Burleson, Daniel Canary, John Caughlin, Scott Christopher, Michael Cunningham, Victoria DeFrancisco, Kathryn Dindia, Norah Dunbar, Renee Edwards, Lisa Farinelli, Cara Fisher, Kory Floyd, Michael Hecht, Susan Jarboe, Susanne Jones, Leanne Knobloch, Pamela Lannutti, Bree McEwan, Tara McManus, Sandra Metts, Claude Miller, Paul Mongeau, Larry Nadler, Sylvia Niehuis, Donna Pawlowski, Sue Pendall, Sandra Petronio, Pam Secklin, Denise Solomon, Brian Spitzberg, Susan Sprecher, Laura Stafford, Glen Stamp, Claire Sullivan, Paul Turman, Richard West, Christina Yoshimura, and Stephen Yoshimura. A special thanks goes to Judee Burgoon (Laura and Walid's doctoral adviser and an exceptional role model) who suggested that we use the term *close encounters* as part of the title.

SAGE Publications would like to thank the following reviewers for their contributions: Rukhsana Ahmed, University of Ottawa; Suzanne Buck, Jack J. Valenti School of Communication/University of Houston; Janie Harden Fritz, Duquesne University; Annelise Ewing Goodman, James Madison University; Sheryl Hurner, CSU Sacramento; Cheryl Pawlowski, The University of Northern Colorado; Leslie Ramos Salazar, California State University, Fresno; Xiaowei Shi, Middle Tennessee State University; Kandi Walker, University of Louisville; Cory Williams, Concord University; Valerie Young, Hanover College; and Nicohlas A. Zoffel, Sierra College.

Finally, we would like to thank all the students we have had in our classes over the years. We use some of their examples in this book, and we have incorporated their feedback into every new edition. Just as importantly, lively dialogue with students has helped sustain our enthusiasm for teaching courses on interpersonal communication and relationships. We hope this book contributes to spirited discussions about relationships in your classrooms as well.

—L. K. G.
—P. A. A.
—W. A. A.

1 CONCEPTUALIZING RELATIONAL COMMUNICATION

Definitions and Principles

> People accomplish a lot by communicating with others. For example, take these three situations. Jake is having trouble with his statistics homework, which is due tomorrow. His friend and roommate, Dave, is a whiz at math, so Jake tries to persuade Dave to stay home (rather than go to a party) and help him. Meanwhile, Su-Lin recently arrived in the United States as an international student and feels a lot of uncertainty about the university and student life. However, after joining a couple of student clubs and getting to know some of her classmates, she starts to feel more comfortable in her new surroundings. Kristi's husband moves out of the house and tells her he wants a divorce. Rather than sitting at home alone, moping around and feeling sorry for herself, Kristi drives over to her parents' house where she receives comfort and support from her mother.

Personal **relationships** are central to being human. McAdams (1988) suggested that "through personal relationships, we may find our most profound experiences of security and anxiety, power and impotence, unity and separateness" (p. 7). People are born into relationships and live their lives in webs of friendships, family networks, romances, marriages, and work relationships. In fact, research shows that when people talk, the most common topics are relationship problems, sex, family, and romantic (or potential romantic) partners (Haas & Sherman, 1982). The capacity to form relationships is innate and biological—a part of the genetic inheritance that has enabled the human race to survive over time. Humans have less potential for survival, creativity,

and innovation as individuals than they do in relationships. Personal relationship experts have begun to unlock the mysteries of these universal human experiences, to assist people with problematic relationships, and to help people achieve greater satisfaction in their close encounters.

As Jake, Su-Lin, and Kristi illustrate, communication plays a central role in relationships. When we need help, comfort, or reassurance, communication is the tool that helps us accomplish our goals. Relationships cannot exist unless two people communicate with each other. "Bad" communication is often blamed for problems in relationships, whereas "good" communication is often credited with preserving relationships. In this introductory chapter, we take a close look at what constitutes both communication and relationships. First, however, we provide a brief history of the field of personal relationships. Then we define and discuss three important terms that are central to this book: (1) **relationships**, (2) **interpersonal communication,** and (3) **relational communication.** The chapter ends with principles of interpersonal and relational communication.

THE FIELD OF PERSONAL RELATIONSHIPS: A BRIEF HISTORY

People have been curious about their relationships for thousands of years, but the formal study of personal relationships is a fairly recent phenomenon. Today we take the study of personal relationships for granted, but a few decades ago the scholarly investigation of relationships was considered unscientific and a waste of resources. In 1975 Senator William Proxmire of Wisconsin publicly criticized two of the finest and earliest relationship researchers, Ellen Berscheid and Elaine Hatfield (formerly Elaine Walster), for their research on love. Proxmire gave the "golden fleece award" for wasteful government spending to the National Science Foundation for supporting Berscheid and Walster's research on love with an $84,000 grant. The senator's objections to "squandering" money on love research were twofold: (1) Scientists could never understand the mystery of love, and (2) even if they did, he didn't want to hear it and was confident that no one else did either (E. Hatfield, personal communication, August 20, 1999). Of course, like many Americans Proxmire had problematic relationships of his own and had just been divorced at the time he gave his "award." Months of harassing phone calls and even death threats to Berscheid and Walster followed (E. Hatfield, personal communication, August 20, 1999).

Now most people, including politicians, realize that close relationships are as important to study as earthquakes or nutrition, especially since having good relationships is associated with better mental and physical health (Ryff, Singer, Wing, & Dienberg Love, 2001; Taylor et al., 2006; Willitts, Benzeval, & Stansfeld, 2004). People now find social scientific knowledge compatible with personal political and religious beliefs. In fact, some churches conduct premarital workshops and marriage encounters based on relationship research. Bookstores and newsstands are crammed with books and magazines that focus on every aspect of relationships, providing advice (of variable quality) on topics such as the "These are the Qualities Men *Actually* Look for in Women" (Keong, 2016) and why "My Husband and I Text More Than We Talk—and That's OK" (Wright, 2015), as well as offering "11 Things You Need to Do to Have a Lasting Relationship" (Moore, 2016), "20 Body Language Signs That Mean He's Into You" (Narins, 2015), and "10 Things You Should Never, Ever Say In a Fight With Your Girlfriend or Wife" (Walgren, 2016), just to name some of the advice in the popular press. One critical function of scientific research on relationships is to provide a check-and-balance system for the popular advice given in the media. Critical consumers can compare the scientific literature to the popular, often inaccurate, advice in magazines, best-selling books, and television shows. Box 1.1 presents one such comparison.

Several major tributaries have contributed to the steady stream of scholarly research on personal relationships. The early pioneers in the field could not have envisioned the vast amount of research on relationships that exists in several disciplines today. The young field of personal relationships has always been transdisciplinary, although it sometimes took years for scholars from different disciplines to discover one another's work. Duck (1988) commented that the field of personal relationships is unusual because it is truly interdisciplinary and has the power to impact people's everyday lives. Scholars from disciplines such as communication, social psychology, child development, family studies, sociology, and anthropology are all in the business of studying human relationships. In particular, research in interpersonal communication, social psychology, and other

BOX 1.1 HIGHLIGHTS
THE IMPORTANCE OF BEING A CRITICAL CONSUMER: COMPARING JOHN GOTTMAN TO JOHN GRAY

People are bombarded with advice about relationships from best-selling books, magazine articles, and talk shows. How accurate is this advice? The answer is, "It depends." Sometimes the advice given in the media is consistent with social scientific research; other times it is not. In a *Psychology Today* article, Marano (1997) put John Gray to the test by comparing his credentials and conclusions to those of John Gottman. John Gray is the author of the number-one best seller in nonfiction, *Men Are From Mars, Women Are From Venus.* John Gottman is one of the premier social psychologists in the study of personal relationships. So how did Gray stack up to Gottman? Here is what *Psychology Today* reported after researching and interviewing both men.

	John Gray	John Gottman
Education	PhD through correspondence school	PhD from the University of Illinois
Licensing	Driver's license	Licensed psychologist
Number of journal articles	None	109
Number of couples formally studied	None	760
The cardinal rule of relationships	Men and women are different.	What people think they do in relationships and what they actually do are very different.
Defining statement	"Before 1950, men were men and women were women."	"It's the everyday mindless moments that are the basis of romance in marriage."
What makes marriage work?	Heeding gender stereotypes	Making mental maps of each other's world
What makes marriage fail?	Gender differences in communication style	Gender stereotypes and reactions to stress
What they say about each other	"John who?"	"I envy his financial success."

Source: Adapted from Marano, H. E. (1997). A Tale of Two Relationship Gurus. In H. E. Marano, *Gottman and Gray: The Two Johns.* © Copyright 1997. www.psychologytoday.com.

disciplines has contributed to the establishment and evolution of the field of personal relationships.

Contributions of Interpersonal Communication Research

The earliest research in this area dates back to the 1950s, but interpersonal communication research began in earnest in the 1960s and 1970s (Andersen, 1982). Previously, communication scholars were preoccupied mainly with public speeches, political rhetoric, and mass communication. In the 1960s scholars realized that most communication takes place in small groups and dyads consisting of close friends, family members, and romantic partners (Miller, 1976). In the early 1970s the first books on interpersonal communication emerged (e.g., McCroskey, Larson, & Knapp, 1971). The study of interpersonal communication thus began with a focus on how people communicate in dyads and small groups.

Scholars also realized that interpersonal communication differs based on the type of relationship people share. Miller and Steinberg (1975) proposed that the defining characteristics of an **interpersonal relationship** are that it is unique, is irreplaceable, and requires understanding of the partner's psychological makeup. By contrast, noninterpersonal or role relationships, like those with store clerks or tech help-line staff, possess few unique qualities, are replaceable, and are relatively impersonal. These shifts in communication scholarship reflected broader societal changes. The youth movement of the 1960s represented a rebellion against a society thought to be impersonal and manipulative. Sensitivity training, encounter groups, and other personal growth movements of the 1960s and 1970s turned people's attention inward to the dyad and to close relationships.

The evolution of interpersonal communication as a primary emphasis in the communication discipline was an outcome of the recognition that relationships are the primary locus for communication. Scholars also realized that relationships are an inherently communicative phenomenon. It is difficult to imagine how human relationships might exist in the absence of communication. Miller (1976) stated, "Understanding the interpersonal communication process demands an understanding of the symbiotic relationship between communication and relational development: communication influences relational development, and in turn (or simultaneously) relational development influences the nature of the communication between parties to the relationship" (p. 15). By the 1980s interpersonal and relational communication research had become increasingly sophisticated and theoretically driven (Andersen, 1982).

Contributions of Social Psychology

Early research in social psychology also laid the groundwork for the scientific investigation of interpersonal relationships, with much of this work focused on social development and personality. From the late 1950s through the mid-1970s, however, social psychologists increasingly began studying interaction patterns related to group and dyadic processes. (For some of the major early works, see Altman & Taylor, 1973; Berscheid & Walster, 1969; Heider, 1958; Thibaut & Kelley, 1959.) This movement was not limited to social psychologists in the United States; in Great Britain, Argyle and his associates spent several decades studying aspects of relationships (see Argyle & Dean, 1965; Argyle & Henderson, 1985).

During the mid-20th century, several highly influential books were published. For example, Thibaut and Kelley's (1959) *The Social Psychology of Groups* eventually led to an explosion of research on social exchange processes in groups and dyads, bringing issues such as rewards (the positive outcomes people get from relationships) and reciprocity (the way one person's behavior leads to similar behavior in another) to the forefront. Berscheid and Walster's (1969) *Interpersonal Attraction* also had a major impact on both interpersonal communication research and the study of dyadic behavior in social psychology. This book focused on emerging relationships between strangers, as did much of the early research in social psychology (see Altman & Taylor, 1973). A short time later, however, relational research began to focus on love, and the study of close relationships began to flourish (see Berscheid & Walster, 1974; Rubin, 1970, 1973). Finally, Altman and Taylor's (1973) *Social Penetration: The Development of Interpersonal Relationships,* which examined the role of self-disclosure in relationships, helped generate research in communication, relationship development, and relationship disengagement.

The prestigious *Journal of Personality and Social Psychology* also included a section on "Interpersonal Processes"; this journal still publishes some of the best research on relationships. However, until the mid-1980s there were no journals that focused exclusively on relationships. In fact, the first professional conference devoted entirely to interpersonal relationships was held in the 1980s, again indicating the youthfulness of the field of personal relationships compared to other academic disciplines (see Kelley, 1986). This conference, which was organized primarily by social psychologists, laid the roots for the creation of two organizations that focused exclusively on personal relationships: the International Network on Personal Relationships (INPR), which was established by Steve Duck; and the International Society for the Study of Personal Relationships (ISSPR), founded by Robin Gilmour and Steve Duck. In 1984 the INPR established the first journal dedicated solely to the study of personal relationships, the prestigious *Journal of Social and Personal Relationships.* A decade later the ISSPR launched a second journal, called *Personal Relationships.* Now these two scholarly societies have merged into one professional association, the International Association for Relationship Research (IARR).

Roots in Other Disciplines

Disciplines such as family studies, sociology, developmental and child psychology, clinical psychology, humanistic psychology, and anthropology also have made important contributions to the field of personal relationships. One study reported that approximately 37% of the research on personal relationships comes from social psychologists, another 37% from communication scholars, and much of the rest from sociologists and family studies scholars (Hoobler, 1999). Sociologists' relationship research often focuses on issues such as cultural values, class,

religion, secularization, divorce, marriage, gender equality, political attitudes, and generational differences—with an eye toward determining how relationships are embedded within the larger society. Family studies scholars examine relationships from a different lens, looking more at the internal dynamics of relationships between family members, either as a family system or as an interpersonal dyad within the broader family structure (e.g., parent–child or spousal relationships). Family scholars also examine developmental issues, such as determining how relationships within one's family of origin influence later relationships in adulthood.

Personal relationship research draws from these different disciplines, so a level of richness and diversity that is often absent in other fields characterizes the field of personal relationships. It is precisely because scholars in the various disciplines—communication, social psychology, sociology, family studies, and so on—have different theoretical and methodological approaches that the field of personal relationships has been so vital and is evolving so quickly (Duck, 1988). Although this book draws on knowledge from various fields, the primary focus is on communication in close relationships, with three terms central to this book: (1) relationships (including role relationships, interpersonal relationships, and close relationships), (2) interpersonal communication, (3) relational communication (see Box 1.2 for definitions of these terms).

BOX 1.2 HIGHLIGHTS
DEFINITIONS OF KEY TERMS

1. *Relationships:*
   a. Role relationships: Two people who share some degree of behavioral interdependence—although people in such relationships are usually interchangeable and are not psychologically or behaviorally unique. One person in a role relationship can easily replace another.

   b. Interpersonal relationships: Two people who share repeated interactions over time, can influence one another, and have unique interaction patterns.
   c. Close relationships: Two people in an interpersonal relationship characterized by enduring bonds, emotional attachment, personal need fulfillment, and irreplaceability.

(Continued)

BOX 1.2 (Continued)

2. *Interpersonal communication:* The exchange of non-verbal and verbal messages between people, regardless of the relationship they share.

3. *Relational communication:* A subset of interpersonal communication focused on the expression and interpretation of messages within close relationships. Relational communication includes the gamut of interactions from vital relational messages to mundane everyday interactions.

RELATIONSHIPS

Think about all the different people with whom you interact in a given day. Do you have relationships with all of them or only some of them? With how many of these people do you have close or personal relationships? Defining the term *relationship* can be tricky. When do we cross the line from interacting with someone to having a relationship? And when do we move from having a casual or functional relationship to having a **close relationship**?

General Types of Relationships

Take a moment to think of all the different relationships you have. Now imagine a piece of paper with a circle representing you in the middle of the page. If you draw additional circles that represent each of the people with whom you have relationships, where would you place those circles in comparison to yourself? You would likely place some individuals nearer to yourself than others based on the closeness you share with each person. How many people would be really close to you, and how many would be near the margins of the paper? Would anyone's circle overlap with yours? Research suggests that among the many relationships most of us have with friends, coworkers, family members, romantic partners, and others, only a select few of those relationships become really close. Most of these relationships stay at an interpersonal level, and others may never really progress beyond a role relationship.

ROLE RELATIONSHIPS According to many relationship scholars, the basic ingredient for having a relationship is that two individuals share some degree of **behavioral interdependence** (Berscheid & Peplau, 1983). This means that one person's behavior somehow affects the other person's behavior and vice versa. Based on this definition, we have relationships with a variety of people, including the salesclerk who helps us make a purchase, the waiter who takes our orders and serves us dinner, and the boss whom we rarely see but whom we depend on for leadership and a paycheck. These basic role relationships are not true interpersonal relationships. Rather, **role relationships** are functional or casual and often are temporary; also, people in such relationships are usually interchangeable and not unique. An interpersonal or close relationship with someone requires more than simple behavioral interdependence.

INTERPERSONAL RELATIONSHIPS In addition to basic behavioral independence, interpersonal relationships require that two individuals influence each other in meaningful ways. This type of **mutual influence** goes beyond basic tasks such as exchanging money for coffee at Starbucks or thanking your hygienist after she cleans your teeth. In interpersonal relationships, influence extends beyond mundane tasks to activities that create connection at a social or emotional level rather than a task level. For example, while helping Jake with his statistics homework, Dave might offer words of encouragement to boost his confidence. After the homework is finished, they may start talking about a political issue and in doing so affect one another's thinking. Knowing that Dave dreads public speaking, Jake may later reciprocate by offering to listen to a speech that Dave is preparing. These tasks take extensive time and effort and include providing emotional support and engaging in self-disclosure rather than just getting something done. Thus, these activities imply that Dave and Jake have moved beyond a simple role relationship.

Interpersonal relationships also have repeated interaction over time. Because they interact with one another frequently, Jake has the time and opportunity to reciprocate by helping Dave, which can strengthen their friendship further. Interactions that are limited in length or frequency rarely develop into interpersonal relationships. Finally, interpersonal relationships are characterized by **unique interaction patterns**. This means that the way Jake communicates with Dave will be different in some ways from how he communicates with other friends. They have a unique relational history, including shared experiences, inside jokes, and knowledge of private information; this history shapes how they communicate with each other.

CLOSE RELATIONSHIPS Close relationships have all the features of interpersonal relationships plus three more: (1) **emotional attachment**, (2) **need fulfillment**, and (3) **irreplaceability.** In a close relationship, we feel emotionally connected; the relationship is the basis of why we feel happy or sad, proud or disappointed. Similarly, close relational partners fulfill critical interpersonal needs, such as the need to belong to a social group, to feel loved and appreciated, or to care for and nurture someone. When a relationship is irreplaceable, the other person has a special place in our thoughts and emotions, as well as in our social network. For example, you may have only one first love and one best friend, and there may be one person in particular whom you reach out to in times of crisis.

It is important to recognize that distinctions between these three types of relationships are often blurred. Our close relationships contain some of the same features as interpersonal and role relationships. For instance, Kristi's close relationship with her mother is partially defined by her role as a daughter.

Behavioral interdependence also characterizes all relationships, but as people move from role to interpersonal to close relationships, interdependence becomes more enduring and diverse (Berscheid & Peplau, 1983). Diverse means that partners are interdependent in many ways, such as needing each other for emotional support, striving to reach shared goals, and influencing each other's beliefs and attitudes. In role relationships, such as those we have with salesclerks or waiters, behavioral interdependence is temporary, and defined by the situation. Need fulfillment is also part of all three relationship types, but the needs that our closest relationships fulfill are more central and personal than the needs other relationships fulfill.

Need Fulfillment in Close Relationships

Researchers suggest that a plethora of human needs are satisfied in close personal relationships, with the three most central interpersonal needs being affection, social inclusion, and behavioral control (Schutz, 1958). In the scenario at the beginning of this chapter, each person used communication to fulfill one of these needs. Kristi went to her mother for affection and social support. Su-Lin joined student clubs and talked with classmates to satisfy inclusion needs. Finally, Jake tried to exert behavioral control by persuading Dave to stay home and help him with his statistics homework.

AFFECTION Throughout life, our need for affection is satisfied through our ability to love other people and through having other people love us (Schutz, 1958). Neglected infants who are never touched suffer from failure-to-thrive syndrome, which can be fatal (Andersen, 2008; Montagu, 1971/1978). Adults who regularly give and receive affection report more psychological and physical health, as well as better relationships (Floyd, 2006). Affectionate communication is a resource that strengthens relationships and makes people feel better about themselves and others. Affection, according to Schutz (1958), occurs in dyads. Inclusion and control, by contrast, can occur either "between pairs of people or between one person and a group of persons" (p. 23). Affection forms the basis for our most powerful and closest relationships (see Chapter 7).

SOCIAL INCLUSION Feeling part of a group is another crucial need (Schutz, 1958). It is through primary group relationships that basic needs such as safety and survival are satisfied. Ruesch (1951) observed the following:

> In the fold of the family, clan or group or in the widest sense of the world, the herd, he [or she] feels secure. Reliance on other members of the group increases his [or her] chance for survival in a troubled world. (p. 36)

Humans evolved as members of hunting and gathering bands of 100 to 200 people (Donald, 1991). This may explain why belonging to groups—from youth groups to corporations, from sports teams to service clubs, from street gangs to fraternities and sororities—is so important to most people. In any case, Schutz (1958) suggested that feeling included is a crucial part of social development that enables us to have successful interactions and associations with other people. A lack of social interaction and inclusion can contribute to loneliness and low self-esteem (Segrin, 1998).

BEHAVIORAL CONTROL The third basic interpersonal need revolves around the desire to feel in control of one's life (Schutz, 1958). People in successful interpersonal relationships share control (Scott & Powers, 1978), including making decisions together involving work, money, sex, children, and household chores. Indeed, a whole body of research suggests that partners who share tasks and resources in a fair manner are more satisfied with their relationships (see Chapter 10). By contrast, partners who believe they lack control or who are denied free choice may deliberately sabotage their relationships, defy rules, and engage in other destructive behavior. For example, if you have a friend who always shows up

late, you might retaliate by leaving before he or she arrives. Prohibition of a relationship by parents sometimes increases the attractiveness of the relationship. According to Cialdini (1988), this effect is based on the idea that scarce objects or people are most attractive. This explains why advertisers offer "limited time offers" and sales "while the supply lasts" and why people who are "hard to get" are more attractive than people who are "easy to get"—except, of course, if they are easy for us to get but hard for others to get.

Relationship Categories

Another way to think about relationships is to categorize them based on type. We do this every day; in our ordinary talk, we refer to some relationships as "friendships," and to others as "romances" or "marriages." We introduce someone as our "best friend," "brother-in-law," "wife," and so forth. These categorizations, although simple, help people understand the relationships we share. Within the broad category of romantic relationships, there are also many subtypes. Indeed, sometimes partners are unsure about which of these subtypes their relationships fall under, especially if their relationship is not "official." When partners are officially dating, other labels, such as "boyfriend," "girlfriend," and "significant other," come with the designation of being an official couple. But sometimes partners just "have a thing" or end up in an "almost relationship" where they repeatedly talk, flirt, and maybe even spend time together or have sexual activity, but never actually date.

When college students think about what constitutes a close relationship, they typically think about dating or romantic relationships. However, as the categories just listed suggest, we live in a network of relationships that includes family members, lovers, acquaintances, coworkers, employers, and so forth. We also have blended relationships, such as having a friend with benefits or a sibling who is also your best friend. Some relationships fit into neat categories such as boyfriend, coworker, wife, or student, but others fit into overlapping categories. As Wilmot (1995) put it, "Relational types are not necessarily mutually exclusive—their boundaries are often fuzzy" (p. 28). Moreover, relationships often move from one category to another, such as when a coworker becomes a friend, a friend becomes a dating partner, or a fraternity brother becomes an employee. In these "fuzzy" relationships, people can be uncertain about how to behave appropriately, especially if they use different relational definitions.

Another way to categorize relationships is based on how typical or mainstream they are. When most people think about a romantic relationship, they think of a man and a woman. When asked to imagine a pair of best friends, most people picture two men or two women as opposed to cross-sex friends. Even in an age where nontraditional families are increasingly common, most people envision the typical family as a mom and a dad with a couple of children. Yet romantic relationships, friendships, and families vary immensely, and diversity is increasing. Researchers have acknowledged this diversity by focusing on a variety of relationship types, including gay, lesbian, and bisexual relationships (Huston & Schwartz, 1995; Kurdek, 1991); polygamy (Altman & Ginat, 1996); cohabitation between unmarried individuals (Cunningham & Antill, 1995); single-parent families, stepfamilies, orphans, and interracial couples (Gaines, 1995; Williams & Andersen, 1998); cross-generational and Internet relationships (Lea & Spears, 1995); long-distance relationships (Rohlfing, 1995); and cross-sex friendships (see Chapter 10).

Despite advances, romantic relationship research on gay men and lesbians lags far behind research on heterosexual romantic relationships, although this gap is not as large as it once was. Peplau and Spalding (2000) reported that of 312 articles published in the *Journal of Social and Personal Relationships* from 1980 to 1993, only three examined any aspect of sexual orientation. Similarly, Wood and Duck (1995) noted that most research has focused on the relationships of young, white, middle-class heterosexuals. To determine if the situation has improved, we conducted a search of articles published in the *Journal of Social and Personal Relationships* and *Personal*

Relationships from 2000 to 2016, using the keywords *gay, lesbian, homosexual, bisexual, transgender, same-sex couple,* and *sexual orientation.* This search produced 43 articles that focused on these issues, which is a significant improvement compared to the 1980s and early 1990s. Nonetheless, these articles still represent a small portion of the research available on romantic relationships. Similarly, although research on intercultural and interracial relationships has increased as these relationships have become more common in the United States, it still lags behind research that focuses mainly on intracultural couples (Kline et al., 2012). As discussed in Box 1.3, people from different cultures may have varying opinions about what constitutes a good relationship. Thus, more research on intercultural couples would be helpful in understanding similarities and differences in relational communication.

In this book we make an effort to include research about various types of understudied relationships. However, because this book is based on existing research, the majority of the discussion necessarily revolves around heterosexual romantic relationships. We also discuss research related to friendships and family relationships, albeit less often, as well as information on cultural differences. So, as you read this book, keep in mind that so-called traditional models of relationships do not apply to all relationships. Nonetheless, many types of relationships have elements in common: connection and conflict, joy and grief, meetings and departures. Indeed, the more scholars study less-common relationships, the more they conclude that all relationships are patches in the same quilt.

Of course, there are important differences sprinkled in with the similarities. Relationships are as unique as the different combinations of patchwork that create a quilt, and individuals in certain types of relationships do encounter particular difficulties that can affect communication processes. For example, Huston and Schwartz (1995), in their research on gay men and lesbians, stated, "The relationships formed by lesbians and gay men are in many ways very similar to heterosexual ones; in

BOX 1.3 AROUND THE WORLD
CULTURE AND EXPECTATIONS ABOUT MARRIAGE

Given the increase in romantic intercultural relationships in the United States and Asia, Kline and her colleagues (2012) set out to determine if young adults from six countries—China, Japan, India, Malaysia, South Korea, and the United States—have different values and expectations about what characterizes "good" versus "bad" marriages.

Kline and colleagues (2012) looked at four concepts related to the qualities people value in relationships in various parts of the world. These concepts are (1) *traditional family–home focus*, where the wife is seen as the nurturer who takes care of the home and children, and the husband is seen as the provider and protector; (2) *mutual love and caring*, which involves being kind, loving one another, and being able to talk together; (3) *respectfulness and gentleness*, which represents a cultural stereotype that the "good wife" is modest, humble, considerate, and respectful to others as well as loyal and of good moral character; and (4) *disrespect and control*, which represents a conception of a "bad" husband or wife as someone who inhibits partner rights or is hurtful by being disrespectful, rude, possessive, or controlling. Kline and others also examined the extent to which young adults from different cultures valued positive relational communication, which included display-

ing trustworthiness, being supportive and understanding, and highlighting similarities showing compatibility.

Results revealed both similarities and differences in what young adults from various cultures value in their relationships. People from China, India, Korea, and the United States all endorsed mutual love and caring as well as positive relational communication as central to a good marriage. Young adults from China and Korea also believed that respectfulness and gentleness were important qualities of a good wife. The lack of a family home focus was more frequently seen as a sign of a bad relationship in China, Korea, and Japan than in the United States. Across all six cultures, disrespect and control was seen as a negative attribute of marriage.

This study shows that people from different cultures all value positive relational communication. However, compared to those from the United States, young adults from some Asian countries hold conceptions of marriage that are linked to more traditional values and religious beliefs. Intercultural couples who have different value systems need to be accepting of one another's beliefs so they can find ways to honor both individuals' cultural traditions while also coming together as a couple.

other ways distinct factors influence relationship formation and survival" (p. 120). Gay and lesbian couples, as well as interracial couples, often have to deal with societal prejudices and pressures with which opposite-sex and same-culture couples do not have to cope.

Characteristics Distinguishing Different Relationship Types

Relationships vary on many characteristics or dimensions. For example, some relationships are more satisfying or committed than others, and some families are traditional whereas others have more liberal values. When it comes to putting relationships into categories, such as friend, romantic partner, or family member, at least five characteristics are relevant: (1) how voluntary the relationship is,

(2) the degree to which people are genetically related, (3) whether the relationship is sexual or platonic, (4) whether the relationship is romantic, and (5) the sex or gender of the partners.

VOLUNTARY VERSUS INVOLUNTARY Relationships can be voluntary or involuntary. People make a conscious choice to be involved in some relationships, but they enter other relationships without volition. For instance, children cannot choose their family; rather, they are born or adopted into relationships with parents, siblings, aunts and uncles, grandparents, and other relatives. People also have little choice in choosing steprelations and in-laws; these relationships often emerge based on other people's choices (e.g., your father or brother gets married).

By contrast, people usually choose their friends. In most Western cultures, people also choose their romantic partners, whereas in some other cultures spouses are selected through arranged marriages, thus making them less voluntary. In many ways, voluntary and involuntary relationships develop differently. When developing friendships and other involuntary relationships, we often use communication to determine whether we want to be in the relationship in the first place. If the conversation flows, similarities are uncovered, and trust develops, then a friendship emerges. With family relationships, the relationship is there regardless of the type of communication we share, although communication will have an enormous impact on the quality of that relationship.

GENETICALLY RELATED VERSUS NONRELATED

The degree to which two people are genetically related also defines the type of relationship they share. Unless someone has an identical twin, people share the most genes (around 50%) with their biological parents and siblings; followed by their biological grandparents, aunts, uncles, nieces, and nephews (around 25%); and their biological first cousins (at around 12.5%). Some researchers have suggested that people communicate somewhat differently depending on how genetically related they are. For example, some studies have shown that people are more likely to give affectionate communication to relatives than nonrelatives, beyond what is predicted by relational closeness (Floyd, 2006; see also Chapter 7). To some extent, the degree of genetic relatedness is also associated with how voluntary or involuntary a relationship is. For instance, even if you do not get along with your cousin, your cousin is your cousin for life, making the relationship involuntary. Genetic relatedness also differentiates biological children from adopted children or stepchildren and helps researchers better understand the dynamics of blended families such as those that include stepsiblings.

SEXUAL VERSUS PLATONIC

Relationships are also characterized by their sexual versus platonic nature. Typically, friendships and relationships with non-spousal family members are platonic, which means they do not include sexual involvement. Dating and marital relationships, by contrast, are usually marked by sexual activity. Of course, friendships can also include sexual activity, as is the case with friends-with-benefits relationships, which are defined in terms of having repeated sexual interaction with someone who is considered a friend but not a romantic partner (Hughes, Morrison, & Asada, 2005). Sexual activity is an important component of many relationships, but it is helpful to remember that platonic relationships can be just as close and satisfying as sexual relationships. Indeed, many people rank their relationships with their children, parents, siblings, and best friends as especially close and satisfying (Argyle & Furnham, 1983).

ROMANTIC VERSUS NONROMANTIC

As the case of friends with benefits illustrates, there is an important distinction between having a sexual relationship and having a romantic relationship. Friends with benefits have sex but not romance. So what does it mean to be in a romantic relationship? Mongeau, Serewicz, Henningsen, and Davis (2006) noted that both romantic relationships and friendships can contain sexual activity and high levels of emotional involvement. The difference is in how the partners mutually define the relationship. Generally, romantic relationships are viewed as being a couple, which may include the possibility of marriage in the future (if they are not already married), as well as sexual exclusivity.

The distinction between emotional closeness and sexual intimacy is reflected in how various relationships develop. Guerrero and Mongeau (2008) suggested that there are three general trajectories or pathways toward developing a romantic relationship. The "traditional" trajectory is acquaintanceship to romantic relationship. Here, two people meet, are physically attracted to one another, start dating, form an emotional attachment, and become a romantic couple. In this case, the sexual and emotional aspects of the relationship tend to develop together. Other times, people follow a trajectory that moves from platonic relationship to romantic relationship. These individuals develop emotional closeness first as friends; later they add sexual intimacy, which often leads them to redefine their relationship as romantic. The third trajectory moves from being friends with benefits to having a romantic relationship. In this trajectory, sexual activity and emotional closeness are usually present in the friends-with-benefits relationship. Thus, these aspects of the relationship are not what changes when the relationship turns romantic. Instead, it is the definition of the relationship that changes. (Although this trajectory does occur, most friends-with-benefits relationships do not turn into romances.)

MALE VERSUS FEMALE OR MASCULINE VERSUS FEMININE Some scholars label sex or gender as a component that defines types of relationships (Wood, 1996). Sex refers to an individual's biological makeup as male or female, whereas gender refers to how masculine, feminine, or androgynous a person is; androgynous individuals possess both feminine and masculine traits (Bem, 1974). Sex is biologically determined, whereas gender is socially and culturally constructed. Sex helps define family relationships into categories such as father–son or father–daughter, or romantic relationships into categories such as lesbian, gay, or heterosexual. Most research on friendship makes these distinctions by comparing male friendships to female friendships, or same-sex friendships to cross-sex friendships (see Chapter 10). Other research focuses on gender by looking at how masculine, feminine, or androgynous individuals are. For example, a romantic couple consisting of a feminine person and a masculine person functions differently from a romantic couple consisting of two androgynous individuals. In this book, we use the term *sex* to refer to biology (male versus female) and the term *gender* to refer to culturally constructed images of men and women as being either masculine or feminine.

PRINCIPLES OF INTERPERSONAL COMMUNICATION

Now that we have defined various relationship types, we turn to a discussion of the kinds of communication that occur in those relationships. The terms *interpersonal communication* and *relational communication* describe the process whereby people exchange messages in different types of relationships. The goal of message exchange is to cocreate meaning, although—as we shall see shortly—not all message exchanges are effective and **miscommunication** occurs frequently. A broader concept than relational communication, interpersonal communication refers to the exchange of messages, verbal and nonverbal, between two people, regardless of the relationship they share. These people could be strangers, acquaintances, coworkers, political candidate and voter, teacher and student, superior and subordinate, friends, or lovers, to name just a few relationship types. Thus, interpersonal communication includes the exchange of messages in all sorts of relationships, ranging from functional to casual to close. Relational communication, by contrast, is narrower in that it typically focuses on messages exchanged in close, or potentially close, relationships, such as those between good friends, romantic partners, and family members. In this section, we focus on six specific principles related to interpersonal communication.

Verbal and Nonverbal Messages

The first principle is that *interpersonal communication consists of a variety of nonverbal and verbal messages that can be exchanged through different channels, including face-to-face and computer-mediated channels.* Although much of our communication consists of verbal messages, nonverbal communication is at least as important as verbal communication (Andersen, 2008). In fact, some studies suggest that 60% to 65% of the meaning in most interactions comes from nonverbal behavior. In addition, when emotional messages are exchanged, even more of the meaning may be gleaned from nonverbal behaviors (see Burgoon, Guerrero, & Floyd, 2010). Words are not always to be trusted. For example, someone can say "I love you" and not really mean it. But the person who spends time with you, gazes into your eyes, touches you lovingly, tunes into your moods, interprets your body language, synchronizes with your behavior, and uses a loving tone of voice sends a much stronger message. Nonverbal actions often do speak louder than words.

Nonverbal communication includes a wide variety of behaviors. In fact, nonverbal behavior is particularly powerful because people can send messages using numerous nonverbal behaviors all at once. For example, Kristi's lip might tremble while she wipes a tear from her cheek, gazes downward, slumps back in her chair, and lets out a sigh. These actions prompt Kristi's mom to reach over and hug her. Similarly, in the photo on this page, several nonverbal cues are being emitted simultaneously. Nonverbal behaviors such as these have been studied with the context of relationships and have been classified into the following categories (Burgoon et al., 2010):

- *Kinesics:* Facial expressions, body and eye movements, including posture, gestures, walking style, smiling, and pupil dilation, among other kinesic cues
- *Vocalics:* Silence and the way words are pronounced, including vocal pitch, loudness, accent, tone, and speed, as well as vocalizations such as crying and sighing
- *Proxemics:* The use of space, including conversational distances and territory
- *Haptics:* The use of touch, ranging from affectionate to violent touch
- *Appearance and adornment:* Physical attributes such as height, weight, and attractiveness, as well as adornments such as clothing, perfume, and tattoos
- *Artifacts and environmental cues:* Objects such as candles and soft music used to set a romantic mood, and ways the environment affects interaction through cues such as furniture arrangement and the size of a room
- *Chronemic cues:* The use of time, such as showing up for a date early or late or waiting a long or short time for someone

Which of these categories of nonverbal behavior are represented in the top photo? The kinesic and

Take a close look at the nonverbal cues in these photos. How do these cues influence your perception of this couple, including the emotions they are experiencing and the type of relationship they share? How is technology affecting their interaction in the second picture?

haptic cues should be easy to pick out. His hand is on her knee and around her back, so you may guess that they are emotionally close. She is closed off and her facial expression is hidden, but it is easy to imagine that she looks sad or upset given that her hands are over her face and he is comforting her. His facial expression is a bit difficult to read. He looks calm. Is there a hint of a smile? Is he trying to be empathetic or act concerned? Kinesic and haptic behavior are also evident in the bottom photo. The couple is in an intimate position. She is leaning against him and his leg is around her. Environmental cues and artifacts (such as the computer and phone) provide contextual information. It looks like they may be purchasing something online since he is holding a credit card and she has a computer on her lap. She looks caught up in her phone conversation, whereas he looks amused about something. There is also a pillow behind his back, which suggests that he may want to be comfortable while engaging in tasks. From these cues, one might guess these individuals are a young romantic couple (perhaps in their 20s), that they live together, and that they get along well and are quite comfortable with one another. This guess may be right or wrong—the point is that we infer a lot about people based on their nonverbal behavior.

Interpersonal communication also consists of many forms of verbal behavior, including verbal content and self-disclosure. Self-disclosure, a vital form of interpersonal communication, is used to reveal personal information to others (see Chapter 6). The use of formal or informal language, nicknames, and present or future tense are also examples of verbal behavior that affects interpersonal interactions. For example, when dating partners first talk about sharing a future, such communication is likely to reflect a shift toward a more committed relationship.

Finally, various channels are used to exchange interpersonal communication. Traditionally, research on interpersonal communication has focused on face-to-face interaction. But in the 21st century communication occurs in a variety of channels that utilize technology. Think of all the different ways you communicated with people yesterday. It is likely that you used your cell phone to call or text someone, visited your social media, sent and received e-mail, and used apps like Snapchat to keep in touch with others. As Spitzberg and Hoobler (2002) noted, "The digital and information revolution has merged into a communications revolution," which consists of new communication technologies such as the Internet, and advances in old technologies, such as phones and computers becoming wireless (p. 72). One implication of this revolution is that people are more accessible to one another. Another implication is that computer-mediated communication can easily be substituted for face-to-face and voice-to-voice communication. Box 1.4 highlights how important technology and computer-mediated communication are in everyday life.

Computer-mediated communication is different from face-to-face communication in some respects. When people communicate via e-mail and text messaging, for example, nonverbal cues are limited. People can insert emoticons like ☺, type in all caps, italicize certain words, and use initialisms such as lol (laugh out loud) to add a nonverbal component, but channels such as e-mail are primarily text based and therefore verbal. Computer-mediated channels also afford communicators more opportunity to control their messages. During face-to-face interaction, it may be difficult to control one's nonverbal reaction or to think of an intelligent-sounding answer to a question. In contrast, when sending a text or e-mail, a person's facial expressions are absent and there is more time to construct, edit, and revise a well-thought-out message. Other computer-mediated channels of communication, such as social networking sites, allow people to communicate in ways that they could not have prior to the digital revolution. For example, people can simultaneously send the same message to many different people using Twitter or e-mail, and they can meet and "chat" with strangers from across a large geographical distance using the Internet. Thus, technology has opened up new ways for people to relate to and interact with one another.

Smartphones and other technology change drastically from generation to generation. In the U.S., most teens (88%) have cell phones, with 73% of them smartphones (Lenhart, 2015a). About a third of teens also use messaging apps such as Kik or WhatsApp, with the average teen sending and receiving around 30 text messages per day (Lenhart, 2015a). U.S. college students involved in romantic relationships send their partners an average of six text messages a day and call them on their cell phones three to four times a day (Duran, Kelly, & Rotaru, 2011). Older adults tend to stick to text messages and just one social media platform (usually Facebook), whereas many younger adults and teens engage a variety of social media platforms on a frequent basis. Figure 1.1 provides data from 2014 and 2015 on the social media platforms that are most popular among teenagers. Each of

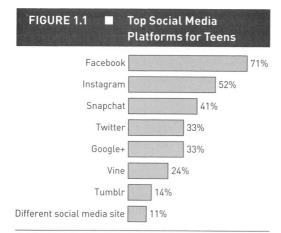

FIGURE 1.1 ■ Top Social Media Platforms for Teens

- Facebook — 71%
- Instagram — 52%
- Snapchat — 41%
- Twitter — 33%
- Google+ — 33%
- Vine — 24%
- Tumblr — 14%
- Different social media site — 11%

Source: "Teens, Social Media & Technology Overview 2015," Pew Research Center, Washington, DC (April 2015), http://www.pewinternet.org/2015/04/09/teens-social-media-technology-2015/pi_2015-04-09_teensandtech_01/.

these platforms has unique features that separate them from each other such that savvy communicators know how and when to use each of them.

For example, an effective communicator might snap a picture of an event to share with a friend but then later text to share details about the experience. Teenage girls are more likely than teenage boys to use Instagram and Snapchat, and the use of Twitter increases as teens get older (Lenhart, 2015a). Of course, the power of these social media platforms extends beyond the teenage world and beyond the United States, as shown in the statistics presented in Box 1.4.

Communication as Inevitable

The second principle is that *one cannot not communicate in face-to-face settings.* In one of the important early works on communication, Watzlawick, Beavin, and Jackson (1967) stated, "Activity or inactivity, words or silence, all have message value: they influence others and these others, in turn, cannot not respond to these communications and thus are themselves communicating" (p. 49). Unless two people simply do not notice each other, some

---

BOX 1.4 TECH TALK
COMMUNICATING TECHNO-STYLE

In today's world, face-to-face interaction is only one of many ways people communicate with one another. Here are some statistics and information about the four most popular social platforms that help illustrate just how prevalent computer-mediated communication is.

- Facebook was created in 2004. By 2016, Facebook had more than 1.3 billion daily users, with 84.5% of these users residing outside North America ("Company Info | Facebook"). The typical Facebook user averages about 20 minutes per day on the social networking site; approximately 66% of users log in at least once per day (Ellison, Steinfield, & Lampe, 2007). Canadian college students who use Facebook spend nearly 40 minutes a day on the social networking site (Christofides, Muise, & Desmarais, 2009).

- Instagram was launched in 2010. By 2016 it had more than 300 million daily users, with over 80% of those users residing outside the United States. More than 95 million photos and videos are posted on Instagram every day ("Instagram Press"). The average user has around 150 followers (Lenhart, 2015a).

- Snapchat became available in 2011 and by 2016 boasted 150 million daily users worldwide. Snapchat is the fastest-growing social media platform, and is especially popular with teens and young adults ("Snapchat Daily").

- Twitter become available in July 2006. More than 1.3 billion accounts have been opened, with about 44% of these accounts currently active (Smith, 2016). Many people browse Twitter for news. In fact, almost a quarter of active accounts on Twitter are owned by journalists, and 83% of world leaders have Twitter accounts. Only 550 million people have sent a tweet on Twitter, suggesting that many people browse the site without posting anything (Smith, 2016). However, Twitter is growing in popularity with teens and young adults (Lenhart, 2015a) who use the site to post pictures, retweet quotes and news, and send subtweets (e.g., messages that are ambiguous but understood by certain people, such as tweeting "I'm done" or "Couldn't be happier after yesterday").

communication is inevitable. Even if someone does not intend to send a message, something that person says or does is often interpreted as meaningful by the other person. This does not mean, however, that everything people do is communication. For communication to occur, a person has to send a message intentionally or a receiver has to perceive and assign meaning to a behavior. For example, if you are blinking while interacting, your friend is unlikely to attach any meaning to such an ordinary, involuntary behavior. Similarly, not all body movements are communication since many go unnoticed. But some movements you make and most words you say will be received and interpreted by others, making it impossible not to communicate at some level (Andersen, 1991).

To illustrate, recall the last time you sat next to a stranger—perhaps at the mall, at the movies, or on a bus. What did you notice about the person? Did you check to see if the person looked friendly or did you notice the stranger's appearance? Did the person look older or younger than you? If you can answer any of these questions, Andersen (1991) argued that communication took place because you perceived and interpreted the stranger's behavior. In our relationships, our partners interpret much of what we do as meaningful. For example, a smile might be perceived as heartfelt or condescending, while a neutral facial expression might be perceived as reflecting boredom or anger. Even silence can communicate a message. For instance, if a close friend stops calling you and fails to return your messages, you will likely suspect that something is wrong. You could attribute your friend's lack of communication to a variety of causes, including being ill, depressed, or mad. In any case, the way you interpret your friend's silence will probably lead you to communicate in particular ways that will further influence the exchange of messages between you and your friend.

Although this principle is most applicable to face-to-face situations, it can also apply to computer-mediated communication. People can choose not to respond to a stranger's post on a website or decide to passively read but not participate in a chat room discussion. In these cases, people are choosing not to communicate and others are unlikely to know it. However, when people delay answering a text message or stop posting on their Facebook timeline for an extended time, others are likely to interpret their inactivity as meaningful. A student once noted that her phone broke when she was in the process of moving. Her computer was packed up, so she wasn't able to access her Facebook or e-mail accounts either. After not hearing from her for about 48 hours, a group of friends came looking for her (first at her old place, then at her new place) to make sure that she was all right.

Interpersonal Communication Goals

The third principle is that *people use interpersonal communication to fulfill goals.* This does not mean that all communication is strategic. As discussed earlier, people often send spontaneous messages that are interpreted by others as meaningful. In addition, much of our communication is relatively mindless and routine (Burgoon & Langer, 1995; Langer, 1989). However, interpersonal communication likely developed as a way to help people meet their everyday goals. Communication helps people make good impressions, connect with others on a social level, and get things done. Even mundane communication, such as saying "hi" to acquaintances when passing by them on campus, fulfills goals related to being civil and polite. Although communication fulfills numerous specific goals, many of those goals fall under one of three overarching categories— **self-presentational, relational,** or **instrumental goals** (Canary & Cody, 1994).

SELF-PRESENTATIONAL GOALS relate to the image we convey. Andersen (2008) claimed that the most common objective of persuasion is selling ourselves. Other scholars contend that people resemble actors on a stage, presenting themselves in the most favorable light (see Chapter 2). Indeed, a central set of communication principles suggests we are only as attractive, credible, competent, or honest as others think we are. Objective personal qualities have little to do with our image, especially when we first meet people. From an interpersonal standpoint, we are what people think we are. Predictably, people spend a lot of time trying to look and act just right for that big date or that important interview. For example, before attending her first student club meeting, Su-Lin might purposely dress like a student from the United States so that she will fit in.

RELATIONAL GOALS have to do with how we communicate feelings about others, including the type of relationships we desire. Canary and Cody (1994) maintained that "nothing brings us more joy than our personal relationships. We spend significant amounts of time, energy and emotion in the pursuit of quality relationships" (p. 6). At every stage in a relationship, we have goals and plans for the future of that relationship. For example, you might want to meet that attractive student in your class, impress your date, avoid the person who won't leave you alone, or spend time with your sister whom you haven't seen all year. Canary and Cody (1994) described three primary sets of relational goals. The first set of goals is activity based and involves doing things with someone, such as attending a party or going skiing. The second is relationship based and involves wanting to initiate, escalate, maintain, or de-escalate a relationship. The third is advice based and involves giving advice to peers and parents.

INSTRUMENTAL GOALS are task oriented. For example, making money, getting good grades, buying a car, getting a ride to school, and completing a homework assignment are all instrumental goals. People often facilitate attainment of instrumental goals by asking for advice or assistance from a friend, getting permission from a parent or boss, eliciting support from a friend, or influencing someone's attitudes or behaviors (Canary & Cody,

1994). Achieving relational goals involves *giving* advice to others; achieving instrumental goals involves *seeking* advice and assistance to meet one's own task-related goals. Thus, in the scenario involving Kristi and her mother, Kristi may reach instrumental goals related to coping with a divorce by asking her mom for advice. Of course, having a goal and reaching a goal are two separate issues. Goals are most likely to be reached when communication is effective.

Effectiveness and Shared Meaning

The fourth principle is that *interpersonal communication varies in effectiveness, with the most effective messages leading to shared meaning between a sender and a receiver.* When one person sends an intentional message, understanding occurs when the receiver attaches approximately the same meaning to the message as did the sender. Of course, such perfectly effective communication may never occur since people typically attach somewhat different meanings to the same messages. It is impossible to get inside people's heads and to think their thoughts and feel their emotions. Thus, it is difficult to truly and completely understand "where someone is coming from." Nonetheless, communication is most effective when the sender and receiver attach very similar meanings to a behavior. Less-effective (or less-accurate) communication occurs when sender and receiver attach different meanings to a behavior.

Guerrero and Floyd (2006) provided a way to think about how different types of messages are more or less effective. In their model (see Figure 1.2), communication necessitates that a sender encodes a message or a receiver decodes a message. Therefore, behaviors falling in the box labeled **unattended behavior** do not qualify as communication. The exchanges in the other boxes are all relevant to interpersonal communication, but the most effective form of communication—**successful communication**—occurs when a sender's message is interpreted correctly by a receiver. For example,

Jake may ask Dave to stay home and help him with his statistics homework, and Dave may understand what Jake wants him to do.

Other exchanges are less effective. Miscommunication occurs when someone sends an intentional message that is misinterpreted by the receiver. For example, you might teasingly say "I hate you" to someone who takes your message literally. **Attempted communication** occurs when someone sends an intentional message that the receiver fails to receive. For example, you might hint that you want to leave a boring party, but your partner fails to get the message and keeps on partying. **Misinterpretation** occurs when someone unintentionally sends a message that is misconstrued by the receiver. You may be scowling because you are in a bad mood after a trying day at work, but your roommate misinterprets your facial expression as showing anger toward her or him. Finally, **accidental communication** occurs when someone does not mean to send a message, but the receiver observes the behavior and interprets it correctly. For example, you might try to hide your joy at acing an exam while a classmate who studied harder than you did poorly, but your classmate sees your nonverbal reaction and correctly assumes you did well. Although such communication is an authentic representation of your feelings, your emotional expression would be ineffective because it communicated a message you did not intend (or want) to send. All of these forms of communication can thus impact the communication process and people's relationships. Certainly,

effectiveness is important to high-quality communication, but it is not an attribute of all interpersonal communication.

Content Versus Relational Information

Another factor influencing whether communication is effective is the extent to which partners have the same relational interpretations of messages. This leads into a fifth principle of interpersonal communication, namely, that *every message contains both content and relational information.* Bateson (1951) observed that messages, whether verbal or nonverbal, send more than literal information: they also tell people something about their relationship: "Every courtesy term between persons, every inflection of the voice denoting respect or contempt, condescension or dependency, is a statement about the relationship between two persons" (p. 213). Building on Bateson's work, Watzlawick and colleagues (1967) discussed two levels of communication. The **content level** of a message conveys information at a literal level whereas the **relational level** provides a context for interpreting the message of a relationship. Both the type of relationship people share and the nonverbal behaviors people use influence the relational level of a message.

The content or literal level of the message, however, should be the same for most people within a given situation. For example, a simple statement, such as, "Hand me your book," contains both a content (namely, the request to hand over the book) and a relational message or messages. The relational

FIGURE 1.2	Types of Communication and Behavior		
	Behavior Not Interpreted	*Behavior Interpreted Inaccurately*	*Behavior Interpreted Accurately*
Behavior Sent With Intention	Attempted communication	Miscommunication	Successful communication
Behavior Sent Without Intention	Unattended behavior	Misinterpretation	Accidental communication

message depends on whether the request is delivered in a harsh, polite, sarcastic, bored, or warm vocal tone. It also depends on the communicator's facial expressions, posture, gestures, use of touch, attire, eye contact, and a host of other nonverbal behaviors. Finally, the context or situation can affect how the relational information in a message is interpreted. Thus, a message can have multiple meanings at the relational level.

Another example may be helpful. Suppose that late on Friday afternoon your romantic partner calls and asks, "So what are we doing tonight?" At the content level, this seems to be a fairly simple question. But at the relational level, this question could be interpreted a variety of ways. You might think, "It sure is nice to know that we always do something together on Friday nights even if we don't plan it in advance." Alternatively, you might think that your partner takes you for granted and assumes that you have nothing better to do than wait around for her or him to call before you make plans. Or if you had argued with your partner the day before, you might think that this is his or her way of making up. Yet another possibility is that you might think your partner always leaves it up to you to decide what to do. Based on which relational information you get from the message, you are likely to react in very different ways.

Symmetry in Communication

Finally, *interpersonal communication can be symmetrical or asymmetrical.* This sixth principle of communication, from Watzlawick and fellow researchers (1967), emphasizes the dyadic nature of communication. That is, communication unfolds through a series of messages and countermessages that contribute to the meaning people attach to a given interaction. Symmetrical communication occurs when people exchange similar relational information or similar messages. For instance, a dominant message may be met with another dominant message. (Jakc says, "Help me with my homework," and Dave responds, "Do it yourself!") Or an affectionate message may be met with another

affectionate message. (Kristi's mother says, "I love you," and Kristi says, "I love you too.") Nonverbal messages can also be symmetrical, as when someone smiles at you and you smile back, or when your date gazes at you lovingly and you touch her or him gently on the arm.

Asymmetrical communication occurs when people exchange different kinds of information. One type of asymmetry arises when people exchange messages that are opposite in meaning. For example, a dominant message such as, "I need you to help me with my homework now!" might be met with a submissive message such as, "Okay, I'll cancel my plans and help you." Or Kristi's declaration of love to her soon-to-be–ex-husband might be met with a guilt-ridden silence and shuffling of feet, after which he says something like, "I'm so sorry that I don't love you anymore." Another type of asymmetry occurs when one person uses more of a certain behavior than another person. For instance, imagine that Su-Lin is from an Asian culture where people generally touch less than do people from the United States. During a social gathering, a new friend of Su-Lin's might casually touch her arm five times, whereas Su-Lin might only initiate touch once. Although there is some symmetry because both Su-Lin and her new friend engage in some touch, the difference in the amount of touch each person initiates constitutes a source of asymmetry. As these examples suggest, the verbal and nonverbal messages that two people send and receive work together to create a unique pattern of communication that reflects their relationship.

PRINCIPLES OF RELATIONAL COMMUNICATION

As mentioned previously, relational communication is a subset of interpersonal communication that focuses on messages exchanged within relationships that are, were, or have the potential to become close. Thus, all of the principles of interpersonal communication apply to communication in relationships. Relational communication includes the entire range of communicative behaviors from vital relational messages to mundane everyday interactions. Relational communication reflects the nature of a relationship at a particular time. Communication constitutes and defines relationships. In other words, communication is the substance of close relationships. Communication is dynamic. Change and contradictions are constant in relationships. Five principles of relational communication are consistent with these ideas.

Relationships Emerge Across Ongoing Interactions

Relationships form not from thin air but across repeated interactions (Wilmot, 1995). Cappella (1988) argued, "Experience and common sense tell us that relationships are formed, maintained and dissolved in interactions with partners. At the same time interactions reflect the kind of relationship that exists between the partners" (p. 325). According to Wilmot (1995), "Relational definitions emerge from recurring episodic enactments" (p. 25). In part, relationships represent collections of all the communication episodes in which two partners have engaged over time, and each episode adds new information about the relationship. In new relationships, each episode may add considerably to the definition of the relationship. Even in well-developed relationships, critical turning points such as a declaration of love, a heated argument, or an anniversary can alter the course of the relationship. The bottom line is this: without communication, there is no relationship.

Relationships Contextualize Messages

In various relationships, messages have different meanings (Wilmot, 1995). For example, a frown from your partner has a different meaning than a frown from a stranger, a touch from your mom does not mean the same thing as a touch from your

date, and disclosure from a coworker communicates something different than disclosure from a good friend. In Wilmot's (1995) words, "Relationship definitions 'frame' or contextualize communication behavior" (p. 27). Thus, the context and relationship are critical to understanding the message. According to Andersen (1989), "It has become axiomatic that no human action can be successfully interpreted outside of its context. The term 'out of context' has become synonymous with meaningless or misleading" (p. 27). This principle reflects the idea that every message contains both a content and a relational meaning.

Communication Sends a Variety of Relational Messages

People send a variety of messages to one another about their relationships. After reviewing the literature from a range of disciplines, Burgoon and Hale (1984, 1987) outlined seven types of relational messages that people communicate to one another: (1) dominance/submission, (2) level of intimacy, (3) degree of similarity, (4) task–social orientation, (5) formality/informality, (6) degree of social composure, and (7) level of emotional arousal and activation. These messages, which have been referred to as the **fundamental relational themes** of communication, all reflect the nature of a relationship at a given point in time. Of these seven dimensions, dominance/submission and level of intimacy are the two main themes that characterize relationships (Burgoon & Hale, 1987). See Box 1.5 for further information on each of these seven themes.

The seven message themes are important within all types of interpersonal interaction but especially in close relationships. In role relationships, relational messages stay fairly constant; people generally follow prescribed rules and scripts. For instance, in manager–employee relationships, a certain level of formality, friendliness, dominance, and task orientation usually prevails across most interactions. By contrast, in close relationships the range and impact of relational messages typically is much greater. For example, a romantic couple might be hostile during an argument and then be intimate when making up, a parent might act with an unusual level of formality and dominance during a serious talk with a child, or friends might have a hard time switching gears and moving from a conversation to a task. Such messages can have a powerful impact on how relational partners view each other and their relationship.

Relational Communication Is Dynamic

Relationships constantly change, as does relational communication. Successful relational partners—whether they are family members, friends, or lovers—learn how to adjust their communication to meet the challenges and changes that they face. For example, a parent's communication style often becomes less authoritative as a child gets older, friends learn to interact with new people in each other's social networks, and spouses may need to find new ways to show affection to each other when they are preoccupied with their children and careers. Long-distance relationships provide a great example of the dynamic nature of relational communication. Partners in long-distance relationships sometimes idealize each other—in part because they are

---

BOX 1.5 HIGHLIGHTS
SEVEN FUNDAMENTAL THEMES OF RELATIONAL COMMUNICATION

1. *Dominance/submission:* Dominance is often defined as the actual degree to which a person influences someone and submission as the actual degree to which a person gives up influence and yields to the wishes of someone else. Dominance is communicated verbally and nonverbally in a variety of ways (see Chapter 12).

2. *Level of intimacy:* Intimacy is a multidimensional construct related to the degree to which people communicate affection, inclusion, trust, depth, and involvement. Intimacy is conveyed in a variety of ways, including through self-disclosure and nonverbal displays of affection and immediacy (see Chapters 6 and 7).

3. *Degree of similarity:* Similarity is achieved through a wide array of verbal cues, such as expressing similar opinions and values, agreeing with each other, reciprocating self-disclosure, and communicating empathy and understanding. Nonverbal cues such as adopting the same posture, laughing together, dressing alike, and picking up someone's accent also communicate similarity.

4. *Task–social orientations:* This message reflects how much people are focused on tasks versus having fun and socializing. People are generally rated as more task oriented when they seem sincere, reasonable, and more interested in completing the task at hand than participating in off-the-topic conversation.

5. *Formality/informality:* When an interaction is formal, people maintain their distance, and the overall tone of the interaction is serious. They are also more likely to feel and look nervous. By contrast, less distance and a more casual approach, including feeling and looking more relaxed, characterize informal interactions.

6. *Degree of social composure:* Social composure relates to the level of calmness and confidence people show in a given interaction. When people are socially composed, they appear sure of themselves. Social composure is conveyed through verbal cues such as making strong, convincing arguments and saying the appropriate words at the right time, as well as nonverbal behaviors such as direct eye contact and fluent speech.

7. *Level of emotional arousal and activation:* This message theme refers to the degree to which an interaction is emotionally charged. It addresses the types of emotion a person experiences and expresses, as well as how much arousal the person feels. Emotional states such as distress, anger, and sadness can sometimes impede communication, whereas emotions such as happiness, excitement, and interest can lead to more effective interpersonal communication.

always on their best behavior when they spend time together. When the relationship becomes proximal, however, their communication may not always be as positive, leading many couples to break up (Stafford & Merolla, 2007).

Dialectic theory also highlights the dynamic nature of relational communication by emphasizing contradictions in messages (see Chapter 5). For example, a person might say, "I can't wait to see you tomorrow night even though it's been good to be away from each other for a while." This seemingly contradictory message ("I want to be with you sometimes but not at other times") reflects the changing nature of the relationship. Therefore, rather than thinking of relationships as hitting a plateau or becoming completely stable, it is better to conceptualize stability as a relative concept. In other words, relationships can be committed and they can include a lot of routine communication, but they are still ever-changing entities.

Relational Communication Follows Both Linear and Nonlinear Patterns

Considerable research has examined how relationships develop over time. In fact, early research on interpersonal communication focused much more on how people begin and end relationships than on how they maintain relationships once they have developed. Some researchers believe that communication follows a linear trajectory (see Chapter 5 for more detail). This means that communication is characterized by increasing self-disclosure and nonverbal affection as a relationship gets closer. Think of this like a diagonal line going upward with the line representing the degree of closeness that is communicated as a relationship moves from being casual to close. If the relationship is ending, the linear approach would predict that there would be a similar line going downward, meaning that closeness is communicated less and less as the relationship de-escalates.

Other researchers believe that relational communication follows a nonlinear trajectory characterized by ups and downs and contradictions (see Figure 1.3 and the turning point approach discussed

in Chapter 5). For example, you might show increasing levels of affection to a new romantic partner until you get into your first big fight. When the fight is over, affection might increase again to a new and even higher level. And sometimes, your communication may be affectionate and distant at the same time, as would be the case if you say, "I like you a lot, but I need some time with my friends this weekend." These types of events would not coalesce to create a nice smooth linear pattern; instead, displays of closeness would spike upward and downward at different times depending on what was being communicated.

Most relationships include communication that reflects both linear and nonlinear patterns of development. Take Su-Lin as an example. Figure 1.3 depicts the trajectory that her relationship with a new roommate might take over the first 12 months of their emerging friendship. Notice that the relationship starts out rather low in terms of self-disclosure and affection but that this type of communication increases as they get to know one another, which is consistent with the linear approach. However, rather than consistently displaying more positive communication with each other, there are times when Su-Lin and her new roommate communicate relatively high and low levels of self-disclosure and affection. One relatively low point may occur during final exam week when they are both studying so hard that they don't talk as much to each other. A high point may occur when they have mutual friends over to their dorm room. Looking at the overall pattern of Su-Lin's relationship with her new roommate, it is clear that self-disclosure and affection have increased somewhat linearly, although there is also some nonlinearity (or up-and-down patterns) embedded within the trajectory.

Of course, relationships do not always follow the pattern depicted for Su-Lin and her roommate. Some relationships take more linear or nonlinear paths than others, but it is difficult to conceive of a relationship where all the progress is linear, or where the relationship is all peaks and valleys with no stability. Beyond self-disclosure and affection, other types of communication also follow patterns. Conflict behaviors, and any of the messages falling

FIGURE 1.3 ■ **Possible Trajectory of a New Relationship**

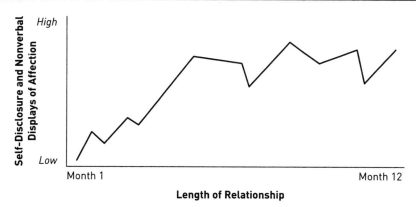

under the relational themes discussed previously (i.e., intimacy, formality, dominance, and so forth), can also be communicated in linear or nonlinear patterns during various points of a relationship's development. The point is that every relationship has a unique trajectory that reflects the dynamic nature of the communication that occurs between two people.

SUMMARY AND APPLICATION

This chapter introduced you to the field of personal relationships and provided information on key concepts that will be discussed throughout this book. After reading this chapter, you should have a better appreciation for the complexity of your relationships and the communication that occurs within them. Communication does not occur in a vacuum. Rather, communication is shaped by contextual and relational factors, and communication both reflects and influences the nature of a given relationship. In the scenarios that opened this chapter, Jake's communication with Dave reflects his expectation that a good friend should help him in a time of need. Su-Lin's communication is shaped by the context of being in a new cultural environment, and Kristi's communication is embedded within a social network that includes her husband and her family.

Communication is essential for accomplishing personal and relational goals, as well as for fulfilling the basic human needs of affection, inclusion, and control. Only through communication can Jake persuade Dave to help him, and only through communication can Dave give Jake the knowledge that he needs to do well on his statistics assignment. It is through communication that Su-Lin will learn about and adapt to the U.S. culture, and it is through communication that her new friends will learn more about her and her culture. The scenario involving Kristi also highlights how communication reflects people's goals and needs—Kristi's husband used communication to inform her that he wanted a divorce; in turn, Kristi searched for comfort by communicating with her mother. While the importance of communication in these scenarios and in everyday life may be obvious to you, it is amazing to think about how much we rely on communication every day in so many ways.

This book is designed to help you better understand how communication functions within your close relationships. We do not provide a blueprint or list of rules for how to communicate effectively in relationships. Instead, we summarize research related to significant relational communication topics in the hope that you will be able to apply the concepts and theories we discuss to your own life. As this chapter has shown, being able to communicate effectively is a key to good relationships, and having good relationships is a key to a happy life.

KEY TERMS

accidental communication (p. 18)

attempted communication (p. 18)

behavioral interdependence (p. 6)

close relationship (p. 6)

content level (p. 18)

emotional attachment (p. 7)

fundamental relational themes (p. 20)

instrumental goals (p. 16)

interpersonal communication (p. 2)

interpersonal relationship (p. 4)

irreplaceability (p. 7)

miscommunication (p. 12)

misinterpretation (p. 18)

mutual influence (p. 6)

need fulfillment (p. 7)

relational communication (p. 2)

relational goals (p. 16)

relational level (p. 18)

relationships (p. 1)

role relationship (p. 6)

self-presentational goals (p. 16)

successful communication (p. 17)

unattended behavior (p. 17)

unique interaction patterns (p. 7)

DISCUSSION QUESTIONS

1. What qualities distinguish your close relationships from your casual relationships?

2. In this chapter, we defined interpersonal communication as the exchange of nonverbal and verbal messages between two people, regardless of their relationship. Do you agree or disagree with this definition of interpersonal communication? What types of behavior should not count as communication?

3. As illustrated by the comparison of John Gottman and John Gray, there is a lot of popular press material on relationships that does not necessarily correspond with what academic researchers have found. Why do you think the public is so fascinated with popular books, talk shows, and magazine articles on relationships? What type of role, if any, do you think relationship researchers should play in this process?

 SAGE edge™

Sharpen your skills with SAGE edge at edge.sagepub.com/guerrero5e.
SAGE edge for students provides a personalized approach to help you accomplish your coursework goals in an easy-to-use learning environment.

2 COMMUNICATING IDENTITY
The Social Self

Emily has a page on Facebook with around 250 people on her friend list. Her favorite quotes are on her page with her personal motto, "carpe diem," featured prominently in her timeline. She posted some quotes in Italian since she is proud of her ethnic background and feels a connection to her relatives who live in Rome. Her page also indicates her current relationship status, which is updated continuously. During a tough stretch with her boyfriend, her status changed from "in a relationship," to "it's complicated" to "single," which caused nearly everyone she knows to "Facebook" her. Emily has posted over 300 pictures; most are of her partying with her friends and sorority sisters or performing in a local dance company. Some are from her trips to Italy. She also has a long history of messages on her timeline with some friends wishing her happy birthday, others making inside jokes, and others reminiscing about the previous night or just saying "hi."

What does Emily's Facebook page say about her? It lets people know if she is dating or not (though the information she posts may or may not be true), gives others a sense of how popular she is (from the number of "friends" on her list), gives strangers a glimpse of who she is, provides a peek into her personal and social life, and facilitates interaction with acquaintances and friends. Whether her **self-presentation** is effective depends on who views her page. Emily's page speaks to her friends in important ways; through her pictures and wall, she identifies herself as a good friend to certain people. Her page communicates to classmates and potential friends; her Facebook profile helps shape their impression of her before they really get to know her. But what if potential employers, professors, or her parents look at her page? Putting our identity out there for everyone to see raises questions about appropriateness, audience analysis, and privacy. Unlike everyday interactions, social networking sites such as Facebook, Instagram, and Twitter are less nimble in creating multiple identities.

The Internet is but one venue where people present and manage their identities. Identity management occurs in face-to-face interaction, in social networking, on the telephone, in text messages, and even in letters and gifts. Research most often focuses on face-to-face contexts that offer a glimpse into how people create and present their identities.

Identity management is chiefly important at the beginning of relationships when people try to make a good initial impression, but is even important in well-developed relationships.

In this chapter, we explore how people use communication to manage their identities in social interaction. First, we briefly discuss the development of personal identities and the role that relationships play in their development. Second, we discuss general principles of identity management, such as whether trying to make a good impression is deceptive and manipulative or is simply a natural, often unconscious process. Finally, we review literature on three perspectives on identity management, including Goffman's (1959) **dramaturgical perspective,** Brown and Levinson's (1987) **politeness theory,** and research on facework.

THE DEVELOPMENT OF PERSONAL IDENTITY

Communication scholars, sociologists, anthropologists, psychologists, and family researchers, among others, study how personal identities affect our lives. People are increasingly concerned about many aspects of their identity: popularity, education, relational partners, cars, resumes, homes, income, bodies, attractiveness, styles, sororities, occupations, health, mental well-being, and happiness. But identity is more than a personal experience: it is inherently social, communicative, and relational. Identity is inextricably interwoven with messages—verbal and nonverbal—we send about ourselves, and with how other people respond to those messages.

Defining Identity

We define **identity** as the person we think we are and communicate to others. Specifically, it is the personal "theory of self that is formed and maintained through actual or imagined interpersonal agreement about what self is like" (Schlenker, 1985,

p. 67). Identity is the sense of self or the "I" that has been a central topic in psychology and communication for years (Brown, 1965). Identity is the self, the face, the ego, and the image we present to others in everyday life. Identity is composed of self-esteem, continuity, distinctiveness, and meaning (Vignoles, Regalia, Manzi, Golledge, & Scabini, 2006).

Human Nature and Identity

Human beings are conscious creatures who reflect on who they are and how they fit into the greater social fabric. Indeed, a universal quality of all human beings regardless of culture is a sense of self as being distinct from others (Brown, 1991; Erikson, 1968). Thus, a sense of identity is a genetic legacy of our species that becomes increasing focused as we develop. Of course, our identities are largely shaped by culture and communication, but our essence as humans includes an individual identity.

Communication and Identity

In large part, our identity is formed in interactions with other people. No force is as powerful in shaping identity as the feedback we get and the self-image we form from observing ourselves behave and interact. Indeed, expressing an identity on a public posting, like Facebook or Instagram, has a stronger impact on our personal identity than sharing our identity with a single friend because of the broad audience we reach (Walther et al., 2011). In short, "A person's identity is forged, expressed, maintained, and modified in the crucible of social life, as its contents undergo the continual process of actual or imagined observation, judgment, and reaction by audiences (oneself and other)" (Schlenker, 1985, p. 68). For example, moral identity is created interactively, within the family that teaches the importance of decency, ethics, and honesty (Hardy & Carlo, 2011). Our identity is shaped in interactions with other people, the image we seek to project, our anticipated interactions, and the way they respond to and judge us.

Social identity theory explains how we develop and maintain our identity. Identity does not exist in a vacuum: it is linked to our membership in social groups as broad as our ethnic, sexual, or religious affiliation or as narrow as small cliques—for example, Italian American, bisexual, Catholic, alumnus of West High School, a resident of the Bronx, a softball player, and a member of "the big four" (a group of childhood friends). Based on Emily's Facebook page, for instance, you would probably associate her with at least two key groups—her sorority and her dance company. A key principle of social identity theory is that membership is characterized by in-group behaviors that signal membership and define someone as being a part of a group (Hogg & Abrams, 1988). Group members may dress a certain way, get similar tattoos, talk with an accent, use particular gestures, play the same sports, or have conversational routines that identify themselves as belonging to the group. To maintain positive views of ourselves, we often think of "our" groups as better than other groups who are considered outsiders. We often think that our way of doing things is superior, what we wear looks best, what we say is smartest, our view of the world is most reasonable, our perspective on a conflict is a sensible one, our values are moral and divine, and our beliefs are correct.

Several factors influence the impact a group has on our identity, including how central the group is to our self-view (Oakes, 1987). For example, an ethnic group association may be important for someone like Emily, who has visited relatives in Rome, but unimportant to those who have little connection to their ethnic roots. Several studies have also shown that minority groups are especially likely to identify with their ethnic backgrounds. African Americans or Latinos, for example, see ethnicity as more central to their identity than do Caucasians (Jackson, 1999). People in minority groups are typically more aware of their membership in that group than are majority members. Why is that? Everyday events remind them of their minority status. Think about how many black dolls you see advertised on television. Not many! Even in stores in African American neighborhoods most dolls are white, leaving little black girls to imagine that their dolls look like them.

Think about examples in your textbooks: How many describe the lives of gay, lesbian, or bisexual individuals? Not many. Despite our efforts to include all sexual orientations in this book, research on gay relationships is not abundant, so gay or lesbian students cannot always relate to our examples of heterosexual relationships. In these cases, group identity is more salient to minority group members because their lives are surrounded by reminders that they don't "fit" into the majority group's way of thinking or doing.

To clarify how identities are formed, Hecht (1993) introduced the **communication theory of identity**. He argued that identity construction can be viewed through four "frames of identity" or "lenses" (see also Hecht, Collier, & Ribeau, 1993; Hecht, Warren, Jung, & Krieger, 2004). First, identity is viewed through a **personal frame**. In this sense, identity is an image we construct within ourselves: We perceive ourselves to possess certain characteristics and not others. Second, identity can be viewed through an **enactment of communication frame**. Identities develop through communication; not all communication messages are designed to create our identity, but identity is a part of all messages. Third, identity can be seen through a **relationship frame** developed through interaction over time that defines us in terms of our relationships. Your identity is shaped by the kind of friend, romantic partner, and son or daughter you are. Moreover, you might act and feel differently about yourself depending on whether you are with your best friend, a first date, your spouse, or your parents. Finally, identity can be viewed through a **communal frame**. Identities are partly a function of the groups we belong to and are constrained by cultural group rules that teach us norms regarding the "right" way to behave. These rules become so ingrained that they affect our identities. "Indeed culture is so basic, learned at such a tender age, and so taken-for-granted that it is often confused with human nature itself" (Andersen, 2000, p. 258). See Box 2.1 for an example of how individualism, which is part of U.S. cultural identity, influences individual identity. Something as deep as ethnicity or culture cannot be easily manipulated. Research suggests that group identity is strongest under conditions of high uncertainty where communal identity serves as a guide to behavior (Grant & Hogg, 2012).

These four frames work together to affect identity development (Hecht, 1993). Recent research has discovered identity gaps both between conflicting frames of identity such as personal and relational frames (Jung & Hecht, 2004) and between different roles within a given frame, such as between a wife and a granddaughter (Kam & Hecht, 2009). All couples routinely deal with identity issues, but interracial or intercultural couples often face special challenges (Williams & Andersen, 1998): they must each deal with who they are as individuals—for example, as a white man and an African American woman (personal frame). They must also deal with how they present themselves to others (enactment frame), what it means to be an interracial couple (relationship frame), and how to best blend their different cultural backgrounds

(communal frame). Scholars are increasingly aware of these identity-related challenges in interracial or interethnic relationships. Studies have shown that the difficulties they face may include differences in language, conflict styles, communication preferences, and sexual scripts, as well as pressure from family and friends to dissolve the relationship (see Gaines & Liu, 2000; Williams & Andersen, 1998). In the past, most U.S. states banned interracial marriages, with Alabama most recently removing that law in 2000 (Hartill, 2001). As a result of ethnic norms and of the societal pressures confronting them, U.S. Census data show that interethnic couples in the United States are more likely than same-ethnicity couples to get divorced (Bramlett & Mosher, 2002). On the other hand, most research finds very few differences in the quality of inter- and intraracial couples, and emphasizes that the differences within an interracial couple, if managed, may help the bond grow between partners in such relationships (Troy, Lewis-Smith, & Laurenceau, 2006).

Cultural and Ethnic Identity

As the prior discussion indicates, culture and ethnicity are central to our core views of ourselves. Most people, but especially people from minority groups, have some sense of ethnic identity, seeing themselves as, for example, African Americans, Asian Americans, or Latin Americans. Some identities relate to a specific country such as Mexican Americans, Swedish Americans, Chinese Americans, Italian Americans, or Filipino Americans. Groups sometimes identify with the concept of race or color and describe themselves as black, brown, or white (Orbe & Drummond, 2009). "Whiteness," of course, does not literally exist and is a cultural construction of many groups who have tended to be more or less privileged in U.S. society (Lipsitz, 2006); it is also really only a function of how far one's ancestors lived away from the equator, because lighter skin was necessary in northern Europe for greater vitamin D absorption (Jablonsky & Chaplin, 2000). But since most voluntary immigrants to the United States during its first 200 years were "white," it became part of the identity of many people from North America and even a term used by the Census Bureau, despite the fact that most "white people" in the United States choose *American* as their primary identity (Orbe & Drummond, 2009). A more accurate term is *European American*, but most European Americans use the terms *white* or *Caucasian* if they have any racial identity at all (Martin, Krizek, Nakayama, & Bradford, 1996).

Terms are complex; there is almost always controversy over the correct term: *Hispanic* versus *Latina(o)* versus *Latin American*; or *black* versus *Afro-American* versus *African American* (Orbe & Drummond, 2009). The safest and most sensitive move in communication is to use the term that people themselves use in establishing their identity. As the United States has become more diverse, people increasingly have become multicultural and identify with two or more groups. Even the U.S. Census Bureau has begun to permit designation of multiple racial categories on the census form.

Recently, an increasing number of European and American young people with unclear identities have become jihadist terrorists or have identified with and volunteered with ISIS. Research shows that young adults with an unclear identity and weak interpersonal relationships are vulnerable and most likely to become jihadists (Meeus, 2015). Not surprisingly, having a core identity and close relationship is protective against conversion to radical religious cults and terrorist groups.

The Image: Creating an Identity

We are known by our image. Few people know the real us, but they know us by the image we project. Few of us get to peek behind the curtain and learn if other people's image is the real deal. From a communication perspective, images constitute reality, a concept not lost on advertisers, sports figures, celebrities, and even the general public. Today many people employ makeup, nose jobs, boob jobs, or other plastic surgery; workouts; cars; and homes to enhance their physical image. And, in our busy and web-based world, we often do not get to learn much more about people than what they look like, what they wear, and what they drive.

Sports figures such as tennis star Serena Williams, golfer Phil Mickelson, gymnast Simone Biles, and forward LeBron James have become idols who exceed their prodigious athletic accomplishments. They have turned themselves into icons that transcend reality. Their pictures are on television, magazines, in airports, and on the Internet. They rise above their human status into symbols of success and credibility as long as they can avoid scandal, slumps, or debilitating injuries that shatter the facade they and their agents have created. Our political leaders are no different. Andersen (2004) stated the following:

> Neither President Bill Clinton nor President George Bush ever saw military combat, but as commanders in chief they frequently appeared with troops in flight jackets and military uniforms. An image of a president supporting the

troops, saluting the flag, or dressed in a military uniform communicates patriotism and exudes leadership. (pp. 255–256)

These images trigger involuntary reactions in people, often called *heuristics* or what Cialdini (1984) calls our "heart of hearts," automatic processes that circumvent criticism and analysis.

"Talkin' 'Bout Your Generation": Millennials and Generation Z-ers' Identity

There have always been shifts in communication patterns based on generation. For example, the baby boomer generation (people born in the late 1940s through the early 1960s) communicated more openly about feelings and sex than did any generation before them. Recent generations, specifically, millennials and those in generation Z, differ from past generations in terms of their technology use. **Millennials**, who were born between 1980 and around 1995, grew up at a time when the use of computer-mediated communication (e.g., e-mail, the Internet, cell phones, and eventually social networking sites) was expanding rapidly. **Generation Z**, which includes those born between 1996 and 2010, grew up immersed in these forms of communication, often carrying cell phones in grade school and having multiple social media accounts by middle school and high school (Williams, 2015b). Instagram and Snapchat are viewed by generation Z as ways to maintain both image and relationships. Williams (2015b) distinguished these two generations this way: "Millennials were digital; their teenage years were defined by iPods and MySpace. But Generation Z is the first generation to be raised in the era of smartphones. Many do not remember a time before social media." Millennials grew up adapting to changing technology; generation Z, on the other hand, are digital natives who navigate their smartphones with great speed and ease. For example, Emily's younger sister, Bella, who is a freshman in college (and a generation Z-er) frequently has several applications open on her phone, and is checking Instagram and stories on Snapchat between texting

turns or sending and receiving snaps. Although Emily, who is a millennial, is tech savvy, Bella is even more proficient in her media use.

Millennials are very comfortable with texting, "Facebooking," "YouTubing," and tweeting, and think of e-mail as old fashioned. More than 80% of millennials text (dangerously, two thirds do so while driving), over 75% of millennials are on Facebook, and each person has typically "friended" hundreds of people (Taylor & Keeter, 2010). Across the world, millennials spend an average of 7 hours online every day, using phones, tablets, or computers (Telephonica Global Millennial Survey, 2014). As a result, social networking and building interpersonal networks are second nature to millennials. As a group, millennials are also more socially confident than their parents' generation, which, when taken to an extreme makes them more self-absorbed, entitled, and narcissistic than any generation before them (Taylor & Keeter, 2010; Twenge, 2006; Twenge & Campbell, 2009).

Millennials are racially diverse compared to previous generations and are more likely to have interracial relationships, including interracial romantic relationships (Keeter & Taylor, 2009; Taylor & Keeter, 2010). They also report less "work ethic" than prior generations and put marriage and having children ahead of their careers, yet they are less likely to be married at an early age than any prior generation (Taylor & Keeter, 2010). Research shows that when millennials view news articles about their generation, they are most likely to selectively read and remember positive items from the news. However, when baby boomers read these same stories about millennials, they are likely to select and remember negative news; negative news about millennials boosted boomers' self-esteem (Knobloch-Westerwick & Hastall, 2010). This suggests that our identity provides us with a biased lens with which to view the identity of our own and other generations.

Research suggests that millennials have created their own identities and rules for how their identities are displayed (Kelsey, 2007; Taylor & Keeter, 2010;

Telephonica Global Millennial Survey, 2014). These rules about image include the following ideas:

- *Image Is Indispensable*. Your public persona is where it's at. An identity as an attractive, sexy, successful, popular person is a basic social need. A person is a brand. This brand is portrayed on one's social media.

- *Entertainment Rules!* Life is about partying, video games, and social networking.

- *Success Is About Consumption*. A measure of success for all people from the United States, particularly millennials, is about material success including clothes, cars, residences, vacations, and toys.

- *Change Is Essential*. Millennials embrace change and have a distain for old, outdated ways of doing things. And millennials throughout the world believe that they can make a difference.

- *Mediated Presence Is Essential*. Being friended on Facebook, being seen even briefly on television, or being featured on YouTube is the path to a popular, positive identity.

- *Everyone Is Present*. Millennials almost continuously text, check mail, and talk on smartphones. A walk through any college campus will show almost a majority of students using an electronic device.

- *No Gatekeepers*. Millennials want to select their own media and create their own messages. In the world of the blogosphere and YouTube, students want to select from a variety of media, not from traditional channels with gatekeepers like television and newspapers.

- *Privacy Is Uncool if Not Impossible*. Millennials believe that in an electronic society with social media, ubiquitous surveillance cameras, video smartphones, and YouTube, privacy may actually be impossible. For millennials, the need to present a desirable personal identity to others and the convenience of social media for maintaining friendships and sharing information trumps concerns about privacy (Krasnova, Spiekermann, Koroleva, & Hildebrand, 2010; Kuss & Griffiths, 2011; Quinn, 2016).

- *Jobs Need to Make a Difference*. Millennials need exciting work that makes a difference in the world. Most millennials would take a pay cut for an interesting, self-directed, and socially responsible job.

Research on generation Z is newer, but there are some important differences between millennials and generation Z-ers (Renfro, 2012; Williams, 2015a, 2015b). This generation has lived under the threat of terrorism all or most of their lives, their early images of people in power include an African American president, and they grew up with gay marriage legal in many states. They are therefore more cautious than millennials in some respects, and have fewer prejudices based on ethnic or cultural background, or on sexual orientation.

In terms of communication, one difference between millennials and generation Z-ers is a renewed concern for privacy (Williams, 2015b). Generation Z has had to contend with the unintended consequences of social media use from an early age. For example, a group of girls were expelled from their high school when a photo of them wearing black t-shirts spelling ni**er went viral (Blakinger, 2016), causing national outrage on social media. This incident also created an identity issue for the school, with students trying to repair the school's image by posting statements saying that these girls did not represent them or the rest of the student body. Incidents such as this have taught generation Z that anything posted on social media can go viral, hurt their reputations, and stay visible for future college admissions or prospective employers to see. This realization has taught generation Z to be selective in what and where they post things (Williams, 2015b). Thus, many generation Z-ers shy away from posting certain information on social media sites such as

Facebook, and instead prefer snapping (which disappears eventually) or using subtweets (ambiguous messages that only certain people will understand) to protect their privacy. Unlike millennials who tend to think that privacy is unattainable, generation Z-ers believe that it is possible, at least to some extent, to protect their privacy.

Generation Z-ers are also very individualistic and less tied to gender roles than any other generation (Williams, 2015a). They tend to have the attitude that people should be who they are and do whatever makes them happy as long as they are not hurting other people. The images that this generation post on Instagram, Twitter, and other social media sites often reflects this individualism, especially for young women and teenage girls who post selfies as a way to express their personalities and cultivate an online identity. Observations about generation Z (e.g., Renfro, 2012; Williams, 2015a, 2015b) also reveal the following characteristics specific to that generation, and, to a lesser extent, about millennials:

- **Social Networks Display Popularity and Extend Beyond One's Social Network.** People are connected globally through social networks. Pictures posted on Instagram or Twitter, for example, can be seen by people from other schools, states, or countries, creating a lasting impression. In high schools, people can become "social media stars" who amass hundreds of likes on their Instagram and Twitter photos, with others wanting to post pictures with them on social media and on their Snapchat stories.

- **Communication Through Technology Is Seamless.** As Renfro (2012) puts it, today's youth are connected to a seamless, cloud-based world of friends, data, and entertainment, mainly through their smartphones. This seamlessness leads generation Z to be flexible and good at multitasking, as well as able to process information quickly. Slower forms of communication, such as e-mail, are rarely used. Generations Z-ers lose interest quickly when information is slow or inaccessible.

- **Visual Communication Is Valued.** Just as they rarely use e-mail, generation Z-ers rarely pick up a phone to talk voice to voice. Instead, Facetime is preferred for a fast-paced conversation. Texting typically allows more in-depth conversation than snapping, but even texting is usually supplemented by emojis that add a visual element to the communication. Some media platforms, such as Instagram, are heavily visual.

- **Instant, Frequent Contact Is Valued.** Social media make interaction with friends just a click away and give users the ability to efficiently maintain, update, and communicate with a large number of friends and acquaintances with whom it would be impossible to communicate in face-to-face settings. Teens value things like "Snapchat streaks" that show they have been consistently in touch with someone (even though the contact may not be in depth). Snapchat stories allow people to see what others are doing at a given moment without being there. Friends can "see" each other every day through social media with little effort.

- **Crowdsourcing Is Used to Elicit Opinions.** Crowdsourcing for generation Z goes beyond going on social media and asking for recommendations for goods or services (e.g., "My car is leaking oil. Anyone know a good mechanic?"). This generation uses social media to get opinions on a variety of things, including whether they should cut their hair or what classes to take. For example, people can post "polls" on Twitter asking people to "vote" on almost anything. Seeing how many favorites or likes a Tweet or Instagram picture receive, respectively, is another way to determine what one's social network prefers and approves of.

- ***People Are Emotionally Attached to Their Social Media.*** Perhaps the worst punishment for a teenager (and especially for a teenage girl) is to take away her cell phone. Renfro (2012) noted that generation Z-ers are emotionally attached to their phones and their social media more than any other generation before them, and that Internet addiction is now classified as a legitimate mental disorder.

Regardless of which generation a person is from, research suggests that, since the mid-20th century, people of all generations have become increasingly preoccupied with their identities. In fact, in the 1960s and 1970s people in the United States became so preoccupied with image and artifice that Herzog (1973) wrote *The B.S. Factor: The Theory and Technique of Faking It in America*, and so self-absorbed that Lasch (1979) wrote *The Culture of Narcissism: American Life in an Age of Diminishing Expectations*. Both books were echoed a dozen years later in a series of Canon EOS Rebel camera commercials themed "Image is everything," displaying Andre Agassi's buff body and long hair. Subsequently, Agassi (2009) revealed that his hair was indeed all image; he was going bald, and his long hair was a wig. The popular culture had thus discovered what communication researchers already knew: *Perceptions are reality.* If you can manipulate other people's perceptions, you can appear to be credible, cool, attractive, rich, whatever—even if you're not.

Social Networking and Identity

Social networking is increasing among all generations, but millennials and generation Z-ers are most likely to use social network sites, especially Facebook, Instagram, LinkedIn, and Snapchat (Duggan, Ellison, Lampe, Lenhart, & Madden, 2015; Ledbetter et al., 2011; Taylor & Keeter, 2010). Although social networking sites are used principally to maintain social networks, they are employed differently by extroverts and introverts (Kuss & Griffiths, 2011). Extroverts use social networking for social enhancement, to improve their

images, and to enhance their face-to-face relationships. Introverts, on the other hand, use social networking as social compensation, to make up for what they lack in face-to-face interaction. However, research indicates that social networking is a complement to face-to-face interaction for most people rather than a substitute for face-to-face communication, even though some social networkers (such as introverts) do substitute social networking for face-to-face interaction (Kujath, 2011).

Aside from the differences between introverts and extroverts, research suggests that there are three different types of social networking site users: (1) broadcasters, (2) interactors, and (3) spies (Underwood, Kerlin, & Farrington-Flint, 2011). While people can fall into any or all of these roles at a given time, most people primarily use social networking for one of these purposes. **Broadcasters** use social networking sites primarily to send one-to-many messages, much like radio or television broadcasters, but interact infrequently on their sites. For example, they might post photos of a life event or let people know where they are and what they are doing. Users of Twitter commonly fit the profile of broadcasters because they have an asymmetric relationship with followers who some have characterized as a community (Takhteyev, Gruzd, & Wellman, 2012). Communicating one's identity is a major focus for broadcasters. **Interactors** primarily use social networking sites to interact and connect with friends and acquaintances on a reciprocal basis and to establish close relationships with friends (Subrahmanyam & Greenfield, 2008; Underwood et. al., 2011). For example, they are likely to message their friends on Facebook and use social networking sites to issue invitations. Interactors also use social networking as a mechanism for making new friends and becoming better acquainted in addition to increasing intimacy with close friends (Hsu, Wang, & Tai, 2011; Raacke & Bonds-Raacke, 2008). Recent research suggests that dating relationships become stronger, more satisfying, and more invested, and last longer when a person publicly indicates he or she is "Facebook official" and in a relationship, post pictures of the partner, and post on the partner's wall (Lane, Piercy, & Carr, 2016; Toma & Choi, 2015). Developing and maintaining relationships is a major focus for interactors online or in face-to-face communication.

Finally, **spies** use sites such as Facebook as identity surveillance (Tokunaga, 2011b). For example, romantic partners might check each other's Facebook pages to monitor their activities with potential rivals. People also use social networking sites to verify information, such as making sure that someone's online profile matches how a person has presented her- or himself. Spying on another's social networking site has benign uses related to uncertainty reduction (see Chapter 4) and the acquaintance process. But it also has a dark side: spying online can constitute cyberstalking (see Chapter 13) and has been used by sex offenders in attempting to create online liaisons with their victims (Dowdell, Burgess, & Flores, 2011).

The dark side of social networking sites can also be more subtle. Facebook and Snapchat perfectly match the needs of millennials and generation Z-ers by working as a feedback loop to create connection and to satisfy narcissistic qualities. Although interaction on social media is beneficial—linking up friends, staying in touch, posting photos—the dark side is the excessive attention seeking, including the use of profanity, nudity, manipulated images; building large friends' collections to boost egos; and the endless seeking of popularity. Research suggests that Facebook promotes mental health by establishing connections among friends, but that it can promote depression when people use it to make evaluative social comparisons with others (Steers, 2016). Studies have compared frequent uses of social media and video games with infrequent users. Frequent users are more likely to have low social community participation, low academic achievement, attention-deficit disorder, depression, substance abuse, poor impulse control, and relationship problems (Andreassen et al., 2016; Kuss & Griffiths, 2011; Tokunaga & Rains, 2016), indicative of addiction to social media. Indeed, engaging in social media during college classes is very common and is associated with the need for relational maintenance, the alleviation of loneliness, and perceived low teacher competence (Ledbetter & Finn, 2016). "Friending" is a crucial part of Facebooking and creates connection, but it can create disconnection when people are "defriended." Research shows that the number of friends creates more social capital and social resources but only up to a point (Ellison et al., 2011); too many friends may make a person seem shallow. See Box 2.2 for more on how the

BOX 2.2 TECH TALK
SIZE MATTERS: IDENTITY AND MEGA-FRIENDING ON FACEBOOK

For many young people, the number of friends they have on a Facebook site is critical to their identity. Research shows that having a large number of friends on Facebook is proportional to a person's happiness, subjective well-being, and positive identity (Kim & Lee, 2011). Moreover, positive self-presentations on your site also lead to more happiness and a positive identity. Mega-friending seems to be of most benefit to people who are low in self-esteem and who recruit numerous friends to compensate for their low self-esteem (Lee, Moore, Park, & Park, 2012). This strategy actually seems to work in bolstering people with low self-esteem.

Similarly, research shows that need-for-popularity, personal vanity, and narcissism are associated with greater Facebook use, recruiting more friends, and increased grooming activity to enhance one's online identity (Utz, Tanis, & Vermeulen, 2012). More narcissistic individuals use Facebook to recruit as many friends as possible, wanting friends to know what they're doing, and having a positive identity on their site (Bergman, Fearrington, Davenport, & Bergman, 2011). Apparently having a lot of friends and looking good on Facebook is today's equivalent of new, fashionable clothes or a hot car!

quantity of Facebook friends is related to both positive and negative personal attributes.

Social networking can cause other problems as well. Among the most common negative events are denying or ignoring a friend request, deletion of a public message, low ranking or no ranking among a person's top friends, disparaging remarks on a person's site, a posted question that is ignored, gossip appearing on a third party's message board, restricted access to a friend's page, and defriending a former friend (Tokunaga, 2011a). These events can certainly strain a relationship or even lead to or mark its termination.

An even bigger problem is the use of social networking sites by sex offenders, who often disguise their "true" identity online and pose as someone else. For example, one of our daughters and her friends "liked" a post by "Winnie the Pooh" that was circulating on Facebook. "Winnie the Pooh" then posted another message saying, "No one wants to play with me and Piglet. Will you play with us?" Some users posted messages saying "yes" and then "Winnie the Pooh" went on their pages and asked them to friend him on his "other" Facebook page. Luckily, the girls were suspicious and "de-liked" him. Who "Winnie the Pooh" really was, and if he (or she) was truly a danger, was never determined, but this example illustrates how easily someone can change her or his identity on social networking sites. Research provides some guidelines for how to recognize possible sexual offenders. In addition to posing as people (or characters) that they are not, sex offenders are often impatient and initiate sexual conversation during their first interaction (Dowdell et al., 2011). They may also use ruses, such as inviting potential victims to nonexistent parties or pretending to provide them with job opportunities, as a way to try to meet (and potentially harm) them in person.

Research also suggests that social networking sites generally bring together people who are similar rather than broadening the diversity of one's social network. The "audience" of Twitter microbloggers are mainly from the same community or travel to the same destinations, suggesting they may constitute an actual as well as a virtual community (Gruzd, Wellman, & Takhteyev, 2011). Indeed, research shows that social networkers are typically composed of people who are similar in terms of ethnicity, religion, politics, age, country of origin, attitude toward children, and sexual orientation, even though people are just as likely to communicate with someone of the opposite sex as the same sex on social networking sites (Thelwall, 2009). In short, social networking is a medium that people generally use to communicate with individuals who are, in most respects, just like them.

Identity, Perception, and Self-Esteem

Our identities help us understand ourselves in relation to the world in which we live. Self-esteem and identity are part of a person's **theory of self** or **vision of self.** Self-esteem refers to how positively or negatively we view ourselves. People with high self-esteem tend to view their traits and behaviors in a positive light, while people with low self-esteem mostly see their traits as negative. Identity defines who we are (see Schlenker, 1985; Vignoles et al., 2006) by specifying the characteristics that define us (African American, student, smart, heterosexual, attractive, introvert) and comparing ourselves to others (smarter than John, not as smart as Haley). Self-esteem is to a large degree a function of the degree to which a person can control one's own life, doing one's duty, benefitting others, and achieving high social status (Becker et al., 2014). Unlike self-esteem, however, one's identity is not only evaluative: it is also a perception of oneself as a person. For example, both Emily and her friend Lindsay may see themselves as partiers who like to have fun. However, Emily may think that partying is a cool aspect of her personality, whereas Lindsay may be depressed because she realizes that partying is interfering with her success in school yet she can't seem to stop going out every night. Thus, while partying is a part of each of their identities, it could contribute to high self-esteem for Emily and to low self-esteem for Lindsay. The focus of this chapter is on identity and identity management rather than on self-esteem, despite their influences on one another.

Expanding Identity

One theory in particular is especially well suited to explain the benefits of relationships. Specifically, A. Aron and E. N. Aron's (1986, 1996) **self-expansion theory** helps explain how identity influences the development of close relationships after first impressions are made. Self-expansion theory is framed around three primary predictions. First, people seek to expand the self, to be more than they are. Studies completed by E. N. Aron and A. Aron (1996) have shown that a fundamental human desire is to broaden our experiences and extend our identities. We do not seem satisfied with a static sense of self. Instead, we seek to develop our sense of self as part of our physical, cognitive, and emotional development. For example, if you are good at oil painting, you might try other kinds of art, such as ceramics or watercolors. If you like reading or television, you may search for new types of books or shows you have not seen previously.

Second, one reason people enter into relationships is the opportunity to expand their identities. An excellent way to expand the self is by becoming close to someone who contributes to our identity development by exposing us to new experiences.

Aron, Aron, and Smollan (1992) found that the more partners defined their relationship as a meshing of both identities, the closer they were likely to be. Figure 2.1 shows the inclusion-of-others-in-self scale that these authors have used in their studies. Research consistently finds that an expansion of self through inclusion of others characterizes close relationships. In a recent study where couples were randomly called over a week's time, the more activating and expanding a couple's activities were at the time of the call, the greater the relational satisfaction and quality (Graham, 2008), suggesting that the effects of self-expansion are continuously being experienced. Finally, relationship interventions designed to mindfully seek new and exciting possibilities with one's partner can dramatically improve relationships (Carson, Carson, Gil, & Baucom, 2007).

Rather than having two completely separate identities, people in close relationships tend to merge identities, allowing each partner's identity to expand through new experiences. In a test of this prediction, Aron, Paris, and Aron (1995) over a 10-week period asked students to list as many self-descriptive words or phrases in response to the question, "Who are you today?" and whether they had fallen in love during the task. Consistent with the theory's prediction, those who fell in love showed a marked increase in the number of self-definitions they listed,

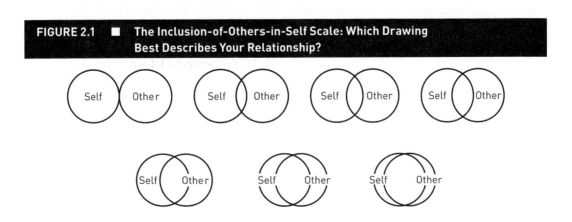

FIGURE 2.1 ■ **The Inclusion-of-Others-in-Self Scale: Which Drawing Best Describes Your Relationship?**

an indication that their identity had expanded. Likewise, consistent with the theory, a breakup of a self-expansive relationship led to a significant contraction of one's working self-concept and a detrimental impact to one's own identity (Lewandowski, Aron, Bassis, & Kunak, 2006). Recent research suggests that falling in love may actually be an instance of the motivation for self-expansion (Aron & Aron, 2016; Lamy, 2016; also see Chapter 8).

Self-expansion theory does not suggest that in strong relationships partners are completely intertwined. The theory emphasizes the importance of self in relationships. Losing one's sense of self or one's individual identity in favor of a relational identity is not what the theory would predict as a "healthy" relationship outcome. Instead, the theory predicts that close relationships are those in which both individuals have strong self-identities that can grow from the new experiences that each partner's identity brings.

A relationship's success depends on the ability of the relationship to expand the partners' experiences and sense of self. A common phenomenon in many relationships is stagnation; that is, over time, the relationship gets bogged down by routine, decreasing satisfaction for both partners. Self-expansion theory offers an interesting explanation and remedy for this common problem. Specifically, A. Aron and E. N. Aron (1986, 1996) argued that relationships stagnate when they stop creating self-expansion. The remedy for stagnation is for partners to help one another find new and exciting experiences that can be incorporated in their identity. Research suggests that infidelity is often associated with insufficient self-expansion with one's primary partner, so need-fulfillment and self-expansion are pursued in an alternative relationship (Lewandowski & Ackerman, 2006). Self-expansion theory also has helped us understand people's connections to their communities, neighborhoods, and social networks (Mashek, Cannady, & Tangney, 2007). This theory, to our knowledge, has not been applied to interracial relationships, though its premises seem especially well suited for the identity-expansion opportunities found there.

Of course, ethnicity is but one aspect of identity that challenges relational partners. Sexual identities hold an important position in individuals' sense of self in relationships. These expressions, including how we initiate relationships with prospective partners, whether we hold hands in public, or if we are comfortable with intimate displays of public affection, are public messages about our relational identity. Such displays are more benign for heterosexual couples since that sexual orientation is more normative. The decisions to initiate a relationship, hold hands, or display public intimacy are far more significant identity issues for gay or lesbian couples. Research suggests that many gay, lesbian, and transgendered people must closet their real identities because of fears of rejection, violence, and misunderstanding, particularly when those real identities conflict with their religious background (Faulkner & Hecht, 2011), though others were able to integrate and reveal their real identities. For most individuals with these identity gaps, except for the most secure, feelings of separation, fear, and alienation were often present. Steinbugler (2005) examined the double trouble of identity in interracial, gay, and lesbian couples. One of her participants (a 28-year-old black, gay, male dating a white, gay, male) reflected on the couple's behavior this way:

> We have a lot of PDA [public displays of affection] but not overt, not loud PDA. It's very quiet. For example, . . . we'll walk and one of us will rub the other on the back. Or if we hold hands it's sort of brief, very brief. (p. 435)

He also noted that he felt more comfortable with these expressions when he knows "for a fact that there are other gay people around" (p. 245). The struggle for ethnic minorities, gay and lesbian people, and other people who are minorities in intolerant societies highlights the struggle between public and private identities.

PRINCIPLES OF IDENTITY MANAGEMENT

Identity affects how we perceive ourselves, how others perceive us, how we behave, and how we evaluate our behavior and relationships. Seven principles provide a summary of this research.

Identity and Hierarchical Structure

The first principle is that *our identities provide us with a hierarchical structure of who we are.* Although we define ourselves in myriad ways, our identity helps organize these various facets into a hierarchical structure that fluctuates according to context (Schlenker, 1985). Our identity includes our relationships (e.g., boyfriend, friend, son), roles (e.g., student, basketball player, law clerk), goals (e.g., live in Europe, get a job helping others), personal qualities (e.g., friendly, honest), accomplishments (e.g., 3.5 GPA, organization president), group or cultural membership (e.g., sorority member, Asian), and appearance (e.g., attractive, wears Abercrombie clothes). Appearance is important among millennials today. One recent study of female athletes, who one would expect would have a positive identity and image, and who must balance fitness and thinness, found that communication from others, particularly their coach, was associated with a positive identity and healthy behaviors (Beckner & Record, 2016). For more on the important role of attraction see Chapter 3.

These facets of our identity vary in the degree to which they centrally define who we are. The more central they are to our definition of self, the more stable they are across our lifetime and the more prominent they are when we present ourselves during interaction. Think back to Emily and her Facebook page. Although its content gives visitors a sense of Emily's identity structure, Emily is probably displaying only part of her identity when she posts that page. Thus, people who view her page might have biased impressions about Emily. For example, they might think that Emily cares for her friends more than her family, when actually the reverse is true.

Identity and the Looking-Glass Self

The second principle is that *the feedback we receive from others helps shape our identities.* Charles Horton Cooley (1922) first developed the notion of the looking-glass self, a metaphor that identity is shaped by feedback from others. He argued that social audiences provide us with an image of ourselves similar to the one we see in a mirror. For example, think of how you came to believe that you were smart enough to go to college. Your identity as an intelligent person was cultivated through interactions with parents, teachers, and peers. Perhaps a specific teacher in high school said you were smart enough to go to college, or your parents gave you positive feedback and encouragement, or a friend kept complimenting you on your ability to learn. Indeed, college itself is a major source of broad exploration and identity reformulation (Beyers & Goossens, 2008), and the effect is bigger for students who reside on college campuses. So, experience in college provides another "mirror" that helps you reform and shape an identity

©iStockphoto.com/karens4

The concept of the looking-glass self describes how our identities are shaped by the way we are seen by others. Do you think the image you have of yourself matches what others see?

that may last a lifetime. Regardless of the source, one or more people likely helped develop your identity. Many parts of our identities are similarly formed through our interactions with significant others and the institutions that shape our lives.

Identity and the Interpretation of Feedback

The third principle is that *our identities help us interpret feedback from others*. Just as people's feedback affects our identities, our identities affect how we perceive others' feedback (Schlenker, 1980). For example, people like Emily who view themselves as extroverts react differently than those who define themselves as introverts when someone says to them, "You're awfully quiet today." The emotions they experience and perceptions of what the statement means, as well as what it says about the sender of the message—and the intent—are influenced by their identity as an introvert or extrovert, and other qualities as well.

Research also suggests that we are likely to interpret feedback from others as consistent with our identity (Swann, 1983; Swann & Read, 1981). For example, people who consider themselves attractive may interpret someone's negative comment about their appearance as an expression of envy rather than a true reflection of their attractiveness. An unattractive person may interpret that statement as consistent with a negative self-image. Moreover, we are generally more likely to remember information consistent with our identity and to discount inconsistent information (Kahneman, Slovic, & Tvesky, 1982). However, research suggests that this tendency applies only to central aspects of our identity and those aspects for which we have strongly held beliefs (Stangor & Ruble, 1989). For less central aspects of self, inconsistent information is more easily dismissed. For example, a young man who adopts an identity as someone who enjoys drinking on weekends may struggle when a friend says that she thinks people who drink are irresponsible. This feedback may influence both his identity development and his relationship with her. For a person who takes

only an occasional drink, her comment would have little effect on his identity or their relationship.

Identity, Expectations, and Behavior

The fourth principle specifies that *identity incorporates expectations and guides behavior*. The central characteristics we think we possess create social expectations for our behavior (Schlenker, 1985) and expectations or self-fulfilling prophecies (Merton, 1948). We tend to behave consistently with our identity. For example, if a person's identity includes being a good student, the individual will behave in identity-consistent ways by studying harder and attending classes regularly. If a person's identity includes being an excellent athlete, the individual's daily workouts become central to that identity. Research has shown that moral identity, whereby a person thinks of her- or himself as a good and ethical person, is associated with behavior that is more moral (Hardy & Carlo, 2011). Notice that these behaviors set up a **self-fulfilling prophecy** that causes persons to behave in a way (often unconsciously) that actually makes it more likely that their behavior will be consistent with their identity.

Identity and Self-Evaluation

The fifth principle is that our *identities and the identities presented by others influence our evaluations of self*. The expectations and behavioral guidelines connected to identity provide people with comparison points against which to judge their performances (Schlenker, 1985; Vignoles et al., 2006). As a result, our identity influences our evaluation of how well or poorly we performed. For example, good students are likely to get upset if they receive a C on an exam or a paper, whereas those who see themselves as poor students might be delighted to receive a C. Interestingly, self-esteem and identity may be most closely connected through this expectation–evaluation link. Unrealistically flattering self-definitions lead to expectations of self that are unlikely to be met, which leads to a string of perceived failures. In addition, when people compare themselves to idealized images, their identities suffer. For example, a research study demonstrated that after viewing either an attractive photo or a successful resume on a social network site, people had more-negative self-images and identities than people that viewed an unattractive photo or a weak resume (Haferkamp & Kramer, 2011). Social comparison of one's identity is alive and well on social networking sites.

Identity and Goal Achievement

The sixth principle is that *identity influences the likelihood of goal achievement.* Achieving goals is facilitated by the presence of qualities that are consistent with that particular goal. Thus, people who see themselves as good students are likely to get better grades because they see studying and attending class as important behaviors to help maintain their identities. The same type of process influences goal achievement in our relationships. For example, the likelihood that Bill will achieve his goal of dating Jeff depends on the extent to which Bill believes he possesses characteristics desired by or appealing to Jeff. If an important aspect of Bill's identity is his sensitivity and Jeff prefers to date a partner who is macho, Bill may feel he has little hope of attracting Jeff. Self-fulfilling prophecies also relate to goal achievement. For instance, if Emily believes that she can become a dancer on Broadway, she is likely to have confidence, be more motivated, and perhaps work harder—all of which will make it easier to achieve her goal.

Identity and Relationships

The final principle is that *our identity influences what social relationships we choose to pursue, create, and maintain.* Years ago, psychologist Eric Erikson (1968) theorized that ego and identity development are essential prerequisites to relational development. Recent research has confirmed this theory. A longitudinal study suggests that development of a strong and stable identity is an essential precondition for the development of intimacy; people with a strong identity at age 15 had a more intimate relationship at age 25 than those who had a weak identity at age 15 (Beyers & Seiffge-Krenke, 2010).

People prefer interactions with people who provide identity-consistent feedback to them (Robinson & Smith-Lovin, 1992). So people who have positive identities prefer to be treated positively, while people who define themselves in negative terms, such as *unintelligent,* unconsciously seek partners who confirm that negative identity. Why is this the case? People distrust feedback that is inconsistent with their identity, so they perceive those who offer contrary feedback as dishonest (Swann, Griffin, Predmore, & Gaines, 1987). The consequences of this tendency can be serious, especially for women who are victims of abuse, who may unconsciously find themselves attracted to individuals who treat them the same way as those who abused them in the past.

Identity-consistent behavior is particularly important in established relationships. Swann, De La Ronde, and Hixon (1994) found that our preference for "authentic" feedback (feedback consistent with our identity) or "positive" feedback (feedback more favorable than our view of self) changes across relationship stages. People in the most intimate marriages preferred authentic feedback, but people in dating relationships preferred feedback that was more positive than their self-image. Evidently, we want others to view us through rose-colored glasses while dating, but prefer authenticity when we are in successful marriages.

Recent studies also suggest that self-disclosure, humor, and entertainment in computer-mediated interaction and social media are prerequisites to online intimacy, much as it is in face-to-face interaction (Jiang, Barazova, & Hancock, 2011; Utz, 2015; Wang & Andersen, 2007). This research suggests that revealing one's true identity online along with positive communication may be particularly vital in long-distance relationships and may accelerate intimacy and romantic relationship development.

In sum, how we view ourselves plays a central role in the interactions we seek, relationships we pursue, and how these interactions and relationships develop. However, we have not yet addressed how we communicate our identity to others, how we maintain our identity despite threats to its validity, and what social rules are in place to help us navigate the pitfalls of identity management. The next section focuses on communication and how identity management influences our behavior across a variety of situations.

COMMUNICATING IDENTITY TO OTHERS

> Antonio: *I hold the world but as the world, Gratiano; A stage where every man must play a part, And mine a sad one.*
>
> Gratiano: *Let me play the fool. . . .*
>
> **—William Shakespeare,**
> *The Merchant of Venice, Act I, Scene I*

Shakespeare's writing popularized the notion that "all the world's a stage," upon which we are merely actors. Scholars have embraced this concept when describing identity management (see Tracy, 1990). Three interrelated theoretical perspectives illuminate how people use communication to present themselves in a positive light: (1) self-presentation, (2) Goffman's (1959, 1967, 1971) dramaturgical approach that suggests people are similar to actors on a stage, and (3) Brown and Levinson's (1987) politeness theory, including preventive and **corrective facework.** Our efforts at self-presentation reflect the things we do to portray a particular image of self (e.g., I'm a rebel, I'm smart, I'm helpless), while the latter two approaches involve activities that are a part of everyday interaction (e.g., politeness, image maintenance, image repair).

General Issues in Self-Presentation

On any given day, you try to portray a particular impression of yourself to your boss, your parents, your teacher, and your romantic partner. This means concealing or minimizing potential faults while maximizing strengths. On Emily's Facebook page, the image she presents to her friends (i.e., as a partier) is likely quite different from the image she wants to display to prospective employers. Emily may be worried or embarrassed to learn that a potential employer looked her up on the web. In the next section, we examine if impression management is hypocritical, manipulative, and deceptive; reflects communication competence; or simply represents the way people unconsciously present themselves to others.

IS SELF-PRESENTATION HYPOCRITICAL, MANIPULATIVE, OR DECEPTIVE? When discussing self-presentation in class, some students think that self-presentation is hypocritical, evidence of insecurity, phony, manipulative, or downright deceptive. These students are uncomfortable with the notion that we are chameleon-like in our behavior, changing according to the audience and situation. Are we trying to deceive people? The answer is sometimes, but not usually. Self-presentation is usually a matter of highlighting certain *aspects* of ourselves for different audiences. We may possess elements of intelligence, sociability, athleticism, crassness, career orientation, and laziness in our identity, but we segregate these elements when communicating to various audiences. This segregation is not usually deceptive if those characteristics are all real aspects of ourselves. For example, Emily may display her social side to her friends and her serious side to teachers and employers. Her family might see both these sides of Emily's personality.

Of course, people fabricate identities. The news is full of people who lead double lives, pad their resumes, or fake their identities in Internet chat rooms and embellish their identities on Facebook. Computer-mediated communication provides more opportunity to fabricate our identity. Research shows that such fabrications have many intentions (Caspi & Gorsky, 2006; Toma, Hancock, & Ellison, 2008; Utz, 2005; Whitty, 2008) and are most likely fabricated by people who are materialistic, have higher self-efficacy, and spend more time on Facebook (Frunzaru & Garbasevschi, 2016). Online sexual predators usually use a false identity (Dowdell et al., 2011). People who are younger, use computers more frequently, and are more tech savvy are more likely to engage in online deception (Caspi & Gorsky, 2006). **Attractiveness deception** is a ubiquitous form of online identity enhancement: for example, men are likely to lie about their height and women about their weight (Toma et al., 2008; Whitty, 2008). People also engage in online deception about age, personality, relational intentions, and relational status (Whitty, 2008). Gender switching is associated with role exploration but is also sometimes used by sexual predators. Some people conceal their online identity because they want to maintain privacy in the online world (Caspi & Gorsky, 2006; Utz, 2005). So how do people resolve discrepancies between online identities and offline identities? Deandrea and Walther (2011) found that people felt such inconsistencies were hypocritical, untrustworthy, and misleading, and were more serious if the perpetrator was an acquaintance rather than a friend. Even seemingly innocuous and trivial self-presentations triggered unfavorable reactions.

All of us employ less-extreme forms of identity manipulation. Have you ever pretended you understood someone, hidden your anger from others, put on a happy face, feigned interest in a boring conversation, or acted as if you liked someone you actually disliked? These are called **display rules** (Andersen, 2008) and are part of face maintenance. Communication researchers have begun to investigate the results of a similar construct, **emotional labor,** where people must display certain attitudes or emotions at work (Rivera, 2015; Tracy, 2005; Tracy & Trethewey, 2005). We act these ways for many reasons, but all those reasons involve a belief in the importance of self-presentation. We may not want people to know that we are angry or sad because we want to keep our composure, we may have an occupation requiring a certain demeanor, we may not show boredom because that would be disrespectful, and we may not express our dislike because that would disrupt group dynamics.

Attempts to manage impressions to advance a desirable image of ourselves sometimes backfire. First, it is stressful to display an inauthentic identity or emotion (Rivera, 2015; Tracy, 2005). A key element of a successful performance is that it is perceived as sincere (Goffman, 1959) and a true reflection of one's personality. Cases in which individuals are caught lying in order to manage their identity actually damage their identity. Research has shown that when deception is detected, it produces detrimental personal and relational consequences (Buller & Burgoon, 1994; O'Hair & Cody, 1994; see also Chapter 13). Indeed, honesty is an important impression that we want to foster because it goes to the core of our identity. Being perceived as inauthentic will likely put in doubt the sincerity of all the other positive qualities that we have successfully portrayed and that accurately reflect who we are.

Exaggerating the truth or putting too much effort into self-presentation can produce negative outcomes. Research on narcissism (self-focusing behavior) has shown that boastful individuals are rated as less socially attractive and less liked than are people who are less self-promoting (Vangelisti, Knapp, & Daly, 1990). Behaviors meant to bolster one's image to receivers can fail if the person is perceived as selfish or insincere. Schlenker (1980, 1984, 1985) discussed a dilemma that people face of having to choose between presenting the best possible image of self and presenting a realistic image. Research shows that online daters had to retain a balance between impression management and authenticity (de Vries, 2016; Ellison, Heino, & Gibbs, 2006) by attempting to present a real but ideal self. The perfect self-presentation strikes a balance between positivity and plausibility.

HOW IS SELF-PRESENTATION RELATED TO COMMUNICATION COMPETENCE? Researchers who study communication competence indicate that socially skilled people have a knack for communicating effectively and appropriately (Spitzberg & Cupach, 1988). Competent communicators usually have more successful lives and relationships. You would probably not have many friends if you acted as formally as you would during a job interview. Similarly, you would probably not be hired if you acted like you do at a party when meeting a prospective employer. Among friends we act relaxed, discuss social activities, get a little crazy, and often trade stories about humorous events. During a job interview, we want to emphasize very different aspects of ourselves—as a reliable colleague, a smart person, and someone who can contribute to the company's development. If we switch gears, does this mean that we are phonies? No. It means we understand that we must fulfill different roles for different audiences. Role flexibility can help us be more effective communicators, as long as we are not manipulating others for evil purposes.

Even among friends we may display various aspects of ourselves. We are more likely to present a favorable impression of ourselves to strangers than to friends. We assume that strangers do not know much about us, so it is important to disclose favorable information about ourselves. By contrast, friends probably already know of our accomplishments, so pointing them out again may be perceived as conceited, thus backfiring; also, close friends can recognize realistic from unrealistic stories, while strangers have difficulty making such a distinction. Tice, Butler, Muraven, and Stillwell (1995) conducted five studies that compared the differences in people's self-presentations to friends and to strangers. They concluded, "People habitually use different self-presentation strategies with different audiences, relying on favorable self-enhancement with strangers but shifting toward modesty when among friends" (Tice et al., 1995, p. 1120). Indeed, one of the charms of close friends is that we can present our most authentic self.

Several studies show that we vary the impression that we want to project based on the relationship or situation. Daly, Hoggs, Sacks, Smith, and Zimring (1983) observed restroom behavior of men and women in restaurants and bars. They recorded the amount of time that people spent preening (e.g., adjusting their clothes, straightening their hair, looking in the mirror) and recorded the relationship with the person they were with. Not surprisingly, those who spent the most time managing

their appearance were in the newest relationships. Research on **affinity-seeking behavior,** actions designed to attract others, found numerous impression management activities that we do early in relationships to increase our partner's attraction to us (Daly & Kreiser, 1994). These include attending to how we look, appearing interested in conversations, emphasizing similarities, and portraying an image as a "fun" person. The recent practice of "sexting" is an attempt to seek affinity by establishing an uninhibited, fun, and sexy identity. However, such images may be a source of great embarrassment, identity damage, and even sexual aggression. Research has shown that "sexters" are often insecure and relationally anxious individuals who overcompensate for these deficiencies by using sexting as a means of increasing interpersonal attraction (Weisskirch & Delevi, 2011). Normally, the way people present themselves to others is flexible and dynamic; people manage their behavior differently depending on the relationship so as to maximize positive impressions and social competence.

TO WHAT EXTENT IS SELF-PRESENTATION A DELIBERATE, CONSCIOUS ACTIVITY? Self-presentation is so commonplace that it becomes routine, habitual behavior that is encoded unconsciously. DePaulo (1992) offered several examples of habitual impression management behavior, including postural etiquette that girls learn as they are growing up and the ritualistic smiles by the first runner-up at beauty pageants. Other examples are the routine exchange of "thank you" and "you're welcome," table manners, and the myriad taken-for-granted politeness strategies. These behaviors were enacted deliberately and consciously at one time but have become habitual, automatic aspects of interaction.

At times, however, even habitual behaviors become deliberate. When we especially want to make a good impression or expect difficulty in achieving a desired impression, self-presentations are more planned and controlled (Leary & Kowalski, 1990; Schlenker, 1985). When you first meet your girlfriend's or boyfriend's parents, you will probably be more aware than usual of your posture, politeness, and other normally habitual impression management behaviors. Your deliberateness in enacting these behaviors may be further heightened if your partner's parents do not approve of the relationship or if you expect resistance from them. Thus, in some circumstances, we are deliberate in using impression management tactics—for example, on first dates, at the dean's office, or in an interview—but most of our self-presentational strategies are relatively habitual and are performed unconsciously.

Even "autonomous" people, who claim not to care about what others think of them, tend to manage their identities in ways that make them more socially competent, providing further evidence that self-presentation is often an unconscious, habitual process. Schlenker and Weigold (1990) compared "autonomous" individuals with individuals who place significant weight on others' attitudes. If self-presentational concerns are irrelevant to autonomous individuals, we would expect their reported attitudes to be unaffected by audiences. Instead, both autonomous and more socially driven people change their attitudes to maintain a certain image of themselves; only the kind of image differs. However, research shows that people who are insensitive to audience characteristics and self-presentation needs are less successful relationally and professionally than those who are sensitive to these issues (Schlenker, 1980).

"Life Is a Stage": The Dramaturgical Perspective

In his classic book, *The Presentation of Self in Everyday Life,* Goffman (1959) advanced a revolutionary way of thinking about identity management—the dramaturgical perspective. Borrowing from Shakespeare, Goffman used the metaphor of theater to describe our everyday interactions. Goffman maintained that we constantly enact performances geared for audiences—with the purpose of advancing a beneficial image of ourselves. In other words, we are concerned about appearances and work to

ensure that others view us favorably. The evidence for this view is strong. Several studies show that some sexually active individuals refrain from using condoms because they are afraid such an action may imply that they (or their partners) are "uncommitted" or "diseased" (Lear, 1997). Holtgraves (1988) argued that gambling enthusiasts pursue their wagering habits partly because they wish to portray themselves as spontaneous, adventurous, and unconcerned about losing money. Snow and Anderson's (1987) yearlong observational study revealed that even homeless people present themselves to their communities in ways that help restore their dignity. For instance, a 24-year-old male who had been homeless for 2 weeks told those authors the following:

> I'm not like the other guys who hang out at the "Sally" [Salvation Army]. If you want to know about street people, I can tell you about them; but you can't really learn about street people from studying me, because I'm different. (p. 1349)

This man clearly made an effort to distance himself verbally from what he considered to be an undesirable identity: being homeless. In fact, distancing was the most common form of self-presentation these authors found among the homeless.

Since Goffman's early work, scholars have outlined certain conditions under which impression management becomes especially important to us (Schlenker, Britt, & Pennington, 1996). Although researchers still consider impression management to be something that is always salient to us, the following three conditions seem to make it especially important.

CONDITION 1: THE BEHAVIOR REFLECTS HIGHLY VALUED, CORE ASPECTS OF THE SELF People are more concerned about successful impression management of central features of our identity than peripheral ones. Our identities are tied to the distinctiveness of ourselves as the person that we assert to establish as our core identity (Vignoles et al., 2006). For example, Emily sees herself as fun loving and outgoing but only moderately career oriented, so she is likely to portray herself as more social than professional. Situations such as planning a party or college reunion are likely to call forth a particularly strong need for Emily to present her distinct self.

CONDITION 2: SUCCESSFUL PERFORMANCE IS TIED TO VITAL POSITIVE OR NEGATIVE CONSEQUENCES

If your success in a cherished relationship depends on your ability to convince your partner of your commitment, the importance of impression management heightens. You might send your partner flowers, give gifts, and say "I love you" more often as ways to show you are a devoted, committed partner. In a similar vein, if you are told that your raise at work depends on teamwork, you may devote more attention to your identity as a team player. Studies show that we are especially motivated to be perceived positively when interacting with attractive or valued others (see Jellison & Oliver, 1983; Schlenker, 1984).

CONDITION 3: THE BEHAVIOR REFLECTS DIRECTLY ON VALUED RULES OF CONDUCT

Particular rules of conduct are especially important. For example, some people strongly believe that engaging in conflict in a public setting is inappropriate (Jones & Gallois, 1989) and violating that norm would be threatening to their desired public identity. Similarly, some people believe that public displays of affection are inappropriate and may act unaffectionately in public. When important relational rules such as these are violated frequently, it not only is very face-threatening, but also often leads to relationship deterioration (Argyle & Henderson, 1984; Metts, 1994).

Three identity factors are prominent in close relationships, especially in early stages, when partners try to make positive first impressions (Swann et al., 1994). In early stages, people typically display central aspects of themselves to their partners (condition 1). Success in these displays can make the difference between attracting or repelling a friend or romantic partner (condition 2). Finally, ground rules are often set as to what types of conduct will be most highly valued (condition 3). To the extent that the three conditions outlined here are salient, people will engage in impression management. Consistent with his dramaturgical perspective, Goffman (1959) referred to social behavior designed to manage impressions and influence others as a performance in front of a set of observers or an audience and in a particular location: a stage.

FRONTSTAGE VERSUS BACKSTAGE As in any theatrical venue, there are two stage locations: front and back. The frontstage is where our performances are enacted, where our behaviors are observed by an audience, and where impression management is particularly important. Conversely, the backstage is where we can let our guard down and do not have to think about staying in character. According to Goffman (1959), the backstage is "where the performer can reliably expect that no member of the audience will intrude" (p. 113). In the backstage and surrounding area, which Goffman referred to as the **wings,** we often find materials such as cologne or perfume, a hairbrush, and a mirror that we use to improve our appearance, increasing the potential success of our self-presentational performance on a first date. We might also ask friends to give us information about the person whom we are about to date. In fact, a primary way that we gain information about someone is by consulting other people (see Baxter & Wilmot, 1984; Berger, 1987). Answers to questions such as, "Is he dating anyone right now?" and "Does she like sports?" can help reduce uncertainty and give people an idea of how to manage their impressions (see Chapter 4). If you learn that someone you want to date is interested in sports, you might portray yourself as a sports enthusiast and invite that person to a college sporting event.

Tedeschi (1986) made a distinction similar to frontstage and backstage by comparing public behavior that is subject to observation and private behavior that is free from such scrutiny. Studies have shown that we often behave differently in public than in private (Baumeister, 1986). Singing is a common example of a backstage behavior. Many people are too embarrassed to sing in front of others (in the frontstage) but, when pressed, admit to singing in the shower or in their cars (which are backstage regions). In a similar vein, hygienic activity, despite its universality, is reserved for backstage regions. Relationships also determine if we are frontstage or backstage. When people are with their closest friends or intimate partners, behaviors that typically are reserved for the backstage are moved to the frontstage. You might not swear in public but do so with your closest friends. Our close friends and family members are backstage, so they get a more authentic and unrehearsed version of us. Again, we are reminded of Emily's Facebook page. The pictures that are posted (some by her, and others of her without her consent) are often things done in backstage settings (with friends, at home, and so forth) but are presented on frontstage and viewed by whoever visits the page. This mixing of backstage and frontstage on webpages is dangerous for identity management.

ROLE, AUDIENCE, AND CONTEXT Whether behaviors occur in the frontstage or backstage depends on the role enacted, the audience being targeted, and the context in which the activities are performed. For example, you might feel free to sing in front of strangers at a karaoke bar in another city but not in a bar that you hang out in regularly in your own town. Similarly, some teenagers manage their use of swearing with parents or other adults to display proper and respectful identity. With their friends, by contrast, they might convey a carefree, rebellious, and "cool" identity that is bolstered by swearing. The only viable criterion on which performance success is judged is whether it successfully advances the image that the performer desires to advance for a particular audience (Baumeister, 1982; Leary, 1995; Schlenker, 1980). When a performance threatens the image that one wants to convey to a certain audience, it is reserved for the backstage. Thinking back to Emily's Facebook page, we see a problem concerning identity management. The page

is a clear identity message, but she has little control over what audiences access it or what gets posted, so identities are merged to Emily's detriment.

Finally, it is important to note the audience's role in the impression-management process. When self-presentation is successful, the audience and "actor" interact to help each other validate and maintain their identities. After all, we can work hard to establish an identity, but it depends on the audience to accept or reject our self-presentation. In fact, Goffman (1967) argued that the validation of another person's identity is a "condition of interaction" (p. 12). In other words, we expect other people to accept our identities and to help us save face when we accidentally display an undesired image. In fact, Goffman (1967) called people who can watch another's "face" being damaged without feeling sorrow, hurt, or vicarious embarrassment "heartless" human beings (p. 11). Moreover, research shows that people who fail to help others save face are often disliked and shunned (see Cupach & Metts, 1994; Schlenker, 1980). Most people know how it feels to be made fun of after an embarrassing event, so instead of laughing, they try to relieve the distress that the embarrassed person is feeling. This leads to the next theory of impression management: politeness theory.

Politeness Theory

As an extension of Goffman's work, Brown and Levinson (1987) developed politeness theory, which focuses on the specific ways that people manage and save face using communication. A large portion of their theorizing was a distinction they made between positive face and negative face.

POSITIVE FACE VERSUS NEGATIVE FACE **Positive face** is the favorable image that people portray to others and hope to have validated by others. It essentially reflects our desire to be liked by others. By contrast, **negative face** reflects our desire to "be free from imposition and restraint and to have control over [our] own territory, possessions, time, space, and resources" (Metts & Grohskopf, 2003, p. 361). Put another way, our positive face is the "best face" we put forward so that others like us, while our negative face is the part of us that wants to do what we want to do or say, without concern about what others would like us to do or say.

Politeness theory revolves around four general assumptions (see Brown & Levinson, 1987; Metts & Grohskopf, 2003). First, threats to positive and negative face are an inherent part of social interaction. People have to deal with a constant struggle between wanting to do what they want (which satisfies their negative face needs) and wanting to do what makes them look good (which satisfies their positive face needs). On some occasions, the same action can satisfy both aspects of face. For example, suppose your best friend asks you to help prepare food for a party he or she is giving. You might agree to help your friend, which supports your positive face needs because it makes you look good. But if you happen to love cooking, your negative face needs also would be satisfied because you are doing exactly what you wanted to do. However, it is much more likely that a behavior will fall somewhere between the two face needs or that supporting one face need may threaten the other. For example, you may agree to help a friend move despite your desire to relax at home. If you attend to your negative face needs by staying home, you would come across as a poor friend and threaten your positive face needs. Central to politeness theory is that positive and negative face needs are managed in every interaction. If you need to go, at what point do you end a conversation and how do you do it? In what tone of voice do you talk to your parents despite your desire to express displeasure? How do you respond to someone's question about what you're doing this weekend in a way that is friendly but doesn't commit yourself to do something you don't want to do?

Second is the assumption that people's positive and negative faces can be either validated or threatened by interaction. Identity is validated when a person's behavior and the receiver's response to that behavior support the individual's desired image. For example, you may validate your identity as a caring partner by taking your significant other for an unexpected dinner after he or she had a long week at work. In return, your partner may validate your identity as a caring partner by saying how much surprises like special dinners are appreciated. In this example, both you and your partner have done things to validate *your* positive face.

A study by Albas and Albas (1988) examined how students validated their positive faces following receipt of a good exam grade. The researchers identified several strategies that "acers" (as they labeled them) used to reveal their grade to others as a way to bolster their positive faces without directly bragging. These strategies included "repressed bubbling" (nonverbal signals of elation), "accidental revelation" (leaving the test facing upward, with the grade in full display), and "question-answer chain" (asking other students how they did, which sets the stage for them to reciprocate with a similar question) (Albas & Albas, 1988, pp. 293–294). In these ways, students who performed well on the test could "publish" that fact to others, thereby supporting their identity as an intelligent person and good student. However, if the person appears to be bragging or fishing for a compliment, these strategies could backfire.

When a person's behavior is at variance with the identity that a person desires to convey, a face-threatening situation occurs. **Face-threatening acts (FTAs)** are behaviors that detract from an individual's identity by threatening either their positive or their negative face desires (Brown & Levinson, 1987). For example, forgetting a dinner date with your significant other is a self-inflicted threat to your positive face—your identity as a caring partner. Your partner may further contribute to this face threat by publicly chiding you for getting stood up at the restaurant. Of course, not all behaviors are equally face-threatening. Certain behaviors cause people to lose more face and lead to more negative personal and relational consequences than others. Indeed, recent research on online communication shows that even minor FTAs lead to negative feelings and retaliatory aggression (Chen, 2015).

The third assumption of politeness theory is that both members of an interaction are motivated to avoid threatening either their own or the interaction partner's face needs. Given our desire to prevent face threats, we normally try to avoid making others look bad (i.e., threatening our positive face) and respect others who refrain from making us look bad. Interactions are typically dances where both partners understand the social expectations that help them maintain each other's face needs. Emily might understand that it is important to respect Lindsay's time and space and not point out her flaws, and she expects Lindsay to do the same for her. Of course, some people enjoy violating social expectations and embarrassing others. How would politeness theory researchers respond to that? They would offer two explanations: First, those people who are also often shunned, socially reprimanded, or disliked by most other people (e.g., seen as bullies, jerks) have little to lose and feel as though they can enhance their status by putting down other people. Second, all threats to face are not equally bad; some are much less severe than others. In fact, this issue forms the basis for the fourth assumption underlying politeness theory: the severity of FTAs depends on several factors.

Research suggests that at least six factors affect the degree to which an FTA is perceived to be severe. The first three factors, identified by Schlenker and his colleagues (Schlenker, Britt, Pennington, Murphy, & Doherty, 1994; Schlenker & Weigold, 1992), focus on behaviors that threaten a person's own face. The remaining three factors, from Brown and Levinson's (1987) politeness theory, focus on behaviors that threaten either one's own or one's partner's face.

1. *The more important the rule that is violated, the more severe the FTA.* For example, forgetting your relational partner's birthday is a greater rule violation than forgetting to call your partner to say you will be late coming home from work.
2. *The more harm the behavior produces, the more severe the FTA.* If you trip and lose your balance, you may feel loss of face; if you trip, fall, and tear your outfit, however, the loss of face will be greater. Similarly, if you get caught telling a lie about something that has serious implications for your relationship, the loss of face will be greater than if you get caught telling a "little white lie."
3. *The more the actor is directly responsible for the behavior, the more severe the FTA.* If a store clerk refuses to accept your credit card because the expiration date is past, it is much less face threatening than if the clerk phones in your card number and is asked to confiscate your card and cut it up because you are late on your payments.
4. *The more of an imposition the behavior is, the more severe the FTA.* You would be more concerned about your negative face if someone asked you to move furniture (a major imposition on your time) than if someone asked you to write down their new phone number (hardly an imposition).
5. *The more power the receiver has over the sender, the more severe the FTA.* If you make a silly comment that your boss misconstrues as an insult, you will probably be more worried than if you make the same silly comment to a friend.
6. *The larger the social distance between sender and receiver, the more severe the FTA.* You will probably worry less about threatening the face of your best friend than that of an acquaintance, because the friendship is more solid and less susceptible to harm from face threats.

Although research has generally supported the validity of these factors, research has shown that the sixth factor, which relates to the social distance between receiver and sender, may not always be true. Holtgraves and Yang (1990, 1992) suggest that in many cases, instead of being *less* concerned about threatening the identity of those close to us, we are actually *more* concerned about doing so. The point is that identity-management concerns become more salient as the consequences of impression-management failure increase.

FACEWORK STRATEGIES Given the importance of facework in people's everyday lives, it should come as no surprise that people use a variety of intricate strategies to manage face needs during interaction. In fact, most, if not all, interactions inherently include examples of facework that help people maintain or repair, or that strategically threaten, their own faces or those of others. Even a simple request ("Since we live so far apart, would you mind meeting at a restaurant that is somewhere halfway between us?") is phrased in a way that respects the positive and negative face needs of the other person. This fact becomes clear if you think of other ways that these requests may be phrased ("I don't want to drive that far. You have to meet me halfway").

Given the many ways that concerns for facework influence our interactions, Brown and Levinson (1987) offered five options that individuals have when considering an FTA. The strategies differ in the degree of balance achieved between the goals of accomplishing a face-threatening task and managing face concerns (see Figure 2.2).

The **bald on-record strategy** is characterized by primary attention to task and little attention to helping the partner save face. It is the most efficient strategy but also the most face threatening. Brown and Levinson (1987) offered the examples of a mother telling her child, "Come home right now!" or someone in need of assistance telling a bystander, "Lend me a hand here!" Bald on-record strategies are typically used when maximum task efficiency is important or where a large difference in power or status exists between actors.

The **positive politeness strategy** is intended to address the receiver's positive face while still accomplishing the task. It includes explicit recognition of the receiver's value and the receiver's contributions to the process and couches the FTA (often a request) as something that does not threaten the identity of the receiver. For example, complimenting someone on attire, haircut, or performance is an example of positive politeness that might precede a request. Similarly, if you want a friend to help you write a resume and cover letter, you might say, "You are such a good writer. Would you help me edit this?"

The **negative politeness strategy** tries to address the receiver's negative face while still accomplishing the task. The key is that receivers not feel coerced into complying, but feel that they are performing the act of their own volition. Often, negative politeness also involves deference on the part of the sender to ensure not being perceived as coercive. For example, you might say to a friend, "I suppose there wouldn't be any chance of your being able to lend me

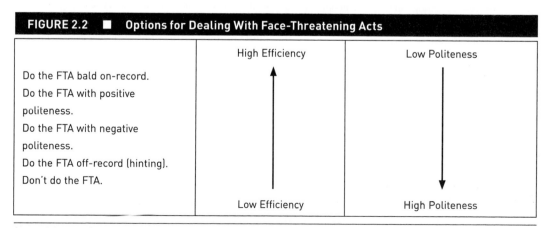

FIGURE 2.2 ■   Options for Dealing With Face-Threatening Acts

	High Efficiency	Low Politeness
Do the FTA bald on-record. Do the FTA with positive politeness. Do the FTA with negative politeness. Do the FTA off-record (hinting). Don't do the FTA.	↑	↓
	Low Efficiency	High Politeness

Source: We thank Sandra Metts for providing this graphic and granting us permission to use it in this book.

Note: FTA = face-threatening acts.

your car for a few minutes, would there?" Brown and Levinson (1987) noted that requests phrased this way clearly emphasize the freedom of the receiver to decline.

The **going off-record strategy** is characterized by primary attention to face and little attention to task. It is an inefficient strategy for accomplishing tasks, but given the importance of face, it may serve the participants well. Examples include hinting, using an indirect nonverbal expression, or masking a request as a joke. For instance, if you want your partner to take you on a vacation, you might comment, "I've always wanted to go on a Caribbean cruise" or "It would be great to get away and go somewhere tropical."

Finally, people can **decide not to engage in the FTA.** Brown and Levinson (1987) noted that individuals often choose to forgo face-threatening tasks completely in favor of preserving face. For example, even if you are upset because your roommate's partner spends the night at your apartment, you might decide to say nothing for fear of embarrassing or angering your roommate (particularly if you do not want your roommate to move out). According to Brown and Levinson (1987), people perform a cost-benefit analysis when deciding what type of strategy to use. Bald on-record strategies are the most efficient but also the most damaging to face and as such may be most damaging to the relationship. However, by going off record, people run a much greater risk that the receiver will not recognize the request or will simply ignore it.

Metts (1992) applied this logic to the predicament of breaking up with a romantic partner. The act of breaking up is face threatening in many ways (see Chapter 15). Suppose Emily tells her current boyfriend, Alex, that she wants to end their relationship, but Alex does not want to break up. This act threatens Alex's negative face because he is being forced to do something he does not want to do. Alex's positive face also is threatened because Emily's request suggests that he is no longer a desirable relational partner. Emily's positive face may also be threatened if she worries that Alex (and perhaps other people) will see her as selfish, egotistical, or uncaring. Her

negative face could also be threatened; she may want to change her relationship status on her Facebook page but feels it would be premature to do so without talking things over with Alex. According to Metts (1992), Emily is likely to use different strategies depending on how face threatening she thinks the breakup will be for both herself and Alex. If she thinks the breakup will be highly distressing, she is likely to use an on-record-with-politeness strategy. Conversely, if Emily thinks the breakup will cause little distress, she is likely to use an off-record strategy (e.g., avoiding the person) or a bald on-record strategy (e.g., blunt statements about wanting to break up).

PREVENTIVE AND CORRECTIVE FACEWORK

Certainly, people often are task driven and perform FTAs with little attention to the consequences of threatening their own or another person's face. But people are more likely to avoid face threats or attempt to repair a damaged face. Research on preventive and corrective facework highlights other ways that concerns for face affect our interactions (Cupach & Metts, 1994).

Preventive facework is characterized by efforts to avoid or minimize potential face threat. Preventive strategies seek to preclude future damage by framing the message in friendlier, softer terms. Studies have identified types of preventive facework in daily interaction. **Disclaimers** are the most common form of preventive facework. Hewitt and Stokes (1975) outlined five general disclaimers that individuals use before saying or doing something that is face threatening: (1) hedging ("I may be way off here, but . . . "), (2) credentialing ("I'm your father, so I'll be straight with you"), (3) sin license ("Well, since we're all disclosing embarrassing situations . . . "), (4) cognitive disclaimer ("I know you're going to think I've lost it, but . . . "), and (5) appeal for suspended judgment ("Hear me out before jumping to conclusions").

Other researchers have included the notion of **verbal self-handicapping** as a method of preventive facework (Higgins & Berglas, 1990)—that is,

FIGURE 2.3 ■ Face Threat/Loss Sequence

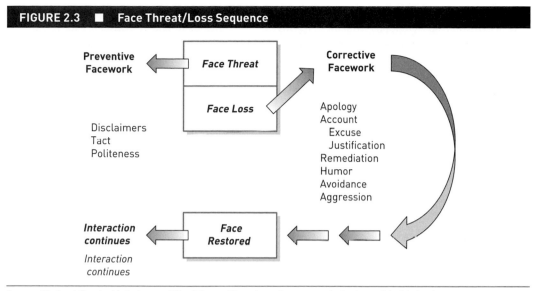

Source: We thank Sandra Metts for providing this graphic and granting us permission to use it in this book.

people will sometimes offer an excuse that serves to minimize the face threat of a potentially poor performance. For example, prior to an important dance competition, Emily may inform her coach of a knee injury she has suffered. This strategic precompetition disclosure serves two functions. If Emily dances her routines well, she bolsters her identity as a "tough" professional who can perform with pain. But if she performs poorly, she has a built-in excuse for her subpar performance. Unfortunately, these self-handicapping tactics often become self-fulfilling prophecies because they offer the individual a reason *not* to do as well as possible. In sum, the various disclaimers all serve to soften the potential face threat that might result from impending action.

Corrective facework is characterized by efforts to *repair* an identity already damaged by something that was said or done. Like preventive facework, corrective facework may be performed by the person whose face was threatened, or by others who are assisting in the protection or repair of the person's face. Of course, preventive and corrective facework are part of a cycle or sequence, as illustrated

in Figure 2.3. Both constantly occur in the course of communication and are interactively achieved in everyday communication.

Embarrassing moments are good examples of situations that often lead to corrective facework because they undermine a person's positive self-image. As Cupach and Metts (1994) argued, people become embarrassed when they are perceived to have acted incompetently—that is, when behavior is judged to be "inappropriate, ineffective, or foolish" (p. 18).

In a comprehensive review of embarrassment research, Miller (1996) outlined 10 types of embarrassing behaviors that typically threaten one's face. The two most common causes of embarrassment were "physical pratfalls or inept performance" and "cognitive errors." The former category includes instances where people appear unnecessarily awkward or incompetent—for example, missing a pole on which you intended to lean, falling over after leaning back too far in a chair, and catching your hair on fire as you light the grill. The latter category includes mistakes in judgment (trying every key before realizing you are at the wrong door), forgetfulness (forgetting your phone number or people's names), lack of attention or "temporary stupidity" (saying something that gives away a secret you are trying to keep for others), or clumsy answers. One of the best sources for examples of clumsy answers is Petra and Petra's 1993 book *The 775 Stupidest Things Ever Said*. One example of clumsy answers in that book is a comment that then vice president of the United States George Herbert Walker Bush gave at a campaign rally: "For 7 1/2 years I've worked alongside President Reagan. We've had triumphs. Made some mistakes. We've had sex . . . uh . . . setbacks."

People typically use corrective facework in response to embarrassing situations such as these, as well as to other situations involving FTAs. You can take the test in Box 2.3 to determine which types of corrective facework you are most likely to use in a particular situation. There are six general corrective strategies for repairing a damaged face (Cupach & Metts, 1994; Schlenker & Weigold, 1992):

1. *Avoidance:* The common thread underlying avoidance behaviors is the goal of distancing oneself or one's partner from the act. Often, distancing occurs when individuals pretend that the act never happened or ignore its occurrence. For example, continuing to walk down the aisle after knocking over a display in a grocery store or glossing over a Freudian slip are instances of avoidance. The hope is that the audience may pay less attention to the act if the actor avoids reference to it.

2. *Humor:* When the consequences of the FTA are relatively small, people often resort to humor as a way to deal with the threat. By using humor after an FTA, people show poise and come across as competent communicators, thereby repairing their damaged faces. Sometimes it is best to laugh at yourself so others will laugh with you, not at you.

3. *Apologies:* Apologies are "admissions of responsibility and regret for undesirable events" (Schlenker & Weigold, 1992, p. 162). In that sense, they may help repair some of the damage to face by emphasizing

the actor's nature as a moral individual who intends to take responsibility for the action. Unlike avoidance, where actors deny responsibility, apologies tie the incident directly to the actor and, as such, may further threaten face—especially if the apology is deemed insincere.

4. *Accounts:* Accounts, or attempts to explain the FTA, come in the form of excuses or justifications. Excuses are explanations that minimize personal responsibility of the actor for the actions. For example, if you engage in a silly fraternity or sorority prank that causes you to lose face, you might excuse your behavior by saying that your friends pressured you into action or that you had consumed too much alcohol. With justifications, actors do not try to distance themselves from the act, but instead "reframe an event by downplaying its negative implications" (Cupach & Metts, 1994, p. 10). Arguing that your behavior at the fraternity or sorority party was "not that big of a deal" or that the prank did not really hurt anyone are examples of justifications for FTAs.

5. *Remediation:* This strategy involves attempts to repair physical damage. For example, you might quickly clean up a coffee spill on the table, or you might zip up your pants once you recognize that your fly is open. Relational partners, especially if sympathetic, often engage in physical remediation as well. For example, if you see a food smudge on your partner's chin, you might wipe it off before other people see it.

6. *Aggression:* In some cases, individuals feel the need to repair their damaged face by using physical force. For example, people may start a physical altercation in response to a put-down or personal attack. In fact, research shows that dating violence often follows a perception of face threats (for a review of violence research, see Gelles & Cornell, 1990). People may also become aggressive when they are embarrassed or violate a norm.

BOX 2.3 PUT YOURSELF TO THE TEST
HOW DO YOU ATTEMPT TO REPAIR FACE?

Imagine yourself in the following situation. You are assigned to work in a group of four students to complete a class project. A number of personal issues interfere with your ability to get things done as quickly and effectively as you usually do, and you fall behind the rest of the group. Midway through the semester, one of the other group members puts you on the spot by saying, "You haven't been doing your share, so I'm afraid that if we give you something important to do you won't get it done on time or you won't do it well." How would you respond to this face-threatening comment? Answer the questions using the following scale: 1 = you would be very unlikely to react that way, and 7 = you would be very likely to react that way.

	Very Unlikely						Very Likely
1. I would ignore it.	1	2	3	4	5	6	7
2. I would apologize.	1	2	3	4	5	6	7
3. I would explain why I hadn't been able to do my fair share.	1	2	3	4	5	6	7
4. I would say something sarcastic or rude to the person who made the comment.	1	2	3	4	5	6	7
5. I would promise to do more than my fair share in the future.	1	2	3	4	5	6	7
6. I would laugh it off and say that I've always been a procrastinator.	1	2	3	4	5	6	7
7. I would change the subject.	1	2	3	4	5	6	7
8. I would admit that I had not done my fair share.	1	2	3	4	5	6	7
9. I would tell everyone why I wasn't able to put forth my best effort.	1	2	3	4	5	6	7
10. I would say something to put down the person who made the comment.	1	2	3	4	5	6	7
11. I would take on a task no one else wanted to do to make it up to everyone.	1	2	3	4	5	6	7
12. I would make fun of myself and my lack of time management.	1	2	3	4	5	6	7

To obtain your results, add your scores for the following items:

Avoidance: Items 1 + 7 =   _____

Apology: Items 2 + 8 =   _____

Account: Items 3 + 9 =   _____

Aggression: Items 4 +10 =   _____

Remediation: Items 5 + 11 =   _____

Humor: Items 6 + 12 =   _____

(Continued)

BOX 2.3 (Continued)

Higher scores indicate a stronger likelihood of using a particular type of corrective facework in this type of situation. How might your use of corrective facework differ on the basis of the situation or the relationship you share with the people around you?

For example, if you accidentally bump into someone while walking through a crowded shopping mall, you might angrily say, "Watch where you're going."

Of course, several of these strategies may be combined in efforts to repair a damaged face. For example, after spilling coffee on the boss's desk, you might say you are sorry (apology), explain that you were distracted by the boss's stimulating presentation (account), and then clean up the mess (physical remediation). Indeed, the more face threatening the act, the more energy will be expended in multiple repair attempts.

In other situations, people are more likely to ignore face threats or to respond with humor. This is especially likely when FTAs are expected. For instance, embarrassing and face-threatening actions are more

expected and accepted at wedding and baby showers. Common activities at baby showers include having people guess how big the mom-to-be's stomach is or what she weighs; at wedding showers, the bride-to-be often receives revealing lingerie. Braithwaite (1995) observed behavior at coed wedding and baby showers to investigate the tactics people used to embarrass others and what tactics people used to respond to face threats. She found that wedding and baby showers are contexts where embarrassment is expected, so these actions are not as face threatening as in other contexts. Yet the dance between embarrassment-producing face threats and face-repairing responses was still evident. Other situations, such as "roasting" someone at a retirement party, may require this same delicate dance.

SUMMARY AND APPLICATION

Our desire to present particular images of ourselves shapes our social interactions and influences our relationships. In this chapter, we outlined the factors that influence identity and the ways in which we communicate this identity to others during initial encounters and in established relationships. A person's identity is based on a complex theory of self that incorporates expectations, self-fulfilling prophecies, and feedback from others. People project a certain identity to the world, and that identity is either accepted or rejected by the audience, causing the identity to be either reinforced or modified. In this chapter, we also emphasized the ways in which other people help us maintain our public identities.

It is important to note that this chapter covered only a small portion of the literature on identity and impression management. Research looking at psychological processes such as self-esteem and self-concept are also relevant to identity and impression management. In this chapter, our focus was on identity management in social and personal relationships. Other researchers have studied self-presentation within different contexts, such as first impressions during employment interviews or self-presentation strategies used by teachers in classrooms. The information posted on Emily's Facebook page functions for both established and new relationships—the page serves to maintain relationships with friends who can click and see all Emily's pictures in which they are featured; the page also serves as an introduction for new friends, acquaintances, and classmates who don't yet know Emily very well.

Interpersonal communication researchers have also studied identity and impression formation within the attraction process. People are attracted to those who convey a positive self-identity while appearing to be modest and approachable. Physical appearance, which plays a key role in impression management, is also one of several bases for attraction in close relationships (see Chapter 3). Emily's Facebook page reflects some of the characteristics that people find attractive, including sociability and popularity. The pictures she and others have posted show viewers what she and her friends look like, and also give viewers an idea of what kinds of activities she and her friends enjoy. The people viewing Emily's Facebook page will perceive her differently depending on how they evaluate the identity she has portrayed. Some people might have a positive impression

of Emily as a popular person, a talented dancer, bilingual, and one who visits exotic places such as Rome. Other people, however, may perceive Emily as a superficial, narcissistic person, more concerned about her large social network than developing high-quality close relationships. Viewers' perceptions would be influenced by their own identities and the characteristics they value in themselves and others. If Emily learns that some people she cares about have a negative impression of her when they view her Facebook page, she might change her postings.

Finally, identity can be expanded and protected within close relationships. Self-expansion theory suggests that relationships provide a venue for one's broadening identity and growing as a person. Facework is also important to project one's own desired image and to protect the positive and negative faces of a relational partner. Indeed, an awareness of the importance of face can go a long way toward helping people understand the development and deterioration of relationships.

KEY TERMS

affinity-seeking behavior (p. 43)
attractiveness deception (p. 42)
bald on-record strategy (p. 49)
broadcasters (p. 33)
communal frame (p. 27)
communication theory of identity (p. 27)
corrective facework (p. 41)
decide not to engage in the FTA (p. 50)
disclaimers (p. 50)
display rules (p. 42)
dramaturgical perspective (p. 26)

emotional labor (p. 42)
enactment of communication frame (p. 27)
face-threatening acts (FTAs) (p. 47)
generation Z (p. 30)
going off-record strategy (p. 50)
identity (p. 26)
interactors (p. 33)
millennials (p. 30)
negative face (p. 46)
negative politeness strategy (p. 49)
personal frame (p. 27)
politeness theory (p. 26)

positive face (p. 46)
positive politeness strategy (p. 49)
preventive facework (p. 50)
relationship frame (p. 27)
self-expansion theory (p. 36)
self-fulfilling prophecy (p. 39)
self-presentation (p. 25)
social identity theory (p. 26)
spies (p. 34)
theory of self (p. 35)
verbal self-handicapping (p. 50)
vision of self (p. 35)
wings (p. 45)

DISCUSSION QUESTIONS

1. Millennials and generation X-ers have different opinions about privacy in the era of social media. How do these generations differ and which perspective is closer to your personal opinion? How well (if at all) do you think people can protect their privacy in today's media-rich world?

2. In this chapter, we discussed ethical issues in identity management. Under what circumstances do you think that techniques used to manage one's positive identity are unethical or deceptive?

3. Think about one of your most embarrassing moments. Did you do facework? If so, what identity-management techniques did you employ? Did people around you help you save face? If so, how?

 SAGE edge™

Sharpen your skills with SAGE edge at edge.sagepub.com/guerrero5e.
SAGE edge for students provides a personalized approach to help you accomplish your coursework goals in an easy-to-use learning environment.

3 DRAWING PEOPLE TOGETHER
Forces of Social Attraction

Sofia is frustrated with her dating life. Even though she considers herself smart and pretty, she always seems to be the single one among her friends, and she is tired of feeling like the third wheel all the time. It seems so easy for her friends to find long-term boyfriends, while she seems to struggle. When she does find a boyfriend, the relationship never lasts very long. At first, Sofia thought her last boyfriend, Diego, was perfect for her. He was extremely good looking and his personality was exactly the opposite of her shy self. He loved to socialize and was flirtatious and fun. Eventually, however, Sofia got tired of trying to keep up with his fast-paced social life, and she became jealous of the women he hung out with even though Diego swore they were only friends. When they broke up, Sofia wondered why she had been so attracted to him in the first place. She also wondered if she was attracted to the wrong type of men. After all, her friends often had good relationships with men whom she didn't find particularly attractive.

Attraction is a force that draws people together. It can occur as quickly as a flash of lightning or develop slowly over time. Sometimes a surge of arousal—with a pounding heart and sweaty palms—accompanies attraction. Other times, a warm, cozy, comfortable feeling accompanies attraction. Of course, attraction is not always mutual; people are often attracted to individuals who are not attracted to them.

The reasons people are attracted to some individuals and not others are complex and dynamic; frequently attraction is hard to explain. Sofia's concerns about being able to find the right person are understandable; she wonders why she always seems to be attracted to the wrong person. She also wonders why her friends are attracted to certain people whom she finds unappealing. After Sofia and Diego break up, she realizes that the qualities that attracted her to him were not enough to sustain their relationship. After an experience such as Sofia's, people sometimes tell themselves that they will never again be attracted to a certain type of person only to later find themselves dating the same type of person.

Although attraction is complex—and the characteristics that attract people to others vary widely—there are fundamental reasons attraction develops. Social scientists have devoted considerable energy to determining the causes of **social attraction.** In this chapter, we review some of the research in this area. Specifically, we focus on how the personal attributes of two individuals work separately and together to affect attraction. We also look at the role that context and the environment play in the attraction process. This chapter provides insight into the many factors that influence to whom you are attracted and why people are or are not attracted to you.

ATTRACTION

Attraction has been defined as "a motivational state in which an individual is predisposed to think, feel, and usually behave in a positive manner toward another person" (Simpson & Harris, 1994, p. 47). This definition embraces many motivations for thinking, feeling, and behaving positively toward someone. For instance, such motivation could stem from thinking that someone is physically attractive, wanting to be someone's friend, wanting to work with someone, or wanting to be someone's lover. These four motivations underlie different types of attraction, as discussed next.

Types of Attraction

Early work identified three main forms of attraction: (1) physical, (2) social, and (3) task (McCroskey & McCain, 1974). **Physical attraction** occurs when we are drawn to people's looks, whether it is someone's body, eyes, hair, attire, or other aspects of a person's appearance. **Social attraction** reflects the feeling that we would like to "hang out" and be friends with someone. When people are socially attractive, we also usually think that they would fit in well with our circle of friends and our family. Finally, **task attraction** refers to our desire to work with someone to fulfill instrumental goals, such as completing a project or making a presentation. For example, think of people with whom you would like to work on a group project; they are probably smart,

hardworking, fair, and friendly. Box 3.1 includes a test you can take to see how attracted you are to someone in these three areas. Researchers have also identified a fourth type of attraction, **sexual attraction,** which reflects the desire to engage in sexual activity with someone and typically is accompanied by feelings of sexual arousal in the presence of the person.

Obviously, these types of attraction are related. In fact, both task and physical attraction can contribute to more general perceptions of social attraction. For example, if you meet someone who is physically attractive, you might decide that this person is also charming and intelligent and thus socially attractive. This tendency to perceive physically attractive people as more sociable is part of the **halo effect**, which is discussed later in this chapter. You also might be socially attracted to certain people, such as roommates and coworkers, because you find them task attractive. This is likely if you are the type of person who attends carefully to tasks and takes your work seriously. Physical and sexual attraction are also related. Indeed, Reyes and colleagues (1999) found that physical attractiveness relates more closely to sexual attraction than it does to social attractiveness—with physical and sexual attraction often occurring together in romantic relationships.

Despite the similarities, these types of attraction are distinguishable. For example, the person you would like to be part of your group project may not always be the first person you would ask to a party. Engineers and accountants often get a "bad rap" for fitting that stereotypic mold of people who are respected for their knowledge but who can be dull socially. In a similar vein, if you had a choice of partners for an important project, you would rarely use someone's physical appearance as the main criterion for selection. And although you might be physically attracted to someone who dresses well and is about the same age as you, this does not necessarily mean that you want to have sex with this person. So, despite some overlap between these types of attraction, there are also definite differences.

BOX 3.1 PUT YOURSELF TO THE TEST
WHAT TYPES OF PEOPLE ATTRACT YOU MOST?

To see what types of people attract you, try rating your closest friends and current or recent romantic partners using this scale. Think about the qualities that attracted you to them when you first met, and rate them accordingly by circling the appropriate number. Perhaps you are more attracted to people based on their ability to help with tasks, their sociability, or their physical appearance, or perhaps all of these types of attraction are important to you. You might also notice that different forms of attraction were present when you first met your close friends versus your romantic partners. Use the following scale to make your ratings:

1 = strongly disagree and 7 = strongly agree.

	Strongly Disagree						Strongly Agree
1. If I wanted to get things done, I thought I could probably depend on her/him.	1	2	3	4	5	6	7
2. I had confidence in her/his ability to get the job done.	1	2	3	4	5	6	7
3. I thought I would enjoy working with her/him on a task.	1	2	3	4	5	6	7
4. I thought this person would be an asset in any task situation.	1	2	3	4	5	6	7
5. I thought this person would take her/his work seriously.	1	2	3	4	5	6	7
6. I thought she/he could be a friend of mine.	1	2	3	4	5	6	7
7. I wanted to have a friendly chat with her/him.	1	2	3	4	5	6	7
8. I thought she/he would be easy to get along with.	1	2	3	4	5	6	7
9. I thought she/he would be pleasant to be with.	1	2	3	4	5	6	7
10. I thought I could become close friends with her/him.	1	2	3	4	5	6	7
11. This person struck me as handsome or pretty.	1	2	3	4	5	6	7
12. I found her/him attractive physically.	1	2	3	4	5	6	7
13. This person looked appealing.	1	2	3	4	5	6	7
14. I thought she/he was good looking.	1	2	3	4	5	6	7
15. I thought she/he had an attractive face.	1	2	3	4	5	6	7

Add Items 1 through 5 to determine your score on task attraction, items 6 through 10 to determine your score on social attraction, and items 11 through 15 to determine your score on physical attraction. Scores range from 5 to 15; the closer your score is to 15, the higher your level of each type of attraction.

Source: In Tardy, C. H. (Ed.), *A Handbook for the Study of Human Communication: Methods and Instruments for Observing, Measuring, and Assessing Communication Processes.* Copyright © 1988. Reproduced with permission of Greenwood Publishing Group, Inc., Westport, CT.

Fatal Attraction

Regardless of whether we are initially attracted to individuals because of their winning personality, their ability to help us accomplish goals, or their good looks, we could eventually discover that the very qualities we once found attractive are not as desirable as first thought. Felmlee (1995, 1998; Felmlee, Orzechowicz, & Fortes, 2010) studied this phenomenon by conducting a number of studies on **fatal attraction**, which she defined as occurring when the very qualities that draw us to someone eventually contribute to relational breakup. That is, certain qualities may seem attractive initially but spell danger ahead. Felmlee asked people to think of the last romantic relationship they were in that ended and then to describe both what initially attracted them to the person and what ultimately led to the breakup.

Felmlee's analysis of the answers led her to some interesting conclusions. First, differences were consistently the most common type of fatal attraction. In other words, being attracted to someone because the person is one's "opposite" might be exciting in the short term, but this novelty is likely to wear thin over time, as it did for Sofia in her relationship with Diego. Second, initially attractive qualities such as being fun, exciting, or easygoing can also contribute to breakups—especially if someone has these qualities to an extreme. For example, if you are attracted to someone primarily because of the person's sense of humor, that attraction could turn to dislike if you realize that your partner can never be serious. Similarly, Diego's attractive, outgoing, flirtatious nature became distressing to Sofia when she saw him socializing with other women and when she preferred to stay at home rather than go out.

Being attracted to a narcissistic person also appears to be a common type of fatal attraction. **Narcissism** is a personality trait that involves a "pervasive pattern of grandiosity, self-focus, and self-importance" (Back, Schmukle, & Egloff, 2010, p. 132), and is part of the "Dark Triad" personality (narcissism, Machiavellianism, and subclinical psychopathy; Qureshi, Harris & Atkinson, 2016). Studies have shown that people are initially attracted to narcissists (Back et al., 2010; Morf & Rhodewalt, 2001; Paulhus, 1998). They appear extroverted, self-confident, charming, agreeable, and competent. They are also "entertaining to watch" (Young & Pinsky, 2006, p. 470). However, as people get to know narcissists, they tend to become less attracted to them. One study even showed that the very characteristics that make narcissists most attractive when people first meet were the same characteristics that were most damaging in the long run (Back et al., 2010). Behaviors that were initially seen as showing confidence and motivation were later viewed as exploitative and self-absorbed. Importantly, Felmlee studied both opposite-sex and same-sex romantic relationships and found the types of fatal attraction traits to be very similar across both.

A FRAMEWORK FOR UNDERSTANDING ATTRACTION

In the rest of this chapter, we attempt to answer this question: What attracts us to others? In line with the available research, we focus mostly on social and physical attraction when addressing this question. As you will see, the answer to this question is complex. Indeed, researchers have found that many factors influence attraction. To organize these factors, we will use a model that is similar to a framework presented by Kelley and colleagues in 1983. Our application of this framework to the attraction process is depicted in Figure 3.1. Kelley argued that four general factors influence how we behave during interactions:

1. **Personal qualities** and preferences that *we* bring to the interaction, including our personality, interpersonal needs, expectations, self-esteem, physical appearance, and level of communication skill, among other qualities. Although not envisioned by early relational scholars, recent technologies have allowed researchers to examine the biological and neurological aspects of attraction, which also

would belong under personal qualities of attraction.

2. ***Qualities of the other*** and preferences that *they* bring to the interaction, including personality, needs, expectations, self-esteem, physical appearance, and level of communication skills, among other qualities.

3. ***Qualities of the pair,*** including similarities and differences between relational partners across a range of characteristics.

4. ***Qualities of the physical or social environment,*** including details of the location in which the interaction takes place (e.g., size, temperature, furniture, public versus private setting) and feedback from friends and family.

PERSONAL QUALITIES

What personal preferences, personality traits, skills, and perceptual biases do we possess that might influence our attraction to others? The considerable research that has focused on this question suggests that our evaluations of a person's reward value, our expectations about a person's behavior, and a number of demographic and personality variables all impact how attractive we find people.

Perceptions of Reward Value

When people enter relationships, they hope to obtain benefits or rewards, such as companionship, affection, sex, fun, and sometimes even financial resources. Therefore, one of the most powerful influences on our attraction to others is our perception of their reward value, which relates to our interpersonal needs and preferences. In fact, ideas

---

FIGURE 3.1   ■   Factors Influencing Interaction and Attraction

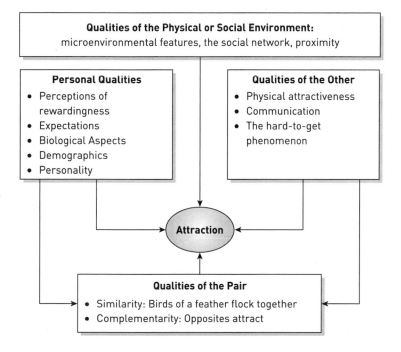

from interdependence theory (see Chapter 14) serve as a foundation for research on attraction. According to this theory, we are attracted to others when we think they offer more rewards than costs. Thus, if someone seems to have a host of positive, rewarding qualities (e.g., a good sense of humor, good looks, a willingness to sacrifice for others) and only a few negative, costly qualities (e.g., being late all the time, pessimistic), attraction should be high. Furthermore, individuals will be perceived as especially attractive if they have more rewards to offer than other people.

Although many of these rewards can also be considered qualities possessed by the other person (e.g., the other person's physical attractiveness) or are associated with qualities of the pair (e.g., similarity in beliefs and attitudes), it is people's own perception of these rewards that are relevant. Because these perceptions are our own and may have no basis in objective reality, they reflect our personal preferences and biases. Anything that impacts our perception of the rewards that others can offer plays a role in determining to whom we are attracted. Additionally, what qualifies as "rewarding" varies from one individual to another. For example, in the scenario that opened this chapter, Sofia may find that the qualities she sees initially rewarding in a prospective partner (e.g., he has a large social network) are actually something that may be harmful for long-term dating success (e.g., he spends all of his time with his friends). So, one key for Sofia is the qualities that she finds attractive and whether those coincide with good attributes for long-term mates.

Expectations

People's perceptions of reward value are influenced by our behavioral expectations. Numerous studies have shown that people's expectations of others play a large role in the attraction process (see Afifi & Burgoon, 2000). This process operates in three ways. First, people's expectations determine what they notice as being unusual or usual, which influences their attraction to others. When people act in unusual ways, others take notice (Burgoon & Hale,

1988). In general, if the unexpected behavior is perceived as rewarding, attraction should increase. By contrast, if the unexpected behavior is perceived as unrewarding, attraction is likely to decrease (Afifi & Burgoon, 2000). Miller-Ott and Kelly (2015) asked ten groups of college students about their expectation related to someone else's use of cell phones when spending time with them. Their expectations differed based on the situation. During dates, undivided attention is expected and the use of cell phones (except for a periodic and short text, with explanation) is seen as an unacceptable. However, when two people are just "hanging out" for an extended period of time (e.g., at a friend's house), expectations for undivided attention/no cell phone use are much more relaxed. Indeed, we often take cell phone use during occasions where we expect undivided attention to be either a reflection of a lack of interest or a lack of sensitivity, with important implications for attraction. In the case of Sofia's selection of partners, she may think about whether she is sufficiently weighting "red flags" when in early stages of attraction. She should not dismiss her expectations of potential dating partners when developing attraction to them. So if a potential partner violates expectations by being on the phone during a date with Sofia, this could decrease attraction and lead Sofia to explore other options.

Second, people's expectations have a way of becoming reality, regardless of the other person's actual behavior, and in so doing influence to whom people are attracted. This suggests that our expectations of other people lead us to treat them in ways that make it more likely that they will confirm our expectations. For example, if Sofia thinks Aaron is a friendly, considerate person, she is likely to treat him with respect, which, in turn, will make Aaron more likely to treat Sofia in a friendly, considerate manner. This also suggests that we tend to perceive people as acting in ways that fulfill our expectations, regardless of their actual behaviors. The extensive research on self-fulfilling prophecies supports these ideas. In one study, new teachers were told that certain students were "smart" and that other students were "less smart" (see Rosenthal & Jacobson, 1968). Although the two groups of students actually were no different from each other, by the end of the semester the teachers' expectations about the students' intelligence translated into different grades and even different IQ scores for the two groups. The students whom the teachers expected to be smart received better grades and had higher IQs than the students saddled with lower teacher expectations despite the initial similarity in ability and intelligence between the two groups.

This important study was followed by a series of studies that investigated why the teachers' expectations resulted in different grades and performance. At least two explanations have been given. First, teachers treated student comments and essays differently. Specifically, when supposedly poor students gave good answers, teachers focused on superficial aspects of their answers and attributed the smart-sounding parts of the responses to luck. By contrast, when supposedly smart students gave poor answers, teachers tended to look for something positive in their responses. For example, if a student labeled as smart commented that a political candidate won a debate because the candidate "was nicer," the teacher might interpret the student's answer to mean that viewers put too much weight on style compared to substance.

Second, the teachers' expectations led them to treat the two groups differently, which eventually influenced the actual quality of the students' work and their performance. Teachers gave mostly positive feedback to the supposedly bright students and mostly negative feedback to the supposedly poor students. Eventually, the students in the "poor group" simply stopped trying, while those in the "bright group" were encouraged to try harder (Rubovits & Maher, 1973).

After these studies on teacher–student interaction were published, numerous other studies showed a similar pattern across a range of contexts, including courtrooms, job interviews, and athletic fields. Expectancy effects have also been found in research on attraction. For example, Snyder, Tanke, and Berscheid (1977) tested the impact of men's perceptions of women's physical attractiveness on the women's behavior. The researchers found that when interacting with men who found them physically attractive, women behaved in a more sociable, likable, and friendly manner than when interacting with men who found them unattractive. Much more recently, Lemay and Wolf (2016) studied whether romantic and/or sexual attraction to a friend produced self-fulfilling outcomes. They discovered that people who had desire for a friend overestimated how much their friend reciprocated that desire, which led them to engage in sexual or romantic initiation efforts. But what is particularly noteworthy is that those efforts often resulted in an increase in their friends' desire, especially when the friend found the initiator attractive to begin with. Unfortunately, misperception of sexual interest is common (Perilloux, 2014), and often results in unwanted sexual attention and/or unwanted or pressured sexual behavior, so it is critical that individuals proceed with sexual advances with caution, always respecting an individual's desires and comfort levels.

Third, research on beliefs about future interaction provides another example of how expectations influence attraction. When people expect to see someone again, they are more likely to find that person attractive, regardless of the individual's behavior, than if they do not have expectations of future interaction (Kellermann & Reynolds, 1990). The expectation of future interaction motivates people to look for positive qualities in someone so that they will look forward to future interactions rather than dread them. That, in turn, makes us see things and act in ways that lead to attraction. Conversely, when people interact with someone whom they do not foresee meeting again, they have little reason to search for positive qualities. In fact, doing so may be depressing, given that they may not have the opportunity to get to know the person better in future interactions. Indeed, people are sometimes motivated to find negative qualities in individuals whom they do not expect to see again. The result is that the chances of attraction are minimized.

Biological Aspects of Attraction

Technology has allowed researchers to begin to focus on the biological and neurological aspects of the attraction process. While there is still a lot we do not yet know, what researchers *have* found out on these fronts is eye-opening and suggests that some of the attraction we feel for others is out of our control. Our bodies, to some extent, dictate to whom we are attracted.

One of the most potent attraction hormones seems to be oxytocin (OT). OT is a chemical released naturally in our bodies that has earned the name "the hormone of love" and the "connection chemical" because of its effects on the attraction process (Kuchinskas, 2009). Specifically, the release of OT creates a warm afterglow, tinting our subsequent experiences with "rose-colored glasses." Studies of high-OT mothers soon after birth showed that they were more likely than low-OT mothers to gaze at the baby's face, use baby talk, touch the child affectionately, and frequently check on the baby (Feldman, Weller, Zagoory-Sharon, & Levine, 2007). To further illustrate the effect of OT, Guastella, Mitchell, and Dadds (2008) nasally injected some participants with a burst of OT and then showed them images of several faces. Participants who received the OT "gazed longer and fixated more frequently" at the eye region of the faces (p. 4). Other studies have shown that OT increases our trust in others, makes us better able to read the emotional states of our interaction partners, contributes to empathy with others, and increases the likelihood of social approach (for review, see De Dreu & Kret, 2016; Guastella et al., 2008; Marazziti, Consoli, Silvestri, & Dell'Osso, 2009). No wonder OT gives a boost to the attraction process. It is also no surprise that drug companies are devoting considerable energy to developing a drug that mimics the effects of naturally produced OT.

Studies of brain activity are also enlightening and suggest that particular regions of the brain are activated during the attraction process. For instance, Fisher, Aron, and Brown (2005) recruited college students who reported being "intensely in love" and used functional magnetic resonance imaging to capture their brain activity as they looked at a picture of their partner. Results showed how the body influences the attraction process by providing a burst of activity to parts of the brain rich in dopamine, the primary pleasure chemical in the human system. That led the researchers to suggest the presence of an "attraction mechanism [that has] evolved to enable individuals to focus their mating energy on specific others" (p. 58). Bartels and Zeki (2004), using a similar procedure but this time with mothers looking at pictures of their children, found that feelings of love not only activate reward centers of the brain, but also deactivate parts of the brain that are associated with critical judgments and negative emotions. To bring this science to life, a documentary filmmaker recently collaborated with researchers at Stanford University's Center for Cognitive and Neurobiological Imaging. Their collaboration resulted in a heartwarming and insightful 12-minute short film tracking several participants in a "Love Competition," in which they were asked to think about someone they loved for five minutes while their brain was being scanned. The person whose brain scan suggested the most intense emotional experiences of love during that period would be crowned the "winner." You may be surprised of the outcome (see film here: https://vimeo.com/130648160; or Google "the Love Competition"). Other research suggests that sexual desire and love activate different regions of the brain and that even different types of sexual desire produce unique neural responses (Cacioppo & Cacioppo, 2016; Diamond & Dickenson, 2012), adding insight into the often-debated question about the overlap between feelings of love and sexual desire. In sum, researchers are increasingly concluding that the attraction process and related emotions are facilitated or hindered by the release of chemicals in the body and by the activation of particular emotion centers in the brain. These processes seem to have a lot more to do with whom we are attracted to and what we do with that attraction than previously believed.

Demographic Characteristics

As we have seen, perceptions and expectations have a direct effect on whom people find attractive. Sex, age, and other demographic variables also affect attraction, although the effects of such variables appear to be somewhat weaker than those connected to expectations. The demographic characteristic that has received the most attention in the attraction literature is sex.

SEX DIFFERENCES One of the most frequently asked questions is whether men and women differ in what qualities they find attractive. The popular belief is that men are primarily attracted by looks whereas women are more often attracted by personality, but the research on this question is somewhat mixed. For example, Feingold (1991) reviewed results from several studies and concluded that "men valued physical attractiveness more than did women, and that women valued similarity more than did men" (p. 357). Similarly, Sprecher (1998a) found that men rated physical attractiveness as a more important reason for attraction than did women, while women rated personality as a more important reason for attraction than did men.

One explanation for these sex differences and others like them (see Hamida, Mineka, & Bailey, 1998) stems from work in evolutionary psychology (also see Chapters 9 and 13). Evolutionary psychologists argue that sex differences in attraction are consistent with our evolution as a species. A central idea in social evolutionary theory is that humans, like all mammalian species, are driven by a desire to advance the species. Because only the strong survive, people are attracted to those whom they consider to be the "strongest" (see Buss, 1994; Schmitt, 2008). Because men and women fulfill different roles in the evolutionary chain, they look for different qualities

in their mating partners. Specifically, theorists argue that women "are looking for men who are willing to commit and who can provide security for them and their offspring" (Pines, 1998, p. 148) whereas men are simply looking for the most attractive (and most potentially fertile) women available.

Evolutionary psychologists suggest that these specialized sex roles evolved over thousands of years and are responsible for many of the sex differences observed today. According to this view, women are attracted to older men with more resources whereas men typically are drawn to younger women in their reproductive prime (Buss, 1994). Also, men are more easily influenced by physical appearance, whereas women attend more closely to personality, resources, and compatibility.

However, sex differences in attraction are not always as clear-cut as these studies suggest. In fact, sex differences between men and women may be exaggerated in studies in which the researchers rely on data from questionnaires. In these studies, respondents rate the extent to which physical appearance is an important part of their attraction to others. Women appear to be more hesitant than men to report that physical attraction is an important part of their selection process. Indeed, when researchers use a different measure to test whether both men and women are more attracted to physically appealing others, they find that men and women are both influenced by physical attraction. Sprecher (1989) conducted a study in which men and women were given a wide range of information about someone of the opposite sex. Of all the information provided, that which was related to the person's physical attractiveness was found to be the most important determinant of attraction for both men and women. However, when Sprecher later asked participants how much the person's physical attractiveness influenced their attraction, men were more willing than women to acknowledge its effect. In sum, as is typical in much of the research that we will discuss in this book, sex differences in social attraction may be overstated. Men and women seem more similar than different in terms of what they find attractive in others. Indeed, a recent review of more than 75 studies with over 30,000 participants combined showed that physical appearance was an equally strong predictor of mate preferences for both men and women (Eastwick, Luchies, Finkel, & Hunt, 2014). In sum, the question of whether the sexes differ in what attracts them to others is more complicated than it may seem: the answer likely depends on the way the question is asked and the method used to answer it.

GENDER DIFFERENCES Rather than studying sex differences, several scholars argue that we need to think of everyone as varying on a continuum of masculine–feminine qualities labeled as "gender orientation" or "sex-role orientation" (Archer, 1989; Bem, 1974). For instance, you may know men whose beliefs and behaviors are relatively feminine and women whose beliefs and behaviors are relatively masculine. Many men and women display a mix of feminine and masculine behaviors and beliefs and are classified as **androgynous** (Bem, 1974). Clearly, socialization affects much behavior. Thus, men who grow up in an environment that encourages emotional expression and that values personal qualities are not expected to behave similarly to or be attracted to the same types of partners as men who grow up in an environment in which emotional expression is discouraged or masculinity is defined by inattention to relationships. The same can be said for women. Mayback and Gold (1994) found that women who agree with "traditional" female roles are more attracted to aggressive, "macho" men than are women whose attitudes toward female roles are more unconventional. More recently, a study that surveyed people from nine countries showed that both men and women are attracted to others who fit stereotypical gender roles (Eastwick et al., 2006). Curiously, though, the opposite was found in one of the few studies of attraction in online dating settings. Specifically, Chappetta and Barth's (2016) experiment showed that participants looking at dating profiles online were more attracted to those profiles that described incongruous gender role

characteristics (e.g., men who described themselves as "intuitive" and women who described themselves as "analytical") than those that fit the gender role stereotypes. One explanation that the authors provided was that the former group may have been perceived as more sincere/more real than those that neatly fit stereotypes. Sure enough, Wotipka and High (2016) showed that college students found less polished/less "perfect" online profiles more attractive than those that they saw as being "too perfect." In other words, we ignore online profiles that we think are "too good to be true."

SEXUAL ORIENTATION AND AGE Two other important demographic characteristics that have received little attention from scholars are sexual orientation and age. The few studies that have examined the impact of these variables suggest that they do not have much effect on the qualities that people seek in their mates. The attraction process appears to be relatively similar, regardless of sexual orientation (Boyden, Carroll, & Maier, 1984; Felmlee et al., 2010). These findings are in stark contrast to the belief held by some in our society that gay or lesbian communities are attracted to partners by sexual motivations to a greater degree than their heterosexual counterparts. In fact, Felmlee and her colleagues found that members of the lesbian, gay, bisexual, transgender, and queer (LGBTQ) community listed fun, sense of humor, intelligence, kindness, and supportiveness as the top five attractive traits in potential partners. In a similar vein, scholars studying aging have found that people show remarkable consistency in whom they find attractive, regardless of age. In fact, people seem to find essentially the same qualities attractive whether they are in their preteen or teen years, or in their 70s or 80s (Aboud & Mendelson, 1998; Webb, Delaney, & Young, 1989). In sum, although these studies did not find differences in attraction due to sexual orientation or age, given the small number of studies it seems premature to dismiss the possibility that differences exist. Yet it also makes sense from an evolutionary perspective that the characteristics that make others attractive to us are not shaped by sexual orientation or age.

Personality

Our personalities influence the types of partners to which we are the most attracted and are the most compatible. Numerous facets of our personalities impact the attraction process. We examine four of these: (1) attachment style, (2) relationship beliefs, (3) self-esteem, and (4) narcissism.

ATTACHMENT STYLE A substantial amount of research has investigated how attachment style functions within relationships (see Chapter 8; see also Birnbaum & Reis 2012 for discussion of attachment theory and sexual attraction). **Attachment styles** reflect how people view themselves and their relationships with others. These views are represented by four attachment styles (Bartholomew, 1990): (1) Secure individuals are comfortable both alone and in relationships, (2) dismissive individuals prefer to be alone and are unmotivated to develop and maintain relationships, (3) fearful avoidant individuals fear intimacy and lack self-confidence, and (4) preoccupied individuals want intimacy and fear being alone.

Attachment style influences to whom we are attracted. For example, Bartholomew (1990) argued that one way people maintain their attachment styles is through the unconscious process of selectively choosing interaction partners who confirm their sense of self and others. This may explain why people who are treated badly as children are attracted to romantic partners who also treat them badly. In a related vein, Sperling and Borgaro (1995) found that preoccupied individuals are more attracted than are securely attached persons to people who provide a hint of positive. Apparently, because preoccupied individuals strongly desire to be in relationships, they grab onto any potential opportunity suggested by someone giving them a compliment. Secure individuals, by contrast, are not so quick to jump at the potential opportunity; other factors influence their relationship choices. So an important piece of the

attraction puzzle with which Sofia is struggling resides in her attachment style and related relational behavior.

RELATIONSHIP BELIEFS Knee (1998) examined how relationship beliefs impact attraction. Two dimensions underlie people's beliefs about the nature of relationships: (1) **destiny beliefs** and (2) **growth beliefs.** Destiny beliefs are based on the idea that first impressions of others are fixed and enduring and that people cannot change. Growth beliefs are based on the belief that impressions of others evolve over time and that people and relationships grow when faced with challenges.

Not surprisingly, studies have found that the process of attraction is quite different for people based on which type of these beliefs they hold (for review, see Knee & Petty, 2013). Those who hold strong destiny beliefs are quick to discount someone whom they see as less than an ideal partner. Conversely, they strongly pursue those with whom they have a "perfect" first encounter. They believe that some people are destined to meet (e.g., "soul mates"), rely heavily on their "gut" instinct to make that assessment, and are attracted only to those for whom they have that sense of destined connection. In contrast, those who hold growth beliefs believe that relationships are always a work in progress and that they require regular work. As a result, "imperfections" in others are not a "deal breaker" when it comes to attraction.

SELF-ESTEEM Several studies have shown that how people feel about themselves strongly influences whom they find attractive. For example, Joshi and Rai (1987) found that people's self-esteem directly relates to their level of attraction to others. That is, those who have high self-esteem consistently find others more attractive than those whose self-esteem is low.

Self-esteem can operate in even more subtle ways. In two studies, Hoyle, Insko, and Moniz (1992) assessed students' self-esteem, asked students to complete a bogus test on intelligence, and then provided them with either positive or negative feedback about their performance. After this feedback, the students talked briefly with another person and completed a survey about their attraction to the interaction partner. The students with low self-esteem were more attracted to the other after being told good news about their performance on the "intelligence test," compared to being told bad news about their performance. In other words, good news made them more attracted to others, perhaps because they associated the person with a rewarding situation or perhaps because they were simply in better moods, felt confident, and were more receptive to their interaction partner's positive qualities.

People with high self-esteem showed the exact opposite pattern in Hoyle and fellow researchers' (1992) study; that is, they were more attracted to others after hearing bad news about their performance on the intelligence test than they were after hearing good news. Why would that be? One explanation is that people with high self-esteem recognize the need to boost their self-image after receiving bad news, and one way to do so is to view others as attractive and to interact with them. In that case, the most likely time that people with high self-esteem are likely to be attracted to others is after experiencing a failure (e.g., doing poorly on an exam).

NARCISSISM Recall that narcissism is defined in terms of having an exaggerated sense of self-importance and a focus on oneself at the expense of others. Campbell (1999) conducted five studies to determine how individuals' degree of narcissism affects their attraction to others. He found big differences between the qualities that are attractive to narcissists and to non-narcissists. Most noticeably, narcissists are attracted to others who admire them, while non-narcissists are drawn to others who exhibit caring qualities. Other studies have found similar results, showing that narcissists are more focused on the short-term rewards they get from relationships, and therefore look for someone who provides them with immediate admiration rather than long-term mutual liking (Emmons, 1989; Morf & Rhodewalt, 2001).

Despite their illusions of self-importance, research suggests that some narcissists have relatively low self-esteem and seek self-esteem boosts. In fact, in Campbell's (1999) study, narcissists were partly drawn to admiring others because of their own need to improve their self-esteem. Narcissists may also protect their self-esteem by downplaying situations where they are rejected. In one study (Rhodewalt & Eddings, 2002), highly narcissistic men were especially likely to elaborate on positive aspects of their dating history if they had been rejected by a potential dating partner—perhaps as a defense mechanism that protected them from feeling bad after being rejected.

OTHER PEOPLE'S QUALITIES

So far, our discussion has focused on personal perceptions and predispositions people have when evaluating others' attractiveness. Of course, other people's qualities increase one's likelihood of being attracted to them. As noted earlier, one view of attraction boils down to a perception that someone can offer us more rewards than costs relative to other potential partners. Thus, the key question becomes this: What qualities do people find especially rewarding? People seem to prefer those who are physically attractive and communicatively skilled. Moreover, people who are perceived to be in high demand and moderately "hard to get" are also highly valued. In this section, we discuss these variables, starting with the quality that has received the most attention—physical attractiveness.

Physical Attractiveness

Studies have consistently shown that physical attractiveness is one of the top two predictors of social attraction (Dion, 1986; Little, 2015). For example, Sprecher (1989) found that the more physically attractive the other person was, the more attracted participants were to the person. Similarly, Johnson, Afifi, and Duck's (1994) research on first dates among dating club members showed that, more than any other quality, people's physical attractiveness determined whether their dates found them socially attractive. These findings may not be surprising, but the more interesting question may be what specific "looks" we find attractive.

The answer to that question is too complex to be fully addressed here, and in some ways is culturally determined (see Box 3.2), but several studies have yielded some insights. One feature that has been shown to strongly influence women's attraction to men is height. In fact, studies have found that women tend to find very short men unattractive as potential mates even when the researcher assigns them a whole host of other rewarding qualities, such as a positive personality, intelligence, and high earning potential (Jackson &

Ervin, 1992; Pierce, 1996). Tall women also seem to be at an advantage but less than their male counterparts (Hensley, 1994). Across many different cultures, when men are being evaluated, a strong jawline, broad shoulders, and a hip-to-waist ratio of slightly less than one (i.e., a waist just slightly smaller than the hips) contribute to judgments of physical attractiveness. For women, a soft jawline and an hourglass figure (i.e., a waist significantly smaller than the chest and hips) is preferred (Buss, 1989, 1994; Singh, 1995). Both men and women also value physical fitness and an athletic build in their dating partners. In the United States, overweight people are usually not considered attractive, but the link between weight and attractiveness varies by culture (see Box 3.2).

BOX 3.2 AROUND THE WORLD
WHEN BEAUTY IS (AND IS NOT) IN THE EYE OF THE BEHOLDER

Some attributes associated with beauty appear to hold across the globe while others are determined by cultural and individual preferences.

Personal and Cultural Preferences:

Coloring: Preferences often vary on the basis of what is perceived as scarce in a particular culture or coculture (e.g., dark skin and hair is more prized in places where light hair and skin is common and vice versa). So in countries like India, many women avoid the sun to look lighter whereas in the United States light-skinned women want to look tan.

Weight: Preferences regarding weight vary by culture, especially for women. In most industrialized countries, such as the United States, thinness is prized because it indicates that a person has the resources needed to eat healthy foods and stay in shape. However, in other places, such as the Ivory Coast, plumpness is prized because it is associated with wealth and having enough to eat.

Height: Although the preference for tall men has been found in many cultures, there are differences in how much

this attribute is valued. Preferences related to women's height vary quite a bit as a function of culture and personal preference. In general, men prefer women who are shorter than they are whereas women prefer men who are taller than they are. Thus, a person's own height influences who that person finds attractive.

Universal Preferences:

Body and facial symmetry: When two sides of a face or body mirror each other, a person is rated as more physically attractive.

Body proportionality and the golden ratio: The golden ratio of f (Phi), or 1 to 1.618, is an index of attractiveness (e.g., bodies are rated as more proportional if the distance from the navel to the bottom of the feet is 1.618 times the distance from the navel to the top of the head; faces are rated as more proportional if the width of the lips is 1.618 times the width of the nose, among other comparisons).

Waist-to-hip ratio: For women, the ideal ratio is 0.70 (the waist is 70% the size of the hips). For men, the ideal ratio is about 1.0 (hips and waist about the same size).

(Continued)

Koinophilia: Faces are rated as more attractive when they have "average" features—with studies showing that a computer composite of multiple faces is perceived as more attractive than any single face.

Facial neoteny and maturity: Faces are rated as more attractive when they are characterized by a combination of babylike and mature features that represent youth and sexuality (e.g., a woman with large eyes, full lips, and high cheekbones or a man with large eyes, a small nose, and strong jawline).

Source: Information compiled from Guerrero and Floyd (2006).

Perhaps preoccupation with looks seems unfair, and people should be judged by their inner character rather than their outward appearance. This may be true, but the research suggests that, fair or not, people use outward appearances to make judgments about people's inner character. Specifically, research has shown that people often associate good looks with a wide range of other positive qualities. This tendency, often called the "halo effect" or the "what-is-beautiful-is-good" stereotype, leads people to believe that physically attractive individuals are more likely to succeed, and are more sociable, popular, intelligent, and competent than their less-attractive counterparts (Dion, 1986; Dion, Berscheid, & Walster, 1972; Hatfield & Sprecher, 1986b). The halo effect means that people are drawn to attractive individuals because most people are looking for someone who offers the "complete package." Because looks are a shortcut for other positive traits, physically attractive people receive more positive attention from others throughout life (Dion, 1972), often develop more-positive self-esteem (Nell & Ashton, 1996), and may actually develop some of the skills people assume they have (Chaiken, 1979).

The halo effect helps explain why good looks are so important in the attraction process. Social evolutionary theorists offer a complementary explanation for why physical attractiveness matters. Specifically, they argue that people's attraction to particular physical traits is due to the genetic drive to mate with the fittest person possible (Buss, 1994). Physical fitness, especially body shape and size, is perceived to be an outward sign of health and fertility. Thus, although cultural standards for beauty vary, social evolutionary theorists predict that some preferences cut across cultures (see Box 3.2). For example, physical attributes related to health and fertility, such as a clear complexion and a physically fit body, have been found to be valued by most cultures around the globe (Buss, 1994). In fact, Buss's classic 1989 study showed remarkable consistency across 37 cultures in what people found to be physically attractive. Langlois and colleagues' (2000) summary of 130 samples found the same physical characteristics of attraction. Specifically, we seem to be unconsciously drawn to features such as body and facial symmetry, body proportionality, and particular waist-to-hip ratios, among many other attributes (for review, see Guerrero & Floyd, 2006).

Judgments of beauty, however, are not always objective. For example, people involved in romantic relationships tend to see members of the opposite sex as less physically attractive, perhaps as a way of maintaining their current relationship (Simpson, Gangestad, & Lerma, 1990). Research testing **interaction appearance theory** has also demonstrated that people perceive others as more physically attractive if they have warm, positive interactions with them (Albada, Knapp, & Theune, 2002). Thus, in some cases relationships and interaction can lead people to revise their initial impressions of people or to regard their relational partners as more physically attractive than an objective observer would judge them to be.

Finally, people may be drawn to physically attractive individuals because they hope to gain rewards through association. For instance, think about when you are with your most attractive friends; perhaps you have more opportunities to meet people and feel more attractive yourself. Research suggests that whether intentional or not, people benefit by interacting with more attractive others. Sigall and Landy (1973), for example, found that people were rated as more attractive when they were with comparatively more attractive individuals than when they were not. The idea here is that some of the attention that physically attractive people get spills over to their friends through what is called the **assimilation effect.**

In sum, most people are attracted to good-looking persons, but what other qualities do we find attractive in potential partners or friends? Is physical appearance all that matters? The answer is a resounding "No." People notice those who are physically attractive and are more likely to initiate communication with attractive people, but that does not guarantee that highly attractive people will continue to be valued after initial attraction fades. In fact, they can be at a disadvantage in trying to live up to the high expectations imposed by the halo effect. Physical appearance only goes so far, and there are other significant qualities that make people attractive.

Interpersonal Communication Skills

Are we so drawn to physically attractive people that their interpersonal communication skills do not matter initially? For years, scholars ignored the role of interpersonal communication in favor of studying the impact of other variables on our attraction. Sunnafrank (1991, 1992) was among the first scholars to study how communication influences attraction. In the mid-1980s, he began a series of studies that added what was, until then, a novel element to

studies of attraction—he actually had participants interact with the person they were rating on attraction. Most previous studies had only shown participants a picture or given them information about some fictitious character. Sunnafrank argued that unless people communicated, experiments would not be representative of the real qualities that people consider when evaluating the attractiveness of others. In fact, he suggested that many of the factors that scholars had found to predict attraction, such as similarity and physical attractiveness, might not matter as much once people started talking to one another. Instead, he claimed, people would be influenced by another's communication style and behavior to determine how attracted they were to each other.

Many studies have supported Sunnafrank's contention. Reyes and fellow researchers (1999) had students view a still picture of an actor and asked them to answer several survey questions, including questions about their attraction to the actor. Then the students watched an interaction in which an opposite-sex actor was either nice or acted like a jerk and answered the questions again. The power of communication was evident. Although physical attractiveness was a primary quality that drew people to the actor prior to watching the interaction, the actor's behavior during the interaction, whether positive or negative, became a primary determinant of their attraction to the actor afterwards; physical attractiveness hardly mattered. Thus, communication plays a key role in determining to whom we are attracted. But what specific communication styles do we find appealing? Some studies provide important clues as to the connection between communication and attraction.

One communication quality that seems to emerge relatively consistently in studies of attraction is warmth. A generally positive attitude and a show of concern for others typically communicates warmth (Folkes & Sears, 1977); nonverbally, such behaviors as smiling, making eye contact, and showing interest in the other person also communicate warmth (Andersen, 1985; Andersen & Guerrero,

1998a; Friedmann, Riggio, & Casella, 1988). In fact, Sprecher (1998a) conducted three studies, all of which revealed that warmth and kindness were rated as the two qualities of the interaction partner that were most responsible for the participant's attraction to the partner. And Burgoon and her colleagues have repeatedly shown that something as simple as showing that you are interested in what your partner has to say makes a strong impact on your attractiveness (Burgoon & Le Poire, 1993).

Sociability and competence are two other communication qualities that have been shown to influence attraction (Krueger & Caspi, 1993). Here, sociability refers to one's ability to communicate easily among a group of people. People who are extroverted and expressive are perceived as highly sociable. Competence is determined by one's level of composure and knowledge. People are often evaluated as competent when they communicate without showing signs of nervousness and seem knowledgeable, although when people go out of their way to seem knowledgeable, they are often rated as unattractive (Vangelisti et al., 1990).

One study specifically asked participants to describe what they thought ideal relational partners would say or do on a first date (Wildermuth, Vogl-Bauer, & Rivera, 2006). More than 1,100 strategies were listed, all of which could be captured by 15 general categories. The most commonly mentioned actions included taking charge in initiating relational events (e.g., getting contact information), identifying positive aspects about their interaction partner, getting their interaction partner to discuss likes and dislikes, and saying and doing things to look their best, among others. It is also worth noting that bragging and the use of humor were the least frequently listed among participants in this study. Of course, what we *think* an ideal partner would say or do and what we actually respond to most favorably do not always match. Indeed, there are occasions in which the use of humor may be very attractive, as we have shown, and occasions in which getting contact information may be seen as too forward or inappropriate.

In contrast to these "softer" qualities of warmth—sociability and competence—some people are drawn to potentially "darker" qualities. For example, several studies have shown that women in particular are attracted to men who show a certain degree of assertiveness or power. This is consistent with social evolutionary theory in that women should be attracted to behavioral expressions of dominance in men because it reflects a reproductive advantage. In other words, women should be subconsciously attracted to the strongest and fittest men who will produce the best offspring. To test this idea, Sadalla, Kenrick, and Vershure (1987) created perceptions of dominance by having male actors take seats close to the subjects. The "nondominant" actors sat up straight and chatted quietly among themselves; the "dominant" actors sat in a very relaxed posture and showed a lack of interest in the women while talking loudly, quickly, and clearly. They found that the women were most attracted to the men who showed these signs of dominance.

Does this mean that women prefer dominant men to nice men? Jensen-Campbell, Graziano, and West (1995) attempted to address the question of whether "nice guys really finish last." They argued that, from an evolutionary perspective, women should also value altruism in men because they want partners who make sacrifices and invest considerable resources in the relationship. This is exactly what they found. First, women were attracted to altruistic men (men who were willing to do something boring so that the woman did not have to) much more than to nonaltruistic men (men who jumped at the opportunity to do something fun and left the boring task to the woman). The study was consistent with the research showing that people are attracted to individuals who are warm and caring. However, men who were altruistic but otherwise unassertive and weak were not very attractive. Men who were assertive or dominant and nonaltruistic were not attractive to the women either. Instead, women found the combination of assertiveness or dominance and altruism most appealing. Thus, strong but altruistic men may be perceived as most attractive.

Interestingly, the same results did not emerge with regard to men's attraction to women. That is, men's levels of attraction were unaffected by a woman's level of dominance, but the men were much more attracted to altruistic women. So, again, the importance of communicating care in interactions shines through; nice men—and women—are generally preferred over ones who are not.

Finally, the timing of positive versus negative behavior seems to influence attraction. Several studies have identified what has been called the **loss–gain effect** (Afifi & Burgoon, 2000; Aronson & Linder, 1965; Sharma & Kaur, 1996). This effect reflects what happens to attraction when a person's behavior moves from positive to negative or from negative to positive. For example, if someone seems very nice to you early in the interaction but then begins to act like a jerk, would you be more attracted to that person than if the person was a jerk from the start? Studies suggest that you would not. In fact, people are more attracted to individuals who are consistently negative than to people who initially behave positively and then switch to negative behavior. People who start out being nice get our hopes up, so the letdown we experience when we discover that they are not nice makes it worse than if they had acted badly from the start. Of course, people are most attracted to those who are pleasant throughout an interaction.

The "Hard-to-Get" Phenomenon

In some situations, the person who acts somewhat hard to get is perceived as attractive. For example, Roberson and Wright (1994) put males in a situation in which they had to try to convince a female stranger (an actor who was actually working for the experimenters) to be their coworker on a project. The men were told that the woman either would be easy to convince, might be difficult to convince, or would be impossible to convince. Results showed that the men rated the woman they were told would be moderately difficult to convince as most attractive. The authors concluded that playing hard to get has its benefits but that it can backfire if the person is seen as unattainable.

Similarly, Wright and Contrada (1986) found that people rated members of the opposite sex as most attractive when they were portrayed as moderately selective rather than as very selective or nonselective. Why is that? Apparently, we are more attracted to individuals who present a bit of a challenge than to those whom we perceive to be too easily attainable or completely unattainable. One reason for this may be that in our effort to shoot for the best possible "catch," we think that we are not shooting high enough if we are attracted to those who are not at least somewhat of a challenge. Consistent with this reasoning, research has shown that we are most likely to be attracted to hard-to-get people if they are easy for us to attract but difficult for others to attract (Walster, Walster, Piliavin, & Schmidt, 1973). One explanation is that when a person is hard for others to attract but easy for you to do so, people view you in a more positive light. In other words, people will likely perceive that you must have outstanding personal qualities if you were able to obtain such a high-quality partner. Another explanation is that scarcer resources, including people, are more valuable.

In sum, in addition to individuals' own personal qualities, many qualities of other people increase or decrease feelings of attraction. However, unique qualities emerge when two people interact with each other. These factors, which we call qualities of the pair, also affect attraction.

QUALITIES OF THE PAIR

When two people interact, the synergy of their interaction creates a certain chemistry that determines their mutual interpersonal attraction. One of the strongest and most important aspects of interpersonal chemistry is the degree to which people are similar to one another. This conclusion is far from new. As early as 1870, Sir Francis Galton, the cousin of Charles Darwin and a scientist best known for his research on intelligence and heredity, concluded that spouses usually are similar on several characteristics. Over the next century, many studies showed that friends and spouses tend to be similar on everything from attitudes and beliefs to height and visual acuity (Byrne, 1992). These studies all reached the same conclusion: The more similar others are to us, the more we will be attracted to them.

Similarity: "Birds of a Feather Flock Together"

Do similar individuals really tend to hang out together as this saying suggests? Think about your friends and dating partners. Do most of them have a lot in common with you? Maybe you like to do the same things, think the same way, or have similar personalities. Or perhaps you come from similar backgrounds. This preference for similarity has been shown to hold true across a whole host of personal qualities, including demographic characteristics such as race, cultural background, educational level, socioeconomic status, and religion, among other demographic characteristics (Hill, Rubin, & Peplau, 1976; Kandel, 1978). However, similarity has been studied most extensively in the context of similarity among attitudes.

ATTITUDINAL SIMILARITY When people are similar in their attitudes, beliefs, and values, they are said to share attitudinal similarity. People can have perceived similarity (thinking that they are similar to the other person) or actual similarity (actually being similar to the other person), or both. Two people may think they share attitudes and beliefs but later find out that they have very different likes and dislikes. The importance of this distinction quickly became evident to researchers. In one of the first extensive studies of attitudinal similarity, Newcomb (1961) found important differences between actual and perceived similarity. Newcomb gave a group of male undergraduates room and board in exchange for their participation in a study on friendships. The participants were randomly assigned roommates and were given surveys throughout the school year. The results showed that roommates liked one

another more when they were similar. Interestingly, at the beginning of the year, perceived similarity and actual similarity did not match. New roommates were often oblivious to the actual level of similarity they shared, so they relied heavily on their perceptions of similarity to determine liking. As the year went on, however, the actual degree of similarity between roommates gradually became evident. By the end of the year, those who were actually dissimilar did not like one another even though their initial perceptions of similarity had led them to like one another at first.

At about the same time of Newcomb's now famous experiment, Byrne (1961, 1971) began to research the impact of attitudinal similarity attraction, which has contributed greatly to our understanding of the relationship between similarity and attraction. One of his main methods for testing the effect of similarity on attraction was what he labeled the "bogus stranger" method. Byrne would first ask participants a series of questions assessing their likes and dislikes. He would then take the questionnaire to a different room and create answers on another, similar questionnaire that ranged from being almost identical to the participants' answers to very different from the participants' answers. Next, he took the bogus survey back to the participants, told them that the survey belonged to a participant who had already taken part in the study, asked them to read it over, and then rate the extent to which they would be attracted to this bogus stranger. Byrne and his colleagues repeatedly found that participants were more attracted to bogus strangers who were similar to them (Byrne, 1997).

Not surprisingly, the real-life applicability of this method has been challenged; some scholars argue that this similarity effect disappears when two people communicate with each other (Sunnafrank, 1991). Nonetheless, the remarkable consistency of the finding that people are attracted to attitudinally similar individuals is hard to dispute. Thus, the question becomes centered on what it is that makes attitudinal similarity so important.

According to Byrne's (1971) **reinforcement model,** we are attracted to similar others because they reinforce our view of the world as the correct perspective. People do not like it when others challenge the correctness of their own attitudes and values. The best way to avoid such a challenge is to interact with individuals who think the same way. For example, imagine disagreeing about everything with your friends or dating partner; that would get tiresome rather quickly, so you probably avoid people with whom you think that may happen. By contrast, when two people are similar, they usually have more in common to talk about and like to do the same things, which makes interaction enjoyable. Similarities make people's lives much easier, and make people feel that their way is the "right" way since others share their views. The disadvantage, of course, is that people fail to grow very much if all their friends are just like them.

A related argument is that we view people with attitudes similar to our own as trustworthy, and it is that perception of trustworthiness that makes them attractive. Singh and his colleagues (2015) have completed several studies in which they have shown that the impact of similarity on attraction reduces without the benefit of trust. Their argument is that we are attracted to people we perceive as similar to us because we believe that we can trust them.

There is also an important distinction between actual similarity and perceived similarity. Both actual and perceived similarities have important relational implications, as shown in a study by Morry (2005). She studied attraction similarity in ongoing same-sex friendships. Like other researchers, she found similarity to be important but also showed that the happier people were in their friendships, the more similar they reported their friends to be. Importantly, she was able to show that the attraction came *before* the bias toward perceptions of similarity in her study. In other words, we tend to see people to whom we are attracted as being more similar to us than they really are. Relatedly, we see people we dislike as being less similar.

A comprehensive summary of more than 300 studies of attitudinal similarity adds weight to the suggestion that perceived similarity, rather than actual similarity, may be the critical aspect of attraction (Montoya, Horton, & Kirchner, 2008). Researchers have studied the association between attitudinal similarity and attraction in three main ways: asking about attraction (1) to hypothetical others, (2) to a stranger they talked to in the lab, or (3) to someone with which they had a relationship. The authors compared results from all three kinds of methods and concluded that perceived similarity was significantly more important than actual similarity in most situations. Even more impressively, they found that only perceived similarity—not actual similarity—predicted attraction in existing relationships. More recently, Tidwell, Eastwick, and Finkel's (2013) study of speed-daters also showed that perceived similarity, not actual similarity, predicted attraction in that context. This conclusion does not negate the importance of actual similarity, but it does suggest that it is the *perception* of similarity about attitudes, even in its actual absence, that affects whom we are attracted to. But the impact of similarity on attraction has been studied across several characteristics other than attitudes.

If you were told that there were three couples in this picture and that each person was randomly assigned a place to stand, who would you guess was in a relationship with whom? Would your guesses be based on how similar they look or some other criteria? How might stereotypes influence people's guesses and lead them to make wrong assumptions?

SIMILARITY IN COMMUNICATION SKILLS People also have a preference for similarity in communication style. Burleson (1998) examined why people are attracted to others who have similar levels of communication skills and are happier with similarly skilled individuals than with those who are not similarly skilled. What intrigued Burleson was not that very good communicators are attracted to other good communicators, but rather that poor communicators are also drawn to other poor communicators. Why might people with limited communication skills be attracted to others who are similarly limited? Burleson (1998) advanced four possible explanations:

1. *The differential importance explanation:* Communication may not be a very frequent or important activity for those with low communication skill. As a result, low-skill people may not care if their partner is unskilled. In other words, since low-skill people do not engage in communication very often, they may not be looking for a high-skill partner. Other factors affecting attraction may be more important to them.

2. *The "ignorance is bliss" explanation:* Low-skill individuals are not aware that some people communicate better than they do. Because they have relationships with similar others, most of their interactions have been with people with relatively low social skills. As a result, they are happy with the way their low-skill partner communicates.

3. *The "sour grapes" explanation:* People who have poor communication skills are painfully aware of their shortcomings in the social arena. Although they might like to have partners with better skills than they have, they perceive highly skilled communicators to be hopelessly out of their reach. As a result, they settle for partners with lower social skills, figuring these partners are as good as they can get, while downgrading higher-skill people.

4. *The skill-as-culture explanation:* What some people consider to be poor communication, others might actually see as effective communication. Thus, individuals who are defined as low-skill communicators by researchers may be enacting communication behaviors that they and their partners consider to be quite competent. For example, some people might perceive low levels of expressiveness as indicative of incompetence, but an inexpressive dyad might feel most comfortable keeping their emotions hidden.

SIMILARITY IN PHYSICAL ATTRACTIVENESS Another form of similarity that has been studied extensively for its impact on attraction is physical attractiveness. Have you ever noticed, for instance, how people who are dating tend to be similar in terms of physical attractiveness? In fact, people take notice when one member of a romantic couple is much better looking than the other. Fair or not, the automatic assumption is that the less-attractive partner must have other exceptional qualities (e.g., a great personality, wealth, high social standing) that led the more attractive partner to choose this person over better-looking alternatives.

Our tendency to be attracted to people who are similar to us in physical attractiveness has been called the **matching hypothesis** (Berscheid, Dion, Walster, & Walster, 1971). This does not mean that people search for partners who look similar to themselves in terms of physical features—for example, brown-eyed people looking for brown-eyed partners or people with high cheekbones and fair skin looking for partners who have similar bone structure and skin color. Instead, the matching hypothesis predicts that people look for partners who have roughly the same level of overall physical attractiveness as themselves. Thus, even though Sofia is a petite, fair-skinned, green-eyed blonde and Diego is a tall, dark-skinned, brown-eyed brunette, because they are both good looking they fit the matching hypothesis. By contrast, if you think you are fairly good looking but not stunningly beautiful or devastatingly handsome, the matching hypothesis predicts that you will look for a partner who is somewhat above average but not extraordinarily attractive. Interestingly, the matching hypothesis has been shown to hold true across a wide variety of relationship types from friendships to marriages, as well as across cultures (Feingold, 1988).

However, this matching hypothesis appears to be in stark contrast to the research on physical attractiveness. Those studies found that people are most attracted to individuals who are very physically attractive. By contrast, research on the matching hypothesis suggests that people are most attracted to individuals who are similar to them in physical attractiveness. In other words, less-attractive people should be attracted to other similarly less-attractive people rather than to the best-looking ones. These seemingly inconsistent findings lead to two questions: (1) Which of these hypotheses is right? and (2) Why would less-attractive people be attracted to other less-attractive individuals as opposed to more-attractive people?

The answer to both of these questions depends on people's sense of what is ideal and realistic. Ideally, people want to date others who are more attractive than they are, but realistically recognize that physically attractive individuals are likely to have many options and are somewhat selective about whom they date. Recall the research on the hard-to-get phenomenon. These studies showed that people are attracted to individuals who are somewhat hard to get but tend to shy away from individuals who are too selective because they do not want to waste their effort on people they see as too selective, choosy, or conceited. Thus, people may label someone who is much better looking than themselves as conceited and instead select a dating partner who is similar to themselves in terms of physical attractiveness. In short, the matching hypothesis is based on the idea that people want to maximize the attractiveness of their partner by choosing someone who is at least as attractive as themselves while minimizing their chances for rejection by choosing someone who is attainable. Based on this reasoning, both the beautiful-is-good and matching hypotheses appear to have some basis in truth.

SIMILARITY IN MUSICAL PREFERENCES Music plays an important part in our lives. We often identify strongly with certain kinds of music, or artists, and distance ourselves from others. So it should come as no surprise that scholars have studied the way in which our musical preferences are linked to our attractiveness to others. The few studies that have done so consistently show that similarity in musical preferences is linked to attraction. Social bonds are created through shared musical preferences. In fact, Schäfer and colleagues (2016) argue that music's ability to foster human connection is part of its basic function, and that attraction to others with similar musical preferences may have evolutionary advantages for us. But what's the reason behind this attraction to those with similar musical preferences? Is music an indicator of personality? Or are musical choices perceived as even more meaningful? Boer and colleagues (2011) showed that people see others' musical choices as indicators of their values so that similarity in musical tastes seems to express similarity in values—stronger than a mere expression of personality. Consistent with our recognition of the importance of music for connectedness, Denes, Gasiorek, and Giles (2016) showed that college students were more willing to adjust the music playing in their apartment toward the preferences of someone for whom they had romantic interest than someone for whom they did not. In other words, we seem to be quite aware of the ways in which musical preferences are tied to attraction.

SIMILARITY IN NAMES AND BIRTH DATES Evidence suggests that our affinity for similar others may go to absurd lengths. Using the notion of **implicit egotism,** several scholars have shown that we are attracted to others based on similarity on the most arbitrary things. These scholars argue that even similarity in first or last names, in the size of earlobes, or in the date of birth, among other subtle similarities, activate liking for others because these characteristics are subconsciously associated with liking for ourselves (e.g., our names, our earlobe lengths, our birth dates). If this sounds crazy, it is worth pointing out that several studies have observed this trend. For example, Jones, Pelham, Carvallo, and Mirenberg (2004) summarized seven studies they performed that systematically tested this implicit egotism effect. In the end, their studies showed that people were more attracted to others whose arbitrary experimental code assigned by the researchers shared similarities with their birth dates or were subliminally connected to their names. Moreover, their investigation of marriage records showed that people are disproportionately likely to marry someone whose first or last name shares at least some similarity to their own (e.g., their first or last name starts with the same letter) even after accounting for ethnic similarities in names. In a similar vein, Kooti, Magno, and Weber's (2014) analysis of Twitter and Google+ accounts found that we are 10% to 30% more likely to follow others with our same name than we would expect by chance alone. More research is necessary to determine the extent to which implicit egotism plays a role in the attraction process.

Complementarity: Sometimes Opposites Attract

Although the research discussed thus far shows that there is a strong similarity effect when it comes to attraction and liking, this does not mean that people are always similar on every valued characteristic. Sometimes relational partners or good friends also complement one another in some areas. For example, Sofia and her best friend, Beanna, might both be intelligent, have the same major in college, and enjoy winter sports such as ice skating and skiing; but Sofia might be the better student whereas Beanna might be the better athlete. Instead of envying each other's skills, they may be proud of each other's special talents; Sofia may benefit from Beanna's contribution to their tennis team, while Beanna benefits from Sofia's help in studying for an exam. They also might be completely different in some ways. For instance, Sofia might be shy and reserved, carefully thinking before talking, while Beanna is extroverted and impulsive. Likewise, these qualities could complement one another; that is, Sofia might appreciate having Beanna around to help her make new friends, while Beanna might appreciate it when Sofia tells her to think before acting on certain impulses.

As this example suggests, the old saying that "opposites attract" can have some basis in truth. However, **complementarity** seems to be a much better predictor of attraction and liking when it is linked to behavior or resources and not attitudes and values (Strong et al., 1988). When it comes to people's core attitudes and beliefs, similarity seems to be much more important than complementarity. Additionally, as noted previously, sometimes people are initially attracted to someone who is completely unlike them, only to discover that those "opposite" characteristics eventually drive them crazy. This happened in Sofia's relationship with Diego, who was too much an extrovert and player for Sofia. As Felmlee (1998) suggested in her work on fatal attraction, "Be careful what you wish for," because sometimes you might get it and then regret it (p. 235).

Similarity and Complementarity in Initial Versus Committed Relationships

The vast majority of studies on the similarity-attraction link have looked at the advantages or disadvantages of similarity during the initial stages of a relationship's development. However, we know less about the role that similarity plays beyond that stage. Amodio and Showers (2005) examined this issue more closely by having undergraduate students who were in an exclusive dating relationship for at least 3 months complete two surveys 1 year apart. Their results suggest a very important role for commitment in our understanding of the way that similarity operates in ongoing relationships. Specifically, the benefit of similarity for liking and attraction seems to hold primarily for high-commitment couples. Those who reported being highly committed to their relationship benefited from their attribute similarity over time. However, those who reported having low relationship commitment were actually harmed by that similarity.

Amodio and Showers (2005) speculated that dissimilarity may actually be exciting for dating partners we don't see as long-term mates. In essence, you can experience new things with this person while knowing that this person is not someone whom you will be with forever. In contrast, being dissimilar to someone with whom you see yourself in a relationship with for a long time is likely to gnaw at you, eroding that liking over time.

So which characteristic is more attractive—similarity or complementarity? The answer may depend on the goals you have for a relationship with the person. If you hope for or are in a highly committed relationship with your partner, then similarity seems to be a key ingredient to success. But if instead you are looking for a somewhat casual relationship experience without considerable commitment, then dissimilarity or complementarity may, in fact, be more what you should look for. Just keep in mind that those differences may come back to haunt you if your relationship goals change. For example, Sofia may like the excitement of having an outgoing and physically attractive boyfriend like Diego; but if she is interested in pursuing a long-term committed relationship, she may be well advised to look for someone who is more similar to her.

In sum, several studies have shown that similarities in attitudes, likes and dislikes, and physical attractiveness are related to attraction and liking. Some complementary features may also be related to attraction, especially when there is complementarity in behavior (e.g., a shy person paired with an outgoing person) or resources (e.g., a wealthy person paired with a beautiful person). The best relationships may be characterized by both similarity and complementarity, with similarity in important attitudes and values sustaining commitment, and complementarity sustaining excitement. The final influence on people's attraction to others is environmental features.

QUALITIES OF THE PHYSICAL OR SOCIAL ENVIRONMENT

How does the environment or context influence people's attraction to others? The ways the environment can affect attraction and liking may be surprising—the physical environment, our proximity to others, and aspects of our social environment—are all contextual elements that are associated with attraction.

Physical Environment

Research suggests that the environment has subtle effects on attraction and liking (see Andersen, 2008). For example, research on room features and their effects has shown that room temperature (Griffitt, 1970), the presence of music (May & Hamilton, 1980), and even such seemingly irrelevant characteristics as the size of the room, the presence of high ceilings, the linear perspective of the room, the type of couch material, the color of the walls and ceilings, and the lighting may influence whether people are attracted to one another (Andersen, 2008; Burgoon et al., 2010). For example, environments that encourage interaction by providing a cozy atmosphere can promote attraction. Similarly, low lighting and soft colors may make certain people look particularly attractive, while brighter lighting and bolder colors may cause other people to look appealing. Environments that put people face to face in close proximity also enhance attraction (Andersen, 2008).

Byrne and Clore (1970; see also Clore & Byrne, 1974) have also explained the environmental effects on attraction using the **reinforcement affect model,** according to which certain types of environments are more likely to make people feel good. For example, an intimate setting with comfortable chairs and couches, soft wall colors, low lighting, and soft music relaxes people. These environmentally induced positive emotions get transferred to the interactants in that environment. In other words, people unconsciously associate the feelings they experience in a particular environment with the individuals who are part of that environment.

Other studies have shown that under some circumstances, the emotions people experience due to the environment can also be related to attraction. Dutton and Aron (1974) conducted an unusual experiment to test the impact of environmental cues on attraction. They had male participants cross either a stable or a relatively unstable bridge. To make matters worse, the stable bridge was low-lying while the unstable bridge spanned a steep ravine. After crossing the bridges, the participants were met by either a male or female research assistant and told to write a brief story, which was later coded for sexual imagery. The participants also were given the assistant's phone number and invited to call her or him at home if they wanted more information. Amazingly, the researchers found that the men who crossed the unstable bridge and met the female assistant included more sexual images in their stories and were more likely to call the assistant at home. Apparently, their misattributed fear and arousal increased their attraction to the female assistant.

It may seem odd that a negative emotion such as fear can lead to attraction. Why does this happen? Zillman (1978), an emotions theorist, identified the presence of a process called **excitation transfer.** What sometimes happens, Zillman argued, is that people mistake the cause of their emotional arousal. This is especially likely to happen when people experience arousal in response to two different sources in close proximity to each other. In those cases, people mix the two states of arousal together and attribute excitement to the second stimulus. In the Dutton and Aron (1974) study, participants experienced high arousal or anxiety after walking over an unstable bridge and then immediately experienced emotional arousal when they met the female research assistant. In doing so, they may have unconsciously and mistakenly attributed their rapid heartbeats and other signs of intense emotional arousal to the presence of the female assistant, leading them to believe that they were more attracted to her than they objectively might have been. Although this may sound far-fetched (and scholars have challenged the validity of excitation transfer; see Riordan & Tedeschi, 1983), other studies have confirmed this finding (White, Fishbein, & Rutstein, 1981). Apparently, in some cases, people who share scary experiences are more likely to be attracted to each other due to excitation transfer. A hit television show might have offered some evidence for this phenomenon. Midway through season 14 of the hit ABC show *The Bachelor*, Jake (the bachelor) and one of his dates (Vienna) went bungee jumping together off a very high bridge, despite both being afraid of heights.

At the end of the jump, as they dangled at the end of the cord, they had their first kiss. Maybe it should have been predictable at that point, given research on the excitation transfer, that Jake would propose to Vienna at the end of the show. However, the notion of excitation transfer and its association with love does not predict relationship longevity: Jake broke up with Vienna three months after the show aired. Indeed, many of these dating shows have participants go on similar fear-inducing dates. The short-term outcome is often a kiss. The long-term outcome is rarely relational success.

Proximity

Of all the environmental features that impact attraction, proximity has received the most research attention. This is not surprising. Proximity gives people the opportunity to meet and be attracted to one another. Have you ever been attracted to someone who you share classes with or work with, or who lives close to you? If so, then you, too, have been influenced by the impact of proximity on attraction.

Several studies have confirmed that proximity is extremely important in attraction and relationship development. The earliest set of studies was conducted by Festinger, who found that the location of college students' apartments affected who became friends (see Festinger, Schachter, & Back, 1950). Students who lived close to one another were much more likely to become friends than were students who lived in the same building but farther apart. Similarly, Newcomb's (1961) famous dormitory roommates study demonstrated a strong proximity effect during the second year, even though proximity did not affect attraction during the first year. Newcomb's findings were especially intriguing because they suggested that proximity can outweigh similarity as a basis for attraction. Specifically, Newcomb paired half of the male undergraduates with similar others and the other half with dissimilar others (unbeknownst to the participants). Regardless of whether they were similar or dissimilar, the students were more likely to be friends with their roommates than with other dormitory residents.

The tendency for people to develop romantic relationships and friendships with individuals they meet in the workplace has also been attributed primarily to proximity. Indeed, 75% of the organizational members that Dillard and Witteman (1985) surveyed could identify at least one workplace romance involving themselves or someone they knew. This statistic is not surprising, given the amount of time most people spend in the workplace. As Westhoff (1985) put it, "Corporate romance is as inevitable as earthquakes in California" (p. 21). Similarly, a *New York Post* article began with the declaration that the workplace is "the best dating service" around ("The Best," 1988, p. 14). Other times, work associates become close friends (Bridge & Baxter, 1992). Proximity is a major contributor to the development of these friendships, as is similarity and shared tasks (Sias & Cahill, 1998; Sias, Smith, & Avdeyera, 1999).

In sum, the effects of proximity are all around us. We are more likely to be friends with our neighbor than with someone who lives a few miles away, and we are more likely to marry someone we meet at work or school than someone we meet in a bar. This is because we have more opportunities to interact with and become attracted to people whom we see on a frequent basis.

Social Environment

Another factor that impacts attraction is one's social network, including family and friends. For example, have you noticed that what you find attractive in others is often similar to what your friends find attractive? If so, you are not alone. In fact, hundreds of studies have shown that people's attitudes and intentions are strongly influenced by the attitudes of their friends and family (Sheppard, Hartwick, & Warshaw, 1988). Many scholars argue that the attitudes of members of our social circle, known as subjective norms, are the strongest predictor of our own attitudes and intentions. Given that attraction represents an attitude

toward other people, the feedback we receive from friends and family certainly plays an important role in who we find attractive. Interestingly, a person's social network, including the number of friends, attractiveness of friends, and the sense of community among one's friends, are all related to being perceived as attractive on Facebook (see Box 3.3).

In most cases, approval by one's social network promotes attraction and liking. For example, if you meet someone you would like to date and your friends all tell you how wonderful the person is, you are likely to feel even more positively toward this potential dating partner. However, the reverse can also occur. Perhaps you find someone attractive, but after your friends question what you see in the person and discourage you from pursuing a relationship, your attraction decreases. There is one notable exception to this phenomenon, however. Some research has supported the **"Romeo and Juliet" effect,** which predicts that parental interference can strengthen attraction between two people. Specifically, Driscoll, Davis, and Lipetz (1972) found that partners in dating couples reported more love for each other when their parents disapproved of their relationship. Driscoll and fellow researchers retested their hypothesis 10 months later using the same couples and found the same results; parental interference was still positively related to the amount of love couples reported.

There are at least four viable explanations for the Romeo and Juliet effect. First, rebellious young couples may exert their power by defying their parents and becoming romantically involved with their forbidden partner. These feelings of power and excitement may be attributed to their relationship, much as the excitation transfer process suggests. Second, some writers believe that autonomy is so important to young adults that every day is an Independence Day, and differences with parents is a sign of their emerging maturity and independence. Third, as discussed earlier, people may be attracted to individuals who are somewhat challenging or hard to get yet attainable. Finally, if their love is especially strong, the partners can endure disapproval from the social network. Two people who are less in love might be quick to break up when parents and friends disapprove, making it unlikely that they would be together long enough to be in a research study.

Keep in mind that the Romeo and Juliet effect does not always hold true. In Chapter 15 we report that some couples may break up due to disapproval from parents and friends. Similarly, in Chapter 10 we report that involvement in each other's social network helps keep relational partners close. Sometimes interference from others draws people closer together, but other times such interference tears them apart.

BOX 3.3 TECH TALK
ATTRACTION ONLINE

Hundreds of millions of people actively use social networking sites such as Facebook, Instagram, Snapchat, and the like. One of the primary purposes of these sites is to create and/or maintain social bonds. As a result, understanding what aspects of online environments create social attraction is a multimillion dollar endeavor. So what do we know so far?

Several studies have shown that sites that include attractive images of a profile owner lead to greater attraction to that person than those with either no image or with an unattractive image (e.g., Wang, Moon, Kwon, Evans, & Stefanone, 2010). That should come as no surprise, given the impact of attractiveness in attraction in face-to-face settings. It is also worth noting, though, that some evidence shows that females who post sexualized images of themselves as Facebook profiles are rated as less attractive by their female peers than those women whose Facebook profiles are less sexualized (Daniels & Zurbriggen, 2016).

Our friends also play an important role in whether others are attracted to us. The simple listing of the number of friends is related to attraction. Tong, Van Der Heide, Langwell, and Walther (2008) found that the number of Facebook friends was associated in a curvilinear way with social attraction. In other words, there is such a thing as having too many or too few online friends—those with a moderate number of friends (around 300 in the 2008 study; that number would likely be higher now) were rated as more attractive than those with a larger number of friends. The latter may signal insincerity or narcissism, or, alternatively, simply a lack of similarity with the participants, who likely had, on average, a moderate number of friends. And our friends influence attraction by more than their simple numbers. Antheunis and Schouten

(2011) showed that the attractiveness of a profile owner's friends and the positivity of their wall postings were associated with attraction to the profile owner. So, just like offline settings, we are judged by the company we keep, both by whether they are attractive and whether they seem nice. Moreover, Scott (2014) found that individuals who were perceived as popular, based on their staged Facebook profile, including the number of Facebook friends, were perceived to be more physically attractive (despite no difference in actual physical appearance) and also to be more socially attractive.

In addition, though, features of the site itself either heighten or weaken the likelihood of attraction. The more that aspects of the site allow visitors to be immersed in the life of the profile owner, the more they are able to feel "present" in the owner's life, the more that seeds of attraction are allowed to blossom (Farzan, Dabbish, Kraut, & Postmes, 2011), and the more connected they can feel to their friends and family (Oliveira, Huertas, & Lin, 2016). In other words, the more that the online structure can build a sense of community and social presence, the more immersed and attracted visitors will feel in the presence of the right characteristics. It is no wonder, then, that Facebook purchased the leading virtual reality company (Oculus), encourages the "tagging" of friends in pictures, and continues to work on ways to increase the creation of social bonds. Indeed, the success of social networking sites is, in large part, dependent on their ability to create online environments that facilitate social attraction.

SUMMARY AND APPLICATION

Many factors help determine your attraction to friends and romantic partners. Although knowledge of these factors does not guarantee that we will be attracted to the "right people," it helps us better understand why we are attracted to certain people and not others. Awareness of the ways that we stereotype people based on factors such as physical appearance is also important so that we might consider a more complete package of attributes when deciding whether to pursue a relationship with someone.

So what advice does the literature on attraction offer for individuals like Sofia who are having trouble finding the right person? First, as the research on fatal attraction suggests, it is important to understand what is attractive over the long haul. If we are attracted to someone only because the person is opposite to us in some characteristics, research suggests that the attraction may not be lasting. People like Sofia may find themselves in the same types of doomed relationships over and over again because they subconsciously choose partners based on initially attractive qualities that become fatal attractions, rather than the more stable factors of social or relational attraction. Recognizing what qualities lead to fatal attraction in our relationships is the first step in breaking this cycle.

Second, it is important to recognize our own biases and preferences as well as common stereotypes such as the "what is beautiful is good" hypothesis. For example, Sofia may be attracted to especially good-looking men because she perceives them to have an array of positive attributes that they may or may not actually possess. When she discovers their negative attributes, she is likely to be disappointed. If she was less focused on physical appearance, she might find someone with whom she is more compatible on a social and relational level. Sofia might also benefit from taking stock of what she would find rewarding in a long-term relationship. She might decide that qualities such as being able to spend quiet time together would be more

rewarding to her than having a partner who likes to socialize all the time.

Third, it is important to remember that similarity and complementarity are important factors in the attraction process. Similarity in key characteristics that are important to us, such as family values or life philosophies, is a critical part of the recipe for relational success. Indeed, social attraction is only a starting point. After two people who are attracted to each other become initially acquainted, they usually have a long way to go before they develop a truly intimate relationship. Having core similarities will help sustain commitment over the long term. Complementarity can also be beneficial—especially when different abilities help partners get tasks done and different personality traits help sustain novelty. The key might be for differences to be helpful or exciting rather than distracting or distressing. In Sofia and Diego's relationship, their personality differences in sociability were initially appealing but soon become distressing. Thus, this is an area where Sofia might want to look for similarity rather than complementarity.

Finally, it is good to know that chemicals released in our body that take us on a ride, for better or for worse, shape part of the process of attraction. Understanding the ways in which OT and dopamine, among other chemicals, shape our reaction to others is important to increasing our awareness that who we become attracted to may be less in our control than we once thought. After all, we all vary in the basic levels of these chemicals in our body. Moreover, situations and contexts having little to do with the attraction process also change the speed with which these hormones are released.

There is no magical way to determine if someone to whom we are attracted will be a true friend or a long-term romantic partner. There is also no magical formula regarding what to look for in a potential mate. However, the research presented in this chapter summarizes what we know about why we are more attracted to some people than others. Attraction can occur as quickly as a flash of lightning, or it can develop slowly over time. Either way, attraction often provides the initial stepping-stone into new relationships that may become your closest encounters.

KEY TERMS

androgynous (p. 66)
assimilation effect (p. 71)
attachment styles (p. 67)
complementarity (p. 78)
destiny beliefs (p. 67)
excitation transfer (p. 80)
fatal attraction (p. 60)
growth beliefs (p. 67)

halo effect (p. 58)
implicit egotism (p. 77)
interaction appearance theory (p. 70)
loss-gain effect (p. 73)
matching hypothesis (p. 76)
narcissism (p. 60)
physical attraction (p. 58)

reinforcement affect model (p. 79)
reinforcement model (p. 75)
"Romeo and Juliet" effect (p. 81)
sexual attraction (p. 58)
social attraction (p. 58)
task attraction (p. 58)

DISCUSSION QUESTIONS

1. Think about five people in your social network. What initially attracted you to these people? Do all of the qualities you thought of fit into the framework discussed in this chapter, or are there factors you would add to the model?

2. This chapter discussed the importance of proximity in the attraction process. In long-distance relationships, proximity is missing, which has led people to debate whether "absence makes the heart grow fonder" or "out of sight means out of mind." Based on your experiences, which of these sayings is more true?

3. This chapter included a Tech Talk box (Box 3.3) that discussed the predictors of attraction in social networking sites like Facebook and Twitter. Visit the profiles of five people in your social network. What aspects of their profile would make you find them attractive? What aspects would make you find them unattractive? What structural features could the site change to increase your attraction to each person? How closely does this activity match with findings described in the Tech Talk box?

 SAGE edge™

Sharpen your skills with SAGE edge at edge.sagepub.com/guerrero5e.
SAGE edge for students provides a personalized approach to help you accomplish your coursework goals in an easy-to-use learning environment.

4 MAKING SENSE OF OUR WORLD
Managing Uncertainty and Expectancy Violations

Vish sat excitedly waiting for Serena to arrive for their Friday night date. He had spent all day cleaning his apartment and preparing dinner for her. This was going to be a special night that would draw Serena closer to him. They had been friends a long time, but this was their first real date. She was supposed to arrive at 6:00, but 6:00 came and went and no Serena; 6:30, no Serena. That was odd; she had always been on time in the past. He called her cell, but there was no answer. Seven-thirty came and went and still no Serena. By 8:00, he realized that she wouldn't be coming. He was really down. What was going on? Was Serena okay? Was this her way of telling him they were better off just being friends? Why would she do this to him? He went to bed feeling angry and confused, and he was surprised when Serena called in the morning. She sounded like nothing was wrong. "Hi, Vish," she said. "What's up? Did you have fun last night?" Now Vish was even more confused. "What?" he responded with frustration in his voice. "We had plans last night and you blew me off, so no I didn't have fun last night." Serena sounded genuinely surprised. "What do you mean?" she asked. "Our plans were for tonight, not last night!" Vish scanned his mind for any way he could have gotten the night wrong. Was she just trying to make something up to explain her absence last night? Or was it really just a misunderstanding?

This type of scenario may have happened to you. There are times in all relationships when expectations are violated and people experience uncertainty. For example, Vish expected Serena to show up on time (or at least not too late) for their date. When she violated this expectation, he experienced uncertainty about her and their relationship. What will Vish do next? Will he believe Serena, or will questions linger in his mind, fueling uncertainty? If they go out tonight, will he continue looking for clues about whether or not she was telling the truth and whether or not she wants to be more than friends? How he deals with his uncertainty will affect if and how their relationship progresses. It is not surprising that communication researchers have examined how both uncertainty and expectancy violations affect perceptions and behavior. In this chapter, we explore the concepts of uncertainty and expectancy violations. After defining uncertainty, we examine some of the issues raised in **uncertainty reduction theory,** including how scholars have challenged and extended this theory. Next, we summarize three other theories related to uncertainty: (1) **predicted outcome value theory,** (2) the **theory of motivated information management (TMIM),** and (3) **relational turbulence theory.** The chapter ends with a discussion of **expectancy violations theory,** including how the theory has been applied to research on flirtation and sexual activity, first dates, hurtful events, and modality switching, which is the transition from an online to an offline relationship.

UNCERTAINTY

Our experience of the world is inextricably linked to our level of uncertainty. When we receive information that reduces uncertainty, we are more confident that we understand ourselves, other people, our relationships, and the world around us. In most cases, the more information we have about someone, the more we feel we know that person. A lack of information, or information that violates expectations, often increases uncertainty. Given this book's focus on close relationships, our examination of uncertainty relates to relationships, but it is important to realize that uncertainty extends well beyond our relationships with others. For example, job loss creates uncertainty about a wide range of issues, people who become refugees from wars or natural disasters face uncertainty about nearly every aspect of their lives, and so on. These uncertainties impact all aspects of our lives, including relationships.

Uncertainty has been defined as the inability to predict or explain someone's attitudes and/or behaviors (Berger & Calabrese, 1975). More broadly, Brashers (2001) argued that uncertainty occurs when people "feel insecure in their own state of knowledge or the state of knowledge in general [about a topic]" (p. 478). For example, part of Vish's uncertainty might stem from feeling that he doesn't have enough history with Serena to know how she really feels. Thus, high uncertainty occurs when people feel unsure or insecure about their ability to

predict or explain someone's attitudes and behaviors. Low uncertainty occurs when people feel confident in their ability to predict and explain someone's behavior, often because they believe they know someone well. Notice that *being confident and secure* about one's explanations and predictions is the key feature in these definitions.

So far our definition of uncertainty has focused on uncertainty about a partner. However, people also experience uncertainty about themselves and their relationships. In fact, scholars have identified three specific types of relationally-relevant uncertainty (for review, see Knobloch, 2009; Knobloch & Solomon, 1999, 2002, 2005). **Self-uncertainty** occurs when people question their own feelings about how involved they want to be with another person. For example, after Serena failed to show up, Vish may question his own feelings about how much he really likes her. **Partner uncertainty** occurs when people are uncertain about their partner's feelings and intentions, including if the partner reciprocates their feelings (Knobloch & Solomon, 1999). So Vish may wonder if Serena's actions indicate that she is trying to distance herself from him. Finally, **relationship uncertainty** occurs when people have questions about the state of their relationship. In particular, Knobloch and Solomon (1999) noted that people often experience uncertainty about relationship definitions (Are we dating or just friends?), the future of the relationship (Will the relationship last? Can we stay friends if the dating thing doesn't work?), behaviors that are acceptable versus unacceptable with a relationship (Vish may have initially wondered how tolerant he should be about Serena's tardiness), and other behavioral norms (How will the amount of time we spend together change if we become a couple?). See Box 4.1 to complete questions that let you know how much uncertainty you perceive to exist in one of your relationships.

Uncertainty Reduction Theory: Issues and Challenges

In the past 30 years, no fewer than 10 research programs have been developed to better understand

BOX 4.1   PUT YOURSELF TO THE TEST
THE RELATIONAL UNCERTAINTY SCALE

Respond to the following questions by using the following scale: 1 = completely or almost completely certain, 2 = mostly certain, 3 = slightly more certain than uncertain, 4 = slightly more uncertain than certain, 5 = mostly uncertain, and 6 = completely or almost completely uncertain.

Think about a specific relationship. How certain are you about

Self

1. How committed you are to the relationship?   _____

2. How you feel about the relationship?   _____

3. How much you are romantically interested in your partner?   _____

4. Your view of this relationship?   _____

5. Whether or not you want this relationship to last?   _____

6. Your goals for the future of the relationship?   _____

Subdimension total _____

Partner

7. How committed your partner is to the relationship?   _____

8. How your partner feels about the relationship?   _____

9. How much your partner is romantically interested in you?   _____

10. Your partner's view of this relationship?   _____

11. Whether or not your partner wants this relationship to last?   _____

12. Your partner's goals for the future of the relationship?   _____

Subdimension total _____

Relationship

13. What you can or cannot say to each other in this relationship?   _____

14. The norms for this relationship?   _____

15. Whether or not you and your partner feel the same way about each other?   _____

16. The current status of this relationship?   _____

17. The definition of this relationship?   _____

18. How you and your partner would describe this relationship?   _____

19. Whether or not you and your partner will stay together?   _____

20. The future of the relationship?   _____

Subdimension total _____

(Continued)

BOX 4.1 (Continued)

Add up your scores for each dimension. The maximum score for the self-dimension and the maximum score for the partner dimension is 36, and the minimum scores are 6. The maximum score for the relationship dimension is 48, and the minimum score is 8. The higher your score is, the more relational uncertainty you have. (You might want to re-answer these questions later in the semester to see if your uncertainty level changes.)

Source: This is a sampling of the items that make up the relational uncertainty scale (Knobloch & Solomon, 1999).

the role that uncertainty plays in interpersonal interaction (see Afifi & Afifi, 2009 for review). The next part of this chapter describes some of these theories, beginning with one of the earliest communication theories to explain the management of uncertainty—Berger and Calabrese's (1975) uncertainty reduction theory.

Uncertainty reduction theory focused on understanding what happens during initial interactions when two people meet. Berger and Calabrese maintained that the driving force in initial encounters is obtaining information about the other person to get to know her or him better and, ultimately, to reduce uncertainty. The theory offered 7 general predictions and 21 more-specific predictions; however, we focus here on three general issues that provided a foundation for the theory and spawned later research: (1) the motivation to reduce uncertainty, (2) the relationship between communication and uncertainty, and (3) the ways people use communication to strategically reduce uncertainty. As will be shown, some of the original thinking on these issues has been extended and challenged by other researchers. In particular, we now know that uncertainty is important in established relationships as well as in new relationships, and that uncertainty can sometimes be beneficial rather than detrimental in relationships. We also know that the motivation to reduce uncertainty varies based on the situation.

The Motivation to Reduce Uncertainty

One of the primary principles underlying uncertainty reduction theory was that *people generally dislike uncertainty and are therefore motivated to reduce it.* Berger and Calabrese (1975) argued that our reason for behaving the way we do during initial interactions with strangers is simple: we want to get to know them better. Not only do we *want* to get to know them but we *have* to get to know them better so that we can reduce uncertainty and create order in our world. In other words, we dislike situations in which we are unsure about the outcome and we do our best to create predictable environments.

There is a good bit of evidence that supports that claim. From an evolutionary perspective, it makes sense (see Afifi, 2009; Inglis, 2000). Imagine if our ancestors weren't motivated to reduce their uncertainty about where to gather food or who was a friend versus foe? Our species would have not lasted long were we not motivated, at a basic level, to reduce uncertainty. It should not be surprising that a lot of research has shown that uncertainty is associated with anxiety. In fact, brain-imaging studies have shown uncertainty to activate regions of the brain similar to those triggered by anxiety. Uncertainty has also been linked to relational dissatisfaction in some studies. For example, Theiss and Knobloch (2014) studied the romantic relationships of U.S. military service members after a tour of duty. Their results showed that satisfaction in those relationships was negatively associated with self, partner, and relationship uncertainty, with those uncertainties also tied to negative relationship thoughts and behaviors. Even more striking than the link between uncertainty and dissatisfaction is evidence that people who feel uncertain about the positive direction of their close relationship are more likely to think about their partners as "objects," including thinking of them in purely physical terms or considering them as simply there to fulfill a particular goal for the person (Keefer, Landau, Sullivan, & Rothschild, 2014). Finally, Quirk and colleagues (2016) found that uncertainty about one's own commitment to a romantic relationship was tied to the termination of that relationship weeks later.

However, researchers have challenged the notions that people are always motivated to reduce uncertainty and that uncertainty is always undesirable. Health scholars, for example, have shown that people sometimes prefer uncertainty to knowledge (Mischel, 1981, 1988, 1990). When reducing uncertainty might mean eliminating hope for recovery (by discovering that a disease is unmanageable or fatal), uncertainty is cherished because it keeps hope alive. Indeed, Brashers and his colleagues (Brashers, 2001; Hogan & Brashers, 2009), in articulating **uncertainty management theory,** argued that "uncertainty is not inherently good or inherently bad, but something that is managed" (Hogan & Brashers, p. 48). Specifically, they noted that uncertainty can reduce negative emotions (e.g., when not knowing is better than knowing that harm is inevitable), produce neutral emotions (e.g., when it doesn't matter whether you know or don't know more about this issue), and even produce positive emotions (joy over a surprise party). Uncertainty only produces negative emotions, such as anxiety, when not having information is perceived as harmful.

There is considerable evidence supporting Brashers' logic. Take people's sexual behavior as an example. Despite the fact that hundreds of thousands of college students are at high risk of contracting a sexually transmitted infection (STI), only a very small percentage ever get tested for such infections. One reason people give for not getting tested is that they would rather not know if they have an STI. For these people, the uncertainty is preferable to the potential knowledge that they have a stigmatized disease that may change, or even shorten, their life. This attitude is worrisome given that many STIs

are treatable, especially if diagnosed early. Research shows a similar pattern in tests for breast cancer and colon cancer. Only a very small percentage of the population most at risk for these types of cancer actually get regular checkups—again despite the fact that with early detection the consequences in many cases are relatively benign.

Similarly, research suggests that we sometimes prefer to keep a level of uncertainty in our relationships, especially if reducing uncertainty could reveal negative information or lead to negative relational consequences. For example, studies on "taboo topics" that people avoid discussing in relationships show that the future of the relationship is one of the most avoided topics among romantic partners (Baxter & Wilmot, 1985). Studies show that even couples who have been together for many years sometimes avoid seeking information and reducing uncertainty. For example, one study included long-term dating couples in which one of the partners would be graduating from college in a few months (Afifi & Burgoon, 1998). Many of these couples avoided having the "dreaded discussion" about their future. Perhaps many were worried about their future together and feared that the relationship might change after graduation. In this case, uncertainty might be perceived as a better alternative than finding out that the relationship could be at risk.

Research on **dialectics theory** (see also Chapter 5) also supports the idea that people sometimes find uncertainty exciting rather than confusing or anxiety-provoking. According to dialectics theory, people have opposing interpersonal needs. For example, people want to be close and connected to others, but they also want independence. People want to share things about themselves, but they also want to keep some information private. Similarly, people want both certainty (predictability) and uncertainty (novelty) in their relationships. People don't like situations in which they know everything about their partner, hear the same stories again and again, or go through the same intimacy routines, because it is boring. But they also don't like situations in which they can't predict what their partner is going to do from day to day, because that produces stress. Instead, people want a bit of certainty and a bit of uncertainty. As a result, people often swing back and forth between wanting more excitement/novelty and wanting more stability/predictability in their relationships.

Studies on cross-sex friendships also suggest that uncertainty is often accepted and even preferred in ongoing relationships. Some cross-sex friendships are full of ambiguity regarding issues such as whether romantic potential exists (O'Meara, 1989). In these cross-sex friendships "sensitive" topics—especially about the relationship—are typically avoided (Afifi & Burgoon, 1998; Knight, 2014).

In some cases, uncertainty can make us miserable; in other cases, uncertainty is exciting and gives us more choices.

In fact, the current and future status of the relationship is the most commonly avoided topic in cross-sex friendships. Guerrero and Chavez (2005) found that individuals were especially likely to avoid discussing the status of their relationship when they were romantically attracted to their cross-sex friend but feared that their friend did not reciprocate their feelings. Thus, people sometimes prefer uncertainty when they fear that information-seeking might confirm their worst fears—for example, that the relationship does not have a future. Alternatively, the maintenance of relational uncertainty is at the crux of some relationships. For example, Knight (2014) found that friend-with-benefit relationships have a "no strings attached" ethos that strongly discourages its participants from engaging in relational talk or explicitly managing uncertainty therein. In other words, people vary in their motivation to reduce uncertainty, as well as their dislike of uncertainty, based on relationship types and circumstances. Moreover, there are cultural-level norms that can also shape people's responses to uncertainty, as summarized in Box 4.2.

The Relationship Between Communication and Uncertainty

Another central idea underlying uncertainty reduction theory is that *people communicate to get information and reduce uncertainty, especially during initial encounters with others.* Berger and Calabrese (1975) claimed that because we dislike situations in which we are not sure about the outcome, we act as naive scientists who gather information and sort through alternative explanations to better understand people. In initial interactions we ask one another basic questions to establish commonalities and to gain understanding, because this type of information helps us get acquainted and reduces uncertainty. As others tell us about themselves, we feel more confident in our ability to predict how they think and act. As a result, we feel more comfortable in the interaction. Initially, however, we ask "superficial" questions and engage in small talk. But small talk is important because this type of communication

BOX 4.2 AROUND THE WORLD
UNCERTAINTY IN OTHER COUNTRIES

Although research has shown that uncertainty and ambiguity vary at the individual level, some cultures tolerate uncertainty better than others. Some cultures are accepting of ambiguity whereas other cultures, called *uncertainty-avoidant cultures*, steer clear of uncertainty at all cost (Andersen, 2008; Hofstede, 2001). Uncertainty-avoidant cultures tend to be located in or have origins in the Mediterranean region, and often limit individual rights. Countries with the highest levels of uncertainty avoidance are Greece, Portugal, Belgium, Japan, Peru, France, Chile, Spain, Argentina, and Turkey (Hofstede, 2001). You can compare countries on uncertainty avoidance, among other dimensions at https://geert-hofstede.com/tools.html. Over the past century, most of these countries have had dictatorships that decreased freedom and reduced uncertainty by imposing harsh rules and preventing social change. People in these countries tend to follow tradition and are uncomfortable with uncertainty.

By contrast, countries lowest in uncertainly avoidance and most tolerant of ambiguity tend to be stable liberal democracies, often with considerable equality and individual freedom. The countries lowest in uncertainty avoidance and highest in tolerance are Singapore, Denmark, Sweden, Hong Kong, Ireland, Great Britain, India, the Philippines, the United States, Canada, and New Zealand. This list is dominated by Northern European and South Asian cultures, many of which were originally part of the British empire. These low-uncertainty-avoidant countries have a long history of democratic rule that is likely to be both the cause and an effect of uncertainty avoidance.

A culture's level of uncertainty avoidance has profound effects on people's relationships. For example, women's dating decisions and sexual behavior is more tightly regulated in uncertainty-avoidant cultures countries. However, it would be a mistake to assume that one approach to uncertainty avoidance is inherently superior to another, or that cultural differences on uncertainty avoidance are tied to better political or economic systems.

helps give us a sense of how the other person acts and thinks. In addition, by sticking to superficial topics, we can keep some things about ourselves private until we know the other person better and feel more comfortable disclosing more information about ourselves.

According to uncertainty reduction theory, the more information we have about someone, the more we "know" her or him, the better we should be able to predict that person's attitudes and behaviors. Thus, as communication increases, uncertainty about an interaction partner should decrease. We should be more certain about someone after spending 20 minutes with that person than after spending 5 minutes because we will have had four times as much time to seek information about him or her. A study by Douglas (1990) confirmed this by having pairs of unacquainted college students interact for 2 minutes, 4 minutes, or 6 minutes.

After the interactions, the participants completed a measure of confidence in their ability to predict the other person's behavior and attitudes. The uncertainty levels of those who interacted for 6 minutes were much lower than the levels of those who interacted for just 2 minutes. Douglas also found that students who asked more questions were more confident in their predictions, suggesting that the amount of communication (in terms of responses to questions) was related to decreases in uncertainty. Other researchers extended the interaction time to a maximum of 16 minutes and obtained relatively similar results for the first 6 minutes but did not find that uncertainty decreased significantly from the 8th to the 16th minute of interaction (Redmond & Virchota, 1994). Apparently, people gather information rather quickly during initial interactions and then stick with their initial impressions.

Studies have shown somewhat similar patterns for online interactions. For example, Antheunis, Valkenburg, and Peter (2010) studied member experiences on a popular Dutch social network site (www.Hyves.nl), and found that members who had the least uncertainty about other people they knew on the site had also asked them the most questions. A study of online dating (Gibbs, Ellison, & Lai, 2011) found a link between disclosure and uncertainty reduction. Their study examined people's use of uncertainty reduction strategies when meeting prospective partners on websites such as eHarmony. Subscribers to these sites reported that they were more likely to have engaged in personal disclosure with a prospective dating partner if they had also tried to reduce uncertainty about that person.

Despite these findings, research shows that information sometimes *increases* uncertainty, especially in established relationships. Some early work in this area came from Planalp and Honeycutt's research on uncertainty-increasing events. Planalp and Honeycutt (1985) conducted a study to determine when people in established relationships experienced uncertainty. They asked students whether they could recall a time when they learned something surprising about a friend, spouse, or dating partner that made them question the relationship. Ninety percent of the respondents in this study were able to recall such an instance, thus strongly supporting the claim that particular behaviors can increase, rather than decrease, uncertainty, even in developed relationships. The researchers then categorized the responses into six uncertainty-increasing behaviors:

1. *Competing relationships* included the discovery that a friend or dating partner wanted to spend time with someone else.

2. *Unexplained loss of contact or closeness* occurred when communication and/or intimacy decreased for no particular reason.

3. *Sexual behavior* included discovering that a friend or dating partner engaged in sexual behavior with another person.

4. *Deception* involved discovering that friends or dating partners had lied, fabricated information, or been misleading.

5. *Change in personality/value* occurred when people realized that their friends or dating partners were different from what they used to be.

6. *Betraying confidences* included instances in which people's friends or dating partners disclosed private information to others about them without their consent.

For all six types of behavior, the participants felt less able to predict their friend or dating partner's attitudes and behaviors following these events than they had before these events took place. In other words, they felt as if they "knew them less" following the unexpected behavior than they did prior to it. Studies confirm the high incidence of such uncertainty-increasing behaviors in close relationships. For example, one study found that 80% of marriages included uncertainty-increasing events (Turner, 1990). As we will discuss later, though, it is important to note that not all uncertainty-increasing behaviors are as dramatic as the six found in this research. Something as banal as someone showing up late to an important date may be sufficient to increase one's uncertainty about that person.

The method that Planalp and Honeycutt (1985) used is worth noting. They asked participants to think about something "surprising." In fact, earlier, Berger (1993) had argued that unexpected (or surprising) behaviors increase uncertainty, and this study seems to support his claim. When people do something unexpected, we are sometimes *less* able to predict their attitudes and behaviors—for example, Vish's uncertainty about Serena increased after his night alone waiting for her. If they had actually agreed to get together the next day, then Serena's uncertainty about Vish also likely increased because she may be surprised by his absentmindedness and his anger.

These sorts of examples led Berger (1993) to claim that unexpected behaviors always lead to increases in uncertainty. But let's examine that claim. Think about behaviors that fit in any of the six uncertainty-increasing categories. It is easy to see how they might increase uncertainty, but might they not also *reduce* uncertainty in some cases? Couldn't these behaviors sometimes make us feel as if we now know how the person *really* is? To illustrate, suppose a friend lied to you about his past. The fact that he lied about such an important issue may tell you a lot about the kind of person he is. Discovering that lie may not increase your uncertainty but actually reduce it. Similarly, Serena might think that she now knows the *real* Vish after she hears him react the way he did on the phone. These counterexamples suggest that in some cases communication decreases uncertainty, but in other cases communication increases uncertainty.

General Strategies for Reducing Uncertainty

Uncertainty reduction theory also suggests that *people communicate in strategic ways in an attempt to reduce uncertainty.* Specifically, Berger and his colleagues identified three general ways people go about reducing uncertainty in initial encounters.

PASSIVE STRATEGIES People who rely on unobtrusive observation of individuals are using passive strategies (Berger, 1979, 1987) that involves behaviors such as looking at someone sitting alone to see if a friend or date comes along, observing how a person interacts with others, or paying attention to the kinds of clothes a person wears. Based on observation, you might make assumptions about someone's age, relational status (Is the person physically close to someone? Is he or she wearing a ring?), and personality, among many other characteristics. On social network sites, we may reduce uncertainty passively about someone by searching through posted pictures or checking when she or he was last active on the site, among other strategies (Fox & Anderegg, 2014).

Passive observations are likely to be effective and informative when they are conducted in an informal setting, like a party, rather than in a formal setting, like a classroom or business office (Berger & Douglas, 1981). Moreover, people usually make more accurate judgments when watching someone interact with others than when the person is sitting alone. Most people's communication is constrained in formal settings because rules in these situations are fairly strict, so their behavior is not particularly informative. For example, it is unusual to see people behave inappropriately in a fancy restaurant or during a business meeting. By contrast, people act in unique, personal ways at an informal party or in many online settings because the "rules" are less rigid. Therefore, it is more informative, and consequently much more uncertainty reducing, to observe someone in an informal, as opposed to a formal, setting. Unfortunately, there's also a dark side to passive uncertainty reduction: When passive observation strategies become compulsive, stalking or relational intrusion is the result (see Chapter 13).

ACTIVE STRATEGIES Often our strategies for uncertainty reduction are more active. Berger and Calabrese (1975) identified two forms of active uncertainty reduction strategy. One type involves manipulating the social environment and then observing how someone reacts. The information seeker may not be part of the manipulated situation, although he or she sets up the situation. These tactics are like mini-experiments conducted with the intent of gaining information about the target person. For example, one student of ours used an active strategy on her boyfriend by creating a fake online profile of an attractive woman, contacting him, and seeing if he would respond to flirtation. (In case you are wondering, he ignored the contact from the fake profile.) Several other students in our classes have admitted using similar active uncertainty-reduction strategies with dating partners (e.g., flirting with someone else to see how their partner reacts) or leaving their relational partner alone with a flirtatious friend to see what the partner would do. Serena could also have been using a form of this strategy if she intentionally decided to stand Vish up to see how he would react, thereby reducing her uncertainty about his personality and his commitment.

This information-seeking strategy is useful because it helps reduce uncertainty without the need to rely on more direct methods. Of course, such manipulative attempts could backfire in the long run, making the person look paranoid and/or communicating distrust to her or his partner.

The second type of active uncertainty reduction strategy involves asking third parties (i.e., friends, family members) about the person in question. We often ask friends if they have heard anything about a particular person of interest or ask for help interpreting something that person did. In fact, one study found that 30% of the information we have about someone comes from asking others (Hewes, Graham, Doelger, & Pavitt, 1985). For example, before trying to turn his relationship with Serena romantic, Vish may have asked their mutual friends if they knew if she was interested in anyone, whether she ever mentioned any interest in him, or whether they thought she'd consider going out with him as more than a friend.

INTERACTIVE STRATEGIES The third general type of uncertainty reduction strategy is interactive (Berger, 1979, 1987). Interactive strategies involve direct contact between the information seeker and the target. Common interactive strategies include asking questions, encouraging disclosure, and relaxing the target. We are especially likely to ask such questions the first time we meet someone. In studies of behavior during initial interactions, researchers have found that the frequency of question-asking drops over time, coinciding with decreases in our level of uncertainty (Douglas, 1990; Kellermann, 1995).

It is important to note, though, that the questions being asked in initial interactions are usually very general. Research suggests that we hesitate to ask questions about intimate issues until we have a close relationship with the person and even then may avoid asking direct questions (Bell & Buerkel-Rothfuss, 1990). Indeed, Fox and Anderegg's (2014) study of uncertainty-reduction strategies on Facebook found that interactive

strategies such as liking a picture, sending a message through Messenger, or commenting on a picture were significantly more common as relationships got closer. Studies have also shown that people sometimes disclose information about themselves with the specific hope that their disclosure will encourage the other person to do the same (Berger, 1979). Again, though, we generally use disclosure as an uncertainty-reduction strategy only after we reach a certain level of comfort in being able to predict the other person's attitudes and behaviors and enough trust to disclose ourselves. This comfort level typically is reached through the general questions that are so common during initial interactions. Finally, people sometimes try to relax the target so that she or he feels comfortable revealing information. People sometimes offer drugs or alcohol to achieve this effect. However, examples of less-manipulative strategies include creating a comfortable environment that is conducive to talking, smiling a lot, or acting interested to get the other person talking (Berger, 1979).

As these examples suggest, interactive strategies are not limited to verbal communication. We often reduce our uncertainty about someone through nonverbal cues (Kellermann & Berger, 1984). For instance, if you smile at and make eye contact with someone across a room, and the person motions you to come over, a clear message has been sent and received. That one motioning gesture provides considerable information and uncertainty reduction. Vish communicated much of his feelings to Serena just through his voice—angry intonation and abruptness, both nonverbal components. In fact, nonverbal behaviors can be the primary method of communicating our thoughts and feelings about other people and our relationships with them (see summaries in Andersen, 2008; Burgoon et al., 2010). For example, research on sexual behavior (see Chapter 9) has shown that the primary way people go about discovering whether a partner is interested in escalating sexual activity—and reducing uncertainty about a person's sexual desires—is through nonverbal cues. Although much of the research on interactive uncertainty reduction methods has focused on verbal strategies, people often engage in nonverbal behavior to help reduce uncertainty. Research has also focused mostly on how people reduce uncertainty in live or face-to-face interactions, even though people also engage in uncertainty-reduction strategies online (see Box 4.3 for details).

Of course, whether in online or face-to-face contexts, people can use multiple strategies to reduce uncertainty—either over time or during a single interaction. Let's imagine that Vish did this when he first met Serena. Suppose he was a new university student and didn't know many people yet. He is at a party with a classmate who nods and smiles at Serena from across the room. Vish observes Serena and her group of her friends for a few minutes. They are laughing and having a good time, so they seemed approachable (passive strategy). Because Vish is a bit shy, he asks his classmate acquaintance if he knows her. When he says "yes," Vish asks him to go over and see if they can join them (active strategy). His classmate goes over, talks to them for a minute, and then waves Vish over. After Vish joins the group, he starts to feel comfortable and begins engaging in conversation with Serena and her friends (interactive strategy).

BOX 4.3 TECH TALK
UNCERTAINTY REDUCTION ONLINE

Uncertainty reduction is just as important when people are communicating online as when they are communicating face to face. Several scholars have now examined ways that people reduce uncertainty in computer-mediated contexts and found that people use the three general strategies of passive, active, and interactive that were identified in the original uncertainty-reduction theory (Fox & Anderegg, 2014; Tong, 2013). Ramirez, Walther, Burgoon, and Sunnafrank (2002) also found another online strategy—extractive—that is unique to computer-mediated contexts. Examples of each of these strategies are as follows:

Passive: Getting information through unobtrusive online observation, such as looking at text or photos on a person's Facebook page, reading the messages someone posted on a forum, or checking out someone's YouTube channel

Active: Viewing the pages of a person's "friends" on Facebook to see what people are saying about her or him, or saving a person's e-mail or text messages to check for consistency with what other people are saying (e.g., If someone is self-described as "fun," do friends' posts support this description?)

Interactive: Engaging in direct communication, such as asking the person questions online, sending the person an e-mail, or phoning the person to get to know her or him better

Extractive: Using noninteractive strategies such as conducting an online background check, searching for someone on Google, or comparing the profiles that a person posted on various websites

Research on online dating (Gibbs et al., 2011) has shown that interactive strategies, such as directly questioning someone over the phone or online, are the most common way that subscribers to services such as eHarmony or match.com reduce uncertainty about potential dating partners. However, the participants in this study also reported using passive, active, and extractive strategies. Extractive strategies, such as conducting a Google search, were mentioned least often, perhaps because people need to have verified a person's name and other information before they can use most extractive strategies.

In addition to online information-seeking about potential or current partners, Tong (2013) found several strategies that people use to gather information about ex-partners. In particular, some individuals used their ex-partner's Facebook page to gather information about their social activity (e.g., what they are up to, who they hang out with), learn about new romantic partners, and see what they say to others through posts. The ability to monitor activity and posts on social networking sites without others knowing makes them particularly valuable for information gathering, unfortunately sometimes with a dark side.

Secret Tests

On the heels of Berger and colleagues' work on uncertainty-reduction strategies during initial interactions, relational scholars examined things that people do to reduce uncertainty in close relationships. Baxter and Wilmot (1985) labeled some of those uncertainty-reduction strategies as "secret tests." According to their research, there are at least seven strategies people can use to reduce their uncertainty about their partner's commitment to the relationship:

1. *Asking-third-party tests:* This strategy relies on feedback from social network members. This test is virtually identical to one of the active strategies described earlier. For example, a week after the "date that never was," Vish might ask Serena's best friend how she is feeling about the whole thing.

2. *Directness tests:* This strategy involves talking about issues with the partner and includes strategies such as asking questions and discussing things the person feels uncertain about. This test is similar to the interactive strategies described earlier. Here Vish would go directly to Serena and ask her how she is feeling about it. Unlike the other "secret" tests listed here, this strategy involves direct communication.

3. *Triangle tests:* This strategy is intended to test the partner's commitment to the relationship by creating three-person triangles. *Fidelity checks* (such as seeing if the partner responds to a fictitious "secret admirer" note) and *jealousy tests* (such as flirting with someone else to see how the partner responds) are two examples of triangle tests.

4. *Separation tests:* This strategy relies on creating physical distance between relational partners. Two primary methods are having a long period of physical separation (such as seeing if your relationship can survive a summer of not seeing each other) and ceasing contact for an extended period of time to see how long it takes for your partner to call.

5. *Endurance tests:* This strategy increases the costs or reduces the rewards for the other person in the relationship. One such test, known as "testing limits," involves seeing how much a partner will endure. For instance, someone might dress sloppily, become argumentative, arrive late for dates, or fail to call at a designated time to see if the partner stays committed despite these irritations. Another test, known as "self putdowns," involves criticizing oneself to see if the partner responds by offering positive feedback. For example, Chan may say that he feels overweight in the hope that Hong will try to convince him that he looks great, thus indicating her support for him.

6. *Public presentation tests:* This strategy involves monitoring a partner's reaction to the use of certain relational labels or actions. It is most commonly used in early relationship stages. It is typified by the first public presentation of a partner as your "boyfriend" or "girlfriend" (whereas before, the partner may have been introduced only as a "friend"), or by holding hands on a date, then observing the partner's reaction. Public presentation tests that might occur later in the relationship include asking someone to wear a ring or a sports or letterman's jacket, or asking someone to spend the holidays with your family.

7. *Indirect suggestion tests:* This strategy uses hints or jokes to bring up a topic without taking responsibility. The partner's response provides insight into her or his feelings about the issue. For example, Allison might joke about moving in with Peter to check his reaction to the issue. Allison may have been truly thinking about moving in, but the fact that she said it as a joke gives her an "out" that allows her to save face if Peter rejects the idea. Or Allison could say, "I wonder what color our kid's eyes will be" and observe Peter's reaction. These tactics allow Allison to seek information about

Peter's attitudes toward cohabiting with her or his interest in marriage.

These categories of secret tests were derived from interviews with college students who were asked to discuss information acquisition strategies that they used in one of three relationship types: (1) a platonic opposite-sex friendship, (2) an opposite-sex friendship with romantic potential, or (3) a romantic relationship. Beyond identifying these secret tests, Baxter and Wilmot's (1985) study revealed an important point about our relationship behavior—namely, the vast majority of uncertainty reduction strategies in relationships are indirect. The study refuted the image of relationships as completely open and of partners as totally direct. In fact, only 22% of the students who reported on a romantic relationship listed direct strategies as a tactic they used to reduce their uncertainty. By contrast, 34% said they used triangle tests, and 33% reported using endurance tests in their romantic relationships. Especially interesting is the extent to which indirectness was used in friendships with romantic potential. Consistent with research showing these relationships to be ambiguous and uncertain (O'Meara, 1989), the students who were reporting on a relationship with romantic potential were more likely than those reporting on the other relationship types to mention separation tests and indirect suggestion tests as information-seeking strategies. Perhaps this is because relationships with romantic potential are still developing and are more prone to uncertainty than are stable friendships or existing romantic relationships.

People are also more likely to use indirect secret tests in the early stages of dating relationships, when using direct information-seeking strategies may be riskier than they are later in the relationship (Bell & Buerkel-Rothfuss, 1990). For example, Emmers and Canary (1996) found that when romantic couples wanted to repair their relationship after encountering an uncertainty-increasing event such as deception or infidelity, they used direct or interactive strategies more often than passive or active strategies. Some people did nothing to reduce uncertainty, which reinforces the notion that sometimes people prefer uncertainty to certainty, and sometimes other forces, besides uncertainty, influence whether or not people feel a need to seek information through communication. Predicted outcome value theory and the TMIM provide further insight into these types of situations.

Predicted Outcome Value Theory

An alternative to uncertainty reduction theory, called predicted outcome value theory (Sunnafrank, 1986, 1990), suggests that people are not driven by a need to reduce uncertainty in all cases. Instead, whether or not people seek more information depends on whether **outcome values** are positive or negative. The theory is grounded in two main ideas: (1) that people are motivated to maximize rewards and minimize costs and (2) that people's judgments about likely future outcomes guide their behavior. In this theory, outcome values relate to predictions about how rewarding or unrewarding future interactions with a particular person would be. People are judged as having a **high outcome value** when they are perceived to be more rewarding than other potential partners. For example, when Vish first met Serena, he might have perceived her to be more self-confident and fun than other women he had met. This perception of Serena's high outcome value would lead Vish to want to get to know her. When people have a **low outcome value,** they are perceived to be less rewarding than other potential partners. Suppose that when Vish first approached Serena she seemed cold and arrogant. Obviously, if Vish had perceived Serena this way, he would have little desire to reduce uncertainty with her, he would have been much less likely to want to be friends with her, and he would have likely looked for a more rewarding person to hang out with.

According to Sunnafrank's theory, we initially reduce uncertainty as a way of finding out how we feel about a person or an interaction. After that, the positive or negative outcome value becomes the driving force behind seeking further information. Thus, when someone reveals negative information during an initial encounter, we are likely to predict negative outcome values and to cut off communication with that person. Put another way, when outcome values are positive, we are motivated to seek information; when outcome values are negative, we decrease communication and stop seeking information. Thus, according to predicted outcome theory, the relationship between uncertainty reduction and attraction might be best stated as follows: When uncertainty is reduced by learning positive information about someone, attraction increases; when uncertainty is reduced by learning negative information about someone, attraction decreases. Although predicted outcome value theory focuses on initial interaction, this reasoning applies to more-developed or well-established relationships. Think back to the scenario with Vish and Serena. Vish's belief that Serena stood him up could dramatically affect his perception of how rewarding it would be to interact with her in the future. If Vish reduced uncertainty by concluding that a relationship with Serena would be filled with late arrivals, forgotten dates, anxiety, or frustration, his feelings of attraction would decrease.

Studies support the idea that predicted outcome values are an important predictor of communication in initial encounters. People are more likely to engage in positive communication when their partner has a high outcome value. They are also more likely to attempt to continue interaction and communicate in future. By contrast, people restrict information and work to discourage future interaction when a partner has a low outcome value (Sunnafrank, 1986). In one study, students engaged in brief first conversations with another student at the beginning of the semester (Sunnafrank & Ramirez, 2004). The level of outcome value the students associated with their conversational partner after these brief, early interactions predicted later communication and relationship development. Specifically, when a student evaluated the conversational partner as having high reward value, he or she was much more likely to develop a relationship with the partner over the course

of the semester. Another study produced similar findings for roommates: roommates who had positive initial interactions with each other, and therefore more positive predicted outcome values, tended to live together longer (Marek, Wanzer, & Knapp, 2004).

Predicted outcome value theory has also been applied to ongoing relationships. A study by Ramirez, Sunnafrank, and Goei (2010) investigated how a couple's relationship changes following an unexpected event. They reasoned that when unexpected events occur, people adjust their predicted outcome values. These adjustments, then, lead to corresponding changes in liking, attraction, amount of communication, and information seeking. Their study also showed that people report more uncertainty in response to unexpected negative events compared to unexpected positive events. However, changes in predicted outcome values were better predictors of changes in liking and communication than was uncertainty.

The Theory of Motivated Information Management

The TMIM (Afifi & Morse, 2009; Afifi & Weiner, 2004) also helps explain why people seek information in some situations and not others. This theory is based on the idea that people prefer certainty in some situations and uncertainty in other situations. The TMIM starts by recognizing that individuals are only motivated to manage their uncertainty levels when they perceive *a discrepancy* between the level of uncertainty they have about an important issue and the level of uncertainty they want. In other words, someone may be uncertain about an issue but be comfortable with that state—in which case he or she would not deliberately engage in information management.

Consistent with predicted outcome value theory, the TMIM proposes that people who feel a discrepancy between actual and desired uncertainty use an "evaluation phase" to decide whether to reduce the discrepancy. The person's decision depends on (1) the **outcome expectancy,** referring to whether the outcome of the information search is expected to be positive or negative; and (2) the **efficacy assessment,** focusing on whether people feel able to gather information and cope with it. These two perceptions determine whether people seek information directly, seek information indirectly, avoid information (actively or passively), or reassess their level of uncertainty. The TMIM also explicitly notes the role of the information provider in this exchange, arguing that the provider goes through a similar process of information management in trying to decide what information to give and how to give it (see Figure 4.1).

Several studies have successfully tested the TMIM (for review, see Afifi, 2015; Lancaster, Dillow, Ball, Borchert, & Tyler, 2016; Rauscher &

Hesse, 2014). The theory has accurately predicted whether people seek information about relationship history and sexual health from their partner, whether teenagers talk to their divorced or nondivorced parents about the parent's relationship, whether marital partners talk to each other about finances, and whether adult children talk to their parents about family health history and eldercare preferences, among other issues. In all these cases, two patterns were found. First, some people (albeit a minority) wanted more uncertainty, not less, or were satisfied with elevated uncertainty levels. Second, those who wanted to reduce uncertainty generally did so only when their expectations and efficacy assessments encouraged a search for information. However, the surprising overarching pattern of findings is

FIGURE 4.1   ■   Model of Theory of Motivated Information Management Predictions

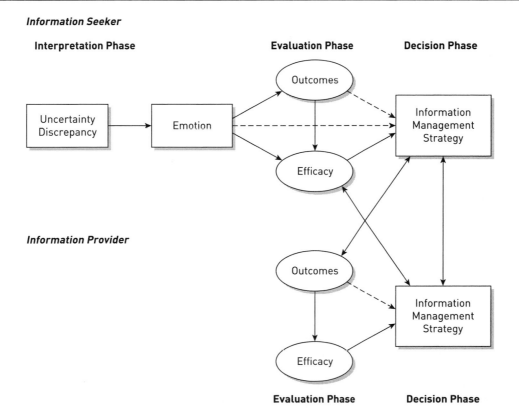

that we generally avoid seeking information when we most desire the reduction of uncertainty (see Afifi & Robbins, 2014). In that sense, the findings in these studies, and as predicted by TMIM, are in stark contrast to the early predictions stemming from uncertainty reduction theory—that we almost always seek information when we are uncertain. It is clear that scholars need to better understand the conditions under which uncertainty leads us to seek information and those under which it discourages such action.

Relational Turbulence Theory

So far the theories we have discussed have focused on why, how, and when people are motivated (or not motivated) to use communication to reduce uncertainty. Solomon and her colleagues took a different twist on answering the "when" question by proposing that, in romantic relationships, the transition from casual dating to commitment is a "turbulent" period in relationship development that is often fraught with uncertainty. This is the central idea in the **model of relational turbulence** (Solomon & Knobloch, 2001, 2004). The turbulence during this transition period comes from partners' efforts to renegotiate their level of interdependence (see Chapter 14) and is a function of two primary factors: (1) uncertainty associated with the question of whether or not to increase commitment (e.g., is this "the" person?), and (2) irritations from partners who block the person's other goals (e.g., limiting the partner's independence and ability to do what he or she wants to do).

Prior to the turbulence model, most scholars believed that uncertainty gradually decreased across relationship stages as partners became better acquainted. However, the turbulence model suggests that relational uncertainty peaks in the middle stages of relationships. Relational doubts are highest when couples are deciding whether to escalate their casual relationship into a more committed relationship. It is also important to note that different types of uncertainty may characterize different stages of a relationship. Uncertainty about another person's general beliefs, attitudes, and behavior may dominate initial encounters whereas uncertainty about the relationship and the partner's feelings and intentions may govern the transition from a casual to a more committed relationship. The relational turbulence model focuses on the latter.

So far, some studies show the predicted upturn in uncertainty when relationships are escalating, but others reveal that uncertainty gradually decreases as relationships develop, much as the original uncertainty reduction theory predicted (for review, see Knobloch, 2007a, 2007b). In short, the longer you are with your partner, the less uncertainty you have about her or him. The findings for irritations across relational stages have been more consistent with the escalating stage of a relationship marked by increased irritation as predicted by the model of relational turbulence. Across studies, increased uncertainty was shown to accompany increased irritation. The inconsistency in these findings suggests that some couples experience relatively smooth transitions from casual to committed relationships, without irritations, whereas others experience considerable turbulence and associated irritations and uncertainty.

While the specific prediction about increases in uncertainty across relationship stages has not always panned out, the model has been a very useful tool for understanding important events within relationships, and relationship events, more generally. For example, Theiss, Knobloch, Checton, and Magsamen-Conrad (2009) asked dating couples to report on their relationships and their relational and partner uncertainty once a week for 6 weeks along with the extent to which the partner made it difficult for them to achieve their goals (i.e., partner interference) and any hurtful things that their partner did or said. Their analyses showed that the degree of uncertainty in the relationship and the extent to which the partner interfered with their goals predicted the hurtfulness of the event and any relational deterioration that resulted. A study by McLaren, Solomon, and Priem (2011) applied the turbulence model to people's reactions to a romantic partner's hurtful message, such as being insulted or criticized. They found that people who reported experiencing more uncertainty and interference from a hurtful message also reported more relational turbulence, more intense hurt, and more negative emotion. And Ellis and Ledbetter (2015) found the model to predict how couples fared in long-distance relationships. Not surprisingly, physical distance in relationships increased the times in which the partner was perceived to be blocking goals, but the negative effects of that interference were greatly diminished in couples who spoke regularly about closeness and how much they missed one another. In other words, specific kinds of maintenance behaviors seem to overcome the uncertainty and relational turbulence that comes with many long-distance relationships.

Finally, Steuber and Solomon (2008) coded 438 online messages posted by husbands or wives managing their infertility diagnoses. Both relational uncertainty and partner interference were evident in the messages. For instance, one person described her experience of relational uncertainty this way:

> Once he [her husband] found out the problem was not him (my right tube was blocked) he told me that he shouldn't have to go to any appointments with me because "it's your problem, not mine"! . . . I don't understand why he is being like this, normally . . . he's very loving and supportive. (Steuber & Solomon, 2008, p. 842)

Another participant described the unique aspects of partner interference, and related relational difficulties, that infertility treatment sometimes bring into a marriage:

> But last night [her husband] came home with a cold and did not feel like performing his part. Yeah on the most important night of the month. I lost it and just started crying and all the stress that was building up just came out. It was pretty bad. (Steuber & Solomon, 2008, p. 844)

The uncertainty and relational difficulties that come with turbulence-producing episodes are evident from these people's words and highlight the challenges that couples sometimes face. Thus, the turbulence model may not only be applicable to couples transitioning from casual to committed relationships but also to couples who are dealing with a crisis event that produces higher-than-usual levels of uncertainty.

This broader sense of the model's application led its primary authors to publish an update that builds on the model's successes and introduces the relational turbulence theory (RTT) (Solomon, Knobloch, Theiss, & McLaren, 2016). The revision focuses on three primary theoretical positions: (1) Instead of thinking of relational uncertainty and partner interference as equivalent factors impacting relational processes and cognitions, the RTT focuses on the way that each distinctively impacts our thoughts and feelings; (2) the RTT offers a set of explanations for how cognition, emotions, and communication outcomes impact one another in close relationships; and (3) the RTT gives us a better picture of how a series of experiences create a sense of chaotic relationships, with significant implications for individuals and their relationships. Together, these changes lead to seven statements or propositions (P) about relational experiences:

P1: Relational uncertainty makes understanding of specific relational events more difficult and, as such, leads people to form more biased interpretations of those events.

P2. Goal interruptions from a partner, especially those involving everyday routines, make us emotionally charged and cause more intense emotional responses.

P3: Biased interpretations of events, of the sort described in P1, causes people to respond communicatively in more extreme ways than is otherwise the case.

P4: Intense emotional responses, of the sort described in P2, cause people to respond communicatively in more extreme ways than is otherwise the case.

P5: The experience of events through biased interpretations, intense emotions, and characterized by extreme communicative responses create a sense of relational chaos that leads partners to perceive their relationship as turbulent.

P6: Perceptions of the relationship as turbulent leads the individual to be preoccupied with the sense of chaos, affecting a variety of personal, relational, and social outcomes.

P7: Perceptions of the relationship as turbulent negatively impacts the ease with which partners can work smoothly together, affecting a variety of personal, relational, and social outcomes.

Together, these seven propositions lead to a clearer and more specific picture of the ways in which relational uncertainty and disruptions create a cascade of perceptions and experiences that shape our individual and relational lives.

EXPECTANCY VIOLATIONS

Uncertainty is also connected to another important area of communication research—that of expectancy violations. As Berger (1979) suggested, behaviors that deviate from expectations are likely to increase a person's motivation to reduce uncertainty. This is because expectancy-violating behaviors make it difficult for people to predict and explain someone's behavior. It is not surprising that considerable research has been conducted on expectancy violations in relationships. In this section, we discuss Burgoon's (1978; Burgoon & Hale, 1988) expectancy violations theory, as well as related research on expectancy violations in contexts such involving sexual activity between cross-sex friends, first dates, and hurtful events in romantic relationships. As you will see, some of this research has used the concepts of expectancy violations and uncertainty together to help explain how people communicate in relationships.

Expectancy Violations Theory

How do people react when they encounter unexpected behavior? Burgoon has attempted to answer this question by developing and testing expectancy violations theory (Burgoon, 1978; Burgoon & Hale, 1988; Burgoon, Stern, & Dillman, 1995). In its earliest form, the theory focused on how people react to violations of personal space. Later, however, the theory was extended to encompass all types of behavioral violations, positive and negative. An expectancy violation occurs whenever a person's behavior is different from what is expected.

People build expectancies largely through interpersonal interaction. By observing and interacting with others, people reduce uncertainty and form expectancies about how people behave under various circumstances. These expectations can be either predictive or prescriptive. **Predictive expectancies** tell people what to expect in a given situation based on what normally occurs in that particular **context** and/or relationship (Burgoon et al., 1995). For example, based on Serena's past promptness, Vish would have been surprised had she been even 10 minutes late. His expectations for "on-time arrival" are very different for other people he knows, though—people who are consistently 30 minutes late, for example. Predictive expectancies are generally based on the norms or routines that typically occur within a given context and/or relationship. **Prescriptive expectancies,** by contrast, tell people what to expect based on general rules of appropriateness (Burgoon et al., 1995). So, cultural norms would have led Vish to expect a call from Serena before the date had she known that she wasn't going to be able to make it.

According to expectancy violations theory, three factors affect expectancies: (1) communicator characteristics, (2) relational characteristics, (3) and context. Communicator characteristics refer to individual differences, including age, sex, ethnic background, and personality traits. For instance, you might expect an elderly woman to be more polite than an adolescent boy, or you might expect your extroverted friend to be outgoing at a party and your introverted friend to be quiet and reserved.

Relational characteristics refer to factors such as how close we are to someone, the type of relationship we share (platonic, romantic, business), and what types of experiences we have shared together. Hearing "I love you" from a romantic partner might be an expected behavior, but hearing the same words from a casual acquaintance might be highly unexpected. Similarly, certain types of intimate touch are usually expected in romantic relationships but not in platonic ones. Finally, context includes both the social situation and cultural influences. Clearly, different behavioral expectations exist depending on the situation. For example, if you are in church attending a funeral, you expect people to act in different ways from how they would act in the same church attending a wedding. Behavioral expectations may also shift depending on whether you are at work or out for a night on the town with friends. Similarly, expectations differ based on culture. For example, you might expect someone to greet you by kissing your face three times on alternating cheeks if you are in parts of the Middle East, but not if you are in the United States.

What happens when expectancies are violated? Maybe your platonic friend touches you in an overly intimate fashion, or maybe you expect to be greeted affectionately by a European friend but the friend offers only a stiff handshake. According to expectancy violations theory, your response will be contingent on at least two factors: (1) the positive or negative interpretation of the behavior and (2) the rewardingness of the partner.

THE POSITIVE OR NEGATIVE INTERPRETATION OF THE BEHAVIOR When unexpected events occur, people often experience heightened arousal and uncertainty, leading them to search for an explanation (Burgoon & Hale, 1988). To do this, people pay close attention to their partner and the situation to ascertain the meaning of the unexpected behavior and interpret it as positive or negative. As part of this process, the unexpected behavior is compared to the expected behavior. When the unexpected behavior

is perceived to be more satisfying than the expected behavior, a positive violation has occurred. For example, if Serena had shown up on Friday night, she may have been positively surprised by the care Vish took in cleaning his apartment and preparing her dinner since he normally does not go to such trouble. By contrast, when the unexpected behavior is perceived to be less positive than the expected behavior, a negative violation has occurred (for review, see Floyd, Ramirez, & Burgoon, 2008). So if Vish ends up telling Serena to forget about getting together over the weekend, Serena might be surprised because she expected Vish to be reasonable and understand that the mix-up was a simple mistake.

Expectancy violations can have positive or negative relationship consequences. When positive violations occur, people are likely to be happier and more satisfied with their relationships. When negative violations occur, however, people might become angry and dissatisfied with their relationships (Burgoon et al., 1995; Levitt, 1991; Levitt, Coffman, Guacci-Franco, & Loveless, 1994). But not all expectations are fair to relational partners, a reality that sometimes harms relationships. One such example when people expect their relationship partners to understand their needs and feelings without having to be told: mind reading expectations. Given that many of us have likely experienced such expectations at some point in our lives, we can relate to Wright and Roloff's (2015) finding that such unrealistic expectations are likely to lead to negative expectancy violations (i.e., we expect our partner to respond in a particular way but our partner does not know that we want him to respond that way so he doesn't) and relational dissatisfaction. Clarity about expectations within relationships is always recommended.

THE REWARDINGNESS OF THE PARTNER Sometimes people cannot determine the valence of a behavior simply by comparing the unexpected behavior to what they expected. This is because some behaviors are ambiguous; they can be positive in some situations and negative in others, depending on who enacts them. For example, imagine that you are working on a class project with several classmates. Because they are always together, you assume that two of the classmates, Terry and Alex, are a couple. However, Terry approaches you after the group meeting, smiles warmly, touches your arm, and asks you out on a date. You are surprised and ask, "Aren't you with Alex?" Terry replies, "Oh no, Alex and I are just really good friends."

How might you respond to Terry's unexpected behavior? The smile, touch, and request are not inherently positive or negative. Instead, the interpretation of these unexpected behaviors may depend on how rewarding you perceive Terry to be. If you see Terry as attractive, charming, and intelligent, you likely will see the expectancy violation as positive and reciprocate by accepting the date. If, however, you see Terry as a deceitful person who is going behind Alex's back, you probably will see the expectancy violation as negative and refuse the date. In this case, it is not the behavior per se that is positive or negative; instead, it is the combination of the behavior and the rewardingness of the partner.

Interestingly, research on expectancy violations theory has shown that nonrewarding communicators are evaluated the most favorably if they stay within the norms and avoid violating expectations (Burgoon & Hale, 1988). For example, suppose you have to work on a project with a coworker whom you dislike. The two of you do not talk to each other much, but so far you have tried to keep your relationship civil. If the coworker suddenly starts asking you to go to lunch with her and telling you her life's story, you will probably evaluate her even more negatively because you will see her as pushy and overbearing. Similarly, if the coworker starts pointedly ignoring you and makes sarcastic remarks while you are speaking, you will likely evaluate her even more negatively as a mean, rude person. Notice that whether the expectancy violation involves behaviors that are more friendly or less friendly, you might still perceive the coworker negatively. This is because

people tend to interpret unexpected behavior as consistent with their initial impressions of someone. To produce a more positive result, the coworker would be better off remaining civil and gradually becoming less distant. Such behavior would confirm your expectations and perhaps lay a foundation for a better relationship.

With rewarding communicators, however, expectancy violations theory suggests that positive violations actually produce better outcomes than expectancy-confirming behaviors (Burgoon et al., 1995; Burgoon & Hale, 1988). When positive violations occur, people feel "bright emotions" such as joy, excitement, and relief. When expectancies are confirmed, people also feel bright emotions, but they are less intense. Finally, when negative violations occur, people feel "dark emotions," such as sadness, anger, and disappointment (see also Levitt, 1991). Positive violations are met with reciprocity, which means that the person receiving the unexpectedly positive behavior will respond by engaging in more positive behavior. Clearly, positive expectancy violations can be beneficial in close relationships even though they may create uncertainty and reflect a lack of predictability. Floyd and colleagues (2008) put it this way:

> When unexpected events occur, . . . they force us to admit that our predictions were wrong and they can cause us to feel uncertain about the future. Expectancy violations theory concedes that expectancy violations often do produce more negative outcomes than expectancy confirmations. However, it parts ways with other theories by suggesting that under certain circumstances, expectancy violations can produce outcomes that are actually more positive than those produced by expectancy confirmations. (p. 506)

Types of Expectancy Violations in Close Relationships

Given that expectancy violations can be beneficial or harmful to relationships, a sensible next question to ask is this: Do certain behaviors tend to function as positive or negative expectancy violations in people's day-to-day relationships? In past research, such as that by Planalp and Honeycutt (1985), researchers focused primarily on negative events. Afifi and Metts (1998) extended this research by asking people in friendships and romantic relationships to think about the last time their friend or partner did or said something unexpected. They emphasized that the unexpected event could be either positive or negative. Participants reported on events that had occurred, on average, 5 days earlier. Some of the behaviors reported were relatively mundane, and others were quite dramatic. In addition to varying substantially in terms of severity, these reported violations differed in the extent to which they were seen as positive or negative and, just as importantly, the extent to which they increased or decreased uncertainty. Unlike earlier researchers, Afifi and Metts (1998) found that many expectancy violations reduce uncertainty by providing important information about a person. The outcome was a list of nine general categories of expectancy violations that commonly occur in relationships:

1. *Criticism or accusation:* Actions that are critical of the person or that accuse her or him of some type of offense

2. *Relationship escalation:* Actions that confirm or intensify the commitment of the person to the relationship, such as saying "I love you" or giving expensive gifts

3. *Relationship de-escalation:* Actions that imply a desire to decrease the intimacy level in the relationship, such as reducing communication and spending more time apart

4. *Uncharacteristic relational behavior:* Actions that are not consistent with the way the person defines the relationship, such as members of cross-sex friendships asking their supposedly platonic friend for a sexual relationship

5. *Uncharacteristic social behavior:* Actions that do not have relational implications but that simply are not expected from that

person in that context, such as a mild-mannered person raising her or his voice during an argument with a salesperson

6. *Transgressions:* Actions that are violations of taken-for-granted rules of relationships, such as having an affair, being disloyal, sharing private information with other people, and being deceitful

7. *Acts of devotion:* Actions that imply that the person really views the partner and/or the relationship as being special, such as going "above and beyond the call of duty" to help that individual through a difficult time

8. *Acts of disregard:* Actions that imply that the person considers the partner and/or the relationship as unimportant, such as showing up late or being inconsiderate

9. *Gestures of inclusion:* Actions that show an unexpected desire to include the partner in the person's activities or life, such as disclosing something very personal or extending an invitation to spend the holidays with his or her family

McLaughlin and Vitak (2012) further advanced thinking about expectation violations by studying norms and expectation violations on Facebook. Participants cited the overuse of new status updates, overly personal or emotional disclosures, engaging in private conflict over a public channel, and tagging people in pictures without their permission as examples of negative violations. Positive violations included things like learning about similarities with others through their Facebook posts, or discovering information that they considered positive (e.g., the person is moving closer) through someone's Facebook updates or posted pictures. Bevan, Ang, and Fearns (2014) added Facebook unfriending as a form of online negative expectancy violation studied by scholars, and Miller-Ott and Kelly (2015) found that college students have clear expectations for when cell phone use when with others is appropriate and when it negatively violates expectations.

Expectancy Violations and Uncertainty in Specific Contexts

The concepts of expectancy violations and uncertainty have been helpful in understanding specific processes that occur in relationships, including sexual activity, first dates, hurtful events, and modality switches. These types of events can decrease or increase uncertainty, depending on the circumstances.

FLIRTATION AND SEXUAL ACTIVITY Research has examined how expectancies and uncertainty are related to flirtation and sexual activity. In a study of reactions to flirtation, Lannutti and Cameron (2007) asked college partygoers to participate in a study. Some of the women in the study had been drinking and others had not. The researchers presented the participants with scenarios depicting a man coming up and flirting with them. Depending on the scenario they read, the man was portrayed as either very attractive or very unattractive. The scenarios also varied in terms of flirting behavior; the man was said to put his arm around the woman's shoulder, to touch her thigh, or to try to kiss her. All of these behaviors have been found to be unexpected, but the kiss attempt was rated as the most unexpected, followed by the thigh touch.

There was also a *social lubrication effect*. This effect occurs when alcohol makes interaction less stressful and more enjoyable (Park, 2004). By extension, women who have been drinking expect the people around them to be more social, thereby making mildly flirtatious behaviors more enjoyable and expected. This was the case in Lannutti and Cameron's (2007) study. Women who had not been drinking evaluated the situation where the man was portrayed as putting his arm around her as more unexpected than did women who had been drinking. But the attractiveness level of the man was the biggest influence on women's interpretations of flirtatious behavior; unattractive men were evaluated more negatively than attractive men regardless of the type of touch. The most positive evaluations were of attractive men who touched the thigh as opposed

to attempting to kiss the woman. This suggests that attractive men are likely to be evaluated somewhat positively when they use unexpectedly flirtatious behavior—but of course, only up to a point.

Other studies have investigated uncertainty and expectancy violations as they relate to sexual activity in both cross-sex friendships and romantic relationships. A study of sexual initiation with otherwise-platonic opposite-sex friends (Afifi & Faulkner, 2000) showed that participants generally rated those experiences (friends with benefits) as unexpected and that their impact depended on whether the event was seen as positive or negative and whether it increased or decreased uncertainty. Friends were most likely to perceive that their relationship was damaged when the sexual contact increased uncertainty and was evaluated negatively. In another investigation, Bevan (2003) compared sexual resistance in cross-sex friendships and dating relationships. Her study revealed that resisting sexual attempts was perceived as more normative (less unexpected) and as a more relationally important expectation violation in cross-sex friendships, as compared to dating relationships. The logic here is that such resistance essentially defines the relationship in the context of cross-sex friendships ("Okay, we're not going to move the relationship to that level"), making it especially important. In addition, because sexual activity is not typical in such relationships, resistance is more expected than in romantic relationships. Mongeau, Knight, Williams, Eden, and Shaw (2013) found that friends with benefits varied dramatically on the extent to which they were either primarily experienced as friendships or primarily as outlets for uncommitted sexual activity, but with uncertainties as an important dimension in almost all cases.

EXPECTATIONS AND GOALS ON FIRST DATES Expectations and goals also influence the success of first dates. Some of the most common goals people have for first dates include having fun, reducing uncertainty, investigating romantic potential, developing friendship, and engaging in sexual activity

(Mongeau, Serewicz, & Therrien, 2004). Of these, having fun and reducing uncertainty are the most common goals. The goals partners have influence the expectations and communication that characterize first dates. When partners have similar expectations, the goals of both individuals are more likely to be fulfilled, leading to a "good" date.

Take Vish and Serena as an example. Imagine that Vish gets over his earlier disappointment and goes out with Serena the following night. Both Vish and Serena believe that they have already established closeness at a friendship level. Their priority, then, is to determine if there is sexual chemistry and the potential for a romantic relationship. During their date, they show affection to one another, share personal stories, and spend considerable time kissing, which helps them both decide that the relationship does indeed have romantic and sexual potential. On the other hand, imagine that Serena is still uncertain about Vish as a person and potential friend, whereas Vish's goal is to determine romantic potential and to engage in sexual activity. In this case, Vish and Serena's different goals could put them at cross-purposes, with both being frustrated that they could not reach their individual goals. As Mongeau and colleagues (2004) put it, "What constitutes a 'good' or 'bad' date, then, depends on the compatibility of partners' goals" (p. 143).

The goals that people have also depend on the type of relationship they share prior to the first date. Some people enter a first date as strangers or acquaintances, whereas others are already good friends. Strangers and acquaintances are more likely than friends to have the goals of reducing uncertainty about the person and developing a friendship. By contrast, friends are more likely than strangers or acquaintances to have goals of investigating romantic potential and engaging in sexual activity (Mongeau et al., 2004). Friends are also more likely to expect high levels of intimacy and affection on first dates (Morr & Mongeau, 2004). The goal of having fun appears to be salient regardless of the type of relationship.

In line with uncertainty reduction theory, when people are relatively unacquainted, their primary goal during a first date is to seek information and reduce uncertainty. During the beginning stages of a relationship, people often exchange rather superficial information as part of the getting-acquainted process. However, once people have developed a friendship and exchanged in-depth information with one another, their goal on a first date may be to focus on other forms of intimacy that are yet undeveloped, such as romantic or sexual intimacy. Having fun may be an important goal in first dates because it reduces uncertainty in a positive manner by showing that a person is rewarding, and as predicted outcome value theory suggests, people are more likely to develop close relationships with people who they regard as rewarding (Sunnafrank & Ramirez, 2004).

Finally, some research has examined sex differences in goals and expectations about sexual activity on first dates. This research suggests that men expect and desire more sexual activity on first dates than do women (Mongeau & Carey, 1996; Mongeau et al., 2004). However, the differences in sexual expectations for men versus women are not very large. College-age men tend to expect heavy kissing, whereas college-age women tend to expect light kissing (Mongeau & Johnson, 1995; Morr & Mongeau, 2004). Some studies also show that men are likely to have higher sexual expectations for dates that are initiated by women, even though these expectations are not likely to be met (Mongeau & Johnson, 1995; Muehlenhard & Scardino, 1985). A man's expectation of more sexual activity on dates initiated by women may be due to the perception that a woman who initiates a first date is more liberal, open, and attracted to him, but in actuality, dates initiated by women tend to be characterized by the same or less sexual activity than dates initiated by men. This exemplifies a situation where more certainty leads to the wrong expectations (e.g., men have more certainty about a woman's intentions, yet their heightened expectations for sexual activity are violated).

HURTFUL EVENTS Research has also used expectancy violations theory to examine how people respond to uncertainty-evoking or hurtful events, such as deception, infidelity, or other forms of betrayal. Cohen (2010) compared friends' likely responses to three types of expectancy violations: (1) moral, (2) trust, and (3) social. **Moral violations** occur when a person's behavior deviates from what is considered right. Behaviors such as drinking, using drugs, acting violent, and cheating during a game are all moral violations of expectancies. **Trust violations** occur when a person behaves in a way that is deceptive or betrays trust. Examples of trust violations include revealing a friend's secret, breaking promises, concealing important information, and putting on an act to impress or manipulate others. Finally, **social violations** occur when people fail to act in relationally appropriate ways and instead engage in rude, cold, critical, or condescending behavior. In Cohen's study, people reported that trust and social violations were worse than moral violations, even though they would feel less close to a friend who committed any of these violations. Women tended to have stronger reactions than men; they reported a greater reduction in closeness following violations than men did.

Malachowski and Frisby (2015) followed up on this work with a study that focused on the role played by relational uncertainty on forgiveness and change in relationship closeness after a hurtful event. The study asked participants to report on the most hurtful event that occurred in a current romantic relationship, then, two months later, contacted participants again for a follow-up. The study's results showed that self-uncertainty (i.e., the extent to which participants were certain that they were committed to the relationship) shaped the outcome of the hurtful experience. When people were confident in their own commitment, they were more willing to forgive their partner and the relationship suffered less damage. Those results somewhat mirror what Knobloch (2005) found in her study of responses to uncertainty-increasing events in close relationships. Participants were better able

to withstand uncertainty-increasing events if they reported high levels of relational closeness.

MODALITY SWITCHES Modality switching occurs when people who have previously communicated exclusively online begin to interact face to face. The switch from an online to an offline relationship can be a significant turning point in a relationship, leading to either increased or decreased closeness. Ramirez and his colleagues have suggested that the concepts of uncertainty and expectancy violations help explain why some relationships grow closer after a modality switch whereas others become more distant. In the first of two studies, Ramirez and Zhang (2007) found that if people had been interacting for a short time online, the shift to face-to-face interaction decreased uncertainty, but if they had been interacting exclusively online for an extended time, the move to face-to-face interaction actually increased uncertainty. They used the idea of an idealization effect (Walther, 1996) to explain this finding.

According to the **idealization effect,** people who communicate exclusively online for an extended period of time tend to idealize one another and have high expectations about what their relationship would be like if they were to interact in person. Face-to-face interaction then leads people to make more realistic assessments, which often lead to disappointment. Interestingly, this phenomenon is similar to the idealization effect found in long-distance relationships. As discussed in Chapter 10, long-distance partners often have high expectations for how great their relationship will be once they live in the same area, but when they move closer to one another they become disillusioned because the relationship does not live up to their expectations.

To determine whether expectations could help explain how people react to modality switches, Ramirez and Wang (2008) conducted an experiment. They had previously unacquainted dyads work together online for either 3 or 6 weeks, following which some dyads met face to face while others stayed online. Compared to the people who continued communicating only online, the dyads who switched modalities rated the information they received during their last meeting as more unexpected. However, whether the unexpected behavior was seen as positive or negative was dependent on the length of time they had interacted online. People who had interacted online for a relatively short time (3 weeks), evaluated the communication that occurred during their final meeting as more

positive and uncertainty reducing if they met face to face versus online. But the opposite pattern emerged for people who had interacted online for a longer time (6 weeks): those people reported evaluating the information exchanged during their final meeting as more negative and more uncertainty increasing when face to face versus online. These findings support the idea that people idealize others and build up more positive expectations the longer they interact online before meeting someone.

SUMMARY AND APPLICATION

Uncertainty and expectancy violations play important roles in the way people communicate with others. In initial interactions with strangers and acquaintances, people often feel motivated to reduce uncertainty through communication. Even in close, developed relationships, people sometimes feel strongly motivated to reduce uncertainty. Behaviors that are unexpected, such as Serena not showing up for the date, are especially likely to lead to uncertainty. So people who are in a situation like Vish's should recognize that their feelings of uncertainty are natural. However, there are also circumstances when people feel unmotivated to reduce uncertainty. For example, if Vish is uncertain about Serena's feelings for him, he might prefer uncertainty rather than finding out that she isn't attracted to him, or jeopardizing their friendship by asking her how she feels about him. According to the TMIM, Vish will be more motivated to reduce uncertainty if he wants to know how Serena feels, if he believes he can get the information he is searching for, and if he can cope with whatever he finds out.

If Vish decided to reduce his uncertainty, there are several strategies he can use. He can reduce uncertainty by passively observing Serena with others, manipulating the social environment, questioning third parties, or interacting with her directly. In established relationships, people also report using a variety of "secret tests" to

help them determine their partner's intentions. People in established relationships also use a number of direct strategies, including using direct communication, showing closeness or being romantic, and engaging in destructive communication or conflict. The strategies that Vish uses may be dependent on the type of relationship he shares with Serena. If, previous to Friday night, Vish had characterized his friendship with Serena as close and satisfying, he would be likely to use direct and positive strategies to reduce uncertainty rather than distancing or avoidant strategies. However, if he is worried that Serena might not reciprocate his desire to turn their friendship romantic, he would probably use more indirect strategies to try to reduce uncertainty.

The stage of the relationship may also matter. The relational turbulence model suggests that couples are especially likely to experience uncertainty and irritation during the transition from a casual to a committed relationship. The same logic applies to relationships moving from friendship toward romance. Given that Vish had planned the date with the hope of increasing closeness with Serena, their relationship may be at a transition point, which could intensify the frustration and uncertainty that Vish is experiencing. If Vish and Serena had a long-standing committed romantic relationship, Vish might have more readily accepted her explanation of a misunderstanding about the day of the date.

The scenario between Vish and Serena illustrates another important point about uncertainty. For Vish and Serena, there is a danger that the uncertainty they are both experiencing could seep into the fabric of their relationship and feelings for one another. After their Saturday morning conversation, Vish may still not be convinced that Serena is telling the truth about mixing up the night of their date. At the very least, this might lead Vish to question if he trusts Serena. For her part, Serena might be frustrated that Vish does not believe her and incredulous because he got the dates mixed up. As a result, Serena might reduce her uncertainty by reevaluating Vish as an unreasonable, forgetful, and paranoid person, thereby decreasing her attraction toward him— both as a friend and as a potential romantic partner.

Expectancy violations also produce uncertainty. Interestingly, however, expectancy violations can be beneficial to relationships when they are interpreted positively. In other words,

when unexpected behavior is perceived to be better than expected behavior, people experience positive outcomes despite the initial discomfort they might have felt at not being able to accurately predict their partner's behavior. Vish's initial attempt to plan a special date and turn their relationship romantic may have been successful in positively violating Serena's expectations and promoting increased feelings of attraction and closeness. Moreover, to the extent that Vish and Serena generally perceive one another to be rewarding, they would be likely to put aside any negative feelings about the misunderstanding and move forward in their relationship.

As the situation between Vish and Serena illustrates, uncertainty-increasing events can be critical turning points in relationships. How partners cope with uncertainty, including whether or not they are motivated to manage uncertainty, affects the future course of the relationship. Hopefully the research in this chapter gave you a clearer picture of why these experiences occur and how best to deal with them.

KEY TERMS

context (p. 102)

dialectics theory (p. 89)

efficacy assessment (p. 99)

expectancy violations theory (p. 86)

high outcome value (p. 97)

idealization effect (p. 108)

low outcome value (p. 97)

model of relational turbulence (p. 100)

moral violations (p. 108)

outcome expectancy (p. 98)

outcome values (p. 97)

partner uncertainty (p. 86)

predicted outcome value theory (p. 86)

predictive expectancies (p. 102)

prescriptive expectancies (p. 102)

relational turbulence theory (p. 86)

relationship uncertainty (p. 86)

self-uncertainty (p. 86)

social violations (p. 108)

theory of motivated information management (TMIM) (p. 86)

trust violations (p. 108)

uncertainty (p. 86)

uncertainty management theory (p. 89)

uncertainty reduction theory (p. 85)

DISCUSSION QUESTIONS

1. According to uncertainty reduction theory, people are driven by the need to reduce uncertainty during initial encounters. Do you agree with this idea? Are there certain circumstances that make uncertainty reduction an especially salient goal?

2. Think about the last few times someone violated your expectations—either positively or negatively. Does expectancy violations theory help explain how you reacted to these expectancy violations? Why or why not?

3. Think about a relationship in which you felt uncertainty about your own levels of commitment. How did that uncertainty impact your behavior? Did it influence what you did or did not discuss with the other person?

 SAGE edge™

Sharpen your skills with SAGE edge at edge.sagepub.com/guerrero5e.
SAGE edge for students provides a personalized approach to help you accomplish your coursework goals in an easy-to-use learning environment.

5 CHANGING RELATIONSHIPS
Stages, Turning Points, and Dialectics

When Anne and Connor meet at a Sierra Club meeting, they discover they have much in common. They both have degrees in biology, love animals, and enjoy outdoor activities. Anne is a caretaker at the local zoo, and Connor teaches science at a middle school. For the first two months, their relationship goes smoothly. They text every day, spend considerable time together, and Facetime almost every night if they haven't seen each other during the day. They decide to make their relationship exclusive. Connor assumes that Anne would want to spend Thanksgiving with him. When she says she'd rather be with her family, Connor feels hurt and becomes distant. After a week of silence, Connor calls Anne and apologizes. They resume their relationship, and a month later, Connor tells Anne he loves her and hopes to marry her someday. She responds that she feels the same way. Six months later, Anne suggests they move in together. Connor, however, hesitates. He worries that living together before marriage could cause them to take their relationship for granted. He also knows that his family would never approve. Their disagreement about living together leads to a big argument; after which, Anne starts to realize her values and future plans are radically different from Connor's. She wants him to put their connection first. He wants her to consider his family more. They gradually spend more and more time apart, texting and talking less, until eventually Connor meets someone new. Anne is hurt but also a little relieved—it had become increasingly clear to her that they were not as compatible as she once thought they were. It was probably better to end the relationship now.

The processes related to developing and ending relationships have interested communication researchers for decades. Researchers have tried to unlock the mysteries of how communication propels relationships toward more closeness yet also causes relationships to fall apart. In Anne and Connor's case, getting to know one another was easy. Maintaining the relationship, however, was harder. Clearly, communication played a vital role in both the development and deterioration of their relationship. Various theories of communication help explain the trajectories that Anne and Connor's relationship took. A trajectory describes the road or path that something takes. Relationship trajectories can be smooth or bumpy. People can move their relationships forward, backward, or sideways, or in many different directions at once. The only certainty is that each relationship has a unique trajectory that is more complex and nuanced than any one theory of communication can explain.

In this chapter, we describe some of the communication skills necessary to form and develop relationships. Then we discuss three different perspectives that help describe how relationships change over time: (1) the stage model approach, (2) the turning point approach, and (3) dialectics theory. Stage models describe various stages that relationships go through as people develop their relationships and then, in some cases, break up (e.g., Altman & Taylor, 1973; Knapp & Vangelisti, 2008). The turning point approach takes a different perspective by focusing on the major events that shape people's relationships in positive and negative ways. Finally, dialectics theory suggests that rather than conceptualizing relationships in terms of stages, people should view relationships as constantly changing.

COMMUNICATION SKILLS

Relationships don't just develop out of thin air. People must advance and nurture them. Some people are shy or worry about rejection, making it more difficult for them to establish new relationships. Other people are overzealous about forming new relationships, using excessive self-disclosure or being overly pushy—and, as a result, scaring potential new friends or romantic partners away. Given these complexities, there are essential communication skills and strategies that can help people form and develop new relationships. Buhrmester, Furman, Wittenberg, and Reis (1988) identified five types of communication skills that help people build relationships with new friends and romantic partners: (1) relationship initiation, (2) self-disclosure, (3) emotional support, (4) negative assertion, and (5) conflict management skills. To see how skilled you are in these five areas, take the test in Box 5.1.

SKILL IN RELATIONSHIP INITIATION Skill in initiating relationships is crucial if people are going to get to know one another. People skilled in relationship initiation know how to approach others and make good first impressions. They feel comfortable introducing themselves and striking up conversations with new acquaintances. They are also effective in issuing invitations and making suggestions for things to do with new friends. The ability to initiate relationships is a vital skill for forming new friendships. Two studies that have looked at first-year students during the first few weeks of their college experience suggest even further benefits from having these skills (McEwan & Guerrero, 2010; Shaver, Furman, & Buhrmester, 1985). In these studies, the students who were more skilled at initiating relationships and issuing invitations reported being better adjusted to college life and building more rewarding social networks at their new university.

SKILL IN SELF-DISCLOSURE Self-disclosure involves revealing personal information about oneself to others. As discussed in more detail later in this chapter, people skilled at self-disclosure gradually increase the depth of their disclosure so it becomes more personal. They know how to self-disclose in appropriate ways that allow them to get to know others without scaring them off. For instance, if Connor had approached Anne when he first met her, immediately told her that he thought she was beautiful, and then launched into a rant about his frustrations with the lack of progress on environmental issues, Anne might have viewed Connor's self-disclosure as premature and inappropriate. Instead, Connor started out by introducing himself and sharing impersonal information. As they got to know one another, both Anne and Connor felt comfortable sharing more personal information with one another. People who possess self-disclosure skills tend to be well liked (Fehr, 2008). They also perceive themselves to have more friends with whom to hang out and socialize (McEwan & Guerrero, 2010), suggesting that they build stronger social networks than those who have less skill in self-disclosure.

BOX 5.1 PUT YOURSELF TO THE TEST
INTERPERSONAL SKILLS RELATED TO FORMING AND DEVELOPING RELATIONSHIPS

People have different ways of communicating. For the following items, rank how well you feel you can perform each type of communication, being as honest as possible. Answer the questions using the following scale: 1 = you are poor at the behavior described and would avoid doing it if possible and 5 = you are extremely good at the behavior and would be comfortable in that situation.

		Poor at this				Good at this
1.	Asking or suggesting to someone new that you get together and do something.	1	2	3	4	5
2.	Telling someone you don't like a certain way he/she has been treating you.	1	2	3	4	5
3.	Helping someone work through his/her thoughts and feelings about a major life decision.	1	2	3	4	5
4.	Being able to admit you might be wrong when a disagreement begins to build into a serious fight.	1	2	3	4	5
5.	Confiding in a new friend and letting him/her see your softer, more sensitive side.	1	2	3	4	5
6.	Being able to put resentful feelings aside during a fight.	1	2	3	4	5
7.	Finding and suggesting things to do with new people you find interesting.	1	2	3	4	5
8.	Turning down an unreasonable request.	1	2	3	4	5
9.	Saying no when someone asks you to do something you don't want to do.	1	2	3	4	5
10.	When having a conflict with someone, really listening to his or her complaints and not trying to "read" his/her mind.	1	2	3	4	5
11.	Being an interesting and enjoyable person when first getting to know people.	1	2	3	4	5
12.	Standing up for your rights when someone is neglecting you or being inconsiderate.	1	2	3	4	5
13.	Letting a new companion get to know the "real you."	1	2	3	4	5
14.	Introducing yourself to someone you might like to get to know.	1	2	3	4	5
15.	Letting down your protective outer shell and trusting others.	1	2	3	4	5
16.	Being a good and sensitive listener for someone who is upset.	1	2	3	4	5
17.	Refraining from saying things that might cause a disagreement to build into a big fight.	1	2	3	4	5
18.	Telling others things that secretly make you feel anxious or afraid.	1	2	3	4	5
19.	Being able to do and say things to support another person when she/he is feeling down.	1	2	3	4	5
20.	Presenting a good first impression to people with whom you might like to become friends.	1	2	3	4	5

BOX 5.1

21.	Telling someone that she/he has done something that hurt your feelings.	1	2	3	4	5
22.	Being able to show empathetic concern even when the other person's concern is uninteresting to you.	1	2	3	4	5
23.	When angry, being able to accept that the other person has a valid point of view even if you don't agree with that view.	1	2	3	4	5
24.	Knowing how to move a conversation beyond superficial talk to really get to know each other.	1	2	3	4	5
25.	Being able to give advice in ways that are well received.	1	2	3	4	5

Add up the following items for your score on each skill.

Relationship initiation skills: Items 1 + 7 + 11 + 14 + 20 = _____

Negative assertion skills: Items 2 + 8 + 9 + 12 + 21 = _____

Self-disclosure skills: Items 5 + 13 + 15 + 18 + 24 = _____

Emotional support skills: Items 3 + 16 + 19 + 22 + 25 = _____

Conflict management skills: Items 4 + 6 + 10 + 17 + 23 = _____

Higher scores mean that you possess more of a particular skill. The highest possible score for a given skill is 35; the lowest possible score is 7.

Source: Copyright ©1988 by the American Psychological Association. Reproduced with permission. Buhrmester, D., Furman, W., Wittenberg, M. T., & Reis, H. T. (1988). Five domains of interpersonal competence in peer relationships. *Journal of Personality and Social Psychology, 55,* 991–1008. No further reproduction or distribution is permitted without written permission from the American Psychological Association.

SKILL IN THE PROVISION OF EMOTIONAL SUPPORT Being able to provide others with emotional support is another key skill related to formation, as well as continuation, of close relationships (see Chapter 7). This skill involves being able to listen empathetically to people's problems and concerns, as well as being able to offer advice that is well received by others. Effective emotional support also entails being warm and responsive to others rather than trying to tell people what to do. Indeed, Fehr (2008) described **responsiveness** as a major determinant of whether or not people form relationships. According to Fehr, responsiveness is a communication style that shows care, concern, and liking. People are attracted to others who have this type of warm, other-centered communication style. In addition to being perceived as more responsive, individuals who are skilled in emotional support tend to develop friendship networks that are rich in personal resources, such as having friends whom they trust and can turn to for help in times of trouble (McEwan & Guerrero, 2010). A study by Shelton, Trail, West, and Bergsieker (2010) confirmed that responsiveness is important in developing both interracial and intraracial friendships. In their study, self-disclosure was most effective in developing friendships when it was accompanied by responsiveness.

SKILL IN NEGATIVE ASSERTION As relationships develop, people begin to reveal negative aspects of their personalities more often. Sometimes there is also a struggle for control or power within a relationship. Buhrmester and colleagues (1988) suggested that skill in negative assertion helps people to navigate these potentially problematic situations while "saving face." Recall from Chapter 2 that one part of saving face involves being perceived as able to make one's own decisions without being controlled by another person. Skill in negative assertion helps people accomplish this. Negative assertions include being able to say no to a friend's request, stand up for one's rights within a relationship, and tell a partner when one's feelings are hurt. If negative assertions are stated in a constructive rather than a critical manner, they can help people avoid relationship problems. In McEwan and Guerrero's (2010) study on first-year students forming new friendships, students who reported being skilled in negative assertion were more likely to have joined groups or clubs to make friends. Thus, skills in negative assertion may help people navigate group settings and form friendships.

SKILL IN CONFLICT MANAGEMENT As discussed in detail in Chapter 11, skill in conflict management is vital in both established and developing relationships. During the initial stages of relationship development, people are usually on their best behavior and refrain from engaging in conflict. However, as relationships get closer, people feel freer to disclose negative information and assert differing opinions, which makes conflict more likely. According to Buhrmester and associates (1988), people who are skilled in conflict management are better able to listen to their partner, understand their partner's perspective (even if they disagree with it), and refrain from communicating hostile feelings during conflicts. As for skill in negative assertion, McEwan and Guerrero (2010) found that the students who reported being skilled in conflict management were more likely to have joined groups as a way of forming new friendships.

RELATIONSHIP STAGES

The skills that were previously discussed help explain how people use communication to form close relationships. Stage models help explain the process of developing relationships. One of the earliest and most important stage theories is Altman and Taylor's (1973) social penetration theory (see also Chapter 6). According to this theory, as partners get closer, they move through four stages of relationship development. The first stage, called *orientation,* involves superficial disclosure that allows people to get to know one another in a nonthreatening manner. The second stage, called *exploratory affective exchange,* focuses on broadening the range of topics that people talk about so they can determine what they have in common and decide whether or not to further develop a relationship. The third stage, called *affective exchange,* occurs when people start to disclose about more personal topics, such as emotions and vulnerabilities. Partners reach the final stage, *stable exchange,* when they feel free to disclose almost all of their thoughts, feelings, and experiences with one another. Social penetration theory also addresses how relationships de-escalate and end through the process of *social depenetration.* The social depenetration process is the mirror image of social penetration in that self-disclosure becomes less personal and less frequent.

The staircase model (Knapp & Vangelisti, 2008) expanded social penetration theory by describing 10 specific stages relevant to relationship development and disengagement. Within the staircase model, there are five steps leading upward, called the "coming together stages," with each of these steps representing increasing closeness. There are also five steps leading downward, called the "coming apart stages," with each of these steps representing decreasing closeness (see Figure 5.1). The coming apart stages exemplify the *reversal hypothesis,* which suggests that people undo closeness by decreasing communication. Thus, the coming apart stages are seen as the "reverse" of the coming together stages.

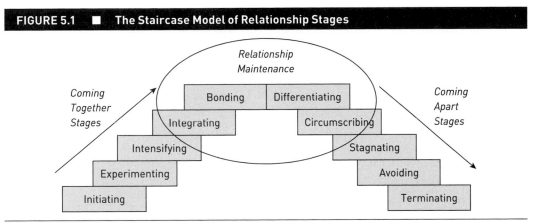

FIGURE 5.1 ■ The Staircase Model of Relationship Stages

Source: The authors created this model based on information in Knapp, M. L., & Vangelisti, A. L. (2008). *Interpersonal communication and human relationships* (6th ed.). Boston: Allyn & Bacon.

Notice, however, that the top four stages are circled in the model. This is because people in established relationships don't always stay on one stage. Instead, they use communication that exemplifies the top stages in both the coming together and coming apart stages. Sometimes they communicate intimacy and closeness, but other times they want distance and autonomy.

Next, we use the 10 stages in Knapp and Vangelisti's staircase model as a way to organize the research related to the various stages that couples (and to a lesser extent, friends) go through as their relationships develop and deteriorate. The types of communication that people use to develop, maintain, and end relationships have changed over the years since this model was first introduced. The typical script for developing relationships used to be that two people would meet, exchange numbers, talk voice-to-voice on the phone, get to know each other on a date, and then perhaps start "going steady" or dating exclusively. Now the sequence is more like this: Two people meet face to face or online, check each other out via social media, exchange phone numbers or Snapchat addresses (often by friending the person on social media and then requesting information through direct messaging), Snapchat and/or text the person for a

while, hang out and do something casual (either alone or in a group), and maybe eventually date (Fox & Warber, 2013). Breakups have changed as well. Because early relationships can be developed through snapping and texting, it is easier to "ghost" someone to break up—which means that one person simply vanishes. They stop texting and snapping and may even delete you from their social media. If former friends or romantic partners do not delete each other from social media, they might see images of each other on an almost daily basis, which can affect how fast a person heals and moves on following a breakup. Although the process of dating has changed, the basic stages proposed by Knapp still provide a good structure for describing how communication changes as people grow closer and further apart.

The "Coming Together" Stages

INITIATING Most stage theories include an initial interaction or beginning stage that focuses on when people meet either in face-to-face contexts or online. Sometimes this stage lasts for two or three more encounters, particularly if each interaction is short in duration. This stage involves exchanging superficial information that allows strangers and new acquaintances to get to know each other a bit without making themselves vulnerable. In Knapp and Vangelisti's (2008) staircase model, the initiating stage involves greeting each other and exchanging bits of information, such as one's name, occupation, or major. The information exchanged during this stage is usually positive; participants try to make a good impression by following rules of social politeness.

A greeting or question followed by a reply is typical of this stage (Knapp & Vangelisti, 2008), which often evolves into a back-and-forth exchange of superficial information that helps people reduce uncertainty about each other. For example, when Connor first met Anne he said, "Hi, I haven't seen you at our meetings before. Is this your first time coming?" Anne responded, "Yeah. Have you been coming for long?" Connor said he'd been to a couple of other meetings but was also fairly new. Then they exchanged names and continued talking about rather superficial topics, such as what happens at the Sierra Club, until the meeting was called to order. At the end of meeting, Connor told Anne it was fun talking to her and asked to add her on his Snapchat. This short conversation helped Connor and Anne reduce uncertainty and set a foundation for future interactions. Sometimes people never progress beyond this stage. Think of people with whom you work or take classes. You may recognize some of these people but rarely talk to them in depth. When you see these casual acquaintances, you likely exchange a quick greeting and reply ("Hi, how are you?" "Fine, thanks") but nothing more, which indicates that you have not moved past the initiating stage.

Initial interactions may play a key role in determining whether people like Anne and Connor develop their relationship further. Indeed, some researchers have argued that people determine their feelings for one another quickly during initial encounters (Berg & Clark, 1986). They then communicate differently based on whether they like the person or not. According to predicted outcome value theory, during initial encounters people make decisions about how rewarding they expect a relationship to be (see Chapter 4). These initial impressions can have lasting effects on how a relationship develops. In one study, undergraduate students were paired with a stranger of the same sex to talk for between 3 and 10 minutes on the first day of class (Sunnafrank & Ramirez, 2004). After this initial interaction, students recorded their perceptions of how rewarding it would be for them become involved in a relationship with the person they just met. The students were surveyed again later in the semester and were much more likely to report developing a relationship with someone they initially perceived to be rewarding. They were also more likely to have sat near them during class, communicated with them frequently, and felt high levels of social attraction and liking. This study demonstrated that the first few minutes of initial encounters have a big influence on if, and how, relationships develop.

EXPERIMENTING Regardless of how people first meet, if their relationship is to progress they need to move beyond the exchange of superficial information. Yet revealing personal information is risky and can make people feel vulnerable. One easy low-risk way to find out information is to check a person's social media. In the early stages of relationships, people are particularly likely to scroll through someone's pictures on social media sites such as Facebook, Twitter, or Instagram as a way to learn more about that person (Fox & Anderegg, 2014). It is also an easy way to check someone's relationship status (Fox, Warber, & Makstaller, 2013). Small talk is another way to help determine whether or not to pursue a closer relationship with someone. This type of self-disclosure involves talking about a lot of different topics, but not getting into much depth on any one topic (Altman & Taylor, 1973). In other words, people explore potential topics by increasing breadth (i.e., the number of topics they discuss) first and then only increasing depth (e.g., the intimacy level of the communication) if they feel comfortable with each other. Indeed, *small talk* is the primary mode of communication during the experimenting stage (Knapp & Vangelisti, 2008).

Small talk allows people to fulfill a number of goals simultaneously, including discovering common interests, seeing if it would be worthwhile to pursue a closer relationship, reducing uncertainty in a safe manner that does not make them vulnerable, and allowing them to maintain a sense of connection with other people without putting themselves at much risk for hurt or rejection. In some relationships, however, common interests are not a prerequisite for getting closer. Sometimes differences between people are intriguing, leading people to seek out more information. Indeed, a study of intercultural friendship showed that both similarities and differences can prompt people to get to know one another better

(Sias et al., 2008). Box 5.2 contains more information on how intercultural friendships develop.

Many people also use Snapchat and texting in the early stages of relationship development. Indeed, using Snapchat has been likened to small talk. In a study of college students (Bayer, Ellison, Schoenebeck, & Falk, 2016), Snapchat was primarily seen as a way to send selfies and share small moments throughout one's day. They noted that many of the messages sent on Snapchat are comparable to the type of small talk that occurs between acquaintances. People use Snapchat to maintain close relationships with friends, romantic partners, and families, but they also use it as a testing ground

BOX 5.2 AROUND THE WORLD
DEVELOPING FRIENDSHIPS WITH PEOPLE FROM OTHER CULTURES

A study by Sias and her colleagues (2008) explored how people from different cultures develop friendships with one another. Their study included college students from a wide variety of countries, all of whom were friends with someone from a different country. They noted that there are several barriers to developing intercultural friendships, including having different "first" languages and diverse cultural experiences and values, all of which can lead to misunderstanding and frustration. However, there are also several advantages to intercultural friendships, including novelty and the ability to expand one's horizons by gaining cultural knowledge and broadening one's perspective.

So how do people capitalize on the advantages of intercultural friendships while overcoming the barriers? The participants in Sias and colleagues' (2008) study mentioned three positive factors that helped move their intercultural relationships from acquaintanceships to friendships:

- *Cultural similarities*: Stressing things that their cultures have in common (e.g., "We are both from Europe," or "We both think people from the United States do some things a lot differently from how we do them.")

- *Cultural differences:* Discovering differences that are interesting and serve as conversation starters (e.g., "Wow. I can't believe how much vacation people in France get. You are so lucky.")

- *Targeted socializing:* Being able to do new things as a result of one's association with an intercultural friend (e.g., "I got to go to a Chinese New Year celebration.")

They also mentioned two positive factors that helped make their friendships closer after their initial development:

- *Humor and play:* After working through language differences, some of those differences, such as the use of slang, become humorous or function as an inside joke (e.g., using U.S. slang such as "Yo man, what's up?").

- *Unique language:* Coming up with unique vocabulary that signifies we have a special relationship (e.g., using a specific mix of Japanese and English words when conversing).

Prior intercultural experience was another factor that influenced friendship development at different points—such as when they were moving from acquaintances to friends as well as when they were moving from friends to best friends. Specifically, people said that they were more open to having an intercultural friend if they had been involved with people from other cultures in the past or if they were curious about people from other cultures.

In sum, this study suggests that intercultural friendships develop in ways that help people embrace their differences and discover their similarities. Being open to the experience of getting to know someone from another culture is the first step in this process.

for potential relationships. Sending snaps is a relatively low-risk way to see if someone is interested as well as to learn mundane information about that person. So, when Connor sent Anne a Snapchat a couple of days after they met, he was happy when she snapped a selfie back. This allowed them to keep in contact, which eventually led to a bit of texting. By the time the next meeting came along, it seemed natural for them to find each other and sit together.

Of course, in some cases, people in this stage decide they have little in common or do not find each other very interesting, leading them to either remain casual friends or terminate the relationship. Anne may have snapped Connor back a couple of times to be polite but then stopped. Or Connor might have decided that even though they had a lot in common there was not enough of a spark there after all. Indeed, most of people's interpersonal relationships probably stay at this stage—or do not venture far beyond it. Think about all the acquaintances and casual friends you have. Chances are that your conversations with them are composed mainly of small talk rather than more intimate disclosures.

INTENSIFYING With a select few individuals, people emerge from the experimenting stage feeling that there is potential for a close relationship. They move from wanting to get to know the person better to wanting the relationship with that person to be closer. How close is sometimes unclear at the beginning of this stage, but there is a sense that something good could develop so people invest more time and energy into getting to know each other on a deeper level. So how do people move relationships from casual to closer? According to social penetration theory, people increase the depth of their self-disclosure and start exchanging information on an emotional level (Altman & Taylor, 1973). The beginning of this stage is often marked by longer, more in-depth conversations as partners start to reveal more personal information and trust each other.

Besides in-depth disclosure, other types of communication common in this stage include displaying affectionate nonverbal communication to each other (see Chapter 7); using nicknames or forms of endearment, saying "we" instead of "I" ("We should go down to Mexico sometime"), and making statements that reflect positive regard and commitment, such as saying "I love you" or "You are my very best friend." Declarations such as these usually first occur at the end of the intensifying stage and then continue into the next two stages as couples integrate and bond. As relationships intensify, people are also more likely to "favorite" or comment on their partner's pictures or timeline posts (Fox & Anderegg, 2014). So, Anne might go to Connor's Instagram page and like a few of his pictures and then comment on the most recent one. Use of computer-mediated communication also tends to change so that the two people have a routine. Romantic couples report using more forms of computer-mediated communication as their relationships intensify (Bryant & Marmo, 2012). For example, they might start out with snapping but then add texting and eventually Facetiming. They also report routines, such as sending a good-morning Snapchat or texting most nights before they go to sleep.

Work by Tolhuizen (1989) gives further insight into how people intensify their relationships. In his research, Tolhuizen found 15 different intensification strategies; Box 5.3 lists the strategies. The three most common strategies are increased contact, relationship negotiation (which involves talking about the relationship), and social support and assistance (which involves asking someone for advice and/or comfort). Nearly 40% of the people Tolhuizen surveyed described increased contact as an important intensification strategy, while 29% and 26% mentioned relationship negotiation and social support/assistance, respectively. Thus, these three strategies appear to be fairly common ways of intensifying various relationships. The other strategies listed in Box 5.3 appear to play more minor roles in the intensification process, but they still represent important means by which people escalate their relationships.

The more two people use the strategies in Box 5.3, and the more frequently they have in-depth conversations with one another, the more likely

BOX 5.3 HIGHLIGHTS
TOLHUIZEN'S STRATEGIES FOR INTENSIFYING RELATIONSHIPS

1. *Increased contact* includes seeing or calling the person more often (39.2%).

2. *Relationship negotiation* includes openly discussing the state of the relationship and the feelings the partners have for one another (29.1%).

3. *Social support and assistance* involves asking people for support, advice, and comfort (26.1%).

4. *Increased rewards* include doing favors and making sacrifices for one another, such as helping someone move or helping with household tasks (17.6%).

5. *Direct definitional bid* involves asking the partner to make a definite commitment, such as seeing each other exclusively, moving in together, or getting married (16.1%).

6. *Tokens of affection* include sending flowers, cards, and gifts, as well as exchanging rings (16.1%).

7. *Personalized communication* includes using idiomatic communication, such as special nicknames and inside jokes, as well as listening empathically (15.1%).

8. *Verbal expressions of affection* include uttering declarations such as "I love you" and "I hope we are always this close" (14.1%).

9. *Suggestive actions* include flirting, trying to get someone jealous, and playing "hard to get" (13.1%).

10. *Nonverbal expressions of affection* include gazing at the partner lovingly, touching the partner, and smiling (12.1%).

11. *Social enmeshment* involves getting to know and spending more time with the partner's family and friends, sometimes through activities such as spending a holiday together (11.6%).

12. *Acceptance of definition bid* involves redefining the relationship through actions such as saying "yes" when the partner asks for more commitment or agreeing to date exclusively, move in together, or get married (9.5%).

13. *Personal appearance* involves changing one's physical appearance to please the partner by engaging in behaviors such as trying to lose weight, changing one's hairstyle, or dressing particularly well (9.5%).

14. *Sexual intimacy* involves engaging in increasingly intimate behavior, often including sexual relations (8%).

15. *Behavioral adaptation* involves changing one's behavior to please the partner, perhaps by trying to secure a better job or to criticize the partner less and compliment the partner more (7.5%).

Note: The percentages in this table represent the percentage of people in a study by Tolhuizen (1989), who described or reported using each strategy. Because people were allowed to describe as many strategies as they deemed relevant, the percentages add up to more than 100%.

the relationship will develop into something really close and special. However, people sometimes start to intensify relationships but stop before reaching the next stage. For example, you can probably recall a time when you got close to a friend for a couple of weeks or so, but then you both got busy with other things and the friendship never developed beyond that. For potential dating partners, the intensifying stage can be confusing. Most people have had "almost relationships" where everything seemed to be intensifying but then fizzled out. The two people might be texting and snapping, and even spending some time together, but then one or both people cuts things off before a truly close relationship develops. College and high school students sometimes say they have a "thing" but are not officially dating. Eventually some of these relationships become official whereas other do not. When a relationship becomes official or a friendship stabilizes to the point that others recognize it, they have moved into the integrating stage.

INTEGRATING By the time two people reach the integrating stage in romantic relationships, they have already become close and are ready to show that closeness to others by presenting themselves as a "dyad" or "couple." This type of presentation is not limited to romantic couples; friends often present themselves as a unified team as well. The key here is that the two people have developed a relational identity; they see themselves as part of a dyad with some aspects of their personalities and experiences overlapping (Knapp & Vangelisti, 2008). Another key is that they have gone public. For romantic couples this can be accomplished in several ways, including calling one another "boyfriend," "girlfriend," or "significant other"; making the relationship "Facebook official"; or using couple photos as profile pictures. Being Facebook official is seen as a milestone for some couples because it signifies that they are exclusive and committed and want others to respect that. According to Fox et al. (2013), most couples have a discussion about the state of their relationship before declaring it official on social media, thus it signifies a conscious process of escalating the relationship to something serious. When dating relationships become exclusive, people are also more likely to integrate into their partner's social media, including "friending" the partner's friends and family on Facebook and following them on Instagram or Twitter (Fox & Anderegg, 2014). Once this "coupling" has occurred, people outside the relationship see them as a couple. It is easy to see when this has taken place. For example, imagine that Connor attends a party alone and several people stop and ask him, "Where's Anne?" This indicates that people in Connor's social network regard Anne and Connor as a couple; they expect to see the two of them together. Connor and Anne may also start to receive joint invitations to parties or combined Christmas gifts, and their mutual friends have a presence on their social media, which shows that other people see them as a committed couple.

Although self-disclosure is likely to be very high in both the intensifying and integrating stages, it may fall short of complete disclosure. As noted previously, in social penetration theory, the final stage of relationship development is the *stable exchange stage* in which people disclose openly about *almost* everything. However, achieving a true state of stable exchange is very difficult. Even in our closest relationships we tend to keep some secrets from our partner (Vangelisti, 1994a). Baxter and Wilmot (1984) found that 91% of the partners in romantic couples they surveyed said that there was at least one topic that they never discussed with their relational partner. Common taboo topics included the state of the relationship, past relationships, and sexual experiences. Thus, although stable exchange may seem like a worthy goal, it is probably an unrealistic one. Partners may exchange intimate information on a regular basis, but very few actually share 100% of their thoughts and feelings.

In any case, complete self-disclosure is probably not the best prescription for a happy relationship. Later in Chapter 6, we emphasize that many people have strong needs for privacy and autonomy. As Hatfield suggested, too much self-disclosure may rob us of our sense of privacy and make us feel overly dependent on others. In addition, it can be nice to keep some mystery in our relationships. This is not to say that people should purposely hide important information from their close relational partners. They should, however, feel that they have the right to control private information and to keep certain innermost thoughts and feelings undisclosed (Petronio, 2002). This helps explain why a stable rate of exchange is difficult to achieve—even in relationships that are exceptionally close.

BONDING In the final stage of the "coming together" side of the staircase model, partners find a way to declare their commitment publicly to each other, usually through the formalization of the relationship. Making future plans and promises, and taking vows, are also part of the bonding stage (Avtgis, West, & Anderson, 1998). Perhaps the most obvious way of institutionalizing a romantic relationship is through marriage. Getting married shows commitment and also makes it harder to leave the relationship. Most people cannot simply walk away from a marriage. There are possessions to divide, perhaps children to provide for, and a socially shared history that is hard to leave behind. Marriage can also be thought of as a social ritual in that two people come together before family and friends to declare their love for each other. Such a public declaration cements their bond even further. Importantly, before same-sex couples had the legal right to marry, they often had public commitment ceremonies uniting them as life partners in front of friends and family. These ceremonies underscore how important public commitment is to most couples.

Other types of relationships also reach the bonding stage, although the formalization of these relationships is more difficult. Friends and family members, however, can make public, enduring commitments to one another in many different ways. For instance, if you get married, the people you choose to stand up as your bridesmaids or groomsmen will be an important part of this critical life event, and they will hold that place in your memory forever. By choosing them, you are telling your social network that these people have a special place in your life. Similarly, if you have a child and choose godparents, these individuals will be part of a very important social ritual that publicly lets others know you value and trust them. Some friendship rituals, such as becoming blood brothers or getting matching tattoos, may also be ways to show a permanent bond.

The "Coming Apart" Stages

DIFFERENTIATING This stage occurs when people begin to behave as individuals rather than as a couple and emphasize difference at the expense of similarities. Partners may start doing things separately, and they may also argue about their differences and start noticing more incompatibilities (Avtgis et al., 1998). For example, after Anne discovered that she and Connor had different opinions regarding cohabitation, she started to realize that they had radically different opinions regarding other issues as well. During the differentiating

After years of protests, debates, and controversy, the Supreme Court made same-sex marriage in the United States legal in all 50 states on June 26, 2015. Based on what you read about the bonding stage, why do you think people fought so hard for same-sex couples to have the right to marry?

stage, people also report feeling lonely, confused, and inadequate (Avtgis et al., 1998). Rather than validating one another's positions and feelings, partners are questioning one another.

Of course, many relational partners go through the differentiating phase without proceeding toward relational termination. Sometimes people simply need to assert their individuality and autonomy. Indeed, Avtgis and colleagues (1998) found that people in this stage sometimes reported compromising to try to balance their needs for autonomy and closeness. Extended differentiation, however, can lead couples to feel disconnected, especially when differences are perceived to outweigh similarities (Welch & Rubin, 2002). In many ways, the differentiating stage is the reversal of the integrating stage; instead of wanting to be seen as a unit, partners want to be seen as individuals. Thus, just as coupling behavior helps define the integrating stage, *uncoupling* behavior helps define the differentiating stage (Welch & Rubin, 2002).

CIRCUMSCRIBING This stage occurs when communication becomes constricted in both depth and breadth. In some ways, the superficial communication that takes place during this stage is similar to small talk, except that the communicators are using talk (and avoidance of talk) to distance themselves from each other instead of to learn more about each other. Communication can be constricted at any stage of a relationship and does not necessarily mean that a relationship is in trouble. However, when partners begin to feel that they have nothing to talk about, it could be a sign that the relationship is declining. In particular, Avtgis and colleagues (1998) found that the circumscribing stage was characterized by talk about mundane, everyday issues. The type of communication people engage in can also shift to media that are less suited for in-depth conversation. Facetime might be replaced by texting, and texting might be replaced with a quick Snapchat. Tolstedt and Stokes (1984) found that during breakups self-disclosure decreased in terms of the topics partners discussed, and the content of self-disclosure became more negative, which is consistent with the description of this stage. However, contrary to the reversal hypothesis, depth of disclosure actually increased. This may

be because some couples have intense arguments and discussions as they move toward relational termination.

If circumscribing is a persistent pattern of communication, the closeness that people once felt may seem to be eroding, leading people to feel frustrated, distant, and misunderstood while in this stage. In some cases, people also begin to pursue separate activities and start to act indifferent when around each other (Avtgis et al., 1998). However, efforts to reconnect can be still be successful. Indeed, many couples find themselves in this stage at times as part of a larger pattern of wanting some privacy in their relationships. Some circumscribing can be normal and healthy in relationships since partners in established relationships already know a lot about one another and do not need to disclose all the time to feel close. Problems arise when people settle in this stage and continue engaging in small talk without any in-depth disclosure.

STAGNATING During the third stage, the relationship seems to be at a standstill. Communication becomes tense and awkward, and the relationship is itself virtually a taboo subject. Avtgis and colleagues (1998) found that couples in this stage tend to give short answers to questions, see discussion about their relationship as "reruns" of past conversations, and perceive relationship talk as futile. At this point, people often feel that they already know what their partner will say or that the outcome of interaction will always be negative. Therefore, communication is seen as unproductive and unpleasant. For example, Anne and Connor reached a standstill about whether to live together or not. Anne felt that their relationship would not progress if they couldn't take this step, whereas Connor felt that it would be the wrong move for multiple reasons. They tried to agree to disagree, but communication started to become strained on other issues as well because they just didn't seem to be as compatible as they once thought they were.

Communication on social media can also reflect that a relationship is stagnating. Because the couple is not communicating as much with each other, they may be reaching out to others more often. A study examining pre- and post-breakup communication patterns on Twitter (Garimella, Weber, & Dal Cin, 2014) showed that the number of tweets directed toward the partner decreased prior to a breakup, whereas the number of tweets directed toward others increased. Partners are also less likely to retweet each other's tweets or like one another's photos and comments on various social media during the stagnating stage. Their social network might notice that they are posting less (or no) photos of each other on social media and their Snapchat stories.

The stagnating stage is also characterized by a group of distinct and somewhat contradictory emotions, such as feeling unwanted, sentimental, and bored (Avtgis et al., 1998). Couples are sometimes sentimental about their "old" relationship even though they are bored in the "current" relationship. Eventually they may cease physical contact and affection (Avtgis et al., 1998), which will likely lead them into the next stage—avoiding. Nonetheless, some couples who reach this stage eventually find a way to revive their relationship. Others, like Anne and Connor, give up hope and, quickly or gradually, move to the avoiding stage.

AVOIDING This stage is best defined in terms of physical separation. Communication becomes even less frequent; statements such as "I don't know" and "I don't care" characterize this stage (Avtgis et al., 1998). People also report feeling annoyed, nervous, and helpless in this stage (Avtgis et al., 1998). If possible, relational partners move into separate physical environments and try not to encounter each other, or they just start spending less time with each other, like Anne and Connor did.

If physical separation is not possible, the partners simply ignore each other. For example, spouses who have young children and cannot afford to live apart might move into separate bedrooms until a more permanent solution can be reached. According to Avtgis and colleagues (1998), people in this stage also stay busy with separate activities and engage in everyday activities, such as eating or getting ready for work alone or in silence. In any case, the goal in the avoidance stage is to achieve as much physical and psychological distance as possible.

This avoidance extends to social media. As during the stagnating stage, there is likely a decrease in the number of posts and tweets directed toward or mentioning the partner during this time. In addition, a "stonewalling" effect can also be present on Twitter (Garimella et al., 2014) such that the proportion of tweets directed to or about the partner is skewed, with one partner mentioning the other a lot more than vice versa. This could indicate that one partner is trying to save the relationship, while the other is avoiding. During this stage, one or both of the partners may also use more depressed words or phrases in their tweets (Garimella et al., 2014). For example, Anne might tweet, "What's the point anymore?" hoping that her friends will ask her what is wrong and offer her support. Conner might similarly tweet "Ugh" as a way to vent frustration. One or both partners may also change their relationship status to "It's complicated" if they are on Facebook or delete a tag to their partner on their Twitter or Instagram page. They might also delete some or all of their pictures with each other and replace a "couple profile picture" with a selfie or a photo with friends. These actions can signal that a relationship is moving toward termination.

TERMINATING In this final stage, relational partners end contact, often after discussing what went wrong and talking about the details of the breakup. In some cases, partners also negotiate what their post-breakup relationship will look like. For example, romantic partners may decide whether or not they can still be friends and spouses may discuss what their relationship will be in terms of raising their children after they divorce. In Garimella et al.'s (2014) study, when people broke up there was also an exodus of their ex-partner's friends and family on their Twitter accounts. This can go both ways: When Anne and Connor break up, Anne might stop following Connor's family and friends, and they may also unfollow her. Sometimes people also use the mute function on Twitter so that they do not have to see an ex's (or an ex's social network's) tweets even though they are still shown as following them. And, of course, people can take more extreme action by blocking an ex from their social media accounts. The terminating stage also tends to be marked by somewhat ambivalent emotions, such as feeling sad but relieved, or lonely but hopeful (Avtgis et al., 1998), and these emotions are sometimes communicated on social media sites like Twitter (Garimella et al., 2014).

Terminating a long-term relationship can be tough (see Chapter 15). Although partners may quickly be able to separate from each other physically, it might take longer to separate psychologically. Individuals develop their own self-interests and social networks as a way of distancing themselves from their past relationship and moving on with their lives. They may delete their ex from their social media, either temporarily or permanently, so that they have space to heal. If communication does occur at this stage, it is usually tense, awkward, and hesitant until both partners have closure and are able to move on.

The Ordering and Timing of Stages

Before leaving our discussion of the staircase model, it is important to note that people do not always move through these stages in an orderly manner. Knapp has argued that his 10 stages outline the typical pattern of relational development and decline for many couples but that variations frequently take place (Knapp & Vangelisti, 2008). Couples, or friends, might go through the stages in a different order, or they might skip some stages entirely. For example, some romantic couples meet, fall in love at first sight, and quickly get married. Other couples move in together after only a few dates. However, a pattern of rapid escalation is atypical, and when people skip stages or move too quickly through them, they might later go back and engage in communication appropriate for that stage. Take a couple who meets and soon gets married as an example. Their friends and family might be surprised at the news of their marriage, and the newlyweds may need to work on merging their social networks and gaining

acceptance as a couple. In this case, some of the processes that typically occur during the integrating stage would be occurring after the bonding stage. The phenomenon of ghosting, or disappearing from a relationship, usually involves going through the first three coming-together stages, but then having one person move straight into the avoiding or terminating stage somewhere in the middle of the intensifying stage. Ghosting has become more common because it is fairly easy (although not particularly kind) to disappear from a person's social media and stop texting if the relationship had not yet become official. Other studies have shown that on-again, off-again relationships, which involve repeatedly getting together and breaking up, only to get back together again, are fairly common (Dailey, Hampel, & Roberts, 2010; on-again off-again relationships are discussed in more detail in Chapter 14). As these examples show, relationships can follow many different trajectories.

TURNING POINTS

A turning point is "any event or occurrence that is associated with change in a relationship" (Baxter & Bullis, 1986, p. 469). Turning points can also be thought of as major relational events. Interestingly, most of the scenes in romantic movies and novels consist of significant relational events or turning points. This is probably because turning points help tell the story of relational change. Rather than focusing on the more mundane events that occur on a day-to-day basis, the turning point approach emphasizes those events that stand out in people's minds as having the strongest impact on their relationships. Couples tell stories about turning points to their social networks (such as "how we met"), and turning points are often remembered through celebrations and mementos, such as anniversaries and pictures (Baxter & Pittman, 2001). This is not to say that mundane events are unimportant. Indeed, mundane events help shape the way people see their relationships even if such events sometimes go unnoticed and unappreciated. These mundane events can

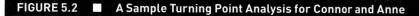

FIGURE 5.2   ■   A Sample Turning Point Analysis for Connor and Anne

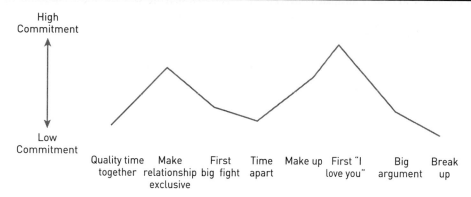

be thought of as part of the regular road on which a relationship travels. Turning points, by contrast, are the detours relationships sometimes take.

The turning point approach is quite different from stage approaches to relationship development and disengagement even though turning points can mark entry into new stages. Social penetration theory, for example, suggests that relationships develop fairly smoothly and gradually as people's communication becomes more intimate and personal. By contrast, according to the turning point approach, relationships can follow a choppier path, with both positive and negative events affecting their course. To determine the path that relationships take, scholars ask people to identify the events that changed their relationships. They can then create a map, which is referred to as a **turning point analysis** (Baxter & Bullis, 1986; Bullis, Clark, & Sline, 1993). As shown in Figure 5.2, these maps do not usually depict a smooth, gradual increase in commitment or closeness. Instead, this approach reveals a rockier road that includes all of the important ups and downs that influence the growth and in some cases the demise of close relationships.

Research suggests that both the turning point approach and stage approaches have merit; some relationships follow a linear, gradual pattern of developing intimacy; and other relationships are characterized by periods of extreme growth or decline or by a random pattern of highs and lows. For example, Johnson and her colleagues examined how friendships develop and deteriorate (Johnson et al., 2004; Johnson, Wittenberg, Villagran, Mazur, & Villagran, 2003). They found that between 40% and 50% of friendships fit the linear pattern— closeness increased gradually as friends developed their relationships and closeness decreased gradually in friendships that ended. The other 50% to 60% of friendships developed and deteriorated in a nonlinear manner. Various types of turning points are related to closeness and commitment in romantic relationships, family relationships, and friendships (Baxter, 1986; Baxter, Braithwaite, & Nicholson, 1999; Bullis et al., 1993; Golish, 2000; Johnson et al., 2003, 2004). Next, we discuss some of the most common turning points that have been identified by researchers.

Communication-Based Turning Points

Although most turning points include some level of communication, the act of communication itself constitutes a turning point in many cases. For example, get-to-know time includes initial interactions and focuses on the quantity rather than the quality of communication and time spent together. First meetings and first dates typify this turning point (Bullis et al., 1993). By contrast, quality communication focuses on special times when two people have a high-quality interaction, such as having an especially long and intimate conversation. Both forms of communication are often integral to the story of romantic relationships. For instance, people often ask how a couple met. Connor might reply that "we met at a Sierra Club meeting and hit it off right away." Anne might tell people, "I knew we had something special on our first date when we sat under the stars together under a blanket and talked for hours." Communicative events can also be turning points in family relationships. In a turning point study of relationships between adult children and their parents, communication issues such as finally talking about something important or feeling listened to were identified as turning points that increased closeness (Golish, 2000). Friends also identify self-disclosure about feelings and discovery of positive personality traits as turning points that help develop closeness (Johnson et al., 2004).

Activities and Special Occasions

Other turning points involve engaging in activity and spending quality time with others. For romantic partners, occasions such as meeting the family and going on trips together are common turning points (Bullis et al., 1993). For family members, turning points includes vacations, holiday rituals, and special occasions such as graduations. A study on blended families showed that quality time together is strongly related to bonding (Baxter et al., 1999). Blended families occur when two previously separate families merge together into one family, as is often the case when divorced or widowed parents remarry. In the study by Baxter and her colleagues, turning points related to holidays and special events made people feel like the blended family was "more of a family" about two thirds of the time. Turning points involving activity, such as going on vacation together, were related to feeling more like a family 100% of the time. Similarly, turning points that involve engaging in special activities together are related to closeness in friendships. In

fact, Johnson and colleagues (2003) found that activity sharing was the most common turning point in friendships.

Events Related to Passion and Romance

Some turning points mark particular junctures in the development of one's relationship based on the level of passion or romance that is present. Passionate events include the first kiss, the first time a couple exchanges the words "I love you," the first sexual encounter, and other passionate phenomena such as falling in love at first sight (Bullis et al., 1993). According to research by Metts (2004), the order that passionate event turning points occur can affect relationship development; people were more likely to escalate their relationships and feel positively about one another when saying "I love you" preceded having sex. **Romantic relationship transitions** refer to the "point or period in time when a relationship changes from being either platonic or nonexistent to being romantic" (Mongeau et al., 2006, p. 338). Some passionate events, such as love at first sight, are romantic relationship transitions. Likewise, when friends or acquaintances turn their previously platonic relationships romantic, an important change has occurred.

Events Related to Commitment and Exclusivity

Although some passionate events, such as saying "I love you," are a huge turning point, implying some level of commitment, other turning points more directly reflect how committed two people are to each other and their relationship. Exclusivity occurs when people decide to date only each other and drop all other rivals. Somewhat related to exclusivity (or the lack thereof) is the turning point of external competition, which occurs when a person feels threatened by a third party or an activity that is taking up a lot of the partner's time. Sometimes an ex-spouse or former girlfriend or boyfriend reemerges; other times, a new rival starts to compete for the partner's affections; and still other times responsibilities related to work, school, or childcare, or time spent with friends interfere with the relationship. External competition can reinforce or threaten partners' levels of commitment toward one another. Finally, romantic couples can show serious commitment by events such as moving in together or getting married.

Changes in Families and Social Networks

While marriage can change the structure of a couple's relationship, other turning points often involve changes in a family's structure. For blended families, changes in the household configuration are a primary turning point (Baxter et al., 1999). Children may have to deal with a new stepparent, parents with new stepchildren, and children with new stepsiblings. Contrary to the storyline in shows such as *The Brady Bunch,* the transition from one's family of origin to a blended family is often fraught with problems and confusion. New family members constitute a turning point in other types of relationships. For example, a new baby changes the dynamics of a family for both the parents and any siblings. In Golish's (2000) study of adult children's relationships with their parents, some people said that a new baby brought them closer together. For example, a father and son may feel more emotionally connected when the son has his first baby and the father, as a consequence, has his first grandchild. Other times, sibling rivalry or jealousy may occur when a new baby becomes part of the family. In friendships, interference from a romantic partner can sometimes cause conflict and decreased closeness between friends (Johnson et al., 2004). As a case in point, imagine that Anne's best friend starts to feel increasingly left out and neglected as Anne spends more and more time with Connor.

Proximity and Distance

Another set of turning points deals with physical separation and reunion. In Bullis and colleagues' (1993) study of romantic partners, physical separation was reported when people were apart, often involuntarily, due to vacations, business trips, and school breaks. Reunions occurred when the period of physical separation was over and the couple was together again. Adult children also report that **physical distance** is an important turning point in their relationship with their parents (Golish, 2000). When children move out of the house, they sometimes feel that their relationship with their parents improves because the parents now perceive their offspring as an adult. So far, the turning points under this category focus on physical distance. However, the desire for psychological distance and autonomy can also mark a significant turning point in parent–child relationships. In her study on parents and children, Golish identified rebellion as a turning point that occurs when teenagers express a need for autonomy from their parents. Friends also identify turning points related to proximity and distance. For example, friends often recall that becoming roommates was a significant turning point in their relationship that led to either increased or decreased closeness. Friends who ended their relationship often indicate that turning points such as not living together anymore and an increase in distance were markers of relationship decline (Johnson et al., 2004).

Crisis and Conflict

The challenges that people face are often significant turning points in their relationships with one another. Bullis and her colleagues identified disengagement and conflict, which includes a couple's first big fight, attempts to de-escalate or withdraw from the relationship, and actual relational breakups, as major relational turning points. Conflict is also a significant turning point in friendships (Johnson et al., 2004). Researchers examining turning points for both families and friends talk about times of crisis as significant turning points (Baxter et al., 1999; Golish, 2000; Johnson et al., 2004). These include illnesses, death, accidents, and major financial problems. In Baxter and colleagues' study of blended families, 72% of people reported that these crisis-related turning points brought the family closer together. A crisis situation can also lead to the turning point called

sacrifice or support, which includes being there to support and comfort each other in crises, such as dealing with the death of a loved one or helping one regain confidence after an embarrassing failure (Bullis et al., 1993; Johnson et al., 2004). Similarly, although conflict can decrease closeness and commitment, couples sometimes make up and feel more connected than ever. Thus, making up is another important turning point in many relationships. Baxter and Bullis (1986) noted that there is not always a perfect correspondence between conflict and making up. Sometimes the conflict is viewed as more significant than the making-up session than vice versa.

Perceptual Changes

Sometimes people report that a turning point does not have a specific cause. Instead, they simply report that their attitudes toward the partner changed, even though they cannot figure out exactly why. When attitudes and perceptions become more positive, the turning point is called **positive psychic change** (Bullis et al., 1993). For example, Anne might suddenly see Connor as more physically attractive and sexually appealing (a positive psychic change) without being able to pinpoint why. In another case, labeled **negative psychic change,** attitudes and perceptions become more negative. A person might suddenly see the relationship as boring even though nothing else has really changed.

THE DIALECTICAL PERSPECTIVE

Like the turning point approach, the **dialectical perspective** provides an alternative to the view of relationships as a series of linear stages; people move both toward and away from an optimal level of closeness. Indeed, the dialectical perspective suggests that relationships do not always progress in a smooth, linear fashion, and that partners do not always travel in the same direction or at the same pace. Every relationship experiences ups and downs, and no relationship stays the same from start to finish. Theories

taking a dialectical perspective capture the dynamic nature of relationships and describe some of the common tensions that are reflected in interpersonal communication.

According to the dialectical perspective (see Baxter, 2010; Baxter & Montgomery, 1996), relationships are never completely stable but are constantly changing. Therefore, they should not be thought of in terms of stages. As Baxter (1994) stated, "A healthy relationship is a changing relationship" (p. 234). Think about your close relationships. Wouldn't they be boring if they were always the same? Doesn't communication reflect the changing ways that you think about one another and construct meaning in your relationships? The dialectical perspective embraces the ever-changing nature of relationships. According to this perspective, relationships are fluid and dynamic rather than stable. Therefore, it is more helpful to think of relationships in terms of patterns of communication that reflect the ebb and flow of closeness, rather than stages that reflect a particular level of closeness at a particular time.

The dialectical perspective also suggests that tensions between seemingly contradictory needs, such as wanting both independence and closeness, help shape the changing nature of a relationship. Tension is at the heart of the dialectical perspective; a push and pull toward different needs is seen as both healthy and inevitable. Some scholars have described dialectic tensions as competing needs within relationships. For example, Fehr (1996) described the tug-of-war of dialectical tensions this way:

> We have to juggle our need for dependence with our need to be independent; wanting to be completely open versus wanting to protect ourselves by not revealing everything; wanting to have a lot in common, but not so much that the relationship feels boring and predictable. (p. 156)

If two people can manage these competing needs successfully, they will be more likely to sustain a happy and healthy relationship.

Other scholars have situated these tensions within communication. Most notably, Baxter's

(2010) **relational dialectics theory** focuses on **discursive tensions,** which can be thought of as messages that have two seemingly contradictory meanings. Baxter and Braithwaite (2008) gave the following example of a college student telling a friend, "Well, I'm kinda, like, seeing him, but we're not, ya know, serious" (p. 26). This statement displays a discursive tension between connection ("I'm seeing him") and autonomy ("but we're not serious"). Importantly, these contradictions are not viewed as problematic, but rather as a necessary and inevitable part of communication. Two theories in particular from the dialectical perspective—Baxter's relational dialectics theory and Rawlins's application of dialectics to friendships—allow deeper understanding and application of how these tensions function within relationships.

Relational Dialectics Theory

The central idea in relational dialectics theory is that "all of communication is rife with the tension-filled struggle of competing discourses" (Baxter & Braithwaite, 2008, p. 352). People express different perspectives through their interaction with one another. The meaning-making process then involves communicating and making sense of these differing viewpoints. Within relational dialectics theory, communication is viewed as the means by which people make sense of the social world. Thus, communication gives meaning to people's relationships.

There are various discursive tensions in relationships, such as pulls and pushes between similarity and dissimilarity (Baxter & West, 2003), old and new family structures in stepfamilies (Braithwaite, Baxter, & Harper, 1998), and fortune and misfortune (Krusiewicz & Woods, 2001). Of the many tensions that exist in various relationships, Baxter (2006) identified the dialectics of integration, certainty, and expression as "the big three" (p. 137). Each of these dialectics can be expressed as an internal or an external tension, as shown in Figure 5.3. *Internal manifestations* refer to the tensions that people express about their relationships with one another (e.g., "I love you, but I need my space sometimes"). *External manifestations* refer to tensions that people in a relationship, group, or family express in regard to their interaction with others who are outside that relationship or group (e.g., "I want to go to Thanksgiving dinner at your house but I also want to spend time alone with you"). The three major discursive tensions—(1) integration, (2) certainty, and (3) expression—manifest both internally and externally.

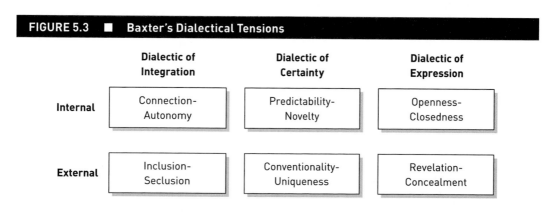

FIGURE 5.3 ■ Baxter's Dialectical Tensions

	Dialectic of Integration	Dialectic of Certainty	Dialectic of Expression
Internal	Connection-Autonomy	Predictability-Novelty	Openness-Closedness
External	Inclusion-Seclusion	Conventionality-Uniqueness	Revelation-Concealment

Source: From Werner, C. M., Altman, I., Brown, B. B., & Ganat, J. Celebrations in personal relationships: A transactional/dialectical perspective. In S. Duck (Ed.), *Social context and relationships* (pp. 109–138). Copyright © 1993. Reprinted with permission of SAGE, Inc.

THE DIALECTIC OF INTEGRATION The dialectic of integration refers to the tension between social integration and social division. That is, people talk about being connected to relational partners and social groups, but they also talk about being self-sufficient and doing things on their own. Baxter (2006) related an effective analogy that one of her students used to describe how the dialectic of integration functions within families. This student "referred to her family as a hand: individual fingers whose strength rests in their capacity to function independently yet which unite to form the strength of a single fist" (Baxter, 2006, p. 135). In this analogy, the fingers represent division (or independence) whereas the hand represents integration.

The internal manifestation of this dialectic has been called the **connection-autonomy** tension (Baxter, 1993). This tension, which is the most fundamental relational dialectic, is expressed when people communicate in ways that reflect both closeness and distance (or independence). For example, at one point in their relationship, Connor might have said, "I'm glad you want to move in together. I love being with you. But I think we both need time on our own before getting married someday." Such a statement includes elements of both autonomy (Connor expresses his need for "time on my own") and closeness (he says he loves being with Anne). The external manifestation of the integration dialectic is the **inclusion-seclusion** tension. Couples or groups often communicate in ways that stress the importance of spending time with other people, but they also communicate in ways that suggest they want to keep to themselves. A study of lesbian couples provides a useful example of this tension (Suter, Bergen, Daas, & Durham, 2006). One couple explained that although they usually celebrate their anniversary alone (seclusion), they invited friends and family to help them celebrate their 10th anniversary (inclusion) because they considered it to be an especially important milestone in their relationship.

THE DIALECTIC OF CERTAINTY This dialectic reflects the tension between the forces of certainty, stability, and routine, and the forces of surprise,

change, and newness. The internal manifestation of this dialectic is **predictability-novelty.** For example, imagine that Connor and Anne had a history of going together to the movies Saturday nights. One evening while searching the Internet to see what is playing, Connor commented, "It's nice that we always have a movie date on Saturdays (predictability), but maybe we should change things up tonight (novelty)." Successfully negotiating the predictability-novelty tension is important because boredom is one of the top reasons couples break up (Hill et al., 1976); thus, excitement is vital in relationships. The external manifestation of the certainty dialectic is **conventionality-uniqueness.** This tension focuses on how people communicate in ways that show consistency or inconsistency with the larger social group. Baxter (2006) shared an example given by one of her students, who said, "The [Jones] are the [Jones]: the same from one generation to the next, but different, too" (p. 136). This statement reflects some conventionality or sameness across generations but also some unique aspects of each generation. Similarly, when a couple gets married, they may adopt some of their parents' traditions for celebrating holidays, while also creating some of their own.

THE DIALECTIC OF EXPRESSION This dialectic reflects "the interplay of discourses of openness, disclosure, and candor with the competing discourses of discretion, privacy, and secrecy" (Baxter, 2006, p. 136). The internal manifestation of this dialectic, **openness-closedness,** refers to communication that occurs within a dyad or group. One of Baxter's (2006) students described her family as being able to say anything they want to one another but as also knowing when they should refrain from saying something. The external contradiction, **revelation-concealment,** refers to the tension between keeping information private and sharing it with the social network. In Suter and colleagues' (2006) study, many lesbian couples expressed this tension. One of these couples discussed how they felt closeted but also wanted to share their relationship with others.

MANAGING DIALECTICAL TENSIONS Relational dialectics theory also addresses how dyads and families manage these tensions. As noted previously, the contradictions that discursive tensions represent should not be viewed as good or bad but rather as a vibrant and dynamic part of the communication process. Through communication, people can manage these tensions in productive ways that help relationships evolve and change in positive ways. According to work by Baxter (1990), there are four general ways to manage dialectical tensions: (1) **selection,** (2) **separation,** (3) **neutralization,** and (4) **reframing.**

Selection involves talking about the tensions in a way that values one side of the dialectic over the other. For example, at one point, Anne and Connor might have promised each other that they would always be completely open and honest about everything. This way of managing a dialectic tension can sometimes be successful, but it can also lead to problems if one person wants to engage the other side of the dialectic later. For instance, when Anne realizes how different they are, she might keep some of her thoughts to herself so that they don't get into an argument. When Connor pushes her to state her feelings, she might say, "I don't want to talk about it," to which Connor might reply, "I thought we promised to always be open with each other." As this example illustrates, selection may not always be a very practical way to manage dialectical tensions. Other times, it may be quite successful. Box 5.4 includes information on how selection—along with neutralization and separation—is used to manage conflict over cell phone communication.

Neutralization occurs when couples avoid fully engaging either side of the dialectical tension. There are two strategies for accomplishing neutralization. The first, **moderation,** involves striving to reach a "midpoint," such that couples engage both sides of the dialectic but only to a certain extent. For example, Anne might reveal some information about her relationship with Connor to others but still keep the details private. She could tell her best friend, "Oh,

yeah, we got into a fight" without offering more information. In this case, Anne is being somewhat open, but her disclosure is lacking in depth. Second, couples can use **disqualification,** which involves being ambiguous so that neither side of the dialectic is engaged. This includes tactics such as changing the topic or avoiding an issue. For example, Anne might change the subject when someone asks her whether she and Connor decided to move in together. Or she might avoid engaging in behavior that is either too predictable or too novel when interacting with Connor.

Separation occurs when people favor each side of the dialectic at different times. There are two ways to accomplish this. First, couples can use **cyclic alternation** by moving from one side of the dialectic to the other alternately. For example, when Anne and Connor started feeling disconnected from each other, they could have expressed a need to get away alone together somewhere (and perhaps plan a romantic getaway). Conversely, if they start feeling smothered, one of them might stress the importance of spending some time apart. Not engaging in cyclic alternation could have left their relationship unbalanced, such that needs for one side of the dialectic were being met but not the other. Indeed, it seems that a lack of connection is the main reason Anne and Connor broke up.

Another way to accomplish separation is through **topical segmentation,** which involves emphasizing different sides of the dialectic depending on the topic or context. When they started having problems, Anne and Connor might have decided to reveal positive information about their relationship to others but conceal negative information. So, if Anne's best friend asked how things were going between her and Connor, Anne might have replied, "Great, we have even talked about moving in together" without telling her about the conflict over whether they should live together or not. Couples using topical segmentation might also decide to keep certain activities separate (e.g., playing golf or shopping with friends) while engaging in others together (e.g., going to a favorite restaurant or watching television).

BOX 5.4 TECH TALK
AUTONOMY-CONNECTION TENSION IN CELL PHONE COMMUNICATION

In a study by Duran et al. (2011), the autonomy/connection dialectic was cast as relevant to cell phone communication. They noted that cell phones provide people with *perpetual contact* (Katz & Aakhus, 2002), which means that partners can contact each other anytime they want. Although this accessibility may increase social connection, it also threatens autonomy because people have less control over when others can contact them. As Duran and colleagues (2011) stated, mobile phones may tie people "too tightly to their romantic partners" or people may "enjoy the potential for constant connection" that cell phones provide (p. 21). As dialectics theory suggests, this tension is evident in communication when people say things like, "You don't need to call me so much" or "Why did it take so long for you to text me back?"

In Duran and others' (2011) study, 61% of the college students they surveyed reported having conflict in their romantic relationships about cell phone communication that revolved around issues of autonomy or connection. The most common conflict issues related to autonomy and connection were as follows:

- My partner doesn't answer calls or texts (23%).

- My partner doesn't call or text enough (19%).

- My partner calls or texts too much (11%).

- My partner doesn't return calls or texts (10%).

- My partner monitors my calls or texts to check for communication with potential rivals (9%).

- My partner calls/texts others while with me (8%).

Of these, not answering calls or texts, not calling or texting enough, and monitoring a partner's calls and texts were related to higher levels of tension over autonomy/connection in a relationship.

This study also investigated how individuals deal with conflict about cell phone communication. People employed the selection strategy most often, followed by neutralization and then separation. A common *selection* strategy was to emphasize one end of the dialectic by calling or answering more or by deciding not to pick up when a partner repeatedly called or texted. An example of a *neutralization* strategy was for people to be open about who they were communicating with so that their partner would not need to monitor their calls and texts. Finally, *separation* strategies involved making rules such as not calling or texting at certain times.

The final general way to manage dialectical tension is through reframing, a sophisticated strategy that involves talking about tensions so that they seem complementary rather than contradictory. For example, when he started noticing that Anne was becoming more distant, Connor might have told her, "It's okay that we're spending more time apart. It makes the time we spend together even more special." Or Anne might have told Connor, "We don't need to tell each other everything all the time; we already know each other so well that some things can go left unsaid." Such statements demonstrate a recognition that seemingly contradictory forces— like connection and autonomy or openness and closedness—can work together to make relationships healthier and more productive. Reframing is a particularly effective way of managing dialectical tensions, so perhaps if Anne and Connor had used this type of communication, they would have stood a better chance of sustaining their relationship.

Dialectical Tensions in Friendships

Although applicable to a variety of relationships, Baxter's work on dialectics has focused primarily on romantic relationships. Yet researchers have also looked at dialectics within the context of friendships (Bridge & Baxter, 1992; Rawlins, 1989, 1992, 1994). In particular, Rawlins's (1992) investigation of friendship took a dialectical perspective. He argued that six main dialectical tensions characterize friendships, as well as other types of relationships.

Two of Rawlins's dialectics—**independent-dependent** and **expressive-protective**—are similar to those identified as autonomy-connection and openness-closedness by Baxter, except that they focus more on needs friends have than discursive tensions. Specifically, the independent-dependent dialectic refers to the tension between wanting the freedom to pursue individual activities and depending on someone for help and support. For example, you might want to ask your friend, who is a math major, to help you with your trigonometry homework, but you might also want to prove that you can do the work on your own. The expressive-protective dialectic focuses on how much friends express versus keep information private. After interviewing pairs of close friends, Rawlins (1983a, 1983b) concluded that this is a central tension that exists in friendships. In order for a friendship to be close, people must disclose personal information. However, if friends disclose too much, they open themselves up to potential criticism and rejection (see also Chapter 6).

The remaining four dialectics differ from those proposed by Baxter. The **judgment-acceptance** dialectic involves being able to accept friends for who they are versus feeling free to offer criticism and advice. This is a common tension. For example, imagine that a good friend of yours has been in a dead-end job for 2 years after graduation. Should you accept that your friend isn't very ambitious, or should you suggest that your friend go out and look for something better? You avoid insulting your friend if you do the former, but in the long run you might help your friend if you do the latter. The choice is indeed a dilemma.

The **affection-instrumentality** dialectic refers to whether friends focus more on feelings of warmth or on instrumental tasks. When friendships are based only on instrumental goals (e.g., wanting help with homework), the relationship may seem impersonal. Conversely, when friendships are based on affection without instrumental benefits, people might feel that some of their goals are not being fulfilled. Rawlins (1992) suggested that although both men and woman want both types of benefits, men value instrumentality more, while women value affection more.

The **public–private** dialectic involves how relationships are negotiated in public versus private. Rawlins (1992) argued that friendships are negotiated primarily in private, yet some aspects of the relationship are made public. For example, you might call your friend silly nicknames like "bubble-head" or "monkey face" in private but not in public. In high school, if you invited an unpopular person to your house, you might not have told the other kids at school. But if the homecoming king and queen came over, you likely would have told everyone. Cross-sex friends might show affection to one another in private but not in public because they don't want other people to think they have romantic feelings for one another.

Finally, the **ideal-real** dialectic reflects the tension between what the friendship "ought to be" and what the relationship "really is." People want an ideal friendship, but most people know that the ideal relationship is a fantasy and that no friend is perfect. In high school, some kids wish they could be friends with a certain student who is especially popular, athletic, talented, or beautiful. However, their "real" friends have a mix of positive and negative characteristics. There may also be tension between trying to live up to idealistic expectations and wanting to be oneself.

SUMMARY AND APPLICATION

This chapter focused on three different perspectives about the paths, or trajectories, that relationships take. The relationship stage approach suggests that relationships typically follow a linear pattern; people become increasingly close as their relationships develop and increasingly distant as

their relationships deteriorate. In contrast, the turning point approach suggests that relationships are characterized by a more nonlinear path; both positive and negative events influence the level of satisfaction and commitment that people experience in their relationships. Rather than being seen as a staircase that moves toward or away from intimate communication, relationships are viewed as a series of ups and downs; intimate communication waxes and wanes at different points in the relationship. Finally, the dialectical perspective suggests that instead of being composed of neat and tidy stages, relationships are fluid and ever-changing; communication helps partners better understand and manage the competing forces (such as autonomy and connection) within their relationships. Of course, these perspectives do overlap. Within the staircase model, the stages of integrating, bonding, differentiating, and circumscribing are all at the top of the staircase—with couples in stable relationships moving among these stages as they negotiate tensions related to autonomy/connection and openness/closedness. Similarly, turning points such as saying "I love you," getting married, and moving away from someone may mark movement into different stages.

At this point, it is important to recognize that every relationship follows a unique trajectory. Some relationships may develop linearly; others may not. Similarly, some breakups might be forecast by decreasing levels of intimate communication whereas others might be connected to an especially negative turning point. In many cases, stages do not define a relationship. Instead, it is the communication within the relationship that defines it, and part of that communication involves expressing and managing tensions, such as the struggle between wanting both autonomy and connection in relationships.

Connor and Anne's relationship provides a good example of how these various theories might work together to explain the trajectory of a relationship. Their relationship develops smoothly and in a linear fashion for the first two months. Then they have their first big fight followed by a period of withdrawal and then making up. When they resume their relationship, they follow a fairly linear path toward increasing closeness for a while. Then a new turning point occurs when Anne raises the issue of cohabitation. This issue uncovers areas of major disagreement from which the relationship cannot recover. Perhaps, more importantly, dialectical tensions, such as the struggle between privileging their own connection versus their connections with their families, surface and are not managed in productive ways. The connection that Anne wants, both in terms of living together and in terms of sharing common goals, seems to disappear along with the relationship. As predicted by the staircase model, intimate communication decreases, and the relationship eventually ends. This combination of gradually increasing and decreasing closeness, marked by some turbulence due to turning points and dialectical tensions, is probably fairly common in premarital relationships. In more enduring relationships, turning points and dialectical tensions are likely more central since they are at the heart of ongoing relationships.

As the dialectical perspective reminds us, it is important to understand that partners may not always want or need the same things. Two people can be in different stages or have different needs. One person may be trying to reach the intensifying stage of Knapp's model, while the other is content to stay at the experimenting stage. Similarly, two people might map the turning points in their relationship differently. Anne might see the night they spent talking under the stars as the beginning of their romantic relationship whereas Connor might regard their first kiss as the start of their romance. Anne might have started the process of differentiating before Connor, and she might have moved through the coming apart stages faster even though he was the one who found someone new. They may also have viewed the tensions in their relationship differently. Anne might have viewed Connor's refusal to live together as evidence that he cared more about approval from others than his connection with her. In truth, he may have seen not living together as an important way of ensuring their future connection with one another as well as with their families. Connor may have welcomed it when Anne stopped spending as much time with him, perhaps thinking that she agreed with him and thought they both needed more autonomy. She, for her part, may have hoped that he would miss her and try to strengthen their connection.

Perhaps Anne and Connor could have saved their relationship had they communicated more effectively. Or perhaps they were better off going their separate ways. Either way, the path that their fictional relationship took probably sounds somewhat familiar to you—although the details are unique. This illustrates that relationship trajectories follow somewhat predictable paths, although no two relationships are exactly the same. Theories that focus on relationship stages provide a useful blueprint of how close relationships typically unfold over time. Yet every relationship follows its own path. Turning points help us understand the twists and turns in the path whereas dialectical tensions help us understand that the path is always changing. The uniqueness of each path is what makes the journey worthwhile.

KEY TERMS

affection-instrumentality (p. 135)
connection-autonomy (p. 132)
conventionality-uniqueness (p. 132)
cyclic alternation (p. 133)
dialectical perspective (p. 130)
discursive tensions (p. 131)
disqualification (p. 133)
expressive-protective (p. 134)
ideal-real (p. 135)
inclusion-seclusion (p. 132)

independent-dependent (p. 134)
judgment-acceptance (p. 135)
moderation (p. 133)
negative psychic change (p. 130)
neutralization (p. 133)
openness-closedness (p. 132)
physical distance (p. 129)
positive psychic change (p. 130)
predictability-novelty (p. 132)
public–private (p. 135)

reframing (p. 133)
relational dialectics theory (p. 131)
responsiveness (p. 115)
revelation-concealment (p. 132)
romantic relationship transitions (p. 128)
sacrifice or support (p. 130)
selection (p. 133)
separation (p. 133)
topical segmentation (p. 133)
turning point analysis (p. 127)

DISCUSSION QUESTIONS

1. Texting, snapping, and social media have all influenced how relationships develop and end. Based on your experiences, how do these forms of communication change as your romantic relationships and friendships get closer or fall apart? How do you use these forms of communication differently to communicate to friends versus romantic partners?

2. Which dialectical tensions are most common in your relationships? Have you experienced any tensions that are not mentioned in this chapter? How do you prefer to manage those tensions?

3. This chapter discusses three different perspectives for describing relationship trajectories. The perspectives differ in terms of how linear versus nonlinear they are, as well as the extent to which closeness or intimacy is perceived to be a stable characteristic of relationships. How does each perspective differ on these issues? Which perspective do you think best explains the trajectory that most relationships take, and why?

SAGE edge™

Sharpen your skills with SAGE edge at edge.sagepub.com/guerrero5e.
SAGE edge for students provides a personalized approach to help you accomplish your coursework goals in an easy-to-use learning environment.

6

REVEALING AND HIDING OURSELVES

Self-Disclosure and Privacy

Camila and her fiancé, Khaled, have an especially close relationship. Since they first met during their sophomore year of college, they have told each other almost everything. Camila can remember the long conversations they had in the early days of their relationship. They spent lots of time hanging out and getting to know each other. On the nights they could not be together, they Facetimed until one of them fell asleep. They were both falling in love and wanted to know every single detail about each other. Khaled told Camila about his childhood and some of the prejudices he had experienced as a Muslim American growing up post–9/11. Camila told Khaled about her struggle to figure out what career to pursue after graduation and her doubts about her ability to succeed no matter what field she chose. They supported each other through all the trials of the next two and a half years of college and moved in together after graduation. But there was one thing that Khaled did not know about Camila. When she was in elementary school, both Camila and her sister, Sara, had been sexually abused by their uncle. The girls had talked about it with each other as teenagers and had seen a therapist, but they had never told anyone else. Not even their parents knew. Their uncle was dead, and they did not want to hurt anyone in the family. But now that Camila has accepted Khaled's marriage proposal, she feels guilty that he doesn't know. She is sure that Khaled will still love and accept her, but will he be hurt that she had hidden something so important from him for so long? And what about Sara? They had made a pact not to talk about the abuse with anyone but each other. Would she be betraying Sara if she told Khaled, or would Sara understand?

As Camila's predicament illustrates, even in the closest relationships there are times when people keep information secret. Camila's relationship with Khaled is built on openness and trust, yet she has kept a big secret from him. What would you do if you were Camila? Would you tell him about the abuse, or would you continue to keep that information private? If you decided to tell him, could you

disclose the information in a way that would help him understand why you had kept it secret from him for so long? If you decided not to tell him, would you continue feeling guilty about keeping a secret from him? In close relationships, people expect their partners to be open and tell them everything, but this does not always happen.

As discussed in Chapter 5, scholars have used a dialectical perspective to explain how people navigate between expressing some parts of themselves to others, while keeping other parts of themselves private (Baxter & Montgomery, 1996; Petronio, 2000, 2002; Rosenfeld, 2000). According to the dialectical perspective, people have strong needs for both openness and secrecy. Rosenfeld (2000) put it this way:

> I want to be open because I want to share myself with others and get the benefits of such communication, such as receiving social support, the opportunity to think out loud, and the chance to get something off my chest. I do not want to be open because I might be ridiculed, rejected, or abandoned. Open or closed; let others in or keep others out? Every interaction has the potential for raising the tension of holding both desires simultaneously. It is not that one desire "wins" and the other "loses." Rather, they exist simultaneously. Interpersonal life consists of the tension between these opposites. (p. 4)

The push and pull of the forces of disclosure and privacy is evident in all types of interpersonal communication, even with cell phones. Indeed, people say that the feature they like most about their cell phones is that they can contact people whenever they want, but the feature they like least is that other people can also contact them whenever they want (Baron, 2008). In this chapter, we explore both ends of the openness-closedness dialectic by looking at how people express themselves through **self-disclosure,** as well as how people maintain privacy by setting boundaries, using **topic avoidance,** and keeping secrets.

SELF-DISCLOSURE

Communication is the primary vehicle for developing relationships and creating feelings of connection and closeness. In fact, much of the research on relationship development has examined how self-disclosure helps people move from being strangers to being close friends or lovers. Traditionally, self-disclosure has been defined as verbal communication that reveals something about a person to others. However, some researchers have also included aspects of nonverbal communication as self-disclosure. For example, if someone is wearing a religious symbol such as a cross or a particular type of scarf they are disclosing information about themselves and their affiliations. Some scholars also regard certain types of photos, especially when posted online on sites like Facebook, to be self-disclosive if they give people information about a person's activities or whereabouts (Mazer, Murphy, & Simonds, 2007). Most self-disclosure, however, is verbal. Some self-disclosure, such as talking about where you grew up or what your major is, is fairly impersonal; other self-disclosure, such as talking about your future hopes and childhood insecurities, is much more intimate. As discussed in Chapter 5, as relationships develop, increases in personal self-disclosure typically characterize communication. As relationships deteriorate, self-disclosure usually decreases.

Dimensions of Self-Disclosure

One of the first theoretical explorations of self-disclosure was developed by Altman and Taylor (1973). According to their **social penetration theory,** self-disclosure usually increases gradually as people develop their relationships. Self-disclosure can be conceptualized in terms of six dimensions: (1) **depth,** (2) **breadth,** (3) **frequency,** (4) **duration,** (5) **valence,** and (6) **veracity** (Altman & Taylor, 1973; Gilbert, 1976; Tolstedt & Stokes, 1984).

DEPTH AND BREADTH According to social penetration theory, the dimensions that are most central to the process of relationship development are depth and breadth. Depth refers to how personal or deep the communication is whereas breadth captures how many topics a person feels free to discuss. As relationships develop, they tend to increase in breadth and then depth. In fact, according to social penetration theory, it is helpful to visualize the process of self-disclosure during relationship development as the slow unpeeling of an onion, as Figure 6.1 illustrates. An onion has a rather thin and flimsy outer layer, but as you peel through the various layers, they get harder, with the core of the onion very tightly bound.

Similarly, Altman and Taylor (1973) suggested that there are three basic layers of self-disclosure: (1) a superficial layer that is easy to penetrate; (2) a social or personal layer that is easy for most friends, family members, and lovers to penetrate; and (3) a very intimate layer, or core, that is seldom revealed, and then only to people who are completely trusted. At the superficial layer, people reveal commonplace facts about themselves that are not threatening in any way. For example, telling someone your name, major, hometown, zodiac sign, and favorite color are benign self-disclosures. At the social or personal level, people typically reveal more about their likes and dislikes and hopes and fears, but they still keep their deepest hopes and fears a secret. For example, you might tell most of your friends that you'd like to marry a certain kind of person, that you had an unhappy childhood, or that you are worried about getting a job when you graduate from college. But you might not tell them all the intimate details related to these topics. At the core, people share all the personal details that make them who they are. Within the core are people's most secret, intimate feelings. For example, you might disclose negative childhood experiences that you would normally prefer not to think about, and you might confess all of your fears and insecurities about succeeding in your chosen profession. You might also reveal intimate, positive feelings about people by telling them how much they mean to you and how lost you would be without them.

FREQUENCY AND DURATION The next two dimensions focus on frequency (how often people self-disclose) and duration (how long people self-disclose). Various types of encounters can be characterized differently based on these dimensions. For example, when you have to work on a class project with someone you don't know well, you might need

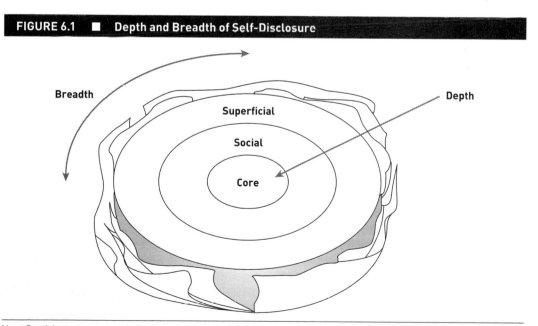

FIGURE 6.1   ■   Depth and Breadth of Self-Disclosure

Note: Depth increases as people disclose about more intimate topics, while breadth increases as people talk about a wider range of topics. Different topics can be thought of as occupying different "wedges" of the onion.

to get together with this person frequently in order to complete the class assignment. Although your self-disclosure with this person would probably be described as low in depth and breadth, it would likely be high in frequency—at least until you complete the project. Of course, if you began to develop a close relationship with your classmate, the depth and breadth of your self-disclosure would probably increase so that you'd be talking about more varied and more personal topics in addition to discussing the assignment. This example illustrates an important point: Frequent self-disclosure can lead to liking and relationship development.

It is possible for people to have self-disclosures of limited frequency but long duration. A common example of this is the "stranger on the plane" (or train) phenomenon. When you sit down next to someone on a plane, you might chat with the person for the entire duration of the flight. You might even disclose intimate details about your life to your seatmate, figuring that you probably won't see this person again, so you are not really making yourself vulnerable. Thus, it is the limited frequency of the interaction that allows you to confidently engage in self-disclosure that is high in both depth and duration. Online interactions can be similar to the "stranger on the plane" phenomenon in some ways. Studies have shown that people tend to disclose more information, including more in-depth information, online compared to face-to-face encounters. For example, one study showed that people were more willing to declare their romantic intentions toward someone over e-mail than face to face (Joinson, 2003). One reason for this is that rejection may be easier to handle online. Other research suggests that people might use higher levels of disclosure when communicating with acquaintances online versus face to face because there is more anonymity and communication is more controllable (Mesch & Beker, 2010).

In other cases, people engage in frequent but short disclosures. For example, coworkers might talk every day but only for limited amounts of time during a coffee break. One study showed that the

duration of face-to-face interaction is more strongly related to closeness in friendships than is the frequency of interaction (Emmers-Sommer, 2004). This same study showed that friendships regarded as especially close and intimate tend to be characterized by high levels of in-depth communication. Thus, friends do not need frequent contact to stay close as long as they periodically have long, in-depth conversations.

VALENCE AND VERACITY The final two dimensions relate to the specific content revealed by the self-disclosure. Valence refers to the positive or negative "charge" of the self-disclosure. For example, if you disclose your dreams, your warm feelings for someone, or your happiest childhood memories, the self-disclosure has a positive valence. By contrast, if you disclose your fears, your hostile feelings for someone, or your unhappiest childhood memories, the self-disclosure has a negative valence. Valence is a crucial dimension of self-disclosure because it helps determine how people feel about one another. Think about friends who call you all the time to complain about their lives. Their self-disclosure might be full of breadth and depth, but instead of feeling closer to your friend, you might end up feeling depressed and want to avoid such conversations in the future.

Similarly, some research has shown that couples show an increase in depth of self-disclosure when they are continually arguing or when their relationship is in decline (Tolstedt & Stokes, 1984). The types of comments they typically make, however, are negatively valenced ("I wish I'd never met you," "Why don't you ever listen to me?" "You make me feel unimportant"). Thus, high depth alone does not tell the whole story. Depth and valence work together to create the emotional climate of a self-disclosure. Of course, some negatively valenced self-disclosure can draw people closer. For example, when two individuals feel comfortable enough to reveal their deepest fears, worst failures, and most embarrassing moments, they probably have developed a particularly close relationship. The key is to limit the number of negatively valenced disclosures relative to the number of more positively valenced disclosures.

Veracity refers to how honest or deceptive self-disclosure is. True self-disclosure is honest in that it reveals something real about oneself to others. However, there are times when people give false or misleading information to others that passes as self-disclosure. For example, when people like others, they sometimes exaggerate their positive personal qualities to try to make a positive first impression. When first meeting someone to whom they are attracted, they often exaggerate how successful they are, perhaps by describing their job as more high powered than it actually is (Rowatt, Cunningham, & Druen, 1998, 1999). Alternatively, they may exaggerate or hide certain aspects of their appearance through the use of clothing or makeup. One study of online daters showed that the less physically attractive people are in person, the more likely they are to enhance their photos and exaggerate their physical attributes on their dating profiles (Toma & Hancock, 2010). Of course, information that looks like self-disclosure but is actually deceptive can backfire, leading to lower levels of trust that hinder relationship development. Honest self-disclosure is the only real path for developing closeness. Indeed, studies have shown that when people met online, they were more likely to have a successful offline relationship if their online disclosure had been honest and in-depth (Baker, 2005; McKenna, Green, & Gleason, 2002). Dishonest representations are risky; they might open the door to someone finding you more attractive initially, but that door may shut when they find out the truth.

Most research on the dimensions of self-disclosure has been conducted in face-to-face contexts. However, a growing body of research has examined how self-disclosure operates in mediated contexts by looking at the dimensions of depth, breadth, and frequency (see Box 6.1).

BOX 6.1 TECH TALK
DEPTH, BREADTH, FREQUENCY, AND VALENCE OF SELF-DISCLOSURE IN COMMUNICATION TECHNOLOGIES

Besides communicating face to face, people self-disclose using a variety of communication technologies, including voice calling, texting, social networking, and e-mailing. Research has shown that the dimensions of self-disclosure play an important role in how people use self-disclosure to develop and maintain happy relationships using these communication technologies.

In general, when people are first getting to know one another, they tend to disclose in greater depth and breadth when using communication technologies than when communicating face to face (Ruppel, 2015). There are two primary explanations for this. First, people are likely to be less self-conscious or worry about rejection when communicating via communication technologies compared to face-to-face. Second, people may compensate for the reduced nonverbal behavior in communication technologies by upping their use of verbal disclosure. However, in ongoing relationships people disclose more in person, with people reporting less depth and breadth in their text messages and phone calls than in their face-to-face interactions (Ruppel, 2015).

Other research has focused on how dimensions of disclosure in communication technologies function to maintain relationships. Hollenbaugh and Ferris (2014) found that people who are concerned with maintaining relationships with people in their social network tend to use Facebook disclosure that is high is breadth and frequency. Similarly, Boyle and O'Sullivan (2016) found that dating partners reported more intimacy when they used communication technologies to disclose in addition to disclosing face to face. High levels of breadth and positive valence were most important for promoting intimacy. Using communication technologies such as texting to engage in frequent disclosure that is high in breadth may help people feel present and accessible to one another throughout the day (Pettigrew, 2009).

However, some research suggests that it is also important for technology-assisted disclosure to be high in depth.

(Continued)

BOX 6.1 (Continued)

Rains, Brunner, and Oman (2016) looked at disclosures over a week to a friend across e-mail, voice calls, text messages, instant messages, and posts on social networking sites. When people received a high frequency of disclosures from a friend, they tended to report less liking and satisfaction to the extent that a high percentage of those messages were superficial. Thus, the combination of high frequency and low depth was problematic in friendships, suggesting that if you disclose frequently to someone via communication technologies, it is important that some of those messages be high in depth. McEwan and Horn (2016) found a similar trend for text messaging in romantic relationships. Their study showed that texting frequently is related to satisfaction and closeness as long as some of the texts are focused on maintaining the relationship rather than on more superficial matters.

For example, texts can show positivity (e.g., sharing something funny that happened) or assure your partner that you care (e.g., saying ILY or sending a heart) and show both depth and positive valence, which contribute to satisfaction.

Taken together, these studies suggest that the disclosure dimensions of frequency, breadth, depth, and valence all play a role in how communication technologies are used to develop and maintain relationships. High frequency and breadth, as well as positive valence, help people stay connected with various members of their social networks. However, in our close relationships, some of our disclosures via communication technology should also contain high levels of depth. If not, the relationship may not be as satisfying as it could be.

Self-Disclosure and Liking

Because self-disclosure makes people vulnerable, the act of self-disclosure conveys both trust and closeness. Self-disclosure also helps people uncover similarities and reduce uncertainty about one another (see Chapter 4). When the information people exchange is favorable, people will want to get to know each other even more. Thus, according to social penetration theory, self-disclosure typically increases gradually as people get to know, like, and trust one another. If people do not develop trust or liking, self-disclosure will not progress very far, and the relationship will stagnate or terminate.

Many studies have examined the relationship between self-disclosure and liking or closeness. In a statistical review of 94 studies, Collins and Miller (1994) tested the **disclosure-liking hypothesis**, which predicts that when a sender discloses to a receiver, the receiver will like the sender more. They found support for this hypothesis, although this relationship appears to be stronger among acquaintances than strangers. Similar findings have emerged for studies looking at online disclosure. For example, Jiang and colleagues (2011) varied online disclosure

so that some people received in-depth disclosure whereas other people received general information from someone posing as another student. When people received more in-depth disclosure, they reported feeling more liking and closeness to their partner. Collins and Miller's statistical review also supported the **liking-disclosure hypothesis,** which predicts that people will disclose more to receivers they like. Thus, people are more likely to disclose to close relational partners and to people to whom they are attracted than people they dislike.

Of course, not all disclosure leads to increased liking. Scholars have identified several circumstances that affect whether self-disclosure leads to liking or disliking, including the timing of the disclosure, how personalistic disclosure is, the channel or means by which someone discloses, and the partner's response to disclosure.

THE TIMING OF SELF DISCLOSURE When self-disclosure violates normative expectations, it will not lead to liking (Derlega, Metts, Petronio, & Margulis, 1993). Sometimes people disclose too much information too quickly or disclose negative information that leads others to dislike them

(Bochner, 1984; Parks, 1982). As Derlega and colleagues (1993) observed, "Highly personal, negative disclosure given too soon inhibits liking unless some strong initial attraction already exists" (p. 31). Self-disclosure is usually a gradual process; the depth of disclosure reflects the level of closeness in a relationship. Therefore, too much disclosure too early can scare people away.

PERSONALISTIC VERSUS NONDIRECTED DISCLOSURE Self-disclosure is a better predictor of liking when receivers think that their partner only discloses information to certain special people. If senders are perceived to disclose information indiscriminately, the self-disclosure may be seen as less valuable, and liking may not result. Self-disclosure is valuable to the extent that people think that it is directed at them because they are trustworthy and have a close relationship (or the potential for a close relationship) with the sender. Taylor, Gould, and Brounstein (1981) called this type of communication **personalistic disclosure**. Personalistic disclosure is also important in computer-mediated contexts; people are especially likely to feel increased liking and closeness toward an online partner when they believe that disclosure was prompted by something special about them or their relationship (Jiang et al., 2011). In other words, they think that the disclosure was directed specifically at them rather than just general information they would share with a lot of different people. Blogs and social networking sites are also good examples of this. As Jang and Stefanone (2011) suggested, the information people post on blogs is often **nondirected disclosure** that is sent to large groups of people rather than individuals and is therefore considered less personal. Similarly, there is a difference between posting a self-disclosive statement on your Facebook timeline versus sending a direct message on Facebook to a specific friend. The latter message would be more likely to signal closeness than the former.

THE CHANNEL Research also suggests that the communication channel—such as face-to-face or mediated—influences how much disclosure leads to liking. As noted previously, there is evidence that people actually disclose more personal information in mediated contexts—such as social networking sites and blogs—than in face-to-face contexts, especially when they are first getting to know one another (e.g., Tidwell & Walther, 2002; Valkenburg & Peter, 2009). One reason for this may be that people need verbal self-disclosure to get to know one another in mediated contexts, especially since they do not have access to information from nonverbal cues. According to Walther's (1996) hyperpersonal model, people develop stronger impressions of one another in mediated contexts compared to face-to-face contexts because they over-rely on the limited, mostly verbal, information that they exchange. These stronger impressions can then lead to exaggerated feelings of closeness and liking compared to what they might experience in face-to-face contexts. Jiang and colleagues (2011) described this as an **intensification effect**; personal self-disclosure produces more intense feelings of closeness and liking in computer-mediated contexts than in face-to-face contexts.

THE RECEIVER'S RESPONSE Scholars have also noted that "disclosure will not lead to liking if it is responded to in a negative manner" (Derlega et al., 1993, p. 32). If a sender discloses sensitive information and the receiver dismisses the information or responds in an unkind or critical manner, both sender and receiver are likely to feel negatively about the interaction and about each other. As shown later in this chapter, people are less likely to disclose to others if they fear negative judgment or unresponsiveness. Usually, however, receivers match the intimacy level of a sender's self-disclosure, as the literature on reciprocity of self-disclosure suggests.

Reciprocity of Self-Disclosure

For relationships to flourish in the initial stages, self-disclosure must be reciprocated. Extensive research has focused on the reciprocity or matching of self-disclosure, starting with Jourard's (1959, 1964) pioneering work on patterns of self-disclosure.

Jourard believed that reciprocal self-disclosure, which he termed the **dyadic effect,** is the vehicle by which people build close relationships (see also Altman & Taylor, 1973; Gouldner, 1960). Reciprocal self-disclosure occurs when a person reveals information and the partner responds by offering information that is at a similar level of intimacy. For example, when Camila and Khaled were first getting to know one another, they started out by exchanging rather superficial information, but then Khaled shared some stories about his childhood with Camila, and she reciprocated by telling him some equally personal information about herself. This illustrates Jourard's idea that self-disclosure usually begets more self-disclosure. In other words, people are likely to respond to high levels of self-disclosure by revealing similarly personal information. Of course, there are exceptions to this rule. For example, you might not want to continue a conversation with someone because you don't want to "lead the person on," or you might decide that the other person's level of self-disclosure is inappropriate and makes you uncomfortable. In these cases, you are less likely to reciprocate self-disclosure.

Nonetheless, research suggests that people typically feel a natural pull toward matching the level of intimacy and intensity present in their conversational partner's self-disclosure. In a statistical review of 67 studies involving 5,173 participants, Dindia and Allen (1992) concluded that the evidence overwhelmingly supports the tendency for people to reciprocate self-disclosure. People typically match the intimacy level of their conversational partner's self-disclosure regardless of the context (face to face versus via telephone or the Internet), the type of relationship (strangers versus intimates), or the amount of liking or disliking (Dindia, Fitzpatrick, & Kenny, 1997; Henderson & Gilding, 2004; Hosman & Tardy, 1980). Individuals who violate the norm of reciprocity are perceived as cold, incompetent, unfriendly, and untrustworthy (Bradac, Hosman, & Tardy, 1978). The timing of reciprocity also makes a difference in initial interactions. Researchers used an experiment to compare two situations (Sprecher, Treger, Wondra, Hilaire, & Wallpe, 2013). In the first situation, people took turns asking questions and disclosing across two interactions. In the second situation, people asked questions in one interaction and listened, and then disclosed in the other interaction (or vice versa). Sprecher et al. (2013) found that people in the first situation reported more liking, which shows that having shorter turns while disclosing reciprocally is important within initial interactions.

Although immediate reciprocity is highly preferred in initial encounters when people are first getting to know one another, in long-term close relationships reciprocity is often delayed. For example, a husband might disclose his social anxieties to his wife, who simply listens patiently. Subsequently, the wife might reciprocate by sharing some of her deepest fears while the husband assumes the listening role. Immediate reciprocity is not necessary because long-term partners know that they will have opportunities to reciprocate in the future.

Reciprocity is the norm in face-to-face encounters, but not always in mediated contexts. In particular, when people disclose on blogs or social networking sites, they do not usually expect a response unless their disclosure is directed to a particular person. A study on blogs (Jang & Stefanone, 2011), for example, showed that people were much more likely to reciprocate personalistic disclosures than nondirected disclosures. If receivers believe a message on a blog is intended for a general audience, they may not feel obligated to respond—either by acknowledging the message or by reciprocating with self-disclosure on the blog or in a later conversation. On social networking sites like Facebook and Twitter, it is also likely that people are more likely to reciprocate disclosive statements sent via direct messaging rather than those placed on a timeline for all one's friends to see.

Risks Associated With Self-Disclosure

Despite its benefits, disclosing personal information is risky. When we tell other people our innermost thoughts and feelings, we become vulnerable and open ourselves up to criticism. The vulnerability associated with self-disclosure may be stronger in face-to-face contexts, where people risk receiving immediate negative feedback and are less able to control their communication (Caplan, 2003). Indeed, some researchers have argued that people who lack the social skills necessary to communicate effectively in face-to-face contexts prefer to self-disclose online. As McKenna and colleagues (2002) put it, people "who have the social skills needed to communicate themselves well and effectively have little need to express their true selves or 'Real Me' over the Internet. The rest of us should be glad that the Internet exists" (p. 12).

A study by Ledbetter and others (2011) tested this idea by investigating how attitudes toward online self-disclosure and attitudes toward social connection work together to predict disclosure on Facebook. In this study, people who reported a preference for online communication over face-to-face communication were unlikely to disclose on Facebook. This finding might represent an overall tendency not to disclose. In other words, people who would rather disclose online than in a face-to-face context may generally not like to disclose much personal information, regardless of the context. Ledbetter and his colleagues also found that people who believed that online communication is important for social connection reported more self-disclosure on Facebook but only if they also reported that they did *not* have a preference for online communication compared to face-to-face communication. This suggests that the people who disclose the most on Facebook have two characteristics. First, they believe that online communication is an essential tool for forming and developing social connections. Second, they do not have a preference for online communication over face-to-face communication, which means that they are comfortable in face-to-face settings and likely have good communication skills. To see how much of each of these characteristics you possess, complete the test in Box 6.2.

While communicating online may decrease some of the risks and vulnerabilities associated with self-disclosure, it cannot erase them all. Regardless of the communication channel, self-disclosure carries some inherent risks that lead people to avoid talking about certain topics. Some of the most common reasons people avoid intimate self-disclosure include (1) fear of exposure or rejection, (2) fear of retaliation or angry responses, (3) fear of loss of control, and (4) fear of losing one's individuality (Hatfield, 1984; Petronio, 2002).

FEAR OF EXPOSURE OR REJECTION Sometimes people worry that too much self-disclosure will expose their negative qualities and cause others to think badly of them, like them less, and even reject or abandon them. Hatfield (1984) put it this way:

> One reason, then, that all of us are afraid of intimacy, is that those we care most about are bound to discover all that is wrong with us—to discover that we possess taboo feelings . . . have done things of which we are deeply ashamed. (p. 210)

Hatfield gave an excellent example of how revealing one's real self can lead to rejection and abandonment when she told the story of one of her former graduate students. This young European woman was beautiful, intelligent, and charming; in fact, many men fell madly in love with her. Of course, she was not perfect—she had insecurities and self-doubts, just as we all do. But she put on a bright, charming facade in order to fit the perfect image that people had of her. The problem was that whenever she got close enough to a man to admit her insecurities, she fell off the pedestal that he had put her on. It was impossible to meet the high expectations of these men. When her perfect image was shattered, they lost interest.

FEAR OF RETALIATION OR ANGRY ATTACKS People also worry that their partners might become angry or use what they disclose against them. For example, you might worry that your relational partner will retaliate or withdraw from the relationship if you confess to a one-night stand, admit telling a lie,

BOX 6.2 PUT YOURSELF TO THE TEST
ATTITUDES TOWARD ONLINE COMMUNICATION

	Disagree					Agree	
1. I feel less nervous when sharing personal information online compared to in person.	1	2	3	4	5	6	7
2. If I couldn't communicate online, I would feel "out of the loop" with my friends.	1	2	3	4	5	6	7
3. I feel like I can be more open when I am communicating online versus in person.	1	2	3	4	5	6	7
4. If I lost Internet access, I think I would probably lose contact with many of my friends.	1	2	3	4	5	6	7
5. I feel like I can sometimes be more personal during Internet conversations than face-to-face conversations.	1	2	3	4	5	6	7
6. Without the Internet, my social life would be drastically different.	1	2	3	4	5	6	7
7. When online, I feel more comfortable disclosing personal information to a member of the opposite sex than I would in person.	1	2	3	4	5	6	7
8. I would communicate less with my friends if I couldn't talk with them online.	1	2	3	4	5	6	7
9. I feel less shy when I am communicating online versus face to face.	1	2	3	4	5	6	7
10. Losing Internet access would change my social life dramatically.	1	2	3	4	5	6	7
11. I feel less embarrassed sharing personal information with another person online than face to face.	1	2	3	4	5	6	7
12. Online communication is an important part of my social life.	1	2	3	4	5	6	7
13. It is easier to disclose personal information online than in person.	1	2	3	4	5	6	7

To obtain your results, first add your scores for odd-numbered items. Then divide by 7. This is your score for Attitudes Toward Online Self-Disclosure. Your score will range from 1 to 7. The higher your score, the more you prefer disclosing personal information online rather than face to face. Next, add your scores for the even-numbered items. Then divide by 6. This is your score for Attitudes Toward Online Social Connection. This score will also range from 1 to 7. The higher your score, the more you believe that online communication is important for being socially connected with people. According to Ledbetter and colleagues' (2011) study, if you scored *low* on the first scale (Attitudes Toward Online Self-Disclosure) and *high* on the second scale (Attitudes Toward Online Social Connection), you are especially likely to use a social networking site like Facebook, Twitter, or MySpace as a communication tool.

Source: This is a revised version of The Online Communication Scale, adapted from Ledbetter, A. M. (2009). Measuring online communication attitude: Instrument development and validation. *Communication Monographs, 76,* 463–486. Copyright © 2009.

or recount happy experiences you had with a former relational partner. One of our students once told us that he was secretly in love with his brother's fiancée. The two brothers had always had a very close but competitive relationship, and he worried that disclosing his feelings could lead to anger, suspicion, and even **confrontation.** He also worried that his brother's fiancée would end up hurt, confused, and maybe angry. In other cases, people use the intimate information we share with them as ammunition against us. For example, if you tell your best friend that you sometimes only pretend to pay attention to people, your friend might later accuse you of being selfish and of not really listening when he or she is disclosing personal problems.

FEAR OF LOSS OF CONTROL People also worry that if they engage in too much self-disclosure, they will lose control of their thoughts and feelings or the thoughts and feelings of others. For example, Khaled fell in love with Camila after only a couple weeks, but he did not tell her he loved her then because he knew he might scare her away. Similarly, Camila might be afraid that if she starts talking to Khaled about the abuse she experienced as a child, she will break down and cry uncontrollably. People may also fear losing control of information, especially if they think that the receiver might share the information with others without their permission (Petronio, 2002; Phillips & Metzger, 1976). Additionally, people may worry that if they disclose personal weaknesses to their partner, they will lose their ability to influence the partner (Petronio, 1991).

FEAR OF LOSING INDIVIDUALITY Some people fear losing their personal identity and being engulfed by the relationship. According to Hatfield (1984), one of the "most primitive fears of intimacy" is that we could "literally disappear" if we become too engulfed in a relationship (p. 212). Consistent with the dialectical perspective, this fear represents the push and pull that many people feel between the competing forces of wanting to be closely connected to others and wanting to be independent and self-sufficient. The idea here is that if we tell people

too much about ourselves, we risk losing our uniqueness and mysteriousness. Moreover, if we maintain high levels of self-disclosure, we may come to a point where there is nothing left to share. In this case, we may feel that we are part of a group or dyad, rather than a unique individual with some private, secret thoughts and feelings. We may even feel a need to "escape" from our relational partner in order to find privacy and assert our independence.

PRIVACY

As the risks associated with self-disclosure suggest, there are times when people do not want to disclose personal information. **Communication privacy management (CPM)** theory helps explain how individuals maintain privacy boundaries (Petronio, 1991, 2002, 2013). The theory is rooted in the assumption that people set up **boundary structures** as a way to control the risks inherent in disclosing private information. Private information is considered "any information that makes people feel some level of vulnerability" (Child, Duck, Andrews, Butauski, & Petronio, 2015, p. 350). These boundary structures are based on three principles associated with private information: (1) **privacy ownership**, (2) **privacy control**, and (3) **privacy turbulence.** See Figure 6.2 for a pictorial representation of this model.

Privacy Ownership

According to CPM, our private information is first and foremost *ours*. We should be able to decide with whom we share that information, if anyone. Indeed, there have been very distressing examples of people's reactions to losing the ownership of their privacy, as illustrated by the suicide of a college student whose sexual encounter with a same-sex partner was recorded without his knowledge or permission through a webcam (http://www.newyorker.com/magazine/2012/02/06/the-story-of-a-suicide). NOTE: If you or a friend are in crisis and considering suicide, seek help right away. Call the National Suicide Prevention

FIGURE 6.2   ■   Critical Aspects of Private Information

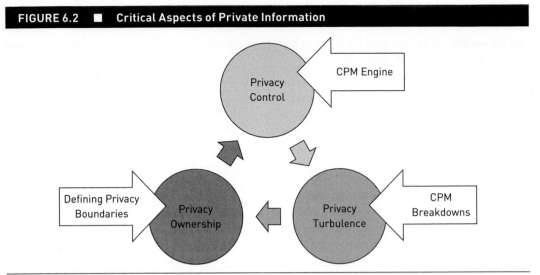

Source: Sandra Petronio; *Journal of Family Communication 2013*, 13, 6-14. DOI: 10.1080/15267431.2013.743426. Copyright © 2013 Taylor & Francis Group, LLC.

Lifeline at 1-800-273-8255 for assistance or visit the American Foundation for Suicide Prevention at www.afsp.org for more information.

When we decide to share our private information with others, those people become **authorized co-owners** (also known as "boundary insiders"), with responsibility to maintain that exclusive ownership unless granted permission to do otherwise. This issue of ownership and co-ownership is becoming increasingly important because a growing percentage of our private information is now co-owned, and because our norms and expectations of privacy have changed. The management of this ownership can be seen in individuals' decisions about which pictures to post and/or what information to disclose on their social media sites (Child & Starcher, 2016). Posting information or images immediately makes a large number of people co-owners of that private information, with related risks. Indeed, decisions about whose friend requests to accept are integral to our privacy ownership efforts (Frampton & Child, 2013; Mullen & Hamilton, 2016). Your decision about whether to accept a "friend request" from another

student in your class, from your boss, or from your uncle all have implications for the boundaries of your information ownership, especially if available restrictions to content accessibility (e.g., who can view what is on your social media sites) are not carefully monitored. That sort of monitoring is an example of strategies related to the next principle of CPM: privacy control.

Privacy Control

Petronio (2013) discusses privacy control as the "engine of CPM." This principle speaks to the idea that people feel strongly about having control over their own private information. We not only want to decide who, if anyone, is allowed to co-own our private information, but we also want to be able to control what aspects of that information (if any) they are allowed to share with others and how the information is framed. For example, secrets held by an entire family (like not telling anyone outside the family they are on welfare) require that all family members agree to keep the relevant information private, which means that they must coordinate their boundary structures and rules on that particular issue. In a similar vein, someone who cheats on a romantic partner must either implicitly (and naively) assume or explicitly discuss a degree of boundary coordination with the sexual partner to keep the incident a secret. To help maintain coordinated boundary structures, people usually develop penalties for group or dyad members who violate the boundary structure (Petronio, 1991, 2002). Boundary coordination becomes especially salient when the information is revealed to someone who is not a part of the original group. For example, Camila and Sara may want to keep the abuse they experienced between just the two of them since they are the only two who can truly understand what they went through. If Camila decides to tell Khaled what happened to her, she may feel obligated to inform Sara of her decision before disclosing the information to Khaled, perhaps even to seek her permission (privacy ownership). If Khaled is told, the addition of a new member into the secret-keeping group may necessitate additional boundary structure coordination, and the rules must often be made explicit to the new member (privacy control). So Camila may tell Khaled not to tell another living soul what happened to her, and never even to mention it in front of Sara. In other words, even after we decide to share information with others, making them authorized co-owners, we still want to control whether that information is spread farther and how, if at all, it is framed when shared with others. Who do you tell about your breakup? How do you want the story of the breakup told? And what strategies do you use to see to it that your privacy on this issue is maintained and that you maintain control over the "story"? Even if you want to spread the information widely and you have little concern over ownership (privacy ownership), you probably still want to make sure that the "story" about your breakup (e.g., who is to blame, what happened, why) is told a certain way (privacy control).

Privacy Turbulence

The third principle is that co-owners of information sometimes undergo privacy turbulence. Privacy turbulence occurs when new events force renewed boundary management (Petronio, 1991; 2013). There are situations in which old boundary structures may need to be either fortified or renegotiated. For example, when people's lives change, topics previously avoided (e.g., the future of the relationship) may become acceptable topics (e.g., after a marriage proposal). Similarly, once a previous boundary structure is violated (e.g., when a secret is first disclosed), a radical change in the nature of the new structure may occur (e.g., the once-secret information becomes a commonplace disclosure). When the boundary expectations held by the original owner of the information are violated, confidentiality is considered to have been compromised. This breach is the sort of event that creates privacy turbulence.

Pederson and McLaren (2016) studied how people who had experienced a hurtful event managed that information with others. One of the unfortunate outcomes of that process was that they were sometimes hurt again by an "authorized co-owner" (a friend who they had told about the hurtful incident) telling others without permission. That privacy breach created **boundary turbulence** by forcibly reshaping the boundaries of who now owned that information and what they may know about it. That turbulence, in turn, likely affects the person's willingness to reveal private information to others (ownership control) and their concern about the loss of control over information once revealed (privacy control).

Although medical settings are not contexts where most people expect confidentiality breaches, Petronio and Reierson (2009) identified several examples of such violations by medical personnel. For instance, patients are sometimes frustrated by the loss of control over their medical information once it enters the realm of a medical team, especially within teaching hospitals where the case may become an occasion to test medical students' knowledge. Patients may feel violated by a loss of control over sensitive information. The result may be boundary restructuring in future encounters with physicians—a dangerous outcome since it may involve concealment of important information as a way to prevent a potential privacy breach. The ways in which individuals negotiate privacy boundaries thus can be both complex and challenging.

Influences on Rules for Privacy Management

CPM theorists also acknowledge that our decisions about privacy ownership, privacy control, and even our management of privacy turbulence is impacted by five main factors that shape our notions of privacy: (1) *culture,* (2) *personality,* (3) *the relationship,* (4) *biological sex,* and (5) *motivations.* First, each culture has different rules regarding privacy and self-disclosure (see Box 6.3). For example, some cultures have relatively loose rules regarding what

topics are appropriate to discuss with strangers; other cultures are more restrictive. For example, cultures differ in terms of ownership over health information. Certain cultures, including in some Asian and Middle Eastern countries, have a family-centric tradition of health information disclosure, whereby physicians give information about a patient's health only to a patient's family. The family then decides what, if anything, to tell the patient. In contrast, countries such as the United States have strict laws that ensure that health information belongs only to the patient.

Second, personality guides disclosure decisions. Some people are highly self-disclosive and expressive, whereas other people are much more private. Third, a host of relational factors, such as attraction, closeness, and relationship type (friends

BOX 6.3 AROUND THE WORLD
PRIVACY MANAGEMENT AND CULTURE

Cultures vary dramatically in the extent to which individuals' privacy is promoted. One dimension that seems to separate cultures on this front is communal-individual norms. In communal cultures, individuals play a secondary role to the good and rights of the community (e.g., the family). In contrast, individualistic cultures generally prioritize individuals over community members. This difference affects privacy expectations and disclosure norms in many ways. For example, studies have shown that some communal cultures treat an individual's health information and health decisions as community owned. Physicians either withhold diagnosis information or first inform family members who then decide what to reveal to the patient (Hamadeh & Adib, 1998). Compare that to norms in the United States, where laws require the disclosure of medical information to the patient, and only the patient.

Privacy may also be difficult to maintain in cultures that are highly communal because of the realities of the living contexts. Communal cultures often expect all family members to live under one roof, often with very little space. Under these conditions, the privacy of one's bedroom evaporates. When one shares a room with four or

more siblings or relatives, it is difficult to maintain privacy. Famously, some people from communal cultures share generally private marital successes and challenges with family members. For instance, sheets taken from the bed after the first marital sexual episode may be displayed publicly, as evidence that the marriage has been consummated. Uncles or aunts may also be brought in as mediators to help solve marital conflicts in the family. Clearly, **privacy maintenance** is difficult in these contexts. A norm is established where community members, typically all with close connections to one another, look out for each other. So a teenager who tries to escape with a girlfriend to a remote location for privacy often discovers that the rendezvous was far less private than he expected, because others in the community saw them going to that location and then immediately shared the information with the parents.

Given the decreased status of the individual, vis-à-vis the community, in communal cultures, individuals' perceptions of the appropriateness of revealing personal struggles is very different from those of people from more individualistic cultures. Therapists have long been

BOX 6.3 (Continued)

aware of the need to be sensitive to cultural differences on this front (Sue & Zane, 1987). People often consider therapists in the United States to be safe havens to reveal dark personal secrets, and research has shown that such disclosures to therapists can be very beneficial. This benefit, though, is unlikely to be realized in communal cultures, where therapists' offices are not shielded from the strongly held notion that personal disclosures and the difficulties they sometimes reveal are selfish and inappropriate. In other words, even people who go to therapists for help may be unwilling to engage in the necessary disclosure because of a sense, accurate or not, that they will be perceived by the therapist as overly focused on themselves.

Implications of cultural differences in individualism and collectivism has also been shown to have implications for privacy concerns on social media sites. In a comparison of attitudes of people in Germany and in the United States, Krasnova, Veltri, and Günther (2012) found that trust in the members of the social networking sites played a stronger role in shaping online self-disclosure decisions for participants in the United States than it did for those in Germany. Reed, Spiro, and Butts (2016) completed an even more

comprehensive examination of privacy and is impacts on disclosure decisions on social media by examining 200,000 randomly selected Facebook users across 30 countries. Their results showed strong differences across countries in users' disclosure preferences on Facebook (as defined by four different privacy settings).

Finally, much of our understanding of family strengths comes from an assumption that parents and children should disclose to one another. While that may be true in individualistic cultures, some communal cultures are founded on a premise of a certain distance between parent and child. As such, both parents and their children may perceive personal disclosures to one another as too intimate of an exercise. The patterns we have discussed here point out an interesting reality: We have argued that disclosure is linked to privacy—the less one discloses, the more privacy one has. However, we have also pointed to the reality of communal cultures, where both privacy and disclosure are low in some cases. What gives? What is the relationship between privacy and disclosure? These are interesting and important questions that do not yet have clear answers, but one thing is clear: People's experience with privacy goes beyond simple disclosure patterns.

versus coworkers), impact the dynamics of privacy and self-disclosures. As mentioned previously, people tend to disclose more with individuals they like than with those they dislike. Fourth, sex differences, although usually small, can nonetheless influence privacy boundaries. As discussed later in this book, women's rules for disclosing information sometimes differ from men's: women tend to disclose somewhat more than men, particularly on intimate topics (see Chapter 7). Finally, individuals' motivations can affect how they manage privacy boundaries. For instance, people who are motivated to make friends may disclose more than those who are motivated to accomplish a task, and people who worry about getting hurt or rejected might avoid self-disclosure that could make them vulnerable. CPM recognizes that the ways in which we create disclosure boundaries

are influenced by these many factors, which shape when, where, and to whom we disclose information.

Negotiating Privacy in Relationships: Challenges and Violations

The central feature of CPM is its recognition that we cherish our rights to privacy and our ability to control information. But perhaps the most interesting questions revolve around information ownership issues. Ask yourself: What information does your romantic partner (present or future) have a right to know—your past dating history, financial status, job history, whether you have a sexually transmitted infection (STI), details about your parents' relationship, or none of the above? Do you have the right to decide whether to disclose these types of information or not? Now ask yourself this: What information about your parents do you have the right to know—the quality of their relationship, their health and well-being, or what they did in college? Put yourself in Khaled's shoes. Does he have a right to know everything about Camila? Or does Camila have a right to keep some information private?

To address real-world privacy right challenges that people face, Petronio, Sargent, Andea, Reganis, and Cichocki (2004) used CPM to study family and friends who serve as informal health care advocates for patients. Their results showed some of the privacy-related difficulties that physicians, patients, and extended family members face in these situations. Physicians in the United States are often uncomfortable giving information to someone other than the patient, and advocates sometimes worry that the information they receive could depress or worry the patient and undermine the treatment. Advocates also struggle about whether to keep certain patient information private (by not divulging it to the physician) or whether to reveal private information for the sake of the patient's health. In the end, most advocates put the patient's health needs over their privacy needs.

This struggle for privacy emerges in many different contexts and relationships. Given that adolescence is a time when we generally try to establish our own identities separate from that of our family, it is not surprising that privacy struggles occur with some frequency in families with teenage children. Teenagers may believe they have a right to be independent and to maintain their privacy, but parents may believe that their teens still need guidance and protection. In this sense, the boundary coordination rules in families can be complex, and their negotiation can be very difficult. In general, though, these privacy struggles decrease once children "leave the nest" (e.g., for college). Parents' privacy violations at that stage reflect a failure to recognize the children's "right" to independence at a time when their sense of autonomy is beginning to flourish (McGoldrick & Carter, 1982). The consequences of privacy violations at that stage may be particularly damaging to the parent–child relationship, but how common are they, and what form do they take?

To answer these questions, Petronio and Harriman (1990) asked college students to describe recent instances of privacy violations by their parents and how they responded. All of the students were able to describe at least one example, and 96% of them described at least three such incidences, suggesting that parents' privacy violations are a fairly common occurrence for college students. Eight types of parental privacy violations were reported: (1) asking personal questions about the student's life, (2) giving unsolicited advice, (3) making unsolicited remarks about the student's life, (4) opening the student's mail without permission, (5) going through the student's belongings without permission, (6) entering the bathroom without knocking, (7) eavesdropping on face-to-face conversations with others, and (8) using a second telephone line to listen in on a phone conversation without permission. Moreover, two general reactions were reported: (1) confrontation, where the child openly challenges the guilty parent (asking the parent to stop the privacy violation, confronting the parent with evidence), and (2) evasion, where the child changes the behavior to protect privacy but does not discuss it directly with the parents. Petronio and Harriman found that students were more likely to react in a confrontational manner when they caught their parents secretly trying to invade their privacy than when their parents invaded their privacy by asking questions or giving unsolicited advice. Not surprisingly, the authors noted that these sorts of privacy violations and the resultant confrontation were related to decreased trust and a drop in the quality of the parent–child relationship.

TOPIC AVOIDANCE AND SECRET KEEPING

So far, we have discussed how people violate others' privacy. On the other side of the coin are ways that people maintain privacy by managing information. Two information-management strategies—(1) topic avoidance and (2) secret keeping—are related in that they are both efforts to erect privacy barriers around information, but they are different in that they often involve varying degrees of shared knowledge. Topic avoidance simply reflects cases where someone intentionally avoids discussing a particular topic. People in relationships avoid discussing topics of which they are both aware—Khaled and Camila may avoid talking about the time during sophomore year when they were miserable after having their first big fight and breaking up for a week. Secret keeping, in contrast, involves intentional efforts to keep information away from others, such as Camila and Sara's decision not to disclose their abuse to anyone but each other. (See Afifi, Caughlin, & Afifi, 2007, for further discussion of the difference between topic avoidance and secrets.)

Both topic avoidance and secret keeping are common in all types of close relationships. Baxter and Wilmot (1984) found that over 95% of the college students in their study could name at least one topic that they considered to be "taboo" or off limits in their friendships or dating relationships. Relatedly, most studies of secret keeping have found that nearly everyone keeps at least some information secret from partners, family members, or friends (see Finkenauer, Kubacka, Engels, & Kerkhof, 2009; Vangelisti, 1994a; Wegner, 1992). Given the similarities between topic avoidance and secret keeping, the research in the two domains is reviewed together although we periodically focus on each separately, as appropriate.

Topics Commonly Avoided or Kept Secret

Although people can avoid talking about almost anything, some topics are more likely to be avoided than others. Guerrero and Afifi's (1995a, 1995b) summary of the available research revealed six general topics that are commonly avoided in close relationships: (1) relationship issues (e.g., relationship norms, the state and future of the relationship, the amount of attention to the relationship), (2) negative experiences or failures (e.g., past experiences that may be considered socially unacceptable or were traumatic), (3) romantic relationship experiences (e.g., past or present romantic relationships

and dating patterns), (4) sexual experiences (e.g., past or present sexual activity or sexual preferences), (5) friendships (e.g., current friendships with others, the qualities of the friendship, the activities engaged in together), and (6) dangerous behavior (e.g., behaviors that are potentially hurtful to oneself). Golish and Caughlin's (2002) study of avoidance between parents and their children led to the addition of six more topics: (1) everyday activities (e.g., school, daily events), (2) other family members (e.g., talking about the other parent or stepparent, siblings), (3) money, (4) deep conversations, (5) drinking or drugs, and (6) religion. Of course, no one study will capture all the possible issues that may be avoided in relationships, so it is best to think of these as ones that are commonly avoided. For example, given that most studies in this area used college students, adolescents, and young married couples, they likely underrepresent some of the topics avoided by older adults. They also mostly reflect white, middle-class populations, thereby under-representing topics that may be more salient to communities of color or to individuals belonging in other socioeconomic groups.

If we turn to common topics that people keep as secrets, we find that they fit within the same category types described for avoided topics. For instance, one-night stands, a socially stigmatized illness, an alcoholic father's behavior, or a real dislike for someone are all among the sort of things one might keep as a secret. Of course, it is also worth noting that the content of secrets may be positive—although probably not the first thing we think of when discussing secrets. Yet, you may keep secret the surprise birthday party you are planning for your best friend, the vacation plans you made for yourself and your romantic partner, or a gift you purchased for your child. These are positive examples of secret keeping.

Consistent with the notion that most information kept secretive is negative in some way, Caughlin, Afifi, Carpenter-Theune, and Miller's (2005) study of secret keeping in romantic relationships and friendships revealed that the three most common secrets were dating or sexual history (22% kept this secret from a dating partner or friend), an affair (held by 18% of the sample), and personality or opinion conflicts (held by 14% of the people in the study). In a study of family secrets, Vangelisti and Caughlin (1997) showed that finances—which include issues related to money, business holdings, and other assets owned by family members—were the most often kept secrets by families, followed by substance abuse, and then premarital pregnancy.

Families are a common context for secret keeping. Karpel (1980) discussed three forms of secrets particularly relevant to family units that differ in the complexity of the required boundary coordination (to use CPM terminology). The first form of secrets is **whole-family secrets,** which are held by the entire family and kept from outsiders. For example, sadly, Armstrong (1978) described a common tendency to keep a child's sexual abuse by a family member secret from all those outside the immediate family, assuming that the family is aware of the abuse. This tendency may explain why Camila and Sara are so reluctant to share their past abuse with anyone but a professional therapist.

Karpel's (1980) second form of secrets, **intrafamily secrets,** occurs when some family members have information they keep from other members. This is the case for Camila and Sara, who have kept information about their abuse from everyone, including close family members such as their parents and aunt. Originally, Camila's sexually abusive uncle may have told her and Sara to "keep it our little secret," thereby hiding the abuse from other family members (Cottle, 1980). Other intrafamily secrets can be benign or even positive, such as Camila and Sara keeping the surprise gift they are getting for their parents' anniversary a secret from everyone until they open it.

The third form of secrets, **individual secrets,** occurs when information is held by a single individual and kept secret from other family members (Karpel, 1980). For example, Khaled might not have told any of his family members about some of the harassment he received at school after 9/11. Individual secrets may or may not be shared outside

of the family. So even though Khaled didn't tell his family, he may have talked to Camila about how hurtful it was for him when some of the kids harassed him at school.

Reasons for Topic Avoidance and Secret Keeping

People engage in topic avoidance and secrecy for a myriad of reasons. Many of these reasons fall under three general motivations: (1) relationship-based, (2) individual-based, and (3) information-based (Afifi & Guerrero, 2000; Caughlin & Vangelisti, 2009).

RELATIONSHIP-BASED MOTIVATIONS Paradoxically, people can use topic avoidance to strengthen or to disengage from a relationship. In fact, contrary to research conducted in the 1970s and early 1980s that touted the benefits of complete openness and self-disclosure, more recent studies on topic avoidance suggest that one of the most important reasons for not being completely open/disclosive is a concern for maintaining the relationship (Afifi & Guerrero, 2000; Parks, 1982). Baxter and Wilmot (1985) found that the desire for **relationship protection** was the single biggest motivator leading to avoidance of a particular issue with a relational partner. Similarly, Hatfield (1984) and Rosenfeld (1979) noted that fear of abandonment often explained someone's decision to avoid certain topics or keep something a secret. In other words, if people are worried that their partner will disapprove, they will likely keep something to themselves.

This motivation is not restricted to romantic relationships. Friends and family members also withhold information that could harm their relationships. Afifi and Guerrero (1998) found that males were more likely than females to claim relationship protection as a reason for topic avoidance in their friendships and that people avoided certain topics with male friends more than with female friends because of this concern. In family relationships, Guerrero and Afifi (1995a) found that individuals were more likely to be driven by a desire to protect the relationship when avoiding topics with their parents, as opposed to their siblings. In an extension of this research, Golish and Caughlin (2002) found that relationship protection was more often a reason underlying avoidance with stepparents than with fathers, and with fathers than with mothers. Thus, although relationship protection is an important reason underlying decisions to avoid disclosure, it seems especially relevant to some close relationships.

In contrast to the desire to protect and sustain the relationship, some people avoid discussing certain topics or keep secrets in hopes of destroying the relationship or preventing it from becoming closer. This motivation has been labeled relationship destruction or **relationship de-escalation** (Afifi & Guerrero, 2000). Although much less work has focused specifically on this motivation, several lines of research support the idea that people use topic avoidance or secrets to terminate a relationship or to prevent it from becoming more intimate. For instance, during the breakup stages of relationships, partners may distance themselves from the other by shutting down communication and withholding previously shared information (see Chapters 5 and 15). Another way to think about this motivation is how it works, for example, when someone you dislike wants to become friends with you. You might strategically avoid discussing personal topics with this person so that intimacy cannot develop.

INDIVIDUAL-BASED MOTIVATIONS People also avoid discussing certain issues to protect themselves. Chapter 2 highlighted the importance people place on protecting their public identities. Literally hundreds of studies have shown that people work hard to project and maintain a positive image. Not surprisingly, then, one of the main reasons people avoid discussing certain issues is that disclosure on certain topics may make them "look bad." Afifi and Guerrero (2000) labeled this motivation **identity management**. In fact, across four studies—spanning sibling, parent–child, stepparent–child, friendship, and dating relationships—the fear of embarrassment and criticism, fueled by feelings of

vulnerability, was the leading reason given for topic avoidance (Afifi & Guerrero, 1998; Guerrero & Afifi, 1995a, 1995b; Hatfield, 1984). Together, these studies suggest that the primary reason people avoid discussing certain issues is the fear that disclosure will threaten their identities. Relationship protection is a close second. Apparently, people decide that it is better not to talk about something if it might make others perceive them negatively. If a person's identity is on the line, disclosure often is not worth the risk.

Besides this concern over public identity, people may avoid specific topics as a way to maintain privacy. This motivation, which Afifi and Guerrero (2000) termed *privacy maintenance,* is rooted in individuals' needs for privacy and autonomy. Given the importance of privacy maintenance in people's lives, one way that people maintain privacy is to avoid disclosure about certain topics. For example, you may become annoyed with a friend who wants to know all the details about your romantic relationship or who constantly asks you how well you did on exams or term papers. In response, as a way to protect your privacy, you may refuse to answer your friend's questions and avoid bringing up any related topics in the future.

INFORMATION-BASED MOTIVATIONS The final set of reasons people choose to avoid disclosure or keep information to themselves is based on the information they expect to receive from the other person. In particular, people may choose to avoid disclosure because they suspect that the other person will find the disclosure trivial, not respond in a helpful way, or lack the requisite knowledge to respond. Afifi and Guerrero (2000) labeled these types of motivations **partner unresponsiveness**. For example, if you have a problem for which you need advice, but you think your friend will be unable to provide you with much help or will not care enough to really listen, you will likely avoid discussing that problem with your friend. Studies have found that people are especially likely to avoid discussing problems with men for this reason (Afifi

& Guerrero, 1998; Guerrero & Afifi, 1995a, 1995b). In fact, a study by Burke, Weir, and Harrison (1976) found that 23% of wives, compared to only 10% of husbands, avoided disclosure because of a belief that their spouse would be unresponsive. This finding is consistent with later research on social support; that research shows that women generally are better listeners than men (Derlega, Barbee, & Winstead, 1994). Consistent with the negative implications of partner unresponsiveness for disclosure, perceptions of support are associated with less secret-keeping and avoidance. In that vein, Tilton-Weaver's (2014) study of 874 seventh and eighth graders across two years found that their perceptions of their parents' supportiveness was one of the strongest predictors of their secret-keeping from parents one year later. Adolescents who perceive their parents to be supportive appear to be significantly less likely to keep secrets from them.

People also engage in topic avoidance or secret keeping when they believe that talking about a particular topic would be futile or a "waste of time." Afifi and Guerrero (2000) labeled this motivation **futility of discussion**. Although this motivation has received less attention than the others, it may play an important role in people's decisions to withhold information. For example, believing that your partner or friend is so entrenched in her or his position as to make discussion meaningless certainly will motivate topic avoidance, but it may also be especially detrimental to relational success. Knowing that your partner will never understand why you loaned a lot of money to a friend, for instance, may make you keep that information secret.

Recent research has revealed another important information-based motivation for avoidance and secrecy—but one that is less focused on failings of the "other" and more on the self. This motivation revolves around one's own **communication inefficacy** (Afifi, 2010; Afifi & Robbins, 2014; Afifi & Steuber, 2009). Specifically, people often avoid a topic or keep something secret because they don't feel they have the communication skills to bring up the topic or maintain discussion in a competent and

effective manner. They may not know how to start the conversation or think they'll freeze once the discussion starts. In either case, the motivation to just stay quiet in these cases is strong.

Collectively, these motivations account for many of the reasons that people maintain strict information boundaries within their relationships. It is also important to keep in mind that people often avoid topics or keep secrets for several reasons, not just one, and that the reasons are often related. Knobloch and Carpenter-Theune (2004) found that people who avoided topics with their partner because of concerns that discussion would damage their image also worried that talking about the issue would harm the relationship. Indeed, these two motivations—(1) identity management and (2) relationship protection—are the most commonly cited reasons for information management and tend to work together to prohibit disclosure. Other research has uncovered more specific reasons why people keep information to themselves. For example, Golish and Caughlin (2002) found several specific reasons why parents and children use topic avoidance with one another, including lack of contact (especially in the case of divorced families), the emotional pain of discussion, and simple dislike for the person.

How People Engage in Topic Avoidance

Most studies of topic avoidance have involved asking people to rate how much they avoid discussing a certain topic with a particular person on a scale that ranges from "I always avoid discussing this issue with this person" to "I never avoid discussing this issue with this person." Recently, however, scholars have started investigating specific ways people practice topic avoidance rather than just measuring the degree of topic avoidance.

Dailey and Palomares (2004) identified eight general strategies for avoiding disclosure, varying in directness and politeness. Examples of avoidance tactics perceived as direct and impolite include abruptly saying something like "you should go" or simply leaving the conversation when a topic comes up. Other strategies for avoiding disclosure are more subtle and polite, such as using a cliché to avoid expressing true feelings (e.g., "that's the way the ball bounces" or "it is what it is") or giving a hesitant response to signal discomfort about the topic, hoping the other helps out by switching topics. In one study, college students who had frequent contact with their parents recalled their response when their parent last asked them about a topic they wanted to avoid (Mazur & Hubbard, 2004). Participants offered 10 different avoidance strategies, ranging from telling a lie (i.e., avoiding through deception), to showing anger or irritation, to appearing disinterested or uncomfortable.

Topic Avoidance During Relationship Transitions

People can engage in topic avoidance at any time. Sometimes topic avoidance is embedded in a relationship, such as spouses avoiding talking about politics because they know they cannot change each other's minds and will only argue. Other times, topic avoidance is a one-time occurrence. For instance, perhaps you are in a bad mood and don't want to talk about something, but later you end up sharing everything with your partner. Even though topic avoidance can occur at any time, there appear to be certain transition points in relationships, and two in particular, that are marked by higher overall levels of topic avoidance.

TOPIC AVOIDANCE IN ESCALATING ROMANTIC RELATIONSHIPS Researchers have examined how relationship stage affects the times when people are most likely to avoid certain topics. The assumption for a long time was that people most avoided disclosure in the beginning stages of dating relationships, when intimacy was still somewhat low and topics were considered sensitive. Knobloch and Carpenter-Theune (2004), however, found that the most avoidance in dating relationships usually occurs in the middle stages of development, when intimacy is moderate. Their rationale is that people are most likely to fear that discussing a topic will harm the relationship, make them look bad, or have other

negative consequences when a relationship is shifting from casual to serious. They also reasoned that this transition time is accompanied by increased uncertainty about the relationship and how one's partner might react to certain disclosures. Their findings supported these predictions: People who reported moderate levels of intimacy were the most uncertain about their relationships and also the most likely to avoid topics with their partner.

TOPIC AVOIDANCE DURING FAMILY TRANSITIONS Studies of family communication have also shown times in the parent–child relationship when avoidance is particularly high. Not surprisingly, young people are most likely to avoid topics with their parents during their middle teenage years (Guerrero & Afifi, 1995b). Mid-adolescence is a time when teens try to separate themselves from their parents, and keeping information private from parents is an important way for teens to develop a unique sense of self. Less avoidance occurs when children go to college or leave their parent's home. Another time when avoidance is high is during and shortly after a divorce. Studies have found that children from divorced families are more likely to avoid issues with their parents than are those from intact families, especially if the child feels caught between loyalties to each of the parents. A common reaction in these cases is for the child to shut down and avoid expressing feelings so as not to betray either parent (Afifi, 2003; Afifi & Schrodt, 2003; Golish & Caughlin, 2002).

Consequences of Topic Avoidance

Avoidance is common, but what about the consequences of avoidance? Can avoidance have positive consequences for individuals and relationships? As mentioned earlier in the chapter, some scholars say yes (Altman, Vinsel, & Brown, 1981; see also dialectics theory, Chapter 5), but most researchers still find that avoidance is a symptom of an unsatisfying relationship. For example, Dailey and Palomares (2004) studied three different relationship types—(1) dating relationships, (2) mother–child relationships, and (3) father–child relationships—and found lower satisfaction across all three relationships when individuals avoided discussing their concerns about the relationship with their partner. Importantly, though, avoidance on another topic—personal failures—was not associated with lower satisfaction. Therefore, one possibility is that avoidance is harmful to relationships only when it is about issues that are directly relevant to the relationship itself. The conclusion here would be that avoidance about relationally relevant issues harms the relationship while avoidance of non-relationally relevant issues has little effect. However, in complete contrast to that prediction, Caughlin and Afifi (2004) found that people who avoided a topic in order to protect their relationship tended not to experience negative consequences.

One explanation for these seemingly contradictory findings may lie in Afifi and Joseph's (2009) **standards for openness hypothesis**. This hypothesis extends earlier work (Caughlin & Golish, 2002) showing that people's perceptions of how much their partner is avoiding influences satisfaction more than a partner's actual avoidance. In this most recent explanation, Afifi and Joseph (2009) argued that the perception of a partner's avoidance is harmful to relationship satisfaction to the extent that it comes across as a sign of a bad relationship. In other words, if people associate openness with having a good relationship, they will think there is a problem if they perceive their partner to be less than open. Since women often have higher expectations of openness in relationships than men, and are often more attuned to shifts in their partner's openness, women are more likely to become dissatisfied in the face of perceived partner avoidance than men. Thus, women may be more likely than men to perceive topic avoidance and to experience negative relationship consequences associated with topic avoidance. The effects for topic avoidance hold both similarities and differences to those found for secret keeping.

Consequences of Secret Keeping

Secret keeping can have positive or negative consequences. Sharing a secret can communicate trust and show that a relationship is close. On the other hand, having a secret kept from you can make you feel left out. Thus, there are both negative and positive consequences involved in secret keeping—with complexities related to various relationship contexts.

NEGATIVE CONSEQUENCES OF SECRET KEEPING

Research on the effects of secret keeping on individuals has focused on how keeping information secret influences people's thought patterns through a process called **hyperaccessibility** (Wegner, 1989, 1992; Wegner & Erber, 1992; Wegner, Lane, & Dimitri, 1994). Because secrets require people to avoid disclosing information to others, people often try to suppress the information and thoughts related to that secret. The reasoning here is that if people suppress thoughts about a secret, they will be less likely to disclose secret information because it will not be "on their minds." However, thought suppression is not usually successful and can even backfire. The strong impact of thought suppression can be illustrated by a simple example. Here it goes: *Do not think of dancing elephants.* Now that you have been asked not to think about dancing elephants, you will probably have dancing elephants on your mind as you read this section. The simple request for people to suppress a thought about a particular thing, regardless of how innocent the request or how irrelevant the thing, has been shown to increase their thinking about it. In fact, that information is often all they can think about. So no matter what, please don't imagine dancing elephants as you read on.

In their study of thought suppression, Wegner, Schneider, Carter, and White (1987) asked students not to think of a white bear and then had them ring a bell every time they thought of the bear. Rather than suppress the thought of the white bear, the students, on average, thought of the bear more than once per minute over a 5-minute period. Several subsequent studies have confirmed that the desire to suppress a thought does the exact opposite, bringing it to the forefront of our thoughts and thus making it *hyperaccessible.*

But is this hyperaccessibility permanent? Don't those thoughts eventually fade? According to Wegner and associates (1987), the hyperaccessibility of the suppressed thought decreases over time if one removes oneself from contact with the relevant information or secret. This scenario can be applied to Camila's situation. Children who were sexually abused may eventually stop thinking about the "secret" if they are separated long enough from the abusing adult, but the thoughts will come flooding back as soon as the possibility of seeing that adult surfaces. Since Camila's uncle is dead, seeing Sara, who went through a similar experience, or her aunt, who was married to the abuser but likely did not know of his actions, may trigger terrible memories. This triggering of thoughts that are normally suppressed is called the **rebound effect.** The rebound effect may also make it difficult for people to keep other secrets, such as infidelity. In this case, the unfaithful person may be away from the partner or lover at work long enough to successfully suppress the thought of infidelity, but seeing the partner or lover will immediately serve as a reminder of the thought being attempted to suppress. The hyperaccessibility of the thought will make it difficult for the unfaithful person to keep the infidelity a secret and is likely to result in more guilt about the affair or more anxiety about being caught.

The **fever model of self-disclosure** (Stiles, 1987; Stiles, Shuster, & Harrigan, 1992) can explain these effects. According to this model, people who are distressed about a problem or who think about a problem a lot are much more likely to reveal thoughts and feelings about the problem than are those who are not experiencing anxiety about an issue. If given the opportunity, people who are feeling highly anxious about something are likely to disclose more about it than people who are not. This model, when combined with Wegner's research on the hyperaccessibility of secrets, may explain why people so often reveal secrets to others. Their hyperaccessibility

(especially during times when the secret information is "rebounding") makes the level of stress and anxiety so high that individuals have to find an outlet. The result frequently is the selection of someone they consider to be a confidant.

Afifi and Caughlin's (2006) research has shown another consequence of the secret keeping and rumination mix. At two points in time, they asked students about a secret they were keeping from a friend or dating partner and found secret keeping was harmful for self-esteem. Although it was the first study to show this link, the association makes sense, especially for individually held secrets, in which the information being concealed is often something that people regret and something that makes them question themselves. Given the negative impact that low self-esteem has on individuals and relationships, the fact that secret keeping promotes rumination about a negative aspect of self may be one of its most damaging consequences.

The maintenance of secrets has been shown to have additional negative consequences. First, keeping secrets negatively impacts the quality of interactions with the person from whom the secret is being kept (e.g., Brown-Smith, 1998). Knowing that you have to keep a secret from someone can lead to awkwardness. Or you might just avoid the person so that there is no chance the secret can slip out. Second, secrets encourage concealment of relational problems and can lead to deception. Hiding a secret from others requires the secret keepers to put on an "air" that everything is fine and that the secret keepers share a happy relationship. This pretense can cause personal and relational stress (Karpel, 1980). For example, growing up, Camila may have had to act as if she didn't fear her uncle when the extended family got together. Concealing her feelings likely added even more stress to her life. On some occasions, she may have decided to pretend she was sick so she wouldn't have to see her uncle. Sometimes the maintenance of secrets results in the spinning of lies to cover up the information. The consequence is often a web of deception that must be continuously tended. If discovered, the deception is often considered a serious relational transgression that erodes trust (see Chapter 13). Yet, in some cases, such as Camila's, uncovering a secret can be the first step toward recovering from a traumatic event. Khaled and her parents would likely understand why she kept the information secret and help her deal with the scars left from the sexual and emotional abuse.

In addition to stress, suppressing information can lead to depression, delinquency, aggression, and low self-esteem, as shown in a study of 10- to 14-year-olds from the Netherlands who were keeping secrets from their parents (Frinjs, Finkenauer, Vermulst, & Engels, 2005). Family-held secrets can also create power imbalances. Given that knowledge often is equated with power, family members who know the secrets have power over those who do not (Imber-Black, 1993). When children know secret information about their parents, the typical power structure in families is sometimes irreversibly altered, changing the family dynamics forever (Brown-Smith, 1998). For example, imagine a child

knowing about a parent's adulterous affair and holding that parent hostage with the information. Any disciplinary power that the parent has over that child is undermined by the fear that the secret will be disclosed.

The power structure of families has been studied to better understand to whom children are likely to disclose individual secrets (see Chapter 12). Afifi, Olson, and Armstrong (2005) found that children were least likely to disclose secrets to the parent whom they saw as having the greatest punitive power. So while holding a parent's secret may decrease the parent's power, children who hold individual secrets are especially likely to fear repercussions from powerful family members and, as such, continue concealment from those people.

Another possible consequence of family secrets is the development of what Karpel (1980) called a **split loyalty pattern.** Secret keepers are often put in a bind of having to choose between being loyal to other secret holders or being loyal to friends or family members who may be hurt by not knowing the secret. Camila is caught in this bind. She feels guilty about not telling Khaled, but she also worries that telling Khaled would betray her sister. Split loyalties create lose-lose situations, ruin relational dynamics, tear families apart, and destroy friendships.

Source: ©iStockphoto.com/cthoman

Are you still thinking of dancing elephants?

DigitalVision/DigitalVision/Thinkstock

Secrets can serve a bonding function. Even young children feel privileged and special when someone shares a secret with them.

Discussing the situation with Sara and telling her she wants Khaled to know may be Camila's best option. If Sara objects, she might suggest telling Khaled about her own experiences without disclosing what Sara went through.

POSITIVE CONSEQUENCES OF SECRET KEEPING
Although most of the research suggests that keeping secrets has negative consequences, there are cases when secret keeping has positive consequences. Although some studies have shown it is harmful for early adolescents to keep secrets from their parents, other studies have found secret keeping beneficial in middle adolescence. Specifically, 14- to 18-year-olds are usually in the midst of developing their own identities. As discussed in research on avoidance, an important developmental event is the ability of children this age to form their own identities separate from their parents. Keeping secrets seems to perform that function, and as such, some types of secret keeping may be developmentally advantageous for children at this stage (Finkenauer, Engels, & Meeus, 2002).

Another way that secret keeping may be beneficial is that it sometimes increases cohesion among holders of the secret. Secrets kept by a whole family, spouses, dating partners, friends, or members of a group may bring the secret holders closer together because of the bond of trust they share. Research by Vangelisti (1994a) and Vangelisti and Caughlin (1997) supports this conclusion. Students in these studies reported that the existence of whole family secrets often improved relationships, perhaps by creating a special bond between members who were trusted to keep secrets. Thus, secret keeping can sometimes be beneficial rather than harmful to relationships.

Consequences of Revealing Secrets

There are no doubt various consequences of keeping a secret, but what are the consequences of revelation? Derlega and Grzelak (1979) noted five reasons why people eventually reveal private information: (1) to achieve catharsis, (2) to clarify their own interpretation of events, (3) to get validation from others that they are still a good person, (4) to make the relationship closer, or (5) to control others. Each of these reasons has different consequences—positive and negative.

POSITIVE CONSEQUENCES OF REVEALING SECRETS Although it is impossible to say with certainty when someone should or should not disclose a secret, Kelly and McKillop (1996) made several recommendations for when to do so. Their research led them to identify three reasons people might want to consider revealing secrets; these include if revealing the secret (1) reduces psychological or physical problems, (2) helps deter hyperaccessibility, or (3) leads to resolution of secrets. First, there is considerable evidence that secret keeping is stressful and wears on secret keepers psychologically and physiologically (see Pennebaker, 1990). Spiegel (1992) has found that individuals with life-threatening illnesses who reveal private information in therapy sessions have a longer life expectancy than those who do not. Pennebaker's research on social support also suggests that the mere act of disclosing distressful information makes people feel better.

Second, as noted previously, keeping information secret makes secrets salient. As Wegner and colleagues (1994) put it, "The secret must be remembered, or it might be told. And the secret cannot be thought about, or it might be leaked" (p. 288), thus creating the two conflicting cognitive processes discussed earlier. Disclosing the secret frees the secret keeper from having to suppress it and makes it no longer hyperaccessible, thereby decreasing anxiety.

Third, without disclosing the secret, secret keepers cannot work toward a resolution of issues underlying the secret. Sharing the information may provide the individual with insight into the secret and allow a much-needed regained sense of control over life events (see Pennebaker, 1990). The secret keeper often has an unbalanced view of the situation and may benefit from the perspective of the recipient of the disclosure. Silver, Boone, and Stones (1983) found that female victims of incest who were able to reveal the secret to a confidant were much more likely to feel better about themselves and their lives than those who were unable to do so. Afifi and Caughlin (2006) showed that those who revealed their secret across an 8-week period experienced a significant increase in self-esteem. It is also worth noting that Caughlin and others (2005) found that those who revealed secrets often reported partner reactions that were less negative than they had originally feared. So one benefit of disclosing may be that one gains the advantages of catharsis and resolution without the feared destruction of the relationship.

NEGATIVE CONSEQUENCES OF REVEALING SECRETS These positive consequences of revealing a secret should be weighed against the possible negative consequences. Specifically, three considerations can be assessed: Kelly and McKillop (1996) suggested that people might consider keeping a secret if revelation would (1) elicit a negative reaction from the listener or (2) help a person maintain a privacy boundary; Petronio (1991) suggested that people might decide to keep secrets if revealing private information would (3) be seen as a betrayal by others.

First, given the typically negative nature of secrets, there is always a possibility that the recipient of the information will react with disapproval or shun the discloser. In fact, Lazarus (1985) reported that confidants often distance themselves following the disclosure of a negative secret. Coates, Wortman, and Abbey (1979) showed that people who disclose secret problems to others are considered less attractive than those who suppress such disclosure. When people have kept negative information to themselves as a way to manage their identities, they are especially likely to put stock in the listener's reaction when they finally reveal the secret. Disconfirming reactions may worsen what is likely an already diminished sense of self.

Work on disclosure of abuse demonstrates this point especially well. Dieckman (2000) interviewed female victims about their decision to tell others about their abuse. Her interviews highlighted the difficulty associated with disclosure and the importance of the response. Victims of abuse often hesitate to tell others about their experience because they fear being perceived as "weak" or being ridiculed for staying in the relationship. Indeed, Crocker and Schwartz (1985) found that many people responded to disclosures of abuse by telling the discloser that they "would never put up with that kind of treatment" and asking them why they didn't "just leave." Since victims typically disclose past abuse for the purpose of self-expression or validation, responses like those can diminish the discloser's ability to cope with the situation. Rather than helping disclosers, such responses often lower their self-esteem and discourage future disclosure. Their already low sense of self falls even lower because the response they feared the most—ridicule—is the response they received. Worse yet, the discloser might decide to keep the information secret once again, rather than risking more ridicule. As this example illustrates, the listener's response to sensitive self-disclosure is of paramount importance.

Second, preserving personal boundaries is critical to people's identities, as conveyed in the communication boundary management theory discussed in this chapter. To the extent that secrets make up part of the personal boundaries of individuals, secret keeping may help people maintain a sense of independence. Some scholars have even argued that secret keeping serves a developmental function by helping people manage their personal identity (Hoyt, 1978). By contrast, revealing the secret erodes the personal boundaries being tightly held by the secret keeper. In a related vein, keeping secrets greatly increases a person's control over the information. By contrast, the decision to disclose a secret requires boundary coordination and leaves the individual vulnerable to betrayal of confidences. The information is no longer solely the person's own, and the individual has less control over how the information is spread.

Third, sometimes secrets are shared between two or more people, and revealing the secret to someone outside the dyad or group will be seen as a betrayal. Indeed, research reported in Chapter 13 suggests that betraying confidences is one of the most common relational transgressions in friendships, romantic relationships, and family relationships. If a confidence has been betrayed, revealing a secret often has a significant cost. Trust is eroded, and future self-disclosures from the person who feels betrayed are less likely. As such, another negative consequence of revealing secrets may be severe sanctions by other secret keepers. To ensure that a member of a group of secret keepers is not tempted to disclose the secret, groups will often make explicit boundary rules or threaten individuals with severe penalties for revealing the secret (Petronio, 1991).

The diversity of potential positive and negative consequences makes it difficult to determine when to disclose a secret and when not to do so. Kelly and McKillop (1996) developed a decision-making model for revealing secrets that takes into account the primary consequences associated with the revelation of individually held secrets; Figure 6.3 shows the model. In a similar vein, Petronio (1991) noted that the answers to five questions typically determine what people will disclose and to whom they will disclose it: (1) How badly do you need to reveal the information? (2) What do you think will be the outcome of the disclosure? (3) How risky will it be to tell someone the information? (4) How private is the information? and (5) How much control do you have over your emotions? These questions reflect a variety of issues raised in this chapter, as well as capturing the essence of Kelly and McKillop's model. Clearly, then, issues of anxiety, hyperaccessibility, and informational control play a key role in determining whether the revelation of secrets is likely to produce positive or negative outcomes.

FIGURE 6.3 ■ Decision-Making Model for Revealing Secrets

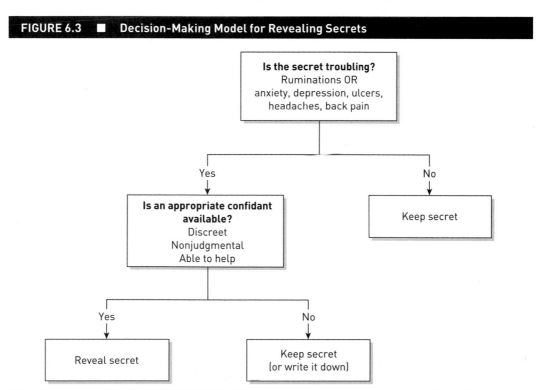

Source: From Kelly, A. E., & McKillop, K. G., Consequences of revealing personal secrets, in *Psychological Bulletin, 120.* Copyright © 1996, the American Psychological Association. Reprinted with permission.

SUMMARY AND APPLICATION

People have an innate need to express themselves to others. Yet they have an equally strong need to keep certain aspects of themselves private. This chapter examined types of communication that help people fulfill both of these needs, starting with self-disclosure. Although people can learn things about others by observing their reactions and assessing their appearance, one of the best ways to get to know someone is through self-disclosure. Self-disclosure occurs when people reveal something about themselves to others, usually through verbal communication. Most close relationships, such as the one shared by Khaled and Camila, are developed primarily through the exchange of self-disclosure. As relationships develop, the amount of breadth, and then depth, increases as people feel closer to one another. Self-disclosure also varies in terms of frequency, duration, valence, and veracity.

In relationships like Khaled and Camila's, self-disclosure leads to more liking and closeness. However, not all self-disclosure is equal in terms of its ability to foster a closer, more satisfying relationship. Self-disclosure needs to be gradual and appropriate given the context of a relationship. When disclosure is too personal or occurs too early in a relationship, negative reactions can follow. Disclosure is also more likely to lead to liking when it is perceived to be personalistic rather than indiscriminant, and when it is reciprocated. Some research also suggests that the link between self-disclosure and liking is intensified when people communicate online rather than in person. In some cases, instead of leading to increased liking and closeness, self-disclosure leads to criticism, retaliation, loss of control, or a loss of individuality. Indeed, one of the paradoxes of self-disclosure is that by revealing ourselves to others we open the possibility of getting close to others, but we also open ourselves up to rejection. People who are not skilled at communication may prefer to self-disclose online where the risks are smaller.

Even in the best of relationships, people want privacy at times, as CPM theory suggests. For example, Camila and her sister, Sara, feel that they "own" the information about the abuse they experienced as children. Therefore, it is important that they are able to construct boundaries to protect that information and control whom has access to it. Privacy can be maintained a number of different ways, including by engaging in topic avoidance and keeping secrets. Commonly avoided topics include finances, drug use, personal failures, topics that emphasize differences between people, and sexual history. People have different motivations for avoiding topics and keeping secrets. Understanding what those motivations are may be the first step in deciding whether or not to reveal information.

For instance, Camila might realize that when she was a child she avoided talking about the sexual abuse she suffered because she was afraid of her uncle and was deeply ashamed. Even after her uncle died, she continued to feel that she was somehow responsible for the abuse or that she should have at least stopped her uncle from harming her sister. When she digs deep, she might also realize that she is afraid to tell Khaled. She doesn't think he will judge her, but she can't be 100% sure he won't, and she feels as guilty about having that suspicion as she does about not telling him. Eventually Camila may understand that she was an innocent victim. She may also recognize that now her main motivation for keeping the abuse a secret is that she does not want to re-live the emotional pain, not that she thinks Khaled will judge her. Through these types of realizations, Camila may come to believe that she can share her secret with Khaled, and that he will support her through the emotional pain and help her heal old wounds. However, if Camila decides to keep this information a secret, it is her right to do so.

The research in this chapter also provides other helpful information about when to reveal a secret.

When people are feeling high levels of uncertainty and ruminating about a secret all the time, they might consider telling their secret to someone to relieve their stress. People also decide whether or not to reveal a secret based on how supportive and nonjudgmental they think the listener will be. Ultimately, this might be what leads Camila to reveal her secret to Khaled—she knows he loves her and she can trust him. If she thought otherwise, she'd be more likely to keep the information private. After sharing her secret, positive consequences could follow. Camila may feel less stress and guilt, her self-esteem may be bolstered because of Khaled's supportive response, and their relationship may be closer because they now know they can truly trust each other even with their darkest secrets.

As Camila's predicament illustrates, the tug-of-war between the forces of disclosure and privacy can wage in even the closest of relationships. In fact, the process of negotiating privacy boundaries can be especially delicate and complex when our relationships are particularly close. This is because many people subscribe to an ideology of intimacy (Parks, 1982). In other words, many people think that openness is the hallmark of close relationships and that any attempts to maintain privacy will hinder the development and maintenance of intimacy. Camila probably felt this way since she experienced guilt about not revealing information about her past to Khaled. The research in this chapter, however, suggests that it is normal and healthy to erect privacy boundaries. Individuals need privacy as well as connection. Relational partners who are always together and constantly sharing every bit of information with each other may lose their individual identities and become engulfed by the relationship. Thus, the hallmark of satisfying relationships may actually be the maintenance of individual identities in the midst of a close, connected relationship.

KEY TERMS

authorized co-owners (p. 150)

boundary structures (p. 149)

boundary turbulence (p. 151)

breadth (p. 140)

communication inefficacy (p. 158)

communication privacy management (CPM) (p. 149)

confrontation (p. 149)

depth (p. 140)

disclosure-liking hypothesis (p. 144)

duration (p. 140)

dyadic effect (p. 146)

fever model of self-disclosure (p. 161)

futility of discussion (p. 158)

frequency (p. 140)

hyperaccessibility (p. 160)

identity management (p. 157)

individual secrets (p. 156)

intensification effect (p. 145)

intrafamily secrets (p. 156)

liking-disclosure hypothesis (p. 144)

nondirected disclosure (p. 145)

partner unresponsiveness (p. 157)

personalistic disclosure (p. 145)

privacy control (p. 149)

privacy maintenance (p. 152)

privacy ownership (p. 149)

privacy turbulence (p. 149)

rebound effect (p. 161)

relationship de-escalation (p. 157)

relationship protection (p. 156)

self-disclosure (p. 140)

social penetration theory (p. 140)

split loyalty pattern (p. 162)

standards for openness hypothesis (p. 160)

topic avoidance (p. 140)

valence (p. 140)

veracity (p. 140)

whole-family secrets (p. 156)

DISCUSSION QUESTIONS

1. This chapter includes a discussion of some of the conditions that make it more or less likely that self-disclosure will lead to liking and relational closeness. Which of these conditions do you think are most important, and why? Do you agree that people tend to disclose more online than in face-to-face contexts? Why or why not?

2. In this chapter, we discussed several studies suggesting that most close relational partners consider certain topics to be "taboo" and keep certain secrets from each other. Based on your personal experiences, do you agree or disagree? What types of topics are taboo in your relationships?

3. How hard is it for you to keep a secret? Do you agree with the idea that attempts to suppress thoughts about a secret actually make it harder to keep the secret?

 SAGE edge™

Sharpen your skills with SAGE edge at edge.sagepub.com/guerrero5e.
SAGE edge for students provides a personalized approach to help you accomplish your coursework goals in an easy-to-use learning environment.

7 COMMUNICATING CLOSENESS
Affection, Immediacy, and Social Support

Luke treasures his close relationships. Aside from his family, there are two people he feels especially close to—his girlfriend, Macie, and his best friend, Dan. When they are together, Macie brightens Luke's day. They spend a lot of time together talking, touching, comforting, and listening to one another. Best of all, he can tell Macie anything, and she listens and supports him. If he is sad or upset, she has a way of cheering him up, and she always seems to make him feel good about himself. Luke's connection with Dan is different but nonetheless special. They have a long history together. In high school, they were teammates on the track and football teams, and in college, they were both on their university's debate team. Today they take ski trips and run together, and they have great conversations about everything—business, sports, politics, and life in general. Unlike with his other male friends, Luke can talk to Dan about anything, even Macie. They are like brothers.

As Luke's relationships with Macie and Dan illustrate, close relationships come in many forms. People have close relationships with family members, friends, and romantic partners. All of these relationships play vital roles in people's lives. As Andersen and Guerrero (1998a) put it, "The brightest side of life's experience often occurs in close . . . relationships during the exchange of warm, involving, immediate messages" (p. 303).

Communication helps people develop and sustain feelings of closeness. Communication also reflects the unique qualities associated with people's closest relationships. For example, although Luke's close relationships with Macie and Dan both play vital roles in his life, these two relationships also differ in important ways.

If Luke kept a diary of the behaviors that he used to communicate closeness to Dan and Macie, what types of behaviors would likely be similar and different across these two relationships? What behaviors might be more characteristic of his best friendship with Dan? Which might be reserved for his romantic relationship with Macie?

To answer these and other questions, this chapter focuses on three specific types of communication that help foster and sustain closeness in relationships—(1) **affectionate communication,** (2) immediacy, and (3) social support. First, definitions of different types of closeness are provided. Next, theory and research on affectionate communication, immediacy, and social support is reviewed.

Together, the research in these three areas paints a picture of how people develop and reinforce feelings of closeness and connection in their relationships.

CLOSENESS IN RELATIONSHIPS

What makes relationships like the ones Luke shares with Dan and Macie so special? It is the level of closeness that sets these relationships apart. Closeness is a multifaceted concept that has different meanings. Sometimes the term *close,* or *closeness,* refers to spatial proximity (e.g., living near or standing next to someone). Other times closeness refers to the type of relationship people share or the way people feel about each other. Researchers have tried to distinguish between various types of closeness, including physical, emotional, and **relational closeness.**

Physical Closeness

Physical closeness refers to the amount of spatial proximity and physical contact people have. Engaging in behaviors such as touching, sitting next to each other, and putting one's head on another's shoulder all indicate physical closeness. Spending time with someone, even if it is just sitting in a car together listening to the radio or being reunited at the end of the day, contributes to physical closeness. For example, in a study on closeness in married couples, one of the wives said that she "felt that closeness when he [her husband] came back early from work, unexpectedly, and we spent the whole evening together, just the two of us" (Ben-Ari & Lavee, 2007, p. 634). In some relationships, sexual interaction is another common form of physical closeness. However, even in marital relationships, sexual interaction does not appear to be as central to the concept of closeness as affectionate communication (Ben-Ari & Lavee, 2007).

Emotional Closeness

Emotional closeness has been defined as having a sense of shared experiences, trust, enjoyment, concern, and caring in a relationship (Lee, Mancini,

& Maxwell, 1990). Sharing and caring are fundamental to both the experience and the expression of emotional closeness. In Ben-Ari and Lavee's (2007) study of married couples, "Sharing thoughts, experiences, and feelings appeared both as a conception of closeness ('closeness *is* wanting to share with her') and an expression of it ('*when we are close* we have deep conservations')" (p. 633). Caring involves showing concern and providing support for another. Sharing involves the reciprocal disclosure of intimate information. Studies have shown that high levels of self-disclosure and social support characterize close friendships (Feeney, 1999; Parks & Floyd, 1996).

Relational Closeness

Relational closeness is the interdependence people share (Kelley et al., 1983). Interdependent partners exchange resources; influence one another's thoughts, behaviors, and emotions; and meet each other's needs. Especially strong, enduring, and diverse levels of interdependence characterize close relationships (Kelley et al., 1983). For example, Luke and Macie might discuss major life decisions together, learn valuable life lessons from each other, and become emotionally attached to one another's families. In these ways, and more, they have become interdependent. Some scholars have also conceptualized closeness in terms of the degree to which two individuals overlap (Aron & Aron, 1986; Aron, Mashek, & Aron, 2004; see also Chapter 2). In these studies, a circle represents each person. The degree to which two people's circles overlap then indicates their level of closeness. As is the case with emotional closeness, relational closeness is associated with caregiving and social support. Interdependent individuals rely on each other; what matters to one person matters to the other person.

Communicating Closeness

Communication is also an integral part of closeness (Andersen, Guerrero, & Jones, 2006). Ben-Ari and Lavee (2007) asked married couples to describe what closeness meant to them. The participants in this study often mentioned communication. For example, Michael, a 43-year-old man who had been married for 13 years, described closeness this way:

> I had a busy day with meetings one after the other all day long, I knew I would come home late in the evening. I had a small break between meetings in the middle of the day so I rushed home, gave her a big hug, a kiss, and I brought her a flower. . . . For me, this is closeness. (Ben-Ari & Lavee, 2007, p. 627)

As Michael's response suggests, many forms of physical closeness, such as hugs and rushing home to be with someone, reflect emotional or relational closeness. These three forms of closeness overlap even though they each have their distinct qualities. For example, you can be emotionally close without being physically close. Some of the couples in Ben-Ari and Lavee's (2007) study made this point; one wife said that "being emotionally close to her husband did not mean that she needed to be around him physically" (pp. 634–636). There are also important distinctions between emotional closeness, which is rooted more in feelings, and relational closeness, which is rooted more in behavioral patterns that foster interdependence.

Closeness is reflected in three specific types of communication: affectionate communication, immediacy behavior, and social support (Andersen & Guerrero, 1998a; Rittenour, Myers, & Brann, 2007; Weigel & Ballard-Reisch, 2002). These three types of communication each highlight a different aspect of closeness. Work on affectionate communication focuses on how people portray feelings of fondness and positive regard to one another. Research on immediacy examines behavior that increases both physical and emotional closeness. Finally, the literature on social support emphasizes concern and caring. All three areas of research show that communication is vital in creating and sustaining close relationships.

AFFECTIONATE COMMUNICATION

Affection is both a need and an emotion (Pendell, 2002). As noted in Chapter 1, affection is a basic human need. People want to feel accepted and cared for by others. This need for affection is met through interpersonal interaction and forging mutually supportive relationships (Prager & Buhrmester, 1998; Rubin & Martin, 1998). As an emotion, affection is rooted in feelings of fondness, caring, and positive regard that have developed for someone over time (Floyd & Morman, 1998).

Affectionate communication is behavior that portrays feelings of fondness and positive regard to another (Floyd, 2006). Affection and affectionate communication occur in a wide variety of close relationships, including those between friends, family members, and romantic partners (Floyd & Ray, 2003; Pendell, 2002; Salt, 1991). Affectionate communication is a key to establishing relationships and keeping them close. In fact, affectionate communication often acts as a "critical incident" that facilitates the establishment of close relationships (King & Christensen, 1983; Owen, 1987). The absence of affectionate communication, conversely, can reflect decreased emotional closeness and propel a relationship toward de-escalation (Owen, 1987). Floyd (2006) also noted that there is a **paradox of affection** because "although affection is often intended and usually perceived by others to be a positive communicative move, it can backfire for a number of reasons and produce negative outcomes" such as distress and relationship dissolution (p. 2). For instance, showing affection too early in a relationship can scare potential friends and romantic partners away.

Affection Exchange Theory

To better understand how affectionate communication functions in various relationships, Floyd (2001, 2002, 2006) developed **affection exchange theory**. This theory is based on the idea that affectionate communication is a biologically adaptive behavior that evolved because it helps people provide and obtain valuable resources necessary for survival.

Thus, the theory draws on Darwin's (1872/1998) principle of selective fitness, which specifies that people who adapt best to their environment have the best chance to survive, procreate, and pass their genes on to the next generation. Pendell (2002) expressed a similar belief about the adaptive value of affection, stating that "intimate relationships, pair bonding, and affection are basic human biological adaptations evolved for the purpose of reproduction and protecting the young" (p. 91).

PRINCIPLES OF AFFECTION EXCHANGE THEORY Affection exchange theory contains three overarching principles that illuminate how affectionate communication is adaptive. First, affectionate communication is theorized to facilitate survival because it helps people develop and maintain relationships that provide them with important resources. For example, centuries ago, humans fared better if they had people to help feed them and protect them if attacked. Today, resources gained from one's social network, such as having a friend help with homework or a parent finance one's education, are helpful for surviving daily life as well as gaining the resources necessary to attract potential mates.

Second, people who display affectionate communication are more likely to be perceived as having the skills necessary to be a good parent, thereby increasing their ability to attract potential mates and have reproductive opportunities. As noted in Chapter 3, people are generally attracted to those who are warm and caring. When looking for a long-term romantic partner, both men and women usually want someone who they believe will be a nurturing and responsible parent for any children they might have.

Third, people are motivated to show affection to people who serve at least one of two basic evolutionary needs—(1) **viability** and (2) fertility (Floyd & Morr, 2003). Viability relates to the motivation to survive, whereas fertility relates to the motivation to procreate and pass on one's genes. At an unconscious level, these needs motivate people to show affection to those with whom they share a genetic or sexual relationship. For example, parents are motivated to show affection to their children because "the

benefits associated with receiving affection make the children more suitable as mates, thereby increasing the chances that the children will themselves reproduce and pass on their genes to yet a new generation" (Floyd & Morman, 2001, p. 312). People who grew up in affectionate families are also more likely to be affectionate adults who develop emotionally close relationships with their own spouse and children. People are also motivated to show affection to nieces, nephews, siblings, and cousins who share their genetic material. Thus, the goal is not necessarily to reproduce oneself but rather to pass on one's genes either directly or indirectly through one's relatives (Hamilton, 1964). Finally, people are motivated to show affection to sexual partners who can help them achieve the goal of procreation. Of course, people can also receive valuable resources from their broader social networks, which include friends, in-laws, and acquaintances, but according to affection exchange theory, the motivation to exhibit affectionate behavior is strongest in relationships that have the most potential to fulfill viability or fertility needs.

BENEFITS OF GIVING AND RECEIVING AFFECTION In affection exchange theory, affectionate communication is cast as a valuable resource that is essential for survival and procreation. One reason affectionate communication helps people survive and attract others is because giving and receiving affection is related to better mental and physical health. In fact, people who regularly receive affection are advantaged in almost every way compared to people who receive little affection; they are happier, more self-confident, less stressed, less likely to be depressed, more likely to engage in social activity, and in better general mental health (Floyd, 2002). Giving affection has similar benefits. People who readily show affection to others report more happiness, higher self-esteem, less fear of intimacy, less susceptibility to depression, and greater relational satisfaction (Floyd et al., 2005).

A substantial body of research also provides compelling evidence that giving and receiving affection is associated with better physical health.

Floyd and his colleagues (2005) demonstrated a physiological link between affection and bodily changes. When people gave or received affection, adrenal hormones associated with stress tended to decrease, while oxytocin (OT) (a hormone associated with positive moods and behaviors) tended to increase (Floyd, 2006). Other health benefits of affection include lower resting blood pressure, lower blood sugar (Floyd, Hesse, & Haynes, 2007), lower heart rate, a less exaggerated hormonal response to stress (Floyd, Mikkelson, Tafoya, et al., 2007), and healthier changes in cortisol levels (Floyd & Riforgiate, 2008). In one study, people in married or cohabiting relationships were either given instructions to kiss more over a 6-week period or were given no instructions about how to behave. Those who were told to kiss more reported less stress, more relational satisfaction, and healthier levels of cholesterol at the end of the study (Floyd et al., 2009). Even writing about the affection that one feels toward close friends, relatives, and romantic partners reduces cholesterol levels (Floyd, Mikkelson, Hesse, & Pauley, 2007). To see how affectionate you are, take the test in Box 7.1. People who score higher on the affectionate communication index tend to possess better mental and physical health, even after controlling for the amount of affection received from others.

BOX 7.1 PUT YOURSELF TO THE TEST
THE AFFECTIONATE COMMUNICATION INDEX

Circle the number that represents how much you agree with how each statement describes you. Answer the questions using the following scale: 1 = you strongly disagree and 7 = you strongly agree.

	Strongly Disagree					Strongly Agree	
1. I consider myself to be a very affectionate person.	1	2	3	4	5	6	7
2. I am always telling my loved ones how much I care about them.	1	2	3	4	5	6	7
3. When I feel affection for someone, I usually express it.	1	2	3	4	5	6	7
4. I have a hard time telling people that I love them or care about them.	1	2	3	4	5	6	7
5. I'm not very good at expressing affection.	1	2	3	4	5	6	7
6. I am not a very affectionate person.	1	2	3	4	5	6	7
7. I love giving people hugs or putting my arms around them.	1	2	3	4	5	6	7
8. I don't tend to express affection to other people very much.	1	2	3	4	5	6	7
9. Anyone who knows me well would say that I'm pretty affectionate.	1	2	3	4	5	6	7
10. Expressing affection to other people makes me uncomfortable.	1	2	3	4	5	6	7

To calculate your score: First, give yourself 30 points. Second, add up your responses to questions 1, 2, 3, 7, and 9 and put the total on the first line below. Third, add up your responses to questions 4, 5, 6, 8, and 10 and put the total on the second line below. A score at or close to 0 means that you are highly unaffectionate; a score at or close to 60 means that you are highly affectionate.

My score: 30 plus _____ minus _____ = _____

                              (line 1)   (line 2)

Communicating Affection

There are numerous ways to communicate affection (Pendell, 2002). Floyd and Morman (1998), however, argued that it is useful to categorize affectionate communication into one of three categories: (1) direct verbal behavior, (2) direct nonverbal behavior, or (3) indirect nonverbal behavior. The types of affectionate communication that fall under each category differ in terms of how they are encoded and decoded.

DIRECT AND VERBAL AFFECTIONATE COMMU-NICATION Many verbal behaviors, such as saying "I care about you" or leaving a sticky note that says "I love you," are direct ways of communicating affection. People usually encode direct and verbal expressions of affection with the intent of communicating affection to someone, and others easily decode these messages as clear and unambiguous expressions of affection. Verbal statements of affection are also usually more precise than nonverbal expressions. As Floyd (2006) put it, "There is an enormous qualitative difference between saying 'I like you' and 'I'm in love with you,' a distinction that may not be conveyed quite as accurately through nonverbal behaviors" (p. 32). Of course, words are not always completely unambiguous. The statement "I love you" could mean "I love you as a friend" or "I love you as a potential romantic partner," and it could be seen as sincere or insincere, thoughtful or rash. Nonetheless, verbal statements provide people with a channel for communicating affection in a relatively direct and precise manner.

Several types of verbal behavior communicate affection, including self-disclosure, **direct emotional expressions,** compliments and praise, and **assurances** (Pendell, 2002). Self-disclosure, which involves revealing the self to others (see Chapter 6), allows people to develop shared knowledge about one another, and this shared knowledge leads to emotional and relational closeness (Prager & Roberts, 2004). In fact, when people are asked to describe how "close" or "intimate" friendships differ from more casual friendships, self-disclosure

is the most common response (Monsour, 1992). Direct emotional expressions involve expressing feelings by using phrases such as "I love you," "You make me happy," and "You're fun to be around." These statements are the most direct and least ambiguous way to communicate affection to someone, but they are also risky because they open a person up to rejection. In some cases, compliments and praise communicate positive regard and liking (Pendell, 2002). Compliments can also strengthen feelings of affection and emotional closeness because they make people feel good about themselves and their relationships. Finally, assurances, which have also been termed *relationship talk,* are direct messages about people's commitment level in a relationship. As noted in Chapter 10, assurances have been conceptualized as a relational maintenance behavior but are also expressions of affection. Statements such as "I want to see you again," "I can't imagine my life without you," and "I hope our friendship never ends" are symbols of emotional closeness that reflect how much people care about and value each other (Floyd, 2006; King & Sereno, 1984).

DIRECT AND NONVERBAL AFFECTIONATE COMMUNICATION Many nonverbal behaviors, such as hugging someone, are direct and nonverbal expressions of affection because others commonly interpret them as communicating affection (Floyd & Morman, 2001). According to the **social meaning model of nonverbal communication,** some nonverbal behaviors have strong consensual meanings across different contexts (Burgoon & Newton, 1991). For example, smiling usually signals friendliness, and hugs usually communicate affection regardless of the situation in which people find themselves. Of course, there are exceptions to these rules. Sometimes a smile is fake, condescending, or sarcastic, and a hug is an obligatory rather than an affectionate move. The social meaning model, however, suggests that people recognize the exceptions to the rule because they do not look only at one nonverbal cue but rather a constellation of nonverbal cues that work in concert to communicate a message. A condescending smile, therefore, will look different from a friendly smile, and an obligatory hug will look (and feel) different from a genuinely affectionate hug.

Although a wide variety of nonverbal behaviors can communicate affection, three classes of behavior in particular have been found to do so in a relatively unambiguous manner that is consistent with the social meaning model—(1) physical closeness, (2) eye contact, and (3) vocal behavior. Physical closeness involves touch and close distancing. Floyd and Morman's (1998) measure of affectionate communication includes several types of touch—holding hands, hugging, kissing, massaging someone, and putting one's arm around another's shoulders—as well as sitting close to one another. Similarly, Pendell (2002) listed physical closeness and a wide variety of tactile behaviors as nonverbal indicators of affection, including friendly roughhousing or mock aggression, hand squeezes, shaking hands, cuddling, snuggling, lap sitting, picking someone up, gently cleaning someone, and fondling. Eye contact also communicates affection in a relatively direct and unambiguous fashion, especially when it is prolonged and mutual, and when it is used alongside other behaviors that reflect positive emotions, such as smiling (Floyd & Morman, 1998; Pendell, 2002). In one study, strangers were paired in opposite sex dyads. Each person was told to look at the partner's hands for 2 minutes, look into the partner's eyes for 2 minutes, or count the number of times the partner blinked (Kellerman, Lewis, & Laird, 1989). People reported greater liking when they had both been told to look at each other, which demonstrates that mutual gaze is related to liking. Finally, **vocalic behavior,** such as speaking tenderly or in a warm voice, laughing with someone, talking faster when excited, and using a moderate amount of talk time (i.e., not speaking more or less than one's partner) are related to affection and liking (Palmer & Simmons, 1995; Pendell, 2002). Women are also rated as more affectionate if they speak in a somewhat high-pitched voice (Floyd & Ray, 2003).

INDIRECT AND NONVERBAL AFFECTIONATE COMMUNICATION According to Floyd and Morman (2001), there are two types of affectionate communication that are indirect and nonverbal expressions of affection: (1) **support behaviors** and (2) **idiomatic behaviors.** Although these behaviors are frequently interpreted as communicating affection, sometimes they are not. The situation and the relationship people share often help determine whether or not these behaviors are construed as expressions of affection. Support behaviors involve giving someone emotional or instrumental support. For example, friends and relatives might show support to a new mother by bringing her food, offering to babysit, giving her child care advice, buying savings bonds for the new baby, and listening patiently when she complains about being overly tired. Although these types of actions do not communicate affection directly, they likely let the young mother know that people love and care for her.

Idiomatic behaviors "have a specific meaning only to people in a particular relationship" (Burgoon et al., 2010, p. 331). The primary reason romantic couples use idioms is to communicate affection (Bell, Buerkel-Rothfuss, & Gore, 1987). Hopper, Knapp, and Scott (1981) gave several examples of idioms in romantic relationships, including twitching noses to signal "you're special" and twisting wedding rings to warn "don't you dare do or say that!" Idioms can be used in other types of relationships as well. For example, Dan might sometimes tease Luke by acting like he is sprinkling something over his head. This gesture may have a special meaning for the two of them because it leads them to recall an event they attended together where Luke ended up with cake crumbs all over his head. Other people—even Macie—will not understand the meaning of this gesture unless Dan or Luke shares it with them. And even if Luke explains it to Macie, since she was not there, she might not fully understand its meaning.

IMMEDIACY BEHAVIOR

As the previous section suggests, affectionate communication is essential for establishing and sustaining emotional closeness. Immediacy behaviors play a complementary and equally important role in developing and maintaining close relationships. **Immediacy behaviors** are actions that signal warmth, communicate availability, decrease psychological or physical distance, and promote involvement between people (Andersen, 1985). These behaviors have also been called **positive involvement behaviors** (Guerrero, 2004; Prager, 2000) because they show both positive affect and high levels of involvement in an interaction.

Immediacy (or positive involvement) is a broader concept than affection. Affection and affectionate communication are rooted in feelings of fondness and positive regard that have developed toward someone over time (Floyd, 2006). Immediacy, in contrast, is a style of communicating that is used across a wide variety of interactions to express involvement and positivity without necessarily expressing affection. For example, a person who uses behaviors such as eye contact, smiling, and handshaking with a prospective employer during a job interview would probably be labeled as immediate but not affectionate. Nonetheless, increases in immediacy provide a foundation for creating and sustaining close relationships (Andersen, 2008), and there is some overlap between immediacy behavior and affectionate communication.

Verbal Immediacy

Most research on immediacy has focused on nonverbal behaviors. However, certain verbal behaviors also reflect immediacy. **Verbal immediacy** is a function of several stylistic features of language that reflect the closeness of a relationship (see Andersen, 1998a), including word choice, forms of address, depth of disclosure, and relationship indicators.

WORD CHOICE Inclusive pronouns, such as *we*, are perceived to indicate more interdependence than using exclusive pronouns, such as *I* or *you and me*

(Weiner & Mehrabian, 1968). Prager (1995) suggested that more immediate pronoun use (*this* and *these* versus *that* and *those*), adverb use (*here* versus *there*), and verb tense (present versus past), as well as the use of the active as opposed to the passive voice, all contribute to greater verbal immediacy and perceptions of closeness. Bradac, Bowers, and Courtwright (1979) maintained that verbal immediacy builds positive relationships and likewise that being in a close, emotionally connected relationship leads to more verbal immediacy.

FORMS OF ADDRESS Casual forms of address ("Chris" as opposed to "Dr. Rodriguez") also imply a closer relationship (King & Sereno, 1984), as do nicknames (Bell et al., 1987; Hopper et al., 1981). Using inappropriately informal names or disliked nicknames, however, is not a way to establish a close relationship. For example, calling your boss "Bud" when he prefers "Mr. Johnson" or calling your date by a nickname that might be considered derogatory or sexist, such as "sweet cheeks" or "sugar daddy," is not an effective way to build a strong relationship. As noted earlier, personal idioms can be a way to express affection and emotional closeness in a relationship. Special greetings, secret nicknames, sexual euphemisms, mild teases, and unique labels for the relationship often are a source of emotional closeness that also increases the immediacy level of an interaction (Bell et al., 1987; Hopper et al., 1981). Of course, the use of some of these terms in a public setting may be a source of embarrassment and cause a loss of closeness.

DEPTH OF DISCLOSURE Close relationships are characterized by deep rather than superficial interactions. In close relationships, partners "can communicate deeply and honestly . . . sharing innermost feelings" (Sternberg, 1987, p. 333). Self-revealing statements that convey vulnerable emotions are especially conducive to emotional closeness (Prager & Roberts, 2004). Self-disclosure plays an essential role in relationship development because, as people become closer, they share their innermost thoughts and feelings (see Chapter 6). Only by sharing personal information, thoughts, and feelings can two people get to know each other well enough to develop an emotionally close relationship and build interdependence. Therefore, the depth with which people explore various topics and self-disclose to one another is sometimes considered to be an indicator of the immediacy level within an interaction (Andersen, 1998a). For example, when responding to a friend who asks, "How've you been?" the level of depth in Luke's answer may reflect the emotional closeness of the friendship. If the friendship is casual, Luke might say he's fine even if he has been feeling terrible lately. If the friendship is moderately close, Luke might say, "Not that great, I've been overwhelmed with work and sick with the flu, but I'll be okay." In contrast, if talking to Dan or Macie, Luke would feel free to go into much more depth about his recent trials and tribulations, including asking for help.

RELATIONSHIP INDICATORS The language partners use to refer to each other suggests a certain public, relational image that is an index of the closeness between them. For example, cohabitors may describe themselves along a continuum that includes roommate, friend, boyfriend or girlfriend, and partner—which signals increasing levels of immediacy and emotional closeness. Similarly, when individuals call someone their "best friend" in public, this label sends a strong message about the closeness of the relationship. The first time Luke referred to Macie as his "girlfriend" in public was probably a milestone because the nature of their relationship was made clear to both Macie and others, suggesting that Luke and Macie are a "pair," have a special bond, and are dating each other exclusively. When Macie inserted the phrase, "In a Relationship with Luke" on her Facebook page, it further clarified the level of closeness and commitment that characterizes their relationship. This type of language is considered immediate because it emphasizes that there is a special level of psychological and physical closeness between Luke and Macie.

Nonverbal Immediacy

Verbal immediacy is undoubtedly important, yet nonverbal immediacy appears to be even more critical for sending messages related to emotional closeness. Some scholars even contend that nonverbal immediacy is a stronger predictor of emotional and relational closeness than self-disclosure. Montgomery (1988) stated, "The nonverbal mode of expression appears to be more closely linked to relational quality than the verbal mode" (p. 348). Similarly, Prager (2000) suggested that nonverbal behavior makes a major contribution to the level of closeness that people experience in their relationships, "probably due to its relatively involuntary character. People's facial expressions, voice tones, postures and gestures can reveal unspoken emotions and intentions and can override efforts at impression management" (p. 232). Clearly, nonverbal communication is a vital component within close relationships.

Although the specific behaviors that communicate nonverbal immediacy are reviewed separately in the following sections, it is important to remember that nonverbal behaviors are often processed as a *gestalt* (Andersen, 1985, 2008). In other words, rather than focusing on single behaviors, people usually take the whole package of nonverbal behaviors into consideration when assigning meaning and determining how much immediacy is being communicated. In addition, nonverbal communication is interpreted within a broader social context. Eye contact reflects closeness sometimes but intimidation other times. Similarly, a smile might be perceived as friendly in one context and condescending in another.

VISUAL OR OCULESIC BEHAVIORS Eye behavior, or **oculesics,** helps establish emotional closeness. The eyes have been said to be "the windows to the soul," and eye contact is widely recognized as an invitation to communicate (Andersen, 2008). Increased eye contact is a sign of intimacy and attraction (Andersen, 1985; Exline & Winters, 1965; Ray & Floyd, 2006). People engage in the highest levels of eye contact with friends, dating partners, and people they like (Coutts & Schneider, 1976; Exline & Winters, 1965). Romantic partners, in particular, appear to use high levels of eye contact to communicate relational and emotional closeness (Guerrero, 1997). Eye contact is also a sign of attentiveness and involvement. Pupil dilation is also related to attraction. In an imaginative study, Hess and Goodwin (1974) showed people two virtually identical pictures of a mother holding her baby; however, in one photo, the eyes were retouched to appear dilated, while in the other photo they were constricted. People thought the mother with the dilated pupils seemed to love her baby more. Interestingly, only a few of these people accurately identified the eyes as the source of their attributions, which suggests that pupil dilation is processed as an immediacy cue but only at very low levels of awareness. Of course, low light, candlelit dinners, and dusk have always been associated with romance and closeness, perhaps in part due to subtle cues like pupil dilation.

SPATIAL OR PROXEMIC BEHAVIORS **Proxemics,** or the way people use space in interpersonal communication, signals the level of closeness in a relationship. In a classic book about proxemics in North America, Hall (1968) identified the distance ranging from touch to 18 inches as the *intimate zone.* The people we most often let into this zone are those with whom we have intimate relationships, such as our children, our closest friends, family members, and romantic partners. Immediacy is also communicated proxemically via body angle. Facing someone directly is immediate, while sitting or standing at a 45-degree angle is less immediate and positioning oneself side by side or back-to-back with another person is even less so. Women are more likely to use a direct, face-to-face body orientation than men (Guerrero, 1997); this is one of several ways that women seem to be more nonverbally immediate than men. Communicating eye to eye also increases perceptions of immediacy and closeness (Andersen, 1985). For example, toddlers are often placed in high chairs so they are face to face with the rest of the family at the dinner table.

Such placement increases the overall immediacy level of the family's interaction during dinner.

TACTILE OR HAPTIC BEHAVIORS Physical contact, or **haptics,** is a key immediacy behavior that reflects closeness. In a study of airport arrivals and departures, Heslin and Boss (1980) found a strong association between the amount of tactile intimacy recorded by observers and the closeness of the relationship reported by couples. Another study found that observers perceived higher levels of closeness for touching couples than for nontouching couples (Kleinke, Meeker, & LaFong, 1974). Similarly, Guerrero and Andersen's (1991) study of couples' tactile communication in theater and zoo lines revealed that high levels of touch were associated with a more serious, accelerating relationship. Emmers and Dindia (1995) found that this was true for private touch as well. Thus, a high level of touch usually occurs when couples are in the process of escalating their relationships from casual to committed. Hugs and kisses are a particularly immediate and affectionate form of communication, as is touch to the face (Andersen, 2008; Andersen et al., 2006; Floyd, 2006; Guerrero & Floyd, 2006).

BODY MOVEMENT OR KINESICS Kinesics comprises body movements such as smiling, body positions, and posture. Over several decades, researchers have found that the frequency and intensity of smiling is the single best predictor of interpersonal closeness, liking, and warmth (Argyle, 1972; Bayes, 1970; Ray & Floyd, 2006; Reece & Whitman, 1962). Smiles are a universal sign of positive affect that signal approachability and availability for communication. Open body positions free of obstruction by objects or limbs are also considered immediate. People are most likely to cross their arms, hide their face, or stand behind objects when they lack trust, feel vulnerable, and do not want to interact. In contrast, Beier and Sternberg (1977) reported that "close" couples used more open leg positions than did couples who were less close or who were experiencing conflict. Like good dancers, intimate couples show high levels of coordinated movement, called **body synchrony.** The good "vibes" resulting from smooth interaction with and adaptation to one's partner are a vital part of communicating immediacy and closeness (Guerrero & Floyd, 2006; Morris, 1977). In one study, when people were asked to signal liking to another person, one of the behaviors they employed was postural matching (Ray & Floyd, 2006). For example, Luke and his best friend, Dan, frequently match postures; they lean forward together at a bar, both put their feet up while watching a game, and both throw their heads back when they laugh.

VOCALIC COMMUNICATION Words have meaning, but changes in pitch, volume, rate, and tone of voice—or **vocalics**—are sometimes more important than words. Shifts in vocal pitch, rate, amplitude, and duration are associated with positive interpersonal affect (Beebe, 1980; Scherer, 1979). Certain vocalic behaviors, such as baby talk, are especially immediate. Adults often use baby talk, a high-pitched, highly varied imitation of children's speech, to communicate with infants and small children (Andersen, 2008). Baby talk includes real words ("You're a little sweetie") and nonsense sounds ("kutchy-kutchy-koo"). Such talk has been found to aid the development of conversational skills, as well as more emotionally connected parent–child relationships (Ferguson, 1964). Interestingly, lovers like Luke and Macie sometimes privately employ baby talk during their most intimate interactions perhaps because intimate behaviors related to courtship are often submissive, nonthreatening, and childlike (see Chapter 9).

CHRONEMIC BEHAVIORS The way people use time, or **chronemics,** communicates a lot about their relationships. In North America and parts of Europe, time is a precious commodity that is spent, saved, wasted, or invested as though it were money. Studies show that chronemic cues send messages related to immediacy and closeness (Andersen, 1984). Spending time with another person sends the message that the person is important and reflects a desire to develop

or maintain a close relationship. Egland, Stelzner, Andersen, and Spitzberg (1997) found that the best way to signal relational closeness is to spend time with one's partner. Similarly, being on time, waiting for a late partner, sharing conversation time, replying to texts and Snapchats in a timely manner, and devoting time to work on the relationship all play a role in the level of emotional closeness partners feel for one another.

COGNITIVE VALENCE THEORY

As noted previously, engaging in affectionate or immediate communication carries risks. Sometimes people respond positively to such behavior; other times people respond negatively. **Cognitive valence theory (CVT)** helps explain why people respond to increases in immediacy positively in some cases and negatively in others by examining six cognitive valencers: (1) culture, (2) personality, (3) the rewardingness of the partner, (4) the relationship, (5) the situation, and (6) temporary states. **Cognitive valencers** can be thought of as templates or knowledge structures that people use to help them evaluate behavior as appropriate or inappropriate and welcome or unwelcome. The six cognitive valencers identified in CVT also influence how people give and receive affection (Pendell, 2002). The overall theory includes interpersonal perception, physiological arousal, social cognition, and relational outcomes (Andersen, 1985, 1989, 1998a). (See Figure 7.1 for a depiction of the theory.)

Behavior

All close relationships begin with one person increasing immediacy via nonverbal or verbal communication (see the behavior column in Figure 7.1). As Andersen (1998a) explained, "Relationships do not occur in the absence of human contact. They begin, develop, thrive and disengage as communicative acts" (p. 40). Thus, using Dan and Luke to help illustrate, Dan would try to develop a closer friendship with Luke by increasing immediacy through

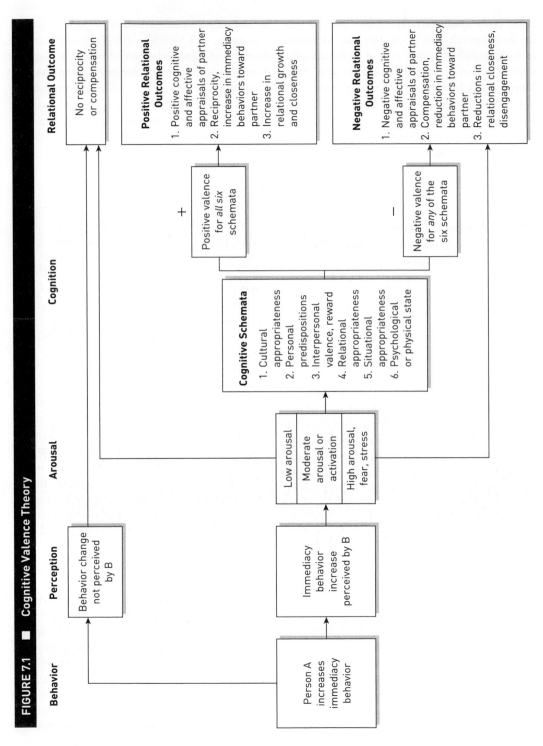

FIGURE 7.1 ■ Cognitive Valence Theory

verbal or nonverbal communication. As noted earlier, Dan would have a variety of verbal behaviors at his disposal, including personal forms of address and expressions of relational closeness such as telling Luke that he respects his athletic performance and is glad they are teammates. Usually, nonverbal communication plays a substantial role in promoting relational closeness, so Dan also might engage in behaviors such as smiling, making eye contact, touching, or hanging out with Luke.

Perception

Behaviors by themselves do not increase closeness; one's partner must notice the behaviors (see the perception column in Figure 7.1). Andersen (1989) indicates that expressions of closeness have "no communicative significance" unless perceived by one's partner (p. 8). Such perceptions need not be conscious but must register in the mind of the receiver. Words spoken to no ear and smiles perceived by no eye do not communicate and have no chance of increasing closeness. So Dan might smile and comment to Luke that he enjoys being teammates. But if Luke's mind is on something else, Dan's attempt to develop a closer friendship will fail.

Arousal

If Luke notices Dan's immediacy behavior, he will respond physiologically and possibly cognitively and behaviorally. Nonverbal immediacy behaviors are stimulating and increase physiological arousal (see the arousal column in Figure 7.1). In his summary of 24 studies on the relationship between immediacy behaviors and arousal, Andersen (1985) concluded, "The research generally supports a positive relationship between immediacy and increases in arousal" (p. 15). Increases in multichanneled immediacy behavior, such as more eye contact, smiles, and touch, increase physiological arousal (Andersen, Guerrero, Buller, & Jorgensen, 1998). Sometimes arousal change is accompanied by positive emotions and other times by negative emotions. Take Luke and Dan again as an example. If Dan hugs

Luke after he scores a goal during a soccer game, Luke might feel heightened arousal, joy, and pride because Dan's gesture affirms that he is highly valued as both a friend and teammate. On the other hand, Luke might experience a high level of arousal if he is embarrassed by Dan showing him high levels of immediacy in public, especially since heterosexual men are often homophobic and regard such displays of affection as unmasculine (Floyd, 2006).

Many studies have shown that rapid arousal increases are aversive and frightening (see Andersen, 2008, for a summary). For example, a threatening-looking stare by a stranger with a menacing facial expression likely prompts high arousal and the impulse to flee in a receiver. As a consequence, CVT predicts that negative relational outcomes will occur when arousal levels are very high. By contrast, when a friend says hi on the way to class, no arousal will occur because this behavior is highly routine and represents no real increase in immediacy. The most interesting reactions occur in relation to moderate increases in immediacy. For example, when receiving a smile from an attractive person or personal self-disclosure from a friend, moderate arousal is likely to occur. Moderate arousal has been shown to stimulate cognitive processes, which in turn influence how people respond to increases in immediacy behavior.

Cognition

For the sake of example, imagine that Dan's friendly behavior leads Luke to experience a moderate increase in arousal. In this case, CVT predicts that Luke's response to Dan's behavior will be contingent on how he cognitively appraises the situation. Specifically, CVT suggests that Luke will evaluate Dan's increase in immediacy based on how appropriate Dan's behavior is in relation to the six cognitive valencers shown in Figure 7.1.

CULTURE Andersen (2008) argued that culture is so foundational in our lives that we often confuse it with human nature itself. We determine if something is appropriate in our culture, and that gives us a basis for reacting to it. For instance, kissing the wife of a friend goodbye would often be appropriate in the United States but not in Arab countries. If a behavior is appropriate, it can be positively valenced; if the behavior is culturally inappropriate, it will be negatively valenced. Within U.S. culture, Dan's smile and self-disclosure would probably be perceived as appropriate and so would be positively valenced. However, if Dan's self-disclosure was too immediate for a male in U.S. culture, it could be valenced negatively. See Box 7.2 for more on how culture affects a specific type of nonverbal immediacy—touch.

PERSONALITY Personal predispositions make up one's personality. People differ in their sociability, extroversion, and attitudes toward touch and the degree to which they approach or avoid new

experiences or sensations (see Andersen, 1993, 1998a). A hug or a personal disclosure may be appreciated by one person but not by another. Thus, people will valence the same behavior differently based on their personality. If Luke is an outgoing, friendly person, he might welcome Dan's self-disclosure. However, if Luke is shy and introverted, he might be nervous and uncomfortable hearing something personal about Dan. In the former case, Luke would likely react positively to Dan's self-disclosure; in the latter, he would likely react negatively.

REWARDINGNESS The degree to which people find someone rewarding influences how they react to that person's increase in immediacy behavior (Burgoon & Hale, 1988). Rewardingness, which is also called **interpersonal valence,** refers to the degree to which someone is considered attractive. Recall from Chapter 3 that people can be attractive

---

BOX 7.2 AROUND THE WORLD
TO TOUCH OR NOT TO TOUCH: A QUESTION OF CULTURE

Culture has a considerable effect on the degree to which people from different countries use touch. A number of studies have shown that the least touch occurs in Asian countries, including Myanmar—formerly Burma—China, Hong Kong, Japan, South Korea, the Philippines, Taiwan, Thailand, and Vietnam (e.g., Jones, 1994; McDaniel & Andersen, 1998). People from Northern European cultures, such as Finland, Norway, and Sweden, as well as people from Germany and Great Britain, also exhibit relatively low levels of touch, although not as low as their Asian counterparts. In contrast, the most touch tends to occur in two regions in the world: (1) the region around the Mediterranean Sea, which includes the southern parts of France, Italy, Portugal, and Spain, along with Greece and the Northern part of Africa, and (2) the Americas south of the United States, which includes Mexico, the Caribbean, and South America. People from Eastern Europe, including Russia, Hungary, and Romania, also tend to be touch oriented, as do those from Arab countries. However, in Arab countries, there is more touch between members of the same sex, especially in public. In fact, it is commonplace to see male friends holding hands in parts of the Middle East. So where does the United States fit in? Recent

research suggests that the United States, Australia, and Canada are somewhere in the middle; people in these countries touch one another less than do people in the Mediterranean area, South America, Eastern Europe, and the Middle East but more than do people in Asian and Northern European countries.

However, it is important to keep in mind that the studies looking at culture and touch behavior have been conducted in public places, such as restaurants and airports. There is reason to believe that these differences may not always translate to private settings. For example, in Japan, which is considered a low-touch culture, parents frequently touch their children; in fact, some children sleep with their parents until they are about 7 or 8 years old. This would be considered out of the ordinary in the United States. In Australia, as part of an effort to encourage high levels of touch between mothers and their babies, laws were passed that limited the use of infant seats that can be moved directly from cars to strollers. These examples show that although there is variability in the ways people from different cultures use touch, touch is still a universal way to express affection and communicate emotional closeness.

based on physical attributes (e.g., how beautiful they are, what clothes they wear), social qualities (e.g., how friendly they are), and instrumental qualities (e.g., how good they are at performing certain tasks). In general, people who are physically attractive, have high social standing, possess positive personality traits, and are similar to the receiver are regarded as highly rewarding. Thus, people react differently to changes in immediacy on the basis of who their partner is. Andersen (1993) noted that "positive perceptions of another person's values, background, physical appearance and communication style are the primary reasons why we initiate and maintain close relationships" (p. 25). For example, a touch from a disliked other is judged very differently from a touch from a highly attractive date. Similarly, if Luke likes Dan and thinks he is good guy, he is likely to react positively when Dan increases immediacy. By contrast, if Luke thinks Dan is a pest who is no fun to be around, or has negative qualities such as abrasiveness, he is likely to react negatively.

THE RELATIONSHIP The most important valencer that influences how people react to increases in immediacy is the relationship (see Andersen, 1998a, 2008). People are able to easily classify relationships with others as friend, coworker, best friend, lover, fiancé or fiancée, parent, boss, roommate, and so on. These relational definitions create parameters regarding the appropriateness or inappropriateness of immediacy increases. Too much touch or self-disclosure on a first date is often a turnoff, yet the same amount of touch or self-disclosure from a fiancé or fiancée would be warmly accepted. In the right relationship, almost any immediacy behavior will be valenced positively. In the wrong relationship, even mild displays of immediacy can be negatively valenced and cause adverse relational outcomes. Luke and Dan have been close friends for years, so Luke will probably expect a high level of in-depth self-disclosure. But if Luke did not know Dan at all, Luke would likely react negatively to Dan's disclosure of personal information to him.

THE SITUATION The situation, or the context in which immediacy behavior occurs, is vital in determining how people respond to increases

in immediacy (Andersen, 1993). High levels of immediacy in the classroom, boardroom, bathroom, and bedroom produce distinctly different reactions. Some settings, such as living rooms, hot tubs, and hotel rooms, are highly conducive to immediacy. Other situations are highly formal with immediacy behaviors limited to handshakes or polite smiles. Passionately kissing one's date goodnight in a private place has entirely different connotations than engaging in the same behavior in front of one's parents. The bottom line is this: Immediacy must be situationally appropriate. If Dan increases immediacy with Luke during a private conversation, his self-disclosure is likely to be regarded positively. But if he increases immediacy while Luke is in the middle of an important conversation with Macie, his self-disclosure is likely to be regarded negatively.

TEMPORARY STATES Everyone has bad days and good days—intellectually, emotionally, and physically. Temporary states are short-term internal conditions that make individuals feel and react differently at various times (Andersen, 1993). Many things affect a person's temporary state or mood, including having a fight with the boss, being criticized (or complimented) by a friend, getting a bad night's sleep, partying too much, and receiving a pay raise. A classic example of negative-state valencing is a person's response to an affectionate spouse: "Not tonight, dear. I have a headache." Negative physical or emotional states generally lead to negative valencing of immediacy behavior whereas positive states generally lead to positive valencing. Thus, Luke is more likely to react positively to Dan's increase in immediacy if he is alert, feeling well, and in a good mood.

Relational Outcomes

As noted earlier, relationships are fragile, and few relationships reach high levels of emotional and relational closeness. CVT provides one explanation for why this is so. Negative valencing for *any* of the six cognitive valencers can lead to decreased relational closeness. When immediacy increases are valenced negatively, a host of aversive outcomes follow, including appraising one's partner negatively, reducing immediacy behaviorally (perhaps by moving away), and maybe even disengaging from the relationship. Positive valencing of the immediacy behavior, by contrast, results in more favorable appraisals of one's partner, reciprocity of immediacy behaviors, and greater relational and emotional closeness. Thus, increasing immediacy behavior is not without risk, but the benefits can outweigh the potential costs if a more enjoyable, closer relationship is desired. Dan's original attempt to become friends with Luke might have resulted in rejection, but luckily Dan ended up developing a rewarding and emotionally close relationship with a new friend.

SUPPORTIVE COMMUNICATION

Friends, relatives, and romantic partners also communicate emotional closeness and show interdependence by being there for each other in times of distress. As discussed in Chapters 10 and 14, making sacrifices for one another and providing social support are key ways of sustaining closeness and maintaining relationships. When people want to establish a closer friendship, they both give and receive more social support (Sanderson, Rahm, Beigbeder, & Metts, 2005). Supportive communication has been

defined as "verbal and nonverbal behavior produced with the intention of providing assistance to others perceived as needing that aid" (Burleson & MacGeorge, 2002, p. 374). Several different types of supportive communication have been identified (Cutrona & Suhr, 1992). **Emotional support** involves expressing caring, concern, and empathy. **Esteem support** is used to bolster someone's self-worth by making that person feel valued, admired, and capable. **Informational support** entails giving specific advice, including facts and information that might help someone solve a problem. **Tangible aid** occurs when people provide physical assistance, goods, or services, such as babysitting someone's children or helping someone complete a task. Finally, **network support** involves directing someone to a person or group who can help them because they have had similar experiences. As these types of supportive communication show, some support focuses on making the distressed person feel better, whereas other forms of supportive communicate focus on solving problems. Of course, people can use multiple types of supportive communication to try and help a distressed person.

People feel distress in reaction to a wide variety of situations. In S. M. Jones' (2000) study of distressing events among college students, the following

People give and receive support different ways, including providing tangible aid such as a father helping his son with homework; esteem support such as a coach giving a player a trophy to say "good job"; informational support, such as a doctor giving medical advice to a patient; network support, such as bringing a friend to a support group; and emotional support, such as giving a friend a hug.

Credits, clockwise from top left: ©iStockphoto.com/monkeybusiness images, ©iStockphoto.com/asiseeit, ©iStockphoto.com/sturti, ©iStockphoto.com/g-stockstudio, ©iStockphoto.com/AntonioGuillem

were most frequently described as distressing: problems in a romantic relationship, college performance (grades), friend or roommate problems, family problems, work-related stress, family illness, death, and personal illness or injury. A follow-up study by Jones (2006) demonstrated that these situations vary in terms of the type of distress they produce—with sadness related to death and breakups, hurt related to breakups, and helplessness related to personal illness or injury.

Regardless of the type of distress one is experiencing, a key question is as follows: How can people provide the most helpful support to someone who is distressed or needs help? Support is only likely to relate to emotional and relational closeness when it is effective. In some cases, giving support can backfire. Indeed, research on the dark side of social support shows that attempts at supportive communication sometimes make a situation worse (Albrecht, Burleson, & Goldsmith, 1994). In Chapter 2, we discussed how important it is for people to project an identity of themselves that is positive and autonomous. People usually want others to see them as strong and independent rather than weak and dependent. When attempts at supportive communication come across as pity or suggest that a person is incapable of handling a situation alone, they can make the distressed person feel worse. This may be especially true for informational support, which is commonly known as advice. People often react negatively to unsolicited advice or advice that seems pushy (Goldsmith & Fitch, 1997). Advice can also be threatening if it implies that the advice giver is more knowledgeable and capable than the person receiving the advice. Indeed, Goldsmith and MacGeorge (2000) found that advice is only perceived as effective if it does not threaten the receiver's face.

Providing other forms of social support can also be problematic in the context of close relationships, where people sometimes want to spare the feelings of their partner rather than tell the truth. For example, if Dan suffers a serious injury to his leg, Luke may tell him that it will "heal with time" to try to make him feel better. Such assurances could lead Dan to downplay his injury and put off seeking therapy that will help his leg heal. This illustrates another potential problem with supportive communication in relationships—people sometimes feel obligated to comfort others and give advice even if they do not have the proper knowledge to do so. In this case, no advice is usually better than bad advice. Attempts at supportive communication can cause other problems in relationships as well. The distressed person may worry about being judged or criticized, and the support giver may become overburdened. Some researchers believe that seeking support online helps reduce some of these negative effects, as discussed in Box 7.3.

Of course, supportive communication can be highly effective during face-to-face interaction. The question, then, becomes what makes some attempts at supportive communication more effective than others? Communication researchers and social psychologists have started to answer this question by focusing on how different kinds of communication make distressed individuals feel better or worse. Researchers have also examined whether reductions in distress are long- or short-lasting. In other words, do some types of supportive communication lead people to feel better only for a short time while others lead to long-term reductions in distress?

The Dual Process Model of Supportive Communication

The dual process model of supportive communication (Bodie & Burleson, 2008; Burleson, 2009) addresses these and other issues by outlining the process that occurs when people receive and respond to supportive messages. In this model, the person attempting to provide support is called the "helper" and the person receiving help is called the "recipient." As shown in Figure 7.2, the process starts when the helper sends a supportive message. After this, two different pathways can occur depending on whether or not the recipient is motivated and able to process the message. Hence, this theory is called a "dual process" model.

BOX 7.3 TECH TALK
THE LURE OF ONLINE SUPPORT

In the 21st century, people have many options for seeking social support. In addition to communicating face to face, people can seek support by participating in online chat rooms, discussion boards, and other forums on the World Wide Web. According to Walther and Boyd (2002), Usenet is a common forum for seeking social support, with Internet users joining various newsgroups related to a specific topic (such as divorce) and then reading, posting, and replying to messages on the site. Walther and Boyd suggested that seeking social support online has at least four advantages that help reduce some of the potential problems associated with giving and receiving social support in personal relationships.

First, people are attracted to online social support because it affords them *social distance*. When people seek support from relational partners, they worry about being judged. They also worry that their partner may not be objective or might try too hard to make them feel better. These concerns are not as relevant when seeking support from more objective third parties online.

Second, *anonymity* is a plus when seeking support online. Sometimes people want to keep an issue private without anyone in their social network knowing about it. Other times, they just want to be able to express themselves without anyone knowing who they are. Online environments give people the ability to say anything they want while keeping their identity private.

Third, people have more control over *interaction management* when seeking support online compared to face to face. People can take the time they need to construct a carefully worded message. They also don't need to worry about being interrupted or being too shy to talk. If they don't like a reply, they don't have to read the rest of it.

Fourth, *access* is another advantage associated with online support. People can receive online support anytime they want it, day or night. They can also connect with people who have expertise in a particular area or who have had experiences similar to their own, which is often not the case when seeking support from a relational partner.

Together, these advantages help explain why seeking online social support can be especially attractive. As Walther and Boyd noted, sometimes face-to-face communication is not the best option, especially if the issue a person wants to discuss is personal, delicate, and requires informational as well as emotional support. In those cases, online communication can provide an attractive alternative to face-to-face communication.

In the first path, the recipient is unmotivated or unable to process the message. For example, Luke might try to comfort Macie after she finds out that her aunt has been diagnosed with breast cancer, but Macie might prefer not to talk about it and be too upset to really process what Luke is saying. In this case, the dual process model suggests that whether or not Macie feels better is dependent on environmental cues. Environmental cues include characteristics of the setting and the helper. Perhaps Macie is comforted just by having Luke there with her—in which case she might feel a little better, but only temporarily. If, however, Macie is too distraught to notice Luke's presence, she is unlikely to feel better despite his trying to comfort her.

In the second path, the recipient is motivated and able to process the message. In this case, whether or not Macie feels better is dependent on the quality of the message. According to the model, messages are effective when they help the recipient reappraise the situation so that it seems less distressing. This means that the supportive message does not directly influence whether the recipient feels better. Instead, the supportive message might help the recipient to reappraise the situation as less distressing. As Burleson and Goldsmith (1998) put it, "Although the words and deeds of others may facilitate a reappraisal of a stressful circumstance, no one can directly alter or modify the appraisals of another" (p. 258). Instead, the only way to reduce someone's distress is to change the way she or he feels about the situation.

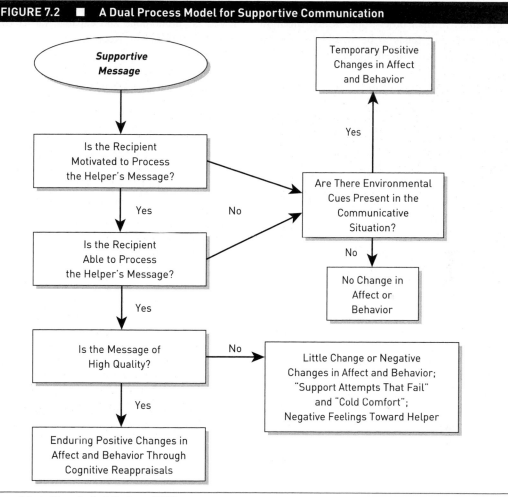

FIGURE 7.2 ■ A Dual Process Model for Supportive Communication

Source: Adapted from Bodie & Burleson (2008).

Imagine that Luke tells Macie, "Don't worry, honey. Lots of women get breast cancer and live through it." Will this help Macie reappraise the situation and feel better? If Macie already knows the statistics, maybe not. She might think, "I don't care about lots of women. I just care about my aunt." If that is the case, Luke's message would be ineffective. However, if his message prompts Macie to think about other women she knows who are breast cancer survivors, it might help her to reappraise the situation as somewhat less threatening, thereby reducing her distress. As this example

suggests, there is no "magic bullet" message that will always be effective (Burleson & Goldsmith, 1998). The same message can be effective in one situation but not another, depending on whether or not it leads to reappraisal. This also means that it not usually effective for helpers to tell recipients what they should do or how they should act or feel. Instead, recipients need to figure this out for themselves. Helpers are more likely to facilitate reappraisals by engaging in certain behaviors compared to others, but there is no sure bet when it comes to giving effective support. Nonetheless, research suggests that certain types of support tend to be more effective than others. Specifically, the most effective support tends to be invisible or person-centered and nonverbally immediate.

Invisible Support

As noted earlier, a number of mental and physical health benefits are associated with giving and receiving affection. Thus, it seems logical to expect that receiving social support would have similar benefits. The research on this, however, is mixed. People report better health when they have large social networks and perceive that resources are available, yet people sometimes report worse health when they perceive that their partner provided them with actual support (Bolger & Amarel, 2007). Too much support can also be detrimental, especially when the receiver feels obligated to reciprocate and provide others with support. For example, one study showed that if people engage too much on social networking sites, they can feel "social overload" (Maier, Laumer, Eckhardt, & Weitzel, 2015). So if Macie regularly tweets and posts photos on Instagram, to the extent that others show their support for her postings, she may feel obligated to like or retweet other people's postings. As noted earlier in this chapter, supportive communication has another dark side: recipients may think people see them as weak or unskilled, and they may worry about being judged by the helper. For their part, helpers may feel overburdened or worry about giving the "wrong" advice. Yet in other cases, supportive communication helps people reappraise situations and reduce stress. Supportive communication also helps people maintain relationships (see Chapter 10). These types of contradictory findings led Bolger, Zuckerman, and Kessler (2000) to propose the **invisible support phenomenon.**

The invisible support phenomenon suggests that support attempts that go unnoticed by recipients are the "most effective in reducing distress" and promoting good health (Bolger & Amarel, 2007,

p. 458). This may be because people want to be viewed as autonomous and capable, rather than dependent and needy. Receiving too much support, or receiving support from an unskilled partner, may draw too much attention to a person's problems, thereby exacerbating distress and lowering self-esteem (Shrout, Herman, & Bolger, 2006). In addition, when too much support is received, people may feel obligated to reciprocate by being supportive in the future. The invisible support phenomenon may also reflect that "support is rooted in the everyday fabric of relationships, in the routine interactions that people have with their friends and partners, interactions that are not necessarily viewed as acts of support" (Bolger & Amarel, 2007, p. 459; see also Leatham & Duck, 1990). Thus, affectionate communication may provide indirect forms of support that are superior to more direct expressions of support.

Recent studies have supported but qualified the invisible support phenomenon. Bolger and Amarel (2007) conducted three studies to determine whether invisible support was superior to visible support. In these studies, participants were told that they would be delivering a speech. A confederate who was working for the researcher pretended to be another participant in the study who had been assigned to write an essay rather than a speech. At some point, the researcher walked in and asked, "Do you have any questions for me before we move on?" The confederate then provided either invisible or visible support. In the first study, informational support, which entails giving concrete advice (e.g., telling the participant to be sure to summarize the speech at the beginning and the end) was provided in the visible support condition. In the invisible support condition, the confederate simply asked the researcher if summarizing at the beginning and the end was a good idea.

The second study focused on emotional support, which involves helping the partner feel better without necessarily trying to solve the problem. In the visible support condition, the confederate told the participant, "Look, you've got nothing to worry about, you'll do fine. I'd understand if you were nervous, but really I think it's going to be okay" whereas in the invisible support condition the confederate told the researcher that the participant "is going to do fine, she's got nothing to worry about, but I still don't know what I'm supposed to do" (Bolger & Amarel, 2007, p. 464). As hypothesized, larger increases in distress occurred when people were given visible rather than invisible support. Therefore, invisible support was more effective than visible support.

The third study added the idea that some messages imply that the participant either does or does not seem capable of coping with the situation (e.g., "You look like you need help" versus "I can tell you don't need any help, but I do.") This study showed that when visible messages implied that the participant needed help, they were actually less effective than no message at all. The most effective message, on the other hand, was invisible and implied that the participant was capable of handling the situation. Specifically, this message involved telling the researcher, "Well, I don't think she needs any help, but I could use some help. Should I structure my essay in a certain way? Like to summarize what I'm going to say at the beginning, and to end with a definite conclusion?" Notice that this message provided informational support in a nonthreatening, invisible way.

Support may also be especially effective when it is perceived as responsive and is delivered by a helper who is empathetic. Responsiveness refers to the degree to which a message communicates understanding, caring, and validation of one's partner (Maisel & Gable, 2009). This is related to both emotional support and esteem support, which were defined earlier in this chapter. In a study designed to determine whether responsiveness might help explain why some forms of visible support are perceived as ineffective, Maisel and Gable had cohabiting couples complete questionnaires for 2 weeks every night before they went to bed. Like past work, they found that invisible support was generally more effective than visible support. However, the level of perceived responsiveness also made a difference. In fact, visible support had positive effects when it was considered to be responsive, whereas invisible support had negative effects when it was considered to be unresponsive. The worst support occurred when both the recipient and the support provider agreed that the support was low in responsiveness. This study suggests that the way support is communicated is critical, regardless of whether support is visible or invisible. Another study showed that helpers are more likely to provide effective invisible support when they possess empathetic accuracy (Howland, 2016). This means that they are able to interpret and understand how the receiver is feeling, which allows them to provide sensitive invisible support.

Of course, it is not always possible to give invisible support all the time. Take Macie and Luke as an example. If Macie starts crying after talking to her aunt, it would be difficult for Luke to respond using only invisible support. Seeing her cry would likely prompt him to offer support that was clearly a response to her behavior. But Luke could provide invisible support in other ways. Knowing that Macie is having a hard time dealing with the news, he might do some special things for her, like cook her favorite dinner or be extra affectionate while they are watching a funny movie together. The movie might even help Macie take her mind off the situation (at least temporarily). If Luke engages in these supportive behaviors in a casual way, they could be "invisible" to Macie as support behaviors.

Other times, however, Luke may want to provide Macie with visible forms of support that will help her describe and explain how she feels, which, hopefully, will lead her to reappraise the situation and feel a little better. Both emotional and informational support could be important in the reappraisal process, as could network support whereby Luke directs Macie to information about the high survival rate of women who, like Macie's aunt, detect breast cancer in the early stages. Thus, although invisible support may be optimal in some situations, visible support may be optimal in others. Communication researchers have identified several features that may help make visible attempts at support more effective, including person-centeredness and immediacy.

Person-Centered Messages

One way to provide responsive, high-quality support is to use **person-centered messages** (Applegate, 1980; Burleson, 1982, 2003). When messages are highly person-centered, they acknowledge, elaborate on, and validate the feelings and concerns of the distressed person. Comforting messages can be ranked as high or low in quality based on how person-centered they are (Burleson, 1982, 1984; S. M. Jones, 2000). Highly person-centered messages help distressed people gain a perspective on their feelings. These messages also legitimize the distressed person's feelings. Suppose that Luke tells Macie, "I'm so sorry to hear that. It must be so hard for you. Your aunt is such a wonderful person. And she is strong, too. It sounds like they caught it early, so she will be okay, don't you think?" Notice that the highly person-centered response conveys understanding ("It must be so hard for you") and empathy ("I'm so sorry to hear that") while also helping the distressed person think about the event in a different way (by emphasizing that she will be okay). The question at the end of this message also gives Macie an opportunity to describe and explain how she is feeling, which may also help her reappraise the situation.

Moderately person-centered messages acknowledge the distressed person's feelings, but these messages do not help the distressed person contextualize or elaborate on the situation. For example, imagine that Luke said, "Don't worry, she'll be okay," or "It will be all right. I know your aunt and she'll beat this." Notice that these messages provide simple explanations and solutions that do not allow for much elaboration or reappraisal. These types of messages, which are frequently used by people in the helper role, provide support that is okay but not great.

Finally, messages that are low in person-centeredness (sometimes called *position-centered messages*) implicitly or explicitly deny the legitimacy of the distressed person's feelings, sometimes by blaming the distressed person for the situation and other times by changing the topic or the focus. For example, Luke might tell Macie, "You shouldn't be worried. It is Stage 1, so it is curable." In this case, Luke would be denying the legitimacy of Macie's feelings by saying that she shouldn't be worried. Instead, it would be much better to validate and empathize with Macie's feelings. In other cases, people blame the person for their own predicament. Most people are sensitive enough not to do this when it comes to serious issues. For instance, if Luke told Macie, "I knew this might happen. Cancer runs in your family and your aunt never gets herself checked," most people would agree that Luke is pretty cold and unfeeling. In yet other cases, people avoid talking about the issue. Perhaps Luke has a hard time dealing with sickness so he says, "Let's get our minds off this and go to the beach or somewhere."

Not surprisingly, several studies have shown that people who use highly person-centered messages provide the best comfort and are perceived the most positively (Burleson & Samter, 1985a, 1985b; Jones & Burleson, 1997; Jones & Guerrero, 2001). Highly person-centered messages are perceived as the most appropriate, effective, helpful, and sensitive. These messages are likely to be effective in expressing care and concern, but perhaps more importantly, they might help the distressed person reevaluate the situation so that the event seems less distressing (Burleson & Goldsmith, 1998; S. M. Jones, 2000). Highly person-centered messages also have lasting effects. These lasting effects appear to occur one of two ways (High & Solomon, 2016). One way is that the highly person-centered message is immediately evaluated as supportive, leading the receiver to reappraise the situation and feel better. The other way is that the highly person-centered message is invisible at first but then has effects later. For example, initially Macie might be too stressed out and depressed to carefully process Luke's support messages about her aunt, but those messages still make an impact later. Other times people might not want to be supported, and therefore might rebel against the messages they hear. Later, however, they might realize that the information was helpful.

Nonverbal Immediacy

Of course, when comforting someone, it is important to use both nonverbal and verbal strategies. Jones and Guerrero (2001) investigated whether nonverbal immediacy behaviors and verbal person-centeredness work together to influence the quality of comforting behavior. They trained people to enact high, moderate, and low levels of nonverbal immediacy and person-centeredness and then had them listen and react to people's distressing stories. They found that both nonverbal immediacy behaviors and person-centeredness had strong effects on comforting quality. When distressed people interacted with someone who used high levels of nonverbal immediacy and high levels of person-centeredness, they reported feeling the best. When high person-centered messages were paired with low levels of nonverbal immediacy, or conversely, when low person-centered messages were paired with high levels of nonverbal immediacy, overall comforting quality decreased. Not surprisingly, comforters who used low levels of both nonverbal immediacy and person-centeredness were least effective at alleviating distress.

Other studies have also highlighted the important role nonverbal immediacy plays in providing high-quality, successful comforting (Jones, 2004; Jones & Burleson, 2003). Dolin and Booth-Butterfield (1993) asked students how they would comfort a roommate who was distressed because of a recent relational breakup. The students reported that they would use the following behaviors most frequently, with percentages showing how often a behavior was mentioned in the students' descriptions:

- *Hugs* (41.9%): Giving the person a whole-body hug or hugging him or her around the shoulder
- *Close proxemic distancing* (40.9%): Sitting down next to the person or leaning closer
- *Facial expression* (38.7%): Looking empathetic, sad, or concerned
- *Attentiveness* (37.7%): Listening carefully and nodding as the person talked about the distressing event
- *Increased miscellaneous touch* (34.4%): Using all forms of touch other than hugs or pats, such as holding the person's hand or stroking the person's hair
- *Pats* (26.9%): Using short, repetitive, movements such as patting the distressed person's arm or shoulder
- *Eye contact* (23.7%): Looking directly at the distressed person, particularly while the person was talking

In addition to these behaviors, Dolin and Booth-Butterfield (1993) found a few other nonverbal comforting strategies that were reported less often. Some students described behaviors related to weeping, such as crying with the distressed person or offering a "shoulder to cry on." Some said that they would engage in emotional distancing behavior, such as trying to remain uninvolved, getting comfortable, or fixing a cup of coffee. Presumably these strategies would keep the individual from experiencing too much negative affect while talking to the distressed person. Other students reported that they would engage in instrumental activities, such as getting the distressed person a tissue or something to eat. Still others indicated that they would show concern through warm vocal tones and empathetic gestures. For example, if the distressed person was angry, the individual in the comforting role might clench her or his fist to mirror the distressed person's anger.

As shown in the list above, touch is a particularly powerful mode for communicating comfort and support. Consistent with the idea of invisible support, Robinson, Hoplock, and Cameron (2015) found that "haptic support represents a unique form of support that does not rely on individuals' abilities to articulate their needs or to interpret another's accurately" (p. 835). In their study, one member of a couple was subjected to a stress-inducing task. Without even consciously being aware of it, the stressed partner often engaged in touch-seeking behavior and their partner then touched them. Effective support was provided naturally without partners necessarily even noticing the behavior.

Considered together, these studies suggest that when people want to do a good job comforting someone, they should pay attention to both their verbal and nonverbal behavior. In some cases, nonverbal forms of social support may be especially effective because they are somewhat "invisible." In other words, people can comfort someone without directly offering them advice or providing commentary on their situation. When a distressed person wants to talk, it is important for comforters to listen instead of changing the topic or focusing the discussion on themselves. When people can disclose their distressing circumstances freely to others, it helps them vent their negative emotion and possibly think through and reassess the problem, which can contribute to psychological and physical well-being (Burleson & Goldsmith, 1998; Pennebaker, 1989; Pennebaker, Colder, & Sharp, 1990). It is also important to remain positive when comforting a distressed person since people tend to match the affect that their partner expresses using immediacy cues (Jones & Wirtz, 2007).

SEX DIFFERENCES IN THE EXPERIENCE AND EXPRESSION OF CLOSENESS

Sex differences in closeness are important to consider. People sometimes expect women to be more affectionate and to provide more social support than men, and a number of studies confirm that women are generally more nonverbally immediate than men (Burgoon & Bacue, 2003). Yet it should not be presumed that men and women are completely different. Rather, men and women both achieve closeness and appreciate closeness, though in somewhat different ways. Indeed, research shows that men and women are far more similar than different in how they achieve emotional and relational closeness in both same-sex and opposite-sex relationships.

Perceptions of Closeness

Certainly, both men and women have the potential to develop very close relationships. Despite popular literature suggesting that men and women are from different planets, research has shown that men and women are far more similar than different. As noted in Chapter 10, according to Dindia, a more apt metaphor than "men are from Mars, and women are from Venus" is "men are from North Dakota, and women are from South Dakota" (Wood & Dindia, 1998). Both men and women believe that emotional communication is more important for developing close relationships than are instrumental or task-oriented skills (Burleson, Kunkel, Samter, & Werking, 1996). Perhaps surprisingly, this appears to be true in male friendships, female friendships, cross-sex friendships, and romantic relationships. As Burleson and fellow researchers (1996) discovered, "Affectively oriented communication skills appear to be important for both genders in the conduct of intimacy—regardless of whether intimacy is realized in same-sex friendship or opposite-sex romances" (p. 218).

Several other studies have demonstrated that there are few, if any, differences in closeness levels for men and women. In one study, college students reported similar levels of closeness in their same-sex versus cross-sex friendships (Johnson et al., 2003). Similarly, a study of committed Canadian couples produced almost identical reports of emotional, social, intellectual, and recreational intimacy for men and women (McCabe, 1999). Emotional intimacy referred to how much individuals felt their partner was there for them, social intimacy referred to how much people enjoyed spending time with their partner, intellectual intimacy referred to how much the partner helped expand and clarify one's thoughts, and recreational intimacy referred to how much they enjoyed doing activities together. In a study of Australian men's and women's friendships, there were no sex differences for behavioral or cognitive closeness, which suggests that men's and women's friendships are equally interdependent (Polimeni, Hardie, & Buzwell, 2002). There was, however, a small sex difference for emotional closeness; women reported more trust, affection, and caring in their same-sex friendships compared to men.

Despite the lack of sex differences found in some studies, some scholars have claimed that females have closer relationships than males, starting in childhood (Meurling, Ray, & LoBello, 1999). Others have argued that the finding that females have closer relationships than males may be due to the fact that researchers have employed a "feminine" definition of closeness (Wood & Inman, 1993). Most of the data on differences in closeness between men and women comes from research claiming that in the United States women disclose more than men (Floyd, 1995). But disclosure is only one type of closeness. Parks and Floyd (1996) pointed out that for decades, scholars have thought of close relationships as emotional, feminine, and affectionate rather than instrumental, masculine, and logical. Because men's relationships are somewhat lower in emotional expression and self-disclosure, men were thought not to have very close relationships. However, there is little actual evidence for a difference in the closeness of men's and women's friendships. In fact, Parks and Floyd (1996) found no support for the hypothesis that women are more likely than men to label their relationships as "intimate" or "close."

Communication of Closeness

When sex differences do emerge, they tend to revolve around how men and women communicate closeness in their same-sex friendships. Females are more likely to have **expressive friendships** that involve using emotionally charged nonverbal and verbal communication during conversations, showing nonverbal affection, talking about fears, and shopping (Floyd, 1995; Helgeson, Shaver, & Dyer, 1987; Monsour, 1992). Studies also suggest that girls show more trust and loyalty, more dependence on friends, and a greater tendency to discuss their relationships with friends than do boys (Meurling, Ray, & Lobello, 1999; Sharabany, Gershoni, & Hoffman, 1981). Similarly, Floyd (2006) reported a series of studies that show that in general, women

express more affection than men in same-sex dyads, even though men increase their level of affection to nearly the same level as women in cross-sex friendships. Another study showed that women use more emotional nonverbal cues, such as emoticons and descriptions of nonverbal behaviors (e.g., typing in *sigh*) than men do when providing social support via e-mail (Ledbetter & Larson, 2008).

Males, in contrast, are more likely to have **agentic friendships** that focus on companionship and shared activities (Rawlins, 1982). Sharing adventures, telling stories, doing physical labor, working on a joint project, taking a fishing trip, and serving in the army are all experiences that develop and sustain closeness in their own way. Floyd (1995) found that among college students, males are more likely than females to develop closeness through shaking hands, drinking together, and talking about sex. These action-oriented behaviors may be just as valid a path to high levels of closeness as self-disclosure or emotional expression.

The distinction between expressive and agentic friendships was illustrated in a study by Caldwell and Peplau (1982) who asked men and women to choose whether they would rather "just talk" or "do some activity" with a same-sex friend. Women preferred talking, 57% to 43%, whereas men overwhelmingly preferred activity, 84% to 16%. However, this distinction does not mean that women friends never do activities together; they do. Nor does it mean that men never get together just to talk; sometimes they do. The distinction simply means that given a preference, more women would want to get together just to talk whereas more men would want to get together to engage in an activity.

Preferences for Same-Sex Versus Cross-Sex Friendships

In much of the research on friendships, there is an implicit assumption that people's closest friendships tend to be with members of the same sex. Recent research casts doubt on this assumption. Specifically, Baumgarte and Nelson (2009) found that college students were just as likely to prefer having a close friendship with someone of the opposite sex as someone of the same sex. Like past work, this study showed that women's same-sex friendships were generally perceived to be higher in closeness, common interests, caring, and trust than men's same-sex friendships. However, this difference disappeared or reversed when preferences for same-sex versus cross-sex friendships were considered. For example, women who preferred cross-sex friendships reported that they were just as interested in sharing activities as talking with their male friends. These women also rated their friendships with men as more caring,

supportive, and trusting than their friendships with women. This study suggests that the increased prevalence of cross-sex friendships may be closing the gap between men's and women's communication styles. As Baumgarte and Nelson (2009) put it, stereotypes of women as expressive and men as agentic may be "relevant primarily to those who hold a strong preference for same-sex friendship. Those who prefer cross-sex friendship either make much weaker distinctions based on the sex of their friends, or they hold values that reflect a reversal of these stereotypes" (p. 915).

SUMMARY AND APPLICATION

As this chapter has emphasized, people communicate closeness in various ways. Luke is very close to both Macie and Dan, but closeness is communicated somewhat differently in these two relationships. Luke's relationship with Macie emphasizes deep conversations, lots of time spent together, long eye contact, and romantic touch as manifestations of emotional and relational closeness. Luke communicates closeness to Dan in different ways through playing ball and skiing, debating political issues, discussing their careers, and sharing a ball game and some refreshments on a Sunday afternoon. Although these differences reflect stereotypes about the type of behavior that is appropriate in romantic relationships versus male friendships, there are also many ways that Luke displays closeness similarly to Dan and Macie. He frequently uses immediacy behaviors such as smiling, using idioms, and speaking in a warm, confidential voice with both of them.

Indeed, to have truly close relationships with both Macie and Dan, Luke needs to break away from stereotypical behavior. For example, to sustain emotional closeness with Macie, it is essential that Luke do things that men often forget to do, such as listening during conversations and

looking at Macie when she is talking. For her part, it is important Macie remember to share in Luke's activities, such as skiing or watching a ball game. She may need to try some activities that Luke likes even though she never attempted them before. And, Luke and Dan may need to have periodic talks that include in-depth self-disclosure. They should also not be afraid to show each other affection through verbal, nonverbal, or supportive behavior.

Indeed, real connection is impossible without communication. As CVT suggests, closeness is created by two people through a series of moves and countermoves. Luke cannot develop or sustain a close relationship by himself; instead, "it takes two to tango." It is also important to remember that close relationships occur in a larger context. Luke needs to understand that factors such as Dan's or Macie's cultural background, the context or situation of their interaction, Dan's and Macie's moods and states, their personality, their level of rewardingness, and, of course, the stage of their relationship can all influence whether immediate communication is accepted or rejected. As Luke and Macie developed their relationship and became closer, it was important for them to define where they were in their relationship. Saying "I love you," giving rings, and planning a future together were important ways to express affection and develop emotional and relational closeness. However, Luke and Macie were careful not to make such moves too early in their relationship. They waited until there was a mutual level of affection so that they wouldn't scare each other off. Understanding the six cognitive valencers can help partners like Macie and Luke be better equipped to know when (and when not) to increase immediacy with each other.

The research in this chapter also provides you with some guidelines for how to provide more effective social support to others, even though there is no magic bullet when it comes to relieving the distress of others. Supportive communication is only effective if it helps people reappraise the situation in a way that reduces distress. Luke, like the rest of us, may find himself giving both invisible and visible (but hopefully person-centered and immediate) social support to family and friends, including Macie and Dan. At the moment, providing effective supportive communication to Macie

would be especially important since she is dealing with a family crisis. For his attempts at social support to be effective, Luke should focus on listening to and validating Macie's feelings and concerns. He should also offer emotional support so that Macie feels cared for and loved. Other types of supportive communication may also be helpful. For example, Luke might give tangible aid by going with Macie to drive her aunt to doctor's appointments. He might also give her network support by helping her find credible information on breast cancer and telling her about discussion boards where she could go to communicate with others who are in a similar situation to hers. When providing these types of support, Luke should be sure to imply that Macie is fully capable of dealing with the situation on her own and that he is only trying to be helpful. Finally, the best social support occurs in the context of emotionally close relationships where people feel safe, secure, and supported, so Luke is in a good position to help Macie cope with her distress. Hopefully, the research in this chapter has put you in a good position as well.

KEY TERMS

affection exchange theory (p. 171)

affectionate communication (p. 169)

agentic friendships (p. 193)

assurances (p. 174)

body synchrony (p. 179)

chronemics (p. 179)

cognitive valence theory (CVT) (p. 179)

cognitive valencers (p. 179)

direct emotional expressions (p. 174)

emotional closeness (p. 170)

emotional support (p. 184)

esteem support (p. 184)

expressive friendships (p. 193)

haptics (p. 178)

idiomatic behaviors (p. 175)

immediacy behaviors (p. 176)

informational support (p. 184)

interpersonal valence (p. 182)

invisible support phenomenon (p. 188)

kinesics (p. 178)

network support (p. 184)

oculesics (p. 177)

paradox of affection (p. 171)

person-centered messages (p. 190)

physical closeness (p. 170)

positive involvement behaviors (p. 176)

proxemics (p. 178)

relational closeness (p. 170)

social meaning model of nonverbal communication (p. 174)

support behaviors (p. 175)

tangible aid (p. 184)

verbal immediacy (p. 176)

viability (p. 172)

vocalic behavior (p. 175)

vocalics (p. 179)

DISCUSSION QUESTIONS

1. Which of the three types of closeness discussed in this chapter—(1) physical, (2) emotional, or (3) relational—do you think is most important within close relationships? Why? Also, how do you think these three types of closeness vary based on relationship type, such as relatives versus friends or lovers?

2. Do you agree or disagree with the principles guiding affection exchange theory? How might the theory explain patterns of affectionate communication in relationships between friends or adopted children and their parents?

3. If you want to give friends or loved ones effective social support, what should you say and do? What might you avoid saying or doing? Do you agree or disagree with the idea that invisible support is often more effective than visible support? Explain your reasoning.

 SAGE edge™

Sharpen your skills with SAGE edge at edge.sagepub.com/guerrero5e.
SAGE edge for students provides a personalized approach to help you accomplish your coursework goals in an easy-to-use learning environment.

8 MAKING A LOVE CONNECTION
Styles of Love and Attachment

Gabriela and Brian have been dating for several months. Although they care deeply for one another, problems have started to surface in their relationship. Brian wishes Gabriela would show him more affection. Every time they get really close, she seems to pull away. She also seems to put her career ahead of their relationship. Just last week, she cancelled their Saturday night date so she could spend extra time working on an advertising campaign. Sometimes Brian wonders if he cares more for Gabriela than she cares for him. Gabriela, in contrast, wants Brian to give her more space. She doesn't understand why he needs her to say "I love you" so often. Shouldn't he understand how she feels without her having to tell him all the time? After all, she always makes sure to fit some quality time with Brian into her busy schedule, and they do all sorts of activities together—golfing, skiing, and watching old movies. Sometimes Gabriela wonders if she can devote enough time to the relationship to satisfy Brian. Maybe she's just not ready for the level of commitment he wants.

Who do you relate to more—Gabriela or Brian? Gabriela is focused on her career. She expresses love by engaging in activity, and she values her autonomy. Brian, on the other hand, is more focused on the relationship. He expresses his feelings by saying "I love you" and showing affection. Are Gabriela and Brian's attitudes toward love fairly common? What other attitudes do people have about love? How do they know if they are really in love? Finally, can two people such as Gabriela and Brian—who have such different needs, priorities, and communication styles—be happy together?

The literature on love and attachment helps answer these questions.

In this chapter, we examine different styles of love and attachment. Before doing so, we define love and discuss two major perspectives on how people experience various types of love: (1) Sternberg's triangle of love and (2) Lee's love styles. Next, we discuss different ways that people communicate love. Finally, we discuss **attachment theory**. Attachment is an important part of various loving relationships, including relationships between family members, romantic partners, and close friends.

WHAT IS LOVE?

When love is shared, it is one of the most wonderful human experiences. When love is not returned, people feel rejected and miserable. Researchers have spent considerable energy investigating love. Some of this research has focused on answering basic questions, addressed in the upcoming sections, and including the following: Is loving a distinctly different experience than **liking**? How do people meet and fall in love? And are there different types of love?

LOVING VERSUS LIKING

Some researchers have tried to distinguish loving from liking. Rubin (1970, 1973, 1974) suggested that there are qualitative, rather than quantitative, differences between loving and liking. In other words, liking someone a lot does not necessarily translate into loving someone. Loving is more than an abundance of liking, and loving and liking are related but distinctly different concepts. People can, in some cases, love others without liking them very much. In general, however, individuals tend to like the people they love. For example, Rubin (1970, 1973) found that people *like* their close friends and dating partners about equally, but *love* their dating partners more than their friends. Romantic partners who are "in love" and plan to marry also report loving each other more than dating partners who do not have concrete plans for the future. Thus, romance and commitment appear to be important in many love relationships.

Liking and loving can be distinguished from each other by certain feelings and relationship characteristics (Davis & Roberts, 1985; Davis & Todd, 1982, 1985; Rubin, 1973). Some of the key characteristics defining liking are affection, respect, trust, feeling comfortable together, and enjoying each other's company. Love is a deeper and more intense bond than liking because it is characterized by stronger attachment, a level of caring that includes making sacrifices for one another, and emotional and behavioral interdependence. **Passion** is also a key ingredient in some love relationships. Passion includes being fascinated by the loved one, feeling that the relationship is unique and exclusive, and experiencing strong sexual desire. Of course, love also occurs in nonromantic relationships such as those between parents and children or best friends. In these cases, the levels of attachment, caring, and interdependence are especially high.

Love as a Triangle

Sternberg's (1986, 1988) triangular theory of love also distinguishes between liking and different types of love. This theory includes three components related to love—(1) **intimacy,** (2) passion, and (3) commitment—pictured as sides of a triangle. According to Sternberg, liking occurs when a person experiences high levels of intimacy but relatively low levels of passion and commitment in a relationship. Love occurs when intimacy combines with passion or commitment. The most complete type of love, **consummate love,** is based on having high levels of all three components (see Box 8.1).

INTIMACY: THE "WARM" COMPONENT Intimacy is based on feelings of emotional connection and closeness and has therefore been called the "warm" part of love. Among the three sides of Sternberg's (1986) triangle, intimacy is seen as most foundational to both love and liking. Liking is defined by intimacy alone. When passion is combined with intimacy, people experience **romantic love**. This type of love often characterizes initial stages of dating relationships, when two people are sexually attracted to each other and feel an intimate connection but have not yet fully committed themselves to the relationship. When commitment is combined with intimacy, **friendship love** emerges. This type of love transcends relationship type (Fehr & Russell, 1991). In other words, love for family members and friends fits this description, as does love between romantic partners who have been together for a long

BOX 8.1 HIGHLIGHTS
SELECTED LOVE TRIANGLES

Types of Love	Intimacy	Passion	Commitment
Liking	+	−	−
Infatuation	−	+	−
Romantic love	+	+	−
Friendship love	+	−	+
Empty love	−	−	+
Consummate love	+	+	+

time or consider themselves to be best friends more than lovers. Many scholars consider these two types of love to be universal and to have existed throughout time (Berscheid, 2010). When these two types of love are experienced together so that a relationship contains high levels of intimacy, passion, and commitment, people achieve consummate love.

Sternberg theorized that intimacy is moderately stable over the course of a relationship. However, he made an important distinction between latent and manifest intimacy. **Latent intimacy** refers to internal feelings of closeness and interpersonal warmth, which are not directly observable by others. This type of intimacy is what we feel inside. **Manifest intimacy** refers to how people communicate affection and closeness to someone, such as disclosing intimate feelings to a partner or spending extra time together. According to Sternberg (1986), latent intimacy is likely to increase and then reach a plateau as a relationship develops. Once two people have reached a high level of latent intimacy, their level of psychological and emotional connection usually remains high unless the relationship starts to deteriorate. Manifest intimacy, by contrast, is likely to grow during the initial stages of a relationship, reach

its peak when people are in the process of moving the relationship from casual to serious, but then decline over time as people feel less of a need to show one another how they feel.

Research has shown some support for Sternberg's predictions. Acker and Davis (1992) found that couples felt more intimacy and closeness as their relationships became more serious; however, behavioral (or manifest) intimacy decreased as the relationship progressed. Guerrero and Andersen (1991) found a similar pattern for touch in public settings. Couples in serious dating relationships touched more than married couples, yet spouses felt just as close to each other as did daters. Emmers and Dindia (1995) found a similar pattern for private touch. Even though married couples used less touch to manifest intimacy, they still experienced very high levels of latent intimacy. Every couple is different, but Figure 8.1 shows the general pattern of latent and manifest intimacy over time. This pattern explains why couples who are escalating their relationships or have recently become "official" often show each other more affection through behaviors such as touch, flirting, and staying up all night and talking, than do couples who have been together for a while.

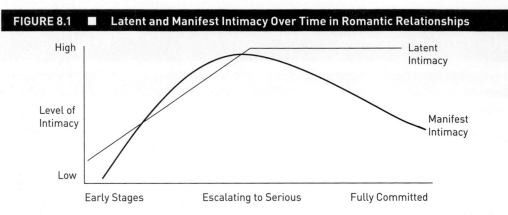

FIGURE 8.1 ■ Latent and Manifest Intimacy Over Time in Romantic Relationships

Established couples usually feel just as close as new couples, but they are past the honeymoon stage and feel less of a need to communicate intimacy overtly. This can be helpful for couples to know; as they become more committed, partners should expect a drop in manifest intimacy but understand that the level of latent intimacy is probably still high.

PASSION: THE "HOT" COMPONENT According to Sternberg (1986, 1988), passion is the "hot" component of love that consists of motivation and arousal. However, passion is not limited to sexual arousal. Friends can experience excitement through activities or by just being together. Passion also includes motivational needs for affiliation, control, and self-actualization. Thus, parents can feel a passionate love for their children that includes an intense desire for them to achieve success and happiness. In romantic relationships, however, passion is often experienced primarily as sexual attraction and arousal. When people have this type of passion without much intimacy or commitment, they are experiencing **infatuation.** Infatuated individuals idealize the objects of their affection and imagine that their lives would be wonderful if they could develop a relationship with that person. Some researchers also argue that infatuation is blind because people downplay dissimilarities and other potential problems when they are infatuated with someone (McClanahan,

Gold, Lenney, Ryckman, & Kulberg, 1990). Because infatuation is based on the "hot" component of the love triangle, it is not surprising that infatuated individuals often fall in and out of love quickly, as their passion heats up and then cools down.

Passion is also relatively unstable as relationships progress, with passion levels often fluctuating greatly during the course of a relationship. Passion and romance tend to be high during the initial stages of a relationship but then level off as the relationship becomes more predictable and less arousing (Hatfield & Sprecher, 1986a; Sternberg, 1986). This is not to say that long-term romantic relationships are devoid of passion. As Sternberg (1986) suggested, highly committed couples are likely to cycle back and forth in terms of passion. A romantic weekend away or a candlelight dinner followed by stargazing in a hot tub can provide an important passionate spark to a long-term relationship. Sternberg's point is that these types of events occur less often in developed relationships because it is hard to sustain a high level of passion all of the time. Acker and Davis (1992) found that people feel and desire less passion as they grow older, which suggests that passion may be more characteristic of young romances and the reproductive years than mature relationships. However, Acker and Davis also found that while women were more passionate in new relationships compared to established relationships, men showed fairly high levels of passion regardless of whether the relationship was new or old.

COMMITMENT: THE "COOL" COMPONENT The third component of Sternberg's (1986, 1988) love triangle is commitment/decision. This component refers to the decision to love someone and the commitment to maintain that love. Because commitment is based on cognition and decision making, Sternberg referred to it as the "cool" or "cold" component. Commitment is undoubtedly an important part of love for many people. In a study by Fehr (1988), college-aged students rated how closely various words or phrases, such as *affection* and *missing each other when apart,* relate to love. Of the 68 words and phrases Fehr listed, the word *trust* was rated as most central to love. *Commitment* ranked 8th overall, suggesting that it is also highly central to love. The other two components of the triangular theory of love were also important, although less central, with *intimacy* ranking 19th and *sexual passion* rating 40th. Fehr (1988) also had college-aged students rate words and phrases describing the concept of commitment. *Loyalty, responsibility, living up to one's word, faithfulness,* and *trust* were the top five descriptors of commitment, suggesting that commitment involves being there for someone over the long haul.

Of the three components of the love triangle, commitment is most stable over time. In long-term relationships, commitment typically builds gradually and then stabilizes (Acker & Davis, 1992). Commitment also appears to play an important role in keeping a relationship satisfying and stable. In the Acker and Davis study, intimacy, passion, and commitment were all related positively to satisfaction, but commitment, followed by intimacy, were the strongest predictors of satisfaction. Hendrick, Hendrick, and Adler (1988) conducted a study to determine whether commitment, relational satisfaction, or investment of time and effort was the best predictor of relational stability. They found that commitment was the best predictor of whether dating couples would still be together two months later. Thus, commitment

is not only a part of most love relationships but also a stabilizing force within these relationships.

Yet commitment alone is not enough to keep a relationship happy. When individuals experience **empty love**, they have commitment but relatively low levels of intimacy and passion. Some long-term relationships fall into this category. For instance, if partners no longer feel attached to each other but stay together for religious reasons or because of the children, their love might be characterized as empty. In other cases, empty love characterizes the beginning of a relationship. For example, spouses in arranged marriages may begin their relationships with empty love. Intimacy and passion may, or may not, emerge later.

Finding Love and Falling in Love

Although arranged marriages are rare in Western cultures, they are still common in parts of Africa, Asia, and the Middle East (Batabyal, 2001). Worldwide, more than half of all marriages are arranged, and in India, almost 90% of marriages are (Harden, 2016). A small percentage of these marriages involve force rather than free choice, but most modern arranged marriages allow the prospective bride and groom to make the final decision regarding whether or not they will marry. Families and friends act as matchmakers or well-wishers who search for a suitable partner for their loved one. If the social network agrees, two people meet and courtship may ensue. Research has shown that couples in modern arranged marriages are, on average, as satisfied with their relationships as are couples in marriages based on personal choice (Myers, Madathil, & Tingle, 2005).

In some ways, modern arranged marriages are not that different from pre-20th-century relationships in the United States. Mongeau, Hale, Johnson, and Hillis (1993) noted that at the end of the 19th century, courtship involved men "calling" on women at their homes. The "call" often involved the woman inviting the man over for dinner or tea in the presence of her family. Around the beginning of the 20th century, dating started to replace calling. Dating involved two people going somewhere outside of the home together, often to have dinner out and go to a concert, play, or social event. This shift from calling to dating also entailed a change in who initiated the get-acquainted process. With calling, a woman's family largely controlled the situation—they could invite the man over and decide what food and home entertainment they would provide. With dating, men usually controlled the situation—they asked the woman out, provided transportation, and paid for the date. This also marked a shift in how people met and fell in love; personal attraction started to outweigh family approval and practical concerns as reasons to explore having a romantic relationship with someone.

Much has changed from the beginning of the 20th century until now. Rosenfeld and Thomas (2012) conducted a study to determine how married couples in the United States met. They surveyed over 3,000 married individuals of different ages and backgrounds. Around 25% of married couples who met in 1940 reported that their family had facilitated their meeting. Families become less influential than friends throughout the rest of the 20th century, so that the percentage of couples who reported meeting through friends rose from 21% in 1940 to a high of around 40% in the 1980s and 1990s. Other ways of meeting one's spouse, such as in high school, through neighbors, or through one's church, have also declined, whereas meeting one's spouse in college has become more common. Between 1995 and 2005, the Internet was a fast-growing way of meeting. In fact, 22% of married couples who met in 2009 said that they got together through the Internet, making the Internet one of most common ways to meet one's spouse. The most frequently mentioned way to meet was still through friends (although this way of meeting had dropped to under 30% by 2009); the Internet and meeting at a public place such as a restaurant or bar tied for second place. The Internet was an even more common way for same-sex couples to meet; over 60% of same-sex couples who were interviewed in 2009 reported that they met online. (To learn more about the advantages and disadvantages of looking for love online, see Box 8.2.)

Of course, meeting and falling in love are two very different things. Most people meet a lot of potential partners but only fall in love with a few if that. Indeed, lasting romantic relationships are distinguished from other types of love relationships by the process of falling in love or being "in love." In one study, college students were asked to write the names of members of their social network under four categories: (1) friends, (2) people they love, (3) people they are in love with, and (4) people whom they feel sexual desire toward (Meyers & Berscheid, 1997). The students were told that they could place a person's name in more than one category. Most students only put one person in the "in love" category, and that person was also listed in the "friend" and "sexual desire" categories, which suggests that being in love is related to both intimacy and passion, as Sternberg (1986, 1988) predicted in his triangular theory of love.

So how do people fall in love? A study by Aron, Dutton, Aron, and Iverson (1989) attempted to answer this question by contrasting the experience of "falling in love" with the experience of "falling in friendship." In some ways, this distinction is similar to the differences between love and liking discussed earlier in this chapter. However, falling in love and being in love are distinctly different from loving someone; falling in love and being "in love" imply a romantic connection. Falling in friendship can involve liking or loving someone but not in a romantic way. Aron and his colleagues found that falling in love was facilitated most by reciprocal liking (self-disclosure and other actions that show feelings are mutual) and noticing the partner's desirable characteristics (such as a good personality and attractive appearance). Other studies have confirmed that reciprocal liking and desirable characteristics are central to the process of falling in love (Pines, 2001; Riela, Rodriguez, Aron, Xu, & Acevedo, 2010; Sprecher et al., 1994). Falling in friendship, on the other hand, is more strongly related to perceived similarity and being in proximity to one another (Aron et al., 1989).

BOX 8.2 TECH TALK
LOOKING FOR LOVE IN ONLINE PLACES

Looking for love online is now commonplace, but does it actually improve your chances of finding love? Based on the research, the answer seems to be yes and no. A review of the research on online dating suggests looking for love online is different from traditional dating in three important ways: (1) level of access, (2) type of communication, and (3) degree of matching (Finkel, Eastwick, Karney, Reis, & Sprecher, 2012).

Access is an advantage in that you can meet people online who you would never otherwise meet. You can also meet people at times that are convenient for you rather than trying to coordinate schedules. You are no longer limited to meeting people who live near you or go to school with you. Physical proximity is unnecessary. However, access also means that you might be choosier, thinking that there is an unlimited supply of possible partners waiting to meet you out in cyberspace.

There are also advantages and disadvantages when it comes to communicating online. One big advantage is that you can gain information and reduce uncertainty about someone without investing the time to meet face to face. This can help you narrow the field. However, people do not always present themselves authentically on the Internet. People also tend to overinterpret social cues and see potential partners more positively when communicating online versus face to face. Both the ease with which people can misrepresent themselves and the overinterpretation

of social cues can lead people to be disappointed when they meet in person. Another issue is that online communication is missing some of the nonverbal elements that characterize face-to-face communication, including timing and feedback. Therefore, it can be hard to determine if you will "click" and be "in sync" with someone based only on online communication.

In terms of matching, you have probably seen commercials promising that their dating site will help you find your "perfect match" by connecting you to someone who is compatible with you in almost every way. Finkel and his colleagues (2012) cautioned, however, that the methods these companies use to match people are in-house and not verifiable by social scientists. They also note that people might expect to find their perfect soulmate by using these sites, which can lead to disappointment. Also, sometimes people match on paper but do not click in person.

So what does the research on online dating tell us so far? It seems that online dating is a pathway to love for some people, but like any other way of starting a relationship, it is successful in some cases but not others. The research suggests, however, that if you meet someone online and think that there is a possibility for a relationship to develop, it is important to get together in a face-to-face context sooner rather than later, so that unrealistic expectations don't develop.

LOVE STYLES

When people fall in love, they can communicate their feelings in a variety of ways, including through self-disclosure, emotional responses, and time spent together. Two perspectives in particular describe different styles of loving. The first focuses on different **ideologies** that people hold about love. The second focuses on different styles of communicating love.

Lee's Love Styles

Lee (1973, 1977, 1988) argued that people have various ideologies when it comes to love. These ideologies can be thought of as collections of beliefs, values, and expectations about love. Lee also contended that there are three primary styles of loving, much as there are three primary colors. When mixing paint, the primary colors are red, blue, and yellow. Mixing these three colors can create any color in the rainbow. Lee

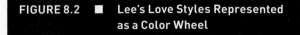

FIGURE 8.2 ■ Lee's Love Styles Represented as a Color Wheel

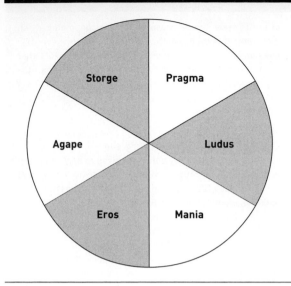

Note: The primary styles are shaded; the secondary styles are composed of the aspects of the two primary styles adjacent to them.

conceptualized styles of loving in a similar manner. He proposed that the primary love styles are **eros,** or romantic love; **storge,** or friendship love; and **ludus,** or game-playing love. Just as the primary colors can be blended to create a multitude of different hues, Lee theorized that elements of the three primary styles of love can combine to create a vast number of love styles. Of the many possible combinations, Lee suggested that three are the most common: (1) **mania,** or possessive love; (2) **agape,** or compassionate love; and (3) **pragma,** or practical love. Figure 8.2 depicts Lee's love styles as a color wheel.

Each style of love is defined by both positive and negative characteristics. The more strongly and exclusively a person identifies with a single style, the more likely the person is to experience some of the negative characteristics associated with that style. Most people, however, report identifying with a combination of styles—with one or two styles experienced most strongly. Box 8.3 gives a scale by which you can determine your own love style.

EROS: ROMANTIC LOVE Eros, which has also been termed romantic or **passionate love**, is rooted in feelings of affection, attraction, and sexual desire. It is also closely related to being "in love" and feeling secure in relationships (Galinha, Oishi, Pereira, Wirtz, & Esteves, 2014; Lee, 1988). Individuals with the eros style look for partners who are physically attractive and good lovers (Lee, 1988; Levine, Aune, & Park, 2006). They are eager to develop intense, passionate relationships and often experience intense emotional highs and lows. They also feel substantial arousal and desire physical contact. Because they possess strong feelings of attraction, eros lovers develop a sense of intimacy and connectedness relatively quickly. These individuals are "intense communicators" who show high levels of self-disclosure, are able to elicit similarly high levels of self-disclosure from their partners, and display high levels of touch and nonverbal affection (Taraban, Hendrick, & Hendrick, 1998, p. 346). They are also good at coping with stress, which contributes to feeling satisfied in their relationships (Vedes et al., 2016). When eros lovers want to intensify their relationships, they tend to use strategies such as increasing contact, giving tokens of affection (e.g., sending gifts or flowers), and changing their behavior to please their partner (Levine et al., 2006). Compared to other types of lovers, eros lovers also report a stronger desire to increase closeness with their partners (Goodboy & Booth-Butterfield, 2009). Romantic love is also related to engaging in everyday forms of routine communication, such as asking about each other's day or discussing current events or television shows (Tagawa & Yashida, 2006).

Eros is a central part of many love relationships. This type of love is common in the initial stages of romantic relationships. Eros love can also evolve into a more friendship-based and secure style of love as the relationship progresses (Hendrick et al., 1988). Some level of eros also keeps relationships exciting and passionate. However, too much eros can have negative effects. For example, if you are only interested in someone because of the person's beauty, the attraction may fade quickly. Also, some eros lovers have trouble

BOX 8.3 PUT YOURSELF TO THE TEST
WHAT IS YOUR LOVE STYLE?

To determine your dominant love style, rate yourself on each of these statements according to the following scale: 1 = strongly disagree and 5 = strongly agree.

		Strongly Disagree				Strongly Agree
1.	My partner and I were attracted to each other immediately when we first met.	1	2	3	4	5
2.	My partner and I have the right physical chemistry.	1	2	3	4	5
3.	The physical part of our relationship is intense and satisfying.	1	2	3	4	5
4.	My partner and I were meant for each other.	1	2	3	4	5
5.	My partner fits my ideal standards of physical attractiveness.	1	2	3	4	5
6.	I try to keep my partner a little uncertain about my commitment to her/him.	1	2	3	4	5
7.	I believe that what my partner doesn't know about me won't hurt her/him.	1	2	3	4	5
8.	I could get over my relationship with my partner pretty easily.	1	2	3	4	5
9.	When my partner gets too dependent on me, I back off.	1	2	3	4	5
10.	I enjoy playing the field.	1	2	3	4	5
11.	It is hard for me to say exactly when our friendship turned into love.	1	2	3	4	5
12.	To be genuine, our love first required caring.	1	2	3	4	5
13.	Our love is the best kind because it grew out of a close friendship.	1	2	3	4	5
14.	Our love is really a deep friendship, not a mysterious or mystical emotion.	1	2	3	4	5
15.	Our love relationship is satisfying because it developed from a good friendship.	1	2	3	4	5
16.	I considered what my partner was going to become in life before committing myself to her/him.	1	2	3	4	5
17.	I tried to plan my life carefully before choosing a partner.	1	2	3	4	5
18.	In choosing my partner, I believed it was best to find someone with a similar background.	1	2	3	4	5
19.	An important factor in choosing my partner was whether she/he would be a good parent.	1	2	3	4	5
20.	Before getting very involved with my partner, I tried to figure out how compatible our goals were.	1	2	3	4	5

(Continued)

BOX 8.3 (Continued)

21.	If my partner and I broke up, I don't know how I would cope.	1	2	3	4	5
22.	It drives me crazy when my partner doesn't pay enough attention to me.	1	2	3	4	5
23.	I'm so in love with my partner that I sometimes have trouble concentrating on anything else.	1	2	3	4	5
24.	I cannot relax if I suspect that my partner is with someone else.	1	2	3	4	5
25.	I wish I could spend every minute of every day with my partner.	1	2	3	4	5
26.	I would rather suffer myself than let my partner suffer.	1	2	3	4	5
27.	I am usually willing to sacrifice my own wishes to let my partner achieve her/his goals.	1	2	3	4	5
28.	Whatever I own is my partner's to use as she/he pleases.	1	2	3	4	5
29.	When my partner behaves badly, I still love her/him fully and unconditionally.	1	2	3	4	5
30.	I would endure all things for the sake of my partner.	1	2	3	4	5

Add up the following items to get your score on each love style.

Eros: Items 1–5 _____

Ludus: Items 6–10 _____

Storge: Items 11–15 _____

Pragma: Items 16–20 _____

Mania: Items 21–25 _____

Agape: Items 26–30 _____

Higher scores mean that you possess more of a particular love style. The highest possible score for a given style is 25; the lowest possible score is 5.

Source: This is an abbreviated, modified version of Hendrick and Hendrick's (1990) love attitudes scale.

adjusting after the initial "hot" attraction begins to cool or after they discover that the partner, who seemed perfect at first, cannot possibly live up to their unrealistically high expectations. Still, research suggests that maintaining some degree of eros is beneficial in a relationship. Hendrick and associates (1988) found that dating couples were more likely to stay together if the partners were high in eros and low in the ludic, game-playing style of love, which suggests that passion and commitment are both important in many love relationships.

STORGE: FRIENDSHIP LOVE This type of love, which is also called **companionate love,** is based on high levels of intimacy and commitment but comparatively low levels of passion (Sternberg, 1986, 1988). Grote and Frieze (1994) defined friendship love as "a comfortable, affectionate, trusting love for a likable partner, based on a deep sense of friendship and involving companionship and the enjoyment of common activities, mutual interests, shared laughter" (p. 275). Friendship love has been called the glue that keeps relationships together because it is thought to be enduring. People who identify with storgic love also report feeling good about themselves and their relationships (Galinha et al., 2014). However, Berscheid (2010) cautioned that storgic love is based on shows of similarity, reciprocal self-disclosure, shared activities, and mutual validation. If these activities wane, friendship love will also wane.

Storgic lovers have relationships based on affection, shared values and goals, and compatibility (Lee, 1988). Physical attraction is not as important as security, companionship, task sharing, and joint activity. Indeed, when asked what they find attractive in potential romantic partners, storgic individuals endorse personality characteristics, such as intelligence, understanding, a good personality, compassion, and communication skills rather than physical characteristics (Levine et al., 2006). Although these relationships are not very exciting, they are dependable and stable. Levine and colleagues found that people with a storgic style tended not to report using secret tests, which are indirect, sometimes sneaky ways of trying to find out information, such as asking third parties what they know, seeing if your partner gets jealous when you flirt with someone, or taking a break to find out if your partner will miss you (see Chapter 4 for more on secret tests). Presumably, storgic lovers do not need to use secret tests because their relationships tend to be secure with little uncertainty.

For storgic individuals, love often is framed as a partnership or a lifelong journey. Thus, it is important that the two individuals want the same things—perhaps a home and family, or perhaps independence and the ability to travel together to exotic places. Like a person with an old pair of blue jeans, storgic lovers feel extremely comfortable with each other, and emotions tend to be positive but muted. Unlike some other love styles, storgic lovers do not experience many intense emotional highs or lows. Yet this type of love tends to last. Because storgic lovers trust each other and do not require high levels of emotional stimulation and arousal, they are able to withstand long separations. For example, military couples may be better able to withstand their time apart if they are storgic lovers. Although they are likely to be sad when parted from each other, their trust and relational security keeps them from being distressed. Other types of lovers (e.g., erotic, manic) feel much higher levels of distress because their relationships are fueled by physical attraction and the physical presence of the loved one. Of course, it is important to keep in mind that although trust and security can provide a safety net for a relationship, too much stability can lead to predictability and boredom. Thus, bringing excitement and emotion to the relationship is often the biggest challenge for storgic lovers.

LUDUS: GAME-PLAYING LOVE Ludic lovers see relationships as fun, playful, and casual; they view relationships as games to be played and are less committed and less securely attached to relationships than are people with other love styles (Galinha et al., 2014). They also have difficulty coping with stress in their relationships, presumably because they like to keep their relationships casual and fun (Vedes et al., 2016). Like eros lovers, they look for partners who are physically attractive and good lovers (Levine et al., 2006). The opening lines ludic lovers report using highlight the game-playing aspect of this love style. Specifically, Levine and associates found that ludus was associated with using cute or flippant opening lines when meeting people, such as saying, "Someone like you should be arrested for being too beautiful." The lack of commitment that characterizes the ludic style is also reflected in their communication; ludic lovers are less likely to report using increased contact, relationship talk, or bids for commitment (e.g., agreeing to have an exclusive relationship) than are people with other love styles (Levine et al., 2006), which makes sense since they also report desiring less closeness with their partners than do people with other love styles (Goodboy & Booth-Butterfield, 2009). When ludic lovers do want to intensify their relationships, their preferred strategies are to be more affectionate and sexually intimate. Compared to the other love styles, individuals with the ludic style are also the least likely to value communication skills related to emotional support and comfort within their relationships (Kunkel & Burleson, 2003).

Because they avoid commitment and prefer to play the field rather than settle down with one person (Lee, 1988), ludic lovers are also more likely to have on-again off-again relationships and to use certain types of secret tests. Levine and fellow researchers (2006) found that rather than using direct communication, ludic lovers reported trying to get information indirectly by asking third parties, checking for fidelity or jealousy, and increasing the costs in the relationship to see if the partner will still stick around. Ludic lovers also tend to use negative strategies to try to maintain their relationships, such as making the partner jealous or being unfaithful (Goodboy, Myers, & Members of Investigating Communication, 2010). People with the ludic style also share relatively little personal information with their partners and are slow to develop intimate relationships (Hendrick & Hendrick, 1986). Some ludic lovers are self-sufficient individuals who put personal goals and activities ahead of their relationships, similar to how Gabriela was described at the beginning of this chapter. Many students and recent college graduates adopt the ludic style, especially if they feel they are not ready for a highly committed romantic relationship. Instead, they may feel that school or career takes precedence over relational involvements. When these individuals are ready and when they meet the right person, they are likely to move out of the ludic style and into a more committed style of loving.

MANIA: POSSESSIVE LOVE The manic style is a combination of eros and ludus, and therefore contains elements related to passion and game-playing. Manic lovers tend to be more demanding, dependent, possessive, and jealous than people with other love styles (Lee, 1973, 1988). They often feel a strong need to be in control and to know everything that the partner is doing. The classic song "Every Breath You Take," written by Sting and recorded by his band, the Police, exemplifies the manic lover's desire to monitor "every breath you take, every move you make, every bond you break." Manic lovers feel high levels of physical attraction and passion for their partners (Hendrick et al., 1988). Perhaps surprisingly, manic lovers are not interested in finding partners who are intelligent or good lovers; instead, they want sensitive partners who understand their feelings (Levine et al., 2006). Finding a sensitive partner who can cope with the emotional highs and lows that manic lovers often experience may be advantageous. Manic lovers often want to spend every minute with the partner, and any perceived lack of interest or enthusiasm by the partner, or any physical separation, results in extreme emotional lows. By contrast, when the beloved person reciprocates affection, the manic lover experiences an emotional high. A sensitive partner may be equipped to cope with these reactions while satisfying the manic partner's needs.

The emotional highs and lows associated with mania are also reflected in communication. Manic individuals report using a lot of communication aimed at intensifying the closeness within their relationships (Levine et al., 2006). They also report using secret tests relatively frequently, including triangle tests designed to make the partner jealous or see if the partner will be faithful, and endurance tests designed to see if the partner will stay with them even if they behave badly (Levine et al., 2006). In an effort to maintain their relationships, manic lovers also tend to use some negative behaviors, such as trying to make the partner feel jealous, spying on the partner, and engaging in destructive conflict designed to control the partner (Goodboy et al., 2010). Of course, not all manic lovers engage in these potentially destructive behaviors. Many people experience a mild form of mania—they feel jealous when their partners flirt with an ex-boyfriend or ex-girlfriend; they find themselves constantly thinking about the partner; and their happiness seems to depend, at least in part, on having a relationship with the person they love. When these thoughts and feelings become extreme, a more negative form of mania emerges.

AGAPE: COMPASSIONATE LOVE Agapie revolves around caring, concern, and tenderness, and is more focused on giving than receiving (Lee, 1988; Sprecher & Fehr, 2005). People with this style cope with stress in a positive fashion that helps keep their relationships satisfying (Vedes et al., 2016). The agapic style contains elements of both eros and storge (Lee, 1973). An agapic lover has a deep, abiding, highly passionate love for a partner—although not only in a physical sense. The storge side of agapic love stresses the enduring and secure nature of the relationship, which helps explain why agapic individuals are able to love their partners unconditionally. These individuals look for partners with a host of positive personal characteristics, including a sense of humor, intelligence, understanding, compassion, caring, communication skills, and sensitivity (Levine et al., 2006).

Once in a relationship, agapic lovers are motivated by an intense concern for their partner's well-being. They are willing to make sacrifices for their partner, even at the expense of their own needs and desires. For example, an agapic husband might decide not to pursue having a large family (even though he really wants one) if his wife had a difficult first pregnancy. Agapic love is associated with prosocial behavior, with agapic (as well as manic) lovers reporting that they use the most communication designed to intensify their relationships (Levine et al., 2006). Unlike those with the manic style, however, agapic lovers tend not to use secret tests in their relationships. This pattern of communication reflects the intense, passionate part of agapic love that is related to eros, combined with the stable part of agapic love that is related to storge. Although this description might make agapic love seem ideal, there are some drawbacks to this style. Agapic lovers sometimes seem to be "above" everyone else. Their partners often have trouble matching their high level of unconditional love, which can lead to feelings of discomfort and guilt. In addition, agapic lovers sometimes put their partners on too high of a pedestal, leading their partners to worry that they cannot live up to such an idealized image. Agapic love may also have an easier time flourishing in relationships that are considered fair and equitable (Berscheid, 2010). So if one partner is doing all the giving and the other is doing all the receiving, levels of agapic love may drop off.

PRAGMA: PRACTICAL LOVE The pragmatic style combines elements of both storge and ludus. As Lee (1988) explained, storge comes into play because pragmatic lovers are seeking a compatible partner. Undertones of the ludus style also are evident in many pragmatic lovers, who typically avoid emotional risk taking and commit to a relationship only after careful thought and considerable time. Pragmatic lovers search for a person who fits a particular image in terms of vital statistics, such as age, height, religion, and occupation, as well as preferred characteristics, such as being a loyal partner or having the potential to be a good parent. In Levine and colleagues' (2006) study, the pragma love style was also associated with looking for a partner who had money and was successful. Lee (1988) used a computer dating service metaphor to help describe the pragma style. If you went to a dating service, you might indicate that you are looking for a petite brunette who is Jewish, likes sports, and has a stable job. Or you might request a college-educated male who is older than you, has a good sense of humor, and loves children. In either case, you would have specified vital statistics that are most important to you.

Pragmatic lovers have a "common-sense, problem-solving approach to life and love" that is reflected in their communication style (Taraban et al., 1998, p. 346). For example, when meeting a potential partner, individuals with the pragma style tend to use direct opening lines, such as simply stating their name and introducing themselves (Levine et al., 2006). When they want to intensify a relationship, they are likely to engage in social enmeshment strategies, such as getting to know their partner's friends and family. Such a strategy is practical because it gives people insight into how they would fit in the partner's social network if the relationship became serious. Pragma lovers' practical side is also reflected in their television viewing; they prefer watching the news over family dramas or movies with a love theme (Hetsroni, 2012). Practical lovers try to present a positive personal appearance when they want to escalate their relationships (Levine et al., 2006). As a way of obtaining additional information to help them decide if a partner is right for them, pragmatic lovers sometimes engage in secrets tests such as seeing if the partner gets jealous, spending time apart to see if they miss each other, and publicly presenting the partner to check for reactions (Levine et al., 2006). For example, a pragmatic lover might introduce her new love interest as "my really good friend" to see if he objects or wants to be called her "boyfriend." Practical lovers also use spying to get information and try to maintain their relationships (Goodboy et al., 2010). The practical nature of this style has benefits; people tend to match themselves up with those with whom they are compatible. But if love is based only on practical concerns, it can be lifeless and dull. Some level of intimacy and passion is required to put the spark into a relationship. For pragmatic lovers, intimacy and passion sometimes develop after realistic concerns have laid the foundation for the relationship.

DIFFERENCES DUE TO SEX AND CULTURE

Lee's original work, as well as subsequent research, suggests that the tendency to identify with the various love styles differs somewhat for men versus women. Studies have shown women from the United States and Portugal score higher than men on pragma (Bernardes, Mendes, Sarmento, Silva, & Moreira, 1999; Hendrick & Hendrick, 1986), while men tend to score higher in ludus and agape (Bernardes et al., 1999; Kunkel & Burleson, 2003; Sprecher & Toro-Morn, 2002). The finding that women tend to be more pragmatic is in line with other research showing that women are rational lovers who are choosier about their partners. The finding that men tend to identify with ludus fits with

research showing that men are generally less committed to relationships than are women. Yet studies have also found that men generally fall in love faster than do women (Huston, Surra, Fitzgerald, & Cate, 1981; Kanin, Davidson, & Scheck, 1970) and that they usually say "I love you" first in heterosexual romantic relationships (Owen, 1987; Tolhuizen, 1989), which could help explain why some studies have shown men to be more agapic than women. Together these seemingly contradictory findings suggest that although men may hesitate to make a strong commitment, when they do fall in love, they do it more quickly and emotionally than do women.

As noted previously, some types of love tend to be experienced similarly across different cultures. For example, Jankowiak and Fischer (1992) tested the idea that romantic (or erotic) love is a product of Western culture. Contrary to this idea, they found romantic love to exist in 147 of the 166 cultures sampled. Based on these data, Jankowiak and Fischer suggested that romantic love is nearly universal. Friendship love also appears to cross cultural boundaries—many people from many different cultures around the globe embrace the warmth and security that storgic love offers. Other studies have shown that young adults from the United States, Russia, Japan (Sprecher et al., 1994) Portugal (Neto, 1994), and Israel (Hetsroni, 2012) are similar in terms of their love styles. There is also similarity in how love styles are related to satisfaction in relationships. Across various European cultures, agape and eros lovers tend to be satisfied in their relationships, whereas mania lovers tend to be dissatisfied (Rohmann, Führer, & Bierhoff, 2016).

There are some cultural differences in love styles, however. A study comparing people from France and the United States (Murstein, Merighi, & Vyse, 1991) found that the French were higher on agape whereas people from the United States scored higher on storge and mania. People from cultures that endorse arranged marriages believe more strongly in pragmatic love than do people from cultures where people marry for love alone. In arranged marriages, the parents, often with the community, match their children based on perceived compatibility and an equitable exchange of resources, which makes practical love highly relevant. Research conducted in India, for example, has shown that people who believe in arranged marriages tend to value the conjugal love that emerges from a socially sanctioned and family-approved union more than they value romantic love (Gupta, 1976). Couples in arranged marriages also report a larger increase in love over time compared to nonarranged marriages (Gupta & Singh, 1982), which suggests that love can develop and grow in some relationships that begin purely on the basis of practical love.

In addition to being more prevalent in countries where arranged marriages are common, pragma is also a popular love style in China, where people tend to endorse both pragmatic and agapic types of love more than people from the United States (Sprecher & Toro-Morn, 2002). Although many people in the United States do identify with the agapic love style (Levine et al., 2006), it is even more prevalent in Asian cultures where people focus on group harmony and cohesiveness rather than individual needs. People in the United States and East Asian countries may also emphasize different aspects of the agapic style; those from the United States value unconditional love and those from China, Japan, and South Korea value caregiving (Kline, Horton, & Zhang, 2008). There are also differences in how love is communicated across cultures, as discussed in Box 8.4.

BOX 8.4 AROUND THE WORLD
COMMUNICATING LOVE AMERICAN AND NON-AMERICAN STYLE

Love is a universal emotion, so it should be communicated the same way across different cultures, right? Well, not always. Research has shown that love is communicated both similarly and differently across cultures.

Similarity Across Cultures

Self-disclosure, social support, and shared experiences are related to love across cultures. One study showed that dating relationships characterized by either friendship or romantic love contain higher levels of self-disclosure than same-sex or cross-sex friendships for both U.S. and Japanese college students (Kito, 2005). Another study investigated how people in China, Japan, South Korea, and the United States communicate love to their friends and spouses (Kline et al., 2008). Across all these countries, people reported expressing love to friends by sharing common experiences, being supportive, and engaging in open discussion. With spouses, people also reported communicating love through physical intimacy and verbal statements, such as saying "I love you" and "I miss you."

Differences Across Cultures

Certain verbal and nonverbal expressions of love may be valued more in some cultures than others. In individualistic cultures, such as the United States, where self-expression and individual feelings are valued, people are especially likely to verbalize their love by saying "I love you" (Wilkins & Gareis, 2006). People from Latino cultures also appear to say "I love you" to their romantic partners, friends, and family more than do people from other non-U.S. cultures (Wilkins & Gareis, 2006), such as Germany (Gareis & Wilkins, 2011). In contrast, nonverbal expressions of love may be valued more in cultures where people pay especially close attention to subtle contextual cues, which is the case in many Asian and European countries. For example, Gareis and Wilkins (2011) found that over 80% of Germans believed that nonverbal expressions of love are more common than verbal expressions, compared to only 45% of people from the United States. Germans also noted that subtle cues, such as gaze, most often accompanied verbal expressions of love, whereas people from the United States mentioned hugs and kisses more often.

Culture may affect the activities people see as expressing love. Activities are valued differently across cultures. People in more developed countries have more leisure time whereas those in less developed countries may work together more often. One study demonstrated that there are subtle differences in the types of activities that people in the United States versus East Asian countries saw as expressing love in their marriages. For spouses from the United States, sports, food preparation, and shopping were key activities. For East Asians, talking and food preparation were most important.

Ways to Communicate Love

There is also individual variability in how people communicate love. For example, in addition to thinking about love differently, Gabriela and Brian vary in how they prefer to communicate love to each other. Researchers have worked to identify the various ways people communicate love. In one study, the top five ways were (1) saying "I love you" to one's partner; (2) doing special things for one's partner; (3) being supportive, understanding, and attentive; (4) touching one's partner; and (5) simply being together (Marston, Hecht, & Robers, 1987). Of these, saying "I love you" was the most common response, with 75% of respondents mentioning it. The researchers also asked, "How does your partner communicate love to you?" The top five responses were similar to those listed previously. Saying "I love you" again emerged as the most common answer, with 70% of the participants identifying this strategy. The next most common responses were showing love through touch and sexual contact, being supportive, doing favors or giving gifts, and engaging in behaviors that show togetherness. Other less-frequently mentioned behaviors included communicating emotion, engaging in eye contact, and smiling. Together these findings show that love is communicated and received in a variety of ways but that verbally telling our partners we love them is a particularly important way of expressing love. This may explain why Brian wishes that Gabriela would tell him she loves him more often.

In his bestselling book, Chapman (1995) suggested that there are five **love languages** that represent preferred ways of communicating and receiving love. These five love languages revolve around (1) words of affirmation, (2) quality time, (3) gifts and tokens of affection, (4) acts of service, and (5) physical touch. As such, these languages include many of the behaviors found in the Marston et al. (1987) study mentioned above. Researchers have tested to see whether Chapman's love languages represent a valid way of classifying different ways of

communicating love. These studies have generally confirmed that they do (Egbert & Polk, 2006; Polk & Egbert, 2013). In addition, Marston, Hecht, and their colleagues identified **love ways** that represent different styles of communicating and experiencing love (Hecht, Marston, & Larkey, 1994; Marston & Hecht, 1994; Marston, Hecht, Manke, McDaniel, & Reeder, 1998; Marston et al., 1987). Chapman's five love languages are described next. These descriptions are augmented by related work from the research on love ways by Marston and Hecht.

1. *The Language of Affirmation and Support*: Communicating love through affirmation commonly includes being encouraging, supportive, and complimentary (Chapman, 1995). For example, Brian might send Gabriela a text that says "good luck" before she makes an important presentation, and Gabriela might respond with a smiling Snapchat that says, "Thanks, you're the best" with a red heart. The work on love ways suggests that people who use this type of affirming communication tend to regard relationships as partnerships where people build one another up. Such partnerships increase energy and intensify emotion, which help maintain the relationship.

2. *The Language of Time Together*: For some people, spending time together participating in shared activities is an essential way to express love (Chapman, 1995). Marston et al. (1987) identified a similar love way that involves engaging in joint activities and feeling strong and self-confident. People who prefer communicating love this way are likely to engage in activities such as spending their free time together, having deep conversations, going places, and being alone as a couple. When couples are highly committed, they are also likely to communicate love this way by planning

future activities together, such as vacations or holidays with family (Marston et al., 1987).

3. *The Language of Gifts and Tokens of Affection*: This way of communicating love includes doing things such as bringing one's partner flowers or a surprise gift (even if there is no special occasion), creating and posting a collage of pictures on Instagram for an anniversary, and giving one's partner personal items to wear such as a ring or watch (Chapman, 1995). People who prefer this way of communicating love also tend to be well integrated into each other's social networks (Egbert & Polk, 2006), perhaps because both private and public demonstrations of togetherness and affection are important to them. They want their partner, as well as other people, to know how strong their bond is.

4. *The Language of Physical Touch*: Holding hands, cuddling, sitting close to one another, and engaging in sexual activities are just a few ways that people communicate love through physical contact. Marston et al.'s work on love ways suggests that when love is grounded in touch, it is also experienced through physical reactions such as feeling warm all over, getting nervous, and losing one's appetite. Although physical contact is considered to be a defining characteristic of most romantic relationships, Chapman (1995) suggests that for some people physical connection is the most important ingredient for maintaining relationships and keeping them satisfying.

5. *The Language of Acts of Service*: This love language involves helping with necessary tasks by doing things such as washing one's partner's car, helping with housework or homework, and running errands for one's partner. Egbert and Polk (2006) found that

people who preferred showing love through acts of service also reported that they share tasks and engage with their partner's social network as ways to maintain their relationships. Although some people see acts of service as a primary way of communicating love, others do not. This can cause misunderstanding. For example, Brian might wash Gabriela's car as a way to communicate love, but she might see washing the car as a routine chore rather than an act of love and therefore not appreciate his action as much as he expected.

Indeed, understanding each other's preferred way of communicating love may help partners maintain happy relationships. Chapman (1995) believes that most people favor one or two of the love languages, and that it is critical for people to recognize their partner's style so they can give them what they need. Other research suggests that people often value aspects of all or most of the love languages (Egbert & Polk, 2006). Regardless of whether people have one or more love language preferences, Marston and Hecht (1994) provide helpful advice for communicating love in ways that maximize relational satisfaction. First, they suggest that people recognize that their partner's preferred communication might be different from their own. For example, if Brian expresses love through physical touch and likes to hug and hold hands in public, he should not necessarily expect Gabriela to want the same. In fact, Gabriela might dislike showing affection in public and prefer to cuddle in private or to show her love through time together engaging in shared activities. Second, people should be careful not to overvalue particular elements of their own way of communicating loving. For example, since Gabriela prefers to express her love through time and activities, she might worry if she and Brian start to develop different sports interests or argue about which old movies to watch. If this happens, Gabriela should recognize that other aspects of their relationship may still reflect their love for one another. Finally, people should avoid statements like, "If you really loved me, you'd give me more space" (as Gabriela might say) or, "If you really loved me, you'd tell me more often" (as Brian might say). Instead, Brian and Gabriela should focus on the various other ways that they express love for one another. Remember that any two people bring different ideologies and expectations about love to the relationship. The key may be to appreciate what each partner brings to the table, rather than wishing that the table was set in a different way.

ATTACHMENT THEORY

So far, we have shown that scholars classify love in many different ways. Lee's six styles of love are based largely on ideology. Love languages are based on how people express love through verbal and nonverbal communication. Attachment theorists take yet another approach in studying love. According to attachment theorists such as Hazan and Shaver (1987), love is best conceptualized as a process of attachment, which includes forming a bond and becoming close to someone. Attachment theory takes a social-developmental approach, stressing how interactions with others affect people's attachment style across the life span. Children first learn to develop attachments through communication with caregivers. As children grow, they develop a sense of independence that is rooted in security. Finally, security in adulthood is based on being self-sufficient when necessary, while also having the ability to provide care and support for another adult in a love relationship that functions as a partnership (Ainsworth & Bowlby, 1991).

Communication plays a central role in attachment theory (Guerrero, 2014a). Communication is one of the key causes of attachment style. People's communication with others leads them to think about themselves and others in ways that lead them to develop particular attachment styles.

Communication is also a result of one's attachment style. As discussed later in this chapter, people with different attachment styles vary along a wide array of communication variables, including self-disclosure, emotional expression, caregiving, conflict behavior, and nonverbal behavior just to name a few. People also report different levels of relational satisfaction depending on their attachment style and the attachment style of their partner. Some research suggests that communication plays an important role here, too. Partners with certain attachment styles may be happier in their relationships because they are better communicators.

The Propensity for Forming Attachments

Originally, attachment theory was studied within the context of child-caregiver relationships (Ainsworth, 1969; Ainsworth, Blehar, Waters, & Wall, 1978; Ainsworth & Wittig, 1969; Bowlby, 1969, 1973, 1980). Later, researchers extended the theory to adult romantic relationships (Hazan & Shaver, 1987). Although parent–child and romantic relationships have received the most attention, attachment theory applies to all types of close relationship, including friendships and sibling relationships. Because people usually want to be part of a social group and to be loved and cared for by others, attachment theorists believe that people have a natural tendency to try to develop close relational bonds with others throughout the life span.

In childhood, the need to develop attachments is an innate and necessary part of human development (Ainsworth, 1991). According to Bowlby (1969, 1973, 1980), attachment is an essential component within a larger system that functions to keep children in close proximity to caregivers, which protects children from danger and provides them with a **secure base** from which to explore their world. For example, toddlers may feel free to try the slides and swings at the playground if they know that a caregiver is close by to act as a secure base if they get hurt or need help. Similar to the way soldiers return to a military base to get supplies or reinforcements, children use their caregivers as secure bases that allow them to feel comfortable exploring their surroundings. Exploration of the environment eventually leads to self-confidence and autonomy. Thus, one goal of the attachment system is to give children a sense of both security and independence. Another goal is to help children develop a healthy capacity for intimacy.

In adulthood, attachment influences the type of relationship a person desires. For example, some people (like Gabriela) might want a relationship that is emotionally reserved, while others (like Brian) might desire a relationship that is emotionally charged. Bowlby (1977) and Ainsworth (1989, 1991), who pioneered research on child-caregiver attachments, both believed that attachment typifies intimate adult relationships, with Bowlby (1977) arguing that attachment is characteristic of all individuals from the cradle to the grave. The type of attachment individuals form depends on their cognitive conceptions of themselves and others. These cognitions, or **internal working models,** influence orientations toward love, intimacy, and interpersonal interaction in adult relationships.

Internal Working Models and Attachment Styles

According to attachment theorists, people have different styles of attachment depending on how they perceive themselves and others. These perceptions, which are called internal working models, are cognitive representations of oneself and potential partners that reflect an individual's past experiences in close relationships and help an individual understand the world (Bowlby, 1973; Bretherton, 1988; Collins & Read, 1994). Models of both self and others fall along a positive-negative continuum. A positive self-model is "an internalized sense of self-worth that is not dependent on ongoing external validation"

(Bartholomew, 1993, p. 40). Thus, individuals who hold positive self-models view themselves as self-sufficient, secure, and lovable. Those holding negative self-models see themselves as dependent, insecure, and unworthy of love and affection. Positive models of others reflect expectations about how supportive, receptive, and accepting people are, as well as how rewarding it is to be in an intimate relationship. Individuals with positive models of others see relationships as worthwhile and possess *approach* orientations toward intimacy. Individuals with negative working models of others see relationships as relatively unrewarding and possess *avoidant* orientations toward intimacy.

Depending on individuals' configurations of internal working models—that is, the "mix" of how positive or negative their models of self and others are—they develop different attachment styles. An attachment style is a social interaction style that is consistent with the type and quality of relationship one wishes to share with others, based on working models of self and others (Bartholomew, 1990). Attachment styles include one's own communication style, the way one processes and interprets others' behavior, and the way one reacts to others' behavior (Guerrero & Burgoon, 1996). Attachment styles are also associated with "relatively coherent and stable patterns of emotion and behavior [that] are exhibited in close relationships" (Shaver, Collins, & Clark, 1996, p. 25).

Attachment Styles in Childhood

Early communication with primary caregivers shapes children's internal models of themselves and others and sets the stage for later attachments (Ainsworth et al., 1978; Bowlby, 1977). Although new interactions with significant others continue to modify the way people see themselves and relational partners, the first two to three years of life (and especially the first year) are critical in developing these internal models. By the time a baby is about 6 weeks old, the infant already shows a preference for the primary caregiver—usually the mother. For example, if a 2-month-old baby is crying, she might be best comforted by her mother. At around 14 to 20 months old, toddlers are usually attached to their mothers and feel separation anxiety when they leave. At this time, babysitters may have trouble with their charges, who often become distressed when they realize their mother who functions as their secure base is not around. Some of our students have reported experiences like this, where a niece or nephew who used to be fine when alone with them suddenly seems nervous and starts crying or looking around for her or his mom.

Most children emerge from the first two years of life with secure, healthy attachments to caregivers (Ainsworth et al., 1978; Bowlby, 1969). If this is the case, they have developed positive models of both themselves and others. Not all children are so lucky. About 30% of children develop insecure attachment styles because they have negative models of themselves or others. Bowlby's original work showed that children who were raised in institutions and deprived of their mother's care for extended periods of time were more likely to develop insecure attachments (Bowlby, 1969, 1973). Ainsworth and her colleagues later demonstrated that the type of care children receive at home influences their attachment style (Ainsworth, 1969, 1982, 1989; Ainsworth & Eichberg, 1991; Ainsworth et al., 1978; Ainsworth & Wittig, 1969). They delineated three types of infant attachment: (1) secure, (2) avoidant, and (3) anxious ambivalent.

SECURE CHILDREN The majority of children fall into the secure category. Secure children tend to have responsive and warm parents, to receive moderate levels of stimulation, and to engage in synchronized interaction with their caregivers. The fit between the caregiver and the child is crucial. Caregivers may need to adjust their style of communication to accommodate the child. Thus, one child may need a lot of cuddling and reassurance while another may prefer to be left alone. This helps

Although mothers are often considered to be the primary caregiver, the way fathers communicate affection also has profound effects on a child's attachment style.

explain why children from the same family environment may develop different attachment styles. Children who develop secure attachments to a caregiver are more likely to feel free to explore, approach others, and be positive toward strangers than are insecure types. Secure children are also likely to protest separation and then to show happiness when reunited with their caregivers. These children tend to develop positive models of self and others.

AVOIDANT CHILDREN Some insecure children develop an **avoidant attachment style** (Ainsworth et al., 1978). Avoidant children tend to have caregivers who are either insensitive to their signals or try too hard to please. In addition, avoidant children are often either over- or understimulated, which leads to physiological arousal and a flight response. When overstimulated, they retreat from social interaction to avoid being overloaded. When understimulated, they learn how to cope without social interaction. Because their caregivers are not able to fulfill their needs, they develop negative models of others. These children stay within themselves, seldom explore their environment, and are rarely positive toward strangers. They tend not to protest separation from caregivers and show little emotion when the caregiver returns.

ANXIOUS-AMBIVALENT CHILDREN Other insecure children develop an **anxious-ambivalent
attachment style** (Ainsworth et al., 1978). These
children tend to be the product of inconsistent
caregiver communication; sometimes the caregiver is appropriately responsive, and other times
the caregiver is neglectful or overstimulating.
Anxious-ambivalent children often have caregivers who are preoccupied with their own problems,
such as relational conflict, divorce, or substance
abuse. Instead of blaming the caregiver (or the
caregiver's situation) for this inconsistency, they
blame themselves and develop self-models of
doubt, insecurity, and uncertainty. Anxious-
ambivalent children often are tentative when
exploring their environment in the presence of
their caregivers and fearful of exploration if alone.
They protest separation from caregivers vehe-
mently yet are both relieved and angry when the
caregiver returns. This contradiction is reflected in
their label—they are anxious upon separation and
ambivalent when the caregiver returns. Sometimes

these children develop positive models of others
because they do receive some comfort and security
from caregivers.

Attachment Styles in Adulthood

Attachment styles are also relevant in adult relationships. Hazan and Shaver (1987) conceptualized love as
an attachment process that is "experienced somewhat
differently by different people because of variations in
their attachment histories" (p. 511). Using Ainsworth
and colleagues' (1978) three attachment styles as a
guide, Hazan and Shaver (1987) proposed that adults
can have secure, avoidant, or anxious-ambivalent
attachments to their romantic partners similar to those
they had with caregivers. Shortly after Hazan and
Shaver (1987) published their groundbreaking work,
Bartholomew (1990) proposed a four-category system
of attachment. She argued that the working models a
person holds about self and others combine to produce
four, rather than three, attachment styles: (1) secure,
(2) preoccupied, (3) dismissive, and (4) fearful (see
Figure 8.3), as described next.

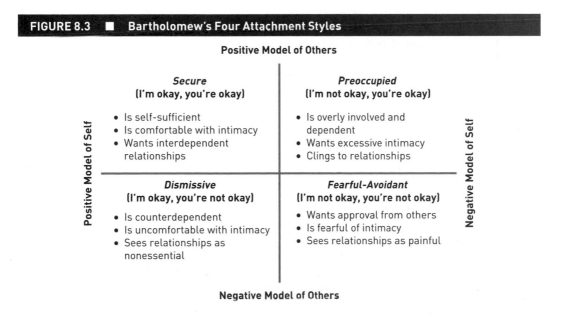

FIGURE 8.3 ■ Bartholomew's Four Attachment Styles

Positive Model of Others

Secure
(I'm okay, you're okay)
- Is self-sufficient
- Is comfortable with intimacy
- Wants interdependent
  relationships

Preoccupied
(I'm not okay, you're okay)
- Is overly involved and
  dependent
- Wants excessive intimacy
- Clings to relationships

Dismissive
(I'm okay, you're not okay)
- Is counterdependent
- Is uncomfortable with intimacy
- Sees relationships as
  nonessential

Fearful-Avoidant
(I'm not okay, you're not okay)
- Wants approval from others
- Is fearful of intimacy
- Sees relationships as painful

Positive Model of Self

Negative Model of Self

Negative Model of Others

Source: Adapted from Guerrero (1996).

SECURE: THE PROSOCIAL STYLE Individuals with a **secure attachment style** have positive models of themselves and others ("I'm okay and you're okay"). Secure individuals feel good about themselves and their relationships, and they display "high self-esteem and an absence of serious interpersonal problems" (Bartholomew, 1990, p. 163). These individuals have the capacity for close, fulfilling relationships. They are likely to have realistic expectations, be satisfied with their relationships, and be comfortable depending on others and having others depend on them. Although they value relationships, they are not afraid of being alone.

Secure individuals have a communication style that displays social skill and promotes healthy relationships (Guerrero & Jones, 2005). They seek social support when distressed and know how to provide support and comfort to their relational partners (Kunce & Shaver, 1994; Weger & Polcar, 2002). In general, their communication tends to be pleasant, attentive, and expressive (Guerrero, 1996; Le Poire, Shepard, & Duggan, 1999), and they smile at, laugh with, and touch their romantic partners more than do individuals with other attachment styles (Tucker & Anders, 1998). When secures are distressed, they are usually able to express their negative feelings appropriately and seek support from others (Feeney, 1995; Simpson & Rholes, 1994). They cope with feelings of anger, jealousy, and sadness by behaving in ways that bolster their self-esteem and help maintain relationships (Guerrero, 1998; Guerrero, Farinelli, & McEwan, 2009; Sharpsteen & Kirkpatrick, 1997). In conflict situations, secure individuals are more likely than individuals with other attachment styles to compromise and solve problems (Bippus & Rollin, 2003; Pistole, 1989), especially if their partner is also secure (Domingue & Mollen, 2009). Secure individuals also employ high levels of relational maintenance behavior, such as engaging in romantic activities, talking about commitment, and sharing activities (Bippus & Rollin, 2003; Guerrero & Bachman, 2008; Simon & Baxter, 1993). In a study of Iranian couples, secure individuals reported using the word *we* more often as a way of being nice and emphasizing

commitment (Sadeghi, Mazaheri, & Moutabi, 2011). A study of married couples also showed that secure individuals were most likely to express positive emotions—such as love, pride, and happiness—to their spouses (Feeney, 1999).

PREOCCUPIED: THE EMOTIONAL STYLE Individuals with a **preoccupied attachment style** have positive models of others but negative models of themselves ("You're okay but I'm not okay"). These individuals are overly dependent on relationships. As Bartholomew (1990) put it, preoccupied individuals are characterized by "an insatiable desire to gain others' approval and a deep-seated feeling of unworthiness" (p. 163). Their relational identities often are much stronger than their self-identities; they need to have a relationship with someone to feel worthwhile. In fact, preoccupied individuals report feeling lost and unable to cope in the absence of a close relationship. They also are likely to cling to their relationships in times of trouble and to resist any attempts by a partner to de-escalate or terminate close relationships.

Preoccupied individuals exhibit mixed messages that reflect their high need for intimacy coupled with low self-confidence. In everyday interactions, they often appear pleasant, attentive, and expressive (Guerrero, 1996). However, when they become anxious their communication sometimes becomes unpleasant and self-focused. In one study, preoccupied individuals exhibited low levels of enjoyment when talking about relationship issues with their romantic partners (Tucker & Anders, 1998). In another study, preoccupied individuals were expressive but showed low levels of composure and altercentrism (a focus on the partner) when discussing a conflict issue (Guerrero & Jones, 2005). Preoccupied individuals are also overly sensitive and have trouble controlling their emotions (Guerrero & Jones, 2003). In their quest to develop intimacy, they sometimes disclose intimate information too quickly (Bartholomew & Horowitz, 1991; Mikulincer & Nachshon, 1991). Sometimes preoccupied individuals display demanding behavior in an attempt to hang onto their relationship or change their partners (Bartholomew & Horowitz, 1991; Guerrero & Langan, 1999). In conflict situations, they tend to engage in controlling behavior and to nag and whine (Creasey, Kershaw, & Boston, 1999; O'Connell-Corcoran & Mallinckrodt, 2000). Similarly, they tend to express anger using aggressive or passive-aggressive behaviors (Feeney, 1995; Guerrero et al., 2009). They also avoid discussing deception with their partners, which is perceived as an ineffective communication strategy (Jang, 2008).

FEARFUL: THE HESITANT STYLE Individuals with a **fearful attachment style** have negative models of both themselves and others ("I'm not okay and you're not okay"). Some of the **avoidants** in Hazan and Shaver's (1987) system fall in this category, as do a few of the anxious-ambivalents, particularly when they have negative views of both others and themselves. The key characteristic of fearful avoidants is that they are afraid of hurt and rejection, often because they have experienced painful relationships in the past. Fearful individuals usually want to depend on someone but find it difficult to open up to others. As Bartholomew (1990) put it, fearful individuals "desire social contact and intimacy, but experience pervasive interpersonal distrust and fear of rejection" (p. 164).

Fearful individuals tend to avoid social situations and potential relationships because they fear rejection. Even when in relationships, they tend to be hesitant to communicate emotions or to initiate escalation of the relationship. Bartholomew (1990) noted the paradoxical nature of fearful individuals' actions and desires: By refusing to open up to others, they undermine their chances for building the very type of trusting relationship they desire. Their communication style reflects their fear and lack of trust. Guerrero (1996) found that fearful individuals were less fluent and used larger proxemic distances than individuals with other attachment styles. Other studies suggest that fearful individuals possess less social skill than people with other attachment styles. They tend to lack assertiveness

(Anders & Tucker, 2000) and to appear uncomposed (Guerrero & Jones, 2005). They also have difficulty expressing emotions and responding to the emotions of others (Guerrero & Jones, 2003). Fearful individuals are both anxious and avoidant, and research shows that people who possess these two characteristics report using less relational maintenance behavior (e.g., showing affection, being positive and cheerful) in their relationships (Guerrero & Bachman, 2006). Fearful individuals also have difficulty confronting conflict issues; instead, they tend to withdraw or accommodate the partner (Pistole, 1989).

DISMISSIVE: THE DETACHED STYLE Individuals with a **dismissive attachment style** have positive models of themselves but negative models of others ("I'm okay but you're not okay"). Many of the avoidants in Hazan and Shaver's system would fall here. Dismissives can best be characterized as counterdependent. In other words, they are so self-sufficient that they shun close involvement with others. Some researchers suggest that counterdependence is a defensive strategy that allows people to feel good about themselves without opening themselves up to the criticisms and scrutiny of others. Dismissives neither desire nor fear close attachments but rather lack the motivation to build and maintain intimate relationships (Bartholomew, 1990). They place a much higher value on autonomy than on relationships and tend to focus on less-personal aspects of their lives, such as careers, hobbies, and self-improvement (Bartholomew, 1990).

Not surprisingly, dismissive individuals possess a highly avoidant attachment style. Yet unlike fearful individuals, dismissives are composed and self-confident (Anders & Tucker, 2000; Guerrero & Jones, 2005). Dismissive individuals generally exhibit less disclosure, conversational involvement, and affection than individuals with the secure or preoccupied style (Bartholomew & Horowitz, 1991; Guerrero, 1996). They report relatively low levels of relational maintenance behaviors, such as being romantic and giving assurances that they are committed to the relationship (Guerrero & Bachman, 2008; Simon & Baxter, 1993), and their partners see them as relatively uncaring and unsupportive (Kane et al., 2007). People who are high in avoidance and low in anxiety (which is what defines dismissive individuals) also report using less cell phone communication with their romantic partners (Jin & Peña, 2010). Dismissives also are seen as fairly dominant. They tend to interrupt their partners more than do those with other attachment styles (Guerrero & Langan, 1999), and they report low levels of accommodation and tend to withdraw during conflict (Feeney, Noller, & Roberts, 2000). When dismissives experience emotional distress, they often deny their feelings and insist on handling their problems without help from others (Bartholomew, 1993). As Simpson and Rholes (1994) put it, dismissives "distance themselves from others emotionally. Over time they come to see themselves as fully autonomous and immune to negative events" (p. 84).

As the descriptions above show, people communicate differently based on their attachment style. (Box 8.5 summarizes some of the key attachment-style differences in communication.) People with different attachment styles also use technology differently. Secure individuals tend to use high levels of communication, including texting, snapping, and social media, as well as high levels of face-to-face communication. Studies have shown that attachment security is related to sending more text messages (Drouin & Landgraff, 2012), whereas avoidance, which is typical of dismissive and fearful attachment, is related to texting and talking on the phone less (Morey, Gentzler, Creasy, Oberhauser, & Westerman, 2013). However, researchers have also shown that individuals with insecure attachment styles are likely to rely more on texting than on other forms of communication (such as face-to-face interaction) to maintain their relationships (Luo, 2014). Taken together, this research suggests that secure individuals report high levels of texting because they communicate a lot with their partners through their phones and in person. Insecure individuals report less texting overall; nevertheless,

texting represents a higher share of their overall communication than does face-to-face interaction. This may be because texting is perceived as less intimate and less threatening than face-to-face communication (Luo, 2014). Interestingly, people with insecure attachment styles are more likely to engage in sexting, which involves sending sexual images or texts to one's partner via one's cell phone, than people with secure attachment styles (Drouin & Landgraff, 2012; Weisskirch & Delevi, 2011). These individuals may feel more of a need to use such messages to maintain their relationships than do secure individuals.

There are also attachment style differences in Facebook usage. Individuals who have attachment anxiety (especially preoccupieds) are likely to look at their partners' Facebook accounts to check up on them; this type of surveillance often fuels jealousy (Marshall, Bejanyan, Di Castro, & Lee, 2013). These individuals also tend to check social media frequently, use it to express negative feelings, and to be concerned with the impressions they make on Facebook. In contrast, individuals with avoidant attachment (especially dismissives) tend to use Facebook less frequently (Oldmeadow, Quinn, & Kowert, 2013).

Attachment and Relational Satisfaction

As the descriptions of the four attachment styles suggest, security is associated with relational satisfaction. In fact, both one's own security and the partner's security make a difference. In one of the first studies of adult attachment, Hazan and Shaver (1987) found that secure individuals reported having happier and more trusting relationships than insecure individuals. Individuals with negative models of self or others tend to report less satisfaction (Collins & Read, 1990; Feeney, 1995; Feeney, Noller, & Callan, 1994; Feeney, Noller, & Roberts, 1998; Simpson, 1990). In some studies, researchers have asked both partners in romantic couples to rate their own attachment style and relational satisfaction. These studies have shown that one person's attachment style predicts

BOX 8.5 HIGHLIGHTS
ATTACHMENT-STYLE DIFFERENCES IN COMMUNICATION

	Secure	Preoccupied	Fearful	Dismissive
Conflict Behavior	Most compromising and adept with problem solving	Demanding, exhibits dominating behavior, nagging, whining	Accommodating, responds passively	Withdrawing, less accommodating, more interrupting
Maintenance Behavior	Highest level of maintenance	High level of maintenance	Relatively low level of maintenance	Less maintenance overall, especially less romance and assurances
Emotional Expression	Readily expresses emotions in a direct, prosocial manner	Expresses negative emotions using aggression or passive aggression	Inhibits the expression of negative emotions	Experiences and expresses emotions (negative and positive) the least
Self-Disclosure	High levels of appropriate disclosure, able to elicit disclosure from others	High levels of disclosure that is sometimes inappropriate or indiscriminate	Low levels of disclosure, especially with strangers or acquaintances	Low levels of disclosure
Nonverbal Intimacy	Relatively high levels of facial and vocal pleasantness, laughter, touch, and smiling	Mix of positive and negative nonverbal cues, depending on situation	Relatively low levels of facial and vocal pleasantness, expressiveness, and smiling	Relatively low levels of facial and vocal pleasantness, expressiveness, and smiling
Social Skill	Assertive, responsive to others, able to provide effective care and comfort	Overly sensitive, difficulty controlling emotional expression	Trouble expressing self and being assertive, exhibits anxiety cues such as lack of fluency and long response latencies	Trouble expressing self and comforting others

how satisfied the other person is. Specifically, Kane and fellow researchers (2007) found that men were happier when their partners were low in attachment anxiety (which is related to having a positive model of self), and women were happier when their partners were low in attachment avoidance (which is related to having a positive model of others). Guerrero and associates (2009) found that people were most likely to report high levels of relational satisfaction when their partners were high in security and low in both dismissiveness and preoccupation. Other studies have shown that relationships tend to be especially satisfying if both partners are secure (Senchak & Leonard, 1992).

Researchers have also tried to determine why secure attachment is related to being in a happier relationship. Communication provides one answer to this important question. Feeney and colleagues (2000) explained that communication may be "the underlying mechanism" that explains why secure partners have better relationships (p. 198). According to this reasoning, secure individuals engage in patterns of communication that promote closeness and cooperation, whereas insecure individuals engage in communication patterns that are more distant or demanding. Indeed, numerous studies have shown couples that include at least one insecure partner tend to exhibit negative communication patterns (Pearce & Halford, 2008). Several studies also support the idea that communication helps explain the link between attachment and relationship satisfaction. For example, Kane and colleagues (2007) found that security was related to caregiving and that caregiving helped predict why some partners were more satisfied with their relationships than others. Other studies have shown that the affectionate communication, constructive conflict behavior, and self-disclosure that secure partners use is related to being happier in one's relationship (Feeney et al., 2000; Morrison, Urquiza, & Goodlin-Jones, 1997).

Emotional communication provides another explanation for why people are more satisfied with relationships that include secure partners. Feeney and colleagues (1998) found that women reported being happier in relationships with secure men because those men tended to communicate sadness and other emotions directly and openly, allowing them to work out problems. Guerrero and colleagues (2009) found different patterns of emotional communication and relational satisfaction for people who had secure, dismissive, and preoccupied partners. People reported that their secure partners engaged in more prosocial emotional communication, such as discussing feelings in an open and calm manner, which led to more relationship satisfaction. Individuals perceived dismissive partners as using more detached communication, such as avoiding talking about their emotions, which was related to less satisfaction. Finally, people viewed their preoccupied partners as using more aggressive and passive-aggressive expressions of anger, which was related to less satisfaction. Thus, the manner in which people communicate emotions helps explain why individuals are more satisfied with secure partners.

Stability and Change in Attachment Styles Across the Life Span

By now, it may not be difficult to guess what attachment styles Brian and Gabriela have. (To assess your own attachment style, take the test in Box 8.6.) Brian appears to be somewhat preoccupied. He worries that he might care more for Gabriela than she cares for him. He also appears to desire high levels of overt affection in his relationships. Gabriela, on the other hand, seems somewhat dismissive. She wonders if she can commit enough time and energy to her relationship, and her priority seems to be her personal goals. If Gabriela and Brian stay together, are their attachment styles likely to change or stay the same during the course of their relationship? Have they had these attachment styles since childhood or could they have developed these styles recently? Finally, do they have the same attachment styles with their friends and family as they have with each other? Research investigating how stable attachment styles are across time suggests that the answer to all of these questions is "it depends." Studies have shown that around 25% to 30% of adults experience changes in their attachment style toward romantic partners (Davila, Burge, & Hammen, 1997; Davila, Karney, & Bradbury, 1999; Feeney & Noller, 1996). Similarly, in a study on adolescent friendships, 35% of high school students reported a change in attachment style from one year to the next (Miller, Notaro, & Zimmerman, 2002). These studies suggest that although attachment styles are fairly stable, they can be modified by new experiences.

EXPLANATIONS FOR STABILITY At least two forces work to stabilize a person's attachment style. First, communication with caregivers has an especially strong effect on a person's social development, including the attachment style a person develops. Bowlby (1969, 1973) believed that early interactions with caregivers provide a mental blueprint for thinking about oneself and others that carries into adulthood. An avoidant child thus has many obstacles to overcome to develop into a secure adult, including learning to trust others and being comfortable with closeness. Similarly, an anxious-ambivalent

BOX 8.6 PUT YOURSELF TO THE TEST
WHAT IS YOUR ATTACHMENT STYLE?

This questionnaire asks you to think about your general attitudes toward yourself, others, and relationships. Please rate yourself on each of these statements according to the following scale: 1 = strongly disagree and 7 = strongly agree.

		Disagree					Agree	
1.	I fit in well with other people.	1	2	3	4	5	6	7
2.	I worry that people don't like me as much as I like them.	1	2	3	4	5	6	7
3.	I would like to trust others, but I worry that if I open up too much people might reject me.	1	2	3	4	5	6	7
4.	Sometimes others seem reluctant to get as close to me as I would like.	1	2	3	4	5	6	7
5.	I worry a lot about the well-being of my relationships.	1	2	3	4	5	6	7
6.	I feel smothered when a relationship takes too much time away from my personal pursuits.	1	2	3	4	5	6	7
7.	I worry about getting hurt if I allow myself to get too close to someone.	1	2	3	4	5	6	7
8.	I would like to have closer relationships, but getting close makes me feel vulnerable.	1	2	3	4	5	6	7
9.	I tend not to take risks in relationships for fear of getting hurt or rejected.	1	2	3	4	5	6	7
10.	I rarely worry that I don't "measure up" to other people.	1	2	3	4	5	6	7
11.	Achieving personal goals is more important to me than maintaining good relationships.	1	2	3	4	5	6	7
12.	I avoid getting too close to others so that I won't get hurt.	1	2	3	4	5	6	7
13.	I am confident that other people will like me.	1	2	3	4	5	6	7
14.	I worry that others do not care about me as much as I care about them.	1	2	3	4	5	6	7
15.	I wonder how I would cope without someone to love me.	1	2	3	4	5	6	7
16.	I rarely worry that others might reject me.	1	2	3	4	5	6	7
17.	Being independent is more important to me than having a good relationship.	1	2	3	4	5	6	7
18.	I am confident that others will accept me.	1	2	3	4	5	6	7
19.	I find it relatively easy to get close to people.	1	2	3	4	5	6	7
20.	Pleasing myself is much more important to me than getting along with others.	1	2	3	4	5	6	7
21.	I need relational partners to give me space to do "my own thing."	1	2	3	4	5	6	7
22.	I sometimes worry that my relational partners will leave me.	1	2	3	4	5	6	7

(Continued)

BOX 8.6 (Continued)

23.	It is easy for me to get along with others.	1	2	3	4	5	6	7
24.	I frequently pull away from relational partners when I need time to pursue my personal goals.	1	2	3	4	5	6	7
25.	I need to be in a close relationship to be happy.	1	2	3	4	5	6	7

Add up the following items and then divide by the number shown to get your score on each attachment style.

Security: Items 1+10+13+16+18+19+23 / 7 =   _____

Preoccupation: Items 2+4+5+14+15+22+25 / 7 =   _____

Dismissiveness: Items 6+11+17+20+21+24 / 6 =   _____

Fearful: Items 3+7+8+9+12 / 5 =   _____

Higher scores mean that you possess more of a particular attachment style. The highest possible score for a given style is 7; the lowest possible score is 1.

Source: Adapted from Guerrero et al. (2009).

child needs to become self-confident and self-sufficient to achieve security. Such changes are possible but require time, effort, and the cooperation and patience of others.

A second source of stability is called the **reinforcement effect** (Bartholomew, 1993). According to this perspective, people communicate in cycles that reinforce their attachment style. For example, because secure individuals are self-confident and readily approach others, they are more likely to make friends and develop relationships, causing them to feel even better about themselves and others. Preoccupied individuals, by contrast, continually reach for higher levels of intimacy. Perhaps you have had a partner like this—someone who wanted to meet your family right away, told you how much she or he loved you on the third date, or wanted to move in with you after your first month together. A common reaction to these premature declarations of love and commitment is to try to de-escalate the relationship, which only makes the preoccupied person engage in more excessive intimacy and closeness. This process reinforces that individual's negative model of self ("My partner doesn't love me as much as I love her") and positive model of others ("Everything would be great if only I could get him to love me").

Fearful and dismissive individuals suffer from similarly paradoxical interaction patterns. More than anything else, fearful individuals need to build a secure, happy relationship to help them feel better about themselves and others. However, their fear of pain and rejection keeps them from reaching out to others and developing the kind of intimate relationship that would bring them out of their protective shells. Dismissives display similarly negative self-reinforcing patterns. If dismissives continually avoid highly committed relationships and refuse to ask others for help and support, they reinforce their view that other people are unnecessary and they should rely only on themselves. They miss the opportunity to discover ways in which committed relationships can enrich, rather than impede, personal satisfaction.

EXPLANATIONS FOR CHANGE There are four primary explanations for change in attachment styles (Feeney et al., 2000). First, significant events such as divorce, marriage, reunion after a long separation, development of a new relationship, or the death of a loved one may modify a person's attachment style. For example, a fearful man may become more secure after reuniting with his ex-wife, and a secure young woman may become more dismissive when she heads off to college and away from those who love her. Research has also shown that women report less attachment anxiety and avoidance over time if they are in a stable relationship (Givertz & Safford, 2011). Second, a person's attachment style may be affected by a partner's style, as several studies have shown (e.g., Guerrero & Bachman, 2008; Le Poire et al., 1999). For example, Givertz and Safford (2011) showed that men's attachment styles become increasingly avoidant if their relationship is characterized by demand-withdrawal conflict. (This type of conflict occurs when one person demands change and the other person withdraws, see Chapter 11.) In the case of Gabriela and Brian, their opposing needs could cause them to become more dismissive and preoccupied, respectively. When Gabriela expresses a need for

more space, Brian might feel a lack of closeness and crave more intimacy. When Brian expresses a need for more affection, Gabriela might pull away and retreat into her personal activities.

Third, people may have different attachment styles depending on relationship type (Baldwin & Fehr, 1995; Cozzarelli, Hoekstra, & Bylsma, 2000; Pierce & Lydon, 2001). For example, Gabriela might have a dismissive attachment orientation toward Brian and her father but a secure attachment orientation toward her mother and friends. The movie *Good Will Hunting* provides a good example of how attachment orientations sometimes vary on the basis of relationship type. Will exhibits classic fearful behavior with romantic partners—he avoids commitment because he is afraid of being hurt and abandoned as he was as a child in the foster care system. However, within his close-knit group of male friends, Will displays a secure attachment style. Finally, some researchers have suggested that stability (or instability) of attachment style is a personality characteristic; some people are more susceptible to change than others. So Gabriela's attachment style could be more likely to change based on life events (e.g., what's happening at work) than Brian's.

SUMMARY AND APPLICATION

People approach loving relationships in a variety of ways. Every person has a unique set of perceptions, expectations, and preferences that contribute to that individual's love and attachment styles. When two people's styles interact within the context of a close relationship, another unique relational pattern emerges. Partners should realize that what works in one of their relationships might not necessarily work in others and that it is difficult for two people to fully meet each other's expectations.

The attitudes Gabriela and Brian have about love and relationships are fairly common. From the description at the beginning of this chapter,

Gabriela has a dismissive attachment style and communicates love through activity-sharing. Brian has a preoccupied attachment style and communicates love through affection and verbal expression. Of course, most people do not fall neatly into a love or attachment category. Take another look at Figure 8.3. Where would you fall on the dimensions representing positive versus negative models of self and others? You could fit squarely within a given category or you could fall on the border between categories. For instance, Gabriela might have an extremely positive model of self and only a slightly negative model of others, and Brian might be on the border between preoccupation and security. Moreover, the interaction between Brian and Gabriela's styles is likely to produce a unique set of behaviors. Styles of love and attachment reflect some important differences in how people approach and communicate in close relationships, but it is crucial to see ourselves and others as complex individuals who do not always fit a particular profile.

People with different relational needs and communication styles, like Brian and Gabriela, can often work together to build happy relationships. One key to a successful relationship is for relational partners to help each other grow as individuals. For example, preoccupied individuals like Brian may need to make an effort to give their partners more space, while dismissive individuals like Gabriela may need to work on showing more affection. At the same time, individuals in relationships with people who have insecure attachment styles should be patient and understanding, rather than demanding more or less intimacy than their partners are comfortable giving. Relational partners should also understand and appreciate each other's ways of

loving. For example, Brian may feel more secure if he realizes that Gabriela is showing that she cares for him when she plans activities for them to do together.

In the scenario at the beginning of this chapter, Brian also wonders if Gabriela really loves him. This is a difficult question to answer. Liking and loving differ in both quantitative and qualitative ways. Loving is typically characterized by more attachment, caring, and commitment than liking, and love between romantic partners is also usually characterized by feelings of passion. Yet it is hard to quantify love, and there is no simple answer to the seemingly straightforward question: What is love? Love is a complex and variable phenomenon that defies simple definition. Indeed, instead of simply asking what love is, it may be more appropriate to ask, "What is love to me and to my partner, and how does love function in the unique relationship we share?" Thinking about these issues may be especially helpful to relational partners like Gabriela and Brian, who have different styles of loving and attachment.

KEY TERMS

agape (p. 204)
anxious-ambivalent attachment style (p. 217)
attachment theory (p. 197)
avoidants (p. 219)
avoidant attachment style (p. 216)
companionate love (p. 207)
consummate love (p. 198)
dismissive attachment style (p. 219)
empty love (p. 201)
eros (p. 204)
fearful attachment style (p. 219)
friendship love (p. 198)
ideologies (p. 203)

infatuation (p. 200)
internal working models (p. 215)
intimacy (p. 198)
language of acts of service (p. 213)
language of affirmation and support (p. 212)
language of gifts and tokens of affection (p. 213)
language of physical touch (p. 213)
language of time together (p. 212)
latent intimacy (p. 199)
liking (p. 198)
love languages (p. 212)

love ways (p. 212)
ludus (p. 204)
mania (p. 204)
manifest intimacy (p. 199)
passion (p. 198)
passionate love (p. 204)
pragma (p. 204)
preoccupied attachment style (p. 218)
reinforcement effect (p. 224)
romantic love (p. 198)
secure base (p. 214)
secure attachment style (p. 218)
storge (p. 204)

DISCUSSION QUESTIONS

1. How would you distinguish loving from liking? Do you think the difference between loving and liking is more quantitative or qualitative? Why?

2. Do you think people's love styles and love languages change throughout their lives? If so, what factors do you think account for this change? How might culture affect people's love styles beyond what was discussed in this chapter?

3. According to attachment theory, parent–child communication forms the basis for personality development, including the capacity to have close, intimate adult relationships with others. To what extent do you agree or disagree that early communication with parents shapes a person's life? What other events and interactions have shaped your attachment style?

 SAGE edge™

Sharpen your skills with SAGE edge at edge.sagepub.com/guerrero5e.
SAGE edge for students provides a personalized approach to help you accomplish your coursework goals in an easy-to-use learning environment.

9 COMMUNICATING SEXUALLY
The Closest Physical Encounter

Although Brittany, Sarah, and Taylor are sorority sisters, their sex lives could not be more different. Brittany has been seeing the same man for 4 years and has an active sex life. She believes her boyfriend, Chris, is completely faithful, but she insisted they both get tested to be sure they do not have sexually transmitted infections (STIs). She is on the pill and tries to be as responsible about sex as possible, yet she has never discussed her active sex life with her parents. Though she loves Chris, she is not entirely sure he is the "one" for her. Sarah is deeply religious and has chosen to remain a virgin until after marriage. Sometimes she feels strange because most of the girls in the house are not virgins. She enjoys sexual activity with her boyfriend but always makes sure that they stop well short of sexual intercourse. Occasionally, her sisters are unkind and call Sarah frigid or prudish, which makes Sarah feel that her values are out of the mainstream. Taylor dated men but recently admitted to herself and the world that she has always been more attracted to women. She announced to her sisters that she is a lesbian and is in a committed, monogamous relationship with her partner, Leslie. Most of the women in the house accepted her fully; however, she has heard a few homophobic comments and caught some of her sisters exchanging strange glances when she mentions Leslie.

Sex is one of the most rewarding and difficult issues people face. In this chapter, we focus on sexual behavior and its importance in human relationships. Also, we examine communication related to the development of sexual attitudes and beliefs, initiation and refusal of sexual activity, coercion and harassment, and safe sex in short- and long-term relationships. The research clearly demonstrates that communication is essential for healthy sexual relationships and sexual satisfaction. Many close relationships are platonic, but some of our closest encounters are sexual, including romances and marriages. Most studies focus on sexual relationships between men and women; however, we make an effort to include the existing research about relationships between gay men, lesbians, and bisexuals. Also, most studies focus on attitudes and behaviors of U.S. couples; in other countries, sexual attitudes and behaviors may be quite different. Finally, the physiology of sex and sexual desire is beyond the scope of this chapter, although excellent books on these topics are available (see Regan & Berscheid, 1999).

SEX IN RELATIONSHIPS

Research shows that sexual interaction, including intimate kissing, touching, and sexual intercourse, is a vital part of dating and marital relationships. Although people experience some ambivalence about sex in premarital relationships (O'Sullivan & Gaines, 1998), sexual involvement is typical in most dating relationships (Twenge, Sherman, & Wells, 2015). For most people, sex, attraction, desire, romance, and love are closely intertwined. Differences in sexual interaction often exist based on the type of relationship people share, including short-term versus long-term and gay versus straight. Men and women also differ in their sexual attitudes and behaviors.

Sex in Short-Term and Early Dating Relationships

Short-term sex occurs when a couple has sex without having an emotionally close relationship. Most short-term sex takes the form of hook-ups or one-night stands. **Hook-ups** are spontaneous, casual sexual encounters with an acquaintance or a stranger who is not a regular dating partner with no expectations of a long-term relationship, although not all hook-ups culminate in sexual intercourse (Bogle, 2008; Heldman & Wade, 2010; Mongeau & Wiedmaier, 2011). Hook-ups are intended as one-night stands but may become more enduring relationships. Since the turn of the century, hook-ups have become an increasingly common form of relational and sexual interaction engaged in by a majority of college students. Contrary to the stereotype that only men seek short-term sexual relationships, research shows that women also engage in short-term mating strategies for many of the same reasons as men: sexual desire, sexual experimentation, physical pleasure, and alcohol or drug use (Buunk, Dijkstra, Fetchenhauer, & Kenrick, 2002; Reid, Elliott, & Webber, 2011). Because hook-ups are often motivated primarily by

sexual desire, they are not likely to transform into serious romantic relationships (Jonason, 2012).

Recent research has suggested that dating is not dead; it is still common on college campuses and considered to be a higher quality relationship than a hook-up. Thirty percent of students describe themselves as in a committed dating relationship (Mongeau & Wiedmaier, 2011). Research has generally shown that women are less positive and more negative about hook-ups than men (Campbell, 2008; Heldman & Wade, 2010; Mongeau & Wiedmaier, 2011), although both women and men are more positive than negative (Owen & Fincham, 2011). One study suggests that hook-ups do often lead to a date and that in the hook-up scenario women have considerable agency and control over the situation and its consequences (Reid et al., 2011). However, the sexual script and sexual practices are more ambiguous in hook-ups, particularly for women, and the types of sex that are engaged are often difficult negotiations (Backstrom, Armstrong, & Puentes, 2012).

Although hook-ups and one-night stands are increasingly common, premarital sex typically occurs in dating relationships between people who share some relational and emotional intimacy. In these relationships, people seek to experience sexual attraction, sexual arousal, and relational closeness (Mongeau et al., 2004; O'Sullivan & Gaines, 1998). Research suggests that first sex is a turning point in relationships for better or worse (Metts, 2004; Reissing, Anduff, & Wentland, 2012). Both men and women experience a variety of positive and negative emotions in early sexual encounters, but females are more likely than males to experience negative emotions such as sadness, guilt, or embarrassment whereas males are more likely to experience more anxiety but also more positive emotions such as pleasure, happiness, pride, and excitement (Cupach, Metts, & Hoffman, 2012; Sprecher, 2014). Situational factors, such as drinking alcohol, can also prompt sexual involvement in both hook-ups and long-term relationships (Heldman & Wade, 2010; Klein, Geaghan, & MacDonald, 2007;

Morr & Mongeau, 2004; Sprecher & McKinney, 1993) as can special occasions such as prom or anniversaries. In the eyes of both men and women, alcohol consumption by women increased dating intimacy, but alcohol use by men decreased dating intimacy (Ip & Heubeck, 2016).

In the past two decades **friends with benefits** have become more prevalent (see also Chapter 10). These are sexual but nonromantic relationships among friends or acquaintances. About a quarter of all college students have had a "friends-with-bene-fits" relationship, and they are equally prevalent among urban and rural high school and college students (Eisenberg, Ackard, Resnick, & Neumark-Sztainer, 2009; Letcher & Carmona, 2015). There are numerous subtypes of these relationships including "true" friends who have sex, serial hook-ups, and various types of transitions in and out of relationships (Knight, Wiedmaier, Mongeau, Eden, & Roberto, 2012; Mongeau, Knight, Williams, Eden, & Shaw, 2013) but true friends, defined as close friends having sex are the most common. (See Chapter 10 for a more detailed discussion of the different types of friends-with-benefits relationships.) There is little risk of harmful psychological outcomes in friends-with-benefits relationships (Eisenberg et al., 2009) and most people in friends-with-benefits relationships have sexually permissive attitudes (Akbulut & Weger, 2016). Some of these relationships transition from friends with benefits to a conventional romantic relationship (VanderDrift, Lehmiller, & Kelly, 2012). However, most friends-with-benefits relationships are placeholders until a more serious romantic relationship comes along (Jonason, 2012).

Sex in Long-Term Relationships

Criteria for long-term romantic partners differ from those for a first date or a short-term sexual encounter. In long-term relationships, both men and women place a high value on qualities such as interpersonal skill, emotional stability, responsiveness, affection, and family orientation, and less value on physical attraction (Buunk et al., 2002). Women throughout the world prefer long-term partners higher in social and economic status than themselves (Buunk et al., 2002; Fales et al., 2016). But sex itself is important; in long-term relationships, "sexual desire is a distinguishing feature and a prerequisite of the romantic love experience" (Regan & Berscheid, 1999, p. 126). In short-term sexual encounters, by contrast, sexual desire is often present without love or intimacy, though even in short-term sexual encounters intimacy is positively correlated with sexual satisfaction (Birnie-Porter & Hunt, 2015).

The most satisfying sex takes place in long-term romantic relationships, not in hook-ups or short-term dating relationships (DeLamater & Hyde, 2004; Heldman & Wade, 2010; Willetts, Sprecher, & Beck, 2004). Married people have higher levels of sexual satisfaction than dating or cohabiting couples (Sprecher & Cate, 2004), although engaged couples have the highest level of sexual satisfaction (Birnie-Porter & Hunt, 2015). Sexual intimacy evolved to keep mates interested in one another (Buss, 1988b; Hendrick & Hendrick, 2002). A couple's ongoing sexual interest promotes bonding, cooperation, and a stable environment for childrearing (Buss, 1994; Sprecher & Cate, 2004). Sex is best when it is motivated by wanting to feel good about oneself, please one's partner, or promote intimacy. Sex is not as pleasurable or relationship enhancing when prompted by motives such as preventing one's partner from getting upset, avoiding conflict, or preventing one's partner from losing interest (Impett, Peplau, & Gable, 2005).

Although men's sexual desire peaks in their early 20s and women's in their 30s, the association between relational and sexual satisfaction is high throughout life, even for seniors (Howard, O'Neill, & Travers, 2006; Taylor & Gosney, 2011). The amount of sex declines as couples age, but sexual satisfaction does not (DeLamater & Hyde, 2004, Howard et al., 2006; Willetts et al., 2004). Research shows that as women age into midlife and the senior years, feeling attractive is associated with sexual desire, enjoyment, frequency of sexual activity, and ability to reach orgasm (Koch, Mansfield, Thurau, & Carey, 2005).

Both men and women view sexual desire and satisfaction as vital to true romantic love (Holmberg, Blair, & Phillips, 2010; Regan, 1998; Regan & Berscheid, 1999; Sprecher & Cate, 2004) with physical contact—including touching, kissing, and sexual intercourse—seen as an essential part of expressing that love (Christopher & Kissler, 2004; Regan & Berscheid, 1999). People with high levels of sexual desire in their relationships report higher levels of excitement, connection, love, and relational satisfaction (Byers, Demmons, & Lawrence, 1998; Christopher & Kissler, 2004; Hendrick & Hendrick, 2002; Sprecher & Regan, 1996). Interestingly, the positive association between sexual satisfaction and relational satisfaction also exists in China, suggesting the cross-cultural strength of this association (Reined, Byers, & Pan, 1997). If the relationship is satisfying and if neither partner feels coerced or obligated to have sex, their first experience of sexual intercourse usually has a positive effect on the relationship (Cate, Long, Angera, & Draper, 1993). This is not to say that sex always makes a relationship better, but high-quality sex can contribute to a good relationship. Of course, many other factors also contribute to relational satisfaction, such as commitment, love, and compatibility. Recent research shows that teens experience more relational and sexual satisfaction when they meet face to face rather than online, and when they know the partner better before having sex (Blunt-Vinti, Wheldon, McFarlane, Brogan, & Walsh-Buhi, 2016), suggesting that traditional romantic dating patterns still lead to the best outcomes.

Sex Differences

Sex is an important part of a good relationship, but men and women are not identical in their sexual inclinations and behaviors. Biologically, women invest more time and resources in becoming a parent. For women, reproduction involves finding a mate, having sex, going through pregnancy and childbirth, nursing and nurturing the baby, and in most cases raising the child to adulthood; for men, only finding a mate and having sex are biological imperatives (Trost & Alberts, 2006). This may be why women are much choosier than men about who to have a one-night stand with. For many men, the ideal short-term mate is physically attractive (Buunk et al., 2002; Fales et al., 2016; Greitemeyer, 2005; Van Straaten, Engels, Finkenauer, & Holland, 2008), but men are willing to compromise on traits such as intelligence and status. For women, the ideal short-term partner is physically attractive, somewhat older, more experienced, self-confident, intelligent, interpersonally responsive, and has a steady income, (Buunk et al., 2002; Fales et al., 2016; Trost & Alberts, 2006).

Men and women also differ in terms of sexual desire and sexual attraction. Studies consistently show that men have a stronger sex drive than women (DeLamater & Hyde, 2004; Holmberg & Blair, 2009; Vohs, Catanese, & Baumeister, 2004) and that they experience greater sexual arousal in response to a short-term sexual opportunity than women do (Stone, Shackelford, & Goetz, 2011). Among first-year college students, men had an equal amount of reward from either oral or vaginal sex while women found vaginal sex more rewarding (Lefkowitz, Vasilenko, & Levitt, 2016). For men, sexy looks, erotic situations, and friendly social behaviors promote sexual desire (Benuto & Meana, 2008; Buunk et al., 2002; Cupach & Metts, 1995; Greitemeyer, 2005; Regan, 2004). Women, in contrast, are sexually attracted to men who are relationally oriented, emotionally connected, and who show tenderness and intimacy with them. Indeed, studies show that women's sexual desire is more dependent on feelings, the type of relationship they share with the partner, the potential for intimacy and humor, and the status and intelligence of the man (McCall & Meston, 2006), whereas men's desire is more influenced by physical attraction, sexual pleasure, and erotic qualities (Buunk et al., 2002; Greitemeyer, 2005; Metts, 2004; Regan, 2004; Regan & Berscheid, 1995, 1999).

BOX 9.1 TECH TALK
CYBERSEXUALITY

Online sexual interaction has become increasingly common. In 2012, the Internet Filter Learning Center reported that about 12% of all Internet content contained pornography, and that 40 million people in the United States view Internet pornography on a regular basis, of which 72% are male. And the United States is not alone. According to the Internet Filter Learning Center, every second 28,258 Internet users around the world view pornography. An analysis by country of searches using the words *porn* and *XXX* revealed that the United States was not even in the top 10. The most searches with the keyword *porn* were in South Africa, Ireland, and New Zealand. The most searches for *XXX* were in Bolivia, Chile, and Romania. Another study (Twohig, Crosby, & Cox, 2009) revealed that around half of the college-aged men they surveyed (compared to less than 3% of the college-aged women they surveyed) reported viewing Internet pornography at least once in the past 3 months.

Some people think Internet pornography has contributed to a degeneration of morals, a deterioration of personal relationships, and can lead to Internet sexual addiction (Griffiths, 2012). One recent study showed that pornography consumption was related to flirting with others and being less committed to one's partner and less commitment was related to infidelity (Lambert, Negash, Stillman, Olmstead, & Fincham, 2012). Other people think such sites are a form of safe sex that prevents STIs and unwanted pregnancies. Twohig and others' (2009) research suggests that viewing Internet pornography is problematic for some people but not others.

Of great concern are risqué or sexual posts by high school and college students on websites or Facebook. Of even greater concern are risky portrayals of sexuality on dating websites. One study showed young men who were exposed to pornography were less likely to use a condom than were those who were not (Luder et al., 2011). Another study of a teen dating website revealed that over 15% of female posts contain explicit sexuality or nudity (Pujazon-Zazik, Manasse, & Orrell-Valente, 2012), putting them in danger from cyberstalkers and sexual predators. Many teens and young adults fail to consider that sexual postings are available widely to friends as well as enemies, predators, teachers, and potential employers. So as with anything you put on the Internet, think before you post.

Research suggests the female sex drive is more socially flexible, culturally responsive, and adaptable than the male sex drive, which is more predictable and consistent, less shaped by culture, and somewhat stronger (Baumeister, 2000; Diamond, 2012; Vohs et al., 2004; Wells & Twenge, 2005); although research suggests that men and women are more similar than different in their sex drives (Benuto & Meana, 2008). Some women seem to do fine without sex, while other women are highly sexual, depending on circumstances (Baumeister, 2000) and are more satisfied with their sexual relationships than men regardless of how much sex they are having (Holmberg & Blair, 2009). Numerous studies show individual women vary in sex drive over time. For example, a woman may have a stronger sex drive when she is in an intimate relationship than when she is not involved with anyone. Men, by contrast,

have a more consistent sex drive that operates regardless of their relational involvement with someone. Heterosexual women are aroused by a greater variety of stimuli (e.g., affectionate behaviors, romantic context) than are heterosexual men, who are more likely to be aroused primarily by sights and thoughts of attractive women (Chivers & Bailey, 2005; Chivers, Soto, & Blanchard, 2007) and have a stable erotic compass. Of course, the popularity of Viagra and Cialis suggests that men's sex drive is also somewhat variable.

Female sexuality is also more varied across different sociocultural settings than is male sexuality. Baumeister (2000) cited ethnographic studies that report much greater cross-cultural variation in sexual behavior for females than for males. For example, in some cultures, women have premarital sex while in others they do not. A worldwide survey reveals that in countries where women have more equality they engage in more casual sex, have more partners in their lifetime, and have sex at an earlier age (Baumeister & Mendoza, 2011). Studies also show that women are less likely to reveal their true sexual attitudes than are men if social norms require them to hide their sexual interest so as to not appear "loose" (DeLamater & Hyde, 2004).

Men and women also think about sex differently. Men have greater expectations for sex on dates (Mongeau, Jacobsen, & Donnerstein, 2007; Mongeau & Johnson, 1995) and may feel social pressure and gain status by having sex (Sweeney, 2014). Men also think about sex more often, as much as every few seconds (Fisher, Moore, & Pittinger, 2012; Vohs et al., 2004); although they also think more about food and sleep than women do. Men are more motivated to date to have sexual relations, less willing to live without sex (Mongeau et al., 2004; Regan & Berscheid, 1995), more liberal in sexual attitudes (Benuto & Meana, 2008), and are more likely to think of the advantages of sexual relations rather than the disadvantages (Kisler & Christopher, 2008). Men are more likely than women to regret *not having* a sexual relationship; women regret sexual action and inaction equally (Roese et al., 2006).

Studies also show differences in sexual behavior as well. Men tend to look at women longer and more sexually than women look at men (Lykins, Meana, & Strauss, 2008). Men are also more likely to engage in short-term mating opportunities, particularly with physically attractive women (Van Straaten et al., 2008), more likely to want a friends-with-benefits relationship (Akbulut & Weger, 2016), and to view pornographic material on the Internet. When women do view pornography on the Internet, they tend to keep it secret (Internet Filter Learning Center, 2012). (See Box 9.1 for more information on cybersex, including sex differences.) Men have more sex partners (Willetts et al., 2004), are less monogamous, and are more likely to believe that monogamy is a sacrifice (Schmookler & Bursic, 2007). Interestingly, the first act of sexual intercourse between two people usually has a much more positive effect on the relationship for women than for

men, assuming that the sex was a voluntary act reflecting love and commitment (Cate et al., 1993).

Sex in Same-Sex Relationships

Significant minorities of people are not sexually attracted to members of the opposite sex but rather have same-sex attractions. Like Taylor, who we introduced in the opening scenario, most homosexuals have early recollections of same-sex attraction and a clear sense that they were different from the majority as early as preschool. Research suggests that throughout the world, most gay men and lesbians experienced some degree of gender nonconformity as children (Crooks & Baur, 1999). Studies show that sexual attraction is more than mere preference; gay men show the most sexual response to gay scenes, bisexual men to bisexual scenes, and straight men to heterosexual interactions (Cerny & Janssen, 2011; Rosenthal, Sylva, Safron, & Bailey, 2011).

Because men and women differ in their sexual attitudes and behaviors, it is not surprising that relationships between lesbians, gay men, and heterosexuals also differ to some degree. Yet there are major similarities between heterosexual, gay, and lesbian relationships as well (Holmberg & Blair, 2009; Holmberg et al., 2010). Like heterosexual couples, the vast majority of lesbians and gay men want intimacy and long-term committed relationships (Frost & Gola, 2015; Peplau, Fingerhut, & Beals, 2004). Even when same-sex marriage was illegal in most states, the majority of lesbians and gay men would have married their partner if it was legal (Peplau et al., 2004). Interestingly, some studies have shown that gay men and lesbians report higher levels of sexual satisfaction than do heterosexual couples (Holmberg & Blair, 2009).

Despite increasingly progressive attitudes about homosexuality and bisexuality in the United States, gay and lesbian relationships are still not readily accepted or understood by many segments of society (Callender, 2015; Peplau et al., 2004). This may be the reason, even today, that gays and lesbians are more likely to meet partners for dates and hookups online (Kuperberg & Padgett, 2015) rather than in bars or at parties. Growing up gay in a heterosexual, homophobic world is not easy, and most problems for gay men and lesbians come from adverse reactions of society. Even today, publicly gay men experience more anxiety and depression than do closeted men (Pachankis, Cochran, & Mays, 2015). Adolescence is a tough time for all young people, as indicated by the high teenage suicide rate. The rate is even higher for gay teens, who may need counseling as they adjust to their sexual orientation and to the attitudes of those around them.

SEX IN LESBIAN RELATIONSHIPS Compared to heterosexual couples and gay male couples, lesbians report the highest level of relational satisfaction (Kurdek, 2008) and the lowest level of sexual victimization (Johnson, Matthews, & Napper, 2016). Over 75% of lesbian couples are monogamous; fidelity is especially important to lesbians (Blumstein & Schwartz, 1983); moreover, monogamy in lesbian couples has increased over the past 40 years (Gota et al., 2011). Unlike men, lesbians are less attracted to women based on physical attraction. Sexual activity for lesbians declines over time, leading to concerns and even jokes about the "lesbian bed death" (Peplau et al., 2004; Van Rosmalen-Nooijens, Vergeer, Lagro-Janssen, 2008). Although the frequency of sexual relations is associated with increased satisfaction in lesbian couples (Peplau et al., 2004), lesbians have sex less frequently than male gay couples, heterosexual daters, or married couples (Blumstein & Schwartz, 1983), which is consistent with variability in all women's sexual desire (Diamond, 2012). Women generally are taught to be selective in choosing sexual partners, to take a reactive rather than proactive role in sexual situations, and to act as gatekeepers who decide whether sexual activity will take place. Lesbians must renegotiate these gender roles so that they feel comfortable initiating sex. Moreover, since men have a more consistent sex drive than women (Baumeister, 2000), with no man to initiate sex, sex is less likely to occur. Among lesbian women, acceptance of oneself as a lesbian is

associated with sexual satisfaction (Henderson, Lehavot, & Simoni, 2009). Finally, lesbians may be satisfied with nongenital sex since, like heterosexual women, lesbians value physical contact, such as hugging and cuddling, and are likely to consider these ends in and of themselves rather than a prelude to sex (Blumstein & Schwartz, 1983).

Prior research suggests that between a quarter and third of lesbians have been married to men (Boon & Alderson, 2009). Some may be bisexual, others may be testing their heterosexual orientation, and still others may be concealing their homosexual orientation. According to Bell and Weinberg (1978), relational satisfaction is low in such marital relationships, and most end in separation or divorce. Over 75% of lesbians have had at least one sexual encounter with a man (Reinisch & Beasley, 1990), and numerous young women who report being only attracted to men still report sexual activity with other women (McCabe, Brewster, & Tillman, 2011). As discussed previously, research suggests that women are more sexually variable than men and have an easier time accepting various sexual orientations and conditions, including homosexuality or abstinence (Baumeister, 2000).

SEX IN RELATIONSHIPS BETWEEN GAY MEN According to the Kinsey report, although about one third of all men have engaged in homosexual behavior at one time in their lives, only about 8% have had exclusively gay relationships for 3 or more years, and only 4% have been exclusively gay throughout their lives. About two thirds of gay men have had sex with a woman, and 10% to 15% of gay men may be more accurately viewed as bisexual (Reinisch & Beasley, 1990).

On average, gay men have more sex partners and engage in sex more often than lesbians or heterosexuals (Blumstein & Schwartz, 1983; Kelly, Bimbi, Nanin, Iziennicki, & Parsons, 2009; Parsons et al., 2008). Because women often act as sexual gatekeepers, the absence of a woman in a relationship probably reduces restraint and increases sexual frequency. Gay men are also more likely than lesbians or heterosexuals to be in non-monogamous relationships. In the 1970s and 1980s, over 80% of gay men were nonmonogamous, but by 2000 that number had dropped to less than 60% (Blumstein & Schwartz, 1983; Gota et al., 2011). Long-term relationships among gay men are much more common than the media would have us believe. The Kinsey data suggest that virtually all gay men have had a steady, highly committed gay relationship that lasted 1 to 3 years (Reinisch & Beasley, 1990) and for those gay men in long-term relationships, satisfaction increases over time (Kurdek, 2008). Furthermore, some evidence suggests that gay men, like heterosexual men and women, have become more monogamous since the AIDS epidemic first emerged in the 1980s (Gota et al., 2011; Sprecher & Regan, 2000).

Gay men may have difficulty negotiating sexual initiation precisely because it is typically a male prerogative. In short, some gay men resent the other male's initiation and refuse sex, which can lead to conflict. Gay men have more sex than other couple types since either partner can feel free to initiate sex (Blumstein & Schwartz, 1983; Parsons et al., 2008), and most gay men are highly satisfied with their sexual relationships. How to initiate sex may sometimes be difficult, since kissing, which is a more feminine behavior, is often the gateway to sexual relations and is most likely in lesbian relationships, moderately likely in heterosexual relationships, and least likely in gay relationships between men (Blumstein & Schwartz, 1983).

SEXUAL ATTITUDES

Deciding if and when to have sex is a personal choice influenced by many factors, including levels of commitment and passion, alcohol consumption, and moral values. Sexual behavior is strongly related to people's attitudes, for people may be born with a number of sexual preferences and proclivities, but most attitudes and beliefs about sex are learned. For example, a person might be physically aroused and curious when thinking about having sex, but moral attitudes and beliefs might stop the individual from acting on the impulse to have sex.

The social norms of one's culture also influence people's sexual attitudes. Attitudes toward sexuality, particularly premarital and female sexuality, became increasingly liberal in the United States during the 20th century (Sprecher & McKinney, 1993; Twenge et al., 2015; Wells & Twenge, 2005). The best data on changes in sexuality come from a study by Wells and Twenge (2005) that aggregated over 500 studies including over 250,000 participants. Throughout most of the century, premarital sex was considered unacceptable, particularly for women. But "premarital sexual activity has become normative for today's youth. Rates of sexual intercourse for teens have increased dramatically since the early 1960s" (Christopher & Roosa, 1991, p. 11).

Positive attitudes toward sexual activity, especially among females, steadily increased from 1965 to 2012 (Twenge et al., 2015; Wells & Twenge, 2005). In the 1950s, only 13% of teenage girls were sexually active whereas by the 1990s, 47% were sexually active. Before 1970, the average age for first sexual intercourse for men was 18 and for women was 19; by the late 1990s, this average had dropped to age 15 for both genders (Wells & Twenge, 2005). Similarly, before 1970, less than half of teenagers had engaged in oral sex, but by the 1990s over two thirds of both men and women had engaged in oral sex. In the late 1950s, only 12% of young women approved of premarital sex, and by the 1980s about three quarters approved. The only sexual behavior not increasing is the number of partners, which has remained fairly constant over the years, especially since news of the AIDS epidemic in the 1980s (Wells & Twenge, 2005). But times have changed; by the 21st century, over 80% of men and women have had premarital sexual intercourse (Willetts et al., 2004).

The revolution in sexual attitudes that began in the 1960s was due to a number of factors. The 1960s was a revolutionary era for all types of values, including those associated with politics, music, the environment, civil rights, and women's rights. In the 1960s, images of sexuality were widely depicted in the mass media through magazines, books, and movies, and to a lesser degree, television. Perhaps the biggest factor was the birth control pill—the first simple and effective technology that permitted sex without reproduction. For the first time in human history, women could have sexual relationships without risking pregnancy. Scholars suggest that the sexual revolution of the 1960s and 1970s was mainly a change in women's values, with men remaining much the same (Baumeister, 2000). Today, teens and young adults are much more sexually active than they were before the sexual revolution of the 1960s.

Researchers have identified three types of sexual attitudes held by people today (Sprecher & McKinney, 1993). Some people have a **procreational orientation,** which reflects the belief that producing offspring is the primary purpose of sexual intercourse. Other people have a **relational orientation,** which holds that sexual intercourse is a way of expressing love and affection, and developing greater relational intimacy. Still others have a **recreational orientation,** viewing sex as a primary source of fun, escape, excitement, or pleasure. The procreational orientation, the position taken by most major religions, is associated with traditional, conservative cultural values. The relational orientation, which is equated with moderate sexual values, is widespread in the United States. People with this orientation disapprove of casual sex but usually approve of premarital sex in the context of a committed or loving relationship. The recreational orientation is a sexually liberal view holding that sex is appropriate between consenting adults regardless of their relationship (or lack thereof).

These orientations are not mutually exclusive; many people's sexual attitudes are some combination of procreational, relational, and recreational. Indeed, most married couples in the United States embrace elements of all three values within their relationship at different times. By contrast, attitudes toward premarital sex vacillate between a relational orientation and a somewhat recreational orientation in the United States but are rarely procreational.

Research has shown that couples are more likely to endorse increased sexual activity, including sexual intercourse, as the relationship becomes closer (Sprecher, McKinney, Walsh, & Anderson, 1988). For several decades, people in the United States have subscribed primarily to a relational orientation through the practice of **serial monogamy** (Christopher & Roosa, 1991; Sorensen, 1973). These couples are sexually active only with each other (monogamy) and do not engage in other sexual relationships until the current relationship ends.

While a lot of research has focused on the dark side of premarital sex, such as disease, pregnancy, and abortion, positive outcomes also occur. Most premarital sex takes place in an intimate and committed relationship that provides support and often leads to marriage (Christopher & Roosa, 1991). In fact, early research showed that serial monogamists, people who have one sexual relationship at a time, overwhelmingly loved each other and had healthy, caring sexual relationships (Sorensen, 1973). Moreover, serial monogamists had the highest school grades, were most likely to use birth control, enjoyed sex more, and were generally better adjusted than were either promiscuous adventurers or virgins. Recent research has shown that adolescents who engage in normative sexual behavior are better adjusted psychologically and more positive about life than are adolescents who are sexually inexperienced (Vrangalova & Savin-Williams, 2011).

Although most college students are sexually experienced, some choose to remain virgins. In a study of sexual behavior of college students, Sprecher and Regan (1996) found that 11% of men and 13% of women were virgins; although virtually all of the virgins reported experiencing sexual desire. Thus, Sarah, who we introduced at the beginning of this chapter, is not alone in her virginity. Women like Sarah give several reasons for being a virgin, including the absence of a long-term or love relationship, fear of negative consequences such as pregnancy or STIs, personal beliefs and values, and feelings of inadequacy or insecurity. All of these reasons are stronger for women than for men. In Sprecher and

Regan's study, virgins reported a mixture of pride and anxiety about their status; although positive emotions outweighed negative ones. Women were more likely to be proud and happy about keeping their virginity, while men were more likely to be embarrassed about it. Men are reluctant virgins; most are virgins because their partner is not willing (Sprecher & Treger, 2015). Virgins and adolescents who have not engaged in oral sex are more likely to be traditionally religious, and religious individuals are more positive about their status as virgins than less religious virgins (Burris, Smith, & Carlson, 2009; Sprecher & Regan, 1996; Vazsonyi & Jenkins, 2010). Interestingly, however, for young adults, spirituality, when defined as a search for sacredness and transcendence, is associated with increased sexual activity (Burris et al., 2009).

Developing Sexual Attitudes and Beliefs

Aside from historical forces, how do people develop sexual attitudes and beliefs? We have already touched on one important source—culture. Sexual attitudes and knowledge come from many other sources as well, including mass media, parents, peers, and past relationships (Andersen, 1993). These factors influence more than sexual attitudes; they also influence sexual behavior and communication about sex.

CULTURE Culture influences sexual attitudes. Andersen (1998a) argued that "the most basic force that molds and shapes human beings, other than our membership in the human race itself, is culture" (p. 48). Culture is resistant to change, and people usually adopt the values and attitudes of their parents and their culture unless very strong countervailing forces come into play. Children of immigrants, for example, are caught between two sets of cultural values—(1) those of their parents and (2) those of their peers. Sexual attitudes change slowly across each generation and still show cultural influences after 100 or more years of cultural assimilation. In the United States, African Americans have the most permissive sexual attitudes, followed by whites, while people from Asian, Latino, and

Middle Eastern cultures have the most conservative sexual orientations (Sprecher & McKinney, 1993). Among white Americans, particularly women, and to a lesser degree among African Americans, talking about sexual intimacy is quite common and is believed to be the heart and soul of a good relationship (Crooks & Baur, 1999). By contrast, Asian Americans and Hispanic Americans tend to be more reluctant to discuss their sexual relationship. In interethnic couples, these differences require considerable understanding and adaptation by the partners. For more on how culture impacts sexual attitudes and behaviors, see Box 9.2.

THE MEDIA Both the mass media and social media are important sources of sexual information. Research has shown that 29% of interactions on prime-time television depict sexual issues that emphasize male sexual roles and a recreational rather than a procreational sex orientation (Ward, 1995). Most of these interactions depict sex as a competition and equate masculinity with being sexual. The media also influences **sexual scripts** for communicating about sex. Magazines are an important information source about sex and sexual issues. Starting in 1953 with the publication of *Playboy,* people from the United States were introduced to open nudity on newsstands and perhaps, more importantly, to the "playboy" philosophy that rejected limits on sexual expression, condoned any form of consensual sex, and was critical of the institution of marriage (D'Emilio & Freedman, 1988). Similarly, publication of Helen Gurley Brown's (1962) *Sex and the Single Girl* in the early 1960s urged young women to reconsider the taboo against premarital sex. Research suggests that when young males view men's movies and men's magazines it affects the way they think about sex and behave by fostering male sexual privilege, having more sexual partners, and rejecting abstinence before marriage (Ward, Epstein, Caruthers, & Merriwether, 2011). But media facilitates healthy sex practices, too. Viewing dramas that feature frank discussions about sex facilitate sexual communication among viewers

BOX 9.2 AROUND THE WORLD
SEXUALITY AND CULTURE: THE ABNORMAL IS NORMAL

Every culture has at least one thing in common: Its residents engage in sexual behavior since sex is necessary for procreation. Cultures that did not engage in sexual intercourse are all extinct. But much of the similarity ends there! Cultures differ widely in the time, place, motivation, and appropriateness for sexual interaction. As we discuss in this chapter, couples from the United States have sex to recreate, relate, and procreate. Of course, many young people in the United States, especially males, adopt a recreational orientation to sex if they are not in an exclusive romantic relationship. When partners develop a close relationship, they usually move to a more relational orientation with sex seen as a way to create and maintain closeness in their relationship.

In some cultures in other parts of the world, people have a purely procreational orientation toward sex. This is particularly true in cultures with fundamentalist religious beliefs (Andersen, 2011a). In Islamic cultures, among Hindus, and among truly fundamentalist Christians, virginity at marriage is expected, particularly for women. In the United States, virginity at marriage is increasingly uncommon (Andersen, 2008). At the other end of the spectrum are Northern European countries that are far more liberal than the United States about premarital sex, single parenthood, and nudity.

Sex is treated very differently by different cultures and different individuals. Since sexual behavior is so diverse, a significant relational challenge is to find a partner who is sexually compatible or at least accommodating to your personal sexual beliefs and behaviors. Sex is an extremely personal act, and we all have our own personal and cultural beliefs about what is appropriate and satisfying.

---

that promoted open conversations about sex 2 weeks after viewing (Moyer-Guse, Chung, & Jain, 2011).

Sexual material on the Internet is a concern of parents, educators, and politicians. Cybersex may be a negative influence with increasingly bizarre or violent effects, or it may be a harmless form of safe sex with beneficial cathartic effects for adults (see Box 9.1 earlier in this chapter). Research suggests that adolescent and young adult women on social media sites may flaunt sexuality, disclose excessively, and risk connection with predators (Theil-Stern, 2009). The practice of "sexting" is widespread among teens and young adults creating legal issues regarding pornography, causing potential image problems for sexters in the future, creating a potential jaded view of sexuality and encouraging sexual predators (Lenhart, 2009). On the other hand, over 20% of young adults turn to online information about sexual health that may be hard to talk about face to face, so like other media, the Internet and social media may have negative and positive effects on the development of sexual attitudes and behavior.

PARENTS Children learn about sex and relationships from their parents both indirectly and directly. Indirectly, parents serve as models for children. If parents are affectionate or sexual toward each other, children will expect their own romantic relationships to include affection or sex. Kids pick up attitudes about sex from their families through modelling and body language. As a result, people raised with more conservative family values are more erotophobic and experience more sexual guilt and anxiety (Simpson, Wilson, & Winterheld, 2004). Children of more religious parents are less likely to engage in risky sexual behaviors and have less sexually permissive peers (Landor, Simons, Simons, Brody, & Gibbens, 2011). Loving, involved parents have positive effects on their children's sexual behavior including delayed sexual intercourse, greater condom use, more sexual autonomy, greater likelihood of sex occurring only in an existing relationship, and less anxiety on the part of the child (Afifi, Joseph, & Aldeis, 2008; Parkes, Henderson, Wight, & Nixon, 2011). Parents also influence their children directly by talking to them about sex, particularly when it occurs during the early teen years, yet parent–child communication about sex is rare (Byers, 2011; Fisher, 2004; Warren, 1995), and teenagers often feel uncomfortable talking to parents about sex, primarily because the parents issue orders or warnings rather than frankly discussing sexual thoughts and feelings (Brock & Jennings, 1993). As a result, parents are amazingly unaware of their teenage offspring's sexual behavior (Fisher, 2004). Within families, teens report being most comfortable talking to a same-sex older sibling or same-sex parent about sex (Guerrero & Afifi, 1995b), and mothers and daughters are more likely to talk about sex than are fathers and sons (Fisher, 2004).

PEERS Rogers (1995) showed that most diffusion of information about a variety of topics, including sexually related ones, occurs interpersonally between people who are similar to one another. Sprecher and McKinney (1993) showed that peers have more influence on people's sexual standards than parents. Male adolescents are notorious for instilling attitudes about what constitutes a physically attractive woman, what constitutes masculine behavior, and the importance of sexual conquests. Females share all manner of relational and sexual information with one another regarding birth control methods, and the quality of individual males as potential mates. Sexual attitudes and behaviors are also modelled by friends and then imitated.

PAST RELATIONSHIPS Many attitudes about sex result from prior relational experiences. People who have learned to trust others and to be comfortable with closeness tend and more monogamous in their sexual relationships (Simpson & Gangestad, 1991). Moreover, having a partner who provides consistent, loving, physical contact helps build an individual's self-esteem and sets up positive expectations for future relationships (Hazan & Zeifman, 1994). In contrast, people who are uncomfortable with closeness and have had unsatisfying sexual relationships in the past will be more likely to desire short-term, casual sex than committed relationships (Brennan & Shaver, 1995; Stephan & Bachman, 1999). Frequent, casual sex has trade-offs. Research

shows that people with many casual sexual partners are more likely to have close friends, less likely to experience loneliness, but more likely to have experienced relational aggression and sexually based prejudice (Vrangalova & Bukberg, 2015). Those who have been hurt in past love relationships are less likely to experience highly passionate or obsessive love in the future (Stephan & Bachman, 1999). Together, these findings suggest that people who have had positive sexual experiences in committed relationships are most likely to expect future relationships to be monogamous and sexually satisfying. Past sexual relationships can also affect attraction. Sprecher and Regan (2000) concluded the following:

> In general, research indicates that low to moderate levels of current or past sexual activity and the restriction of sexual activity to committed relationships are more likely to increase one's desirability as a partner than is a history of many sexual partners or casual sexual activity. (p. 219)

COMMUNICATION ABOUT SEX

Along with sexual attitudes, the way people communicate about sex can influence the course that a relationship takes as well as how satisfied couples are. Research on courtship patterns and flirtation provides insight on how romantic and sexual relationships develop. Studies have also shown how communication about sex keeps relationships satisfying. Work on sexual scripts often focuses on how communication is used to initiate and refuse sex. Finally, research on **pillow talk** describes how people communicate following sexual encounters.

Courtship and Flirtation

When people flirt, they typically use indirect communication strategies to convey their interest and attraction, especially when they are in the early stages of a relationship. Nonverbal flirtation displays are more common than verbal cues (Beres, Herold, & Maitland, 2004). Gazes, smiles, warm vocal tones, and close distances are key flirtatious behaviors (Givens, 1978, 1983; Moore, 1985; Muehlenhard, Koralewski, Andrews, & Burdick, 1986). Indirect nonverbal cues are often used because they provide protection from potential rejection. The receiver can simply ignore these nonverbal cues without having to verbally reject the flirtatious person. The flirtatious person can deny flirting and simply feign friendliness. Sometimes, of course, direct verbal strategies are used, such as telling people they look sexy or talking about sex. These more direct strategies, however, are more likely to be used in an established romantic relationship. There are also differences in people's motivations and style of flirting (Hall, Carter, Cody, & Albright, 2010). Five different flirting styles—the **traditional flirting style,** the **physical flirting style,** the **sincere flirting style,** the **playful flirting style,** and the **polite flirting style**—are described in Box 9.3.

Scheflen's (1965, 1974) model of the courtship process sought to explain how various nonverbal behaviors unfold over time to signal availability and sexual interest. Scheflen's model includes five stages, with the earlier stages characterized by the most indirect communication. The courtship behaviors in this model often reflect attentiveness, approachability, and submissiveness. Thus, potential partners must gain one another's attention and signal that they are available for communication. Submissive behaviors that communicate a desire for intimacy are particularly useful during the courtship process because they are seen as a nonthreatening, playful way to convey sexual interest. Some submissive behaviors, such as stroking someone's hair in a comforting way, also mirror those used in parent–child relationship to convey caring and intimacy.

THE ATTENTION STAGE The goal of the first stage in Scheflen's model, the **attention stage,** is to get the other person's attention and to present oneself in the best possible light—either strategically or accidentally. When Taylor met Leslie with a group at dinner, she made sure she was in a good location to

BOX 9.3 HIGHLIGHTS
THE FIVE FLIRTING STYLES

People take different approaches to flirting based on their attitudes and goals. Hall and his colleagues (2010) identified five styles. You likely identify more strongly with one or two or these than the others. Your style might also vary based on who you are flirting with and what your goals are.

The Traditional Style: This style is based on the traditional belief that men chase whereas women respond to men's advances. Men communicate their interest more verbally than women. Women show interest primarily through nonverbal cues. People endorsing this style believe that "Men should make the first move" and their behavior is guided by social norms.

The Physical Style: This style is based on communicating sexual and romantic interest, and likely includes more references to physical appearance as well as more touching and sexual innuendo. People endorsing this style believe that they are good at showing their sexual interest to others and they are motivated by romantic interest.

The Sincere Style: This style is based on creating an emotional bond, and is often perceived as an honest and effective way to make a real connection with someone. People endorsing this style say that they "really look for an emotional connection with someone" and are motivated to get to know the person better.

The Playful Style: This style is based on the idea that flirting can be fun and does not necessarily need to be tied to starting a relationship with someone. People endorsing this style say they flirt with people who they are not really interested in, they flirt to feel good about themselves, and they don't take flirting seriously.

The Polite Style: This style revolves around caution and the idea that expression of sexual interest is inappropriate. People who endorse this style are typically conservative and believe that "being too physical can be a turn-off." Sometimes they also assume that the other person does not want a relationship with them.

converse with her. At the table, she made sure that she was seated near her to encourage interaction. Throughout history, people have practiced the art of gaining attention as a precursor to courtship. In 19th-century America, it was common for women to drop something, such as a glove or handkerchief, in front of a man whom they wanted to get to know. The man, if polite, was obliged to retrieve the dropped item and to turn his attention to the woman. Similarly, men commonly asked to be formally introduced to a woman—often by a relative or friend—before pursuing a conversation. Any place where singles gather, we are likely to see a variety of attention-getting strategies, such as Taylor positioning herself in Leslie's view and trying to catch her eye. These behaviors are indirect, including demure glances, tentative smiles, anxious movements such as twisting the ring on one's finger, and primping behavior such as fixing one's hair, applying lipstick, or straightening one's tie.

THE COURTSHIP READINESS STAGE During the **courtship readiness stage,** or what is sometimes referred to as the *recognition stage,* the initiator of the flirtation determines whether the other person is approachable for interaction. For example, if Taylor's eye contact and friendliness is met with Leslie's cold stare or annoyed glance, or is ignored, the courtship process will end. Similarly, if Leslie is busy interacting with other people, Taylor will probably hesitate to approach unless she receives a fairly clear signal of interest. Typical flirting behaviors include sustained mutual gaze and smiling, raised eyebrows, direct body orientation, head tilts in the direction of the other person, and nervous laughter. More grooming behavior also tends to occur in this stage, with people tucking in their stomachs, arranging their clothing and hair, and wetting their lips as they prepare to approach one another.

THE POSITIONING STAGE If Taylor and Leslie are attracted to each other, they will engage in a series of positioning behaviors that signal availability for interaction while indicating to others that

they are, at least temporarily, a "couple" and so should be left alone. Close distancing and face-to-face body orientation are typical in the **positioning stage**, as are forward leans. Partners also gaze and smile at each other and display interest and animation through gestures and expressive voices. If the relationship is progressing, hand-holding is a common romantic or sexual escalation event (O'Sullivan, Cheng, Harris, & Brooks-Gunn, 2007). If the setting is quiet, Taylor and Leslie may lower their voices to draw each other closer. In this stage, communication becomes more synchronized; that is, turn taking becomes smoother, and partners engage in similar behaviors such as crossing their legs. Although there is a marked increase in the intimacy of communication at this stage, some submissiveness and ambiguity still remain. For example, if Taylor and Leslie gaze for too long into each other's eyes, they might feel embarrassed, avert their eyes, and laugh nervously.

THE INVITATIONS AND SEXUAL AROUSAL STAGE Taylor and Leslie are very attracted to each other and are moving into the fourth stage—the **invitations and sexual arousal stage**. The beginning of this stage is marked by subtle touch and sexual contact. For example, Taylor might put her hand on Leslie's knee or stroke her back to see how she responds. More subtle signs of intimacy include grooming the partner, performing carrying and clutching activities, and acting sexually provocative (Burgoon et al., 2010; Givens, 1978; Scheflen, 1965). Widespread among primates including humans, grooming behaviors include adjusting a partner's clothing, pushing a stray strand of hair out of someone's eyes, and affectionate stroking touches that appear to have functional qualities (Dunbar, 2010). These seemingly innocuous behaviors release oxytocin (OT) and endorphins, chemicals that are keys to bonding, trust, and pleasure. Carrying and clutching behaviors include carrying someone's bags or books, holding hands, and leaning on someone's arm for support, behaviors that promote trust and reciprocity. Sexually provocative actions include dancing in a suggestive way, revealing body parts by unbuttoning one's shirt or crossing one's leg to expose more thigh, and touching the partner in intimate places.

THE RESOLUTION STAGE If Taylor's invitation is accepted and sexual interaction occurs, Taylor and Leslie have reached the final stage, the **resolution stage.** Of course, determining whether the invitation is accepted is not always easy, especially if the behaviors used in the sexual arousal and invitations stage were indirect and ambiguous. When people move through the courtship stages rapidly, the intent of both partners might be unclear. Perhaps Leslie was just being friendly while Taylor was interested in a sexual relationship. Sometimes people engage in sexual teasing, a behavior that is more commonly used by women (Meston & O'Sullivan, 2007) and which can be misconstrued as real sexual interest.

Some studies have shown that men are more likely than women to see flirtatious behaviors as seductive, whereas women often see these same behaviors as ways of being friendly and expressing innocent attraction (Abbey, 1982, 1987; Abbey & Melby, 1986). To complicate matters even further, research has shown that people flirt for a variety of reasons, only one of which is to signal sexual interest. For example, people may flirt because they see it as playful fun, they want to make a third party jealous, they want to develop their social skills, or they are trying to persuade someone to do something for them (Afifi, Guerrero, & Egland, 1994; Koeppel, Montagne-Miller, O'Hair, & Cody, 1993). Thus, when someone is flirting, the person may or may not be showing sexual interest.

In longer courtships, couples spend considerable time in the sexual arousal and invitations stage, with sexual intimacy increasing slowly over time. Partners are more likely to be direct about their intentions, but misunderstandings can still occur. Sometimes one person is ready to have sex before the other, and one partner may view intimate touch as a way to express closeness while the other sees it as a prelude to sex. Partners must negotiate if and when sex occurs, often through both verbal and

nonverbal communication. If one or both of the partners does not want to have sex, they are entering the first four of Scheflen's stages are referred to as **quasi-courtship** rather than courtship. Misinterpretation of flirtatious cues is likely, given that the first three of four stages often look the same, regardless of whether they are quasi-courtship or true courtship stages.

It is important to note that these courtship stages provide only a rough guide for how people signal romantic interest and increase sexual involvement. Couples are unique and progress at different speeds. A relatively small number of couples have sex on a first date or shortly after the partners meet; most couples wait until some level of intimacy has developed before having sex. With this in mind, Christopher and Cate (1985) identified four types of couples. **Rapid-involvement couples** have high levels of physical arousal and have sex on the first date or shortly thereafter. For these partners, sexual intimacy often precedes psychological intimacy. **Gradual-involvement couples** let sexual involvement increase gradually as the relationship develops and becomes more psychologically intimate. Sexual involvement moves through stages with sexual involvement increasing as the partners move from a first date, to a casually dating relationship, to a more serious, committed relationship. **Delayed-involvement couples** wait until the two people consider themselves to be a committed couple to become sexually involved. For these couples, psychological intimacy precedes sexual intimacy. **Low-involvement couples** usually wait to have sex until the partners are engaged or married. Research suggests that most couples in the United States define themselves as falling under either the gradual- (31%) or delayed-involvement (44%) category, with around 17% identifying themselves as low involvement and 7% classifying themselves as rapid involvement (Christopher & Cate, 1985; Sprecher & McKinney, 1993). These findings correspond with research showing that most people have a relational orientation toward sex.

Communication, Sexual Satisfaction, and Relational Satisfaction

Beyond courtship, the relational orientation suggests that established couples use sexual interaction to express love, attraction, and desire to one another. Yet even couples who are in love can be dissatisfied with their sexual relationships. Some relational partners think sex is a taboo topic and so do not talk about their sexual desires and preferences (Baxter & Wilmot, 1985). Yet studies suggest that communication about sex is extremely important. Research shows that sexual self-disclosure is associated with a satisfying and rewarding relationship (MacNeil & Byers, 2009). Frank, Anderson, and Rubinstein (1979) found that about half of husbands and three fourths of wives reported having some sexual difficulty in their marriages, and that these difficulties were increased by poor communication skills.

Direct communication about sex facilitates satisfaction. Sexual satisfaction and relationship satisfaction are positively correlated across a variety of relationship types (Birnie-Porter & Hunt, 2015; Henderson et al., 2009), but communication appears to tie these two forms of satisfaction together. Indeed, Cupach and Comstock (1990) found that good communication about sex leads to greater sexual satisfaction, which in turn contributes to more relational satisfaction. Research also suggests that men prefer clear, instrumental disclosure about sex because it leads to greater sexual understanding and, in turn, to more sexual satisfaction (MacNeil & Byers, 2005, 2009). Indeed, indirect communication about sex decreases sexual satisfaction for both men and women (Theiss, 2011), whereas direct communication increases both sexual satisfaction and overall relational satisfaction (Montesi, Fauber, Gordon, & Heimberg, 2010). If you are currently in a sexual relationship, you can access your level of sexual communication satisfaction by taking the test in Box 9.4.

A common misconception is that men enjoy sexual intercourse more than women. The reality is that heterosexual men and women both enjoy intercourse. Contrary to the stereotype, some research suggests that women may actually enjoy intercourse more than men (Blumstein & Schwartz, 1983). In close, committed relationships, most women enjoy sexual intercourse because of the extreme intimacy and closeness it reflects. Although some women may not want to have sex as often as men, when they do have high-quality sex, they report finding it extremely pleasurable. A study of university students (Higgins, Mullanax, Trussell, Davidson, & Moore, 2011) found that the vast majority of both males and females experienced high or very high levels of sexual satisfaction and rarely felt uncomfortable or guilty about having sex. This study found that lack of guilt, frequency of orgasm, and comfort with one's sexuality were positively associated with sexual satisfaction for both men and women. Indeed, nonverbally expressing sexual pleasure during sex is associated with one's own and one's partner's sexual satisfaction (Babin, 2013). Other studies have shown that sex can reduce stress and enhance feelings of well-being (Shrier, Shih, Hacker, & de Moor, 2007; Wright, Parkes, Strange, Allen, & Bonell, 2008).

Another common misconception is that the most important predictor of sexual satisfaction is how often a couple has sex. Nearly 90% of married individuals report that they are sexually satisfied, with couples varying considerably in how often they have sex; indeed, most studies show little or no relationship between amount of sex and satisfaction (Blumstein & Schwartz, 1983; Sprecher & Cate, 2004). Frequency of sex is not as important as the quality of the sex and the match between two people's needs during sexual activity (Sprecher & Regan, 2000). When partners have similar attitudes about sex, they are happier with their sex lives. Therefore, if they believe that cuddling is more important than sex, they might have sex less often than a couple who believes that sex is the ultimate expression of intimacy; yet both couples would be satisfied.

It is also important to recognize that sexual satisfaction is not the *best* predictor of relational satisfaction in most relationships. As Sprecher and Regan (2000) put it, "Neither the quality nor the quantity of sex might be as important as other non-sexual forms of intimacy in the prediction of relationship satisfaction including expressed affection and supportive communication" (p. 223). These authors noted that sexual dissatisfaction and incompatibility alone are usually not enough to destroy an otherwise close, caring relationship. Only when these sexual problems are "symptomatic of other relational problems" are they likely to lead to conflict and relational termination. The message here is clear: Sexual satisfaction is an important part of romantic relationships, but other factors, such as love, supportiveness, and compatibility, are usually even more important.

BOX 9.4 PUT YOURSELF TO THE TEST
SEXUAL COMMUNICATION SATISFACTION

Think about a current sexual relationship, and rate your communication about sex using the following scale: 1 = strongly disagree and 7 = strongly agree.

		Strongly Disagree					Strongly Agree
1.	I tell my partner when I am especially sexually satisfied.	1	2	3	4	5	6	7
2.	I am satisfied with my partner's ability to communicate her or his sexual desires to me.	1	2	3	4	5	6	7
3.	I let my partner know things that I find pleasing during sex.	1	2	3	4	5	6	7
4.	I do not hesitate to let my partner know when I want to have sex with him or her.	1	2	3	4	5	6	7
5.	I tell my partner whether or not I am sexually satisfied.	1	2	3	4	5	6	7
6.	I am satisfied with the degree to which my partner and I talk about the sexual aspects of our relationship.	1	2	3	4	5	6	7
7.	I am not afraid to show my partner what kind of sexual behavior I like.	1	2	3	4	5	6	7
8.	I would not hesitate to show my partner what is a sexual turn-on for me.	1	2	3	4	5	6	7
9.	My partner shows me what pleases her or him during sex.	1	2	3	4	5	6	7
10.	My partner tells me when he or she is sexually satisfied.	1	2	3	4	5	6	7
11.	I am pleased with the manner in which my partner and I communicate with each other about sex.	1	2	3	4	5	6	7
12.	It is never hard for me to figure out if my partner is sexually satisfied.	1	2	3	4	5	6	7

Add up your answers. A score of 84 indicates maximum sexual communication satisfaction. A score of 12 indicates the lowest level of sexual communication satisfaction possible. Since research shows that sexual communication satisfaction increases as relationships develop, you might want to take this test later in the relationship to see if your score changes.

Source: "The Sexual Communication Satisfaction Scale," From Wheeless, Lawrence R., Wheeless, Virginia Eman, and Baus, Raymond (1984). Sexual communication, communication satisfaction, and solidarity in the development stages of intimate relationships, in *Western Journal of Speech Communication. 48* (3, Summer), 217–230. Used with permission of the Western States Communication Association.

Sexual Scripts

Scripts are social information that is deployed in everyday interaction. Cultural forces define with whom, when, where, and in what relationships sexual behavior may appropriately be initiated and conducted (Regan & Berscheid, 1999). Sexual scripts most often revolve around the initiation and acceptance or refusal of sexual advances. The North American script casts men as initiators and women as gatekeepers who refuse or accept dates or sexual invitations, particularly in new relationships (Byers, 1996; Mongeau et al., 2004). As Hinde (1984) commented, men seek to propagate widely while women seek to propagate wisely. Research indicates that both men and women are comfortable asking for dates and initiating sexual interaction (Kelley & Rolker-Dolinsky, 1987); although many women think their sexual initiatives might threaten men. However, women are more likely to initiate sexual interaction in well-developed relationships as opposed to developing relationships.

Negotiating sexual activity in a developing relationship can be difficult because both individuals have multiple goals including managing impressions, providing relational definitions, satisfying sexual desire, following sexual standards or morals, and avoiding disease or pregnancy (Cupach & Metts, 1991). Most sexual initiation attempts are indirect and communicated through nonverbal behavior and flirtation (Andersen, 2008), which may be why face-to-face initiation leads to more relational and

sexual satisfaction than online relationship initiation (Blunt-Vinti et al., 2016). Regardless of the medium, friendly behaviors—particularly those by women—are misinterpreted by men as sex-initiating behaviors. To avoid sexually coercive situations (discussed later in this chapter), individuals need to verbally articulate their disinterest, and their partners need to respect their wishes.

INITIATION STRATEGIES Both men and women use persuasive strategies and scripts to initiate dating and sexual relationships. These strategies typically fall into five categories: (1) **hinting and indirect strategies**, (2) **expressions of emotional and physical closeness**, (3) **pressure and manipulation**, (4) **antisocial acts**, and (5) **logic and reasoning** (Christopher & Frandsen, 1990; Edgar & Fitzpatrick, 1988, 1993).

Sexual relations are sensitive and ego threatening, so hinting and indirect strategies can be useful. Romantic conversations are full of indirect communication such as compliments, sexual innuendo, hints, and nonverbal communication. Such ploys are safe because if the partner does not respond sexually, little face is lost. As Edgar and Fitzpatrick (1988) noted, when one person wants to have sex, the situation can be emotionally charged, and an opportunity to save face is welcome. Both men and women are most comfortable with sexual involvement if emotional and physical closeness is present; this is particularly true for women. Establishing a close relationship and sending reassuring relational messages results in increased sexual activity (Christopher

& Frandsen, 1990). Doing special things for your partner, telling your partner how much you like her or him, flattering your partner, and sharing time and space with your partner are ways to enhance emotional closeness and initiate sexual activity.

Another sexual influence tactic is logical reasoning by persuading someone that it is advantageous to become sexually involved. This strategy uses logic or negotiates the timing or degree of sexual involvement to overcome a partner's concerns (Christopher & Frandsen, 1990). For example, if Brittany is afraid of getting pregnant or contracting an STI, Chris might make reassuring statements about the effectiveness of condoms or suggest that they both get tested for STIs before having sex. These types of tactics are associated with greater sexual activity in a relationship over the long term, although they may limit or postpone sexual involvement in the short term (Christopher & Frandsen, 1990).

Not surprisingly, men are more likely to use pressure and manipulation to gain sexual compliance than women (Christopher & Frandsen, 1990). These strategies encompass a wide variety of coercive tactics, such as repeated requests for sex, threats to break off or de-escalate the relationship, the use of drugs or alcohol to reduce resistance to sex, and outright deception. These tactics seldom increase the frequency of sexual activity in a relationship (Christopher & Frandsen, 1990) and can lead to relational dissatisfaction or de-escalation.

Evidence suggests that antisocial acts are unsuccessful in initiating sex in a relationship (Christopher & Frandsen, 1990). These strategies encompass a wide assortment of tactics, including intentionally trying to make the partner jealous (Fleischmann, Spitzberg, Andersen, & Roesch, 2005), pouting or holding a grudge to try to get one's way, and sexual harassment. Such acts may lead to relational termination and even legal action in some cases.

REFUSING AND ACCEPTING SEXUAL INVITATIONS

The power to refuse and regulate sex is mainly a woman's prerogative. Across the world, women are more judicious and less casual in their choices about sex than men (Buss, 1994). Men are poor at turning down sex and have few refusal strategies in their repertoire; women regard men's refusals as insincere, unexpected, and upsetting (Metts, Cupach, & Imahori, 1992). This does not imply that women have license to ignore men's refusals; men should be taken as seriously as women when they decline to have sex.

Research suggests that women are well prepared with sexual-compliance-resisting scripts and use multiple resistance strategies (Lannutti & Monahan, 2004; Metts et al., 1992). Women often use indirect strategies because these are perceived as polite; however, more direct strategies seem to be more effective for refusing unwanted sex. Moreover, most men have experienced receiving sexual rejection messages and find them relatively predictable and not particularly disconcerting (Metts et al., 1992). This is useful information for women who use indirect strategies to refuse sex when they are worried about hurting the partner's feelings. Direct strategies are more effective, and thankfully, they are unlikely to be taken personally by men (Motley & Reeder, 1995).

In committed dating relationships, both men and women accept the majority of sexual initiations by their partner (Byers, 1996). In Byers' study, only about 20% of initiations were refused by the partner with about the same percentage for men and women. These data suggest that sex in committed dating relationships is not adversarial and that contrary to the stereotype, in developed relationships, women are more likely to be facilitators of sexual interaction than gatekeepers. In investigating sexual activity among heterosexual daters over a 1-month period, Byers and Lewis (1988) found that nearly half of the couples reported disagreements caused by the man's desire to increase sexual involvement. However, disagreements occurred during just 7% of all dates. Disagreements about sex did occur occasionally over the course of a month, but most dates were free of such disagreements. When sex is refused from a long-term dating partner, the refusal is both unexpected and viewed negatively (Bevan, 2003).

Once sexual activity becomes fairly regular, shared dyadic scripts emerge to guide sexual interaction. In well-developed relationships, women feel freer to initiate touch, affection, and sexual behavior (Cupach & Metts, 1995; Guerrero & Andersen, 1991). Brown and Auerbach (1981) found that wives increased their initiation of sexual activity by about 1% per year of marriage. Several studies have shown that stages of sexual involvement are fairly well scripted, starting with kissing and moving to hand to breast, hand to genitals, oral sex, sexual intercourse, and orgasm in the ideal case (DeLamater & Hyde, 2004; Morris, 1977). This script is generally followed both within a single sexual encounter and across a series of dates with only occasional variation.

Saying "no" to sex in a long-term relationship is often difficult because partners do not want to hurt one another's feelings, but everyone has the right to refuse sex no matter how close the relationship. It is important for long-term partners to say "no" in a tender and supportive manner with clear verbal communication. Research has shown that most refusals are done verbally and that the best refusals maintain both the relationship and the partner's face (Cupach & Metts, 1991). For example, telling your partner that you are "really tired" or "not feeling well" is better than saying that you are not feeling much sexual desire for her or him at the moment. When refusals are accompanied by assurances of future activity ("We'll have more time for each other this weekend"), they are also accepted more gracefully.

Pillow Talk

Many studies have examined people's communication before sex including seduction, hitting on a person, flirting, come-ons, propositions, pressure, booty calls, requests, and of course, turn-downs, turn-offs, rejection messages, declines, and refusals. But until recently few have looked at communication following sex.

This gap has been filled by researchers doing studies on pillow talk and postcoital behavior. Pillow talk is the tranquil, intimate conversation that takes place after sexual intercourse or sexual climax (Denes, 2013). Pillow talk is often accompanied by relaxation, physical and psychological closeness, cuddling, and pleasant conversation, including expressions of affection and liking (Denes, 2012). Pillow talk often involves disclosure. Research shows that partners who orgasmed engaged in increased self-disclosure, particularly positive disclosure, and found greater benefits from disclosing than partners who did not experience orgasm (Denes & Afifi, 2014).

Pillow talk and nonverbal interaction following sex may have a chemical basis in the release of oxytocin and serotonin. Oxytocin is a chemical released during affectionate communication (see Chapter 7), by women during breast feeding, and by both men and women following orgasm. The presence of oxytocin (sometimes known as the "love hormone") along with individuals' biological ability to process oxytocin, is related to how much disclosure occurs following sexual intercourse (Denes, 2015); more oxytocin, more disclosure. A different sort of relationship has been found between testosterone and post-sex communication (Denes, Afifi, & Granger, 2016). Higher testosterone levels were associated with disclosure being perceived as less beneficial and riskier, and the disclosures that did occur were less intentional and less positive. Moreover, higher levels of testosterone were associated with more negative thoughts and more negative disclosure for those people who did not orgasm, indicating that this group does not obtain as many benefits of post-sex communication. It may be that people with lower levels of testosterone are more nurturing and are more likely to employ pillow talk as a way to bond and connect with their partner.

Interestingly, alcohol consumption was negatively associated with pillow talk and deep disclosure; in addition, the disclosure was perceived as less beneficial (Denes & Afifi, 2014). There may also be a difference in romantic relationship sex as opposed to hookups or one-night stands. For long-term partners, the postcoital period is one of connection and intimacy, but for short-term sexual interactions, such as one-night stands or hookups, it may be about regrets, disentanglement, or even dealing with embarrassment. Post-coital regrets are more common for alcohol-induced than marijuana-induced sexual encounters (Palamar, Acosta, Ompad, & Friedman, 2016). Of course, sometimes post-coital conversations are about pregnancy, disease, cheating, and other negative topics.

Pillow talk is often accompanied by affectionate nonverbal interaction following sex like cuddling, kissing, and sweet tones of voice. Cuddling, kissing, and caressing are affectionate nonverbal behaviors that can occur after sex and result in greater sexual and relational satisfaction (Muise, Glang, & Impett, 2014). Pillow talk sometimes takes the form of baby talk and couples that employ baby talk have greater intimacy and attachment to one another (Bombar & Littig, 1996). The sweet tones of voice used by lovers may be reminiscent of the intimacy of infancy. Both men and women engage in kissing before and after sex, but men are more likely to initiate kissing before sex and women after sex (Hughes & Kruger, 2010). Sex makes some people sleepy and although this is partly a physical response, your partner may feel disrespected if you snooze off and post-sexual behavior doesn't include cuddling, caressing, and pillow talk.

SEXUAL COERCION AND HARASSMENT

Most people associate sex with pleasure, intimacy, relational closeness, and desire. However, sex has its dark side as well. Negative aspects of sex include sexual dysfunction, sexual abuse, rape, sexual coercion, and sexual harassment. In this section, we focus on coercion and harassment because communication is at the heart of these types of problematic interaction.

Sexual Coercion

Sexual coercion occurs when an individual pressures or forces another to engage in sexual activity or generally unacceptable practices, with physical force the most unacceptable (Struckman-Johnson & Struckman-Johnson, 1991). Verbal insistence is the most common and least aversive method of coercion

(Murnan, Perot, & Byrne, 1989). Women generally find sexual coercion to be less acceptable than men (Christopher, Owens, & Strecker, 1993; Struckman-Johnson & Struckman-Johnson, 1991). Coercive strategies are generally unsuccessful in gaining sexual compliance (Christopher & Frandsen, 1990).

Sexual coercion is far too common. News headlines about sexual coercion and rape on college campuses are an almost daily occurrence; these news stories and books have created a national outcry. Research has shown that in the majority of sexually coercive situations, a man is the perpetrator. Over 50% of college women report having been victims of sexual coercion (Byers, 1996), and over 95% of all women report having engaged in some form of unwanted sexual activity (Muehlenhard & Cook, 1988). Other studies have shown that over 20% of college women report having been forced to engage in sexual intercourse, and 35% to 46% of women report having unwanted sex as a result of sexual persuasion or coercion, typically from a partner the woman knew fairly well (Byers, 1996; Muehlenhard & Cook; 1988; Murnan et al., 1989; O'Sullivan & Allgeier, 1998). If unwanted sexual penetration in any form is used as a standard, the most recent data suggest about 20% of college women have been raped (Muehlenhard, Peterson, Humphreys, & Jozkowski, 2016). Women report experiencing sexual coercion on about 7% of all dates (Byers & Lewis, 1988) and 50% of college women reported that they had engaged in at least one unwanted sexual activity. Sometimes women have unwanted sex to please their partners; other times they are pressured or forced to have sex. Worst of all, almost two thirds of sexual assaults occur with regular relational partners (Christopher & Kissler, 2004). Recent research on 30,000 college students shows that gay men and bisexual men and women are the most common targets of sexual coercion and victimization (Johnson et al., 2016).

As Charlene Muehlenhard, a leading sex researcher in the Psychology Department and Women, Gender, and Sexuality Studies Department at the University of Kansas, and her colleagues have pointed out, the issue of sexual consent on campus is filled with complexities (Muehlenhard, Peterson, Humphreys, & Jozkowski, 2016). Decisions about how to communicate consent/nonconsent are often sequential and contingent. While nonconsent is usually communicated verbally, nonconsent often begins with less-explicit nonverbal cues (Muehlenhard et al., 2016). Nonverbal cues, such as turning the lights back on or moving someone's hand, may be too subtle, but even verbal cues are often counterbalanced with confusing positive relational maintenance cues.

For many people, especially women, two goals may conflict: maintain the relationship but stop the sexual advance (Muehlenhard et al., 2016). Women sometimes fail to send sexual resistance messages because they fear the relational consequences of turning down their partner (Motley & Reeder, 1995). The reality is, men rarely disrupt or terminate a relationship because a woman resists sexual escalation. In fact, Motley and Reeder (1995) found that men rarely are hurt, offended, or angered when women use direct sexual resistance messages. Because women seldom are rejected in their attempts to sexually escalate a relationship, they are more likely to be hurt and upset if they are rejected. They project these feelings onto men, who rarely share their hurt and anger over being sexually rejected. Many men, on the other hand, have considerable experience with sexual rejection and have learned coping strategies to deal with rejection short of relational de-escalation or breakup.

Another source of confusion is that a majority of both men and women believe that not resisting is usually a consent cue (Muehlenhard et al., 2016). Yet one of the most common reactions of women to sexual advances or coercion is no response (Byers, 1996). The prevalence of a party culture on most campuses and alcohol can compound the situation since it may impair a woman's ability to resist and makes sexual coercion seem more acceptable to some men (Abbey, 2011; Muehlenhard et al., 2016).

In most situations in which men pursue sex and women refuse, men halt their sexual advances (Byers, 1996). About 15% of the time, however, the man does not believe the woman's refusal really means no (Byers & Wilson, 1985). Men often perceive that the woman's refusal is only token resistance (Muehlenhard & Cook, 1988). Research has shown that men often do not perceive indirect resistance messages on the part of women as real resistance (Motley & Reeder, 1995). Indeed, Motley and Reeder suggested that women need to be much more direct in communicating sexual resistance and that men should listen more carefully to understand women's resistance messages.

When token resistance is used, the situation is confusing and dangerous. Both men and women use token resistance, but contrary to the stereotype, men are more likely to use it than women (O'Sullivan & Allgeier, 1994). As noted previously, a sexual initiator should not ignore a request to stop. If, however, an initiator has learned that stop does not really mean stop, "real" requests to stop may be ignored, leading to problems ranging from relational disagreements to sexual assault. Thus, it is best to stop and ask for clarification if you think your partner might be engaging in token resistance. Unless your partner explicitly says "yes" and not "no," you should avoid further sexual activity. Clearly, men should never try to second-guess a woman's motivation for saying "no." As Andersen (2008) stated, when people misinterpret nonverbal cues or ignore explicit verbal cues in favor of nonverbal cues that erroneously appear positive, sexual harassment or date rape can follow. Therefore, "stop" always means stop, and "no" always means no.

In about 10% of sexually coercive situations, the woman is the aggressor and the man is the target. Among college students, about one third of men reported an episode of pressured or forced sex since the age of 16 (Byers, 1996; Struckman-Johnson & Struckman-Johnson, 1994), and in the vast majority of these cases, the perpetrator of coercion was a woman. O'Sullivan and Allgeier (1998) reported that over a 2-week period, 26% of college men engaged in an unwanted sexual act and almost 9% had unwanted sexual intercourse. Struckman-Johnson (1988) found that 16% of the men in her sample reported an incident of forced sexual intercourse. Muehlenhard and Cook (1988) studied over 1,000 men and women in introductory college psychology courses and found that more men (62.7%) than women (46.3%) reported having unwanted sexual intercourse. Although men generally have less negative reactions to being the target of coerced sexual encounters than women, one fifth of the men in a study by Struckman-Johnson and Struckman-Johnson (1994) had a strong negative reaction to the experience.

Studies have shown that women are not very sensitive to male refusals to have sex. O'Sullivan and Byers (1993) found that when met with a refusal to have sex, 97% of women still tried to influence the man to have sex. Women are not used to being refused, and they find such refusals unpredictable, constraining, and uncomfortable (Metts et al., 1992). Men may have neither experience in nor well-developed scripts for saying "no," and believe it is unmanly to refuse sex (Metts et al., 1992). They also engage in unwanted intercourse due to peer pressure, inexperience, sex-role concerns, and popularity factors (Muehlenhard & Cook, 1988). Of course, both men and women often experience ambivalence about having sex, so some of these cases of unwanted sex probably represent situations where mixed feelings were present.

You should never assume that someone is using token resistance. "No" means no, and "stop" means stop.

Sexual Harassment

Sexual harassment occurs when inappropriate sexual comments, behaviors, or requests create a hostile work or school environment or when a person feels pressure to have sex to avoid negative consequences. Harassment is too common in the workplace, among friends and acquaintances (Keyton, 1996). Although men sometimes experience sexual harassment, research shows that women experience it far more. In fact, studies suggest that one out of every two working women was sexually harassed (Swan, 1997). A study by Hesson-McInnis and Fitzgerald (1997) of 4,385 women employed by the federal government found 1,792 reported they were sexually harassed at least once in the past 2 years. This problem was even worse for minority women; Hargrow (1997) found that over 80% of the working African American women she surveyed reported experiencing sexual harassment. Sexual harassment is a serious problem; it in turn negatively affects job satisfaction, health, and psychological well-being (Glomb et al., 1997).

Describing the behaviors that constitute sexual harassment is complicated. What some people see as harassment, others might see as sexy or innocent fun. Moreover, women sometimes perceive behaviors to be more sexually harassing than do men, especially if they have recently entered the workforce (Booth-Butterfield, 1989). In any case, research suggests that certain verbal and nonverbal behavior should be avoided. Dougherty, Turban, Olson, Dwyer, and Lapreze (1996) noted that some behaviors, such as making lewd comments or grabbing someone's breasts or buttocks, are blatantly harassing. Marks and Nelson (1993) found that potentially inappropriate touching by professors was seen as more harassing than inappropriate verbal comments. Less sexually oriented forms of touch, such as on the shoulder or around the waist, are not perceived to be as harassing as verbal comments. Dougherty and colleagues (1996) compared people's interpretations of potentially harassing situations involving touch behavior (putting an arm around a female coworker's shoulder) and verbal behavior (asking a female coworker how her love life was and if she'd had any exciting dates lately). They found that the verbal comment was perceived as more harassing than the touch.

More specifically, Lee and Guerrero (2001) compared types of touch to determine which were perceived as most harassing. They excluded blatantly harassing touches, such as grabbing breasts or buttocks or kissing someone on the mouth, and instead focused on more ambiguous forms of touch. Of the eight types of touch they studied, touching the face was perceived as most harassing, followed by an arm around the waist. Lee and Guerrero subsequently theorized that types of touch that invade people's personal space are particularly threatening. The face is an especially vulnerable part of the body, and letting someone touch it requires trust. Interestingly, not everyone saw these types of touch as harassing. In fact, while about one third of the participants "agreed strongly" that face touch was sexually harassing, another one third "disagreed strongly." This suggests that some forms of touch are seen as harassing by some people but not others, which leads to confusion and misunderstanding.

When people encounter sexual harassment, they can respond using passive, assertive, or retaliatory strategies. Passive responses, also referred to as *indirect strategies*, involve ignoring the harassment or appeasing the harasser. **Assertive responses** involve telling the harasser to stop the behavior, with statements such as "Please stop bothering me," "I'm not interested in you that way," "I'm seeing someone else so I'd appreciate it if you'd stop asking me out," and "Your behavior is inappropriate and unprofessional." Assertive responses also involve issuing warnings, such as threatening to talk to the harasser's supervisor. Finally, **retaliatory responses** involve punishing or getting revenge on the harasser, usually by harassing the person back, making derogatory comments about the harasser to others, or getting the harasser in trouble.

Unfortunately, there is not always an effective way of responding to sexual harassment. Swan (1997) found that people who viewed sexual harassment experiences as highly upsetting were

most likely to use coping strategies. When people used assertive strategies, they reported feeling better about their jobs and themselves. By contrast, when people used passive or retaliatory strategies, they reported feeling even worse. Retaliatory responses diminished job satisfaction, and passive responses diminished job satisfaction and psychological well-being. However, some studies also have shown that assertive strategies can exacerbate the problem (Schneider, Swan, & Fitzgerald, 1997). Bingham and Burleson (1989) found that although sophisticated verbal messages were more effective at stopping sexual harassment than unsophisticated ones, neither type of message was very effective. Because sexual harassment often involves a power imbalance, it is a particularly difficult situation. If the victim uses passive strategies, the individual remains powerless, and the harassment is likely to continue. But if the victim uses direct strategies, the powerful person might resent being told how to act and retaliate by demoting the victim or making the work environment even more unpleasant. Even so, research suggests that assertive strategies are most effective. If these strategies do not work, the victim may need to talk with the harasser's supervisor.

COMMUNICATION AND SAFE SEX

So far we have discussed how communication about sex can enrich a romantic relationship. We have also examined some highly problematic aspects of sexual interaction, including coercion and harassment. Another problematic issue is unsafe sex. The safest form of sex in relationships is no sex. Abstinence is the best way to avoid unwanted pregnancy, AIDS, and other STIs. But total abstinence from sex is unusual, unrealistic, precludes most romantic relationships, and fails to work with the high percentage of adolescents who are not virgins (Rasberry & Goodson, 2009). Thus, additional safe sex practices are imperative. Unfortunately, being in a close relationship inadvertently puts partners at risk since trust is higher and, as a result, safe sex is practiced less in the closest relationships (Noar, Zimmerman, & Atwood, 2004). Worse yet, information and communication about STIs are far less common than they should be; although many publications give excellent advice for safe sex and AIDS prevention (Centers for Disease Control and Prevention, 1997; Larkin, 1998). STIs are epidemic in the United States; 65 million Americans have an incurable STI such as genital herpes or HIV (Noar et al., 2004). Box 9.5 provides a list of likely familiar rules to help avoid AIDS and other STIs. (For more information about HIV/AIDS, contact your campus health service or county health department.)

BOX 9.5 HIGHLIGHTS
GENERAL RULES OF SAFE SEX PRACTICES

1. *Practice abstinence.* Although complete abstinence is unlikely for most adults, about 12% of the college-age population are virgins who have had no high-risk sexual activity (Sprecher & Regan, 1996). Abstinence is the most effective policy when it comes to preventing STIs.

2. *Practice secondary abstinence.* Secondary abstinence involves starting to abstain from sex after having previously been sexually active. Research shows that this practice is popular with more religious young people and those who believe that abstinence is normative. Unfortunately, conventional abstinence education appears to decrease the likelihood of secondary abstinence (Rasberry & Goodson, 2009).

3. *Avoid high-risk sex.* HIV and other STIs are spread by exchanging bodily fluids. Intercourse is particularly dangerous. One episode of unsafe sex with an HIV positive person puts you at risk for catching the virus. Multiple unsafe sex episodes put you at even greater risk (Hammer, Fisher, Fitzgerald, & Fisher, 1996).

4. *Use condoms.* During sexual intercourse, a new latex condom offers good protection from the transmission of HIV. Old condoms and "off brand" condoms offer poor protection because they may break or leak. Condoms made from animal membranes (skins) are porous and offer less protection against HIV transmission. Although condoms do not offer complete protection, when condoms are used properly, they are highly successful in preventing HIV/AIDS even with an infected partner (Centers for Disease Control and Prevention, 1997; Noar et al., 2004).

5. *Get tested.* If you are uncertain whether you have been exposed to HIV, get tested. Only about 1% of those who are tested show the presence of HIV, so the test is likely to relieve you of concern that you have the virus. If you are HIV positive, you need to get treated immediately. With the proper treatment, many people who are HIV positive live many symptom-free years and even decades. Your campus health center or county department of health typically does HIV tests that are either anonymous or confidential. You can also use an HIV home test kit.

6. *Limit your partners.* Another good preventive technique is to limit yourself to a single partner who was previously a virgin, has been strictly monogamous, or has been tested for HIV since her or his last sexual encounter like Brittany and Chris did. Remember, when you have sex with your partner, you are exposing yourself to risk from every person who has had sex with your partner in the past. Having sex only in the context of a monogamous infection-free sexual relationship provides you with protection and may be the healthiest form of sexual activity (Noar et al., 2004).

7. *Really know your partners.* A partner you know, respect, and trust is the safest person with whom to have a sexual relationship, but this can be misleading. It is risky to have sex with a new acquaintance, with someone whose sexual history you do not know, or with a partner you do not trust. Research shows that people make flawed judgments about who is a safe partner. People erroneously believe that having sex with healthy looking, attractive people; friends; or people similar to themselves is safe (Noar et al., 2004); sometimes it is not. Research also shows that people find it difficult to discuss safe sex and condom use during a sexual encounter with a new acquaintance (Rosenthal, Gifford, & Moore, 1998). Again, people who fail to communicate about safe sex are literally risking their health.

8. ***Avoid intoxication.*** Research shows that binge drinkers engage in more sexual activity with a wider variety of partners (Mongeau & Johnson, 1995) than do heavy drug users, although drug use also increases risk of STIs. Studies also show that people are most likely to lapse in safe sex practices when under the influence of alcohol and drugs. Binging on alcohol or using drugs is a major predictor of failure to use condoms and of catching STIs (Hammer et al., 1996; Lindley, Barnett, Brandt, Hardin, & Burcin, 2008). Alcohol use, sex while intoxicated, and unsafe sex are prevalent on college campuses, especially with members of sororities and fraternities (Scott-Sheldon, Carey, & Carey, 2008).

9. ***Be honest.*** It is essential to report unsafe sex outside your relationship to your partner so that appropriate steps can be taken. Obviously, telling your partner about past sexual activity or recent infidelities can be uncomfortable and harm your relationship. But in the long run, it is far better to warn your partner of possible dangers than to save yourself from discomfort or conflict.

As some of the rules listed in Box 9.5 suggest, communication is an essential ingredient in promoting safe sex. Unsafe sex can occur with any partner—even one you know well. It is therefore always best to be proactive about safe sex with every partner. This requires communicating with partners about past sexual experiences and talking about safe sex practices, such as those discussed in the following section. Unfortunately, many people are complacent when they have sex with someone they know well (Hammer et al., 1996; Noar et al., 2004; Rosenthal et al., 1998). They believe that being well acquainted with someone means that they are free of STIs. Recent research suggests that 99% of one college sample were confident in their assessment that their partner did not have an STI despite research showing that over one third of college students have an STI (Afifi & Weiner, 2006). Brittany, in our chapter opener, made an intelligent decision: before she got sexually involved with Chris, she insisted they both get tested for STIs. They waited to have sex until they were both found free of STIs.

Many sexually active people believe that they can tell if a partner is lying to them about safe sex behaviors. In actuality, research has shown that people cannot tell when someone is lying about sexual behavior or HIV status (Swann, Silvera, & Proske, 1995). Particularly dangerous is the truth bias, whereby individuals tend to assume that people they like are telling them the truth (see Chapter 13). Trust is important in relationships, but is it worth your health to trust someone who could be wrong about her or his HIV status?

Another danger is people's lack of condom use, even though they know that condoms help prevent STIs. Using condoms consistently, meaning *every time* you have sexual intercourse, is the only effective way to prevent STIs during intercourse (Noar et al., 2004). Studies show that only about one third of couples use any form of contraception during intercourse (Willetts et al., 2004). Many couples decline to use condoms because they limit spontaneity and reduce sensation (Hammer et al., 1996). Yet about one third of the males in Hammer and colleagues' study reported that sharing the act of putting on a condom can actually bring the couple closer and is arousing. Research suggests that when a woman verbally suggests use of a condom, romanticism, emotional closeness, expectation for sexual relations, and condom use are maximized (Alvarez & Garcia-Marques, 2011).

Logically people should use condoms to prevent STIs, but in real relationships, factors other than logic influence condom use. Managing identity, not wanting to seem promiscuous, not wanting to destroy a romantic moment, not liking the feel of condoms, and believing a partner is "safe" are factors that influence decision making regarding whether to use condoms (Afifi, 1999; Galligan & Terry, 1993). Knowledge of the risk reduction effects of condoms are a major motivator for people to use them, but women were less likely to use a condom when they feared it would destroy the romance of the moment

(Galligan & Terry 1993). Afifi (1999) reported that when attachment to a partner is high and suggesting condom use will be perceived as a lack of trust, condom use decreased. Of course, suggesting condom use may not always be perceived negatively by one's partner; rather, it may be seen as a sign of caring and of responsibility.

These findings underscore the importance of communication; partners should have frank discussions about safe sex before becoming sexually involved. Almost any communication strategy increases the likelihood of condom use, but discussing pregnancy prevention or suggesting condom use "just to be safe" are the most effective strategies, because talking about AIDS can make people uncomfortable (Reel & Thompson, 1994). By contrast, discussing the sexual history of the partners, negotiating monogamy, and requesting that the partner use a condom can promote safe sex (Cline, Freeman, & Johnson, 1990). However, Cline et al. found that those who discuss safe sex are only a little more likely to engage in safe sex practices than are those who do not. Therefore, it is crucial that partners do more than talk about safe sex practices: they must also take appropriate action to protect one another.

SUMMARY AND APPLICATION

Sex is a vital part of most romantic relationships. Partners who have similar sexual attitudes and high-quality sexual interaction are likely to be satisfied with their sex lives. Sexual satisfaction is associated with relational satisfaction, although it is important to remember that other factors, such as affection, love, and compatibility, are more important. Similarly, partners who are knowledgeable about sex are generally happier with their sex lives.

The research discussed in this chapter can help people like Taylor, Sarah, and Brittany in at least two ways. First, research on sexual attitudes can help them better understand their sexual selves. Second, research on sexual communication can help them improve how they talk about sex with their partner, both before and after engaging in sexual activity. In terms of sexual attitudes, Taylor has accepted and embraced her homosexuality. Sex is important in lesbian relationships, but nonverbal affection may be even more important to Taylor and Leslie. When Taylor hears homophobic comments and sees strange looks on the faces of her sorority sisters

when she mentions Leslie, she has every right to be upset. But Taylor might be consoled by recognizing that people have different attitudes and preferences regarding sex whether they are homosexual or heterosexual. For instance, Sarah sometimes struggles with derogatory comments that people direct at her because she is a virgin.

For her part, Sarah should be comforted by the fact that about 12% of college students (and 13% of women college students) are virgins and that people who remain virgins because of strong moral beliefs and values are usually happy and proud of their virginity. Indeed, if Sarah gave up her virginity for the sake of pleasing her boyfriend or conforming to social norms, she might very well regret her decision. Research suggests that Sarah should refuse sexual advances in a direct manner, using clear verbal communication. Her boyfriend might use a wide variety of strategies to try to convince her to have sex, including pressure, manipulation, or antisocial behaviors, but research suggests that these strategies are likely to backfire or result in less relational satisfaction, so they should be avoided. Research also suggests that Sarah's boyfriend will accept her decision.

Because she refuses to have sex, Sarah is in the position of being the sexual gatekeeper in her relationship with her boyfriend. Even in relationships that turn sexual, women tend to be in the gatekeeping position at the beginning of the relationship, with men cast in the role of sexual initiator. Socially accepted scripts for sexual communication are typically followed in the early stages of relationships. However, as the relationship develops, women usually feel freer to initiate sex. Unique, individual sexual scripts replace socially normative scripts in developed relationships.

Finally, communication plays an important role in promoting sexual satisfaction. Couples who tell each other their sexual preferences and communicate their needs, desires, and aversions are much more likely to be happier with their sex life, as are those who engage in cuddling and self-disclosure following sex. Communication is also critical for promoting safe sex and avoiding STIs or an unplanned pregnancy, as Brittany's communication with her boyfriend exemplifies. Although Brittany does not talk about her sex life with her parents, she learned how to be sexually responsible from them. Parents should talk to their children about sex in a supportive, nondefensive manner rather than issuing warnings. Partners like Brittany and Chris should also talk to each other openly and honestly about their past sexual experiences and the need to practice safe sex. However, it is important to remember that safe sex *talk* is not enough; safe sex *behaviors* promote healthy lives.

KEY TERMS

antisocial acts, as a sexual initiation strategy (p. 245)
assertive responses (p. 251)
attention stage (p. 240)
courtship readiness stage (p. 241)
delayed-involvement couples (p. 242)
expressions of emotional and physical closeness, as a sexual initiation strategy (p. 245)
friends with benefits (p. 230)
gradual-involvement couples (p. 242)
hinting and indirect strategies, as a sexual initiation strategy (p. 245)

hook-ups (p. 229)
invitations and sexual arousal stage (p. 241)
logic and reasoning, as a sexual initiation strategy (p. 245)
low-involvement couples (p. 242)
physical flirting style (p. 240)
pillow talk (p. 239)
playful flirting style (p. 240)
polite flirting style (p. 240)
positioning stage (p. 241)
pressure and manipulation, as a sexual initiation strategy (p. 245)
procreational orientation (p. 236)

quasi-courtship (p. 242)
rapid-involvement couples (p. 242)
recreational orientation (p. 236)
relational orientation (p. 236)
resolution stage (p. 242)
retaliatory responses (p. 251)
scripts (p. 245)
serial monogamy (p. 236)
sexual scripts (p. 237)
sincere flirting style (p. 240)
traditional flirting style, (p. 240)

DISCUSSION QUESTIONS

1. In this chapter, we presented data suggesting that most couples wait until some emotional intimacy or commitment has developed before engaging in sex. We also reported a study indicating that around 10% to 15% of college students are virgins. Based on the conversations you have had with friends, do you think these numbers hold true for your school? Why might these estimates differ depending on the group of people responding?

2. Based on what you learned in this chapter, what strategies would you use to protect yourself from sexual coercion or harassment? Why do you think people misinterpret supposed sexual cues so often?

3. Why do you think people practice unsafe sex even though they know the risks involved? What communication strategies might partners use to ensure that they engage in safe sex?

 SAGE edge™

Sharpen your skills with SAGE edge at edge.sagepub.com/guerrero5e.
SAGE edge for students provides a personalized approach to help you accomplish your coursework goals in an easy-to-use learning environment.

10 STAYING CLOSE
Maintaining Relationships

After 3 years of serious dating, Yasser proposes to Rachel and she accepts. They move in together and start planning their wedding, with Rachel doing the bulk of the work. Although she loves Yasser and is excited about the prospect of marrying him, she starts to worry that getting married could change things. When she was in middle school, her parents divorced after several years of bitter fighting. To add fuel to her worries, a good friend of hers recently announced that she and her husband were separating after only 2 years of marriage. Sometimes it seems to Rachel that everyone is getting divorced. Yasser assures her that things will be different for them. After all, they love each other and have a great relationship. And Yasser's parents have been happily married for nearly 30 years, so he has seen how two people can work together to maintain a successful relationship. Rachel wonders what their secret is. How do Yasser's parents manage to keep their relationship so happy, and can she and Yasser do the same?

In fairy tales, everyone lives "happily ever after," as if happiness was bestowed on them with the flick of a magic wand. In real life, however, there is no magic recipe for a happy relationship. So what can couples like Rachel and Yasser do to keep their relationships happy? How might getting married change their relationship? Maintaining relationships requires effort and perseverance. The road to a successful relationship can be full of potholes and detours, but "staying on course" and maintaining important relationships is a worthwhile endeavor. In fact, because having a close relationship is a key determinant of overall happiness (Carr & Springer, 2010), people who have trouble maintaining close relationships with others often are lonely and depressed, and they may doubt their self-worth (Segrin, 1998). Married people tend to report being happier and more satisfied with their lives than do single people (Carr, Freedman, Cornman, & Schwarz, 2014), yet 45% to 50% of first marriages in the United States end in divorce (Lansford, 2009). In 2008, estimates suggested that for every two people who got married in the United States, another person got divorced (Tejada-Vera & Sutton, 2009). Studies also show that marital satisfaction drops after parenthood, providing another maintenance challenge (Twenge, Campbell, & Foster, 2003). Given these facts, Rachel's concerns are certainly understandable and justified.

The research on **relational maintenance** provides important information on behaviors that couples like Yasser and Rachel can use to promote relational satisfaction and longevity. In this chapter, we look at several areas of research related to maintenance. First, we define relational maintenance and discuss specific types of behaviors people use to maintain a variety of close relationships, including romantic relationships and friendships. We also discuss some of the special challenges people face when trying to maintain cross-sex friendships, friends-with-benefits relationships, long-distance relationships, and cohabiting relationships. The chapter ends with a discussion of **equity theory,** which focuses on how benefits and fairness help keep relationships satisfying and stable.

DEFINING RELATIONAL MAINTENANCE

People maintain things that they care about. They take their cars in for routine maintenance service and repair mechanical problems when they occur. They maintain their homes by keeping them clean, mowing the lawn, trimming the hedges, and painting the walls. They maintain their good images at work by trying to be punctual, professional, presentable, and well organized. Similarly, people usually try to maintain and mend their relationships with others through contact and communication. As you may already know or will learn, maintaining a relationship is far more challenging than maintaining a car or a home.

Relational maintenance has been defined in various ways. According to Dindia and Canary (1993), there are four common definitions. First, *relational maintenance involves keeping a relationship in existence.* Although some relationships are kept in existence through extensive contact, others require minimal effort. For example, social networking sites such as Facebook and Twitter allow people to

keep in touch with one another without having to invest time and effort into communicating with each individual "friend" one-on-one. Similarly, you might send holiday or birthday cards to people who you do not have much contact with during the course of the year as a way of keeping a relationship in existence. Second, *relational maintenance involves keeping a relationship in a specified state or condition, or at a stable level of intimacy, so that the status quo is maintained* (Ayres, 1983). For example, friends might work to keep their relationship from becoming romantic, or sisters might try to keep their relationship as close as ever despite living in different cities. Third, *relational maintenance can involve keeping a relationship in satisfactory condition.* Dating and married couples often try to rekindle the romance in their relationships to keep them satisfying. They might have a candlelit dinner or spend a weekend away together. Similarly, friends might plan a weekend ski trip together to catch up with each other and have fun. Fourth, *relational maintenance involves keeping a relationship in repair.* The idea here is that people work to prevent problems from occurring in their relationships, and to fix problems when they do occur.

As Dindia and Canary (1993) stated, these four components of relational maintenance overlap. A critical part of keeping a relationship satisfying is preventing and correcting problems, and an important part of keeping a relationship in existence is keeping it satisfying. In a broad sense, relational maintenance can be defined as *keeping a relationship at a desired level* (Canary & Stafford, 1994). For some relationships, the desired level may be a casual friendship, professional association, or acquaintanceship, with occasional e-mails or contact through social networking sites such as Facebook being all that is necessary. For other relationships, physical and emotional closeness are desired, which typically requires more sustained maintenance efforts. It is also important to recognize that keeping a relationship at a desired level does not necessarily mean that a relationship remains at the same level of closeness over time. As people's desires change, the way they define and maintain their relationships also changes.

Maintenance is a dynamic process that involves continually adjusting to new needs and demands.

BEHAVIORS USED TO MAINTAIN RELATIONSHIPS

So *how* do people maintain their relationships? Scholars began addressing this important question in the 1980s (Ayres, 1983; Bell, Daly, & Gonzalez, 1987; Dindia & Baxter, 1987; Duck, 1988; Shea & Pearson, 1986). Since then, much has been learned about behaviors people use to maintain various types of relationships. Although various scholars have advanced different lists of behaviors used to maintain relationships, most maintenance behaviors can be characterized based on three distinctions: (1) how prosocial or antisocial they are, (2) their channel or **modality,** and (3) whether they are employed strategically or routinely.

Prosocial Maintenance Behaviors

The majority of behaviors used to maintain relationships are prosocial, positive behaviors that promote relational closeness, trust, and liking. Stafford and Canary (1991) asked dating and married couples what they did to maintain their relationships and keep them satisfying. Five primary maintenance strategies, all of which are prosocial, emerged: (1) positivity, (2) openness, (3) assurances, (4) social networking, and (5) task sharing. A summary of the research showed that couples who regularly use these five maintenance behaviors tend to have relationships characterized by high levels of satisfaction, commitment, liking, and love (Ogolsky & Bowers, 2013). Couples who use high levels of these five prosocial maintenance behaviors also tend to have overlapping identities, which may lead them to want to work together and to share resources (Ledbetter, Stassen-Ferrara, & Dowd, 2013). Other researchers have identified supportiveness, joint activities, romance, humor, and constructive conflict as additional prosocial behaviors that are commonly used to maintain certain relationships (Afifi, Guerrero, & Egland, 1994; Dainton & Stafford, 1993; Stafford,

2003). These maintenance behaviors are described further in Box 10.1.

As mentioned previously, people who use high levels of prosocial maintenance behavior tend to be satisfied with their relationships (Stafford, 2003; Weigel & Ballard-Reisch, 2008). **Relational satisfaction** refers to the "pleasure or enjoyment" that people derive from their relationships (Vangelisti & Huston, 1994, p. 173). Some studies have shown that positivity, assurances, and social networking are especially important for predicting how satisfied couples are with their relationships (Dainton, Stafford, & Canary, 1994; Stafford & Canary, 1991; Weigel & Ballard-Reisch, 2001). In one study, people reported being the most satisfied in their relationships when their partners used higher levels of positivity and assurances than they expected them to use (Dainton, 2000). High levels of positivity and social networking are important in family relationships as well (Morr Serewicz, Dickson, Morrison, & Poole, 2007). Spending time together is also important because it creates feelings of companionship, cohesion, and openness (Egland et al., 1997; Reissman, Aron, & Bergen, 1993). Likewise, when partners share tasks in a fair and equitable manner, they tend to feel closer and more satisfied with their relationships (Canary & Stafford, 1994; Guerrero, Eloy, & Wabnik, 1993).

Not surprisingly, relationships characterized by high levels of prosocial maintenance also tend to be stable and committed. In a study by Guerrero et al. (1993), college-aged daters were surveyed near the beginning of the semester and then 8 weeks later. People who reported using more prosocial maintenance behaviors at the beginning of the study were more likely to have become more serious or stayed at the same intimacy level by the end of the eight weeks. Those who reported using low levels of prosocial maintenance behavior were likely to have de-escalated or terminated their relationships by the end of the 8 weeks. In another study, Ramirez (2008) had married couples complete two surveys that were spaced around 2 weeks apart. Couples who reported using more prosocial maintenance were more personally committed to their marriage when surveyed two weeks later, with personal commitment defined

BOX 10.1 HIGHLIGHTS
PROSOCIAL MAINTENANCE BEHAVIORS

Behavior	Definition and Examples
Positivity	Making interactions pleasant and enjoyable (e.g., giving compliments, acting cheerful)
Openness and routine talk	Talking and listening to one another (e.g., self-disclosing, sharing secrets, asking how the partner's day went)
Assurances	Giving each other assurances about commitment (e.g., assuring the other you still care, talking about the future)
Social networking	Spending time with each other's social network (e.g., going to family functions together, accepting each other's friends)
Task sharing	Performing routine tasks and chores relevant to the relationship together (e.g., sharing household chores, planning finances together)
Supportiveness	Giving each other social support and encouragement (e.g., providing comfort, making sacrifices for the partner)
Joint activities	Engaging in activities and spending time together (e.g., hanging out together, playing sports, shopping together)
Romance and affection	Revealing positive, caring feelings for each other (e.g., saying "I love you," sending flowers, having a romantic dinner)
Humor	Using inside jokes, humor, and sarcasm (e.g., using funny nicknames, laughing together)
Constructive conflict management	Managing conflict in constructive ways that promote problem solving and harmony (e.g., listening to one another's positions, trying to come up with acceptable solutions)

as the extent to which a person was devoted to the partner and desired to remain in the relationship. Similarly, spouses use more prosocial maintenance behavior when they are both committed to their marriage (Weigel & Ballard-Reisch, 2008).

Even though prosocial maintenance behaviors are associated with greater commitment and relational stability, couples do not use these behaviors consistently throughout their relationships. In a summary of the research on relational maintenance, positivity, openness, and assurances actually decreased slightly the longer a couple had been together (Ogolsky & Bowers, 2013). Couples may use the highest levels of relational maintenance when they are moving their relationship from casual to committed, or when they are trying to rekindle or repair their relationship. Once a relationship is secure and committed, relational maintenance is still important, but partners may not feel the need to work quite as hard on the relationship all the time.

Antisocial Maintenance Behavior

In contrast to the prosocial maintenance behaviors that are related to commitment and satisfaction,

scholars have identified a set of antisocial or negative behaviors that are sometimes used to maintain
relationships, although they tend not to increase
(and may even decrease) relational satisfaction.
These behaviors tend to discourage interaction or
try to change the partner in some way; are often
coercive, manipulative, or controlling; and include
ultimatums, threats, and becoming distant (Dindia,
1989, 2003; Dindia & Baxter, 1987). Although it
might seem puzzling that negative behaviors such as
these would be used to try to maintain relationships,
keep in mind that antisocial behaviors only qualify
as maintenance when they are used specifically for
that purpose. Antisocial maintenance behaviors
are unlikely to be used to try to keep a relationship
satisfying, but they may be used for other mainte-
nance-related reasons, such as trying to control
a partner who might break up with you, trying to
force someone to see you as more attractive or desirable, or trying to avoid conflict.

Antisocial maintenance behaviors may also be
used to try to keep a relationship at a given level of
intimacy or closeness, as Ayres (1983) suggested
is often the case when people use **avoidance** as a
maintenance strategy. For example, you might avoid
talking about how attracted you are to a friend if
you worry that such a revelation could harm your
friendship (Afifi & Burgoon, 1998); you might distance yourself from a friend who has a crush on you
to signal that you are not interested (Eden & Veksler,
2010); or you might refrain from arguing with your
partner on a particular topic if you think it could
damage your relationship. In other cases, people use
avoidance to keep their relationships at a casual level.
For instance, if you are uncomfortable becoming
close friends with a coworker or classmate, you might
avoid personal topics of conversation when talking
with this individual. In cross-sex friendships, people
sometimes avoid flirting and instead talk about their
romantic relationships with others as maintenance
strategies that help keep the relationship platonic
(Guerrero & Chavez, 2005; Messman, Canary, &
Hause, 2000). Box 10.2 further explains these and
other antisocial maintenance behaviors.

Antisocial maintenance behaviors are sometimes
designed to alter the partner's feelings or keep the
partner in the relationship. At times, people use **jealousy induction** as a maintenance strategy for one
or both of these purposes (Dainton & Gross, 2008;
Fleischmann et al., 2005). The idea here is that jealousy might spark feelings of love and possessiveness,
making a partner more likely to stay in the relationship. Spying or surveillance may also function to
maintain relationships by providing information
that reduces uncertainty about rival relationships
and helps a jealous person compete with potential
rivals (Dainton & Gross, 2008; Guerrero & Afifi,
1999). Dainton and Gross also identified infidelity,
allowing control, and destructive conflict as negative behaviors that can be used to try to maintain
relationships (see Box 10.2).

Obviously, antisocial behaviors such as jealousy
induction, spying, infidelity, and destructive conflict can backfire, leading to more problems or to
breakup rather than relational maintenance. Some
of these antisocial maintenance behaviors may even
represent desperate attempts to hang onto a relationship that is in trouble. For example, jealousy induction is often used when people are worried that their
partner is interested in someone else (Guerrero &
Andersen, 1998b), and people who do not have the
communication skills to solve problems in a constructive manner sometimes use controlling strategies (Christopher & Lloyd, 2000). Not surprisingly,
people who report using the antisocial maintenance
behaviors of allowing control, destructive conflict,
jealousy induction, and infidelity also report low
levels of relational satisfaction (Dainton & Gross,
2008). Thus, although behaviors such as avoidance,
no flirting, and talking about others can be effective and appropriate at times and can even lead to
more relational satisfaction, many antisocial maintenance behaviors could have destructive effects on
relationships.

Modality of Maintenance Behavior

Modality refers to the channel of communication; for
example, is a message sent by words, facial expression,

BOX 10.2 HIGHLIGHTS
ANTISOCIAL MAINTENANCE BEHAVIORS

Behavior	Definition and Examples
Avoidance	Evading the partner in certain situations or on certain issues (e.g., planning separate activities, respecting each other's privacy)
No flirting	Refraining from flirting with someone to clearly communicate that you are not interested in pursuing a romantic relationship (e.g., being standoffish when someone flirts with you)
Talking about others	Talking about someone else to signal that you already have a special relationship with another person (e.g., repeatedly mentioning your significant other, explaining why someone is your "best" friend)
Jealousy induction	Attempting to make your partner jealous (e.g., leaving a note from a "secret admirer" out for your partner to see, flirting with someone in front of your partner)
Spying	Getting information about your partner without his or her knowledge (e.g., looking through your partner's text messages, asking your partner's friends for information)
Infidelity	Engaging in sexual activity with someone else (e.g., making out with someone else so your partner knows you have other alternatives, sleeping with someone else to get rewards that you are missing in your current relationship)
Allowing control	Focusing exclusively on the partner (e.g., ignoring your friends so you can spend time with your partner, letting your partner make all the decisions)
Destructive conflict	Using destructive conflict to control the partner (e.g., yelling at your partner if she or he does not do what you want, starting arguments so you can tell your partner how she or he should act)

voice tone, computer, or letter? Some researchers consider mediated communication, such as e-mail or text messaging, to be a special category of maintenance behavior based on its modality. However, mediated communication is not listed as a separate category in Boxes 10.1 or 10.2 because most maintenance behaviors can be employed in either face-to-face or mediated contexts. For example, friends can call and then catch up by having lunch or they can exchange e-mails. Similarly, individuals can spy on their partners by following them or by checking their

Facebook page. Mediated forms of maintenance behavior include communicating via social networking services (such as Twitter or Facebook), e-mail, text messaging, snapping, blogging, the telephone, and cards and letters (Canary, Stafford, Hause, & Wallace, 1993; Herring, Scheidt, Bonus, & Wright, 2005; Marmo & Bryant, 2010; Wright, 2004). In fact, one study showed that college students text their romantic partners an average of six times a day and call them on their cell phones three to four times a day (Duran et al., 2011). As discussed in Box 10.3, cell phones also play an important role in maintaining relationships.

Although people can enact various maintenance strategies through these different modalities, the same behavior may be interpreted differently depending on whether it occurs in face-to-face versus mediated contexts. Imagine receiving a holiday greeting card from a friend online versus in the mail. Now imagine receiving the card with a pre-typed signature versus a real signature. Which card is more personal? All three cards would likely help maintain the friendship, but each card would send a somewhat different message. Another example is discussing the nature of one's relationship. When couples engage in this type of relationship talk in a face-to-face context, they usually report being happy in their relationships. However, when couples discuss the nature of their relationship when texting, they tend to be less satisfied with their relationships (Brody & Peña, 2015). This may be because texting provides a relatively nonintimate context for discussing this type of serious issue. Some maintenance behaviors are also enacted differently depending on their modality. Take task sharing as an example. People can accomplish some task sharing, such as working together on a written project, through mediated communication. But other forms of task sharing, such as washing and drying the dishes together, can only be accomplished in face-to-face settings.

Mediated forms of communication are especially important for maintaining certain types of relationships, including friendships, online relationships, and long-distance relationships. In terms of friendships, Marmo and Bryant (2010) examined how acquaintances, casual friends, and close friends use Facebook to maintain their relationships. People in all of these friendship groups reported using strategies such as writing on each other's walls and commenting on each other's photos to keep in contact. Facebook users also reported sending messages related to assurances and positivity. For example, if someone posts a comment saying she's having a particularly hard day, her friends are likely to respond with comments expressing support and empathy (Marmo & Bryant, 2010). The importance of positivity is highlighted by some of the implicit rules that govern how friends interact on Facebook. According to these rules, people expect others to present themselves and their friends positively (in messages, photos, etc.) on Facebook and to refrain from posting anything that could hurt a person's image (Bryant & Marmo, 2010, 2012). Another unwritten rule, which is reflected in reports of actual behavior, is that close friends should engage in more maintenance behavior on Facebook than casual friends, who should engage in more maintenance behavior than acquaintances (Marmo & Bryant, 2010). However, maintaining a relationship using Facebook alone may not be enough. One study showed that contact via Facebook was sufficient for maintaining acquaintanceships and casual friendships, but not enough for close friends and romantic partners, who also needed to use other means, such as talking face to face or on the phone, to maintain the high intimacy levels in their relationships (Bryant & Marmo, 2012).

Researchers have also studied relational maintenance in online relationships. Wright (2004) found that openness and positivity were the most frequently used maintenance behaviors in these relationships. Rabby (2007) compared maintenance in four types of relationships: (1) **Virtual relationships** were defined in terms of the partners having communicated only online. (2) **Pinocchio relationships** occur when partners first meet online but then start meeting in person (i.e., they become "real"). (3) **Cyber emigrant relationships** are those in which partners first meet in person but then start communicating primarily online. (4) Finally, communication in real-world relationships starts and continues primarily in face-to-face contexts. In Rabby's study, people in the virtual-only group reported using the least maintenance behavior. However, if people in the virtual-only group were highly committed to their partner, they used just as much relational maintenance as did people in the other three groups. This suggests that

BOX 10.3 TECH TALK
CELL PHONES AND RELATIONSHIP MAINTENANCE

Research has shown that teens and young adults, in particular, see their cell phones as critical for maintaining relationships and keeping in contact with members of their social network (e.g., Yates & Lockley, 2008). Cell phones also play an important role in maintaining marriages, with Pew research from 2008 revealing that over 70% of married individuals in the United States in 2008 said that both they and their spouse had cell phones and that they communicated with one another via cell phone at least once a day. The more often people communicate using their cell phone, the more likely they are to report being satisfied with their relationship (Schwartz, 2008; Yin, 2009). In contrast, Yin's (2009) research suggested that text messaging, especially in the absence of talking to one another on the phone, is negatively related to satisfaction in long-distance romantic relationships. So text messaging may be seen as a less personal form of communication than talking on one's cell phone.

Studies also suggest that cell phone communication is most likely to be related to satisfaction when people follow certain rules. Duran and colleagues (2011) found that about one third of couples had rules for how to communicate via their cell phones. These rules often related to the content, timing, and frequency of cell phone communication. A related study by Miller-Ott, Kelly, and Duran (2012) identified six rules about cell phone communication that people sometimes set up in their relationships:

- *Contact with others:* Not talking or texting others when spending time together

- *Call times:* Not calling too late or early or during other specified times (e.g., during work hours)

- *Availability expectations:* Setting expectations for call-back times (e.g., expecting a call or text back within an hour; not expecting one's partner to have her or his cell phone on when at work)

- *Relational issues:* Casting certain topics, such as having an argument or talking about a serious relationship issue, as inappropriate for text messaging

- *Repetitive contact:* Giving the partner an appropriate amount of time to text or call back without leaving another message

- *Monitoring partner usage:* Not checking the partner's phone log

In Miller-Ott and others' (2012) study, couples who had set rules about contact with others and relational issues (see above) reported being happier with their cell phone communication. Moreover, couples who reported having rules about relational issues, repetitive contact, and monitoring partner usage reported being more satisfied with their relationships. Therefore, setting rules about cell phone communication—and following those rules—may contribute to keeping a relationship happy.

---

maintenance behavior is more strongly related to commitment than modality.

Mediated forms of maintenance behavior are also common in long-distance relationships between romantic partners, family members, and friends (Rabby & Walther, 2003; Rohlfing, 1995). In fact, social networking sites, such as Facebook and Twitter, are marketed as ways to maintain relationships or keep in touch with friends. Mediated communication can also be used to terminate a relationship, as can be the case if someone is "de-friended" on Facebook. Failure to answer an e-mail or even failing to send a

greeting card for birthdays or holidays may be also perceived as a sign that someone does not want to maintain a relationship (Dindia, Timmerman, Langan, Sahlstein, & Quandt, 2004). Some types of maintenance behaviors are especially amenable to mediated communication and therefore more likely to be used in long-distance relationships. In one study, people reported using computer-mediated forms of communication related to positivity and social networking as ways to maintain their long-distance relationships. In contrast, openness and shared tasks were more likely to occur in face-to-face contexts (Dainton & Aylor, 2002).

©iStockphoto.com/asiseeit

Communicating with friends using Snapchat and social networking sites may be sufficient for maintaining acquaintanceships and casual friendships, but additional modes of communication are usually necessary to maintain our closest relationships.

Strategic and Routine Maintenance Behaviors

In addition to modality, maintenance behaviors can be distinguished by how strategic versus routine they are (Canary & Stafford, 1994; Dindia, 2003; Duck, 1986). **Strategic maintenance behaviors** are intentionally designed to maintain a relationship. For example, if you have an argument with your best friend, you might call with the intent of apologizing and repairing the situation. On Mother's Day, you might send your mom a bouquet of flowers so that she knows you are thinking of her. If you live far away from a loved one, you might call twice a week at a designated time or send the loved one a few Snapchats to keep in touch. These types of actions are deliberate and intentionally designed to maintain a positive relationship with someone.

Routine maintenance behaviors are less strategic and deliberate. They are used without the express purpose of maintaining the relationship, yet they still help people preserve their bonds with one another. Behaviors such as task sharing and positivity are especially likely to be used routinely rather than strategically (Dainton & Aylor, 2002). For example, roommates might share household responsibilities as a routine or habit. One roommate might do grocery shopping, pay bills, and vacuum and dust the apartment, and the other roommate might water the plants, clean the bathroom, and do the cooking. Similarly, Yasser and Rachel might routinely engage in positivity by appearing happy when one partner arrives home from work and using polite communication such as saying "thank you" when doing favors for one another. Duck (1994) argued that routine talk is more important than strategic behavior for maintaining relationships. Other researchers have demonstrated that routine maintenance is a somewhat better predictor of relational satisfaction and commitment than strategic maintenance (Dainton & Aylor, 2002). Thus, maintaining a relationship does not always require conscious "work." Sometimes maintenance rests in seemingly trivial behaviors that people enact rather mindlessly on a day-to-day basis.

Naturally, the line between strategic and routine maintenance behaviors is sometimes blurred. Many people cannot really tell if a given behavior is strategic or routine. Moreover, the same behavior can be strategic in some situations and routine in others. For example, holding your romantic partner's hand at the movie theater might be a habitual routine; you always hold your partner's hand at the movies. After an argument, however, reaching for your partner's hand might be a strategic move designed to repair the relationship and to restore intimacy. Strategic maintenance behaviors also may be used to prevent a relationship from becoming too intimate, to escalate or de-escalate the level of intimacy in the relationship, or to restore intimacy to repair a relationship. Both routine and strategic behaviors can contribute to relational maintenance in terms of keeping the relationship close and satisfying.

MAINTENANCE BEHAVIOR IN ROMANTIC RELATIONSHIPS

Maintenance behaviors vary based on the type of relationship people share. People maintain all types of relationships, but most research has focused on maintaining romantic relationships. Openness, assurances, and positivity seem to be more common in romantic relationships than in other types of relationships (Canary et al., 1993). Cohabiting romantic partners use many routine maintenance behaviors, including task sharing, joint activities, and routine talk, more than most friends do. Thus, when Rachel and Yasser move in together after getting married, they may begin to use more routine maintenance behaviors.

Changes in Maintenance Over the Course of Romantic Relationships

Of course, Rachel and Yasser do not have to wait to get married to see changes in how they maintain their relationship. Changes have occurred from the time they first met until they became engaged, and more changes are likely to occur after they get married. Stafford and Canary (1991) compared couples at four relationship stages: (1) casually dating, (2) seriously dating, (3) engaged, and (4) married. They found that (1) married and engaged couples reported using more assurances and task sharing than did dating couples, (2) engaged and seriously dating couples reported using more openness and positivity than married or casually dating couples, and (3) married couples reported the most social networking. Adding to these findings, Dainton and Stafford (1993) compared the reports of maintenance behavior in dating versus marital relationships. They found that spouses shared more tasks than daters. Daters, however, engaged in more mediated communication, such as calling each other on the phone, exchanging cards and letters, and so forth. Another study showed that couples report less openness but more social networking, task sharing, and constructive conflict management the longer they are together (Dainton & Aylor, 2002).

These results make sense. As couples become more committed, partners may feel freer to provide assurances, and they may, by necessity, share more tasks, especially if they are living together. Similarly, couples may need to integrate social networks as the relationship becomes more committed and people come to view them as a "couple." However, openness and positivity may peak before romantic partners become fully committed. Once married, spouses may not feel the need to disclose their innermost

feelings all the time—in part because they have already told each other so much about themselves. Spouses may also express more negativity once they have the security of marriage. When spouses are still in the "honeymoon stage," they are more likely to be on their best behavior and to "put on a happy face." Moreover, the daily interaction that comes from living together makes it difficult for married couples to be positive all of the time. Complaints and conflicts are likely to occur, even in the best relationships.

In marriages, relational maintenance may follow a curvilinear pattern; in other words, spouses may use more maintenance behavior in the early and later years of marriage (Weigel & Ballard-Reisch, 1999). One explanation for this finding is that couples put considerable effort in their marriages during the honeymoon stage. Imagine how Rachel might act during the early years of her marriage with Yasser. Because being married is novel and exciting—and because she is concerned about making her marriage a success—she may be especially likely to engage in maintenance behavior. As the marriage progresses, she and Yasser may become preoccupied with their children and careers, leaving less time to devote to one another. Eventually, however, Weigel and Ballard-Reisch's research suggests that their level of maintenance will rebound, perhaps when their children are older or they settle into a comfortable work routine.

Maintenance in Gay and Lesbian Relationships

In addition to using the prosocial maintenance behaviors listed earlier, gay and lesbian couples use some unique strategies to maintain their relationships. Haas and Stafford (1998) found that partners in same-sex romantic relationships reported that it is important to live and work in environments that are supportive and not judgmental of their relationships. Similarly, same-sex couples emphasized the importance of being "out" in front of their social networks. Spending time with friends and family members who recognize and accept their relationship was a key relational maintenance behavior, as was being able to introduce each other as "my partner." Some gay and lesbian couples also reported modeling their parents' relationships. Gay and lesbian couples tend to see their relationships as similar to heterosexual relationships in terms of commitment and communication but dissimilar in terms of nonconformity to sex-role stereotypes.

In a later study, Haas and Stafford (2005) found that although same-sex romantic relationships were characterized by many of the same maintenance behaviors as opposite-sex marriages, subtle differences existed. Sharing tasks was the most commonly reported maintenance behavior for both types of relationships. However, gay and lesbian couples reported using more maintenance behaviors that show bonding, such as talking about the commitment level in their relationships. Haas and Stafford argued that bonding communication was especially necessary in gay and lesbian relationships because, at the time of the study, these relationships were not legally validated the way marriages were.

MAINTENANCE BEHAVIOR IN SAME-SEX FRIENDSHIPS

Even though friendships are extremely important, people usually don't work as hard to maintain their friendships as their romantic relationships (Dainton, Zelley, & Langan, 2003; Fehr, 1996). Perhaps this is because people take a more casual approach to friendships. People are taught that romantic relationships require a spark to get started and that the spark needs to be rekindled from time to time if the relationship is to stay strong. Friendships, on the other hand, are expected to be maintained with little effort most of the time. In fact, most people would think it was odd if Rachel was worried about maintaining a relationship with her best friend rather than her future spouse.

Nonetheless, friendships require maintenance. Fehr (1996) suggested that three maintenance behaviors are particularly important in friendships: (1) openness, (2) supportiveness, and (3) positivity.

Afifi, Guerrero, and Egland (1994) found that all three of these behaviors are associated with relational closeness in same-sex friendships between both men and women. Several studies have shown that openness, which includes both routine talk and intimate self-disclosure, is the cornerstone of all good friendships (Canary et al., 1993; Rose, 1985; Rosenfeld & Kendrick, 1984). Other maintenance behaviors, such as joint activities and affection, differ somewhat in importance depending on whether the friends are men or women.

Talking Versus Doing

Many studies have compared, directly or indirectly, how female versus male friends maintain their relationships. One common finding is that women tend to "talk" more while men tend to "do" more (Barth & Kinder, 1988; Sherrod, 1989). Wright (1982) referred to women's friendships as "face to face" because of the focus on communication, and men's friendships as "side by side" because of the focus on activity. This sex difference, albeit small, appears early in life and extends to mediated communication such as texting and online gaming. In a study on teens (Lenhart, 2015b), video games were found to play "a crucial role in the development and maintenance of [teen] boys' friendships." Teenage boys felt more connected to one another when they played video games together either in person or online, with 71% of boys saying that one of the ways they communicate with their friends is while playing games, compared to only 31% of girls. In contrast, teenage girls engage in more texting (62% to 48%) as well as more instant messages (32% to 23%) to stay connected to friends than do boys. Snapchat is by far the most common form of instant messaging teens use, but instant messaging includes a variety of applications, including WhatsApp, Facebook Messenger, and AOL Instant Message (O'Reilly, 2015). These differences between boys and girls reflect research showing that girls focus primarily on talk whereas boys focus primarily on activity. However, because they use many of the same social media, such as Snapchat and Twitter, teen boys and girls develop similar patterns in how they use the technology on their smartphones to develop and maintain their relationships.

Males and females are similar in other ways too: Research shows that both men and women value self-disclosure in their relationships (Afifi et al., 1994; Floyd & Parks, 1995; Monsour, 1992; Parks & Floyd, 1996), but women disclose to one another a bit more. Similarly, both men and women value spending time with one another, even though men tend to engage in more focused activities than women. Supporting this, Fehr (1996) reviewed research showing that men and women spend similar amounts of time with their friends. The difference is that men engage in more activities, such as playing sports. In other words, women get together more often just to talk and spend time with one another, whereas men get together more often to do something specific, such as surf, play golf, or watch a game. Of course, sometimes men get together just to talk, and sometimes women get together to play sports. In fact, one study found no difference in how much male and female friends reported engaging in shared activities (Floyd & Parks, 1995). The difference between men's and women's activities is more subtle than dramatic; therefore, the talking versus doing distinction may be overstated.

Men and Women Are From the Same Planet

Taken as a whole, the research suggests that some sex differences exist in how men and women maintain their friendships. However, these differences are not dramatic; men and women are generally more similar than dissimilar, and when differences are found, they tend to be small (Andersen, 1998b; Canary & Hause, 1993). Everyone wants friends to talk to, do things with, and turn to in times of trouble, regardless of gender. In fact, both men and women see their friendships as one of the most important sources of happiness in their lives (Fehr, 1996; Rawlins, 1992). Box 10.4 examines the issue of whether men and women really are from "different planets."

MAINTENANCE BEHAVIOR IN CROSS-SEX FRIENDSHIPS

Cross-sex friendships can be very rewarding (Werking, 1997). Both men and women like to get the perspective of the "other sex," and many people perceive cross-sex friendships as fun and exciting. However, cross-sex friendships can be confusing and ambiguous at times. Think about your friends of the opposite sex. Do you sometimes wonder if they are physically attracted to you? Do you wonder what it would be like to get involved with them romantically? If one or both of you are heterosexual, these types of questions are likely to surface, even if only in your mind.

Challenges in Cross-Sex Friendships

As a result of this ambiguity, cross-sex friends sometimes face special challenges. O'Meara (1989) discussed four challenges that men and women face when they want to be "just friends" with one another. Three of these challenges—(1) the emotional bond challenge, (2) the sexual challenge, and (3) the public presentation challenge—are especially relevant to maintaining cross-sex friendships.

THE EMOTIONAL BOND CHALLENGE This challenge stems from men and women being socialized to see one another as potential romantic partners rather than platonic friends. This can lead to uncertainty regarding whether cross-sex friends have romantic feelings for each other. It may also be confusing to feel close to opposite-sex friends without also feeling romantic toward them. We grow up believing that when we feel close to an age-appropriate person of the opposite sex, we should also be able to fall in love with that person. For example, have you ever had a good friend of the opposite sex whom you thought was wonderful yet for whom you did not have romantic feelings? If so, you may have wondered how you could be so close without becoming romantic. This is because the line between emotional closeness and romantic attraction can be blurred in some cross-sex friendships. In contrast, heterosexual same-sex friends expect emotional closeness without romantic attraction.

BOX 10.4 HIGHLIGHTS
ARE MEN AND WOMEN REALLY FROM DIFFERENT PLANETS?

If you watch television talk shows or read popular books on relationships, you have probably been introduced to the idea that men and women are very different from each other and that these differences can cause relational problems. For example, Deborah Tannen's popular 1990 book *You Just Don't Understand: Women and Men in Conversation* is built around the idea that boys and girls grow up in different cultures, with girls learning to communicate in ways that are confirming and create intimacy and boys learning to communicate in ways that enhance independence and power. According to Tannen, women and men have difficulty communicating with one another because of "cultural misunderstanding."

John Gray's 1992 best seller *Men Are From Mars, Women Are From Venus*, discussed in Chapter 1, takes this argument a step farther by conceptualizing men and women as inhabitants of different planets. He put it this way:

> Men and women differ in all areas of their lives. Not only do men and women communicate differently but they think, feel, perceive, react, respond, love, need, and appreciate differently. They almost seem to be from different planets, speaking different languages and needing different nourishment. (p. 5)

According to Gray, these "interplanetary differences" are responsible for all the problems that people have in their opposite-sex relationships.

Most relationship researchers, however, do not take a position as extreme as Gray's. Some take a position similar to Tannen's in that they believe a different cultures

perspective can help explain communication differences between men and women (see Wood, 1994, 1996). According to this view, boys and girls grow up primarily playing in same-sex groups. Therefore, they learn different sets of rules and values, leading to distinct communication styles.

Some researchers, however, disagree with the different cultures perspective (Dindia, 1997). Instead, they believe that men and women are remarkably similar and that sex differences are small. These researchers are quick to point out that boys and girls grow up in a similar cultural environment, interacting with a variety of people, including teachers and family members, of both sexes. As Dindia has put it, "Men are from North Dakota, and women are from South Dakota."

What do you think? Andersen (1998b) summarized his take on the debate as follows:

> The actual research on sex differences has led to one major, overall conclusion: Men and women are far more similar than different. They are not from different metaphoric planets or cultures. They are all earthlings with goals, hopes, dreams, emotions, fears, and communication behaviors that are a whole lot more similar than they are different. Of course, South Dakotans probably believe that North Dakotans are from another planet. From close range, differences are more obvious than similarities and they are certainly more newsworthy and sensational! From any vantage point other than Dakota, North and South Dakotans look pretty similar. (p. 83)

THE SEXUAL CHALLENGE This challenge involves coping with the potential sexual attraction that can be part of some cross-sex relationships. In the classic movie *When Harry Met Sally,* Harry declares that men and women cannot be friends because "the sex part always gets in the way." Although Harry's statement is extreme, it is true that cross-sex friends (particularly if both are heterosexual) are likely to think about sexual issues related to each other. In one study (Halatsis & Christakis, 2009), about 50% of the participants reported

having experienced sexual attraction toward a cross-sex friend. This percentage is higher for men, who tend to see their cross-sex friends as potential sexual partners far more often than do women (Abbey, 1982; Abbey & Melby, 1986; Shotland & Craig, 1988). Research has also shown that sex between friends is not uncommon. Although most cross-sex friends see themselves as strictly platonic (Guerrero & Chavez, 2005), nearly half of the college students surveyed in one study admitted to having had sex with a nonromantic friend (Afifi & Faulkner, 2000).

These students also reported experiencing feelings of uncertainty after having sex with their friend. Later in this chapter, and also touched on in Chapter 1, we discuss the phenomenon of friends with benefits, which refers to nonromantic relationships between friends who have sex. Clearly, potential sexual attraction can complicate cross-sex friendships.

THE PUBLIC PRESENTATION CHALLENGE This challenge arises when other people assume there is something romantic or sexual going on in a cross-sex friendship. Cross-sex friends are sometimes careful about how they present their friendship to others and may be asked to explain the nature of their relationship to others. If you have a close cross-sex friend, you can probably relate to this. Have people ever asked you questions such as, "Are you really just friends?" or "Do you love her or him?" or "Have you ever slept together?" Romantic partners may also be suspicious and jealous of your close cross-sex friends leading to other complications.

Some scholars have criticized O'Meara's four challenges for being applicable only to cross-sex heterosexual friendships. However, these challenges are also applicable to homosexual same-sex friends. Additionally, when one friend is homosexual and the other is heterosexual, these challenges may apply regardless of whether the friends are of the same or the opposite sex.

Coping With Romantic Intent

In cross-sex friendships that include at least one heterosexual partner, these challenges can make relational maintenance a complex and delicate matter (Werking, 1997). Two studies provide a closer look at how **romantic intent,** or the desire to move the friendship toward a romantic relationship, is related to maintenance behavior. The first of these studies (Guerrero & Chavez, 2005) examined four types of cross-sex friendships that differ in terms of romantic intent. Individuals in the *strictly platonic* group said that neither they nor their partner wanted the friendship to become romantic. Individuals in the *mutual romance* group said that both they and their partner wanted the friendship to become romantic. Individuals in the *desires-romance* group said that

they wanted the friendship to become romantic, but their partner wanted it to stay platonic. Finally, individuals in the *rejects-romance* group said that they wanted the friendship to stay platonic, but their partner wanted it to become romantic. In the second of these studies (Weger & Emmett, 2009), both friends reported on the degree of romantic intent that they felt toward their cross-sex friend. Together, these studies suggest that cross-sex friends report different levels of some maintenance behaviors depending on their romantic intentions.

Friends who have romantic intentions are especially likely to report using prosocial maintenance behavior. In Guerrero and Chavez's (2005) study, friends in the mutual romance group said they used the most maintenance behaviors, which suggests that increases in maintenance behavior might mark a move from friendship toward romance. Those in the desires-romance group also reported relatively high levels of maintenance, with one notable exception: People who desired romance but believed that their friend did not were the least likely to report talking about the relationship with their friend, perhaps because they feared rejection and worried that confessing their feelings could jeopardize the friendship. In Weger and Emmett's (2009) study, people who had romantic intentions toward their cross-sex friend were likely to report engaging in routine relationship activity, support and positivity, and flirtation, and were unlikely to report talking about the relationship with other people.

Individuals who reported low levels of romantic intent reported somewhat different patterns of maintenance behavior. In Guerrero and Chavez's (2005) study, individuals in both the rejects-romance and strictly platonic groups reported using less joint activity and flirtation but more talk about outside relationships, such as referring often to their boyfriend or girlfriend. This suggests that individuals who want to keep the relationship platonic refrain from flirting with each other so as not to lead each other on. They also limit their public appearances by showing up at parties separately and engaging in less joint activity in public settings. This may be a way of managing O'Meara's public presentation challenge; if they limit the amount of time they spend together, others are less likely to see them as a potentially romantic couple. Finally, individuals in the rejects-romance and strictly platonic groups are especially likely to talk about their boyfriends, girlfriends, or spouses (assuming that they are already in another romantic relationship), perhaps as a way of signaling that they are already taken.

Keeping Friendships Platonic

Although some cross-sex friends have to deal with the sexual and romantic challenges O'Meara proposed, most cross-sex friends define their relationships as strictly platonic (Guerrero & Chavez, 2005; Messman et al., 2000). There are at least six reasons why people in cross-sex friendships want to maintain the status quo and keep their relationships platonic (Messman et al., 2000). First, people report that it is important to safeguard the relationship; people worry that a shift toward romance could hurt the quality of their friendship or result in a breakup. Second, people reveal that they are not attracted to their friend in a romantic or sexual way. Third, people say that there would be network disapproval if they became romantically involved with their friend; people in their social network might get upset. Fourth, people keep friendships platonic because one or both members of the friendship are already involved in another romantic relationship. Fifth,

people experience risk aversion, which involves feeling uncertain about the partner's reaction and worrying about potentially being hurt or disappointed. Finally, people take a time-out, meaning they do not want a serious romantic relationship with anyone at the present time.

Of these six reasons, safeguarding the relationship was the most common, followed by lack of attraction and network disapproval. Risk aversion and time-out were least common. Sex differences for keeping friendships platonic also exist. Women are more likely than men to want to safeguard the relationship and to say they are not attracted to their friend in a romantic way (Messman et al., 2000).

People also use different maintenance behaviors depending on their reason for keeping the friendship platonic. In particular, people who want to safeguard the relationship are most likely to report using openness, positivity, joint activities, and supportiveness in their friendships. People were most likely to say they used avoidance if they reported risk aversion, network disapproval, and time-out as reasons for keeping the relationship platonic. Finally, people who were unattached to their friend reported that they avoided flirting as a way to maintain the relationship. To determine why you may keep one of your friendships platonic rather than romantic, take the test in Box 10.5.

BOX 10.5 PUT YOURSELF TO THE TEST
WHY DO YOU KEEP ONE OF YOUR CLOSE CROSS-SEX FRIENDSHIPS PLATONIC?

Think about why you have kept a relationship with a good friend (of the opposite sex if you are heterosexual or the same sex if you are gay) platonic. Rate the following reasons using this scale: 1 = strongly disagree and 7 = strongly agree.

	Strongly Disagree						Strongly Agree
I keep our friendship platonic because:							
1. My friend might reject me.	1	2	3	4	5	6	7
2. My friend and/or I are already dating someone else.	1	2	3	4	5	6	7
3. I do not want to risk losing our friendship.	1	2	3	4	5	6	7

(Continued)

BOX 10.5 (Continued)

4.	My friend is not the kind of person I want to be involved with in a romantic way.	1	2	3	4	5	6	7
5.	At this time, I am not ready for a romantic relationship with anyone.	1	2	3	4	5	6	7
6.	My friend might end up hurting my feelings.	1	2	3	4	5	6	7
7.	Other people would be upset if our relationship turned romantic.	1	2	3	4	5	6	7
8.	I value this person as a friend too much to change things.	1	2	3	4	5	6	7
9.	I think of this person *only* as a friend.	1	2	3	4	5	6	7
10.	My friend and/or I are already romantically involved with someone else.	1	2	3	4	5	6	7
11.	This person is not sexually attractive to me.	1	2	3	4	5	6	7
12.	I don't want to date anyone at this time.	1	2	3	4	5	6	7
13.	I am not sure that the romantic feelings I have for my friend are mutual.	1	2	3	4	5	6	7
14.	Some of my friends or family would be upset with me if our friendship turned romantic.	1	2	3	4	5	6	7
15.	My friend and/or I already have good romantic relationships with someone else.	1	2	3	4	5	6	7
16.	Getting romantic could cause problems within our social network.	1	2	3	4	5	6	7
17.	Getting romantic could ruin our friendship.	1	2	3	4	5	6	7
18.	I'm not interested in a romantic relationship right now.	1	2	3	4	5	6	7

To obtain your results, average your scores for the following items:

Emotional uncertainty: Items 1 + 6 + 13 = _____

Network disapproval: Items 7 + 14 + 16 = _____

Safeguard relationship: Items 3 + 8 + 17 = _____

Not attracted: Items 4 + 9 + 11 = _____

Time-out: Items 5 + 12 + 18 = _____

Third party: Items 2 + 10 + 15 = _____

Higher scores indicate stronger reasons for keeping your friendship platonic.

Source: Adapted from Messman, Canary, & Hause (2000).

MAINTENANCE CHALLENGES IN OTHER RELATIONSHIPS

Cross-sex friends are not the only individuals who sometimes face special challenges in their relationships. Scholars have also identified friends-with-benefits relationships, long-distance relationships, and cohabiting relationships as especially challenging to maintain.

Friends-With-Benefits Relationships

In contrast to platonic friendships, some friends decide to have sex but stay friends rather than become a romantic couple. This type of relationship, which has been called a **friends-with-benefits relationship** in television shows and the popular press, is fairly common on college campuses. Across various studies, between 47% and 68% of college students report that they are currently or had previously been involved in at least one relationship characterized as friends with benefits (Afifi & Faulkner, 2000; McGinty, Knox, & Zusman, 2007; Mongeau, Ramirez, & Vorrell, 2003; Reeder, 2000). The distinguishing characteristic of a friends-with-benefits relationship is that two people are having sex but do not consider themselves a romantic couple.

Although most studies have examined friends-with-benefits relationships as a form of cross-sex friendship, these relationships also occur between same-sex friends who are gay, lesbian, or bisexual. They can also take many shapes and forms. Mongeau and his colleagues (2013) described seven types of friends-with-benefits relationships:

- *True Friends* (26.1%): Close friends who add sex to their friendship but don't consider themselves a couple even though they care about each other as friends
- *Network Opportunism* (14.5%): Partners within the same social network who are not particularly close but serve as a "sexual backup" if neither of them are with anyone else
- *Just Sex* (12.4%): Sexual partners whose interaction revolves almost exclusively around

planning and having sex without any real emotional connection

- *Transition Out/Ex-Sex* (11.2%): Former romantic partners who are no longer an official couple but continue or resume their sex relationship sometime after they break up
- *Intentional Transition In* (8.4%): Partners decide to start out in a friends-with-benefits relationship with the intention of becoming a couple if everything goes well and then they successfully make the transition to a romantic relationship
- *Unintentional Transition In* (7.6%): Partners intend to keep the relationship as friends with benefits but end up emotionally attached and become a couple
- *Failed Transition* (6.8%): One or both partners enter the friends-with-benefits relationship with the intention of eventually becoming a couple, but instead they do not move beyond being friends with benefits.

The percentages after each type represent the percentage of college students who described their most recent friends-with-benefits relationship this way. The total does not equal 100% because some of the descriptions did not fit neatly into one category. For example, in an on-again off-again relationship, what starts out as a transition out (ex sex) may turn into an intentional or unintentional transition back in. As can be seen, only a little more than half of friends-with-benefits relationships are between two people who consider themselves to be friends (ranging from casual to close friends). Just over one third of friends-with-benefits relationships are between people who either had, intend to have, or end up in a romantic relationship with their partner. Moreover, of those who intend to move their friends-with-benefits relationship to a romantic relationship, only a little more than half succeed.

College students have described several advantages and disadvantages associated with friends-with-benefits relationships. These advantages differ based on the type of friends-with-benefits relationship people share. The overriding theme of the advantages is that a person is able to have "sex with a trusted other while avoiding commitment" (Bisson & Levine, 2009, p. 68), although this is mainly an advantage for those who are true friends, in the same network, just friends, or exes. Lack of commitment was mentioned as an advantage by almost 60% of students in Bisson and Levine's study. A smaller percentage of students (7.3%) listed "becoming closer" as an advantage. This is likely an advantage for those who intend to become a couple or for those in an on-again off-again relationship. Nearly 9% said that there were no advantages associated with friends-with-benefits relationships, even though they had participated in one.

In terms of disadvantages, students worried that unreciprocated romantic feelings, jealousy, or hurt might develop, all of which could harm the friendship. Concern about developing romantic feelings was the top disadvantage, with over 65% of students mentioning this possibility. Some students also listed lack of commitment as a disadvantage rather than an advantage, and others noted the possible negative consequences of having sex as a disadvantage. These disadvantages reflect the different types of friends-with-benefits relationships. For partners who do not want to be more than friends, unreciprocated feelings is likely a top concern, but for those who want the relationship to turn into more, lack of commitment would be seen as a disadvantage.

There may also be differences in how men and women view the advantages and disadvantages associated with friends-with-benefits relationships. In one study, women were more likely to emphasize the "friends" part of the relationship by focusing on emotions, whereas men were more likely to emphasize the "benefits" part of the relationship by focusing on sex (McGinty et al., 2007).

Given that many participants in friends-with-benefits relationships worry about the possibility of developing romantic feelings, it is not surprising that about half the participants in Bisson and Levine's (2009) study experienced some uncertainty about their friends-with-benefits relationship. Sources of uncertainty included how they should label their relationship, how their relationship might change in the future, how they felt about each other now that they were having sex, whether they could stay friends, and how they could maintain their relationship. Despite this uncertainty, 76% of the students in the study said that they did not initiate any discussion about these issues, and 66% reported that they never negotiated any ground rules for the relationship.

When friends with benefits do talk about these issues, they appear to focus on establishing rules that help them maintain their relationship so that neither party gets hurt. According to research by Hughes and colleagues (2005), the most common rule in friends-with-benefits relationships involves staying emotionally detached. Friends with benefits often agree not to get jealous or fall in love with one another (Hughes et al., 2005). This rule is probably only important in friends with benefits who fit the categories of true friends, just sex, network opportunism, and sometimes transition out. Other rules for maintaining these friendships include negotiations about sexual activity (e.g., agreeing to use condoms), communication (e.g., making rules about calling one another, being honest about other relationships), secrecy (e.g., agreeing not to tell common friends that they have sex), permanence (e.g., agreeing that the sexual part of the relationship is only temporary), and the friendship (e.g., agreeing to value the friendship over the sexual relationship).

Although many of these maintenance rules help friends with benefits maintain the status quo, this type of relationship sometimes ends completely, returns to friendship only (no sex), or turns into a romantic relationship (Hughes et al., 2005). Friends with benefits often keep the sexual aspect of their relationship private, yet Hughes and her colleagues found that these friendships are more likely to continue if their broader network of friends is accepting of the type of relationship they have. Of course, these types of friendships can be fraught with all kinds of challenges, including one friend wanting the relationship to turn romantic while the other person does not, or an ex using sex to try to get a former partner back when the partner just wants a friends-with-benefits relationship. Compared to other types of relationships, the friends-with-benefits relationship is probably one of the most challenging to maintain.

Long-Distance Relationships

Long-distance relationships can also be challenging to maintain. Many people have been in at least one long-distance romantic relationship, and virtually everyone has been in a long-distance relationship of some sort, whether it be with a friend or family member. With more individuals pursuing higher education, more couples having dual professional careers, and more people immigrating to the United States, the number of romantic partners separated by large distances is increasing. Within the college student population, between 25% and 50% of romantic relationships are long distance (Stafford, 2005) and approximately 3 million happily married couples in the United States are living apart at any given time (Bergen, Kirby, & McBride, 2007). Military couples, who make up part of this group, commonly face months of separation followed by reunions.

A primary challenge for maintaining long-distance romantic relationships is the lack of face-to-face communication (Stafford & Merolla, 2007), which is believed to be the glue that holds romantic relationships together. How, then, can couples stay close if partners are unable to engage in much face-to-face communication? Distance also prevents partners in long-distance relationships from displaying nonverbal affection, sharing most activities or tasks, and engaging in the same type of daily routine talk as couples in proximal relationships do. Indeed, studies show that people in long-distance relationships generally use less maintenance behavior, such as openness, assurances, and

joint activities, than people in geographically close relationships (Johnson, 2001; Van Horn et al., 1997). Yet many long-distance couples maintain happy relationships. In fact, studies suggest that individuals in romantic long-distance relationships are just as happy and maybe even more "in love" with their partners than are people in proximal romantic relationships (Dargie, Blair, Goldfinger, & Pukall, 2015; Stafford & Merolla, 2007; Stafford & Reske, 1990). Similarly, friends in long-distance relationships report as much relational satisfaction as friends in geographically close relationships (Johnson, 2001).

The concept of **idealization** has been offered as an explanation for why some long-distance relationships stay satisfying despite the lack of face-to-face interaction (Stafford & Reske, 1990). Idealization occurs when people describe their relationship and their partner in glowing, overly positive terms that sometimes reflect unrealistic expectations (Stafford & Merolla, 2007). This type of idealization keeps people committed to their relationships; dating couples are more likely to believe that they will get married one day if they idealize each other (Stafford & Reske, 1990). At first, it may seem counterintuitive that long-distance couples would idealize their relationships more than proximal couples would, but considering that people in such relationships were usually close before separating, these findings make sense. Moreover, partners in romantic long-distance relationships often think about how great their lives would be if they could be with their partners more of the time, making idealization more likely (Stafford & Reske, 1990); in this case, "absence indeed makes the heart grow fonder." Idealization may also be fueled by some of the communication patterns that typically occur in long-distance relationships, including reliance on mediated communication and the tendency to be on one's best behavior when together.

People in long-distance relationships often compensate for the lack of face-to-face communication by increasing their use of texting, snapping, and social media to maintain their relationships. Studies have shown that romantic couples (Billedo, Kerkhof, & Finkenauer, 2015) and friends (Vitak, 2014) who are in long-distance relationships use Facebook to maintain closeness more than do people who live near one another. Vitak (2014) identified four ways people use Facebook to maintain relationships: (a) supportive communication such as liking posts, (b) sharing interests, such as joining common Facebook groups, (c) passive browsing, such as scrolling through the partner's timeline, and (d) social information seeking, such as checking for updates. The latter two types of maintenance can provide information that is helpful when having voice-to-voice phone conversations or Facetiming. Using Skype is also related to being satisfied in a long-distance relationship (Kirk, 2013), presumably because it allows people to talk in real time while seeing one another.

Maintenance through media such as texting and social media may offer a skewed perception of a partner's communication style, in part because people can control their communication more in mediated contexts than they can in face-to-face contexts (Stafford & Merolla, 2007), which can lead to more-intimate interactions and more idealization. For example, partners likely pick up the phone when they feel like talking, something over which each partner has almost complete control. Moreover, if someone is not in the mood to talk, it is easy to let the call go to voicemail, or to ask the partner to call back at another time. One study found that, in long-distance relationships, texts, video chats, and phone calls are usually rated as highly intimate because partners focus on presenting themselves in a positive light and reducing uncertainty (Jiang & Hancock, 2013). Similar findings have been found for Internet-based relationships (Wright, 2004). People who send electronic messages showing positivity and openness tend to be regarded favorably by their Internet partners.

As these examples illustrate, individuals in long-distance relationships are typically on their best relational behavior when they are together. Compared to those in geographically close relationships, people in long-distance relationships tend to engage in less joint activities, task sharing, and social networking (Dainton & Aylor, 2001; Johnson, 2001), especially if they have limited contact with one another. However, when people in a long-distance relationship do get together, they often plan shared activities more carefully; work hard to treat each other in a fair and equitable manner; and have long, in-depth discussions. People in long-distance relationships often prepare well in advance for weekend visits and present an image of themselves that may not be consistent with the day-to-day reality of their lives. Dinner reservations are made, work calendars are cleared, and plans with friends and family are often suspended so the partners can spend quality time alone. Partners in proximal relationships seldom make such accommodations for each other. Thus, compared to partners in proximal relationships, partners in long-distance relationships often perceive that their communication is more restricted but of higher quality (Stafford & Reske, 1990). As Johnson (2001) stated, it may be the quality rather than the quantity of communication that is most important when it comes to maintaining long-distance relationships.

Although idealization helps long-distance partners maintain their relationships, it can also lead to difficulties when the relationship becomes proximal (Stafford & Merolla, 2007). Suddenly, the once seemingly perfect partner needs to study or write a report for work when the other partner wants to spend quality time together, and the sensitive issues that were never discussed over Facetime lead to conflict in actual face-to-face interaction. Stafford and Merolla found that long distance couples who moved close to one another were twice as likely to break up as those who remained apart. The more long-distance couples had idealized each other and their relationship, the more likely they were to break up after they moved near one another. This research suggests that partners in long-distance relationships may need to work to keep their expectations realistic so that they are not disappointed once the relationship becomes proximal. Some level of idealization is healthy in both proximal and long-distance relationships (Murray, Holmes, & Griffin, 1996), but too much idealization in long-distance relationships appears to make the transition to a proximal relationship more difficult (Stafford & Merolla, 2007).

Interestingly, military couples who often cycle back and forth between living together and living apart have some particularly helpful strategies and perspectives for dealing with separation and reunion. Army wives reported some paradoxes in how they would maintain their relationships before, during, and after their husbands' deployment (Maguire, Heinemann-LaFave, & Sahlstein, 2013). Some recognized that there could be too much communication while they were separated. For example, if they shared too much while they were separated they would have less to talk about when reunited. One of the wives also noted that it was hard to stay connected on WebCam because she couldn't reach out and touch her husband, and another said that when her husband sent her gifts, it just made her miss him more. Wives also reported activities such as focusing on themselves and writing their thoughts and feelings down in a journal as ways to cope with the separation. These types of maintenance strategies may help reduce idealization in couples who endure repeated separations.

In sum, the good news is that long-distance relationships are as stable and satisfying, and perhaps more emotionally intense, than are proximal relationships (Van Horn et al., 1997). The bad news is that friends and romantic partners in long-distance relationships sometimes get frustrated with their lack of face-to-face communication (Rohlfing, 1995). Romantic partners in long-distance relationships also need to ensure that their positive perceptions of each other are not a function of idealization. This may be the biggest challenge facing long-distance partners who wish to maintain their relationships.

Cohabiting Relationships

Cohabitation, or living together without being married, can also pose some special challenges when it comes to maintaining relationships. Most couples initially view cohabitation as a transitional period that occurs between dating and marriage, or as a sort of precursor to marriage, and most couples in the United States live together for at least a short time before marrying (Rhoades, Stanley, & Markman, 2012). In a large survey of cohabiting and dating couples, Willoughby, Carroll, and Busby (2011) found that 92.5% of cohabiting couples were planning to marry each other someday, but not necessarily soon. Yet studies suggest that fewer than half of cohabiting partners end up getting married to each other. In a study conducted from 2006 to 2010 by the National Center for Health, around 40% of the couples who were cohabiting at the beginning of the study were married three years later, around 32% were still living together but not married, and about 27% were no longer together ("Key Statistics," 2015).

The question then becomes this: Are cohabiting couples less likely to maintain their relationships than couples who do not live together before marriage? In line with this question, much of the research on cohabitation has focused on determining whether cohabitation is beneficial or harmful to long-term relationships. Researchers have compared couples who married without cohabiting first to couples who cohabited before getting married. Researchers have also compared cohabiting couples who marry to those who do not. These studies have focused on a number of issues, including relationship stability, relational quality, and communication patterns.

RELATIONSHIP STABILITY In general, marital relationships are more stable than cohabiting relationships. Some scholars have argued that cohabitation represents a looser bond than marriage because cohabitation involves more autonomy, less commitment, and fewer social and legal barriers to dissolution than does marriage (Thorton, Axinn, & Teachman, 1995). For instance, a cohabiting couple is less likely to share property than a marital couple, and cohabiting couples can break up without having to file any legal paperwork. The **selection effect** provides another explanation for the instability found in some cohabiting relationships (Lillard, Brien, & Waite, 1995). According to the selection effect, people who choose to cohabit rather than marry have certain preexisting personal characteristics and attitudes that make it less likely that their relationships will last. These attitudes include greater acceptance of divorce and premarital sex, stronger needs for autonomy, and more negative feelings about marriage (Cunningham & Antill, 1994; Lillard et al., 1995; Rindfuss & VandenHeuvel, 1990). Willoughby and his colleagues (2011) summarized research showing that throughout the 21st century in the United States there has been a consistent pattern with couples who cohabit before marriage more likely to divorce than couples who do not; and this pattern is found in other cultures as well. However, the timing of cohabitation makes a difference. Couples who wait to move in together until after they are engaged are less prone to divorce than couples who move in together without being engaged (Rhoades, Stanley, & Markman, 2009).

RELATIONAL QUALITY Some studies have shown that married couples who do not live together prior to marriage are more satisfied with their relationships than are cohabiting couples or couples who transition from cohabitation to marriage (Nock, 1995; Stafford, Kline, & Rankin, 2004). Other studies found no difference (Yelsma, 1986). Brown and Booth (1996) found that cohabitors who planned to get married were just as satisfied with their relationships as married couples, whereas cohabitors who did not plan to marry were less satisfied. Similarly, Willoughby et al. (2011) demonstrated that couples who waited to move in together until they

were engaged had better marriages than those who moved in earlier. Another study showed that when couples make the transition from dating to cohabiting there is a decline in satisfaction but an increase in commitment. There are also more constraints keeping the couple from breaking up (Rhoades et al., 2012). Shared bills and possessions, a common social network, and a more public display of commitment all work to keep cohabiting couples together.

Importantly, time in the relationship may be a better predictor of relational satisfaction than whether a couple lived together before marriage. Satisfaction levels appear to decrease over time in marriages regardless of whether couples cohabited or not (Stafford et al., 2004). This same pattern has been found in relationships between cohabiting gay and lesbian couples. In one study, satisfaction dropped during the first year that gay and lesbian couples lived together but then rebounded again after they had lived together 11 years or longer (Kurdek, 1989). Couples who move directly toward marriage may still be in the honeymoon phase of their relationships, and, therefore, might still be on their best behavior, using a lot of prosocial maintenance behaviors. Those who cohabited before marriage may have already moved beyond the honeymoon stage. Thus, some of the differences that researchers have found may be due more to time in the relationship than whether a couple had cohabited (Stafford et al., 2004).

COMMUNICATION PATTERNS Time may also be a better predictor of communication patterns than whether a couple cohabited or not. Stafford and her colleagues (2004) compared three types of couples at two points in time over a 5-year period: (1) cohabiting couples who had not married, (2) transitioned couples who had moved from cohabiting to marriage, and (3) married couples. Across all three types of couples, people reported less satisfaction, less sexual interaction, more conflict, and more heated arguing over time. There were also some small differences in communication among the three types of couples. Cohabiting couples reported the most conflict, followed by transitioned couples. Married couples reported the least conflict. Cohabiting couples were also more likely to report violent behavior, such as hitting or throwing something, than either transitioned or married couples.

Other studies have found similar results. Brownridge and Halli (2000) reported that couples who lived together before marriage were 54% more likely to engage in violent behavior than couples who did not live together prior to marriage. Another study showed that cohabiting couples have more conflict than married couples (Nock, 1995). However, these differences may be strongest when the comparison is between married couples and cohabiting couples who do not plan to marry. Cohabiting couples who plan to marry do not differ from married couples in terms of conflict or violence (Brown & Booth, 1996).

Together, these studies suggest that cohabiting relationships are most likely to be characterized by satisfaction and high-quality communication when the couple plans to marry. In addition, it is important that partners have congruent perceptions about the future of the relationship and when they will marry. Willoughby and his colleagues (2011) classified couples into the following four groups:

- *Engaged, Incongruent* (around 59% of cohabiting couples): The couple plans to marry but each partner has different perceptions about when and how soon this will happen.
- *Engaged, Fast* (around 19% of cohabiting couples): The couple plans to marry and both agree that it will be soon.
- *Engaged, Slow* (around 14% of cohabiting couples): The couple plans to marry and both agree that it will not be for a while.
- *Not Engaged* (around 7.5% of cohabiting couples): The couple has no plans to marry.

The couples who were in the engaged/fast and engaged/slow groups fared the best in terms of relational satisfaction and better communication. This suggests that partners who are engaged and have a similar view of when they will marry have the easiest time maintaining their relationships. Unfortunately, though, in Willoughby et al.'s (2011) study most partners did not have congruent perspectives on when they would marry. It is important to remember that cohabiting relationships that are characterized by positive interaction and low levels of destructive conflict are usually as stable and satisfying as happy marriages (Brown, 2000). Therefore, using some of the prosocial maintenance behaviors discussed earlier, such as positivity and constructive conflict management, may be especially important for sustaining cohabiting relationships.

EQUITY THEORY

Equity also plays an important role in maintaining many types of relationships and may be especially important when people live together. Equity theory focuses on determining whether the distribution of resources is fair to both relational partners (Deutsch, 1985). Equity is measured by comparing the ratio of contributions (or costs) and benefits (or rewards) for each person. The key word here is *ratio*. Partners do not have to receive equal benefits (e.g., receiving the same amount of love, care, and financial security) or make equal contributions (e.g., investing the same amount of effort, time, and financial resources) as long as the ratio between these benefits and contributions is similar.

For example, as they prepare for their upcoming wedding, Rachel might put a lot more effort into planning and making the arrangements than Yasser, but having a certain type of wedding may also be more important to Rachel than to Yasser. Thus, even though Rachel is making more contributions, she is also getting more benefits when it comes to planning the wedding. To put it in numeric terms, Rachel may be making 10 contributions to planning the wedding, but she will also reap 20 benefits. Yasser, on the other hand, may be making five contributions, but getting only 10 benefits. Their ratios of 10 to 20 and 5 to 10 are equitable—they both get two benefits for each contribution they make in connection to their wedding.

When determining how equitable or inequitable a relationship is, it is also important to consider that both equity and **inequity** occur at general levels as well as specific levels (Henningsen, Serewicz, & Carpenter, 2009). **General equity** (or inequity) represents an overall assessment of balance between two people's benefits and contributions. **Specific equity** focuses on the balance between people's benefits and contributions in a specific area, such as physical attractiveness, financial resources, social status, ability to influence each other, and supportiveness. A relationship can be unbalanced in terms of specific equity but balanced overall. For example, Yasser and Rachel's relationship is unequal but equitable when it comes to the wedding plans, but it may not be equitable in other areas. When it comes to the household chores, Rachel may do more than Yasser, leading her to feel frustrated at times. Yet Yasser may work harder to maintain their relationship by doing special things for Rachel, such as fixing her a nice dinner or rubbing her back and shoulders when she is tired after a long day's work. In terms of relational maintenance, then, Yasser does more than Rachel. Because each of them makes more contributions in some areas than others, their level of general equity may be balanced.

Principles of Equity Theory

Since Yasser and Rachel have an equitable relationship, they are likely to experience more satisfaction and commitment than a couple in an inequitable relationship would, largely because people feel distress when inequity is perceived to exist (Adams, 1965; Walster, Berscheid, & Walster, 1973; Walster, Walster, & Berscheid, 1978). Five principles help explain why benefits and equity are associated with relational satisfaction and commitment (Canary & Stafford, 2001; Guerrero, La Valley, & Farinelli, 2008; Walster, Walster, & Berscheid, 1978):

1. Individuals try to maximize their benefits so that the benefits they receive in their relationships outweigh their costs and contributions.
2. People in groups and dyads develop rules for distributing resources fairly.
3. Within groups and dyads, people will reward those who treat them equitably and punish those who treat them inequitably.
4. When individuals are in inequitable relationships, they will experience distress. This distress will lead them to try to restore equity, such that the more distress they experience, the harder they will try to alleviate that stress.
5. Individuals in equitable relationships experience more satisfaction. They also engage in more prosocial communication, including relational maintenance behavior, than do individuals in inequitable relationships.

These principles have been tested and supported for people in the United States and other Western cultures. In other cultures, equity may operate differently (see Box 10.6).

BENEFITS OF EQUITY Around half of spouses report that their marriages are equitable (Peterson, 1990). Partners who perceive equity tend to be satisfied with and committed to their relationships. Early work on equity theory showed that individuals who perceived their dating relationships to be equitable reported being happier and more content than those who perceived their dating relationships to be inequitable (Walster, Walster, & Traupmann, 1978). Later work on married couples showed that people who perceive equity or see themselves as overbenefited are happier than those who perceive themselves as underbenefited (Buunk & Mutsaers, 1999; Guerrero et al., 2008). Couples who perceive equity also tend to report more commitment to their relationships (Crawford, Feng, Fischer, & Diana, 2003). Equity in specific areas is also related to satisfaction and commitment. For example, one study showed that when partners are equitable in how much they influence one another, they report more

BOX 10.6 AROUND THE WORLD
EQUITY ACROSS DIFFERENT CULTURES

Some researchers have suggested that equity and equality are valued differently depending on how fairness is conceptualized within a culture. People in Australia, North America (excluding Mexico), and Western Europe prefer equity, which means that they believe resources should be distributed based on the contributions people make. In contrast, people in Asia and Eastern Europe prefer **equality,** which means that they believe resources should be distributed equally among people regardless of their contributions (Carson & Banuazizi, 2008; Leung, 1988; Powell, 2005). For example, one study showed that people from the United States preferred equity more than people from Korea (Kim, Park, & Suzuki, 1990). Another study showed that inequity was related to anger and decreased liking for

people from the United States but not for people from Korea (Westerman, Park, & Lee, 2007). Yum and Canary (2009) examined the link between equity and relational maintenance behavior, such as being positive and open, in six countries—China, the Czech Republic, Japan, South Korea, Spain, and the United States. This link was strongest in the United States, followed by Spain. In these countries, people reported using more prosocial communication to maintain relationships that were perceived as equitable. However, equity was not related to maintenance behavior in China, the Czech Republic, Japan, or South Korea. These findings highlight that while equity is an important concept in the United States and other Western cultures, it is somewhat less important in other cultures.

satisfaction and commitment in their relationship (Weigel, Bennett, & Ballard-Reisch, 2006).

Communication patterns may contribute to the satisfaction that couples in equitable relationships experience. For instance, couples and friends in equitable relationships report using more relational maintenance behavior than those in inequitable relationships (Canary & Stafford, 2001; Messman et al., 2000; Stafford & Canary, 2006). In particular, the maintenance behaviors of positivity, openness, and assurances are related to equity. Couples in equitable relationships also say that they express anger, guilt, and sadness in more constructive ways than do couples in inequitable relationships (Guerrero et al., 2008). For example, they talk about their anger in an assertive manner without resorting to aggression.

When relationships are inequitable, one individual is **overbenefited** and the other is **underbenefited** (Walster, Walster, & Berscheid, 1978). The overbenefited individual receives more benefits or makes fewer contributions, or both, than does the partner, so that the ratio between them is unbalanced. In simple terms, this person is getting the "better deal." In the scenario depicting Rachel as

doing more household chores than Yasser, Yasser is overbenefited. The underbenefited individual, by contrast, receives fewer benefits or makes greater contributions than does the partner, so that the ratio between them is not balanced. This person is getting the "worse deal," as Rachel is when it comes to doing the household chores. Theoretically, inequity should always entail one person being overbenefited and the other person being underbenefited. However, perception does not always match reality. Because people tend to overestimate their own contributions to relationships, both dyadic members might think they are underbenefited even though this is not actually the case. For example, in a classic study by Ross and Sicoly (1979), husbands and wives rated the degree to which they had responsibility for various activities, such as caring for the children, washing the dishes, and handling the finances, on a scale from 0 (no responsibility) to 150 (complete responsibility). Thus, if a husband and wife split the task of doing the dishes evenly, both should have rated their responsibility at the 75-point midpoint. However, the results suggested that 73% of the spouses overestimated the amount of work they did; when their ratings were summed and averaged across all the activities, they totaled over 150 points. (Apparently, a lot of dishes were being cleaned twice!) As this example illustrates, relational partners like Rachel and Yasser might both perceive themselves to be underbenefited, but in reality, it would be impossible for each person to be getting a worse deal than the other.

CONSEQUENCES OF UNDERBENEFITED INEQUITY According to equity theory, whether people are over- or underbenefited, they experience increases in distress and decreases in satisfaction and happiness (Walster, Walster, & Berscheid, 1978). Of course, underbenefited individuals experience a different kind of stress than overbenefited individuals. As you might suspect, underbenefited individuals are usually more distressed than overbenefited individuals (Canary & Stafford, 1994). They also report the least relational satisfaction (Buunk & Mutsaers, 1999; Guerrero et al., 2008). When people are underbenefited, they tend to feel cheated, used, and taken for granted, and they experience anger or sadness (Walster, Walster, & Traupmann, 1978). Men may be particularly likely to be angry when they are underbenefited, while women may be especially likely to be sad, disappointed, or frustrated (Sprecher, 1986, 2001). Both men and women report expressing anger more aggressively when they are in the underbenefited position (Guerrero et al., 2008).

Underbenefited individuals also report that both they and their partners use less prosocial forms of communication. In a study on relational maintenance behaviors, underbenefited husbands reported that their wives used less positivity, offered fewer assurances, and shared fewer tasks than did overbenefited husbands and husbands in equitable relationships (Canary & Stafford, 1992). Therefore, people may feel underbenefited if they do not receive adequate amounts of relational maintenance. Another study showed that the more women are underbenefited, the less likely they are to use positivity and social networking (Ledbetter et al., 2013). People who are underbenefited in terms of supportiveness

or physical attractiveness put less effort into comforting their partners when they are distressed (Henningsen et al., 2009). These studies suggest that people who are underbenefited might not feel like exerting much effort into maintaining a dissatisfying or unfair relationship. Doing so could make them even more underbenefited.

CONSEQUENCES OF OVERBENEFITED INEQUITY Overbenefited individuals tend to experience less distress than their underbenefited counterparts but more distress than individuals who are in equitable relationships (Guerrero et al., 2008; Sprecher, 1986, 2001; Walster, Walster, & Traupmann, 1978). People who perceive themselves as overbenefited may also feel smothered and wish that their partner would spend less time doing things for them. One study showed that overbenefited wives tend to express guilt by apologizing and doing nice things for their husbands (Guerrero et al., 2008). Another study showed that people who are overbenefited in terms of the balance of supportiveness in their relationship report using the most sophisticated comforting strategies when their partner is distressed (Henningsen et al., 2009). Thus, when people perceive themselves to be overbenefited, they might use prosocial behaviors to try to balance their relationships by increasing their partner's rewards. Yet some research shows that people in the overbenefited position use less relational maintenance behavior. For example, Ledbetter et al. (2013) found that the more overbenefited people were, the less likely they were to use social networking and task sharing. Both of these activities involves spending time together, so perhaps overbenefited individuals avoid these behaviors so as not to feel overwhelmed or smothered in a relationship where they already get a high level of benefits.

Not surprisingly, some overbenefited men and women feel quite content with their relationships and not guilty at all (Hatfield, Greenberger, Traupmann, & Lambert, 1982; Traupmann, Hatfield, & Wexler, 1983). One study even showed that people are increasingly happy the more overbenefited they are (Buunk & Mutsaers, 1999). People may need to be highly overbenefited before they experience distress and guilt. By contrast, being even somewhat underbenefited can lead to anger and frustration. In any case, if people perceive enough inequity, feelings of anger, sadness, and guilt may pervade the emotional fabric of the relationship and threaten its stability.

Reducing Distress in Inequitable Relationships

What happens when relational partners experience inequity and distress? According to Walster, Walster, and Berscheid (1978), they will be motivated to reduce inequity and the accompanying distress. There are three general ways to do this. The first two ways can help people maintain their relationships—they can either restore actual equity or adjust their perceptions. The third option is to leave the relationship.

RESTORING ACTUAL EQUITY People can attempt to restore actual equity by changing their behavior. For example, the overbenefited partner might contribute more to the relationship, whereas the underbenefited partner might do less. Alternatively, the underbenefited partner might ask the overbenefited partner to do more. Some research suggests that underbenefited people are more likely to ask their partners to change their behaviors to restore equity, whereas overbenefited people are more likely to change their own behavior (Westerman et al., 2007). This makes sense from an equity theory standpoint. Underbenefited individuals probably feel that they are already in a disadvantaged position, so why should they change their behavior? Overbenefited individuals, on the other hand, may change their behavior to make the relationship more equitable, thereby protecting the benefits they gain from being in the relationship.

ADJUSTING PSYCHOLOGICAL EQUITY People can also attempt to restore psychological equity. Recall that to some extent equity is "in the eye of the beholder" in that perceptions are as important as actions. To restore equity, people sometimes reassess their costs and benefits and decide that they are actually getting a fairer deal than they first thought. For instance, if Rachel gets really frustrated about putting more effort into the household chores, she might take a minute and reflect on all he does for her. She might realize that Yasser actually does a lot for her. He massages her when her back and shoulders hurt, even if he is bone tired, and he regularly proofreads reports before she submits them to her boss, just to double-check that everything is right. When she thinks about all the special things he does for her—both on a routine basis and as a special treat—she recognizes that in actuality she is getting a fair deal. Sometimes mental adjustments such as these represent the situation more accurately than an initial assessment. However, there is also a potential danger in using this strategy. Individuals might continually readjust their perceptions even though the situation is, in actuality, inequitable. If this happens, a person might remain stuck in the underbenefited or overbenefited position.

LEAVING THE RELATIONSHIP Sometimes people temporarily leave as a way to try to restore equity. For example, Rachel could leave for a few days so that Yasser realizes how messy the place would be if she were not there to clean it up. Another way to restore equity, which is sometimes a last resort, is to end the relationship entirely. This is most likely to occur when people are receiving few benefits and making considerable contributions to the relationship, as explained next.

Combined Influence of Benefit-Cost Ratios and Equity

Although equity relates to a host of positive processes in relationships, equity does not tell the whole story. To be highly satisfied, a couple also needs to be in a relationship in which benefits outweigh costs. **Costs** include people's contributions, such as the time and effort they put into accomplishing tasks and maintaining their relationships, as well as the negative consequences of being in a relationship, such as having conflict and losing opportunities. Studies by Cate and his associates showed that the overall level of benefits (or rewards) associated with a relationship is more important than equity (Cate & Lloyd, 1988; Cate, Lloyd, & Henton, 1985; Cate, Lloyd, & Long, 1988). Some level of inequity might be inconsequential if both partners are receiving enough benefits. Thus, relationships that are characterized by equity as well as high levels of benefits are most likely to be satisfying. Relationships that are inequitable with benefits outweighing costs should also be satisfying, especially if the benefits are high and the inequity is fairly small. By contrast, relationships that are equitable with costs outweighing benefits are likely to be perceived as fair but somewhat dissatisfying. Finally, inequitable relationships in which costs outweigh benefits are the least satisfying.

Let's take a look at some examples that illustrate how equity and benefit-cost levels work together. Imagine that Joe and Darren are in a satisfied, committed relationship. Suppose that Joe receives 25 benefits for every 5 contributions he makes to his relationship with Darren. This means that Joe has a benefit-contribution ratio of 25:5. Darren has a ratio of 50:10. Is their relationship equitable or inequitable? Because both Joe and Darren are receiving five benefits per contribution, their relationship is equitable. Notice that for the relationship to be equitable, Joe and Darren do not have to be receiving the exact same number of benefits, nor do they have to be making the same number of contributions. Instead, the ratios between each person's benefits and contributions must be the same. Notice also that their benefits outweigh their costs. Thus, Darren and Joe's relationship is equitable and rewarding and as a consequence satisfying.

In other cases, relationships can be equitable without being particularly rewarding. Imagine that Garrett has a benefit-contribution ratio of 15:30 while Sophia has a benefit-contribution ratio of 10:20. Both individuals are getting one benefit for every two contributions they make, so the relationship is equitable. But would Garrett and Sophia have a satisfying relationship? The answer seems to be yes and no. They might be satisfied in that both are getting a fair deal but dissatisfied because they are not maximizing their benefits, which, as discussed previously, is the first principle of equity theory. It would be better to be in a relationship where benefits outweigh costs even if that relationship was somewhat inequitable. In this case, if they wanted to maintain their relationship, it might be wise for Garrett and Sophia to increase their use of prosocial maintenance behavior so that they would both be receiving more benefits.

SUMMARY AND APPLICATION

The research on relational maintenance offers couples such as Rachel and Yasser advice about how to keep their relationship strong. Both routine and strategic maintenance are related to satisfaction, but routine behavior may be a little more important. Therefore, it is essential that Yasser and Rachel settle into a routine that includes prosocial maintenance behaviors, such as asking about each other's day and sharing tasks in a fair and equitable manner. For married couples, positivity and assurances appear to be especially effective maintenance behaviors. Rachel therefore might try to compliment Yasser once in a while and to act cheerful and optimistic. Rachel might periodically offer Yasser assurances that she loves him and is committed to their relationship. Yasser should do the same. The couple should also focus on doing things together such as joint activities and social networking, as maintenance behavior. Engaging in these activities creates a partnership, reinforces similarity, and allows couples to have fun together.

Rachel wondered if getting married would change their relationship. It likely would.

Long-term committed relationships, such as marriage, tend to contain less openness but more social networking, task sharing, and constructive conflict management. Although Rachel and Yasser may engage in especially high levels of maintenance at the beginning of their marriage, these levels are likely to drop over time, especially if they have children. Later in life, however, maintenance behaviors may show a resurgence when they retire or their children leave the nest, giving Rachel and Yasser more time to spend together. Cohabiting before their marriage could also change their relationship. Research suggests that couples who cohabit before marrying sometimes have more conflict and are more likely to divorce than couples who do not live together before marriage. However, Rachel and Yasser are much less likely to experience these problems because they are engaged and already planning a wedding, rather than cohabiting without being seriously committed to one another.

As the wedding approaches, Rachel may get absorbed in the planning and, as a result, pay less attention to Yasser. This is why routine maintenance is so important: Routine patterns of prosocial maintenance behavior help sustain relationships even when couples have little time to focus on one another. Yasser might feel a little neglected, and Rachel may feel overworked because she is doing a disproportionate share of the wedding planning and the household chores. This is where equity theory comes in. One of the cornerstones of a happy relationship is that partners believe that resources are being shared in an equitable manner, such that there is a fair distribution of benefits and costs in a relationship. It is also important that both partners are getting more benefits than costs. For Rachel and Yasser, there may be inequity in some areas. Rachel is doing more of the wedding planning and household chores. Yasser generally does more favors and other special things for Rachel. But when everything is considered together, the relationship is balanced. Even more importantly, both Yasser and Rachel are receiving more benefits than costs as a result of being in a relationship together. Keeping benefits high in comparison to costs, sustaining equity, and using prosocial maintenance behavior are some of the secret ingredients that help couples like Yasser's parents maintain a happy relationship across the years.

KEY TERMS

avoidance (p. 261)

costs (p. 283)

cyber emigrant relationships (p. 263)

equality (p. 281)

equity (p. 279)

equity theory (p. 258)

failed transition, as a type of friends-with-benefits relationship (p. 273)

friends-with-benefits relationship (p. 273)

general equity (p. 280)

idealization (p. 275)

inequity (p. 280)

intentional transition in, as a type of friends-with-benefits relationship (p. 273)

jealousy induction (p. 261)

just sex, as a type of friends-with-benefits relationship (p. 273)

modality (p. 259)

network opportunism, as a type of friends-with-

benefits relationship (p. 273)

overbenefited (p. 281)

Pinocchio relationships (p. 263)

relational maintenance (p. 258)

relational satisfaction (p. 259)

romantic intent (p. 270)

routine maintenance behaviors (p. 265)

selection effect (p. 278)

specific equity (p. 280)

strategic maintenance
behaviors (p. 265)

transition out, as a type of
friends-with-benefits
relationship (p. 273)

true friends, as a type
of friends-with-benefits
relationship
(p. 273)

underbenefited (p. 281)

unintentional transition in,
as a type of friends-with-
benefits relationship
(p. 273)

virtual relationships (p. 263)

DISCUSSION QUESTIONS

1. How challenging do you think it is to maintain
    different types of cross-sex friendships,
    including friends with benefits? How might the
    type of cross-sex friendship (or friends-with-
    benefits relationship) make a difference in how
    you would maintain it?

2. Based on the information in this chapter,
    what five pieces of advice do you think would
    be most important to share with someone
    like Rachel who wants to maintain a
    relationship? How might your advice change if

Rachel's marriage would be long-distance
at times?

3. How important do you think equity is in
    relationships? Think about your relationships
    with romantic partners, friends, and family
    members. Have you had any conflict about
    equity (or fairness) in any of those relationships?
    If so, what did you have conflict about? Finally,
    do you agree that it is more important for
    benefits to outweigh costs than for a relationship
    to be equitable?

 SAGE edge™

Sharpen your skills with SAGE edge at edge.sagepub.com/guerrero5e.
SAGE edge for students provides a personalized approach to help you accomplish your coursework
goals in an easy-to-use learning environment.

11 COPING WITH CONFLICT
When Relational Partners Disagree

Mary and Doug catch their teenage daughter, Amanda, smoking after school with her friends. Because Mary is convinced that Amanda's friends are a bad influence on her, she wants to ground Amanda for a month, making her come home immediately after school. Doug, however, thinks grounding will be more of a punishment for the parents than Amanda because she will be moping around the house complaining all the time and arguing with her twin sister, Megan. Instead, Doug proposes that they deduct the cost of a carton of cigarettes from Amanda's weekly allowance for the next 6 months. Mary objects, saying that she does not want Amanda to be motivated to change her behavior because of money. Both parents feel strongly that their punishment is best, leading to a disagreement.

If you were Amanda's parent, how would you want to handle this situation? From Amanda's perspective, which punishment would most likely be effective? Are there other types of punishment—besides grounding or reducing Amanda's allowance—that might actually be more effective? What conflict management styles might Mary and Doug use to deal with this situation, and are there any conflict behaviors that are especially destructive?

Contrary to popular perception, conflict is not inherently good or bad. Depending on how people manage conflict, disagreement can either make a relationship stronger or weaker. Indeed, the literature on interpersonal conflict demonstrates that people have a variety of options for dealing with conflict. Some of these options involve cooperating and managing conflict productively and effectively. Other options are aggressive and competitive, which can lead to distress and exacerbation of the problem. Effective conflict management is essential for maintaining a healthy and happy relationship.

In this chapter, we examine how relational partners cope with disagreement. First, we define conflict and discuss the role conflict plays in close relationships, including those between spouses, family members, friends, and romantic partners. Next, we turn our attention to how people communicate during conflict situations. We review six conflict styles—(1) **competitive fighting,** (2) **compromising,** (3) **collaborating,**

(4) **indirect fighting,** (5) **avoiding,** and (6) **yielding.** We also discuss patterns of communication, such as negative reciprocity and demand-withdraw. The chapter ends with practical rules for constructive conflict management.

CONFLICT IN RELATIONSHIPS

Think about all the positive and negative experiences you have had with close friends, family members, and romantic partners. As you reflect on these experiences, can you think of a close relationship of yours that has not included some conflict or disagreement? If you can, that relationship is the exception to the rule.

Defining Conflict

Notice that we asked you to try and think of a close relationship that did not include some level of conflict or disagreement. When people think about "conflict" in their relationships, they usually imagine angry voices, name-calling, and relationship problems. However, conflict is more synonymous with the term *disagreement* than with yelling or arguing. People can engage in conflict by using positive forms of communication during disagreements, such as collaboration and compromise. Voices can be calm, negative emotions muted, positions can be validated, and relationships can be strengthened instead of weakened. In line with these ideas, Hocker and Wilmot (2013) defined **conflict** as "an expressed struggle between at least two interdependent parties who perceive incompatible goals, scare resources, and interference from others in achieving their goals" (p. 13).

When people are interdependent, a lack of compatibility can interfere with each person's ability to reach personal goals. Understandably, some forms of incompatibility are more important than others. Hocker and Wilmot (2013) argued that incompatibility will likely lead to a struggle when rewards are scarce. The various issues linked to conflict in different relationships, as listed in Box 11.1,

BOX 11.1 HIGHLIGHTS
COMMON CONFLICT ISSUES IN VARIOUS RELATIONSHIPS

Parents and Young Children	Parents and Teenagers	Siblings	Married Couples
Possessions	Curfew	Possessions	Household Labor
Caretaking*	Friends	Privacy	Money and Possessions
Hurtful Behavior**	Dating Patterns	Parental Attention	Jealousy/Possessiveness
Rules and Manners	Privacy	Territory	Sex
Need for Assistance***	Lifestyle Choices		Children

Sources: Canary, Cupach, & Messman (1995); Dunn (1983); Dunn & Kendrick (1982); Eisenberg (1992); Gottman (1994); Mead, Vatcher, Wyne, & Roberts (1990).

*Caretaking refers to tasks such as having to take a bath.
**Hurtful behavior refers to behaviors such as calling a sibling names.
***Need for assistance refers to demands to be helped or left alone, such as a child not wanting any help brushing teeth.

highlight incompatibility as the central theme. In addition, conflict is most likely when incompatible goals are important to both people and are difficult to obtain because there is interference from one another or from others. For example, you can imagine Amanda (a teenager) wanting to stay out later than her parents want her to (curfew); Amanda and her sister, Megan, arguing about who gets more space in the bedroom closet they share (territory); and Amanda's parents arguing over how to best discipline her for smoking (children). In all of these cases, someone is interfering with someone else's goals. Amanda's parents are preventing her from staying out as late as she wants and Megan is trying to limit her closet space. Mary and Doug are getting in the way of how they each think Amanda should be punished.

Frequency of Conflict in Various Relationships

Conflict is most likely to occur in the context of close relationships. In a study by Argyle and Furnham (1983), people rated different relationships in terms of frequency of conflict and degree of emotional and relational closeness. Spouses reported the most closeness but also the most conflict. Indeed, most romantic couples have between one and three disagreements per week, with one or two disagreements per month being particularly unpleasant (Canary et al., 1995). Unhappy couples often experience much more conflict; one study found that distressed couples reported having 5.4 conflicts over a 5-day period (see Canary et al., 1995). Yet another study showed that conflict increased as relational partners became more committed and interdependent (Lloyd & Cate, 1985). Together these studies make an important point: Although too much conflict may reflect relational problems, some level of conflict is normal and healthy in close relationships. As we shall see later, the way people manage conflict is even more important than the frequency of conflict. In Argyle and Furnham's study, family relationships, including parents and children or siblings, were also high in both conflict and closeness. Conversely,

relationships between neighbors were low in both conflict and closeness. Across the life span, conflict is more likely to occur within family and romantic relationships than friendships or work relationships (Sillars, Canary, & Tafoya, 2004). In parent–child relationships, the most conflict tends to occur when children are toddlers or teenagers. One study showed that disputes between mothers and their 18- to 36-month-old children occurred around seven times per hour, with about half of these disputes being brief and the other half lasting longer and being more competitive (Dunn & Munn, 1987). During the teenage years, around 20% of parents and adolescents complain that they have too much conflict with one another. When children reach late adolescence and early adulthood, conflict typically declines (Paikoff & Brooks-Gunn, 1991).

Like conflict between parents and children, conflict between siblings is often intense during early childhood and adolescence (Arliss, 1993). Same-sex siblings of about the same age are particularly likely to engage in frequent, competitive fighting. In fact, adolescent siblings are unlikely to compromise with one another. Instead, their conflict often ends in a standoff or in intervention by another family member or friend (Laursen & Collins, 1994). Yet siblings also share a unique bond. They usually know each other most of their lives; the sibling relationship predates romantic relationships and typically outlives parent–child relationships. Many siblings not only survive stormy periods of conflict but also develop a close and special bond as adults.

Effects of Conflict on Relationships

The way people manage conflict is more important than how much people disagree. Of course, when partners argue a lot, it could be a sign that there are unresolved problems in the relationship. Frequent arguing is also associated with more use of aggressive communication, with aggressive communication tied to low levels of relationship satisfaction. One study found that wives who reported high levels of marital conflict were almost one and a half times more at risk for divorce than were wives who reported less conflict (Orbuch, Veroff, Hassan, & Horrocks, 2002). However, the destructiveness of conflict was an even more potent predictor of divorce, and this finding was consistent across both husbands and wives, with couples who reported yelling, exchanging insults, and criticizing one another more likely to divorce (Orbuch et al., 2002). Couples who argue frequently and in an aggressive manner also report reduced commitment (Knee, Patrick, Vietor, & Neighbors, 2004).

Marital conflict can have harmful effects on children as well as spouses. Children who witness their parents engaging in frequent, aggressive conflict are more likely to have trouble interacting with their peers and performing at their full potential in school (Buehler et al., 1997; Sillars et al., 2004). Research on this **spillover effect** suggests that these negative effects arise because parents who engage in dysfunctional conflict are also likely to have dysfunctional parenting styles (Davies & Cummings, 1994). A **socialization effect** is also likely to occur, with children adopting conflict styles similar to their parents' conflict styles (Koerner & Fitzpatrick, 2002; Reese-Weber & Bartle-Haring, 1998). A study by Kitzmann and Cohen (2003) examined several aspects of interparental conflict: frequency (how often parents argue in front of them), intensity (how mad parents get when they argue with each other), perceived threat (how scared children get when their parents argue), and resolution (how long parents stay mad at each other beyond the actual argument). Their results showed that children in Grades 3 through 6 were less likely to report having a high-quality relationship with a best friend if their parents had trouble resolving their conflicts. Frequency, intensity, and threat were less predictive of poor friendship quality than resolution, underscoring how important it is for parents to manage conflict rather than holding grudges and remaining angry. Studies have also shown that children actually fare better when feuding parents divorce compared to when they stay together and engage in increasingly negative patterns of conflict communication (Caughlin & Vangelisti, 2006).

Despite these negative effects, conflict can be beneficial when it is managed productively. Gottman's (1979, 1994) research shows that satisfied couples are more likely to discuss issues of disagreement, whereas dissatisfied couples are likely to minimize or avoid conflict. By confronting disagreement, relational partners can manage their differences in ways that enhance closeness and relational stability (Braiker & Kelley, 1979; Canary et al., 1995; Lloyd & Cate, 1985). Couples who handle conflict in a calm, collaborative fashion tend to be satisfied with their relationships and are less likely to divorce (McGonagle, Kessler, & Gotlib, 1993). A study by Siegert and Stamp (1994) examining the effects of a couple's "first big fight" also underscores the important role that conflict plays in relationship development. Partners who stayed together after the fight gained a greater mutual understanding of their feelings, felt they could solve problems together, and were confident that they would both be willing to make sacrifices for each other. By contrast, partners who broke up after the fight reported feeling uncertain about their relationship. During the fight, many people discovered negative information about their partners, and many felt that future interaction would be tense and uncomfortable. More than anything, however, the way partners perceived and handled conflict predicted whether their first big fight would signal the end of their relationship or a new beginning. In addition, the way partners manage conflict is a better predictor of relational satisfaction than is the experience of conflict itself. Being able to resolve conflict so that both parties are satisfied with the outcome is also predictive of relational satisfaction (Cramer, 2002).

CONFLICT STYLES

Considerable research has focused on the strategies or styles that people use to deal with conflict in organizations (Blake & Mouton, 1964; Putnam & Wilson, 1982; Rahim, 1986; Rahim & Bonoma, 1979) and in relationships between friends, lovers, and roommates (Fitzpatrick & Winke, 1979; Klein & Johnson, 1997; Sillars, 1980; Sillars et al., 2004). Research in both these areas suggests that conflict styles can be distinguished by two dimensions: cooperation and directness (Rahim, 1986; Sillars et al., 2004). Cooperative conflict takes both partners' goals into account, whereas uncooperative conflict focuses on one person trying to win the argument. Direct conflict involves engaging in conflict and talking about issues, whereas indirect conflict involves avoiding discussion of conflict. Researchers have developed several typologies of conflict styles from these dimensions, with some scholars identifying three styles (e.g., Putnam & Wilson, 1982; Sillars, 1980), other scholars finding four styles (e.g., Klein & Johnson, 1997; Sillars et al., 2004), and still other scholars discovering five styles (e.g., Blake & Mouton, 1964; Rahim, 1986). A review of the strategies in these typologies suggests that there are six styles of conflict: (1) competitive fighting, (2) compromising, (3) collaborating, (4) indirect fighting, (5) avoiding, and (6) yielding (see Figure 11.1). Notice that only two of these six styles are labeled as "fighting." This is because only two of the styles are inherently competitive and aggressive. The other styles all represent nonaggressive ways to express disagreement and manage conflict. To determine your own conflict style, complete the scale in Box 11.2.

Competitive Fighting

Competitive fighting is direct and uncooperative (Blake & Mouton, 1964). This style has been called *direct fighting* (Sillars et al., 2004), *distributive* (Sillars, 1980), *dominating* (Rahim, 1986), *controlling* (Putnam & Wilson, 1982), and *contentious* (Klein & Johnson, 1997; Pruitt & Carnevale, 1993). As these labels suggest, people with a competing style try to control the interaction so they have more power than their partner. They attempt to achieve a win-lose situation, wherein they win and their partner loses. In their attempts to achieve dominance, individuals who employ competing strategies use several tactics: confrontational remarks, accusations, personal criticisms, threats, name-calling, blaming the partner, sarcasm, and hostile jokes (Sillars et al., 2004).

Imagine that Mary and Doug both used competitive fighting when trying to determine how to punish Amanda. They might cling stubbornly to their own perspectives, with each arguing that their method is superior to the other partner's. Mary might accuse Doug of being too selfish to put up with Amanda being at home all the time because she is grounded, and Doug might claim that Mary's past attempts at grounding Amanda have been unsuccessful and that "everyone knows" she is too lenient. The conflict could very well escalate, with Mary and Doug yelling at each other and calling each other

FIGURE 11.1 ■ Interpersonal Conflict Styles

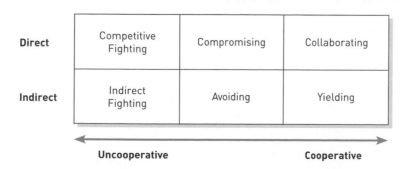

BOX 11.2 PUT YOURSELF TO THE TEST
WHAT IS YOUR CONFLICT STYLE?

Think about the last few times you and a relational partner disagreed. How did you behave? Use the following scale to determine your typical conflict style: 1 = strongly disagree and 7 = strongly agree.

	Strongly Disagree						Strongly Agree
1. I discuss the problem to try to reach a mutual understanding.	1	2	3	4	5	6	7
2. I keep arguing until I prove my point.	1	2	3	4	5	6	7
3. I show my partner that I am angry or upset without saying a word.	1	2	3	4	5	6	7
4. I sometimes sacrifice my own goals so my partner can meet her or his goals.	1	2	3	4	5	6	7
5. I try to find a new solution that will satisfy both our needs.	1	2	3	4	5	6	7
6. I usually try to win arguments.	1	2	3	4	5	6	7
7. I do not like to talk about issues of disagreement.	1	2	3	4	5	6	7
8. I am willing to give up some of my goals in exchange for achieving other goals.	1	2	3	4	5	6	7
9. I try to get all my concerns and my partner's concerns out in the open.	1	2	3	4	5	6	7
10. I try to get back at my partner by giving the silent treatment or holding a grudge.	1	2	3	4	5	6	7
11. I usually try to forget about issues of disagreement so I don't have to confront my partner.	1	2	3	4	5	6	7
12. I try to think of a solution that satisfies some of both our needs.	1	2	3	4	5	6	7
13. Sometimes I find myself attacking my partner.	1	2	3	4	5	6	7
14. I use facial expressions to let my partner know I am angry or upset.	1	2	3	4	5	6	7
15. It is important to get both our points of view out in the open.	1	2	3	4	5	6	7
16. Sometimes I criticize my partner to show that he or she is wrong.	1	2	3	4	5	6	7
17. I try to meet my partner halfway.	1	2	3	4	5	6	7
18. If the issue is very important to my partner, I usually give in.	1	2	3	4	5	6	7
19. I attempt to work with my partner to find a creative solution we both like.	1	2	3	4	5	6	7
20. I tend to show negative feelings through nonverbal communication, such as rolling my eyes.	1	2	3	4	5	6	7

21. I usually let my partner take responsibility for bringing up conflict issues.	1	2	3	4	5	6	7
22. I would rather not get into a discussion of unpleasant issues.	1	2	3	4	5	6	7
23. I give in to my partner to keep my relationship satisfying.	1	2	3	4	5	6	7
24. I try to make my partner see things my way.	1	2	3	4	5	6	7
25. I avoid bringing up certain issues if my arguments might hurt my partner's feelings.	1	2	3	4	5	6	7
26. I might agree with some of my partner's points to make my partner happy.	1	2	3	4	5	6	7
27. I am likely to give my partner cold or dirty looks as a way of expressing disagreement.	1	2	3	4	5	6	7
28. I avoid talking with my partner about disagreements.	1	2	3	4	5	6	7
29. I try to find a "middle ground" position that is acceptable to both of us.	1	2	3	4	5	6	7
30. I believe that you have to "give a little to get a little" during a disagreement.	1	2	3	4	5	6	7

To obtain your results, add your scores for the following items:

Yielding: Items 4 + 18 + 23 + 25 + 26 =   _____

Avoiding: Items 7 + 11 + 21 + 22 + 28 =   _____

Collaborating: Items 1 + 5 + 9 + 15 + 19 =   _____

Competitive fighting: Items 2 + 6 + 13 + 16 + 24 =   _____

Compromising: Items 8 + 12 + 17 + 29 + 30 =   _____

Indirect fighting: Items 3 + 10 + 14 + 20 + 27 =   _____

Higher scores indicate that you possess more of a particular conflict style.

names. Even if one of them eventually yields, the desired win-lose outcome likely will be only temporary (Kilmann & Thomas, 1977). In the long run, Mary and Doug's relationship could be harmed, leading to a lose-lose situation for both.

As this example illustrates, the competing strategy is usually associated with poor communication competence and reduced relational satisfaction (Canary & Spitzberg, 1987, 1989, 1990; Gross & Guerrero, 2000; Sillars, 1980). People who use competing strategies are typically ineffective in meeting their goals and inappropriate in their treatment of their partner. There are exceptions to this, however. In relationships where a power differential exists, such as those between managers and employees or between parents and children, strategies related to competitive fighting are sometimes effective. For instance, if a father wants to prevent his son from engaging in dangerous behavior, he might force him to stay home while his friends attend a rowdy party. The competing strategy is most useful when immediate compliance is necessary (Hocker & Wilmot, 2013). The competing strategy may also be useful when it is important to deal with a particular conflict issue. For instance, if one partner does not want to talk about a critical problem (e.g., how to deal with the financial fallout of the wife being laid off from her job), the other partner may engage in competing behaviors to force the partner to confront the issue. In other cases (e.g., finding out one's partner flirted with an ex-lover all night at a party), people may be justified in expressing anger or leveling accusations at their partners. Usually, however, competitive fighting leads to a conflict escalation and harms relationships, especially if positive communication does not counterbalance verbal aggression (Canary & Lakey, 2006).

Compromising

The compromising style is direct and moderately cooperative (Blake & Mouton, 1964; Kilmann & Thomas, 1977; Rahim, 1986). Compromise involves searching for a fair, intermediate position that satisfies some of both partner's needs. With compromise, people need to give something up to reach a solution that will meet at least some of their goals. Thus, compromise usually leads to a part-win-part-lose situation. Indeed, people who compromise talk about "splitting the difference" and "meeting the partner halfway." According to Hocker and Wilmot (2013), compromising behaviors include appealing to fairness, suggesting a trade-off, maximizing wins while minimizing losses, and offering a quick, short-term resolution to the conflict. Mary and Doug could reach this type of resolution by deciding to ground Amanda for 2 weeks instead of a month and deduct cigarette money from her allowance for 3 months instead of 6. This way, Mary and Doug both get to administer the punishment they perceive as appropriate, but neither applies the punishment for as long as they originally proposed. In short, they get to keep something but they also have to give up something.

Research suggests that the compromising style is generally perceived to be moderately appropriate

and effective (Gross & Guerrero, 2000). Although this style is not as effective or appropriate as the collaborating style that is discussed next, there are situations in which compromising is best. Suppose a couple is arguing over whom to ask to be godparents for their son. The husband wants his sister and brother to be godparents, while the wife prefers her favorite aunt and uncle. Assuming their son can only have two official godparents, the couple might decide to put names in a hat, with one slip of paper appointing the aunt and brother as godparents and the other designating the sister and uncle. Such a compromise is likely to be seen as fair by all parties. As Hocker and Wilmot (2013) described, most people perceive compromising to be a reasonable, fair, and efficient strategy for managing conflict, even though it requires some sacrifice and hampers the development of creative alternatives. When a compromise is seen as unfair, it can lead to dissatisfaction. In one study, violent couples actually used more compromise than satisfied couples (Morrison, Van Hasselt, & Bellack, 1987). Thus, although compromise is usually a moderately effective conflict strategy, if couples have to compromise too often, they may feel that their needs are not being met and their problems are never truly resolved.

Collaborating

The collaborating style is direct and cooperative (Blake & Mouton, 1964). This style has been called *integrating* (Rahim, 1986; Sillars, 1980), *solution oriented* (Putnam & Wilson, 1982), *problem solving* (Klein & Johnson, 1997; Pruitt & Carnevale, 1993), and *negotiation* (Sillars et al., 2004). As these labels suggest, the collaborating style focuses on cooperative problem solving that helps people find creative solutions that satisfy both partners' needs and lead to a win-win situation. Collaborating is a better option than compromising because both people have met their goals rather than each person having to give up something in order to get something. Another difference between the compromising and collaborating styles is that compromising usually involves modifying preexisting solutions, whereas collaborating involves creating new solutions. The collaborating style opens lines of communication, increases information seeking and sharing, and maintains relationships for future interaction (Hocker & Wilmot, 2013). Tactics associated with the collaborating style include expressing agreement, making descriptive or disclosive statements, being supportive, accepting responsibility, brainstorming ideas, and soliciting partner opinions (Sillars et al., 2004).

So how might Mary and Doug use a collaborating style? A starting point would be to share their concerns and search for a creative way to teach Amanda about the dangers of smoking. By using collaborative tactics, Doug might discover that Mary's main motivation is to keep Amanda away from the "bad" crowd she has been spending time with lately. Mary might discover that Doug's main objection to grounding is that it will not teach Amanda anything about the negative consequences of smoking. Doug might also realize that reducing Amanda's allowance by the cost of several cartons of cigarettes will only teach Amanda about the monetary cost of smoking, not the health risks. They might agree that it would be better if they required Amanda to volunteer some time after school at the local hospital, where she can help patients with lung cancer. Such a disciplinary action will keep Amanda away from her new friends (meeting Mary's needs) while also teaching Amanda about the risks associated with smoking (meeting Doug's needs). In fact, this new solution might address each of their concerns better than their original plans would have.

Of the six styles, the collaborating style is evaluated as the most effective and appropriate in managing conflict (Canary & Spitzberg, 1987, 1989, 1990; Gross & Guerrero, 2000; Gross, Guerrero, & Alberts, 2004). Couples who use collaborating styles and show positive affect during conflict are likely to be happier, and children benefit from parents who use this conflict style (Caughlin & Vangelisti, 2006; Koerner & Fitzpatrick, 2006). Collaborating is related to perceptions of competence and relational satisfaction because it gives each individual access to the partner's views of so-called incompatible goals,

allowing disputants to reach understanding and to co-construct meaning. When such understanding occurs, problems can be defined, and a solution that integrates the goals and needs of both parties can be reached (Tutzauer & Roloff, 1988). In one study, parents and children reported being more satisfied with their relationships if they reported using the collaborating style to cope with conflict (La Valley & Guerrero, 2012). In another study, people reported using cooperative strategies to manage conflict in online relationships if the relationship was close and they wished to continue interacting with their partner in the future (Ishii, 2010). In some cases, it may be easier to be collaborative online because people have more time to think things through before communicating.

Indirect Fighting

Sillars and his colleagues (2004) refer to conflict behaviors that are indirect and uncooperative as indirect fighting. These behaviors have also been called *passive aggression* (Guerrero, 2013) and *active distancing* (Bachman & Guerrero, 2006a) and are related to patterns of negative withdrawal (Gottman, 1994). Examples of indirect fighting include failing to acknowledge or validate the partner's concerns, ignoring the partner, holding a grudge, using a whiny voice, giving the partner cold or dirty looks, angrily leaving the scene, rolling one's eyes, and administering the silent treatment (Guerrero, 2013; Sillars et al., 2004). All of these behaviors express aggression or disagreement in an indirect manner that can shut down discussion about the conflict issue.

For instance, rather than discussing optimal punishment in a calm manner that facilitates cooperation, Doug and Mary might show hostility through indirect behaviors. Doug might try to explain his philosophy—that Amanda needs to learn there are consequences associated with smoking—in a condescending tone that makes Mary feel he is talking to her as if she is a child. Mary's response may be to sigh, roll her eyes, and cross her arms over her chest in a defensive manner.

Doug might then complain, in a hostile voice, that Mary isn't even listening. Such tactics could result in one or both of the partners leaving the scene in frustration. In this type of scenario, the indirect behaviors often provoke metaconflict, which we defined earlier as conflict about how people disagree. Mary might demand, "Stop talking to me as if I'm a child," and Doug might complain, "We never get anywhere because you don't listen to me." Metaconflict often sidetracks partners away from discussing the issue at hand—in this case, how to best teach Amanda a lesson about smoking.

Indirect fighting may be especially destructive when partners use these behaviors to avoid confronting problems (Sillars et al., 2004). A study of conflict in parent–child relationships showed that people report using more indirect fighting when their partner has an avoidant personality type (La Valley & Guerrero, 2012). Therefore, people may resort to indirect fighting when they feel that they are being dismissed or ignored by their partners. Indirect fighting reflects a level of hostility that is not found in other indirect styles of conflict management. As discussed next, avoiding is more neutral than indirect fighting, and yielding is more cooperative. Indirect fighting is related to many of the same negative outcomes as the competitive fighting, including relationship dissatisfaction and a failure to resolve conflicts. However, indirect fighting may be even more detrimental to relationships than competitive fighting because it is an indirect strategy. At least competitive fighting involves engaging in direct, verbal communication that might bring important issues to the forefront. As you will learn later in this chapter, behaviors associated with indirect fighting, such as rolling one's eyes, sounding disgusted or fed up, and ignoring one's partner, have been identified as signs of unproductive conflict that can lead to relationship decline (Gottman, 1994). People who employ indirect fighting are also perceived as less effective and appropriate than are those who use cooperative strategies (Guerrero, 2013).

Avoiding

Avoiding is an indirect style of conflict that is regarded as somewhat neutral in terms of how cooperative versus uncooperative it is. This style has also been called *inaction* (Klein & Johnson, 1997; Pruitt & Carnevale, 1993) and *nonconfrontation* (Putnam & Wilson, 1982). When using the avoiding style, people refrain from arguing and refuse to confront their partners in any meaningful way. Avoiding tactics are fairly common. Studies have shown that roommates frequently report using the avoiding style in their conflicts (Sillars, 1980), and 63% of college students report withholding at least one complaint from their dating partners (Roloff & Cloven, 1990). People who use the avoiding strategy engage in tactics such as denying the conflict, being indirect and evasive, changing or avoiding topics, acting as if they don't care, making irrelevant remarks, and joking to avoid dealing with the conflict (Hocker & Wilmot, 2013).

Imagine that Mary and Doug deal with their disagreement by using the avoiding style. Neither of them wants to confront the issue, so they avoid talking about how to best handle the situation with Amanda. Perhaps they both punish Amanda their own way, without consulting the other, making Amanda suffer two punishments instead of one. Or perhaps they both decide not to do anything, letting Amanda "off the hook" for smoking. Either way, the use of avoidance would lead to a lose-lose situation, with little being accomplished. Consistent with this example, several studies have shown that the avoiding style is evaluated as inappropriate and ineffective (Canary & Spitzberg, 1987, 1989, 1990; Gross & Guerrero, 2000; Gross et al., 2004).

Occasionally, though, avoidance may be beneficial. Roloff and Ifert (2000) described five conditions that influence whether avoidance has a positive or negative effect on relationships. First, avoidance may be an effective strategy for certain types of couples. Couples who find it difficult to engage in conflict without resorting to aggression may find avoidance preferable to engagement. Second, avoidance is more acceptable when accompanied by expressions of positive affect. So if Doug says, "I'm too tired to talk about this anymore, honey" with a warm voice and genuine smile, Mary might empathize with him rather than feeling dismissed. Third, people are most likely to respond positively to avoidance when the topic is of little importance to both people. As Hocker and Wilmot (2013) noted, the avoidant style can be used to acknowledge that a relationship is more important than a particular issue.

Fourth, individuals are more likely to find avoidance acceptable if it is their decision to avoid discussion about a particular topic. When people feel their partners are pressuring them to keep quiet about relational issues that are bothering them, avoidance may have an especially harmful effect on the relationship. Finally, when people are socially skilled communicators, they may be able to recognize when avoidance is appropriate versus inappropriate. For example, imagine that Doug is staunchly conservative and Mary is extremely liberal. If they are socially skilled, they might be flexible enough to "agree to disagree" when it comes to political issues but to confront conflict issues revolving around Amanda and her twin sister, Megan.

Yielding

The yielding style is cooperative and indirect (Klein & Johnson, 1997; Pruitt & Carnevale, 1993; Sillars, 1980). People who use this style forgo their own goals and desires in consideration of the partner (Kilmann & Thomas, 1977). This style has also been labeled *obliging* (Rahim, 1986) and *accommodating* (Blake & Mouton, 1964). Papa and Canary (1995) noted that this type of response is adequate and comfortable; it does not cause further disagreement or escalation of conflict. However, the yielding style glosses over differences, plays down disagreements, and trivializes conflict, making effective conflict management difficult. Hocker and Wilmot (2013) described several specific yielding tactics, including putting aside one's own needs to please the partner, passively accepting the partner's decisions, and making conciliatory statements.

Mary or Doug might engage in any or all of these tactics as part of a yielding response. Suppose Doug decides to give in to Mary and grounds Amanda. He might tell Mary that she is right, that he'll just have to deal with having Amanda at home, and that he loves his family and hopes it works out. Doug may yield for many different reasons. Perhaps he really does believe that Mary knows best when it comes to disciplining Amanda. Or perhaps he decides that it is not worth arguing over and he will simply let Mary have her way. Yet another possibility is that he feels threatened or coerced. In their research on the **chilling effect,** Cloven and Roloff (1993) found that people are likely to avoid voicing their opinions and complaints when they feel powerless or fear that their partner will act aggressively toward them (see also Chapter 12).

Yielding occurs for many different reasons, so it can be perceived as both competent and incompetent (Gross & Guerrero, 2000). Yielding behavior is cooperative and appropriate when one person feels strongly about an issue and the other person does not. In such cases, it is appropriate for the person who feels less strongly to give in to the partner. Yielding may also be an appropriate strategy when two people cannot agree but a decision must be made. For instance, if Mary and Doug are arguing over who is going to pick Amanda up after a party (each believes it is the other's turn), one of them might give in so that Amanda will have a safe ride home.

However, most research suggests that although the yielding style is sometimes appreciated by one's partner, it is generally ineffective (Gross & Guerrero, 2000; Papa & Canary, 1995). People who use the yielding style are unlikely to achieve personal goals, which could strain their relationship. According to Hocker and Wilmot (2013), repeatedly yielding puts a person in a powerless position. Perhaps this is why people seldom report yielding when the conflict issue is important to them. Sillars (1980) examined how often roommates reported using yielding strategies. He had students recall significant disagreements with their roommates and describe how they and their roommates communicated. Only 2% of the students reported using yielding strategies during their most significant roommate disagreements. By contrast, 33% of students perceived their roommates to have yielded during these same disagreements. Sillars suggested that the discrepancy occurred because students reported on a disagreement that was significant to them, which made it less likely that they would yield. Their roommates, conversely, may not have seen these disagreements as significant and so were willing to concede the issue. This finding suggests that yielding is more common when people do not care much about an issue.

PATTERNS OF CONFLICT INTERACTION

Although people have tendencies to manage conflict in particular ways, people often use different strategies depending on the situation, the type of conflict, and the channel of communication. (See Box 11.3 for how people sometimes switch from one channel of communication to another to help manage conflict.) Conflict strategies are not mutually exclusive. In other words, people can use more than one strategy during a single conflict interaction. For example, Doug and Mary may begin with the intention of communicating in a cooperative, direct manner but become increasingly competitive as they both stubbornly hang on to their original positions. They might also exhibit different conflict styles altogether. Perhaps Mary favors indirect fighting whereas Doug prefers to yield. As these examples illustrate, understanding various conflict styles in isolation does not paint a very good picture of how conflict interaction unfolds. This is why researchers have sought to understand common patterns of conflict within relationships. Next, we discuss four such patterns: (1) negative reciprocity, (2) demand-withdraw, (3) the **four horsemen of the apocalypse,** and (4) accommodation.

Negative Reciprocity

Despite the fact that indirect and competitive fighting usually have negative effects on relationships,

people use these strategies more frequently than cooperative strategies (Canary et al., 1995; Sillars, 1980). This may be because of the **principle of negative reciprocity,** a pattern whereby aggression begets more aggression. Once one person uses competitive or indirect fighting, the other person is likely to follow suit. Patterns of negative reciprocity have even been found online. In a study looking at **flaming,** which is defined as a "hostile expression of emotions" online through means such as "swearing, insults, and name-calling," Lee (2005) noted that "once started, flaming begets more flaming" (p. 393). People can also "flame" nonverbally by doing things like typing an insulting word or phrase in bold or all caps, or putting exclamations after statements such as "How can anyone be so stupid?!!!!!"

Whether people are face to face or communicating online, hostile behaviors tend to be reciprocated during conflict (Gottman, 1994; Krokoff, Gottman, & Roy, 1988). Alberts and her colleagues (Alberts, 1989; Alberts & Driscoll, 1992) found that if a partner launches a complaint, the other partner is likely to fire back with a countercomplaint. Moreover, individuals in dissatisfying relationships were twice as likely as individuals in satisfying relationships to respond to complaints by denying the validity of the complaint or by escalating the hostility of the interaction (Alberts & Driscoll, 1992). Patterns of negative reciprocity also distinguish couples who are dissatisfied and violent from those who are dissatisfied but nonviolent. Violent couples are most likely to engage in high levels of negative reciprocity and low levels of **positive reciprocity** (Smith, Vivian, & O'Leary, 1990).

In conflict interaction, negative reciprocity appears to be more common than positive reciprocity. In a classic study, Gaelick, Brodenshausen, and Wyer (1985) studied how perceptions of a partner's behavior influence patterns of reciprocity during conflict. They found that people enact positive behaviors when they perceive their partner is expressing affectionate emotions and negative behavior when they perceive their partner is expressing hostile emotions. However, negative

BOX 11.3 TECH TALK
MOTIVES FOR CHANNEL SWITCHING DURING CONFLICT INTERACTION

When people think about interpersonal conflict, they usually think of two people arguing face to face. However, in the 21st century considerable conflict occurs in computer-mediated contexts, such as through texting, snapping, and other forms of instant messaging. A study by Scissors and Gergle (2013) found that conflicts that start within a mediated channel (such as texting) often continue face to face, sometimes face-to-face conflict is abandoned in favor of discussing the issue via a mediated channel, and other times people go back and forth between channels. For instance, the topic could come up while texting, be discussed further face to face, and then revisited and finally resolved with an exchange of text messages. This study also found the following four motivations for switching channels during conflict:

To Avoid Conflict Escalation: Conflict might be started in a mediated channel to ease into a discussion before moving it to a face-to-face context, or it might move from texting or instant messaging to face to face because one party believes he or she is being misinterpreted. Other times moving from face to face to texting can minimize conflict escalation because messages are shorter, and people have more time to think before replying, all of which can result in a calmer discussion.

To Manage Emotion: Sometimes people move from face to face into mediated channels because they feel more in control of their emotions when texting or instant messaging than when talking face to face. They can represent their emotions in a photo or an emoji, which may make them feel less vulnerable than they would expressing emotions face to face. Similarly, people sometimes feel they can more carefully express their feelings through a channel such as text because they would not get overwhelmed and

blurt out the wrong thing. Other times, people feel that the depth of their emotions can be expressed better in face-to-face communication or that the delay in text messages will make them more anxious or angry.

To Adjust to Partner Preferences: Sometimes people accommodate to each other's channel preferences in an effort for the discussion to progress more smoothly. For example, if Doug does not like to argue on text, he might read Mary's message and not respond, prompting her to call him or wait until she gets home to talk. If Amanda prefers to deal with conflict issues through text, Mary and Doug might send her a group chat to discuss something that is bothering them.

To Resolve the Conflict: Conflict does not always get resolved during a single interaction. Sometimes channel switching helps provide a concluding segment to a conflict. In Scissors and Gergle's (2013) study, some people felt that face-to-face communication is necessary if a conflict is truly to be resolved, so moving from a mediated context to face to face was a way to conclude the conflict. Other times people felt that summarizing or apologizing using texting after a face-to-face conversation was a helpful way to resolve and shut down the conflict. So Amanda might text her parents the next day and say she is sorry for smoking and reiterate that she accepts their punishment.

These motivations suggest that channel switching can be very useful for managing conflict. Being aware of the advantages and disadvantages of different channels, such as face to face versus texting versus snapping, as well as understanding what channels your partner is most comfortable with, can lay the foundation for productive problem solving.

---

reciprocity was the main pattern for two reasons. First, people exhibit more negative than positive emotion in conflict situations. Second, and perhaps more importantly, people perceived their partners were expressing hostility even when they were not. For instance, imagine that Mary offers her view using a neutral voice, but Doug interprets

her tone to be condescending. This could set off a chain of negativity, even though Mary's initial comment was not meant to be hostile.

Patterns of negative reciprocity can be set off by a variety of hostile behaviors, including sarcasm, personal criticism, name-calling, yelling, and unfair accusations. Four other tactics have been found to be especially likely to divert attention away from the conflict issue while escalating negativity— (1) **gunnysacking,** (2) **kitchen sinking,** (3) bringing third parties into the argument, and (4) **mind reading**. Gunnysacking occurs when people store up old grievances and then dump them on their partner during a conflict (Bach & Wyden, 1970). Rather than discussing each issue when it first surfaces, issues are placed in a metaphorical gunnysack and presented all at once. Kitchen sinking is similar to gunnysacking. However, instead of storing up complaints, people rehash their old arguments when they get into a new argument (Bach & Wyden, 1970). Because gunnysacking and kitchen sinking involve multiple attacks, partners are likely to feel defensive and overwhelmed, making it difficult to discuss any of the issues productively.

Bringing third parties into an argument can also promote defensiveness. There are at least four ways that people do this. First, people mention things that other people said as a form of evidence ("Your sister warned me you can be really picky"). Such comments are especially hurtful and hard for receivers to defend because they cannot confront the person who supposedly made them. Second, people can badmouth the partner's friends or family by making comments such as "I guess your erratic behavior shouldn't surprise me—your whole family acts that way." Statements like these make people particularly defensive. Not only do they have to defend themselves but they have to defend their friends or family. Third, individuals compare their partner unfavorably to other people ("None of my other girlfriends ever complained about that"), which is an especially frustrating type of personal attack. Fourth, people can make their conflicts public by telling their social networks, or, worse yet, taking the conflict online. Doing so tends to create drama, which makes problems worse. In a study based on interviews with teenagers, Marwick and Boyd (2014) defined **drama** as "interpersonal conflict that takes place in front of an active, engaged audience, often on social media" (p. 1191). For example, two people may post

comments (either directly to the person or as a subtweet) that others will favorite, retweet, or comment on, creating a public war that only exacerbates problems.

Mind reading occurs when people assume that they know their partner's feelings, motives, and behaviors. Gottman (1994) gave the following examples to illustrate mind reading: "You don't care about how we live" and "You get tense in situations like this one" (p. 2). Imagine someone saying these things to you even though they were not true. Your partner would be assuming that you do not care and that you get tense instead of listening and verifying how you really feel. Because your partner's guesses are wrong, defensiveness is likely to ensue and you are likely to be frustrated and even offended that your partner could misinterpret you so much. Gottman also noted that mind reading statements often include words such as *always* or *never*. As such, mind reading violates two principles of fair fighting: (1) it is often based on jumping to conclusions and (2) it is usually based on overgeneralizations. Conversational data collected by Alberts and Driscoll (1992) on complaints illustrates this point. In this scenario, Charles is upset because Cindy assumed that if he did a favor for her, he would hold it against her in some way. He tells her that he does not mind doing favors for her and would not expect anything in return. Eventually, Charles says this to Cindy:

> When you tell me what I was going to say, it's almost always wrong. I mean it's wrong, and it's infuriating and it drives me nuts. Like you really know me so well, that you know exactly what I'm going to say. And it's never ever true. It's never the correct answer. It's what you want to believe I'm going to decide. (Alberts & Driscoll, 1992, p. 404)

Regardless of what specific behaviors couples use, those who engage in patterns of negative reciprocity report less relational satisfaction (Gottman, 1979). Dissatisfied couples also become increasingly hostile during discussions about problems or conflict issues, while satisfied couples maintain a consistently lower level of hostility (Billings, 1979; Gottman & Levenson, 1992). This does not mean that couples in satisfying relationships never display negative reciprocity. On the contrary, research suggests that negative reciprocity is a fairly common pattern in conflict interaction. The key appears to be the percentage of behaviors that are negative versus positive. Gottman's (1994) research demonstrates that happy couples tend to engage in about five positive behaviors for every negative behavior, whereas the ratio of negative-to-positive behaviors was about one to one for unhappy couples.

Demand-Withdraw

Researchers have identified another common but dysfunctional conflict sequence called the **demand-withdraw interaction pattern** (Gottman & Levenson, 1988; Sagrestano, Heavey, & Christensen, 2006). This pattern occurs when one person wants to engage in conflict or makes demands on a partner and the other wants to avoid it. The person in the demanding position is likely to be in a less powerful position (relative to the partner) and tends to be dissatisfied with something. By contrast, the person in the withdrawing position is likely to be in a more powerful position and to be happy with the status quo. Married couples are more likely to engage in the demand-withdrawal pattern when one partner desires more closeness or involvement in the home and the other partner desires more autonomy (Sagrestano et al., 2006). This pattern has been found in several different cultures (see Box 11.4).

The demand-withdrawal pattern can move in both directions—increased demands can lead to more withdrawal, but increased withdrawal can also lead to more demands (Klinetob & Smith, 1996). In fact, couples who use the demand-withdrawal pattern may have problems of **punctuation** (Watzlawick et al., 1967), with each partner "punctuating" the cause of the conflict differently. One partner might say, "I have to nag you all the time

---

BOX 11.4 AROUND THE WORLD
DEMAND-WITHDRAW IN DIFFERENT COUNTRIES

Demand-withdraw is a common pattern of conflict interaction around the world. People from Australia, Brazil, Italy, Pakistan, Taiwan, and the United States all report being less satisfied and more distressed within their relationships if their conflict is characterized by the demand-withdraw pattern (Christensen, Eldridge, Catta-Preta, Lim, & Santagata, 2006; Noller & Feeney, 1998; Rehman & Holtzworth-Munroe, 2006). In contrast, across different cultures, couples who report using constructive conflict patterns that include compromising and collaborating report high levels of relational satisfaction.

Despite these consistencies, there are also some differences between cultures. In the study by Christensen and colleagues, Brazilians reported higher levels of demand-withdraw than did people from Italy, Taiwan, and the United States. There are also differences in how people from different countries engage in demanding behavior.

For example, compared to U.S. wives, Pakistani wives tend to be less assertive when demanding change (Rehman & Holtzworth-Munroe, 2006). In fact, Pakistani husbands were more likely than Pakistani wives to engage in behavior that was aggressive and demanding, and Pakistani wives were more likely than Pakistani husbands to engage in withdrawal. This pattern is opposite to that found in some studies of couples from the United States, where wives are more likely to demand and husbands are more likely to withdraw. One possible explanation for these findings is that the power structure in marriage is different in some countries than others, with women less likely to be aggressive and more likely to withdraw in non-equalitarian cultures where men have considerably more power than women. In these non-equalitarian cultures, gender roles may outweigh other factors to determine who is more demanding versus withdrawing.

because you always withdraw," whereas the other partner might say, "I have to withdraw because you are always nagging me." Notice that both partners blame the other for their behavior.

The demand-withdrawal pattern is most likely to occur when the conflict engager uses either competitive or indirect fighting. Engagers who use cooperative strategies are rarely perceived as demanding (Heavey, Christensen, & Malamuth, 1995). Because the demand-withdrawal pattern consists of uncooperative behavior, it is generally seen as an incompetent form of dyadic communication (Christensen & Shenk, 1991; Gottman & Levenson, 1988). Yet the effect this pattern of conflict communication has on relationships is not clear. Some studies have shown that couples characterized by the demand-withdrawal pattern are more likely to be dissatisfied with their relationships and, eventually, to break up. Yet other studies have shown that couples who use the demand-withdrawal sequence are likely to report increased relational satisfaction over time (Caughlin & Vangelisti, 2006). It may be that couples who break free from this sequence end up reporting more satisfaction because important changes were made in their relationships, whereas those who repeatedly follow this pattern become increasingly dissatisfied.

A more consistent finding is that women are more likely to do the demanding whereas men are more likely to do the withdrawing (Caughlin & Vangelisti, 1999; Christensen & Shenk, 1991; Gottman, 1994; Heavey, Layne, & Christensen, 1993). Imagine if Doug approaches Mary to discuss Amanda's punishment, but Mary tells him she does not want to talk about it anymore. Would this situation seem more believable if it were reversed— with Mary wanting to talk about the problem and Doug retreating? The research suggests it would, and that women may be in the demanding role more often because they are more likely to want to institute change in their relationships. However, this sex difference reverses if the conflict involves something the man wants to change (Kluwer, De Dreu, & Buunk, 1998; Sagrestano et al., 2006). In fact, a recent study looking at marital conflict in the home showed that husbands and wives were equally likely to be in either the demander or withdrawer role and that demand-withdrawal sequences were most likely when couples were discussing relationship issues that one partner had initiated (Papp, Kouros, & Cummings, 2009). So if Doug thinks it is unfair that he always ends up having to tell his daughters what their punishments are, he would probably be in the demanding role when he and Mary discuss who will tell Amanda that she must volunteer at the hospital. Finally, some evidence suggests that couples characterized by husband-to-wife violence are more likely than nonviolent couples to exhibit rigid patterns of husband demand and wife withdrawal (Caughlin & Vangelisti, 2006). Olson (2002b) also found that couples who spontaneously engage in reciprocal violence during conflict are often caught in a demand-withdraw conflict pattern.

Overall, then, research has shown that the demand-withdrawal pattern is more prevalent in relationships where violence is present and, in such relationships, men are just as likely to be the demanders and women are just as likely to be the withdrawers (Babcock, Waltz, Jacobson, & Gottman, 1993; Berns, Jacobson, & Gottman, 1999; Holtzworth-Munroe, Smutzler, & Stuart, 1998; Ridley & Feldman, 2003). To manage conflict constructively and maintain a happy relationship, couples must learn to break this cycle. The person in the demanding role needs to be patient and persistent without becoming aggressive or violent. The person in the withdrawing role needs to listen and try to understand and empathize with the partner. With effort, the cycle can be broken and the relationship can become more satisfying.

The Four Horsemen of the Apocalypse

Gottman's extensive research on the causes of divorce uncovered another especially destructive pattern of conflict called "the four horsemen of the apocalypse." According to Gottman (1994), couples who divorce are likely to exhibit a conflict pattern that includes the following four types of communication: (1) criticism, (2) defensiveness, (3) contempt, and (4) stonewalling, with contempt and stonewalling particularly toxic to relationships (Gottman, 1994; Lisitsa, 2013b). Gottman's research suggests that within the first three minutes of an interaction, the presence of these forms of communication can predict divorce with an accuracy rate of over 90%. The Gottman Institute offers antidotes or alternatives for the four horsemen that will lead to communicating in a more positive manner (Lisitsa, 2013a). The four horsemen and their antidotes are described next, with examples shown in Box 11.5.

CRITICISMS VERSUS COMPLAINTS Criticisms are personal attacks that blame someone else for a problem. **Complaints,** on the other hand, focus on a specific behavior. Gottman (1994) noted that often complaints are healthy. If relational partners never complained, they would be unable to improve their relationships by changing problematic behavior. Criticisms, in contrast, are not healthy. Because they focus on attacking and blaming the partner, they lead people to feel hurt and rejected, and therefore often trigger an escalation of conflict that includes the other more-deadly horsemen. Criticisms can revolve around personal characteristics, including negative remarks about personality or appearance. For example, Amanda might tell Megan, "You are an inconsiderate and rude sister" or "If you weren't so fat your clothes wouldn't take up so much closet space." Criticism can also focus on performance (Alberts, 1988). In this case, someone dislikes the way something was done. For example, Doug might complain that Mary does not do a good job helping Amanda with her geometry homework by saying, "You're not explaining that very well. The way you described the theorem is confusing. Do you even know what you're doing?" This type of complaint can be frustrating because it implies that someone is not doing something the proper way. Indeed, Mary might respond by getting up from the table and telling Doug to help her himself!

As you can probably guess, the antidote to a criticism is a complaint that focuses on a specific behavior without assigning blame. Luckily, research has shown that behavioral complaints are more common than criticisms revolving around

---

BOX 11.5 HIGHLIGHTS
EXAMPLES OF THE FOUR HORSEMEN OF THE APOCALYPSE AND THEIR ANTIDOTES

Negative Behavior

Criticism:
"I can't believe how much space you hog up in the closet. You are so inconsiderate and rude!"

Defensiveness:
"Well, if you weren't on your cell phone all the time maybe we could actually spend some quality time together without having to do anything special."

Contempt:
"I need some damn help! All you do is sit there on your butt watching T.V. while I fix dinner and tend to the kids. I worked just as hard, actually harder, than you did today. You are just lazy and self-absorbed."

Stonewalling:
"Just stop yacking and let me watch T.V. I'm really not interested in anything you have to say."

Antidote

Complaint:
"I think it's important that we divide the closet space evenly. I don't like when my clothes are all scrunched together."

Accepting Responsibility:
"You're right. I should make more of an effort to plan things for us to do together. When things at school settle down I promise I will."

Showing Respect:
"I know that you're tired after working all day and your job is really important. I'm tired too. I would really appreciate it if you could help with dinner and then we can both relax."

Physiological Self-Soothing:
"Let's take a break and calm down. In about a half an hour we can regroup and talk again when we're both in a better frame of mind to try to work this out."

personal characteristics, appearance, or performance (Alberts, 1988, 1989), yet when people are upset or frustrated about something, it is easy for them to blame the other person and fall into personal criticism. Focusing on the behavior, however, will be more productive in the long run.

DEFENSIVENESS VERSUS ACCEPTING RESPONSIBILITY People become defensive when they feel a need to protect themselves and ward off personal attacks, such as the types of criticism mentioned above. **Defensiveness** involves defending oneself by communicating "it's not me, it's you." Gottman (1994) listed several defensive forms of communication, including denying responsibility for a problem, making excuses, issuing counter-complaints, whining, making accusations to deflect responsibility from oneself, and mind reading. Other behaviors discussed previously, such as gunnysacking and kitchen-sinking, can also be used in an attempt to deflect the blame from oneself and direct it toward one's partner.

Defensiveness is a natural response to being attacked, but in most conflict situations both partners have some responsibility for the issues that are causing problems. So the antidote for defensiveness is to fight the impulse to defend oneself and instead accept at least partial responsibility. The Gottman Institute gives this example to illustrate the difference between responding defensively versus accepting responsibility: A wife asks her husband, "Did you call Betty and Ralph to let them know that we're not coming tonight as you promised this morning?" The husband could respond defensively by saying, "I was just too darn busy today. As a matter of fact, you know just how busy my schedule was. Why didn't you just do it?," or he could accept responsibility by saying, "Oops, I forgot. I should have asked you this morning to do it because I knew my day would be packed. Let me call them right now" (Lisitsa, 2013b). Notice that the defensive response deflects blame on the wife, while the second response not only admits responsibility, but also promises action to remedy the situation.

CONTEMPT VERSUS SHOWING RESPECT Showing contempt is one of the most destructive forms of communication that can occur in a relationship. **Contempt** communicates an air of superiority and is often the byproduct of long-standing problems in a relationship. When people feel they cannot solve their relational issues and their relationship is stagnating, they are often frustrated and perceive their partner as the problem. This can lead to contemptuous behaviors that go beyond blame and criticism. Nonverbal behaviors, such as sighing while someone is talking or rolling one's eye communicate contempt. So do many other forms of communication. As Gottman (1994) stated:

> Contempt is also easy to identify in speech. It involves any insult, mockery, or sarcasm or derision, of the person. It includes disapproval, judgment, derision, disdain, exasperation, mockery, put downs, or communicating that the other person is absurd or incompetent. Three types of contempt are hostile humor, mockery, or sarcasm. In this form of contempt, there may be derision, a put down, or cold hate. There is often a definite sense of distance, coldness, and detachment in this category of behavior. (p. 25)

Statements such as "you're crazy" or "You can't do anything right" are prototypical ways of communicating contempt. The Gottman Institute also gives the example of a wife coming home after an exhausting day and seeing her husband lounging on the couch. When she asks him to help her with dinner he replies by saying he's too tired, after which she lights into him and says: "You're 'tired'?! Cry me a river. . . . I've been with the kids all day, running around like mad to keep this house going and all you do when you come home from work is flop down on that sofa like a child and play those idiotic video games. I don't have time to deal with another kid. . . . Just try, try to be more pathetic" (Lisitsa, 2013b). Notice that the insults are not only more pointed than typical criticism (e.g., she calls him a pathetic child), but they imply that she is superior to him.

The antidote for contempt is to try and put yourself in your partner's place and show some respect, which is the opposite of contempt. This can be difficult, but to get respect people need to show respect. Not feeling respected can be toxic in a relationship.

STONEWALLING VERSUS PHYSIOLOGICAL SELF-SOOTHING Stonewalling usually occurs after a conflict pattern (including criticism, defensiveness, and contempt) has become pervasive in the relationship. At this point, one or both people shut down and withdraw from the interaction. Interaction seems futile and the withdrawing partner usually experiences heightened anxiety and a rapid pulse rate such that he or she just wants to get away. Partners are no longer trying to work problems out and instead avoid each other, tune out, act busy, and generally separate from each other. Sometimes one partner engages in stonewalling behavior while the other is still trying to fix things, which leads to the demand-withdrawal type of pattern discussed previously in this chapter. Although it usually takes time for stonewalling to occur, once it does it tends to become a habit. If this habit is not broken, Gottman's research suggests that relationships become stagnant and couples are likely to break up.

The antidote for stonewalling is **physiological self-soothing**. This method involves taking a break from the conflict, usually by telling your partner that you are feeling too much emotion and need to step away for a while to calm down and regain your thoughts. The Gottman Institute suggests that the break be at least 20 minutes long so that you can calm down sufficiently and let go of any negative feelings that could lead to defensiveness or contempt (Lisitsa, 2013a). Doing something pleasant during the break, such as reading or watching a T.V. show you enjoy, can be helpful so that you can regroup and go back to the discussion in the right frame of mind.

When emotions kick in and couples find themselves stonewalling, they should take a break from one another and do something pleasant for around 20 to 30 minutes so that they can calm down and be in a positive frame of mind to resume discussion.

Accommodation

For people to be able to successfully substitute the antidotes for the four horsemen of the apocalypse, they need to be able to engage in accommodation. Rusbult's work helps explain why some couples are more able to do this than others using the idea of the **accommodation principle** (Rusbult, Bissonnette, Arriaga, & Cox, 1998; Rusbult, Verette, Whitney, Slovik, & Lipkus, 1991). This principle rests on three ideas. First, people have a tendency to retaliate or withdraw when their partner engages in negative behavior. This is consistent with the conflict patterns discussed previously. Negative behavior begets more negative behavior, demand leads to withdrawal and withdrawal leads to demand, and criticism and contempt lead to defensiveness and eventually stonewalling. Second, accommodation occurs when people able to overcome these initial tendencies and engage in cooperative rather than uncooperative communication to maintain their relationships. Third, couples in satisfying, committed relationships more often use accommodation than couples in uncommitted or dissatisfying relationships (Rusbult, Olsen, Davis, & Hannon, 2001).

Several studies have supported the accommodation principle (e.g., Campbell & Foster, 2002; Duffy & Rusbult, 1986; Rusbult & Zembrodt, 1983; Wieselquist, Rusbult, Foster, & Agnew, 1999). These studies demonstrate that accommodation is most likely to occur in relationships characterized by high levels of commitment, satisfaction, and trust. However, accommodation may not always have positive effects on relationships. Rusbult and her colleagues (2001) noted that accommodation can cause relational problems, including power imbalances. As with the yielding strategy, if only one person is doing the accommodating (or yielding), that person may be in a powerless position that could eventually lead to relational dissatisfaction. Thus, the key to successful accommodation may be that it prompts a pattern of positive reciprocity, with both partners eventually engaging in cooperative strategies. This does not mean that all conflict behaviors need to be cooperative; indeed, it may be hard to refrain from using some uncooperative forms of communication when a conflict issue is particularly contentious. It does mean, however, that it is critical for partners to break escalating cycles of negativity by engaging in and responding positively to accommodation. Some research has even shown that couples who fail to reciprocate positive messages are more likely to report interpersonal violence (Smith et al., 1990).

There are many ways to accommodate a partner's negative behavior, including refraining from reacting angrily, using appropriate humor, or showing positive affect. Alberts and Driscoll's (1992) data on conversational complaints provide a nice example of accommodation that leads to a more productive interaction. They gave an example of a man (we'll call him Aaron) who complains to a woman (we'll call her Beth) that he cannot find his possessions because she always moves them when she cleans the house. The end of their conversation went this way:

Aaron: But, I mean, it's not like you do it on purpose. It's because you're absentminded.

Beth: Uh-huh. Yeah.

Aaron: And it's not like I don't do it either.

Beth: Yeah, I mean, I agree that things have to have their place . . . if you put them in their place, then you know where they are and it saves you a lot of worry.

Aaron: Well, then, there's really no disagreement.

Beth: Yeah, that's the way things should be. It's just that sometimes we do things that are contrary to the things we agree on.

Notice that Aaron engaged in a personal attack when he called Beth "absentminded." Yet instead of reciprocating his hostility, Beth accommodated by expressing agreement (perhaps because she agreed that she did not do it "on purpose"). This led Aaron to admit that he sometimes does the same thing, which paved the way to ending the disagreement.

Being able to respond to negativity with positivity promotes relational satisfaction. In one study, couples in which people were nice only when the partner was nice were more likely to separate either one and a half, two and a half, or five years later than were couples in which the two people were nice regardless of whether their partners acted positively or negatively. As this study demonstrated, it is important for people to be positive when the partner is sad, angry, or inexpressive, as well as when the partner is happy. Gottman's (1994) recommendation that couples counterbalance every one negative statement with five positive statements appears to be very sound advice.

EXPLANATIONS FOR CONFLICT PATTERNS

Questions likely follow as to why patterns such as negative reciprocity and demand-withdrawal are so common. If people care about their relationships, why don't they try to defuse a negative situation by accommodating and reacting with positivity? Sometimes people do respond positively, but often they find it hard to refrain from negativity because of emotions they feel, attributions they make, or their lack of communication skills. Complementing the discussion in this section,

Box 11.6 provides rules for fair fighting that help people avoid falling into the trap of negative reciprocity during conflict.

Emotional Flooding

During conflict situations, people often naturally experience aversive emotions, such as anger, hurt, and guilt (Guerrero, 2013). Earlier in this chapter, we defined conflict as occurring when people have incompatible goals. Similarly, people feel negative emotion when someone or something blocks or disrupts their goals. So, if Mary feels that Doug's plan for punishing Amanda interferes with her goal to teach Amanda the "right" kind of lesson about smoking, Mary is likely to feel frustrated and perhaps even angry. Interestingly, moderate levels of emotion may be helpful during conflict situations (T. S. Jones, 2000). When people feel low levels of emotion, they are unlikely to put much effort into resolving conflict issues. On the other hand, especially intense emotion is counterproductive during conflict interactions.

During conflict situations, negative emotions may become so intense that people automatically resort to the fight-or-flight response. Gottman

(1994) suggested that **emotional flooding** occurs when people become "surprised, overwhelmed, and disorganized" by their partner's "expressions of negative emotion" (p. 21). When this happens, people often experience high levels of physiological arousal (including increased heart rate and higher blood pressure), have difficulty processing new information, rely on stereotyped thoughts and behaviors, and respond with aggression (fight) or withdrawal (flight). Thus, flooding contributes to negative patterns of communication that involve both uncooperative behavior and avoidance.

Several communication behaviors are associated with flooding. According to Gottman's (1994) research, if one partner becomes defensive, stubborn, angry, or whiny, the other partner is likely to experience emotional flooding. Other behaviors act as buffers against emotional flooding. If one partner expresses joy, affection, or humor during a conflict interaction, the other partner is less likely to experience emotional flooding. Situational variables also play a role. Zillman's (1990) work on the excitation transfer suggests that people who are highly aroused (due to either stress or physical exertion) before engaging in conflict are more likely to react

---

BOX 11.6 HIGHLIGHTS
TEN "RULES" FOR CONSTRUCTIVE CONFLICT MANAGEMENT

Based on the situation, there are various ways to manage conflict effectively. However, based on the research reviewed in this chapter, the following 10 "rules" should serve people well in most conflict situations.

1. Avoid gunnysacking or bringing in everything but the kitchen sink.

2. Do not bring other people into the conflict unless they are part of the conflict.

3. Attack positions, not people (no name-calling, button pushing, or violence).

4. Avoid making empty relational threats.

5. If necessary, postpone conflict until your emotions cool down.

6. Try to understand your partner's position by practicing active listening and avoiding mind reading.

7. Use behavioral complaints rather than personal criticisms.

8. Try to accommodate rather than get defensive when you feel like you are being attacked.

9. Try to validate your partner's position by expressing agreement and positive affect rather than stonewalling or escalating conflict.

10. For every one negative statement or behavior, use five positive statements or behaviors.

aggressively—presumably because they are experiencing emotional flooding. When people experience emotional flooding, they sometimes say things they don't really mean, or things they wish they could take back. For example, relational partners who are experiencing intense emotion might call each other names or make statements such as "I hate you" or "I wish I never met you." In the moment, such statements seem true because people are filled with negative emotion. However, when they calm down, they realize they actually care deeply for each other. Other times, people make these kinds of statements to get a kind of emotional revenge. They know that they don't really hate the partner, but by saying "I hate you" they hope to hurt the partner the way they themselves feel hurt.

When feeling hurt and uncertain, people sometimes lash out by engaging in **button pushing** or making empty relational threats. When people engage in button pushing, they purposely say or do something they know will be especially hurtful to the partner. This could entail bringing up a taboo topic, insulting the partner with an offensive name, or looking away when the partner is talking. The key is that the button pusher knows the words or behavior will bother the partner.

Empty threats involve suggestions to do something that the speaker does not really intend to do. For instance, someone might say, "If you see her again, I'll break up with you" or "I can't stand this anymore; I want a divorce" when the speaker in each case actually has no intention of terminating the relationship. Empty threats have at least two negative consequences. First, if someone does not follow through on these threats, the person will lose face, and the partner may think the person is bluffing during future interactions when this time the individual is really serious. As the old fairy tale warns, it is not wise to "cry wolf" too many times. Second, if someone threatens to end a relationship without really intending to, this could plant a seed for relationship termination. Research suggests that people go through a cognitive process of psychological separation before terminating close relationships

(Duck, 1988). Therefore, if one partner continues talking about ending the relationship, the other partner might think about being single or about better relational alternatives. If this happens, the partner who delivered the threats moved the possibility of breaking up to the forefront of the other partner's mind. Thus, empty relational threats are more likely to backfire than to solve problems.

Because people tend to become defensive or aggressive when they are emotionally flooded, it is advisable to avoid discussing conflict issues until both partners have calmed down. However, conflict should not be put off indefinitely. If necessary, couples might need to schedule a time to talk about issues that are bothering them. In the interim, each partner might want to write down their feelings. To illustrate, one of our students once told us about a writing technique that she and her husband used when they were feeling really angry with each other. From their past experiences, they knew it was likely that conflict would escalate if they confronted each other when their emotions were running high. They thus decided to vent their negative emotions by going to different rooms and writing letters to each other. Later, after they had calmed down, they would each read the letters to themselves and decide whether to share them with the spouse. This student said that neither of them ever ended up sharing the letters but instead always tore them up. The letters were usually filled with things they did not really mean, such as exaggerations, name-calling, or unfair accusations. But these letters helped her and her husband put their conflict issues in perspective and enabled them to move on and discuss their problems in a calmer fashion.

Attributions

People like to be able to explain the behavior of others, particularly during significant events such as conflict episodes. To do this, people make attributions. In their book on interpersonal communication, Fisher and Adams (1994) defined an **attribution** as "a perceptual process of assigning reasons or causes to another's behavior" (p. 411).

This definition is consistent with Heider's (1958) conception of people as "naive scientists" who study one another's behavior and make judgments about why they act the way they do. People are especially likely to make attributions about negative behavior, including the uncooperative types of behaviors that often occur during conflict (Roloff & Miller, 2006). Three specific types of attributions have been studied extensively (Kelley, 1973). First, people attribute a person's behavior to personal versus situational causes. When people make personal attributions, they believe that the cause of another person's behavior is rooted in their personality. By contrast, when people make situational attributions, they believe that the other person's behavior was affected by external factors, such as context or situation. For example, Doug might be upset because Mary ran out and got his birthday present at the last minute, causing them to be late for their dinner reservation. He could attribute Mary's behavior to personality factors (Mary is forgetful and disorganized) or to situational factors (Mary has been especially busy with work and has had to drive Amanda to the hospital every day after work).

Second, people make attributions about behavior being stable versus unstable. In other words, is Mary usually too busy to prepare for Doug's birthday? After many years of marriage, Doug might determine that her last-minute behavior is atypical and that she usually finds the time to buy him a nice gift no matter how busy she gets. Third, people make attributions about how global versus specific the cause of a behavior is. The more global a cause is, the greater number of behaviors and situations it applies to. For instance, the extra tasks with which Mary has been occupied might have caused her to put off doing things she normally does, or perhaps she just forgot about getting Doug a present.

Research on the **attribution hypothesis** has shown that patterns of attribution are related to conflict escalation and lower levels of satisfaction (Fincham, Harold, & Gano-Phillips, 2000). As Figure 11.2 shows, people in happy relationships tend to make **relationship-enhancing attributions**

by attributing negative behavior such as complaints, whining, and nagging to causes that are external, unstable, and specific. By contrast, people in unhappy relationships tend to make **distress-maintaining attributions** by attributing negative behavior to internal, stable, and global causes (Bradbury & Fincham, 1990; Brehm & Kassin, 1990; Harvey, 1987; Holtzworth-Munroe & Jacobson, 1985). In general, people make more positive attributions about their own behavior than their partner's behavior during conflict, but partners in dissatisfying relationships are especially likely to blame their partners (Sillars, Roberts, Leonard, & Dun, 2000).

Since Doug and Mary are happily married, their pattern of attributions would most likely be relationship enhancing. For instance, if Mary becomes aggressive when Doug doesn't agree with her, he might think this: "She's just especially upset because her grandfather died of lung cancer and she's worried about Amanda. We can usually talk about disciplining our daughters without getting into a heated argument." On the other hand, if they were a dissatisfied couple, Doug might think this: "Mary is so stubborn. She always thinks she's right! We never agree about how to discipline our daughters—or anything else for that matter!"

As these examples suggest, when people attribute negative behavior to internal, stable, and global causes (as people in dissatisfying relationships tend to do), they are more likely to use uncooperative conflict behaviors, such as indirect and competitive fighting (Davey, Fincham, Beach, & Brody, 2001; Schweinle, Ickes, & Bernstein, 2002). This can lead to negative spirals in dissatisfying relationships. Couples in dissatisfying relationships are also more likely to pay attention to negative behaviors than positive behaviors and to attribute positive behaviors to negative causes. In some cases, these attributions represent habitual but inaccurate ways of perceiving the partner's behavior.

In other cases, negative attributions may be accurate. Amanda might resist her parents' advice about smoking because she is stubborn and rebellious

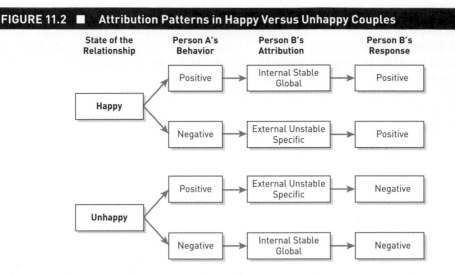

FIGURE 11.2 ■ Attribution Patterns in Happy Versus Unhappy Couples

(a personal cause), and Megan and Amanda might continually fight over family possessions, such as the phone and computer, because they both want privacy and autonomy (a stable cause). In conflict situations such as these, identifying the causes may be essential for managing the conflict (Roloff & Miller, 2006). Therefore, it is essential—although difficult—to sort out inaccurate attributions from accurate attributions so that the true causes of conflict can be identified.

Communication Skill Deficits

In addition to emotional flooding and cognitive attributions, some people simply do not have the communication skills necessary to engage in constructive conflict. These individuals are likely to feel helpless and defensive when attacked by others because they cannot respond effectively. Thus, they resort to aggressive behaviors or withdrawal, which can contribute to negative spirals of behavior. People with communication or social skill deficits are also more likely to report using violence in their relationships (Christopher & Lloyd, 2000). These deficits include having difficulties in the following areas: general emotional expression, anger management, social support seeking and giving, and problem solving. Men with communication skill deficits are also less likely to make

relationship-enhancing attributions for their partner's behavior (Holtzworth-Munroe & Hutchinson, 1993; Holtzworth-Munroe & Smutzler, 1996).

ARGUMENTATIVENESS VERSUS AGGRESSIVENESS Another important communication skill is the ability to engage in logical argument. Infante and his colleagues distinguished between **argumentativeness** and **verbal aggressiveness** (Infante, 1987; Infante, Chandler, & Rudd, 1989; Infante & Rancer, 1982). Argumentativeness refers to conflict styles that focus on logical argument and reasoning: People with argumentative styles confront conflict directly by recognizing issues of disagreement, taking positions on controversial issues, backing up claims with evidence and reasoning, and refuting views contrary to their own. Argumentativeness is an important social skill. People who are skilled in argument do not have to resort to name-calling, accusations, or other negative tactics. Instead, they can present their positions in a skilled and convincing manner. Rather than attacking their partner, they attack their partner's position.

Verbal aggressiveness involves attacking the other person's self-concept, often with the intention of hurting the other person. Verbally aggressive people engage in such tactics as teasing, threatening, and criticizing the partner's character or appearance

(Infante, Sabourin, Rudd, & Shannon, 1990). Infante's research has shown that people resort to these types of tactics when they are unskilled in argumentation. Partners in violent marriages are more likely to report high levels of verbal aggression and low levels of argumentativeness than are those in nonviolent marriages (Infante et al., 1989, 1990).

The following example illustrates how difficult it is to deal with someone who is verbally aggressive: Amanda and Megan are starting to think about where to apply for college, so they watch a news report on admission requirements at various universities. After the report, the sisters begin discussing their differing opinions on affirmative action.

Amanda: I can't believe they are going to prohibit affirmative action at State.

Megan: If you ask me, it's about time they did.

Amanda: You mean you are against affirmative action?

Megan: Let's put it this way: I think people should be admitted to universities based on their qualifications rather than their skin color.

Amanda: So you are a racist who hates minorities.

Megan: That's not true. I don't like discrimination in any form. I just think universities should make exceptions based on factors other than race. Poor white students are also disadvantaged. Maybe a policy that admits students based on where they rank in their particular high school would be fairer. That way, all students who are economically disadvantaged, including minority students, would get help.

Amanda: And I suppose you think that white men are discriminated against, too. I thought you were smarter than that. How can you be so gullible?

If you did not have a strong opinion about affirmative action policies before reading Amanda and Megan's comments, you may have been persuaded by Megan's arguments because they focused on her position rather than attacking Amanda as a person. In short, Megan used argumentative communication. By contrast, Amanda used verbal aggression when she called Megan a racist, implied she was unintelligent, and asked how she could be so gullible. If Amanda had used argumentative communication,

you might have been persuaded by her argument rather than Megan's. This example also illustrates how verbally aggressive communication can lead to negative spirals. Put yourself in Megan's place. If the conversation continued—and you kept being attacked personally—would you have been tempted to retaliate by using verbal aggression yourself? Most people have a hard time remaining neutral in the face of personal attacks, partly due to emotional flooding.

EFFECTIVE LISTENING The ability to listen to others is another critical skill for effective conflict management. When people practice effective listening, they are better able to understand their partner's thoughts and feelings, and, ultimately, to empathize with their concerns. Such understanding plays a vital role in collaboration and compromise. In fact, studies have shown that people with listening and decoding skills (the ability to figure out what the partner is feeling) tend to be more satisfied in their relationships (Guerrero & Floyd, 2006).

Active listening is very challenging in conflict situations. For instance, think about the last heated argument you had with someone. How carefully did you listen to what the person said? If you felt attacked or became defensive, chances are that you did not really listen to the other person very carefully. Instead, you were probably thinking about what you would say next. Your mind may have been racing as you thought about how to defend yourself, and your emotions may have been so turbulent that you became preoccupied with your own thoughts and feelings and "tuned the other person out." Ironically, if the other person was not practicing active listening either, all the counterarguments you spent so much time creating would never really be heard.

Active listening thus requires effort and concentration. The experts on listening and negotiation give the following advice for improving active listening skills (Stark, 1994; Steil, Barker, & Watson, 1983; Stiff, Dillard, Somera, Kim, & Sleight, 1988):

1.   *Let your partner speak*. Refrain from arguing your case or interrupting until your partner finishes stating her or his position. If you spend noticeably more time talking than

your partner, this probably means that you need to talk less and encourage your partner to talk more.

2. *Put yourself in your partner's place*. Enter a conflict situation with specific goals regarding what you would like to learn from your partner. As Gottman (1994) emphasized, if people want to understand and empathize with each other, they need to create **mental maps** of each other's thoughts and feelings. By listening actively, people can see things from their partner's perspective.

3. *Don't jump to conclusions*. Don't assume you know what your partner will say or why they will say it. Making such assumptions can lead you to interpret your partner's statements in a way that is consistent with your preexisting beliefs—even if your preexisting beliefs are wrong.

4. *Ask questions*. Ask questions that allow your partner to clarify and explain her or his position. Be sure to phrase these questions in a positive manner so you don't sound sarcastic or condescending.

5. *Paraphrase what your partner says*. Paraphrase what you hear to confirm that you have really heard what your partner is trying to tell you. When partners paraphrase, they summarize each other's positions. This way partners have the opportunity to correct misinterpretations and to further clarify their positions.

SUMMARY AND APPLICATION

Conflict is inevitable in close relationships. The closer you are to someone, the more likely you will encounter disagreements. Disagreements can have positive or negative effects on relationships. When differences are handled cooperatively, conflict can improve relationships by helping partners solve problems and understand each other. But when negative patterns of conflict communication become pervasive, including those involving the four horsemen of the apocalypse, relational partners are likely to become less satisfied and committed and to feel less emotional closeness. When spouses argue, their conflict style can also impact their children's well-being. Children whose parents repeatedly engage in hostile patterns of conflict are less likely to have good peer relationships and more likely to use uncooperative conflict styles themselves. Conflict between parents and children also has a socializing effect on children. So if Amanda disagrees with her parents regarding her punishment, the way her parents communicate with her will likely influence how

Amanda deals with conflict in other relationships in the future.

Doug and Mary have many options for dealing with conflict. They could engage in communication that is cooperative or uncooperative, direct or indirect. Although six separate styles of conflict are described in this chapter, Doug and Mary could use a variety of styles during a conflict interaction and each could use different styles of communication. Mary might be more direct than Doug, and Doug might be more cooperative than Mary. In addition, conflict interaction is a two-way street. It takes two people to escalate conflict; it also takes two people to cooperate.

Engaging in cooperative conflict requires communication skills. Many people use uncooperative strategies, such as competitive fighting and indirect fighting, which cause conflicts to escalate. It follows that negative patterns of conflict communication can develop in relationships. For example, some relational partners get caught in patterns of negative reciprocity, demand-withdrawal, or the four horsemen of the apocalypse. If Doug and Mary notice that their conflict interactions are characterized by plenty of personal criticism, contempt, defensiveness, or stonewalling, their relationship could be in trouble. Using the antidotes for the four horsemen of the apocalypse and engaging in patterns of accommodation, which involve responding to negative behavior with positive behavior, help diffuse negativity and promote cooperation.

Using the collaborating style would provide Mary and Doug with the best option for disciplining Amanda effectively. Mary and Doug would be more likely to reach a collaborative solution if they avoided destructive patterns of conflict communication and remained focused on their goals. The studies reviewed in this chapter point to several rules for constructive conflict management, which Mary and Doug would be advised to follow. These rules are summarized in Box 11.6 and provide a blueprint for communicating effectively during conflict situations, as do the antidotes described in Box 11.5.

Although the advice in this chapter probably makes sense to you, it may be hard for Mary and Doug (or any two people) to follow it all of the time. Even if you have good intentions and know how you *should* act during a conflict situation, when your emotions are running high, it is difficult not to violate some of these rules. If you find yourself engaging in some destructive tactics during conflict situations, do not panic—even experts in negotiation make mistakes. Recognizing these mistakes is a first step toward managing conflict in ways that keep your relationships satisfying.

KEY TERMS

accommodation principle (p. 305)

argumentativeness (p. 310)

attribution (p. 308)

attribution hypothesis (p. 309)

avoiding (p. 288)

button pushing (p. 308)

chilling effect (p. 297)

collaborating (p. 287)

competitive fighting (p. 287)

compromising (p. 287)

complaints (p. 303)

conflict (p. 288)

contempt (p. 304)

criticisms (p. 303)

defensiveness (p. 304)

demand-withdraw interaction pattern (p. 301)

distress-maintaining attributions (p. 309)

drama (p. 300)

emotional flooding (p. 307)

empty threats (p. 308)

flaming (p. 298)

four horsemen of the apocalypse (p. 298)

gunnysacking (p. 300)

indirect fighting (p. 288)

kitchen sinking (p. 300)

mental maps (p. 312)

mind reading (p. 300)

physiological self-soothing (p. 305)

positive reciprocity (p. 298)

principle of negative reciprocity (p. 298)

punctuation (p. 301)

relationship-enhancing attributions (p. 309)

socialization effect (p. 290)

spillover effect (p. 290)

stonewalling (p. 305)

verbal aggressiveness (p. 310)

yielding (p. 288)

DISCUSSION QUESTIONS

1. Do you tend to avoid or engage in conflict? Which of the six conflict styles discussed in this chapter best fits you? Does your style of communication stay fairly consistent, or does it vary a lot depending on the situation and the partner?

2. Think of times when you have used criticism, defensiveness, contempt, and stonewalling during a conflict. Now that you have read the research on the four horsemen of the apocalypse, what would you say or do differently? Try to recall what you said and then come up with a phrase you could have used to implement the antidote.

3. When people are in the midst of interpersonal conflict, they often are flooded with emotions. This makes it difficult to "fight fairly." Which of the rules for constructive conflict management do you think is most difficult to follow? Do you have any additional suggestions that might help your classmates learn to manage conflict in more constructive ways?

 SAGE edge™

Sharpen your skills with SAGE edge at edge.sagepub.com/guerrero5e.
SAGE edge for students provides a personalized approach to help you accomplish your coursework goals in an easy-to-use learning environment.

12 INFLUENCING EACH OTHER
Dominance and Power Plays in Relationships

Tyler is a pretty laid-back individual who really loves his girlfriend, Ashley. Ashley loves Tyler too, but she would like him to get a better job and go back to school. Their love life is good in all respects except when Ashley hassles him about school and work. Tyler defends his lifestyle and his current job, but when Ashley's persuasion becomes more strident, Tyler withdraws and Ashley gets mad, shops excessively, and their sex life goes downhill. Ashley is smart and beautiful, and Tyler worries that she has better alternatives, especially since she is graduating with a communication degree from college and already has better job offers than his entry-level position.

As illustrated by Ashley and Tyler's situation, **power** struggles characterize many relationships, with partners trying to influence or change the other. Power is a crucial aspect of social relationships. The philosopher Bertrand Russell (1938) once remarked, "The fundamental concept in social science is Power in the same sense that Energy is the fundamental concept in Physics" (p. 10). But there is a dark side to power; as historian Lord Acton (1887/1972) famously observed, "Power corrupts and absolute power corrupts absolutely" (p. 335). Whether power is a force for good or evil, power abhors a vacuum, and close relationships are no exception. Power exists in all relationships: Someone takes the initiative to start a relationship, or decide how to spend money, initiate sex, accept or reject the initiation, take out the garbage, or clean the bathroom. At some level, power is a factor in every friendship, romance, marriage, and family.

Power is so prevalent in relationships that scholars have labeled **dominance** and submission as a basic, core dimension of social relationships and interpersonal communication (Burgoon & Hale, 1984; Mast, 2010). When power imbalances exist, couples like Ashley and Tyler must find ways to communicate their needs in constructive rather than controlling ways. What options do they have for influencing one another? Are some forms of communication more effective than others? And perhaps most important, how can they achieve a more balanced, egalitarian relationship? This chapter addresses these and other questions by examining how issues of power, control, and influence play out in close relationships. First, we define power and outline six principles of power. Next, we review the literature on influence goals and examine specific verbal tactics and nonverbal power behaviors. Finally, we focus on issues of power and equality in families.

DEFINING POWER AND RELATED TERMS

Power refers to an individual's ability to control or influence others to do what the individual wants (Berger, 1985; Mast 2010), as well as a person's ability to resist influence. In relationships, people often exert power by controlling valuable resources (Ellyson & Dovidio, 1985). First, relational partners can grant or withhold resources, such as money and possessions, affection, sex, or time spent together (Fitzpatrick & Badzinski, 1994). For example, Ashley gives Tyler extra affection to reward good behavior and withholds affection to punish negative behavior. Second, power is part of the decision-making process when relational partners determine how to spend valuable resources such as time and money. Relational partners exercise power when they divide tasks such as washing the dishes, balancing the checkbook, and doing the driving on a road trip. Relational partners exercise power when they decide what kind of car to buy, how to spend their time together, and where to go on vacation. In interpersonal relationships, power reflects the ability to affect the behavior, emotions, or decisions of one's partner (Berger, 1985).

Power is a basic feature of relationships because humans want to have autonomy, control their lives, and be free agents (Lammers, Stoker, Rink, & Galinsky, 2016). Free agents have **agency,** an empowering aspect of experience where a person is able to freely control the surrounding environment, including social interaction and relationships (McAdams, 1985). This is why people often feel the need to "change" their relational partners so they fit their conceptions of how a perfect partner should behave. Uncontrolled agency leads to dominance.

Ideally, power motivates, energizes, and enables a person without diminishing or subjugating other people. Negative forms of power, such as harassment or coercion, destroy intimacy and produce unstable and dissatisfying relationships. The key to using power productively is for partners to use their influence for the good of the relationship and to keep the decision-making process fair and equitable. In short, both people in a relationship should have a voice.

Dominance refers to the expression of power used to gain or maintain influence over another (Mast, 2010). As we will discuss in this chapter, dominant behaviors include verbal communication such as commands and other "one-up" messages (*"We* are going to *my* family's home for Thanksgiving this year") as well as nonverbal communication such as using a loud voice while maintaining high levels of eye contact. But, using a certain behavior doesn't always make someone dominant. Dominance is determined by submissive responses; it is not dominance unless it works (Burgoon et al., 2010). If demanding to spend Thanksgiving with one's family is met with a response such as "I'm not going—you can go by yourself," or if the strategy of using a loud voice with steady eye contact fails to get a partner's attention, dominance did not occur.

Dominance is also multidimensional (Burgoon, Johnson, & Koch, 1998). People who are regarded as interpersonally dominant tend to possess at least some combination of the following characteristics: poise, panache, self-assurance, and the ability to control conversation. It is these qualities that combine to make them influential, which is the key to being dominant. People who have **poise** are smooth and appear calm during stressful situations. **Panache** is the elusive quality that some people have that draws others in. There is something about the person that commands attention and makes them memorable. **Self-assurance** relates to a person's focus, drive, and leadership qualities. **Conversational control** refers to an individual's ability to manage a conversation by doing things such as regulating who talks and how long the interaction will last. Finally, people who possess some combination of these characteristics have **influence,** or the ability to persuade others to think and act in certain ways, which is the hallmark of interpersonal dominance. To see how someone you know measures up on these five characteristics, take the test in Box 12.1.

Intuitively, one might think that powerful people always engage in more dominant behaviors but this is not the case. **Dyadic power theory** suggests that most dominance would be displayed by people in equal power positions because they deal with conflict and struggle for control (Dunbar & Abra, 2010). Within this theory, **relative power** is the amount of power people have in comparison to one another. If you have high relative power, you are more dominant than your partner. If you have low relative power, your partner is more dominant than you. If you have equal relative power, you influence one another the same amount. Recent research shows that when couples were equal in power, as opposed to unequal, they were more likely to complain to their partner, to perceive complaints as less threatening, and were likely to expect positive outcomes from these episodes (Worley & Samp, 2016) supporting dyadic power theory. However, mulling about conflicts and complaints has been shown in a number of studies to have negative personal and relational implications (Cloven & Roloff, 1993, also see Chapter 11).

Social influence involves changing someone's thoughts, emotions, or behaviors (Burgoon et al., 2010). Sometimes social influence results from strategic communication, when one person tries to change another person's attitudes, beliefs, feelings, or behaviors. Other times indirect influence occurs. Dominant behaviors can be part of the social influence process, although they do not have to be. The person who ultimately affects a change in the other person is influential and has exerted power, either directly or indirectly.

POWER PRINCIPLES

Whether power is exercised through dominance or subtle forms of influence, it occurs within a social and relational context. Six principles of power describe how power functions within our interactions with others.

Power as a Perception

The first principle is that *power is a perception*. People can use powerful communication, but if others don't perceive or accept their power, their behavior is not dominant. Others are powerful only to the extent we believe they are powerful. When power is perceived to be illegitimate and undeserved people will resist and even overthrow the power structure (Lammers, Galinsky, Gordijn, & Otten, 2008).

Some people have **objective power** but fail to influence other people. Objective power is the authority associated with factors such as position, strength, weaponry, and wealth. Presidents, defensive linemen, nuclear nations, and millionaires have objective power, but their actual power is diminished if people fail to perceive their power. People who employ power cues and act powerfully tend to be perceived as powerful (Hall, Coats, & LeBeau, 2005; Magee, 2009), contributing to enhanced perceptions of power. Cultural power stereotypes create social knowledge, although they may contain only a "kernel" of truth (Hall et al., 2005). For instance, using direct gaze while talking is powerful but people think it is more powerful than it really is. Also, people who seek power overestimate power motivations of other people and are hyperaware of communication cues that can be used to influence others or resist power (Mast, Hall, & Ickes, 2006). In general, powerful people are more accurate in assessing the messages and emotions of other people (Hall, Mast, & Latu, 2015; Mast & Darioly, 2014). This is particularly true for people with dominant personalities that are empathic and responsible rather than egotistical and aggressive.

BOX 12.1 PUT YOURSELF TO THE TEST
HOW INTERPERSONALLY DOMINANT IS SOMEONE YOU KNOW?

If you are curious about how interpersonally dominant someone you know is, take this test to find out. You can reference a friend, a romantic partner, or a family member. You might also have them take the test with you in mind. Then you can compare perceptions and see if you have similar relative power.

	Strongly Disagree						Strongly Agree
1. This person has a dramatic communication style.	1	2	3	4	5	6	7
2. This person tends to take charge of conversations.	1	2	3	4	5	6	7
3. This person shows a lot of poise during stressful situations.	1	2	3	4	5	6	7
4. This person is very expressive during conversations.	1	2	3	4	5	6	7
5. This person often influences me to do or think things differently.	1	2	3	4	5	6	7
6. This person makes her or his presence felt when interacting with others.	1	2	3	4	5	6	7
7. This person is more of a leader than a follower.	1	2	3	4	5	6	7
8. This person usually does more talking than listening.	1	2	3	4	5	6	7
9. This person is usually relaxed and at ease.	1	2	3	4	5	6	7
10. This person has a way of communicating that makes her/him memorable.	1	2	3	4	5	6	7
11. This person stays focused during conversation.	1	2	3	4	5	6	7
12. This person seems ambitious and driven.	1	2	3	4	5	6	7
13. This person has a natural talent for winning people over.	1	2	3	4	5	6	7
14. This person is very smooth when talking.	1	2	3	4	5	6	7
15. This person regulates whether conversation keeps going.	1	2	3	4	5	6	7
16. This person shows a lot of grace in social situations.	1	2	3	4	5	6	7
17. This person is usually successful in persuading others.	1	2	3	4	5	6	7
18. This person seems like he/she is the type of person that takes charge of things.	1	2	3	4	5	6	7
19. This person has a lot of influence on people.	1	2	3	4	5	6	7
20. This person seems in control of the conversation around her/him.	1	2	3	4	5	6	7

Add up your responses as follows. Items 3 + 9 + 14 + 16 = *Poise*; Items 1 + 4 + 6 + 10 = *Panache*; Items 2 + 8 + 15 + 20 = *Conversational Control*; Items 7 + 11 + 12 + 18 = *Self-Assurance*; Items 5 + 13 + 17 + 19 = *Influence*. Scores for each dimensions of dominance will range from 4 to 28. The higher the score, the more a person is perceived to possess that component of dominance.

Source: Adapted from Burgoon et al., 1998.

The opposite can occur as well; some people become influential or dominant though they do not overtly use powerful behavior. People such as Mahatma Gandhi, Martin Luther King Jr., and Mother Teresa demonstrated that people of humble means and little objective power can be influential and wield real power when they stand for something that large groups of followers believe. Similarly, our relational partners are only as powerful (or as powerless) as we perceive them to be, regardless of their level of objective power.

The way people perceive themselves is also important. Thinking of one's self as powerful does not ensure that one will be powerful, but thinking of yourself as powerless virtually guarantees powerlessness. People who are confident and appear self-assured are likely to manifest more power and are more influential than people who lack confidence (Burgoon et al., 2010; Dunbar & Burgoon, 2005). People who feel powerless often get trapped in bad relationships because they do not have the confidence to assert themselves to change the situation. Moreover, powerful people tend to have a more positive and stable self-concept and as a result are perceived as more authentic by others (Kraus, Chen, & Keltner, 2011).

Power as a Relational Concept

A second principle is that *power exists in relationships*. Power is a relational concept; one individual cannot be dominant without someone else being submissive. In relationships, the issue is often how much relative power a person has in comparison to one's partner (Mast, 2010). Most romantic relationships are characterized by small imbalances of power (Dunbar, Bippus, & Young, 2008; Dunbar & Burgoon, 2005). In heterosexual relationships, men have traditionally been perceived as the more powerful partner (Sprecher & Felmlee, 1997), although this is changing. Studies suggest that people are happiest in equalitarian relationships (DeMaris, 2007; Lively, Steelman, & Powell, 2010). However, some non-equalitarian relationships can be harmonious if the submissive person defers to the preferences and wishes of the dominant person, helps them to pursue their goal, and adopts their goals as their own, thereby facilitating relational coordination and satisfaction (de Kwaadsteniet & van Dijk, 2010; Laurin et al., 2016). It needs to be the submissive person's choice, however. And if one person is submissive all the time, it could be problematic. Fortunately, in many relationships, partners are submissive in some situations but assertive in others.

Partners who display annoying dominance through unwanted touch and resource control have a history of problematic social-emotional development and concurrent relational problems (Ostrov & Collins, 2007). But the balance of power in relationships is often dynamic. Partners in close and satisfying relationships often influence each other at different times in various arenas. For example, in a single day, a wife may persuade her husband to invest in a certain stock and which babysitter to call. He may decide what movie they see that night and what restaurant to visit for dinner. Interestingly, men are more likely than women to perceive the world to be hierarchical and organized in pecking orders and power structures (Mast, 2005).

In close relationships, influence is inevitable—even desirable. Partners who exercise little influence over each other may not really be a couple, but virtual strangers in the same household. Partners in close relationships are interdependent; the action of one person affects the other. As we will see in this chapter, the way in which power is used and communicated is crucial. When partners perceive that power is fairly distributed and they are receiving adequate resources from each other, they have greater relational satisfaction (see Chapter 10).

Power as Resource Based

A third principle is that *power usually represents a struggle over resources; scarce and valued resources create more intense and protracted power struggles*. People bring numerous resources to their relationships. Most early research on power focused on money and social standing as resources (Berger,

1985). Defined in this way, men typically have more power than women. Recently, the gap between men's and women's earnings has narrowed as more women than men graduate from college and cultivate well-paying careers. As women bring more financial resources to relationships, their power is increasing.

Research from numerous countries shows that when married men and women have more equal income, women have more decision-making power, share in money management, and do less housework (Kan, 2008; Yodanis & Lauer, 2007). Young mothers who are dependent for housing on boyfriends or partners suffer from low power and autonomy (Clark, Burton, & Flippen, 2011). Similarly, unequal access to money in a marital relationship and keeping money in separate accounts is associated with more male control and less female relationship satisfaction (Vogler, Lyonette, & Wiggins, 2008).

Income also appears to be an important source of power for gay men and lesbians. Studies show that in gay relationships, the older man, who typically earns more money, has more power (Blumstein & Schwartz, 1983; Harry, 1984; Harry & De Vall, 1978). Early research on lesbian relationships found no differences in power based on income (Blumstein & Schwartz, 1983); lesbians reported that it was important for both partners to earn money so that neither partner would be financially dependent on the other. However, more recent research on lesbian relationships shows that the woman who earns more has more power (Peplau & Fingerhut, 2007; Reilly & Lynch, 1990).

However, money is only one resource that people bring to relationships. Research on power in families has been criticized for focusing on income and social prestige (Berger, 1985; McDonald, 1981). Other resources—such as communication skill, physical attractiveness, advice, social support, a sense of humor, parenting ability, sexual rewards, affection, companionship, and love—are exchanged in relationships (see Chapter 14). When resources are defined as more than financial, women wield

considerable power in their relationships. Gottman and Carrere (1994) argued that in public interactions, or interactions with strangers, men typically act more dominant and are more influential than women. However, in private interactions, especially with relational partners, women typically are more dominant and influential. As Gottman and Carrere (1994) put it, "Women's public tentativeness and deference, the acceptance of a subordinate role and politeness in stranger groups does not hold in marriages" (p. 211). In close relationships, women confront conflict more readily and are more demanding, expressive, and even coercive (Gottman, 1979). No gender difference has been observed in social dominance in long-term dating relationships (Ostrov & Collins, 2007). Likewise, women are *not* passive in marriages, as gender stereotypes may suggest. Interestingly, in high status positions, men and women exhibit few power differences but in low-status positions, men are much more likely to employ power strategies than women (Kesher, Kark, Pomerantz-Zorin, Koslowsky, & Schwarzwald, 2006).

Women also tend to be more powerful during sexual interactions. The decision to escalate a relationship sexually in almost all societies has been a women's prerogative (Byers, 1996). Virtually every theory, based on either biology or socialization, suggests that women have more negative attitudes toward casual sex than men (Browning, Kessler, Hatfield, & Choo, 1999). Studies have shown that the more powerful partner can refuse sex, and this finding is true in gay, lesbian, and heterosexual romances (Blumstein & Schwartz, 1983). Thus, in dating relationships, sexual escalation and access is an arena where women exert considerable power. However, more submissive women are more likely to consent to casual sexual behavior, particularly unusual sexual behavior (Browning et al., 1999).

In relationships, some resources are scarcer than others. According to the **scarcity hypothesis,** people who possess limited resources or have resources that are in high demand have the most power. For example, you may be attracted to several different people, but if you are in love with one of them, that person will have the most power. People with more information about another person perceive increased power because they have a scarce resource (Baldwin, Kiviniemi, & Snyder, 2009). But a scarce resource leads to power only if it is valued. For one person, money and position may be important, so a partner who is rich and successful is seen as possessing a scarce and valuable resource. For another person, religious beliefs and family values might be perceived as scarce and therefore valuable resources to possess. Regardless of which resources are valued, in the 21st century, access to technology also helps determine who has more power. Indeed, for some there is a "digital divide" between those who have access to resources via technology and those who do not (see Box 12.2).

Power as Having Less to Lose

A fourth principle is that *the person with less to lose has greater power*. People who are dependent on their relationship or partner are less powerful, especially if they know their partner has low commitment and might leave them. This phenomenon has been termed **dependence power** (Samp & Palevitz, 2014; Samp & Solomon, 2001); the dependent person feels greater relational threats in face-to-face communication or via social media. Dependence power is also related to a person's alternatives. According to interdependence theory, **quality of alternatives** refers to the types of relationships and opportunities people could have if they were not in their current relationship (see Chapter 10). In the opening example, if Ashley is attractive to many other men, but

---

BOX 12.2 TECH TALK
POWER, STATUS, AND THE DECREASING DIGITAL DIVIDE

As a college student, you may think that everyone uses the Internet, texts, and uses social networking sites as much as you do, but this is not the case. The digital divide, although decreasing, divides our society into technological "haves" and "have-nots." Data from the Pew Research Center has shown that when it comes to Internet use, this divide has decreased, with around 50% of adults in the United States using the Internet in 2000, but about 84% using it in 2015 (Perrin & Duggan, 2015). There are still generational differences in Internet use, with 58% of those over 65 years old reporting Internet use, compared to 96% of those under 30 years old. The status differences between those on the two sides of the digital divide are apparent when looking at Internet use as a function of education and income. Specifically, the Pew Research Center data showed that people who made less than $30,000 a year and those who did not finish high school were less likely to report using the Internet than those with higher incomes and more education (Perrin & Duggan, 2015). There are similar patterns for cell phones. Although 92% of people living in the United States own a cell phone, more expensive, powerful phones are reserved for those who are more educated and

have higher incomes. The 68% of the population who have smartphones tend to be younger, more educated, and have more income than those who do not (Anderson, 2015). Both Internet use and smartphones are also more prevalent in countries with developed versus undeveloped economies (Poushter, 2016), which shows that the digital divide extends to countries. Importantly, people on the unconnected side of the digital divide have less access to information, economic trends, or high tech jobs and are often reconciled to low paid and increasingly obsolete occupations with little job mobility and low personal or political power. Fortunately, the digital divide is decreasing, partly because people have a diverse array of devices beyond a desktop computer, which was once the only option. Today people can connect wirelessly from smartphones, laptops, and tablets, with more devices on the drawing board. They can also connect to the Internet in libraries and other public places. Although many devices are expensive and even elitist, basic technological devices and services have become more affordable over the years. This appears to be closing the digital divide and giving people more power to enter the information economy and connect with friends.

Tyler is not as attractive to other women, Ashley is the scarcer resource and has more power than Tyler.

The **principle of least interest** suggests that if a difference exists in the intensity of positive feelings between partners, the partner who feels most positive is at a power disadvantage (Sprecher, Schmeeckle, & Felmlee, 2006). For example, if you are in love with your partner but your partner is not in love with you, your partner has more power. If you are less interested in the relationship than your partner, you have more power. When the least interested partner makes requests, such as requesting money or sex, the more interested partner is likely to comply rather than risking the relationship. By contrast, if the more interested partner makes a request, the less interested partner does not have to comply to maintain the relationship.

Studies of both heterosexual and lesbian couples confirms the principle of least interest (Caldwell & Peplau, 1982; Peplau & Campbell, 1989; Sprecher et al., 2006; Sprecher & Felmlee, 1997). Sprecher and Felmlee found that for both men and women, the partner with less emotional involvement in the relationship had greater power and control in the relationship. They also found that men are generally less emotionally invested in their relationships than women, which suggests the balance of power generally favors men. In lesbian relationships, Caldwell and Peplau found that women who were more committed and involved in the relationship than their partners tended to have less power. Longitudinal research has shown that a partner with less emotional involvement has more power, but equal emotional involvement was associated with greater relational satisfaction and stability (Sprecher et al., 2006).

In line with the principle of least interest, when one person in a relationship values autonomy over closeness, that person tends to have more power. Harter and her colleagues (1997) described three relationship orientations: (1) self-focused autonomy, (2) other-focused connection, and (3) mutuality. People who emphasize autonomy value their independence over closeness. Those who emphasize connection do the opposite—they value closeness over independence. Finally, about three fourths of couples have a mutuality orientation value that balances independence with relational closeness. The other couples are characterized by one partner having a mutuality orientation and the other partner having either an autonomy- or connection-focused style. Neff and Harter (2002) showed people tend to be more subordinate if their partner values self-focused autonomy. Conversely, people are more likely to be dominant if their partner values other-focused connection. Equality was most likely in relationships where both partners value mutuality.

Power as Enabling or Disabling

A fifth principle is that *power can be enabling or disabling*. Power is part of the human spirit that infuses us with agency and potency and helps us achieve success. However, excessive power or frequent power plays often cripple close relationships. Few people like being dominated or manipulated and often respond to power plays with resistance, stubbornness, and defiance (McAdams, 1985). Research shows that explicit (but not implicit) dominance displays hurt women's likability (Williams & Tiedens, 2016). Men with very high power needs often have problematic love relationships; both men and women with high power needs have few intimate friendships (McAdams, 1985), and their partners experience increased negative emotions (Langner & Keltner, 2008). Research suggests that high testosterone interacts with high power to produce unfair and sometime corrupt resource allocations (Bendahan, Zehnder, Pralong, & Antonakis, 2015). Like powerful nations, powerful people must be careful not to overuse their power. Power can corrupt but only for people with a poor moral identity; for those with a strong moral identity and a sense of right and wrong, power can motivate people to use power for good and enrich their positive moral identity (DeCelles, DeRue, Margolis, & Ceranic, 2012). Both personal power and personal choice are protective against pressure, situational stress, low self-esteem, and excessive influence by others (Galinsky, Magee, Gruenfeld, & Whitson, 2008; Inesi, Botti, Dubois, Rucker, & Galinsky, 2011). Research shows that people are more likely to have an enduring influence on others when they use dominant behavior that reflects social skill rather than intimidation (Guerrero & Floyd, 2006). Communicating power through self-confident, expressive, composed behavior is most successful in achieving goals and maintaining good relationships.

In contrast, power is disabling when it leads to destructive patterns of communication. Three such patterns are (1) **emotional insensitivity,** (2) the chilling effect, and (3) the **demand-withdrawal pattern.** Emotional insensitivity occurs if a person fails to tune in to the emotions or feelings of other people. Regrettably, powerful people often ignore other people's feelings (Moeller, Ewing Lee, & Robinson, 2011) and treat other people like objects or animals, a process called dehumanization (Lammers & Staple, 2011). This may be an advantage for soldiers or surgeons who have to be stoical and insensitive in carrying out their jobs, but insensitivity on the part of the powerful can lead to resentment, self-centeredness, and relational problems. A series of studies suggests that many powerful individuals are more, not less **interpersonally sensitive** and **empathic** than less powerful people (Côté et al., 2011; Mast, Jonas, & Hall, 2009) **suggesting** that insensitivity is a choice powerful people make, not a deficit in their skill level.

The chilling effect occurs when less powerful people hesitate to communicate grievances to their partner (Roloff & Cloven, 1990). Researchers have identified conditions conducive to the chilling effect and power dynamics within relationships. First, people are susceptible to the chilling effect when they are dependent on a relational partner but perceive that their partner is uncommitted (Cloven & Roloff, 1993; Roloff & Cloven, 1990; Solomon, Knobloch, & Fitzpatrick, 2004). The chilling effect is less likely to occur in committed relationships. Second, people who are afraid of losing their partners often respond to relationship problems by withdrawing support and withholding

complaints (Roloff, Soule, & Carey, 2001). Third, partners are likely to withhold grievances to avoid negative relational consequences, such as conflict or partner aggression (Cloven & Roloff, 1993). These conditions are related to dependence power (Solomon & Samp, 1998). Research on both European-Americans and Mexican-Americans shows that power discrepancies are associated with a lack of self-expression that negatively impacts physical health (Neff & Suizzo, 2006). The chilling effect has harmful effects on relationships; problems habitually stay unsolved, power differentials increase, stress increases, and relational satisfaction erodes. The chilling effect is often the result of a highly controlling partner and can result in a woman experiencing sexual victimization, uncomfortableness with requesting condom use, reduced condom use, unwanted pregnancy, and domestic violence (Catallozzi, Simon, Davidson, Breitbart, & Rickart, 2011).

Power dynamics can also lead to a demand-withdrawal pattern, which can be disabling and destructive (Baucom et al., 2015; Christensen & Heavey, 1990; see also Chapter 11). This pattern occurs when one person makes demands, and their partner gets defensive and withdraws. When people feel powerless, they sometimes enact demanding behavior to try to change their partner's behavior. In the scenario at the beginning of this chapter, Ashley is portrayed as the "demander." She is frustrated that Tyler lacks ambition, so she tries to get him to go back to school and find a better job. Tyler is portrayed as the "withdrawer" who unsuccessfully tries to defend himself and then withdraws, perhaps to avoid further conflict. Although Ashley might have other types of power in her relationship, she seems powerless when it comes to influencing Tyler on an issue. People are most likely to be in the demanding position when, like Ashley, they are seeking compliance or change from their partner (Sagrestano et al., 2006). Women are more likely than men to seek such change, as well as to be in a less powerful position; therefore, they tend to be in the demanding role. A recent meta-analytic summary of the demand/withdrawal

Patterns such as the chilling effect and demand-withdraw sequences often reflect power imbalances in relationships. When couples stop talking, they are unable to manage problems and restore an equitable balance of power.

pattern found that both wives and husbands can be the demander, and either can be the withdrawer (Schrodt, Witt, & Shimkowski, 2014). Patterns of demand-withdraw are found in both satisfying and dissatisfying relationships, but the negative effect on the relationship and on marital communication are greater in distressed couples than in nondistressed couples (Schrodt et al., 2014). But when such patterns occur repeatedly, they erode relational satisfaction (Heavey et al., 1995). The demand-withdrawal pattern results in short-term decreases in relational satisfaction for both partners, though in the long run it can actually increase relational satisfaction for women (Caughlin, 2002).

Power as a Prerogative

The sixth principle is that *the partner with more power can make and break the rules.* According to this **prerogative principle,** powerful people can violate norms, break relational rules, and manage interactions without as much cost as less powerful people. In fact, in many cases, powerful individuals actually enhance their positive images when they display power (Guerrero & Floyd, 2006).

In organizations, people with higher status and power usually can arrive late to a meeting without penalty, while subordinates may be reprimanded. Similarly, high-status individuals, such as presidents or CEOs, can dress casually if they want (Burgoon et al., 2010). In families, parents may be able to eat while sitting on the new leather sofa, but children might be told to eat their food at the table. Powerful males and females overinterpret the sexual interest of less powerful people and may treat them in more sexual ways (Kunstman & Maner, 2011). In romantic relationships, the person who cares least can get away with arriving late for dates, forgetting birthdays or anniversaries, or even dating other people. These actions may reinforce the powerful person's dependence power; such actions show that one person is more dedicated to the relationship than the other.

Powerful people have the prerogative to initiate relationships; traditionally males are initiators. However, a series of studies show that when women's sense of personal power increases, women are as likely as men to make the effort to initiate a relationship and to use direct communication, rather than indirect, relationship initiation strategies (MacGregor & Cavallo, 2011). The more powerful person also is entitled to manage both verbal and nonverbal interactions. As discussed later, powerful people can initiate conversations, change topics, interrupt others, and terminate discussions more easily than less powerful people. Imagine that you are in a hurry to get to your next class and someone stops you and initiates a conversation. Would you be likely to chat for a moment or to brush them off and rush to class? According to the prerogative principle, you would be likely to stop and chat with someone you found powerful or attractive (e.g., your professor or someone you want to date). Similarly, in high school, the popular kids get to decide where to go and what to talk about, with the less popular kids following. In romantic relationships, the person with the most power decides which relational topics can be discussed and which are taboo.

The power prerogative is also evident in non-verbal behavior (Andersen, 2008; Burgoon et al., 2010). Take touch as an example. In interactions between teachers and students or supervisors and subordinates, who has the prerogative to initiate touch? Research shows that the teachers and supervisors are most likely to initiate touch because they have more power in these relationships. By contrast, if students or subordinates initiate touch, it may be perceived as inappropriate. Some research suggests that in heterosexual romantic relationships, men have more nonverbal power in the initial stages of the relationship. As a result, they have the prerogative to ask the woman out and to initiate behavior such as hand-holding and sex. Guerrero and Andersen (1994) found that men were more likely than women to initiate touch in casual dating relationships, but women tend to initiate touch more than men in marriages.

Together, these six principles indicate that relational partners negotiate power based on perceptions of each other and characteristics of their relationship. In close relationships, partners often share power, with each person exerting influence at certain times and accommodating the partner's wishes at other times. Thus, designating one person as "powerful" and the other as "powerless" can be misleading. In addition, when trying to influence each other, relational partners have goals that affect the power dynamic.

INTERPERSONAL INFLUENCE GOALS

Most communication is influential. Thus, when we ask someone for a favor, when we advertise a product, or when we campaign for political office, we are trying to influence people's attitudes or change their behavior. Other times, we try to resist such influence. This is particularly true in close relationships—for example, parents try to prevent their kids from smoking; dating partners initiate or refuse sexual involvement; and spouses influence each other about when and whether to have children or to buy a new

house. As Dillard (1989) stated, "Close personal relationships may be the social arena that is most active in terms of sheer frequency of influence attempts" (p. 293). Most interpersonal influence attempts are goal driven. In other words, people enact influence attempts to try to achieve particular goals (Berger, 1985). Dillard's (1989) research suggests that most influence goals fall into the six categories.

Making Lifestyle Changes

The most frequent—and some of the most important—influence attempts in close relationships involve the desire to change the behavior patterns of a partner, friend, or family member, which Dillard (1989) called giving advice about lifestyles. Examples of these influence goals might include trying to prevent conflict between your partner and your friends, getting a close friend to terminate a romantic relationship that you think is bad for her, persuading your dad to quit smoking, or convincing your brother not to move to Ohio for a job. Dillard's (1989) research indicated that lifestyle-change messages are usually logical, positively presented, and direct.

Gaining Assistance

A more routine but important kind of influence attempt involves gaining assistance. Examples of these messages might include getting your spouse to proofread your term paper, getting a friend to drive you to another city to see your girlfriend, borrowing money from your parents, and petitioning the university to readmit you. These influence attempts may be less significant than lifestyle changes, but they are personally and relationally important. When romantic partners, friends, or family members assist you, their actions say something powerful about your relationship—namely, that they value and support you. Messages designed to gain assistance are often indirect. People often attempt to gain assistance via hints or suggestions (Dillard, 1989). Instead of saying, "Get me a blanket and a bowl of popcorn," the person might hint by saying, "I'm kind of cold and hungry. A soft blanket and some warm popcorn would really feel good right now."

Sharing Activities

A critical type of relational influence attempt involves offers to share time and space (Egland et al., 1997). As discussed in Chapter 10, shared activities play a crucial role in maintaining relationships. Joint activities enable people to spend time together, show common interests, enjoy companionship, and develop intimacy. Shared activities are an important form of intimacy in male friendships because men do not usually develop intimacy via self-disclosure. Examples of these messages include offers to run or bike together, party together, shop, or go on vacation. Many of these activities are attempts to increase relationship closeness; if the other person agrees to the persuasive overture, the relationship can escalate or become more exclusive. Activities requiring people in romantic relationships to spend time together, especially alone time, signal commitment or exclusivity, like a private vacation or visiting a partner's home for Thanksgiving. Sometimes requests for shared activity are direct, but more often they are indirect and appeal more to emotion than logic (Dillard, 1989).

Initiating Sexual Activity

A common form of interpersonal influence is initiating sexual interaction. This is true in dating, cohabiting, marital, gay, and lesbian couples (see Chapter 9 for a longer discussion of sexual initiation and resistance). The principle of least interest, which was previously discussed, means that the person who desires sex the most will have the least power and the person who can take it or leave it has the most power. In dating and cohabiting relationships, men usually initiate sex (Morgan & Zurbriggen, 2007), though in marital relationships the woman may suggest or request sex more (see Chapter 9). Lesbian relationships may have less sex because sexual initiation is not in most women's sexual scripts.

Condom use is another situation where power and sexuality intersect. More powerful partners can put their partner at risk by coercing or persuading a partner to have unprotected sex. Studies show that teenage women, particularly African American and Hispanic women, who experience partner dominance and intimate violence are less likely to use condoms consistently (Catallozzi et al., 2011; Teitelman, Ratcliffe, Morales-Aleman, & Sullivan, 2008). Empowering young women to resist sexual coercion and keeping them free of abusive partners may be areas where interpersonal power is a matter of life and death.

Changing Political Attitudes

Some people are more political than others, but nearly everyone gets involved in political issues at one time or another. Convincing someone to take stands, support causes, or join movements are acts of political persuasion. Examples include talking someone into joining a union, persuading someone to vote for a political candidate, getting someone to register to vote, or convincing someone to boycott a sexist movie. By participating with you, friends or partners show their support for your cause and demonstrate that their attitudes align with yours, which can contribute to relational closeness. When relational partners seek to change each other's political attitudes, they often use indirect appeals for involvement that are low in coerciveness so as not to threaten each other's autonomy (Dillard, 1989).

Giving Health Advice

An important reason for exerting power and influence is to help partners improve their mental or physical health. For example, we may want our partner to get exercise or to take vitamins. We may advise a friend to abandon an abusive relationship or tell our teenage brother to drive carefully and party safely. We might tell a troubled colleague to seek counseling or recommend that a sick friend go to the doctor.

Of course, the way people give health advice may make a difference in terms of whether the advice is followed. If the persuader is too judgmental or demanding, the receiver may resist exercising, refuse to seek help, or rebel by engaging in dangerous behavior. **Psychological reactance** or **boomerang effects** can occur when a parent, friend, or spouse is controlling or demanding (Shen & Dillard, 2005) and is common among defensive adults and most teenagers. Such influence attempts may cause the other person to become defensive and resistant and continue to engage in unhealthy behavior, or worse, engage in more unhealthy behavior than before. One study showed that wives' control efforts on their husband's cancer treatments had no positive effects and some negative effects on his health behavior and negative effects on the couple's interactions (Helgeson, Novak, LePore, & Eton, 2004). A comprehensive summary of recent research suggests that positive control by close relational allies leads to better health outcomes, but it is only true for positive control, such as persuasion and positive reinforcement, but not for negative control, such as criticism or pressuring (Craddock, vanDellen, Novak, & Ranby, 2015). Some research on inconsistent nurturing suggests that partners who alternate patterns of punishing or reinforcing their partners may actually perpetuate drug and alcohol abuse (Le Poire, Hallett, & Erlandson, 2000). Conversely, socially supportive communication had positive effects. Messages that express concern without being critical may be best. Dillard (1989) found that most successful messages aimed at giving health advice are direct and logical.

Changing Relationships

A common form of influence among close friends is providing relationship advice. For instance, you may urge a friend to dump her cheating boyfriend, ask a friend to join your church, or suggest to a romantic partner that "we just be friends." Because the stakes are high, such influence attempts can be problematic, and whether they are accepted or not, may signal major changes in a relationship. Think about when you wanted to change either your own or a friend's relationship. Maybe you wanted a platonic

friendship to turn romantic but were afraid that communicating romantic desire might ruin your friendship (see Chapter 10). Or maybe you were afraid to give relational advice to a friend because you worried about getting caught in the middle. The prototypical example of this is if you see a friend's romantic partner out with someone else. If you tell your friend what you saw, your friend might side with the partner and accuse you of being jealous or making things up. If you keep silent, your friend might be hurt in the long run. Giving relational advice is a tricky proposition. When people try to influence others to change their relationships, they usually use direct communication, logical appeals, and large doses of positivity (Dillard, 1989).

VERBAL POWER PLOYS

Traditionally, power and persuasion have been thought of as verbal activities. But in reality, communication that is powerful and persuasive consists of a combination of verbal and nonverbal cues.

Verbal Influence Strategies

Studies show that relational partners can choose from an assortment of strategies to influence each other, often called **compliance-gaining strategies** (Miller & Boster, 1988; Miller, Boster, Roloff, & Siebold, 1977; Wiseman & Schenck-Hamlin, 1981) or **influence strategies** (Falbo & Peplau, 1980). Research suggests that both prosocial and coercive control strategies may enhance personal emotional well-being and physical health and may have evolved to enable people to have better personal control and social positioning (Hawley, 2014; Massey-Abernathy & Byrd-Craven, 2016). Skilled communicators have an arsenal of strategies to deploy to influence particular people for particular purposes. People in more stable and equitable relationships use fewer verbal power strategies than people in unstable or inequitable relationships (Aida & Falbo, 1991), presumably because there is less they want to change. Research has also shown that powerful people are more likely to be persuasive than less powerful people, regardless of the strategies they use (Levine & Boster, 2001). For individuals who are low in power, the best strategy may be to phrase requests using a positive, polite tone (Levine & Boster, 2001).

DIRECT REQUESTS An obvious **interpersonal influence** strategy is the **direct request** (Wiseman & Schenck-Hamlin, 1981), also known as the **simple request** or asking (Falbo & Peplau, 1980). Studies show that this is the most common strategy for both men and women, most likely used by a person who feels powerful and supported (Levine & Boster, 2001; Morgan & Zurbriggen, 2007; Sagrestano, 1992). Interestingly, research has shown that in intimate relationships direct requests initially are not positively perceived or thought to be effective but 12 months later direct, positive, messages produced the most change (Overall, Fletcher, Simpson, & Sibley, 2009). Examples of direct requests include asking your boyfriend or girlfriend, "Could you turn down the stereo, please?" or saying, "I really wish you wouldn't swear in public." While these are not very sophisticated or strategic messages, they are usually effective, particularly in relationships with high levels of mutual respect and closeness. Indeed, in a study of unmarried heterosexual and gay couples, Falbo and Peplau (1980) found that the most satisfied couples typically use direct strategies. Similarly, in a study of married couples, Aida and Falbo (1991) found that satisfied couples used more direct and fewer indirect strategies than did unsatisfied couples.

BARGAINING A **bargaining strategy** involves agreeing to do something for someone if the person does something in return. In addition to bargaining (Falbo & Peplau, 1980; Howard, Blumstein, & Schwartz, 1986), this type of influence attempt has been called *promising* (Miller et al., 1977; Wiseman & Schenck-Hamlin, 1981) and the *quid pro quo strategy*. For example, one partner agrees not to watch football on Sunday if the other gives up smoking; then each partner is giving up something in return for a concession. Sometimes individuals using bargaining to persuade a partner will mention past favors or debts owed by the partner (Wiseman & Schenck-Hamlin, 1981). Sometimes people use bargaining to reward their partner prior to a persuasive request; this is called **pregiving** (Miller et al., 1977). Howard and fellow researchers (1986) found that more occupationally and relationally equal couples tended to bargain more than unequal ones. In unequal relationships, the more powerful person does not need to bargain to gain compliance, while the less powerful person lacks resources to use in the bargaining process. In unequal relationships, less powerful people are more likely to negotiate and bargain than more powerful people (Levine & Boster, 2001).

AVERSIVE STIMULATION Also called the **negative affect strategy** (Falbo & Peplau, 1980), **aversive stimulation** (Miller et al., 1977; Wiseman & Schenck-Hamlin, 1981) involves whining, sulking, complaining, crying, or acting angry to get one's way, hoping the receiver will eventually comply just to stop the aversive behavior. This strategy is unsophisticated and is viewed as childish because it is used by toddlers and small children. Sagrestano (1992) found that people perceived aversive stimulation as the second most negative and unpleasant power strategy among the 13 strategies she tested (**withdrawal** ranked first). Research on adolescent couples reveals that girls often use shaming or humiliating behaviors on their immature partner as power ploys, though final decisions are often made by the male partner in adolescent dyads (Bentley, Galliher, & Ferguson, 2007).

INGRATIATION Often called positive affect (Falbo & Peplau, 1980), liking (Miller et al., 1977), **ingratiation** (Wiseman & Schenck-Hamlin, 1981), "kissing up," or "sucking up," this strategy involves using excessive kindness to get one's way. A husband buying his wife flowers before asking for forgiveness or an athlete repeatedly complimenting her coach are examples of ingratiation. A person using ingratiation wants to be perceived as likable so that another person will want to be compliant. Research suggests that prosocial behavior is not necessarily altruistic; it may have evolved in humans to enhance personal power and control resources (Hawley, 2014). Of course, ingratiation strategies can backfire if they are perceived as insincere. Canary and Cody (1994) discussed the concept of **illicit ingratiation** that occurs when a person acts nice merely to gain compliance. Ingratiation is persuasive only if it is seen as honest rather than manipulative. Relatedly, during power struggles interactants equal in power use more humor than those unequal in power probably as a way of releasing tension and diffusing conflict (Dunbar, Banas, Rodriguez, Liu, & Abra, 2012).

HINTING Called **indirect requests,** suggesting (Falbo & Peplau, 1980), or **hinting** (Wiseman & Schenck-Hamlin, 1981), this strategy involves implying a request without ever coming out and stating one. For example, Ashley might hint to Tyler that lots of people are returning to college this fall after taking a break from school. A wife who mentions to her husband how nice it would be to take a vacation may be hinting that she wants to go somewhere for their anniversary. While this is a polite strategy, its effectiveness depends on the perceptiveness of one's partner. If the partner does not pick up on the hint, this strategy will fail. In other cases, the partner might understand what the sender is hinting at but nonetheless ignore the request. When the request is made in such an indirect manner, the partner's responsibility for responding diminishes.

MORAL APPEALS These compliance-gaining messages, which are also called **positive altercasting** and **negative altercasting** (Miller et al., 1977), take one of two forms. **Positive moral appeals** suggest that a good or moral person would comply with the request ("An understanding partner wouldn't nag me about school," says Tyler). **Negative moral appeals** suggest that only bad or immoral people would fail to comply ("Only an unambitious or unintelligent person would pass up an opportunity to complete his education," says Ashley). Both positive and negative moral appeals associate certain behaviors with the basic "goodness" of the

receiver. Such a strategy also ties into an individual's identity as a basically good person. As discussed in Chapter 2, people generally prefer to act consistent with their positive self-identities. So if Ashley sees herself as an understanding girlfriend and Tyler sees himself as an ambitious and intelligent person, they might be more likely to comply in response to moral appeals. But such appeals can also exacerbate conflict and lead to defensiveness, especially if a receiving partner perceives being attacked at a personal level (see Chapter 14).

MANIPULATION Manipulation is a set of strategies used to get one's way by making the partner feel guilty, ashamed, or jealous (Fleischmann et al., 2005; Wiseman & Schenck-Hamlin, 1981), including passive-aggressive strategies (see Chapter 13). Manipulation includes making a relational partner feel guilty for going on vacation without you or ashamed for flirting with another person. Suggesting the availability of other partners is manipulative and threatening but could be an effective strategy if a partner becomes jealous. If your partner fails to spend enough time with you at a party, you might flirt with someone hoping that your partner will get jealous and be more attentive to you. Such strategies can backfire because people dislike being manipulated. Manipulative strategies are perceived of as a special kind of aversive stimulation. Strategies that cause people to experience negative affect are seen as childish. Worse, a person may get turned off by manipulation and just avoid the manipulator. So by flirting with someone at a party, your partner simply might ignore you or leave with someone else rather than giving you the attention you want.

WITHDRAWAL Closely related to both aversive stimulation and manipulation are a set of strategies variously called distancing, avoidance (Guerrero, Andersen, Jorgensen, Spitzberg, & Eloy, 1995), withdrawal (Falbo & Peplau, 1980), or **passive aggression** that occur when people give their partners the silent treatment, ignore them, or limit communication with them. A woman in one of our classes gave a good example of withdrawal as an influence strategy. She had dated her fiancé for 6 years and thought he would give her an engagement ring for Christmas. When she failed to get a ring, she gave her fiancé the silent treatment until he asked what was wrong; eventually he bought her the ring. This might not be the best strategy. Over time, he began to wonder whether he would have proposed if she had not manipulated him. Worse, this strategy does not always work. Sometimes a partner gets fed up with being ignored and moves on. Sagrestano (1992) found withdrawal was perceived as the most negative of the 13 power strategies. Still, the withdrawal strategy can be effective in some situations. Sometimes people hesitate to bring up a sensitive subject, and by withdrawing, they let the partner be the one who initially asks, "What's wrong?" and starts the conversation. Or people might miss their partner and appreciate them more after spending time apart.

DECEPTION Some people use lies or **deception** as a compliance-gaining strategy (Wiseman & Schenck-Hamlin, 1981). People make false promises when they have no intention of keeping them. People exaggerate or make up information to gain compliance. For example, a teenager who wants a later curfew might tell his parents that all his friends get to stay out past midnight when few of them actually do. Aside from the ethical issues related to this strategy, it is a risky relational maneuver. Discovery of deception may result in a loss of trust and the deterioration of the relationship (see Chapter 13). Even if the relationship survives the discovery of deception, the partner may become suspicious or guarded, making persuasion difficult in the future.

DISTRIBUTIVE COMMUNICATION With **distributive strategies** or **antagonistic strategies,** people attempt to blame, hurt, insult, or berate their partner in an effort to gain compliance (Guerrero et al., 1995; Sillars, Coletti, Parry, & Rogers, 1982; Wiseman & Schenck-Hamlin, 1981). These strategies are sometimes called **bullying** (Howard et al., 1986), are usually ineffective, and often lead to escalated conflict (see Chapter 11)

and relational deterioration (Jayamaha & Overall, 2015). Howard and associates (1986) reported that contrary to some stereotypes, both men and women and both masculine and feminine people are likely to use distributive strategies. Unfortunately, distributive and aggressive strategies sometimes actually work in getting one's way and may have evolved as human resource control behavior (Hawley, 2014).

THREATS Threats such as faking a breakup, failing to cooperate with a partner until the partner gives in, or threatening to withhold resources such as money or information are typically ineffective. Howard and colleagues (1986) found that both men and women assert authority through self-serving threats. People also may engage in fake violence, issue violent warnings, and act as if they are going to hurt their partner but then not do so. A girl might shake her fist in front of her brother's face without hitting him to illustrate what might happen if he does not stop teasing her. People are more likely to use threats such as these when the partner is perceived to be low in power (Levine & Boster, 2001).

Relational Control Moves: One-Ups and One-Downs

Rogers and her associates developed a classic method to determine dominance and control in relational communication (Rogers & Farace, 1975; Rogers & Millar, 1988). In any conversation, messages can be coded as dominant and controlling, or **one-up messages**; deferent or accepting, or **one-down messages**; or neutral, **one-across messages**. The focus is on the *form* of the conversation, not the content. Consider the following interaction between teenage sisters:

Marissa: You've been on the phone for an hour—get off! (one-up)

Nicole: Okay. (one-down)

Marissa: Now! (one-up)

[Nicole tells her friend she will call her later and hangs up.]

Marissa: Thank you. (one-down)

Nicole: Ask a little more nicely next time. (one-up)

Coding a person's verbal behavior can reveal if the individual is domineering or submissive. Researchers can also study how the behavior of one partner impacts the relationship. For example, Rogers and Millar (1988) reported that when wives were domineering, both husbands and wives tended to experience less relational satisfaction. More significantly, by looking at patterns of one-up and one-down messages, we can determine the nature of the relationship between two people. This coding method represented a major conceptual breakthrough. A pair of utterances, called a **transact,** can be coded as symmetrical or **complementary.** If people engage in a pattern where one person uses mostly one-ups and the other person uses mostly one-downs, the pattern is complementary with one person dominant and the other person submissive. If both people use the same moves, it is **symmetrical behavior**. When two people repeatedly use one-up moves, it is called **competitive symmetry.** When two people repeatedly use one-down moves, the pattern is called **submissive symmetry.** Along with these variations, much conversation is neutral in terms of control. When both partners exchange these one-across messages, the pattern is termed **neutral symmetry.** And when a one-up or one-down message is paired with a one-across message, a **transition** has occurred. Box 12.3 provides examples of these five interaction patterns. Research has shown that spouses who report dyadic inequality in their marriages have more competitive symmetry (Rogers & Millar, 1988).

However, all interactions do not fall neatly into these categories. Take the interaction between Marissa and Nicole. At the outset of the interaction, Marissa is the dominant sister, but by the end of the interaction, Nicole asserts herself. It is also important to consider nonverbal communication and the context when interpreting one-up and one-down statements. A statement such as "You sure are in a good mood today" is often considered a one-down message but as a one-up message if delivered in a sarcastic tone of voice.

Powerful and Powerless Speech

Investigators have identified characteristics associated with **powerful speech** that occur when speakers focus mainly on themselves, dominate conversations, redirect the conversation away from topics others are discussing, and interrupt (Fitzpatrick & Badzinski, 1994). Men are more likely than women to use powerful speech (Kalbfleisch & Herold, 2006; Leaper & Robnett, 2011), though it is dependent on the topic (Palomares, 2009). Falbo and Peplau (1980) found that women used more indirect strategies such as hinting whereas men used more direct strategies such as open communication. Women were more likely to use unilateral strategies such as pouting or negative affect whereas men were more likely to use bilateral strategies such as debate or negotiation. Two meta-analytic reviews of nearly 60 combined studies show that men tend to use more powerful language than women including fewer hedges, disclaimers, and tag questions, but the size of the gender effect is small (Leaper & Robnett, 2011; Timmerman, 2002). Results showed that women are more likely to use less powerful speech because they are more polite and interpersonally sensitive rather than because they are low in assertiveness. In a study of e-mail language use, Palomares (2009) reported no sex difference in the use of powerful language on gender-neutral topics. Nonetheless, research has shown that more powerful speech creates more credibility and persuasive power, enabling males and other users of powerful language to be more influential (Burrell & Koper, 1998).

It is important to note that differential use of strategies appears to be less a function of sex or gender than one of power or powerlessness. Cowan, Drinkard, and MacGavin (1984) found that both men and women use more indirect and unilateral strategies when communicating with a power figure. By contrast, both females and males are more direct and bilateral when communicating with a power equal. Kollock, Blumstein, and Schwartz (1985) found that the more powerful person in the relationship interrupts the partner more, regardless of sex or sexual orientation. Also, whether men or women use powerful verbal behavior depends on the topic. A study by Dovidio, Brown, Heltman, Ellyson, and Keating (1988) revealed that on traditionally male topics, such as working on a car, men engage in more verbal power strategies, such as speech initiation and total time talking. However, women use more of these verbal power strategies when discussing traditionally female topics such as cooking or raising children. Women physicians who use more total talk time, talked while engaged in other activities, and spoke in a louder voice were perceived as significantly more dominant (Mast, Hall, Cronauer, & Cousin, 2011).

Studies report that women use more **powerless speech** than men (Giles & Wiemann, 1987). Powerless speech occurs when people use tag questions or hedges. Tag questions involve asking people to affirm that one is making sense or that they understand. For example, you might ask, "You know what I mean, don't you?" Hedges refer to statements that give the sender or receiver an "out." Statements such as "I'm not sure this is right but . . . " and questions such as "You did say you'd help me with this, didn't you?" exemplify hedges. Although women use powerless speech more often than men, such speech is not always submissive. Sometimes women use tag questions and hedges in creative ways to get more information, accomplish goals, and improve their relationships (Giles & Wiemann, 1987). In addition, speaking is a skill that can be taught, and many women have learned to use more powerful speech (Timmerman, 2002).

NONVERBAL POSITIONS OF POWER

Verbal communication signals power, but nonverbal communication is an even richer source of power

---

BOX 12.3 HIGHLIGHTS
EXAMPLES OF TRANSACTS

Complementarity

Ashley: If you really don't want to go back to school, it's okay. (one-down)

Tyler: I won't go back no matter what you say. (one-up)

Marissa: We should pool our money together to buy something for Mom and Dad's anniversary. (one-up)

Nicole: Okay. How much do you think I should give? (one-down)

Competitive Symmetry

Tyler: Stop nagging me about school. (one-up)

Ashley: Then get off your butt and look for a better job. (one-up)

Submissive Symmetry

Nicole: What should we buy Mom and Dad for their anniversary? (one-down)

Marissa: I don't know. You decide. (one-down)

Neutral Symmetry

Marissa: They have been married 23 years. (one-across)

Nicole: Grandma and Grandpa were married for over 50 years before Grandpa died. (one-across)

Transition*

Tyler: I wish you would stop talking about graduation all the time. (one-up)

Ashley: Hey, did you see *American Idol* last night? (one-across)

Nicole: I wonder if there are tickets left for that concert Mom said she'd like to go to. (one-across)

Marissa: If you want me to, I can check. (one-down)

---

*Transitions include all combinations of one-across messages paired with one-up or one-down messages, regardless of order.

messages. The animal kingdom is a nonverbal world and is replete with dominance displays and pecking orders. Competition for mates, food, and territory can be fierce and deadly. Animals evolved power cues that establish dominance hierarchies without the need for deadly combat, and these pecking orders are all established nonverbally. Humans have more complex power structures, and these are mostly nonverbal in nature (Andersen, 2008). Moreover, research suggests that perceptions of power are more influential than the actual power people possess (Hall et al., 2005). Power is communicated via many forms of nonverbal communication, as introduced in Chapter 1. Thus, it is important to remember that the context and the relationship between people help determine if these behaviors are perceived as powerful.

Physical Appearance

Before a word is ever uttered, people make judgments about power from others' physical appearance. Research shows that more physically attractive people are more influential and that women are most likely to use physical attraction to increase power or persuasion (Davies, Goetz, & Shackelford, 2008). Formal, fashionable, and expensive clothes also indicate power and dominance (Andersen, 2008; Bickman, 1974; Morris, 1977). Research suggests that wearing high-status brand clothing induces more submissive behavior in interaction partners in both male and female dyads (Fennis, 2008). Similarly, expensive shoes and the trendiest workout or basketball shoes are major status symbols that imply power (Andersen, 2008). Women's clothing, once inflexibly prescribed, is now quite varied. Women can dress informally or formally in modest or sexy attire and in feminine or masculine styles. Men's clothing, by contrast, is proscribed more rigidly and generally must be modest, masculine, and appropriate to the occasion (Kaiser, 1997). Despite the greater variability of women's clothing, when women violate norms by dressing in inappropriate attire perceived as too trendy, sexy, nerdy, or masculine, they produce more negative reactions than

men who violate clothing norms. Uniforms convey the power associated with an occupation (surgeon, police officer), but uniforms also convey powerlessness because they strip away individuality and other status symbols (e.g., jewelry) (Joseph & Alex, 1972). Clothing color also makes a difference. Black athletic uniforms, for instance, may be associated with power and aggression (Frank & Gilovich, 1988).

Studies show that the mesomorphic or muscular body is associated with power. Likewise, height is related to power and confidence (Andersen, 2008; Burgoon et al., 2010). Physical dominance is conveyed by height and broad shoulders and is related to perceptions of power, attractiveness, and mate value, particularly in women's perceptions of men (Bryan, Webster, & Mahaffey, 2011). This **principle of elevation** (Guerrero & Floyd, 2006) suggests that fair or not, height or vertical position is associated with power. This is why powerful people are often seated in elevated positions. Kings and queens sit on thrones, judges sit above the courtroom; by contrast, people bow to show submission. In interpersonal interactions, people exercise power by looming over someone who is seated (Andersen, 2008). Height differentials are also related to use of space. Moving in close and standing over someone is often perceived as intimidating. The greater height and muscle mass of men, compared to women, is an explanation for the traditional dominance and oppression women experience at the hands of men. Traditional ideals of the tall, dark, and handsome man and the petite woman have perpetuated this stereotype (Andersen, 2004). However, physical appearance is most important during initial interactions; once a relationship is established, its effects diminish (Andersen, 2008).

Spatial Behavior

The study of interpersonal space and distance, called **proxemics**, reveals how the use of space reflects and creates power (Andersen, Gannon, & Kalchik, 2013). Invading someone's space and "getting in someone's face" are powerful, intimidating behaviors. In the United States, most people interact at about arm's length, but powerful people, such as superiors communicating with subordinates, or parents talking to children, can invade another's space (Carney, Hall, & LeBeau, 2005; Henley, 1977; Remland, 1981). Subordinates, by contrast, must respect the territory of their superiors. As the prerogative principle suggests, powerful individuals can violate personal space norms by invading other people's space or by remaining spatially aloof. Others, in turn, view these violations as dominance displays (Burgoon & Dillman, 1995; Hall et al., 2005; Mast et al., 2011).

A higher status person can give someone the "cold shoulder" by adopting an indirect body orientation and not facing that person. A husband who reads the paper during a conversation with his wife or the teenager who texts while talking to her parents may be exercising power but are often perceived as rude. Direct, open body positions convey immediacy and intimacy (see Chapter 6) but also are indicants of confidence and power (Carney et al., 2005; Hall et al., 2005; Mast et al., 2011).

Eye Behavior

The study of eye behavior, called oculesics, reveals numerous power behaviors, including staring, gazing while speaking, and failing to look when listening. People perceived as powerful are also looked at more by others, a principle we call **visual centrality.** Eye contact is usually affiliative and friendly, but staring is powerful, rude, and intrusive (LaFrance & Mayo, 1978). Looking less while listening is the prerogative of the powerful; low-status individuals must remain visually attentive. Direct eye contact while speaking is perceived as a dominant, intimidating, behavior (Andersen, 2004; Carney et al., 2005; Hall et al., 2005). Recent research shows that direct eye contact by women communicates greater power with no loss of likability (Williams & Tiedens, 2016). Although eye contact while speaking is dominant, eye contact while listening is a submissive behavior. This finding led Exline, Ellyson, and Long (1975) to develop the **visual dominance ratio,** a function of the time spent looking while

speaking divided by the time spent looking while listening. A high score indicates interpersonal dominance. Shy, submissive people often break eye contact when confronted with direct gaze (Andersen, 2004). Similarly, excessive blinking is perceived as weak and submissive (Mehrabian, 1981).

Body Movements

Kinesics, the study of body movement, reveals that several body positions, facial expressions, and gestures can communicate power and status. Expansive body positions with arms and legs apart and away from the body and the hands-on-hips positions convey power and dominance (Andersen, 2004; Hall et al., 2005; LaFrance & Mayo, 1978; Remland, 1982). Superiors can sprawl and even invade another's personal space (Andersen, 2008). Powerful people can lean back to relax or lean forward to make a point; submissive people usually must remain still and attentive. In most situations, relaxation rules (Andersen, 2004). Interestingly, couples that are equal in power tend to display harmonious synchronized nonverbal behavior indicative of respect and connection (Dunbar & Mejia, 2013).

Gestures, especially grand, sweeping ones and those directed at other people, create perceptions of dominance, dynamism, and panache (Burgoon et al., 1998; Carney et al., 2005; Dunbar & Abra, 2010; Hall et al., 2005). Pointing at someone or wagging one's finger in another person's face is a powerful but hostile move (Remland, 1981; Scheflen, 1972). Such gestures are intrusive acts, much like invading a person's space or, as we discuss next, brashly or rudely touching another person.

Some facial expressions, such as a deep frown or a scornful sneer, are dominant and threatening. A jutting jaw, narrowed eyes, and a face reddened with anger are facial expressions that communicate dominance (Andersen, 2008; Carney et al., 2005; Henley, 1977). Conversely, expressions of fear and sadness are perceived as signs of lower power (Carney et al., 2005). Facial expressiveness and skill at facial expressiveness is thought to be dominant (Carney et al., 2005; Hall et al., 2005) and associated with more power (Dunbar & Burgoon, 2005). Because smiling often conveys submissiveness and the absence of threat, it is usually an appeasing gesture in both humans and other primates (Andersen & Guerrero, 1998b; Hall et al., 2005). Women smile more and by doing so, send friendly, nonthreatening messages (Andersen, 2008). Smiling women are also more likely to be interrupted by their partner than either unsmiling women or men (Kennedy & Camden, 1983). However, smiling can convey dominance in some situations. When smiling is used with other power cues, dominant smiles convey confidence, power, and social skill (Burgoon & Bacue, 2003; Dunbar & Abra, 2010; Hall et al., 2005; Hall, Coats, Smith LeBeau, 2006; Huang & Galinsky, 2010).

Touch

The study of interpersonal touch, haptics, has shown that while touch is usually an affectionate, intimate behavior, it can be used to display one's power (Andersen et al., 2013). The initiation of touch is perceived as more dominant than receiving or reciprocating touch, because the person who initiates touch is controlling the interaction (Carney et al., 2005; Hall et al., 2005; Major & Heslin, 1982). Among casual daters, men are more likely to initiate touch, presumably because social norms dictate that men have the prerogative to try to escalate intimacy in the early stages of relationships. Women, however, initiate touch more often in marital relationships (Guerrero & Andersen, 1994; Stier & Hall, 1984). Guiding another person through a door, physically restraining an individual, and touching someone in an intimate place are all indicative of high power (Andersen, 2008). But caution is advised; charges of sexual harassment and even sexual assault can be the consequences of excessive or inappropriate touch (Lee & Guerrero, 2001). Even when the sender means to send a message of affiliation, the receiver can perceive touch as inappropriate or harassing. While early research (Henley, 1977) indicated that touch was a highly dominant, powerful behavior used by men to maintain gender difference, more recent research finds little support for this view and

suggests that touch is more affiliative than dominant (Andersen, 2008; Burgoon & Dillman, 1995; Hall et al., 2005; Stier & Hall, 1984). Indeed, when touch is used to communicate power, women touch more while discussing feminine topics (Smith, Vogel, Madon, & Edwards, 2011), denying Henley's gender politics hypothesis. Longitudinal research suggests that receiving intrusive and negative forms of touch early in life is associated with poor romantic relationship quality, conflict, and aggression later in life (Ostrov & Collins, 2007).

The Voice

The content of spoken words is the subject of verbal communication, but voice tones and intonations are in the realm of nonverbal communication, called vocalics or **paralinguistics.** Social status can be detected from one's voice fairly accurately (Andersen, 2008), with higher-class speakers having clearer articulation and sharper enunciation of consonants. Similarly, fewer filled pauses, like *ah* or *um* and other speech errors, are associated with greater status and power (Carney et al., 2005; Hall et al., 2005). Listeners can make fairly accurate judgments about people's levels of dominance by listening to samples of their voices (Scherer, 1972). Vocal variation, which is perceived as an immediate, affiliative behavior (see Chapter 7), is also perceived as more powerful (Hall et al., 2005). Generally, louder, deeper, and more varied voices are perceived as more dominant (Andersen, 2008; Cheng, Tracy, Ho, & Henrich, 2016; Dunbar & Abra, 2010; Hall et al., 2005). Some recent research suggests higher-pitched voices are actually more dominant and also are perceived as more dominant (Ko, Sadler, & Galinsky, 2015; Tusing & Dillard, 2000), and louder and slower speech rates are viewed as more dominant than softer or faster speech rates. More expressive speech is rated as more dominant. When people are making an important point, they might vary their pitch and talk slowly but loudly and deliberately. Other research suggests that moderately fast voices are perceived as confident and powerful because they suggest that the speaker knows about the subject and needs no time to think (Burgoon et al., 2010; Hall et al., 2005). Together this research suggests that both slower and faster voices can be considered dominant under certain circumstances. In close relationships, departures from normal modes of interaction may signal dominance. For instance, when people who are normally soft spoken raise their voices, even slightly, dominance is communicated.

Time

The study of the interpersonal use of time, chronemics, has revealed that the way people employ time tells a lot about how powerful and dominant they are. Speaking time is related to dominance, especially for men (Mast, 2002). Powerful people are allowed to speak longer and have more speaking turns, which gives them more opportunity to influence others. Waiting time also reflects power; waiting is the fate of the powerless, as people are generally waiting for the powerful. The powerless wait in long lines for welfare checks and job interviews while the rich and powerful have reservations and can relax in luxurious lounges on the rare occasions when they must wait (Henley, 1977). Doctors are notorious for exercising their power prerogative to keep patients waiting, and many executives let people "cool their heels" as a ploy before negotiating a business deal. However, keeping relational partners waiting may be a bad idea because it signals their lack of importance and could be perceived as inconsiderate.

In contrast, spending time with relational partners is one of the most meaningful signs of love. Time spent together shows that a relationship is valued. Egland and colleagues (1997) found that among all the behaviors that convey understanding, equality, and intimacy, spending time together is the most important. Conversely, like being late, people who spend little time with children, friends, or spouses are communicating that the relationship is of little importance to them.

Artifacts

Artifacts are ultimate status symbols. Having a big house, luxury cars, and expensive toys are signs of power, particularly in our status-conscious, materialistic society. Some status symbols are indirect, such as the largest office, the reserved parking space, and the most expensive and slimmest briefcase (Korda, 1975). Similarly, giving expensive or rare gifts to loved ones is a sign of their status and importance in one's life.

POWER AND INFLUENCE IN FAMILIES

Power is part of the fabric of family relationships. Although equality is often the goal, parents sometimes have more knowledge than their children, and one spouse sometimes has more financial resources than the other. Some of the main power issues that surface in parent–child relationships, in romantic relationships, and in marriages reveal significant considerations for our close relationships.

Parent and Child Relationships

Parents need power. No one believes that a 2-year-old is capable of making important decisions. Parents must control the behavior of their young children, but control should be inversely related to age. Clearly, the youngest children need the most control. Teenagers still need considerable control and guidance, but parents are kidding themselves if they believe they can start to become strong parents during the teen years. Indeed, most parents decrease their power and dominance over their children from early to late adolescence (De Goede, Branje, & Meeus, 2009). Attempts to crack down on an unruly teen who has developed no moral foundation will usually result in conflict and defiance. A strong foundation laid in early childhood helps children to become good decision makers and responsible teens. Indeed, the whole enterprise of parenting involves the gradual relinquishing of authority, from total control over an infant or toddler to minimal control over a young adult. Gibran (1923/1970) famously said the following:

> Your children are not your children. They come through you but not from you. And though they are with you, yet they belong not to you. You are the bows from which your children as living arrows are sent forth. Let your bending in the archer's hand be for gladness. (pp. 18–19)

Gibran's quote highlights two junctures at which power is especially important in parent–child relationships: (1) at the beginning, when parents are raising infants and very young children, and (2) during the teenage years, when children assert their independence. Although parents need to control young children, parents are not always more influential than their offspring. As anyone who has seen a mother trying desperately to calm a crying infant or a father trying to get his toddler to eat her vegetables can attest, young children can have a huge impact on their parents' behavior. Yingling (1995) put it this way:

> That parents influence their infants is beyond dispute, but infants' influence on parents has begun to receive attention as well. . . . At some point in the first year, infants begin to recognize the power of their interactive behaviors to influence the primary relationship. However, interactive effects begin even before that recognition. (p. 35)

Without consciously intending to, newborns persuade parents to feed them in the middle of the night, change their diapers around the clock, and soothe them when they are upset. As infants get older, they learn to manage social interactions through crying, cooing, and smiling, and by the time they are toddlers, they are particularly good at using the word *no* to assert themselves (Lewis & Rosenblum, 1974). Later, children continue to use strategies to influence their parents and siblings. Firstborns are influential and act as positive and negative role models for younger siblings whereas those born second are influenced to both model and differentiate from their older siblings, but firstborns reported little influence from a younger sibling (Whiteman & Christiansen, 2008).

Naturally, parents use much more sophisticated influence strategies than their young children. Classic work by Baumrind (1971, 1991) suggests that there are three general approaches to parenting: (1) authoritarian, (2) permissive, and (3) authoritative.

Authoritarian parents are demanding, directive, and nonresponsive. They control and monitor their children's behavior continuously so that it conforms to strict standards of order. In being nonresponsive, they expect their children to obey them without question. Authoritarian parents do not believe that they need to explain reasons behind disciplinary actions to their children—their word is "law" and is not to be questioned.

Permissive parents, by contrast, are undemanding, nondirective, and responsive. These parents relinquish most authority and let their children regulate their own behavior in most situations. If they punish their children, they are lenient penalties. Permissive parents try to be responsive to their children by showing them support and giving them encouragement. Unlike the authoritarian parent, who acts like a dictator, the permissive parent acts more like a friend and the child is given considerable, often excessive power.

Authoritative parents blend aspects of the authoritarian and permissive styles. These parents are demanding and directive but also responsive. Authoritative parents have clear standards and expectations for how their children should behave, and these standards are communicated to the children in terms they can understand. These parents set limitations, but they also allow their children some freedom and privacy. Authoritative parents are responsive in that they generally avoid harsh punishments and focus instead on reasoning with their children and providing support. The authoritative parent is more like a benevolent teacher than either a dictator or friend. Although the parent has more power than the child, the child still has a voice in the decision-making process, and parents and children mutually influence each other.

Hoffman's (1980) work identified two similar styles of parenting: (1) **power assertion** and (2) induction. Power assertion, similar to the authoritarian style, refers to parents who believe that they should be in complete control and can demand compliance without having to explain why. The prototypical dialogue that characterizes this style is when a parent issues a directive ("You cannot go to Olivia's party"), the child asks for an explanation ("Why not?"), and the parent asserts authority without giving an explanation ("Because your father and I say you can't go—that's why not"). Power assertion strategies can also include threats, spankings or other physical punishment, and harsh verbal reprimands.

The **inductive philosophy** of parenting is similar to the authoritative style. When parents use induction, they believe that it is critical that they provide children with reasons for their disciplinary actions. They explain their decisions in the hope that the children will learn how to make good decisions on their own. For example, if Lauren was told that she could not go Olivia's party, her parents would explain why. Perhaps Lauren's parents know that Olivia's parents will not be home and that some of the kids are bringing beer, or perhaps Lauren had violated her curfew the last three times she went to a party. In any case, Lauren's parents would explain their thinking, and Lauren would have the opportunity to reason with them.

Inductive parenting strategies are more effective because they involve explanation and reasoning. Burleson, Delia, and Applegate (1992) argued that such strategies are **reflection enhancing** because they encourage children to think about their misconduct, including how their actions affect themselves and others. Studies show that children, from toddlers to teenagers, who are disciplined using the authoritative or inductive style have higher self-esteem, are more morally mature, engage in more prosocial and cooperative behavior, show more

communication competence, and are more accepted by their peers than are children who are disciplined using other styles (Baumrind, 1991; Buri, Louiselle, Misukanis, & Mueller, 1988; Burleson et al., 1992; Hart, DeWolf, Wozniak, & Burts, 1992; Hoffman, 1970; Kennedy, 1992).

Of course, authoritarian or power assertive strategies might be necessary in some cases. Steinmetz (1979) found that power strategies often lead to more rapid compliance than do inductive strategies. Similarly, studies have shown that power assertive strategies are efficient when parents are seeking immediate, short-term compliance (Grusec & Kuczynski, 1980; Kuczynski, 1984). Thus, when a mother is worried that her young son might hurt himself by crossing the street without looking or by using drugs, an authoritarian strategy might be most effective in the short term, with inductive explanations given later.

SEPARATION AND INDIVIDUATION As children grow older and become more independent, a moral foundation based on explanations and reasoning rather than commands helps them make better decisions. Such a foundation is particularly important during adolescence when teenagers become more independent and sometimes rebel against their parents' authority (Andersen, 2004; De Goede et al., 2009). By their early teens, most children depend more on their friends than their parents when it comes to making decisions and asking for advice (Steinberg & Silverberg, 1986). Indeed, teens will engage in risky behaviors like alcohol, tobacco, drugs, and sex in order to gain social status among their peers (Agan et al., 2015). Similarly, teens yield much less to their parents and insist on making their own decisions much more often when they reach mid-adolescence (Steinberg, 1981). The teen years are a transition between the time when children are heavily dependent on their parents and the time when teenagers become responsible, independent young adults. Scholars have referred to this transition period as a process of **separation and individuation** whereby teenagers distance themselves, to some degree, from their parents and develop an individual identity apart from the family structure (Guerrero & Afifi, 1995b).

During this transition period, power struggles between parents and teenagers are inevitable. Teenagers are ready to express independence before parents are ready to relinquish authority or before the teens can make responsible adult decisions. This can lead to a period of "storm and stress" characterized by emotional distance between parents and children and increased conflict (Kidwell, Fischer, Dunham, & Baranowski, 1983; Paikoff & Brooks-Gunn, 1991; Steinberg, 1987). Researchers have found that parent–child interaction during the teen years is often marked by less warmth (Paikoff & Brooks-Gunn, 1991; Steinberg, 1981), more interruptions by teens (Jacob, 1974), and less open communication (Guerrero & Afifi, 1995b).

Some adolescent-parent relationships are stormier than others. If children gradually show that they are responsible enough to make their own decisions and parents gradually relinquish authority, the transition from child to young adult can be marked by more cooperation and mutual respect than rebellion. Along these lines, Hill and Holmbeck (1986) argued that adolescence is a time of family regrouping, as parents and teenagers renegotiate rules and role relationships. Hill and Holmbeck also argued that the process of separation and individuation does not preclude close relationships between parents and children. Instead, this period of transition often leads to a redefinition of the parent–child relationship from an authority-based relationship, characterized by unequal power, to one characterized by mutual friendship and respect. Furthermore, Grotevant and Cooper (1985) found that by age 17 most teens had begun renegotiating relational rules and roles with their parents. The key to a successful transition lies partially with the parents, who need to let adolescents become more individuated while still providing a supportive and caring environment (Campbell, Adams, & Dobson, 1984; Papini, Sebby, & Clark, 1989).

Traditional Versus Egalitarian Marriages

Relationships are complex, and maintaining any long-term relationship is difficult (see Chapter 10). Although there is no one formula for an ideal romantic relationship, evidence suggests that peer relationships characterized by respect and relative equality are healthier, more satisfying, and more likely to succeed. This is true for both friendships and dating relationships (Roiger, 1993). However, equality may be harder to achieve in marriages than in many friendships or dating relationships because spouses typically share money and possessions and have to divide household chores. This division is not usually equitable; most working married women in the United States and throughout the world are still responsible for the majority of household chores and an even larger percentage of child care (Bauer, 2016). This difference persists into later life; studies suggest that wives have lower satisfaction and lower power than do husbands (Bulanda, 2011). Interestingly, most women think their relationships are equitable despite their greater contributions to household labor (Braun, Lewin-Epstein, Stier, & Baumgartner, 2008). Trying to find a fair way to share resources and divide labor can lead to power struggles within even the best of marriages.

When studying issues of equality, social scientists have described two different types of marriages: (1) traditional and (2) egalitarian (Steil, 2000). According to Steil, **traditional marriages** are "based on a form of benevolent male dominance coupled with clearly specialized roles. Thus, when women are employed, the responsibility for family work is retained by the women, who add the career role to their traditionally held family role" (p. 128). Of course, some women in traditional marriages are not employed or only work part-time so that they can devote considerable time to managing the house and raising the children.

Some couples are very happy in traditional marriages (Fitzpatrick, 1988). However, in the 21st century, most women are not satisfied with traditional gender roles, and dual-career households are the rule rather than the exception. In dual-career marriages (as well as other close relationships in which people live together), partners need to negotiate roles related to household responsibilities rather than rely on traditional gender roles. Thus, although various types of marriages can be fulfilling, studies show that the best chance for happiness occurs in marriages in which the balance of power is nearly equal (Aida & Falbo, 1991; DeMaris, 2007; Schwartz, 1994; Steil, 2000; Thompson & Walker, 1989). In an **egalitarian marriage,** also called **peer marriage** or sharing marriage (Schwartz, 1994), "Both spouses are employed, both are actively involved in parenting, and both share in the responsibilities and duties of the household" (Steil, 2000, p. 128). Combining money into a single pool and making collaborative decisions on how to spend it are also associated with more relational satisfaction (Vogler et al., 2008).

Egalitarian marriages are often more intimate than traditional marriages. Most egalitarian marriages are deep and true friendships, as well as romances. Furthermore, emotionally bonded spouses are likely to achieve equality in their relationships. Research conducted in Scandinavia by Thagaard (1997) showed that "close emotional ties between spouses are linked to the interpretation of the relationship in terms of equality. The perception of equality is based on the ability to influence the relationship beginning with one's own values" (p. 373). Aida and Falbo (1991) found that partners in egalitarian marriages used fewer dominant power strategies than partners in traditional marriages, perhaps because they could influence each other without power plays. Moreover, a study of relationships in 32 countries, found that female empowerment was linked to more equal division of household chores (Knudsen & Waerness, 2008). When partners influence each other in equal, independent relationships, they use more diverse and egalitarian influence strategies than do traditional couples (Mannino & Deutsch, 2007; Witteman & Fitzpatrick, 1986).

Partners in traditional, unequal relationships, by contrast, are more likely to use blatant power strategies such as verbal aggression and less likely to use compliance-gaining strategies (Witteman & Fitzpatrick, 1986). They also use less open communication. Studies have compared couples in interdependent, egalitarian marriages to those in more separate, isolated marriages. Those in equalitarian marriages with equal power were more likely to express complaints and talk about relational problems than those in separate or traditional style marriages (Solomon et al., 2004; Worley & Samp, 2016). In fact, chronically powerless individuals are likely to seek revenge on a powerful person following an episode where they experience an episode of high power (Strelan, Weick, & Vasiljevic, 2014).

Equality has also been associated with better mental health whereas inequality is sometimes associated with lesser mental health. Among couples with troubled marriages, inequality is likely to be associated with depression symptoms in the less powerful partner (Bagarozzi, 1990). Even people in troubled marriages who have an equal power structure are less likely to have severe mental or emotional problems. Halloran (1998) suggested that inequality in close relationships is a cause of both depression and low-quality marriages. Moreover, this pattern leads to a vicious cycle. As one spouse becomes depressed, the other spouse must take over more control of the family, leading to greater inequality. In their major review of justice and love relationships, Hatfield, Rapson, and Aumer-Ryan (2008) concluded the following:

> In the end, fairness and equity matter. Scientists have found this to be the case for most couples—single, living together, married; affluent or poor; dating for a few weeks or married for 20 years. In all of these groups, the degree of reward, fairness, and equity are linked to sexual satisfaction, marital happiness, contentment, satisfaction, and marital stability. (p. 425)

Equality of marriage does not simply "happen." It takes commitment by both partners. As Schwartz (1994) observed, "Social forces and

BOX 12.4 AROUND THE WORLD
GLOBAL VARIATIONS IN GENDER EQUALITY

Cultures have many different philosophies about power. The Scandinavian countries of Northern Europe have relatively little social class structure; people have similar levels of power, and there is little difference between the status of men and women. The most gender equal countries in the world are Sweden, Norway, the Netherlands, Denmark, and Finland, all Northern European liberal democracies with a long history of equal rights for women. If you visit these countries, it will be hard to find instances of gender discrimination. The very perception of power differs across culture. One study found that Germans are more sensitive to differences in people's status than Americans or Arabs (Bente, Leuschner, Al Issa, & Blascovich, 2010).

Other countries display more power distance, with highly structured social classes and great differences between the status of men and women (Andersen, 2011b). When one of your authors was research director of the Japan-US Telecommunication Research Institute, of the hundreds of telecommunication executives he worked with, only one was a woman. Likewise, in countries like Mexico, Venezuela, Austria, and Switzerland, women are considered less powerful than men and are often expected to defer to their male partners (Andersen, 2011b; Hofstede, 2001). For examples, a wife is expected to move if her husband has a job opportunity somewhere far way, but husbands are not expected to do the same for their wives. In these countries, it is easy to find cases of gender discrimination (as defined in the United States), and it is easy for women from the United States to unknowingly violate cultural rules about the place and role of women.

While gender equality does not exist to the same degree in the United States as it does in Northern Europe, most of the United States is closer to Sweden than it is to Japan when it comes to the equality of men and women in relationships. But here is the catch: People from the United States come from every country and culture on Earth, and your romantic partner may have completely different values regarding the role of men and women in close relationships. It is important to select romantic partners with similar values about gender equality or to negotiate differences early in a relationship. In a culture as diverse as the United States, one should never assume that a person has the same values as you do when it comes to gender and power in close relationships.

psychological processes tenaciously maintain marriage along the old guidelines. Women still look to men to provide larger and more predictable income that establishes the family's social class and creature comforts" (p. 8). Several forces conspire against equality. Here in the second decade of the new millennium, women in the United States still earned less than 80% of what men earn, creating a power discrepancy and dependence on the part of many wives. Childbearing typically impacts a woman's career and earning power more than her husband's. Perhaps even more important, in terms of household labor, most so-called egalitarian relationships are not really so equal after all. In heterosexual relationships, women still tend to do more of the household work than men, when even both partners are working. Centuries of hierarchical relationships do not disappear overnight, nor do the power structures that exist in most families. While great progress has been made in elevating the status of women, sources of inequality still exist that will take additional years and effort to break down. Culture is another force that impacts how equal men and women are in relationships (see Box 12.4).

In the marriages and relationships between gay men and especially between lesbians, sharing of tasks is more equal throughout the world (Bauer, 2016; Goldberg & Perry-Jenkins, 2007; Kurdek, 2007; Shechory & Ziv, 2007). Like heterosexual couples, more equal division of labor is associated with greater relational satisfaction in both gay and lesbian couples (Kurdek, 2007). This is in contrast to heterosexual couples, where women still do the majority of household tasks (see Chapter 10).

SUMMARY AND APPLICATION

Power and influence are present in almost every human relationship, including Tyler and Ashley's. Whether somebody is persuading a roommate to take out the trash, asking one's child to be home at a certain time, or deciding if and when to marry a dating partner, some level of interpersonal influence is present. Power is a perception. But people do not automatically have power; rather, power is granted to people. Resources such as money, social standing, and love give people the ability to be powerful, especially when these resources are scarce, but ultimately, people are only as influential as others let them be.

In Tyler and Ashley's relationship, they can assert power and try to influence one another using a variety of verbal and nonverbal strategies. Some are ineffective, like Tyler's withdrawal behavior when he refuses to discuss relationship issues, or like Ashley's constant nagging, which she knows does no good. Tyler and Ashley are at their best when they use a large assortment of influence strategies they have in their repertoire and when they select appropriate strategies in a given situation that are the most effective at persuasion.

Power is tied to issues of authority and equality. Child dependence and parental authority initially mark parent–child relationships. Gradually, however, parents relinquish control and children assert their independence—a process that prepares children to be responsible young adults. In marriage, the husband typically has more concrete resources (e.g., income, occupational status) than the wife, which can reduce her power base. Women who have higher-status careers than their husbands are perceived by others as having more power but also as less likeable and less likely to be satisfied in their marriage (Hettinger, Hutchinson, & Bosson, 2014). Ashley, like the aforementioned couple, has better job offers than Tyler does, and will be more independent and powerful as a result. In fact, Ashley's ambition and Tyler's laziness may create a power imbalance and threaten the equality and stability of the relationship. Ashley thus has

dependence power that makes her more powerful in the relationship. Hopefully they will resolve this power discrepancy, as research shows that both men and women are usually happier and the relationship is stronger in egalitarian marriages than in traditional marriages where one partner is more powerful.

Power and equality certainly are important in relationships. As discussed in Chapters 10 and 14, relationships function best when people experience more rewards than costs and when they feel that they are being treated fairly. Ashley feels that Tyler is not trying hard enough and that the relationship sometimes has a poor cost-benefit ratio. This is true not in just heterosexual relationships, but gay men and lesbians also believe that it is important to have an egalitarian relationship. Achieving equality, however, is a difficult task. Ashley and Tyler need to equally value the different resources they bring to the relationship. One strength in Ashley and Tyler's relationship is that they have the power to influence decisions without getting their way at the expense of the partner. And if Tyler is less ambitious about his career, perhaps he can do more of the household tasks such as cleaning and home repair to provide balance between the partners.

It is important for Tyler and Ashley to realize some facts about power. Power is a perception that is simultaneously a reality for a person. If Tyler believes Ashley is too powerful or controlling in the relationship, they both have to deal with that perception and either the perception or behavior must change to resolve that discrepancy.

Tyler is right to be concerned about the future of the relationship. People with considerable resources—like Ashley's beauty, occupational status, and intelligence—have more power since they have more alternatives. And like so many women today, who are graduating from college in greater numbers than are men, her excellent job offers give her the ability to be self-sufficient and powerful in ways beyond traditional sources of feminine power such as sex and beauty.

KEY TERMS

agency (p. 316)
antagonistic strategies
(p. 330)
authoritarian parents (p. 337)
authoritative parents (p. 337)
aversive stimulation (p. 328)
bargaining strategy (p. 328)
boomerang effects (p. 327)
bullying (p. 330)
competitive symmetry (p. 331)
complementary (p. 331)
compliance-gaining strategies
(p. 327)
conversational control (p. 316)
deception (p. 330)
demand-withdrawal pattern
(p. 323)
dependence power (p. 321)
direct request (p. 328)
distributive strategies (p. 330)
dominance (p. 315)
dyadic power theory (p. 317)
egalitarian marriage (p. 340)
emotional insensitivity
(p. 323)
empathic (p. 323)
hinting (p. 329)
illicit ingratiation (p. 329)
indirect requests (p. 329)
inductive philosophy (p. 338)

influence (p. 317)
influence strategies (p. 327)
ingratiation (p. 328)
interpersonal influence (p. 328)
interpersonally sensitive
(p. 323)
manipulation (p. 329)
negative affect strategy
(p. 328)
negative altercasting (p. 329)
negative moral appeals
(p. 329)
neutral symmetry (p. 331)
objective power (p. 317)
one-across messages
(p. 330)
one-down messages (p. 330)
one-up messages (p. 330)
panache (p. 316)
paralinguistics (p. 335)
passive aggression (p. 329)
peer marriage (p. 340)
permissive parents (p. 337)
poise (p. 316)
positive altercasting (p. 329)
positive moral appeals (p. 329)
power (p. 315)
power assertion, as a parenting
style (p. 338)
powerful speech (p. 331)

powerless speech (p. 332)
pregiving (p. 328)
prerogative principle
(p. 324)
principle of elevation (p. 333)
principle of least interest
(p. 322)
proxemics (p. 333)
psychological reactance
(p. 327)
quality of alternatives (p. 321)
reflection enhancing (p. 338)
relative power (p. 317)
scarcity hypothesis (p. 320)
self-assurance (p. 316)
separation and individuation
(p. 338)
simple request (p. 328)
social influence (p. 317)
submissive symmetry (p. 331)
suggesting (p. 323)
symmetrical behavior (p. 331)
threats (p. 330)
traditional marriages (p. 339)
transact (p. 331)
transition (p. 331)
visual centrality (p. 334)
visual dominance ratio
(p. 334)
withdrawal (p. 328)

DISCUSSION QUESTIONS

1. Think about the three most powerful famous people you know about. Now think about the three most powerful people you have known personally. What characteristics make (or made) these individuals powerful?

2. In your relationships, do you agree or disagree with some scholars that men have more power than women? On the basis of what you have read in this chapter, how do you think relative power and sex differences in power influence relationship satisfaction and decision making? Does this seem to apply to your own romantic relationships?

3. In this chapter, we discussed a number of strategies people use to gain compliance in their relationships. Which persuasive strategies do you personally think are most effective? Is your experience consistent with the research?

 SAGE edge™

Sharpen your skills with SAGE edge at edge.sagepub.com/guerrero5e.
SAGE edge for students provides a personalized approach to help you accomplish your coursework goals in an easy-to-use learning environment.

13 HURTING THE ONES WE LOVE
Relational Transgressions

Ava and Preston get into a big argument and he storms out of her apartment. After a couple of days pass, Ava tries to get a hold of Preston to work things out, but he doesn't answer his cell phone or text her back for a week, so Ava knows he's avoiding her. A few days later, Ava is at a party with friends trying to get her mind off Preston when she runs into an old boyfriend, Jack. One thing leads to another and they have a one-night stand. Ava feels guilty—she isn't sure if Preston broke up with her or not—and she feels even worse when he calls her a couple of days later, says he's sorry, and wants to make up. Ava panics. She loves Preston and doesn't want to lose him. She only hooked up with Jack because she was feeling miserable about Preston not talking to her. Ava thought he didn't love her anymore. Now she doesn't know what to do. Should she tell Preston what happened? Will he still want to be with her if she does? She wants to be honest, but she is afraid that if she tells him he'll break up with her.

If you were in Ava's place, what would you do? And if you were Preston, would you understand or not? Either way, you would probably feel betrayed. Research on the dark side of relationships suggests that Ava and Preston's situation is not unusual. People commonly experience problems such as infidelity, **jealousy,** and deception in their close relationships (Cupach & Spitzberg, 1994; Spitzberg & Cupach, 1998). Hurtful words are sometimes exchanged, and people say things that they don't mean or wish they never said. No relationship is perfect, so understanding these kinds of events can help people navigate the turbulent waters that can flood even the best of relationships at times. Later in this book, we also discuss how people can repair some of the damage that these turbulent times can cause (see Chapter 14).

In this chapter, we focus on understanding various aspects of the dark side of relational communication—with an emphasis on how partners hurt one another. First, we discuss hurt feelings in the context of relationships. Then we review research related to **hurtful messages,** deception, infidelity, jealousy, **obsessive relational intrusion (ORI)** (which are stalking-type behaviors), and violence.

HURT FEELINGS IN RELATIONSHIPS

Think about the last few times you felt emotional pain. Chances are that you had close relationships with the people who directly or indirectly inflicted that pain. In one study, people described a situation that led them to experience hurt feelings (Leary, Springer, Negel, Ansell, & Evans, 1998). Of the 168 participants in this study, only 14 described situations involving strangers or acquaintances; the other 154 all described situations involving close relational partners, such as romantic partners, family members, or good friends. Scholars have noted the paradoxical nature of hurt—the people with whom we share the strongest emotional connection have the power to hurt us in ways that other people cannot. Dowrick (1999) put it this way:

> It is one of life's most terrible ironies that betrayal can be as connective as love. It can fill your mind and color your senses. It can keep you tied to a person or to events as tightly as if you were bound, back to back—or worse, heart to heart. The person you want to think of least may become the person you think of constantly. (p. 46)

The most intense hurt feelings arise when a partner's words or actions communicate **devaluation** (Feeney, 2005). Devaluation involves feeling unappreciated and unimportant. A person can feel devalued at the individual or relational level. For example, if a good friend says she's not surprised that you failed an exam because you're not very smart, you might feel hurt because your friend does not value your intellect. At a relational level, devaluation is a perception that one's partner does not perceive the relationship to be as close, important, or valuable as one would like (Leary et al., 1998). Examples of relationship devaluation include someone breaking up with you, saying "I don't love you anymore," or choosing to spend time with other people instead of you. Researchers have focused on two particular forms of behavior that cause people to feel devaluated: (1) **relational transgressions** and (2) hurtful messages.

Relational Transgressions

Relational transgressions occur when people violate implicit or explicit relational rules (Metts, 1994). For example, many people believe that romantic partners should be sexually faithful and that all close relational partners should be emotionally faithful, loyal, and honest. When people violate these standards of faithfulness, loyalty, and honesty, they also devalue the partner and the relationship (Feeney, 2005). Many different kinds of behavior qualify as relational transgressions—the key is that the behavior violates a relational rule in a way that inflicts hurt on the partner. The top relational transgressions identified by college students are (1) having sex with someone else, (2) wanting to or actually dating others, and (3) deceiving others about something significant (Metts, 1991). Other transgressions include flirting with or kissing someone else, being physically violent, keeping secrets from the partner, becoming emotionally involved with someone else, and betraying the partner's confidence (Jones & Burdette, 1994; Roscoe, Cavanaugh, & Kennedy, 1988).

Transgressions can cause irreparable harm to a relationship. In Jones and Burdette's (1994) study, 93% of people who had been betrayed by their partners said that their relationships had been damaged as a result of the transgression. Therefore, Ava is right to worry about Preston's reaction. Leary and his colleagues (1998) examined a wider variety of hurtful events than betrayals. Nonetheless, 42% of their participants said that the hurtful event had permanently harmed their relationships. In friendships, betrayal leads to less acceptance, trust, and respect (Davis & Todd, 1985). In fact, when people are betrayed by a friend, they often recast the friend's entire personality to frame the friend in a more negative light (Wiseman, 1986).

Similarly, the social network may view a person more negatively after a transgression has occurred. For example, Preston might be hurt and angry that Ava would have a one-night stand with her ex-boyfriend so soon after their argument. He might tell his friends that they never officially broke up and that Ava betrayed him. His friends are likely to be less accepting of Ava after this incident, making it more difficult for them to reconcile. Here is where communication can come into play. A study by Vallade and Dillow (2014) looked at two different ways that people communicate with members of their social networks about relational transgressions that occur with their partner—**transgression-maximizing messages** and **transgression-minimizing messages**. Transgression-maximizing messages highlight the negative aspects of the transgression as well as the partner's role in causing that negativity. Specific forms of transgression-maximizing messages include blaming the partner and talking about how hurt one is. Transgression-minimizing messages, on the other hand, focus on downplaying the severity of the transgression by using strategies such as saying that the partner's behavior was unintentional, explaining or justifying the partner's behavior, or saying that it is not a big deal. Not surprisingly, people in happier relationships are less likely to use transgression-maximizing messages, and people who use transgression-maximizing messages are more likely to see a decline in the quality of their relationship. The exception was when people said their partner took responsibility for the transgression. This actually led to an increase in relationship quality. The social network may be more willing to give the friend's partner another chance if the partner admits responsibility and the social network believes that the transgression will not reoccur.

Hurtful Messages

Hurtful messages, which are words that elicit psychological pain, constitute a particular type of transgression because they violate rules about how people should treat each other in relationships. As Vangelisti (1994b) argued, "Words have the ability to hurt or harm in every bit as real a way as physical objects. A few ill-spoken words . . . can strongly affect individuals, interactions, and relationships" (p. 53). People report more distancing and less relational closeness when their partner frequently uses hurtful messages (Vangelisti, 1994b;

Vangelisti & Young, 2000). Messages perceived to be intentional are especially hurtful and damaging to relationships (McLaren & Solomon, 2008; Mills, Nazar, & Farrell, 2002; Vangelisti, 1994b; Vangelisti & Young, 2000). For example, if you think someone said something to purposely hurt your feelings, you are likely to be more upset than if you thought the comment was not intended to hurt you. You are also more likely to distance yourself from someone who frequently uses hurtful messages (McLaren & Solomon, 2008). This holds true for messages received via texting as well. Jin (2013) found that when college students receive hurtful text messages from a friend, they are more likely to be hurt and to distance themselves from that friend if they believe the message was sent with the intention of hurting them. Messages are more or less hurtful based on the topic they address and the form of communication they take. One study showed that hurtful messages are less psychologically painful when they are lightened through humor (Young & Bippus, 2001). Another study suggested that messages focusing on relationship issues are even more hurtful than those focusing on personality traits (Vangelisti, 1994b).

Some people recover more quickly after receiving hurtful messages than others. In particular, Miller and Roloff (2014) found that people vary in the degree to which they take conflict and hurtful messages personally. The more personally people take negative comments, the more likely they are to ruminate about what was said and to experience residual hurt. This makes it difficult to let go of the pain, and makes people more likely to avoid their partner or seek revenge on them. Similarly, people vary in the extent to which they tend to see messages as intentional and hurtful (McLaren & Solomon, 2014). This tendency makes hurtful messages more damaging. In addition, McLaren and Solomon found that relationship history makes a difference. Hurtful messages inflict more pain when a person has experienced hurt in past relationships. A pattern of frequent hurtful messages in one's current relationships is also predictive of more relationship damage. Taken together, these studies suggest that people who take things personally, have a history of being hurt in relationships, and receive frequent hurtful messages in their current relationship are especially susceptible to the negative effects of hurtful messages.

Types of Hurtful Messages

To determine the specific types of messages people find hurtful, Vangelisti (1994b) identified 10 types of hurtful messages (see Box 13.1) from college students' reports. The most common were evaluations, accusations, and informative statements (Vangelisti, 1994b). Research has also examined hurtful messages between parents and children. In one study, children (ages 7 to 10) and parents were asked to describe a time when a hurtful message had occurred in the context of their parent–child relationship (Mills et al., 2002). Children described situations

involving discipline or disregard, whereas mothers described situations involving misconduct or disregard. Under the category of disregard, children mentioned issues such as sibling favoritism, teasing, criticism, rebuffs, and statements showing disrespect. Similarly, mothers wrote about times they felt criticized, rebuffed, or disrespected. Together, these studies demonstrate that feeling devalued is a central component of hurtful messages for young children as well as adults.

Responses to Hurtful Messages

Research has uncovered three general ways that people respond to hurtful messages: (1) **active verbal responses,** (2) **acquiescent responses,** and (3) **invulnerable responses.** These responses occur in both adult relationships (Vangelisti & Crumley, 1998) and parent–child relationships (Mills et al., 2002).

BOX 13.1 HIGHLIGHTS
HURTFUL MESSAGES

Evaluation	Negative judgments of worth, value, or quality (e.g., "This relationship has been a waste of my time").
Accusation	Charges about a person's faults or actions (e.g., "You are a selfish and rude person").
Informative statement	Disclosure of unwanted information (e.g., "I only dated you because I was on the rebound").
Directive	Directions or commands that go against one's desires or imply negative thoughts or feelings (e.g., "Don't call me anymore").
Expressions of desire	Statements about one's preferences or desires (e.g., "I wish you were more like your brother").
Threat	A declaration of intent to inflict punishment under certain conditions (e.g., "If you see him again I'll break up with you").
Question	Inquiry or interrogation that implies a negative judgment (e.g., "Aren't you finished with school yet?").
Joke	A witticism or prank that insults the partner (e.g., "I guess your wife wears the pants in the family and you wear the skirt").
Deception	A statement that is untrue or distorts the truth (e.g., One partner says, "Trust me, I didn't do it" when the other partner knows this is false).

Source: Definitions adapted from Vangelisti (1994b).

ACTIVE VERBAL RESPONSES Active verbal responses focus on confronting one's partner about hurtful remarks. Some active verbal responses are more positive than others. For example, questioning the partner and asking for an explanation are active verbal responses that may help partners understand one another. Other active verbal responses, such as sarcasm and verbal attacks on the partner, can lead to an escalation of negativity. Active verbal responses are the most frequently reported response in both adult relationships and parent–child relationships (Mills et al., 2002). People may be especially likely to use active verbal responses when they are in satisfying relationships (Vangelisti & Crumley, 1998). Couples in satisfying relationships may talk to one another more, which could help them repair the psychological damage caused by hurtful messages. Couples in happy relationships may also be better able to withstand the use of more negative active verbal responses than couples in unhappy relationships.

ACQUIESCENT RESPONSES Instead of talking about the hurtful message, people sometimes use acquiescent responses, which involve giving in and acknowledging the partner's ability to inflict hurt. For example, people might cry, apologize ("I'm sorry I make you feel that way"), or concede ("Fine, I won't see him anymore"). People use acquiescent responses when they are deeply hurt by something a close relational partner said (Vangelisti & Crumley, 1998). To that end, the quickest way for people to stop emotional pain may be to give in and acknowledge their feelings.

INVULNERABLE RESPONSES Invulnerable responses also avoid talking about the hurtful message and involve acting unaffected by the hurtful remark. For instance, you might ignore the hurtful message, laugh it off, become quiet, or withdraw. Both acquiescent and invulnerable responses may be more likely than active verbal strategies when people become flooded with emotion and have difficulty talking about their feelings.

DECEPTION

As noted previously, deception has been mentioned as a type of hurtful message. Deception has also been cast as a major relational transgression that often leads to feelings of betrayal and distrust (O'Hair & Cody, 1994). Therefore, if Ava keeps her one-night stand secret, she will double her betrayal—in addition to having been unfaithful, she would also be concealing her actions, which is considered to be a form of deception. Deception violates both relational and conversational rules and is often considered to be a negative violation of expectancies (Aune, Ching, & Levine, 1996). Most people expect friends and loved ones, as well as strangers, to be truthful most of the time. In fact, McCornack (1992) argued that expecting others to be truthful is a basic feature of conversations (see also Grice, 1989). If people did not expect that most conversations are truthful, talking to others would simply be too difficult and unproductive. For example, if you were always suspicious and had to question the veracity of every statement you heard, it would be virtually impossible to get to know people.

On a given day, however, it is highly likely that you or someone you are talking to will engage in some form of deception. Studies have found that people report lying in approximately 25% of their daily interactions in both face-to-face (DePaulo, Kashy, Kirkendol, Wyer, & Epstein, 1996) and computer-mediated communication situations (George & Robb, 2008); although some studies suggest that deception is slightly higher in face-to-face than mediated contexts (Lewis & George, 2008). Other research suggests that people lie about different things when meeting in person versus online. Specifically, Lewis and George (2008) found that people were most likely to lie about where they lived and their salary in face-to-face contexts and their physical appearance and interests in computer-mediated contexts. Deception is also fairly common in romantic relationships. A diary study by Guthrie and Kunkel (2013) showed that people averaged about five deceptions a week with a romantic partner. Almost 45% of the deception they reported was in the form of lies, followed by exaggerations (almost 20%) and half-truths (about 17%). Another study showed that more than one third of college students who had been in a committed dating relationship admitted to lying while sexting their partner (Drouin, Tobin, & Wygant, 2014). Common lies revolved around what they were wearing or doing; women were more likely than men to lie while sexting.

Types of Deception

Lying is only one way relational partners deceive each other. Deception includes all communications or omissions that serve to distort or omit the truth. Buller and Burgoon (1994) defined deception as intentionally managing verbal or nonverbal messages so that a receiver will believe or understand something in a way that the sender knows is false. Notice that the word *intentionally* is part of this definition. For example, if you truly believe that the big basketball game between your college and a rival school starts at 6:00 p.m. when it really starts at 7:00 p.m., it would not be deception if you told your friend the incorrect time. Instead, this type of misinformation might be termed a *mistake*. But when people intentionally mislead others or conceal or misrepresent the truth, deception has occurred.

There are five primary types of deception: (1) **lies,** (2) **equivocations,** (3) **concealments**, (4) **exaggerations**, and (5) **understatements**. Lies, also called *falsifications* or *fabrications*, involve making up information or giving information that is the opposite of (or at least very different from) the truth (Ekman, 1985). For example, if you are single and someone you find unattractive approaches you at a bar and asks if you are married, you might say you are. Equivocation or evasion (Bavelas, Black, Chovil, & Mullett, 1990; O'Hair & Cody, 1994) involves making an indirect, ambiguous, or contradictory statement, such as saying that your friend's new hairstyle (which you hate) is the "latest fashion" when you are asked if you like it. Concealment or omission involves omitting information one knows

is important or relevant to a given context (Buller & Burgoon, 1994; O'Hair & Cody, 1994; Turner, Edgley, & Olmstead, 1975). Ava would be doing this if she decided not to tell Preston about her one-night stand.

The last two forms of deception are opposites. Exaggeration or overstatement involves stretching the truth a little—often to make oneself look better or to spice up a story (O'Hair & Cody, 1994; Turner et al., 1975). The prototypical example of exaggeration involves job interviews: People often make their skills and experiences sound better than they actually are. Understatement or minimization, on the other hand, involves downplaying aspects of the truth. For instance, Ava might tell Preston she met up with her old boyfriend but not tell him details.

Motives for Deception

People engage in deception for many reasons. Metts (1989; Metts & Chronis, 1986) described three major motivations for deception in close relationships. First, relational partners have partner-focused motives, such as using deception to avoid hurting the partner, to help the partner maintain self-esteem, to avoid worrying the partner, and to protect the partner's relationship with a third party. For example, if you say that your best friend's new hairstyle looks great when you really think it looks awful, your deceptive behavior probably has a partner-focused motive. Sometimes partner-motivated deception is seen as socially polite and relationally beneficial. Indeed, not engaging in deception when you hate your friend's new hairstyle might violate relational expectations and hurt your friend's feelings. Partner-focused deceptions also tend to be altruistic. In other words, they benefit someone else rather than the deceiver. People report using more partner-focused lies with close relational partners than strangers (Ennis, Vrij, & Chance, 2008). Similarly, people are more likely to use partner-focused lies in relationships characterized by high levels of interdependence (Kam, 2004).

Second, people deceive due to **self-focused motives**, such as wanting to enhance or protect their self-image, or wanting to shield themselves from anger, embarrassment, criticism, or other types of harm. So if a job applicant exaggerates his qualifications during an employment interview or a child avoids telling her mother that she failed an exam because she doesn't want to be punished, deception is based on self-focused motives. This type of deception is usually perceived as a much more significant transgression than partner-focused deception because the deceiver is acting for selfish reasons rather than for the good of the partner or the relationship. Indeed, across different cultures, self-motivated deception is perceived as more unacceptable than partner-motivated deception (Mealy, Stephan, & Urrutia, 2007; Seiter, Bruschke, & Bai, 2002). People also report feeling more guilt and shame when deceiving to benefit themselves rather than their partner (Seiter & Bruschke, 2007).

Finally, people have relationship-focused motives for deceiving a partner. Here, the deceiver wants to limit relational harm by avoiding conflict, relational trauma, or other unpleasant experiences. For example, Ava's primary reason for concealing her one-night stand might be to safeguard her relationship. She is scared that if Preston finds out he will break up with her. Notice, however, that in this case, as well as in other cases involving relationship-focused motives, partner- and self-focused motivations may also come into play. By not telling Preston, Ava may also be protecting herself from judgment and possible abandonment (a self-focused motive) while protecting Preston from feeling hurt and jealous (a partner-focused motive). The key is whether someone is using deception primarily to protect the relationship, rather than only to protect either oneself or the partner.

People associate different motives for deception with different levels of acceptability and guilt. Deception is perceived as the most acceptable and the least guilt-provoking when it is motivated out of concern for others. In contrast, deception is perceived to be less acceptable and more guilt-provoking when people use it to affiliate with someone, benefit someone else, protect their privacy, or

avoid conflict (Seiter & Bruschke, 2007; Seiter et al., 2002). There are cultural differences in the motives and acceptability of deception as well, as shown in Box 13.2.

Sometimes, relationally motivated deception is seen as beneficial within a relationship. Other times, however, such deception only complicates matters. Metts (1994) used the following excerpt from an advice column to illustrate how deception can make a bad situation even worse:

Dear Abby: My husband and I were planning a 40th anniversary celebration, but I called it off three months ago when I learned from someone that my husband had had an affair with a young woman while he was stationed in Alameda, California, during World War II. The affair lasted about a year while he was waiting to be shipped out, but never was. When I confronted him with the facts, he admitted it, but said it was "nothing serious." . . . I am devastated. I feel betrayed, knowing I've spent the last 37 years living with a liar and a cheat. How can I ever trust him again? The bottom has fallen out of my world. (p. 217)

In this situation, even if the deception was motivated by relational concerns, such as wanting to avoid conflict and even divorce, it compounded the problem in the long run. As Metts (1994) observed, "In this case, the act of infidelity is only the first blow; the 37 years of omission is the second, and probably more devastating, hit" (p. 217). Preston might feel the same if he found out that Ava had a one-night stand years after it happened. Even if Preston understands that his actions led her to think he no longer loved her and that the one-night stand didn't mean anything to her, he would feel doubly betrayed because she hadn't trust him enough to confide in him.

A more recent study (Guthrie & Kunkel, 2013) found five more specific motives for deception in romantic relationships. First, people use deception to *maintain the relationship*. Examples include denying

BOX 13.2 AROUND THE WORLD
DECEPTION IN INDIVIDUALISTIC VERSUS COLLECTIVISTIC CULTURES

Do people around the world share the same values and beliefs about deception? Research suggests that the answer to this question is yes *and* no. Most studies looking at cultural differences in deception have compared people from North America (the United States and Canada) with people from Asian cultures, such as China and Taiwan. People from the U.S. mainland have also been compared to people from American Samoa. Taken together, this research suggests that people from collectivistic cultures generally view deception as more acceptable than do people from individualistic cultures like the United States (Seiter et al., 2002).

People from collectivistic cultures value group harmony and belong to strong integrated groups. They also prioritize group needs and social norms over individual desires and preferences. By contrast, people from individualistic cultures value personal freedom, privacy, and the right to speak one's mind. Individual goals and beliefs guide behavior more than social norms (Hofstede, 1980; Triandis, 1989). The United States is the most individualistic culture in the world. Many Asian cultures, as well as American Samoa, are considered to be collectivistic cultures.

Research suggests that people's motives for deception vary by culture. In a study by Aune and Waters (1994), American Samoans reported more motivations for deceiving than did North Americans. Specifically, American Samoans were more motivated to deceive when they thought deception would benefit their family or group, appease an authority figure, protect their relationship, protect their image, and avoid conflict, among other motivations. The only motivations for deception that were endorsed more by North Americans than American Samoans were concern for a partner's physical or mental state and wanting to keep information private.

People may experience different emotions when deceiving depending on their culture. In one study, people from China and the United States read a number of scenarios involving deception and were asked how much guilt and shame they would feel if they used deception in each situation (Seiter & Bruschke, 2007). The scenarios included many different motivations for deception (as described previously) and many different relational contexts (e.g., boss, parent, teacher, friend, spouse, stranger). Across all of the relationships except for those with teachers, people from China reported that they would feel *less* guilt and shame than did people from the United States. In another study, children from Taiwan and China were more likely than Canadian children to feel good after lying about good deeds that they had done (Lee, Xu, Fu, Cameron, & Chen, 2001). These findings may explain why Cody, Lee, and Chao (1989) found that Chinese people did not communicate many negative feelings while lying. Studies have also shown that people from collectivistic cultures such as Korea are more likely to engage in deception, both in business negotiations and other forms of face-to-face communication (Lewis & George, 2008; Triandis et al., 2001).

What can we learn from this? Does this research mean that people from the United States tend to be more honest? No, that would be an overly simplistic analysis of these findings. People from Asian cultures such as China and Korea may be more concerned with "providing the appropriate information at the appropriate time and context with the appropriate persons" than engaging in "honest and truthful communication" (Gao & Ting-Toomey, 1998, p. 64). For people from collectivistic cultures, goals such as maintaining group harmony, protecting one's family, showing respect for authority figures, and avoiding conflict may be valued more than direct and open communication. In contrast, people from individualistic cultures such as the United States may see truthful communication as paramount (Seiter et al., 2002). It is also critical to recognize that cultural differences related to deception are small. The reasons people engage in deception are a far better predictor of how acceptable and guilt-provoking deception is than culture is (Seiter et al., 2002).

being attracted to someone or saying you had a good time even when you did not. The goal in these cases is to preserve the relationship and avoid unnecessary conflict. Second, people reported being deceptive to *manage face needs* for both themselves and their partners. In other words, they engaged in deception to make themselves or their partner look good. Examples include lying about how good the partner looked or saying that you did better on a test than you actually did. Third, people used deception to *negotiate dialectical tension*. For example, in Chapter 5 you learned about the dialectical tension of autonomy-connection. The tension here is between wanting to be autonomous and do things on your own, versus wanting to be connected to someone you feel close to. A person might lie and say that she already has plans as a way to gain some autonomy without making the partner feel badly. Another dialectic revolves around privacy versus expression. If you want to manage this dialectic by getting privacy, you might lie and say you promised a friend that you would not tell a secret. Fourth, people use deception to *establish relational control*. Examples include trying to control your partner's actions by exaggerating to make her or him feel guilty (e.g., "I spent hours planning this so you have to come" when you really did not do that much) or acting like you have better options than you actually do to make your partner jealous. Finally, some people use deception because they need to *continue previous deception*. In other words, they lie or conceal in order to prevent being caught in a previous lie.

Deception Detection

The letter about the husband who cheated on his wife might spark questions about how he got away with deceiving her for so long. One might think that there must have been clues that he had had an affair or that he was concealing something from her. In reality, however, it is difficult to detect deception in everyday conversations with relational partners unless one partner says something that is blatantly false or that contradicts information the other partner knows. This is not to say that most people can successfully deceive their partners all the time. In fact, it is difficult to hide serious relational transgressions such as infidelity over a long period. However, in day-to-day conversations about relatively minor issues, deception often occurs without one partner suspecting that anything is amiss.

Detecting deception is difficult because there are no completely reliable indicators of deception.

Although behaviors such as speech hesitations and body shifts often accompany deception, these behaviors can indicate general anxiety, shyness, or discomfort in addition to deception (Andersen, 2008; Burgoon et al., 2010). Also, stereotypic behaviors such as eye behavior are often controlled during deception. When people lie to you, for instance, they know to look you straight in the eye, which makes eye contact an unreliable cue for detecting deception (Hocking & Leathers, 1980). Perhaps the most reliable method for detecting deception is to compare a person's normal, truthful behavior with that individual's current behavior. If the person's behavior is noticeably different—either more anxious or more controlled—perhaps deception is occurring. There is not, however, a foolproof method for detecting deception.

It may be easier to detect deception in certain contexts than others. In one study, people were instructed to deceive or tell the truth using face-to-face communication, videoconferencing, audio-conferencing, or text. Receivers did the best job discriminating between truthful and deceptive messages in the audio- and videoconferencing contexts. They did the worst job when the message was delivered via text (Burgoon, Stoner, Bonita, & Dunbar, 2003). It may be difficult to detect deception in text-only contexts because it is easier for deceivers to control what they say. Also, deceivers do not have to worry about leaking emotions through nonverbal communication when they are using e-mail or text messaging. Despite this, research suggests that people actually prefer engaging in deception using face-to-face communication rather than computer-mediated communication (Carlson & George, 2004), perhaps because they can better monitor their partner's reactions and make adjustments if their partner seems suspicious.

People often assume they are better able to detect deception by close relational partners than strangers or acquaintances. Research, however, suggests that this is not the case. Comadena (1982) found that friends and spouses are better at detecting deception than acquaintances. However, Comadena also found that friends are superior to spouses, suggesting that the ability to detect deception does not increase as a relationship becomes closer. Other studies have shown that romantic partners have trouble detecting deception; accuracy rates are only slightly better than chance (Levine & McCornack, 1992; Stiff, Kim, & Ramesh, 1992). In one study, people reported that their romantic partners accepted about half of their deceptive messages as truthful (Boon & McLeod, 2001). People in close relationships experience both advantages and disadvantages when it comes to detecting deception.

ADVANTAGES OF RELATIONAL CLOSENESS

Because comparing "normal" behavior to deceptive behavior is important in the deception detection process, close relational partners have an advantage over strangers: They have knowledge of the partner's typical communication style. Burgoon and her colleagues (2010) called this type of knowledge **behavioral familiarity.** Close friends, family, and romantic partners are familiar with one another's honest behavior; therefore, deviations from this behavior can tip them off that something is amiss. Relational partners also have the advantage of **informational familiarity** (Burgoon et al., 2010). In other words, you know certain information about your relational partner, so your partner cannot lie to you about that information. You can tell a stranger that you have three children instead of one, but obviously you cannot get away with telling such a lie to family members or friends.

DISADVANTAGES OF RELATIONAL CLOSENESS

Despite these advantages, deception is difficult to detect in close relationships for at least two reasons. First, people have a **truth bias.** People expect others to be honest, so they enter conversations without suspicion and do not look for deceptive behavior. Truth biases are especially strong within close relationships and with people whom we like. People who are socially attractive are generally seen as less deceptive, and when they are caught deceiving, people usually attribute their motives for deception to more benign causes (Aune et al., 1996). McCornack

and Parks (1986) argued that the truth bias makes close relational partners overly confident in the truthfulness of each other's statements, causing them to miss much of the deception that occurs. Even in the face of seemingly deceptive information, relational partners can be influenced by the truth bias (Buller, Strzyzewski, & Comstock, 1991; McCornack & Parks, 1986). Indeed, Kam (2004) found that relationship interdependence was associated with a stronger truth bias and lower accuracy in detecting deception.

The second reason close relational partners might have trouble detecting deception is that the deceiver may exert **behavioral control**. People try to control their nervous or guilty behaviors to appear friendly and truthful. Several deception researchers have demonstrated that regardless of whether deceivers are interacting with friends or strangers, they try to control their behavior so that they seem honest (see Ekman & Friesen, 1969; Zuckerman, DePaulo, & Rosenthal, 1981). However, this may be particularly true for close relational partners, who have more to lose if the deception is discovered. Buller and Aune (1987) found that when people deceived friends or romantic partners, they became friendlier and showed less anxiety as the interaction progressed than when they deceived strangers. In comparison to deceiving strangers, people tried harder to look truthful when deceiving relational partners—in part by "putting on a happy face" and hiding nervousness. Another study suggested that people may feel less guilty when deceiving spouses and friends compared to parents or teachers (Seiter & Bruschke, 2007). Therefore, romantic partners and friends may not have to work as hard to hide guilty feelings.

Effects of Deception on Relationships

Paradoxically, research shows that deception can help people develop and maintain relationships, but it can also lead to conflict and relationship breakup. Most people believe that honesty is an absolutely essential ingredient in the recipe for close, healthy relationships. Yet people can identify situations where it is important, even ethical, to deceive their partner (Boon & McLeod, 2001). For example, if Preston overhears someone saying something really negative about Ava, he might decide not to tell her because it would hurt her feelings too much. Partner-focused deceptions such as these are often regarded as acceptable and appropriate, and can help maintain positive relationships.

Cole (2001) discussed two other ways that deception is associated with the development and maintenance of relationships. First, deception may help couples avoid arguments, thereby promoting relational harmony. For example, a mother who is mediating an argument between her two sons may try to sound even-handed even though she thinks one of the sons is more to blame. Similarly, your best friend might understate how hurt she feels when you receive an honor that she wanted so you won't feel badly.

Second, deception allows people to downplay their faults and accentuate their virtues, which may help them develop and maintain relationships (Cole, 2001). Two lines of research support this idea. Work on the benefit of positive illusions (Murray et al., 1996) suggests that people who hold idealized images of one another are most satisfied in their relationships. So if Ava exaggerates by telling Preston, "You are ten times more attractive than Jack," her exaggeration would contribute to his positive illusions and perhaps lead him to feel less threatened by Ava's former relationship with Jack.

Work on date initiation also supports the idea that people use deception to emphasize their positive qualities and minimize their negative qualities. According to research reviewed by Rowatt et al. (1999), 46% of men and 36% of women admit that they have lied to initiate a date with someone. In a study on deception in the early stages of dating (Tooke & Camire, 1991), men were more likely than women to exaggerate (or lie about) how successful they were and to act more committed and sincere than they actually were. Women, in contrast, were more likely to try to enhance their appearance by engaging in behaviors such as wearing clothing that made them look thinner and using makeup to exaggerate desirable facial features. Furthermore, people are most likely to lie when initiating dates with potential partners who are very physically attractive (Rowatt et al., 1999).

With Internet dating on the rise, people may have more opportunities than ever before to deceive dating prospects on these issues. A study by Ellison and colleagues (2006) looked at how people present themselves in online dating situations. Online daters reported feeling a tension between wanting to be accurate and truthful yet also wanting to present a positive image that is attractive to others. To resolve this tension, online daters often present images that reflect their ideal self or a potential future version of themselves. For example, a woman might say that she is a world traveler when she has only been to a couple of countries in Europe, or a man might say that he is an avid skier and golfer even though he only does these types of activities occasionally.

Of course, deceiving a partner about one's positive versus negative qualities can backfire. Eventually a deceiver is seen more accurately, which may lead to disappointment and disillusion. It is thus important to remember that deception can have negative consequences for relationships. When people uncover a significant deception, they usually feel a host of negative emotions, including anxiety, anger, and distress (e.g., McCornack & Levine, 1990). People who use deception frequently in their relationships report lower levels of commitment, intimacy, and closeness. Similarly, when people perceive their partners as dishonest, they report less relational satisfaction and commitment (Cole, 2001). Deception is also a leading cause of conflict (see Chapter 11) and relationship breakup (see Chapter 15).

Finally, some deceptions are not only harmful to people's relationships but also to their health. Lucchetti (1999) found that one third of sexually active college students avoided talking about their sexual history with their partners, even though many of them knew that talking would help them have safer sex. Around 20% of these same college students reported that they had intentionally misrepresented their sexual history to their partner.

As discussed in Chapter 9, people lie about their sexual history for a variety of reasons, including not wanting to appear promiscuous (especially if one is female), wanting to appear more experienced (especially if one is male), and not wanting to talk about past sexual partners.

INFIDELITY

Another reason people misrepresent their sexual history is that they want their partner to see them as someone who will be faithful to them. This is because fidelity and sexual exclusivity are highly valued in most committed romantic relationships in the United States. Thus, when infidelity occurs, it is especially hurtful (Malachowski & Frisby, 2015) and tends to have a particularly strong negative effect on relationships (Feeney, 2004). In another study, **sexual infidelity,** along with relationship breakup, were rated as the least forgivable of several hurtful events in dating relationships (Bachman & Guerrero, 2006b). The way people discover sexual infidelity also makes a difference. Afifi, Falato, and Weiner (2001) compared four methods of discovery: (1) finding out from a third party, (2) witnessing the infidelity firsthand, such as walking in on the partner with someone else, (3) having the partner admit to infidelity after being questioned, and (4) having the partner confess without being asked. People who found out through a third party or by witnessing the partner's infidelity firsthand were the least likely to forgive their partners and the most likely to say that their relationships had been damaged. People were most likely to forgive their partners when they confessed on their own. This research suggests that it might be wise for Ava to tell Preston what happened. If he found out later through a third party or got suspicious and questioned Ava until she confessed, he would be less likely to forgive her than if she had come to him and confessed on her own.

Types of Infidelity

Researchers have made a distinction between sexual and **emotional infidelity.** Sexual infidelity refers to "sexual activity with someone other than one's long-term partner" (Shackelford & Buss, 1997, p. 1035). Most people in the United States disapprove of sexual infidelity (Weinbach, 1989; Weis & Slosnerick, 1981), yet studies suggest that around 20% to 40% of dating and cohabiting relationships are marked by at least one incident of sexual infidelity (Guerrero, Spitzberg, & Yoshimura, 2004; Wiederman & Hurd, 1999). Rates of sexual infidelity are lower for married couples; estimates suggest that between 13% and 18% of married individuals admit to having at least one extramarital affair over the course of their marriage (Blow & Hartnett, 2005). Across all types of romantic relationships, men are more likely than women (Blow & Hartnett, 2005; Sprecher & McKinney, 1993), and gay men are more likely than lesbians or heterosexuals, to have sexual affairs (Blumstein & Schwartz, 1983). Both gay men and lesbians, however, may react even more strongly to sexual infidelity than do heterosexual individuals (Dijkstra, Barelds, & Groothof, 2013). Emotional infidelity, on the other hand, refers to emotional involvement with another person, which leads one's partner to channel "emotional resources such as romantic love, time, and attention to someone else" (Shackelford & Buss, 1997, p. 1035). Suspecting that your partner loves or confides in someone else more than you, if confirmed, is an example of emotional infidelity.

Researchers have also discussed the concept of **communicative infidelity** (Tafoya & Spitzberg, 2007). Communicative infidelity occurs when people engage in sexual activity with a third party to communicate a message to their partner. People sometimes use communicative infidelity to send messages related to jealousy, sex, or revenge (Tafoya & Spitzberg, 2007). For example, suppose that Ava purposively tried to make Preston jealous by sleeping with her ex-boyfriend. Or maybe she was mad because he was ignoring her, so having a one-night stand seemed like a good way to get his attention and get back at him at the same time. Other times, people engage in communicative infidelity as a way to signal to their partner that they are dissatisfied with the sexual activity in their current relationship. Tafoya and Spitzberg's work also showed that communicative infidelity is more acceptable and justifiable under certain circumstances—such as engaging in infidelity in response to one's partner having sex with someone else or partners saying that they are no longer in love.

Finally, some researchers have studied **online infidelity**, which is defined as "romantic or sexual contact facilitated by Internet use that is considered to violate relationship rules regarding faithfulness" (Hertlein & Piercy, 2008, p. 484). Contact is typically maintained primarily through conversations via e-mail or through virtual communities such as interactive games or chat rooms (Young, Griffin-Shelley, Cooper, O'Mara, & Buchanan, 2000). Of course, communication in these relationships can eventually move to texting and face-to-face interaction. Online infidelity can be sexual, emotional, or both, and includes a wide variety of behaviors, such as flirting and talking dirty, touching one's self in provocative ways, sending nudes, sharing sexual thoughts, and engaging in deep disclosure (Henline, Lamke, & Howard, 2007). Behavior on social media sites, such as Facebook and Twitter, can also be perceived as infidelity. In a review of the literature on Facebook infidelity, "friending an ex-partner or ex-spouse, friending attractive members, sending private messages to the opposite sex, commenting on attractive users' pictures, not having up the correct relationship status on their profile, and not allowing their partner to be their friend on Facebook" were all identified as possible indicators of infidelity (Cravens, Leckie, & Whiting, 2013, p. 328). However, these behaviors are not always viewed as forms of infidelity. In fact, 8.1% of participants in Henline et al.'s (2007) study said that there is no such thing as online infidelity because it is not real. Perhaps because of the lack of real physical contact online, both men and women are more threatened by emotional online infidelity than sexual online infidelity, and believe that a real affair is more likely to start if there is an emotional connection (Henline et al., 2007).

Given the prevalence of infidelity, it is important to ask why people engage in acts of infidelity in the first place. Research on sexual infidelity suggests that dissatisfaction with the current relationship is the leading cause (Hunt, 1974; Roscoe et al., 1988; Sheppard, Nelson, & Andreoli-Mathie, 1995). Other common causes of infidelity include boredom, the need for excitement and variety, wanting to feel attractive, sexual incompatibility with one's partner, and trying to get revenge against the partner (Buunk, 1980; Fleischmann et al., 2005; Roscoe et al., 1988; Wiggins & Lederer, 1984). Less research has examined causes of emotional infidelity, yet it is likely that emotional infidelity is related to feeling dissatisfied with the communication and social support a person is receiving in the current relationship. People engage in online infidelity for many of the same reasons, but online infidelity often has the added attraction of being anonymous, convenient, and secret. In addition, there is a wider range of potential partners available on the Internet (Hertlein, 2012; Young et al., 2000).

Behavioral Cues to Infidelity

Researchers have uncovered specific behavioral cues that trigger suspicion about infidelity. In one study (Shackelford & Buss, 1997), undergraduate students described the cues that would lead them to suspect that their partners were (1) being sexually unfaithful (sexual infidelity) or (2) falling in love with someone else (emotional infidelity). Fourteen types of behavior were found to trigger suspicion. As illustrated in Box 13.3, some of these cues were associated more with suspicions of sexual infidelity, while others were associated more with suspicions of emotional infidelity. Still other cues were associated with sexual and emotional infidelity about equally.

While most of the behaviors that trigger suspicion about sexual infidelity are related to observed changes in a partner's sexual behavior, most of the behaviors that trigger suspicion about emotional infidelity are the opposite of those that people use to maintain their relationships. As discussed in Chapter 10, self-disclosure, routine talk, and positivity are key behaviors that help keep a relationship satisfying. Thus, when partners stop using these behaviors and instead act emotionally distant, apathetic, and argumentative, people suspect that something is amiss. Integrating social networks and spending time together are also important maintenance behaviors (see Chapter 10), so when partners start spending more time with a third party (and less time with you), suspicions are likely to arise. In short, it appears that when people feel their partners are no longer working to maintain the relationship, they may suspect this lack of effort is due to emotional infidelity, or worse yet, both emotional and sexual infidelity.

There are also sex differences in how people perceive possible cues to infidelity. In Shackelford and Buss's (1997) study, women were more likely than men to see suspicious behaviors as indicative of infidelity (see Box 13.3). Perhaps this is because, in the United States, men are somewhat more likely than women to have extradyadic affairs (Sprecher & McKinney, 1993) or because women are better encoders of information than men (Burgoon et al., 2010).

Sex Differences in Reactions to Infidelity

Research has also examined sex differences in reactions to sexual versus emotional infidelity. Much of the research, which comes out of evolutionary psychology (Buss, 1989, 1994), suggests that men and women react to emotional and sexual infidelity differently because they have different priorities related to reproduction. Women know they are the parent of a child, but men are sometimes uncertain about paternity and therefore are more concerned about sexual infidelity. Women, on the other hand, according to this perspective, should be more worried about emotional infidelity because they are especially concerned with protecting their most important resource, their relationship. Thus, the **evolutionary hypothesis for infidelity** predicts that men should get more upset over sexual infidelity than emotional infidelity whereas women should get more upset over emotional infidelity than sexual infidelity.

Studies supporting this evolutionary hypothesis have generally used one of two methods (Guerrero et al., 2004). The first of these methods involves having men and women imagine that their partner either engaged in sexual activity or was in love with someone else and then measuring their level of distress. In these studies, men show greater psychological and physiological distress when they imagine their partner engaging in sexual infidelity, whereas women display more distress when they imagine their partner in love with someone else (Buss, Larsen, Westen, & Semmelroth, 1992; Wiederman & Allgeier, 1993). The second method involves having people choose which would make them more upset—their partner having a one-night stand or their partner falling in love with someone else. When this method is used, men identify sexual infidelity as more upsetting whereas women identify emotional infidelity as more upsetting (Becker, Sagarin, Guadagno, Millevoi, & Nicastle, 2004; Trost & Alberts, 2006). Also consistent with principles from evolutionary psychology, men get less upset about a female's lesbian affair compared to a heterosexual affair since pregnancy would not be an issue; however, women get more upset about a partner's homosexual affair (Confer & Cloud, 2010).

Despite these findings, the evolutionary hypothesis has been challenged. Some researchers have argued that sex differences in reactions to sexual and emotional infidelity are better explained by the **double-shot hypothesis** than the evolutionary hypothesis (DeSteno & Salovey, 1996). According to this view, both men and women get most upset when their partners have engaged in both sexual and emotional infidelity. Therefore, when people are forced to choose between whether sexual or emotional infidelity is more upsetting, they will choose the event that is most likely to imply that both types of infidelity are occurring. Men choose sexual infidelity as more upsetting because they assume that their girlfriends or wives would not have sex with a man unless they were also connected to him emotionally. According to this reasoning, if Preston found out that Ava had a one-night stand with Jack, he would likely think that

BOX 13.3 HIGHLIGHTS
EXAMPLES OF CUES TO INFIDELITY

Behaviors Leading Primarily to the Suspicion of Sexual Infidelity	
Indirect physical signs	Smelling someone's perfume or cologne on the partner's clothing
Direct revelations	Walking in on the partner with someone else or the partner confesses
Changes in sexual behavior	Noticing that the partner acts differently during sex
Exaggerated affection	Perceiving that the partner is acting especially affectionate because he or she feels guilty about being with someone else
Sexual disinterest	Noticing that the partner seems less interested and excited about having sex
Behaviors Leading Primarily to the Suspicion of Emotional Infidelity	
Relationship dissatisfaction	The partner reveals that she or he is no longer in love or wants to pursue other alternatives.
Emotional disengagement	The partner seems to be distancing herself or himself emotionally.
Passive rejection	The partner becomes more inconsiderate or inattentive than usual.
Negative communication	The partner is uncharacteristically angry, critical, or argumentative.
Reluctance to spend time together	The partner starts to spend less time one-on-one and to separate his or her social network.
Reluctance to talk about a certain person	The partner seems reluctant or nervous to talk about a particular person.
Guilty communication	The partner acts like he or she has done something wrong.
Behaviors Leading to the Suspicion of Both Sexual and Emotional Infidelity	
Apathetic communication	The partner seems to be putting less effort into the relationship.
Increased contact with third party	The partner seems to be focusing more time and attention on another person.

Source: Information compiled and adapted from Shackelford and Buss (1997).

she still had strong feelings for her ex, thereby leading him to suspect both sexual and emotional infidelity. Women, on the other hand, choose emotional infidelity because they believe that their boyfriends or husbands are likely to have had sex with a woman with whom they have a strong emotional attachment. By this reasoning, if the situation was reversed and it was Preston who had the one-night stand, Ava would not automatically assume that Preston was attached to the other woman on an emotional level. But if she found out he was in love with another woman, she would suspect that he was having sex with her.

Researchers supporting the double-shot hypothesis have also argued that the sex difference only emerges when using a forced-choice format (DeSteno, Bartlett, Salovey, & Braverman, 2002). In other words, if people report how jealous or upset they are on a scale (e.g., from 1 to 10 with 10 being the most jealous), instead of choosing which type of infidelity is more upsetting, then the sex difference disappears. DeSteno and associates had people use scales and found that both men and women reported more jealousy in response to sexual infidelity than emotional infidelity. Similarly, Parker (1997) found that both women and men perceived sexual infidelity as more threatening than verbal intimacy when people rated the degree of threat for each situation using a scale. These findings suggest that the evolutionary hypothesis should be revised so that it does *not* predict that men or women will be higher on sexual or emotional infidelity, but instead predicts that men, in comparison to women, will perceive sexual infidelity as worse than emotional infidelity (Edlund & Sagarin, 2009). In other words, both men and women rate sexual infidelity as highly upsetting, women rate emotional infidelity as highly upsetting, and men rate emotional infidelity as moderately upsetting.

JEALOUSY

When people suspect or discover infidelity, they commonly become jealous. Interestingly, jealousy is often the result of a relational transgression such as a partner having an affair or spending extra time with someone else. But jealousy is also seen as a transgression in its own right when a partner's suspicions are unwarranted (Metts, 1994). For example, imagine that Ava told Preston about her one-night stand, explained that she thought he was breaking up with her, apologized, and promised it would never happen again. Months go by and Ava is completely faithful, yet Preston is always suspicious and checking up on her. If this possessive behavior continues, Ava might see Preston's lack of trust as a relational transgression.

Characteristics of Jealousy

Now imagine that Ava confesses. Would Preston be jealous? According to the literature, it depends on whether or not he believes Jack is a threat to their relationship. **Romantic jealousy** occurs when people believe that a third party threatens the existence or quality of their romantic relationship. This threat can be imagined or real. There are also different types of jealousy. The first two forms of jealousy shown in Box 13.4 pertain to romantic relationships. The remaining five forms of jealousy, which were identified by Bevan and Samter (2004), can occur in romantic relationships, friendships, and family relationships. Jealousy can be triggered by a multitude of behaviors. When people notice that their partner seems interested in others, spends more time away, communicates with former romantic partners, or seems preoccupied with work, jealousy may ensue (Sheets, Fredendall, & Claypool, 1997).

Scholars have also discussed how social networking sites, such as Twitter and Facebook, can trigger jealousy. When asked to describe their jealousy experiences on Facebook, young adults mention that the accessibility of information and the lack of context on Facebook can lead to jealousy (Muise, Christofides, & Desmarais, 2009). On Facebook and other social networking sites, information is typically exchanged openly. People can see pictures that their partner is tagged in, comments that their partner makes, and comments made about their partner—among other information. Such information highlights the various social connections that a person has, which can lead to jealousy.

The lack of context, or ambiguity, of messages on Facebook is another issue. Many Facebook messages can be interpreted a number of different ways. For example, if someone ends a message with a smiley face or series of hearts, what does that mean? Indeed, a research study showed that people responded with more jealousy when a Facebook message on their partner's wall included a winking face compared to just plain text (Fleuriet, Cole, & Guerrero, 2014). One of the young men in Muise and colleagues' (2009) study explained how both the amount and ambiguity of information on Facebook affects him by writing, "I have enough confidence in her [his partner] to know my partner is faithful, yet I can't help but second-guess myself when someone posts on her wall. . . . It can contribute to feelings of you not really 'knowing' your partner" (p. 443). These kinds of thoughts can lead to what Muise and colleagues referred to as a feedback loop, where exposure to information on a partner's social networking site leads to increased surveillance (e.g., checking their site more often), which then leads to even more jealousy. In the study by Muise and colleagues, just over 10% of the young adults they surveyed wrote about having a Facebook addiction—in part because they felt compelled to check their partner's page for information about her or him. Snapchat has been shown to be even more jealousy-inducing than Facebook, presumably because Snapchat is more private, and people use it more than Facebook to flirt and explore potential relationships (Utz, Muscanell, & Khalid, 2015). Similarly, people have stronger jealous reactions if they see private messages exchanged through direct messages versus a message posted publicly on a social networking site (Cohen, Bowman, & Borchert, 2014).

Jealousy is different from two related constructs: (1) **envy** and (2) rivalry (Bryson, 1977; Guerrero & Andersen, 1998a; Salovey & Rodin, 1986, 1989). Jealousy occurs when people worry that they might lose something they value, such as a good relationship or high-status position, due to interference from a third party. The prototypical jealousy situation involves fearing that someone will "steal" a romantic partner away. Envy, by contrast, occurs when people want something valuable that someone else has. Prototypical envy situations involve feelings of resentment toward someone who seems to have a better life—often because the person has stronger relationships; is better looking; is intelligent and talented; or has more stature, money, or possessions. Rivalry occurs when two people are competing for something that neither one of them has. A prime example of rivalry involves siblings who are competing to be seen as "best" in the eyes of their peers,

parents, and other adults (Dunn, 1988a, 1988b). As these examples and Figure 13.1 illustrate, who possesses the desired relationship or commodity differentiates jealousy, envy, and rivalry.

The triangle of Ava, Preston, and Jack helps illustrate the differences between jealousy and envy. Imagine that Ava comes clean and tells Preston what happened. Preston gets upset. He knows that Jack was Ava's first love and remembers her saying that he is ambitious and smart. The thought of her being with him again drives him crazy. On the basis of the previously given definitions, would you characterize Preston as jealous or envious? Preston would be experiencing jealousy if he is worried that he might lose Ava to Jack. However, Preston might also be experiencing envy because he wishes he could have been Ava's first love. He might also worry that Ava thinks Jack is more intelligent than he is. Assuming that Jack is still in love with Ava, he might be envious of Preston's relationship with her. Now pretend that Ava is not currently in a relationship with either man and that they both want to date her exclusively. If this were the case, Preston and Jack would be experiencing rivalry. As this example shows, jealousy, envy, and rivalry sometimes coexist within the same set of relationships.

Experiencing Romantic Jealousy

When people perceive a third-party threat to their romantic relationships, they are likely to experience a number of cognitions and emotions. On the cognitive side, jealous individuals typically make appraisals regarding the source and severity of the threat. On the emotional side, jealous individuals tend to experience a cluster of jealousy-related emotions.

JEALOUS THOUGHTS White and Mullen (1989) described primary and secondary cognitive appraisals that tend to occur as jealous feelings develop. **Primary appraisals** involve general evaluations about the existence and quality of a rival relationship, including the degree of the threat from the third party. For example, Preston might ask himself questions like this: "Has Ava been seeing Jack

BOX 13.4 HIGHLIGHTS
DIFFERENT TYPES OF JEALOUSY

Romantic jealousy	Worrying that a potential rival might interfere with the existence or quality of the romantic relationship
Sexual jealousy	Worrying that a rival is having or wants to have sex with one's partner
Friend jealousy	Feeling threatened by the partner's relationships with friends, such as worrying that your closest friend has a new "best friend"
Family jealousy	Feeling threatened by the partner's relationships with family, such as worrying that your spouse is closer to her or his mother than you
Activity jealousy	Worrying that the partner's activities, such as work, hobbies, or school, are interfering with the relationship
Power jealousy	Perceiving that one's influence over the partner is being lost to others
Intimacy jealousy	Believing that one's partner is engaging in more intimate communication, such as disclosure and advice seeking, with someone else

FIGURE 13.1 ■ Differences Between Jealousy, Envy, and Rivalry Based on Possession of a Desired Relationship or Commodity

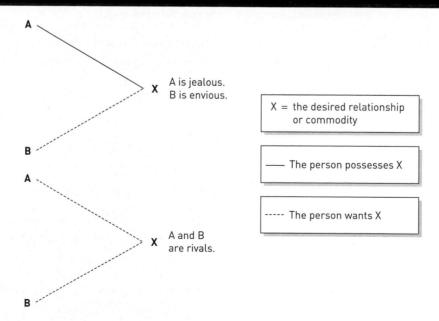

behind my back?" and "Could Ava still love Jack?" **Secondary appraisals** involve more specific evaluations of the jealousy situation, including possible causes and outcomes. White and Mullen (1989) described four types of secondary appraisals that people use to gather information and interpret the situation. First, jealous people assess motives ("Why did Ava hook up with Jack?"). Second, they compare themselves to the rival ("Jack might be smarter than I am, but I'm more athletic and caring"). Third, they evaluate their alternatives ("If Ava dumps me for Jack, who would I want to date? Would I rather be on my own than date someone who has been unfaithful to me?"). These questions would help prepare Preston—or anyone else dealing with jealousy or infidelity—for a possible breakup or reconciliation. Finally, jealous people assess their potential loss ("How devastating would it be if Ava and I broke up?").

According to White and Mullen (1989), jealous individuals make appraisals so that they can plan coping strategies and assess outcomes. For example, if Preston decides that Ava could be attracted to Jack because he is ambitious and likely to be successful, he might compensate by putting more effort into his own career. If Ava responded favorably to Preston's intensified career pursuits, Preston would likely continue those behaviors. But if Preston's behavior change does not have the desired effect (perhaps Ava complains that Preston is so focused on his career that he is ignoring her), he is likely to try a different strategy.

JEALOUS EMOTIONS In addition to making cognitive appraisals, jealous individuals usually experience combinations of emotions. The emotions most central to jealousy are fear and anger (see Guerrero & Andersen, 1998a, 1998b; Sharpsteen, 1991). People are jealous because they fear losing their relationship, and they are often angry at their partner for betraying them. Sometimes jealous individuals are also angry at the rival, particularly if the rival is someone they know; other times, they feel irritated or annoyed but not really angry (Guerrero, Trost, & Yoshimura, 2005).

Beyond fear and anger, other aversive emotions such as sadness, guilt, hurt, and envy often mark jealousy (Fitness & Fletcher, 1993; White & Mullen, 1989). Sadness occurs near the end of some jealousy episodes when people are feeling gloomy and lonely because a breakup seems inevitable or has just occurred (Sharpsteen, 1991). Sometimes jealous individuals feel guilty because they wrongly accused their partners of misdeeds. Other times, people feel guilty because they think that their own negative qualities or actions caused the partner to become interested in someone else. For example, Preston might think that if he hadn't been so cold and ignored her for so long, she never would have been with Jack. Envy can be part of the jealousy experience, especially when the rival has positive qualities that the jealous person does not possess.

Sometimes jealousy leads to positive emotions such as increased passion, love, and appreciation (Guerrero & Andersen, 1998b; Guerrero et al., 2005). For example, think about how you might feel if you saw someone flirting with your romantic partner. The fact that someone else sees your partner as attractive might make you feel more passionate and loving toward your partner (Pines, 1992; White & Mullen, 1989). Recent research shows that people sometimes intentionally induce jealousy to achieve two goals: to make their partner value the relationship more and to get revenge (Fleischmann et al., 2005). Pines (1992) also argued that jealousy can lead people to appreciate their partners more, to become more committed to the relationship, and to work harder to maintain the relationship. Other researchers have argued that jealousy is closely related to love because people would not get jealous if they did not care about their partners (Salovey & Rodin, 1985). However, inducing jealousy is a dangerous strategy because jealousy often leads to relationship dissatisfaction and sometimes even violence (Guerrero & Andersen, 1998a).

Communicative Responses to Jealousy

Just as jealousy can involve a wide range of thoughts and emotions, so, too, can jealousy be expressed many different ways. Guerrero and her colleagues have identified many different communicative responses to jealousy, which have been described generally as constructive, destructive, avoidant, and rival-focused (Guerrero et al., 1995; Guerrero, Hannawa, & Babin, 2011).

There are two types of constructive responses: **integrative communication** and **compensatory restoration**. Integrative communication is direct, nonaggressive communication that involves disclosing feelings, such as having a calm discussion about hurtful behaviors and trying to reach an understanding so that jealousy is avoided in the future. Compensatory restoration is behavior aimed at improving the primary relationship or oneself, including trying to look more physically attractive and giving the partner gifts or extra attention. The idea here is to show the partner that he or she will be happier staying in the current relationship than trying something new.

Three specific responses are classified as destructive: **negative communication**, **counter-jealousy induction**, and **violent communication**. Negative communication comprises aggressive and passive-aggressive communication that reflects negativity, such as arguing, being sarcastic, acting rude, ignoring the partner, giving cold or dirty looks, and withdrawing affection. Counter-jealousy induction involves taking actions to make the partner feel jealous too, such as flirting with someone else or talking about a rival in a positive way in front of the partner. Violent communication encompasses both threats and actual violence, such as hitting, shoving, or threatening harm.

Two responses are avoidant: **silence** and **denial.** Silence is about decreasing communication, often by getting quiet and not talking as much as usual. This is different from passive-aggressive responses, such as giving the silent treatment, which are a form of negative communication. Denial is about pretending not to be jealous. Sometimes people do not want to admit feeling jealous because they are worried about looking weak or insecure, so they will act as if nothing is bothering them or deny feeling jealous if asked about it.

Finally, sometimes communication about jealousy is directed at the rival instead of the partner. There are four rival-focused responses: **signs of possession, derogating competitors, surveillance,** and **rival contacts.** Signs of possession involve publicly displaying the relationship so people know that the partner is taken by doing things such as kissing the partner in front of rivals and introducing the partner by names such as "girlfriend," "husband," or "significant other." Derogating competitors is communication designed to cast the rival in a bad light. For example, jealous people might make negative comments about potential rivals to their partners, including telling the partner about their bad traits. The idea here is to show that a relationship with the rival would not be as good as the partner imagines. As such, derogating competitors complements compensatory restoration. One response shows that the current relationship is good, whereas the other response makes the case that the rival relationship would not be good. Surveillance can take many forms, such as checking the partner's or rival's social media, looking at the partner's text messages, or checking up on the partner. The goal here is to seek information about the potential rival relationship. Finally, rival contacts occur when the partner talks directly to the rival. For example, if Preston suspects that Ava is still talking to Jack, he might call Jack and ask him about it.

The most common responses are integrative communication and negative communication. In addition to these specific responses, it is important to consider how much emotion people express when communicating jealousy. For example, a person could be cold and stoic when using integrative communication or show anxiety and sadness. Showing genuine, nonthreatening emotion is preferable.

People use different communicative responses to jealousy based on their goals and emotions (Bryson, 1977; Guerrero & Afifi, 1998, 1999;

Guerrero et al., 2005). When people want to maintain their relationships and feel annoyance rather than anger, they report using constructive responses. People who fear losing their relationships tend to report compensatory restoration. In contrast, people who are more concerned with maintaining their self-esteem deny their jealous feelings. When people are motivated to reduce uncertainty about their relationship, they report using integrative communication, surveillance, and rival contacts, which all represent ways of seeking information. People tend to use destructive responses when they feel jealous anger and want revenge against their partners.

Jealousy and Relational Satisfaction

Although jealousy can be a sign of love and attachment, it can also be both a symptom and a cause of relational distress. In fact, research has shown that jealous thoughts and feelings generally are associated with relational dissatisfaction (Andersen, Eloy, Guerrero, & Spitzberg, 1995; Buunk & Bringle, 1987; Guerrero & Eloy, 1992; Salovey & Rodin, 1989). However, jealousy is experienced in many relationships that remain satisfying. The key seems to be managing jealousy in a productive way. Refraining from using destructive communicative responses is especially important. One study showed that the more jealousy people feel, the more likely they are to use destructive communication such as yelling and accusing their partner. However, when jealous individuals use high levels of destructive communication, they tend to be unhappy in their relationships. In contrast, when people use low levels of destructive communication, they tend to be happy (Guerrero, 2014b). In this study, feeling jealous did not predict satisfaction nearly as well as knowing whether or not the jealous person reacted destructively.

Among the many communicative responses to jealousy listed in Box 13.5, only the two constructive responses appear to be consistently associated with relational satisfaction. All the other responses usually make the problem worse; although some studies have shown that counter-jealousy induction and signs of possession can be effective in certain circumstances (Buss, 1988a; Fleischmann et al., 2005). Indeed, Guerrero (2014b) found that women reported being more satisfied in their relationship if their partner used signs of possession and refrained from using destructive communication when jealous. Integrative communication involves talking about jealousy in a constructive manner, often by disclosing feelings and renegotiating relational rules and boundaries. Afifi and Reichert (1996) found a positive association between integrative communication and relational satisfaction in jealous situations. Research by Andersen et al. (1995), however, found that integrative communication was only associated with relational satisfaction when people expressed their emotions while communicating with their partner. Showing that one is hurt and upset but still making an effort to talk issues over in a fair and rational manner may be one key to preserving relational satisfaction in the face of a jealous threat. Refraining from engaging in destructive communication is the other key. To see which communicative responses to jealousy you use most, take the quiz in Box 13.5. The more you use the constructive responses (integrative communication and compensatory communication) rather than the destructive responses (negative communication, counter-jealousy induction, and violent communication), the more likely you are to be happy in your relationships.

Sex Differences in Jealous Emotions and Communication

Research findings on sex differences in jealous emotions are mixed, but some studies suggest that women experience more hurt, sadness, anxiety, and confusion than men perhaps because they blame themselves for the situation more often (Becker et al., 2004; Bryson, 1976). By contrast, men have been found to deny jealous feelings and to focus on bolstering their self-esteem more than women (Buunk, 1982; White, 1981). These differences are small, but they suggest that women are somewhat

BOX 13.5 PUT YOURSELF TO THE TEST
COMMUNICATIVE RESPONSES TO JEALOUSY

Add the items to find your score, which will range from 3 to 21. The higher the score, the more you tend to use each jealousy response.

		Never						Always
Think about the last few times you have felt jealous in a relationship. When I felt jealous I								
1.	Flirted with or talked about others to make my partner jealous	1	2	3	4	5	6	7
2.	Denied feeling jealous	1	2	3	4	5	6	7
3.	"Checked up" on my partner more than usual	1	2	3	4	5	6	7
4.	Tried to show my partner that I loved her/him	1	2	3	4	5	6	7
5.	Became silent	1	2	3	4	5	6	7
6.	Used physical force with my partner	1	2	3	4	5	6	7
7.	Made sure rivals knew my partner is "taken"	1	2	3	4	5	6	7
8.	Gave my partner cold or dirty looks	1	2	3	4	5	6	7
9.	Confronted the rival	1	2	3	4	5	6	7
10.	Made hurtful or mean comments to my partner	1	2	3	4	5	6	7
11.	Explained my feelings to my partner	1	2	3	4	5	6	7
12.	Pointed out the rival's bad qualities	1	2	3	4	5	6	7
13.	Let my partner know that I was mad	1	2	3	4	5	6	7
14.	Let rivals know that my partner and I are in a relationship	1	2	3	4	5	6	7
15.	Shared my jealous feelings with my partner	1	2	3	4	5	6	7
16.	Tried to find out what my partner was doing when she/he wasn't with me	1	2	3	4	5	6	7
17.	Got quiet and didn't say much	1	2	3	4	5	6	7
18.	Told my partner how much she/he means to me	1	2	3	4	5	6	7
19.	Said mean things about the rival	1	2	3	4	5	6	7
20.	Acted like I wasn't jealous	1	2	3	4	5	6	7
21.	Pretended nothing was wrong	1	2	3	4	5	6	7
22.	Stopped talking	1	2	3	4	5	6	7
23.	Tried to be the "best" partner possible	1	2	3	4	5	6	7

BOX 13.5 (Continued)

		1	2	3	4	5	6	7
24.	Made negative comments about the rival	1	2	3	4	5	6	7
25.	Showed my partner extra affection when rivals were around	1	2	3	4	5	6	7
26.	Kept closer tabs on my partner	1	2	3	4	5	6	7
27.	Pushed, shoved, or hit my partner	1	2	3	4	5	6	7
28.	Talked to the rival	1	2	3	4	5	6	7
29.	Discussed the situation with my partner	1	2	3	4	5	6	7
30.	Tried to make my partner feel jealous too	1	2	3	4	5	6	7
31.	Threatened to harm my partner	1	2	3	4	5	6	7
32.	Acted like I was interested in someone else	1	2	3	4	5	6	7
33.	Discussed issues with the rival	1	2	3	4	5	6	7

To obtain your results, add your scores for the following items:

Counter-jealousy Induction: Items 1 + 30 + 32 = _____

Negative Communication: Items 8 + 10 + 13 = _____

Violent Communication: Items 6 + 27 + 31 = _____

Compensatory Restoration: Items 4 + 18 + 23 = _____

Integrative Communication: Items 11 + 15 + 29 = _____

Silence: Items 5 + 17 + 22 = _____

Denial: Items 2 + 20 + 21 = _____

Surveillance: Items 3 + 16 + 26 = _____

Signs of Possession: Items 7 + 14 + 25 = _____

Derogating Competitors: Items 12 + 19 + 24 = _____

Rival Contact: Items 9 + 28 + 33 = _____

more focused on the relationship whereas men are more focused on individual concerns.

Sex differences in communicative responses to jealousy are more consistent, although relatively small. Jealous women report using integrative communication, expressing emotion, enhancing their appearance, and using counter-jealousy inductions more often than jealous men. In contrast, jealous men more often contact the rival, restrict the partner's access to potential rivals, and give gifts and spend extra money on the partner (Buss, 1988a; Guerrero & Reiter, 1998). An evolutionary perspective can partially explain these findings: Men focus on competing for mates and showing resources whereas women focus on creating social bonds and showcasing their beauty (Buss, 1988a).

UNREQUITED LOVE

Jealousy occurs when people are worried about losing a relationship that they have. Other times people are worried that they will never have a relationship with the person they desire. Such is the case with **unrequited love,** whereby one person, the would-be lover, wants to initiate or intensify a romantic relationship, but the other person, the rejector, does not (Baumeister & Wotman, 1992; Baumeister, Wotman, & Stillwell, 1993; Bratslavsky, Baumeister, & Sommer, 1998). Unrequited love can characterize several types of situations. Sometimes the two people do not know one another well even though one of them feels "in love" with the other; other times, they may be good friends but one person wants to intensify the relationship further and the other person does not; and still other times unrequited love occurs in the initial stages of a relationship or after a breakup. For example, after going on a few dates, one person may fall in love, but the other might want to stop dating altogether (see Chapter 15). Unrequited love also occurs in established or de-escalating relationships when one partner ceases to love the other. Rejection is usually more unpleasant and hurtful when it comes from a romantic partner as opposed to a friend or acquaintance (Young, Paxman, Koehring, & Anderson, 2008).

When unrequited love strikes, the would-be lover has two general options: (1) to keep quiet about the feelings or (2) to try to win the partner's love (Baumeister et al., 1993). Either way, there are considerable risks for the would-be lover. On the one hand, approaching the loved one could lead to rejection, humiliation, or, in the case of an established friendship, the de-escalation or termination of the relationship. On the other hand, keeping quiet could cost the person any opportunity to win the other person over or escalate the relationship.

Situations of unrequited love are difficult for both people, but perhaps surprisingly, Baumeister and his colleagues discovered that rejectors typically report experiencing more negative emotions than do would-be lovers. According to their research,

would-be lovers perceive the situation as having either extremely positive or negative outcomes whereas most rejectors perceive only negative outcomes. Although it is flattering to be the object of someone's affection, the rejector typically feels guilty for being unable to return the would-be lover's sentiments. If the would-be lover is persistent, the rejector may feel frustrated and even victimized (Baumeister et al., 1993). The appropriate way to communicate rejection is also unclear, since it is difficult to reject advances without hurting the would-be lover's feelings. Would-be lovers, by contrast, have a much clearer script for how to behave. Baumeister and colleagues (1993) put it this way:

> The would-be lover's script is affirmed and reiterated from multiple sources; for example, one can probably hear a song about unrequited love in almost any American house within an hour, simply by turning on the radio. A seemingly endless stream of books and movies has portrayed aspiring lovers persisting doggedly to win the hearts of their beloveds. Many techniques are portrayed as eventually effective. If one is rejected in the end, the familiar script calls for heartbroken lovers to express their grief, perhaps assign blame, accept the failure, and then go on with their lives. (p. 379)

For example, songs like Taylor Swift's 2009 hit "You Belong With Me" include storylines where the underdog would-be lover eventually prevails. The rejector, however, does not have a clearly defined cultural prescription for how to deal with the would-be lover. Movies and novels often portray rejectors as "aloof, casual, teasing, or sadistic heartbreakers," but in real life, most rejectors are concerned with helping the would-be lover save face (Baumeister et al., 1993, p. 391). Thus, many rejectors resist making harsh statements such as "I'm not attracted to you" and instead rely on polite, indirect communication strategies, such as saying that they value the friendship too much to ruin it by pursuing a romantic relationship or that they are too busy to date anyone at this time. Folkes (1982) found that rejectors try to let other people down easily and avoid hurting their feelings.

The problem with polite or indirect messages is that they can be misinterpreted (Cupach & Metts, 1991). Would-be lovers may cling to the hope that since the rejector did not dismiss them directly, a love relationship is still possible. For example, would-be lovers who receive a message such as "I'm not interested in dating anyone right now, but I want to stay friends" might hear this as "There might be a chance of a love relationship in the future since I like you." Eventually, the rejector may have to resort to harsher and more direct messages if the would-be lover persists (Metts, Sprecher, & Regan, 1998). When clear sexual advances are made, women are likely to be verbally direct, and most men accept their refusals (Metts et al., 1998).

Although there is not a clear script for how to best reject someone, research suggests that some rejection messages are more inappropriate than others depending on the relationship between the would-be-lover and the rejector. A study by Young et al. (2008) examined several types of rejection messages, including ambiguous or "off-record" strategies (e.g., "I like you, but I'm really busy right now"); direct "on-record" strategies that blame situational constraints for the rejection (e.g., "I'm interested in someone else"); and direct "on-record" strategies that blame the self for the rejection (e.g., "It wouldn't work because I'm not right for you"). The would-be lovers in this study rated the ambiguous off-record strategies as especially inappropriate for friends to use, perhaps because such messages left them wondering whether or not to pursue a romantic relationship in the future. Friends may also expect more directness in their relationships. When the rejector was a romantic partner, would-be lovers rated on-record strategies that blamed situational constraints as the most inappropriate. Given that they are already in a romantic relationship, would-be lovers are often surprised to have their attempts at escalation rebuffed, and perhaps even more surprised that the rejector blames external factors such

as a third party. Finally, would-be lovers rated on-record strategies that blamed the self as the most inappropriate message for acquaintances to use. Since the two people don't yet know one another well, it may seem premature for the rejector to assume that something personal (age, disposition, values, etc.) would stand in the way of the desired relationship. The would-be lover may feel that the potential relationship was rejected without giving it a fair chance.

OBSESSIVE RELATIONAL INTRUSION

Sometimes the would-be-lover does not accept rejection and instead persistently pursues the object of her or his affection. This type of persistent pursuit has been called ORI. ORI refers to unwanted behaviors that invade someone's privacy and are used for the purpose of trying to get close to someone (Cupach & Spitzberg, 1998). ORI includes annoying behavior, such as repeated calls or texts; malicious behavior, such as spreading false rumors; **stalking** behaviors, such as following someone everywhere; and even violent behavior, such as kidnapping or assault. As this list suggests, stalking is a form of ORI behavior. Stalking behaviors constitute repeated and unwanted contact that is threatening and/or fear-provoking (Spitzberg & Hoobler, 2002). Not all stalking is ORI behavior because ORI centers on the pursuit of intimacy, and stalking can be used for other purposes, such as trying to scare an enemy. Similarly, ORI behaviors that do not threaten or produce fear are *not* stalking. About 20% of college students have been stalked; "rates of unwanted relationship pursuit that do not quite rise to the level of causing threat or fear are likely to be substantially higher" (Spitzberg, Cupach, Hannawa, & Crowley, 2014, p. 29). Thus, ORI, and to a lesser extent, stalking, are fairly prevalent.

Cupach and Spitzberg (1998) surveyed 876 people to determine what types of ORI behaviors are most common. The top five behaviors were (1) calling and arguing, (2) calling and then hanging up, (3) constantly asking for "another chance," (4) watching or staring at the loved one from a distance, and (5) making exaggerated claims about affection for the loved one. Stalking behaviors were much less common. According to Spitzberg and Hoobler (2002), the most extreme cases of ORI, such as stalking, tend to occur when the people involved are former relational partners. So it is more likely that Ava would be stalked by Jack (or another former relational partner) than a stranger. Researchers have also examined ORI behaviors in mediated contexts, such as e-mail or Facebook, and found that many of the messages are similar; they are just delivered in a different format. See Box 13.6 for more information on ORI in these mediated contexts.

Reasons People Use Obsessive Relational Intrusion Behavior

Relational goal pursuit theory helps explain ORI (Cupach & Spitzberg, 2004; Spitzberg et al., 2014). According to this theory, people expend energy to develop or reinitiate relationships to the extent that they perceive a relationship is desirable and attainable. Relationships are perceived as especially

---

BOX 13.6 TECH TALK
OBSESSIVE RELATIONAL INTRUSION IN CYBERSPACE

According to Spitzberg and Hoobler (2002), the digital information revolution has made people more accessible while also increasing the potential for interpersonal intrusion. They conducted a series of studies to see how people engage in cyber-ORI. The most common cyber-ORI behaviors focused on **hyperintimacy**, which involves sending repeated and unwanted messages of interest and affection. For example, 31% of people reported being sent unwanted tokens of affection, such as poetry, electronic greeting cards, or songs. Other commonly reported ORI behaviors included receiving excessively disclosive or "needy" messages, receiving pornographic or sexually harassing messages, having private information exposed to others, and having the intrusive person pose as someone else. Hyperintimacy messages are also a common type of ORI behavior in non-cyber contexts.

Another potentially intrusive cyber behavior has become common during the past few years—social media stalking. Although stalking a person's social media—such as their Facebook, Twitter, or Instagram accounts—is not, in itself, an ORI behavior (partly, at least, because it is hidden from the target), it often occurs as part of a pattern of ORI. In two studies involving more than 400 Facebook users, Joinson (2008) found that "virtual people watching" was the second most common use for Facebook (after maintaining contact with friends) and that the motivation of "social investigation," which includes "stalking other people," was among the best predictor of both frequency of visits to Facebook and number of Facebook friends.

Other research has focused on SNUPE-ing, otherwise known as "social network's use for prying electronically" (Phillips & Spitzberg, 2010). There are three general types of surveillance via social networks: (1) *obsessive* (e.g., "I could seem preoccupied with checking on my partner's social network site"), (2) *covert* (e.g., "I have asked friends to use their cameras or phones to photograph my partner and tag a photo of my partner to a social networking site so I would know what my partner was up to"), and (3) *problematic* (e.g., "My partner and I have had conflicts about what I discovered on his or her social network site").

It is also worth noting that individuals often engage in what some have called *lurking* on friends and family members' social networking sites without the sort of preoccupation or manipulative covert behaviors described here. For instance, you might look at your friends' newly uploaded photo albums simply as a way to keep in touch with their lives. Or you might glance though someone's friend list to see if there is anyone whom you want to befriend on Facebook. In fact, these sorts of lurking behaviors, and the relationship maintenance function they serve, are exactly what many users say they most appreciate about social networking sites and likely do not fit in the category of intrusive behaviors.

desirable when being with a particular person is linked to more general life goals, such as happiness. For example, imagine that Preston breaks up with Ava. Ava is devastated and starts thinking she will never love anyone the way she loves Preston, that he is the only one who can make her happy, and that life without him will be miserable. This type of **goal-linking** fuels Ava's thoughts and emotions so that she sees having a relationship with Preston as vitally important and desirable. (The goals that are linked are as follows: Getting Preston back = having a happy life.) As long as the desired relationship is perceived to be attainable, people will continue pursuing their goal. Given that Ava previously had a happy relationship with Preston, she is likely to think that she can regain what she lost so she will continue to pursue him. But if at some point she realizes that there is nothing she can do to get him back, relational goal pursuit theory predicts that she will give up and seek an alternative goal.

Unfortunately, however, people sometimes continue to believe that a relationship is attainable even though it is not. In these cases, ORI is likely to occur. In fact, episodes of ORI typically increase in intensity as the object of attention tries to fortify privacy boundaries—for example, by taking pains to avoid the pursuer. At first, ORI behaviors are usually prosocial, indirect, and only mildly annoying (Cupach & Spitzberg, 2004, 2008). The pursuer might act flirtatious, try to spend time with the desired partner, and text or call frequently. If these ORI behaviors are unsuccessful, the pursuer will sometimes employ more invasive violations of privacy, such as surveillance, harassment, and infiltration into the desired person's social network. Such behaviors are typically perceived as aggravating and inconvenient. Finally, in some cases, ORI becomes particularly volatile, frightening, and creepy—with pursuers stalking their victims and engaging in coercive and even violent behavior (Cupach & Spitzberg, 2004).

So why do some pursuers continue to use ORI behaviors rather than abandoning their goal and seeking an alternative relationship? Cupach and Spitzberg (1998, 2004, 2008) suggested four general reasons: (1) cultural scripts, (2) the ambiguity of communication, (3) rumination, and (4) a shift in motivation.

Cultural scripts often portray people as "playing hard to get." These scripts also suggest that if people try hard enough, they will eventually win the affection of the person they love. Think about the movies you have seen where one of the main characters is in love with someone who seems out of reach. Most of the time, these characters end up with the person of their dreams. These types of cultural scripts work against the realization that a relationship is unattainable.

Ambiguous communication may also keep hope alive. As noted in Chapter 9, during courtship people engage in ambiguous flirtatious behavior that is safe and helps them save face if they are rejected. Similarly, as noted earlier in this chapter, people often use indirect strategies to reject people because they worry about hurting their feelings. Rather than seeing these strategies as polite ways of rejecting them, pursuers may fail to correctly interpret rejection signals and continue to believe that the desired relationship is attainable.

Rumination is a symptom of being frustrated that you cannot get what you want (Spitzberg et al., 2014). For example, Ava wants to be happy, she thinks she cannot be happy without Preston, and Preston is resisting getting back together, leading her to experience frustration and to constantly think about what she cannot have. Rumination is often accompanied by a flood of negative emotion, which leads people to redouble their efforts to get what they want so they can start feeling better (Spitzberg et al., 2014). This cycle of rumination can be difficult to break as people try harder and harder to reach their goal.

Finally, sometimes there is a **shift in motivation** where people abandon relationship pursuit and instead try to get revenge against their partner for rejecting them. This shift sometimes marks the beginning of more aggressive ORI behaviors (Cupach & Spitzberg, 2008). When this shift occurs, ORI sometimes escalates to stalking, wherein someone repeatedly harasses another person in a way that threatens the individual's safety (Meloy & Gothard, 1995). Studies suggest that the vast majority of stalkers (i.e., about 75%) have had a previous relationship with their victims, and about half are former romantic partners (Cupach & Spitzberg, 2004). And, strikingly, the average stalking episode lasts nearly 2 years. One individual described her experience as "pure hell" that "just kept going on and on and on and on" (Draucker, 1999, p. 478).

Consequences of Obsessive Relational Intrusion Behavior

Not surprisingly, the toll that this sort of constant threat takes on victims' psychological and physiological health is tremendous. Even moderate forms of ORI, though, can have devastating psychological consequences for the person being pursued (Cupach & Spitzberg, 2000). The most obvious consequence of ORI episodes is extreme and repeated experiences of fear associated with the target's loss of control over individual physical and psychological privacy (Mullen & Pathe, 1994). This fear often results in the target making drastic attempts to regain privacy, including equipping house and car with alarm systems, changing phone numbers and addresses, and even changing jobs. In fact, Wallace and Silverman (1996) argued that the effects of stalking are often similar to those experienced by victims of posttraumatic stress disorder.

A key question, then, is how can the desired person thwart ORI behavior? Cupach and Spitzberg (2008) identified five general ways that people cope with ORI behavior: (1) *passive* (waiting for the pursuer to tire of the target, lose interest, or give up),(2) *avoidant* (not answering phone calls and staying away from the pursuer), (3) *aggressive* (being mean or rude, threatening to harm the pursuer if the target is not left alone), (4) *integrative* (communicating disinterest

directly, negotiating relationship rules and boundaries), and (5) *help seeking* (asking others for assistance in preventing ORI behavior). Cupach and Spitzberg (2008) concluded that the success of each strategy varies dramatically but found that confrontation and the clear outlining of relationship rules and boundaries (i.e., integrative strategies) had the greatest likelihood of success. If ORI becomes violent or crosses the line into stalking, it is usually imperative to seek help from others.

RELATIONAL VIOLENCE

Violence can occur in the context of ORI when one person wants a relationship and the other person does not. Indeed, the media details sensational cases where scorned lovers decide that if they cannot have the person they love, no one else will either. Despite the attention these cases receive, violence is one of the least common ORI behaviors, and violence is more likely to occur in established relationships than in relationships between a would-be-lover and a rejector. Research suggests that about 16% of married couples, 35% of cohabiting couples, and 30% of dating couples can recall at least one incidence of interpersonal violence in their relationship over the past year (Christopher & Lloyd, 2000). Gay and lesbian couples report violence rates that are about the same as married couples; although they report using milder forms of violence than straight couples (Rohrbaugh, 2006). The most common types of interpersonal violence in romantic relationships include pushing or shoving one's partner, forcefully grabbing one's partner, and shaking or handling one's partner roughly (Marshall, 1994). Sibling relationships also tend to involve violence. Around 36% of siblings report engaging in acts of moderately severe violence during childhood and adolescence, such as kicking and hitting with objects. Even more siblings (around 64%) report that they have engaged in less severe forms of violence, such as shoving and pushing (Straus & Gelles, 1990). Next, we discuss two patterns of violence—common couple violence and **intimate terrorism**—that have been studied in the context of romantic relationships.

Common Couple Violence

Common couple violence occurs when conflict spins out of control and partners resort to using violence as a way to vent their emotions and try to control the conflict (Johnson, 1995; McEwan & Johnson, 2008). This type of violence tends to be reciprocal—one person commits a violent act and the other person retaliates with more violence (Hamel, 2009; Johnson, 1995). Because common couple violence is reciprocal, men and women tend to engage in this type of violence about equally (Graham-Kevan & Archer, 2003; Hamel, 2009; Johnson, 1995; Olson, 2002b). Most of the time, common couple violence includes less severe forms of violent behavior, such as throwing objects, grabbing, shoving, pushing, or slapping (Johnson & Leone, 2005; Olson, 2004). Other times, common couple violence gets out of control, escalating into more severely violent behaviors, including hitting, beating, or using a weapon against the partner (Johnson & Leone, 2005).

There are two general patterns of common couple violence in relationships. Some couples show a pattern of **repeated common couple violence.** Episodes of this type of violence occur once every 2 months or so (Johnson, 1995). For these couples, conflicts that are especially serious tend to escalate into violence on a fairly regular basis. More couples, however, report a pattern of **isolated common-couple violence.** These types of episodes are rare and only occur when a conflict gets especially emotional and aggressive. To examine these patterns, a large national survey about violence against women was conducted. Only 1% of people who reported that common couple violence had occurred at some point in their relationship said that an incident had occurred within the past 12 months (Johnson & Leone, 2005). In other words, some people could recall at least one time when they had experienced common couple violence in their relationship, but it was rare enough that it had not occurred in the past year. Some of the couples who experience isolated

common couple violence discuss their violent behavior, deem it inappropriate, and vow that it will not happen again. These types of discussions decrease future episodes of common couple violence (Olson, 2002b).

Common couple violence often occurs alongside other aggressive forms of communication or when people feel ignored (Olson, 2002a, 2002b; Olson & Braithwaite, 2004). Hamel (2009) concluded that common couple violence occurs when partners are motivated to communicate rather than control their anger but have trouble communicating effectively. Emotions often take over, and people have trouble controlling their behavior. Similarly, Olson argued that people often resort to this form of violence when they get frustrated and feel that they cannot communicate what they want to their partner (Olson, 2002b; Olson & Braithwaite, 2004). Common couple violence can also surface when people use violence to gain their partner's attention or keep their partner from leaving the scene of the conflict (Olson, 2002a, 2002b; Olson & Braithwaite, 2004). This can result in a struggle with one partner using violence to try and keep an argument going, either to try to win the argument or out of frustration of the issue remaining unresolved, and the other

Violence is always unacceptable. Research suggests that people sometimes resort to violent behavior when they lack the interpersonal skills necessary to solve relational problems.

partner using violence to try to get away and end the argument.

Intimate Terrorism

Whereas common couple violence is spontaneous and often fueled by emotion, intimate terrorism is a strategic and enduring pattern that involves using violence to control a partner (Johnson & Ferraro, 2000). For example, an individual may use violence to keep a partner from talking to rivals, control what a partner wears, or force a partner to engage in certain sexual behaviors. Common couple violence is also reciprocal, meaning both partners become violent. In contrast, intimate terrorism is unidirectional; one partner is the perpetrator and the other partner is the victim. If victims of intimate terrorism engage in violence, it is usually to protect or defend themselves from being attacked.

The classic movie, *Sleeping With the Enemy,* provides a good portrayal of a relationship marked by intimate terrorism. In the movie, Julia Roberts plays Laura, a woman who is controlled by her violent husband. After Laura is polite and friendly toward a waiter at a restaurant, her husband beats her for being flirtatious. He also expects her to keep his house immaculately clean to the point that the towels in the bathroom have to be hung just right and the food in the pantry and cabinets has to be perfectly organized with the labels facing outward. If things are out of order, Laura knows he will hurt her. Laura's husband also has sex with her after beating her. Laura does what he wants out of fear, until she fakes her death and (at least temporarily) escapes. Eventually he finds her, and she shoots him before he can kill her.

The scenario depicted in *Sleeping With the Enemy* also illustrates another common aspect of intimate terrorism—perpetrators of intimate terrorism often cycle between being violent and being especially nice, apologetic, and generous (Shackelford, Goetz, Buss, Euler, & Hoier, 2005; Walker, 2000). For example, after hurting their partner, perpetrators might buy their partner flowers or expensive gifts, like the jewelry that Laura's husband gives her in the movie. They also tell their victims that they get violent because they love them so much and don't want to lose them. These kinds of explanations feed into fairy tale notions of love as all-consuming, which can, unfortunately, lead some people to accept some level of violence in their relationships because they see violence as an inevitable side effect of having strong feelings for someone (Wood, 2001). One study showed that violent husbands were especially likely to engage in certain types of behavior, such as pleading for their partners to stay with them, saying that they can't live without their partners, and monopolizing their partners' time so rivals do not have access to them (Shackelford et al., 2005). These behaviors, which simultaneously communicate love and control, are often part of intimate terrorism.

Consistent with the storyline in *Sleeping With the Enemy,* men are more likely to use intimate terrorism than women. In a study by Graham-Kevan and Archer (2003), 87% of intimate terrorism cases involved men as the perpetrators and women as the victims. Of course, there are times when women are the perpetrators (Hines & Douglas, 2010). The key to defining intimate terrorism is not that men tend to be the perpetrators and that women tend to be the victims but rather that one partner is using violence to try to control the other. Another key to defining intimate terrorism is that it is an enduring pattern (Johnson & Leone, 2005). Studies have shown that violence occurs about once a week in relationships characterized by intimate terrorism (Johnson, 1995), which is about eight times more often than in relationships characterized by repeated common couple violence. Even more disturbingly, intimate terrorism tends to become more frequent and more severe over time as perpetrators become more controlling and possessive (Graham-Kevan & Archer, 2003; Johnson & Ferraro, 2000).

SUMMARY AND APPLICATION

In a perfect world, people would never hurt one another. But the world is full of imperfect people leading imperfect lives. Coping with relational transgressions and hurt feelings is a difficult challenge that many relational partners face. Sometimes the damage from infidelity, deception, or other transgressions is too great, and the relationship ends. Other times, people work out their problems and improve their relationships. Chapter 14 addresses some of the ways that people can repair their relationships following hurtful events.

For now, you should understand that close relational partners, including romantic couples, friends, and family members, sometimes hurt one another by what they say and do. People are especially likely to experience hurt if they feel devalued. Criticism, insults, and other evaluative statements threaten a person's self-esteem, especially when delivered by someone who is supposed to love and care for you. Similarly, actions like deception and infidelity violate trust and relational rules about how people should behave in close, caring relationships. Infidelity is one of the most serious and upsetting relational transgressions, so Ava should be concerned about Preston's reaction. She should also be concerned about concealing this information from him. Even if she believes she is keeping her one-night stand secret to protect their relationship, she is also protecting herself from Preston's anger and the possibility of a breakup, which could be construed as a self-focused motive. Research in this chapter also suggests that Preston will be less likely to forgive Ava if he finds out from a third party rather than hearing it from her.

Regardless of how Ava tells him, if Preston finds out, he is likely to feel upset and jealous. Indeed, finding out that your partner had a one-night stand with an ex-lover may be especially threatening. Research has shown that men (as well as women) react strongly to sexual infidelity. Men do not react as strongly to emotional infidelity, but given that Jack and Ava used to have an emotional

connection, Preston may assume that Ava still has feelings for him. This is consistent with the double-shot hypothesis, which predicts that men view sexual infidelity as especially threatening because they assume that their female partners wouldn't have sex with another man unless they also had an emotional connection to him.

If Preston feels jealous and wants to work things out, he should use integrative communication and express his feelings rather than destructive responses such as negative communication and violence. He should also appraise the situation to determine the level of threat that Jack actually poses. He might conclude that there were extenuating circumstances, and that if they had never argued, or if he had stopped ignoring her sooner, Ava would never have had the one-night stand. In this case, Preston might realize that Ava loves him and not Jack, so the threat would dissipate. On the other hand, Preston may conclude that a part of Ava is still in love with Jack and that their temporary separation was an excuse for her to try to get back together with him. In that case, the threat would intensify. The larger the perceived threat, the stronger jealous emotions are, and the more difficult it is to use constructive forms of communication, like integrative communication, as opposed to destructive forms of communication, like yelling or counter-jealousy inductions.

Finally, we could imagine endings to Ava's story that would involve ORI or violence. Perhaps Jack is still in love with Ava, and their one-night stand renews his desire to try and get back together with her. Although Ava tells him that she loves Preston and not him, Jack may continue to hope that they could get back together. He might use mildly intrusive behaviors, such as calling or texting her repeatedly or stopping by her work. Eventually it could escalate with Jack telling Preston about their one-night stand, spying on her, or even becoming violent. Violence has no place in a relationship. Some are fooled into thinking that violence can stem from love and wanting to be with someone so much that you can't control yourself. But a healthy relationship is built on prosocial communication and effective conflict management (see Chapters 10 and 11). By using these tools, as well as the repair strategies discussed in Chapter 14, couples like Ava and Preston can try to work through relational transgressions and get their relationships back on track.

KEY TERMS

acquiescent responses (p. 348)
active verbal responses (p. 348)
ambiguous communication (p. 371)
behavioral control (p. 354)
behavioral familiarity (p. 354)
communicative infidelity (p. 356)
compensatory restoration (p. 364)
concealments (p. 350)
counter-jealousy induction, as a communicative response to jealousy (p. 364)
cultural scripts (p. 371)
denial, as a communicative response to jealousy (p. 364)
derogating competitors (p. 364)
devaluation (p. 346)
double-shot hypothesis (p. 358)
emotional infidelity (p. 356)
envy (p. 361)
equivocations (p. 350)
evolutionary hypothesis for infidelity (p. 358)
exaggerations (p. 350)

goal-linking (p. 371)
hurtful messages (p. 345)
hyperintimacy (p. 370)
informational familiarity (p. 354)
integrative communication (p. 364)
intimate terrorism (p. 373)
invulnerable responses (p. 348)
isolated common couple violence (p. 373)
jealousy (p. 345)
lies (p. 350)
negative communication, as a communicative response to jealousy (p. 364)
obsessive relational intrusion (ORI) (p. 345)
online infidelity (p. 357)
primary appraisals (p. 361)
relational goal pursuit theory (p. 370)
relational transgressions (p. 346)
repeated common couple violence (p. 373)
rival contacts (p. 364)

romantic jealousy (p. 360)
rumination (p. 371)
secondary appraisals (p. 363)
self-focused motives (p. 350)
sexual infidelity (p. 356)
shift in motivation (p. 371)
signs of possession, as a communicative response to jealousy (p. 364)
silence, as a communicative response to jealousy (p. 364)
stalking (p. 369)
surveillance (p. 364)
transgression-maximizing messages (p. 347)
transgression-minimizing messages (p. 347)
truth bias (p. 354)
understatements (p. 350)
unrequited love (p. 368)
violent communication, as a communicative response to jealousy (p. 364)

DISCUSSION QUESTIONS

1. Under what circumstances, if any, do you think it is okay to deceive a friend or relational partner? When would you feel betrayed if your friend or partner deceived you?

2. Think about the last time you or someone you know was jealous. Which of the communicative responses to jealousy did you or the person know use? Did these responses make the situation better or worse?

3. On television and in the news, we often hear about cases involving ORI or stalking. Have you or people you have known ever experienced this problem? What strategies might you use to stop such behavior? Why is stopping such behavior so difficult?

SAGE edge™

Sharpen your skills with SAGE edge at edge.sagepub.com/guerrero5e.
SAGE edge for students provides a personalized approach to help you accomplish your coursework
goals in an easy-to-use learning environment.

14 HEALING THE HURT
Relationship Repair and Reconciliation

Tia and Jamal are deeply in love and plan to marry after Tia finishes graduate school. During a conversation with a mutual friend, Jamal discovers that Tia recently had lunch with her ex-boyfriend, Robert, and then spent time alone with him in his apartment. Tia had told Jamal that she had been out with friends that night. Jamal is flooded with negative thoughts and emotions. Robert was Tia's first love, and her friends always talk about him as if he's perfect, saying he's hot, athletic, and smart. Jamal can't help but wonder if Tia is still into him. And why would she lie unless she had something to hide? Jamal confronts Tia later that evening, calls her a liar, and says he can't trust her anymore. Tia defends herself by saying that she is completely over Robert, they met by chance and decided to "catch up" over lunch and then continued their conversation at his place. Tia says, "It didn't mean anything, and I knew it would just upset you. I told him that I love you, and we are engaged. I think it was good for us to both get closure." Jamal is not sure what to believe at this point and a larger argument ensues. They both think they are right and stubbornly stop talking to each other. Eventually Tia tells Jamal that if he can't trust her, they should break up. He is devastated, but agrees to break up after all his attempts to reconcile fail. After about a month, Jamal starts dating someone new, but he still misses Tia. When Tia sees Jamal with someone new on his Snapchat stories, she realizes that she is not over him. In fact, it makes her realize why Jamal felt so jealous. She decides to contact him. They talk and agree to give things another try. To do so, they know that they will both need to work on being honest and trusting each other.

Like Tia and Jamal, many couples encounter situations that threaten the continuation of their relationships. Of course, problems can occur in any relationship, including those between romantic partners, friends, or family members. The question then becomes this: Is the relationship worth saving? And if it is, how can partners move beyond the problem and repair their relationship? Getting a relationship back on track after a serious transgression or conflict can be a difficult challenge, as Fincham (2000) described using the metaphor of "kissing porcupines":

Imagine two porcupines huddled together in the cold of an Alaskan winter's night, each providing life-sustaining warmth to the other. As they draw ever closer together, the painful prick from the other's quills leads them to instinctively withdraw—until the need for warmth draws them together again. This "kiss of the porcupines" is an apt metaphor for the human condition, and it illustrates two fundamental assumptions. . . . Humans harm each other and humans are social animals. (p. 2)

As Fincham (2000) put it, acceptance of these two assumptions results in the following challenge: "how to maintain relatedness with fellow humans in the face of being harmed by them" (p. 2). This chapter addresses this issue by examining several areas of theory and research. First, we discuss two related models that explain some of the conditions that make it more likely that partners will stay together following relational harm—the investment model and the accommodation model. Next, we describe some of the remedial behaviors that people use to try to repair their relationships after a transgression has occurred, followed by a discussion of **forgiveness** and forgiving communication. The final sections of this chapter focus on relationship reconciliation, on-again off-

again relationships, and relationship redefinition, which can all occur after a breakup.

THE INVESTMENT MODEL OF RELATIONSHIP-MAINTAINING BEHAVIOR

The investment model is an extension of Thibaut and Kelley's (1959) interdependence theory. According to interdependence theory, relational partners become interdependent and committed to one another through the exchange of valuable resources, such as love and possessions (Kelley, 1979; Rusbult, Drigotas, & Verette, 1994). Every relationship has a unique pattern of interdependence that is based on the specific **rewards** and costs partners exchange as well as the degree to which they are dependent on one another to reach their goals.

The investment model has been expanded and applied to situations calling for relationship repair. This model, which Rusbult and colleagues (1994) called the **investment model of relationship-maintaining behavior,** rests on the idea that commitment helps buffer relationships against the destruction that hurtful events and conflict can

FIGURE 14.1 ■ The Investment Model of Relationship-Maintaining Behavior

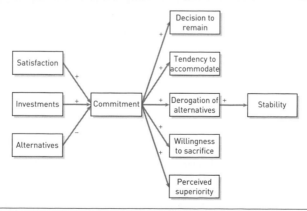

Source: From Rusbult, Caryl E., Drigotas, Stephen M., & Verette, Julie, "The Investment Model: An Interdependence Analysis of Commitment Processes and Relationship Maintenance Phenomena." In Daniel J. Canary & Laura Stafford (eds.), *Communication and Relational Maintenance.* Used with permission from Elsevier.

cause. As shown in Figure 14.1, the first part of the model focuses on how satisfaction, **investments,** and alternatives work together to predict how committed a person is in a relationship. The second part of the model suggests that people in highly committed relationships get through difficult times by employing five types of pro-relationship behavior. The various parts of this model are discussed next.

Commitment

According to the investment model, satisfaction, investments, and alternatives predict how committed people are to their relationships. Satisfaction is highest when people are in rewarding relationships that exceed their expectations. Investments are "resources that become attached to a relationship and would decline in value or be lost if the relationship were to end" (Rusbult et al., 1994, p. 119). Finally, the quality of alternatives refers to the types of alternatives that people perceive they have outside of a current relationship (Thibaut & Kelley, 1959). The combination of high satisfaction, high investment, and low quality alternatives makes relationships more resilient when problems occur. In contrast, if people are dissatisfied, have made few investments into their relationships, or have good quality alternatives, they are less committed and their relationships are more fragile in the face of relationship threats.

SATISFACTION In both independence theory and the investment model, satisfaction is based on two things. First, rewards must outweigh costs. Second, the reward-cost ratio (or **outcome**) in the relationship must be as good as or better than expected. Different types of rewards and costs characterize relationships. Sprecher (1998b) defined rewards as "exchanged resources that are pleasurable and gratifying" and costs as "exchanged resources that result in a loss or punishment" (p. 32). Rewards and costs play an important role in both friendships and romantic relationships. In one study, people rated their friendships as especially close when they felt they were receiving rewards such as affection and support (Tornblom & Fredholm, 1984). For romantic couples, exchanging love and information is related

to increased intimacy and satisfaction (Lloyd, Cate, & Henton, 1982). Other rewards include being able to pool financial resources, having someone to raise children with, and being with someone who is fun. Costs include having to pay someone else's expenses, being with someone who is disagreeable, and giving up a job opportunity for the sake of the relationship. Relationship transgressions and conflict are also part of the costs of a relationship, so for relationships to survive, these types of negative events must be counterbalanced by rewards. To get a general idea of how rewarding one of your relationships is, complete the scale found in Box 14.2.

Interdependence theory and the investment model use the term *outcome* to refer to the ratio of rewards to costs. When rewards outweigh costs, the outcome is positive; when costs outweigh rewards, the outcome is negative. Put another way, rewards minus costs equal the outcome. To illustrate, suppose that Jamal perceives that he is receiving 10 rewards and 20 costs in his relationship with Tia. According to interdependence theory, Jamal then has a negative outcome ($10 - 20 = -10$). In economic terms, his relationship with Tia is characterized by a deficit. In contrast, Tia may perceive that she is receiving 30 rewards and incurring only 10 costs. Her outcome would then be positive ($30 - 10 = +20$); Tia would be getting a profit from being in a relationship with Jamal. Of course, in real life, rewards and costs are very hard to quantify, and some rewards and costs are more important than others. One reward—such as having someone who provides unconditional love and support—may be valuable enough to outweigh several smaller costs. The critical point here is that people mentally compare costs and rewards to determine whether they are in a positive or negative relationship.

Knowing whether the relationship has a positive or negative outcome is not enough. Some people expect highly rewarding relationships, so outcomes have to be particularly positive for them to be happy. Other people expect their relationships to be unrewarding, so a slightly positive outcome or even an outcome that is not as negative as expected might be all that is needed to make them happy.

To account for the influence of expectations, interdependence theory includes the concept of **comparison level,** which involves the expectation of the kinds of outcomes a person expects to receive in a relationship (Thibaut & Kelley, 1959). This expectation is based on the person's past relational experiences and personal observations of other people's relationships. For example, if Tia has had really good relationships in the past and her parents and friends all tend to have happy relationships, she would have a high comparison level. Thus, even if her outcome in her relationship with Jamal was positive, it might still be lower than what she expected, leading her to be unhappy. Consistent with the idea of comparison levels, one study demonstrated that women are less likely to rate their current relationship as committed and satisfying if their past relationships were especially close (Merolla, Weber, Myers, & Booth-Butterfield, 2004). Perhaps this is why Robert is such a threat to Jamal—Jamal knows that Tia once had an especially close and satisfying relationship with him, and he worries that he might not live up to the comparison.

Comparison levels also influence how much positive behavior people expect from their partners. Dainton (2000) conducted two studies looking at comparison levels, relational satisfaction, and maintenance behaviors. Maintenance behaviors included actions such as showing commitment to the partner, being positive and cheerful around the partner, and sharing tasks in a fair manner (see Chapter 9). These behaviors can be thought of as "rewards" in a relationship. Dainton's research showed that people tended to be satisfied with their relationships when they perceived their partner to use high levels of rewarding maintenance behavior. Satisfaction was also higher when people reported that their partner used more maintenance behavior than they expected them to. In other words, people were happiest when their partner engaged in lots of rewarding behavior that met or exceeded their comparison level.

INVESTMENTS Like satisfaction, investment can lead to more commitment in a relationship. Investments can be classified as either intrinsic or extrinsic (Rusbult, 1983). **Intrinsic investments** are those that are put directly into the relationship, including time, effort, affection, and disclosure. **Extrinsic investments** are resources or benefits that are developed over time as a result of being in the relationship, such as material possessions, enmeshment within a common social system, and an identity that is attached to being in a relationship. People put more investments into relationships to which they feel a strong commitment (Matthews, 1986). These investments then make it difficult to walk away from a relationship, which strengthens commitment even more. If two people do end a highly invested relationship, they will probably feel that all the time and effort they put into their relationship was a waste. They also might feel that they now have to start over, find someone new, and make adjustments to their identity and social image. These challenges make the prospect of ending a long-term, heavily invested relationship a daunting one.

Several studies have demonstrated that investments help predict commitment (Le & Agnew, 2003). These studies have shown that investments, along with satisfaction and the quality of alternatives, influence whether people are committed to and stay in their relationships with friends and romantic partners (Drigotas & Rusbult, 1992; Duffy & Rusbult, 1986; Guerrero & Bachman, 2008; Rusbult, 1980, 1983), as well as whether people stay at their jobs (Farrell & Rusbult, 1981; Rusbult & Farrell, 1983). For example, Rusbult (1983) looked at dating relationships over a 7-month period. She found that daters who reported increases in satisfaction and investment, as well as decreases in the quality of alternatives, were the most committed to their relationships. These people were also likely to be together at the end of the 7-month period. By contrast, daters who reported decreases in satisfaction and investment, as well as increases in the quality of alternatives, tended to experience less commitment and to voluntarily leave the relationship sometime during the seven-month period.

Another study examined abusive relationships by interviewing women at shelters (Rusbult & Martz, 1995). Women who went back to their abusive partners usually had large investments in the relationship and low-quality alternatives. Women in this situation may believe that it is better to stay in the relationship than to be alone or to move on to another—potentially worse—relationship. They may be dependent on their partner for financial resources or self-esteem. They also may not want to face the possibility that they have put a lot of time and effort into a bad relationship. Therefore, they may work even harder to improve their relationship by trying to change their own and their partner's behavior. This continuous investment, however, keeps them trapped within the dissatisfying relationship. Thus, while high levels of investment keep people in relationships, it does not always ensure that relationships are satisfying.

QUALITY OF ALTERNATIVES The quality of alternatives also helps explain why people sometimes stay in dissatisfying relationships. Alternatives can include pursuing other relationships or being on one's own. Some people perceive that they have good alternatives. Perhaps many other attractive people would be interested in them, and perhaps they would be happier alone than in their current relationship. Other people perceive that they have poor alternatives. Perhaps they are dependent on their partner for financial support and cannot afford to leave the relationship, or they can envision no attractive alternative relationships, or they view themselves as unlovable and think that if they leave their partner they will be alone for the rest of their lives.

When people have good alternatives, they tend to be less committed to their relationships. By contrast, when people have poor alternatives, they tend to be highly committed to their relationships (Crawford et al., 2003). A simplistic example of the way alternatives function might be observed during the month before the senior prom. Suppose that Rosa, a high school senior, has been dating Carlos for the past year. She is considering breaking up with him sometime before they both leave for college, but she is not sure when. If Rosa thinks that two or three boys she finds attractive are likely to ask her to the prom, she might break

up with Carlos sooner (assuming that going to the prom is important to her). But if Rosa thinks that no one "better" than Carlos is going to ask her to the prom, she is likely to stay with him—at least temporarily.

On a more serious note, some individuals stay in unsatisfying and even abusive relationships because they have poor alternatives. For example, a man might decide that it is better to stay in his unhappy marriage rather than risk losing custody of his children. In a study on predictors of divorce, people reported being much more likely to leave their spouses when they had appealing alternatives (Black, Eastwood, Sprenkle, & Smith, 1991). Research also suggests that abused women who are dependent on their husbands for financial support are more likely to stay in their marriages (Pfouts, 1978; Rusbult & Martz, 1995). These women—many of whom have little education, few work skills, and no means of transportation—often see their abusive relationships as a better alternative than being poor, hungry, and unable to support their children (Rusbult & Martz, 1995).

Pro-Relationship Behaviors

The next part of the model (see Figure 14.1) focuses on pro-relationship behaviors. According to the model, if people are highly committed to their relationship, they are likely to use five pro-relationship behaviors when they encounter problems in their relationships—(1) deciding to remain in the relationship, (2) accommodating the partner, (3) derogating alternatives, (4) showing a willingness to sacrifice, and (5) perceiving relationship superiority. If they are uncommitted to their relationship, they are unlikely to use any of these behaviors, and the relationship is more likely to de-escalate or end.

DECIDING TO REMAIN The first and perhaps most important step is the decision to remain in the relationship. People who encounter serious problems or conflict in their relationships sometimes give up or decide it would be better to end the relationship.

Without a commitment by the partners to stay in the relationship and work through problems, the relationship is unlikely to survive. In one study, couples who were committed to one another were less likely to report exiting the relationship following a relational transgression, such as their partner betraying or lying to them (Menzies-Toman & Lydon, 2005). In the studies reported earlier on betrayal, couples were less likely to de-escalate their relationships if they had reported high levels of satisfaction and investment earlier (e.g., Guerrero & Bachman, 2008).

ACCOMMODATING THE PARTNER People have a natural tendency to respond to negative events with more negativity or to avoid the person who has hurt them. This has been called a "fight or flight" response, with people wanting to retaliate against or get away from people who make them feel bad. However, when people are in a highly committed relationship, they are more likely to curb this tendency and accommodate their partner by engaging in more positive behavior. For example, when Jamal calls Tia a liar and says he can't trust her, she may feel frustrated and lose her temper, but because she loves him and values their relationship she makes an effort to calm down quickly and then tell him she's sorry. Being able to accommodate the partner by acting constructively rather than destructively is especially important because it helps break negative cycles and prevents further escalation of negative behavior.

DEROGATING ALTERNATIVES Commitment also leads people to derogate their alternatives. In other words, committed people tend to find reasons to downgrade potential alternative partners. For example, in a study by Johnson and Rusbult (1989), when highly committed individuals were matched up with attractive partners via computer-assigned dates, they found ways to derogate their computer dates, especially if they were highly attractive. When people derogate their alternatives, it also keeps them more committed to their relationships because they perceive their quality of alternatives to be relatively

low. Derogating alternatives can also function as a motivation to repair a relationship since the current relationship, even with its problems, may seem preferable to other options.

SHOWING A WILLINGNESS TO SACRIFICE People in highly committed relationships are also more willing to make sacrifices for each other. Sacrifices can be thought of as special types of investments that involve putting aside one's own immediate self-interest and focusing on the best interests of the relationship. The willingness to make sacrifices has been found to be an important factor in maintaining high-quality relationships. People are more likely to make sacrifices for their partner or their relationship when they are committed and satisfied, have made large investments, and have low-quality alternatives (Van Lange et al., 1997). Making sacrifices sometimes involve helping a relational partner through a crisis situation. One study showed that college students see their closest friends as a significant source of comfort, encouragement, and social support (Burleson & Samter, 1994). Willingness to sacrifice is also important because it is difficult for two people to get everything each one wants within the constraints of the relationship. For example, spouses have to make hard decisions regarding their careers, children, and so forth. If the wife's new promotion means that the family will have to move somewhere that is unappealing to the husband, the couple will have to make some type of compromise or sacrifice. Or, if the husband wants to have only one child and the wife wants at least three, something will have to give. In short, because both people cannot always have everything their own way, it is essential that relational partners be willing to sacrifice their own preferences for the overall good of the relationship.

PERCEIVING RELATIONSHIP SUPERIORITY Relational partners who are highly committed to each other perceive their relationship to be superior to other relationships. This can be thought of as a "relationship-enhancing illusion" (Rusbult et al., 1994, p. 129). For highly committed relationships, "the grass is rarely greener" on the other side. People tend to see their own relationships as having more positive and fewer negative characteristics than the relationships of others. This bias is particularly strong in highly committed relationships (Rusbult, Van Lange, Wildschut, Yovetich, & Verette, 2000). People might say and think things like, "We give each other a lot more freedom than most couples do" and "Our relationship doesn't have as many problems as the average relationship has." This type of thinking leads to positive attitudes about the relationship and sets the tone for behaving constructively and making more sacrifices. In relationships that are low in commitment and satisfaction, such positive thinking is less likely—the "grass on the other side" may indeed seem greener.

The investment model has proven to be a powerful theory for explaining the role that commitment plays in the process of maintaining and repairing relationships. Two people are most likely to become committed to each other when they are satisfied with the relationship, have low-quality alternatives, and have made sizable investments. Once a couple is highly committed, the relationship is maintained through several types of pro-relationship activities, including remaining in the relationship through good times and bad, accommodating the partner by resisting the urge to retaliate, derogating alternatives, being willing to sacrifice for the good of the relationship, and perceiving the relationship to be superior to the relationships of others. These forces help couples maintain their relationships and provide motivation for repairing relationships when problems arise.

THE MODEL OF ACCOMMODATION

Researchers have expanded on the idea that people in committed relationships are more likely to accommodate their partners and repair their relationships by proposing a **model of accommodation** (Rusbult, Johnson, & Morrow, 1986; Rusbult et al., 1991). This model describes four general ways that people respond to problems or dissatisfying events in their relationships and

predicts that people will be more likely to use constructive responses when they are committed to their relationships. In the original model, the four basic response choices that people have for dealing with problems in their relationships are (1) **exit,** (2) **neglect,** (3) **voice**, and (4) **loyalty** (Rusbult, 1987; Rusbult & Zembrodt, 1983). As Figure 14.2 shows, each of these responses is defined by whether it is constructive or destructive and whether it is passive or active. The behaviors that fall under each of these categories have been expanded by other researchers who have looked at how people try to repair their relationships after a transgression or other negative event has occurred (e.g., Brandau-Brown & Ragsdale, 2008; Emmers & Canary, 1996; Guerrero & Bachman, 2008). Thus, the responses shown in Figure 14.2 represent a more comprehensive account of how victims respond to hurtful events than was represented in the original model.

Destructive Behaviors

Two main types of behavior have been identified as destructive and passive: (1) neglect and (2) **punishment.** Neglect behaviors involve standing by and letting conditions in the relationship get worse—such as ignoring the partner, spending less time together, treating the partner poorly, and avoiding any discussion of relational problems. These types of behaviors are sometimes part of a larger pattern of avoidance that signals the de-escalation of a relationship (Roloff & Cloven, 1994). Brandau-Brown and Ragsdale identified a related set of behaviors called punishment that focus on balancing the relationship by evening the score and forcing the partner to act to restore closeness. Punishment includes passive-aggressive behaviors such as sulking, pouting, giving the silent treatment, and withholding favors or affection. Bachman and Guerrero (2006a) uncovered a similar category of behaviors, called active distancing, which people use in response to hurtful events.

Two other behaviors have been identified as destructive and active: (1) exit and **antisocial communication.** Exit behaviors include actions

FIGURE 14.2 ■ Responses to Dissatisfaction and Hurtful Events in Relationships		
	Destructive	**Constructive**
Active	*Exit* (leaving the relationship) *Antisocial Communication* (insults, yelling, retribution)	*Voice* (problem solving, relationship talk) *Prosocial Communication* (affection, assurances)
Passive	*Neglect* (letting things get worse) *Punishment* (passive aggressive behaviors)	*Loyalty* (waiting for things to get better)

Source: From Rusbult, Caryl E., Drigotas, Stephen M., & Verette, Julie, "The Investment Model: An Interdependence Analysis of Commitment Processes and Relationship Maintenance Phenomena." In Daniel J. Canary & Laura Stafford (eds.), *Communication and Relational Maintenance.* Used with permission from Elsevier.

such as threatening to break up, moving out of the house, and getting a divorce. Communication scholars have also included antisocial communication in the destructive/direct quadrant in Rusbult's model (Bachman & Guerrero, 2006a). Antisocial communication, such as insults, yelling at one's partner, and seeking revenge contribute to cycles of negative behavior in relationships and can exacerbate rather than repair problems in relationships (Roloff & Cloven, 1994).

According to the accommodation model, when encountering a relationship problem, people are more likely to engage in destructive responses such as neglect, punishment, exit, and antisocial communication when their relationships are characterized by low levels of commitment and satisfaction. This idea has been supported by research. In one study (Guerrero & Bachman, 2008), people who had been betrayed by their partners reported using more antisocial communication if they had been dissatisfied with their relationship before the betrayal had occurred. In another study (Bevan, 2008), people were more likely to report communicating about jealousy using antisocial

communication when they had invested into their relationship but the relationship was dissatisfying. In this case, the destructive response may reflect the frustration that often stems from investing in a relationship that is no longer satisfying. Finally, Brandau-Brown and Ragsdale (2008) found that married individuals who reported using punishment as a relationship repair strategy tended to report low levels of personal commitment to their relationships. Using destructive behavior, such as exit, punishment, neglect, and antisocial communication, exacerbates problems rather helping to repair the relationship.

Constructive Behaviors

Constructive behaviors, by contrast, help people repair their relationships. Many different relational repair strategies are constructive and active. In the original model of accommodation, the term *voice* described behaviors that revolve around discussion and problem solving, including talking about problems in a polite manner, seeking help from others, and changing negative behavior (Rusbult et al., 1986). Bachman and Guerrero (2006a) found a similar strategy, which they termed *integrative communication.* Other strategies, which we are calling **prosocial communication,** focus more on reestablishing closeness and connection rather than solving problems. For example, people try to repair their relationships by being more affectionate, spending more time together, stressing commitment, saying "I love you" more, and doing favors for one another (Bachman & Guerrero, 2006a; Brandau-Brown & Ragsdale, 2008; Emmers & Canary, 1996). These behaviors are also related to feeling hopeful. Specifically, Merolla (2014) looked at how two forms of hope are related to behaviors that people use when they are dealing with problems in their relationships. *Dispositional hope* refers to a person's general tendency to feel hopeful and optimistic across situations. *Relationship-specific hope* refers to a person's feelings of hope in a particular relationship. Both forms of hope are related to using more prosocial communication such as voice.

There is another type of constructive response, but this response, called loyalty, is passive rather than active. Partners who use loyalty optimistically wait for positive change by hoping things will improve, standing by the partner during difficult times, and supporting the partner in the face of criticism. Some people who use loyalty may also minimize the importance of the transgression, see problems in the relationship as rare, or change their perception so that the behavior is no longer seen as a transgression (Roloff & Cloven, 1994). Although constructive, some scholars believe that loyalty is less effective at repairing relationships than voice or prosocial behavior. Voice involves directly confronting issues and solving problems whereas loyalty often leaves issues unresolved (Guerrero & Bachman, 2008; Rusbult, Olsen, Davis, & Hannon, 2001). Prosocial behavior involves actively working to fix the relationship and restore it to a more intimate state whereas loyalty involves letting events unfold without trying to improve things. Thus, loyalty may be a good strategy if used alongside more active strategies like voice and prosocial behavior, but it may be ineffective if used alone. Finally, it is also important to note that

although constructive behaviors like loyalty and voice may help preserve the relationship, sometimes it is better to exit a bad relationship than work to improve it (Rusbult, Arriaga, & Agnew, 2001).

The model of accommodation suggests that people are more likely to react constructively to negative events if their relationship is committed and satisfying. Several studies have found this. For example, Brandau-Brown and Ragsdale (2008) showed that people who are highly committed to their relationships are especially likely to use strategies such as being open, emphasizing how much they love their partner, and spending time together as ways of repairing their relationships. Having low-quality alternatives was also related to using these types of prosocial behaviors. Guerrero and Bachman (2008) focused on how people respond to relational betrayals. In their study, people reported responding with more constructive communication (similar to voice and prosocial communication) if they had been satisfied with and invested in the relationship prior to the betrayal. People also reported using less vengeful communication if they were highly invested in the relationship. Another study suggested that betrayers are more likely to use constructive strategies, such as apologizing and promising to change—if they are still committed to their relationship— and that people are most likely to stay with their partners following betrayals if they still regard their relationship as satisfying (Ferrara & Levine, 2009). Finally, a study by Bevan (2008) showed that people tend to discuss jealousy in a constructive manner (similar to voice) if they are committed to and invested in their relationship. Together these studies suggest that satisfaction, investment, quality of alternatives, and commitment are all related to using constructive communication to try to repair relationships after negative events such as betrayals and jealousy.

These studies also suggest that the investment model may not always operate the way that it is depicted in Figure 14.2 or in the model of accommodation. Take another look at Figure 14.2.

Notice how satisfaction, investment, and low quality of alternatives are supposed to lead to commitment, and then commitment is supposed to lead to pro-relationship behaviors. The accommodation model makes a similar prediction: Satisfaction, investment, and low quality of alternatives are theorized to lead to more commitment, which then leads to more constructive and less destructive communication. However, studies on jealousy and betrayal demonstrate that satisfaction, investment, and commitment all lead *directly* to constructive communication. In other words, satisfaction can have a positive effect on communication that is separate from commitment. Indeed, these studies suggest that satisfaction, in particular, tends to be a stronger predictor of whether couples communicate constructively and stay together following negative events than commitment (Bevan, 2008; Ferrara & Levine, 2009; Guerrero & Bachman, 2008).

Finally, research suggests that attachment style influences how people react to negative events in their relationships. People with **secure attachment styles** are independent but also value being in close relationships with others. There are three types of insecure attachment: (1) dismissive, (2) preoccupied, and (3) fearful. Dismissive individuals are highly independent to the point that they prioritize their own activities over their relationships. In other words, they value their independence over their relationships. Preoccupied individuals, in contrast, value relationships over independence to the point that they rely on their relationships with others to make them feel good about themselves. Finally, fearful individuals do not feel good about themselves or their relationships. They have low self-esteem and worry that partners will reject or leave them, often because they have been hurt in past relationships (see Chapter 8 for a much more detailed description of attachment styles).

Ragsdale, Brandau-Brown, and Bello (2010) looked at how attachment style affects relational repair strategies used by remarried individuals. They found three types of repair strategies. Two are constructive strategies: (1) affection and assurances (e.g., kissing, hugging, talking about the future) and (2) positivity (e.g., acting cheerful and affectionate while also avoiding criticism). The other one—punishments (e.g., giving the partner the cold shoulder, leaving without telling the partner when one would return)—is destructive. Ragsdale and colleagues (2010) found that people with a secure attachment style reported using more of all three repair strategies than did fearful individuals. Securely attached individuals also used more affection and assurances than dismissive individuals.

Attachment has also been related to the use of voice, exit, neglect, and loyalty behaviors in heterosexual romantic relationships. People with a secure attachment style are unlikely to use exit and neglect (Gaines et al., 1997; Scharfe & Bartholomew, 1995) and likely to use voice (Scharfe & Bartholomew, 1995). On the other hand, people with preoccupied and fearful attachment styles are more likely to use destructive behaviors like neglect and exit. Similar findings have emerged for same-sex couples (Gaines & Henderson, 2002). However, these findings may not generalize to intercultural couples, since Gaines and Henderson (2002) failed to find differences in destructive or constructive responses to negative events based on attachment style when they sampled interethnic and interracial couples. Intercultural couples may develop unique ways to deal with relational problems that transcend personality differences such as attachment styles. For more on how intercultural couples are unique in maintaining and repairing their relationships, see Box 14.1.

REMEDIAL STRATEGIES

The model of accommodation focuses on how people respond to negative events in their relationships. **Remedial strategies,** on the other hand, focus on specific behaviors that people engage in to try and fix their relationship after they have done something wrong. So in our scenario at the beginning of this chapter, Jamal could respond to Tia's deception by using destructive behavior (such as exit,

BOX 14.1 AROUND THE WORLD
COPING WITH CULTURAL STRESSORS: YOUR CULTURE OR MY CULTURE?

Most of the research on how people respond to negative events has focused on relationships between people from the same culture. Increasingly, however, people in the United States and around the world are marrying partners from cultures different from their own. Some researchers have noted that these couples face special challenges due to differences in communication style, beliefs, values, customs, and worldviews. The extended family might also disapprove of the ways that intercultural couples handle certain issues. Other researchers have noted that some intercultural couples cope with these challenges in ways that help them become closer. In fact, Heller and Wood (2007) found that some intercultural couples obtain more mutual understanding than same-culture couples. So how do some intercultural couples manage negative events in ways that create closeness and help them maintain and repair their relationships in the face of special challenges?

A study by Bustamante, Nelson, Henriksen, and Monakes (2011) addressed this issue by interviewing intercultural couples about their marriages. In this study, intercultural marriages were defined as being composed of partners who belong to different national or ethnic groups. The couples in this study mentioned several culture-related stressors that had led to problems in their relationships, including having different philosophies about raising children, having different time orientations (e.g., one partner being more punctual and organized and the other more laid back and spontaneous), having different gender role expectations, and

feeling external pressure from their families about the "right" way to do things.

Couples also reported several coping mechanisms that helped them deal with these stressors:

- *Gender role flexibility*: They talked about expectations and responsibilities in ways that allowed them to deviate from traditional cultural norms and create flexibility.

- *Humor about differences*: They let the little things pass and were able to laugh and joke in ways that minimized their differences. For example, "One Persian male participant jokingly said to his Mexican American wife: 'Kabob is in my blood, just like Enchilada is in your blood'" (Bustamante et al., 2011, p. 160).

- *Cultural deference*: One partner tended to defer more to the cultural norms of the other. Those who deferred usually saw themselves as more "multicultural" than their partner, and therefore thought it was easier for them to adapt than it would be for their partner.

- *Recognizing similarities*: Couples emphasized similarities even in the midst of differences. For example, even if they had different opinions about raising children, they might agree that they both have strong family values.

- *Cultural reframing*: Some couples were able to create a "third culture" for the relationship that extended, blended, and transformed their individual cultural orientations into something new that bonded them together. Instead of your culture versus my culture, it becomes "our culture."

punishment, neglect, and antisocial communication) or constructive behavior (such as voice, prosocial communication, and loyalty). Tia, for her part, may use more specific remedial strategies to try and repair the damage that her behavior has caused.

Remedial strategies are attempts to correct problems, restore one's positive face, or repair the relationship. Remedial strategies are not magic bullets. If you have engaged in a relational transgression, such as cheating on your partner, lying, or breaking a promise, you cannot erase your offense with the wave of a magic wand, and your relationship might

never again be the same even if your partner forgives you. However, research on discovered deception (Aune, Metts, & Hubbard, 1998), sexual infidelity (Mongeau, Hale, & Alles, 1994), social predicaments (Cupach, 1994), and forgiveness (Kelley, 1998) suggests that people use various remedial strategies when they have committed a transgression.

Apologies and Concessions

Apologizing and admitting guilt is one of the most obvious and frequently used remedial strategies. However, not all apologies are equal. Apologies can vary from a simple statement such as "I'm sorry" to more elaborate forms of apology that include expressing guilt and remorse, derogating oneself, promising to make up for the bad behavior, and promising never to engage in the transgression again (Cupach, 1994; Schlenker & Darby, 1981). When people have committed serious transgressions, elaborate apologies are more successful than simple ones (Darby & Schlenker, 1982, 1989). In general, apologies are most effective when they are perceived as sincere, elicit empathy, and are given voluntarily. Morse and Metts (2011) also found that "apologies that indicate remorse, acknowledge the severity of the offense, and promise better conduct in the future" promote both forgiveness and reconciliation (p. 252).

Sincere apologies can lead the victim to perceive the transgressor as a generally good and thoughtful person despite the hurtful event. In Kelley's (1998) study, 31% of victims indicated that they forgave their partners because they acted in ways that showed remorse or accepted responsibility, such as apologizing for their actions. Victims are also more likely to say that they used explicit forgiveness and engaged in positive communication toward the transgressor if the transgressor made a sincere apology (Bachman & Guerrero, 2006b; Gracyalny, Jackson, & Guerrero, 2008). Acknowledging wrongdoing is also an

essential part of a sincere and effective apology (Fehr & Gelfand, 2010). When offenders acknowledge wrongdoing they admit to violating important rules or norms. For example, an offender might say, "What I did was bad" or "I was wrong and I know it."

Apologies are also more likely to be effective if the victim feels empathy for the transgressor. Empathy involves showing concern and compassion. When offenders display empathy, they communicate that they understand the victim's feelings and are sorry for hurting them. It may seem odd that a victim should feel empathy when the victim is the one who was hurt. However, if the transgressor expresses negative emotions—such as guilt, remorse, and even fear of losing the partner—the victim might feel badly for the transgressor. As McCullough, Worthington, and Rachal (1997) put it, empathy can lead to "an increased caring" for the transgressor that "overshadows the salience" of the hurtful action and leads to forgiveness (p. 333). The relationships between apologies, empathy, forgiveness, and communication are depicted in Figure 14.3. People who value close personal relationships and see their identity as intertwined with their partner's identity are especially likely to see empathy as a key ingredient in an effective apology (Fehr & Gelfand, 2010).

FIGURE 14.3 ■ Model of the Forgiveness Process

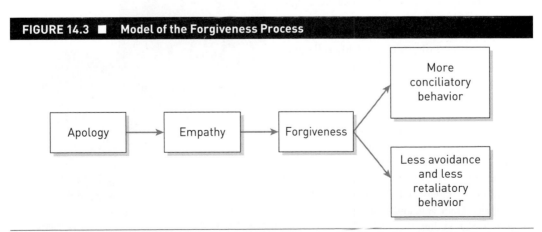

Finally, it is important that the apology is perceived as voluntary rather than forced. Studies have shown that people are more likely to forgive their partners for engaging in infidelity if they confess on their own and concede their guilt (Afifi et al., 2001; Mongeau et al., 1994). In fact, in Mongeau and associates' study, concessions emerged as the most effective strategy for repairing a relationship following infidelity. However, if the apology and accompanying confession are offered after someone is accused of a transgression, the apology loses its effectiveness because it seems forced rather than honest. Of course, many people do not want to apologize and admit guilt if their partner does not know about the transgression (Mongeau & Schulz, 1997). But if they wait until the partner accuses them (as would be the case if Tia apologizes), their apology might be seen as the result of being caught rather than a free admission of guilt.

Appeasement

Types of appeasement, or compensation, behaviors have appeared in the literature on remedial strategies (Waldron & Kelley, 2008). For instance, people who seek forgiveness often use ingratiation strategies such as promising to make up for what they did (Kelley, 1998). When people are caught deceiving their partners, they sometimes use soothing strategies that are designed to appease the target. Specifically, Aune and his colleagues (1998) found that people used remedial strategies such as complimenting the partner, trying to be more attentive to the partner, spending more time with the partner, saying "I love you" more often, and buying the partner gifts and flowers. With all of these strategies, the transgressor seeks to "compensate" for the hurtful behavior by being particularly nice and helpful. Tia uses an indirect appeasement strategy when she says, "I told [Robert] that I love you, and we are engaged." After they got back together, she might also show Jamal more affection to convince him that he is the one she loves.

Appeasement has been found to be a fairly effective strategy—although some research suggests that apologies are even more effective (Waldron & Kelley, 2008). Other research suggests that promising to compensate for one's actions is an important part of an effective apology (Fehr & Gelfand, 2010). For example, when apologizing the transgressor might offer to do favors for the hurt individual or promise to be a better partner in the future. In this way, the transgressor tries to compensate for the costs he or she has brought to the relationship by being more rewarding. People who are highly autonomous and goal-driven tend to see promises to compensate as a particularly important part of apologies (Fehr & Gelfand, 2010).

When people report that their partner used appeasement, they are more likely to say that they granted forgiveness using nonverbal displays, such as hugs or smiles (Gracyalny et al., 2008). However, they are also more likely to say that forgiveness was conditional (Gracyalny et al., 2008). Waldron and Kelley (2008) suggested that appeasement (or compensation) is sometimes used

Saying "I'm sorry" seems easy, but sometimes it's not enough. In the case of serious transgressions, apologies are usually most effective when they are voluntary, acknowledge wrongdoing, elicit empathy, and include promises to behave better in the future.

as part of the bargaining process that is associated with conditional forgiveness. So instead of arguing and holding a grudge, Jamal could have told Tia that he would forgive her if she is sure that he is the one she loves and if she promises never to lie to him about something important like that again. Tia might have engaged in appeasement strategies (e.g., spending extra time with him, giving him a special gift) to meet his conditions and prove her love for him. If they had engaged in these strategies, perhaps they would not have broken up. Appeasement is more likely when transgressions are severe. The same is true for conditional forgiveness. In general, severe transgressions require more remediation—with the hurt individual wanting to see proof that the partner is sorry and will not engage in similarly hurtful actions in the future.

Explanations

When transgressors try to explain why they engaged in an untoward act, they are using **excuses** or **justifications** to account for their behavior. When transgressors use excuses, they try to minimize responsibility for their negative behavior by focusing on their inability to control their own actions or by shifting the blame to others (Aune et al., 1998; Cupach, 1994; Mongeau & Schulz, 1997). For example, Tia might offer an excuse by saying, "I didn't know I was going to run into Robert; it just happened. And then it made sense to go to his place and talk about some of the issues that we had never resolved." Tia could also blame Robert by saying, "He insisted that we have lunch and then he really wanted to talk somewhere in private. I went along with it because I was afraid of hurting his feelings." When transgressors use justifications, they try to minimize the negative implications of the transgression by denying their behavior was wrong or that the transgression was severe (Aune et al., 1998; Cupach, 1994; Mongeau & Schulz, 1997). Tia offers a justification when she says that there is nothing wrong with spending time with an ex-boyfriend and that Robert does not mean anything to her anymore.

Explanations can play an important role in repairing relationships, yet the degree to which they are effective varies. Waldron and Kelley (2008) argued that explanations provide information that "is crucial in deciding whether forgiveness is warranted and whether the relationship can be mended" (p. 115). However, explanations are generally not as effective as apologies or appeasements and can even be negatively related to forgiveness (Gracalny et al., 2008). The quality of the explanation makes a difference. Some explanations are more plausible and forgivable than others. Explaining that you talked with an ex-lover at a party because he or she seemed depressed, for instance, is probably a better explanation than saying you were so drunk you couldn't help flirting with her or him.

Denials

With explanations, transgressors admit some responsibility for their hurtful actions. However, with denials, transgressors argue that they should not be held accountable for their behavior or that a transgression never occurred. Some scholars believe denials are a special type of excuse, one that is good enough for the transgressor to feel that a relational rule has not been broken. The television show *Friends* provides a great example of denial as a remedial strategy. Ross and Rachel have been dating for some time when they get into an argument and agree to "take a break." That night, Ross has sex with another woman. When Rachel finds out about Ross's one-night stand, she is very upset. Ross, however, denies he has done anything wrong because they were "on a break." Ross refuses to take any blame because he does not see his behavior as a transgression. This example illustrates the complexity of relational transgressions—what is perceived as a transgression by one party might not necessarily be perceived as a transgression by the other. Not surprisingly, Mongeau and his colleagues (1994) found denials to be an ineffective remedial strategy that was likely to aggravate rather than repair the relationship. Gracalny and her associates (2008) also found that denials were associated with more de-escalation and a greater likelihood of relationship breakup.

Avoidance and Evasion

Avoidance and evasion, or silence, involve efforts to avoid discussing the transgression. Transgressors who use this strategy often report that talking about the problem only makes it worse and it is better to let the transgression fade into the background of the relationship and be minimized (Aune et al., 1998). Transgressors using this strategy might also refuse to give an explanation for their behaviors. If avoidance and evasion are used after an apology and forgiveness has been granted, it may be effective. But if the primary strategy is avoidance and evasion, the problem might be left unresolved and could resurface in the future. Because relational transgressions often lead to relational change, which sometimes includes the altering of rules and boundaries, avoidance and evasion may not be a particularly effective strategy in the long run. Indeed, Mongeau and colleagues (1994) found that avoidance (or silence) was an ineffective strategy for repairing relationships after infidelity had occurred, and Morse and Metts (2011) showed that avoidance was negatively associated with forgiveness.

Relationship Talk

Relationship talk involves talking about the transgression within the larger context of the relationship. Aune and associates (1998) discussed two specific types of relationship talk. The first, which they called **relationship invocation,** involves expressing attitudes or beliefs about the relationship or using the qualities of the relationship as a backdrop for interpreting the transgression. For example, transgressors might say, "Our relationship is strong enough to survive this," or "I love you too much to lose you over something like this." In Tia's case, she might have told Jamal that their relationship is much better than Robert and hers ever was. The second type of relationship talk, **metatalk** (Aune et al., 1998), involves explicitly discussing

the transgression's effect on the relationship. For instance, after conceding that she was wrong to lie to Jamal, Tia might say that she wants Jamal to trust her in the future. This might lead Tia and Jamal into a discussion about rules of honesty in their relationship. They might also discuss the future of their relationship, and the type of marriage they want to have.

FORGIVENESS

As mentioned earlier, remedial strategies such as offering a sincere apology and using appeasement make forgiveness and relational repair more likely. Forgiveness plays a critical role in repairing a relationship after a transgression occurs (Emmers & Canary, 1996).

What Forgiveness Means

But what does it mean to forgive someone? Waldron and Kelley (2008) defined forgiveness as a relational process that has four characteristics: (1) acknowledgment of harmful conduct, (2) an extension of undeserved mercy, (3) an emotional transformation, and (4) relationship renegotiation.

ACKNOWLEDGMENT OF HARMFUL CONDUCT

For forgiveness to even be necessary, one or both partners must acknowledge that there has been wrongdoing. Behavior that requires forgiveness in one relationship may be acceptable in another relationship. For example, Tia lied and said she was with friends because she was afraid Jamal would get upset if he knew she was with Robert. This tells us that Tia understood that the unwritten (and perhaps unspoken) rules of their relationship dictated that she should not spend extended time with Robert. If, however, there was no such "rule," and both Tia and Jamal instead had an understanding that they could spend as much time with ex-boyfriends and ex-girlfriends as they wanted, then there would be no need for forgiveness because no wrongdoing occurred and Tia would not have felt compelled to lie.

EXTENSION OF UNDESERVED MERCY Second, the hurt person must make a decision to extend mercy to the partner. The idea that such mercy is undeserved is highlighted by Freedman and Enright (1996), who stated, "There is a decidedly paradoxical quality to forgiveness as the forgiver gives up the resentment, to which he or she has a right, and gives the gift of compassion, to which the offender has no right" (p. 983). The decision to forgive sets the process of forgiveness in motion and makes statements such as "I forgive you" meaningful (Fincham, 2000). You have probably been in a situation, for instance, when someone told you "I forgive you" but you did not really believe it. When this happens, people doubt that the hurt person has truly made the decision to forgive them.

EMOTIONAL TRANSFORMATION Forgiveness involves an emotional transformation that allows hurt individuals to let go of negative feelings (Boon & Sulsky, 1997; Waldron & Kelley, 2008). When individuals are hurt, their natural reaction is to get revenge, seek restitution, or avoid the person who hurt them (McCullough et al., 1997). Forgiveness entails getting rid of these impulses and instead feeling positively about oneself and the partner. In line with this emotional transformation, hurt individuals report engaging in more positive forms of communication, such as talking over issues and calmly renegotiating relationship rules, once they have forgiven their partner (Bachman & Guerrero, 2006b; McCullough et al., 1998). In contrast, when people do not forgive their partners, they tend to engage in more vengeful communication (e.g., arguing, name-calling), de-escalation (e.g., breaking up, dating others), and avoidance. Being able to transform one's emotions also has benefits for the hurt person. One of the participants in Kelley's (1998) study on forgiveness wrote, "I began to realize that this anger was not only torturing him, but myself as well. It was eating me up inside and making me more of an angry person. Why should I suffer for what he has done?" (p. 264).

RELATIONSHIP RENEGOTIATION Sometimes the hurt individual is motivated to reconcile with the partner. Other times the relationship de-escalates or ends even though forgiveness is granted. Either way, forgiveness entails renegotiating the nature of one's relationship, including rules and expectations for future behavior. In a study examining the relational consequences of forgiveness, Kelley (1998) found that around 28% of participants indicated that their relationship had returned to "normal" after forgiveness was granted, around 36% reported that their relationship had deteriorated, and around 32% reported that their relationship had strengthened. Thus, forgiveness does not always entail reconciliation. For example, you might forgive your friend for lying to you but still not feel as close to her as you once did. Reconciliation can also occur without forgiveness. Jamal might not forgive Tia if she meets with Robert again, but he might value their relationship enough to stay with her anyway.

Forgiving Communication

The way people communicate forgiveness is connected to how partners renegotiate their relationships following hurtful events. People communicate forgiveness in a variety of ways. Waldron and Kelley (2005) identified five specific ways people show forgiveness following a partner's relational transgression: (1) explicit forgiveness, (2) nonverbal display, (3) minimization, (4) discussion, and (5) conditional forgiveness. To determine the strategy you used to grant forgiveness the last time you forgave someone after being hurt, take the test in Box 14.2.

EXPLICIT FORGIVENESS Explicit forgiveness, which is the most common way to communicate forgiveness (Kelley, 1998), involves making a direct statement, such as "I forgive you." Making such a statement appears to have positive consequences for relationships. Explicit forgiveness is the clearest way to communicate forgiveness to a transgressor and convey that one wants to repair the relationship (Scobie & Scobie, 1998). When the hurt person

BOX 14.2 PUT YOURSELF TO THE TEST
WAYS TO COMMUNICATE FORGIVENESS

Think about the last time you forgave a relational partner (e.g., a good friend, family member, romantic partner) after he or she hurt your feelings. Use the following scale to determine which strategies you used the most: 0 = not used at all, 4 = used moderately, and 7 = used extensively.

	Not Used at All		Used Moderately			Used Extensively		
1. I gave my partner a look that communicated forgiveness.	0	1	2	3	4	5	6	7
2. I told my partner I had forgiven him or her, but I really didn't forgive my partner until later.	0	1	2	3	4	5	6	7
3. I joked about it so my partner would know he or she was forgiven.	0	1	2	3	4	5	6	7
4. I initiated discussion about the transgression.	0	1	2	3	4	5	6	7
5. I told my partner I forgave her or him.	0	1	2	3	4	5	6	7
6. I gave my partner a hug.	0	1	2	3	4	5	6	7
7. I told my partner not to worry about it.	0	1	2	3	4	5	6	7
8. I discussed the transgression with my partner.	0	1	2	3	4	5	6	7
9. The expression on my face said "I forgive you."	0	1	2	3	4	5	6	7
10. I told my partner I would forgive him or her only if things changed.	0	1	2	3	4	5	6	7
11. I told my partner it was no big deal.	0	1	2	3	4	5	6	7
12. I touched my partner in a way that communicated forgiveness.	0	1	2	3	4	5	6	7
13. I told my partner I would forgive her or him if the transgression never happened again.	0	1	2	3	4	5	6	7

To obtain your results, average your scores for the following items:

Nonverbal display: Items (1+6+9+12) / 4 =   _____

Conditional forgiveness: Items (2+10+13) / 3 =   _____

Minimization: Items (3+7+11) / 3 =   _____

Discussion: Items (4+8) / 2 =   _____

Explicit forgiveness: Item (5) =   _____

Higher scores indicate that you used more of a particular strategy.

Source: Adapted from Waldron & Kelley (2005).

verbally says, "I forgive you" (or something similar), both partners also have more closure and the relationship has a better chance of strengthening instead of declining (Waldron & Kelley, 2005).

NONVERBAL DISPLAY Sometimes people display forgiveness nonverbally through behaviors such as smiles, hugs, or head nods. These types of nonverbal displays are likely to be used when people want to repair the relationship, indicate that a transgression is not that serious, or avoid confrontation (Gracyalny et al., 2008; Kelley, 1998). Nonverbal displays often occur as part of a conciliatory pattern of communication with the transgressor engaging in constructive communication, such as making apologies and showing affection, and the victim reciprocating by showing forgiveness nonverbally (Gracyalny et al., 2008).

DISCUSSION The discussion-based approach involves "explicit acknowledgment of the transgression, mutual perspective-taking, and dialogue" (Waldron & Kelley, 2005, p. 735). People who use this strategy often grant forgiveness within the context of a deeper discussion of the hurtful event and its consequences for the relationship. Thus, discussion can include renegotiating relationship rules, explaining why and how the transgression occurred, and expressing feelings to one another.

MINIMIZING APPROACH When people use the minimizing approach, they emphasize that the hurtful event was not that "big of a deal" and that the partner should not worry about it anymore. Minimization is most likely when the transgression is not very serious (Guerrero & Bachman, 2008). So Jamal might be likely to use minimization (e.g., "Okay, it doesn't seem like that big of a deal") if he believes Tia's lunch with Robert was innocent. People may also use minimizing strategies when they do not want to invest any more time and energy into dealing with the issue (Waldron & Kelley, 2008). Jamal might decide that he has thought enough about Robert and wants to move on. If, on the other

hand, he continues to be suspicious of Tia's motives, he might use conditional forgiveness (e.g., "It's okay, as long as you promise not to see him again").

CONDITIONAL FORGIVENESS Conditional forgiveness is used when people grant forgiveness contingent on the partner's behavior. As such, conditional forgiveness is an "if/then" strategy. The victim may make statements such as "I will only forgive you if you do X or Y." Conditional forgiveness was shown in a classic episode of the popular television series *Friends* when Ross's new wife, Emily, told Ross that she would only forgive him for saying Rachel's name during their wedding ceremony if he promised to never see Rachel again. Some scholars have pointed out that conditional forgiveness is often a temporary state and that relationship deterioration is more likely when forgiveness is granted with conditions (Waldron & Kelley, 2005), as it was for Ross and Emily. Yet conditional forgiveness may be the only appropriate course of action, at least initially, when a person has been deeply hurt. As Fincham (2000) noted, forgiveness is contingent not only on the hurt person's change in motivation but also on the offending person's change in behavior. If a person does not think a partner's behavior will change, forgiveness is unlikely.

Indeed, one study showed that behavior change was the most important ingredient when friends, romantic partners, and family members wanted to rejuvenate their relationships after they had become less close (Wilmot & Stevens, 1994). In this study, there were two pathways to relationship rejuvenation. The first pathway involved implicit relational moves. People who used this pathway did not talk about the issues that caused a decline in their relationship, but one or both partners changed their behavior. For example, instead of talking to Jamal about what happened, Tia might simply try to show him that she loves him by spending more time with him and being open and honest about all her current activities. The other pathway to relationship rejuvenation involved **explicit relational talk.**

People who used this pathway had a "big relationship talk" to discuss issues and then one or both of the partners changed their behavior. So Tia and Jamal might sit down and discuss both her behavior and his reaction. She might promise not to lie to him and he might promise not to act possessive. In both pathways, behavior change is critical. Therefore, it is no surprise that people often forgive with conditions as a way of increasing the odds that behavior change will occur.

Conditions That Promote or Impede Forgiveness and Forgiving Communication

As Fincham's (2000) porcupine analogy suggests, forgiveness is not always easy, nor should it be. Forgiveness can help heal a relationship, but it cannot always save it. And in some cases, it may be better not to save the relationship. For instance, people who forgive too readily might stay in abusive relationships (Katz, Street, & Arias, 1995). So how do people determine—consciously or unconsciously—whether to forgive or not, and which, if any, forms of forgiving communication they should use? Some research suggests that women may generally be more forgiving than men (Miller, Worthington, & McDaniel, 2008). Research also demonstrates that victims are more likely to grant forgiveness and use positive communication with their partner if (1) the seriousness of the transgression does not prohibit forgiveness and (2) the relationship was of high quality prior to the transgression.

THE SERIOUSNESS OF THE TRANSGRESSION

It probably goes without saying that people are less forgiving when a transgression is especially serious (Bennett & Earwaker, 1994; Girard & Mullet, 1997). But what might be less obvious is that victims sometimes reassess the transgression as less serious if they decide to stay in the relationship. In Kelley's (1998) study, 44% of victims forgave their partners after reframing the situation so that the transgression seemed less severe. For example, they came to understand why the transgressor had behaved in a certain way or realized that the transgressor had not intended to hurt them.

The seriousness of a transgression also relates to how much a behavior violates relationship expectations. For example, hurtful events vary in the extent to which someone considers them unacceptable. When people consider a hurtful event to be a highly negative violation of their expectations, they are less likely to forgive their partner and less likely to engage in positive forms of communication, including explicit forgiveness, nonverbal displays, and minimization (Bachman & Guerrero, 2006a; Guerrero & Bachman, 2010). Even if people do forgive their partner, they are likely to do so with conditions (Guerrero & Bachman, 2010; Waldron & Kelley, 2005). Recall the situation between Jamal and Tia. Jamal might be upset that Tia lied to him, but he is unlikely to regard this transgression as one of the worst things Tia could do if he believes her when she says they met by accident and just talked. Therefore, he would be more likely to forgive Tia for her deception. On the other hand, if Tia really was having an affair with Robert, Jamal would be much more likely to see that as a highly negative violation of a relationship rule—and as a consequence, be much less likely to forgive her.

RELATIONSHIP AND PARTNER CHARACTER-ISTICS

People are also more likely to forgive their partners and engage in positive communication when they are in high-quality relationships with rewarding partners, as suggested earlier in this chapter when we discussed the investment model. In Kelley's (1998) study, 35% of victims indicated that forgiveness was granted because they wanted to repair their relationship. Love was a motivation behind forgiveness for another 15% of the participants. People are also likely to evaluate transgressions as less serious, to forgive their partners, and to engage in more positive communication, such as nonverbal displays of forgiveness, if they perceive their partner to be socially attractive and rewarding (Aune et al., 1996; Bachman & Guerrero, 2006a; Guerrero & Bachman, 2010). Forgiveness may also be especially likely when victims perceive their partner to be more rewarding than they perceive themselves to be (Sidelinger & Booth-Butterfield, 2007). In addition, people are more likely to report using positive communication and discussion-based forgiveness following relational transgressions when their relationships are highly committed and emotionally involved (Guerrero & Bachman, 2010; Menzies-Toman & Lydon, 2005; Roloff et al., 2001). Finally, people in committed, satisfying relationships tend to evaluate their partner's transgressions as less serious than do those in less satisfying, less committed relationships (Menzies-Toman & Lydon, 2005; Young, 2004).

RELATIONAL RECONCILIATION

So far we have discussed various ways that people can repair relationships following a negative event or transgression. Forgiveness is part of the road to relationship repair, but as noted earlier, forgiveness and reconciliation are not the same. You can forgive someone without reconciling with them. For example, you might forgive your partner for cheating on you, but that doesn't necessarily mean that you want the relationship to continue. Reconciliation is also different from repair (Patterson & O'Hair, 1992). Repair strategies focus on fixing problems and saving a relationship when problems occur. Reconciliation, on the other hand, involves getting back together and rebuilding a relationship after a breakup or a falling out.

Reconciliation is not uncommon. One study showed that almost 75% of college students had broken up and then reconciled with a romantic partner at least once (Bevan & Cameron, 2001). National-level data have shown that about 10% of couples who are currently married were separated and then reconciled at one point during their marriage (Wineberg, 1994), and 44% of women report trying to reconcile with their husbands after being separated (Wineberg, 1995). More recent data from divorcing parents demonstrates that around 25% of these individuals believe

that with hard work their marriages could still be saved (Doherty, Willoughby, & Peterson, 2011). People break up and then reconcile for a variety of reasons, many of which are connected to concepts such as rewards and costs. For example, people are more likely to reconcile with an ex-partner if they have poor quality alternatives and continue to feel attached to their ex (Dailey, Rossetto, Pfiester, & Surra, 2009). They are also more likely to reconcile if they spend time with their ex-partner (often because they are still part of the same social network) and start to see their positive qualities. Time together as friends can also help ex-partners learn to communicate more effectively (Dailey, Rossetto et al., 2009), making them more optimistic that they can work things out if they give the relationship another try.

Whether or not people are successful in reconciling depends on a number of factors. According to one study, couples who have similar religious beliefs and those who cohabited before marriage are more likely to reconcile after being separated (Wineberg, 1994). Communication can also influence whether or not people get back together after a breakup.

Reconciliation Strategies

Two studies, in particular, have examined the types of communication people report using when they want to reestablish a romantic relationship. In the first study (Patterson & O'Hair, 1992), individuals who were in relationships that had ended but then got back together were interviewed to determine what they had done to facilitate reconciliation. For the second study (Bevan, Cameron, & Dillow, 2003), students thought about a breakup that they had been through and then indicated what strategies they would use if they wanted to get back together with their partner. Together, these studies suggest that people use a variety of reconciliation strategies, including explanation and disclosure, relationship references, promises, stage-setting, vulnerable appeals, and direct requests.

EXPLANATION AND DISCLOSURE In Bevan and colleagues' (2003) research, explanation was the most frequently mentioned reconciliation strategy; around 49% of participants said they would explain how they felt and why they wanted to get back together. A similar strategy called mutual interaction was identified by Patterson and O'Hair (1992). This strategy involves communicating openly about why the relationship ended, how old problems can be fixed, and why it would be a good idea to reconcile. Open communication that includes explanations and disclosure is the key to this strategy, which seems to be important in reconciling all types of relationships, from romantic to family. Indeed, in a study looking at fathers and sons who reconciled their relationships, this type of communication was the most frequently mentioned determinant of successful reconciliation (Katz, 2002).

RELATIONSHIP REFERENCES Another common strategy is to remind the former partner of all the positive aspects of the former relationship. In Bevan and colleagues' (2003) study, around one third of the students said that they would use this strategy with their former boyfriend or girlfriend if they wanted to reestablish the relationship. For example, one student said, "I would remind him of all the good times we've had together" (Bevan et al., 2003, p. 129). This type of strategy plays up the reward value of the former relationship. As noted earlier in this chapter, people are more likely to stay and work through problems if they believe that their relationship is generally rewarding and satisfying. People may also be more likely to reconcile with a partner if they believe that the relationship could once again be rewarding.

PROMISES Promises are another reconciliation strategy related to rewards. However, instead of reminding the ex-partner about the positive aspects of the former relationship, the strategy of promises involves telling the partner how good the future relationship would be. For example, one of the students in Bevan and colleagues' (2003) study said, "I would promise that I would try to make it better

in the future if she would" (p. 129). Like relationship references, the promising strategy seems designed to convince the ex-partner that their reestablished relationship would contain more benefits than costs. This strategy is also similar to appeasement, which as mentioned earlier in this chapter is one of the best remedial strategies to use when trying to repair a relationship.

STAGE-SETTING Around 31% of the students in Bevan and colleagues' (2003) study reported that before talking to the partner in person, it is important to "set the stage." This can be done by calling the partner on the phone and saying, "I need to see you." Stage-setting can also reduce uncertainty and give people a feel for whether or not their former partner is amendable to a reconciliation attempt (see Chapter 4). Going on Facebook to check an ex-partner's relationship status and posting friendly messages on their timeline may also help set the stage for possible reconciliation. (For other ways that Facebook is used to reestablish and repair relationships, see Box 14.3.)

VULNERABLE APPEALS When people use vulnerable appeals, they let their ex-partners know how much they miss them and want to be with them again. These types of statements make people vulnerable. Not only do they open a person up for rejection, but they also put a person in a powerless position. For example, imagine that Robert told Tia that he regrets breaking up with her and is miserable every time he thinks of her with Jamal. Then he appeals to her by saying that it would mean the world to him if she would give him another chance. This puts Tia in the powerful position of being able to make the decision as to whether to reestablish the relationship or not. (Of course, this is also an unenviable position since Tia probably won't want to hurt his feelings.) Vulnerable appeals can be successful. They communicate regret and may erase doubts about how much one ex-partner cares for the other. They can also lead to empathy, which as mentioned earlier in this chapter, can promote forgiveness and reconciliation. In Bevan

BOX 14.3 TECH TALK
RECONNECTION AND RELATIONAL REPAIR ON FACEBOOK

Research has shown that computer-mediated communication, including social networking sites like Facebook, are commonly used to help people maintain relationships (Tong & Walther, 2010b). Less research has examined how Facebook is used to reestablish and repair relationships. Yet in a study by Joinson (2008), people described "re-acquiring lost contacts" as one the top three reasons they enjoyed using Facebook. In another study (Pempek, Yermolayeva, & Calvert, 2009), undergraduate students were asked what aspects of Facebook they find most interesting. The #1 answer, mentioned by almost 22% of the students, was the ability to reconnect and reestablish relationships with people with whom they had lost touch, such as friends from high school, elementary school, summer camps, and sports teams. The participants in these studies noted that Facebook allowed them to reconnect with people whom they had not seen in a while or had lost contact with. Indeed, when old friends are on Facebook, it is usually easy to locate them. Therefore, Facebook allows people to reestablish connections with people who might otherwise be difficult to find.

Facebook may also facilitate reconciliation and repair in other ways. An easy and convenient way to announce to others that you have reconciled with a relational partner is to change your "relationship status" on Facebook. Posting current photos of yourself and your formerly estranged partner can also let others know that you are back together. Relational repair also takes place on Facebook. For example, after an argument, "liking" a friend's Facebook posts and photos is a subtle signal that you want everything to be okay between you. Sometimes people also post messages or quotes on their timelines that could have hidden messages for certain viewers. For example, a student once mentioned posting the quotation, "To err is human, to forgive is divine" on her timeline after breaking a promise to a friend. She hoped her friend would read the message and forgive her. As this example illustrates, Facebook and other technologies have opened up new avenues for people to seek repair and reconciliation in their relationships.

and colleagues' (2003) study, around 20% of the students reported that they would be likely to use a similar strategy called ingratiation, which involved saying things like "I miss your heart, your humor, your warmth, and your love" (p. 129).

DIRECT REQUESTS In Bevan and colleagues' (2003) study, about 17% of participants said that they would use a direct request to try to reconcile. For example, one of the participants in this study reported being likely to say, "Would you like to try dating again?" This strategy is likely used with some of the other strategies mentioned here. People might build up to a direct request by first setting the stage, or they may engage in explanation and disclosure, along with referencing the positive aspects of the relationship, before directly asking the ex-partner to get back together. Direct requests are also risky in that they open the person who wants to reconcile up to rejection. In contrast to reconciliation being facilitated by a direct request, some couples say that

they reestablished their relationships spontaneously. In fact, Patterson and O'Hair (1992) noted that many couples say that reconciliation happened naturally over time when they let go of their anger and started spending more time together.

ADDITIONAL STRATEGIES Although these are some of the most common ways that people attempt reconciliation, this list is not exhaustive. Patterson and O'Hair (1992) also mentioned ultimatums as a reconciliation strategy, where one person tells the other, "This is it. It's now or never," to try to force a decision about reconciliation. Other times people use persistence, such as patiently waiting for the ex-partner to come back or continually asking the ex-partner to give the relationship another chance. Persistence can cross over into obsessive relational intrusion (ORI) behaviors, which are unwanted behaviors that people use to try to get close to someone by invading their privacy (Cupach & Spitzberg, 1998; see Chapter 13). Obviously, being overly persistent to the point of becoming obsessive or intrusive often backfires, leading an ex-partner to back away rather than reconcile. Finally, studies have also mentioned third parties as facilitators of reconciliation (Bevan et al., 2003; Patterson & O'Hair, 1992). Sometimes friends and family want to see a couple back together. If that is the case, they might bring them together, talk positively about each partner in front of the other, and point out all the good qualities of their former relationship. Other times, one or both of the ex-partners will ask third parties to intervene. For example, in Bevan and colleagues' (2003) study, one of the students said, "I might get my friends to drop hints" that I might want to get back together (p. 129).

Reintegration in the Social Network

Third parties play other roles in the process of reconciliation. Imagine that one or more of the previously given strategies work and you get back together with your ex-partner. Everything is great, right? Well, maybe not. Sometimes reconciling with one's partner is only the first step. The reconciled relationship is part of a larger social network, and repair work often needs to be accomplished if the couple hopes to be accepted and supported by their family and friends. McBride (2010) studied this issue by examining how people communicate with family members about reconciling with a romantic partner.

When a person undergoes a breakup, the social network is usually supportive and occasionally may have even encouraged the breakup. Imagine that after ending their relationship Tia and Jamal complain about each other's behavior to their friends and family, who support them and tell them they did the right thing by breaking up. When Tia sees Jamal with the new girl on his Snapchat stories she gets jealous and upset. She vents to her sister and friends about how he didn't seem to have any problem moving on. Then when they want to get back together, their friends and families are not so sure they should. Tia's friends give her a hard time for "just falling back into his arms" after everything

that happened. Jamal's friends say he's "whipped" because he will forgive Tia no matter what she does.

So how do people like Tia and Jamal save face when reconciling with someone after a breakup? This question was addressed in a study by McBride (2010). He found that people use several different strategies to help save face in this situation. For example, people update friends and family members so they won't be surprised when they hear about the reconciliation. Sometimes updating also involves setting rules about how family and friends should talk about the reconciliation and treat the partner. For example, Tia might tell her mom, "We are back together now, so be nice to him." Jamal might tell his best friend, "Let's not talk about the breakup anymore. It's my life and I would appreciate it if you don't judge me." In cases where the social network is especially disapproving, people might hedge about the status of the relationship by saying things like, "We're together again, but we're going to take it slow and see how it goes." People also give accounts for reconciliation, such as excusing or justifying their own behavior ("It was my fault for lying to Jamal") as well as their partner's behavior ("He had a right to date someone else after we broke up.") These types of accounts are not necessary if the social network accepts and supports the reconciliation (McBride, 2010). Overall, it is important for reconciled couples to seek the support of their social network, since not having such support can be problematic and sometimes leads to breaking up again in the future (see Chapters 10 and 15).

ON-AGAIN OFF-AGAIN RELATIONSHIPS

After Tia and Jamal reconcile, the trajectory of their relationship could go a multitude of ways. They might stay together and marry eventually, give it one more try and then break up for good, or they could break up and get back together several more times in the future. Indeed, on-again off-again relationships, which are sometimes called cycling relationships, are more prevalent today than ever before. A study by Dailey, Pfiester, Jin, Beck, and Clark (2009) found that about two thirds of college students reported being in at least one **on-again off-again relationship**, which was defined as breaking up and then getting back together at least once. The off-again part of these relationships tended to last around 1 to 2 months. Research also suggests that two to five renewals are common (Halperin, 2012), meaning that on-again off-again couples tend to break up and get back together two to five times before either breaking up for good (which is more common) or staying together permanently. Indeed, in Dailey, Pfiester et al.'s (2009) study, 75% of those in on-again off-again relationships reported that they had broken up and reconciled two or more times.

There are many reasons why on-again off-again relationships are prevalent. Some studies suggest that social media play a role (Halperin, 2012). It is more difficult to forget an ex and move on if you stay connected to their social media and see their tweets, Instagram pictures, or Snapchat stories all the time. Looking at an ex's photos on social media may even trigger the release of hormones such as oxytocin (OT) and dopamine, which are associated with attachment and excitement, respectively. This could have happened to Tia when she saw Jamal with a new woman. Another study looked at the reasons couples get back together after a breakup (Dailey, Jin, Pfiester, & Beck, 2011). By far the most common reason was lingering feelings; partners missed each other and realized that they still cared, as was the case for Tia and Jamal. Other reasons included wanting someone to hang out with, feeling comfortable falling back into old habits with an ex, realizing the partner is "the one," wanting to give the relationship one more try before giving up on it, thinking that the partner has changed in a way that makes her or him more appealing, seeing the ex as a better alternative than dating someone new, believing that the breakup was a mistake, feeling bad about breaking up with and hurting one's ex, and finding it difficult to walk away permanently because of shared memories and experiences.

Although couples who get back together for more positive reasons, such as having lingering feelings or realizing their partner is "the one," are more likely to stay together longer, overall, couples in on-again off-again relationships tend to report more problems than those in stable relationships. On-again off-again relationships are generally characterized by less positive behavior, such as validating each other and communicating understanding, as well as more negative behavior, such as conflict and aggression, than stable dating relationships (Dailey, Pfiester, et al., 2009). Family and friends also become less supportive of these relationships the more the couple breaks up and gets back together. Moreover, the more times couples cycle back and forth between being together and breaking up, the more uncertainty they feel about the relationship (Dailey, Rossetto, et al., 2009). When these couples experience high levels of uncertainty during an "on" stage, they are less likely to renew the relationship if they break up again (Dailey et al., 2011). However, if people experience high uncertainty when they are in the "off" stage, they are more likely to get back together, presumably because they are uncertain of whether they should have broken up and want to see how they feel when they get back together (Dailey et al., 2010).

The way couples in on-again again-off again relationships communicate also depends on the type of relationship they have. Five common types of on-again off-again dating relationships were identified by Dailey, McCracken, Jin, Rossetto, and Green (2013): **habitual**, **mismatched**, **capitalized on transition**, **gradual separators**, and **controlling**. These are displayed in Box 14.4. Think about your own on-again off-again relationships or those of your friends. Do they fit one of these categories or perhaps have elements of two of them? If they do, then you might be able to predict some other aspects of their relationships.

Of the five types of on-again off-again relationships, those who capitalize on the transition are most likely to communicate effectively and

Habitual: The couple breaks up and gets back together without thinking much about what happened during transitions. They see the relationship as comfortable, easy, and convenient, and find themselves falling into their old patterns. They often miss the companionship that the relationship provided when they were together and find it easier to renew their relationship than find or try something new with someone else.

Mismatched: There is unequal involvement in these relationships, sometimes over time. For example, one partner may tend to withdraw but then come back. Or one partner might not act very into the relationship but then fight to get her or his ex back. Differences in personality and what they want from the relationship may drive this inconsistency, but if these issues are resolved they may renew the relationship.

Capitalized on Transition: Transition time is used to reflect about problems, sort out one's feelings, figure out what one wants, improve oneself, or get one's partner to change. Thus, transitions are productive and mark a period of change and possible improvement that could eventually help the partners relate better to one another when they get back together.

Gradual Separators: During each transition partners grow farther apart from one another, interest wanes, and the relationship fades out over time as the "on" periods get shorter. Partners might initially have trouble letting go of each other, but each "off" period gives them more certainty that they should break up until they finally have closure and are able to move on.

Controlling: One partner consistently wants the relationship and the other partner (who controls the trajectory of the relationship) goes in and out. The partner who is consistent sees renewals as continuing evidence that they are meant to be together, but the controlling partner is less certain. Sometimes the controlling partner becomes more aggressive during and following breakups to try and discourage future attempts at renewal.

stay together. These couples use their "off" time productively. Transitions are used to test the relationship and try to improve themselves as individuals and then, when they renew, as a couple. They tend to have less conflict, more relational improvement, and more lingering feelings after they get back together (Dailey et al., 2013). Perhaps surprisingly, mismatched couples also fare relatively well upon renewal. They tend to discuss their breakups and renewal openly with one another and carefully think about whether they should get back together. Their discussions tend to be explicit and may include details of what they want and need if the relationship is to work out (Dailey et al., 2013).

Couples in a controlling on-again off-again relationship tend to have the worst outcomes. Their breakups are more one-sided and messier, and they tend to get back together without as much thought. These relationships are sometimes characterized by a repeated pattern of one person breaking it off and

then getting drawn back into the relationship. This makes it hard to determine whether the breakup will be temporary or permanent, which can lead to a lack of closure. The person who consistently wants the relationship always thinks he or she has a chance to win the partner back. These couples also report conflict patterns that are more ineffective and aggressive, along with higher levels of relational stress, compared to couples in other types of on-again off-again relationships (Dailey et al., 2013). The prognosis for gradual separators is also poor, even though their relationships are less turbulent. These couples do not show much dedication or resolve to make the relationship work so, not surprisingly, the relationship fades out over time. The final breakup tends to give gradual separators the closure they need; they tried but the relationship gradually fell apart.

Habitual on-again off-again relationships fall somewhere in the middle. This is probably because partners who get back together for convenience and comfort have not always worked on the issues that drove them apart initially. Yet they are still at ease with one another and enjoy the companionship that their relationship affords when they are "on." If these couples want to make their relationships last over the long haul, at some point they will need to address the issues that led them to break up once or multiple times.

RELATIONAL REDEFINITION

Finally, instead of breaking up and getting back together again, some romantic relationships shift from a romance to a friendship, or from spouses to coparents. Indeed, Koenig Kellas, Bean, Cunningham, and Cheng (2008) noted that people usually do not make a clean break after breaking up, especially if they were in a long-term relationship and had a shared social network. If mutual respect and admiration exists between partners, a platonic friendship may emerge. Traditional relational dissolution models fail to explain relationships that remain after the romance has ended; although some researchers have studied postbreakup relationships (Lannutti & Cameron, 2002; Masheter, 1997). Lannutti and Cameron's research on gay, lesbian, and heterosexual couples demonstrated that all couple types employ relational redefinition and many are able to transition to nonsexual relationships. Gay and lesbian couples report higher levels of satisfaction, contact, and emotional intimacy with their former partners than straight couples, who report lower satisfaction, closeness, and contact with their former partners. Research shows that even 10 years after divorce, half of all divorced couples report contact with their former spouse (Fischer, De Graaf, & Kalmijn, 2005). Contact is especially likely if the couple has children together, had a relatively long marriage, or hold liberal social values.

Relationships between former spouses can take different forms, including being coparents without being friends and having a unilateral friendship (i.e., only one former spouse regards the other as a friend). Many former spouse stay connected through a social network that includes joint children and family get-togethers. Some former spouses become (or remain) good friends after their divorce. Ahrons (1994) used the concept of *perfect pals* to describe postdivorce friendships that are close and satisfying. Most couples who describe themselves as perfect pals reported that although their divorces were not amicable, they were also not adversarial. Many of these couples said that they grew closer in some ways after the divorce. They reported confiding in and doing favors for each other, regularly talking, and actively coparenting their children; they also saw their friendship as close and irreplaceable. According to Ahrons, about 12% of coparents describe themselves as having this type of friendship 5 years after their divorce. Masheter's (1997) research showed that some former spouses without children also develop or maintain close friendships after divorce.

What about postbreakup relationships between individuals who were dating rather than married? Some ex-partners manage to stay friends, but others do not. In one study, around 60% of ex-couples who remained friends after breaking up showed a pattern of relationship decline over time (Koenig Kellas et al., 2008)—with their commitment to the friendship decreasing in the months after breaking up. In contrast, about 21% of ex-couples said that they became better friends over time after breaking up whereas about 7% indicated that there was little change in their friendship over time.

Ex-partners who build strong friendships after breaking up appear to have different experiences than those who do not. In Koenig Kellas and colleagues' (2008) study, ex-partners who redefined their new platonic friendships in positive ways tended to experience some of the following events in their relationships: engaging in reflective talk, becoming friends or best friends, exchanging social support, and communicating forgiveness. Engaging in reflective talk involves discussing the old romantic relationship, bringing up old memories, and getting closure. Becoming friends or best friends occurs when ex-partners realize that they really can be "just friends" and, in some cases, even best friends. Social support involves being able to count on an ex-partner to help you out or comfort you. Finally, forgiveness involves apologizing and forgiving each other for past transgressions that occurred in the old romantic relationship.

The study by Koenig Kellas and her colleagues also identified some events that were related to an unsuccessful transition from a romantic relationship to a postbreakup friendship. These included awkward or uncomfortable conversations, arguments, one-sided attempts to reestablish a romantic relationship, jealousy-provoked interaction, harassment, negative feelings about the ex-partner being involved with someone new, and being ignored by the ex-partner. This suggests that it is difficult for ex-romantic partners to make the transition to being just friends if one of them still has romantic feelings for the other or can't let go of old issues that lead to conflict. Unlike many ex-spouses, former dating partners sometimes have the freedom to decide whether to redefine their relationship or terminate it completely.

SUMMARY AND APPLICATION

Relationships are seldom problem free. As the analogy of the kissing porcupines suggests, people want warmth and connection, but they also want to avoid being hurt. When conflict, transgressions, and other problems occur, some people decide that the relationship is no longer rewarding enough, so they pull away before investing any more time and energy into saving it. Other times, like Fincham's (2000) kissing porcupines, people decide to draw back together despite the pain, hoping that they will not be "pricked" again.

Repairing a damaged relationship is no easy task, and some relationships are regarded as more worthy of saving than others. According to the investment model, rewards, costs, the quality of alternatives, satisfaction, investments, and commitment all influence whether or not a person will work to save a troubled relationship. In Tia and Jamal's case, most of these factors are in their favor. At the beginning of the scenario, they are in love and have always regarded their relationship as highly rewarding with few costs. They are satisfied with their relationship and plan to get married after Tia finishes graduate school, so they also have a high level of commitment. Over the past couple of years, they have both invested time, energy, and other resources into their relationship, so they both have a stake in making sure things work out. The

factors that could work against them are Tia lying, Jamal's jealousy of Robert, and Tia's reaction to Jamal dating someone else while their relationship was in the "off" stage. If Tia or Jamal had seen these alternative partners as attractive and viable, then their feelings for one another may have faded and they would never have gotten back together. However, in line with the investment model of relationship maintenance, they both eventually derogate their alternatives and regard one another as their best option, which paves the way for them to renew their relationship.

During their initial confrontation about Robert, it is somewhat surprising that Jamal engaged in antisocial communication because their relationship was otherwise satisfying. When people are satisfied and committed in their relationships, they are likely to use strategies such as voice, prosocial communication, and loyalty to cope with dissatisfaction in their relationships. However, even in happy relationships people often feel a pull to either "fight" or "flee" in response to hurtful events, so Jamal's reaction is understandable. If he had given himself more time to reflect about the situation, he would probably have used more-constructive communication. Engaging in open discussion (voice) might have reaffirmed to Jamal that Tia was still completely committed to him and they might have stayed together instead of going into an "off" stage. Tia tried to communicate in ways that foster relationship repair during their initial argument by explaining her actions. However, her attempt at relational repair would have stood a better chance at being successful had she also apologized and used appeasement strategies and relationship invocation to show Jamal how much he and their relationship mean to her.

Unfortunately for Tia and Jamal, instead of using these positive strategies they engaged in antisocial behaviors and broke up for a while. They missed each other and decided to reconcile. Part of the reconciliation process involved explanation and discussion. Another part involved forgiveness. Research suggests that it is best to use clear and direct communication when offering forgiveness. They both did this when they explicitly said "I forgive you" after apologizing for hurting each other. Jamal was able to move from feeling a need to retaliate against or avoid Tia, to wanting to be with Tia and to use positive forms of communication. Because they temporarily broke up, they also had the task of explaining

their reconciliation to their social network. They preempted the Facebook announcement of their reconciliation by telling family and friends that they were getting back together and explaining how much they missed and loved each other, and that it was all a big misunderstanding. Therefore, their friends and family were supportive when they got back together.

As Jamal and Tia's story suggests, transgressions and other relationship problems can be a bump in the relationship road or a detour sign; it depends on how committed and satisfied partners are, the seriousness of the offense, the strategies used to cope with the problem, and how willing the partners are to forgive each other. Tia and Jamal's reconciliation was prompted by lingering feelings, which shows that they missed one another. During their "off" period, they took time to figure out what they both wanted and improved themselves before they transitioned back into the relationship. These signs all suggest that Tia and Jamal have a chance to build a happy relationship that lasts, despite their recent breakup.

KEY TERMS

antisocial communication (p. 384)

capitalized on transition, as a type of on-again off-again relationship (p. 401)

comparison level (p. 381)

controlling, as a type of on-again off-again relationship (p. 401)

excuses (p. 391)

exit, as a coping strategy (p. 384)

explicit relational talk (p. 395)

extrinsic investments (p. 381)

forgiveness (p. 379)

gradual separators, as a type of on-again off-again relationship (p. 401)

habitual, as a type of on-again off-again relationship (p. 401)

intrinsic investments (p. 381)

investment model of relationship-maintaining behavior (p. 379)

investments (p. 380)

justifications (p. 391)

loyalty, as a coping strategy (p. 384)

metatalk (p. 392)

mismatched, as a type of on-again off-again relationship (p. 401)

model of accommodation (p. 384)

neglect, as a coping strategy (p. 384)

on-again off-again relationship (p. 401)

outcome (p. 380)

prosocial communication (p. 386)

punishment (p. 384)

relationship invocation (p. 392)

remedial strategies (p. 387)

rewards (p. 379)

secure attachment style (p. 387)

voice, as a coping strategy (p. 384)

DISCUSSION QUESTIONS

1. The investment model suggests that a variety of factors influence how people respond to the negative events that occur in relationships. These factors include the ratio of rewards versus costs in the relationship, overall satisfaction level, quality of alternatives, investments, and commitment. Which of these factors do you think is most important in determining whether couples stay together following a hurtful event? How are these factors related to the various types of communication discussed in this chapter (voice, prosocial communication, exit, antisocial communication, neglect, punishment, and loyalty)?

2. Think about the hurtful events you have experienced in your relationships. Why did you choose to forgive some people and not others? Are some hurtful events more forgivable than others? What variables do you think are most important in determining whether or not you forgive someone?

3. In this chapter you learned about five different types of on-again off-again relationships. What other types of communication besides those mentioned in this chapter might differentiate these couples? What do you think each type of couple needs to change to ensure that they do not keep repeating the on-again off-again cycle? How might you know that it is better to break up than to stay in this type of relationship?

 SAGE edge™

Sharpen your skills with SAGE edge at edge.sagepub.com/guerrero5e.
SAGE edge for students provides a personalized approach to help you accomplish your coursework goals in an easy-to-use learning environment.

ENDING RELATIONSHIPS
Disengagement and Termination

Kaley is crushed. "I've never been hurt so badly in my life," she tells her friend Aaliyah. "I am a complete basket case since Nick left me. It was so out of the blue." Since Nick broke up with Kaley last week, she has suffered greatly. She can't sleep at night. She has missed work. She can't study. Worse, she left desperate, pleading text messages on Nick's phone that must make him think she is a psycho. The only thing that seems to help is having long talks with Aaliyah while they go shopping or have lunch. For Nick, the breakup was building for years. He thinks that Kaley is too traditional, too religious, not spontaneous enough, and too preoccupied with money and social media. When they talked about these issues, it became clear to Nick that they were way too different. The gap between their values and goals was just too wide to bridge. He felt like he was losing his "real self" by trying to be someone he is not to please Kaley. Finally, he ended the relationship despite feeling terrible about hurting someone he loved. Nick wished there was a nicer way to break up. At first, he thought Kaley would get the hint when he spent more time with his friends and withdrew affection from her. When she didn't get the hint, he eventually had to tell her straight out that he wanted to break up. Kaley insisted that they could work it out, but Nick was firm that his decision was made and it was definitely over.

In Paul Simon's classic song "Fifty Ways to Leave Your Lover," breakups sound so easy. We are told to "Slip out the back, Jack. Make a new plan, Stan. You don't need to be coy, Roy. Just set yourself free." Rarely, however, is it that easy. For a person in either Kaley's or Nick's position, breakups are some of the most difficult episodes in life. For decades, relationship researchers who have examined the ends of relationships have come to understand how and why relationships end and the central role played by communication before, after, and during relationship breakups.

The goal in this chapter is to provide a better understanding of the relational disengagement process. Think about relationships in your own life that have ended. Some probably ended abruptly, while others disintegrated slowly. You and your partner may have had different perceptions of how and why the relationship ended, like Kaley and Nick. It was probably painful to end some relationships and a relief to end others. To help disentangle the complexity of relationship disengagement, this chapter focuses on four areas of relational disengagement research. First, we examine the reasons that relationships end. Second, we review phases that people often go through during a breakup, while also acknowledging that some people do not go through these phases; instead, their relationship ends suddenly. Third, we discuss 15 communication strategies people use to leave their partners. Finally, we take a look at the aftermath of relational disengagement.

WHY RELATIONSHIPS END

All relationships end. Regardless of whether they are brief or close encounters, last 60 days or 60 years, are friendships or marriages, all relationships end eventually. Sometimes they end voluntarily through our personal choice. Other times they end involuntarily because someone breaks up with us, moves away, or dies. Conville (1991) suggested that "disintegration is everywhere. . . . Disintegration is a process that is triggered when the relationship is out of kilter" (p. 96). Baxter (1982) stated, "The breaking up of a relationship is a phenomenon known to most and dreaded by all. It accounts for some of our most intense and painful social experiences" (p. 223). Worse, it is relatively common; 85% of adults in the United States have experienced a romantic relationship breakup (Battaglia, Richard, Datteri, & Lord, 1998). The deep positive and negative feelings we experience in our relationships are connected: There are no highs without lows. Khalil Gibran (1923/1970) described these two sides of love:

> When love beckons to you follow him, though his ways are hard and steep, and when his wings enfold you, yield to him, though the sword hidden among his pinions may wound you. And when he speaks to you believe in him, though his voice may shatter your dreams as the north wind lays waste the garden. Even as love crowns you so shall he crucify you. Even as he is for your growth so is he for your pruning. (p. 12)

The fact that relationships end, often painfully, prevents some people from developing close relationships. By denying themselves the opportunity to feel both the joys and the sorrows of relationships, these people miss an important secret of life: Not feeling anything at all is worse than feeling bad. Avoiding relationships prevents people from experiencing the deepest involvements and emotions humans can have.

People become deeply enmeshed in close relationships (Baxter, 1982). Relationships exist in a web of close ties, emotional connections, financial deals, sexual relations, friendship networks, possessions, homes, memories, identities, families, and sometimes offspring. When a relationship dies, many of these ties die as well. The loss of these networks and relational resources compounds the emotional pain of relational loss. Given how painful the end of relationships can be, you might wonder why relationships end.

Relationships end in many ways, but most couples—unmarried or married, straight or gay—show substantial similarities in how they break up (Kurdek, 1991). In a vast study of U.S. couples, Blumstein and Schwartz (1983) found that lesbians are most likely to break up, followed by gay men, then heterosexual cohabitators; married couples were most stable of all couple types, but when they broke up, they did so for many of the same reasons as other couples. Some variables one would think are associated with relational breakups, such as attachment style, self-esteem, and amount of conflict, do not predict breakups very well (Cate, Levin, & Richmond, 2002; Le, Dove, Agnew, Korn, & Mutso, 2010). What does predict breakups?

National data from a 17-year study of married people gives us some clues (Amato & Previti, 2003). Individuals who divorced during this study told researchers why their marriage ended. Box 15.1 shows the top 10 reasons they gave for divorcing. Women reported that their divorces were due to infidelity, alcohol or drug abuse, physical or **psychological abuse,** and their partner not meeting his family obligations. Men were more likely to report divorcing due to personality problems, lack of communication, or loss of love.

Other predictors of divorce emerged in this study, including unhappiness in one's marriage,

BOX 15.1

THE TOP 10 REASONS PEOPLE GIVE FOR DIVORCING

1. Infidelity/interest in a third party (21.6%) "I wouldn't put up with his cheating."

2. Incompatibility/lack of shared interests (19.2%) "We didn't agree on sex, friends, goals, or anything."

3. Drinking or drug use (10.6%) "He drank too much."

4. Grew apart (9.6%) "Our priorities changed; we weren't the same people."

5. Partner's personality (9.1%) "She was selfish and only thought of herself."

6. Lack of communication (8.7%) "We didn't talk anymore."

7. Physical or psychological abuse (5.8%) "Our relationship started to get violent."

8. Loss of love (4.3%) "I guess I didn't love him anymore."

9. Not meeting family responsibilities (3.4%) "He didn't do his share around the house or with the kids."

10. Work problems (3.4%) "He was too preoccupied with work all the time."

Source: Amato, P. R., & Previti, D. (2003). People's reasons for divorcing: Gender, social class, the life course, and adjustment. *Journal of Family Issues, 24*, 602–626.

wishing to pursue better alternatives, undergoing personal change (e.g., therapy, a midlife crisis) that leads one to want to do new things, financial problems, interference from family or one's social network, physical or mental illness, and immaturity (e.g., getting married too young). Other researchers have identified money or financial problems as a cause of divorce (Bradford, 1980; Lampard, 2014; Parker & Drummond-Reeves, 1993; Safron, 1979) and problems in gay and lesbian separations (Kurdek, 1991). Few relational problems revolve around how much money a couple makes. Instead, problems seem to stem from money management—with the values surrounding spending and saving producing considerable turmoil for couples (Blumstein & Schwartz, 1983). Getting married young is more likely to result in divorce, due to immaturity, lack of money, perceptions of being tied down too early in life, and marrying to escape an unhappy home environment (Huston, 2009). The probability of divorce within the early years of marriage decreases from 40% for 18- to 19-year-olds to 24% for individuals 25 or older (Clarke-Stewart & Brentano, 2006). In relationships, experience matters.

Culture also matters. Just as people from different cultures date, love, and marry differently, they also break up differently. In the United States and in most of Europe, dating, marriage, and divorce are matters of free choice and up to the individual. But that is not the case in much of the world. Dating and marriage are regulated by strong cultural and religious rules in many countries. In some cultures, the family helps decide who a person will marry and may virtually prohibit separations or divorces. Although divorce is increasing throughout most of the world and common in some cultures, it is quite rare in others (see Box 15.2 for more information on divorce throughout the world).

Social network disapproval and stressful events can also lead to breakup. Dating partners are more likely to break up if their social networks or parents disapprove of their relationship (Felmlee, Sprecher, & Bassin, 1990; Sprecher & Felmlee, 1992). Having separate friendship networks can also signal that a relationship is in danger (Metts & Cupach, 1986; Vaughn, 1986)—as can problems getting along with in-laws (Safron, 1979). Relational stressors and traumas are associated with relational breakups in both dating and marital relationships. One study showed that couples experiencing a miscarriage had a 22% greater chance of divorcing and couples experiencing stillbirth have a 40% greater chance of divorcing in the subsequent 10 years (Gold, Sen, & Hayward, 2010).

BOX 15.2 AROUND THE WORLD
DIVORCE: THE CONSEQUENCES OF CULTURE

Divorce rates around the world vary dramatically. In the United States and many European countries, a third to half of all marriages end in divorce ("Divorces and Crude Divorce Rates," 2008; "Divorce Rates," 2011). From 2002 to 2006, the highest divorce rates were in Sweden, the United States, Belarus, and Finland, which all had rates over 50%. In contrast, India, Sri Lanka, and Japan had divorce rates less than 2% during the same time period.

Marriages and divorces in Europe and United States are mostly voluntary, which is a characteristic of individualistic cultures (Andersen, 2011b). But in much of the world and much of recorded history this was not the case. Over the past several millennia, most marriages

were arranged by families and tribes. This practice is still widespread throughout much of the world, although it has been modified in many places so that the prospective bride and groom have some choice in the outcome. In modern arranged marriages, family members and friends act as matchmakers and set people up, but the prospective bride and groom choose whether to marry or not.

The success rate of these marriages is high—less than 10% of arranged marriages end in divorce. In many cultures, love-based marriages are considered strange and risky. We have no idea if all or most of these arranged marriages are happy, but they do last (Coontz, 2005). Indeed, in these cultures, breaking up is hard to do.

Although not mentioned in Amato and Previti's (2003) study, boredom or lack of excitement is also an important reason for breakups, especially in dating relationships (Hill et al., 1976). Nearly 10% of the participants in one study noted the absence of magic and romance as a primary cause for relational termination (Baxter, 1986). Interestingly, this was a factor for 19% of the men but only 5% of the women, suggesting that men are less practical partners. Honeycutt, Cantrill, and Allen (1992) found that disengagers commonly thought about their relationship as boring. Considering that our interpersonal relationships are one of our greatest sources of joy and excitement, when they begin to bore us, the end could be near.

People often complain that a relationship is "smothering" or "suffocating" them and they need their space, freedom, or autonomy. In studies of dating relationships, the need for autonomy and independence is often one of the top three predictors of breakups (Baxter, 1985; Hill et al., 1976). In Baxter's study, this was the primary reason given by around 24% of men and 44% of women. Rhoades, Stanley, & Markman (2010) found that "feeling trapped" in a relationship was a leading predictor or relational

termination. Research by VanderDrift and Agnew (2012) reveals that independence, self-improvement, or self-expansion is a central need in relationships and that if unfulfilled leads to relational termination. Similarly, one of the five most common general issues leading to relational breakups in gay and lesbian couples was excessive fusion, which is a loss of individuality because of the relationship (Kurdek, 1991).

Infidelity and Interest in a Third Party

Extramarital or extrarelational sex is often detrimental to a relationship and may lead to termination. Although the reverse is often true: Unhappy relationships lead to extrarelational sex. Research suggests that sexual betrayal is common in all type of relationships but particularly during dating (Feldman & Cauffman, 1999). For every type of couple, gay or straight, the relationship is less likely to survive when one partner is having sex outside the relationship (Blumstein & Schwartz, 1983; Lampard, 2014). Gagnon (1977) reported that nearly 40% of the time, having an extramarital sexual relationship had an effect on the decision to divorce, and 14%

to 18% of the time, these affairs had a major effect. In other studies, extramarital affairs were a factor in the breakups of 21% to 55% of the couples studied (Amato & Previti, 2003; Bradford, 1980; Parker & Drummond-Reeves, 1993).

As Amato and Previti (2003) suggested, women are more likely than men to cite infidelity as a reason for breakups. Cupach and Metts (1986) found that while extrarelational affairs were associated with breakups for both married and unmarried couples, affairs were a more salient concern for women than for men. They suggested that for men, an affair is a form of self-gratification, whereas women see affairs as a violation of the relationship, a more central reason for a breakup. However, the type of affair is critical. People can engage in sexual infidelity (having sex with someone else), emotional infidelity (falling in love with someone else), or both. Relative to women, men find it more difficult to forgive sexual infidelity than emotional infidelity and are more likely to terminate a relationship following a partner's sexual infidelity (Shackelford, Buss, & Bennett, 2002). The reverse was true for women, who were more likely than men to break up as a result of their partner's emotional infidelity. However, more recent research suggests that both emotional and sexual infidelity are associated with relationship breakups for women (Negash, Cui, Fincham, & Pasley, 2014).

The concept of emotional infidelity suggests that rivals can threaten relationships even if sexual infidelity has not occurred. Perhaps this is why jealousy is such a prevalent emotion and a major cause of relational violence (see Chapter 13). Hill and colleagues (1976) reported that one of the top 10 reasons for terminating a dating relationship for both men and women was interest in someone else. Similarly, Metts and Cupach (1986) reported that a common disengagement theme was third-party involvement, particularly for women. Unfaithfulness was a primary reason for terminating relationships in 16% of the accounts in Baxter's (1986) study on breakups, and the availability of attractive alternative partners makes relational breakups more likely (Felmlee

et al., 1990; Rusbult, Zembrodt, & Gunn, 1982). Interestingly, when people have few good prospects as alternative partners or are unaware of alternatives, they are more likely to stay with their current partner (Miller, 1997; Simpson, 1987). These findings correspond with social exchange theory principles (see Chapter 13). Young couples are particularly vulnerable to breakups caused by infidelity (Huston, 2009), although it is not the only reason why younger couples break up more frequently.

Incompatibility

Despite the oft-repeated folk wisdom that "opposites attract," a more valid cliché is "birds of a feather flock together" (see Chapter 3). Dozens of studies show that the more two people have in common, the more likely they are to stay together. Think of your close friends. You probably have many things in common, including interests, political opinions, and religious values. Similarities are also important in romantic relationships. Personality similarities lead to longer relationships and fewer breakups; spouses who are alike in extraversion, attractiveness, and interest in art are less likely to divorce (Bentler & Newcomb, 1978; Cody, 1982). In Baxter's (1986) heterosexual dating study, the second most common reason for breakups was a difference in beliefs, attitudes, and values—a factor mentioned by nearly one third of the respondents. Metts and Cupach (1986) found that value dissimilarity commonly led to relational disengagement. In a statistical summary of factors leading to divorce, Karney and Bradbury (1995) concluded that attitude dissimilarity was one of the most important factors leading to relational dissatisfaction and divorce.

Although interethnic dating relationships and marriages can be successful and rewarding, they are at greater risk for breakups. Lack of similarity in attitudes, activities, and interests, as well as differences in ethnic, religious, and socioeconomic backgrounds, can precipitate relational breakups (Cate et al., 2002; Felmlee et al., 1990; Lampard, 2014). This is primarily due to the prejudiced influences of family, friends, and society in general that puts greater strain on an interethnic couple (Williams & Andersen, 1998). In a classic study on dating relationships, Hill and associates (1976) found that the fourth most important factor leading to breakups was differences in background. Similarly, although age-discrepant relationships can be very happy, large age differences are statistically related to breakups (Bentler & Newcomb, 1978).

Differences in educational background, intelligence, emotional involvement, and health also pose problems for relationships. In Hill and colleagues' (1976) study, differences in intelligence were among the top reasons for dating breakups. When one partner continues education and the other partner does not, the couple may have less in common (Scott & Powers, 1978). Even among otherwise satisfied couples, differences in partners' health status greatly increase the chance of divorce, even among otherwise satisfied couples (Karraker & Latham, 2015; Wilson & Waddoups, 2002). Relationships also benefit from similar levels of emotional involvement. In over half of dating relationships, one person is more emotionally involved than the other. Breakups are easier for the least involved person according to the principle of least interest (see Chapter 12). Thus, asymmetrical levels of emotional involvement are a risk factor for relational breakups (Sprecher et al., 2006).

Sexual incompatibility is also important. Conflicting sexual attitudes are a key contributor to breakups in heterosexual dating relationships (Hill et al., 1976), marriages (Cleek & Pearson, 1985; Safron, 1979), and gay and lesbian relationships (Kurdek, 1991). As discussed in Chapter 9, sex is a central feature of marriages, romances, and many dating relationships that can lead to relational problems. Partners may differ over the desired frequency of sexual relations, types of sexual behaviors, and the initiation of sex. In dating relationships, engagements, marriages, and gay relationships, fighting about sex is associated with relational breakups (Blumstein & Schwartz, 1983); although there is little association between how much sex a couple has and how long the partners stay together. Frequency is less important than compatibility.

Alcohol and Drugs

Alcohol and drugs have been cited as one of the top 10 reasons for marital breakup in several studies (e.g., Amato & Previti, 2003; Lampard, 2014; Safron, 1979) and were a factor in 45% of the divorces (Parker & Drummond-Reeves, 1993). Alcohol and drug abuse may lead to violence, addiction, problems with the law, the squandering of money, and problems at work—any of which can greatly strain a relationship. Alcohol and drug abuse can also lead to codependency in relationships. Le Poire, Hallett, and Giles (1998) argued that the partners of alcoholics and drug addicts often become codependent, letting their partner's behavior affect their own behavior. Many codependents become obsessed with controlling their partner's negative behaviors and with nurturing the partner. According to Le Poire and colleagues (1998), codependents often show a mix of punishing and reinforcing behaviors. Sometimes, they try to get their partner to stop using drugs or alcohol through punishment (e.g., verbal confrontation, threats to leave). Other times, however, they reinforce the partner's behavior by doing things such as keeping the children out of the way and taking care of the partner when the partner is ill. Although codependency may keep people in relationships for a while, in the long run, codependent behavioral patterns may put considerable strain on relationships.

Growing Apart

Some relationships wither away (Lampard, 2014; Metts & Cupach, 1986). Waning of relationships is often due to different interests, such as the dissimilarities between Kaley and Nick discussed at the start of this chapter. Relationships also wither from reduced quality and quantity of communication, distance, reduced efforts to maintain the relationship, or competition from hundreds of relationships in today's fast-paced world. Dating relationships will deteriorate and terminate as commitment wanes (Le et al., 2010). Recent research suggests that less dedication, fewer material restraints (like sharing a debt or owning a pet), lower commitment, and feelings of being trapped predict breaking up (Rhoades et al., 2010; VanderDrift & Agnew, 2012).

In marriages, people often cannot pinpoint when they started growing apart. Atrophy is a gradual process. Spouses get absorbed in their everyday lives—working and raising children—and forget to give each other the attention they deserve. In marriages characterized by atrophy, marital happiness slowly declines (Sternberg, 1987). Feelings of intimacy and passion diminish and disappear as partners grow farther and farther apart. Owen (1993) found that many relationship breakups were characterized by atrophy. Typical metaphors for relationship endings were "It was like a flower that blossomed and then withered," "I could see the relationship rot each day," and "The relationship faded into the sunset" (pp. 271–272).

Loss of Love

Many factors cause relationship breakups, but one thing is clear: Love prevents breakups. A recent meta-analysis of psychological research found lack of love is a strong predictor of relationship breakups (Le et al., 2010). Love is lost in many ways. Some people experience **chronic dissatisfaction** in their relationships. Temporary dissatisfaction may cause couples to repair and maintain their relationship (see Chapters 10 and 14), but couples with a history of dissatisfaction are at risk for divorce (Kurdek, 1993). Love is linked with feelings of joy, warmth, contentment, and passion. Being with people we love promotes good feelings. Chronic dissatisfaction eats away at good feelings, so we seek happiness elsewhere. Longitudinal research shows most daters with steady levels of satisfaction remain in their relationships; in contrast, daters with fluctuating levels of satisfaction tend to leave their relationships (Arriaga, 2001).

Relationship disillusionment occurs when a person's positive illusions about their partner and relationships fade (Huston, 2009; Lee, Rogee, & Reis, 2010; Niehuis & Bartell, 2006). Loss of love is related to disillusionment. When people are falling in love, they often see their partners and relationships through "rose-colored glasses." These positive illusions during courtship and early marriage are hard to maintain once the honeymoon stage is over (Murray et al., 1996; Swann et al., 1994). A recent statistical summary suggests that loss of positive illusions is a leading reason for dating relationship breakups (Le et al., 2010). Disillusionment predicts divorce and dating breakups better than personality variables do (Huston, 2009; Niehuis & Bartell, 2006; Niehuis & Huston, 2002). Disillusionment causes decreases in love and affection, loss of emotional attachment, and disappointment in the relationship and partner. Disillusionment is strong when people have unrealistic expectations about their relationship during courtship or early marriage. In fact, several studies suggest that people experience disillusionment and subtle, implicit negative evaluations during the early stages of premarital and marital relationships even though they report particularly high levels of affection and passion (Le et al., 2010; Niehuis & Huston, 2002). To see if your relationship is characterized by disillusionment, take the test in Box 15.3.

Equity Issues Related to Family Obligations

Issues related to equity or fairness in family responsibilities is a common reason for marital breakups (Amato & Previti, 2003); some studies cast this as an equality issue for women (Safron, 1979). In Amato and Previti's (2003) study, women cited having a partner who does not meet family obligations as a reason for divorce about three and a half times more than men did. Equity is also important in dating relationships (see Chapter 14). In Baxter's (1986) study of heterosexual dating relational breakups, equity was a primary factor in the breakup for 17%

BOX 15.3 PUT YOURSELF TO THE TEST
RELATIONSHIP DISILLUSIONMENT SCALE

Circle the number that best represents how much you agree or disagree with each statement, using the following scale: 1 = strongly disagree and 7 = strongly agree.

	Strongly Disagree						Strongly Agree
1. I am very disappointed in my relationship.	1	2	3	4	5	6	7
2. I am very disappointed in my partner.	1	2	3	4	5	6	7
3. My partner used to be my best friend, but now I sometimes don't like her or him as a person.	1	2	3	4	5	6	7
4. This relationship is not at all what I expected it to be; I feel very disappointed.	1	2	3	4	5	6	7
5. I used to think I was lucky to be with someone like my partner; now I'm not so sure that I am so lucky.	1	2	3	4	5	6	7
6. I used to love spending time with my partner, but now it is starting to feel like a chore.	1	2	3	4	5	6	7
7. I feel tricked, cheated, or deceived by love.	1	2	3	4	5	6	7
8. The relationship is not as enjoyable as I had expected it to be.	1	2	3	4	5	6	7
9. If I could go back in time, I would not have gotten involved with my partner.	1	2	3	4	5	6	7
10. My partner used to be on her or his best behavior when with me, but now he or she doesn't bother trying to impress me.	1	2	3	4	5	6	7
11. My partner seems to be an entirely different person now.	1	2	3	4	5	6	7

Add up your responses. A score of 11 represents a lack of disillusionment, whereas a score of 77 represents the highest possible level of disillusionment.

Source: From Niehuis, S., & Bartell, D., The marital disillusionment scale: Development and psychometric properties. *North American Journal of Psychology 8*, 69–83, copyright © 2006. Reprinted and adapted with permission of the North American Journal of Psychology and the author.

of the women and 5% of the men. In Blumstein and Schwartz's (1983) study, a major factor in relational breakups revolved around men's opinions about working women. Specifically, if the man objected to the woman working, or if he was unhappy about her job, the couple was more likely to terminate their relationship. Research also suggests that employment may make women more independent and increase their likelihood of leaving a troubled marriage (Kalmijn & Poortman, 2006).

Working women are often under considerable stress, especially if they have children and are trying to run a household. In the popular press, this problem is referred to as the *superwoman syndrome*. Women are supposed go to work and then home and tend to their families and homes. Because women are the primary caregivers at home, they are always working—at the office or at home. Hochschild (1997; Hochschild & Machung, 1989), for example, has shown that women typically do about 70% of the household chores. Moreover, only 20% of dual-career couples report a fair distribution of labor exists in their home. For the other 80% of couples, the woman is usually responsible for the majority of homemaking and child care chores. When this type of inequity exists, it is a major source of tension in the relationship. A longitudinal study of marital breakups found that women's perception of inequality and a sense of being underbenefited increased the risk of divorce significantly (DeMaris, 2007). The association between women's perceived inequity held even when objective indicants such as actual contributions to the relationship were controlled.

COMMUNICATION AS A CAUSE OF RELATIONAL BREAKUP

Poor communication is also a common culprit predicting relational breakups; several studies report it as the number one cause of divorce (Bradford, 1980; Cleek & Pearson, 1985; Parker & Drummond-Reeves, 1993). This includes too much communication, too little communication, low-quality communication, negative communication, and communication that is not mutually constructive. In Amato and Previti's (2003) study, lack of communication and psychological abuse (which involves engaging in hurtful communication) were among the top predictors of divorce. Gottman and Levenson (2000, 2002) found that the type of communication that predicts divorce depends on the length of one's marriage. Specifically, couples who divorce within 5 to 7 years tend to report high levels of destructive marital conflict, whereas those who divorce within 10 to 12 years report a loss of intimacy and connection. Recent longitudinal research found that dysfunctional conflict during the first year of marriage was related to relational breakups 3, 7, and 16 years later (Birditt, Brown, Orbuch, & McIlvane, 2010). (See Chapter 11 for a more detailed discussion of destructive communication patterns used during conflict.)

Withdrawal

Withdrawal is a common reason for relationship breakups that can reflect a lack of intimacy and connection. Baxter (1986) found that low levels of supportiveness—and particularly a lack of listening—was a major factor in over one fourth of the relational breakups she studied. As discussed in Chapter 11, stonewalling occurs when individuals fail to discuss important issues with their partners (Christensen & Shenk, 1991; Gottman, 1993; Gottman & Levenson, 1992). Men use this type of dysfunctional communication more often than women (Clements, Cordova, Markman, & Laurenceau, 1997).

Many studies have examined the demand-withdrawal sequence (also discussed in Chapter 11), which is associated with separation (Christensen & Shenk, 1991). This sequence occurs when one person makes a demand and the partner responds by withdrawing from communication. People in the demanding position are dissatisfied and want to change something in their relationship. Children of divorced parents more frequently report that their mother and father engaged in demand-withdrawal patterns than children of nondivorced parents (Afifi & Schrodt, 2003). Furthermore, Honeycutt and colleagues (1992) had disengaged couples recall behaviors that contributed to relational disengagement. These behaviors included spending less time together, avoiding each other in public settings, and making excuses for not going out together.

Negative Communication

All couples have conflicts and disagreements. In fact, as dating partners become more loving and committed, conflict increases, presumably because of increased interdependence (Lloyd & Cate, 1985). Research shows that it is not the presence or absence of conflict that determines whether a couple will be satisfied and stay together; it is how partners deal with conflict that is more important (see Chapter 11). In a series of studies spanning 15 years, Clements and colleagues (1997) reported that in their earliest interactions, partners who eventually broke up, dealt with their disagreements in a destructive fashion with common fights, name-calling, criticisms, and accusations. Research by Filsinger and Thomas (1988) found that negative interpersonal communication predicted disengagement a year and a half later. In a major statistical summary of the research on divorce, Karney and Bradbury (1995) reported that one of the most prevalent factors leading to divorce was negative behavior. One study found that a common path to disengagement was rules violation, where one partner engages in inappropriate behavior (Metts & Cupach, 1986). For example, if relational partners had agreed to call if they are going to be late or not to swear at each other during disagreements, violations of these rules can lead to dissatisfaction and, perhaps, disengagement.

Conflict increases as dating relationships become more committed and rises even more sharply for partners contemplating a breakup or deciding to terminate their relationship (Lloyd & Cate, 1985). Thus, there may be an optimal level of conflict in a relationship beyond which the relationship is threatened. In short, some conflict may be normal and even healthy for relationships (see Chapter 11). But high levels of conflict may be detrimental, particularly if issues resurface because they were not discussed in a constructive manner.

Increased negative emotional expression and decreased positive emotional expression put heterosexual, gay male, and lesbian couples at risk for dissolution (Dailey et al., 2009; Gottman, 1993; Gottman et al., 2003; Gottman & Levenson, 1992; Karney & Bradbury, 1995). Karney and Bradbury (1995) found that reciprocity of negative behaviors was the most detrimental factor in a marriage. Honeycutt and fellow researchers (1992) reported that couples recalled various forms of aversive communication—such as arguing about little things, disagreeing, verbally fighting, criticizing the partner, and making sarcastic comments—as behaviors that led to the breakup of their relationships. Surprisingly, Gottman (1993) reported that husbands' anger was unrelated to divorce. However, husbands who became defensive, showed contempt, or used stonewalling were more likely to divorce. Similarly, wives who criticized, became defensive, and showed contempt were more likely to see their relationships end. Gottman and his colleagues focused on communication patterns that prevent rather than predict divorce (Gottman, Gottman, & DeClaire, 2006); some of their advice for preventing divorce is presented in Box 15.4.

Lack of Openness and Intimacy

Even though couples need autonomy and privacy (see Chapter 5), open disclosure is still imperative for relationships. Partners who stay together, rather than break up, report much higher levels of self-disclosure early in their relationships (Berg & McQuinn, 1986). Sprecher (1987) found that dating couples who engaged in more self-disclosure were more likely to be together 4 years later. Similarly, a recent summary of psychological research found that lack of self-disclosure was associated with breaking up in dating relationships (Le et al., 2010). Openness is particularly important to women's evaluation of their partners. In Baxter's (1986) study, 31% of the women, compared to only 8% of the men, mentioned lack of openness as a major factor in relational termination. In a study on memories of relationship breakups, Honeycutt and his colleagues (1992) reported that many people remember decreases in

BOX 15.4 HIGHLIGHTS
COMMUNICATION THAT HELPS PREVENT DIVORCE: THE MARRIAGE MASTERS

Based on research conducted in his "love lab" at the University of Washington, John Gottman, along with coauthors Julie Schwartz Gottman and Joan DeClaire, explained that some people are "marriage masters" while others are "marriage disasters." The difference between being a master versus a disaster rests, in large part, on how people communicate. If you are a marriage master, you are more likely to do the following:

- *Soften the start up.* Gottman and colleagues noted that it would be ludicrous to expect two people to live together without complaining but that complaints can be communicated in a respectful manner that expresses your needs without criticizing your partner. When complaints are posed gently and without insults, the partner is more likely to listen and compromise.

- *Tell your partner what you want, rather than what you don't want.* It is easy to tell your partner, "I hate when you leave your dirty socks everywhere" or "You are so rude when you roll your eyes at me." But it is more constructive to tell your partner that you would like some help keeping the house clean and want to be taken seriously when you are talking.

- *Listen for statements of need and respond with open-ended questions.* Active listening can be a challenge during arguments, but try to look beyond the complaints and criticisms and focus on what your partner needs. Ask your partner questions such as, "What's bothering you?" or "How can I help?" when appropriate. This can get productive discussion rolling.

- *Accept your partner's emotional bids.* Your partner reaches out for emotional connection in various ways, including giving compliments, smiling, and sitting next to you while watching TV. Marriage masters turn toward their partners and reciprocate positivity, rather than turning away (ignoring) or turning against (reacting with hostility) them, even when they aren't in the best of moods.

- *Express appreciation.* We all have a natural tendency to retaliate or get angry when we are criticized or attacked, but we don't always reward our partner's positive behavior. If your partner is being attentive or putting effort into your relationship, take the time to thank your partner or offer a compliment.

- *Repair conversations.* If a conversation is getting difficult, marriage masters know how to diffuse the negativity by engaging in behaviors such as apologizing, smiling, or making a funny comment. Marriage masters also know how to cool down when they are flooded with negative emotions, sometimes by taking a break from the conversation.

- *Establish rituals for connection.* Some of the most common complaints that couples have are that they do not have enough time for one another because they are busy with work, children, household chores, and other responsibilities. Therefore, it is important to set aside time to be together alone as a couple—just to talk or to get away on a romantic date or getaway.

- *Accept influence.* Marriage masters are also open to accepting advice and being persuaded by their partners. Stubbornly holding on to one's own positions can be harmful, especially if it prevents partners from growing at both a personal and a relational level. Gottman's research suggests marriages are happier when husbands are willing to listen to and be influenced by their wives.

Source: Information compiled from Gottman et al. (2006).

verbal and nonverbal intimacy as the starting point for relational decline. Couples at risk for eventual disengagement may stop expressing intimate feelings and decrease acts of physical intimacy such as hugs, kisses, and touches.

Abusive Communication

Researchers have tested the "common sense" hypothesis that people are likely to break up with partners who are physically or psychologically abusive (Rhatigan & Street, 2005). **Physical abuse** is violent behavior such as grabbing, pushing, kicking, biting, slapping, and punching whereas psychological abuse is hurtful communication, such as insults, name-calling, and personal criticism. Not surprisingly, research shows that physical and psychological abuse are related to less relational satisfaction, less commitment, and more likelihood of relationship termination (Lampard, 2014; Rhatigan & Street, 2005). Physically battered women are more likely to report that they intend to leave their violent partners when they are also psychologically abused (Arias & Pape, 2001), suggesting that both physical and psychological abuse are important determinants of breakups. People are also likely to break up with partners who abuse their children (Amato & Previti, 2003).

Unfortunately, some people stay in abusive relationships. One study found that battered women stay with their husbands for three reasons: (1) financial dependency, (2) a family history of violence, and (3) psychological factors such as low self-esteem or blaming oneself for their partner's violence (Kim & Gray, 2008). Another study found similar reasons— with women more likely to stay in violent relationships if they were financially dependent, needed their spouse to help with child care, were afraid of being lonely or of being harmed if they left, thought a breakup would be socially embarrassing, had poor support from their social network, or hoped the relationship would change for the better (Hendy, Eggen, Gustitus, McLeod, & Ng, 2003).

Sometimes, people use abuse to try to control their partner and prevent a breakup. Such is the case with intimate terrorism, the intentional use of violence as a means of intimidating and controlling one's partner (Johnson, 1995). This is chronic violence that tends to be more severe than more common forms of violence that occur occasionally when people lose control during the heat of an argument (see Chapter 14). Intimate terrorism is asymmetrical—one partner is the perpetrator and the other is the victim—whereas other forms of violence in relationships are often reciprocal. Though intimate terrorism is used by both men and women, studies suggest that women

are most likely to be victims (Johnson, 1995). This type of violence tends to be more severe and enduring than violence that arises spontaneously during conflict (Graham-Kevan & Archer, 2003). Although victims of intimate terrorism often fear their partner's reaction, they are more likely to end their relationship than are victims of more common forms of violence (Johnson & Leone, 2005).

One surprising finding is that personality factors played little role in relationship breakups. For example, introverts have no greater likelihood of breaking up than extroverts; agreeable people are no less likely to disengage than less agreeable people. Even more surprising, relationship researchers' favorite variable—attachment styles—had virtually only small impact on relationship breakups, with anxious and avoidance individuals only slightly more likely to break up (Le et al., 2010).

THE DISENGAGEMENT PROCESS

Researchers have created several models of how relationships come apart. Most thinking in this area suggests that relationships pass through several phases as people disengage from one another—as if descending a staircase from close relationships to breakups. For example, Knapp and Vangelisti's (2008) staircase model predicts that relationships are characterized by more avoidance and less intimate communication as they fall apart (see Chapter 5). Other researchers have suggested that instead of slowly disintegrating, relationships sometimes go through sudden changes more akin to falling off a balcony than descending stairs. This perspective is embodied by **catastrophe theory** approaches to disengagement. Next we discuss two theories of the disengagement process that reflect both of these general approaches—Duck's (1982, 1988; Rollie & Duck, 2006) process of relational dissolution and catastrophe theory.

A Process Model of Relational Dissolution

A leading model of relational breakups was developed by Duck (1982, 1988), who viewed relational dissolution as a set of distinct but connected phases. Recently, this model was revised to focus more on the communication processes occurring during relationship breakups (Duck, 2005). According to Duck's model, five processes are likely to occur as people disengage from relationships—(1) intrapsychic, (2) dyadic, (3) social, (4) grave-dressing, and (5) resurrection. Moreover, couples can go through several of these processes (particularly the first two) without breaking up. In fact, many couples recognize and resolve relational problems during the intrapsychic and dyadic processes that help them reevaluate their relationships. When partners find themselves embroiled in social processes, however, the relationship might be likely to derail.

INTRAPSYCHIC PROCESSES Relational dissatisfaction triggers the **intrapsychic processes phase** that involve reflecting on the negative aspects of the relationship and comparing these flaws with costs of leaving the relationship. Beyond reflection, the intrapsychic process involves preparing to talk to the partner about problems. Duck (2005) noted that these processes "not only provide a psychological engine for rumination but also affect communicative activity; in particular, they promote a social withdrawal, so that the person can nurse perceived wounds and take stock of the partner and the relationship" (p. 211). At that point, people sometimes realize that their problems are not as bad as they once thought. However, mulling or ruminating about relational problems often make them worse rather than better (Cloven & Roloff, 1993; Saffrey & Ehrenberg, 2007); thinking about dissolving a relationship is an independent predictor of an eventual breakup (VanderDrift, Agnew, & Wilson, 2009). Vaughn (1986) claimed that "uncoupling begins with a secret. One of the partners starts to feel uncomfortable with the relationship" (p. 11). This is what happened to Nick, whom we introduced at the start of this chapter. The relationship was changing him in ways that made him feel uncomfortable. Dissatisfied partners face a dilemma of whether to discuss such feelings and thoughts with their

relational partner or to withdraw. Often they withdraw initially while they are mulling and deciding what to do. A breakup is not inevitable at this stage; the partner is often seeking to resolve problems and maintain the relationship. But when people begin to think that withdrawing from the relationship would be justified, they are likely to engage in dyadic processes that could either repair the relationship or propel it toward dissolution.

DYADIC PROCESSES The **dyadic processes phase** occurs when dissatisfied partners communicate negative thoughts and feelings. Partners attempt to negotiate and reconcile the differences to avert a relationship breakup. Fights, arguments, and long discussions characterize this phase. According to Rollie and Duck (2006), people sometimes experience shock and surprise when a partner airs concerns. Partners can also experience a dramatic reconciliation as a result of dyadic processes. Research on breakups and on-again off-again relationships shows that transitions are initiated and facilitated by "state of the relationship" talk (Dailey, Rossetto, McCracken, Jin, & Green, 2012). Specific topics about conflict and expectations for future behavior are often discussed as individuals continue to weigh the costs and rewards associated with being in the relationship. Partners may also renegotiate rules, promise to change, or improve their behavior. In other cases, they may decide the relationship is not worth saving. This is what happened for Nick. He tried to talk to Kaley about their differences, but he concluded that they were just too different to be able to make their relationship work.

SOCIAL PROCESSES "Going public" about the distress and problems within one's relationship marks the **social processes phase** (Rollie & Duck, 2006). Couples talk to their social networks and investigate alternatives to the current relationship. Even when couples do not have a need to "label" a relationship, the social network may seek clarity through the use of a label (Dailey, Brody, & Knapp, 2015), such as wanting to know if they are still "officially dating."

Partners attempt to save face and receive support by telling their side of the story to friends and family, as Kaley did when she turned to Aaliyah for comfort. They are also likely to develop a story to convince their network, and themselves, that they are doing the right thing (Duck, 1982). Often nonverbal behaviors such as looking depressed or sounding upset reveal to others that something is wrong in the relationship (Vaughn, 1986). Initially the individual's network may try to prevent a breakup, but when the outcome seems inevitable, they help facilitate the breakup by providing interpersonal and emotional support and taking the initiating partner's side in any disputes. When members of the person's social network take their friend's side, it helps convince the breakup initiator that breaking up is the right decision. A word of caution is in order here, though: If people complain too loudly about their partners to others, the social network may have a hard time accepting them back into the fold if the partners change their minds and get back together. As Rollie and Duck (2006) explained, it is difficult to backtrack and repair the relationship once people have engaged in these types of social processes.

GRAVE-DRESSING PROCESSES The communication that occurs during the **grave-dressing processes phase** focuses on coping with a breakup in a socially acceptable manner. Think about the stories you tell about a relationship breakup. If you are the breakup initiator, you might emphasize that you handled the breakup in a sensitive and caring manner. If you are the person who was dumped, you might assure people that you are strong and will be okay. In other cases, you might note that the breakup was inevitable or mutual. Rollie and Duck (2006) noted that people create and tell plausible stories about the breakup to let other people know that they are still desirable partners. Rather than telling only one breakup story, people alter their stories based on the audience. So although Kaley confesses to Aaliyah that she is crushed that Nick broke up with her, her story may change when

she communicates with a group that includes an attractive man. Now she might downplay her hurt feelings saying something like, "Yeah, I was surprised and hurt, but I'll get over it. I guess it just wasn't meant to be. Something better must be out there waiting for me." These types of accounts are vital for obtaining closure and engaging in resurrection processes.

RESURRECTION PROCESSES As Rollie and Duck (2006) explained, the end of a relationship often marks the beginning of something new during the **resurrection processes phase**. After a breakup, people often visualize what their future will look like without their old relationship. To prepare for that future, they construct and communicate a new image of themselves as wiser as a result of their experiences. For example, Kaley may eventually realize that she would be better off finding a partner who shares her values. Nick may have learned that he should not have strung Kaley on for as long as he did. Both may emerge with a sense that they are now better equipped to find a compatible partner and to communicate their needs more clearly. Resurrection processes also include revising stories about the former relationship and the breakup. Right after the breakup there are often bitter feelings, but as time passes, people reframe their partner and the relationship in more positive terms. So while Nick might still acknowledge that he and Kaley had grown apart, he might also note that she is one of the sweetest and most genuine women he has ever known. Such an account paints both Kaley and Nick in a positive light, since it shows that Nick does not hold a grudge and can appreciate Kaley's good qualities despite their differences.

CATASTROPHE THEORY

Catastrophe theory provides an alternative way to describe and explain breakups by suggesting that relationships do not always de-escalate gradually but instead sometimes experience sudden death (Davis, 1973). Like earthquakes building along a silent fault line or a violent storm near the quiet eye of a hurricane, relationship stability can be shattered by rapid cataclysmic events. Of course, fault lines are rarely silent, and subtle signs such as falling air pressure and increased humidity accompany looming hurricanes. Likewise, signs of an impending relational catastrophe exist, but people often fail to see them or deny them, as did Kaley in the opening vignette of the chapter. As Vaughn (1986) stated, "Partners often report that they are unaware, or only remotely aware, even at the point of separation, that the relationship is deteriorating. Only after the other person is gone are they able to look back and recognize the signals" (p. 62).

Breakups are often precipitated by a critical incident leading to rapid disengagement (Baxter, 1984; Bullis et al., 1993; Cupach & Metts, 1986; Lampard, 2014). These incidents range from discovering infidelity, to big arguments or physical violence, to finding differences in values, such as the realization that one partner hates pets and the other person loves them. In about 25% of the relationships in Baxter's (1984) study, partners reported that a single critical incident led to a breakup. Interestingly, Bullis and associates (1993) reported that few disengagements were premeditated. Instead, disengagements often are nonstrategic turning points in relationships that occurred quickly, more in line with a catastrophe model of breakups than a stage model.

Even when no critical incident can be singled out, relationships sometimes dissolve rapidly. Wilmot (1995) discussed the "point of no return" in every relationship, where one or both of the partners know for sure it's over. Wilmot maintained that in these cases "sometimes people just disappear, without any warning or indication of their discomfort with the relationship" (p. 119). Similarly, Davis (1973) talked about sudden relational death, which occurs when a person abruptly decides the relationship is over, falls in love with someone else, or suffers a trauma such as partner abuse. According to Wilmot (1995), sudden death can be likened to an execution rather than a slow death of the relationship. The breakup often occurs without face-to-face communication, but the initiator may enlist the help of a friend to tell the partner the relationship is over or terminate the relationship via a letter, phone call, or text message.

Catastrophe theory, positing that events are discontinuous rather than linear, explains many events in nature (Isnard & Zeeman, 1977; Tesser & Achee, 1994). Sometimes human behavior, including behavior in relationships, flows along a smooth, geometric plane. Like hikers on a path next to a cliff, the relationship can slip off the edge of the trail to a lower level—with catastrophic discontinuities for the relationship. Catastrophe theory has been successfully applied in many contexts, including mood changes, conflict during arguments, stock market behavior, and hostilities among nations (Zeeman, 1977). Relational researchers could thus benefit from catastrophe theory to predict sudden death of relationships.

FIFTEEN WAYS TO LEAVE YOUR PARTNER

Although there are not 50 ways to leave your lover, as the Paul Simon song suggests, research shows at least 15 strategies by which people terminate relationships. These strategies differ based on whether they are direct or indirect and if they are unilateral or bilateral (Baxter, 1982, 1984). Direct strategies rely mainly on face-to-face verbal communication whereas indirect strategies employ more subtle, indirect communication, including nonverbal communication. Unilateral strategies involve one person deciding to break up whereas bilateral strategies are a joint decision to terminate the relationship.

Most breakups are unilateral not bilateral, and most people end relationships using indirect, not direct, strategies. Baxter (1979b) found that 71% of all disengagement strategies were indirect and implicit. In a study of breakup accounts, Baxter (1984) found that 76% of couples employed indirect as opposed to direct communication strategies. When direct strategies were used, they were usually unilateral "dumps" not negotiated dialogues (Baxter, 1979a). Most sex differences regarding breakups are minimal, but Wilmot, Carbaugh, and Baxter (1985) reported that females are more likely to use direct strategies than males.

Although indirect strategies are used often to end both casual and close relationships, they are particularly likely to be used in casual relationships when couples have less to negotiate (Baxter, 1979b, 1982, 1984, 1985; Perras & Lustig, 1982; Thieme & Rouse, 1991; Wilmot et al., 1985). Breakups are stressful, so disengagers try to minimize their pain and anxiety through indirect rather than direct communication. In light of the fact that "ending a relationship is perhaps one of the most face-threatening situations we encounter" (Cupach & Metts, 1994, p. 81), people are most likely to use indirect strategies that minimize guilt and embarrassment. A recent study of breakups among Italian college students found that indirect, abstract messages are most commonly employed (Menegatti & Rubini, 2014). Indirect strategies are sometimes used on social networking sites as well. Instead of telling someone that you no longer want to be friends, you might defriend that person on Facebook or delete them from Snapchat and hope that he or she "gets the message." People can also use social networking sites to break up with someone (by changing their status) or to announce to their social network that a relationship is over. See Box 15.5 for more on relationship disengagement via social networking sites.

Indirect strategies send neither clear nor kind messages. In Baxter's (1984) study, only 22% of recipients of indirect disengagement messages believed the relationship was over. Worse, relational partners were most likely to express regrets about the relationships when indirect rather than direct disengagement strategies were used (Baxter, 1979b). Baxter (1979b) suggested that "hints" and other indirect breakup strategies may actually create uncertainty, prolong the termination process, and be more painful for the participants.

Individuals can terminate their relationships using a single strategy or a complex array of both direct and indirect strategies. For people like Nick, who are concerned about hurting their partner,

finding a strategy that is both effective and sensitive is challenging. As you read about the strategies in Figure 15.1, you will likely recognize some of them from your own breakups. We do not intend for this section to be a "how-to" guide for breaking up. As the research presented in this chapter shows, breakups can be emotionally distressing and the strategies you use to end a relationship can contribute to distress. We hope, however, that by learning about the ways that people break off relationships you will better understand the disengagement process—and perhaps will be a little more sensitive the next time you find yourself initiating a breakup.

Unilateral and Indirect Strategies

AVOIDANCE The most common, least direct, relational disengagement strategy is avoidance, where people literally "just slip out the back, Jack." Many studies report avoidance as a primary disengagement strategy (Baxter, 1982; Cody, 1982; Emmers & Hart, 1996; Perras & Lustig, 1982), which can range from complete evasion to decreased contact. Baxter (1979a) found decreased frequency of contact with a partner to be one of the two most common indirect disengagement strategies. In Baxter's (1984) study of disengagement accounts, 66% of the couples using indirect strategies used avoidance-based withdrawal strategies. An extreme type of avoidance is called **ghosting**. This occurs when a person simply disappears from someone's life, as if they were never a part of it. Ghosting may be more common today than ever before due to the prevalence of texting and social media. Two people might be snapping, texting, and perhaps hang out a few times, and then one person might stop contact. Snapchats are not opened and texts go answered. There is a lack of closure; the person who was ghosted often wonders what went wrong. Avoidance tactics such as ghosting are most likely when there is little likelihood of being friends in the future, when emotional connection is low, when there are fewer formal ties, when the perceived faults of the partner are high, and when the dumper has an avoidant attachment

BOX 15.5 TECH TALK
UNFRIENDLY DEFRIENDING AND PROFILE PITFALLS

Actions such as defriending someone on Facebook, unfollowing someone on Twitter, or deleting someone from Snapchat are decisions with huge relational consequences. The consequences of blocking someone are even greater. When people get defriended, they are likely to believe the relationship is over (Bevan, Pfyl, & Barclay, 2012). So when you decide to defriend someone, realize that this could trigger the beginning of the end of a relationship.

People are defriended (or worse yet blocked) for a variety of reasons. Some of these reasons have to do with their online behavior, such as posting too much, posting things that are polarizing (such as strong political messages), posting things that are inappropriate, and posting things that are mundane (such as updates about what someone ate or where they are) (Sibona & Walczak, 2011). You may be flooded with too many posts and want to slim down what you are receiving. In these cases, defriending someone may start the process of relational disengagement even though your intention was to manage the communication you were receiving rather than to end the relationship in large part. This is, in part, because the person who was defriended might be rejected or offended. Twitter introduced the "muting" function to help solve this problem. Muting allows you to continue to appear on a person's list of followers without receiving their tweets or retweets.

Other reasons have to do with the relationship outside of social media. For example, you might defriend or block someone after a breakup or after someone engaged in negative behavior toward you (Sibona & Walczak, 2011). You might also defriend or block someone on social media to get back at her or him after a conflict or a breakup. You

might think that this is a way to hurt someone you are mad at. However, this strategy can backfire since the person who was deleted or blocked may then see the relationship as permanently over or feel like they are being manipulated, both of which can make reconciliation less likely. Of course, if a person wants to communicate that a relationship is completely over, defriending or blocking someone can be an effective way to move on. Indeed, seeing an ex on social media sites can cause more hurt and in some cases even keep partners cycling in and out of relationships.

People can also use social networking sites to break up with romantic partners. Changing your Facebook relationship status from "in a relationship" or "engaged" to "single" is a clear (although not very brave) way to end a relationship. Research in this chapter shows that the most successful and sensitive way to end a relationship is with a direct, supportive, face-to-face interaction. Other actions on social media can also disrupt and even terminate close relationships. Facebook users experience numerous relationship status disputes over profile choices that can be very consequential, leading to arguments and even relationship terminations (Papp, Danielewicz, & Cayemberg, 2012). For example, changing your profile picture so that it features you with your friends instead of you with your romantic partner can communicate an intentional or unintentional message. And worse, research shows Internet terminations can lead to stalking, cyberstalking (Fox & Tokunaga, 2015), and even interpersonal violence on rare occasions. So the next time you defriend someone or change your relationship status on a social networking site like Facebook, think about the consequences. In many cases, it is advisable to talk with people face to face before defriending them or breaking up with them in such a public way.

---

style (Banks, Altendorf, Greene, & Cody, 1987; Collins & Gillath, 2012). It may also be easier for the dumper to break up this way since he or she avoids confrontation, but, as mentioned above, the person who was dumped is likely to feel a lack of closure if avoidance is the only breakup strategy used.

The world of social media provides new methods of unilateral and indirect breakups, defriending, and changes in relationships status. Defriending

or removing someone from your list of friends on a social networking site like Facebook may not terminate a relationship altogether, but it is likely to come very close to doing so. Facebook users consider defriending to be a form of relational termination that sparks emotional distress and rumination (Bevan et al., 2012). People can also refuse dates using online communication including avoidance (e.g., not opening a message) and automated

FIGURE 15.1 ■ Disengagement Strategies		
	Unilateral	**Bilateral**
Indirect	• Avoidance • Relational ruses • Withdrawal of support and affection • Pseudo de-escalation • Cost escalation	• Fading away
Direct	• The direct dump • Dating other people • Justification • The relationship-talk trick • Threats and bullying • Positive tone • De-escalation	• The blame game • The negotiated farewell

rejections (e.g., "I'm no longer on the dating scene") (Tong & Walther, 2010a).

Becoming "Facebook official," publicly indicating on a social networking site that a couple is partnered, is an official sign of a committed relationship that leads to increased relational satisfaction (Papp et al., 2012). Changing one's relationship status to single is a termination message.

Not surprisingly, research shows that avoidance is a fairly ineffective way to end a relationship. Both parties experience a loss of face (Metts, 1997) and it is difficult for former relational partners to experience closure. When avoidance strategies are used, "the breakup is particularly dissatisfying for the disengager and the partner," even in short-term or relatively casual relationships (Metts, 1997, p. 387). Several studies have found that avoidance strategies are the least effective, most protracted, and most distressing way to end a relationship (Baxter & Philpott, 1980). Nick's initial use of this strategy may have unwittingly extended the breakup process because Kaley failed to recognize his indirect attempts to end their relationship.

RELATIONAL RUSES Unfortunately, disengagers sometimes use strategies that are downright unethical or manipulative, such as **relational ruses.** In

Baxter's (1982) study, a common indirect communication strategy, labeled *manipulation attempts,* included behaviors such as leaking the impending breakup to a friend or asking a third party to announce the disengagement. Other forms of manipulation include pretending to be interested in someone else and asking friends to persuade the partner to end the relationship first. Manipulation is less likely to be used as a disengagement strategy in close relationships (Baxter, 1982). Research also has shown that relationships that are ended through manipulation are unlikely to evolve into cordial postromantic relationships such as a friendship (Metts, Cupach, & Bejlovich, 1989).

WITHDRAWAL OF SUPPORTIVENESS AND AFFECTION A common disengagement strategy involves withdrawing positive forms of communication such as social support, emotional support, affection, and immediacy. **Social support withdrawal** means the disengager is unavailable to discuss problems or provide comfort and compassion. One study reported that the withdrawal of social support was the most common relationship disengagement strategy in relationships of less than 2 years (Baxter, 1979b). As noted in Chapter 7, social support is an important part of close relationships. We expect our friends and loved ones to be there when we need them. If they are unavailable or make no effort to help us, they send an indirect but clear message that they do not value the relationship. Likewise, people expect their close friends and romantic partners to provide us with positive, affectionate communication. During relational disengagement, nonverbal communication becomes less warm, involving, and immediate (Wilmot et al., 1985). In healthy interpersonal relationships, relational partners touch, engage in eye contact, employ positive facial expressions, and maintain close interpersonal distances (see Chapter 7). Conversely, a lack of these behaviors provides a powerful, implicit message that psychological distance is widening. Increasingly nonimmediate behavior is a virtually certain sign of relational distress and movement toward disengagement. Unfortunately, Kaley did not see these signs and was surprised at what she considered the "suddenness" of the breakup with Nick.

PSEUDO DE-ESCALATION This strategy is a false declaration to the other party that the relationship would profit from some distance that masquerades as **de-escalation** but is usually a disguised relational breakup (Baxter, 1985). A person might say, "Let's just put a little space into the relationship" or, "Let's just be friends for a while" when the person really means, "This relationship is over." The intent is often to let the other party down easily. Though this strategy may be more humane than the relational ruses that were previously described, **pseudo de-escalation** is essentially a deceptive, unethical behavior that shows little regard for one's partner. Baxter (1984) found this strategy comprised 22% of indirect breakup strategies, but pseudo de-escalation was highly ineffective since only 9% of the receivers of such a message got the clue that the relationship was actually over. The rest of the participants harbored false hope that the relationship would eventually be revitalized.

COST ESCALATION Also called Machiavellianism strategies (Baxter, 1979c; Perras & Lustig, 1982), **cost escalation** (Baxter, 1984; Emmers & Hart,

1996; Thieme & Rouse, 1991) is an attempt to make the relationship unattractive to one's partner. Disengagers may drink or smoke excessively or be deliberately messy, obnoxious, rude, argumentative, demeaning, or disloyal so that the partner comes to dislike the disengager and becomes more amenable to a breakup. In one account of a breakup, the "dumper" stated: "I thought I would be an 'asshole' for a while to make her like me less" (Baxter, 1985, p. 249). In another study, cost escalation was the most commonly used disengagement strategy, employed by 31% of the respondents (Thieme & Rouse, 1991). But in Baxter's (1984) study, cost escalation was employed by only 12% of the couples using indirect strategies. Ironically, cost escalation can be beneficial in some breakups, especially if the "dumpee" is happy to break off the relationship after the costs have been escalated.

Unilateral and Direct Strategies

THE DIRECT DUMP The most common direct communication strategy is the simple statement that the relationship is over (Baxter, 1984; Dailey, Pfiester, et al., 2009; Thieme & Rouse, 1991). This strategy is sometimes called the open-and-honest approach, where people forthrightly communicate their desire to end the relationship (Baxter, 1982; Perras & Lustig, 1982). It has also been called the **fait accompli approach** (Baxter, 1979b, 1984) since this tactic gives the partner no choice or chance for a response. Research has found that texting a direct dump to a partner is considered the least compassionate and fortunately the least likely way to way to break off a relationship directly (Sprecher, Zimmerman, & Abrahams, 2010).

Often this strategy emphasizes the negative consequences of not breaking up, which helps the partner accept the breakup. Baxter (1984) reported that fait accompli resulted in 81% of the receivers of such messages accepting the breakup and offering no resistance, probably because of the perceived futility of countering such a direct message. It is very disconcerting to receive the direct dump—to suddenly be told that the relationship is over. This is

Breaking up with someone via computer-mediated communication—such as texting that you want to breakup, changing your relationship status on Facebook, or blocking your partner on social media or Snapchat—is usually particularly hurtful. Communicating face-to-face shows more respect, gives both people more closure, and keeps the door open for staying friends.

what Kaley perceived to have happened, when actually Nick had been trying to signal that he wanted to break up. As the scenario between Kaley and Nick illustrates, people sometimes use the direct dump after other subtler strategies have failed.

DATING OTHER PEOPLE Sometimes, rather than break up completely, a disengager recommends dating other people. This strategy, which is sometimes called **negative identity management** (Banks et al., 1987; Cody, 1982; Metts, 1997), imposes one person's solution on the other person at the expense of the recipient's feelings. For example, the person initiating the breakup might say, "I told him that I was going to date other people and that he should also date other people." By using this strategy, the dumper at least communicates directly to the partner. However, although this strategy is direct, its underlying meaning is unclear. Sometimes dating other people represents a temporary hiatus from an intense, intimate relationship that will rekindle.

Often, however, this announcement is a disengagement message.

JUSTIFICATION This common strategy includes explanations for why the relationship is ending, why the partner is dissatisfied, or for changes that have occurred in the partners or in the relationship (Banks et al., 1987; Cody, 1982; Dailey, Pfiester, et al., 2009). Unlike the direct dump, justification recognizes the need to provide a reason for the breakup to one's partner. It attempts to save face for both partners. This strategy is often used in highly intimate and committed relationships where friendship networks of the partners overlap (Banks et al., 1987).

Research shows that justifications enable the rejected person to accept the relationship's end. Thieme and Rouse (1991) found a significant association between the number of reasons given for a breakup and the rebuffed person's acceptance that the relationship is over. Of course, if the justification focuses on the rejected individual's faults, then hurt feelings and lowered self-esteem will follow. But when justifications focus on the initiator of the breakup and general relationship issues, more positive outcomes are likely.

One common type of justification in dating relationships revolves around desire for autonomy. Sometimes people feel too dependent on each other and they feel a loss of independence and individuality. As a result, they de-escalate or disengage using a strategy Cody (1982) called relationship faults or **appeals to independence.** Young lovers often provide a rationale focused on independence because they are unsure they are ready to settle down with one person. Partners may also point to external factors, such as needing to concentrate more on school or one's career, as reasons for decreasing interdependence. This strategy is often less threatening than others because it centers on the needs of the breakup initiator (for more space or freedom) or external events (e.g., school, work) rather than on faults of the person who is being dumped. Often the reason for leaving the relationship is framed in situational terms—"At this point in my life, I'm not ready to settle down yet" or "Right now I have time only for school."

THE RELATIONSHIP-TALK TRICK Some disengagers talk about relationship "problems" as a guise for a relationship breakup. Baxter (1984) reported this strategy was used in 27% of direct breakups. This strategy is rarely an honest attempt to discuss and solve problems in the relationship. More often it is an insincere attempt to talk about the relationship in a way that leads to the conclusion that the problems are insurmountable and that a breakup is imminent. In other words, the breakup initiator intentionally structures the relational talk to show that the partners are better off going their separate ways. Like cost escalation, this strategy can be hurtful in some instances but beneficial in others. If the person initiating the breakup convinces her or his partner that the relationship is not worth saving, both partners can walk away feeling that although they tried, the relationship just could not be saved.

THREATS AND BULLYING Another direct, unilateral strategy involves threatening the partner. Baxter (1984) defined threats and bullying as manipulation attempts to get a partner to break up. Sometimes people use these strategies when a partner refuses to accept the breakup. For example, if a wife wants a divorce and her husband stubbornly refuses, she might threaten to take the children out of state if he doesn't comply with her wishes. Sometimes threats are part of the fabric of the breakup itself; people may tell their soon-to-be former partner not to divulge information about them or the breakup—and threaten to get revenge if they do. Obviously, these types of breakup strategies are very destructive. Threats and bullying can make the "dumped" person feel powerless at a time when the individual's self-esteem is likely to be fragile. These types of strategies are also likely to destroy any chances a couple has to reconcile or remain friends following the breakup.

POSITIVE TONE Sometimes unilateral breakups are accomplished using a **positive-tone strategy** that is designed to lessen the "dumped" person's hurt feelings and make him or her feel better about the breakup (Banks et al., 1987; Baxter, 1982; Cody, 1982; Perras & Lustig, 1982). For instance, Nick could have told Kaley that even though their relationship is over, he has no regrets about the time he spent with her. He might also have appealed to fatalism by saying things such as "It's nobody's fault. It just wasn't meant to be." Other times, the fairness approach is adopted. Nick might have said something like the following: "If I stayed in this relationship, it wouldn't be fair to you. You deserve someone who loves you the way you deserve to be loved." Apologies and compliments can also be part of a positive-tone strategy. Nick might tell Kaley that he is sorry and doesn't want to hurt her, but his heart isn't in the relationship anymore. He might also tell her that he still thinks she is a beautiful and intelligent woman and wishes that it could have worked out. Like some of the indirect strategies discussed earlier, one danger of using the positive-tone strategy is that the person being dumped may hold onto hope that the relationship might somehow survive—or at least rebound. Thus, it is important to emphasize that the breakup is impending for this strategy to be both effective and sensitive.

DE-ESCALATION De-escalation strategies avoid a complete breakup, at least initially, by scaling back a relationship or taking a break to figure things out. Thus, this strategy can result in a break rather than a breakup, and is fairly common in on-again off-again relationships (Dailey, Pfiester, et al., 2009). Unlike pseudo de-escalation, these strategies are an honest attempt to improve the relationship by de-escalating it (Banks et al., 1987; Cody, 1982). Usually the de-escalator recommends relational separation temporarily or recommends that "we just be friends" (Cody, 1982)—a strategy most people, especially men, hate to hear (Hill et al., 1976). Other options include trial separation, moving out of the same living space, or spending less time together. Recent research found that a person who has an anxious attachment style is likely to use a strategy that keeps open the option of getting back together (Collins & Gilath, 2012). Sometimes people think if they spend time apart, they will appreciate each other more. Other times, they think they might get along if they didn't live together. De-escalation provides a new beginning for some relationships as couples transition from romantic partners to friends or from cohabitating to dating, but research suggests de-escalation is usually a giant step along the path of complete disengagement. Indeed, research suggests that most married couples who legally separate end up getting divorced.

Bilateral and Indirect Strategy

FADING AWAY In Baxter's research, only one strategy emerged as both bilateral and indirect, called **fading away.** Sometimes both people in a relationship recognize that the relationship is at a standstill, and they gradually drift apart and lose contact. This is common in the case of friends who lose touch over the years (Baxter, 1979b) and when relational partners are separated from each other for long stretches of time. In long-distance relationships, people sometimes come to feel like strangers due to the limited contact they have with one another. Words may not be necessary to end the relationship; instead, the couple may simply sense that it is over. For example, one of our students told the following story of her relational breakup:

> We only saw each other a couple times since moving away from our hometown to attend different colleges. At first, we called each other frequently, but over time the calls slowed down, and we seemed to have less and less to say to each other. After spending some awkward time together during Thanksgiving weekend, he drove me to the airport. When I left to board the plane, we hugged briefly, and it was clear that the relationship was not the same—it was over.

In some ways, fading away is the antithesis of catastrophic breakups. Fading away has no dramatic incident preceding the breakup but rather a slow and gradual descent.

Bilateral and Direct Strategies

THE BLAME GAME Sometimes dissatisfaction leads to a competitive blame game that eventually results in a breakup. Cycles of negativity become a prevalent pattern; both partners become dissatisfied, and the relationship is charged with negative emotion. When partners talk about their problems, they end up complaining and blaming each other rather than taking responsibility. Eventually, when they agree to break up, they argue over the reasons and blame each other for the relationship's demise (Cody, 1982; Dailey, Rossetto, et al., 2009). Both partners may claim that the impending breakup is the other's fault, and both may feel justified in ending the relationship. In fact, partners use blaming so that leaving the relationship is an option that helps them both save face. This strategy can be beneficial in that it provides both partners with a reason to exit the relationship. However, breakups of this kind are messy, since conflict and disagreement are likely to prevail to the bitter end.

THE NEGOTIATED FAREWELL A common method of relational disengagement, especially for long-term couples, uses problem-solving and negotiation (Dailey, Rossetto, et al., 2009; Emmers & Hart, 1996; Metts, 1997; Sprecher et al., 2010). Some couples may also need to divide up possessions, negotiate child custody and financial issues, and determine how they can both live within a joint social network. The key to the negotiated farewell is that both parties are willing to try to be fair to each other during the disengagement process (in direct contrast to the attitude of those playing the blame game). The goal of the negotiated farewell is to leave the relationship "well" rather than on a sour note. Relational partners report that talking through a breakup is the most commonly used strategy (Sprecher et al., 2010). This strategy is most often used when there are high levels of relational intimacy and commitment, and the partners' interpersonal networks are overlapping (Baxter, 1982; Cody, 1982). When negotiating the breakup, couples using this strategy may also use the positive-tone strategy we discussed earlier. Not surprisingly, this is one of the least distressing ways to end a relationship.

OUTCOMES: THE RESULTS OF RELATIONSHIP ENDINGS

Losing a relational partner is devastating. During the breakup, the world can look bleak and hopeless—especially if you did not initiate it. While the experience is often negative, most people move on with their lives and eventually find some positive outcomes associated with the loss.

Negative Outcomes of Relational Breakups

Most relational breakups are characterized by distress, and immediate reactions to breakups are negative. Partners often feel that the world is about to end, and long-term negative consequences may persist.

NEGATIVE EMOTIONS A common result of relational breakups is the presence of negative emotions. Breakups are one of the most distressing, traumatic events we experience, particularly for the unwilling partner in the breakup. As Duck (1988) stated, "There is very little pain on earth like the pain of a long-term personal relationship that is falling apart" (p. 102). Studies have shown that depression, anger, hurt, guilt, confusion, and frustration are common feelings during a relational breakup. In one-sided breakups, most partners experience negative emotions, regardless of whether they initiated the breakup or whether they are female or male (Boelen & Reijntjes, 2009; Hebert & Popadiuk, 2008; Kurdek, 1991; Park, Sanchez, & Brynildsen, 2011; Simpson, 1987; Wang et al., 2015; Wilmot et al., 1985). In Owen's (1993) study of relationship accounts, respondents described breakups as emotional injuries: "He left a huge hole in my heart," "My heart felt like a dart board," and "I was torn to shreds." Contrary to intuition, some early research found that men experience more initial distress than women after an unwanted breakup (Hill et al., 1976). This is not to minimize women's distress after breakups. Studies have found *both* sexes experience

emotional distress following unwanted breakups (Metts et al., 1989; Perilloux & Buss, 2008; Wilmot et al., 1985). Indeed, women who were rejected experienced more sadness, confusion, and fear than men who were rejected (Perilloux & Buss, 2008; Wrape, Jenkins, Callahan, & Nowlin, 2016). Nonetheless, breakups are one of life's most traumatic experiences for men and women alike.

Several factors predict how much distress people experience after a relational breakup. Social support from friends and economic resources can cushion the distress (Moller, Fouladi, McCarthy, & Hatch, 2003; Vangelisti, 2002; Yildirim & Dimir, 2015). But continued connection and attachment to one's ex-partner is associated with less emotional adjustment and more distress (Fagundes, 2012). People are more depressed by a breakup when their love for their partner was deep, when they were highly committed to the relationship, when their partner was physically attractive, when they didn't want the relationship to end, when their partner did want the relationship to end, and when they brood or ruminate excessively about what went wrong in the relationship (Fagundes, 2012; Saffrey & Ehrenberg, 2007; Sprecher, Felmlee, Metts, Fehr, & Vanni, 1998). Negative thoughts about the breakup, particularly self-blame, are highly associated with grief, depression, and anxiety following a breakup (Boelen & Reijntjes, 2009). In fact, both positive and negative thought about one's ex-partner may increase distress (Brenner & Vogel, 2015) since positive thoughts may make people long for the past relationship. Certainly knowing the reason for the breakup eased the breakup adjustment (Yildirim & Dimir, 2015). People who felt emotionally close to their ex-partner, had high relational satisfaction, were in the relationship for a long time, and had little control over the breakup also tend to experience high levels of distress (Frazier & Cook, 1993; Simpson, 1987; Sprecher et al., 1998). Following a breakup people find it much more difficult to pursue their personal goals (Gomillion, Murray, & Lamarche, 2015). Chapter 2 illustrated how relationships create self-expansion; during breakups, individuals who experienced the greatest self-expansion as a result of their relationship suffered the greatest contraction, loss of possibilities, and reduced self-esteem during a breakup (Lewandowski et al., 2006). People who define their self-worth in terms of their relationship suffer the most emotional distress and are most likely to engage in obsessive pursuit of their former partner (Park et al., 2011; see Chapter 13 for a discussion of obsessive relational behavior).

While distress typically is greater for the victim of an unwanted breakup (Perilloux & Buss, 2008; Yildirim & Dimir, 2015), the emotional distress experienced by the initiator of the breakup should not be underestimated. Like Nick, many people feel badly about having to initiate a breakup. Initiators may feel guilt, shame, embarrassment, stress, loss of positive reputation, and ambivalence about the breakup. Also, they may repeatedly be reminded of the breakup by their social network and may have to provide accounts and justifications for their actions.

LONELINESS The loss of a relationship often produces intense feelings of loneliness. In gay and lesbian relationships, Kurdek (1991) found loneliness was the second most common emotional reaction following a breakup. Moreover, a breakup is a double whammy: Not only have the partners lost the most important person in their lives but they lost the person they would usually turn to for comfort following such a loss. It is natural for people to feel lonely after a relationship breakup. According to Segrin (1998), loneliness is the result of a discrepancy between one's actual and desired level of social interaction. When an intimate relationship ends, this discrepancy increases. Suddenly there is a wider gap between how much intimacy someone wants and how much intimacy the person receives. But individuals are likely to feel less loneliness after a breakup if they are surrounded by friends and family members who care about them (Segrin, 1998).

Interestingly, loneliness can also be a motivation for breaking off a relationship. As discussed previously, people sometimes initiate breakups because they are dissatisfied or bored with their relationships. They long for the connection that they felt early in their relationships when they were first getting to know each other and everything was exciting and new. Breaking up an old relationship and searching for a new one that better fulfills one's needs is often an impetus for breakup. Indeed, one reason for divorce is the hope of finding a happier relationship, and most divorced people do remarry. Unfortunately, a divorce is even more likely in a second marriage than a first (Argyle & Henderson, 1988).

FINANCIAL CONSEQUENCES Divorce or separation is commonly a financial disaster. The costs of maintaining dual residences, paying lawyers, selling a home quickly, to mention but a few problems, makes divorce one of the worst things a person can experience financially. Single moms and "deadbeat dads" are a major source of poverty in this country. Also, men who pay alimony and child support often feel financially strapped (Hendrick & Hendrick, 1992); it is difficult to start a new family with financial burdens of one's old family still on one's shoulders.

Unfortunately, one factor keeping many long-term partners in negative and even abusive relationships is financial dependency. Like married couples, Kurdek (1991) found that one of the problems facing gay and lesbian couples after a breakup involved finances. Cohabiters, regardless of their sexual orientation, are particularly likely to experience financial difficulties as they move out of each other's homes and lives. Like emotional dependency, financial dependency often traps people in unhealthy relationships.

EFFECTS ON CHILDREN What effect does a breakup have on the children of a divorcing couple? Sadly, children seem to fare worse in divorced families than in families in which their parents were continuously and happily married. Amato and Keith (1991) published a statistical summary of prior research on the effects of parental divorce on children's well-being as adults. Based on information from 81,000 people, they reported that divorce is generally associated with a host of negative consequences. Adults from divorced homes are more likely to be depressed; less satisfied with life; less likely to have satisfying relationships; more likely to get divorced themselves; and more likely to have lower socioeconomic status, less income, and poorer physical health than adults from nondivorced families. The authors concluded the following: "These results lead to a pessimistic conclusion: the argument that parental divorce presents few problems for children's long-term development is simply inconsistent with the literature on this topic" (Amato & Keith, 1991, p. 54). Even worse news is that these negative effects are consistent across dozens of studies. The good news, though, is that the effects tend to be small, and when both parents maintain positive relationships with their children, the effects are smaller still. There is some evidence that boys cope better if they live with their father and that girls cope better if they live with their mother (see Hendrick & Hendrick, 1992). Additionally, recent research suggests that in divorced families, siblings support one another, providing children with increased resilience to weather stressful breakups (Jacobs & Sillars, 2012). Children of divorced couples are more likely to be sexually active and irresponsible than children of married parents (Orgilés, Espada, Johnson, Huedo-Medina, & Carratalá, 2012). Despite these gloomy findings, research suggests that it is often better for a child to suffer through a divorce than to live with parents who are constantly fighting (Booth & Edwards, 1989; see also Chapter 11).

Research has also supported the **intergenerational transmission of divorce,** the fact that children of divorced parents are about one to two times more likely to get divorced than children of nondivorced couples (Gahler, Hong, & Bernhardt, 2009; Segrin, Taylor, & Altman, 2005; Wolfinger, 1999). Segrin and his colleagues (2005) summarized some of the reasons why this occurs. First, children of divorced parents may have negative attitudes toward commitment and marriage; they may learn that "marriage is a miserable experience, and . . . therefore

avoid the behavior" (p. 362). Second, children of divorced parents are likely to have witnessed negative, dysfunctional conflict, which adds to the perception of marriage as a stressful experience. Third, some research suggests that couples who divorce are less likely to have effective communication skills than couples who stay together. Certainly this is not always the case—some couples are communicatively competent and simply realize they are not compatible. Nonetheless, children of divorced parents may fail to learn skills related to successful marital communication, making them more susceptible to divorce and other failed relationships. All three of these explanations—(1) negative marital attitudes, (2) dysfunctional parental conflict, and (3) lack of communication skills—have been shown by researchers to relate to the intergenerational transmission of divorce; the study by Segrin and his colleagues suggests that negative attitudes toward marriage and commitment may be the most important.

Research also suggests that "feeling caught" between one's parents leads to negative outcomes such as anxiety and depression (Buchanan, Maccoby, & Dornbusch, 1991, 1996). As Afifi and Schrodt (2003) explained, "Children who feel caught between their parents often describe themselves as being 'put in the middle,' 'torn,' or forced to defend their loyalty to each of their parents" (p. 142). Children are more likely to feel caught in the middle when their parents argue in front of them and disclose negative information about one another. When children feel caught in the middle between divorced parents, they are likely to avoid talking about the state of their family in front of their parents (Golish & Caughlin, 2002), presumably because they do not want to start conflict or appear to be supporting one parent over the other. Children who feel caught in the middle report less satisfaction and closeness in their relationships with their parents (e.g., Afifi & Schrodt, 2003). These findings suggest that it is critical for parents to avoid having their children take sides. Parents who talk to and about one another in a respectful, positive manner are likely to foster a postdivorce environment that is more comfortable for themselves and their children.

HEALTH CONSEQUENCES Studies have shown that separation and divorce threaten people's health. Divorced people have a higher incidence of heart problems, cancer, liver disease, pneumonia, and a host of other diseases (Argyle & Henderson, 1988). Divorce has also been linked to a variety of emotional and physical disorders, psychiatric illness, suicide, excessive drinking, weight gain, and interpersonal violence (Hendrick & Hendrick, 1992; Wang et al., 2015). The breakup of dating relationships can also lead to psychological stress. Monroe, Rohde, Seeley, and Lewinsohn (1999) found that relational breakups were predictive of the onset of a major depressive disorder during adolescence. Najib, Lorberbaum, Kose, Bohning, and George (2004) documented changes in brain activity after a romantic relationship breakup consistent with the pattern associated with chronic depression. Similarly, the death of a partner can affect the grieving person's physical health. When people are depressed, stressed, or grieving, their bodies may be more susceptible to physical ailments, such as ulcers, heart problems, and even the common cold.

Healing After a Separation

Because relationship loss can be personally devastating, it is important to understand what factors influence recovery from the distress, loneliness, and depression that often accompanies a breakup. Mutually negotiated breakups, goodwill toward one's ex, and disclosive communication among ex-partners result in the fewest bad feelings (Lambert & Hughes, 2010; Wilmot et al., 1985) and generally are the easiest from which to recover. Men and women employ similar strategies after they are dumped, including discussions about the breakup, crying, pleading with the ex-partner, and avoiding the ex-partner; the only sex difference is that women tend to go shopping more than men during their recovery (Perilloux & Buss, 2008). Recovery from a unilateral breakup is difficult or impossible

when one person wants the relationship to continue (Frazier & Cook, 1993). Being asked by an ex-partner to be a friend on Facebook and accepting it is associated with increased anxiety and depression, especially for men (Tsai, Shen, & Chiang, 2015). So, if a relationship is really over, it is important to stop dwelling on it and to move on with one's life. Of course, this is more easily said than done. Counterintuitively, one recent study found that people with a secure attachment style had the *most* difficulty with their postdivorce relationships, probably because the experience violated the generally positive predispositions of securely attached people (Lambert & Hughes, 2010). Research has found that the most anxiously attached and insecure people, who have difficulty detaching from a former relationship, may benefit from the prospect of dating a new partner (Speilmann, McDonald, & Wilson, 2009). For these individuals, dating someone on the rebound can substantially promote recovery following a breakup. Several recent studies (Brumbaugh & Fraley, 2015; Yildirim & Dimir, 2015) found that people who rebounded into a new relationship after a romantic breakup had greater personal adjustment, more confidence in their desirability, and more resolution over their relationship with their ex-partner; moreover, the quicker they began new relationships, the greater their psychological and relational health.

Studies suggest that breakups are more protracted and distressing when indirect termination strategies are employed (Baxter & Philpott, 1980). Lack of closure about a relational termination is associated with poorer recovery, more preoccupation with the relationship, and more relational regret (Saffrey & Ehrenberg, 2007). Positively toned communication leads to a less satisfying postdivorce relationship since it may send out mixed signals regarding if the relationship is really over (Lambert & Hughes, 2010). It is more humane and honest to tell someone, in direct and positive terms, that the relationship is over, as Nick eventually did. Only then can the recovery process begin. Research suggests that disclosing one's feelings to others, or even writing about them, is a therapeutic activity that can aid recovery from a breakup (Lepore & Greenberg, 2002; Pennebaker, 1990; Slotter & Ward, 2015). Therefore, Kaley is taking a step in the right direction by shopping with Aaliyah while they discuss her core feelings about the breakup.

Positive Outcomes of Relational Breakups

Despite the trauma associated with breakups, it is not unusual for one or both partners to actually have positive feelings about a separation (Wilmot et al., 1985). One of the most common outcomes in Kurdek's (1991) study of gay and lesbian relationships was increased happiness following the breakup. Indeed, it is often a relief to be out of a bad or dangerous relationship. Sometimes a breakup can provide relief from relational ambiguity or conflict. Not infrequently, a person moves on to a more satisfying relationship following a breakup. Kurdek (1991) found that relief from conflict was one of the most common outcomes of separation in gay and lesbian relationships. In addition, Kurdek found that personal growth was the most commonly cited positive outcome of relational breakups. Of course, some relationships continue to be problematic after the breakup, especially if one person cannot let go. For example, in our opening scenario, Kaley leaves pleading messages on Nick's answering machine. Such messages are highly unlikely to change the situation. Instead, they make Nick feel guiltier and Kaley feel even worse about herself.

One positive outcome of relationship breakups is personal growth that can occur in the relationship's aftermath (Hebert & Popadiuk, 2008; Tashiro & Frazier, 2003). Several kinds of postrelational growth include personal positives, such as increased self-confidence and being able to handle life on one's own; relational positives, such as having learned how to communicate in a relationship and the importance of not jumping into a relationship too quickly; environmental positives, such as concentrating more on school or work or relying on friendship networks more; and future positives, such as knowing what one wants in a relational partner (Tashiro & Frazier, 2003). Eventually, Kaley may experience some of these benefits following her breakup. She may learn that she can cope temporarily without a romantic partner, and perhaps she'll devote more time to other activities that she finds personally rewarding.

Ending any relationship—especially a bad relationship—also represents an opportunity to form a new relationship. But many people make the mistake of leaping head first into a new relationship, which can land them in another relationship destined to fail. Thus, rapid expressions of love and affection in a new relationship are often a turnoff because people doubt whether someone can already like them that much (Sternberg, 1987) and suspect that they are just being used to recover from the loss. New relationships, then, should evolve slowly and naturally.

SUMMARY AND APPLICATION

Relationships end for many reasons. Sometimes people consciously choose to take their lives in a new direction. Other times relationships wither away, partners physically separate due to school or careers, or death occurs. In each case, coping with the loss of a significant relationship is difficult. Both Kaley and Nick feel badly that their relationship has ended. Nick is likely to feel guilty since he initiated the breakup, but he may also feel relief because Kaley finally got the message that the

relationship is over. Kaley will likely have a more difficult time, partly because the breakup seemed sudden to her. Seeking social support from friends like Aaliyah is a first step toward understanding the breakup and moving forward.

Understanding why a breakup occurred can also be helpful. Researchers have identified specific reasons for relationship breakups. Often, communication is the culprit. Avoidance, negative communication, and lack of openness are common communication problems that cause breakups. Gottman's research shows that stonewalling (or avoidance) is a strong harbinger of divorce. Kaley or Nick may have noticed some of these communication patterns in their relationship. If they had worked on their communication, it is possible (although not certain) that their relationship could have improved. Dissimilarity and sexual incompatibility can also precipitate relational breakups, as can financial issues, inequity, disillusionment, and alcohol or drug abuse. The most common reason for the termination of dating relationships is boredom. People simply miss the excitement that once was present in their relationships but that somehow dimmed over time. Sometimes this boredom leads people to look elsewhere and to develop an interest in alternative partners. Still others feel smothered by their relationships and break up to achieve autonomy and independence.

Regardless of why a relationship ends, research has shown that people often experience a host of negative outcomes following relational termination, including emotional, physical, and financial distress. If the person did not want the relationship to end, the individual might feel rejected and fearful of starting a new relationship. The person who initiated the relational breakup often feels guilt. The strategy people use to end their relationships can make a difference. Direct strategies are usually preferred, especially if they include positive communication. Thus, the best way for Nick to break up may have been to use the positive-tone strategy. He could have told Kaley that their relationship meant a lot to him, complimented her, and told her how sorry he was that it wasn't going to work out. Of course, for this strategy to be effective, Nick would need to communicate his desire to break off the relationship—despite his positive regard for her—very clearly. Direct, definitive statements delivered with a positive tone may be the best strategy when breakups are unilateral. The negotiated farewell is the optimal strategy when breakups are bilateral. Such strategies allow a person to get over the breakup more quickly, which opens up the possibility of finding new partners and exploring uncharted relational territory.

KEY TERMS

appeals to independence (p. 426)

catastrophe theory (p. 418)

chronic dissatisfaction (p. 413)

cost escalation (p. 425)

de-escalation (p. 425)

dyadic processes phase (p. 419)

fading away (p. 428)

fait accompli approach (p. 425)

ghosting (p. 422)

grave-dressing processes phase (p. 420)

intergenerational transmission of divorce (p. 431)

intrapsychic processes phase (p. 419)

negative identity management (p. 426)

physical abuse (p. 417)

positive-tone strategy (p. 427)

pseudo de-escalation (p. 425)

psychological abuse (p. 408)

relational ruses (p. 424)

relationship disillusionment (p. 413)

resurrection processes phase (p. 420)

social processes phase (p. 419)

social support withdrawal (p. 424)

DISCUSSION QUESTIONS

1. How does computer-mediated communication—such as texting, Snapchat, and social media platforms like Facebook, Twitter, and Instagram—influence the process of breaking up with someone? Based on your experiences and those of your friends, what do you see as the advantages and disadvantages of (a) breaking up with someone using computer-mediated communication, and (b) deleting or blocking someone from your social media after a breakup?

2. Of the 15 specific breakup strategies mentioned in this chapter, which do you think are the least pleasant or ethical, and why? Describe the most positive way that you think someone can initiate a unilateral breakup.

3. How might you help a friend get over a relationship breakup?

 SAGE edge™

Sharpen your skills with SAGE edge at edge.sagepub.com/guerrero5e.
SAGE edge for students provides a personalized approach to help you accomplish your coursework goals in an easy-to-use learning environment.

GLOSSARY

- **Accidental communication:** Occurs when a message is unintentionally sent but the receiver nonetheless observes the behavior and interprets it correctly.

- **Accommodation principle:** Occurs when people are able to overcome the initial tendency to retaliate in response to negative behavior and instead engage in cooperative communication to maintain their relationship.

- **Acquiescent responses:** Responses that involve giving in, and acknowledging that the partner hurt you.

- **Active verbal responses:** Responses that focus on confronting the partner about her or his hurtful remarks; they can be positive or negative.

- **Affection exchange theory:** A theory that is based on the idea that affectionate communication is a biologically adaptive behavior that evolved because it helps people provide and obtain valuable resources necessary for survival.

- **Affectionate communication:** Behavior that portrays feelings of fondness and positive regard for another.

- **Affection-instrumentality:** The tension between focusing more on feelings of warmth or on functional tasks.

- **Affinity-seeking behavior:** Actions designed to attract or be liked by other people.

- **Agape:** One of Lee's secondary love styles. Based on a combination of eros and storge, it involves having a compassionate style of love that revolves around caring, concern, and tenderness, and is more focused on giving than receiving.

- **Agency:** An empowering aspect of experience where a person is able to freely control the surrounding environment, including social interactions and relationships.

- **Agentic friendships:** Friendship that focuses mostly on companionship and shared activities (especially applicable to male friendships).

- **Ambiguous communication:** The use of indirect strategies that may hold multiple meanings.

- **Androgynous:** Displaying a mix of feminine and masculine behaviors and beliefs.

- **Antagonistic strategies:** Actions that attempt to blame, hurt, insult, or berate others.

- **Antisocial acts, as a sexual initiation strategy:** Tactics such as intentionally trying to make the partner jealous, pouting, holding a grudge, and/or sexually harassing someone.

- **Antisocial communication:** Communication that is hostile or disruptive to a relationship.

- **Anxious-ambivalent attachment style:** A social interaction style where someone tends to be overinvolved, demanding, and dependent on their partner; someone who uses this style tends to value relational closeness over autonomy.

- **Appeals to independence:** Efforts to de-escalate or disengage from the relationship. They typically occur when people feel they are losing independence and individuality.

- **Argumentativeness:** A style that focuses on logical argument and reasoning. People with argumentative styles confront conflict directly by recognizing issues of disagreement, taking positions on controversial issues, backing up claims with evidence and reasoning, and refuting views contrary to their own.

- **Assertive responses:** Empowered communication that exerts control over a situation in an effective and appropriate manner.

- **Assimilation effect:** The idea that people benefit (gain attention) from being around physically attractive others.

- **Assurances:** A maintenance behavior that involves making statements that show commitment to the relationship, such as talking about the partners' future together.

- **Attachment styles:** Social interaction styles that reflect the kind of bond an individual has with someone, based on how positively or negatively individuals view themselves and others.

- **Attachment theory:** A social-developmental approach that helps account for how interactions between children and their caregivers initially shape people's attachment styles and, as a result, how they communicate in relationships across the life span.

- **Attempted communication:** When someone sends an intentional message that the intended receiver fails to receive.

- **Attention stage:** The first stage of the courtship process. Involves getting someone's attention, often by using shy and ambiguous behavior, such as fleeting eye contact and tentative smiling.

- **Attractiveness deception:** A form of online identity enhancement where people lie about their physical characteristics to seem more attractive.

- **Attribution:** A perceptual process of assigning reasons or causes to one's own behavior or that of others.

- **Attribution hypothesis:** According to this hypothesis, people in happy relationships tend to make relationship-enhancing attributions, whereas people in unhappy relationships tend to make distress-maintaining attributions.

- **Authoritarian parents:** Demanding, directive, controlling, and nonresponsive parents.

- **Authoritative parents:** Demanding, directive, and responsive parents.

- **Authorized co-owners:** Also called *boundary insiders*, these are people who we share private information with under the assumption that they will keep the information private unless we grant them permission to do otherwise.

- **Aversive stimulation:** Also called *negative affect strategy*, involves whining, pouting, sulking, complaining, crying, or acting angry to get one's way.

- **Avoidance:** A strategy intended to distance oneself from someone or not engage in a particular topic. Examples include intentionally choosing not to bring up a particular topic, physically withdrawing from someone, giving someone the silent treatment, ignoring someone, or limiting communication with someone.

- **Avoidant attachment style:** A social interaction style where the person is uncomfortable getting close to or depending on others. Children with avoidant attachment styles engage in limited social interaction. Adults with avoidant attachment styles value autonomy over relational closeness.

- **Avoidants:** See *avoidant attachment style.*

- **Avoiding:** An indirect conflict style that is neither inherently cooperative nor inherently uncooperative, and involves tactics such as avoiding a topic, changing the subject, or agreeing to disagree.

- **Bald on-record strategy:** Communication strategy that involves primary attention to task through direct communication, with little or no attention to helping the partner save face.

- **Bargaining strategy:** Agreeing to do something for someone if the person does something in return.

- **Behavioral control:** Exerting one's power in an interpersonal relationship. It is also a strategy whereby people try to control their nervous or guilty behaviors to appear friendly and truthful.

- **Behavioral familiarity:** Having knowledge of the partner's typical communication style.

- **Behavioral interdependence:** One person's behavior affects another person's behavior, beliefs, or emotions, and vice versa. The basic requirement for all relationships.

- **Body synchrony:** High levels of coordinated movement between close friends or intimate couples.

- **Boomerang effects:** When persuasion attempts backfire, resulting in receivers changing their attitude or behavior in the opposite direction from what the persuader intended.

- **Boundary structures:** Rules that guide who has access to and can share private information.

- **Boundary turbulence:** Occurs when information that was intended to be private goes public so that old boundary structures need to be fortified or renegotiated.

- **Breadth:** The number of topics about which people feel free to disclose.

- **Broadcasters:** When referring to how people communicate via social networking sites, this term refers to people who primarily use sites such as Facebook and Twitter to send one-to-many messages (or announcements) rather than using these sites to interact with others in a back-and-forth fashion.

- **Bullying:** Blaming, hurting, insulting, ridiculing, or berating another person.

- **Button pushing:** Purposely saying or doing something you know will be especially hurtful or upsetting to a friend or partner.

- **Capitalized on transition, as a type of on-again off-again relationship:** Couples in on-again off-again relationships who get back together after doing things to improve their relationship, such as reflecting about problems, sorting out feelings, improving themselves, or getting the partner to change.

- **Catastrophe theory:** An alternative to the stage models of relational disengagement that suggests that some relationships occur suddenly after a catastrophic event such as infidelity or deception.

- **Chilling effect:** Occurs when a less powerful person stays silent on an issue or avoids engaging someone in conflict because of the possible negative consequences associated with speaking up, such as having the more powerful person become aggressive or leave the relationship.

- **Chronemics:** The nonverbal use of time, such as showing up for a date early or late or waiting a long or short time for someone.

- **Chronic dissatisfaction:** Partners being continuously dissatisfied with their relationship, making them more likely to seek happiness elsewhere.

- **Close relationship:** Two people in an interpersonal relationship characterized by enduring bonds, emotional attachment, and personal need fulfilment.

- **Cognitive valence theory (CVT):** A theory that predicts how and why people respond to increases in immediacy.

- **Cognitive valencers:** Templates or knowledge structures that people use to help them evaluate behavior as appropriate or inappropriate, and welcome or unwelcome.

- **Collaborating:** A direct and cooperative conflict style that involves creative problem solving and finding new solutions that meet both parties' needs.

- **Communal frame:** The component of the communication theory of identity that captures the aspects of our identity that are tied to the groups and communities to which we belong.

- **Communication inefficacy:** When people believe that they don't have the communication skills to bring up a topic or maintain discussion in a competent and effective manner.

- **Communication privacy management:** A theory that helps explain how and why individuals maintain privacy boundaries. The theory focuses on control over information as a central aspect of disclosure decisions.

- **Communication theory of identity:** A theory that focuses on how identities are managed. Identity construction can be viewed through four frames of identity (personal, enactment, relationship, and communal).

- **Communicative infidelity:** Engaging in sexual activity with a third party to communicate a message to one's partner (e.g., to make them jealous, to get revenge).

- **Companionate love:** Also called *friendship love,* it is based on high levels of intimacy and commitment but comparatively low levels of passion.

- **Comparison level:** How one's relationship compares to expectations about the kinds of outcomes a person thinks he or she should receive in a relationship.

- **Compensatory restoration:** Behavior aimed at improving the primary relationship or oneself in an effort to show one's partner how good the relationship is compared to the rival relationship.

- **Competitive fighting:** A direct and uncooperative conflict style that often involves using verbally aggressive behaviors such as name-calling.

- **Competitive symmetry:** When two people repeatedly use one-up power moves in conversation.

- **Complaints:** Communication about a specific behavior or behaviors that a person finds annoying or problematic.

- **Complementarity:** Differences in behavior, attitudes, or values between two people in a relationship.

- **Complementary:** When discussed in relation to attraction, this is when two people possess different or opposite traits that work together well.

- **Compliance-gaining strategies:** Strategies that are intended to influence others to comply with a request.

- **Compromising:** A direct and moderately cooperative conflict style that involves giving up some things you want to get other things you want.

- **Concealments:** A form of deception that involves omitting information one knows is important or relevant to a given context.

- **Conflict:** A disagreement between two interdependent people who perceive that they have incompatible goals.

- **Confrontation:** Direct communication about a particular issue.

- **Connection-autonomy:** The dialectical tension that focuses on how people struggle between their need for closeness and their need for distance (or independence) in their relationship.

- **Consummate love:** The most complete form of love based on intimacy, passion, and commitment.

- **Contempt:** Communication that conveys an air of superiority and often conveys a lack of respect.

- **Content level:** This part of a message conveys information at a literal level. "What are we doing tonight?" is a question about tonight's activities at the content level.

- **Context:** The social situation and cultural influences of a setting.

- **Controlling, as a type of on-again off-again relationship:** Relationships where one partner consistently wants the relationship and the other partner (who controls the trajectory of the relationship) goes back and forth between wanting and not wanting the relationship.

- **Conventionality-uniqueness:** This dialectical tension focuses on how people communicate in ways that show consistency or inconsistency with the larger social group.

- **Conversational control:** An individual's ability to manage a conversation by doing things such as regulating who talks and how long the interaction will last.

- **Corrective facework:** Efforts to repair an identity damaged by something that was said or done.

- **Cost escalation:** An attempt to make the relationship unattractive to one's partner. Also called *Machiavellianism strategies*.

- **Costs:** Exchanged resources that result in a loss or punishment.

- **Counter-jealousy induction, as a communicative response to jealousy:** Action taken to make the partner feel jealous too, such as flirting with someone else.

- **Courtship readiness stage:** Also called the *recognition stage*, this is the second stage in the courtship process where one person typically approaches the other. Both parties often use timid or ambiguous behaviors as they try to gauge the other person's interest level.

- **Criticisms:** Personal attacks that blame someone else for a problem.

- **Cultural scripts:** Communication routines that arise from cultural practices and are typically done automatically without thought.

- **Cyber emigrant relationships:** Partners who first meet in person but then communicate primarily online.

- **Cyclic alternation:** A way of managing dialectical tensions that involves moving from one side of a dialectic to the other alternately.

- **Deception:** Intentionally managing verbal and/or nonverbal messages so that a receiver will believe or understand something in a way that the sender knows is false.

- **Decide not to engage in the FTA:** Avoiding the topic so that a potential receiver's face is not threatened.

- **De-escalation:** An effort to decrease relational closeness while avoiding a complete breakup.

- **Defensiveness:** Communication designed to defend oneself against attacks by deflecting blame to someone or something else.

- **Delayed-involvement couples:** Couples who wait until they are a committed couple before they become sexually involved.

- **Demand-withdraw interaction pattern:** See *demand-withdrawal pattern*.

- **Demand-withdrawal pattern:** Also called a *demand-withdraw interaction pattern*. Occurs when one person wants to engage in conflict or demands change whereas the other partner wants to avoid the topic and/or the demanding person and maintain the status quo.

- **Denial, as a communicative response to jealousy:** Pretending not to be jealous or falsely denying feeling jealous.

- **Dependence power:** Reliance on a relationship or partner for power, with people who are dependent on their relationship for power having lower status than people who are not.

- **Depth:** The extent to which self-disclosure is highly intimate or personal.

- **Derogating competitors:** Communication designed to cast the rival in a bad light, such as making mean comments about a rival.

- **Destiny beliefs:** People's belief that they and their romantic partner are meant for each other and that first impressions about that destiny are fixed and enduring (in contrast to *growth beliefs*).

- **Devaluation:** Feelings of being unappreciated and unimportant, leading to hurt feelings.

- **Dialectical perspective:** A perspective built around the idea that relationships are never completely stable but are constantly changing as people manage seemingly contradictory tensions (such as autonomy vs. connection); integral to dialectics theory.

- **Dialectics theory:** See *dialectical perspective*.

- **Direct emotional expressions:** Directly and unambiguously expressing feelings by using phrases such as "I love you" and "You make me happy" when expressing affection.

- **Direct request:** Simply asking for something.

- **Disclaimers:** Something that individuals say before saying or doing something face threatening such as hedging and credentialing and sin license, cognitive disclaimers, and appeals for suspended judgments.

- **Disclosure-liking hypothesis:** The more we disclose to someone, the more we start to like that person.

- **Discursive tensions:** Messages that have two seemingly contradictory meanings.

- **Dismissive attachment style:** An attachment style based on positive models of self and negative models of others. With this style, autonomy is valued over closeness in relationships.

- **Display rules:** Manipulation and control of emotional expressions such as pretending you understood someone, hiding your anger or sorrow from others, and putting on a happy face when you are sad.

- **Disqualification:** A strategy for managing dialectical tensions that involves being ambiguous so that neither side of the dialectic is engaged. This strategy is a form of neutralization.

- **Distress-maintaining attributions:** Negative behavior is attributed to causes that are internal, stable, and global.

- **Distributive strategies:** People attempt to blame, hurt, insult, or berate their partner in an effort to gain compliance or win an argument.

- **Dominance:** The display or expression of power through behavior.

- **Double-shot hypothesis:** An alternative explanation (compared to the evolutionary hypothesis) for why men get more upset in response to sexual infidelity and women get more upset in response to emotional infidelity. Based on the idea that men assume that women are emotionally connected to men with whom they have sex and women assume that men would like to (or are) having sex with women to whom they are emotionally attached.

- **Drama:** In the context of social media, drama is interpersonal conflict that takes place in front of an active, engaged audience.

- **Dramaturgical perspective:** A perspective suggesting that the world is a stage, people are actors, and we enact performances geared for particular audiences, with performances enacted to advance beneficial images of ourselves.

- **Duration:** How long people engage in self-disclosure or personal conversation with someone.

- **Dyadic effect:** A reciprocal pattern of self-disclosure that occurs when a person reveals information and his or her partner responds by offering information that is at a similar level of intimacy.

- **Dyadic power theory:** The idea that most dominance is displayed by people in equal power positions as they deal with conflict and struggle for control.

- **Dyadic processes phase:** The third phase in the relational dissolution process. These processes focus on how a couple deals with issues that are causing dissatisfaction in their relationship, and can include conflict, avoidance, and/or problem-solving.

- **Efficacy assessment:** Whether people believe they are able to gather the information for which they are searching and then cope with that information.

- **Egalitarian marriage:** A relationship where both spouses are employed, both are actively involved in parenting, and both share in the responsibilities and duties of the household.

- **Emotional attachment:** The feeling in close relationships of being emotionally connected to someone, where the relationship is a primary source of one's emotions.

- **Emotional closeness:** Having a sense of shared feelings, experiences, trust, enjoyment, concern, and caring in a relationship.

- **Emotional flooding:** Occurs when people become surprised, overwhelmed, and disorganized by their partner's expressions of negative emotion during a conflict situation, causing them to feel high levels of arousal that can inhibit effective conflict management.

- **Emotional infidelity:** Emotional involvement with another person to the extent that emotional resources such as romantic love, time, and attention are diverted to that person rather than to one's primary partner.

- **Emotional insensitivity:** When a person fails to tune in to the emotions or feelings of other people.

- **Emotional labor:** A term that describes the effort it takes to show a different emotion than the one being felt. It is generally used to describe that effort in the context of jobs that require manipulation of emotion expression (e.g., servers, first responders).

- **Emotional support:** Helping someone feel better without necessarily trying to solve the problem.

- **Empathic:** The capacity to understand and experience the same emotions as other individuals.

- **Empty love:** Love based on commitment alone rather than on intimacy and passion.

- **Empty threats:** Threatening to do something (like break up with your partner) that you do not really intend to do.

- **Enactment of communication frame:** The component of the communication theory of identity that captures the ways in which we directly or indirectly express our identities to others.

- **Envy:** Wanting something you value that someone else has.

- **Equality:** The belief that resources should be distributed equally among people regardless of their contributions.

- **Equity:** When two people are getting a fair deal in terms of the benefits and costs they are getting as a result of being in a relationship with each other.

- **Equity theory:** A relational perspective for determining whether the distribution of resources is fair to both relational partners.

- **Equivocations:** A deceptive form of communication that involves making an indirect ambiguous statement, such as saying that your friend's new hairstyle (that you hate) is the "latest fashion" when you are asked if you like it.

- **Eros:** One of Lee's primary love styles. Also called *romantic love* or *passionate love*, it is rooted in feelings of affection, attraction, and sexual desire.

- **Esteem support:** Used to bolster someone's self-worth by making the person feel valued, admired, and capable.

- **Evolutionary hypothesis for infidelity:** Men should get more upset over sexual infidelity than emotional infidelity whereas women should get more upset over emotional infidelity than sexual infidelity, because men and women have different priorities related to mating and parenting (men are concerned with paternal certainty; women are concerned with keeping valued resources).

- **Exaggerations:** A form of deception that involves stretching the truth, often to make oneself look better or to spice up a story.

- **Excitation transfer:** Occurs when emotions caused by one event spill over onto and influence the evaluation of a second event that occurs very soon thereafter.

- **Excuses:** Minimizing responsibility for negative behavior by focusing on the inability to control one's own actions or by shifting the blame to others.

- **Exit, as a coping strategy:** Active, destructive behaviors that are used to decrease closeness or end a relationship.

- **Expectancy violations theory:** A theory that predicts how people will react to unexpected interpersonal behavior based on social norms, expectations, and the reward value of other communicators.

- **Explicit relational talk:** Direct interpersonal communication about interpersonal relationships.

- **Expressions of emotional and physical closeness, as a sexual initiation strategy:** Displaying love, affection, and emotional closeness as a way to initiate sexual activity with someone.

- **Expressive friendships:** Close relationships that involve using emotional nonverbal and verbal communication during conversations, showing nonverbal affection, and having deep conversations (especially applicable to female friendships).

- **Expressive-protective:** The dialectical tension between expressing information versus keeping it private.

- **Extrinsic investments:** Resources or benefits that are developed over time as a result of being in a relationship, such as material possessions, enmeshment within a common social system, and an identity that is attached to being in a relationship.

- **Face-threatening acts (FTAs):** Behaviors that detract from an individual's identity by threatening either that person's positive or negative face desires.

- **Fading away:** A disengagement strategy where both relational partners recognize that the relationship is at a standstill, and they gradually drift apart and lose contact.

- **Failed transition:** Friends-with-benefits relationship where one or both partners enter the arrangement with the intention of eventually becoming a couple; instead they do not move beyond being friends with benefits.

- **Fait accompli approach:** A disengagement strategy that involves breaking up with someone in a direct fashion, often by unequivocally stating that the relationship is over.

- **Fatal attraction:** When the very qualities that draw us to someone eventually contribute to relational breakup.

- **Fearful attachment style:** An attachment style based on negative models of self and negative models of others. People with this style want to have close relationships, but they are afraid that if they get too close to someone they will get hurt.

- **Fever model of self-disclosure:** When people are distressed about a problem or think about a problem a lot, they are especially likely to reveal their thoughts and feelings or to tell a secret.

- **Flaming:** Hostile expression of emotions online through means such as swearing, insulting, and name-calling.

- **Forgiveness:** A relational process that has four characteristics: (1) acknowledgment of harmful conduct, (2) an extension of undeserved mercy, (3) an emotional transformation, and (4) relationship renegotiation.

- **Four horsemen of the apocalypse:** A destructive conflict pattern that includes the following four behaviors: (1) complaints/criticisms, (2) contempt/disgust, (3) defensiveness, and (4) stonewalling.

- **Frequency:** As a dimension of self-disclosure, this refers to how often people self-disclose.

- **Friends-with-benefits relationship:** A sexual but nonromantic relationship between friends or acquaintances.

- **Friends with benefits:** Friends or acquaintances who decide to have a sexual relationship but not be a romantic couple.

- **Friendship love:** Love based on intimacy and commitment that has little passion.

- **Fundamental relational themes:** Messages that reflect the nature of a relationship, such as dominance/submission, intimacy, degree of similarity, task/social orientation, formality/informality, social composure, and emotional activation.

- **Futility of discussion:** A motive for topic avoidance that involves believing it is pointless to talk about something.

- **General equity:** An overall assessment that two people's benefits and contributions are balanced.

- **Generation Z:** Individuals born between 1996 and 2010 who grew up immersed in communication technologies.

- **Ghosting:** A term that refers to stopping all contact (e.g., texting, snapping, seeing each other) as a way to break up or signal that one is no longer interested in someone.

- **Goal-linking:** Being with a particular person is linked to more general life goals, such as happiness; makes a relationship more desirable.

- **Going off-record strategy:** A strategy that involves giving primary attention to face and little attention to task.

- **Gradual separators, as a type of on-again off-again relationship:** Couples that grow farther apart from one another during their "off" phases so that the relationship fades out over time as the "on" periods get shorter.

- **Gradual-involvement couples:** Couples who let sexual activity increase progressively as the relationship develops and they become more psychologically intimate.

- **Grave-dressing processes phase:** The fourth stage of the relational dissolution process. Involves the public presentation of the break-up, often includes communication that helps people save face.

- **Growth beliefs:** Beliefs that impressions of others and attractions to others evolve over time, and that people and relationships grow when faced with challenges (in contrast to *destiny beliefs*).

- **Gunnysacking:** Occurs when people store up old grievances and then dump them on their partner during a conflict.

- **Habitual, as a type of on-again off-again relationship:** Couples who break up and get back together without thinking much about what happened during transitions. Instead, they fall into old habits because the relationship is comfortable, easy, and convenient.

- **Halo effect:** The process whereby people think another person has favorable qualities based on another irrelevant quality (e.g., people who are attractive are smart).

- **Haptics:** The study of the use of touch, ranging from affectionate to violent touch.

- **High-outcome value:** A judgment that someone is highly rewarding and a relationship with that person would be a positive experience.

- **Hinting:** Implying a request without ever coming out and stating it. Also called *indirect requests* or *suggesting*.

- **Hinting and indirect strategies, as a sexual initiation strategy:** Indirect communication such as compliments, sexual innuendo, hints, and nonverbal communication that shows interest in engaging in sexual activity.

- **Hook-ups:** Sexual activity, ranging from making out to having sex, without commitment.

- **Hurtful messages:** Words that elicit psychological pain.

- **Hyperaccessibility:** When particular memories are especially accessible to us, or when they are at the tip of our thoughts. This typically occurs in the context of secrets when, in certain contexts, the information in those secrets becomes hyperaccessible.

- **Hyperintimacy:** Sending repeated and unwanted messages of interest and affection.

- **Idealization:** The process where people think about and describe their relationship and their partner in glowing, overly positive terms that sometimes reflect unrealistic expectations.

- **Idealization effect:** According to this hypothesis, people who communicate exclusively online for an extended period of time tend to idealize one another and have high expectations about what their relationship would be like if they were to interact in person, which can lead to disappointment when they communicate face to face and are able to make more-realistic assessments.

- **Ideal-real:** The dialectical tension between what the friendship or relationship "ought to be" and what it "really is."

- **Identity:** The person we think we are and the self we communicate to others.

- **Identity management:** The process people use to project and maintain a positive image to others.

- **Ideologies:** Collections of beliefs, values, and expectations about life, including love.

- **Idiomatic behaviors:** Behaviors that have a specific meaning only to people within a particular relationship.

- **Illicit ingratiation:** When a person acts nice merely to gain compliance.

- **Immediacy behaviors:** Actions that signal warmth, communicate availability, decrease psychological or physical distance, and promote involvement between people.

- **Implicit egotism:** States that we are attracted to others based on similarity on arbitrary things, such as names and birthdates.

- **Inclusion-seclusion:** A dialectical tension that is expressed when dyads communicate in ways that stress the importance of spending time with other people, but also spending time alone with each other.

- **Independent-dependent:** A dialectical tension between wanting the freedom to pursue individual activities and depending on someone for help and support.

- **Indirect fighting:** An indirect and uncooperative conflict style that involves using passive-aggressive behaviors such as rolling one's eyes or pulling away from one's partner.

- **Indirect requests:** An implied influence attempt that involves suggesting or hinting without ever making a direct request.

- **Individual secrets:** Confidences where information is held by a single individual and kept secret from others.

- **Inductive philosophy:** A parenting philosophy that involves providing children with reasons for disciplinary actions.

- **Inequity:** An imbalanced relationship in terms of the benefits each person is getting and costs each person is paying, such that one person is getting a better deal than the other (i.e., more benefits, lower costs, or both).

- **Infatuation:** A form of incomplete love based on passion only.

- **Influence:** The ability to persuade others to think and act in certain ways.

- **Influence strategies:** Specific behaviors that people use to try to get others to think and/or act in certain ways.

- **Informational familiarity:** Knowing certain information about your relational partner, such as your partner's age or educational background, preventing your partner from being able to lie to you about those things.

- **Informational support:** Giving specific advice, including facts and information that might help someone solve a problem.

- **Ingratiation:** Using excessive kindness or doing favors for someone to gain popularity or get one's way.

- **Instrumental goals:** Goals related to tasks, such as making money, getting good grades, buying a car, getting a ride to school, and completing a homework assignment.

- **Integrative communication:** A style of communication that is direct and nonaggressive and typically involves problem solving.

- **Intensification effect:** The idea that personal self-disclosure produces more-powerful feelings of closeness and liking in computer-mediated contexts than in face-to-face interaction.

- **Intentional transition in, as a type of friends-with-benefits relationship:** Relationship where partners who start out in a friends-with-benefits relationship intend to become a couple and then actually do.

- **Interaction appearance theory:** The perspective that explains why people perceive others as more physically attractive if they have warm, positive interactions with them.

- **Interactors:** When used to describe a type of user of a social networking site, this term refers to people who use sites such as Twitter and Facebook primarily to interact and connect with friends and acquaintances on a reciprocal basis and to establish close relationships.

- **Intergenerational transmission of divorce:** The idea that divorce increases the likelihood that children in that same family will ultimately end up divorced. Children of divorced parents are more likely to get divorced than are children of nondivorced parents.

- **Internal working models:** Cognitive representations of oneself and potential partners that reflect an individual's past experiences in close relationships and that help that individual understand the world.

- **Interpersonal communication:** The exchange of nonverbal and/or verbal messages between two people, regardless of the relationship they share (a broader term than *relational communication*).

- **Interpersonal influence:** The process of one person influencing another person's thoughts and/or behaviors, including getting someone to change a position and getting someone to do something.

- **Interpersonal relationship:** A connection between two people who share repeated interactions over time, can influence one another, and who have unique interaction patterns.

- **Interpersonal valence:** The degree to which someone is considered attractive and rewarding.

- **Interpersonally sensitive:** A person who is empathic and understanding, and who connects with another person's perspective.

- **Intimacy:** The part of relationships based on feelings of emotional connection and closeness and has been called the warm part of love.

- **Intimate terrorism:** A strategic, enduring pattern that involves using violence to control a partner.

- **Intrafamily secrets:** Confidences where some family members have information they keep from other family members.

- **Intrapsychic processes phase:** The first phase of the dissolution model. Involves thinking about the positive and negative aspects of a relationship to evaluate whether you want to stay in it or possibly break up.

- **Intrinsic investments:** Resources that are put directly into the relationship, including time, effort, affection, and disclosure.

- **Investment model of relationship-maintaining behavior:** The perspective that commitment leads people to use behaviors that help them maintain their relationships even when problems or dissatisfaction occur. This model is an extension of the original investment model, which focuses on how satisfaction, investments, and alternatives predict commitment.

- **Investments:** Resources tied to a relationship that would decline in value or be lost if the relationship were to end.

- **Invisible support phenomenon:** The idea that attempts at support that go unnoticed by recipients are the most effective in reducing distress and promoting good health.

- **Invitations and sexual arousal stage:** The fourth stage in the courtship process. In this stage partners focus on showing sexual attraction to one another, often by subtle touch and sexual contact.

- **Invulnerable responses:** Responses that involve acting unaffected by something, such as acting like a hurtful remark did not bother you.

- **Irreplaceability:** The perception that a person has a special place in your thoughts and emotions, as well as in your social network, such that no one else can take that person's place. Irreplaceability helps distinguish close relationships from other types of relationships.

- **Isolated common couple violence:** Inappropriate physical aggression that occurs on rare occasions in a relationship when conflicts become especially heated.

- **Jealousy:** Thoughts and feelings about losing something you value, such as a good relationship, due to interference from a rival.

- **Jealousy induction:** Intentionally trying to make your partner jealous.

- **Judgment-acceptance:** The dialectical tension between accepting a friend for who he or she is versus feeling free to offer criticism and advice.

- **Just sex, as a type of friends-with-benefits relationship:** Sexual partners whose interaction revolves almost exclusively around planning and having sex without any real emotional connection.

- **Justifications:** When used as a remedial strategy, this involves trying to minimize the negative implications of your actions by denying your behavior was wrong or saying that what you did isn't that bad.

- **Kinesics:** Body movement including facial expressions and eye behavior, such as posture, gestures, walking style, smiling, and pupil dilation, among other related cues.

- **Kitchen sinking:** When people rehash groups of old arguments when they get into a new argument so that there are too many issues to deal with at once.

- **Language of acts of service:** This love language involves helping with necessary tasks by doing things such as helping with housework and running errands for one's partner.

- **Language of affirmation and support:** This love language involves being encouraging, supportive, and complimentary.

- **Language of gifts and tokens of affection:** This love language involves giving gifts and doing special things for one's partner.

- **Language of physical touch:** This love language involves communicating love mainly through physical contact.

- **Language of time together:** This love language involves spending time together talking and participating in shared activities.

- **Latent intimacy:** Internal feelings of closeness and interpersonal warmth that are not directly observable by others.

- **Lies:** Made-up information or information that is the opposite of (or at least very different from) the truth. Lies are also called *falsifications* or *fabrications*.

- **Liking:** A feeling or connection characterized by affection and respect. According to the triangular theory of love, liking occurs when people experience high levels of intimacy and low levels of commitment and passion.

- **Liking-disclosure hypothesis:** According to this hypothesis, we are more likely to disclose information to people we like.

- **Logic and reasoning, as a sexual initiation strategy:** Persuading someone that it is advantageous and/or safe to become sexually involved.

- **Loss-gain effect:** Attraction lessens when a person's behavior moves from positive to negative. In fact, people are less attracted to those who initially enact positive behavior and then enact negative behavior than they are to those who consistently enact negative behavior.

- **Love languages:** Five languages that represent preferred ways of communicating and receiving love.

- **Love ways:** The seven categories of physiological and behavioral responses to love, created by Marston and colleagues, which represents the experiences of over 90% of lovers.

- **Low-outcome value:** A judgment that someone is more costly than rewarding and a relationship with that person would be a negative experience.

- **Low-involvement couples:** Couples who wait until they are engaged or married before having sex.

- **Loyalty, as a coping strategy:** Passive, constructive behaviors that involve waiting for positive change by hoping that things will improve, standing by the partner during difficult times, and supporting the partner in the face of criticism.

- **Ludus:** One of Lee's primary love styles, also called *game-playing love*. Ludus is based on having low levels of commitment and seeing relationships as fun, playful, and casual.

- **Mania:** One of Lee's secondary love styles, based on a combination of eros and ludus. Mania involves having a possessive style of loving.

- **Manifest intimacy:** External manifestations of closeness and affection that involve communication, such as hugging or kissing.

- **Manipulation:** A set of strategies used to get one's way by doing things such as making the partner feel guilty, ashamed, or jealous.

- **Matching hypothesis:** Our tendency to be attracted to people who are similar to us in terms of level of attractiveness.

- **Mental maps:** Thinking about how your partner is feeling and trying to understand his or her perspective.

- **Metatalk:** Talking about the way you communicate.

- **Millennials:** The generation that was born between 1980 and around 1995. Millennials grew up at a time when the use of computer-mediated communication was expanding rapidly.

- **Mind reading:** Occurs when people assume (often mistakenly) that they know their partner's feelings, motives, and behaviors.

- **Miscommunication:** Someone sending an intentional message that is misinterpreted by the receiver.

- **Misinterpretation:** Someone unintentionally sending a message that is misinterpreted by the receiver.

- **Mismatched, as a type of on-again off-again relationship:** These relationships are characterized by unequal involvement in terms of how motivated and committed partners are at different times during the course of the relationship.

- **Modality:** The channel of communication.

- **Model of accommodation:** A model that describes how people respond to problems or dissatisfying events in their relationships using neglect, exit, voice, or loyalty.

- **Model of relational turbulence:** An approach that tries to explain the way partners communicate during periods of turbulent changes in a relationship such as the transition from casual dating to commitment or a partner's diagnosis of a chronic illness.

- **Moderation:** A strategy for managing dialectical tensions that involves striving to reach a midpoint such that couples engage both sides of the dialectic but only to a certain extent. Moderation is a form of neutralization.

- **Moral violations:** Behavior that deviates from what is considered right or moral.

- **Mutual influence:** Two people affect one another in meaningful ways. Mutual influence increases as relationships move beyond role relationships to become interpersonal or close.

- **Narcissism:** A personality trait that involves a pervasive pattern of grandiosity, self-focus, and self-importance.

- **Need fulfillment:** When a partner fulfills critical interpersonal needs, such as the need to belong to a social group, to feel loved and appreciated, or to care for and nurture someone.

- **Negative affect strategy:** Also called *aversive stimulation,* involves whining, pouting, sulking, complaining, crying, or acting angry to get one's way.

- **Negative altercasting:** Negative compliance-gaining strategies where one person's positive motivations are questioned.

- **Negative communication, as a communicative response to jealousy:** Aggressive and passive-aggressive communication that reflects negativity, such as arguing, being sarcastic, acting rude, ignoring the partner, giving cold or dirty looks, and withdrawing affection.

- **Negative face:** The part of us that wants to be free from imposition and restraint and to have control over our own resources.

- **Negative identity management:** A sender imposes her or his solution on a receiver at the expense of the receiver's feelings.

- **Negative moral appeals:** The suggestion that only bad or immoral people would fail to comply.

- **Negative politeness strategy:** A set of tactics intended to save the receiver's negative face while still accomplishing the task.

- **Negative psychic change:** A turning point that occurs when attitudes and perceptions become more negative.

- **Neglect, as a coping strategy:** Passive, destructive behaviors that involve standing by and letting conditions in the relationship get worse.

- **Network opportunism, as a type of friends-with-benefits relationship:** Partners within the same social network who are not particularly close but who serve as a sexual backup if neither of them is with someone else.

- **Network support:** Directing someone to a person or group who can help them, often because they have had similar experiences.

- **Neutral symmetry:** When both partners exchange one-across messages in conversation.

- **Neutralization:** A way of managing dialectic tension that involves avoiding full engagement of either side of the dialectical tension through moderation (striving to reach a midpoint) or disqualification (being ambiguous so that neither side of the dialectic is engaged).

- **Nondirected disclosure:** Disclosure that is sent to large groups of people rather than to individuals and is therefore considered less personal.

- **Objective power:** The authority associated with tangible factors such as position, strength, weaponry, and wealth.

- **Obsessive relational intrusion (ORI):** Unwanted behaviors that invade someone's privacy and that are used for the purpose of trying to get close to someone.

- **Oculesics:** Eye behavior. This behavior helps establish emotional closeness.

- **On-again off-again relationship:** Also called *cycling relationships,* these relationships are defined by breaking up and then getting back together at least once.

- **One-across messages:** Neutral messages that are neither dominant nor submissive.

- **One-down messages:** Deferent, submissive, or accepting messages.

- **One-up messages:** Dominant or controlling messages.

- **Online infidelity:** Romantic or sexual contact facilitated by Internet use that is considered to violate relationship rules regarding faithfulness.

- **Openness-closedness:** The dialectical tension that focuses on how people struggle between their need to be open with relational partners while also wanting to keep some information to themselves.

- **Outcome:** A person's calculation of the rewards in a current relationship minus the costs for being in that same relationship.

- **Outcome expectancy:** Predictions about the outcome of an information search as positive or negative.

- **Outcome values:** Predictions about how rewarding or unrewarding future interactions with a particular person would be.

- **Overbenefited:** The state of getting a better deal than your partner in terms of receiving more benefits, making fewer contributions, or both, so that the ratio of benefits to contributions favors you more than your partner.

- **Panache:** An elusive quality that some people have that commands attention, draws others in, and makes them memorable.

- **Paradox of affection:** Although affection is often intended and usually perceived by others to be a positive communicative move, it can backfire and produce negative outcomes such as distress and relationship dissolution.

- **Paralinguistics:** The study of the voice, including voice qualities like pitch, volume, rate, and accent.

- **Partner uncertainty:** Occurs when a person is uncertain about a partner's feelings and intentions, including whether the partner reciprocates the individual's feelings.

- **Partner unresponsiveness:** When a person perceives that a partner will be unhelpful or insensitive to the individual's needs.

- **Passion:** Interpersonal excitation that is often, but not always, sexual. The hot component in Sternberg's triangular theory of love, involving motivation and arousal.

- **Passionate love:** Also called *eros* or *romantic love,* it is based on intimacy, passion, and low commitment.

- **Passive aggression:** Indirect ways of communicating hostility, such as giving a partner the silent treatment, withholding affection, or rolling one's eyes.

- **Peer marriage:** Both spouses are employed, both are actively involved in parenting, and both share in the responsibilities and duties of the household.

- **Permissive parents:** Undemanding, nondirective, and overly responsive parents.

- **Personal frame:** The component of communication theory of identity that captures the personal characteristics we perceive in ourselves (e.g., smart, athletic, nice).

- **Personalistic disclosure:** Disclosure that people think is directed at them because they are trustworthy and have a close relationship with the sender.

- **Person-centered messages:** Communication that acknowledges, elaborates on, and validates the feelings and concerns of a distressed person.

- **Physical abuse:** Violent behaviors such as grabbing, kicking, biting, slapping, and punching.

- **Physical attraction:** Being drawn to a person's looks, including someone's body, eyes, hair, attire, or other aspects of a person's appearance.

- **Physical closeness:** The amount of spatial proximity and physical contact people have.

- **Physical distance:** The amount physical space between people.

- **Physical flirting style:** Focuses on communicating sexual and romantic interest through behavior such as touch and sexual innuendo.

- **Physiological self-soothing:** The antidote to stonewalling, this involves taking a break from the conflict to calm down and regain one's thoughts.

- **Pillow talk:** Tranquil, intimate conversation that takes place after sexual intercourse or sexual climax.

- **Pinocchio relationships:** Partners first meet online but then start meeting in person (i.e., they become "real").

- **Playful flirting style:** Flirting that is fun rather than serious; not usually intended to start a relationship with someone.

- **Poise:** Appearing smooth and calm during stressful situations.

- **Polite flirting style:** Flirting where touch and other types of behavior that could be interpreted as inappropriate are avoided.

- **Politeness theory:** Brown and Levinson's extension of Goffman's work, which focuses on the specific ways that people manage and save face using communication.

- **Positioning stage:** The third stage in the courtship process. It involves signaling availability for interaction while indicating to others that two people are, at least temporarily, a couple that should be left alone by using behaviors such as close distancing, touch, and face-to-face body orientation.

- **Positive altercasting:** Compliance-gaining strategies that suggest a good person would behave in a particular way.

- **Positive face:** The favorable image that people hope to portray to others and to have validated by others. The best face we put forward so that others will like us.

- **Positive involvement behaviors:** Also called *immediacy behaviors*, these behaviors show both positive affect and high levels of involvement in an interaction.

- **Positive moral appeals:** Telling someone that a good or moral person would comply with a certain request.

- **Positive politeness strategy:** A strategy addressing the receiver's positive face while still accomplishing the task.

- **Positive psychic change:** A turning point that occurs when attitudes and perceptions become more positive.

- **Positive reciprocity:** A pattern where both partners engage in cooperative or immediate behavior.

- **Positive-tone strategy:** When used to break up, this strategy is designed to lessen the dumped person's hurt feelings and make her or him feel better about the breakup.

- **Power:** An individual's perceived ability to control or influence as well as to resist the influence attempts of others.

- **Power assertion, as a parenting style:** Occurs when parents demand compliance from their children without thinking they have to explain why.

- **Powerful speech:** Speakers using this style "own" what they are saying, dominate conversations, redirect the conversation away from topics others are discussing, and interrupt others.

- **Powerless speech:** A weak form of speech in which people use tag questions and hedges to qualify what they are saying.

- **Pragma:** One of Lee's secondary love styles, based on a combination of storge and ludus, pragma involves having a practical style of love that focuses on finding a person who has specific desired characteristics.

- **Predictability-novelty:** The dialectical tension that focuses on how people struggle between their needs for stability and change in their relationships.

- **Predicted outcome value theory:** A theory based on the idea that people only seek to reduce uncertainty about someone if they see that person as rewarding.

- **Predictive expectancies:** What type of behavior people think *will* occur in a situation based on personal knowledge about someone (vs. prescriptive expectancies).

- **Pregiving:** When used as a persuasive strategy, this involves someone doing a favor for another person prior to asking for a return favor.

- **Preoccupied attachment style:** An attachment style based on negative models of self and positive models of others. People with this style desire excessive closeness and need relationships to validate their self-worth.

- **Prerogative principle:** Powerful people can violate norms, break relational rules, and manage interactions without as much penalty as powerless people.

- **Prescriptive expectancies:** What type of behavior people think *should* occur in a situation based on social and cultural norms (vs. predictive expectancies).

- **Pressure and manipulation, as a sexual initiation strategy:** Using coercive tactics such as repeated requests for sex, threats to break off or de-escalate the relationship, the use of drugs or alcohol to reduce resistance to sex, and/or deception to initiate sexual activity with someone.

- **Preventive facework:** Efforts to avoid or minimize potential face threat or to thwart future damage by framing the message in friendlier, softer terms.

- **Primary appraisals:** Initial evaluations about whether feelings are good or bad, warranted or not warranted, and so on. When applied to jealousy, primary appraisals evaluate the existence and quality of a rival relationship, including how much of a threat the third party is.

- **Principle of elevation:** This principle states that height or vertical position is associated with power.

- **Principle of least interest:** The idea that when a difference exists in the intensity of positive feelings between partners, the partner who feels more positive feelings is at a power disadvantage.

- **Principle of negative reciprocity:** This principle states that aggression or negative expressions beget more of the same.

- **Privacy control:** The idea that people want control over their personal information, including who knows personal information, and both whether and how those people share the information with others.

- **Privacy maintenance:** People may avoid specific topics as a way to maintain privacy.

- **Privacy ownership:** This states that people own their personal information and if they share that information with others, those people have a responsibility to keep it private unless granted permission to do otherwise.

- **Privacy turbulence:** Occurs when new events force renewed boundary management; in other words, events force people to think about how their private information is being managed and whether they need to change who has access to it.

- **Procreational orientation:** The belief that producing offspring is the primary purpose of sexual intercourse.

- **Prosocial communication:** Positive behaviors that promote relational closeness, trust, and liking.

- **Proxemics:** The way people use space, including conversational distances and territory.

- **Pseudo de-escalation:** A deceptive, unethical breakup strategy where a person says that she or he wants to decrease closeness but actually wants to end the relationship altogether.

- **Psychological abuse:** Hurtful communication such as insults, name-calling, and personal criticisms.

- **Psychological reactance:** A theory that maintains that influence attempts may backfire or boomerang, thereby causing resistance to the request.

- **Public–private:** The dialectical tension that focuses on how people struggle between acting certain ways in the presence of others and other ways when alone.

- **Punctuation:** When both partners think that their negative communication is caused by the other person's behavior (e.g., I think I act demanding because you withdraw, and you think that you withdraw because I act demanding).

- **Punishment:** Trying to balance the relationship by engaging in negative behavior (such as withdrawing affection) that might lead the partner to act to restore closeness.

- **Quality of alternatives:** How one's relationship compares to the kinds of outcomes a person thinks he or she could have by exploring other options (such as starting a new relationship or being alone).

- **Quasi-courtship:** Engaging in courtship-like behaviors (such as flirting with each other) without such behavior leading to sexual involvement.

- **Rapid-involvement couples:** Couples who have high levels of physical arousal and have sex on the first date or shortly thereafter.

- **Rebound effect:** When discussed as part of thought suppression, this is the idea that people can temporarily suppress thoughts about a negative event if they are away from the event (or the person who caused it), but those thoughts will come flooding back as soon as something triggers their memory.

- **Recreational orientation:** As a sexual attitude, the belief that sexual intercourse is primarily a source of fun, escape, excitement, or pleasure.

- **Reflection enhancing:** Behaviors that encourage children to think about their misconduct, including how their actions affect themselves and others.

- **Reframing:** A sophisticated way of managing dialectical tension that involves talking about tensions so that they seem complementary rather than contradictory.

- **Reinforcement affect model:** Certain types of environments make people feel good; people unconsciously associate those good feelings with the people with whom they are interacting in the environment.

- **Reinforcement effect:** When discussed in attachment theory, this means that people communicate in cycles that reinforce their positive or negative models of self and others, leading one's attachment style to stay fairly consistent over time.

- **Reinforcement model:** A perspective used to explain that people are attracted to similar others in part because similarity reinforces and validates our beliefs and values.

- **Relational closeness:** Being interdependent in terms of exchanging resources and intimacy; meeting each other's needs; and influencing one another's thoughts, behaviors, and emotions.

- **Relational communication:** A subset of interpersonal communication that focuses on the expression and interpretation of messages within close relationships. Relational communication includes the gamut of interactions from vital relational messages to mundane everyday interactions.

- **Relational dialectics theory:** A perspective that indicates people have opposing interpersonal needs that exist in dynamic tension, that these tensions are evident in discourse, and that the success of relationships depends on how we manage these tensions.

- **Relational goal pursuit theory:** A theory built on the idea that people expend energy to develop or reinitiate relationships to the extent that they perceive a relationship is desirable and attainable.

- **Relational goals:** Relational objectives or states that we pursue and that often motivate our communication choices.

- **Relational level:** The relational level of a message provides a context for interpreting communication within the broader context of a relationship. Nonverbal cues are a primary part of the relational level of a message.

- **Relational maintenance:** Efforts to keep a relationship at a specified state or at a desired level of closeness.

- **Relational orientation:** As a sexual attitude, the belief that sexual intercourse is a way of expressing love and affection and developing greater relational intimacy.

- **Relational ruses:** A breakup strategy that involves using indirect manipulative strategies to end a relationship, such as having a third party leak the news of the impending breakup.

- **Relational satisfaction:** Pleasure or enjoyment that people derive from their relationships. In interdependence theory, relational satisfaction is defined as having a relationship where rewards exceed costs at a level that meets or exceeds expectations.

- **Relational transgressions:** Actions that violate implicit or explicit relational rules (e.g., infidelity, deception).

- **Relational Turbulence Theory:** A theory that explains how cognition, emotion, and communication impact one another to shape experiences of relationship as either chaotic or smooth.

- **Relationship de-escalation:** The process of decreasing closeness in a relationship.

- **Relationship disillusionment:** People's positive perceptions about their partners and their relationships start to fade.

- **Relationship frame:** The component of the communication theory of identity that captures the aspects of our identity that are tied to our relationships with other people.

- **Relationship invocation:** Expressing attitudes or beliefs about the relationship or using the qualities of the relationship as a backdrop for interpreting a relational transgression.

- **Relationship protection:** As a motivation for topic avoidance, when people avoid talking about things because they think talking about them will harm their relationship.

- **Relationship uncertainty:** A lack of confidence in the ability to predict the current or future state of the relationship.

- **Relationship-enhancing attributions:** Negative behavior is attributed to causes that are external, unstable, and specific.

- **Relationships:** Ongoing interactions between people that result in interpersonal, affective, and behavioral connections.

- **Relative power:** One person's level of power in comparison to someone else's level of power.

- **Remedial strategies:** Attempts to correct problems, restore one's positive face, and/or repair a relationship.

- **Repeated common couple violence:** Physical aggression that occurs intermittently in a relationship when conflicts get especially heated.

- **Resolution stage:** The fifth and final stage in the courtship process. This stage is defined by having sex, and separates courtship (which includes sex) from quasi-courtship (which does not).

- **Responsiveness:** A communication style that shows care, concern, and liking.

- **Resurrection processes phase:** The fifth and final stage of the relational dissolution process, wherein people move on by visualizing their future without their old relationship and learning from their past experiences.

- **Retaliatory responses:** Trying to get back at someone or get revenge on someone.

- **Revelation-concealment:** A dialectical tension that involves the push and pull between wanting to reveal aspects of your relationship to others, but also wanting to keep parts of your relationship private.

- **Rewards:** Exchanged resources that are pleasurable and gratifying.

- **Rival contacts:** Direct communication with a potential rival by a jealous person.

- **Role relationship:** Two people who share some degree of behavioral interdependence, although people in such relationships are usually interchangeable and are not psychologically or behaviorally unique.

- **Romantic intent:** Desire to move the friendship toward a romantic relationship.

- **Romantic jealousy:** When people believe that a third party threatens the existence or quality of their primary love relationship.

- **Romantic love:** Also called *eros* or *passionate love*. It is based on intimacy and passion, and low commitment.

- **Romantic relationship transitions:** The periods of time when a relationship changes from being either platonic or nonexistent to being romantic, or vice versa.

- **"Romeo and Juliet" effect:** The notion that parental interference or disapproval of their children's romantic relationship can strengthen the attraction between those two people.

- **Routine maintenance behavior:** Everyday behaviors that help people preserve their bonds with one another.

- **Rumination:** Repeated mulling over certain information or behavior.

- **Sacrifice or support:** Being there to help and comfort someone in crises, such as dealing with the death of a loved one or helping someone regain confidence after an embarrassing failure.

- **Scarcity hypothesis:** The notion that hard-to-get resources are especially desirable. People have the most power when the resources they possess are hard to come by or in high demand.

- **Scripts:** Social information about how one should act in a particular situation.

- **Secondary appraisals:** Evaluations about the causes and consequences of one's feelings. When applied to jealousy, secondary appraisals include comparing oneself to the rival, thinking about what would happen if the relationship were to end, and so on.

- **Secure attachment style:** A social interaction style based on positive models of self and positive models of others. People with this style are comfortable getting close to and depending on others, seldom worry about being abandoned, and strive for a balance of autonomy and closeness in relationships.

- **Secure base:** In attachment theory, this is the idea that children feel secure about exploring their environment when a preferred caregiver is present to go back to if they need help or are uncomfortable. (The preferred caregiver is the secure base.)

- **Selection:** A way of managing dialectic tension that involves talking about the tension in a way that values one side of the dialectic over the other (e.g., openness over closedness).

- **Selection effect:** People who choose to cohabit rather than marry have certain preexisting personal characteristics and attitudes that make it less likely that their relationships will last.

- **Self-assurance:** Confidence that emanates from a person's focus, drive, and leadership qualities.

- **Self-disclosure:** Revealing personal information about oneself to others.

- **Self-expansion theory:** A theory that maintains that people have relationships to grow and extend their own selves.

- **Self-focused motives:** Reasons to act in particular ways focused on personal benefits or consequences.

- **Self-fulfilling prophecy:** A prophecy that occurs when an expectation exists that an event will happen and a person behaves in a way (often unconsciously) that actually makes it more likely that the anticipated event will occur.

- **Self-presentation:** The things we do to portray a particular image of self.

- **Self-presentational goals:** Motivations that relate to the image we want to convey.

- **Self-uncertainty:** When people question their own feelings about how involved they want to be with another person.

- **Separation:** A way of managing dialectical tensions that involves favoring each side of the dialectic at different times using either cyclic alternation (moving from one side of the dialectic to the other in a cyclical fashion) or topical segmentation (emphasizing different sides of the dialectic depending on the topic or context).

- **Separation and individuation:** Teenagers distance themselves, to some degree, from their parents and develop an individual identity apart from their family structure.

- **Serial monogamy:** Couples are sexually active only with each other (monogamy) and do not engage in other sexual relationships until the current relationship ends. They may, however, move through a series of such relationships.

- **Sexual attraction:** The desire to engage in sexual activity with someone, typically accompanied by feelings of sexual arousal in the presence of the person.

- **Sexual infidelity:** Engaging in sexual activity with someone other than one's long-term partner.

- **Sexual scripts:** Social information about how to initiate, accept, or refuse sexual advances.

- **Shift in motivation:** In relational pursuit theory, the shift that occurs when someone's motives change from wanting a relationship with someone who does not want them, to getting revenge on that person.

- **Signs of possession, as a communicative response to jealousy:** Public displays designed to show people that one's partner is taken, such as holding the partner's hand.

- **Silence, as a communicative response to jealousy:** Decreasing communication, often by getting quiet and not talking as much as usual, when feeling jealous.

- **Simple request:** Directly asking for something.

- **Sincere flirting style:** The flirting style aimed at creating an emotional bond and making a real connection with someone.

- **Social attraction:** The feeling that we would like to spend time with someone and that the person would fit well into our circle of friends.

- **Social identity theory:** A perspective focusing on the way in which people's identification with groups shapes their behavior, toward both members of that group and members of other groups.

- **Social influence:** Changing someone's thoughts, emotions, or behaviors.

- **Social meaning model of nonverbal communication:** Some nonverbal behaviors have strong consensual meanings across different contexts.

- **Social penetration theory:** A theory that describes how self-disclosure changes as people develop their relationships. It is sometimes referred to as the *onion theory*.

- **Social processes phase:** The fourth phase in the relational dissolution process. In this phase people talk to people in their social network about problems in their relationship, including a possible breakup.

- **Social support withdrawal:** Not using supportive behaviors such as listening, comforting, or just being there for someone.

- **Social violations:** People fail to act in relationally appropriate ways and instead engage in rude, cold, critical, or condescending behavior.

- **Socialization effect:** When related to divorce, this effect suggests that children who have parents who frequently engage in aggressive conflict do worse in school and have trouble interacting with their peers in part because children adopt conflict styles similar to their parents' conflict styles.

- **Specific equity:** The balance between people's benefits and contributions in a specific area, such as physical attractiveness, financial resources, social status, ability to influence each other, and supportiveness.

- **Spies:** When applied to people who use social networking sites, these people primarily use sites like Facebook and Twitter to learn things about others.

- **Spillover effect:** The notion that the emotional state of one member of a dyad or group influences (or spills over into) the emotional states, cognitive states, and behaviors of other members of the dyad/group.

- **Split loyalty pattern:** Those who keep secrets are often put in a bind of having to choose between being loyal to other secret holders or being loyal to friends or family members who may be hurt by not knowing the secret.

- **Stalking:** Repeated and unwanted contact that is threatening and/or fear-provoking.

- **Standards for openness hypothesis:** The idea that people differ in their expectations for how open their partner should be. That difference often falls along sex categories (i.e., women have higher expectations for openness than men).

- **Stonewalling:** When a person builds a metaphorical wall around herself or himself, shuts down, and withdraws from interaction with another person.

- **Storge:** One of Lee's primary love styles, also called *friendship of companionate love*, it is based on high levels of intimacy and commitment but comparatively low levels of passion.

- **Strategic maintenance behaviors:** Behaviors intentionally designed to maintain a relationship.

- **Submissive symmetry:** During dyadic communication, when both people repeatedly use one-down moves in conversation.

- **Successful communication:** A sender's message is interpreted correctly by a receiver. (This is the most effective form of communication.)

- **Suggesting:** Implying something without ever coming out and stating it. It is also called *indirect requests* or *hinting*.

- **Support behaviors:** Giving someone emotional or instrumental support.

- **Surveillance:** Information-seeking behaviors designed to find out about a potential rival relationship, including behaviors such as stalking social media or checking up on the partner.

- **Symmetrical behavior:** During dyadic interaction, when both people in a relationship use the same verbal or nonverbal behavior.

- **Tangible aid:** People provide physical assistance, goods, or services, such as babysitting someone's children or helping someone complete a task.

- **Task attraction:** A person's attraction to another person is based on the perception that it would be good to work with that person.

- **Theory of motivated information management (TMIM):** A theory that examines how people respond to uncertainty. Tries to understand when people will seek information and when they will avoid seeking information based on the difference between desired and actual levels of uncertainty, expected outcomes, the ability to gather information, and the ability to cope with the information that might be discovered.

- **Theory of self:** The idea that our identities help us understand ourselves in relation to the world in which we live, and that the self is made up of self-esteem and identity.

- **Threats:** Tactics such as threatening to walk out on the partner, failing to cooperate with the partner until the partner gives in, or threatening to withhold resources such as money and information.

- **Topic avoidance:** Intentionally averting the discussion of a particular topic.

- **Topical segmentation:** A way of managing dialectical tensions that emphasizes different sides of the dialectic depending on the topic or context.

- **Traditional flirting style:** Flirting based on the traditional belief that men chase whereas women respond to men's advances, and that men communicate their interest more verbally whereas women communicate their interest more nonverbally.

- **Traditional marriages:** Men and women have clearly specialized roles based on gender stereotypes.

- **Transact:** A pair of utterances.

- **Transgression-maximizing messages:** Messages that highlight the negative aspects of the transgression as well as the partner's role in causing that negativity. An example would be blaming the partner or talking about how hurt one is.

- **Transgression-minimizing messages:** Messages that focus on downplaying the severity of the transgression by using strategies such as saying that the partner's behavior was unintentional, explaining or justifying the partner's behavior, or saying that it is not a big deal.

- **Transition:** When a one-up or one-down message is paired with a one-across message.

- **Transition out, as a type of friends-with-benefits relationship:** Also referred to as *ex-sex*. Former romantic partners who are no longer an official couple but continue or resume their sex relationship sometime after they break up.

- **True friends, as a type of friends-with-benefits relationship:** Close friends who add sex to their friendship but don't consider themselves a couple even though they care about each other as friends.

- **Trust violations:** When a person behaves in a way that is deceptive or violates relational rules.

- **Truth bias:** The expectation that others will be honest.

- **Turning point analysis:** A method for plotting turning points on a graph to see how various events are related to changes in a relationship.

- **Unattended behavior:** A behavior (such as a blink) that goes unnoticed by either the sender or the receiver. (This is considered behavior but not communication.)

- **Uncertainty:** The level of confidence a person has in her or his ability to predict particular attitudes, behaviors, or outcomes. High uncertainty equates to being unconfident in one's ability to make those predictions whereas low uncertainty equates to being confident in one's ability to make those predictions.

- **Uncertainty management theory:** A theory based on the idea that uncertainty is neither inherently positive nor inherently negative but something that is managed (vs. *uncertainty reduction theory*).

- **Uncertainty reduction theory:** A theory based on the idea that uncertainty is generally negative and that the driving force in initial encounters is obtaining information about the other person in order to reduce uncertainty about her or him (vs. *uncertainty management theory*).

- **Underbenefited:** The state of getting a worse deal than your partner in terms of receiving fewer benefits, making more contributions, or both, so that the ratio of benefits to contributions favors your partner instead of you.

- **Understatements:** A form of deception that involves downplaying aspects of the truth.

- **Unintentional transition in, as a type of friends-with-benefits relationship:** When partners intend to keep the relationship as friends with benefits but end up getting emotionally attached and become a couple.

- **Unique interaction patterns:** Communicating in ways that reflect a relationship's special history, including shared experiences, inside jokes, and knowledge of private information. Unique interaction patterns help differentiate interpersonal (and close) relationships from role relationships.

- **Unrequited love:** A situation involving a would-be lover who wants to initiate or intensify a romantic relationship and a rejecter who does not.

- **Valence:** Positive or negative feelings or attitudes about messages, people, or relationships.

- **Veracity:** As a dimension of disclosure, this refers to how truthful the information is that someone is disclosing.

- **Verbal aggressiveness:** A style that focuses on attacking the other person's self-concept, often with the intention of hurting the other person. Verbally aggressive people engage in such tactics as teasing, threatening, and criticizing the partner's character or appearance.

- **Verbal immediacy:** Features of language that reflect the closeness of a relationship, including word choice, forms of address, depth of disclosure, and relationship indicators.

- **Verbal self-handicapping:** People will sometimes offer an excuse that serves to minimize the face threat of a potentially poor performance.

- **Viability:** Evolutionary needs related to the motivation to survive.

- **Violent communication, as a communicative response to jealousy:** Threats and actual violence, such as hitting, shoving, or threatening harm that occur in response to jealousy.

- **Virtual relationships:** Partners who have communicated and connected only online.

- **Vision of self:** A person's theory of self, made up of self-esteem and identity.

- **Visual centrality:** People who are perceived as powerful are also looked at more by others due to their interpersonal or physical position.

- **Visual dominance ratio:** A function of the time spent looking while speaking divided by the time spent looking while listening.

- **Vocalic behavior:** See *vocalics*.

- **Vocalics:** Also called *vocalic behavior*, nonverbal paralinguistic communication including silence and the way we say words, including vocal pitch, loudness, accent, tone, and speed, as well as vocalizations such as crying and sighing.

- **Voice, as a coping strategy:** Behaviors that are direct and constructive, such as talking about problems.

- **Whole-family secrets:** Confidences held by the entire family and kept from outsiders.

- **Wings:** Part of Goffman's dramaturgical perspective, the backstage and surrounding area where we can let our guard down and do not have to think about staying in character.

- **Withdrawal:** People avoid and give partners the silent treatment, ignore them, or limit communication with them. This is also known as *avoidance* or *distancing*.

- **Yielding:** An indirect and cooperative conflict style that involves one partner giving into and accommodating the other partner.

REFERENCES

- Abbey, A. (1982). Sex differences in attributions for friendly behavior: Do males misperceive females' friendliness? *Journal of Personality and Social Psychology, 42,* 830–838.

- Abbey, A. (1987). Misperceptions of friendly behavior as sexual interest: A survey of naturally occurring incidents. *Psychology of Women Quarterly, 11,* 173–194.

- Abbey, A. (2011). Alcohol's role in sexual violence perpetration: Theoretical explanations, existing evidence, and future directions. *Drug and Alcohol Review, 30,* 481–489.

- Abbey, A., & Melby, C. (1986). The effects of nonverbal cues in gender differences in perceptions of sexual intent. *Sex Roles, 15,* 283–298.

- Aboud, F. E., & Mendelson, M. J. (1998). Determinants of friendship selection and quality: Developmental perspectives. In W. M. Bukowski & A. F. Newcomb (Eds.), *The company they keep: Friendships in childhood and adolescence* (pp. 87–112). New York: Cambridge University Press.

- Acker, M., & Davis, M. E. (1992). Intimacy, passion, and commitment in adult romantic relationships: A test of the triangular theory of love. *Journal of Social and Personal Relationships, 9,* 21–50.

- Acton, L. (1972). *Essays on freedom and power.* Gloucester, MA: Peter Smith. (Original work published 1887).

- Adams, J. S. (1965). Inequity in social exchange. In L. Berkowitz (Ed.), *Advances in experimental psychology* (Vol. 2, pp. 267–299). New York: Academic Press.

- Afifi, T. D. (2003). "Feeling caught" in stepfamilies: Managing boundary turbulence through appropriate privacy coordination rules. *Journal of Social and Personal Relationships, 20,* 729–756.

- Afifi, T. D., Caughlin, J., & Afifi, W. A. (2007). The dark side (and light side) of avoidance and secrets. In B. H. Spitzberg & W. R. Cupach (Eds.), *The dark side of interpersonal communication* (2nd ed., pp. 61–92). Mahwah, NJ: Lawrence Erlbaum.

- Afifi, T. D., & Joseph, A. (2009). The standards for openness hypothesis: A gendered explanation for why avoidance is so dissatisfying. In T. D. Afifi & W. A. Afifi (Eds.), *Uncertainty, information management, and disclosure decisions: Theories and applications* (pp. 341–362). New York: Routledge.

- Afifi, T. D., Joseph, A., & Aldeis, D. (2008). Why can't we just talk about it? An observational study of parents' and adolescents' conversations about sex. *Journal of Adolescent Research, 23,* 689–721.

- Afifi, T. D., Olson, L., & Armstrong, C. (2005). The chilling effect and family secrets: Examining the role of self protection, other protection, and communication efficacy. *Human Communication Research, 31,* 564–598.

- Afifi, T. D., & Schrodt, P. (2003). "Feeling caught" as a mediator of adolescents' and young adults' avoidance and satisfaction with their parents in divorced and non-divorced households. *Communication Monographs, 70,* 142–173.

- Afifi, T. D., & Steuber, K. (2009). The revelation risk model (RRM): Factors that predict the revelation of secrets and the strategies used to reveal them. *Communication Monographs, 76,* 144–176.

- Afifi, W. A. (1999). Harming the ones we love: Relational attachment and perceived consequences as predictor of safe-sex behavior. *Journal of Sex Research, 36,* 198–206.

- Afifi, W. A. (2009). Uncertainty and information management in interpersonal contexts. In S. Smith & S. Wilson (Eds.), *New directions in interpersonal communication research* (pp. 94–114). Thousand Oaks, CA: Sage.

- Afifi, W. A. (2010). Uncertainty and information management in interpersonal contexts. In S. W. Smith & S. R. Wilson (Eds.), *New directions in interpersonal communication research* (pp. 94–114). Thousand Oaks, CA: Sage.

- Afifi, W. A. (2015). Theory of motivated information management. In C. R. Berger and M. Roloff (Eds.), *International Encyclopedia of Interpersonal Communication.* Hoboken, NJ: Wiley Blackwell.

- Afifi, W. A., & Afifi, T. D. (2009). Avoidance among adolescents in conversations about their parents' relationship: Applying the theory of motivated information management. *Journal of Social and Personal Relationships, 26,* 488–511.

- Afifi, W. A., & Burgoon, J. K. (1998). "We never talk about that": A comparison of cross-sex friendships and dating relationships on uncertainty and topic avoidance. *Personal Relationships, 5,* 255–272.

- Afifi, W. A., & Burgoon, J. K. (2000). The impact of violations on uncertainty and the consequences for attractiveness. *Human Communication Research, 26,* 203–233.

- Afifi, W. A., & Caughlin, J. P. (2006). A close look at revealing secrets and some consequences that follow. *Communication Research, 33,* 467–488.

- Afifi, W. A., Falato, W. L., & Weiner, J. L. (2001). Identity concerns following a severe relational transgression: The role of discovery method for the relational outcomes of infidelity. *Journal of Social and Personal Relationships, 18,* 291–308.

- Afifi, W. A., & Faulkner, S. L. (2000). On being "just friends": The frequency and impact of sexual activity in cross-sex friendships. *Journal of Social and Personal Relationships, 17,* 205–222.

- Afifi, W. A., & Guerrero, L. K. (1998). Some things are better left unsaid II: Topic avoidance in friendships. *Communication Quarterly, 46,* 231–249.

- Afifi, W. A., & Guerrero, L. K. (2000). Motivations underlying topic avoidance in close relationships. In S. Petronio (Ed.), *Balancing the secrets of private disclosures* (pp. 165–180). Mahwah, NJ: Lawrence Erlbaum.

- Afifi, W. A., Guerrero, L. K., & Egland, K. L. (1994, June). *Maintenance behaviors in same- and opposite-sex friendships: Connections to gender, relational closeness, and equity issues.* Paper presented at the annual meeting of the International Network on Personal Relationships, Iowa City, IA.

- Afifi, W. A., & Metts, S. (1998). Characteristics and consequences of expectation violations in close relationships. *Journal of Social and Personal Relationships, 15,* 365–392.

- Afifi, W. A., & Morse, C. R. (2009). Expanding the role of emotion in the theory of motivated information management. In S. W. Smith & S. R. Wilson (Eds.), *New directions in interpersonal communication research* (pp. 87–105). Thousand Oaks, CA: Sage.

- Afifi, W. A., & Reichert, T. (1996). Understanding the role of uncertainty in jealousy experience and expression. *Communication Reports, 9,* 93–103.

- Afifi, W. A., & Robbins, S. (2014). Theory of Motivated Information Management: Struggles with uncertainty and its outcomes. In D. O. Braithwaite & P. Schrodt (eds.), *Engaging Theories in Interpersonal Communication* (2nd ed., pp. 143–156). Thousand Oaks, CA: Sage.

- Afifi, W. A., & Weiner, J. L. (2004). Toward a theory of motivated information management. *Communication Theory, 14,* 167–190.

- Afifi, W. A., & Weiner, J. L. (2006). Seeking information about sexual health: Applying the theory of motivated information management. *Human Communication Research, 32,* 35–57.

- Agan, M. L. F., Costin, A. S., Deutz, M. H. F., Edelsbrunner, P. A., Zalis, L., & Franken, A. (2015). Associations between risk behavior and social status in European adolescents. *European Journal of Developmental Psychology, 12,* 189–203.

- Agassi, A. (2009). *Open: An autobiography.* New York: Knopf.

- Ahrons, C. R. (1994). *The good divorce.* New York: HarperCollins.

- Aida, Y., & Falbo, T. (1991). Relationships between marital satisfaction, resources, and power strategies. *Sex Roles, 24,* 43–56.

- Ainsworth, M. D. S. (1969). Object relations, dependency, and attachment: A theoretical review of the infant-mother relationship. *Child Development, 40,* 969–1025.

- Ainsworth, M. D. S. (1982). Attachment: Retrospect and prospect. In C. M. Parkes & J. Stevenson-Hinde (Eds.), *The place of attachment in human behavior* (pp. 3–30). New York: Basic Books.

- Ainsworth, M. D. S. (1989). Attachments beyond infancy. *American Psychologist, 44,* 709–716.

- Ainsworth, M. D. S. (1991). Attachments and other affectional bonds across the life cycle. In C. M. Parkes, J. Stevenson-Hinde, & P. Marris (Eds.), *Attachment across the life cycle* (pp. 33–51). New York: Tavistock/Routledge.

- Ainsworth, M. D. S., Blehar, M. C., Waters, E., & Wall, S. (1978). *Patterns of attachment: A psychological study of the strange situation.* Hillsdale, NJ: Lawrence Erlbaum.

- Ainsworth, M. D. S., & Bowlby, J. (1991). An ethological approach to personality development. *American Psychologist, 46,* 333–341.

- Ainsworth, M. D. S., & Eichberg, C. (1991). Effects of infant-mother attachment of mother's unresolved loss of an attachment figure, or other traumatic experience. In C. M. Parkes, J. Stevenson-Hinde, & P. Marris (Eds.), *Attachment across the life cycle* (pp. 160–186). New York: Tavistock/Routledge.

- Ainsworth, M. D. S., & Wittig, B. A. (1969). Attachment and the exploratory behaviour of one-year-olds in a strange situation. In B. M. Foss (Ed.), *Determinants of infant behavior* (pp. 113–136). London: Methuen.

- Akbulut, V., & Weger, H. (2016). Predicting responses to bids for sexual and romantic escalation in cross sex friendships. *Journal of Social Psychology, 156,* 98–114.

- Albada, K. F., Knapp, M. L., & Theune, K. E. (2002). Interaction appearance theory: Changing perceptions of physical attractiveness through social interaction. *Communication Theory, 12,* 8–40.

- Albas, D., & Albas, C. (1988). Aces and bombers: The post-exam impression management strategies of students. *Symbolic Interaction, 11,* 289–302.

- Alberts, J. K. (1988). An analysis of couples' conversational complaints. *Communication Monographs, 55,* 184–197.

- Alberts, J. K. (1989). A descriptive taxonomy of couples' complaint interactions. *Southern Communication Journal, 54,* 125–143.

- Alberts, J. K., & Driscoll, G. (1992). Containment versus escalation: The trajectory of couples' conversation complaints. *Western Journal of Communication, 56,* 394–412.

- Albrecht, T. L., Burleson, B. R., & Goldsmith, D. (1994). Supportive communication. In M. L. Knapp & G. R. Miller (Eds.), *Handbook of interpersonal communication* (2nd ed., pp. 419–449). Thousand Oaks, CA: Sage.

- Altman, I., & Ginat, J. (1996). *Polygamous families in contemporary society.* New York: Cambridge University Press.

- Altman, I., & Taylor, D. A. (1973). *Social penetration: The development of interpersonal relationships.* New York: Holt, Rinehart & Winston.

- Altman, I., Vinsel, A., & Brown, B. B. (1981). Dialectical conceptions in social psychology: An application to social penetration and privacy regulation. In L. Berkowitz (Ed.), *Advances in experimental social psychology* (Vol. 14, pp. 107–160). New York: Academic Press.

- Alvarez, M. J., & Garcia-Marques, L. (2011). Cognitive and contextual variable in sexual partner and relationship perception. *Archives of Sexual Behavior, 40,* 407–417.

- Amato, P. R., & Keith, B. (1991). Parental divorce and adult well-being: A meta-analysis. *Journal of Marriage and the Family, 53,* 43–58.

- Amato, P. R., & Previti, D. (2003). People's reasons for divorcing: Gender, social class, the life course, and adjustment. *Journal of Family Issues, 24,* 602–626.

- Amodio, D. M., & Showers, C. J. (2005). "Similarity breeds liking" revisited: The moderating role of commitment. *Journal of Social and Personal Relationships, 22,* 817–836.

- Anders, S. L., & Tucker, J. S. (2000). Adult attachment style, interpersonal communication competence, and social support. *Personal Relationships, 7,* 379–389.

- Andersen, J. F. (1984, April). *Nonverbal cues of immediacy and relational affect.* Paper presented at the annual convention of the Central States Speech Association, Chicago.

- Andersen, P. A. (1982, November). *Interpersonal communication across three decades.* Paper presented at the annual convention of the Speech Communication Association, Louisville, KY.

- Andersen, P. A. (1985). Nonverbal immediacy in interpersonal communication. In A. W. Siegman & S. Feldstein (Eds.), *Multichannel integrations of nonverbal behavior* (pp. 1–36). Hillsdale, NJ: Lawrence Erlbaum.

- Andersen, P. A. (1989, May). *A cognitive valence theory of intimate communication.* Paper presented at the International Network on Personal Relationships Conference, Iowa City, IA.

- Andersen, P. A. (1991). When one cannot communicate: A challenge to Motley's traditional communication postulates. *Communication Studies, 42,* 309–325.

- Andersen, P. A. (1993). Cognitive schemata in personal relationships. In S. Duck (Ed.), *Individuals in relationships* (pp. 1–29). Newbury Park, CA: Sage.

- Andersen, P. A. (1998a). The cognitive valence theory of intimate communication. In M. T. Palmer & G. A. Barnett (Eds.), *Progress in communication sciences: Vol. 14. Mutual influence in interpersonal communication: Theory and research in cognition, affect and behavior* (pp. 39–72). Stamford, CT: Ablex.

- Andersen, P. A. (1998b). Researching sex differences within sex similarities: The evolutionary consequences of reproductive differences. In D. J. Canary & K. Dindia (Eds.), *Sex differences and similarities in communication* (pp. 83–100). Mahwah, NJ: Lawrence Erlbaum.

- Andersen, P. A. (2000). Cues of culture: The basis of intercultural differences in nonverbal communication. In L. Samovar & R. E. Porter (Eds.), *Intercultural communication: A reader* (9th ed., pp. 258–270). Belmont, CA: Wadsworth.

- Andersen, P. A. (2004). *The complete idiot's guide to body language.* New York. Alpha.

- Andersen, P. A. (2008). *Nonverbal communication: Forms and functions* (2nd ed.). Prospect Heights, IL: Waveland Press.

- Andersen, P. A. (2011a). Tactile Traditions: Cultural differences and similarities in haptic communication. In M. Hertenstein (Ed.), *Handbook of touch* (pp. 351–371). London, UK: Springer Publishing.

- Andersen, P. A. (2011b). The basis of cultural differences in nonverbal communication. In L. A. Samovar, R. E. Porter, & E. McDaniel (Eds.), *Intercultural communication: A reader* (13th ed., pp. 293–312). Boston: Wadsworth.

- Andersen, P. A., Eloy, S. V., Guerrero, L. K., & Spitzberg, B. H. (1995). Romantic jealousy and relational satisfaction: A look at the impact of jealousy experience and expression. *Communication Reports, 8,* 77–85.

- Andersen, P. A., Gannon, J., & Kalchick, J. (2013). Proxemic and haptic interaction: The closeness continuum. In J. A. Hall & M. L. Knapp (eds.), *Handbook of Communication Science: Volume 2: Nonverbal Communication.* (295–329). Berlin, Germany: De Gruyter Mouton.

- Andersen, P. A., & Guerrero, L. K. (1998a). The bright side of relational communication: Interpersonal warmth as a social emotion. In P. A. Andersen & L. K. Guerrero (Eds.), *Handbook of communication and emotion: Research, theory, applications, and contexts* (pp. 303–329). San Diego, CA: Academic Press.

- Andersen, P. A., & Guerrero, L. K. (1998b). Principles of communication and emotion in social interaction. In P. A. Andersen & L. K. Guerrero (Eds.), *Handbook of communication and emotion: Research, theory, applications, and contexts* (pp. 49–96). San Diego, CA: Academic Press.

- Andersen, P. A., Guerrero, L. K., Buller, D. B., & Jorgensen, P. F. (1998). An empirical comparison of three theories of nonverbal immediacy exchange. *Human Communication Research, 24,* 501–535.

- Andersen, P. A., Guerrero, L. K., & Jones, S. M. (2006). Nonverbal intimacy. In V. Manusov & M. L. Patterson (Eds.), *The handbook of nonverbal communication* (pp. 259–277). Thousand Oaks, CA: Sage.

- Anderson, M. (2015, October 29). *The demographics of device ownership.* http://www.pewinternet.org/2015/10/29/the-demographics-of-device-ownership/.

- Andreassen, C. S., Billieux, J., Griffiths, M. D., Kuss, D. J., Demetrovics, Z., Massoni, E., & Pallesen, S. (2016). Video games and symptoms of psychiatric disorders: A large scale cross-sectional study. *Psychology of Addictive Behaviors, 30,* 252–262.

- Antheunis, M. L., & Schouten, A. P. (2011). The effects of other-generated and system-generated cues on adolescents' perceived attractiveness on social network sites. *Journal of Computer-Mediated Communication, 16*, 391–406.

- Antheunis, M. L., Valkenburg, P. M., & Peter, J. (2010). Getting acquainted through social network sites: Testing a model of online uncertainty reduction and social attraction. *Computers in Human Behavior, 26*, 100–109.

- Applegate, J. L. (1980). Person-centered and position-centered teach communication in a day care center. *Studies in Symbolic Interactionism, 3*, 59–96.

- Archer, J. (1989). The relationship between gender-role measures: A review. *British Journal of Social Psychology, 28*, 173–184.

- Argyle, M. (1972). Non-verbal communication in human social interaction. In R. A. Hinde (Ed.), *Non-verbal communication* (pp. 248–268). Cambridge, UK: Cambridge University Press.

- Argyle, M., & Dean, J. (1965). Eye contact, distance, and affiliation. *Sociometry, 28*, 289–304.

- Argyle, M., & Furnham, A. (1983). Sources of satisfaction and conflict in long-term relationships. *Journal of Marriage and the Family, 45*, 481–493.

- Argyle, M., & Henderson, M. (1984). The rules of friendship. *Journal of Social and Personal Relationships, 1*, 211–237.

- Argyle, M., & Henderson, M. (1985). The rules of relationships. In S. Duck & D. Perlman (Eds.), *Understanding relationships: An interdisciplinary approach* (pp. 63–84). Beverly Hills, CA: Sage.

- Argyle, M., & Henderson, M. (1988). *The anatomy of relationships*. London: Penguin Books.

- Arias, I., & Pape, K. T. (2001). Psychological abuse: Implications for adjustment and commitment to leave violent partners. In D. K. O'Leary & R. D. Maluro (Eds.), *Psychological abuse in violent domestic relations* (pp. 137–151). New York: Springer.

- Arliss, L. P. (1993). Contemporary family communication: Messages and meanings. New York: St. Martin's Press.

- Armstrong, L. (1978). Kiss daddy goodnight: A speak-out on incest. New York: Doubleday.

- Aron, A., & Aron, E. N. (1986). *Love as the expansion of self: Understanding attraction and satisfaction*. New York: Hemisphere.

- Aron, A., & Aron, E. N. (1996). Self and self-expansion in relationships. In G. J. O. Fletcher & J. Fitness (Eds.), *Knowledge structures in close relationships: A social psychological approach* (pp. 325–344). Mahwah, NJ: Lawrence Erlbaum.

- Aron, A., & Aron, E. N. (2016). Comment: An inspiration for expanding the self-expansion theory of love. *Emotion Review, 8*, 112–113.

- Aron, A., Aron, E. N., & Smollan, D. (1992). Inclusion of other in the self scale and the structure of interpersonal closeness. *Journal of Personality and Social Psychology, 63*, 596–612.

- Aron, A., Dutton, D. G., Aron, E. N., & Iverson, A. (1989). Experiences of falling in love. *Journal of Social and Personal Relationships, 6*, 243–257.

- Aron, A., Mashek, D., & Aron, E. W. (2004). Closeness, intimacy, and including other in the self. In D. Mashek & A. Aron (Eds.), *Handbook of closeness and intimacy* (pp. 27–41). Mahwah, NJ: Lawrence Erlbaum.

- Aron, A., Paris, M., & Aron, E. N. (1995). Falling in love: Prospective studies of self-concept change. *Journal of Personality and Social Psychology, 69*, 1102–1112.

- Aron, E. N., & Aron, A. (1996). Love and expansion of the self: The state of the model. *Personal Relationships, 3*, 45–58.

- Aronson, E., & Linder, D. (1965). Gain and loss of esteem as determinants of interpersonal attraction. *Journal of Experimental Social Psychology, 1*, 156–171.

- Arriaga, X. B. (2001). The ups and downs of dating: Fluctuations in satisfaction in newly formed romantic relationships. *Journal of Personality and Social Psychology, 80*, 764–765.

- Aune, R. K., Ching, P. U., & Levine, T. R. (1996). Attributions of deception as a function of reward value: A test of two explanations. *Communication Quarterly, 44*, 478–486.

- Aune, R. K., Metts, S., & Hubbard, A. S. E. (1998). Managing the outcomes of discovered deception. *Journal of Social Psychology, 138*, 677–689.

- Aune, R. K., & Waters, L. L. (1994). Cultural differences in deception: Motivations to deceive in Samoans and North Americans. *International Journal of Intercultural Relations, 18*, 159–172.

- Avtgis, T. A., West, D. V., & Anderson, T. L. (1998). Relationship stages: An inductive analysis identifying cognitive, affective, and behavioral dimensions of Knapp's relational stages model. *Communication Research Reports, 15*, 280–287.

- Ayres, J. (1983). Strategies to maintain relationships: Their identification and perceived usage. *Communication Quarterly, 31*, 62–67.

- Babcock, J. C., Waltz, J., Jacobson, N. S., & Gottman, J. M. (1993). Power and violence: The relationship between communication patterns, power discrepancies and domestic violence. *Journal of Consulting and Clinical Psychology, 61*, 40–50.

- Babin, E. A. (2013). An examination of predictors of nonverbal and verbal communication of pleasure during sex and sexual satisfaction. *Journal of Social and Personal Relationships, 30*, 270–292.

- Bach, G. R., & Wyden, P. (1970). *The intimate enemy: How to fight fair in love and marriage*. New York: Avon Books.

- Bachman, G. F., & Guerrero, L. K. (2006a). An expectancy violations analysis of relational quality and communicative responses following hurtful events in dating relationships. *Journal of Social and Personal Relationships, 23*, 943–963.

- Bachman, G. F., & Guerrero, L. K. (2006b). Forgiveness, apology, and communicative responses to hurtful events. *Communication Reports, 19*, 45–56.

- Back, M. D., Schmukle, S. C., & Egloff, B. (2010). Why are narcissists so charming at first sight? Decoding the narcissism-popularity link at zero acquaintance. *Journal of Personality and Social Psychology, 98*, 132–145.

- Backstrom, L., Armstrong, E. A., & Puentes, J. (2012). Women's negotiation of cunnilingus in college hookups and relationships. *Journal of Sex Research, 49*, 1–12.

- Bagarozzi, D. A. (1990). Marital power discrepancies and symptom development in spouses: An empirical investigation. *American Journal of Family Therapy, 18*, 51–64.

- Baker, A. J. (2005). *Double click: Romance and commitment among online couples*. Cresskill, NJ: Hampton Press.

- Baldwin, A., Kiviniemi, M., & Snyder, M. (2009). A subtle source of power: The effect of having an expectation on anticipated interpersonal power. *Journal of Social Psychology, 149*, 82–104.

- Baldwin, M. W., & Fehr, B. (1995). On the instability of attachment style ratings. *Personal Relationships, 2*, 247–261.

- Banks, S. P., Altendorf, D. M., Greene, J. O., & Cody, M. J. (1987). An examination of relationship disengagement: Perceptions, breakup strategies and outcomes. *Western Journal of Speech Communication, 51*, 19–41.

- Baron, N. S. (2008). *Always on: Language in an online and mobile world*. New York: Oxford University Press.

- Bartels, A., & Zeki, S. (2004). The neural correlates of maternal and romantic love. *Neuroimage, 21*, 1155–1166.

- Barth, R. J., & Kinder, B. N. (1988). A theoretical analysis of sex differences in same-sex friendships. *Sex Roles, 19*, 349–363.

- Bartholomew, K. (1990). Avoidance of intimacy: An attachment perspective. *Journal of Social and Personal Relationships, 7*, 147–178.

- Bartholomew, K. (1993). From childhood to adult relationships: Attachment theory and research. In S. Duck (Ed.), *Learning about relationships* (pp. 30–62). Newbury Park, CA: Sage.

- Bartholomew, K., & Horowitz, L. M. (1991). Attachment styles among young adults: A test of a four-category model. *Journal of Personality and Social Psychology, 61*, 226–244.

- Batabyal, A. A. (2001). On the likelihood of finding the right partner in an arranged marriage. *The Journal of Socioeconomics, 33*, 273–280.

- Bateson, G. (1951). Conventions of communication. In J. Ruesch & G. Bateson (Eds.), *Communication: The social matrix of psychiatry* (pp. 212–227). New York: Norton.

- Battaglia, D. M., Richard, F. D., Datteri, D. L., & Lord, C. G. (1998). Breaking up is (relatively) easy to do: A script for the dissolution of close relationships. *Journal of Personal and Social Relationships, 15*, 829–845.

- Baucom, B. R., Dickenson, J. A., Atkins, D. C., Baucom, D. H., Fischer, M. S., Weusthaff, S., Hahlweg, K., & Zimmerman, T. (2015). The interpersonal process model of demand/withdrawal behavior. *Journal of Family Psychology, 29,* 80–90.

- Bauer, G. (2016). Gender roles, comparative advantages and life course: The divisions of domestic labor in same-sex and different sex couples. *European Journal of Population, 32,* 99–128.

- Baumeister, R. F. (1982). A self-presentational view of social phenomena. *Psychological Bulletin, 91,* 3–26.

- Baumeister, R. F. (Ed.). (1986). *Public and private self.* New York: Springer-Verlag.

- Baumeister, R. F. (2000). Gender differences in erotic plasticity: The female sex drive as socially flexible and responsive. *Psychological Bulletin, 126,* 347–374.

- Baumeister, R. F., & Mendoza, J. P. (2011). Cultural variations in the sexual marketplace: Gender equality correlates with more sexual activity. *Journal of Social Psychology, 151,* 350–360.

- Baumeister, R. F., & Wotman, S. R. (1992). *Breaking hearts: The two sides of unrequited love.* New York: Guilford Press.

- Baumeister, R. F., Wotman, S. R., & Stillwell, A. M. (1993). Unrequited love: On heartbreak, anger, guilt, scriptlessness, and humiliation. *Journal of Personality and Social Psychology, 64,* 377–394.

- Baumgarte, R., & Nelson, D. W. (2009). Preference for same- versus cross-sex friendships. *Journal of Applied Social Psychology, 39,* 901–917.

- Baumrind, D. (1971). Current patterns of parental authority. *Developmental Psychology Monographs, 4*(1, Pt. 2), 1–103.

- Baumrind, D. (1991). Parenting styles and adolescent development. In R. M. Leder, A. C. Petersen, & J. Brooks-Gunn (Eds.), *Encyclopedia of adolescence* (Vol. 2, pp. 746–758). New York: Garland.

- Bavelas, J. B., Black, A., Chovil, N., & Mullett, J. (1990). *Equivocal communication.* Newbury Park, CA: Sage.

- Baxter, L. A. (1979a). Self-disclosure as a relational disengagement strategy. *Human Communication Research, 5,* 215–222.

- Baxter, L. A. (1979b, February). *Self-reported disengagement strategies in friendship relationships.* Paper presented at the annual convention of the Western Speech Communication Association, Los Angeles, CA.

- Baxter, L. A. (1979c, November). *Relational closeness, relational intent and disengagement strategies.* Paper presented at the annual meeting of the Speech Communication Association, San Antonio, TX.

- Baxter, L. A. (1982). Strategies for ending relationships: Two studies. *Western Journal of Speech Communications, 46,* 223–241.

- Baxter, L. A. (1984). Trajectories of relationship disengagement. *Journal of Social and Personal Relationships, 1,* 29–48.

- Baxter, L. A. (1985). Accomplishing relational disengagement. In S. Duck & D. Perlman (Eds.), *Understanding personal relationships: An interdisciplinary approach* (pp. 243–265). Beverly Hills, CA: Sage.

- Baxter, L. A. (1986). Gender differences in the heterosexual relationship rules embedded in breakup accounts. *Journal of Social and Personal Relationships, 3,* 289–306.

- Baxter, L. A. (1990). Dialectical contradictions in relationship development. *Journal of Social and Personal Relationships, 7,* 69–88.

- Baxter, L. A. (1993). The social side of personal relationships: A dialectical perspective. In S. Duck (Ed.), *Understanding relationship processes* (pp. 139–165). Newbury Park, CA: Sage.

- Baxter, L. A. (1994). A dialogic approach to relationship maintenance. In D. J. Canary & L. Stafford (Eds.), *Communication and relational maintenance* (pp. 233–254). San Diego, CA: Academic Press.

- Baxter, L. A. (2006). Relational dialectics theory: Multivocal dialogues of family communication. In D. O. Braithwaite & L. A. Baxter (Eds.), *Engaging theories in family communication: Multiple perspectives* (pp. 130–145). Thousand Oaks, CA: Sage.

- Baxter, L. A. (2010). *Voicing relationships: A dialogic perspective.* Thousand Oaks, CA: Sage.

- Baxter, L. A., & Braithwaite, D. O. (2008). Relational dialectics theory. In L. A. Baxter & D. O. Braithwaite (Eds.), *Engaging theories in interpersonal communication: Multiple perspectives* (pp. 349–361). Thousand Oaks, CA: Sage.

- Baxter, L. A., Braithwaite, D. O., & Nicholson, J. (1999). Turning points in the development of blended families. *Journal of Social and Personal Relationships, 16,* 291–313.

- Baxter, L. A., & Bullis, C. (1986). Turning points in developing romantic relationships. *Human Communication Research, 12,* 469–493.

- Baxter, L. A., & Montgomery, B. M. (1996). *Relating: Dialogues and dialectics.* New York: Guilford Press.

- Baxter, L. A., & Philpott, J. (1980, November). *Relational disengagement: A process view.* Paper presented at the annual meeting of the Speech Communication Association, New York.

- Baxter, L. A., & Pittman, G. (2001). Communicatively remembering turning points of relationship development. *Communication Reports, 14,* 1–18.

- Baxter, L. A., & West, L. (2003). Couple perceptions of their similarities and differences: A dialectical perspective. *Journal of Social and Personal Relationships, 20,* 491–514.

- Baxter, L. A., & Wilmot, W. W. (1984). "Secret tests": Social strategies for acquiring information about the state of the relationship. *Human Communication Research, 2,* 171–201.

- Baxter, L. A., & Wilmot, W. W. (1985). Taboo topics in close relationships. *Journal of Social and Personal Relationships, 2,* 253–269.

- Bayer, J. B., Ellison, N. B., Schoenebeck, S. Y., & Falk, E. B. (2016). Sharing the small moments: Ephemeral social interaction on Snapchat. *Information, Communication & Society, 19,* 956–977.

- Bayes, M. A. (1970). An investigation of the behavioral cues of interpersonal warmth (Doctoral dissertation, University of Miami, 1970). *Dissertation Abstracts International, 31,* 2272B.

- Becker, D. V., Sagarin, B. J., Guadagno, R. E., Millevoi, A., & Nicastle, L. D. (2004). When the sexes need not differ: Emotional responses to the sexual and emotional aspects of infidelity. *Personal Relationships, 11,* 529–538.

- Becker, M., Vignoles, V. L., Owe, E., Esterbrook, M. J., Brown, R., Smith, P. B., Bond, H. H., Regalia, C., & Manzi, C. (2014). Cultural bases for self-evaluation: Seeing oneself positively in different cultural contexts. *Personality and Social Psychology Bulletin, 40,* 657–675.

- Beckner, B. N., & Record, R. A. (2016). Navigating the thin-ideal in an athletic world: Influence of coach communication on female athletes' body image and health choices. *Health Communication, 31,* 364–373.

- Beebe, S. A. (1980). Effects of eye contact, posture and vocal inflection upon credibility and comprehension. *Australian Scan: Journal of Human Communication, 7–8,* 57–70.

- Beier, E. G., & Sternberg, D. P. (1977). Marital communication: Subtle cues between newlyweds. *Journal of Communication, 27,* 92–97.

- Bell, A. P., & Weinberg, M. A. (1978). *Homosexualities: A study of diversity among men and women.* New York: Simon & Schuster.

- Bell, R. A., & Buerkel-Rothfuss, N. L. (1990). S(he) loves me, s(he) loves me not: Predictors of relational information-seeking in courtship and beyond. *Communication Quarterly, 38,* 64–82.

- Bell, R. A., Buerkel-Rothfuss, N. L., & Gore, K. E. (1987). "Did you bring the yarmulke for the cabbage patch kid?" The idiomatic communication of young lovers. *Human Communication Research, 14,* 47–67.

- Bell, R. A., Daly, J. A., & Gonzalez, C. (1987). Affinity-maintenance in marriage and its relationships to women's marital satisfaction. *Journal of Marriage and the Family, 49,* 445–454.

- Bem, S. L. (1974). The measurement of psychological androgyny. *Journal of Consulting and Clinical Psychology, 42,* 155–162.

- Ben-Ari, A., & Lavee, Y. (2007). Dyadic closeness in marriage: From the inside story to a conceptual model. *Journal of Social and Personal Relationships, 24,* 627–644.

- Bendahan, S., Zehnder, C., Pralong, F., & Antonakis, J. (2015). Leader corruption depends on power and testosterone. *Leadership Quarterly, 26,* 101–122.

- Bennett, M., & Earwaker, D. (1994). Victims' responses to apologies: The effects of offender responsibility and offense severity. *Journal of Social Psychology, 134,* 457–464.

- Bente, G., Leuschner, H., Al Issa, A., & Blascovich, J. J. (2010). The others: Universals and cultural specificities in the perception of status and dominance from nonverbal behavior. *Consciousness and Cognition, 19,* 762–777.

- Bentler, P. M., & Newcomb, M. D. (1978). Longitudinal study of marital success and failure. *Journal of Consulting and Clinical Psychology, 46,* 1053–1070.

- Bentley, C. G., Galliher, R. V., & Ferguson, T. J. (2007). Associations among aspects of interpersonal power and relationship functioning in adolescent romantic couples. *Sex Roles, 57,* 483–495.

- Benuto, L., & Meana, M. (2008). Acculturation and sexuality: Investigating gender differences in erotic plasticity. *Journal of Sex Research, 45,* 217–224.

- Beres, M. A., Herold, E., & Maitland, S. B. (2004). Sexual consent behaviors in same-sex relationships. *Journal of Sexual Behavior, 33,* 475–486.

- Berg, J. H., & Clark, M. S. (1986). Differences in social exchange between intimate and other relationships: Gradually evolving or quickly apparent? In V. J. Derlega & B. A. Winstead (Eds.), *Friendship and social interaction* (pp. 101–128). New York: Springer-Verlag.

- Berg, J. H., & McQuinn, R. D. (1986). Attraction and exchange in continuing and noncontinuing dating relationships. *Journal of Personality and Social Psychology, 50,* 942–952.

- Bergen, K. M., Kirby, E., & McBride, M. C. (2007). "How do you get two houses cleaned?": Accomplishing family caregiving in commuter marriages. *Journal of Family Communication, 7,* 287–307.

- Berger, C. R. (1979). Beyond initial interaction: Uncertainty, understanding, and the development of interpersonal relationships. In H. Giles & R. N. St. Clair (Eds.), *Language and social psychology* (pp. 122–144). Oxford, UK: Basil Blackwell.

- Berger, C. R. (1985). Social power and interpersonal communication. In M. L. Knapp & G. R. Miller (Eds.), *Handbook of interpersonal communication* (pp. 439–499). Beverly Hills, CA: Sage.

- Berger, C. R. (1987). Communicating under uncertainty. In M. E. Roloff & G. R. Miller (Eds.), *Interpersonal processes: New directions in communication research* (pp. 39–62). Newbury Park, CA: Sage.

- Berger, C. R. (1993). Uncertainty and social interaction. In S. A. Deetz (Ed.), *Communication yearbook 16* (pp. 491–502). Newbury Park, CA: Sage.

- Berger, C. R., & Calabrese, R. J. (1975). Some explorations in initial interactions and beyond: Toward a developmental theory of interpersonal communication. *Human Communication Research, 1,* 99–112.

- Berger, C. R., & Douglas, W. (1981). Studies in interpersonal epistemology III: Anticipated interaction, self-monitoring, and observational context selection. *Communication Monographs, 48,* 183–196.

- Bergman, S. M., Fearrington, M. E., Davenport, S. W., & Bergman, J. Z. (2011). Millennials, narcissism, and social networking: What narcissists do on social networking sites and why. *Personality and Individual Differences, 50,* 706–711.

- Bernardes, D., Mendes, M., Sarmento, P., Silva, S., & Moreira, J. (1999, June). *Gender differences in love and sex: A cross-cultural study.* Poster presented at the International Network on Personal Relationships Young Scholars Preconference, University of Louisville, KY.

- Berns, S. B., Jacobson, R. W., & Gottman, J. M. (1999). Demand/withdraw interaction patterns between different types of batterers and their spouses. *Journal of Marital and Family Therapy, 25,* 337–348.

- Berscheid, E. (2010). Love in the fourth dimension. *Annual Review of Psychology, 61,* 1–25.

- Berscheid, E., Dion, K., Walster, E., & Walster, G. W. (1971). Physical attractiveness and dating choice: A test of the matching hypothesis. *Journal of Experimental Social Psychology, 7,* 173–189.

- Berscheid, E., & Peplau, L. A. (1983). The emerging science of relationships. In H. H. Kelley, E. Berscheid, A. Christensen, J. H. Harvey, T. L. Huston, G. Levinger, E. McClintock, L. A. Peplau, & D. R. Petterson (Eds.), *Close relationships* (pp. 1–19). New York: Freeman.

- Berscheid, E., & Walster, E. H. (1969). *Interpersonal attraction.* Reading, MA: Addison-Wesley.

- Berscheid, E., & Walster, E. H. (1974). A little bit about love. In T. L. Huston (Ed.), *Foundations of interpersonal attraction* (pp. 355–381). New York: Academic Press.

- Bevan, J. L. (2003). Expectancy violation theory and sexual resistance in close, cross-sex relationships. *Communication Monographs, 70,* 68–82.

- Bevan, J. L. (2008). Experiencing and communicating romantic jealousy: Questioning the investment model. *Southern Journal of Communication, 73,* 42–67.

- Bevan, J. L., Ang, P. C., & Fearns, J. B. (2014). Being unfriended on Facebook: An application of expectancy violation theory. *Computers in Human Behavior, 33,* 171–178.

- Bevan, J. L., & Cameron, K. A. (2001, November). *Attempting to reconcile: The impact of the investment model.* Paper presented at the annual meeting of the National Communication Association, Atlanta, GA.

- Bevan, J. L., Cameron, K. A., & Dillow, M. R. (2003). One more try: Compliance-gaining strategies associated with romantic reconciliation attempts. *Southern Communication Journal, 68,* 121–135.

- Bevan, J. L., Pfyl, J., & Barclay, B. (2012). Negative emotional and cognitive responses to being unfriended on Facebook: An exploratory study. *Computers in Human Behavior, 28,* 1458–1464.

- Bevan, J. L., & Samter, W. (2004). Toward a broader conceptualization of jealousy in close relationships: Two exploratory studies. *Communication Studies, 55,* 14–28.

- Beyers, W., & Goossens, L. (2008). Dynamics of perceived parenting and identity formulation in late adolescence. *Journal of Adolescence, 31,* 165–184.

- Beyers, W., & Seiffge-Krenke, I. (2010). Does identity precede intimacy? Testing Erikson's theory on romantic development in emerging adults of the 21st century. *Journal of Adolescent Research, 25,* 387–415.

- Bickman, L. (1974). The social power of a uniform. *Journal of Applied Social Psychology, 4,* 47–61.

- Billedo, C. J., Kerkhof, P., & Finkenauer, C. (2015). The use of social networking sites for relationship maintenance in long-distance and geographically close romantic relationships. *Cyberpsychology, Behavior, and Social Networking, 18,* 152–157.

- Billings, A. (1979). Conflict resolution in distressed and nondistressed married couples. *Journal of Consulting and Clinical Psychology, 47,* 368–376.

- Bingham, S. G., & Burleson, B. R. (1989). Multiple effects of messages with multiple goals: Some perceived outcomes of responses to sexual harassment. *Human Communication Research, 16,* 184–216.

- Bippus, A. M., & Rollin, E. (2003). Attachment style differences in relational maintenance and conflict behaviors: Friends' perceptions. *Communication Reports, 16,* 113–123.

- Birditt, K. S., Brown, E., Orbuch, T. L., & McIlvane, J. M. (2010). Marital conflict behaviors and implications for divorce over 16 years. *Journal of Marriage and Family, 72,* 1188–1204.

- Birnbaum, G. E., & Reis, H. T. (2012). When does responsiveness pique sexual interest? Attachment and sexual desire in initial acquaintanceships. *Personality and Social Psychology Bulletin, 38*(7), 946–958.

- Birnie-Porter, C., & Hunt, H. M. (2015). Does relationship status matter for sexual satisfaction? The roles of intimacy and attachment avoidance in sexual satisfaction across five types of ongoing sexual relationships. *Canadian Journal of Human Sexuality, 24,* 174–183.

- Bisson, M. A., & Levine, T. R. (2009). Negotiating a friends with benefits relationship. *Archives of Sexual Behavior, 38,* 66–73.

- Black, L. E., Eastwood, M. M., Sprenkle, D. H., & Smith, E. (1991). An exploratory analysis of the construct of leavers versus left as it relates to Levinger's social exchange theory of attractions, barriers, and alternative attractions. *Journal of Divorce and Remarriage, 15,* 127–139.

- Blake, R. R., & Mouton, J. S. (1964). *The managerial grid.* Houston, TX: Gulf.

- Blakinger, K. (2016, January 26). *Phoenix teens spark outrage after posting shocking pic spelling out the N-word with their shirts.* http://www .nydailynews.com/news/national/phoenix-teens-spark-outrage-posting-racist-pic-article-1.250714.

- Blow, A. J., & Hartnett, K. (2005). Infidelity in committed relationships II. A substantive review. *Journal of Marital & Family Therapy, 31,* 217–233.

- Blumstein, P., & Schwartz, P. (1983). *American couples: Money, work, sex.* New York: Morrow.

- Blunt-Vinti, H. D., Wheldon, C., McFarlane, M., Brogan, N., & Walsh-Buhi, E. R. (2016). Assessing relationship and sexual satisfaction in adolescent relationships formed online and offline. *Journal of Adolescent Health, 58,* 11–16.

- Bochner, A. P. (1984). The functions of human communication in interpersonal bonding. In C. C. Arnold & J. W. Bowers (Eds.), *Handbook of rhetorical and communication theory* (pp. 544–621). Boston: Allyn & Bacon.

- Bodie, G. D., & Burleson, B. R. (2008). Explaining variations in the effects of supportive messages: A dual-process framework. In C. Beck (Ed.), *Communication yearbook 32* (pp. 354–398). New York: Routledge.

- Boelen, P. A., & Reijntjes, A. (2009). Negative cognitions in emotional problems following romantic relationship breakups. *Stress and Health, 25,* 11–19.

- Boer, D., Fischer, R., Strack, M., Bond, M. H., Lo, E., & Lam, J. (2011). How shared preferences in music create bonds between people: Values as the missing link. *Personality and Social Psychology Bulletin, 37,* 1159–1171.

- Bogle, K. (2008). *Hooking up: Sex, dating, and relationships on campus.* New York: NYU Press.

- Bolger, N., & Amarel, D. (2007). Effects of social support visibility on adjustment to stress: Experimental evidence. *Journal of Personality and Social Psychology, 92,* 458–475.

- Bolger, N., Zuckerman, A., & Kessler, R. C. (2000). Invisible support and adjustment to stress. *Journal of Personality and Social Psychology, 79,* 953–961.

- Bombar, M. L., & Littig, L. W. (1996). Babytalk as communication of intimate attachment: An initial study in adult romances and friendships. *Personal Relationships, 3,* 137–158.

- Boon, S., & Alderson, K. (2009). A phenomenological study of women in same-sex relationships who were previously married to men. *The Canadian Journal of Human Sexuality, 18*(4), 149–168.

- Boon, S. D., & McLeod, B. A. (2001). Deception in romantic relationships: Subjective estimates of success at deceiving and attitudes toward deception. *Journal of Social and Personal Relationships, 18,* 463–476.

- Boon, S. D., & Sulsky, L. M. (1997). Attributions of blame and forgiveness in romantic relationships: A policy-capturing study. *Journal of Social Behavior and Personality, 12,* 19–44.

- Booth, A., & Edwards, J. N. (1989). Transmission of marital and family quality over the generations: The effect of parental divorce and unhappiness. *Journal of Divorce, 13,* 41–58.

- Booth-Butterfield, M. (1989). Perceptions of harassing communications as a function of locus of control, work force participation, and gender. *Communication Quarterly, 37,* 262–275.

- Bowlby, J. (1969). *Attachment and loss: Vol. 1. Attachment.* New York: Basic Books.

- Bowlby, J. (1973). *Attachment and loss: Vol. 2. Separation.* New York: Basic Books.

- Bowlby, J. (1977). The making and breaking of affectional bonds. *British Journal of Psychiatry, 130,* 201–210.

- Bowlby, J. (1980). *Attachment and loss: Vol. 3. Loss, sadness, and depression.* New York: Basic Books.

- Boyden, T., Carroll, J. S., & Maier, R. A. (1984). Similarity and attraction in homosexual males: The effects of age and masculinity-femininity. *Sex Roles, 10,* 939–948.

- Boyle, A. M., & O'Sullivan, L. F. (2016). Staying connected: Computer-mediated and face-to-face communication in college students' dating relationships. *Cyberpsychology, Behavior, and Social Networking, 19,* 299–307.

- Bradac, J. J., Bowers, J. W., & Courtwright, J. A. (1979). Three language variables in communication research: Intensity, immediacy and diversity. *Human Communication Research, 5,* 257–269.

- Bradac, J. J., Hosman, L. A., & Tardy, C. H. (1978). Reciprocal disclosures and language intensity: Attributional consequences. *Communication Monographs, 45,* 1–14.

- Bradbury, T. N., & Fincham, F. D. (1990). Attributions in marriage: Review and critique. *Psychological Bulletin, 107,* 3–33.

- Bradford, L. (1980). The death of a dyad. In B. W. Morse & L. A. Phelps (Eds.), *Interpersonal communication: A relational perspective* (pp. 497–508). Minneapolis, MN: Burgess.

- Braiker, H. B., & Kelley, H. H. (1979). Conflict in the development of close relationships. In R. L. Burgess & T. L. Huston (Eds.), *Social exchange in developing relationships* (pp. 135–168). New York: Academic Press.

- Braithwaite, D. O. (1995). Ritualized embarrassment at "coed" wedding and baby showers. *Communication Reports, 8,* 145–157.

- Braithwaite, D. O., Baxter, L. A., & Harper, A. M. (1998). The role of rituals in the management of the dialectical tension of "old" and "new" in blended families. *Communication Studies, 49,* 101–120.

- Bramlett, M. D., & Mosher, W. D. (2002). *Cohabitation, marriage, divorce, and remarriage in the United States* (Vol. 23). Hyattsville, MD: National Center for Health Statistics.

- Brandau-Brown, F. E., & Ragsdale, J. D. (2008). Personal, moral, and structural commitment and the repair of marital relationships. *Southern Communication Journal, 73,* 68–83.

- Brashers, D. E. (2001). Communication and uncertainty management. *Journal of Communication, 51,* 477–497.

- Bratslavsky, E., Baumeister, R. F., & Sommer, K. L. (1998). To love or be loved in vain: The trials and tribulations of unrequited love. In B. H. Spitzberg & W. C. Cupach (Eds.), *The dark side of close relationships* (pp. 307–326). Mahwah, NJ: Lawrence Erlbaum.

- Braun, M., Lewin-Epstein, N., Stier, H., & Baumgartner, M. K. (2008). Perceived equity in the gendered division of household labor. *Journal of Marriage and the Family, 70,* 1145–1156.

- Brehm, S. S., & Kassin, S. M. (1990). *Social psychology.* Boston: Houghton Mifflin.

- Brennan, K. A., & Shaver, P. R. (1995). Dimensions of adult attachment, affect regulations, and romantic relationship functioning. *Personality and Social Psychology Bulletin, 21,* 267–283.

- Brenner, R. E., & Vogel, D. L. (2015). Measuring thought content valence after a breakup: Development of the positive and negative ex-relationship thought scale. *Journal of Counselling Psychology, 62,* 476–487.

- Bretherton, I. (1988). Open communication and internal working models: Their role in the development of attachment relationships. In R. A. Thompson (Ed.), *Nebraska symposium on motivation* (pp. 57–113). Lincoln: University of Nebraska Press.

- Bridge, K., & Baxter, L. A. (1992). Blended friendships: Friends as work associates. *Western Journal of Communication, 56,* 200–225.

- Brock, L. J., & Jennings, G. H. (1993). Sexuality education: What daughters in their 30s wish their mothers had told them. *Family Relationships, 42,* 61–65.

- Brody, N., & Peña, J. (2015). Equity, relational maintenance, and linguistic features of text messaging. *Computers in Human Behavior, 49,* 499–506.

- Brown, D. E. (1991). *Human universals.* Philadelphia: Temple University Press.

- Brown, H. G. (1962). *Sex and the single girl.* New York: Bernard Gies.

- Brown, M., & Auerbach, A. (1981). Communication patterns in the initiation of marital sex. *Medical Aspects of Human Sexuality, 15,* 105–117.

- Brown, P., & Levinson, S. (1987). *Politeness: Some universals in language usage.* Cambridge, UK: Cambridge University Press.

- Brown, R. (1965). *Social psychology.* New York: Free Press.

- Brown, S. L. (2000). Union transitions among cohabitors: The significance of relationship assessments and expectations. *Journal of Marriage and the Family, 62*, 833–846.

- Brown, S. L., & Booth, A. (1996). Cohabitation versus marriage: A comparison of relationship quality. *Journal of Marriage and the Family, 58*, 668–678.

- Browning, J. R., Kessler, D., Hatfield, E., & Choo, P. (1999). Power, gender and sexual behavior. *The Journal of Sex Research, 36*, 342–347.

- Brownridge, D. A., & Halli, S. S. (2000). "Living in sin" and sinful living: Toward filling a gap in the explanation of violence against women. *Aggression and Violent Behavior, 5*, 565–583.

- Brown-Smith, N. (1998). Family secrets. *Journal of Family Issues, 19*, 20–42.

- Brumbaugh, C. C., & Fraley, R. C. (2015). Too fast, too soon? An empirical investigation into rebound relationships. *Journal of Social and Personal Relationships, 32*, 99–118.

- Bryan, A. D., Webster, G. D., & Mahaffey, A. L. (2011). The big, the rich, and the powerful: Physical, financial, and social dimensions of dominance in mating and attraction. *Personality and Social Psychology Bulletin, 37*, 365.

- Bryant, E. M., & Marmo, J. (2010). Relational maintenance strategies on Facebook. *Kentucky Journal of Communication.* http://kycommunication.com/jenniferpdf/Bryant.pdf.

- Bryant, E. M., & Marmo, J. (2012). The rules of Facebook friendship: A two-stage examination of interaction rules in close, casual, and acquaintance friendships. *Journal of Social and Personal Relationships, 29*, 1013–1035.

- Bryson, J. B. (1976, September). *The nature of sexual jealousy: An exploratory paper.* Paper presented at the annual meeting of the American Psychological Association, Washington, DC.

- Bryson, J. B. (1977, September). *Situational determinants of the expression of jealousy.* Paper presented at the annual meeting of the American Psychological Association, San Francisco, CA.

- Buchanan, C. M., Maccoby, E. E., & Dornbusch, S. M. (1991). Caught between parents: Adolescents' experience in divorce homes. *Child Development, 62*, 1008–1029.

- Buchanan, C. M., Maccoby, E. E., & Dornbusch, S. M. (1996). *Adolescents after divorce.* Cambridge, MA: Harvard University Press.

- Buehler, C., Anthony, C., Krishnakumar, A., Stone, G., Gerad, J., & Pemberton, S. (1997). Intraparental conflict and youth problem behaviors: A meta-analysis. *Journal of Child and Family Studies, 6*, 233–247.

- Buhrmester, D., Furman, W., Wittenberg, M. T., & Reis, H. T. (1988). Five domains of interpersonal competence in peer relationships. *Journal of Personality and Social Psychology, 55*, 991–1008.

- Bulanda, J. R. (2011). Gender, marital power, and marital quality in later life. *Journal of Women and Aging, 23*, 3–22.

- Buller, D. B., & Aune, R. K. (1987). Nonverbal cues to deception among intimates, friends, and strangers. *Journal of Nonverbal Behavior, 11*, 269–290.

- Buller, D. B., & Burgoon, J. K. (1994). Deception: Strategic and nonstrategic communication. In J. A. Daly & J. M. Wiemann (Eds.), *Strategic interpersonal communication* (pp. 191–223). Hillsdale, NJ: Lawrence Erlbaum.

- Buller, D. B., Strzyzewski, K. D., & Comstock, J. (1991). Interpersonal deception: I. Deceivers' reactions to receivers suspicious and probing. *Communication Monographs, 58*, 1–24.

- Bullis, C., Clark, C., & Sline, R. (1993). From passion to commitment: Turning points in romantic relationships. In P. J. Kalbfleisch (Ed.), *Interpersonal communication: Evolving interpersonal relationships* (pp. 213–236). Hillsdale, NJ: Lawrence Erlbaum.

- Burgoon, J. K. (1978). A communication model of personal space violations: Explication and an initial test. *Human Communication Research, 4*, 129–142.

- Burgoon, J. K., & Bacue, A. (2003). Nonverbal communication skills. In B. R. Burleson & J. O. Greene (Eds.), *Handbook of communication and social interaction skills* (pp. 179–219). Mahwah, NJ: Lawrence Erlbaum.

- Burgoon, J. K., & Dillman, L. (1995). Gender, immediacy and nonverbal communication. In P. J. Kalbfleisch & M. J. Cody (Eds.), *Gender, power, and communication in human relationships* (pp. 63–81). Hillsdale, NJ: Lawrence Erlbaum.

- Burgoon, J. K., Guerrero, L. K., & Floyd, K. (2010). *Nonverbal communication.* New York: Pearson.

- Burgoon, J. K., & Hale, J. L. (1984). The fundamental topoi of relational communication. *Communication Monographs, 51*, 193–214.

- Burgoon, J. K., & Hale, J. L. (1987). Validation and measurement of the fundamental themes of relational communication. *Communication Monographs, 54*, 19–41.

- Burgoon, J. K., & Hale, J. L. (1988). Nonverbal expectancy violations: Model elaboration and application to immediacy behaviors. *Communication Monographs, 55*, 58–79.

- Burgoon, J. K., Johnson, M. L., & Koch, P. T. (1998). The nature and measurement of interpersonal dominance. *Communication Monographs, 65*, 308–335.

- Burgoon, J. K., & Langer, E. (1995). Language, fallacies, and mindlessness-mindfulness. In B. R. Burleson (Ed.), *Communication yearbook 18* (pp. 105–132). Thousand Oaks, CA: Sage.

- Burgoon, J. K., & Le Poire, B. A. (1993). Effects of communication expectancies, actual communication, and expectancy disconfirmation on evaluations of communicators and their communication behavior. *Human Communication Research, 20*, 67–96.

- Burgoon, J. K., & Newton, D. A. (1991). Applying a social meaning model to relational message interpretations of conversational involvement: Comparing observer and participant perspectives. *Southern Communication Journal, 56*, 96–113.

- Burgoon, J. K., Stern, L. A., & Dillman, L. (1995). *Interpersonal adaptation: Dyadic interaction patterns.* New York: Cambridge University Press.

- Burgoon, J., Stoner, M., Bonita, J., & Dunbar, N. (2003, January). *Trust and deception in mediated communication.* 36th Hawaii International Conference on Systems Sciences, 44a.

- Buri, J. R., Louiselle, P. A., Misukanis, T. M., & Mueller, R. A. (1988). Effects of parental authoritarianism and authoritativeness on self-esteem. *Personality and Social Psychology Bulletin, 14*, 271–282.

- Burke, R. J., Weir, T., & Harrison, D. (1976). Disclosure of problems and tensions experienced by marital partners. *Psychological Reports, 38*, 531–542.

- Burleson, B. R. (1982). The development of comforting communication skills in childhood and adolescence. *Child Development, 53*, 1578–1588.

- Burleson, B. R. (1984). Comforting communication. In H. Sypher & J. L. Applegate (Eds.), *Communication by children and adults* (pp. 63–104). Beverly Hills, CA: Sage.

- Burleson, B. R. (1998). Similarities in social skills, interpersonal attraction, and the development of personal relationships. In J. S. Trent (Ed.), *Communication: Views from the helm for the twenty-first century* (pp. 77–84). Boston: Allyn & Bacon.

- Burleson, B. R. (2003). The experience and effects of emotional support: What the study of cultural and gender differences can tell us about close relationships, emotion, and interpersonal communication. *Personal Relationships, 10*, 1–23.

- Burleson, B. R. (2009). Understanding the outcomes of supportive communication: A dual-process approach. *Journal of Social and Personal Relationships, 26*, 21–38.

- Burleson, B. R., Delia, J. G., & Applegate, J. L. (1992). Effects of maternal communication and children's social-cognitive and communication skills on children's acceptance by the peer group. *Family Relations, 41*, 264–272.

- Burleson, B. R., & Goldsmith, D. J. (1998). How the comforting process works: Alleviating emotional distress through conversationally induced reappraisals. In P. A. Andersen & L. K. Guerrero (Eds.), *Handbook of communication and emotion: Theory, research, contexts, and applications* (pp. 246–275). San Diego, CA: Academic Press.

- Burleson, B. R., Kunkel, A. W., Samter, W., & Werking, K. J. (1996). Men's and women's evaluations of communication skills in personal relationships: When sex differences make a difference—and when they don't. *Journal of Social and Personal Relationships, 13*, 201–224.

- Burleson, B. R., & MacGeorge, E. L. (2002). Supportive communication. In M. L. Knapp & J. A. Daly (Eds.), *The handbook of interpersonal communication* (3rd ed., pp. 374–424). Thousand Oaks, CA: Sage.

- Burleson, B. R., & Samter, W. (1985a). Consistencies in theoretical and naive evaluations of comforting messages. *Communication Monographs, 52*, 104–123.

• Burleson, B. R., & Samter, W. (1985b). Individual differences in the perception of comforting messages. *Central States Speech Journal, 36,* 39–50.

• Burleson, B. R., & Samter, W. (1994). A social skills approach to relationship maintenance: How individual differences in communication skills affect the achievement of relationship functions. In D. J. Canary & L. Stafford (Eds.), *Communication and relational maintenance* (pp. 61–90). San Diego, CA: Academic Press.

• Burrell, N. A., & Koper, R. J. (1998). The efficacy of powerful/powerless language on attitudes and source credibility. In M. Allen & R. Preiss (Eds.), *Persuasion: Advances through meta-analysis* (pp. 203–216). Creskill, NJ: Hampton Press.

• Burris, J. L., Smith, G. T., & Carlson, C. R. (2009). Religiousness, spirituality, and sexual practices. *Journal of Sex Research, 46,* 282–289.

• Buss, D. M. (1988a). From vigilance to violence: Tactics of mate retention in American undergraduates. *Ethology and Sociology, 9,* 291–317.

• Buss, D. M. (1988b). Love acts: The evolutionary biology of love. In R. J. Sternberg & M. L. Barnes (Eds.), *The psychology of love* (pp. 100–117). New Haven, CT: Yale University Press.

• Buss, D. M. (1989). Sex differences in human mate preferences: Evolutionary hypotheses tested in 37 cultures. *Behavioral and Brain Sciences, 12,* 1–49.

• Buss, D. M. (1994). *The evolution of desire: Strategies of mate selection.* New York: Basic Books.

• Buss, D. M., Larsen, R. J., Westen, D., & Semmelroth, J. (1992). Sex differences in jealousy: Evolution, physiology, and psychology. *Psychological Science, 3,* 251–255.

• Bustamante, R. M., Nelson, J. A., Henriksen, R. A., Jr., & Monakes, S. (2011). Intercultural couples: Coping with culture-related stressors. *The Family Journal, 19,* 154–164.

• Buunk, B. P. (1980). Extramarital sex in the Netherlands: Motivations in social and marital context. *Alternative Lifestyles, 3,* 11–39.

• Buunk, B. P. (1982). Strategies of jealousy: Styles of coping with extramarital involvement of the spouse. *Family Relations, 31,* 13–18.

• Buunk, B., & Bringle, R. G. (1987). Jealousy in love relationships. In D. Perlman & S. Duck (Eds.), *Intimate relationships: Development, dynamics, and deterioration* (pp. 123–147). Newbury Park, CA: Sage.

• Buunk, B. P., Dijkstra, P., Fetchenhauer, D., & Kenrick, D. T. (2002). Age and gender differences in mate selection criteria for various involvement levels. *Personal Relationships, 9,* 271–278.

• Buunk, B. P., & Mutsaers, W. (1999). Equity perceptions and marital satisfaction in former and current marriage: A study among the remarried. *Journal of Social and Personal Relationships, 16,* 123–132.

• Byers, E. S. (1996). How well does the traditional sexual script explain sexual coercion? Review of a program of research. *Journal of Psychology and Human Sexuality, 8,* 7–25.

• Byers, E. S. (2011). Beyond the birds and the bees and was it good for you? Thirty years of research on sexual communication. *Canadian Psychology, 52,* 20–28.

• Byers, E. S., Demmons, S., & Lawrence, K. (1998). Sexual satisfaction within dating relationships: A test of the interpersonal exchange model of sexual satisfaction. *Journal of Social and Personal Relationships, 15,* 257–267.

• Byers, E. S., & Lewis, K. (1988). Dating couples' disagreements over the desired level of sexual activity. *Journal of Sex Research, 24,* 15–29.

• Byers, E. S., & Wilson, P. (1985). Accuracy of women's expectations regarding men's responses to refusals of sexual advances in dating situations. *International Journal of Women's Studies, 4,* 376–387.

• Byrne, D. (1961). Interpersonal attraction and attitude similarity. *Journal of Abnormal and Social Psychology, 62,* 713–715.

• Byrne, D. (1971). *The attraction paradigm.* New York: Academic Press.

• Byrne, D. (1992). The transition from controlled laboratory experimentation to less controlled settings: Surprise! Additional variables are operative. *Communication Monographs, 59,* 190–198.

• Byrne, D. (1997). An overview (and underview) of research and theory within the attraction paradigm. *Journal of Social and Personal Relationships, 14,* 417–431.

• Byrne, D., & Clore, G. L. (1970). A reinforcement model for evaluative responses. *Personality: An International Journal, 1,* 103–128.

• Cacioppo, S., & Cacioppo, J. T. (2016). Demystifying the neuroscience of love. *Emotion Review, 8*(2), 108–109.

• Caldwell, M. A., & Peplau, L. A. (1982). Sex differences in same-sex friendship. *Sex Roles, 8,* 721–732.

• Callender, K. A. (2015). Understanding antigay bias from a cognitive-affective-behavioral-perspective. *Journal of Homosexuality, 62,* 782–803.

• Campbell, A. (2008). The morning after the night before: Affective reactions to one-night stands among mated and unmated men and women. *Human Nature, 19,* 157–173.

• Campbell, E., Adams, R., & Dobson, W. R. (1984). Familial correlates of identity formation in late adolescence: A study of the predictive utility of connectedness and individuality in family relationships. *Journal of Youth and Adolescence, 13,* 509–525.

• Campbell, W. K. (1999). Narcissism and romantic attraction. *Journal of Personality and Social Psychology, 77,* 1254–1270.

• Campbell, W. K., & Foster, C. A. (2002). Narcissism and commitment in romantic relationships: An investment model analysis. *Personality and Social Psychology Bulletin, 28,* 484–495.

• Canary, D. J., & Cody, M. J. (1994). *Interpersonal communication: A goals-based approach.* New York: St. Martin's Press.

• Canary, D. J., Cupach, W. R., & Messman, S. J. (1995). *Relationship conflict.* Thousand Oaks, CA: Sage.

• Canary, D. J., & Hause, K. G. (1993). Is there any reason to research sex differences in communication? *Communication Quarterly, 41,* 129–144.

• Canary, D. J., & Lakey, S. G. (2006). Managing conflict in a competent manner: A mindful look at events that matter. In J. Oetzel & S. Ting-Toomey (Eds.), *The SAGE handbook of communication and conflict* (pp. 185–210). Thousand Oaks, CA: Sage.

• Canary, D. J., & Spitzberg, B. H. (1987). Appropriateness and effectiveness perceptions of conflict strategies. *Human Communication Research, 14,* 93–118.

• Canary, D. J., & Spitzberg, B. H. (1989). A model of perceived competence of conflict strategies. *Human Communication Research, 15,* 630–649.

• Canary, D. J., & Spitzberg, B. H. (1990). Attribution biases and associations between conflicts strategies and competence outcomes. *Communication Monographs, 57,* 139–151.

• Canary, D. J., & Stafford, L. (1992). Relational maintenance strategies and equity in marriage. *Communication Monographs, 59,* 243–267.

• Canary, D. J., & Stafford, L. (1994). Maintaining relationships through strategic and routine interaction. In D. J. Canary & L. Stafford (Eds.), *Communication and relational maintenance* (pp. 3–22). San Diego, CA: Academic Press.

• Canary, D. J., & Stafford, L. (2001). Equity in the preservation of personal relationships. In J. Harvey & A. Wenzel (Eds.), *Close romantic relationships: Maintenance and enhancement* (pp. 133–151). Mahwah, NJ: Lawrence Erlbaum.

• Canary, D. J., Stafford, L., Hause, K. S., & Wallace, L. A. (1993). An inductive analysis of relational maintenance strategies: Comparisons among lovers, relatives, friends, and others. *Communication Research Reports, 10,* 5–14.

• Caplan, S. E. (2003). Preference for online social interaction: A theory of problematic Internet use and psychosocial well-being. *Communication Research, 30,* 625–648.

• Cappella, J. N. (1988). Personal relationships, social relationships and patterns of interaction. In S. Duck (Ed.), *Handbook of personal relationships: Theory, research and interventions* (pp. 325–342). Chichester, UK: Wiley.

• Carlson, J. R., & George, J. F. (2004). Media appropriateness in the conduct and discovery of deceptive communication: The relative influence of richness and synchronicity. *Group Decision and Negotiation, 13,* 191–210.

• Carney, D. R., Hall, J. A., & LeBeau, L. S. (2005). Beliefs about the nonverbal expression of social power. *Journal of Nonverbal Behavior, 29,* 105–123.

• Carr, D., Freedman, V. A., Cornman, J. C., & Schwarz, N. (2014). Happy marriage, happy life? Marital quality and subjective well-being in later life. *Journal of Marriage and Family, 76,* 930–948.

• Carr, D., & Springer, K. W. (2010). Advances in families and health research in the 21st century. *Journal of Marriage and Family, 72,* 743–761.

• Carson, A., & Banuazizi, A. (2008). It's not fair!: Similarities and differences in resource distribution between American and Filipino fifth graders. *Journal of Cross-Cultural Psychology, 39,* 493–514.

• Carson, J. W., Carson, K. M., Gil, K. M., & Baucom, D. H. (2007). Self-expansion as a mediator of relationship improvements in a mindfulness intervention. *Journal of Marital and Family Therapy, 33,* 517–528.

• Caspi, A., & Gorsky, P. (2006). Online deception: Prevalence, motivation, and emotion. *Cyberpsychology and Behavior, 9,* 54–59.

• Catallozzi, M., Simon, P. J., Davidson, L. L., Breitbart, V., & Rickart, V. I. (2011). Understanding control in adolescent and young adult relationships. *Archives of Pediatric Adolescent Medicine, 165,* 313–319.

• Cate, R. M., Levin, L. A., & Richmond, L. S. (2002). Premarital relationship stability: A review of recent research. *Journal of Social and Personal Relationships, 19,* 261–284.

• Cate, R. M., & Lloyd, S. A. (1988). Courtship. In S. Duck (Ed.), *Handbook of personal relationships* (pp. 409–427). New York: Wiley.

• Cate, R. M., Lloyd, S. A., & Henton, J. M. (1985). The effect of equity, equality, and reward level on the stability of students' premarital relationships. *Journal of Social Psychology, 125,* 715–721.

• Cate, R. M., Lloyd, S. A., & Long, E. (1988). The role of rewards and fairness in developing premarital relationships. *Journal of Marriage and the Family, 50,* 443–452.

• Cate, R. M., Long, E., Angera, J. J., & Draper, K. K. (1993). Sexual intercourse and relational development. *Family Relations, 42,* 158–164.

• Caughlin, J. P. (2002). The demand/withdrawal pattern of communication as a predictor of marital satisfaction over time: Unresolved issues and future directions. *Human Communication Research, 28,* 49–85.

• Caughlin, J. P., & Afifi, T. D. (2004). When is topic avoidance unsatisfying? Examining moderators of the association between avoidance and dissatisfaction. *Human Communication Research, 30,* 479–513.

• Caughlin, J. P., Afifi, W. A., Carpenter-Theune, K. E., & Miller, L. E. (2005). Reasons for and consequences of revealing personal secrets in close relationships: A longitudinal study. *Personal Relationships, 12,* 43–60.

• Caughlin, J. P., & Golish, T. (2002). An analysis of the association between topic avoidance and dissatisfaction: Comparing perceptual and interpersonal explanations. *Communication Monographs, 69,* 275–296.

• Caughlin, J. P., & Vangelisti, A. L. (1999). Desire for change in one's partner as a predictor of the demand/withdraw pattern of marital communication. *Communication Monographs, 66,* 66–89.

• Caughlin, J. P., & Vangelisti, A. L. (2006). Conflict in dating and marital relationships. In J. G. Oetzel & S. Ting-Toomey (Eds.), *The SAGE handbook of conflict communication* (pp. 129–157). Thousand Oaks, CA: Sage.

• Caughlin, J. P., & Vangelisti, A. L. (2009). Why people conceal or reveal secrets: A multiple goals theory perspective. In T. D. Afifi & W. A. Afifi (Eds.), *Uncertainty, information management, and disclosure decisions: Theories and applications* (pp. 279–299). New York: Routledge.

• Centers for Disease Control and Prevention. (1997, May 2). Contraceptive practices before and after an intervention promoting condom use to prevent HIV infection and other sexually transmitted diseases among women—Selected U.S. sites, 1993–1997. *MMWR Weekly, 46*(17). www.cdc.gov/mmwr/.

• Cerny, J. A., & Janssen, E. (2011). Patterns of sexual arousal in homosexual, bisexual, and heterosexual men. *Archives of Sexual Behavior, 40,* 687–697.

• Chaiken, S. (1979). Communicator physical attractiveness and persuasion. *Journal of Personality and Social Psychology, 37,* 1387–1397.

• Chapman, G. (1995). *The five languages of love.* Chicago: Northfield.

• Chappetta, K. C., & Barth, J. M. (2016). How gender role stereotypes affect attraction in an online dating scenario. *Computers in Human Behavior, 63,* 738–746.

• Chen, G. M. (2015). Losing face of social media: Threats to positive face lead to an indirect effect on retaliatory aggression through negative affect. *Communication Research, 42,* 819–838.

• Cheng, J. T., Tracy, J. L., Ho, S., & Henrich, J. (2016). Listen, follow me: Dynamic vocal signals of dominance predict emergent social rank in humans. *Journal of Experiment Psychology-General, 145,* 536–547.

• Child, J. T., Duck, A. R., Andrews, L. A., Butauski, M., & Petronio, S. (2015). Young adults' management of privacy on Facebook with multiple generations of family members. *Journal of Family Communication, 15,* 349–367.

• Child, J. T., & Starcher, S. C. (2016). Fuzzy Facebook privacy boundaries: Exploring mediated lurking, vague-booking, and Facebook privacy management. *Computers in Human Behavior, 54,* 483–490.

• Chivers, M. L., & Bailey, J. M. (2005). A sex difference in features that elicit genital response. *Biological Psychology, 70,* 115–120.

• Chivers, M. L., Soto, M. C., & Blanchard, R. (2007). Gender and sexual orientation differences in sexual response to sexual activities versus gender of actors in sexual films. *Journal of Personality and Social Psychology, 93,* 1108–1121.

• Christensen, A., Eldridge, K., Catta-Preta, A. B., Lim, V. R., & Santagata, R. (2006). Cross-cultural consistency of the demand/withdraw interaction pattern in couples. *Journal of Marriage and the Family, 68,* 1029–1044.

• Christensen, A., & Heavey, C. L. (1990). Gender and social structure in the demand/withdrawal pattern of marital conflict. *Journal of Personality and Social Psychology, 59,* 73–81.

• Christensen, A., & Shenk, J. L. (1991). Communication, conflict, and psychological distance in nondistressed, clinical, and divorcing couples. *Journal of Consulting and Clinical Psychology, 59,* 458–463.

• Christofides, E., Muise, A., & Desmarais, S. (2009). Information disclosure and control on Facebook: Are they two sides of the same coin or two different processes? *Cyberpsychology & Behavior, 12,* 341–345.

• Christopher, F. S., & Cate, R. M. (1985). Premarital sexual pathways and relationship development. *Journal of Social and Personal Relationships, 2,* 271–288.

• Christopher, F. S., & Frandsen, M. M. (1990). Strategies of influence in sex and dating. *Journal of Social and Personal Relationships, 7,* 89–105.

• Christopher, F. S., & Kissler, T. S. (2004). Exploring marital sexuality: Peeking inside the bedroom and discovering what we don't know—but should. In J. H. Harvey, A. Wenzel, & S. Sprecher (Eds.), *The handbook of sexuality in close relationships* (pp. 371–384). Mahwah, NJ: Lawrence Erlbaum.

• Christopher, F. S., & Lloyd, S. A. (2000). Physical and sexual aggression in relationships. In C. Hendrick & S. S. Hendrick (Eds.), *Close relationships* (pp. 331–343). Thousand Oaks, CA: Sage.

• Christopher, F. S., Owens, L. A., & Strecker, H. L. (1993). An examination of single men's and women's sexual aggressiveness in dating relationships. *Journal of Social and Personal Relationships, 10,* 511–527.

• Christopher, F. S., & Roosa, M. W. (1991). Factors affecting sexual decisions in premarital relationships of adolescents and young adults. In K. McKinney & S. Sprecher (Eds.), *Sexuality in close relationships* (pp. 111–133). Hillsdale, NJ: Lawrence Erlbaum.

• Cialdini, R. B. (1984). *The psychology of influence.* New York: Quill.

• Cialdini, R. B. (1988). *Influence: Science and practice* (2nd ed.). New York: HarperCollins.

• Clark, S. L., Burton, L. M., & Flippen, C. A. (2011). Housing dependence and intimate relationships in the lives of low-income Puerto Rican mothers. *Journal of Family Issues, 32,* 369–393.

• Clarke-Stewart, A., & Brentano, C. (2006). *Divorce: Causes and consequences.* New Haven, CT: Yale University Press.

• Cleek, M. G., & Pearson, T. A. (1985). Perceived causes of divorce: An analysis of interrelationships. *Journal of Marriage and the Family, 47*, 179–183.

• Clements, M. L., Cordova, A. D., Markman, H. J., & Laurenceau, J. (1997). The erosion of marital satisfaction over time and how to prevent it. In R. J. Sternberg & M. Hojjat (Eds.), *Satisfaction in close relationships* (pp. 335–365). New York: Guilford Press.

• Cline, R. J. W., Freeman, K. E., & Johnson, S. J. (1990). Talk among sexual partners about AIDS: Factors differentiating those who talk from those who do not. *Communication Research, 17*, 792–808.

• Clore, G. L., & Byrne, D. (1974). A reinforcement-affect model of attraction. In T. L. Huston (Ed.), *Foundations of interpersonal attraction* (pp. 143–170). New York: Academic Press.

• Cloven, D. H., & Roloff, M. E. (1993). The chilling effect of aggressive potential on the expression of complaints in intimate relationships. *Communication Monographs, 60*, 199–219.

• Coates, D., Wortman, C. B., & Abbey, A. (1979). Reactions to victims. In I. H. Frieze, D. Bar-Tal, & J. S. Carroll (Eds.), *New approaches to social problems* (pp. 21–52). San Francisco: Jossey-Bass.

• Cody, M. (1982). A typology of disengagement strategies and an examination of the role intimacy and relational problems play in strategy selection. *Communication Monographs, 49*, 148–170.

• Cody, M. J., Lee, W. S., & Chao, E. Y. (1989). Telling lies: Correlates of deception among Chinese. In J. Forgas, & M. Innes (Eds), *Recent advances in social psychology: An international perspective* (pp. 359–368). Amsterdam, The Netherlands: North Holland.

• Cohen, E. L. (2010). Expectancy violations in relationships with friends and media figures. *Communication Research Reports, 27*, 97–111.

• Cohen, E. L., Bowman, N. D., & Borchert, K. (2014). Private flirts, public friends: Understanding romantic jealousy responses to an ambiguous social network site message as a function of message access exclusivity. *Computers in Human Behavior, 35*, 535–541.

• Cole, T. (2001). Lying to the one you love: The use of deception in romantic relationships. *Journal of Social and Personal Relationships, 18*, 107–129.

• Collins, N. L., & Miller, L. C. (1994). The disclosure-liking link: From meta-analysis toward a dynamic reconceptualization. *Psychological Bulletin, 116*, 457–475.

• Collins, N. L., & Read, S. J. (1990). Adult attachment, working models, and relationship quality in dating couples. *Journal of Personality and Social Psychology, 58*, 644–663.

• Collins, N. L., & Read, S. J. (1994). Cognitive representations of attachment: The structure and function of working models. In K. Bartholomew & D. Perlman (Eds.), *Attachment processes in adulthood: Advances in personal relationships* (Vol. 5, pp. 53–90). Bristol, PA: Kingsley.

• Collins, T. J., & Gillath, O. (2012). Attachment, breakup strategies, and associated outcomes: The effects of security enhancement on the selection of breakup strategies. *Journal of Research in Personality, 46*, 210–222.

• Comadena, M. E. (1982). Accuracy in detecting deception: Intimate and friendship relationships. In M. Burgoon (Ed.), *Communication yearbook 6* (pp. 446–472). Beverly Hills, CA: Sage.

• Company Info | Facebook Newsroom. (n.d.). http://newsroom.fb.com/company-info

• Confer, J. C., & Cloud, M. D. (2010). Sex differences in response to imagining a partner's heterosexual or homosexual affair. *Personality and Individual Differences, 50*, 129–134.

• Conville, R. L. (1991). *Relational transitions: The evolution of personal relationships.* New York: Praeger.

• Cooley, C. H. (1922). *Human nature and the social order.* New York: Scribner.

• Coontz, S. (2005). *Marriage, a history: From obedience to intimacy, or how love conquered marriage.* New York: Viking.

• Côté, S., Kraus, M. W., Cheng, B. H., Oveis, C., Van der Löwe, I., Lian, H., & Keltner, D. (2011). Social power facilitates the effect of prosocial orientation on empathic accuracy. *Journal of Personality and Social Psychology, 101*, 217–232.

• Cottle, T. J. (1980). *Children's secrets.* Reading, MA: Addison-Wesley.

• Coutts, L. M., & Schneider, F. W. (1976). Affiliative conflict theory: An investigation of the intimacy equilibrium and compensation hypothesis. *Journal of Personality and Social Psychology, 34*, 1135–1142.

• Cowan, G., Drinkard, J., & MacGavin, L. (1984). The effects of target, age, and gender on power use strategies. *Journal of Personality and Social Psychology, 47*, 1391–1398.

• Cozzarelli, C., Hoekstra, S. J., & Bylsma, W. H. (2000). General versus specific mental models of attachment: Are they associated with different outcomes? *Personality and Social Psychology Bulletin, 26*, 605–618.

• Craddock, E., vanDellen, M. R., Novak, S. A., & Ranby, K. W. (2015). Influence in relationships: A meta-analysis on health-related social control. *Basic and Applied Social Psychology, 37*, 118–130.

• Cramer, D. (2002). Linking conflict management behaviours and relational satisfaction: The intervening role of conflict outcome satisfaction. *Journal of Social and Personal Relationships, 19*, 431–438.

• Cravens, J. D., Leckie, K. R., & Whiting, J. B. (2013). Facebook infidelity: When poking becomes problematic. *Contemporary Family Therapy, 35*, 74–90.

• Crawford, D. W., Feng, D., Fischer, J. L., & Diana, L. K. (2003). The influence of love, equity, and alternatives on commitment in romantic relationships. *Family and Consumer Sciences Research Journal, 13*, 253–271.

• Creasey, G., Kershaw, K., & Boston, A. (1999). Conflict management with friends and romantic partners: The role of attachment and negative mood regulation expectancies. *Journal of Youth and Adolescence, 28*, 523–543.

• Crocker, J., & Schwartz, I. (1985). Prejudice and ingroup favoritism in a minimal intergroup situation: Effects of self-esteem. *Personality and Social Psychology Bulletin, 11*, 379–386.

• Crooks, R., & Baur, K. (1999). *Our sexuality.* Pacific Grove, CA: Brooks/Cole.

• Cunningham, J. D., & Antill, J. K. (1994). Cohabitation and marriage: Retrospective and predictive comparisons. *Journal of Social and Personal Relationships, 11*, 77–93.

• Cunningham, J. D., & Antill, J. K. (1995). Current trends in marital cohabitation: In search of the POSSLQ. In J. T. Wood & S. Duck (Eds.), *Under-studied relationships: Off the beaten track* (pp. 148–172). Thousand Oaks, CA: Sage.

• Cupach, W. R. (1994). Social predicaments. In W. R. Cupach & B. H. Spitzberg (Eds.), *The dark side of interpersonal communication* (pp. 159–180). Hillsdale, NJ: Lawrence Erlbaum.

• Cupach, W. R., & Comstock, J. (1990). Satisfaction with sexual communication in marriage: Links to sexual satisfaction and dyadic adjustment. *Journal of Social and Personal Relationships, 7*, 179–186.

• Cupach, W. R., & Metts, S. (1986). Accounts of relational dissolution: A comparison of marital and non-marital relationships. *Communication Monographs, 53*, 311–334.

• Cupach, W. R., & Metts, S. (1991). Sexuality and communication in close relationships. In K. McKinney & S. Sprecher (Eds.), *Sexuality in close relationships* (pp. 93–110). Hillsdale, NJ: Lawrence Erlbaum.

• Cupach, W. R., & Metts, S. (1994). *Facework.* Thousand Oaks, CA: Sage.

• Cupach, W. R., & Metts, S. (1995). The role of sexual attitude similarity in romantic heterosexual relationships. *Personal Relationships, 2*, 287–300.

• Cupach, W. R., Metts, S., & Hoffman, R. (2012, July). *Affective responses to first sexual experience.* Paper presented at the International Association for Relationship Research, Chicago, IL.

• Cupach, W. R., & Spitzberg, B. H. (Eds.). (1994). *The dark side of interpersonal communication.* Hillsdale, NJ: Lawrence Erlbaum.

• Cupach, W. R., & Spitzberg, B. H. (1998). Obsessive relational intrusion and stalking. In B. H. Spitzberg & W. R. Cupach (Eds.), *The dark side of close relationships* (pp. 233–264). Mahwah, NJ: Lawrence Erlbaum.

• Cupach, W. R., & Spitzberg, B. H. (2000). Obsessive relational intrusion: Incidence, perceived severity, and coping. *Violence and Victims, 15*, 357–372.

• Cupach, W. R., & Spitzberg, B. H. (2004). *The dark side of relationship pursuit: From attraction to obsession and stalking.* Mahwah, NJ: Lawrence Erlbaum.

- Cupach, W. R., & Spitzberg, B. H. (2008). "Thanks but no thanks . . .": The occurrence and management of unwanted relationship pursuit. In S. Sprecher, A. Wenzel, & J. Harvey (Eds.), *Handbook of relationship initiation* (pp. 409–424). New York: Taylor & Francis.

- Cutrona, C. E., & Suhr, J. A. (1992). Controllability of stressful events and satisfaction with spouse support behaviors. *Communication Research, 19*, 154–174.

- Dailey, R. M., Brody, N., & Knapp, J. (2015). Support and influence of friends on dating relationships: Partner and friend perspectives. Personal Relationships, 22, 368–385.

- Dailey, R. M., Hampel, A. D., & Roberts, J. B. (2010). Relational maintenance in on-again/off-again relationships: An assessment of how relational maintenance, uncertainty, and commitment vary by relationship type and status. *Communication Monographs, 77*, 75–101.

- Dailey, R. M., Jin, B., Pfiester, A., & Beck, G. (2011). On-again/off-again dating relationships: what keeps partners coming back? *The Journal of Social Psychology, 151*, 417–440.

- Dailey, R. M., McCracken, A. A., Jin, B., Rossetto, K. R., & Green, E. W. (2013). Negotiating breakups and renewals: Types of on-again/off-again dating relationships. *Western Journal of Communication, 77*, 382–410.

- Dailey, R. M., & Palomares, N. A. (2004). Strategic topic avoidance: An investigation of topic avoidance frequency, strategies used, and relational correlates. *Communication Monographs, 71*, 471–496.

- Dailey, R. M., Pfiester, A., Jin, B., Beck, G., & Clark, G. (2009). On-again/off-again dating relationships: How are they different from other dating relationships? *Personal Relationships, 16*, 23–47.

- Dailey, R. M., Rossetto, K. R., McCracken, A. A., Jin, B., & Green, E. W. (2012). Negotiating breakups and renewals in on-again, off-again dating relationships: Traversing the transitions. *Communication Quarterly, 60*, 165–189.

- Dailey, R. M., Rossetto, K., Pfiester, A., & Surra, C. A. (2009). A qualitative analysis of on-again/off-again romantic relationships: "It's up and down, all around." *Journal of Social and Personal Relationships, 16*, 23–47.

- Dainton, M. (2000). Maintenance behaviors, expectations for maintenance, and satisfaction: Linking comparison levels to relational maintenance strategies. *Journal of Social and Personal Relationships, 17*, 827–842.

- Dainton, M., & Aylor, B. (2001). A relational uncertainty analysis of jealousy, trust, and maintenance in long-distance versus geographically close relationships. *Communication Quarterly, 49*, 172–188.

- Dainton, M., & Aylor, B. (2002). Routine and strategic maintenance efforts: Behavioral patterns, variations associated with relational length, and the prediction of relational characteristics. *Communication Monographs, 69*, 52–66.

- Dainton, M., & Gross, J. (2008). The use of negative behaviors to maintain relationships. *Communication Research Reports, 25*, 179–191.

- Dainton, M., & Stafford, L. (1993). Routine maintenance behaviors: A comparison of relationship type, partner similarity and sex differences. *Journal of Social and Personal Relationships, 10*, 255–271.

- Dainton, M., Stafford, L., & Canary, D. J. (1994). Maintenance strategies and physical affection as predictors of love, liking, and satisfaction in marriage. *Communication Reports, 7*, 88–98.

- Dainton, M., Zelley, E., & Langan, E. (2003). Maintaining friendships throughout the lifespan. In D. J. Canary & M. Dainton (Eds.), *Maintaining relationships through communication: Relational, contextual, and cultural variations* (pp. 79–102). Mahwah, NJ: Lawrence Erlbaum.

- Daly, J. A., Hoggs, E., Sacks, D., Smith, M., & Zimring, L. (1983). Sex and relationship affects social self-grooming. *Journal of Nonverbal Behavior, 7*, 183–189.

- Daly, J. A., & Kreiser, P. O. (1994). Affinity seeking. In J. A. Daly & J. M. Wiemann (Eds.), *Strategic interpersonal communication* (pp. 109–134). Hillsdale, NJ: Lawrence Erlbaum.

- Daniels, E. A., & Zurbriggen, E. L. (2016). The price of sexy: Viewers' perceptions of a sexualized versus nonsexualized Facebook profile photograph. *Psychology of Popular Media Culture, 5*(1), 2–14.

- Darby, B. W., & Schlenker, B. R. (1982). Children's reactions to apologies. *Journal of Personality and Social Psychology, 43*, 743–753.

- Darby, B. W., & Schlenker, B. R. (1989). Children's reactions to transgressions: Effects of the actor's apology, reputation, and remorse. *British Journal of Social Psychology, 28*, 353–364.

- Dargie, E., Blair, K. L., Goldfinger, C., & Pukall, C. F. (2015). Go long! Predictors of positive relationship outcomes in long-distance dating relationships. *Journal of Sex & Marital Therapy, 41*, 181–202.

- Darwin, C. (1998). *The expression of emotion in man and animals*. New York: Oxford University Press. (Original work published 1872).

- Davey, A., Fincham, F. D., Beach, S. R. H., & Brody, G. H. (2001). Attributions in marriage: Examining the entailment model in dyadic context. *Journal of Family Psychology, 15*, 721–734.

- Davies, A. P. C., Goetz, J. C., & Shackelford, T. K. (2008). Exploiting the beauty in the eye of the beholder: The use of physical attraction as a persuasive tactic. *Personality and Individual Differences, 45*, 302–306.

- Davies, P. T., & Cummings, E. M. (1994). Marital conflict and adjustment: An emotional security hypothesis. *Psychological Bulletin, 116*, 387–411.

- Davila, J., Burge, D., & Hammen, C. (1997). Why does attachment style change? *Journal of Personality and Social Psychology, 73*, 826–838.

- Davila, J., Karney, B. R., & Bradbury, T. N. (1999). Attachment change processes in the early years of marriage. *Journal of Personality and Social Psychology, 76*, 783–802.

- Davis, K. E., & Roberts, M. K. (1985). Relationship in the real world: The descriptive approach to personal relationships. In K. J. Gergen & K. E. Davis (Eds.), *The social construction of the person* (pp. 144–163). New York: Springer-Verlag.

- Davis, K. E., & Todd, M. J. (1982). Friendship and love relationships. In E. E. Davis (Ed.), *Advances in descriptive psychology* (Vol. 2, pp. 79–122). Greenwich, CT: JAI Press.

- Davis, K. E., & Todd, M. J. (1985). Assessing friendships: Prototypes, paradigm cases, and relationship description. In S. Duck & D. Perlman (Eds.), *Understanding personal relationships: An interdisciplinary approach* (pp. 17–38). Beverly Hills, CA: Sage.

- Davis, M. (1973). *Intimate relations*. New York: Free Press.

- De Dreu, C. K., & Kret, M. E. (2016). Oxytocin conditions intergroup relations through upregulated in-group empathy, cooperation, conformity, and defense. Biological Psychiatry, 79(3), 165–173.

- De Goede, I. H. A., Branje, S. J. T., & Meeus M. H. J. (2009). Developmental changes in adolescents' perceptions of relationships with their parents. *Journal of Youth and Adolescence, 38*, 75–88.

- de Kwaadsteniet, E. W., & van Dijk, E. (2010). Social status as a cue for tacit coordination. Journal of Experimental Social Psychology, 46, 515–524.

- de Vries, D. A. (2016). Meeting expectations: The effects of expectations on self-esteem following the construction of a dating profile. *Computers in Human Behavior, 62*, 44–50.

- Deandrea, D. C., & Walther, J. B. (2011). Attributions for inconsistencies between online and offline presentation. *Communication Research, 38*, 805–825.

- DeCelles, K. A., DeRue, D. S., Margolis, J. D., & Ceranic, T. L. (2012). Does power corrupt or enable? When and why power facilitates self-interested behavior. *Journal of Applied Psychology, 97*, 681–689.

- DeLamater, J., & Hyde, J. S. (2004). Conceptual and theoretical issues in studying close relationships. In J. H. Harvey, A. Wenzel, & S. Sprecher (Eds.), *The handbook of sexuality in close relationships* (pp. 7–30). Mahwah, NJ: Lawrence Erlbaum.

- DeMaris, A. (2007). The roles of relationship inequity in marital disruption. *Journal of Social and Personal Relationships, 24*, 177–195.

- D'Emilio, J., & Freedman, E. B. (1988). *Intimate matters: A history of sexuality in America*. New York: Harper & Row.

- Denes, A. (2012). Pillow talk: Exploring disclosures after sexual activity. *Western Journal of Communication, 76*, 91–108.

- Denes, A. (2013). Engaging pillow talk: The challenges of studying communication after sexual activity. *International Journal of Communication, 7*, 2495–2506.

• Denes, A. (2015). Genetic and individual influences on predictors of disclosure: Exploring variation in the oxytocin receptor gene and attachment security. *Communication Monographs, 82*, 113–133.

• Denes, A., & Afifi, T. D. (2014). Pillow talk and cognitive decision-making processes: Exploring the influence of orgasm and alcohol on communication after sexual activity. *Communication Monographs, 81*, 333–358.

• Denes, A., Afifi, T. D., & Granger, D. A. (2016). Physiology and pillow talk: Relationships between testosterone and communication post sex. *Journal of Social and Personal Relationships, 33*, 1–28.

• Denes, A., Gasiorek, J., & Giles, H. (2016). "Don't touch that dial": Accommodating musical preferences in interpersonal relationships. *Psychology of Music, 44*, 1193–1201.

• DePaulo, B. M. (1992). Nonverbal behavior and self-presentation. *Psychological Bulletin, 111*, 203–243.

• DePaulo, B. M., Kashy, D. A., Kirkendol, S. E., Wyer, M. M., & Epstein, J. A. (1996). Lying in everyday life. *Journal of Personality and Social Psychology, 70*, 979–995.

• Derlega, V. J., Barbee, A. P., & Winstead, B. A. (1994). Friendship, gender, and social support: Laboratory studies of supportive interactions. In B. R. Burleson, T. L. Albrecht, & I. G. Sarason (Eds.), *Communication of social support: Messages, interactions, relationships, and community* (pp. 136–151). Thousand Oaks, CA: Sage.

• Derlega, V. J., & Grzelak, J. (1979). Appropriateness of self-disclosure. In G. Chelune (Ed.), *Self-disclosure: Origins, patterns, and implications of openness in interpersonal relationships* (pp. 151–176). San Francisco: Jossey-Bass.

• Derlega, V. J., Metts, S., Petronio, S., & Margulis, S. T. (1993). *Self-disclosure*. Newbury Park, CA: Sage.

• DeSteno, D., Bartlett, M. Y., Salovey, P., & Braverman, J. (2002). Sex differences in jealousy: Evolutionary mechanism or artifact of measurement? *Journal of Personality and Social Psychology, 83*, 1103–1116.

• DeSteno, D., & Salovey, P. (1996). Evolutionary origins of sex differences in jealousy? Questioning the "fitness" of the model. *Psychological Science, 7*, 367–372.

• Deutsch, M. (1985). *Distributive justice: A social-psychological perspective*. New Haven, CT: Yale University Press.

• Diamond, L. M. (2012). The desire disorder in research on sexual orientation in women: Contributions of dynamical systems theory. *Archives of Sexual Behavior, 41*, 73–83.

• Diamond, L. M., & Dickenson, J. A. (2012). The neuroimaging of love and desire: Review and future directions. *Clinical Neuropsychiatry, 9*, 39–46.

• Dieckman, L. E. (2000). Private secrets and public disclosures: The case of battered women. In S. Petronio (Ed.), *Balancing the secrets of private disclosures* (pp. 275–286). Mahwah, NJ: Lawrence Erlbaum.

• Dijkstra, P., Barelds, D. P., & Groothof, H. A. (2013). Jealousy in response to online and offline infidelity: The role of sex and sexual orientation. *Scandinavian Journal of Psychology, 54*, 328–336.

• Dillard, J. P. (1989). Types of influence goals in personal relationships. *Journal of Social and Personal Relationships, 6*, 293–308.

• Dillard, J. P., & Witteman, H. (1985). Romantic relationships at work: Organizational and personal influences. *Human Communication Research, 12*, 99–116.

• Dindia, K. (1989, May). *Toward the development of a measure of marital maintenance strategies*. Paper presented at the annual meeting of the International Communication Association, San Francisco, CA.

• Dindia, K. (1997, November). *Men are from North Dakota, women are from South Dakota*. Paper presented at the annual meeting of the Speech Communication Association, Chicago, IL.

• Dindia, K. (2003). Definitions and perspectives on relational maintenance communication. In D. J. Canary & M. Dainton (Eds.), *Maintaining relationships through communication: Relational, contextual, and cultural variations* (pp. 1–28). Mahwah, NJ: Lawrence Erlbaum.

• Dindia, K., & Allen, M. (1992). Sex differences in self-disclosure: A meta-analysis. *Psychological Bulletin, 112*, 106–124.

• Dindia, K., & Baxter, L. A. (1987). Strategies for maintaining and repairing marital relationships. *Journal of Social and Personal Relationships, 4*, 143–158.

• Dindia, K., & Canary, D. J. (1993). Definitions and theoretical perspectives on relational maintenance. *Journal of Social and Personal Relationships, 10*, 163–173.

• Dindia, K., Fitzpatrick, M. A., & Kenny, D. A. (1997). Self-disclosure in spouse and stranger interaction: A social relations analysis. *Human Communication Research, 23*, 388–412.

• Dindia, K., Timmerman, L., Langan, E., Sahlstein, E. M., & Quandt, J. (2004). The function of holiday greetings in maintaining relationships. *Journal of Social and Personal Relationships, 21*, 577–593.

• Dion, K. K. (1972). Physical attractiveness and evaluations of children's transgressions. *Journal of Personality and Social Psychology, 24*, 207–213.

• Dion, K. K. (1986). Stereotyping based on physical attractiveness: Issues and conceptual perspectives. In C. P. Herman, M. P. Zanna, & E. T. Higgins (Eds.), *The Ontario symposium: Vol. 3. Physical appearance, stigma, and social behavior* (pp. 7–21). Hillsdale, NJ: Lawrence Erlbaum.

• Dion, K. K., Berscheid, E., & Walster, E. (1972). What is beautiful is good. *Journal of Personality and Social Psychology, 24*, 285–290.

• Divorce rates around the world. (2011, January 13) Free Republic. www.freerepublic.com/focus/f-religion/2656530/posts.

• Divorces and crude divorce rates, by urban/rural residence: 2002–2006. (2008, July 21). United Nations Statistics Division. http://unstats .un.org/unsd/demographic/products/dyb/ DYB2004/Table25.pdf.

• Doherty, W. J., Willoughby, B. J., & Peterson, B. (2011). Interest in marital reconciliation among divorcing parents. *Family Court Review, 49*, 313–321.

• Dolin, D. J., & Booth-Butterfield, M. (1993). Reach out and touch someone: Analysis of nonverbal comforting responses. *Communication Quarterly, 41*, 383–393.

• Domingue, R., & Mollen, D. (2009). Attachment and conflict communication in adult romantic relationships. *Journal of Social and Personal Relationships, 26*, 678–696.

• Donald, M. (1991). *Origins of the modern mind: Three stages in the evolution of culture and cognition*. Cambridge, MA: Harvard University Press.

• Dougherty, T. W., Turban, D. B., Olson, D. E., Dwyer, P. D., & Lapreze, M. W. (1996). Factors affecting perceptions or workplace sexual harassment. *Journal of Organizational Behavior, 17*, 489–501.

• Douglas, W. (1990). Uncertainty, information-seeking, and liking during initial interaction. *Western Journal of Speech Communication, 54*, 66–81.

• Dovidio, J. F., Brown, C. E., Heltman, K., Ellyson, S. L., & Keating, C. F. (1988). Power displays between women and men in discussions of gender-linked tasks: A multichannel study. *Journal of Personality and Social Psychology, 55*(4), 580.

• Dowdell, E. B., Burgess, A. W., & Flores, J. R. (2011). Online social networking patterns among adolescents, young adults, and sexual offenders. *American Journal of Nursing, 111*, 28–36.

• Dowrick, S. (1999, March–April). The art of letting go. *Utne Reader*, Issue 92, 46–50.

• Draucker, C. B. (1999). "Living in hell": The experience of being stalked. *Issues in Mental Health Nursing, 20*, 473–484.

• Drigotas, S. M., & Rusbult, C. E. (1992). Should I stay or should I go? A dependence model of breakups. *Journal of Personality and Social Psychology, 62*, 62–87.

• Driscoll, R., Davis, K. E., & Lipetz, M. E. (1972). Parental interference and romantic love: The Romeo and Juliet effect. *Journal of Personality and Social Psychology, 24*, 1–10.

• Drouin, M., & Landgraff, C. (2012). Texting, sexting, and attachment in college students' romantic relationships. *Computers in Human Behavior, 28*, 444–449.

• Drouin, M., Tobin, E., & Wygant, K. (2014). "Love the Way You Lie": Sexting deception in romantic relationships. *Computers in Human Behavior, 35*, 542–547.

- Duck, S. (1982). A topography of relational disengagement and dissolution. In S. Duck (Ed.), *Personal relationships 4: Dissolving personal relationships* (pp. 1–30). London: Academic Press.

- Duck, S. (1986). *Human relationships.* Newbury Park, CA: Sage.

- Duck, S. (1988). *Relating to others.* Monterey, CA: Brooks/Cole.

- Duck, S. (1994). Steady as (s)he goes: Relational maintenance as a shared meaning systems. In D. J. Canary & L. Stafford (Eds.), *Communication and relational maintenance* (pp. 45–60). San Diego, CA: Academic Press.

- Duck, S. W. (2005). How do you tell someone you're letting go? A new model of relationship breakup. *The Psychologist, 18,* 210–213.

- Duffy, S. M., & Rusbult, C. E. (1986). Satisfaction and commitment in homosexual and heterosexual relationships. *Journal of Homosexuality, 12,* 1–21.

- Duggan, M., Ellison, N. B., Lampe, C., Lenhart, A., & Madden, M. (2015). Social Media Update 2014. Pew Research Internet Project. http://www.pewinternet.org/files/2015/01/PI_SocialMediaUpdate20144.pdf.

- Dunbar, N. E., & Abra, G. (2010). Observations of dyadic power in interpersonal interaction. *Communication Monographs, 77,* 657–684.

- Dunbar, N. E., Banas, J. A., Rodriguez, D., Liu, S. J., & Abra, G. (2012). Humor use in power-differentiated interactions. *Humor: International Journal of Humor Research, 25,* 469–490.

- Dunbar, N. E., Bippus, A. M., & Young, S. L. (2008). Interpersonal dominance in relational conflict: A view from dyadic power theory. *Interpersona, 2*(1), 1–33.

- Dunbar, N. E., & Burgoon, J. K. (2005). Perceptions of power and dominance in interpersonal encounters. *Journal of Social and Personal Relationships, 22,* 207–233.

- Dunbar, N. E., & Mejia, R. (2013). A qualitative analysis of power-based entrainment and interactional synchrony in couples. *Personal Relationships, 20,* 391–405.

- Dunbar, R. I. M. (2010). The social role of touch in humans and primates: Behavioral function and neurobiological mechanisms. *Neuroscience and Behavioral Review, 34,* 260–268.

- Dunn, J. (1983). Sibling relationships in early childhood. *Child Development, 54,* 787–811.

- Dunn, J. (1988a). Connections between relationships: Implications of research on mothers and siblings. In R. A. Hinde & J. Stevenson-Hinde (Eds.), *Relationships within families: Mutual influences* (pp. 168–180). New York: Oxford University Press.

- Dunn, J. (1988b). Relations among relationships. In S. W. Duck (Ed.), *Handbook of personal relationships* (pp. 193–209). New York: Wiley.

- Dunn, J., & Kendrick, C. (1982). *Siblings: Love, envy, and understanding.* Cambridge, MA: Harvard University Press.

- Dunn, J., & Munn, P. (1987). Development of justification in disputes with another sibling. *Developmental Psychology, 23,* 791–798.

- Duran, R. L., Kelly, L., & Rotaru, T. (2011). Mobile phones in romantic relationships and the dialectic of autonomy vs. connection. *Communication Quarterly, 59,* 19–36.

- Dutton, D. G., & Aron, A. P. (1974). Some evidence for heightened sexual attraction under conditions of high anxiety. *Journal of Personality and Social Psychology, 30,* 510–517.

- Eastwick, P. W., Eagly, A. H., Glick, P., Johannesen-Schmidt, M. C., Fiske, S. T., Blum, A. B., Eckes, T., Freiburger, P., Huang, L., Fernández, M. L., Manganelli, A. M., Pek, J. C. X., Castro, Y. R., Sakalli-Ugurlu, N., Six-Materna, I., & Volpato, C. (2006). Is traditional gender ideology associated with sextyped mate preferences? A test in nine nations. *Sex Roles, 54,* 603–614.

- Eastwick, P. W., Luchies, L. B., Finkel, E. J., & Hunt, L. L. (2014). The predictive validity of ideal partner preferences: A review and meta-analysis. *Psychological Bulletin, 140*(3), 623–665.

- Eden, J., & Veksler, A. E. (2010, April). *He likes me, he loves me not (Part III): Relational maintenance in the context of unrequited attraction.* Paper presented at the Eastern Communication Association Convention, Baltimore.

- Edgar, T., & Fitzpatrick, M. A. (1988). Compliance-gaining and relational interaction: When your life depends on it. *Southern Speech Communication Journal, 53,* 385–405.

- Edgar, T., & Fitzpatrick, M. A. (1993). Expectations for sexual interaction: A cognitive test of the sequencing of sexual communication behaviors. *Health Communication, 5,* 239–261.

- Edlund, J. E., & Sagarin, B. J. (2009). Sex differences in jealousy: Misinterpretation of nonsignificant results as refuting the theory. *Personal Relationships, 16,* 67–78.

- Egbert, N., & Polk, D. (2006). Speaking the language of relational maintenance: A validity test of Chapman's (1992) five love languages. *Communication Research Reports, 23,* 19–26.

- Egland, K. L., Stelzner, M. A., Andersen, P. A., & Spitzberg, B. H. (1997). Perceived understanding, nonverbal communication and relational satisfaction. In J. Aitken & L. Shedletsky (Eds.), *Intrapersonal communication processes* (pp. 386–395). Annandale, VA: Speech Communication Association.

- Eisenberg, A. R. (1992). Conflicts between mothers and their young children. *Merrill-Palmer Quarterly, 38,* 21–43.

- Eisenberg, M. E., Ackard, D. M., Resnick, M. D., & Neumark-Sztainer, D. (2009). Casual sex and psychological health among young adults: Is having "friends with benefits" emotionally damaging. *Perspectives on Sexual and Reproductive Health, 41,* 231–237.

- Ekman, P. (1985). *Telling lies.* New York: Norton.

- Ekman, P., & Friesen, W. V. (1969). Nonverbal leakage and clues to deception. *Psychiatry, 32,* 88–106.

- Ellis, N. K., & Ledbetter, A. M. (2015). Why might distance make the heart grow fonder?: A Relational Turbulence Model investigation of the maintenance of long distance and geographically close romantic relationships. *Communication Quarterly, 63,* 568–585.

- Ellison, N., Heino, R., & Gibbs, J. (2006). Managing impressions online: Self-presentation processes in the online dating environment. *Journal of Computer-Mediated Communication, 11,* 415–441.

- Ellison, N. B., Steinfield, C., & Lampe, C. (2007). The benefits of Facebook "friends": Social capital and college students' use of online social network sites. *Journal of Computer-Mediated Communication, 12,* 1143–1168.

- Ellison, N. B., Steinfield, C., & Lampe, C. (2011). Connection strategies: Social implications of Facebook-enabled communication practices. *New Media and Society, 13,* 873–892.

- Ellyson, S. L., & Dovidio, J. F. (1985). Power, dominance, and nonverbal behavior: Basic concepts and issues. In S. L. Ellyson & J. F. Dovidio (Eds.), *Power, dominance, and nonverbal behavior* (pp. 1–27). New York: Springer-Verlag.

- Emmers, T. M., & Canary, D. J. (1996). The effect of uncertainty reducing strategies on young couples' relational repair and intimacy. *Communication Quarterly, 44,* 166–182.

- Emmers, T. M., & Dindia, K. (1995). The effect of relational stage and intimacy on touch: An extension of Guerrero and Andersen. *Personal Relationships, 2,* 225–236.

- Emmers, T. M., & Hart, R. D. (1996). Romantic relationship disengagement and coping rituals. *Communication Research Reports, 13,* 8–18.

- Emmers-Sommer, T. M. (2004). The effect of communication quality and quantity indicators on intimacy and relational satisfaction. *Journal of Social and Personal Relationships, 21,* 399–411.

- Emmons, R. A. (1989). Exploring the relations between motives and traits: The case of narcissism. In D. M. Buss & N. Cantor (Eds.), *Personality psychology: Recent trends and emerging directions* (pp. 32–44). New York: Springer.

- Ennis, E., Vrij, A., & Chance, C. (2008). Individual differences and lying in everyday life. *Journal of Social and Personal Relationships, 25,* 105–118.

- Erikson, E. H. (1968). *Identity, youth, and crisis.* New York: Norton.

- Exline, R. V., Ellyson, S. L., & Long, B. (1975). Visual behavior as an aspect of power role relationships. In P. Pliner, L. Krames, & T. Alloway (Eds.), *Nonverbal communication of aggression* (pp. 21–52). New York: Plenum Press.

- Exline, R. V., & Winters, L. C. (1965). Affective relations and mutual glances in dyads. In S. Tomkins & C. E. Izard (Eds.), *Affect, cognition, and personality* (pp. 319–350). New York: Springer.

- Fagundes, C. P. (2012). Getting over you: Contributions of attachment theory for postbreakup emotional adjustment. *Personal Relationships, 19,* 37–50.

- Falbo, T., & Peplau, L. A. (1980). Power strategies in intimate relationships. *Journal of Personality and Social Psychology, 38,* 618–628.

- Fales, M. R., Frederick, D. A., Garcia, J. R., Gildersleeve, K. A., Haselton, M. G., & Fisher, H. E. (2016). Mating markets and bargaining hands: Mate preferences for attractiveness and resources in two national studies. *Personality and Individual Differences, 88,* 78–87.

- Farrell, D., & Rusbult, C. E. (1981). Exchange variables as predictors of job satisfaction, job commitment, and turnover: The impact of rewards, costs, alternatives, and investments. *Organizational Behavior and Human Performance, 27,* 78–95.

- Farzan, R., Dabbish, L., Kraut, R., & Postmes, T. (March, 2011). *Increasing commitment to online communities by designing for social presence.* Paper presented at the conference on Computer Supported Cooperative Work and Social Computing, Hangzhou, China.

- Faulkner, S. L., & Hecht, M. L. (2011). The negotiation of closetable identities: A narrative analysis of lesbian, gay, bisexual, transgendered queer Jewish identity. *Journal of Social and Personal Relationships, 28,* 829–847.

- Feeney, J. A. (1995). Adult attachment and emotional control. *Personal Relationships, 2,* 143–159.

- Feeney, J. A. (1999). Adult attachment, emotional control, and marital satisfaction. *Personal Relationships, 6,* 169–185.

- Feeney, J. A. (2004). Hurt feelings in couple relationships: Toward integrative models of the negative effects of hurtful events. *Journal of Social and Personal Relationships, 21,* 487–508.

- Feeney, J. A. (2005). Hurt feelings in couple relationships: Exploring the role of attachment and perceptions of personal injury. *Personal Relationships, 12,* 253–271.

- Feeney, J. A., & Noller, P. (1996). *Adult attachment.* Thousand Oaks, CA: Sage.

- Feeney, J. A., Noller, P., & Callan, V. J. (1994). Attachment style, communication and satisfaction in the early years of marriage. In K. Bartholomew & D. Perlman (Eds.), *Attachment processes in adulthood: Advances in personal relationships* (Vol. 5, pp. 269–308). Bristol, PA: Kingsley.

- Feeney, J. A., Noller, P., & Roberts, N. (1998). Emotion, attachment and satisfaction in close relationships. In P. A. Andersen & L. K. Guerrero (Eds.), *Handbook of communication and emotion: Research, theory, applications and contexts* (pp. 273–505). San Diego, CA: Academic Press.

- Feeney, J. A., Noller, P., & Roberts, N. (2000). Attachment and close relationships. In C. Hendrick & S. S. Hendrick (Eds.), *Close relationships: A sourcebook* (pp. 185–201). Thousand Oaks, CA: Sage.

- Fehr, B. (1988). Prototype analysis of the concepts of love and commitment. *Journal of Personality and Social Psychology, 58,* 281–291.

- Fehr, B. (1996). *Friendship processes.* Thousand Oaks, CA: Sage.

- Fehr, B. (2008). Friendship formation. In S. Sprecher, A. Wenzel, & J. Harvey (Eds.), *The handbook of relationship initiation* (pp. 29–54). Thousand Oaks, CA: Sage.

- Fehr, R., & Gelfand, M. J. (2010). When apologies work: How matching apology components to victims' self-construals facilitates forgiveness. *Organizational Behavior and Human Decision Processes, 113,* 37–50.

- Fehr, B., & Russell, J. A. (1991). The concept of love viewed from a prototype perspective. *Journal of Personality and Social Psychology, 60,* 425–438.

- Feingold, A. (1988). Matching for attractiveness in romantic partners and same-sex friends: A meta-analysis and theoretical critique. *Psychological Bulletin, 104,* 226–235.

- Feingold, A. (1991). Sex differences in the effects of similarity and physical attractiveness on opposite-sex attraction. *Basic and Applied Social Psychology, 12,* 357–367.

- Feldman, R., Weller, A., Zagoory-Sharon, O., & Levine, A. (2007). Evidence for a neuroendocrinological foundation of human affiliation: Plasma oxytocin levels across pregnancy and the postpartum period predict mother-infant bonding. *Psychological Science, 18,* 965–970.

- Feldman, S. S., & Cauffman, E. (1999). Sexual betrayal among late adolescents: Perspectives of the perpetrator and the aggrieved. *Journal of Youth and Adolescence, 228,* 235–258.

- Felmlee, D. H. (1995). Fatal attractions: Affection and disaffection in intimate relationships. *Journal of Social and Personal Relationships, 12,* 295–312.

- Felmlee, D. H. (1998). "Be careful what you wish for . . . ": A quantitative and qualitative investigation of "fatal attraction." *Personal Relationship, 5,* 235–254.

- Felmlee, D. H., Orzechowicz, D., & Fortes, C. (2010). Fairy tales: Attraction and stereotypes in same-gender relationships. *Sex Roles, 62,* 226–240.

- Felmlee, D. H., Sprecher, S., & Bassin, E. (1990). The dissolution of intimate relationships: A hazard model. *Social Psychology Quarterly, 53,* 13–30.

- Fennis, B. M. (2008). Branded into submission: Brand attributes and hierarchization behavior in same-sex and mixed-sex dyads. *Journal of Applied Social Psychology, 38,* 1993–2009.

- Ferguson, C. A. (1964). Baby talk in six languages. *American Anthropologist, 66,* 103–114.

- Ferrara, M. H., & Levine, T. R. (2009). Can't live with them or can't live without them? The effects of betrayal on relational outcomes in college dating relationships. *Communication Quarterly, 57,* 187–204.

- Festinger, L., Schachter, S., & Back, K. (1950). *Social pressures in informal groups: A study of human factor in housing.* New York: Harper.

- Filsinger, E. E., & Thomas, S. J. (1988). Behavioral antecedents of relational stability and adjustment: A five-year longitudinal study. *Journal of Marriage and the Family, 50,* 585–595.

- Fincham, F. D. (2000). The kiss of the porcupines: From attributing responsibility to forgiving. *Personal Relationships, 7,* 1–23.

- Fincham, F. D., Harold, G. T., & Gano-Phillips, S. (2000). The longitudinal association between attributions and marital satisfaction: Direction of effects and role of efficacy expectations. *Journal of Family Psychology, 14,* 267–285.

- Finkel, E. J., Eastwick, P. W., Karney, B. R., Reis, H. T., & Sprecher, S. (2012). Online dating: A critical analysis from the perspective of psychological science. *Psychological Science in the Public Interest, 13,* 3–66.

- Finkenauer, C., Engels, R. C. M. E., & Meeus, W. (2002). Keeping secrets from parents: Advantages and disadvantages of secrecy in adolescence. *Journal of Youth and Adolescence, 31,* 123–136.

- Finkenauer, C., Kubacka, K. E., Engels, R. C. M. E., & Kerkhof, P. (2009). Secrecy in close relationships: Investigating its intrapersonal and interpersonal effects. In T. D. Afifi & W. A. Afifi (Eds.), *Uncertainty, information management, and disclosure decisions: Theories and applications* (pp. 300–319). New York: Routledge.

- Fischer, T. F. C., De Graaf, P. M., & Kalmijn, M. (2005). Friendly and antagonistic contact between former spouses after divorce: Patterns and determinants. *Journal of Family Issues, 26,* 1131–1163.

- Fisher, B. A., & Adams, K. L. (1994). *Interpersonal communication: Pragmatics of human relationships* (2nd ed.). New York: McGraw-Hill.

- Fisher, H., Aron, A., & Brown, L. L. (2005). Romantic love: An fMRI study of a neural mechanism for mate choice. *Journal of Comparative Neurology, 493,* 58–62.

- Fisher, T. D. (2004). Family foundations of sexuality. In J. H. Harvey, A. Wenzel, & S. Sprecher (Eds.), *The handbook of sexuality in close relationships* (pp. 385–409). Mahwah, NJ: Lawrence Erlbaum.

- Fisher, T. D., Moore, Z. T., & Pittinger, M. J. (2012). Sex on the brain? An examination of frequency of sexual cognitions as a function of gender, erotophilia, and social desirability. *Journal of Sex Research, 49,* 69–77.

- Fitness, J., & Fletcher, G. J. O. (1993). Love, hate, anger, and jealousy in close relationships: A prototype and cognitive appraisal analysis. *Journal of Personality and Social Psychology, 65,* 942–958.

- Fitzpatrick, M. A. (1988). *Between husbands and wives: Communication in marriage.* Newbury Park, CA: Sage.

- Fitzpatrick, M. A., & Badzinski, D. M. (1994). All in the family: Interpersonal communication and kin relationships. In M. L. Knapp & G. R. Miller (Eds.), *Handbook of interpersonal communication* (2nd ed., pp. 726–771). Thousand Oaks, CA: Sage.

- Fitzpatrick, M. A., & Winke, T. (1979). You always hurt the one you love: Strategies and tactics in interpersonal conflict. *Communication Quarterly, 27,* 3–11.

- Fleischmann, A. A., Spitzberg, B. H., Andersen, P. A., & Roesch, S. (2005). Tickling the monster: Jealousy induction in relationships. *Journal of Social and Personal Relationships, 22,* 49–73.

- Fleuriet, C., Cole, M., & Guerrero, L. K. (2014). Exploring Facebook: Attachment style and nonverbal message characteristics as predictors of anticipated emotional reactions to Facebook postings. *Journal of Nonverbal Behavior, 38,* 429–450.

- Floyd, K. (1995). Gender and closeness among friends and siblings. *Journal of Psychology, 129,* 193–202.

- Floyd, K. (2001). Human affection exchange: I. Reproductive probability as a predictor of men's affection with their sons. *Journal of Men's Studies, 10,* 39–50.

- Floyd, K. (2002). Human affection exchange: V. Attributes of the highly affectionate. *Communication Quarterly, 50,* 135–152.

- Floyd, K. (2006). *Communicating affection: Interpersonal behavior and social context.* Cambridge, UK: Cambridge University Press.

- Floyd, K., Boren, J. P., Hannawa, A. F., Hesse, C., McEwan, B., & Veksler, A. E. (2009). Kissing in marital and cohabiting relationships: Effects on blood lipids, stress, and relationship satisfaction. *Western Journal of Communication, 73,* 113–133.

- Floyd, K., Hess, J. A., Miz.o, L. A., Halone, K. K., Mikkelson, A. C., & Tusing, K. J. (2005). Human affective exchange: VIII. Further evidence of the benefits of expressed affection. *Communication Quarterly, 53,* 285–303.

- Floyd, K., Hesse, C., & Haynes, M. T. (2007). Human affection exchange: XV. Metabolic and cardiovascular correlates of trait expressed affection. *Communication Quarterly, 55,* 79–94.

- Floyd, K., Mikkelson, A. C., Hesse, C., & Pauley, P. M. (2007). Affectionate writing reduces total cholesterol: Two randomized, controlled trials. *Human Communication Research, 33,* 119–142.

- Floyd, K., Mikkelson, A. C., Tafoya, M. A., Farinelli, L., LaValley, A. G., Judd, J., Davis, K.L., Haynes, M.T., & Wilson, J. (2007). Human affection exchange: XIV. Relational affection predicts resting heart rate and free cortisol secretion during acute stress. *Behavioral Medicine, 32,* 151–156.

- Floyd, K., & Morman, M. T. (1998). The measurement of affection communication. *Communication Quarterly, 46,* 144–162.

- Floyd, K., & Morman, M. T. (2001). Human affection exchange: III. Discriminative parental solicitude in men's affectionate communication with their biological and nonbiological sons. *Communication Quarterly, 49,* 310–327.

- Floyd, K., & Morr, M. C. (2003). Human affective exchange: VII. Affectionate communication in the sibling/spouse/sibling-in-law triad. *Communication Quarterly, 51,* 247–261.

- Floyd, K., & Parks, M. R. (1995). Manifesting closeness in the interactions of peers: A look at siblings and friends. *Communication Reports, 8,* 69–76.

- Floyd, K., Ramirez, A., & Burgoon, J. K. (2008). Expectancy violations theory. In L. K. Guerrero, J. A. DeVito, & M. L. Hecht (Eds.), *The nonverbal communication reader: Classic and contemporary readings* (3rd ed., pp. 503–510). Prospect Heights, IL: Waveland Press.

- Floyd, K., & Ray, G. B. (2003). Human affection exchange: IV. Vocalic predictors of perceived affection in initial interactions. *Western Journal of Communication, 67,* 56–73.

- Floyd, K., & Riforgiate, S. (2008). Affectionate communication received from spouses predicts stress hormone levels in healthy adults. *Communication Monographs, 75,* 351–368.

- Folkes, V. S. (1982). Communicating the causes of social rejection. *Journal of Experimental Social Psychology, 18,* 235–252.

- Folkes, V. S., & Sears, D. O. (1977). Does everybody like a liker? *Journal of Experimental Social Psychology, 13,* 505–519.

- Fox, J., & Anderegg, C. (2014). Romantic relationship stages and social networking sites: uncertainty reduction strategies and perceived relational norms on Facebook. *Cyberpsychology, Behavior, and Social Networking, 17,* 685–691.

- Fox, J., & Tokunaga, R. S. (2015). Romantic partner monitoring after breakups: Attachment, dependence, distress, and post-dissolution online surveillance via social networking sites. *Cyberpsychology, Behavior, and Social Networking, 18,* 491–498.

- Fox, J., & Warber, K. M. (2013). Romantic relationship development in the age of Facebook: An exploratory study of emerging adults' perceptions, motives, and behaviors. *Cyberpsychology, Behavior, and Social Networking, 16,* 3–7.

- Fox, J., Warber, K. M., & Makstaller, D. C. (2013). The role of Facebook in romantic relationship development: An exploration of Knapp's relational stage model. *Journal of Social and Personal Relationships, 30,* 771–794.

- Frampton, B. D., & Child, J. T. (2013). Friend or not to friend: Coworker Facebook friend requests as an application of communication privacy management theory. *Computers in Human Behavior, 29,* 2257–2264.

- Frank, E., Anderson, C., & Rubinstein, D. (1979). Marital role strain and sexual satisfaction. *Journal of Consulting and Clinical Psychology, 217,* 1096–1103.

- Frank, M. G., & Gilovich, T. (1988). The dark side of self- and social perception: Black uniforms and aggression in professional sports. *Journal of Personality and Social Psychology, 54,* 74–85.

- Frazier, P. A., & Cook, S. W. (1993). Correlates of distress following heterosexual relationship dissolution. *Journal of Social and Personal Relationships, 10,* 55–67.

- Freedman, S. R., & Enright, R. D. (1996). Forgiveness as an intervention goal with incest survivors. *Journal of Consulting and Clinical Psychology, 64,* 983–992.

- Friedmann, H. S., Riggio, R. E., & Casella, D. F. (1988). Non-verbal skill, personal charisma, and initial attraction. *Personality and Social Psychology Bulletin, 14,* 203–211.

- Frinjs, T., Finkenauer, C., Vermulst, A. A., & Engels, R. C. M. E. (2005). Keeping secrets from parents: Longitudinal associations of secrecy in adolescence. *Journal of Youth and Adolescence, 34,* 137–148.

- Frost, D. M., & Gola, K. A. (2015). Meanings of intimacy: A comparison of members of heterosexual and same-sex couples. *Analyses of Social Issues and Public Policy, 15,* 382–400.

- Frunzaru, V., & Garbasevschi, D. (2016). Students' Online Identity Management. *Journal of Media Research, 9,* 3–13.

- Gaelick, L., Brodenshausen, G. V., & Wyer, R. S., Jr. (1985). Emotional communication in close relationships. *Journal of Personality and Social Psychology, 49,* 1246–1265.

- Gagnon, J. H. (1977). *Human sexualities.* Glenview, IL: Scott Foresman.

- Gahler, M., Hong, Y., & Bernhardt, E. (2009). Parental divorce and union disruption among young adults in Sweden. *Journal of Family Issues, 30,* 688–713.

- Gaines, S. O., Jr. (1995). Relationships between members of cultural minorities. In J. T. Woods & S. Duck (Eds.), *Understudied relationships: Off the beaten track* (pp. 51–88). Thousand Oaks, CA: Sage.

- Gaines, S. O., Jr., & Henderson, M. C. (2002). Impact of attachment style on responses to accommodative dilemmas among same-sex couples. *Personal Relationships, 9,* 89–93.

- Gaines, S. O., Jr., & Liu, J. H. (2000). Multicultural/ multiracial relationships. In C. Hendrick & S. S. Hendrick (Eds.), *Close relationships: A sourcebook* (pp. 97–108). Thousand Oaks, CA: Sage.

- Gaines, S. O., Jr., Reis, H. T., Summers, S., Rusbult, C. E., Cox, C. L., Wexler, M. O., Marelich, W. D. & Kurland, G. J. (1997). Impact of attachment style on reactions to accommodative dilemmas in close relationships. *Personal Relationships, 4,* 93–113.

- Galinha, I. C., Oishi, S., Pereira, C. R., Wirtz, D., & Esteves, F. (2014). Adult attachment, love styles, relationship experiences and subjective well-being: Cross-cultural and gender comparison between Americans, Portuguese, and Mozambicans. *Social Indicators Research, 119,* 823–852.

- Galinsky, A. D., Magee, J. C., Gruenfeld, D. H., & Whitson, J. A. (2008). Power reduces the press of the situation: Implications for creativity, conformity, and dissonance. *Journal of Personality and Social Psychology, 95,* 1450–1466.

- Galligan, R. F., & Terry, D. J. (1993). Romantic ideals, fear of negative implications and practice of safe sex. *Journal of Applied Social Psychology, 23,* 1685–1711.

- Gao, G., & Ting-Toomey, S. (1998). *Communicating effectively with the Chinese.* Thousand Oaks, CA: Sage.

- Gareis, E., & Wilkins, R. (2011). Love expression in the United States and Germany. *International Journal of Intercultural Relations, 35,* 307–319.

- Garimella, V. R. K., Weber, I., & Dal Cin, S. (2014, November). From "I love you babe" to "leave me alone": Romantic relationship breakups on Twitter. In *International Conference on Social Informatics* (pp. 199–215). Cham, Switzerland: Springer International Publishing.

- Gelles, R. J., & Cornell, C. P. (1990). *Intimate violence in families* (2nd ed.). Newbury Park, CA: Sage.

- George, J. F., & Robb, A. (2008). Deception and computer-mediated communication in daily life. *Communication Reports, 21,* 92–103.

Gibbs, J. L., Ellison, N. B., & Lai, C. H. (2011). First comes love, then comes Google: An investigation of uncertainty reduction strategies and self-disclosure in online dating. *Communication Research, 38*, 70–100.

Gibran, K. (1970). *The prophet.* New York: Knopf. (Original work published 1923).

Gilbert, S. J. (1976). Self disclosure, intimacy, and communication in families. *The Family Coordinator, 25*, 221–230.

Giles, H., & Wiemann, J. M. (1987). Language, social comparison, and power. In C. Berger & S. H. Chafee (Eds.), *Handbook of communication science* (pp. 350–384). Newbury Park, CA: Sage.

Girard, M., & Mullet, E. (1997). Propensity to forgive in adolescents, young adults, older adults, and elderly people. *Journal of Adult Development, 4*, 209–220.

Givens, D. B. (1978). The nonverbal basis of attraction: Flirtation, courtship, and seduction. *Psychiatry, 41*, 346–359.

Givens, D. B. (1983). *Love signals.* New York: Crown.

Givertz, M., & Safford, S. (2011). Longitudinal impact of communication patterns on romantic attachment and symptoms of depression. *Current Psychology, 30*, 149–172.

Glomb, T. M., Richman, W. L., Hulin, C. L., Drasgow, F., Schneider, K. T., & Fitzgerald, L. F. (1997). Ambient sexual harassment: An integrated model of antecedents and consequences. *Organizational Behavioral and Human Decision Processes, 71*, 309–328.

Goffman, E. (1959). *The presentation of self in everyday life.* Garden City, NY: Anchor/Doubleday.

Goffman, E. (1967). *Interaction ritual: Essays on face-to-face behavior.* New York: Pantheon Books.

Goffman, E. (1971). *Relations in public.* New York: Basic Books.

Gold, K. J., Sen, A., & Hayward, R. A. (2010). Marriage and cohabitation after pregnancy loss. *Pediatrics, 125*, E1202–E1207.

Goldberg, A. E., & Perry-Jenkins, M. (2007). The division of labor and perceptions of parental roles: Lesbian couples across the transition to parenthood. *Human Communication Research, 24*, 297–318.

Goldsmith, D. J., & Fitch, K. L. (1997). The normative context of advice as social support. *Human Communication Research, 23*, 454–476.

Goldsmith, D. J., & MacGeorge, E. L. (2000). The impact of politeness and relationship on perceived quality of advice about a problem. *Human Communication Research, 26*, 234–263.

Golish, T. D. (2000). Changes in closeness between adult children and their parents: A turning point analysis. *Communication Reports, 13*, 79–97.

Golish, T. D., & Caughlin, J. (2002). "I'd rather not talk about it": Adolescents' and young adults' use of topic avoidance in stepfamilies. *Journal of Applied Communication Research, 30*, 78–106.

Gomillion, S., Murray, S. L., & Lamarche, V. M. (2015). Losing the wind beneath your wings: The prospective influence of romantic breakup on goal progress. *Social Psychological and Personality Science, 5*, 513–520.

Goodboy, A. K., & Booth-Butterfield, M. (2009). Love styles and desire for closeness in romantic relationships. *Psychological Reports, 105*, 191–197.

Goodboy, A. K., Myers, S. A., & Members of Investigating Communication. (2010). Relational quality indicators and love styles as predictors of negative relational maintenance behaviors in romantic relationships. *Communication Reports, 23*, 65–78.

Gota, G., Green, R.-J., Rothblum, E., Soloman, S., Balsam, K., & Schwartz, P. (2011). Heterosexual, lesbian, and gay male relationships: A comparison of couples in 1975 and 2000. *Family Process, 50*, 353–376.

Gottman, J. M. (1979). *Marital interaction: Experimental investigations.* New York: Academic Press.

Gottman, J. M. (1993). A theory of marital dissolution and stability. *Journal of Family Psychology, 7*, 57–75.

Gottman, J. M. (1994). *What predicts divorce? The relationship between marital processes and marital outcomes.* Hillsdale, NJ: Lawrence Erlbaum.

Gottman, J. M., & Carrere, S. (1994). Why can't men and women get along? Developmental roots and marital inequities. In D. J. Canary & L. Safford (Eds.), *Communication and relational maintenance* (pp. 203–222). San Diego, CA: Academic Press.

Gottman, J. M., Gottman, J. S., & DeClaire, J. (2006). *10 lessons to transform your marriage.* New York: Three Rivers Press.

Gottman, J. M., & Levenson, R. W. (1988). The social psychophysical of marriage. In P. Noller & M. A. Fitzpatrick (Eds.), *Perspectives on marital interaction* (pp. 182–200). Philadelphia: Multilingual Matters.

Gottman, J. M., & Levenson, R. W. (1992). Marital processes predictive of later dissolution: Behavior, physiology, and health. *Journal of Personality and Social Psychology, 63*, 221–233.

Gottman, J. M., & Levenson, R. W. (2000). The timing of divorce: Predicting when a couple will divorce over a 14-year period. *Journal of Marriage and the Family, 62*, 737–745.

Gottman, J. M., & Levenson, R. W. (2002). A two-factor model for predicting when a couple will divorce: Exploratory analyses using 14-year longitudinal data. *Family Process, 41*, 83–96.

Gottman, J. M., Levenson, R. W., Gross, J., Frederickson, B. L., McCoy, K., Rosenthal, L., Ruef, A., & Yoshimoto, D. (2003). Correlates of gay and lesbian couples' relationship satisfaction and relationship dissolution. *Journal of Homosexuality, 45*, 23–43.

Gouldner, A. W. (1960). The norm of reciprocity: A preliminary statement. *Sociological Review, 25*, 161–178.

Gracyalny, M. L., Jackson, D. C., & Guerrero, L. K. (2008, November). *Associations among victim communication, errant partner communication, and forgiveness following hurtful events in dating relationships.* Paper presented at the annual conference of the National Communication Association, San Diego, CA.

Graham, J. M. (2008). Self-expansion and flow in couples' momentary experiences: An experience sampling study. *Journal of Personality and Social Psychology, 95*, 679–694.

Graham-Kevan, N., & Archer, J. (2003). Patriarchal terrorism and common couple violence: A test of Johnson's predictions in four British samples. *Journal of Interpersonal Violence, 18*, 1247–1270.

Grant, F., & Hogg, M. A. (2012). Self-uncertainty, social identity prominence and group identification. *Journal of Experimental Social Psychology, 48*, 538–542.

Gray, J. (1992). *Men are from Mars, women are from Venus: A practical guide to improving communication and getting what you want in your relationships.* New York: HarperCollins.

Greitemeyer, T. (2005). Receptivity to sexual offers as a function of sex, socioeconomic status, and intimacy of the offer. *Personal Relationships, 12*, 373–386.

Grice, H. P. (1989). *Studies in the way of words.* Cambridge, MA: Harvard University Press.

Griffiths, M. D. (2012). Internet sex addiction: A review of empirical research. *Addiction Research and Theory, 20*, 111–124.

Griffitt, W. (1970). Environmental effects on interpersonal affective behaviors: Ambient effective temperature and attraction. *Journal of Personality and Social Psychology, 15*, 240–244.

Gross, M. A., & Guerrero, L. K. (2000). Managing conflict appropriately and effectively: An application of the competence model to Rahim's organizational conflict styles. *International Journal of Conflict Management, 11*, 200–226.

Gross, M. A., Guerrero, L. K., & Alberts, J. K. (2004). Perceptions of conflict strategies and communication competence in task-oriented dyads. *Journal of Applied Communication Research, 32*, 249–270.

Grote, N. K., & Frieze, I. H. (1994). The measurement of friendship-based love in intimate relationships. *Personal Relationships, 1*, 275–300.

Grotevant, H. D., & Cooper, C. R. (1985). Patterns of interaction in family relationships and the development of identity exploration in adolescence. *Child Development, 56*, 415–428.

Grusec, J. E., & Kuczynski, L. (1980). Direction of effects in socialization: A comparison of the parent's versus the child's behavior as determinants of disciplinary techniques. *Developmental Psychology, 16*, 1–9.

Gruzd, A., Wellman, B., & Takhteyev, Y. (2011). Imagining twitter as an imagined community. *American Behavioral Scientist, 55*, 1294–1318.

Guastella, A. J., Mitchell, P. B., & Dadds, M. R. (2008). Oxytocin increases gaze to the eye region of human faces. *Biological Psychiatry, 63*, 3–5.

- Guerrero, L. K. (1996). Attachment-style difference in intimacy and involvement: A test of the four-category model. *Communication Monographs, 63*, 269–292.

- Guerrero, L. K. (1997). Nonverbal involvement across interactions with same-sex friends, opposite-sex friends, and romantic partners: Consistency or change? *Journal of Social and Personal Relationship, 14*, 31–59.

- Guerrero, L. K. (1998). Attachment-style differences in the experience and expression of romantic jealousy. *Personal Relationships, 5*, 273–291.

- Guerrero, L. K. (2004). Observer ratings of nonverbal involvement and immediacy. In V. Manusov (Ed.), *The sourcebook of nonverbal measures: Going beyond words* (pp. 221–235). Mahwah, NJ: Lawrence Erlbaum.

- Guerrero, L. K. (2013). Emotion and communication in conflict interaction. In J. Oetzel & S. Ting-Toomey (Eds.), *Handbook of conflict and communication* (2nd ed., pp. 105–131). Thousand Oaks, CA: Sage.

- Guerrero, L. K. (2014a). Attachment theory: A communication perspective. In D. O. Braithwaite & L. Baxter (Eds.), *Engaging theory in interpersonal communication* (2nd ed. pp.). Thousand Oaks, CA: Sage.

- Guerrero, L. K. (2014b). Jealousy and relational satisfaction: Actor effects, partner effects, and the mediating role of destructive communicative responses to jealousy. *Western Journal of Communication, 78*, 586–611.

- Guerrero, L. K., & Afifi, W. A. (1995a). Some things are better left unsaid: Topic avoidance in family relationships. *Communication Quarterly, 43*, 276–296.

- Guerrero, L. K., & Afifi, W. A. (1995b). What parents don't know: Topic avoidance in parent–child relationships. In T. J. Socha & G. H. Stamp (Eds.), *Parents, children, and communication: Frontiers of theory and research* (pp. 219–246). Mahwah, NJ: Lawrence Erlbaum.

- Guerrero, L. K., & Afifi, W. A. (1998). Communicative responses to jealousy as a function of self-esteem and relationship maintenance goals: A test of Bryson's dual motivation model. *Communication Reports, 11*, 111–122.

- Guerrero, L. K., & Afifi, W. A. (1999). Toward a goal-oriented approach for understanding communicative responses to jealousy. *Western Journal of Communication, 63*, 216–248.

- Guerrero, L. K., & Andersen, P. A. (1991). The waxing and waning of relational intimacy: Touch as a function of relational stage, gender, and touch avoidance. *Journal of Social and Personal Relationships, 8*, 147–165.

- Guerrero, L. K., & Andersen, P. A. (1994). Patterns of matching and initiation: Touch behavior and avoidance across romantic relationship stages. *Journal of Nonverbal Behavior, 18*, 137–153.

- Guerrero, L. K., & Andersen, P. A. (1998a). The dark side of jealousy and envy: Desire, delusion, desperation, and destructive communication. In B. H. Spitzberg & W. R. Cupach (Eds.), *The dark side of relationships* (pp. 33–70). Mahwah, NJ: Lawrence Erlbaum.

- Guerrero, L. K., & Andersen, P. A. (1998b). The experience and expression of romantic jealousy. In P. A. Andersen & L. K. Guerrero (Eds.), *The handbook of communication and emotion: Research, theory, applications, and contexts* (pp. 155–188). San Diego, CA: Academic Press.

- Guerrero, L. K., Andersen, P. A., Jorgensen, P. F., Spitzberg, B. H., & Eloy, S. V. (1995). Coping with the green-eyed monster: Conceptualizing and measuring communicative responses to jealousy. *Western Journal of Communication, 59*, 270–304.

- Guerrero, L. K., & Bachman, G. F. (2006). Associations among relational maintenance behaviors, attachment-style categories, and attachment dimensions. *Communication Studies, 57*, 341–361.

- Guerrero, L. K., & Bachman, G. F. (2008). Communication following relational transgressions in dating relationships: An investment model explanation. *Southern Communication Journal, 73*, 4–23.

- Guerrero, L. K., & Bachman, G. F. (2010). Forgiveness and forgiving communication: An expectancy-investment model. *Journal of Social and Personal Relationships, 27*, 801–823.

- Guerrero, L. K., & Burgoon, J. K. (1996). Attachment styles and reactions to nonverbal involvement change in romantic dyads: Patterns of reciprocity and compensation. *Human Communication Research, 22*, 335–370.

- Guerrero, L. K., & Chavez, A. M. (2005). Relational maintenance in cross-sex friendships characterized by different types of romantic intent: An exploratory study. *Western Journal of Communication, 69*, 341–360.

- Guerrero, L. K., & Eloy, S. V. (1992). Jealousy and relational satisfaction across marital types. *Communication Reports, 5*, 23–31.

- Guerrero, L. K., Eloy, S. V., & Wabnik, A. I. (1993). Linking maintenance strategies to relationship development and disengagement: A reconceptualization. *Journal of Social and Personal Relationships, 10*, 273–283.

- Guerrero, L. K., Farinelli, L., & McEwan, B. (2009). Attachment and relational satisfaction: The mediating effect of emotional communication. *Communication Monographs, 76*, 487–514.

- Guerrero, L. K., & Floyd, K. (2006). *Nonverbal communication in close relationships.* Mahwah, NJ: Lawrence Erlbaum.

- Guerrero, L. K., Hannawa, A. F., & Babin, B. A. (2011). The communicative responses to jealousy scale: Revision, empirical validation, and associations with relational satisfaction. *Communication Methods and Measures, 5*, 223–249.

- Guerrero, L. K., & Jones, S. M. (2003). Differences in one's own and one's partner's perceptions of social skills as a function of attachment style. *Communication Quarterly, 51*, 277–295.

- Guerrero, L. K., & Jones, S. M. (2005). Differences in conversational skills as a function of attachment style: A follow-up study. *Communication Quarterly, 53*, 305–321.

- Guerrero, L. K., & Langan, E. J. (1999, February). *Dominance displays in conversations about relational problems: Differences due to attachment style and sex.* Paper presented at the annual meeting of the Western States Communication Association, Vancouver, BC.

- Guerrero, L. K., La Valley, A. G., & Farinelli, L. (2008). The experience and expression of anger, guilt, and sadness in marriage: An equity theory explanation. *Journal of Social and Personal Relationships, 25*, 699–724.

- Guerrero, L. K., & Mongeau, P. A. (2008). On becoming "more than friends": The transition from friendship to romantic relationship. In S. Sprecher, J. A. Harvey, & A. Wenzel (Eds.), *The handbook of relationship initiation* (pp. 175–194). Thousand Oaks, CA: Sage.

- Guerrero, L. K., & Reiter, R. L. (1998). Expressing emotion: Sex differences in social skills and communicative responses to anger, sadness, and jealousy. In D. J. Canary & K. Dindia (Eds.), *Sex differences and similarities in communication* (pp. 321–350). Mahwah, NJ: Lawrence Erlbaum.

- Guerrero, L. K., Spitzberg, B. H., & Yoshimura, S. M. (2004). Sexual and emotional jealousy. In J. Harvey, A. Wenzel, & S. Sprecher (Eds.), *The handbook of sexuality in close relationships* (pp. 311–345). Mahwah, NJ: Lawrence Erlbaum.

- Guerrero, L. K., Trost, M. L., & Yoshimura, S. M. (2005). Emotion and communication in the context of romantic jealousy. *Personal Relationships, 12*, 233–252.

- Gupta, G. R. (1976). Love, arranged marriage, and the Indian social structure. *Journal of Comparative Family Studies, 7*, 75–85.

- Gupta, U., & Singh, P. (1982). An exploratory study of love and liking and type of marriages. *Indian Journal of Applied Psychology, 19*, 92–97.

- Guthrie, J., & Kunkel, A. (2013). Tell me sweet (and not-so-sweet) little lies: Deception in romantic relationships. *Communication Studies, 64*, 141–157.

- Haas, A., & Sherman, M. A. (1982). Reported topics of conversation among same sex adults. *Communication Quarterly, 30*, 332–333.

- Haas, S. M., & Stafford, L. (1998). An initial examination of maintenance behaviors in gay and lesbian relationships. *Journal of Social and Personal Relationships, 15*, 846–855.

- Haas, S. M., & Stafford, L. (2005). Maintenance behaviors in same-sex and marital relationships: A matched sample comparison. *Journal of Family Communication, 5*, 43–60.

- Haferkamp, N., & Kramer, N. C. (2011). Social comparison 2.0: Examining the effects of online profiles on social networking sites. *Cyberpsychology, Behavior, and Social Networking, 14*, 309–314.

- Halatsis, P., & Christakis, N. (2009). The challenge of sexual attraction within heterosexuals' cross-sex friendship. *Journal of Social and Personal Relationships, 26*, 919–937.

- Hall, E. T. (1968). Proxemics. *Current Anthropology, 9,* 83–109.

- Hall, J. A., Carter, S., Cody, M. J., & Albright, J. M. (2010). Individual differences in the communication of romantic interest: Development of the flirting styles inventory. *Communication Quarterly, 58,* 365–393.

- Hall, J. A., Coats, E. J., & LeBeau, L. S. (2005). Nonverbal behavior and vertical dimension of social relations: A meta-analysis. *Psychological Bulletin, 131,* 898–924.

- Hall, J. A., Coats, E. J., & Lebeau, L. S. (2006). Is smiling related to interpersonal power? Theory and meta-analysis. In D. Hantula (Ed.), *Advances in social & organizational psychology: A tribute to Ralph Rosnow* (pp. 195–214). Mahwah, NJ: Erlbaum.

- Hall, J. A., Mast, M. S., & Latu, I. M. (2015). The vertical dimension of social relationship and accurate interpersonal perception: A meta-analysis. *Journal of Nonverbal Behavior, 39,* 131–163.

- Halloran, E. C. (1998). The role of marital power in depression and marital distress. *American Journal of Family Therapy, 26,* 3–14.

- Halperin, K. (2012, May 26). *On-off couples should stop recycling romance, and call it quits.* http://abcnews.go.com/Health/off-couples-cyclical-couples-call-quits/story?id=16000441.

- Hamadeh, G. N., & Adib, S.M. (1998). Cancer truth disclosure by Lebanese doctors. *Social Science & Medicine, 47,* 1289–1294.

- Hamel, J. (2009). Toward a gender-inclusive conception of intimate partner violence research and theory: Part 2—New directions. *International Journal of Men's Health, 8,* 41–59.

- Hamida, S. B., Mineka, S., & Bailey, J. M. (1998). Sex differences in perceived controllability of mate value: An evolutionary perspective. *Journal of Personality and Social Psychology, 75,* 953–966.

- Hamilton, W. D. (1964). The genetic evolution of social behavior. *Journal of Theoretical Biology, 7,* 17–18.

- Hammer, J. C., Fisher, J. D., Fitzgerald, P., & Fisher, W. A. (1996). When two heads aren't better than one: AIDS risk behavior in college-age couples. *Journal of Applied Social Psychology, 26,* 375–397.

- Harden, S. (2016). *Arranged / Forced Marriage Statistics.* http://www.statisticbrain.com/arranged-marriage-statistics/.

- Hardy, S. A., & Carlo, G. (2011). Moral identity: What is it, does it develop, and is it linked to moral action? *Child Development Perspectives, 5,* 212–218.

- Hargrow, A. M. (1997). Speaking our realities: From speculation to truth concerning African American women's experiences of sexual harassment. *Dissertation Abstracts International, 57*(7-B), 4707.

- Harry, J. (1984). *Gay couples.* New York: Praeger.

- Harry, J., & De Vall, W. B. (1978). *The social organization of gay males.* New York: Praeger.

- Hart, C. H., DeWolf, D. M., Wozniak, P., & Burts, D. C. (1992). Maternal and paternal disciplinary styles: Relations with preschoolers' playground behavioral orientations and peer status. *Child Development, 63,* 879–892.

- Harter, S., Waters, P. L., Pettitt, L. M., Whitesell, N., Kofkin, J., & Jordan, J. (1997). Autonomy and connectedness as dimensions of relationship styles in men and women. *Journal of Social and Personal Relationships, 14,* 148–164.

- Hartill, L. (2001). A brief history of interracial marriage. *Christian Science Monitor, 93,* 15.

- Harvey, J. H. (1987). Attributions in close relationships: Recent theoretical developments. *Journal of Social and Clinical Psychology, 5,* 420–434.

- Hatfield, E. (1984). The dangers of intimacy. In V. J. Derlega (Ed.), *Communication, intimacy, and close relationships* (pp. 207–220). New York: Academic Press.

- Hatfield, E., Greenberger, D., Traupmann, J., & Lambert, P. (1982). Equity and sexual satisfaction in recently married couples. *Journal of Sex Research, 17,* 18–32.

- Hatfield, E., Rapson, R. L., & Aumer-Ryan, K. (2008). Social justice in love relationships: Recent developments. *Social Justice Research, 21,* 413–431.

- Hatfield, E., & Sprecher, S. (1986a). Measuring passionate love in intimate relationships. *Journal of Adolescence, 9,* 383–410.

- Hatfield, E., & Sprecher, S. (1986b). *Mirror, mirror… The importance of looks in everyday life.* Albany, NY: SUNY Press.

- Hawley, P. H. (2014). Ontogeny and social dominance: A developmental view of human power patterns. *Evolutionary Psychology, 12,* 318–342.

- Hazan, C., & Shaver, P. (1987). Conceptualizing romantic love as an attachment process. *Journal of Personality and Social Psychology, 52,* 511–524.

- Hazan, C., & Zeifman, D. (1994). Sex and the psychological tether. In K. Bartholomew & D. Perlman (Eds.), *Advances in personal relationships* (Vol. 5, pp. 151–177). London: Kingsley.

- Heavey, C. L., Christensen, A., & Malamuth, N. M. (1995). The longitudinal impact of demand and withdrawal during marital conflict. *Journal of Consulting and Clinical Psychology, 63,* 797–801.

- Heavey, C. L., Layne, C., & Christensen, A. (1993). Gender and conflict structure in marital interaction: A replication and extension. *Journal of Consulting and Clinical Psychology, 61,* 16–27.

- Hebert, S., & Popadiuk, N. (2008). University students' experiences of nonmarital breakups: A grounded theory. *Journal of College Student Development, 29,* 1–14.

- Hecht, M. L. (1993). 2002—A research odyssey: Toward the development of a communication theory of identity. *Communication Monographs, 60,* 76–82.

- Hecht, M. L., Collier, M. J., & Ribeau, S. (1993). *African American communication: Ethnic identity and cultural interpretations.* Newbury Park, CA: Sage.

- Hecht, M. L., Marston, P. J., & Larkey, L. K. (1994). Love ways and relationship quality in heterosexual relationships. *Journal of Social and Personal Relationships, 11,* 25–43.

- Hecht, M. L., Warren, J., Jung, J., & Krieger, J. (2004). Communication theory of identity. In W. B. Gudykunst (Ed.), *Theorizing about intercultural communication* (pp. 257–278). Thousand Oaks, CA: Sage.

- Heider, F. (1958). *The psychology and interpersonal relations.* New York: Wiley.

- Heldman, C., & Wade, L. (2010). Hook-up culture: Setting a new research agenda. *Sex Research and Social Policy, 7,* 323–333.

- Helgeson, V. S., Novak, S. A., Lepore, S. J., & Eton, D. T. (2004). Spouse social control efforts: Relations to heath behavior and well-being among men with prostate cancer. *Journal of Social and Personal Relationships, 21,* 53–68.

- Helgeson, V. S., Shaver, P., & Dyer, M. (1987). Prototypes of intimacy and distance in same-sex and opposite-sex relationships. *Journal of Social and Personal Relationships, 4,* 195–233.

- Heller, P. E., & Wood, B. (2007). The influence of religious and ethnic differences on marital intimacy: Intermarriage versus intramarriage. *Journal of Marital and Family Therapy, 26,* 241–252.

- Henderson, A. W., Lehavot, K., & Simoni, J. M. (2009). Ecological models of sexual satisfaction among lesbian/bisexual and heterosexual women. *Archives of Sexual Behavior, 38,* 50–65.

- Henderson, S., & Gilding, M. (2004). "I've never clicked this much with anyone in my life": Trust and hyperpersonal communication in online friendships. *New Media & Society, 6,* 487–506.

- Hendrick, C., & Hendrick, S. S. (1986). A theory and method of love. *Journal of Personality and Social Psychology, 50,* 392–402.

- Hendrick, C., & Hendrick, S. S. (1990). A relationship specific version of the love attitude scale. *Journal of Social Behavior and Personality, 5,* 239–254.

- Hendrick, S. S., & Hendrick, C. (1992). *Liking, loving, and relating* (2nd ed.). Pacific Grove, CA: Brooks/Cole.

- Hendrick, S. S., & Hendrick, C. (2002). Linking romantic love with sex: Development of the perceptions of love and sex scale. *Journal of Social and Personal Relationships, 19,* 361–378.

- Hendrick, S. S., Hendrick, C., & Adler, N. L. (1988). Romantic relationships: Love, satisfaction, and staying together. *Journal of Personality and Social Psychology, 54,* 980–988.

- Hendy, H. M., Eggen, D., Gustitus, C., McLeod, K., & Ng, P. (2003). Decision to leave scale. Perceived reasons to stay in or leave violent relationships. *Psychology of Women Quarterly, 27,* 162–173.

- Henley, N. M. (1977). *Body politics: Power, sex, and nonverbal communication.* Englewood Cliffs, NJ: Prentice Hall.

- Henline, B. H., Lamke, L. K., & Howard, M. D. (2007). Exploring perceptions of online infidelity. *Personal Relationships, 14*, 113–128.

- Henningsen, D. D., Serewicz, M. C. M., & Carpenter, C. (2009). Predictors of comforting communication in romantic relationships. *International Journal of Communication, 3*, 351–368.

- Hensley, W. E. (1994). Height as a basis for interpersonal attraction. *Adolescence, 29*, 469–474.

- Herring, S. C., Scheidt, L. A., Bonus, S., & Wright, E. (2005). Weblogs as a bridging genre. *Information Technology & People, 18*, 142–171.

- Hertlein, K. M. (2012). Digital dwelling: Technology in couple and family relationships. *Family Relations, 61*, 374–387.

- Hertlein, K. M., & Piercy, F. P. (2008). Therapists' assessment and treatment of Internet infidelity cases. *Journal of Marital and Family Therapy, 34*, 481–497.

- Herzog, A. (1973). *The B.S. factor: The theory and techniques of faking it in America.* Baltimore: Penguin Books.

- Heslin, R., & Boss, D. (1980). Nonverbal intimacy in arrival and departure at an airport. *Personality and Social Psychology Bulletin, 6*, 248–252.

- Hess, E. H., & Goodwin, E. (1974). The present state of pupilometers. In M. P. Janisse (Ed.), *Pupillary dynamics and behavior* (pp. 209–246). New York: Plenum Press.

- Hesson-McInnis, M. S., & Fitzgerald, L. F. (1997). Sexual harassment: A preliminary test of an integrative model. *Journal of Applied Social Psychology, 27*, 877–901.

- Hetsroni, A. (2012). Associations between television viewing and love styles: An interpretation using cultivation theory. *Psychological Reports, 110*, 35–50.

- Hettinger, V. E., Hutchinson, D. M., & Bosson, J. K. (2014). Influence of professional status on perceptions of romantic relational dynamics. *Psychology of Men and Masculinity, 15*, 470–480.

- Hewes, D. E., Graham, M. L., Doelger, J., & Pavitt, C. (1985). "Second-guessing": Message interpretation in social networks. *Human Communication Research, 11*, 299–334.

- Hewitt, J., & Stokes, R. (1975). Disclaimers. *American Sociological Review, 40*, 1–11.

- Higgins, J. A., Mullanax, M., Trussell, J., Davidson, J. K., & Moore, N. B. (2011). Sexual satisfaction and sexual health among university students in the United States. *American Journal of Public Health, 101*, 1643–1654.

- Higgins, R. L., & Berglas, S. (1990). The maintenance and treatment of self-handicapping: From risk-taking to face-saving—and back. In R. L. Higgins (Ed.), *Self-handicapping: The paradox that isn't* (pp. 187–238). New York: Plenum Press.

- High, A. C., & Solomon, D. H. (2016). Explaining the Durable Effects of Verbal Person-Centered Supportive Communication: Indirect Effects or Invisible Support? Human Communication Research, 42, 200–220.

- Hill, C. T., Rubin, Z., & Peplau, L. A. (1976). Breakups before marriage: The end of 103 affairs. *Journal of Social Issues, 32*, 147–168.

- Hill, J. P., & Holmbeck, G. (1986). Attachment and autonomy during adolescence. In G. Whitehurst (Ed.), *Annals of child development* (Vol. 3, pp. 145–189). Greenwich, CT: JAI Press.

- Hinde, R. A. (1984). Why do the sexes behave differently in close relationships? *Journal of Social and Personal Relationships, 1*, 471–501.

- Hines, D. A., & Douglas, E. M. (2010). Intimate terrorism by women towards men: Does it exist? *Journal of Aggression, Conflict, and Peace Research, 2*, 36–56.

- Hochschild, A. (1997). *The time bind: When work becomes home and home becomes work.* New York: Metropolitan Books.

- Hochschild, A., & Machung, A. (1989). *The second shift: Working parents and the revolution at home.* New York: Viking/Penguin.

- Hocker, J. L., & Wilmot, W. W. (2013). *Interpersonal conflict* (9th ed.). New York: McGraw-Hill.

- Hocking, J. E., & Leathers, D. G. (1980). Nonverbal indicators of deception: A new theoretical perspective. *Communication Monographs, 47*, 119–131.

- Hoffman, M. L. (1970). Power assertion by parents and its impact on the child. *Child Development, 31*, 129–143.

- Hoffman, M. L. (1980). Moral development in adolescence. In J. Adelson (Ed.), *Handbook of adolescent psychology* (pp. 295–343). New York: Wiley.

- Hofstede, G. (1980). Culture and organizations. *International Studies of Management & Organization, 10*, 15–41.

- Hofstede, G. (2001). *Culture's consequences* (2nd ed.). Thousand Oaks, CA: Sage.

- Hogan, T. P., & Brashers, D. E. (2009). The theory of communication and uncertainty management: Implications for the wider realm of information behavior. In T. D. Afifi & W. A. Afifi (Eds.), *Uncertainty, information management, and disclosure decisions: Theories and applications* (pp. 45–66). New York: Routledge.

- Hogg, M. A., & Abrams, D. (1988). *Social identifications: A social psychology of intergroup relations and group processes.* London: Routledge.

- Hollenbaugh, E. E., & Ferris, A. L. (2014). Facebook self-disclosure: Examining the role of traits, social cohesion, and motives. *Computers in Human Behavior, 30*, 50–58.

- Holmberg, D., & Blair, K. L. (2009). Sexual desire, communication, satisfaction, and preferences of men and women in same-sex versus mixed-sex relationships. *Journal of Sex Research, 46*, 57–66.

- Holmberg, D., Blair, K. L., & Phillips, M. (2010). Women's sexual satisfaction as a predictor of well-being in same-sex versus mixed sex relationships. *Journal of Sex Research, 47*, 1–11.

- Holtgraves, T. (1988). Gambling as self-presentation. *Journal of Gambling Behavior, 4*, 78–91.

- Holtgraves, T., & Yang, J. (1990). Politeness as a universal: Cross-cultural perceptions of request strategies and inferences based on their use. *Journal of Personality and Social Psychology, 59*, 719–729.

- Holtgraves, T., & Yang, J. (1992). Interpersonal underpinnings of request strategies: General principles and differences due to culture and gender. *Journal of Personality and Social Psychology, 62*, 246–256.

- Holtzworth-Munroe, A., & Hutchinson, G. (1993). Attributing negative intent to wife behavior: The attributions of maritally violent versus nonviolent men. *Journal of Abnormal Psychology, 102*, 206–211.

- Holtzworth-Munroe, A., & Jacobson, N. S. (1985). Causal attributions of married couples: When do they search for causes? What do they conclude when they do? *Journal of Personality and Social Psychology, 48*, 1398–1412.

- Holtzworth-Munroe, A., & Smutzler, N. (1996). Comparing the emotional reactions and behavioral intentions of violent and nonviolent husbands to aggressive, distressed, and other wife behaviors. *Violence Victims, 11*, 319–339.

- Holtzworth-Munroe, A., Smutzler, N., & Stuart, G. L. (1998). Demand and withdraw communication among couples experiencing husband violence. *Journal of Consulting and Clinical Psychology, 66*, 731–743.

- Honeycutt, J. M., Cantrill, J. G., & Allen, T. (1992). Memory structure of relational decay: A cognitive test of the sequencing of de-escalating actions and stages. *Human Communication Research, 18*, 528–562.

- Hoobler, G. D. (1999, June). *Ten years of personal relationships research: Where have we been and where are we going?* Paper presented at the annual meeting of the International Network on Personal Relationships, Louisville, KY.

- Hopper, M. L., Knapp, M. L., & Scott, L. (1981). Couples' personal idioms: Exploring intimate talk. *Journal of Communication, 31*, 23–33.

- Hosman, L. A., & Tardy, C. H. (1980). Self-disclosure and reciprocity in short- and long-term relationships: An experimental study of evaluational and attributional consequences. *Communication Quarterly, 28*, 20–30.

- Howard, J. A., Blumstein, P., & Schwartz, P. (1986). Sex, power, and influence tactics in intimate relationships. *Journal of Personality and Social Psychology, 51*, 102–109.

- Howard, J. R., O'Neill, S., & Travers, C. (2006). Factors affecting sexuality in older Australian women: Sexual interest, sexual arousal, relationships and sexual distress in older Australian women, *Climacteric, 9*, 355–367.

- Howland, M. (2016). Reading minds and being invisible: The role of empathic accuracy in invisible support provision. *Social Psychological and Personality Science, 7*, 149–156.

- Hoyle, R. H., Insko, C. A., & Moniz, A. J. (1992). Self-esteem, evaluative feedback, and preacquaintance attraction: Indirect reactions to success and failure. *Motivation and Emotion, 16*, 79–101.

- Hoyt, M. F. (1978). Secrets in psychotherapy: Theoretical and practical considerations. *International Review of Psycho-Analysis, 5,* 231–241.

- Hsu, C. W., Wang, C. C., & Tai, Y. T. (2011). The close the relationship the more the interaction on Facebook? Investigating the case of Taiwan users. *Cyberpsychology, Behavior, and Social Networking, 14,* 473–476.

- Huang, L., & Galinsky, A. D. (2010). No mirrors for the powerful: Why dominant smiles are not processed using embodied simulation. *Behavioral and Brain Sciences, 33,* 448.

- Hughes, M., Morrison, K., & Asada, J. K. (2005). What's love got to do with it? Exploring the impact of maintenance rules, love attitudes, and network support on friends with benefits relationships. *Western Journal of Communication, 69,* 49–66.

- Hughes, S. M., & Kruger, D. J. (2010). Sex differences in post-coital behaviors in long- and short-term mating: An evolutionary perspective. *The Journal of Sex Research, 48,* 496–505.

- Hunt, M. (1974). *Sexual behavior in the 1970s.* New York: Playboy Press.

- Huston, M., & Schwartz, P. (1995). The relationships of gay men and lesbians. In J. T. Wood & S. Duck (Eds.), *Understudied relationships: Off the beaten track* (pp. 89–121). Thousand Oaks, CA: Sage.

- Huston, T. L. (2009). What's love got to do with it? Why some marriages succeed and others fail. *Personal Relationships, 16,* 301–327.

- Huston, T. L., Surra, C. A., Fitzgerald, N. M., & Cate, R. M. (1981). From courtship to marriage: Mate selection as an interpersonal process. In S. Duck & R. Gilmour (Eds.), *Personal relationships: Developing personal relationships* (Vol. 2, pp. 53–88). London: Academic Press.

- Imber-Black, E. (1993). Secrets in families and family therapy: An overview. In E. Imber-Black (Ed.), *Secrets in families and family therapy* (pp. 3–28). New York: Norton.

- Impett, A., Peplau, L. A., & Gable, S. L. (2005). Approach and avoidance sexual motives: Implications for personal and interpersonal well-being. *Personal Relationships, 12,* 465–482.

- Inesi, M. E., Botti, S., Dubois, D., Rucker, D. D., & Galinsky, A. D. (2011). Power and choice: Their dynamic interplay in quenching the thirst for personal control. *Psychological Science, 22,* 1042–1048.

- Infante, D. A. (1987). Aggressiveness. In J. C. McCroskey & J. A. Daly (Eds.), *Personality and interpersonal communication* (pp. 157–192). Newbury Park, CA: Sage.

- Infante, D. A., Chandler, T. A., & Rudd, J. E. (1989). Test of an argumentative skill deficiency model of interpersonal violence. *Communication Monographs, 56,* 163–177.

- Infante, D. A., & Rancer, A. S. (1982). A conceptualization and measure of argumentativeness. *Journal of Personality Assessment, 46,* 72–80.

- Infante, D. A., Sabourin, T. C., Rudd, J. E., & Shannon, E. A. (1990). Verbal aggression in violent and nonviolent marital disputes. *Communication Quarterly, 38,* 361–371.

- Inglis, I. R. (2000). The central role of uncertainty reduction in determining behaviour. *Behaviour, 137,* 1567–1599.

- Instagram Press News. (n.d.). https://www.instagram.com/press/?hl=en.

- Internet Filter Learning Center. (2012). *Pornography statistics.* http://internet-filter-review.toptenreviews.com/internet-pornography-statistics.html.

- Ip, S. H. L., & Heubeck, B. G. (2016). Predictors of alcohol consumption on dates and sense of intimacy. *Personal Relationships, 23,* 124–140.

- Ishii, K. (2010). Conflict management in online relationships. *Cyberpsychology, Behavior, and Social Networking, 13,* 365–370.

- Isnard, C. A., & Zeeman, E. C. (1977). Some models from catastrophe theory in the social sciences. In E. C. Zeeman (Ed.), *Catastrophe theory: Selected papers 1972–1977.* Reading, MA: Addison-Wesley.

- Jablonsky, N. G., & Chaplin, G. (2000). The evolution of human skin coloration. *Journal of Human Evolution, 39,* 57–106.

- Jackson, L. A., & Ervin, K. S. (1992). Height stereotypes of women and men: The liabilities of shortness for both sexes. *Journal of Social Psychology, 132,* 433–445.

- Jackson, R. L., II. (1999). *The negotiation of cultural identity: Perceptions of European Americans and African Americans.* Westport, CT: Praeger.

- Jacob, T. (1974). Patterns of family conflict and dominance as a function of child age and social class. *Developmental Psychology, 10,* 1–12.

- Jacobs, K., & Sillars, A. (2012). Sibling support during post-divorce adjustment: An idiographic analysis of support forms, functions, and relationship types. *Journal of Family Communication, 12,* 167–187.

- Jang, C., & Stefanone, M. A. (2011). Non-directed self-disclosure in the blogosphere: Exploring the persistence of interpersonal communication norms. *Information, Communication & Society, 14,* 1039–1059.

- Jang, S. A. (2008). The effects of attachment style and efficacy of communication on avoidance following a relational partner's deception. *Communication Research Reports, 25,* 300–311.

- Jankowiak, W. R., & Fischer, E. F. (1992). A cross-cultural perspective on romantic love. *Ethnology, 31,* 149–155.

- Jayamaha, S. D., & Overall, N. C. (2015). Agents' self-esteem moderates the effectiveness of negative-direct partner regulation strategies. *Personal Relationships, 22,* 738–761.

- Jellison, J. M., & Oliver, D. F. (1983). Attitudinal similarity and attraction: An impression management approach. *Personality and Social Psychology Bulletin, 9,* 111–115.

- Jensen-Campbell, L. A., Graziano, W. G., & West, S. G. (1995). Dominance, prosocial orientation, and female preferences: Do nice guys really finish last? *Journal of Personality and Social Psychology, 68,* 427–440.

- Jiang, L. C., Bazarova, N., & Hancock, J. T (2011). The disclosure-intimacy link in computer-mediated communication: An attributional extension of the hyperpersonal model. *Human Communication Research, 37,* 58–77.

- Jiang, L. C., & Hancock, J. T. (2013). Absence makes the communication grow fonder: Geographic separation, interpersonal media, and intimacy in dating relationships. *Journal of Communication, 63,* 556–577.

- Jin, B. (2013). Hurtful texting in friendships: Satisfaction buffers the distancing effects of intention. *Communication Research Reports, 30,* 148–156.

- Jin, B., & Peña, J. F. (2010). Mobile Communication in romantic relationships: Mobile phone use, relational uncertainty, love, commitment, and attachment styles. *Communication Reports, 23,* 39–51.

- Johnson, A. J. (2001). Examining the maintenance of friendships: Are there differences between geographically close and long-distance friends? *Communication Quarterly, 49,* 424–435.

- Johnson, A. J., Wittenberg, E., Haigh, M., Wigley, S., Becker, J., Brown, K., & Craig, E. (2004). The process of relationship development and deterioration: Turning points in friendships that have terminated. *Communication Quarterly, 52,* 54–68.

- Johnson, A. J., Wittenberg, E., Villagran, M., Mazur, M., & Villagran, P. (2003). Relational progression as a dialectic: Examining turning points in communication among friends. *Communication Monographs, 70,* 230–249.

- Johnson, D. J., & Rusbult, C. E. (1989). Resisting temptation: Devaluation of alternative partners as a means of maintaining commitment in close relationships. *Journal of Personality and Social Psychology, 57,* 967–980.

- Johnson, L. M., Matthews, T. L., & Napper, S. (2016). Sexual orientation and sexual assault victimization among US college students. *Social Science Journal, 53,* 174–183.

- Johnson, M. L., Afifi, W. A., & Duck, S. (1994, June). *Everything you wanted to know about social attraction but were afraid to ask.* Paper presented at the International Communication Association Convention, Sydney, Australia.

- Johnson, M. P. (1995). Patriarchal terrorism and common couple violence: Two forms of violence against women. *Journal of Marriage and the Family, 57,* 283–294.

- Johnson, M. P., & Ferraro, K. J. (2000). Research on domestic violence in the 1990s: Making distinctions. *Journal of Marriage and the Family, 62,* 948–963.

- Johnson, M. P., & Leone, J. M. (2005). The differential effects of intimate terrorism and situational couple violence: Findings from the National Violence against Women Survey. *Journal of Family Issues, 26,* 322–349.

• Joinson, A. N. (2003). *Understanding the psychology of Internet behaviour.* Basingstoke, UK: Palgrave Macmillan.

• Joinson, A. N. (2008, April 5–10). "Looking at," "looking up," or "keeping up with" people? Motives and uses of Facebook. *CHI Proceeding,* Florence, Italy.

• Jonason, P. (2012, July). *Four functions for four relationships: A consensus definition of four romantic and sexual relationships.* Paper presented at the International Association for Relationship Research, Chicago, IL.

• Jones, E., & Gallois, C. (1989). Spouses' impressions of rules for communication in public and private marital conflict. *Journal of Marriage and the Family, 51,* 957–967.

• Jones, J. T., Pelham, B. W., Carvallo, M., & Mirenberg, M. C. (2004). How do I love thee? Let me count the Js: Implicit egotism and interpersonal attraction. *Journal of Personality and Social Psychology, 87,* 665–683.

• Jones, S. E. (1994). *The right touch: Understanding and using the language of physical contact.* Cresshill, NJ: Hampton Press.

• Jones, S. M. (2000). *Nonverbal immediacy and verbal comforting in the social process.* Unpublished doctoral dissertation, Arizona State University, Tempe.

• Jones, S. M. (2004). Putting the person into person-centered and immediate emotional support: Emotional change and perceived helper competence as outcomes of comforting in helping situations. *Communication Research, 32,* 338–360.

• Jones, S. M. (2006). "Why is this happening to me?" The attributional make-up of negative emotions experienced in emotional support encounters. *Communication Research Reports, 23,* 291–296.

• Jones, S. M., & Burleson, B. R. (1997). The impact of situational variables on helpers' perceptions of comforting messages: An attributional analysis. *Communication Research, 24,* 530–555.

• Jones, S. M., & Burleson, B. R. (2003). Effects of helper and recipient sex on the experience and outcomes of comforting messages: An experimental investigation. *Sex Roles, 48*(1/2), 1–19.

• Jones, S. M., & Guerrero, L. K. (2001). The effects of nonverbal immediacy and verbal person-centeredness in the emotional support process. *Human Communication Research, 27,* 567–596.

• Jones, S. M., & Wirtz, J. G. (2007). "Sad monkey see, monkey do": Nonverbal matching in emotional support encounters. *Communication Studies, 58,* 71–86.

• Jones, W. H., & Burdette, M. P. (1994). Betrayal in relationships. In A. L. Weber & J. H. Harvey (Eds.), *Perspectives on close relationships* (pp. 243–262). Needham Heights, MA: Allyn & Bacon.

• Joseph, N., & Alex, N. (1972). The uniform: A sociological perspective. *American Journal of Sociology, 77,* 719–730.

• Joshi, K., & Rai, S. N. (1987). Effect of physical attractiveness upon the inter-personal attraction subjects of different self-esteem. *Perspectives in Psychological Research, 10,* 19–24.

• Jourard, S. M. (1959). Self-disclosure and other cathexis. *Journal of Abnormal Social Psychology, 59,* 428–431.

• Jourard, S. M. (1964). *The transparent self.* New York: Wiley.

• Jung, E., & Hecht, M. (2004). Elaborating the communication theory of identity: Identity gaps and communication outcomes. *Communication Quarterly, 52,* 265–283.

• Kahneman, D., Slovic, P., & Tvesky, A. (Eds.). (1982). *Judgment under uncertainty: Heuristics and biases.* Cambridge, UK: Cambridge University Press.

• Kaiser, S. B. (1997). The social psychology of clothing: Symbolic appearances in context (2nd ed.). New York: Fairchild.

• Kalbfleisch, P. J., & Herold, A. L. (2006). Sex, power, and communication. In K. Dindia & D. J. Canary (Eds.), *Sex differences and similarities in communication* (2nd ed., pp. 299–313). Mahwah, NJ: Lawrence Erlbaum.

• Kalmijn, M., & Poortman, A. R. (2006). His or her divorce? The gendered nature of divorce and its determinants. *European Sociological Review, 22,* 201–214.

• Kam, J. A., & Hecht, M. L. (2009). Investigating the role of identity gaps among communicative and relational outcomes within the grandparent-grandchild relationship: The young-adult grandchildren's perspective. *Western Journal of Communication, 73,* 456–480.

• Kam, K. Y. (2004). *A cultural model of nonverbal deceptive communication: The independent and interdependent self-construals as predictors of deceptive communication motivations and nonverbal behaviors under deception.* Unpublished doctoral dissertation, University of Arizona, Tucson.

• Kan, M. Y. (2008). Does gender trump money? Housework hours of husbands and wives in Britain. *Work, Employment and Society, 22,* 45–66.

• Kandel, D. B. (1978). Similarity in real life adolescent friendship pairs. *Journal of Personality and Social Psychology, 36,* 306–312.

• Kane, H. S., Jaremka, L. M., Guichard, A. C., Ford, M. B., Collins, N. L., & Feeney, B. C. (2007). Feeling supported and feeling satisfied: How one partner's attachment style predicts the other partner's relationship experience. *Journal of Social and Personal Relationships, 24,* 535–555.

• Kanin, E. J., Davidson, K. D., & Scheck, S. R. (1970). A research note on male-female differential in the experience of heterosexual love. *Journal of Sex Research, 6,* 64–72.

• Karney, B. R., & Bradbury, T. N. (1995). The longitudinal course of marital quality and stability: A review of theory, method, and research. *Psychological Bulletin, 118,* 3–34.

• Karpel, M. (1980). Family secrets. *Family Process, 19,* 295–306.

• Karraker, A., & Latham, K. (2015). In sickness and in health? Physical illness as a risk factor for marital dissolution in later life. *Journal of Health and Social Behavior, 56,* 59–73.

• Katz, J., Street, A., & Arias, I. (1995, November). *Forgive and forget: Women's responses to dating violence.* Paper presented at the annual meeting of the Association for the Advancement of Behavior Therapy, Washington, DC.

• Katz, J. E., & Aakhus, M. A. (2002). Conclusion: Making meaning of mobiles—A theory of Apparatgeist. In J. Katz & M. Aakhus (Eds.), *Perpetual contact: Mobile communication, private talk, public performance* (pp. 301–320). Cambridge, UK: Cambridge University Press.

• Katz, S. H. (2002). Healing the father-son relationship: A qualitative inquiry into adult reconciliation. *Journal of Humanistic Psychology, 42,* 13–52.

• Keefer, L. A., Landau, M. J., Sullivan, D., & Rothschild, Z. K. (2014). The object of affection: Subjectivity uncertainty increases objectification in close relationships. *Social Cognition, 32,* 484–504.

• Keeter, S., & Taylor, P. (2009). *The millennials: A portrait of generation next.* Washington, DC: Pew Research Center.

• Kellerman, J., Lewis, J., & Laird, J. D. (1989). Looking and loving: The effects of mutual gaze on feelings of romantic love. *Journal of Research in Personality, 23,* 145–161.

• Kellermann, K. A. (1995). The conversation MOP: A model of patterned and pliable behavior. In D. E. Hewes (Ed.), *The cognitive bases of interpersonal communication* (pp. 181–224). Hillsdale, NJ: Lawrence Erlbaum.

• Kellermann, K. A., & Berger, C. R. (1984). Affect and the acquisition of social information: Sit back, relax, and tell me about yourself. In R. N. Bostrom (Ed.), *Communication yearbook 8* (pp. 412–445). Beverly Hills, CA: Sage.

• Kellermann, K. A., & Reynolds, R. (1990). When ignorance is bliss: The role of motivation to reduce uncertainty in uncertainty reduction theory. *Human Communication Research, 17,* 5–75.

• Kelley, D. (1998). The communication of forgiveness. *Communication Studies, 49,* 255–271.

• Kelley, H. H. (1973). The processes of casual attribution. *American Psychologist, 28,* 107–128.

• Kelley, H. H. (1979). *Personal relationships: Their structures and processes.* Hillsdale, NJ: Lawrence Erlbaum.

• Kelley, H. H. (1986). Personal relationships: Their nature and significance. In R. Gilmour & S. Duck (Eds.), *The emerging field of personal relationships* (pp. 3–19). Hillsdale, NJ: Lawrence Erlbaum.

• Kelley, H. H., Berscheid, E., Christensen, A., Harvey, J. H., Huston, T. L., Levinger, G., McClintock, E., Peplau, L. A., & Peterson, D. R. (1983). Analyzing close relationships. In H. H. Kelley, E. Berscheid, A. Christensen, J. H. Harvey, T. L. Huston, & G. Levinger, (Eds.), *Close relationships* (pp. 20–67). New York: Freeman.

- Kelley, K., & Rolker-Dolinsky, B. (1987). The psycho-sexology of female initiation and dominance. In D. Perlman & S. Duck (Eds.), *Intimate relationships: Development, dynamics and deterioration* (pp. 63–87). Newbury Park, CA: Sage.

- Kelly, A. E., & McKillop, K. J. (1996). Consequences of revealing personal secrets. *Psychological Bulletin, 120,* 450–465.

- Kelly, B. C., Bimbi, D. S., Nanin, J. E., Iziennicki, H., & Parsons, J. T. (2009). Sexual compulsivity and sexual behaviors among gay and bisexual men and lesbian and bisexual women. *Journal of Sex Research, 46,* 301–308.

- Kelsey, C. M. (2007). *Generation MySpace: Helping your teen survive online adolescence.* Boston: Marlowe.

- Kennedy, C. W., & Camden, C. (1983). Interruptions and nonverbal gender differences. *Journal of Nonverbal Behavior, 8,* 91–108.

- Kennedy, J. H. (1992). Relationship of maternal beliefs and childrearing strategies to social competence in pre-school children. *Child Study Journal, 22,* 39–55.

- Keong, L. (2016, May 26). These are the qualities men *actually* look for in women. http://www.marieclaire.com/sex-love/advice/a6601/qualities-guys-look-for-in-girlfriends/

- Kesher, S., Kark, R., Pomerantz-Zorin, L., Koslowsky, M., & Schwarzwald, J. (2006). Gender, status and the use of power strategies. *European Journal of Social Psychology, 36,* 105–117.

- *Key Statistics from the National Survey of Family Growth: C Listing.* (2015, April 20). http://www.cdc.gov/nchs/nsfg/key_statistics/c.htm.

- Keyton, J. (1996). Sexual harassment: A multidisciplinary synthesis and critique. In B. R. Burleson (Ed.), *Communication yearbook 19* (pp. 92–155). Thousand Oaks, CA: Sage.

- Kidwell, J., Fischer, J. L., Dunham, R. M., & Baranowski, M. (1983). Parents and adolescents: Push and pull of change. In H. I. McCubin & C. R. Figley (Eds.), *Stress in the family: Coping with normative transitions* (pp. 74–89). New York: Brunner/Mazel.

- Kilmann, R. H., & Thomas, K. W. (1977). Developing a forced-choice measure of conflict-handling behavior: The "MODE" instrument. *Education and Psychological Measurement, 37,* 309–325.

- Kim, J., & Gray, K. A. (2008). Leave or stay? Battered women's decision after intimate partner violence. *Journal of Interpersonal Violence, 23,* 1465–1482.

- Kim, J., & Lee, J. E. R. (2011). The Facebook paths to happiness: Effects of the number of Facebook friends and self-presentation on subjective well-being. *Cyberpsychology, Behavior, and Social Networking, 14,* 35–364.

- Kim, K. I., Park, H. J., & Suzuki, N. (1990). Reward allocations in the United States, Japan, and Korea: A comparison of individualistic and collectivistic cultures. *Academy of Management Journal, 33,* 188–198.

- King, C. E., & Christensen, A. (1983). The relationship events scale: A Guttman scaling of progress in courtship. *Journal of Marriage and the Family, 45,* 671–678.

- King, S. W., & Sereno, K. K. (1984). Conversational appropriateness as a conversational imperative. *Quarterly Journal of Speech, 70,* 264–273.

- Kirk, A. (2013). The effect of newer communication technologies on relationship maintenance and satisfaction in long-distance dating relationships. *Pepperdine Journal of Communication Research, 1,* Article 2.

- Kisler, T. S., & Christopher, F. S. (2008). Sexual exchanges and relationship satisfaction: Testing the role of sexual satisfaction as a mediator and gender as a moderator. *Journal of Social and Personal Relationships, 25,* 587–602.

- Kito, M. (2005). Self-disclosure in romantic relationships and friendships among American and Japanese college students. *The Journal of Social Psychology, 145,* 127–140.

- Kitzmann, K. M., & Cohen, R. (2003). Parents' versus children's perceptions of interparental conflict as predictors of children's friendship quality. *Journal of Social and Personal Relationships, 20,* 689–700.

- Klein, R. C. A., & Johnson, M. P. (1997). Strategies of couple conflict. In S. Duck (Ed.), *Handbook of personal relationships: Theory, research, and interventions* (2nd ed., pp. 267–486). New York: Wiley.

- Klein, W., Geaghan, T., & MacDonald, T. (2007). Unplanned sexual activity as a consequence of alcohol use: A prospective study of risk perceptions and alcohol use among college freshmen. *Journal of American College Health, 56,* 317–323.

- Kleinke, C. L., Meeker, F. B., & LaFong, C. (1974). Effects of gaze, touch, and use of name on evaluation of "engaged" couples. *Journal of Research in Personality, 7,* 368–373.

- Kline, S. L., Horton, B., & Zhang, S. (2008). Communicating love: Comparisons between American and East Asian university students. *International Journal of Intercultural Relations, 32,* 200–214.

- Kline, S. L., Zhang, S., Manohar, U., Ryu, S., Suzuki, T., & Mustafa, H. (2012). The role of communication and cultural concepts in expectations about marriage: Comparisons between young adults from six countries. *International Journal of Intercultural Relations, 36,* 319–330.

- Klinetob, N. A., & Smith, D. A. (1996). Demand-withdraw communication in marital interaction: Tests of interspousal contingency and gender role hypotheses. *Journal of Marriage and the Family, 58,* 945–957.

- Kluwer, E. S., de Dreu, C. K. W., & Buunk, B. P. (1998). Conflict in intimate vs. non-intimate relationships: When gender role stereotyping overrides biased self-other judgment. *Journal of Social and Personal Relationships, 15,* 637–650.

- Knapp, M. L., & Vangelisti, A. L. (2008). *Interpersonal communication and human relationships* (6th ed.). Boston: Allyn & Bacon.

- Knee, C. R. (1998). Implicit theories of relationships: Assessment and predictions of romantic relationship initiation, coping, and longevity. *Journal of Personality and Social Psychology, 74,* 360–370.

- Knee, C. R., Patrick, H., Vietor, N. A., & Neighbors, C. (2004). Implicit theories of relationships: Moderators of the link between conflict and commitment. *Personality and Social Psychology Bulletin, 30,* 617–628.

- Knee, C. R., & Petty, K. N. (2013). Implicit theories of relationships: Destiny and growth beliefs. In J. A. Simpson & L. Campbell (eds.), *The Oxford handbook of close relationships* (pp. 183–198). New York: Oxford University Press.

- Knight, K. (2014). Communicative dilemmas in emerging adults' friends with benefits relationships: Challenges to relational talk. *Emerging Adulthood, 2,* 270–279.

- Knight, K., Wiedmaier, B., Mongeau, P. A., Eden, J., & Roberto, A. (2012, July). *Diversity among high school friends-with-benefits relationships.* Paper presented at the International Association for Relationship Research, Chicago, IL.

- Knobloch, L. K. (2005). Evaluating a contextual model of responses to relational uncertainty increasing events: The role of intimacy, appraisals, and emotions. *Human Communication Research, 31,* 60–101.

- Knobloch, L. K. (2007a). Perceptions of turmoil within courtship: Associations with intimacy, relational uncertainty, and interference from partners. *Journal of Social and Personal Relationships, 24,* 363–384.

- Knobloch, L. K. (2007b). The dark side of relational uncertainty: Obstacle or opportunity. In B. H. Spitzberg & W. R. Cupach (Eds.), *The dark side of interpersonal communication* (2nd ed., pp. 31–60). Mahwah, NJ: Lawrence Erlbaum.

- Knobloch, L. K. (2009). Relational uncertainty and interpersonal communication. In S. W. Smith & S. R. Wilson (Eds.), *New directions in interpersonal communication research* (pp. 69–93). Thousand Oaks, CA: Sage.

- Knobloch, L. K., & Carpenter-Theune, K. E. (2004). Topic avoidance in developing romantic relationships: Associations with intimacy and relational uncertainty. *Communication Research, 31,* 173–205.

- Knobloch, L. K., & Solomon, D. H. (1999). Measuring the sources and content of relational uncertainty. *Communication Studies, 50,* 261–278.

- Knobloch, L. K., & Solomon, D. H. (2002). Information seeking beyond initial interactions: Negotiating relational uncertainty within close relationships. *Human Communication Research, 28,* 243–257.

- Knobloch, L. K., & Solomon, D. H. (2005). Relational uncertainty and relational information processing. *Communication Research, 32,* 349–388.

- Knobloch-Westerwick, S., & Hastall, M. R. (2010). Please yourself: Social identity effects on selective exposure to news about in- and out-groups. *Journal of Communication, 60,* 515–535.

• Knudsen, K., & Waerness, K. (2008). National context and spouses' housework in 34 countries. *European Sociological Review, 24,* 97–113.

• Ko, S. J., Sadler, M. S., & Galinsky, A. D. (2015). The sound of power: Conveying and detecting hierarchical rank through voice. *Psychological Science, 26,* 3–14.

• Koch, P. B., Mansfield, P. K., Thurau, D., & Carey, M. (2005). Feeling frumpy: The relationships between body image and sexual response changes in midlife women. *Journal of Sex Research, 42,* 215–223.

• Koenig Kellas, J., Bean, D., Cunningham, C., & Cheng, K. Y. (2008). The ex-files: Trajectories, turning points, and adjustment in the development of post-dissolutional relationships. *Journal of Social and Personal Relationships, 25,* 23–50.

• Koeppel, L. B., Montagne-Miller, Y., O'Hair, D., & Cody, M. (1993). Friendly? Flirting? Wrong? In P. J. Kalbfleisch (Ed.), *Interpersonal communication: Evolving interpersonal relationships* (pp. 13–32). Hillsdale, NJ: Lawrence Erlbaum.

• Koerner, A. F., & Fitzpatrick, M. A. (2002). You never leave your family in a fight: The impact of family of origin on conflict behavior in romantic relationships. *Communication Studies, 53,* 234–251.

• Koerner, A. F., & Fitzpatrick, M. A. (2006). Family conflict communication. In J. G. Oetzel & S. Ting-Toomey (Eds.), *The SAGE handbook of conflict communication* (pp. 159–183). Thousand Oaks, CA: Sage.

• Kollock, P., Blumstein, P., & Schwartz, P. (1985). Sex and power in interaction: Conversational privileges and duties. *American Sociological Review, 50,* 34–46.

• Kooti, F., Magno, G., & Weber, I. (2014, November). The Social Name-Letter Effect on Online Social Networks. In *International Conference on Social Informatics* (pp. 216–227). Cham, Switzerland: Springer International Publishing.

• Korda, M. (1975). *Power: How to get it, how to use it.* New York: Ballantine Books.

• Krasnova, H., Veltri, N. F., & Günther, O. (2012). Self-disclosure and privacy calculus on social networking sites: The role of culture. *Business & Information Systems Engineering, 4,* 127–135.

• Krasnova, H., Spiekermann, S., Koroleva, K., & Hildebrand, T. (2010). Online social networks: Why we disclose. *Journal of Information Technology, 25,* 109–125.

• Kraus, M. W., Chen, S., & Keltner, D. (2011). The power to be me: Power elevates self-concept consistency and authenticity. *Journal of Experimental Social Psychology, 47,* 974–980.

• Krokoff, L. J., Gottman, J. M., & Roy, A. K. (1988). Blue-collar and white-collar marital interaction and communication orientation. *Journal of Social and Personal Relationships, 5,* 201–221.

• Krueger, R. F., & Caspi, A. (1993). Personality, arousal, and pleasure: A test of competing models of interpersonal attraction. *Personality and Individual Differences, 14,* 105–111.

• Krusiewicz, E. S., & Woods, J. T. (2001). "He was our child from the moment we walked in that room": Entrance stories of adoptive parents. *Journal of Social and Personal Relationships, 18,* 785–803.

• Kuchinskas, S. (2009). *The chemistry of love: How the oxytocin response can help you find trust, intimacy, and love.* Oakland, CA: New Harbinger.

• Kuczynski, L. (1984). Socialization goals and mother-child interaction: Strategies for long-term and short-term compliance. *Developmental Psychology, 20,* 1061–1073.

• Kujath, C. L. (2011). Facebook and Myspace: Complement or substitute for face-to-face interaction. *Cyberpsychology, Behavior, and Social Networking, 14,* 75–78.

• Kunce, L. J., & Shaver, P. R. (1994). An attachment-theoretical approach to caregiving in romantic relationships. In K. Bartholomew & D. Perlman (Eds.), *Advances in personal relationships: Vol. 5. Attachment processes in adulthood* (pp. 205–237). Bristol, PA: Kingsley.

• Kunkel, A., & Burleson, B. (2003). Relational implications of communication skill evaluations and love styles. *Southern Communication Journal, 68,* 181–197.

• Kunstman, J. W., & Maner, J. K. (2011). Sexual overperception: Power, mating motives, and biases in social judgment. *Journal of Personality and Social Psychology, 100,* 282–294.

• Kuperberg, A., & Padgett, J. E. (2015). Dating and hooking up in college: Meeting contexts, sex, and variation by gender, partner's gender, and class standing. *Journal of Sex Research, 52,* 517–531.

• Kurdek, L. A. (1989). Relationship quality in gay and lesbian cohabiting couples: A 1-year follow-up study. *Journal of Social and Personal Relationships, 6,* 39–59.

• Kurdek, L. A. (1991). The dissolution of gay and lesbian couples. *Journal of Social and Personal Relationships, 8,* 265–278.

• Kurdek, L. A. (1993). Predicting marital dissolution: A 5-year prospective longitudinal study of newlywed couples. *Journal of Personality and Social Psychology, 64,* 221–242.

• Kurdek, L. A. (2007). The allocation of household labor by partners in gay and lesbian couples. *Journal of Family Issues, 28,* 132–148.

• Kurdek, L. A. (2008). Changes in relationship quality for partners from lesbian, gay male, and heterosexual couples. *Journal of Family Psychology, 22,* 701–711.

• Kuss, D. J., & Griffiths, M. D. (2011). Online social networking and addition—A review of the psychological literature. *International Journal of Environmental Research and Public Health, 8,* 3528–3552.

• La Valley, A. G., & Guerrero, L. K. (2012). Perceptions of conflict behavior and relational satisfaction in adult parent–child relationships: A dyadic analysis from an attachment perspective. *Communication Research, 39,* 48–79.

• LaFrance, M., & Mayo, C. (1978). *Moving bodies: Nonverbal communication in social relationships.* Monterey, CA: Brooks/Cole.

• Lambert, A. N., & Hughes, P. C. (2010). The influence of goodwill, secure attachment, and positively toned disengagement strategy on reports of communication satisfaction in non-marital post-dissolution relationships. *Communication Research Reports, 27,* 171–183.

• Lambert, N. M., Negash, S., Stillman, T. F., Olmstead, S. B., & Fincham, F. D. (2012). A love that doesn't last: Pornography consumption weakens commitment to a romantic partner. *Journal of Social and Clinical Psychology, 31,* 410–438.

• Lammers, J., Galinsky, A. D., Gordijn, E. H., & Otten, S. (2008). Illegitimacy moderates the effects of power on approach. *Psychological Science, 19,* 558–564.

• Lammers, J., & Staple, D. A. (2011). Power increases dehumanization. *Group Process and Intergroup Relations, 14,* 113–126.

• Lammers, J., Stoker, J. I., Rink, F., & Galinsky, A. D. (2016). To have control over or to be free from others? The desire for power reflects a need for autonomy. *Personality and Social Psychology Bulletin, 42,* 498–512.

• Lampard, R. (2014). Stated reasons for relationship dissolution in Britain: Marriage and cohabitation compared. *European Sociological Review, 30,* 315–328.

• Lamy, L. (2016). Beyond emotion: Love as an encounter of myth and drive. *Emotion Review, 8,* 97–107.

• Lancaster, A. L., Dillow, M. R., Ball, H., Borchert, K., & Tyler, W. J. C. (2016) Managing information about a romantic partner's relationship history: An application of the Theory of Motivated Information Management. *Southern Communication Journal, 81,* 63–78.

• Landor, A., Simons, L. G., Simons, R. L., Brody, G. H., & Gibbens, F. X. (2011). The role of religiosity in the relationship between parents, peers, and adolescent risky sexual behavior. *Journal of Youth and Adolescence, 40,* 296–309.

• Lane, B. L., Piercy, C. W., & Carr, C. T. (2016). Making it Facebook official: The warranting value of online relationship status disclosures on relational characteristics. *Computers in Human Behavior, 56,* 1–8.

• Langer, E. J. (1989). *Mindfulness.* Reading, MA: Addison-Wesley.

• Langlois, J. H., Kalakanis, L., Rubenstein, A. J., Larson, A., Hallam, M., & Smoot, M. (2000). Maxims or myths of beauty? A meta-analytic and theoretical review. *Psychological Bulletin, 126,* 390–423.

• Langner, C. A., & Keltner, D. (2008). Social power and emotional experience: Actor and partner effects within dyadic interactions. *Journal of Experimental Social Psychology, 44,* 848–856.

• Lannutti, P. J., & Cameron, K. A. (2002). Beyond the breakup: Heterosexual and homosexual post-dissolutional relationships. *Communication Quarterly, 50,* 153–170.

• Lannutti, P. J., & Cameron, M. O. (2007). Women's perceptions of flirtatious nonverbal behavior: The effects of alcohol consumption and physical attractiveness. *Southern Communication Journal, 72,* 21–35.

- Lannutti, P. J., & Monahan, J. L. (2004). "Not now, maybe later": The influence of relationship type, request persistence and alcohol consumption on women's refusal strategies. *Communication Studies, 55,* 362–378.

- Lansford, J. E. (2009). Parental divorce and children's adjustment. *Perspectives on Psychological Science, 4,* 140–152.

- Larkin, M. (1998). Easing the way to safer sex. *Lancet, 351,* 964–967.

- Lasch, C. (1979). *The culture of narcissism: American life in an age of diminishing expectations.* New York: Warner Books.

- Laurin, K., Fitzsimmons, G. M., Finkel, E. J., Carswell, K. L., Vandellen, M. R., Hofmann, W., Lambert, N. M., Estwick, P. W., Fincham, F. D., & Brown, P. C. (2016) Power and the pursuit of a partner's goals. *Journal of Personality and Social Psychology, 110,* 840–868.

- Laursen, B., & Collins, W. A. (1994). Interpersonal conflict during adolescence. *Psychological Bulletin, 115,* 197–209.

- Lazarus, R. S. (1985). The trivialization of distress. In J. C. Rose & L. J. Solomon (Eds.), *Primary prevention of psychopathology: Vol. 8. Prevention in health psychology* (pp. 279–298). Hanover, NH: University Press of New England.

- Le, B., & Agnew, C. R. (2003). Commitment and its theorized determinants: A meta-analysis of the investment model. *Personal Relationships, 10,* 37–57.

- Le, B., Dove, N. L., Agnew, C. R., Korn, M. S., & Mutso, A. A. (2010). Predicting nonmarital romantic relationship dissolution: A meta-analytic synthesis. *Personal Relationships, 17,* 377–390.

- Le Poire, B. A., Hallett, J. S., & Erlandson, K. T. (2000). An initial test of inconsistent nurturing as control theory: How partners of drug abusers assist their partners' sobriety. *Human Communication Research, 26,* 432–457.

- Le Poire, B. A., Hallett, J. S., & Giles, H. (1998). Codependence: The paradoxical nature of the functional-afflicted relationship. In B. H. Spitzberg & W. R. Cupach (Eds.), *The dark side of relationships* (pp. 153–176). Mahwah, NJ: Lawrence Erlbaum.

- Le Poire, B. A., Shepard, C., & Duggan, A. (1999). Nonverbal involvement, expressiveness, and pleasantness as predicted by parental and partner attachment style. *Communication Monographs, 66,* 293–311.

- Lea, M., & Spears, R. (1995). Love at first byte: Building personal relationships over computer networks. In J. T. Wood & S. Duck (Eds.), *Understudied relationships: Off the beaten track* (pp. 197–233). Thousand Oaks, CA: Sage.

- Leaper, C., & Robnett, R. D. (2011). Women are more likely than men to use tentative language, aren't they? A meta-analysis testing for gender differences and moderators. *Psychology of Women Quarterly, 35,* 129–142.

- Lear, D. (1997). *Sex and sexuality: Risk and relationships in the age of AIDS.* Thousand Oaks, CA: Sage.

- Leary, M. R. (1995). *Self-presentation: Impression management and interpersonal behavior.* Madison, WI: Brown & Benchmark.

- Leary, M. R., & Kowalski, R. M. (1990). Impression management: A literature review and two-component model. *Psychological Bulletin, 107,* 34–47.

- Leary, M. R., Springer, C., Negel, L., Ansell, E., & Evans, K. (1998). The causes, phenomenology, and consequences of hurt feelings. *Journal of Personality and Social Psychology, 74,* 1225–1237.

- Leatham, G., & Duck, S. W. (1990). Conversation with friends and the dynamics of social support. In S. W. Duck (Ed., with R. C. Silver), *Personal relationships and social support* (pp. 23–27). London: Sage.

- Ledbetter, A. M. (2009). Measuring online communication attitude: Instrument development and validation. *Communication Monographs, 76,* 463–486.

- Ledbetter, A. M., & Finn, A. N. (2016). Why do students use mobile technology for social purposes during class? Modeling teacher credibility, learner empowerment, and online communication attitude as predictors. *Communication Education, 65,* 1–23.

- Ledbetter, A. M., & Larson, K. A. (2008). Nonverbal cues in e-mail supportive communication: Associations with sender sex, recipient sex, and support satisfaction. *Information, Communication & Society, 11,* 1089–1110.

- Ledbetter, A. M., Mazer, J. P., DeGroot, J. M., Meyer, K. R., Mao, Y., & Swafford, B. (2011). Attitudes toward online social connection and self-disclosure as predictors of Facebook communication and relational closeness. *Communication Research, 38,* 27–53.

- Ledbetter, A. M., Stassen-Ferrara, H. M., & Dowd, M. M. (2013). Comparing equity and self-expansion theory approaches to relational maintenance. *Personal Relationships, 20,* 38–51.

- Lee, H. (2005). Behavioral strategies for dealing with flaming in an online forum. *Sociological Quarterly, 46,* 385–403.

- Lee, J. A. (1973). *The colors of love: An exploration of the ways of loving.* Don Mills, Ontario, Canada: New Press.

- Lee, J. A. (1977). A typology of styles of loving. *Personality and Social Psychology Bulletin, 3,* 173–182.

- Lee, J. A. (1988). Love styles. In R. J. Sternberg & M. L. Barnes (Eds.), *The psychology of love* (pp. 38–67). New Haven, CT: Yale University Press.

- Lee, J. E. R., Moore, D. C., Park, E. A., & Park, S. G. (2012). Who wants to be "friend-rich"? Social compensatory friending on Facebook and the moderating role of public self-consciousness. *Computers in Human Behavior, 28,* 1036–1043.

- Lee, J. W., & Guerrero, L. K. (2001). Types of touch in cross-sex relationships by coworkers: Perceptions of relational and emotional messages, inappropriateness and sexual harassment. *Journal of Applied Communication Research, 29,* 197–220.

- Lee, K., Xu, F., Fu, G., Cameron, C. A., & Chen S. (2001). Taiwan and Mainland Chinese and Canadian children's categorization and evaluation of lie- and truth-telling: A modesty effect. *British Journal of Developmental Psychology, 19,* 525–542.

- Lee, S., Rogee, R. D., & Reis, H. T. (2010). Assessing the seeds of relational decay: Using implicit evaluations to detect the early stages of disillusionment. *Psychological Science, 21,* 857–864.

- Lee, T. R., Mancini, J. A., & Maxwell, J. W. (1990). Sibling relations in adulthood: Contact patterns and motivations. *Journal of Marriage and the Family, 52,* 431–440.

- Lefkowitz, E. S., Vasilenko, S. A., & Leavitt, C. E. (2016). Oral vs. vaginal sex experiences and consequences among first year college students. *Archives of Sexual Behavior, 45,* 329–337.

- Lemay, E. P. Jr., & Wolf, N. R. (2016). Projection of romantic and sexual desire in opposite-sex friendships: How wishful thinking creates a self-fulfilling prophecy. *Personality and Social Psychology Bulletin, 42,* 864–878.

- Lenhart, A. (2009, December 15). Teens and sexting. A Pew Internet & American Life Project report. http://www.pewinternet.org/files/old-media/Files/Reports/2009/PIP_Teens_and_Sexting.pdf

- Lenhart, A. (2015a, April 09). Teens, Social Media & Technology Overview 2015. http://www.pewinternet.org/2015/04/09/teens-social-media-technology-2015/.

- Lenhart, A. (2015b, August 06). Teens, Technology and Friendships. http://www.pewinternet.org/2015/08/06/teens-technology-and-friendships/.

- Lepore, S. J., & Greenberg, M. A. (2002). Mending broken hearts: Effects of expressive writing on mood, cognitive processing, social adjustment, and health following a relationship breakup. *Psychology and Health, 17,* 547–560.

- Letcher, A., & Carmona, J. (2015). Friends with benefits: Dating practices of rural high school and college students. *Journal of Community Health, 40,* 522–529.

- Leung, K. (1988). Theoretical advances in justice behavior: Some cross-cultural inputs. In M. H. Bond (Ed.), *The cross-cultural challenge to social psychology* (pp. 218–220). Newbury Park, CA: Sage.

- Levine, T. R., Aune, K. S., & Park, H. S. (2006). Love styles and communication in relationships: Partner preferences, initiation, and intensification. *Communication Quarterly, 54,* 465–486.

- Levine, T. R., & Boster, F. J. (2001). The effects of power and message variables on compliance. *Communication Monographs, 68,* 28–48.

- Levine, T. R., & McCornack, S. A. (1992). Linking love and lies: A formal test of the McCornack and Parks model of deception detection. *Journal of Social and Personal Relationships, 9,* 143–154.

- Levitt, M. J. (1991). Attachment and close relationships: A life span perspective. In J. L. Gerwitz & W. F. Kurtines (Eds.), *Intersections with attachment* (pp. 183–206). Mahwah, NJ: Lawrence Erlbaum.

- Levitt, M. J., Coffman, S., Guacci-Franco, N., & Loveless, S. C. (1994). Attachment relationships and life transitions: An expectancy model. In M. B. Sperling & W. H. Berman (Eds.), *Attachment in adults: Clinical and developmental perspectives* (pp. 232–255). New York: Guilford Press.

- Lewandowski, G. W., & Ackerman, R. A. (2006). Something's missing: Need fulfillment and self-expansion as predictors of susceptibility to infidelity. *Journal of Social Psychology, 146,* 389–403.

- Lewandowski, G. W., Aron, A., Bassis, S., & Kunak, J. (2006). Losing a self-expanding relationship: Implications for the self-concept. *Personal Relationships, 13,* 317–331.

- Lewis, C. C., & George, J. F. (2008). Cross-cultural deception in social networking sites and face-to-face communication. *Computers in Human Behavior, 24*(6), 2945–2964.

- Lewis, M., & Rosenblum, L. A. (Eds.). (1974). *The effect of the infant on its caregiver.* New York: Wiley.

- Lillard, L. L., Brien, M. J., & Waite, L. J. (1995). Premarital cohabitation and subsequent marital dissolution: A matter of self-selection? *Demography, 32,* 437–457.

- Lindley, L. L., Barnett, C. L., Brandt, H. M., Hardin, J. M., & Burcin, M. (2008). STDs among sexually active female college students: Does sexual orientation make a difference? *Perspectives on Sexual and Reproductive Health, 40,* 212–217.

- Lipsitz, G. (2006). *The possessive investment in whiteness: How white people profit from identity politics.* Philadelphia: Temple University Press.

- Lisitsa, E. (2013a, April 27). *The four horsemen: The antidotes: The Gottman Institute.* https://www.gottman.com/blog/the-four-horsemen-the-antidotes

- Lisitsa, E. (2013b, May 13). *The four horsemen: Contempt: The Gottman Institute.* https://www.gottman.com/blog/the-four-horsemen-contempt/

- Little, A. C. (2015). Attraction and human mating. In V. Zeigler-Hill, L. L. M. Welling, T. F. Shackelford (eds.), *Evolutionary perspectives on social psychology* (pp. 319–332). Heidelberg, Germany: Springer International Publishing.

- Lively, K. J., Steelman, L. C., & Powell, B. (2010). Equity, emotion, and household division of labor. *Social Psychology Quarterly, 73,* 358–379.

- Lloyd, S. A., & Cate, R. M. (1985). The developmental course of conflict in dissolution of premarital relationships. *Journal of Social and Personal Relationships, 2,* 179–194.

- Lloyd, S. A., Cate, R., & Henton, J. (1982). Equity and rewards as predictors of satisfaction in casual and intimate relationships. *Journal of Psychology, 110,* 43–48.

- Lucchetti, A. N. (1999). Deception in disclosing one's sexual history: Safe-sex avoidance or ignorance? *Communication Quarterly, 47,* 300–314.

- Luder, M. T., Pittet, I., Berchtold, A., Akré, C., Michaud, P. A., & Surís, J. C. (2011). Associations between online pornography and sexual behavior among adolescents: Myth or reality? *Archives of Sexual Behavior, 40,* 1027–1035.

- Luo, S. (2014). Effects of texting on satisfaction in romantic relationships: The role of attachment. *Computers in Human Behavior, 33,* 145–152.

- Lykins, A. D., Meana, M., Strauss, G. P. (2008). Sex differences in visual attention to erotic and non-erotic stimuli. *Archives of Sexual Behavior, 37,* 219–228.

- MacGregor, J. C. D., & Cavallo, J. V. (2011). Breaking the rules: Personal control increases women's relationship initiation. *Journal of Social and Personal Relationships, 28,* 848–867.

- MacNeil, S., & Byers, E. S. (2005). Dyadic assessment of sexual self-disclosure and sexual satisfaction in heterosexual dating couples. *Journal of Social and Personal Relationships, 22,* 169–181.

- MacNeil, S., & Byers, E. S. (2009). Role of self-disclosure in the sexual satisfaction of long term sexual couples. *Journal of Sex Research, 46,* 3–14.

- Magee, J. C. (2009). Seeing power in action: The role of deliberation, implementation, and action in inferences of power. *Journal of Experimental Social Psychology, 45,* 1–14.

- Maguire, K. C., Heinemann-LaFave, D., & Sahlstein, E. (2013). "To be so connected, yet not at all": Relational presence, absence, and maintenance in the context of a wartime deployment. *Western Journal of Communication, 77,* 249–271.

- Maier, C., Laumer, S., Eckhardt, A., & Weitzel, T. (2015). Giving too much social support: Social overload on social networking sites. *European Journal of Information Systems, 24,* 447–464.

- Maisel, N. C., & Gable, S. L. (2009). The paradox of received support: The importance of responsiveness. *Psychological Science, 20,* 928–932.

- Major, B., & Heslin, R. (1982). Perceptions of cross-sex and same-sex nonreciprocal touch: It is better to give than to receive. *Journal of Nonverbal Behavior, 6,* 148–162.

- Malachowski, C. C., & Frisby, B. N. (2015). The aftermath of hurtful events: Cognitive, communicative, and relational outcomes. *Communication Quarterly, 63,* 187–203.

- Mannino, C. A., & Deutsch, F. M. (2007). Changing the divisions of household labor: A negotiated process between partners. *Sex Roles, 56,* 309–324.

- Marano, H. E. (1997, November/December). Gottman and Gray: The two Johns. *Psychology Today, 28.*

- Marazziti, D., Consoli, G., Silvestri, S., & Dell'Osso, M. C. (2009). Biological correlates of romantic bonding: Facts and hypotheses. *Clinical Neuropsychiatry, 6,* 112–116.

- Marek, C. I., Wanzer, M. B., & Knapp, J. L. (2004). An exploratory investigation of the relationship between roommates' first impressions and subsequent communication patterns. *Communication Research Reports, 21,* 210–220.

- Marks, M. A., & Nelson, E. S. (1993). Sexual harassment on campus: Effects of professor gender on perception of sexually harassing behaviors. *Sex Roles, 28,* 207–217.

- Marmo, J., & Bryant, E. M. (2010, November). *Using Facebook to maintain friendships: Examining the differences between acquaintances, casual friends, and close friends.* Paper presented at the annual meeting of the National Communication Association, San Francisco, CA.

- Marshall, L. L. (1994). Physical and psychological abuse. In W. R. Cupach & B. H. Spitzberg (Eds.), *The dark side of interpersonal communication* (pp. 281–311). Hillsdale, NJ: Lawrence Erlbaum.

- Marshall, T. C., Bejanyan, K., Di Castro, G., & Lee, R. A. (2013). Attachment styles as predictors of Facebook-related jealousy and surveillance in romantic relationships. *Personal Relationships, 20,* 1–22.

- Marston, P. J., & Hecht, M. L. (1994). Love ways: An elaboration and application to relational maintenance. In D. J. Canary & L. Stafford (Eds.), *Communication and relational maintenance* (pp. 87–202). Orlando, FL: Academic Press.

- Marston, P. J., Hecht, M. L., Manke, M., McDaniel, S., & Reeder, H. (1998). The subjective experience of intimacy, passion, and commitment in heterosexual loving relationships. *Personal Relationships, 5,* 15–30.

- Marston, P. J., Hecht, M. L., & Robers, T. (1987). True love ways: The subjective experience and communication of romantic love. *Journal of Social and Personal Relationships, 4,* 387–407.

- Martin, J. N., Krizek, R. L., Nakayama, T. K., & Bradford, L. (1996). Exploring whiteness: A study of self labels for white Americans. *Communication Quarterly, 44,* 125–144.

- Marwick, A., & Boyd, D. (2014). 'It's just drama': Teen perspectives on conflict and aggression in a networked era. *Journal of Youth Studies, 17,* 1187–1204.

- Mashek, D., Cannady, L. W., & Tangney, J. P. (2007). Inclusion of community in self-scale: A single-item pictorial study of community connectedness. *Journal of Community Psychology, 35,* 257–275.

- Masheter, C. (1997). Former spouses who are friends: Three case studies. *Journal of Social and Personal Relationships, 14,* 207–222.

- Massey-Abernathy, A., & Byrd-Craven, J. (2016). Functional leadership: Bi-strategic controllers high on effortful control show gains in status and health. *Personality and Individual Differences, 97,* 193–197.

- Mast, M. S. (2002). Dominance as expressed and inferred through speaking time: A meta-analysis. *Human Communication Research, 28,* 420–450.

- Mast, M. S. (2005). The world according to men: It is hierarchical and stereotypical. *Sex Roles, 53,* 919–924.

- Mast, M. S. (2010). Interpersonal behaviour and social perception in a hierarchy: The interpersonal power and behaviour model. *European Journal of Social Psychiatry, 21,* 1–33.

- Mast, M. S., & Darioly, A. (2014) Emotional recognition accuracy in hierarchical relationships. *Swiss Journal of Psychology, 73,* 69–75.

- Mast, M. S., Hall, J. A., Cronauer, C. K., & Cousin, G. (2011). Perceived dominance in physicians: Are female physicians under scrutiny? *Patient Education and Counselling, 83,* 174–179.

- Mast, M. S., Hall, J. A., & Ickes, W. (2006). Inferring power-relevant thoughts and feelings in others: A signal detection analysis. *European Journal of Social Psychology, 36,* 468–478.

- Mast, M. S., Jonas, K., & Hall, J. A. (2009). Give a person power and he or she will show interpersonal sensitivity. *Journal of Personality and Social Psychology, 97,* 835–850.

- Matthews, S. (1986). *Friendships through the life course: Oral biographies in old age.* Beverly Hills, CA: Sage.

- May, J. L., & Hamilton, P. A. (1980). Effects of musically evoked affect on women's interpersonal attraction toward and perceptual judgments of physical attractiveness of men. *Journal of Social and Clinical Psychology, 6,* 180–190.

- Mayback, K. L., & Gold, S. R. (1994). Hyperfemininity and attraction to macho and non-macho men. *Journal of Sex Research, 31,* 91–98.

- Mazer, J. P., Murphy, R. E., & Simonds, C. J. (2007). I'll see you on "Facebook": The effects of computer mediated teacher self-disclosure on student motivation, affective learning, and classroom climate. *Communication Education, 56,* 1–17.

- Mazur, M. A., & Hubbard, A. S. E. (2004). "Is there something I should know?" Topic avoidant responses in parent-adolescent communication. *Communication Reports, 17,* 27–37.

- McAdams, D. P. (1985). Motivation and friendship. In S. Duck & D. Perlman (Eds.), *Understanding personal relationships: An interdisciplinary approach* (pp. 85–105). Beverly Hills, CA: Sage.

- McAdams, D. P. (1988). Personal needs and personal relationships. In S. Duck (Ed.), *Handbook of personal relationships: Theory, research, and intervention* (pp. 7–22). New York: Wiley.

- McBride, M. C. (2010). Saving face with family members: Corrective facework after reconciling with a romantic partner. *Journal of Family Communication, 10,* 215–235.

- McCabe, J., Brewster, K., & Tillman, K. (2011). Patterns and correlates of same-sex activity among U.S. teenagers and young adults. *Perspectives on Sexual and Reproductive Health, 43,* 142–150.

- McCabe, M. P. (1999). The interrelationship between intimacy, relationship functioning, and sexuality among men and women in committed relationships. *Canadian Journal of Human Sexuality, 8,* 31–39.

- McCall, K., & Meston, C. (2006). Cues resulting in desire for sexual activity in women. *Journal of Sexual Medicine, 3,* 838–852.

- McClanahan, K., Gold, J. A., Lenney, E., Ryckman, R. M., & Kulberg, G. E. (1990). Infatuation and attraction to a dissimilar other: Why is love blind? *Journal of Social Psychology, 130,* 433–445.

- McCornack, S. A. (1992). Information manipulation theory. *Communication Monographs, 59,* 1–16.

- McCornack, S. A., & Levine, T. R. (1990). When lies are uncovered: Emotional and relational outcomes of discovered deception. *Communication Monographs, 57,* 119–138.

- McCornack, S. A., & Parks, M. R. (1986). Deception detection and relationship development: The other side of trust. In M. L. McLaughlin (Ed.), *Communication yearbook 9* (pp. 377–389). Beverly Hills, CA: Sage.

- McCroskey, J. C., Larson, C. E., & Knapp, M. L. (1971). *An introduction to interpersonal communication.* Englewood Cliffs, NJ: Prentice Hall.

- McCroskey, J. C., & McCain, T. A. (1974). The measurement of interpersonal attraction. *Speech Monographs, 41,* 261–266.

- McCullough, M. E., Rachal, K. C., Sandage, S. J., Worthington, E. L., Brown, S. W., & Hight, T. L. (1998). Interpersonal forgiving in close relationships: II. Theoretical elaboration and measurement. *Journal of Personality and Social Psychology, 75,* 1586–1603.

- McCullough, M. E., Worthington, E. L., & Rachal, K. C. (1997). Interpersonal forgiving in close relationships. *Journal of Personality and Social Psychology, 73,* 321–336.

- McDaniel, E. R., & Andersen, P. A. (1998) Intercultural variations in tactile communication. *Journal of Nonverbal Behavior, 22,* 59–75.

- McDonald, G. W. (1981). Structural exchange and marital interaction. *Journal of Marriage and the Family, 43,* 825–839.

- McEwan, B., & Guerrero, L. K. (2010). Freshmen engagement through communication: Predicting friendship formation strategies and perceived availability of network resources from communication skills. *Communication Studies, 61,* 445–463.

- McEwan, B., & Horn, D. (2016). ILY & can u pick up some milk: Effects of relationship maintenance via text messaging on relational satisfaction and closeness in dating partners. *Southern Communication Journal, 81,* 168–181.

- McEwan, B., & Johnson, S. L. (2008). Relational violence: The darkest side of haptic communication. In L. K. Guerrero & M. L. Hecht (Eds.), *The nonverbal communication reader* (3rd ed., pp. 232–241). Long Grove, IL: Waveland Press.

- McGinty, K., Knox, D., & Zusman, M. E. (2007). Friends with benefits: Women want "friends," men want "benefits." *College Student Journal, 41,* 1126–1131.

- McGoldrick, M., & Carter, E. (1982). The family life cycle. In F. Walsh (Ed.), *Normal family processes* (pp. 167–195). New York: Guilford Press.

- McGonagle, K. A., Kessler, R. C., & Gotlib, I. H. (1993). The effects of marital disagreement style, frequency, and outcome on marital disruption. *Journal of Social and Personal Relationships, 10,* 385–404.

- McKenna, K. Y. A., Green, A. S., & Gleason, M. E. J. (2002). Relationship formation on the Internet: What's the big attraction? *Journal of Social Issues, 58,* 659–671.

- McLaren, R. M., & Solomon, D. H. (2008). Appraisals and distancing responses to hurtful messages. *Communication Research, 35,* 339–367.

- McLaren, R. M., & Solomon, D. H. (2014). Contextualizing experiences of hurt within close relationships. *Communication Quarterly, 62,* 323–341.

- McLaren, R. M., Solomon, D. H., & Priem, J. S. (2011). Explaining variation in contemporaneous responses to hurt in premarital romantic relationships: A relational turbulence model perspective. *Communication Research, 38,* 543–564.

- McLaughlin, C., & Vitak, J. (2012). Norm evolution and violation on Facebook. *New Media & Society, 14,* 299–315.

- Mead, D. E., Vatcher, G. M., Wyne, B. A., & Roberts, S. L. (1990). The comprehensive areas of change questionnaire: Assessing marital couples' presenting complaints. *American Journal of Family Therapy, 18,* 65–79.

- Mealy, M., Stephan, W., & Urrutia, I. C. (2007). The acceptability of lies: A comparison of Ecuadorians and Euro-Americans. *International Journal of Intercultural Relationship, 31,* 689–702.

- Meeus, W. (2015). Why do young people become Jihadists? A theoretical account on radical identity development. *European Journal of Developmental Psychology, 12,* 275–281.

- Mehrabian, A. (1981). *Silent messages: Implicit communication of emotions and attitudes* (2nd ed.). Belmont, CA: Wadsworth.

- Meloy, J. R., & Gothard, S. (1995). Demographic and clinical comparison of obsessional followers and offenders with mental disorders. *American Journal of Psychiatry, 152,* 258–263.

- Menegatti, M. R., & Rubini, M. (2014). Initiating, maintaining, or breaking up? The motivated use of language abstraction in romantic relationships. *Social Psychology, 45,* 408–420.

- Menzies-Toman, D. A., & Lydon, J. E. (2005). Commitment-motivated benign appraisals of partner transgressions: Do they facilitate accommodation? *Journal of Social and Personal Relationships, 22,* 111–128.

- Merolla, A. J. (2014). The role of hope in conflict management and relational maintenance. *Personal Relationships, 21,* 365–386.

- Merolla, A. J., Weber, K. D., Myers, S. A., & Booth-Butterfield, M. (2004). The impact of past dating relationship solidarity on commitment, satisfaction, and investment in current relationships. *Communication Quarterly, 52,* 251–264.

- Merton, R. K. (1948). The self-fulfilling prophecy. *Antioch Review, 8,* 193–210.

- Mesch, G. S., & Beker, G. (2010). Are norms of disclosure of online and offline personal information associated with the disclosure of personal information online? *Human Communication Research, 36,* 570–592.

- Messman, S. J., Canary, D. J., & Hause, K. S. (2000). Motives to remain platonic, equity, and the use of maintenance strategies in opposite-sex friendships. *Journal of Social and Personal Relationships, 17,* 67–94.

- Meston, C. M., & O'Sullivan, L. F. (2007). Such a tease: Intentional sexual provocation within sexual interactions. *Archives of Sexual Behavior, 35,* 531–542.

- Metts, S. (1989). An exploratory investigation of deception in close relationships. *Journal of Social and Personal Relationships, 6,* 159–179.

- Metts, S. (1991, February). *The wicked things you say, the wicked things you do: A pilot study of relational transgressions.* Paper presented at the annual meeting of the Western States Communication Association, Phoenix, AZ.

- Metts, S. (1992). The language of disengagement: A face-management perspective. In T. L. Orbuch (Ed.), *Close relationships loss: Theoretical approaches* (pp. 111–127). New York: Springer-Verlag.

- Metts, S. (1994). Relational transgressions. In W. R. Cupach & B. H. Spitzberg (Eds.), *The dark side of interpersonal communication* (pp. 217–240). Hillsdale, NJ: Lawrence Erlbaum.

- Metts, S. (1997). Face and facework: Implications for the study of personal relationships. In S. Duck (Ed.), *Handbook of personal relationships: Theory, research and interventions* (pp. 373–390). Chichester, UK: Wiley.

- Metts, S. (2004). First sexual involvement in romantic relationships: An empirical investigation of communicative framing, romantic beliefs, and attachment orientation in the passion turning point. In J. H. Harvey, A. Wenzel, & S. Sprecher (Eds.), *The handbook of sexuality in close relationships* (pp. 135–158). Mahwah, NJ: Lawrence Erlbaum.

- Metts, S., & Chronis, H. (1986, May). *An exploratory investigation of relational deception.* Paper presented at the annual meeting of the International Communication Association, Chicago, IL.

- Metts, S., & Cupach, W. R. (1986, February). *Disengagement themes in same and opposite sex friendships.* Paper presented at the annual meeting of the Western Speech Communication Association, Tucson, AZ.

- Metts, S., Cupach, W. R., & Bejlovich, R. A. (1989). "I love you too much to ever start liking you": Redefining romantic relationships. *Journal of Social and Personal Relationships, 6,* 259–274.

- Metts, S., Cupach, W. R., & Imahori, T. T. (1992). Perceptions of compliance-resisting messages in three types of cross-sex relationships. *Western Journal of Communication, 56,* 1–17.

- Metts, S., & Grohskopf, E. (2003). Impression management: Goals, strategies, and skills. In J. O. Greene & B. R. Burleson (Eds.), *Handbook of communication and social interaction skills* (pp. 357–402). Mahwah, NJ: Lawrence Erlbaum.

- Metts, S., Sprecher, S., & Regan, P. C. (1998). Communication and sexual desire. In P. A. Andersen & L. K. Guerrero (Eds.), *Handbook of communication and emotion: Research, theory, applications, and contexts* (pp. 353–377). San Diego, CA: Academic Press.

- Meurling, C. N., Ray, G. E., & LoBello, S. G. (1999). Children's evaluations of classroom friend and classroom best friend relationships. *Child Study Journal, 29,* 79–83.

- Meyers, S. A., & Berscheid, E. (1997). The language of love: The difference a preposition makes. *Personality and Social Psychology Bulletin, 23,* 347–362.

- Mikulincer, M., & Nachshon, O. (1991). Attachment styles and patterns of self-disclosure. *Journal of Personality and Social Psychology, 61,* 321–331.

- Miller, A. J., Worthington, E. L., Jr., & McDaniel, M. A. (2008). Gender and forgiveness: A meta-analytic review and research agenda. *Journal of Social and Clinical Psychology, 27,* 843–876.

- Miller, A. L., Notaro, P. C., & Zimmerman, M. A. (2002). Stability and change in internal working models of friendship: Associations with multiple domains of urban adolescent functioning. *Journal of Social and Personal Relationships, 19,* 233–259.

- Miller, C. W., & Roloff, M. E. (2014). When hurt continues: Taking conflict personally leads to rumination, residual hurt and negative motivations toward someone who hurt us. *Communication Quarterly, 62,* 193–213.

- Miller, G. R. (1976). *Explorations in interpersonal communication.* Beverly Hills, CA: Sage.

- Miller, G. R., & Boster, F. (1988). Persuasion in personal relationships. In S. Duck (Ed.), *Handbook of personal relationships: Theory, research and interventions* (pp. 275–287). Chichester, UK: Wiley.

- Miller, G. R., Boster, F., Roloff, M., & Siebold, D. (1977). Compliance-gaining message strategies: A typology and some findings concerning the effects of situational differences. *Communication Monographs, 44,* 37–51.

- Miller, G. R., & Steinberg, M. (1975). *Between people: A new analysis of interpersonal communication.* Chicago: Science Research Associates.

- Miller, R. S. (1996). *Embarrassment: Poise and peril in everyday life.* New York: Guilford Press.

- Miller, R. S. (1997). Inattentive and contented: Relationship commitment and attention to alternatives. *Journal of Personality and Social Psychology, 73,* 758–766.

- Miller-Ott, A., & Kelly, L. (2015). The presence of cell phones in romantic partner face-to-face interactions: An expectancy violation theory approach. *Southern Communication Journal, 80,* 253–270.

- Miller-Ott, A., Kelly, L., & Duran, R. L. (2012). The effect of cell phone usage rules on satisfaction in romantic relationships. *Communication Quarterly, 60,* 17–34.

- Mills, R. S. L., Nazar, J., & Farrell, H. M. (2002). Child and parent perceptions of hurtful messages. *Journal of Social and Personal Relationships, 19,* 731–754.

- Mischel, M. H. (1981). The measurement of uncertainty in illness. *Nursing Research, 30,* 258–263.

- Mischel, M. H. (1988). Uncertainty in illness. *Image: Journal of Nursing Scholarship, 20,* 225–232.

- Mischel, M. H. (1990). Reconceptualization of the uncertainty in illness theory. *Image: Journal of Nursing Scholarship, 22,* 256–262.

- Moeller, S. K., Ewing Lee, E. A., & Robinson, M. D. (2011). You never think about my feelings: Interpersonal dominance as a predictor of emotion decoding accuracy. *Emotion, 11,* 816–824.

- Moller, N. P., Fouladi, R. T., McCarthy, C. J., & Hatch, K. D. (2003). Relationship of attachment and social support to college students' adjustment following relationship breakup. *Journal of Counseling and Development, 81,* 354–369.

- Mongeau, P. A., & Carey, C. M. (1996). Who's wooing whom II: An experimental investigation of date-initiation and expectancy violation. *Western Journal of Communication, 60,* 195–213.

- Mongeau, P. A., Hale, J. L., & Alles, M. (1994). An experimental investigation of accounts and attributions following sexual infidelity. *Communication Monographs, 61,* 326–344.

- Mongeau, P. A., Hale, J. L., Johnson, K. L., & Hillis, J. D. (1993). Who's wooing whom? An investigation of female-initiated dating. In P. J. Kalbfleisch (Ed.), *Interpersonal communication: Evolving interpersonal relationships* (pp. 51–68). Hillsdale, NJ: Lawrence Erlbaum.

- Mongeau, P. A., Jacobsen, J., & Donnerstein, C. (2007). Defining dates and first date goals: Generalizing from undergraduates to single adults. *Communication Research, 34,* 526–547.

- Mongeau, P. A., & Johnson, K. L. (1995). Predicting cross-sex first-date sexual expectations and involvement: Contextual and individual difference factors. *Personal Relationships, 2,* 301–312.

- Mongeau, P. A., Knight, K., Williams, J., Eden, J., & Shaw, C. (2013). Identifying and explicating variation among friends with benefits relationships. *Journal of Sex Research, 50,* 37–47.

- Mongeau, P. A., Ramirez, A., & Vorrell, M. (2003, February). *Friends with benefits: Initial exploration of sexual, non-romantic relationships.* Paper presented at the annual meeting of the Western States Communication Association, Salt Lake City, UT.

- Mongeau, P. A., & Schulz, B. E. (1997). What he doesn't know won't hurt him (or me): Verbal responses and attributions following sexual infidelity. *Communication Reports, 10,* 143–152.

- Mongeau, P. A., Serewicz, M. C. M., Henningsen, M. L. M., & Davis, K. L. (2006). Sex differences in the transition to a heterosexual romantic relationship. In K. Dindia & D. J. Canary (Eds.), *Sex differences and similarities in communication* (2nd ed., pp. 337–358). Mahwah, NJ: Lawrence Erlbaum.

• Mongeau, P. A., Serewicz, M. C. M., & Therrien, L. F. (2004). Goals for cross-sex first dates: The identification, measurement, and influence of contextual factors. *Communication Monographs, 71*, 121–147.

• Mongeau, P. A., & Wiedmaier, B. J. (2011, November). *Is dating really dead? Investigating the college hookup culture.* Paper presented at the National Communication Association, New Orleans, LA.

• Monroe, S. M., Rohde, P., Seeley, J. R., & Lewinsohn, P. M. (1999). Life events and depression in adolescence: Relationship loss as a prospective risk factor for first onset of major depressive disorder. *Journal of Abnormal Psychology, 108*, 606–614.

• Monsour, M. (1992). Meanings of intimacy in cross- and same-sex friendships. *Journal of Social and Personal Relationships, 9*, 277–295.

• Montagu, A. (1978). *Touching: The human significance of the skin.* New York: Harper & Row. (Original work published 1971).

• Montesi, J. L., Fauber, R. L., Gordon, E. A., & Heimberg, R. G. (2010). The specific importance of communicating about sex to couples' overall sexual and overall relationship satisfaction. *Journal of Social and Personal Relationships, 28*, 591–609.

• Montgomery, B. M. (1988). Quality communication in personal relationships. In S. Duck (Ed.), *Handbook of personal relationships* (pp. 343–362). New York: Wiley.

• Montoya, R. M., Horton, R. S., & Kirchner, J. (2008). Is actual similarity necessary for attraction? A meta-analysis of actual and perceived similarity. *Journal of Social and Personal Relationships, 25*, 889–922.

• Moore, L. (2016, June 03). 11 things you need to do to have a lasting relationship. http://www.elle.com/life-love/sex-relationships/a36840/how-to-make-my-relationship-work-better-tips/.

• Moore, M. M. (1985). Nonverbal courtship patterns in women: Context and consequences. *Ethology and Sociobiology, 6*, 237–247.

• Morey, J. N., Gentzler, A. L., Creasy, B., Oberhauser, A. M., & Westerman, D. (2013). Young adults' use of communication technology within their romantic relationships and associations with attachment style. *Computers in Human Behavior, 29*, 1771–1778.

• Morf, C. C., & Rhodewalt, F. (2001). Unraveling the paradoxes of narcissism: A dynamic self-regulatory processing model. *Psychological Inquiry, 12*, 177–196.

• Morgan, E. M., & Zurbriggin, E. L. (2007). Wanting sex and wanting to wait: Young adults' accounts of sexual messages from first significant dating partners. *Feminism and Psychology, 17*, 515–541.

• Morr, M. C., & Mongeau, P. A. (2004). First date expectations: The impact of sex of initiator, alcohol consumption, and relationship type. *Communication Research, 31*, 3–35.

• Morr Serewicz, M. C., Dickson, F. C., Morrison, J. H. T. A., & Poole, L. L. (2007). Family privacy orientation, relational maintenance, and family satisfaction in young adults' family relationships. *Journal of Family Communication, 7*, 123–142.

• Morris, D. (1977). *Manwatching: A field guide to human behavior.* New York: Harry N. Abrams.

• Morrison, R. L., Van Hasselt, V. B., & Bellack, A. S. (1987). Assessment of assertion and problem-solving skills in wife abusers and their spouses. *Journal of Family Violence, 2*, 227–256.

• Morrison, T. L., Urquiza, A. J., & Goodlin-Jones, B. L. (1997). Attachment, perceptions of interaction, and relationship adjustment. *Journal of Social and Personal Relationships, 14*, 627–642.

• Morry, M. M. (2005). Relationship satisfaction as a predictor of similarity ratings: A test of the attraction-similarity hypothesis. *Journal of Social and Personal Relationships, 22*, 561–584.

• Morse, C. R., & Metts, S. (2011). Situational and communicative predictors of forgiveness following a relational transgression. *Western Journal of Communication, 75*, 239–258.

• Motley, M. T., & Reeder, H. M. (1995). Unwanted escalation of sexual intimacy: Male and female perceptions of connotations and relational consequences of resistance messages. *Communication Monographs, 62*, 355–382.

• Moyer-Guse, E., Chung, A. H., & Jain, P. (2011). Identification with characters and discussion of taboo topics after exposure to an entertainment narrative about sexual health. *Journal of Communication, 61*, 387–406.

• Muehlenhard, C. L., & Cook, S. W. (1988). Men's self-reports of unwanted sexual activity. *Journal of Sex Research, 24*, 58–72.

• Muehlenhard, C. L., Koralewski, M. A., Andrews, S. L., & Burdick, C. A. (1986). Verbal and nonverbal cues that convey interest in dating: Two studies. *Behavior Therapy, 17*, 404–419.

• Muehlenhard, C. L., Peterson, Z. D., Humphreys, T. P., & Jozkowski, K. N. (2016). The complexities of sexual consent among college students: A conceptual and empirical review. *Journal of Sex Research, 53*, 1–31.

• Muehlenhard, C. L., & Scardino, T. J. (1985). What will he think? Men's impressions of women to initiate dates and achieve academically. *Journal of Counseling Psychology, 32*, 560–569.

• Muehlenhard, C. L., Humphreys, T. P., Jozkowski, K. N., & Peterson, Z. D. (2016). The complexities of sexual consent among college students: A conceptual and empirical review. *The Journal of Sex Research, 53*, 457–487.

• Muise, A., Christofides, E., & Desmarais, S. (2009). More information than you ever wanted: Does Facebook bring out the green-eyed monster of jealousy? *CyberPsychology and Behavior, 12*, 441–444.

• Muise, A., Glang, E., & Impett, E. A. (2014). Post sex affectionate exchanges promote sexual and relationship satisfaction. *Archives of Sexual Behavior, 43*, 1391–1402.

• Mullen, C., & Hamilton, N. F. (2016). Adolescents' response to parental Facebook friend requests: The comparative influence of privacy management, parent–child relational quality, attitude and peer influence. *Computers in Human Behavior, 60*, 165–172.

• Mullen, P. E., & Pathe, M. (1994). Stalking and pathologies of love. *Australian and New Zealand Journal of Psychiatry, 28*, 469–477.

• Murnan, S. K., Perot, A., & Byrne, D. (1989). Coping with unwanted sexual activity: Normative responses, situational determinants, and individual differences. *Journal of Sex Research, 26*, 85–106.

• Murray, S. L., Holmes, J. G., & Griffin, D. W. (1996). The benefits of positive illusions: Idealization and the construction of satisfaction in close relationships. *Journal of Personality and Social Psychology, 70*, 79–98.

• Murstein, B. I., Merighi, J. R., & Vyse, S. A. (1991). Love Styles in the United States and France: A cross-cultural comparison. *Journal of Social and Clinical Psychology, 10*, 37–46.

• Myers, J. E., Madathil, J., & Tingle, L. R. (2005). Marriage satisfaction and wellness in India and the United States: A preliminary comparison of arranged marriages and marriages of choice. *Journal of Counseling & Development, 83*, 183–190.

• Najib, A., Lorberbaum, J. P., Kose, S., Bohning, D. E., & George, M. S. (2004). Regional brain activity in women grieving a romantic relationship breakup. *American Journal of Psychiatry, 161*, 2245–2256.

• Narins, E. (2015, February 18). 20 body language signs that mean he's into you. http://www.cosmopolitan.com/sex-love/news/a36457/things-his-body-language-signs-hes-into-you/.

• Neff, K. D., & Harter, S. (2002). The role of power and authenticity in relationship styles emphasizing autonomy, connectedness, or mutuality among adult couples. *Journal of Social and Personal Relationships, 19*, 835–857.

• Neff, K. D., & Suizzo, M. A. (2006). Culture, power, authenticity, and psychological well being within romantic relationships: A comparison of European Americans and Mexican Americans. *Cognitive Development, 21*, 441–457.

• Negash, S., Cui, M., Fincham, F. D., & Pasley, K. (2014). Extradyadic involvement and relationship dissolution in heterosexual women university students. *Archives of Sexual Behavior, 43*, 531–539.

• Nell, K., & Ashton, N. (1996). Gender, self-esteem, and perception of own attractiveness. *Perceptual and Motor Skills, 83*, 1105–1106.

• Neto, F. (1994). Love styles among Portuguese students. *The Journal of Psychology: Interdisciplinary and Applied, 128*, 613–616.

• Newcomb, T. M. (1961). *The acquaintance process.* New York: Holt, Rinehart & Winston.

• Niehuis, S., & Bartell, D. (2006). The marital disillusionment scale: Development and psychometric properties. *North American Journal of Psychology, 8*, 69–83.

- Niehuis, S., & Huston, T. L. (2002, July). *The premarital roots of disillusionment in early marriage.* Paper presented at the International Conference on Personal Relationships, Halifax, Nova Scotia, Canada.

- Noar, S. M., Zimmerman, R. S., & Atwood, K. A. (2004). Safer sex and sexually transmitted infections from a relationships perspective. In J. H. Harvey, A. Wenzel, & S. Sprecher (Eds.), *The handbook of sexuality in close relationships* (pp. 519–544). Mahwah, NJ: Lawrence Erlbaum.

- Nock, S. L. (1995). A comparison of marriages and cohabiting relationships. *Journal of Family Issues, 16,* 53–76.

- Noller, P., & Feeney, J. A. (1998). Communication in early marriage: Responses to conflict, nonverbal accuracy, and conversational patterns. In T. N. Bradbury (Ed.), *The developmental course of marital dysfunction* (pp. 11–43). Cambridge, UK: Cambridge University Press.

- Oakes, P. (1987). The salience of social categories. In J. C. Turner (Ed.), *Rediscovering the social group* (pp. 117–141). New York: Basil Blackwell.

- O'Connell-Corcoran, K., & Mallinckrodt, B. (2000). Adult attachment, self-efficacy, perspective taking, and conflict resolution. *Journal of Counseling and Development, 78,* 473–483.

- Ogolsky, B. G., & Bowers, J. R. (2013). A meta-analytic review of relationship maintenance and its correlates. *Journal of Social and Personal Relationships, 30,* 343–367.

- O'Hair, D. H., & Cody, M. J. (1994). Deception. In W. R. Cupach & B. H. Spitzberg (Eds.), *The dark side of interpersonal communication* (pp. 181–213). Hillsdale, NJ: Lawrence Erlbaum.

- Oldmeadow, J. A., Quinn, S., & Kowert, R. (2013). Attachment style, social skills, and Facebook use amongst adults. *Computers in Human Behavior, 29,* 1142–1149.

- Oliveira, M. J. D., Huertas, M. K. Z., & Lin, Z. (2016). Factors driving young users' engagement with Facebook. *Computers in Human Behavior, 54*(C), 54–61.

- Olson, L. N. (2002a). Compliance gaining strategies of individuals experiencing "common couple violence." *Qualitative Research Reports in Communication, 3,* 7–14.

- Olson, L. N. (2002b). Exploring "common couple violence" in heterosexual romantic relationships. *Western Journal of Communication, 66,* 104–128.

- Olson, L. N. (2004). Relational control-motivated aggression: A theoretically based typology of intimate violence. *Journal of Family Communication, 4,* 209–233.

- Olson, L. N., & Braithwaite, D. O. (2004). "If you hit me again, I'll hit you back": Conflict management strategies of individuals experiencing aggression during conflicts. *Communication Studies, 55,* 271–285.

- O'Meara, J. D. (1989). Cross-sex friendships: Four basic challenges of an ignored relationship. *Sex Roles, 21,* 525–543.

- Orbe, M. P., & Drummond, D. K. (2009). Negotiations of the complicitous nature of US racial/ethnic categorization: Exploring rhetorical strategies. *Western Journal of Communication, 73,* 437–455.

- Orbuch, T. L., Veroff, J., Hassan, H., & Horrocks, J. (2002). Who will divorce: A 14-year longitudinal study of black couples and white couples. *Journal of Social and Personal Relationships, 19,* 179–202.

- O'Reilly, L. (2015, May 26). Here's one sign Snapchat is dominating Facebook and Google when it comes to instant messaging. http://www .businessinsider.com/vodafone-says-snapchat-accounts-for-75-of-instant-messaging-data-in-the-uk-2015-5

- Orgilés, M., Espada, J. P., Johnson, B. T., Huedo-Medina, T. B., & Carratalá, E. (2012). Sexual behavior in Spanish adolescents of divorced parents. *Psicothema, 24,* 211–216.

- Ostrov, J. M., & Collins, W. A. (2007). Social dominance in romantic relationships: A prospective longitudinal study of non-verbal process. *Social Development, 16,* 580–581.

- O'Sullivan, L. F., & Allgeier, E. R. (1994). Disassembling a stereotype: Gender differences in the use of token resistance. *Journal of Applied Social Psychology, 24,* 1035–1055.

- O'Sullivan, L. F., & Allgeier, E. R. (1998). Feigning sexual desire: Consenting to unwanted sexual activity in heterosexual dating relationships. *Journal of Sex Research, 35,* 234–243.

- O'Sullivan, L. F., & Byers, E. S. (1993). Eroding stereotypes: College women's attempts to influence reluctant male partners. *Journal of Sex Research, 30,* 270–282.

- O'Sullivan, L. F., Cheng, M. M., Harris, K. M., & Brooks-Gunn, J. (2007). I wanna hold your hand: The progression of social, romantic, and sexual events in adolescent relationships. *Perspectives on Sexual and Reproductive Health, 39,* 100–107.

- O'Sullivan, L. F., & Gaines, M. E. (1998). Decision-making in college student's heterosexual dating relationship: Ambivalence about engaging in sexual activity. *Journal of Social and Personal Relationships, 15,* 347–363.

- Overall, N. C., Fletcher, G. J. O., Simpson, J. A., & Sibley, C. G. (2009). Regulating partners in intimate relationships: The costs and benefits of different communication strategies. *Journal of Personality and Social Psychology, 96,* 620–639.

- Owen, J., & Fincham, F. D. (2011). Young adults' emotional reactions after hooking up encounters. *Archives of Sexual Behavior, 40,* 321–330.

- Owen, W. F. (1987). The verbal expression of love by women and men as a critical communication event in personal relationships. *Women's Studies in Communication, 10,* 15–24.

- Owen, W. F. (1993). Metaphors in accounts of romantic relationship terminations. In P. J. Kalbfleisch (Ed.), *Interpersonal communication: Evolving interpersonal relationships* (pp. 261–268). Hillsdale, NJ: Lawrence Erlbaum.

- Pachankis, J. E., Cochran, S. D., & Mays, V. M. (2015). The mental health of sexual minority adults in and out of the closet: A population-based study. *Journal of Consulting and Clinical Psychology, 83,* 890–901.

- Paikoff, R. L., & Brooks-Gunn, J. (1991). Do parent–child relationships change during puberty? *Psychological Bulletin, 110,* 47–66.

- Palamar, J. J., Acosta, P., Ompad, D. C., & Friedman, S. R. (2016). A qualitative investigation comparing psychosocial and physical sexual experience related to alcohol and marijuana used among adults. *Archives of Sexual Behavior, 2016,* 45, 1–14.

- Palmer, M. T., & Simmons, K. B. (1995). Communicating intentions through nonverbal behaviors: Conscious and nonconscious encoding of liking. *Human Communication Research, 22,* 128–160.

- Palomares, N. A. (2009). Women are sort of more tentative than men, aren't they? How men and women use tentative language differently, similarly, and counterstereotypically as a function of gender salience. *Communication Research, 36,* 538–560.

- Papa, M. J., & Canary, D. J. (1995). Communication in organizations: A competence-based approach. In A. M. Nicotera (Ed.), *Conflict and organizations: Communicative processes* (pp. 153–179). Albany, NY: SUNY Press.

- Papini, D. R., Sebby, R. A., & Clark, S. (1989). Affective quality of family relations and adolescent identity exploration. *Adolescence, 24,* 457–466.

- Papp, L. M., Danielewicz, J., & Cayemberg, C. (2012). "Are we facebook official?" Implications of dating partners' facebook use and profiles for intimate relationship satisfaction. *Cyberpsychology, Behavior, and Social Networking, 15,* 85–90.

- Papp, L. M., Kouros, C. D., & Cummings, E. (2009). Demand-withdraw patterns in marital conflict in the home. *Personal Relationships, 16,* 285–300.

- Park, C. L. (2004). Positive and negative consequences of alcohol consumption in college students. *Addictive Behaviors, 29,* 311–321.

- Park, L. E., Sanchez, D. T., & Brynildsen, K. (2011). Maladaptive responses to relational dissolution: The role of relationship contingent self-worth. *Journal of Applied Social Psychology, 41,* 1749–1773.

- Parker, B. L., & Drummond-Reeves, S. J. (1993). The death of a dyad: Relational autopsy, analysis and aftermath. *Journal of Divorce and Remarriage, 21,* 95–119.

- Parker, R. (1997). The influence of sexual infidelity, verbal intimacy, and gender upon primary appraisal processes in romantic jealousy. *Women's Studies in Communication, 20,* 1–25.

- Parkes, A., Henderson, M., Wight, D., & Nixon, C. (2011). Is parenting associated with teenagers' early sexual risk-taking, autonomy, and relationship with sexual partners? *Perspectives on Sexual and Reproductive Health, 43,* 30–40.

- Parks, M. R. (1982). Ideology of interpersonal communication: Off the couch and into the world. In M. Burgoon (Ed.), *Communication yearbook 5* (pp. 79–108). New Brunswick, NJ: Transaction Books.

- Parks, M. R., & Floyd, K. (1996). Meanings for closeness and intimacy in friendship. *Journal of Social and Personal Relationships, 13,* 85–107.

- Parsons, J. T., Kelly, B. C., Bimbi, D. S., DiMaria, L., Wainberg, M. L., & Morgenstern, J. (2008). Explanations for the origins of sexual compulsivity among gay and bisexual men. *Archives of Sexual Behavior, 37*, 817–826.

- Patterson, B., & O'Hair, D. (1992). Relational reconciliation: Toward a more comprehensive model of relational development. *Communication Research Reports, 9*, 119–129.

- Paulhus, D. L. (1998). Interpersonal and intrapsychic adaptiveness of trait self-enhancement: A mixed blessing. *Journal of Personality and Social Psychology, 74*, 1197–1208.

- Pearce, Z., & Halford, W. K. (2008). Do attributions mediate the association of attachment and negative couple communication? *Personal Relationships, 15*, 155–170.

- Pederson, J. R., & McLaren, R. M. (2016). Managing information following hurtful experiences: How personal network members negotiate private information. *Journal of Social and Personal Relationships, 33* (7), 961–983.

- Pempek, T. A., Yermolayeva, V, A., & Calvert, S. L. (2009). College students' social networking experiences on Facebook. *Journal of Applied Developmental Psychology, 30*, 226–238.

- Pendell, S. D. (2002). Affection in interpersonal relationships: Not just a fond or tender feeling. In W. B. Gudykunst (Ed.), *Communication yearbook 26* (pp. 70–115). Mahwah, NJ: Lawrence Erlbaum.

- Pennebaker, J. W. (1989). Confession, inhibition, and disease. In L. Berkowitz (Ed.), *Advances in experimental social psychology* (Vol. 22, pp. 211–244). San Diego, CA: Academic Press.

- Pennebaker, J. W. (1990). *Opening up: The healing power of confiding in others.* New York: Morrow.

- Pennebaker, J. W., Colder, M., & Sharp, L. K. (1990). Accelerating the coping process. *Journal of Personality and Social Psychology, 58*, 528–537.

- Peplau, L. A., & Campbell, S. M. (1989). The balance of power in dating and marriage. In J. Freeman (Ed.), *Women: A feminist perspective* (4th ed., pp. 121–137). Mountain View, CA: Mayfield.

- Peplau, L. A., & Fingerhut, A. W. (2007). The close relationships of lesbians and gay men. *Annual Review of Psychology, 58*, 405–424.

- Peplau, L. A., Fingerhut, A., & Beals, K. P. (2004). Sexuality in the relationships of lesbians and gay men. In J. H. Harvey, A. Wenzel, & S. Sprecher (Eds.), *The handbook of sexuality in close relationships* (pp. 349–369). Mahwah, NJ: Lawrence Erlbaum.

- Peplau, L. A., & Spalding, L. R. (2000). The close relationships of lesbians, gay men, and bisexuals. In C. Hendrick & S. S. Hendrick (Eds.), *Close relationships: A sourcebook* (pp. 111–123). Thousand Oaks, CA: Sage.

- Perilloux, C. (2014). (Mis) reading the signs: Men's perception of women's sexual interest. In V. A. Weekes-Shackelford & T. K. Shackelford (eds.), *Evolutionary perspectives on human sexual psychology and behavior* (pp. 119–133). New York: Springer.

- Perilloux, C., & Buss, D. M. (2008). Breaking up romantic relationships: Costs experienced and coping strategies deployed. *Evolutionary Psychology, 6*, 164–181.

- Perras, M. T., & Lustig, M. W. (1982, February). *The effects of intimacy level and intent to disengage on the selection of relational disengagement strategies.* Paper presented at the annual meeting of the Western Speech Communication Association, Denver, CO.

- Perrin, A., & Duggan, M. (2015, June 26). *Americans' Internet Access: 2000–2015.* http://www.pewinternet.org/2015/06/26/americans-internet-access-2000-2015/.

- Peterson, C. C. (1990). Husbands' and wives' perceptions of marital fairness across the family life cycle. *International Journal of Aging and Human Development, 31*, 179–188.

- Petra, R., & Petra, K. (1993). *The 775 stupidest things ever said.* New York: Doubleday.

- Petronio, S. (1991). Communication boundary management: A theoretical model of managing disclosure of private information between marital couples. *Communication Theory, 1*, 311–335.

- Petronio, S. (Ed.). (2000). *Balancing the secrets of private disclosures.* Mahwah, NJ: Lawrence Erlbaum.

- Petronio, S. (2002). *Boundaries of privacy: Dialectics of disclosure.* Albany, NY: SUNY Press.

- Petronio, S. (2013). Brief status report on communication privacy management theory. *Journal of Family Communication, 13*, 6–14.

- Petronio, S., & Harriman, S. (1990, October). *Parental privacy invasion: Tactics and reactions to encroachment.* Paper presented at the annual meeting of the Speech Communication Association, Chicago.

- Petronio, S., & Reierson, J. (2009). Regulating the privacy of confidentiality: Grasping the complexities through communication privacy management theory. In T. D. Afifi & W. A. Afifi (Eds.), *Uncertainty, information management, and disclosure decisions: Theories and applications* (pp. 365–383). New York: Routledge.

- Petronio, S., Sargent, J., Andea, L., Reganis, P., & Cichocki, D. (2004). Family and friends as healthcare advocates: Dilemmas of confidentiality and privacy. *Journal of Social and Personal Relationships, 21*, 33–52.

- Pettigrew, J. (2009). Text messaging and connectedness within close interpersonal relationships. *Marriage & Family Review, 45*, 697–716.

- Pfouts, J. H. (1978). Violent families: Coping responses of abused wives. *Child Welfare, 57*, 101–111.

- Phillips, G. M., & Metzger, N. J. (1976). *Intimate communication.* Boston: Allyn & Bacon.

- Phillips, M., & Spitzberg, B. H. (2010). Speculating about spying on MySpace and beyond: Social network surveillance and obsessive relational intrusion. In K. B. Wright & L. M. Webb (Eds.), *Computer-mediated communication in personal relationships* (pp. 344–367). New York: Peter Lang.

- Pierce, C. A. (1996). Body height and romantic attraction: A meta-analytic test of the male-taller norm. *Social Behavior and Personality, 24*, 143–149.

- Pierce, T., & Lydon, J. E. (2001). Global and specific relational models in the experience of social interactions. *Journal of Personality and Social Psychology, 80*, 613–631.

- Pines, A. (1992). *Romantic jealousy: Understanding and conquering the shadow of love.* New York: St. Martin's Press.

- Pines, A. (1998). A prospective study of personality and gender differences in romantic attraction. *Personality and Individual Differences, 25*, 147–157.

- Pines, A. M. (2001). The role of gender and culture in romantic attraction. *European Psychologist, 6*, 92–102.

- Pistole, M. C. (1989). Attachment in adult romantic relationships: Style of conflict resolution and relationship satisfaction. *Journal of Social and Personal Relationships, 6*, 505–510.

- Planalp, S., & Honeycutt, J. M. (1985). Events that increase uncertainty in personal relationships. *Human Communication Research, 11*, 593–604.

- Polimeni, A., Hardie, E., & Buzwell, S. (2002). Friendship closeness inventory: Development and psychometric evaluation. *Psychological Reports, 91*, 142–152.

- Polk, D. M., & Egbert, N. (2013). Speaking the language of love: On whether Chapman's (1992) claims stand up to empirical testing. *The Open Communication Journal, 7*, 1–11.

- Poushter, J. (2016, February 22). Smartphone ownership and internet usage continues to climb in emerging economies. http://www.pewglobal.org/2016/02/22/smartphone-ownership-and-internet-usage-continues-to-climb-in-emerging-economies/.

- Powell, L. A. (2005). Justice judgments as complex psychocultural constructions: An equity-based heuristic for mapping two- and three-dimensional fairness representations in perceptual space. *Journal of Cross-Cultural Psychology, 36*, 48–73.

- Prager, K. J. (1995). *The psychology of intimacy.* New York: Guilford Press.

- Prager, K. J. (2000). Intimacy in personal relationships. In C. Hendrick & S. S. Hendrick (Eds.), *Close relationships: A sourcebook* (pp. 229–242). Thousand Oaks, CA: Sage.

- Prager, K. J., & Buhrmester, D. (1998). Intimacy and need fulfillment in couple relationships. *Journal of Social and Personal Relationships, 15*, 435–469.

• Prager, K. J., & Roberts, L. J. (2004). Deep intimate connection: Self and intimacy in couple relationships. In D. J. Mashek & A. P. Aron (Eds.), *Handbook of closeness and intimacy* (pp. 43–60). Mahwah, NJ: Lawrence Erlbaum.

• Pruitt, D. G., & Carnevale, P. J. (1993). *Negotiation in social conflict.* Pacific Grove, CA: Brooks/Cole.

• Pujazon-Zazik, M. A., Manasse, S. M., & Orrell-Valente, J. K. (2012). Adolescents' self-presentation on a teen dating web site: A risk-content analysis. *Journal of Adolescent Health, 50,* 517–520.

• Putnam, L. L., & Wilson, C. E. (1982). Communicative strategies in organizational conflicts: Reliability and validity of a measurement scale. In M. Burgoon (Ed.), *Communication yearbook 6* (pp. 629–652). Beverly Hills, CA: Sage.

• Quinn, K. (2016). Why we share: A uses and gratifications approach to privacy regulation in social media use. *Journal of Broadcasting and Electronic Media, 60,* 61–86.

• Quirk, K., Owen, J., Shuck, B., Fincham, F. D., Knopp, K., & Rhoades, G. (2016). Breaking bad: Commitment uncertainty, alternative monitoring, and relationship termination in young adults, *Journal of Couple & Relationship Therapy, 15,* 61–74.

• Qureshi, C., Harris, E., & Atkinson, B. E. (2016). Relationships between age of females and attraction to the Dark Triad personality. *Personality and Individual Differences, 95,* 200–203.

• Raacke, J., & Bonds-Raacke, J. (2008). MySpace and Facebook: Applying the uses and gratifications theory to exploring friend-networking sites. *Cyberpsychology and Behavior, 11,* 169–174.

• Rabby, M. K. (2007). Relational maintenance and the influence of commitment in online and offline relationships. *Communication Studies, 58,* 315–337.

• Rabby, M. K., & Walther, J. B. (2003). Computer mediated effect on relationship formation and maintenance. In D. J. Canary & M. Dainton (Eds.), *Maintaining relationships through communication: Relational, contextual, and cultural variations* (pp. 141–162). Mahwah, NJ: Lawrence Erlbaum.

• Ragsdale, J. D., Brandau-Brown, F., & Bello, R. (2010). Attachment style and gender as predictors of relational repair among the remarried. *Journal of Family Communication, 10,* 158–173.

• Rahim, M. A. (1986). *Managing conflicts in organizations.* New York: Praeger.

• Rahim, M. A., & Bonoma, T. V. (1979). Managing organizational conflict: A model for diagnosis and intervention. *Psychological Reports, 44,* 36–48.

• Rains, S. A., Brunner, S. R., & Oman, K. (2016). Self disclosure and new communication technologies: The implications of receiving superficial self-disclosures from friends. *Journal of Social and Personal Relationships, 33,* 42–61.

• Ramirez, A., Jr. (2008). An examination of the tripartite approach to commitment: An actor-partner interdependence analysis of the effect of relational maintenance behavior. *Journal of Social and Personal Relationships, 25,* 943–965.

• Ramirez, A., Jr., Sunnafrank, M., & Goei, R. (2010). Predicted outcome value theory in ongoing relationships. *Communication Monographs, 77,* 27–50.

• Ramirez, A., Jr., Walther, J. B., Burgoon, J. K., & Sunnafrank, M. (2002). Information-seeking strategies, uncertainty, and computer-mediated communication. *Human Communication Research, 28,* 213–228.

• Ramirez, A., Jr., & Wang, Z. (2008). When online meets offline: An expectancy violations theory perspective on modality switching. *Journal of Communication, 58,* 20–39.

• Ramirez, A., Jr., & Zhang, S. (2007). When on-line meets off-line: The effect of modality switching on relational communication. *Communication Monographs, 74,* 287–310.

• Rasberry, C. N., & Goodson, P. (2009). Predictors of secondary abstinence in U. S. College Undergraduates. *Archives of Sexual Behavior, 38,* 74–86.

• Rauscher, E. A., & Hesse, C. (2014). Investigating uncertainty and emotions in conversations about family health history: A test of the Theory of Motivated Information Management. *Journal of Health Communication, 19,* 939–954.

• Rawlins, W. K. (1982). Cross-sex friendship and the communicative management of sex-role expectations. *Communication Quarterly, 30,* 343–352.

• Rawlins, W. K. (1983a). Negotiating close friendships: The dialectic of conjunctive freedoms. *Human Communication Research, 9,* 255–266.

• Rawlins, W. K. (1983b). Openness as problematic in ongoing friendships: Two conversational dilemmas. *Communication Monographs, 50,* 1–13.

• Rawlins, W. K. (1989). A dialectical analysis of the tensions, functions, and strategic challenges of communication in young adult friendships. In J. A. Anderson (Ed.), *Communication yearbook 12* (pp. 157–189). Newbury Park, CA: Sage.

• Rawlins, W. K. (1992). Friendship matters: Communication, dialectics, and the life course. Hawthorne, NY: Aldine de Gruyter.

• Rawlins, W. K. (1994). Being there and growing apart: Sustaining friendships during adulthood. In D. J. Canary & L. Stafford (Eds.), *Communication and relational maintenance* (pp. 275–294). San Diego, CA: Academic Press.

• Ray, G. B., & Floyd, K. (2006). Nonverbal expressions of liking and disliking in initial interaction: Encoding and decoding perspectives. *Southern Communication Journal, 71,* 45–64.

• Redmond, M. V., & Virchota, D. A. (1994, November). *The effects of varying lengths of initial interaction on attraction and uncertainty reduction.* Paper presented at the annual meeting of the Speech Communication Association, New Orleans, LA.

• Reece, M. M., & Whitman, R. N. (1962). Expressive movements, warmth, and verbal reinforcement. *Journal of Abnormal and Social Psychology, 64,* 234–236.

• Reed, P. J., Spiro, E. S., & Butts, C. T. (2016). Thumbs up for privacy?: Differences in online self-disclosure behavior across national cultures. *Social Science Research, 59,* 155–170.

• Reeder, H. M. (2000). "I like you . . . as a friend": The role of attraction in cross-sex friendship. *Journal of Social and Personal Relationships, 17,* 329–348.

• Reel, B. W., & Thompson, T. L. (1994). A test of the effectiveness of strategies for talking about the effectiveness of condom use. *Journal of Applied Communication Research, 22,* 127–140.

• Reese-Weber, S., & Bartle-Haring, S. (1998). Conflict resolution styles in family subsystems and adolescent romantic relationships. *Journal of Youth and Adolescence, 27,* 735–752.

• Regan, P. C. (1998). Of lust and love: Beliefs about the role of sexual desire in romantic relationships. *Personal Relationships, 5,* 139–157.

• Regan, P. C. (2004). Sex and the attraction process: Lessons learned from science (and Shakespeare) on lust, love, chastity, and fidelity. In J. H. Harvey, A. Wenzel, & S. Sprecher (Eds.), *The handbook of sexuality in close relationships* (pp. 115–133). Mahwah, NJ: Lawrence Erlbaum.

• Regan, P. C., & Berscheid, E. (1995). Gender differences in beliefs about the causes of male and female sexual desire. *Personal Relationships, 2,* 345–358.

• Regan, P. C., & Berscheid, E. (1999). *Lust: What we know about sexual desire.* Thousand Oaks, CA: Sage.

• Rehman, U. S., & Holtzworth-Munroe, A. (2006). A cross-cultural analysis of the demand-withdraw marital interaction: Observing couples from a developing country. *Journal of Counseling and Clinical Psychology, 74,* 755–766.

• Reid, J. A., Elliott, S., & Webber, G. R. (2011). Casual hook-ups to formal dates: Redefining the boundaries of the sexual double standard. *Gender and Society, 25,* 545–568.

• Reilly, M. E., & Lynch, J. M. (1990). Power-sharing in lesbian partnerships. *Journal of Homosexuality, 19,* 1–30.

• Reined, C., Byers, E. S., & Pan, S. (1997). Sexual and relational satisfaction in mainland China. *Journal of Sex Research, 34,* 399–410.

• Reinisch, J. M., & Beasley, R. (1990). *The Kinsey Institute report on sex: What you must know to be sexually literate.* New York: St. Martin's Press.

• Reissing, E. D., Anduff, H. L., & Wentland, J. J. (2012). Looking back: The experience of first sexual intercourse and current sexual adjustment in young heterosexual adults. *Journal of Sex Research, 49,* 27–35.

• Reissman, C., Aron, A., & Bergen, M. R. (1993). Shared activities and marital satisfaction: Causal direction and self-expansion versus boredom. *Journal of Social and Personal Relationships, 10,* 249–254.

• Remland, M. S. (1981). Developing leadership skills in nonverbal communication: A situational perspective. *Journal of Business Communication, 18,* 17–29.

• Remland, M. S. (1982, November). *Leadership impressions and nonverbal communication in a superior subordinate situation.* Paper presented at the annual meeting of the Speech Communication Association, Louisville, KY.

• Renfro, A. (2012, December 05). *Meet generation Z.* http://gettingsmart.com/2012/12/meet-generation-z/.

• Reyes, M., Afifi, W., Krawchuk, A., Imperato, N., Shelley, D., & Lee, J. (June, 1999). *Just (don't) talk: Comparing the impact of interaction style on sexual desire and social attraction.* Paper presented at the joint conference of the International Network on Personal Relationships and the International Society for the Study of Personal Relationships, Louisville, KY.

• Rhatigan, D. L., & Street, A. E. (2005). The impact of intimate partner violence on decisions to leave dating relationships. *Journal of Interpersonal Violence, 20,* 1580–1597.

• Rhoades, G. K., Stanley, S. M., & Markman, H. J. (2009). The pre-engagement cohabitation effect: A replication and extension of previous findings. *Journal of Family Psychology, 23,* 107–111.

• Rhoades, G. K., Stanley, S. M., & Markman, H. J. (2010). Should I stay or should I go? Predicting dating relationship stability from four aspects of commitment. *Journal of Family Psychology, 24,* 543–550.

• Rhoades, G. K., Stanley, S. M., & Markman, H. J. (2012). The impact of the transition to cohabitation on relationship functioning: Cross-sectional and longitudinal findings. *Journal of Family Psychology, 26,* 348–358.

• Rhodewalt, F., & Eddings, S. K. (2002). Narcissus reflects: Memory distortion in response to ego-relevant feedback among high- and low-narcissistic men. *Journal of Research in Personality, 36,* 97–116.

• Ridley, C., & Feldman, C. (2003). Female domestic violence toward male partners: Exploring conflict responses and outcomes. *Journal of Family Violence, 18,* 157–171.

• Riela, S., Rodriguez, G., Aron, A., Xu, X., & Acevedo, B. P. (2010). Experiences of falling in love: Investigating culture, ethnicity, gender, and speed. *Journal of Social and Personal Relationships, 27,* 473–493.

• Rindfuss, R., & VandenHeuvel, A. (1990). Cohabitation: A precursor to marriage or an alternative to being single? *Population and Development Review, 16,* 703–726.

• Riordan, C. A., & Tedeschi, J. T. (1983). Attraction in aversive environments: Some evidence for classical conditioning and negative reinforcement. *Journal of Personality and Social Psychology, 44,* 683–692.

• Rittenour, C. E., Myers, S. A., & Brann, M. (2007). Commitment and emotional closeness in the sibling relationship. *Southern Communication Journal, 72,* 169–183.

• Rivera, K. D. (2015). Emotional taint: Making sense of emotional dirty work at the US Border Patrol. *Management Communication Quarterly, 29,* 198–228.

• Roberson, B. F., & Wright, R. A. (1994). Difficulty as a determinant of interpersonal appeal: A social-motivational application of energization theory. *Basic and Applied Social Psychology, 15,* 373–388.

• Robinson, K. J., Hoplock, L. B., & Cameron, J. J. (2015). When in Doubt, Reach Out: Touch Is a Covert but Effective Mode of Soliciting and Providing Social Support. *Social Psychological and Personality Science, 6,* 831–839.

• Robinson, T., & Smith-Lovin, L. (1992). Selective interaction as a strategy for identity maintenance: An affect control model. *Social Psychology Quarterly, 55,* 12–28.

• Roese, N. J., Pennington, G. L., Coleman, J., Janicki, M., Norman, P. L., & Kenrick, D. T. (2006). Sex differences in regret: All for love or some for lust? *Personality and Social Psychology Bulletin, 32,* 770–780.

• Rogers, E. M. (1995). *Diffusion of innovations* (4th ed.). New York: Free Press.

• Rogers, L. A., & Farace, R. V. (1975). Analysis of relational communication in dyads: New measurement procedures. *Human Communication Research, 1,* 222–239.

• Rogers, L. A., & Millar, F. E. (1988). Relational communication. In S. Duck (Ed.), *Handbook of personal relationships* (pp. 289–305). New York: Wiley.

• Rohlfing, M. E. (1995). "Doesn't anybody stay in one place anymore?" An exploration of the understudied phenomenon of long-distance relationships. In J. T. Wood & S. Duck (Eds.), *Understudied relationships: Off the beaten track* (pp. 173–196). Thousand Oaks, CA: Sage.

• Rohmann, E., Führer, A., & Bierhoff, H. W. (2016). Relationship satisfaction across European cultures: The role of love styles. *Cross-Cultural Research, 50,* 178–211.

• Rohrbaugh, J. B. (2006). Domestic violence in same-gender relationships. *Family Court Review, 44,* 287–299.

• Roiger, J. F. (1993). Power in friendship and use of influence strategies. In P. J. Kalbfleisch (Ed.), *Interpersonal communication: Evolving interpersonal relationships* (pp. 133–145). Hillsdale, NJ: Lawrence Erlbaum.

• Rollie, S., & Duck, S. W. (2006). Divorce and dissolution of romantic relationships: Stage Models and their limitations. In J. H. Harvey & M. Fine (Eds.), *Handbook of divorce and relationship dissolution* (pp. 176–193). Mahwah, NJ: Lawrence Erlbaum.

• Roloff, M. E., & Cloven, D. H. (1990). The chilling effect in interpersonal relationships: The reluctance to speak one's mind. In D. D. Cahn (Ed.), *Intimates in conflict: A communication perspective* (pp. 49–76). Hillsdale, NJ: Lawrence Erlbaum.

• Roloff, M. E., & Cloven, D. H. (1994). When partners transgress: Maintaining violated relationships. In D. J. Canary & L. Stafford (Eds.), *Communication and relational maintenance* (pp. 23–43). San Diego, CA: Academic Press.

• Roloff, M. E., & Ifert, D. E. (2000). Conflict management through avoidance: Withholding complaints, suppressing arguments, and declaring topics taboo. In S. Petronio (Ed.), *Balancing the secrets of private disclosures* (pp. 151–163). Mahwah, NJ: Lawrence Erlbaum.

• Roloff, M. E., & Miller, C. W. (2006). Social cognition approaches to understanding conflict and communication. In J. G. Oetzel & S. Ting-Toomey (Eds.), *The SAGE handbook of conflict communication* (pp. 97–128). Thousand Oaks, CA: Sage.

• Roloff, M. E., Soule, K. P., & Carey, C. M. (2001). Reasons for remaining in a relationship and responses to relational transgressions. *Journal of Social and Personal Relationships, 18,* 362–385.

• Roscoe, B., Cavanaugh, L. E., & Kennedy, D. R. (1988). Dating infidelity: Behaviors, reasons, and consequences. *Adolescence, 89,* 36–43.

• Rose, S. M. (1985). Same- and cross-sex friendships and the psychology of homosociology. *Sex Roles, 12,* 63–74.

• Rosenfeld, L. B. (1979). Self-disclosure avoidance: Why I am afraid to tell you who I am. *Communication Monographs, 46,* 63–74.

• Rosenfeld, L. B. (2000). Overview of the ways privacy, secrecy, disclosure are balanced in today's society. In S. Petronio (Ed.), *Balancing secrets of private disclosure* (pp. 3–17). Mahwah, NJ: Lawrence Erlbaum.

• Rosenfeld, L. B., & Kendrick, W. L. (1984). Choosing to be open: An empirical investigation of subjective reasons for self-disclosing. *Western Journal of Speech Communication, 48,* 326–343.

• Rosenfeld, M. J., & Thomas, R. J. (2012). Searching for a mate: The rise of the Internet as a social intermediary. *American Sociological Review, 77,* 523–547.

• Rosenthal, A. M., Sylva, D., Safron, A., & Bailey, J. M. (2011). Sexual arousal patterns of bisexual men revisited. *Biological Psychology, 88,* 112–116.

• Rosenthal, D., Gifford, S., & Moore, S. (1998). Safe sex or safe love: Competing discourses. *AIDS Care, 10,* 35–47.

• Rosenthal, R., & Jacobson, L. (1968). *Pygmalion in the classroom: Teacher expectation and pupils' intellectual development.* New York: Holt, Rinehart & Winston.

• Ross, M., & Sicoly, F. (1979). Egocentric biases in availability and attribution. *Journal of Personality and Social Psychology, 37,* 273–285.

• Rowatt, W. C., Cunningham, M. R., & Druen, P. B. (1998). Deception to get a date. *Personality and Social Psychology Bulletin, 24,* 1228–1242.

• Rowatt, W. C., Cunningham, M. R., & Druen, P. B. (1999). Lying to get a date: The effects of facial physical attractiveness on the willingness to deceive prospective dating partners. *Journal of Social and Personal Relationships, 16,* 209–233.

• Rubin, R. B., & Martin, M. M. (1998). Interpersonal communication motives. In J. C. McCroskey, J. A. Daly, M. M. Martin, & M. J. Beatty (Eds.), *Communication and personality: Trait perspectives* (pp. 287–307). Cresskill, NJ: Hampton Press.

- Rubin, Z. (1970). Measurement of romantic love. *Journal of Personality and Social Psychology, 16,* 265–273.

- Rubin, Z. (1973). *Loving and liking: An invitation to social psychology.* New York: Holt, Rinehart & Winston.

- Rubin, Z. (1974). Lovers and other strangers: The development of intimacy in encounters and relationships. *American Scientist, 62,* 182–190.

- Rubovits, P. C., & Maher, M. L. (1973). Pygmalion black and white. *Journal of Personality and Social Psychology, 25,* 210–218.

- Ruesch, J. (1951). Communication and human relations: An interdisciplinary approach. In J. Ruesch & G. Bateson (Eds.), *Communication: The social matrix of psychiatry* (pp. 21–49). New York: Norton.

- Ruppel, E. K. (2015). Use of communication technologies in romantic relationships: Self-disclosure and the role of relationship development. *Journal of Social and Personal Relationships, 32,* 667–686.

- Rusbult, C. E. (1980). Commitment and satisfaction in romantic associations: A test of the investment model. *Journal of Experimental Social Psychology, 16,* 172–186.

- Rusbult, C. E. (1983). A longitudinal test of the investment model: The development (and deterioration) of satisfaction and commitment in heterosexual involvements. *Journal of Personality and Social Psychology, 45,* 101–117.

- Rusbult, C. E. (1987). Responses to dissatisfaction in close relationships: The exit-voice-loyalty-neglect model. In D. Perlman & S. Duck (Eds.), *Intimacy relationships: Development, dynamics and deterioration* (pp. 209–237). Newbury Park, CA: Sage.

- Rusbult, C. E., Arriaga, X. B., & Agnew, C. R. (2001). Interdependence in close relationships. In G. J. O. Fletcher & M. S. Clark (Eds.), *Blackwell handbook of social psychology: Interpersonal processes* (pp. 359–387). Oxford: Blackwell.

- Rusbult, C. E., Bissonnette, V. L., Arriaga, X. B., & Cox, C. L. (1998). Accommodation processes during the early years of marriage. In T. N. Bradbury (Ed.), *The developmental course of marital dysfunction* (pp. 74–113). New York: Cambridge University Press.

- Rusbult, C. E., Drigotas, S. M., & Verette, J. (1994). The investment model: An interdependence analysis of commitment processes and relationship maintenance phenomena. In D. J. Canary & L. Stafford (Eds.), *Communication and relational maintenance* (pp. 115–139). San Diego, CA: Academic Press.

- Rusbult, C. E., & Farrell, D. (1983). A longitudinal test of the investment model: The impact on job satisfaction, job commitment, and turnover of variations in rewards, costs, alternatives, and investments. *Journal of Applied Psychology, 68,* 429–438.

- Rusbult, C. E., Johnson, D. J., & Morrow, G. D. (1986). Impact of couple patterns of problems solving on distress and nondistress in dating relationships. *Journal of Personality and Social Psychology, 50,* 744–753.

- Rusbult, C. E., & Martz, J. (1995). Remaining in an abusive relationship: An investment model analysis of nonvoluntary dependence. *Personality and Social Psychology Bulletin, 21,* 558–571.

- Rusbult, C. E., Olsen, N., Davis, J. L., & Hannon, P. (2001). Commitment and relationship maintenance mechanisms. In J. H. Harvey & A. Wenzel (Eds.), *Close romantic relationships: Maintenance and enhancement* (pp. 87–113). Mahwah, NJ: Lawrence Erlbaum.

- Rusbult, C. E., Van Lange, P. A. M., Wildschut, T., Yovetich, N. A., & Verette, J. (2000). Perceived superiority in close relationships: Why it exists and persists. *Journal of Personality and Social Psychology, 79,* 521–545.

- Rusbult, C. E., Verette, J., Whitney, G. A., Slovik, L. F., & Lipkus, I. (1991). Accommodation processes in close relationships: Theory and preliminary empirical evidence. *Journal of Personality and Social Psychology, 60,* 53–78.

- Rusbult, C. E., & Zembrodt, I. M. (1983). Responses to dissatisfaction in romantic involvements: A multidimensional scaling analysis. *Journal of Experimental Social Psychology, 19,* 274–293.

- Rusbult, C. E., Zembrodt, I. M., & Gunn, L. K. (1982). Exit, voice, loyalty and neglect: Responses to dissatisfaction in romantic involvements. *Journal of Personality and Social Psychology, 43,* 1230–1242.

- Russell, B. (1938). *Power: A new social analysis.* London: Allen and Unwin.

- Ryff, C. D., Singer, B. H., Wing, E., & Dienberg Love, G. (2001). Elective affinities and uninvited agonies: Mapping emotion with significant others onto health. In C. Ryff & B. Singer (Eds.), *Emotion, social relationships, and health* (pp. 133–174). New York: Oxford University Press.

- Sadalla, E. K., Kenrick, D. T., & Vershure, B. (1987). Dominance and heterosexual attraction. *Journal of Personality and Social Psychology, 52,* 730–738.

- Sadeghi, M. A., Mazaheri, M. A., & Moutabi, F. (2011). Adult attachment and quality of couples' communication based on observed couple interactions. *Journal of Psychology, 15,* 3–22.

- Saffrey, C., & Ehrenberg, M. (2007). When thinking hurts: Attachment, rumination, and postrelationship adjustment. *Personal Relationships, 14,* 351–368.

- Safron, C. (1979). Troubles that pull couples apart: A *Redbook* report. *Redbook, 83,* 138–141.

- Sagrestano, L. M. (1992). Power strategies in interpersonal relationships. *Psychology of Women Quarterly, 16,* 481–495.

- Sagrestano, L. M., Heavey, C. L., & Christensen, A. (2006). Individual differences versus social structural approaches to explaining demand-withdraw and social influence behaviors. In K. Dindia & D. J. Canary (Eds.), *Sex differences and similarities in communication* (2nd ed., pp. 379–395). Mahwah, NJ: Lawrence Erlbaum.

- Salovey, P., & Rodin, J. (1985, September). The heart of jealousy. *Psychology Today, 19,* 22–25, 28–29.

- Salovey, P., & Rodin, J. (1986). Differentiation of social-comparison jealousy and romantic jealousy. *Journal of Personality and Social Psychology, 50,* 1100–1112.

- Salovey, P., & Rodin, J. (1989). Envy and jealousy in close relationships. In C. Hendrick (Ed.), *Close relationships* (pp. 221–246). Newbury Park, CA: Sage.

- Salt, R. E. (1991). Affectionate touch between fathers and preadolescent sons. *Journal of Marriage and the Family, 53,* 545–554.

- Samp, J. A., & Palevitz, C. E. (2014). Managing relational transgressions as revealed on Facebook: The influence of dependence power on verbal and nonverbal responses. *Journal of Nonverbal Behavior, 38,* 477–493.

- Samp, J. A., & Solomon, D. H. (2001). Coping with problematic events in dating relationships: The influence of dependence power on severity appraisals and decisions to communicate. *Western Journal of Communication, 65,* 138–160.

- Sanderson, C. A., Rahm, K. B., Beigbeder, S. A, & Metts, S. (2005). The link between the pursuit of intimacy goals and satisfaction in close same-sex friendships: An examination of the underlying processes. *Journal of Social and Personal Relationships, 22,* 75–98.

- Schäfer, T., Auerswald, F., Bajorat, I. K., Ergemlidze, N., Frille, K., Gehrigk, J., Gusakova, A., Kaiser, B., Pätzold, R. A., Sanahuja, A., Sari, S., Schramm, A., Walter, C., & Wilker, T. (2016). The effect of social feedback on music preference. *Musicae Scientiae, 20*(2) 263–268.

- Scharfe, E., & Bartholomew, K. (1995). Accommodation and attachment representations in young couples. *Journal of Social and Personal Relationships, 12,* 389–401.

- Scheflen, A. E. (1965). Quasi-courtship behavior in psychotherapy. *Psychiatry, 27,* 245–257.

- Scheflen, A. E. (1972). *Body language and the social order: Communication as behavior control.* Englewood Cliffs, NJ: Prentice Hall.

- Scheflen, A. E. (1974). *How behavior means.* Garden City, NY: Anchor/Doubleday.

- Scherer, K. R. (1972). Judging personality from voice: A cross-cultural approach to an old issue in interpersonal perception. *Journal of Personality, 40,* 191–210.

- Scherer, K. R. (1979). Acoustic noncomitants of emotional dimensions: Judging affect from synthesized tone sequences. In S. Weitz (Ed.), *Nonverbal communication: Readings with commentary* (pp. 249–253). New York: Oxford University Press.

- Schlenker, B. R. (1980). *Impression management: The self-concept, social identity, and interpersonal relations.* Monterey, CA: Brooks/Cole.

- Schlenker, B. R. (1984). Identities, identifications, and relationships. In V. Derlega (Ed.), *Communication, intimacy, and close relationships* (pp. 71–104). San Diego, CA: Academic Press.

- Schlenker, B. R. (Ed.). (1985). *The self and social life.* New York: McGraw-Hill.

- Schlenker, B. R., Britt, T. W., & Pennington, J. (1996). Impression regulation and management: Highlights of a theory of self-identification. In R. M. Sorrentino & E. T. Higgins (Eds.), *Handbook of motivation and cognition: The interpersonal context* (Vol. 3, pp. 118–142). New York: Guilford Press.

- Schlenker, B. R., Britt, T. W., Pennington, J., Murphy, R., & Doherty, K. J. (1994). The triangle model of responsibility. *Psychological Review, 101,* 632–652.

- Schlenker, B. R., & Darby, B. W. (1981). The use of apologies in social predicaments. *Social Psychology Quarterly, 44,* 271–278.

- Schlenker, B. R., & Weigold, M. F. (1990). Self-consciousness and self-presentation: Being autonomous versus appearing autonomous. *Journal of Personality and Social Psychology, 59,* 820–828.

- Schlenker, B. R., & Weigold, M. F. (1992). Interpersonal processes involving impression regulation and management. *Annual Review of Psychology, 43,* 133–168.

- Schmitt, D. P. (2008). Evolutionary approaches to mate choice and relationship initiation. In S. Sprecher, J. Harvey, & A. Wenzel (Eds.), *Handbook of relationship initiation* (pp. 55–74). New York: Taylor & Francis.

- Schmookler, T., & Bursik, K. (2007). The value of monogamy in emerging adulthood: A gendered perspective. *Journal of Social and Personal Relationships, 24,* 819–835.

- Schneider, K. T., Swan, S., & Fitzgerald, L. F. (1997). Job-related and psychological effects of sexual harassment in the workplace: Empirical evidence from two organizations. *Journal of Applied Psychology, 82,* 401–415.

- Schrodt, P., Witt, P. L., & Shimkowski, J. R. (2014). A meta-analytic review of the demand/withdrawal interaction and its associations with individual, relational, and communicative outcomes. *Communication Monographs, 81,* 28–58.

- Schutz, W. C. (1958). *The interpersonal underworld.* Palo Alto, CA: Science and Behavior Books.

- Schwartz, P. (1994). *Peer marriage: How love between equals really works.* New York: Macmillan.

- Schwartz, R. (2008). *Cell phone communication versus face-to-face communication: The effect of mode of communication on relationship satisfaction and the difference in quality of communication.* Unpublished master's thesis, Kent State University, Kent, OH.

- Schweinle, W. E., Ickes, W., & Bernstein, I. H. (2002). Empathic inaccuracy in husband to wife aggression: The overattribution bias. *Personal Relationships, 9,* 141–158.

- Scissors, L. E., & Gergle, D. (2013, February). *Back and forth, back and forth: Channel switching in romantic couple conflict.* In Proceedings of the 2013 Conference on Computer Supported Cooperative Work (pp. 237–248). ACM.

- Scobie, E. D., & Scobie, G. E. (1998). Damaging events: The perceived need for forgiveness. *Journal for the Theory of Social Behavior, 28,* 373–401.

- Scott, G. G. (2014). More than friends: Popularity on Facebook and its role in impression formation. *Journal of Computer-Mediated Communication, 19*(3), 358–372.

- Scott, M. D., & Powers, W. G. (1978). *Interpersonal communication: A question of needs.* Boston: Houghton Mifflin.

- Scott-Sheldon, L. A. J., Carey, K. B., & Carey, M. P. (2008). Health behavior and college students: Does Greek affiliation matter. *Journal of Behavioral Medicine, 31,* 61–70.

- Segrin, C. (1998). Interpersonal communication problems associated with depression and loneliness. In P. A. Andersen & L. K. Guerrero (Eds.), *Handbook of communication and emotion: Research, theory, applications, and contexts* (pp. 215–242). San Diego, CA: Academic Press.

- Segrin, C., Taylor, M. E., & Altman, J. (2005). Social cognitive mediators and relational outcomes associated with parental divorce. *Journal of Social and Personal Relationships, 22,* 361–377.

- Seiter, J. S., & Bruschke, J. (2007). Deception and emotion: The effects of motivation, relationship type, and sex on expected feelings of guilt and shame following acts of deception in United States and Chinese samples. *Communication Studies, 58,* 1–16.

- Seiter, J. S., Bruschke, J., & Bai, C. (2002). The acceptability of deception as a function of perceivers' culture, deceiver's intention, and deceiver-deceived relationship. *Western Journal of Communication, 66,* 158–180.

- Senchak, M., & Leonard, K. E. (1992). Attachment styles and marital adjustment among newlywed couples. *Journal of Social and Personal Relationships, 9,* 51–64.

- Shackelford, T. K., & Buss, D. M. (1997). Cues to infidelity. *Personality and Social Psychology Bulletin, 23,* 1034–1045.

- Shackelford, T. K., Buss, D. M., & Bennett, K. (2002). Forgiveness or breakups: Sex differences in responses to a partner's responses to a partner's infidelity. *Cognition and Emotion, 16,* 299–307.

- Shackelford, T. K., Goetz, A., Buss, D. M., Euler, H. A., & Hoier, S. (2005). When we hurt the ones we love: Predicting violence against women from men's mate retention. *Personal Relationships, 12,* 447–463.

- Sharabany, R., Gershoni, R., & Hoffman, J. E. (1981). Girlfriend, boyfriend: Age and sex differences in intimate friendship. *Developmental Psychology, 17,* 800–808.

- Sharma, V., & Kaur, I. (1996). Interpersonal attraction in relation to the loss-gain hypothesis. *Journal of Social Psychology, 136,* 635–638.

- Sharpsteen, D. J. (1991). The organization of jealousy knowledge: Romantic jealousy as a blended emotion. In P. Salovey (Ed.), *The psychology of jealousy and envy* (pp. 31–51). New York: Guilford Press.

- Sharpsteen, D. J., & Kirkpatrick, L. A. (1997). Romantic jealousy and adult romantic attachment. *Journal of Personality and Social Psychology, 72,* 627–640.

- Shaver, P. R., Collins, N., & Clark, C. L. (1996). Attachment styles and internal working models of self and relationship partners. In G. J. O. Fletcher & J. Fitness (Eds.), *Knowledge structures in close relationships: A social psychological approach* (pp. 25–61). Mahwah, NJ: Lawrence Erlbaum.

- Shaver, P. R., Furman, W., & Buhrmester, D. (1985). Aspects of a life transition: Network changes, social skills and loneliness. In S. W. Duck & D. Perlman (Eds.), *Understanding personal relationships research: An interdisciplinary approach* (pp. 193–219). London: Sage.

- Shea, B. C., & Pearson, J. (1986). The effects of relationship type, partner intent, and gender on the selection of relationship maintenance strategies. *Communication Monographs, 53,* 352–364.

- Shechory, M., & Ziv, R. (2007). Relationships between gender role attitudes, role division, and perceptions of equity among heterosexual, gay, and lesbian couples. *Sex Roles, 56,* 629–638.

- Sheets, V. L., Fredendall, L. L., & Claypool, H. M. (1997). Jealousy evocation, partner reassurance, and relationship stability: An exploration of the potential benefits of jealousy. *Evolution & Human Behavior, 18,* 387–402.

- Shelton, J. N., Trail, T. E., West, T. V., & Bergsieker, H. B. (2010). From strangers to friends: The interpersonal process model of intimacy in developing interracial friendships. *Journal of Social and Personal Relationships, 27,* 71–90.

- Shen, L., & Dillard, J. P. (2005). Psychometric properties of the Hong psychological reactance scale. *Journal of Personality Assessment, 85,* 74–81.

- Sheppard, B. M., Hartwick, J., & Warshaw, P. R. (1988). The theory of reasoned action: A meta-analysis of past research with recommendations for modification and future research. *Journal of Consumer Research, 15,* 325–343.

- Sheppard, V. J., Nelson, E. S., & Andreoli-Mathie, V. (1995). Dating relationships and infidelity: Attitudes and behaviors. *Journal of Sex and Marital Therapy, 21,* 202–212.

- Sherrod, D. (1989). The influence of gender on same-sex friendships. In C. Hendrick & S. S. Hendrick (Ed.), *Close relationships: A sourcebook* (pp. 164–186). Newbury Park, CA: Sage.

- Shotland, R. L., & Craig, J. M. (1988). Can men and women differentiate between friendly and sexually interested behavior? *Social Psychology Quarterly, 51,* 66–73.

- Shrier, L. A., Shih, M., Hacker, L., & de Moor (2007). A momentary sampling study of the affective experience following coital events in adolescents. *Journal of Adolescent Health, 35,* 357–365.

• Shrout, P. E., Herman, C., & Bolger, N. (2006). The costs and benefits of practical and emotional support on adjustment: A daily diary study of couples experiencing acute stress. *Personal Relationships, 13,* 115–134.

• Sias, P. M., & Cahill, D. J. (1998). From coworkers to friends: The development of peer friendships in the workplace. *Western Journal of Communication, 62,* 273–299.

• Sias, P. M., Drzewiecka, J. A., Meares, M., Bent, R., Konomi, Y., Ortega, M., & White, C. (2008). Intercultural friendship development. *Communication Reports, 21,* 1–13.

• Sias, P. M., Smith, G., & Avdeyera, T. (1999, November). *Developmental influences and communication in peer workplace friendships.* Paper presented at the annual meeting of the National Communication Association, Chicago.

• Sibona, C., & Walczak, S. (2011, January). *Unfriending on Facebook: Friend request and online/offline behavior analysis.* Paper presented at the HICSS conference, Honolulu, HI.

• Sidelinger, R. J., & Booth-Butterfield, M. (2007). Mate value discrepancy as predictor of forgiveness and jealousy in romantic relationships. *Communication Quarterly, 55,* 207–223.

• Siegert, J. R., & Stamp, G. H. (1994). "Our first big fight" as a milestone in the development of close relationships. *Communication Monographs, 61,* 345–360.

• Sigall, H., & Landy, D. (1973). Radiating beauty: The effects of having a physically attractive partner on perception. *Journal of Personality and Social Psychology, 28,* 218–224.

• Sillars, A. L. (1980). Attributions and communication in roommate conflicts. *Communication Monographs, 47,* 180–200.

• Sillars, A. L., Canary, D. J., & Tafoya, M. (2004). Communication, conflict, and the quality of family relationships. In A. L. Vangelisti (Ed.), *Handbook of family interaction* (pp. 413–446). Mahwah, NJ: Lawrence Erlbaum.

• Sillars, A. L., Coletti, S. F., Parry, D., & Rogers, M. A. (1982). Coding verbal conflicts: Nonverbal and perceptual correlates of the "avoidance-distributive-integrative" distinction. *Human Communication Research, 9,* 83–95.

• Sillars, A., Roberts, L. J., Leonard, K. E., & Dun, T. (2000). Cognition during marital conflict: The relationship of thought and talk. *Journal of Social and Personal Relationships, 17,* 479–502.

• Silver, R. L., Boone, C., & Stones, M. H. (1983). Searching for meaning in misfortune: Making sense of incest. *Journal of Social Issues, 39,* 81–102.

• Simon, E. P., & Baxter, L. A. (1993). Attachment-style differences in relationship maintenance strategies. *Western Journal of Communication, 57,* 416–430.

• Simpson, J. A. (1987). The dissolution of romantic relationships: Factors involved in relational stability and emotional distress. *Journal of Personality and Social Psychology, 53,* 683–692.

• Simpson, J. A. (1990). The influence of attachment styles on romantic relationships. *Journal of Personality and Social Psychology, 59,* 971–980.

• Simpson, J. A., & Gangestad, S. W. (1991). Individual differences in sociosexuality: Evidence for convergent and discriminant validity. *Journal of Personality and Social Psychology, 60,* 870–883.

• Simpson, J. A., Gangestad, S. W., & Lerma, M. (1990). Perception of physical attractiveness: Mechanisms involved in the maintenance of romantic relationships. *Journal of Personality and Social Psychology, 59,* 1192–1201.

• Simpson, J. A., & Harris, B. A. (1994). Inter-personal attraction. In A. L. Weber & J. H. Harvey (Eds.), *Perspectives on close relationships* (pp. 45–66). Boston: Allyn & Bacon.

• Simpson, J. A., & Rholes, W. S. (1994). Stress and secure base relationships in adulthood. In K. Bartholomew & D. Perlman (Eds.), *Attachment processes in adulthood: Advances in personal relationships* (Vol. 5, pp. 181–204). Bristol, PA: Kingsley.

• Simpson, J. A., Wilson, C. L., & Winterheld, H. A. (2004). Sociosexuality and romantic relationships. In J. H. Harvey, A. Wenzel, & S. Sprecher (Eds.), *The handbook of sexuality in close relationships* (pp. 87–112). Mahwah, NJ: Lawrence Erlbaum.

• Singh, D. (1995). Female judgment of male attractiveness and desirability for relationships: Role of the waist-to-hip ratio and financial status. *Journal of Personality and Social Psychology, 69,* 1089–1101.

• Singh, R., Wegener, D. T., Sankaran, K., Singh, S., Lin, P. K. F., Seow, M. X., Teng, J. S. Q., & Shuli, S. (2015). On the importance of trust in interpersonal attraction from attitude similarity. *Journal of Social and Personal Relationships, 32*(6) 829–850.

• Slotter, E. B., & Ward, D. E. (2015). Finding the silver lining: The relative roles of redemptive narratives and cognitive reappraisal in individuals' emotional distress after the end of a romantic relationship. *Journal of Social and Personal Relationships, 32,* 737–756.

• Smith, D. A., Vivian, D., & O'Leary, K. D. (1990). Longitudinal prediction of marital discord from premarital expressions of affect. *Journal of Consulting and Clinical Psychology, 59,* 790–798.

• Smith, J. C. S., Vogel, D. L., Madon, S., & Edwards, S. R. (2011). The power of touch: Nonverbal communication within marital dyads. *The Counselling Psychologist, 39,* 464–487.

• Smith, K. (2016, May 17). 44 astonishing Twitter stats and facts for 2016: Brandwatch. https://www.brandwatch.com/2016/05/44-twitter-stats-2016/.

• Snapchat daily active users 2016 | Statistia. (n.d.). http://www.statista.com/statistics/545967/snapchat-app-dau/.

• Snow, D. A., & Anderson, L. (1987). Identity work among the homeless: The verbal construction and avowal of personal identities. *American Journal of Sociology, 93,* 1336–1371.

• Snyder, M., Tanke, E. D., & Berscheid, E. (1977). Social perception and interpersonal behavior: On the self-fulfilling nature of social stereotypes. *Journal of Personality and Social Psychology, 35,* 656–666.

• Solomon, D. H., & Knobloch, L. K. (2001). Relationship uncertainty, partner interference, and intimacy within dating relationships. *Journal of Social and Personal Relationships, 18,* 804–820.

• Solomon, D. H., & Knobloch, L. K. (2004). A model of relational turbulence: The role of intimacy, relational uncertainty, and interference from partners in appraisal of irritations. *Journal of Social and Personal Relationships, 21,* 795–816.

• Solomon, D. H., Knobloch, L. K., & Fitzpatrick, M. A. (2004). Relational power, marital schema, and decisions to withhold complaints: An investigation of the chilling effect of confrontation in marriage. *Communication Studies, 55,* 146–167.

• Solomon, D. H., Knobloch, L. K., Theiss, J. A., & McLaren, R. M. (2016). Relational Turbulence Theory: Explaining variation in subjective experiences and communication within romantic relationships. *Human Communication Research, 42,* 507–532.

• Solomon, D. H., & Samp, J. A. (1998). Power and problem appraisal: Perceptual foundations of the chilling effect in dating relationship. *Journal of Social and Personal Relationships, 15,* 191–209.

• Sorensen, R. C. (1973). *Adolescent sexuality in contemporary America.* New York: World Publishing.

• Speilmann, S. S., McDonald, G., & Wilson, A. E. (2009). On the rebound: Focusing on someone new helps anxiously attached individuals let go of ex-partners. *Personality and Social Psychology Bulletin, 35,* 1382–1394.

• Sperling, M. B., & Borgaro, S. (1995). Attachment anxiety and reciprocity as moderators of interpersonal attraction. *Psychological Reports, 76,* 323–335.

• Spiegel, D. (1992). Effects of psychosocial support on patients with metastatic breast cancer. *Journal of Psychosocial Oncology, 10,* 113–120.

• Spitzberg, B. H., & Cupach, W. R. (1988). *Handbook of interpersonal communication competence.* New York: Springer-Verlag.

• Spitzberg, B. H., & Cupach, W. R. (Eds.). (1998). *The dark side of close relationships.* Mahwah, NJ: Lawrence Erlbaum.

• Spitzberg, B. H., Cupach, W. R., Hannawa, A. F., & Crowley, J. P. (2014). A preliminary test of a relational goal pursuit theory of obsessive relational intrusion and stalking. *Studies in Communication Sciences, 14,* 29–36.

• Spitzberg, B. H., & Hoobler, G. (2002). Cyberstalking and the technologies of interpersonal terrorism. *New Media and Society, 4,* 71–92.

• Sprecher, S. (1986). The relation between emotion and equity in close relationships. *Social Psychological Bulletin, 49,* 309–321.

• Sprecher, S. (1987). The effects of self-disclosure given and received on affect for an intimate partner and the stability of the relationship. *Journal of Personal and Social Relationships, 4,* 115–128.

• Sprecher, S. (1989). The importance to males and females of physical attractiveness, earning potential, and expressiveness in initial attraction. *Sex Roles, 12,* 449–462.

- Sprecher, S. (1998a). Insiders' perspectives on reasons for attraction to a close other. *Social Psychology Quarterly, 61*, 287–300.

- Sprecher, S. (1998b). Social exchange theories and sexuality. *Journal of Sex Research, 35*, 32–43.

- Sprecher, S. (2001). A comparison of emotional consequences of and changes in equity over time using global and domain-specific measures of equity. *Journal of Social and Personal Relationships, 18*, 477–501.

- Sprecher, S. (2014). Evidence of change in men's versus women's emotional reactions to first sexual intercourse. A 23-year study in a human sexuality course at a Midwestern university. *Journal of Sex Research, 51*, 466–472.

- Sprecher, S., Aron, A., Hatfield, E., Cortese, A., Potapova, E., & Levitskaya, A. (1994). Love: American style, Russian style, and Japanese style. *Personal Relationships, 1*, 349–369.

- Sprecher, S., & Cate, R. M. (2004). Sexual satisfaction and sexual expression as predictors of relationship satisfaction and stability. In J. H. Harvey, A. Wenzel, & S. Sprecher (Eds.), *The handbook of sexuality in close relationships* (pp. 235–256). Mahwah, NJ: Lawrence Erlbaum.

- Sprecher, S., & Fehr, B. (2005). Compassionate love for close others and humanity. *Journal of Social and Personal Relationships, 22*, 629–651.

- Sprecher, S., & Felmlee, D. (1992). The influence of parents and friends on the quality and stability of romantic relationships: A three-wave longitudinal study. *Journal of Marriage and the Family, 54*, 888–900.

- Sprecher, S., & Felmlee, D. (1997). The balance of power in romantic heterosexual couples over time from "his" and "her" perspectives. *Sex Roles, 37*, 361–378.

- Sprecher, S., Felmlee, D., Metts, S., Fehr, B., & Vanni, D. (1998). Factors associated with distress following the breakup of a close relationship. *Journal of Social and Personal Relationships, 15*, 791–809.

- Sprecher, S., & McKinney, K. (1993). *Sexuality.* Newbury Park, CA: Sage.

- Sprecher, S., McKinney, K., Walsh, R., & Anderson, C. (1988). A revision of the Reiss premarital sexual permissiveness scale. *Journal of Marriage and the Family, 50*, 821–828.

- Sprecher, S., & Regan, P. C. (1996). College virgins: How men and women perceive their sexual status. *Journal of Sex Research, 33*, 3–15.

- Sprecher, S., & Regan, P. C. (2000). Sexuality in a relational context. In C. Hendrick & S. S. Hendrick (Eds.), *Close relationships: A sourcebook* (pp. 217–227). Thousand Oaks, CA: Sage.

- Sprecher, S., Schmeeckle, M., & Felmlee, D. (2006). The principal of least interest: Inequality in emotional involvement in romantic relationships. *Journal of Family Issues, 27*, 1255–1280.

- Sprecher, S., & Toro-Morn, M. (2002). A study of men and women from different sides of earth to determine if men are from Mars and women are from Venus in their beliefs about love and romantic relationships. *Sex Roles, 46*, 131–147.

- Sprecher, S., & Treger, S. (2015). Virgin college students' reasons for and reactions to their abstinence from sex: Results from a 23-year study at a Midwestern US university. *Journal of Sex Research, 52*, 936–938.

- Sprecher, S., Treger, S., Wondra, J. D., Hilaire, N., & Wallpe, K. (2013). Taking turns: Reciprocal self-disclosure promotes liking in initial interactions. *Journal of Experimental Social Psychology, 49*, 860–866.

- Sprecher, S., Zimmerman, C., & Abrahams, E. M. (2010). Choosing compassionate strategies to end a relationship. Effects of compassionate love for a partner and the reason for the breakup. *Social Psychology, 41*, 66–75.

- Stafford, L. (2003). Maintaining romantic relationships: Summary and analysis of one research program. In D. J. Canary & M. Dainton (Eds.), *Maintaining relationships through communication: Relational, contextual, and cultural variations* (pp. 51–77). Mahwah, NJ: Lawrence Erlbaum.

- Stafford, L. (2005). *Maintaining long-distance and cross-residential relationships.* Mahwah, NJ: Erlbaum.

- Stafford, L., & Canary, D. J. (1991). Maintenance strategies and romantic relationship type, gender and relational characteristics. *Journal of Social and Personal Relationships, 8*, 217–242.

- Stafford, L., & Canary, D. J. (2006). Equity and interdependence as predictors of maintenance strategies. *Journal of Family Communication, 6*, 227–254.

- Stafford, L., Kline, S. L., & Rankin, C. T. (2004). Married individuals, cohabiters, and cohabiters who marry: A longitudinal study of relational and individual well-being. *Journal of Social and Personal Relationships, 21*, 231–248.

- Stafford, L., & Merolla, A. J. (2007). Idealization, reunions, and stability in long distance dating relationships. *Journal of Social and Personal Relationships, 24*, 37–54.

- Stafford, L., & Reske, J. R. (1990). Idealization and communication in long-distance premarital relationships. *Family Relations, 39*, 274–279.

- Stangor, C., & Ruble, D. H. (1989). Strength of expectancies and memory for social information: What we remember depends on how much we know. *Journal of Experimental Social Psychology, 25*, 18–35.

- Stark, P. B. (1994). *It's negotiable: The how-to handbook of win/win tactics.* San Diego, CA: Pfieffer.

- Steers, MLN (2016) "It's complicated": Facebook's relationship with the need to belong and depression. *Current Opinion in Psychology, 9*, 22–26.

- Steil, J. M. (2000). Contemporary marriage: Still an unequal partnership. In C. Hendrick & S. S. Hendrick (Eds.), *Close relationships: A sourcebook* (pp. 125–136). Thousand Oaks, CA: Sage.

- Steil, L. K., Barker, L. L., & Watson, K. W. (1983). *Effective listening: Keys to success.* Reading, MA: Addison-Wesley.

- Steinberg, L. D. (1981). Transformations in family relations at puberty. *Developmental Psychology, 17*, 833–840.

- Steinberg, L. D. (1987). Impact of puberty on family relations: Effects of pubertal status and pubertal timing. *Developmental Psychology, 23*, 451–460.

- Steinberg, L. D., & Silverberg, S. B. (1986). The vicissitudes of autonomy in early adolescence. *Child Development, 57*, 841–851.

- Steinbugler, A. C. (2005). Visibility as privilege and danger: Heterosexual and same-sex interracial intimacy in the 21st century. *Sexualities, 8*, 425–443.

- Steinmetz, S. K. (1979). Disciplinary techniques and their relationship to aggressiveness, dependency, and conscience. In W. Burr, R. Hill, R. I. Nye, & I. L. Reiss (Eds.), *Contemporary theories about the family* (Vol. 1, pp. 405–438). New York: Free Press.

- Stephan, C. W., & Bachman, G. F. (1999). What's sex got to do with it? Attachment, love schemas, and sexuality. *Personal Relationships, 6*, 111–123.

- Sternberg, R. J. (1986). A triangular theory of love. *Psychological Review, 93*, 119–135.

- Sternberg, R. J. (1987). *The triangle of love: Intimacy, passion, commitment.* New York: Basic Books.

- Sternberg, R. J. (1988). Triangulating love. In R. J. Sternberg & M. L. Barnes (Eds.), *The psychology of love* (pp. 119–138). New Haven, CT: Yale University Press.

- Steuber, K. R., & Solomon, D. H. (2008). Relational uncertainty, partner interference, and infertility: A qualitative study of discourse within online forums. *Journal of Social and Personal Relationships, 25*, 831–855.

- Stier, D. S., & Hall, J. A. (1984). Gender differences in touch: An empirical and theoretical review. *Journal of Personality and Social Psychology, 47*, 440–459.

- Stiff, J. B., Dillard, J. P., Somera, L., Kim, H., & Sleight, C. (1988). Empathy, communication, and prosocial behavior. *Communication Monographs, 55*, 198–213.

- Stiff, J. B., Kim, H. J., & Ramesh, C. N. (1992). Truth biases and aroused suspicion in relational deception. *Communication Research, 19*, 326–345.

- Stiles, W. B. (1987). "I have to talk to somebody": A fever model of disclosure. In V. J. Derlega & J. H. Berg (Eds.), *Self-disclosure: Theory, research, and therapy* (pp. 257–282). New York: Plenum Press.

- Stiles, W. B., Shuster, P. L., & Harrigan, J. A. (1992). Disclosure and anxiety: A test of the fever model. *Journal of Personality and Social Psychology, 63*, 980–988.

- Stone, E. A., Shackelford, T. K., & Goetz, A. T. (2011). Sexual arousal and pursuit of attractive mating opportunities. *Personality and Individual Differences, 51*, 575–578.

• Straus, M. A., & Gelles, R. J. (1990). How violent are American families? Estimates from the National Family Violence Resurvey and other studies. In M. A. Straus & R. J. Gelles (Eds.), *Physical violence in American families: Risk factors and adaptations to violence in 8,145 families* (pp. 95–112). New Brunswick, NJ: Transaction.

• Strelan, P., Weick, M., & Vasiljevic, M. (2014). Power and revenge. *British Journal of Social Psychology, 53*, 521–540.

• Strong, S. R., Hills, H. J., Kilmartin, C. T., DeVries, H., Lanier, K., Nelson, B. N., Strickland, D., & Meyer C. W. (1988). The dynamic relations among interpersonal behaviors: A test of complementarity and anti-complementarity. *Journal of Personality and Social Psychology, 54*, 798–810.

• Struckman-Johnson, C. (1988). Forced sex on dates: It happens to men too. *Journal of Sex Research, 24*, 234–241.

• Struckman-Johnson, C., & Struckman-Johnson, D. (1991). Men's and women's acceptance of sexually coercive strategies varied by initiator gender and couple intimacy. *Sex Roles, 25*, 661–676.

• Struckman-Johnson, C., & Struckman-Johnson, D. (1994). Men pressured and forced into sexual experience. *Archives of Sexual Behavior, 23*, 93–114.

• Subrahmanyam, K., & Greenfield, P. (2008). Virtual worlds in development: Implications of social networking sites. *Journal of Applied Developmental Psychology, 29*, 417–419.

• Sue, S., & Zane, N. (1987). The role of culture and cultural techniques in psychotherapy: A critique and reformulation. *American Psychologist, 42*, 37–45.

• Sunnafrank, M. (1986). Predicted outcome value during initial interactions: A reformulation of uncertainty reduction theory. *Human Communication Research, 13*, 3–33.

• Sunnafrank, M. (1990). Predicted outcome value and uncertainty reduction theories: A test of competing perspectives. *Human Communication Research, 17*, 76–103.

• Sunnafrank, M. (1991). Interpersonal attraction and attitude similarity: A communication-based assessment. In J. A. Anderson (Ed.), *Communication yearbook 14* (pp. 451–483). Newbury Park, CA: Sage.

• Sunnafrank, M. (1992). On debunking the attitude similarity myth. *Communication Monographs, 59*, 164–179.

• Sunnafrank, M., & Ramirez, A., Jr. (2004). At first sight: Persistent relational effects of get-acquainted conversations. *Journal of Social and Personal Relationships, 21*, 361–379.

• Suter, E. A., Bergen, K. M., Daas, K. L., & Durham, W. T. (2006). Lesbian couples' management of public-private dialectical contradictions. *Journal of Social and Personal Relationships, 23*, 349–365.

• Swan, S. C. (1997). Explaining the job-related and psychological consequences of sexual harassment in the workplace: A contextual model. *Dissertation Abstractions International, 58*(6-B), 3371.

• Swann, W. B. (1983). Self-verification: Bringing social reality into harmony with the self. In J. Suls & G. Greenwald (Eds.), *Psychology perspectives on the self* (Vol. 2, pp. 33–66). Hillsdale, NJ: Lawrence Erlbaum.

• Swann, W. B., De La Ronde, C., & Hixon, G. (1994). Authenticity and positive strivings in marriage and courtship. *Journal of Personality and Social Psychology, 6*, 857–869.

• Swann, W. B., Griffin, J. J., Predmore, S., & Gaines, B. (1987). The cognitive-affective crossfire: When self-consistency confronts self-enhancement. *Journal of Personality and Social Psychology, 52*, 881–889.

• Swann, W. B., & Read, S. J. (1981). Self-verification processes. How we sustain our self-conceptions. *Journal of Experimental Social Psychology, 54*, 268–273.

• Swann, W. B., Silvera, D. H., & Proske, C. U. (1995). Un "knowing your partner": Dangerous illusions in the age of AIDS? *Personal Relationships, 2*, 173–186.

• Sweeney, B. N. (2014). Sorting women sexually: Masculine status, sexual performance, and the sexual stigmatization of women. *Symbolic Interaction, 37*, 369–390.

• Tafoya, M. A., & Spitzberg, B. H. (2007). The dark side of infidelity: Its nature, prevalence, and communicative functions. In B. H. Spitzberg & W. R. Cupach (Eds.), *The dark side of interpersonal communication* (pp. 201–242). Mahwah, NJ: Lawrence Erlbaum.

• Tagawa, N., & Yashida, T. (2006). The effects of daily communication on romantic relationships. *The Japanese Journal of Social Psychology, 22*, 126–138.

• Takhteyev Y., Gruzd, A., & Wellman, B. (2012). Geography of Twitter networks. *Social Networks, 34*, 73–81.

• Tannen, D. (1990). *You just don't understand: Women and men in conversation.* New York: Morrow.

• Taraban, C. B., Hendrick, S. S., & Hendrick, C. (1998). Loving and liking. In P. A. Andersen & L. K. Guerrero (Eds.), *Handbook of communication and emotion: Research, theory, applications, and contexts* (pp. 331–351). San Diego, CA: Academic Press.

• Tardy, C. H. (Ed.). (1988). *A handbook for the study of human communication: Methods and instruments for observing, measuring, and assessing communication processes.* Norwood, NJ: Ablex.

• Tashiro, T., & Frazier, P. (2003). I'll never be in a relationship like that again: Personal growth following romantic relationship breakups. *Personal Relationships, 10*, 113–138.

• Taylor, A., & Gosney, M. A. (2011). Sexuality in older age: Essential considerations for healthcare professionals. *Age and Aging, 40*, 538–543.

• Taylor, D. A., Gould, R. J., & Brounstein, P. J. (1981). Effects of personalistic self-disclosure. *Personality and Social Psychology Bulletin, 9*, 487–492.

• Taylor, P., & Keeter, S. (2010). *Millennials: Confident. Connected. Open to change.* Washington, DC: Pew Research Center.

• Taylor, S. E., Gonzaga, G. C., Klein, L. C., Hu, P., Greendale, G. A., & Seeman, T. E. (2006). Relation of oxytocin to psychological stress responses and hypothalamic-pituitary-and renocortical axis activity in older women. *Psychosomantic Medicine, 68*, 238–245.

• Tedeschi, J. T. (1986). Private and public experiences of the self. In R. Baumeister (Ed.), *Public self and private self* (pp. 1–20). New York: Springer-Verlag.

• Teitelman, A. M., Ratcliffe, S. J., Morales-Aleman, M. M., & Sullivan, C. M. (2008). Sexual relationship power, intimate partner violence and condom use among minority urban girls. *Journal of Interpersonal Violence, 23*, 1694–1712.

• Tejada-Vera, B., Sutton, P. D. (2009). *Births, marriages, divorces, and deaths: Provisional data for 2008. National vital statistics reports, Vol. 57, No. 19.* Hyattsville, MD: National Center for Health Statistics.

• Telephonica Global Millennial Survey: Global Results. (2014). http://survey.telefonica.com/globalreports/assets/Telefonica%20-%20 Global%20Millennial%20Survey.pdf.

• Tesser, A., & Achee, J. (1994). Aggression, love, conformity and other social psychological catastrophes. In R. R. Vallacher & A. Nowak (Eds.), *Dynamical systems in social psychology* (pp. 95–109). San Diego, CA: Academic Press.

• Thagaard, T. (1997). Gender, power, and love. *Acta Sociologica, 38*, 357–376.

• The best dating service? Try the workplace! (1988, February 12). *New York Post*, p. 14.

• Theil-Stern, S. (2009). Femininity out of control on the Internet: A critical analysis of media representations of gender, youth, and MySpace. com in International News Discourses. *Girlhood Studies, 2*, 29–30.

• Theiss, J. A. (2011). Modeling dyadic effects in the associations between relational uncertainty, sexual communication, and sexual satisfaction for husbands and wives. *Communication Research, 38*, 565–584.

• Theiss, J. A., & Knobloch, L. K. (2014). Relational turbulence and the post-deployment transition: Self, partner, and relationship focused turbulence. *Communication Research, 41*, 27–51.

• Theiss, J. A., Knobloch, L. K., Checton, M. G., & Magsamen-Conrad, K. (2009). Relationship characteristics associated with the experience of hurt in romantic relationships: A test of the relational turbulence model. *Human Communication Research, 35*, 588–615.

• Thelwall, M. (2009). Homophily in MySpace. *Journal of the American Society for Information Science and Technology, 60*, 219–231.

• Thibaut, J. W., & Kelley, J. J. (1959). *The social psychology of groups.* New York: Wiley.

• Thieme, A., & Rouse, C. (1991, November). *Terminating intimate relationships: An examination of the interactions among disengagement strategies, acceptance, and causal attributions.* Paper presented at the annual meeting of the Speech Communication Association, Atlanta, GA.

• Thompson, L., & Walker, A. J. (1989). Gender in families: Women and men in marriage, work, and parenthood. *Journal of Marriage and the Family, 51*, 845–871.

• Thorton, A., Axinn, W. G., & Teachman, J. D. (1995). The influence of school enrollment and accumulation of cohabitation and marriage in early adulthood. *American Sociological Review, 60*, 207–220.

• Tice, D. M., Butler, J. L., Muraven, M. B., & Stillwell, A. M. (1995). When modesty prevails: Differential favorability of self-presentation to friends and strangers. *Journal of Personality and Social Psychology, 69*, 1120–1138.

• Tidwell, L. C., & Walther, J. B. (2002). Computer-mediated communication effects on disclosure, impressions, and interpersonal evaluations: Getting to know one another a bit at a time. *Human Communication Research, 28*, 317–348.

• Tidwell, N. D., Eastwick, P. W., & Finkel, E. J. (2013). Perceived, not actual, similarity predicts initial attraction in a live romantic context: Evidence from the speed-dating paradigm. *Personal Relationships, 20*(2), 199–215.

• Tilton-Weaver, L. (2014). Adolescents' information management: Comparing ideas about why adolescents disclose to or keep secrets from their parents. *Journal of Youth and Adolescence, 43*, 803–813.

• Timmerman, L. M. (2002). Comparing the production of power in language on the basis of sex. In M. Allen, R. W. Preiss, B. M. Gayke, & N. Burell (Eds.), *Interpersonal communication research: Advances through meta-analysis* (pp. 73–88). Mahwah, NJ: Lawrence Erlbaum.

• Tokunaga, R. S. (2011a). Friend me or you'll strain us: Understanding negative events that occur over social networking sites. *Cyberpsychology, Behavior, and Social Networking, 14*, 425–432.

• Tokunaga, R. S. (2011b). Social networking site or social surveillance site? Understanding the use of interpersonal electronic surveillance in romantic relationships. *Computers in Human Behavior, 2*, 705–713.

• Tokunaga, R. S., & Rains, S. A. (2016). A review and meta-analysis examining conceptual and operational definitions of problematic internet use. *Human Communication Research, 42*, 165–199.

• Tolhuizen, J. H. (1989). Communication strategies for intensifying dating relationships: Identification, use, and structure. *Journal of Social and Personal Relationships, 6*, 413–434.

• Tolstedt, B. E., & Stokes, J. P. (1984). Self-disclosure, intimacy and the depenetration process. *Journal of Personality and Social Psychology, 46*, 84–90.

• Toma, C. L., & Choi, M. (2015). The couple who Facebooks together stays together: Facebook self-presentation and relationship longevity among college-aged dating couples. *Cyberpsychology Behavior and Social Networking, 18*, 367–372.

• Toma, C. L., & Hancock, J. T. (2010). Looks and lies: The role of physical attractiveness in online dating self-presentation and deception. *Communication Research, 37*, 335–351.

• Toma, C. L., Hancock, J. T., & Ellison, N. B. (2008). Separating fact from fiction: An examination of deceptive self-presentation in online dating profiles, *Personality and Social Psychology Bulletin, 34*, 1023–1036.

• Tong, S. T. (2013). Facebook use during relationship termination: Uncertainty reduction and surveillance. *Cyberpsychology, Behavior, and Social Networking, 16*, 788–793.

• Tong, S. T., Van Der Heide, B., Langwell, L., & Walther, J. B. (2008). Too much of a good thing? The relationship between number of friends and interpersonal impressions on Facebook. *Journal of Computer-Mediated Communication, 13*, 531–549.

• Tong, S. T., & Walther, J. B. (2010a). Just say "no thanks": Romantic rejection in computer-mediated communication. *Journal of Social and Personal Relationships, 28*, 488–506.

• Tong, S. T., & Walther, J. B. (2010b). Relational maintenance and CMC. In K. B. Wright & L. M. Webb (Eds.), *Computer mediated communication in personal relationships* (pp. 98–118). New York: Peter Lang.

• Tooke, W., & Camire, L. (1991). Patterns of deception in intersexual and intrasexual mating strategies. *Ethology and Sociobiology, 12*, 345–364.

• Tornblom, K. Y., & Fredholm, E. M. (1984). Attribution of friendship: The influence of the nature and comparability of resources given and received. *Social Psychology Quarterly, 47*, 50–61.

• Tracy, K. (1990). The many faces of facework. In H. Giles & W. P. Robinson (Eds.), *Handbook of language and social psychology* (pp. 209–226). Chichester, UK: Wiley.

• Tracy, S. J. (2005). Locking up emotion: Moving beyond dissonance for understanding emotional labor discomfort. *Communication Monographs, 72*, 261–283.

• Tracy, S. J., & Trethewey, A. (2005). Fracturing the real-self-self dichotomy. Moving toward crystallized organizational identities. *Communication Theory, 15*, 168–195.

• Traupmann, J., Hatfield, E., & Wexler, P. (1983). Equity and sexual satisfaction in dating couples. *British Journal of Social Psychology, 22*, 33–40.

• Triandis, H. C. (1989). The self and social behavior in differing cultural contexts. *Psychological Review, 96*, 506–520.

• Triandis, H. C., Carnevale, P., Gelfand, M., Robert, C., Wasti, S. A., & Probst, T. (2001). Culture and deception in business negotiations: A multilevel analysis. *International Journal of Cross-Cultural Management, 1*, pp. 73–90.

• Trost, M. R., & Alberts, J. K. (2006). How men and women communicate attraction: An evolutionary view. In D. J. Canary & K. Dindia (Eds.), *Sex differences and similarities in communication* (2nd ed., pp. 317–336). Mahwah, NJ: Lawrence Erlbaum.

• Troy, B. A., Lewis-Smith, J., & Laurenceau, J. (2006). Interracial and intraracial romantic relationships: The search for differences in satisfaction, conflict, and attachment style. *Journal of Social and Personal Relationships, 23*, 65–80.

• Tsai, C. W., Shen, P. D., & Chiang, Y. C. (2015). Meeting ex-partners on Facebook: Users' anxiety and severity of depression. *Behavior & Information Technology, 34*, 668–677.

• Tucker, J. S., & Anders, S. L. (1998). Adult attachment style and nonverbal closeness in dating couples. *Journal of Nonverbal Behavior, 22*, 109–124.

• Turner, L. H. (1990). The relationship between communication and marital uncertainty: Is "her" marriage different from "his" marriage? *Women's Studies in Communication, 13*, 57–83.

• Turner, R. E., Edgley, C., & Olmstead, G. (1975). Information control in conversations: Honesty is not always the best policy. *Kansas Journal of Sociology, 11*, 69–89.

• Tusing, K. J., & Dillard, J. P. (2000). The sounds of dominance: Vocal precursors of perceived dominance during interpersonal influence. *Human Communication Research, 16*, 148–171.

• Tutzauer, F., & Roloff, M. E. (1988). Communication processes leading to integrative agreements: Three paths to joint benefits. *Communication Research, 15*, 360–380.

• Twenge, J. M. (2006). *Generation Me: Why today's young people are more confident, assertive, entitled—and more miserable than ever before.* New York: Free Press.

• Twenge, J. M., & Campbell, W. K. (2009). *The narcissism epidemic: Living in the age of entitlement.* New York: Free Press.

• Twenge, J. M., Campbell, W. K., & Foster, C. A. (2003). Parenthood and marital satisfaction: A meta-analytic review. *Journal of Marriage and Family, 65*, 574–583.

• Twenge, J. M., Sherman, R. A., & Wells, B. E. (2015). Changes in American adults' sexual behavior and attitudes 1972–2012. *Archives of Sexual Behavior, 44*, 2273–2285.

• Twohig, M. P., Crosby, J. M., & Cox, J. M. (2009). Viewing Internet pornography: For whom is it problematic, how, and why? *Sexual Addition & Compulsivity, 16*, 253–266.

• Underwood, J. D. M., Kerlin, L., & Farrington-Flint, L. (2011). The lies we tell and what they say about us: Using behavioural characteristics to explain Facebook activity. *Computers in Human Behavior, 27*, 1621–1626.

• Utz, S. (2005). Types of deception and underlying motivation: What people think. *Social Science Computer Review, 23*, 49–56.

• Utz, S. (2015). The function of self-disclosure on social networking sites: Not only intimate, but also positive and entertaining self-disclosure increase the feeling of connection. *Computers in Human Behavior, 45*, 1–10.

• Utz, S., Muscanell, N., & Khalid, C. (2015). Snapchat elicits more jealousy than Facebook: A comparison of Snapchat and Facebook use. *Cyberpsychology, Behavior, and Social Networking, 18*, 141–146.

• Utz, S., Tanis, M., & Vermeulen, I. (2012). It is all about being popular: The effects of need for popularity on social network site use. *Cyberpsychology, Behavior, and Social Networking, 15*, 37–42.

• Valkenburg, P. M., & Peter, J. (2009). Social consequences of the Internet for adolescents: A decade of research. *Current Directions in Psychological Science, 18*, 1–5.

• Vallade, J. I., & Dillow, M. R. (2014). An exploration of extradyadic communicative messages following relational transgressions in romantic relationships. *Southern Communication Journal, 79*, 94–113.

• Van Horn, K. R., Arnone, A., Nesbitt, K., Desilets, L., Sears, T., Giffin, M., & Brijd, R. I. (1997). Physical distance and interpersonal characteristics in college students' romantic relationships. *Personal Relationships, 4*, 15–24.

• Van Lange, P. A. M., Rusbult, C. E., Drigotas, S. M., Arriaga, X. B., Witcher, B. S., & Cox, C. L. (1997). Willingness to sacrifice in close relationships. *Journal of Personality and Social Psychology, 72*, 1373–1395.

• Van Rosmalen-Nooijens, K. A. W. L., Vergeer, C. M., & Lagro-Janssen, A. L. M. (2008). Bed death and other lesbian sexual problems unraveled: A qualitative study of the sexual health of lesbian women involved in a relationship. *Women and Health, 48*, 339–362.

• Van Straaten, I., Engles, C. M. E., Finkenauer, C., & Holland, R. W. (2008). Sex differences in short-term mate preferences and behavioral mimicry: A semi-naturalistic experiment. *Archives of Sexual Behavior, 37*, 902–911.

• VanderDrift, L. E., & Agnew, C. R. (2012). Need fulfillment and stay-leave behavior: On the diagnosticity of personal and relational needs. *Journal of Social and Personal Relationships, 29*, 228–245.

• VanderDrift, L. E., Agnew, C. R., & Wilson, J. E. (2009). Nonmarital Romantic Relationship Commitment and Leave Behavior: The Mediating Role of Dissolution Consideration. *Personality and Social Psychology Bulletin, 35*, 1220–1232.

• VanderDrift, L. E., Lehmiller, J. J., & Kelly, J. R. (2012). Commitment in friends with benefits relationships: Implications for relational and safe-sex outcomes. *Personal Relationships, 19*, 1–13.

• Vangelisti, A. L. (1994a). Family secrets: Forms, functions, and correlates. *Journal of Social and Personal Relationships, 11*, 113–135.

• Vangelisti, A. L. (1994b). Messages that hurt. In W. R. Cupach & B. H. Spitzberg (Eds.), *The dark side of interpersonal communication* (pp. 53–82). Hillsdale, NJ: Lawrence Erlbaum.

• Vangelisti, A. L. (2002). Interpersonal processes in romantic relationships. In M. L. Knapp & J. A. Daly (Eds.), *Handbook of interpersonal communication* (3rd ed., pp. 643–679). Thousand Oaks, CA: Sage.

• Vangelisti, A. L., & Caughlin, J. P. (1997). Revealing family secrets: The influence of topic, function, and relationships. *Journal of Social and Personal Relationships, 14*, 679–706.

• Vangelisti, A. L., & Crumley, L. P. (1998). Reactions to messages that hurt: The influence of relational contexts. *Communication Monographs, 65*, 173–196.

• Vangelisti, A. L., & Huston, T. L. (1994). Maintaining marital satisfaction and love. In D. J. Canary & L. Stafford (Eds.), *Communication and relational maintenance* (pp. 165–186). San Diego, CA: Academic Press.

• Vangelisti, A. L., Knapp, M. L., & Daly, J. A. (1990). Conversational narcissism. *Communication Monographs, 57*, 251–274.

• Vangelisti, A. L., & Young, S. L. (2000). When words hurt: The effects of perceived intentionality on interpersonal relationships. *Journal of Social and Personal Relationships, 17*, 393–424.

• Vaughn, D. (1986). *Uncoupling: Turning points in intimate relationships.* New York: Oxford University Press.

• Vazsonyi, A. T., & Jenkins, D. D. (2010). Religiosity, self-control, and virginity status in college students from the "bible belt": A research note. *Journal for the Scientific Study of Religion, 49*, 561–568.

• Vedes, A., Hilpert, P., Nussbeck, F. W., Randall, A. K., Bodenmann, G., & Lind, W. R. (2016). Love styles, coping, and relationship satisfaction: A dyadic approach. *Personal Relationships, 23*, 84–97.

• Vignoles, L., Regalia, C., Manzi, C., Golledge, J., & Scabini, E. (2006). Beyond self-esteem: Influence of multiple motives on identity construction. *Journal of Personality and Social Psychology, 90*, 308–333.

• Vitak, J. (2014, February). Facebook makes the heart grow fonder: Relationship maintenance strategies among geographically dispersed and communication-restricted connections. In Proceedings of the 17th ACM conference on Computer supported cooperative work & social computing (pp. 842–853). ACM.

• Vogler, C., Lyonette, C., & Wiggins, R. D. (2008). Money, power, and decisions in intimate relationships. *Sociological Review, 56*, 117–143.

• Vohs, K. D., Catanese, K. R., & Baumeister, R. E. (2004). Sex in "his" versus "her" relationship. In J. H. Harvey, A. Wenzel, & S. Sprecher (Eds.), *The handbook of sexuality in close relationships* (pp. 455–474). Mahwah, NJ: Lawrence Erlbaum.

• Vrangalova, Z., & Bukberg, R. E. (2015). Are sexually permissive individuals more victimized and socially isolated? *Personal Relationships, 22*, 230–242.

• Vrangalova, Z., & Savin-Williams, R. C. (2011). Adolescent sexuality and positive well-being: A group norms approach. *Journal of Youth and Adolescence, 40*, 931–944.

• Waldron, V. R., & Kelley, D. L. (2005). Forgiving communication as a response to relational transgressions. *Journal of Social and Personal Relationships, 22*, 723–742.

• Waldron, V. R., & Kelley, D. L. (2008). *Communicating forgiveness.* Thousand Oaks, CA: Sage.

• Walgren, K. (2016, July 20). 10 things you should never, ever say in a fight with your girlfriend or wife. http://www.menshealth.com/sex-women/things-to-never-say-during-a-fight.

• Walker, L. E. (2000). *The battered woman syndrome* (2nd ed.). New York: Springer.

• Wallace, H., & Silverman, J. (1996). Stalking and post-traumatic stress syndrome. *Police Journal, 69*, 203–206.

• Walster, E., Berscheid, E., & Walster, G. W. (1973). Equity and extramarital sexuality. *Archives of Sexual Behavior, 7*, 127–141.

• Walster, E., Walster, G. W., & Berscheid, E. (1978). *Equity: Theory and research.* Boston: Allyn & Bacon.

• Walster, E., Walster, G. W., Piliavin, J., & Schmidt, L. (1973). "Playing hard-to-get": Understanding an elusive phenomenon. *Journal of Personality and Social Psychology, 26*, 113–121.

• Walster, E., Walster, G. W., & Traupmann, J. (1978). Equity and premarital sex. *Journal of Personality, 36*, 82–92.

• Walther, J. B. (1996). Computer-mediated communication: Impersonal, interpersonal, and hyperpersonal interaction. *Human Communication Research, 23*, 3–43.

• Walther, J. B., & Boyd, S. (2002). Attraction to computer-mediated social support. In C. A. Lin & D. Atkin (Eds.), *Communication Technology and Society: Audience Adoption and Uses* (pp. 153–188). Cresskill, NJ: Hampton Press.

• Walther, J. B., Liang, Y. H., DeAndrea, D. C., Tong, S. T., Carr, C. T., Spottswood, E. L., & Amichai-Hamburger, Y. (2011). The effect of feedback on identity shift in computer-mediated communication. *Media Psychology, 14*, 1–26.

• Wang, H., & Andersen, P. A. (2007, May). *Computer-Mediated Communication in Relationship Maintenance: An Examination of Self-Disclosure in Long-Distance Friendships.* Paper presented at the International Communication Association Convention, San Francisco, CA.

• Wang, L., Seelig, A., Wadsworth, S. M., McMaster, H., Alcaraz, J. E., Crum-Cianflone, N. (2015). *Associations of military divorce with mental, behavioral, and physical health outcomes.* BMC Psychiatry, 15, DOI: 10.1186/s12888-015-0517-7.

• Wang, S. S., Moon, S.-I., Kwon, K. H., Evans, C. A., & Stefanone, M. A. (2010). Face off: Implications of visual cues on initiating friendship on Facebook. *Computers in Human Behavior, 26*, 226–234.

• Ward, L. M. (1995). Talking about sex: Common themes about sexuality in prime-time television programs children and adolescents view most. *Journal of Youth and Adolescence, 5*, 595–615.

- Ward, L. M., Epstein, M., Caruthers, A., & Merriwether, A. (2011). Men's media use, sexual cognitions, and sexual risk behavior: Testing a mediational model. *Developmental Psychology, 47*, 592–602.

- Warren, C. (1995). Parent–child communication about sex. In T. Socha & G. H. Stamp (Eds.), *Parents, children, and communication: Frontiers of theory and research* (pp. 173–201). Mahwah, NJ: Lawrence Erlbaum.

- Watzlawick, P., Beavin, J. H., & Jackson, D. D. (1967). *Pragmatics of human communication.* New York: Norton.

- Webb, L., Delaney, J. J., & Young, L. R. (1989). Age, interpersonal attraction, and social interaction: A review and assessment. *Research on Aging, 11*, 107–123.

- Weger, H., Jr., & Emmett, M. C. (2009). Romantic intent, relationship uncertainty, and relationship maintenance in young adults' cross-sex friendships. *Journal of Social and Personal Relationships, 26*, 964–988.

- Weger, H., Jr., & Polcar, L. E. (2002). Attachment style and person-centered comforting. *Western Journal of Communication, 66*, 64–103.

- Wegner, D. M. (1989). *White bears and other unwanted thoughts.* New York: Viking Press.

- Wegner, D. M. (1992). You can't always think what you want: Problems in the suppression of unwanted thoughts. In M. Zanna (Ed.), *Advances in experimental social psychology* (Vol. 25, pp. 193–225). San Diego, CA: Academic Press.

- Wegner, D. M., & Erber, R. (1992). The hyperaccessibility of suppressed thoughts. *Journal of Personality and Social Psychology, 63*, 903–912.

- Wegner, D. M., Lane, J. D., & Dimitri, S. (1994). The allure of secret relationships. *Journal of Personality and Social Psychology, 66*, 287–300.

- Wegner, D. M., Schneider, D. J., Carter, S. R., III, & White, T. L. (1987). Paradoxical effects of thought suppression. *Journal of Personality and Social Psychology, 53*, 5–13.

- Weigel, D. J., & Ballard-Reisch, D. S. (1999). The influence of marital duration on the use of relationship maintenance behaviors. *Communication Reports, 12*, 59–70.

- Weigel, D. J., & Ballard-Reisch, D. S. (2001). The impact of relational maintenance behaviors on marital satisfaction: A longitudinal analysis. *Journal of Family Communication, 1*, 265–279.

- Weigel, D. J., & Ballard-Reisch, D. S. (2002). Investigating the behavioral indicators of relational commitment. *Journal of Social and Personal Relationships, 19*, 403–423.

- Weigel, D. J., & Ballard-Reisch, D. S. (2008). Relational maintenance, satisfaction, and commitment in marriages: An actor-partner analysis. *Journal of Family Communication, 8*, 212–229.

- Weigel, D. J., Bennett, K. K., & Ballard-Reisch, D. S. (2006). Influence strategies in marriage: Self and partner links between equity, strategy use, and marital satisfaction and commitment. *The Journal of Family Communication, 6*, 77–95.

- Weinbach, R. (1989). Sudden death and the secret survivors: Helping those who grieve alone. *Social Work, 34*, 57–60.

- Weiner, M., & Mehrabian, A. (1968). *Language within language: Immediacy, a channel in verbal communication.* New York: Appleton-Century-Crofts.

- Weis, D. L., & Slosnerick, M. (1981). Attitudes toward sexual and nonsexual extramarital involvement among a sample of college students. *Journal of Marriage and the Family, 43*, 349–358.

- Weisskirch, R. S., & Delevi, R. (2011). "Sexting" and adult romantic attachment. *Computers in Human Behavior, 27*, 1697–1701.

- Welch, S. A., & Rubin, R. B. (2002). Development of relationship stage measures. *Communication Quarterly, 50*, 24–40.

- Wells, B. E., & Twenge, J. M. (2005). Changes in young people's sexual behavior and attitudes, 1943–1999: A cross-temporal analysis. *Review of General Psychology, 9*, 249–261.

- Werking, K. (1997). *We're just good friends: Women and men in nonromantic relationships.* New York: Guilford Press.

- Westerman, C. Y. K., Park, H. W., & Lee, H. E. (2007). A test of equity theory in multidimensional friendships: A comparison of the United States and Korea. *Journal of Communication, 57*, 576–598.

- Westhoff, L. A. (1985). *Corporate romance.* New York: Times Books.

- Wheeless, L. R., Wheeless, V. E., & Baus, R. (1984). Sexual communication, communication satisfaction, and solidarity in the development stages of intimate relationships. *Western Journal of Speech Communication, 48*, 217–230.

- White, G. L. (1981). Jealousy and partner's perceived motives for attraction to a rival. *Social Psychology Quarterly, 44*, 24–30.

- White, G. L., Fishbein, S., & Rutstein, J. (1981). Passionate love: The misattribution of arousal. *Journal of Personality and Social Psychology, 41*, 56–62.

- White, G. L., & Mullen, P. E. (1989). *Jealousy: Theory, research, and clinical strategies.* New York: Guilford Press.

- Whiteman, S. D., & Christiansen, A. (2008). Processes of sibling influence in adolescence: Individual and family correlates. *Family Relations, 57*, 24–34.

- Whitty, M. T. (2008). Revealing the "real" me, searching for the "actual" you: Presentations of self on an internet dating site. *Computers in Human Behavior, 24*, 1707–1723.

- Wiederman, M. W., & Allgeier, E. R. (1993). Gender differences in sexual jealousy: Adaptationist or social learning explanation? *Ethology and Sociobiology, 14*, 115–140.

- Wiederman, M. W., & Hurd, C. (1999). Extradyadic involvement during dating. *Journal of Social and Personal Relationships, 16*, 265–274.

- Wieselquist, J., Rusbult, C. E., Foster, C. A., & Agnew, C. R. (1999). Commitment, pro-relationship behavior, and trust in close relationships. *Journal of Personality and Social Psychology, 77*, 942–966.

- Wiggins, J. D., & Lederer, D. A. (1984). Differential antecedents of infidelity in marriage. *American Mental Health Counseling Association Journal, 6*, 152–161.

- Wildermuth, S. M., Vogl-Bauer, S., & Rivera, J. (2006). Practically perfect in every way: Communication strategies of ideal relational partners. *Communication Studies, 57*, 239–257.

- Wilkins, R., & Gareis, E. (2006). Emotion expression and the locution "I love you": A cross-cultural study. *International Journal of Intercultural Relations, 30*, 51–75.

- Willetts, M. C., Sprecher, S., & Beck, F. D. (2004). Overview of sexual practices and attitudes within relational contexts. In J. H. Harvey, A. Wenzel, & S. Sprecher (Eds.), *The handbook of sexuality in close relationships* (pp. 57–85). Mahwah, NJ: Lawrence Erlbaum.

- Williams, A. (2015a, September 15). How to spot a member of generation Z. http://www.nytimes .com/2015/09/18/fashion/how-to-spot-a-member-of-generation-z.HTml?action= click&contentCollection=Fashion%20%26%20 Style&module=RelatedCoverage&region= EndOfArticle&pgtype=article

- Williams, A. (2015b, September 19). Move over, millennials, here comes generation Z. http:// www.nytimes.com/2015/09/20/fashion/move-over-millennials-here-comes-generation-z .html?_r=0.

- Williams, M. J., & Tiedens, L. Z. (2016). The subtle suspension of backlash: A meta-analysis of penalties for women's implicit and explicit dominance behavior. *Psychological Bulletin, 142*, 165–197.

- Williams, S., & Andersen, P. A. (1998). Toward an expanded view of interracial romantic relationships. In V. Duncan (Ed.), *Toward achieving malt.* Dubuque, IA: Kendall-Hunt.

- Willitts, M., Benzeval, M., & Stansfeld, S. (2004). Partnership history and mental health over time. *Journal of Epidemiology and Community Health, 58*, 53–58.

- Willoughby, B. J., Carroll, J. S., & Busby, D. M. (2011). The different effects of "living together": Determining and comparing types of cohabiting couples. *Journal of Social and Personal Relationships, 29*, 397–419.

- Wilmot, W. W. (1995). *Relational communication.* New York: McGraw-Hill.

- Wilmot, W. W., Carbaugh, D. A., & Baxter, L. A. (1985). Communicative strategies used to terminate romantic relationships. *Western Journal of Speech Communication, 49,* 204–216.

- Wilmot, W. W., & Stevens, D. C. (1994). Relationship rejuvenation: Arresting decline in personal relationships. In D. Conville (Ed.), *Uses of structure in communication studies* (pp. 103–124). Westport, CT: Praeger.

- Wilson, S. E., & Waddoups, S. L. (2002). Good marriages gone bad: Health mismatches as a cause of later life marital dissolution. *Population Research and Policy Review, 21,* 505–523.

- Wineberg, H. (1994). Marital reconciliation in the United States: Which couples are successful? *Journal of Marriage and the Family, 56,* 80–88.

- Wineberg, H. (1995). An examination of ever-divorced women who attempted a marital reconciliation before becoming divorced. *Journal of Divorce & Remarriage, 22,* 129–146.

- Wiseman, J. P. (1986). Friendship: Bonds and binds in a voluntary relationship. *Journal of Social and Personal Relationships, 3,* 191–211.

- Wiseman, R. L., & Schenck-Hamlin, W. (1981). A multidimensional scaling validation of an inductively-derived set of compliance gaining strategies. *Communication Monographs, 48,* 251–270.

- Witteman, H., & Fitzpatrick, M. A. (1986). Compliance-gaining in marital interaction: Power bases, processes and outcomes. *Communication Monographs, 53,* 130–143.

- Wolfinger, N. H. (1999). Trends in the intergenerational transmission of divorce. *Demography, 36,* 415–420.

- Wood, J. T. (1994). *Gendered lives: Communications, gender, and culture.* Belmont, CA: Wadsworth.

- Wood, J. T. (Ed.). (1996). *Gendered relationships.* Mountain View, CA: Mayfield.

- Wood, J. T. (2001). The normalization of violence in heterosexual romantic relationships: Women's narratives of love and violence. *Journal of Social and Personal Relationships, 18,* 239–261.

- Wood, J. T., & Dindia, K. (1998). What's the difference? A dialogue about the differences and similarities between women and men. In D. J. Canary & K. Dindia (Eds.), *Sex differences and similarities in communication* (pp. 19–39). Mahwah, NJ: Lawrence Erlbaum.

- Wood, J. T., & Duck, S. (1995). Off the beaten track: New shores for relationships research. In J. T. Wood & S. Duck (Eds.), *Understudied relationships: Off the beaten track* (pp. 1–21). Thousand Oaks, CA: Sage.

- Wood, J. T., & Inman, C. (1993). In a different mode: Masculine styles of communicating closeness. *Journal of Applied Communication Research, 21,* 279–295.

- Worley, T. R., & Samp, J. (2016). Complaint avoidance and complaint-related appraisals in close relationships: A dyadic power theory perspective. *Communication Research, 43,* 391–413.

- Wotipka, C. D., & High, A. C. (2016). An idealized self or the real me? Predicting attraction to online dating profiles using selective self-presentation and warranting. *Communication Monographs, 83,* 281–302.

- Wrape, E. R., Jenkins, S. R., Callahan, J. L., & Nowlin, R. B. (2016). Emotional and cognitive coping in relationship dissolution. *Journal of College Counselling, 19,* 110–123.

- Wright, C. N., & Roloff, M. E. (2015). You should just know why I'm upset: Expectancy violation theory and the influence of mind reading expectations (MRE) on responses to relational problems. *Communication Research Reports, 32,* 10–19.

- Wright, D., Parkes, A., Strange, V., Allen, E., & Bonell, C. (2008). The quality of young people's heterosexual relationships: A longitudinal analysis of characteristics shaping the subjective experience. *Perspectives on Sexual and Reproductive Health, 40,* 226–237.

- Wright, K. (2015, September 21). My husband and I text more than we talk–and that's OK. http://www.redbookmag.com/life/friends-family/a39833/we-text-more-than-talk/.

- Wright, K. B. (2004). On-line relational maintenance strategies and perceptions of partners within exclusively Internet-based and primarily Internet-based relationships. *Communication Studies, 55,* 239–253.

- Wright, P. H. (1982). Men's friendships, women's friendships, and the alleged inferiority of the latter. *Sex Roles, 8,* 1–20.

- Wright, R. A., & Contrada, R. J. (1986). Dating selectivity and interpersonal attractiveness: Toward a better understanding of the "elusive phenomenon." *Journal of Social and Personal Relationships, 3,* 131–148.

- Yates, S. J., & Lockley, E. (2008). Moments of separation: Gender, (not so remote) relationships, and the cell phone. In S. Holland (Ed.), *Remote relationships in a small world* (pp. 74–97). Oxford, UK: Peter Lang.

- Yelsma, P. (1986). Marriage vs. cohabitation: Couples' communication practices and satisfaction. *Journal of Communication, 36,* 94–107.

- Yildirim, F. B., & Dimir, A. (2015). Breakup adjustment in young adulthood. *Journal of Counselling and Development, 93,* 38–44.

- Yin, L. (2009). Communication channels, social support and satisfaction in long distance romantic relationships. Unpublished master's thesis, Georgia State University, Atlanta, GA.

- Yingling, J. (1995). The first relationship: Infant-parent communication. In T. J. Socha & G. H. Stamp (Eds.), *Parents, children, and communication: Frontiers of theory and research* (pp. 23–41). Hillsdale, NJ: Lawrence Erlbaum.

- Yodanis, C., & Lauer, S. (2007). Money management in marriage: Multilevel and cross-national effects of the breadwinner's role. *Journal of Marriage and the Family, 69,* 1307–1325.

- Young, K. S., Griffin-Shelley, E., Cooper, A., O'Mara, J., & Buchanan, J. (2000). Online infidelity: A new dimension in couple relationships with implications for evaluation and treatment. *Sexual Addiction & Compulsivity: The Journal of Treatment and Prevention, 7,* 59–74.

- Young, S. L. (2004). Factors that influence recipients' appraisals of hurtful communication. *Journal of Social and Personal Relationships, 21,* 291–303.

- Young, S. L., & Bippus, A. M. (2001). Does it make a difference if they hurt you in a funny way? *Communication Quarterly, 49,* 35–52.

- Young, S. L., Paxman, C. G., Koehring, C. L. E., & Anderson, C. A. (2008). The application of a face work model of disengagement to unrequited love. *Communication Research Reports, 25,* 56–66.

- Young, S. M., & Pinsky, D. (2006). Narcissism and celebrity. *Journal of Research in Personality, 40,* 463–471.

- Yum, Y., & Canary, D. J. (2009). Cultural differences in equity theory predictions of relational maintenance strategies. *Human Communication Research, 35,* 384–406.

- Zeeman, E. C. (1977). Catastrophe theory. *Scientific American, 234,* 65–83.

- Zillman, D. (1978). Attribution and misattribution of excitatory reactions. In J. H. Harvey, W. Ickes, & R. F. Kidd (Eds.), *New directions in attribution research* (Vol. 2, pp. 335–368). Hillsdale, NJ: Lawrence Erlbaum.

- Zillman, D. (1990). The interplay of cognition and excitation in aggravated conflict. In D. D. Cahn (Ed.), *Intimates in conflict: A communication perspective* (pp. 187–208). Hillsdale, NJ: Lawrence Erlbaum.

- Zuckerman, M., DePaulo, B. M., & Rosenthal, R. (1981). Verbal and nonverbal communication of deception. In L. Berkowitz (Ed.), *Advances in experimental social psychology* (Vol. 14, pp. 1–59). New York: Academic Press.

AUTHOR INDEX

Aakhus, M. A., 134 *box*
Abbey, A., 164, 242, 249, 269
Aboud, F. E., 66
Abra, G., 317, 334, 335
Abrahams, E. M., 425
Abrams, D., 27
Acevedo, B. P., 202
Achee, J., 421
Ackard, D. M., 230
Acker, M., 199, 200, 201
Ackerman, R. A., 37
Acosta, P., 248
Acton (Lord), 315
Adams, J. S., 280
Adams, K. L., 308
Adams, R., 339
Adib, S. M., 152 *box*
Adler, N., 201
Afifi, T. D., 77, 88, 155, 159, 160, 162, 164,
    238, 247, 415, 431
Afifi, W. A., 62, 68, 73, 88, 89, 90, 98, 99,
    100, 105, 106, 155, 156, 157, 158, 161,
    239, 242, 253, 254, 259, 261, 267, 268,
    269, 273, 339, 364, 365, 390
Agan, M. L. F., 338
Agassi, Andre, 33
Agnew, C. R., 306, 381, 386, 408, 410,
    413, 419
Ahrons, C. R., 403
Aida, Y., 327, 328, 340
Ainsworth, M. D. S., 214, 215, 216, 217
Akbulut, V., 230, 233
Albada, K. F., 71
Albas, C., 47
Albas, D., 47
Alberts, J. K., 231, 295, 298, 300, 303,
    304, 306, 358
Albrecht, T. L., 185
Albright, J. M., 240
Aldeis, D., 238
Alderson, K., 234
Alex, N., 333
Allen, M., 146
Allen, T., 410
Alles, M., 388
Allgeier, E. R., 248, 249, 358
Altendorf, D. M., 423
Altman, I., 4, 9, 113, 116, 118, 120,
    131 *figure*, 140, 141, 146, 159
Altman, J., 431
Alvarez, M. J., 253
Amarel, D., 188
Amato, P. R., 408, 409 *box*, 410, 411, 412,
    413, 415, 418, 430, 431
Amodio, D. M., 78, 79
Anderegg, C., 93, 94, 95 *box*, 118, 120, 122
Anders, S. L., 218, 219

Andersen, P. A., 3, 4, 7, 9, 12, 16, 20, 27,
    28, 28 *box*, 29, 40, 72, 79, 91 *box*, 94,
    169, 170, 171, 176, 177, 179, 181,
    182 *box*, 183, 199, 237, 238 *box*, 245,
    246, 247, 249, 261, 268, 269 *box*, 325,
    329, 333, 334, 335, 338, 353, 361, 363,
    365, 410 *box*, 412
Anderson, C., 243
Anderson, C. A., 368
Anderson, L., 44
Anderson, T. L., 122
Andrea, L., 154
Andreassen, C. S., 34
Andreoli-Mathie, V., 357
Andrews, L. A., 149
Andrews, S. L., 240
Anduff, H. L., 229
Ang, P. C., 105
Angera, J. J., 231
Ansell, E., 346
Antheunis, M. L., 92
Antill, J. K., 9, 278
Antonakis, J., 322
Applegate, J. L., 190, 338
Archer, J., 66, 373, 374, 418
Argyle, M., 4, 11, 45, 178, 289, 430, 432
Arias, I., 396, 418
Arliss, L. P., 289
Armstrong, C., 162
Armstrong, E. A., 229
Armstrong, L., 156
Aron, A., 36, 37, 64, 170, 202, 259
Aron, A. P., 80
Aron, E. N., 36, 37, 170, 202
Aronson, E., 73
Arriaga, X. B., 305, 386, 413
Asada, J. K., 11
Ashton, N., 70
Atkinson, B. E., 60
Atwood, K., 252
Auerbach, A., 247
Aumer-Ryan, K., 340
Aune, K. S., 204, 349, 352 *box*, 354, 388,
    390, 391, 392
Avdeyera, T., 81
Avtgis, T. A., 122, 123, 124, 125, 126
Axinn, W. G., 278
Aylor, B., 264, 265, 276
Ayres, J., 258, 259, 261

Babcock, J. C., 302
Babin, B. A., 364
Babin, E. A., 243
Bach, G. R., 300
Bachman, G. F., 218, 219, 220, 225, 239,
    295, 356, 381, 383, 384, 385, 386, 387,
    393, 395, 396, 397

Back, K., 80
Back, M. D., 60
Backstrom, L., 229
Bacue, A., 192, 335
Badzinski, D. M., 316, 331
Bagarozzi, D. A., 340
Bailey, J. M., 65, 233
Baker, A. J., 143
Baldwin, A., 321
Baldwin, M. W., 225
Ball, H., 99
Ballard-Reisch, D. S., 171, 259, 260,
    266, 281
Banas, J. A., 329
Banks, S. P., 423, 426
Banuazizi, A., 281 *box*
Baranowski, M., 339
Barazova, N., 40
Barbee, A. P., 158
Barclay, B., 423 *box*
Barelds, D. P., 356
Barker, L. L., 311
Barnett, C. L., 253 *box*
Baron, N. S., 140
Bartell, D., 413, 414 *box*
Bartels, A., 64
Barth, J. M., 66
Barth, R. J., 267
Bartholomew, K., 67, 215, 217, 218, 219,
    220, 224, 387
Bartle-Haring, S., 290
Bartlett, M. Y., 360
Bassin, E., 409
Bassis, S., 37
Batabyal, A. A., 201
Bateson, G., 18
Battaglia, D. M., 408
Baucom, D. H., 36, 323
Bauer, G., 339, 341
Baumeister, R. E., 231, 232, 234, 236
Baumeister, R. F., 46, 368
Baumgarte, R., 193
Baumgartner, M. K., 339
Baumrind, D., 337, 338
Baur, K., 233, 237
Baus, R., 245 *box*
Bavelas, J. B., 350
Baxter, L. A., 45, 81, 89, 96, 97, 122, 126,
    127, 128, 129, 130, 131, 132, 133, 134,
    140, 155, 218, 220, 243, 259, 261, 408,
    410, 411, 415, 416, 421, 422, 424, 425,
    427, 428, 432
Bayer, J. B., 119
Bayes, M. A., 178
Beach, S. R. H., 309
Bean, D., 403
Beasley, R., 234, 235

Beavin, J. H., 15–16
Beck, F. D., 230
Beck, G., 401, 425
Becker, D. V., 358, 365
Beckner, B. N., 38
Beebe, S. A., 179
Beier, A. P., 178
Beigbeder, S. A., 184
Bejanyan, K., 220
Bejlovich, R. A., 424
Beker, G., 142
Bell, A. P., 234
Bell, R. A., 94, 97, 175, 176, 259
Bellack, A. S., 294
Bello, R., 387
Bem, S. L., 12, 66
Ben-Ari, A., 170, 171
Bendahan, S., 322
Bennett, K., 411
Bennett, K. K., 281
Bennett, M., 396
Bentler, P. M., 411, 412
Bentley, C. G., 328
Benuto, L., 231, 232
Benzeval, M., 2
Beres, M. A., 239
Berg, J. H., 118, 416
Bergen, K. M., 132, 275
Bergen, M. R., 259
Berger, C. R., 45, 86, 88, 90, 92, 93, 94, 96, 102, 316, 319, 320, 325
Berglas, S., 50
Bergman, J. Z., 34 box
Bergman, S. M., 34 box
Bergsieker, H. B., 115
Bernardes, D., 210
Bernhardt, E., 431
Berns, S. B., 302
Bernstein, I. H., 309
Berscheid, Ellen, 2, 4, 6, 7, 63, 70, 76, 199, 202, 207, 209, 228, 230, 231, 233, 245, 280, 281, 282, 283
Bevan, J. L., 105, 106, 246, 360, 385, 386, 387, 397, 398, 399, 400, 423, 423 box
Beyers, W., 38, 40
Bickman, L., 333
Bierhoff, H. W., 210
Biles, Simone, 29
Billedo, C. J., 276
Billieux, J., 34
Billings, A., 301
Bimbi, D. S., 234
Bingham, S. G., 251
Bippus, A., 218
Bippus, A. M., 319, 347
Birditt, K. S., 415
Birnbaum, G. E., 67
Birnie-Porter, C., 230, 243
Bisson, M. A., 274

Bissonnette, V. L., 305
Black, A., 350
Black, L. E., 382
Blair, K. L., 231, 232, 233, 275
Blake, R. R., 290, 291, 294, 297
Blakinger, K., 31
Blehar, M. C., 214
Blow, A. J., 356
Blumstein, P., 234, 235, 243, 320, 328, 408, 409, 410, 412, 414
Blunstein, P., 356
Blunt-Vinti, H. D., 231, 245
Bochner, A. P., 145
Bodie, G. R., 185
Boelen, P. A., 429
Boer, D., 77
Bogle, K., 229
Bohning, D. E., 432
Bolger, N., 188
Bombar, M. L., 248
Bonds-Raacke, J., 33
Bonita, J., 353
Bonoma, T. V., 290
Bonus, S., 262
Boon, S., 234, 355
Boon, S. D., 354, 393
Boone, C., 163
Booth, A., 278, 279, 431
Booth-Butterfield, M., 191, 204, 208, 250, 381
Borchert, K., 99
Borgaro, S., 67
Boss, D., 178
Boster, F., 327, 330
Boster, F. J., 328
Boston, A., 219
Botti, S., 323
Bowers, J. R., 259, 260
Bowers, J. W., 176
Bowlby, J., 214, 215, 216, 222
Boyd, D., 300
Boyd, S., 186 box
Boyden, T., 66
Boyle, A. M, 143 box
Bradac, J. J., 146, 176
Bradbury, T. N., 222, 309, 411, 416
Bradford, L., 29, 409, 410, 415
Braiker, H. B., 290
Braithwaite, D. O., 54, 127, 131, 373
Bramlett, M. D., 28
Brandau-Brown, F. E., 384, 385, 386, 387
Brandt, H. M., 253 box
Branje, S. J. T., 336
Brann, M., 171
Brashers, D. E., 86, 89
Braun, M., 339
Braverman, J., 360
Brehm, S. S., 309
Breitbart, V., 323

Brennan, K. A., 239
Brenner, R. E., 429
Brentano, C., 409
Bretherton, I., 215
Brewster, K., 234
Bridge, K., 81, 134
Brien, M. J., 278
Bringle, R. G., 365
Britt, T. W., 44, 48
Brock, L. J., 239
Brodenshausen, G. V., 298
Brody, G. H., 238, 309
Brody, N., 263, 419
Brogan, S., 231
Brooks-Gunn, J., 241, 289, 339
Brounstein, P. J., 145
Brown, B. B., 131 figure, 159
Brown, C. E., 332
Brown, D. E., 26
Brown, E., 415
Brown, Helen Gurley, 237
Brown, L. L., 64
Brown, M., 247
Brown, P., 26, 41, 46, 47, 48, 49, 50
Brown, R., 26
Brown, S. L., 278, 279
Browning, J. R., 320
Brownridge, D. A., 279
Brown-Smith, N., 161
Brumbaugh, C. C., 432
Brunner, S. R., 144 box
Bruschke, J., 351, 354
Bryan, A. D., 333
Bryant, E. M., 120, 262, 263
Brynildsen, K., 429
Bryson, J. B., 361, 364, 365
Buchanan, C. M., 431
Buchanan, J., 357
Buehler, C., 290
Buerkel-Rothfuss, N. L., 94, 97, 175
Buhrmester, D., 113, 115 box, 116, 171
Bukberg, R. E., 239
Bulanda, J. R., 339
Buller, D. B., 42, 181, 350, 354
Bullis, C., 126, 127, 128, 129, 130, 421
Burcin, M., 253 box
Burdette, M. P., 346
Burdick, C. A., 240
Burge, D., 222
Burgess, A. W., 34
Burgoon, J. K., 12, 13, 16, 20, 42, 62, 72, 73, 79, 89, 90, 94, 95 box, 102, 103, 104, 174, 175, 182, 192, 215, 241, 261, 315, 316, 319, 324, 325, 333, 334, 335, 336, 350, 353, 354, 358
Buri, J. R., 338
Burke, R. J., 158
Burleson, B. R., 76, 184, 185, 190, 191, 192, 208, 210, 251, 338, 383

Burrell, N. A., 331
Burris, J. L., 237
Bursic, K., 233
Burton, L. M., 320
Burts, D. C., 338
Busby, D. M., 277
Buss, D. M., 65, 69, 230, 246, 356, 357, 358, 365, 367, 374, 411, 429, 430, 432
Bustamante, R. M., 388
Butauski, M., 149
Butler, J. L., 43
Butts, C. T., 153 *box*
Buunk, B. P., 229, 230, 231, 280, 282, 283, 302, 357, 365
Buzwell, S., 192
Byers, E. S., 231, 239, 243, 245, 246, 248, 249, 250, 320
Bylsma, W. H., 225
Byrd-Craven, J., 327
Byrne, D., 74, 75, 79, 248

Cacioppo, J. T., 64
Cacioppo, S., 64
Cahill, D. J., 81
Calabrese, R. J., 86, 88, 90
Caldwell, M. A., 193, 322
Callahan, J. L., 429
Callan, V. J., 220
Callender, K. A., 233
Calvert, S. L., 399 *box*
Cameron, C. A., 352 *box*
Cameron, J. J., 191
Cameron, K. A., 397
Cameron, M. O., 106, 403
Camire, L., 355
Campbell, A., 229
Campbell, E., 339
Campbell, S. M., 322
Campbell, W. K., 30, 68, 257, 306
Canary, D. J., 16, 17, 97, 258, 259, 261, 262, 265, 266, 267, 268, 272 *box*, 280, 281, 282, 289, 290, 293, 294, 295, 296, 297, 298, 329, 384, 386, 392
Cannady, L. W., 37
Cantrill, J. G., 410
Caplan, S. E., 147
Cappella, J. N., 20
Carbaugh, D. A., 422
Carey, C. M., 107, 323
Carey, K. B., 253 *box*
Carey, M., 231
Carey, M. P., 253 *box*
Carlo, G., 26, 39
Carlson, C. R., 237
Carlson, J. R., 353
Carnevale, P. J., 291, 294, 296, 297
Carney, D. R., 334, 335
Carpenter, C., 280
Carpenter-Theune, K. E., 155, 158

Carr, C. T., 34
Carr, D., 257
Carratalá, E., 431
Carrere, S., 320
Carroll, J. S., 66, 277
Carson, A., 281 *box*
Carson, J. W., 36
Carson, K. M., 36
Carter, E., 154
Carter, E. J., 240
Carter, S. R., 160
Caruthers, A., 237
Carvallo, M., 78
Casella, D. F., 72
Caspi, A., 41, 42, 72
Catallozzi, M., 323, 326
Catanese, K. R., 231
Cate, R. M., 210, 230, 231, 233, 242, 243, 284, 289, 290, 380, 408, 411, 416
Catta-Preta, A. B., 301 *box*
Cauffman, E., 410
Caughlin, J. P., 155, 156, 157, 159, 161, 163, 164, 290, 295, 302, 324, 431
Cavallo, J. V., 324
Cavanaugh, L. E., 346
Cayemberg, C., 423 *box*
Ceranic, T. L., 322
Cerny, J. A., 233
Chaiken, S., 70
Chance, C., 350
Chandler, T. A., 310
Chao, E. Y., 352 *box*
Chaplin, G., 29
Chapman, G., 212, 213
Chappetta, K. C., 66
Chavez, A. M., 90, 261, 269, 270, 271
Checton, M. G., 100
Chen, G. M., 47
Chen, S., 319, 352 *box*
Cheng, J. T., 335
Cheng, K. Y., 403
Cheng, M. M., 241
Chiang, Y. C., 432
Chichocki, D., 154
Child, J. T., 149, 150
Ching, P. U., 349
Choi, M., 34
Choo, P., 320
Chovil, N., 350
Christakis, N., 269
Christensen, A., 171, 301, 301 *box*, 302, 323, 415
Christiansen, A., 337
Christofides, E., 15 *box*, 360
Christopher, F. S., 231, 233, 235, 236, 242, 245, 246, 261, 310, 372
Chronis, H., 350
Chung, A. H., 238
Cialdini, R. B., 8, 30

Clark, C., 127
Clark, C. L., 215
Clark, G., 401
Clark, M. S., 118
Clark, S., 339
Clark, S. L., 320
Clarke-Stewart, A., 409
Claypool, H. M., 360
Cleek, M. G., 412, 415
Clements, M. L., 415, 416
Cline, R. J. W., 254
Clinton, Bill, 29
Clore, 70, 79
Cloud, M. D., 358
Cloven, D. H., 296, 297, 317, 323, 384, 385, 386, 419
Coates, D., 164
Coats, E. J., 317, 335
Cochran, S. D., 234
Cody, M., 242, 329, 349, 350, 422, 426, 427, 428
Cody, M. J., 16, 17, 42, 240, 352 *box*, 423
Coffman, S., 103
Cohen, E. L., 108
Cohen, R., 290
Colder, M., 191
Cole, M., 360
Cole, T., 355
Coletti, S. F., 330
Collier, M. J., 27
Collins, N., 215, 220
Collins, N. L., 144, 215
Collins, T. J., 423
Collins, W. A., 289, 319, 320, 335
Comadena, M. E., 353
Comstock, J., 243, 354
Confer, J. C., 358
Consoli, G., 64
Contrada, R. J., 73
Conville, R. L., 408
Cook, S. W., 248, 249, 250, 429, 432
Cooley, Charles Horton, 38
Coontz, S., 410 *box*
Cooper, C. R., 339
Cordova, A. D., 415
Cornell, C. P., 52
Cornman, J. C., 257
Côté, S., 323
Cottle, T. J., 156
Courtwright, J. A., 176
Cousin, G., 332
Coutts, L. M., 178
Cowan, G., 331
Cox, C. L., 305
Cox, J. M., 232 *box*
Cozzarelli, C., 225
Craddock, E., 327
Craig, J. M., 269
Cramer, D., 290

Cravens, J. D., 357
Crawford, D. W., 280, 382
Creasey, G., 219
Creasy, B., 220
Crocker, J., 164
Cronauer, C. K., 332
Crooks, R., 233, 237
Crosby, J. M., 232 box
Crowley, J. P., 369
Crumley, L. P., 348, 349
Cui, M., 411
Cummings, E. M., 290, 302
Cunningham, C., 403
Cunningham, J. D., 9, 278
Cunningham, M. R., 143
Cupach, W. R., 42, 46, 50, 51, 52, 229, 243,
    245, 246, 247, 345, 369, 370, 371, 372,
    388, 389, 391, 399, 409, 411, 412, 421,
    422, 424
Cutrona, C. E., 184

Daas, K. L., 132
Dabbish, L., 82 box
Dadds, M. R., 64
Dailey, R. M., 126, 158, 159, 397, 401, 402,
    416, 419, 425, 426, 428
Dainton, M., 259, 261, 264, 265, 266, 267,
    276, 381
Dal Cin, S., 125
Daly, J. A., 42, 43, 259
Danielewicz, J., 423 box
Daniels, E. A., 82 box
Darby, B. W., 389
Dargie, E., 275
Darioly, A., 317
Darwin, Charles, 74, 172
Datteri, D. L., 408
Davenport, S. W., 34 box
Davey, A., 309
Davidson, J. K., 243
Davidson, K. D., 210
Davidson, L. L., 323
Davies, A. P. C., 333
Davies, P. T., 290
Davila, J., 222
Davis, K. E., 81, 198, 346
Davis, K. L., 11
Davis, M., 420, 421
Davis, M. E., 199, 200, 201
Dean, J., 4
Deandrea, D. C., 42
DeCelles, K. A., 322
DeClaire, Joan, 416, 417 box
De Dreu, C. K., 64, 302
De Goede, I. H. A., 336, 338
De Graaf, P. M., 403
De Kwaadstniet, E. W., 319
DeLamater, J., 230, 231, 233, 247
Delaney, J. J., 66

De La Ronde, C., 40
Delevi, R., 43, 220
Delia, J. G., 338
Dell'Osso, M. C., 64
DeMaris, A., 319, 340, 415
D'Emilio, J., 237
Demmons S., 231
Denes, A., 77, 247
DePaulo, B. M., 43, 349, 354
Derlega, V. J., 144, 145, 158, 163
DeRue, D. S., 322
Desmarais, S., 15 box, 360
DeSteno, D., 358, 360
Deutsch, F., 340
Deutsch, M., 279
DeVall, W. B., 320
De Vries, D. A., 42
DeWolf, D. M., 338
Diamond, L. M., 64, 232, 234
Diana, L. K., 280
Di Castro, G., 220
Dickenson, J. A., 64
Dickson, F. C., 259
Dieckman, L. E., 164
Dienberg, Love G., 2
Dijkstra, P., 229, 356
Dillard, J. P., 81, 311, 325, 326, 327, 335
Dillman, L., 102, 334, 335
Dillow, M. R., 99, 347, 397
Dimar, A., 429
Dimir, A., 430, 432
Dimitri, S., 160
Dindia, K., 146, 178, 192, 199, 258, 259,
    261, 264, 265, 269 box
Dion, K., 76
Dion, K. K., 68, 70
Dobson, W. R., 339
Doelger, J., 94
Doherty, K. J., 48
Doherty, W. J., 397
Dolin, D. J., 191
Domingue, R., 218
Donald, M., 8
Donnerstein, C., 233
Dornbusch, M., 431
Doughtery, T. W., 250
Douglas, E. M., 374
Douglas, W., 91, 93, 94
Dove, N. L., 408
Dovidio, J. F., 316, 332
Dowd, M. M., 259
Dowdell, E. B., 34, 35, 41
Dowrick, S., 346
Draper, K. K., 231
Draucker, C. B., 372
Drigotas, S. M., 379, 381
Drinkard, J., 331
Driscoll, R., 81, 298, 300, 306
Drouin, M., 220, 350

Druen, P. B., 143
Drummond, D. K., 29
Drummond-Reeves, S. J., 409, 411, 415
Dubar, N. E., 329
Dubois, D., 323
Duck, Steven, 2, 5, 9, 68, 149, 188, 259,
    265, 308, 418, 419, 420, 429
Duffy, S. M., 306, 381
Duggan, A., 218
Duggan, M., 33, 321 box
Dun, T., 309
Dunbar, N. E., 241, 317, 319, 334, 335, 353
Dunham, R. M., 339
Dunn, J., 289, 361
Duran, R. L., 14, 134 box, 262, 264 box
Durham, W. T., 132
Dutton, D. G., 80, 202
Dwyer, P. D., 250
Dyer, M., 193

Earwaker, D., 396
Eastwick, P. W., 66, 75, 203 box
Eastwood, M. M., 382
Eckhardt, A., 188
Eddings, S. K., 68
Eden, J., 106, 230, 261
Edgar, T., 245
Edgley, C., 350
Edlund, J. E., 360
Edwards, J. N., 431
Edwards, S. R., 335
Egbert, N., 212, 213
Eggen, D., 418
Egland, K. L., 179, 242, 259, 267, 326, 336
Egloff, B., 60
Ehrenburg, M., 419, 429, 432
Eichberg, C., 216
Eisenberg, M. E., 230
Ekman, P., 350, 354
Eldridge, K., 301 box
Elliott, S., 229
Ellis, N. K., 101
Ellison, N., 42, 355
Ellison, N. B., 15 box, 33, 34, 41, 92, 119
Ellyson, S. L., 316, 332, 334
Eloy, S. V., 259, 329, 365
Emmers, T. M., 97, 178, 199, 384, 386,
    392, 422, 425, 428
Emmers-Sommer, T. M., 142
Emmett, M., 270
Emmons, R. A., 68
Engels, R. C., 155
Engels, R. C. M. E., 162, 163
Engles, C. M. E., 231
Ennis, E., 350
Enright, R. D., 393
Epstein, J. A., 349
Epstein, M., 237
Erber, R., 160

Erikson, Eric, 26, 40
Erlandson, K. T., 327
Ervin, K. S., 69
Espada, J. P., 431
Esteves, F., 204
Eton, D. T., 327
Euler, H. A., 374
Evans, C. A., 82 *box*
Evans, K., 346
Ewing Lee, E. A., 323
Exline, R. V., 177, 178, 334

Fagundes, C. P., 429
Falato, W. L., 356
Falbo, T., 327, 328, 329, 331, 340
Fales, M. R., 230, 231
Falk, E. B., 119
Farce, R. V., 330
Farinelli, L., 218, 280
Farrell, D., 381
Farrell, H., 347
Farrington-Flint, L., 33
Farzan, R., 82 *box*
Fauber, R. L., 243
Faulkner, S. L., 37, 106, 270, 273
Fearns , J. B., 105
Fearrington, M. E., 34 *box*
Feeney, J. A., 170, 218, 219, 220, 221, 222,
    225, 301 *box*, 346, 356
Fehr, B., 113, 115, 130, 198, 201, 209, 225,
    267, 268, 429
Fehr, R., 389, 390
Feingold, A., 65, 77
Feldman, C., 302
Feldman, R., 64
Feldman, S. S., 410
Felmlee, D. H., 60, 66, 78, 319, 322, 409,
    411, 429
Feng, D., 280
Ferguson, C. A., 179
Ferguson, T. J., 328
Ferrara, M. H., 386, 387
Ferraro, K. J., 374
Ferris, A. L., 143 *box*
Festinger, L., 80
Fetchenhaur, D., 229
Filsinger, E. E., 416
Fincham, F. D., 229, 232 *box*, 309, 378, 379,
    395, 396, 411
Fingerhut, A. W., 233, 320
Finkel, E. J., 66, 75, 203 *box*
Finkenauer, C., 155, 162, 163, 231, 276
Finn, A. N., 34
Fischer, E. F., 210
Fischer, J. L., 280, 339
Fischer, T. F. C., 403
Fishbein, S., 80
Fisher, B. A., 308
Fisher, H., 64

Fisher, J. D., 252 *box*
Fisher, T. D., 233, 239
Fisher, W. A., 252 *box*
Fitch, K. L., 185
Fitness, J., 363
Fitzgerald, L. F., 250, 251
Fitzgerald, N. M., 210
Fitzgerald, P., 252 *box*
Fitzpatrick, M. A., 146, 245, 290, 291, 295,
    316, 323, 331, 339, 340
Fleischmann, A. A., 246, 261, 329, 357, 365
Fletcher, G. J. O., 328, 363
Fleuriet, C., 360
Flippen, C. A., 320
Flores, J. R., 34
Floyd, K., 7, 11, 12, 17, 70, 103, 104, 170,
    171, 172, 173, 174, 175, 176, 178, 179,
    181, 193, 268, 311, 323, 324, 333
Folkes, V. S., 72, 369
Fortes, C., 60
Foss, B. M., 95 *box*
Foster, C., 257, 306
Foster, C. A., 306
Fouladi, R. T., 429
Fox, J., 93, 94, 117, 118, 120, 122, 423 *box*
Fraley, R. C., 432
Frampton, B. D., 150
Frandsen, M. M., 245, 246, 248
Frank, E., 243
Frank, M., 333
Frazier, P., 433
Frazier, P. A., 429, 432
Fredendall, L. L., 360
Fredholm, E. M., 380
Freedman, E. B., 237
Freedman, S. R., 393
Freedman, V. A., 257
Freeman, K. E., 254
Friedman, S. R., 248
Friedmann, H. S., 72
Friesen, W. V., 354
Frieze, I. H., 207
Frinjs, T., 162
Frisby, B. N., 108
Frost, D. M., 233
Frunzaru, V., 41
Fu, G., 352 *box*
Führer, A., 210
Furman, W., 113, 115 *box*
Furnham, A., 11, 289

Gable, S. L., 189
Gaelick, L., 298
Gagnon, J. H., 410
Gahler, M., 431
Gaines, B., 40
Gaines, M. E., 229
Gaines, S. O., 9, 28, 387
Galinha, I. C., 204, 207

Galinsky, A., 316, 317, 335
Galinsky, A. D., 323, 335
Galligan, R. F., 253, 254
Galliher, R. V., 328
Galton, Francis, 74
Ganat, J., 131 *figure*
Gangestad, S. W., 70, 239
Gannon, J., 333
Gano-Philips, S., 309
Gao, G., 352 *box*
Garbaesevschi, D., 41
Garcia-Marques, L., 253
Gareis, E., 211 *box*
Garimella, V. R. K., 125, 126
Gasiorek, J., 77
Geaghan, T., 229
Gelfand, M. J., 389, 390
Gelles, R. J., 52, 372
Gentzler, A. L., 220
George, J. F., 349, 352 *box*, 353
George, M. S., 432
Gergle, D., 299 *box*
Gershoni, R., 193
Gibbens, F. X., 238
Gibbs, J., 42
Gibbs, J. L., 92
Gibran, K., 337, 408
Gifford, S., 252 *box*
Gil, K. M., 36
Gilbert, S. J., 140
Gilding, M., 146
Giles, H., 77, 332, 412
Gillath, O., 423
Gilmour, Robin, 5
Gilovich, T., 333
Ginat, J., 9
Girard, M., 396
Givens, D. B., 240, 241
Givertz, M., 225
Glang, E., 248
Gleason, M. E., 143
Glomb, T. M., 250
Goetz, A. T., 231, 374
Goetz, J. C., 333
Goffman, E., 26, 41, 42, 44, 45, 46
Gola, K. A., 233
Gold, J. A., 200
Gold, K. J., 409
Gold, S. R., 66
Goldberg, A. E., 341
Goldfinger, C., 275
Goldsmith, D., 185
Goldsmith, D. J., 186, 190, 192
Golish, T. D., 127, 128, 129, 155, 157,
    159, 431
Golledge, J., 26
Gomillion, S., 429
Gonzalez, C., 259
Goodboy, A. K., 204, 208

Goodlin-Jones, B. L., 222
Goodson, P., 251, 252 *box*
Goodwin, E., 178
Gooper, A., 357
Goossens, L., 38
Gordijn, E. H., 317
Gordon, E. A., 243
Gore, K. E., 175
Gorsky, P., 41, 42
Gota, G., 234, 235
Gothard, S., 372
Gotlib, I. H., 290
Gottman, J. S., 416, 417 *box*
Gottman, John, 3 *box*, 290, 296, 298, 300,
    301, 302, 303, 304, 305, 306, 307, 312,
    320, 415, 416, 417 *box*
Gottman Institute, 303, 304, 305
Gould, R. J., 145
Gouldner, A. W., 146
Gracyalny, M. L., 390, 391, 395
Graham, J. M., 36
Graham, M. L., 94
Graham-Kevan, N., 373, 374, 418
Granger, D. A., 247
Grant, F., 28
Gray, John, 3 *box*, 269 *box*
Graziano, W. G., 72
Green, A. S., 143
Green, E. W., 401, 419
Greenberg, M. A., 433
Greenberger, D., 282
Greene, J. O., 423
Greenfield, P., 33
Greitemeyer, T., 231
Grice, H. P., 349
Griffin, D. W., 277
Griffin, J. J., 40
Griffin-Shelley, E., 357
Griffiths, M. D., 31, 33, 34, 232 *box*
Griffitt, W., 79
Grohskopf, E., 46, 47
Groothof, H. A., 356
Gross, J., 261, 293, 294, 295, 296, 297
Grote, N. K., 207
Grotevant, H. D., 339
Gruenfeld, D. H., 323
Grusec, J. E., 338
Gruzd, A., 33, 35
Grzelak, J., 163
Guacci-Franco, N., 103
Guadagno, R. E., 358
Guastella, A. J., 64
Günther, O., 153 *box*
Gupta, U., 211
Gustilus, C., 418
Guthrie, J., 349, 351

Haas, S. M., 266, 267
Haferkamp, N., 40

Halatsis, P., 269
Hale, J. L., 20, 62, 102, 103, 104, 182, 201,
    315, 388
Halford, W. K., 222
Hall, E. T., 178
Hall, J. A., 240, 317, 323, 332, 333, 334,
    335, 336
Hallett, J. S., 327, 412
Halli, S. S., 279
Halloran, E. C., 340
Halperin, K., 401
Hamadeh, G. N., 152 *box*
Hamel, J., 373
Hamida, S. B., 65
Hamilton, N. F., 150, 172
Hamilton, P. A., 79
Hammen, C., 222
Hammer, J. C., 252 *box*, 253 *box*
Hample, A. D., 126
Hancock, J. T., 40, 41, 143, 276
Hannawa, A. F., 364, 369
Hardie, E., 192
Hardin, J. M., 253 *box*
Hardy, S. A., 26, 39
Hargrow, A. M., 251
Harper, A. M., 131
Harrigan, J. A., 161
Harriman, S., 154
Harris, E., 60
Harris, K. M., 241
Harrison, D., 158
Harry, J., 320
Hart, C. H., 338, 422, 425, 428
Harter, S., 322
Hartill, L., 28
Hartnett, K., 356
Hartwick, J., 81
Harvey, J. H., 309
Hass, A., 1
Hassan, H., 290
Hastall, M. R., 30
Hatch, K. D., 429
Hatfield, Elaine, 2, 70, 71, 122, 147, 149,
    156, 157, 200, 282, 320, 340
Hause, K., 261, 268, 272 *box*
Hause, K. S., 262
Hawley, P. H., 327, 329, 330
Haynes, M. T., 173
Hayward, R. A., 409
Hazan, C., 214, 217, 219, 220, 239
Heavey, C. L., 301, 302, 323, 324
Hebert, S., 429, 433
Hecht, M. L., 27, 28, 37, 212, 213
Heider, F., 4, 309
Heimberg, R. G., 243
Heinemann-LaFave, D., 277
Heino, R., 42
Heldman, C., 229
Helgeson, V. S., 193, 327

Heller, P. E., 388
Heltman, K., 332
Henderson, A. W., 234, 243
Henderson, M., 4, 45, 238, 430, 432
Henderson, M. C., 387
Henderson, S., 146
Hendrick, C., 201, 204, 206, 208, 210, 231,
    430, 431, 432
Hendrick, S. S., 201, 204, 210, 231, 430,
    431, 432
Hendy, H. M., 418
Henley, N. M., 334, 335, 336
Henline, B. H., 357
Henningsen, M. L. M., 11, 280, 282
Henrich, J., 335
Henriksen, R. A. (Jr.), 388
Hensley, W. E., 69
Henton, J. M., 284, 380
Herman, C., 188
Herold, A. L., 331
Herold, E., 239
Herring, S. C., 262
Hertlein, K. M., 357
Herzog, A., 33
Heslin, R., 178, 335
Hess, E. H., 178
Hesse, C., 99, 173
Hesson-McInnis, M. S., 250
Hetsroni, A., 210
Heubeck, B. G., 230
Heudo-Medina, T. B., 431
Hewes, D. E., 94
Hewitt, J., 50
Higgins, J. A., 243
Higgins, R. L., 50
High, A. C., 66
Hilaire, N., 146
Hildebrand, T., 31
Hill, C. T., 74, 132, 410, 411, 412, 427, 429
Hill, J. P., 339
Hillis, J. D., 201
Hinde, R. A., 245
Hines, D. A., 374
Hixon, G., 40
Ho, S., 335
Hochschild, A., 415
Hocker, J. L., 288, 294, 296, 297
Hocking, J. E., 353
Hoekstra, S. J., 225
Hoffman, J. E., 193
Hoffman, M. L., 338
Hoffman, R. K. 229
Hofstede, G., 28 *box*, 91 *box*, 352 *box*
Hogan, T. P., 89
Hogg, M. A., 27, 28
Hoggs, E., 43
Hoier, S., 374
Holland, R. W., 231
Hollenbaugh, E. E., 143 *box*

Holmbeck, G., 339
Holmberg, D., 231, 232, 233
Holmes, J. G., 277
Holtgraves, T., 44, 48
Holtzworth-Munroe, A., 301 *box,* 302, 309, 310
Honeycutt, J. M., 92, 105, 410, 416
Hong, Y., 431
Hoobler, G., 14, 369, 370
Hoobler, G. D., 5
Hoplock, L. B., 191
Hopper, M. L., 175, 176
Horn, D., 144 *box*
Horowitz, L. M., 218, 219
Horrocks, J., 290
Horton, B., 211
Horton, R. S., 75
Hosman, L. A., 146
Howard, J. A., 328, 330
Howard, M. D., 357
Howland, M., 189
Hoyle, R. H., 67, 68
Hoyt, M. F., 164
Hsu, C. W., 33
Huang, L., 335
Hubbard, A. S. E., 159, 388
Huertas, M. L. Z., 82 *box*
Hughes, M., 11, 274
Hughes, P. C., 432
Hughes, S. M., 248
Humphrey, T. P., 248, 249
Hunt, H. M., 230, 243
Hunt, L. L., 66
Hunt, M., 357
Hurd, C., 356
Huston, M., 9, 411, 413
Huston, T. L., 210, 259, 409
Hutchinson, G., 310
Hyde, J. S., 230, 231, 233, 247

Ickes, W., 309, 317
Ifert, D. E., 296
Imahori, T. T., 246
Imber-Black, E., 162
Impett, A., 230
Impett, E. A., 248
Inesi, M. E., 323
Infante, D. A., 310, 311
Inglis, I. R., 88
Inkso, C. A., 67
Inman, C., 193
Ip, S. H. L., 230
Ishii, K., 295
Isnard, C. A., 421
Iverson, A., 202
Iziennicki, H., 234

Jablonsky, N. G., 29
Jackson, D. D., 15–16

Jackson, L. A., 69
Jackson, R. L., 27
Jacob, T., 339
Jacobs, K., 431
Jacobson, J., 233
Jacobson, L., 63
Jacobson, N. S., 302, 309
Jacobson, R. W., 302
Jain, P., 238
James, LeBron, 29
Jang, C., 145, 146
Jang, S. A., 219
Jankowiak, W. R., 210
Janssen, E., 233
Jayamaha, S. D., 330
Jellison, J. M., 45
Jenkins, D. D., 237
Jenkins, S. R., 429
Jennings, G. H., 239
Jensen-Campbell, L. A., 72
Jiang, L. C., 40, 144, 145, 276
Jin, B., 220, 347, 401, 419, 425
Johnson, A. J., 127, 128, 129, 130, 142, 192, 275, 276
Johnson, B. T., 431
Johnson, D. J., 383, 384
Johnson, K. L., 201, 233, 253 *box*
Johnson, L. M., 234
Johnson, M. L., 68, 316
Johnson, M. P., 107, 291, 294, 296, 297, 373, 374, 418
Johnson, S. J., 254
Johnson, S. L., 373
Joinson, A. N., 370 *box,* 399 *box*
Jonas, K., 323
Jonason, P., 229, 230
Jones, J. T., 78
Jones, S. E., 182 *box*
Jones, S. M., 170, 184, 190, 191, 218, 219, 307
Jones, W. H., 346
Jorgensen, P., 181, 329
Joseph, A., 160, 238
Joseph, N., 333
Joshi, K., 67
Jourand, 59, 145, 146
Jozkowski, K. N., 248, 249
Jung, E., 28
Jung, J., 27

Kahneman, D., 39
Kaiser, S. B., 333
Kalbfleisch, P. J., 331
Kalchick, J., 333
Kalmijn, M., 403, 415
Kam, J. A., 28, 350
Kan, M. Y., 320
Kandel, D. B., 74
Kane, H. S., 220, 221, 222

Kanin, E. J., 210
Kark, R., 320
Karney, B. R., 203 *box,* 222, 411, 416
Karpel, M., 156, 161–162
Karraker, A., 412
Kashy, D. A., 349
Kassin, S. M., 309
Katz, J., 396, 398
Katz, J. E., 134 *box*
Kaur, I., 73
Keating, C. F., 332
Keefer, L. A., 89
Keeter, S., 30, 33
Keith, B., 430, 431
Kellerman, J., 175
Kellermann, K. A., 63, 94
Kelley, D., 388, 389, 390, 395, 396
Kelley, D. L., 390, 391, 392, 393, 395, 396
Kelley, H. H., 5, 60–61, 170, 290, 309
Kelley, J. J., 4, 379, 380, 381
Kelley, K., 245
Kelly, A., 62
Kelly, A. E., 163, 164, 165
Kelly, B. C., 234
Kelly, J. R., 230
Kelly, L., 14, 105, 264 *box*
Kelsey, C. M., 30
Keltner, D., 319, 322
Kendrick, W. L., 267
Kennedy, D. R., 346
Kennedy, J. H., 338
Kenny, D. A., 146
Kenrick, D. T., 72, 229
Kerkhof, P., 155, 276
Kerlin, L., 33
Kershaw, K., 219
Kesher, S., 320
Kessler, D., 320
Kessler, R. C., 188, 290
Keyton, J., 250
Khalid, C., 361
Kidwell, J., 339
Kilmann, R. H., 293, 294, 297
Kim, H., 311
Kim, H. J., 354
Kim, J., 34 *box*
Kim, K. I., 281 *box*
Kinder, B. N., 267
King, C. E., 171
King, S. W., 174, 176
Kirby, E., 275
Kirchner, J., 75
Kirk, A., 276
Kirkendol, S. E., 349
Kirkpatrick, L. A., 218
Kisler, T. S., 233
Kissler, T. S., 231, 248
Kito, M., 211 *box*
Kitzmann, K. M., 290

Kiviniemi, M., 321
Klein, R. C. A., 291, 294, 296, 297
Klein, W., 229
Kleinke, C. L., 178
Kline, S. L., 9, 10 *box*, 211, 211 *box*, 278
Klinetob, N. A., 301
Kluwer, E. S., 302
Knapp, J., 419
Knapp, J. L., 98
Knapp, M. L., 3, 42, 71, 113, 116,
    117 *figure*, 118, 122, 126, 175, 418
Knee, C. R., 67, 290
Knight, K., 90, 106, 230
Knobloch, L. K., 86, 88, 88 *box*, 100, 101,
    108, 158, 323
Knobloch-Westerwick, S., 30
Knox, D., 273
Knudsen, K., 340
Ko, S. J., 335
Koch, P. B., 231
Koch, P. T., 316
Koehring, C. L. E., 368
Koenig Kellas, J., 403, 404
Koeppel, L. B., 242
Koerner, A. F., 290, 295
Kooti, F., 78
Koper, R. J., 331
Koralewski, M. A., 240
Korda, M., 336
Korn, M. S., 408
Koroleva, K., 31
Kose, S., 432
Koslowsky, M., 320
Kouros, C. D., 302
Kowalski, R. M., 43
Kowert, R., 220
Kramer, N. C., 40
Krasnova, K., 31, 153 *box*
Kraus, M. W., 319
Kraut, R., 82 *box*
Kreiger, J., 27
Kreiser, P. O., 43
Kret, M. E., 64
Krizek, R. L., 29
Krokoff, L. J., 298
Krueger, R. F., 72
Kruger, D. J., 248
Krusiewicz, E. S., 131
Kubacka, K. E., 155
Kuchinskas, S., 64
Kuczynski, L., 338
Kujath, C. L., 33
Kulberg, G. E., 200
Kunak, J., 37
Kunce, L. J., 218
Kunkel, A., 349, 351
Kunkel, A. W., 192, 208, 210
Kunstman, J. W., 324
Kuperberg, A., 233

Kurdek, L. A., 9, 234, 235, 278, 341, 408,
    409, 410, 412, 413, 429, 430, 433
Kuss, D. J., 31, 33, 34
Kwon, K. H., 82 *box*

LaFong, C., 178
LaFrance, M., 334
Lagro-Janssen, A. L. M., 234
Lahavot, K., 234
Lai, C. H., 92
Laird, J. D., 175
Lakey, S. G., 294
Lamarche, V. M., 429
Lambert, A. N., 432
Lambert, N. M., 232 *box*
Lambert, P., 282
Lamke, L. K., 357
Lammers, J., 316, 317, 323
Lampard, R., 409, 410, 411, 412, 418, 421
Lampe, C., 15 *box*, 33
Lamy, L., 37
Lancaster, A. L., 99
Landau, M. J., 89
Landgraff, C., 220
Landor, A., 238
Landy, D., 71
Lane, B. L., 34
Lane, J. D., 160
Langan, E., 264, 267
Langan, E. J., 219, 220
Langer, E., 16
Langlois, J. H., 70
Langner, C. A., 322
Langwell, L., 82 *box*
Lannutti, P. J., 106, 246, 403
Lansford, J. E., 257
Lapreze, M. W., 250
Larkin, M., 252
Larsen, R. J., 358
Larson, C. E., 3
Larson, K. A., 193
Lasch, C., 33
Latham, K., 412
Latu, I. M., 317
Lauer, S., 320
Laumer, S., 188
Laurenceau, J., 28, 415
Laursen, B., 289
La Valley, A. G., 280, 295, 296
Lavee, Y., 170, 171
Lawrence, K., 231
Layne, C., 302
Lazarus, R. S., 164
Le, B., 381, 408, 413, 416, 418
Lea, M., 9
Leaper, C., 331
Lear, D., 44
Leary, M. R., 43, 46, 346
Leatham, G., 188

Leathers, D. G., 353
Leavitt, C. E., 231
LeBeau, L. S., 317, 334, 335
Leckie, K. R., 357
Ledbetter, A. M., 33, 34, 101, 147, 148 *box*,
    193, 259, 282
Lederer, D. A., 357
Lee, H., 298
Lee, H. E., 281 *box*
Lee, J. A., 197, 203–204, 207, 208,
    209, 214
Lee, J. E. R., 34 *box*
Lee, J. W., 251
Lee, K., 352 *box*
Lee, R. A., 220
Lee, S., 413
Lee, T. R., 170
Lee, W. S., 352 *box*
Lefkowitz, E. S., 231
Lehmiller, J. J., 230
LeMay, E. P., 63
Lenhart, A., 14, 15, 15 *box*, 33, 238, 267
Lenney, E., 200
Leonard, K. E., 221, 309
Leone, J. M., 373, 374, 418
Le Poire, B. A., 72, 218, 225, 327, 412
LePore, S. J., 327
Lepore, S. L., 433
Lerma, M., 70
Leung, K., 281 *box*
Levenson, R. W., 301, 415, 416
Levine, A., 64, 207, 208, 209, 210, 211, 330
Levine, L. A., 408
Levine, T. R., 204, 274, 328, 349, 354, 355,
    386, 387
Levinson, S., 26, 41, 46, 47, 48, 49, 50
Levitt, M. J., 103, 104
Lewandowski, G. W., 37, 430
Lewin-Epstein, N., 339
Lewinsohn, P. M., 432
Lewis, C. C., 349, 352 *box*
Lewis, J., 175
Lewis, K., 246, 248
Lewis, M., 337
Lewis-Smith, J., 28
Lillard, L. L., 278
Lim, V. R., 301 *box*
Lin, Z., 82 *box*
Linder, D., 73
Lindley, L. L., 253 *box*
Lipetz, M. E., 81
Lipkus, I., 305
Lipsitz, G., 29
Lisitsa, E., 303, 304, 305
Littig, L. W., 248
Little, A. C., 68
Liu, J. H., 28
Lively, K. J., 319
Lloyd, S., 261, 372

Lloyd, S. A., 284, 289, 290, 310, 380, 416
LoBello, S., 193
LoBello, S. G., 193
Lockley, E., 264 *box*
Long, B., 334
Long, E., 231, 284
Lorberbaum, J. P., 432
Lord, C. G., 408
Louiselle, P. A., 338
Loveless, S. C., 103
Lucchetti, A. N., 355
Luchies, L. B., 66
Luder, M. T., 232 *box*
Luo, S., 220
Lustig, M. W., 422, 425, 427
Lydon, J. E., 225, 383, 397
Lykins, A. D., 233
Lynch, J. M., 320
Lyonette, C., 320

Maccoby, E. E., 431
MacDonald, T., 229
MacGavin, L., 331
MacGeorge, E. L., 184, 185
MacGregor, J. C. D., 324
Machung, A., 415
MacNeil, S., 243
Madathil, J., 201
Madden, M., 33
Madon, S., 335
Magee, J. C., 317, 323
Magno, G., 78
Magsamen-Conrad, K., 100
Maguire, K. C., 277
Mahaffey, A. L., 333
Maher, M. L., 63
Maier, C., 188
Maier, R. A., 66
Maisel, N. C., 189
Maitland, S. B., 239
Major, B., 335
Makstaller, D. C., 118
Malachowski, C. C., 108, 356
Malamuth, N. M., 302
Mallinckrodt, B., 219
Manasse, S. M., 232 *box*
Mancini, J.A., 170
Maner, J. K., 324
Manke, M., 212
Mannino, C. A., 340
Mansfield, P. K., 231
Manzi, C., 26
Marano, H. E., 3 *box*
Marazziti, D., 64
Marek, C. I., 98
Margolis, J. D., 322
Margulis, S. T., 144
Markman, H. J., 277, 278, 410, 415
Marks, M. A., 250

Marmo, J., 120, 262, 263
Marshall, L. L., 372
Marshall, T. C., 220
Marston, P. J., 212, 213
Martin, J. N., 29, 171
Martz, J., 381, 382
Marwick, A., 300
Mashek, D., 37, 170
Masheter, C., 403
Massey-Abernathy, A., 327
Mast, M. S., 316, 317, 319, 323, 332, 334, 336
Matthews, S., 381
Matthews, T. L., 234
Maxwell, J.W., 170
May, J. L., 79
Mayback, K. L., 66
Mayo, C., 334
Mays, V. M., 234
Mazaheri, M. A., 218
Mazer, J. P., 140
Mazur, M., 127
Mazur, M. A., 159
McAdams, D. P., 1, 316, 322
McBride, M. C., 275, 400
McCabe, J., 234
McCabe, M. P., 192
McCain, T. A., 58
McCarthy, C. J., 429
McClanahan, K., 200
McCornack, S. A., 349, 354, 355
McCraken, A. A., 401, 419
McCroskey, J. C., 3, 58
McCullough, M. E., 389, 393
McDaniel, E. R., 182 *box*
McDaniel, M. A., 396
McDaniel, S., 212
McDonald, G., 432
McDonald, G. W., 320
McEwan, B., 113, 115, 116, 144 *box*, 218, 373
McFarlane, M., 231
McGinty, K., 273, 274
McGoldrick, M., 154
McGonagle, K. A., 290
McKenna, K. Y. A., 143, 147
McKillop, K., 163
McKillop, K. J., 164, 165
McKinney, K., 230, 235, 236, 237, 239, 242, 356, 358
McLaren, R. M., 100, 101, 151, 347
McLaughlin, C., 105
McLeod, B. A., 354, 355
McLeod, K., 418
McIlvane, J. M., 415
McQuinn, R. D., 416
Mealy, M., 351
Meana, M., 231, 232
Meehus, M. H. J., 336

Meeker, F. B., 178
Meeus, W., 29, 163
Mehrabian, A., 176, 334
Mejia, R., 334
Melby, C., 242, 269
Meloy, J. R., 372
Mendelson, M. J., 66
Mendes, M., 210
Mendoza, J. P., 233
Menegatti, M. R., 422
Menzies-Toman, D. A., 383, 397
Merighi, J. R., 210
Merolla, A., 275, 276, 277, 386
Merolla, A. J., 381
Merriwether, A., 237
Merton, R. K., 39
Mesch, G. S., 142
Messman, S. J., 261, 271, 272 *box*, 281
Meston, C. M., 242
Metts, S., 45, 46, 47, 49 *figure*, 50, 51, 51 *figure*, 52, 105, 128, 144, 184, 229, 231, 245, 246, 247, 250, 346, 350, 351, 360, 369, 388, 389, 392, 409, 411, 412, 421, 422, 424, 426, 428, 429
Metzger, N. J., 149
Meurling, C. N., 193
Meyers, S. A., 202
Mickelson, Phil, 29
Mikkelson, A. C., 173
Mikulincer, M., 218
Millar, F. E., 330, 331
Miller, A. J., 396
Miller, A. L., 222
Miller, C. W., 310, 347
Miller, G. R., 3, 4, 327, 328, 329
Miller, L. C., 144
Miller, L. E., 155
Miller, R. S., 51, 411
Miller-Ott, A., 62, 105, 264 *box*
Millevoi, A., 358
Mills, R. S. L., 347, 348, 349
Mineka, S., 65
Mirenberg, M. C., 78
Mischel, M. H., 89
Misukanis, T. M., 338
Mitchell, P. B., 64
Moeller, S. K., 323
Moller, N. P., 429
Mollin, D., 218
Monahan, J. L., 246
Monakes, S., 388
Mongeau, P. A., 11, 106, 107, 128, 201, 229, 230, 233, 235, 253 *box*, 273, 388, 390, 391, 392
Moniz, A. J., 67
Monroe, S. M., 432
Monsour, M., 174, 193, 268
Montagne-Miller, Y., 242

Montagu, A., 7
Montesi, J. L., 243
Montgomery, B. M., 130, 140, 177
Montoya, R. M., 75
Moon, S.-I., 82 *box*
Moore, D. C., 34 *box*
Moore, L., 2
Moore, M. M., 240
Moore, N., 243
Moore, S., 252 *box*
Moore, Z. T., 233
Morales-Aleman, M. M., 326
Moreira, J., 210
Morey, J. N., 220
Morf, C. C., 60, 68
Morgan, E. M., 326, 328
Morman, M. T., 171, 172, 174, 175
Morr, M. C., 107, 172, 230
Morris, D., 247, 333
Morrison, J. H. T. A., 259
Morrison, K., 11
Morrison, R. L., 294
Morrison, T. L., 222
Morrow, G. D., 384
Morr Serewicz, M. C., 259
Morry, M. M., 75
Morse, C. R., 98, 389, 392
Mosher, W. D., 28
Mother Teresa, 319
Motley, M. T., 246, 249
Moutabi, F., 218
Mouton, J. S., 290, 291, 294, 297
Moyer-Guse, E., 238
Muehlenhard, C. L., 107, 240, 248–249, 250
Mueller, R. A., 338
Muise, A., 15 *box*, 248, 360, 361
Mullanax, M., 243
Mullen, C., 150
Mullen, P. E., 361, 363, 372
Mullet, E., 396
Mullett, J., 350
Munn, P., 289
Muraven, M. B., 43
Murnan, S. K., 248
Murphy, R., 48
Murphy, R. E., 140
Murray, S. L., 277, 355, 413, 429
Murstein, B. I., 210
Muscanell, N., 361
Musto, A. A., 408
Mutsaers, W., 280, 282, 283
Myers, J. E., 201
Myers, S. A., 171, 208, 381

Nachshon, O., 218
Najib, A., 432
Nakayama, T. K., 29
Nanin, J. E., 234
Napper, S., 234

Nazar, J., 347
Neff, K. D., 322, 323
Negash, S., 232 *box*, 411
Negel, L., 346
Neighbors, C., 290
Nell, K., 70
Nelson, D. W., 193
Nelson, E. S., 250, 357
Nelson, J. A., 388
Neto, F., 210
Neumark-Sztainer, D., 230
Newcomb, M. D., 411, 412
Newcomb, T. M., 74, 80, 81
Newton, 91, 174
Ng, P., 418
Nicastle, L. D., 358
Nicholson, J., 127
Niehuis, S., 413, 414 *box*
Nixon, C., 238
Noar, S. M., 252
Nock, S. L., 278, 279
Noller, P., 220, 222, 301 *box*
Notaru, P. C., 222
Novak, S. A., 327
Nowlin, R. B., 429

Oakes, P., 27
Oberhauser, A. M., 220
O'Connell-Corcoran, K., 219
Ogolsy, B. G., 259, 260
O'Hair, D., 397, 398, 399, 400
O'Hair, D. H., 42, 242, 349, 350
Oishi, S., 204
Oldmeadow, J. A., 220
O'Leary, K. D., 298
Oliveira, M. J. D., 82 *box*
Oliver, D. F., 45
Olmstead, G., 350
Olmstead, S. B., 232 *box*
Olson, D. E., 250
Olson, L., 162
Olson, L. N., 302, 373
Oman, K., 144 *box*
O'Mara, J., 357
O'Meara, J. D., 97, 268, 270, 271
Ompad, D. C., 248
Orbe, M. P., 29
Orbuch, T. L., 290, 415
O' Reilly, L., 267
Orgilés, M., 431
Orrell-Valente, J. K., 232 *box*
Orzechowicz, D., 60
Ostrov, J. M., 319, 320, 335
O'Sullivan, L. F., 143 *box*, 229, 241, 242, 248, 249, 250
Otten, S., 317
Overall, N. C., 328, 330
Owen, J., 229
Owen, W. F., 171, 210, 413, 429

Pachankis, J. E., 234
Padgett, J. E., 233
Paikoff, R. L., 289, 339
Palamar, J. J., 248
Palevitz, C. E., 321
Palmer, M. T., 175
Palomares, N. A., 158, 159, 331
Pan, S., 231
Papa, M. J., 297
Pape, K. T., 418
Papini, D. R., 339
Papp, L. M., 302, 423 *box*
Paris, M., 36
Park, C. L., 106
Park, E. A., 34 *box*
Park, H. J., 281 *box*
Park, H. S., 204
Park, H. W., 281 *box*
Park, L. E., 429, 430
Park, S. G., 34 *box*
Parker, B. L., 409, 411, 415
Parker, R., 360
Parkes, A., 238
Parks, M. R., 145, 156, 170, 193, 268, 354
Parry, D., 330
Parsons, J. T., 234, 235
Pasley, K., 411
Pathe, M., 372
Patrick, H., 290
Patterson, B., 397, 398, 399, 400
Pauley, P. M., 173
Paulhus, D. L., 60
Pavitt, C., 94
Paxman, C. G., 368
Pearce, Z., 222
Pearson, J., 259
Pearson, T. A., 412, 415
Pederson, J. R., 151
Pelham, B. W., 78
Pempek, T. A., 399 *box*
Peña, J., 263
Peña, J. F., 220
Pendell, S. D., 171, 172, 174, 175
Pennebaker, J. W., 163, 192, 433
Pennington, J., 44, 48
Peplau, L. A., 6, 7, 9, 74, 193, 230, 233, 234, 320, 327, 328, 329, 331
Pereira, C. R., 204
Perilloux, C., 63, 429, 430, 432
Perot, A., 248
Perras, M. T., 422, 425, 427
Perrin, A., 321 *box*
Perry-Jenkins, M., 341
Peter, J., 92, 145
Peterson, B., 397
Peterson, C. C., 280
Peterson, Z. D., 248, 249
Petra, K., 52
Petra, R., 52

Petronio, S., 122, 140, 144, 149, 150 *figure*, 151, 154, 164, 165
Pettigrew, J., 143 *box*
Petty, K. N., 67
Pfiester, A., 397, 401, 425, 426
Pfouts, J. H., 382
Pfyl, J., 423 *box*
Phillips, G. M., 149
Phillips, M., 231, 370 *box*
Philpott, J., 424, 432
Pierce, C. A., 69
Pierce, T., 225
Piercy, C. W., 34
Piercy, F. P., 357
Piliavin, J., 73
Pines, A., 65, 202, 363
Pinsky, D., 60
Pistole, M. C., 218, 219
Pittinger, M. J., 233
Pittman, G., 126
Planalp, S., 92, 105
Polcar, L. E., 218
Polimeni, A., 192
Polk, D., 212, 213
Pomerantz-Zorin, L., 320
Poole, L. L., 259
Poortmann, A. R., 415
Popadiuk, N., 429, 433
Postmes, T., 82 *box*
Poushter, J., 321 *box*
Powell, B., 319
Powell, L. A., 281 *box*
Powers, W. G., 8, 412
Prager, K. J., 171, 174, 176, 177
Pralong, F., 322
Predmore, S., 40
Previti, D., 408, 409 *box*, 410, 411, 412, 413, 415, 418
Priem, J. S., 100
Proske, C., 253
Proxmire, William, 2
Pruitt, D. G., 291, 294, 296, 297
Puentes, J., 229
Pujazon-Zazik, M. A., 232 *box*
Pukall, C. F., 275
Putnam, L. L., 290, 291, 296

Quandt, J., 264
Quinn, K., 31
Quinn, S., 220
Quirk, K., 89
Qureshi, C., 60

Raacke, J., 33
Rabby, M. K., 263, 264
Rachal, K. C., 389
Ragsdale, J. D., 384, 385, 386, 387
Rahim, M. A., 290, 291, 294
Rahm, K. B., 184

Rai, S. N., 67
Rains, S. A., 34, 144 *box*
Ramesh, C. N., 354
Ramirez, A., 95 *box*, 98, 103, 107, 108, 118, 259, 273
Ranby, K. W., 327
Rancer, A. S., 310
Rankin, C. T., 278
Rapson, R. L., 340
Rasberry, C. N., 251, 252 *box*
Ratcliffe, S. J., 326
Rauscher, E. A., 99
Rawlins, W. K., 131, 134–135, 193, 268
Ray, G. B., 171, 175, 177, 178, 179
Ray, G. E., 193
Read, S. J., 39, 215, 220
Record, R. A., 38
Redmond, M. V., 91
Reece, M. M., 178
Reed, P. J., 153 *box*
Reeder, H., 212, 249, 273
Reeder, H. M., 246
Reel, B. W., 254
Reese-Weber, S., 290
Regalia, C., 26
Regan, P. C., 228, 230, 231, 233, 235, 236, 237, 239, 243, 244, 245, 252 *box*, 369
Reganis, P., 154
Rehman, U. S., 301 *box*
Reichert, T., 365
Reid, J. A., 229
Reierson, J., 151
Reijntjes, A., 429
Reilly, M. E., 320
Reined, C., 231
Reinisch, J. M., 234, 235
Reis, H. T., 67, 113, 203 *box*, 413
Reissing, E. D., 229
Reissman, C., 259
Reiter, R. L., 367
Remland, M. S., 334
Renfro, A., 31, 32, 33
Resi, H. T., 115 *box*
Reske, J. R., 275, 276
Resnick, M. D., 230
Reyes, M., 58, 71
Reynolds, R., 63
Rhatigan, D. L., 417, 418
Rhoades, G. K., 277, 278, 413
Rhoads, 410
Rhodes, W. S., 218
Rhodewalt, F., 60, 68
Rholes, W. S., 220
Ribeau, S., 27
Richard, F. D., 408
Richmond, L. S., 408
Rickart, V. I., 323
Ridley, C., 302
Riela, S., 202

Riggio, R. E., 72
Rindfuss, R., 278
Rink, F., 316
Riordan, C. A., 80
Rittenour, C. E., 171
Rivera, J., 72
Rivera, K. D., 42
Robb, A., 349
Robbins, S., 100, 158
Robers, T., 212
Roberson, B. F., 73
Roberto, A., 230
Roberts, J. B., 126
Roberts, Julia, 374
Roberts, L. J., 174, 176, 309
Roberts, M. K., 198
Roberts, N., 220
Robinson, K. J., 191
Robinson, M. D., 323
Robinson, T., 40
Robnett, R. D., 331
Rodin, J., 361, 363, 365
Rodrigues, G., 202
Rodriguez, D., 329
Roesch, S., 246
Roese, N. J., 233
Rogee, R. D., 413
Rogers, E. M., 239
Rogers, L. A., 330, 331
Rogers, M. A., 330
Rohde, P., 432
Rohlfing, M. E., 9, 277
Rohmann, E., 210
Rohrbaugh, J. B., 372
Roiger, J. F., 339
Rolker-Dolinsky, B., 245
Rollie, S., 418, 419, 420
Rollin, E., 218
Roloff, M. E., 103, 295, 296, 297, 310, 317, 323, 327, 347, 384, 385, 386, 397, 419
Roosa, M. W., 235, 236
Roscoe, B., 346, 357
Rose, S. M., 267
Rosenblum, L. A., 337
Rosenfeld, L. B., 140, 156, 267
Rosenfeld, M. J., 202
Rosenthal, A. M., 233, 253
Rosenthal, D., 252 *box*
Rosenthal, R., 63, 354
Ross, M., 281
Rossetto, K., 397, 401, 419, 428
Rossetto, K. R., 401
Rotaru, T., 14
Rothschild, Z. K., 89
Rouse, C., 422, 425, 426
Rowatt, W. C., 143, 355
Roy, A. K., 298
Rubin, R. B., 124, 171
Rubin, Z., 4, 74, 198

Rubini, M., 422
Rubinstein, D., 243
Ruble, D. H., 39
Rubovits, P. C., 63
Rucker, D. D., 323
Rudd, J. E., 310
Ruesch, J., 8
Ruppel, E. K., 143 *box*
Rusbult, C. E., 305, 306, 379, 380, 381,
    382, 383, 384, 386, 411
Russell, Bertrand, 315
Russell, J. A., 198
Rutstein, J., 80
Ryckman, R. M., 200
Ryff, C. D., 2

Sabourin, T. C., 310
Sacks, D., 43
Sadalla, E. K., 72
Sadeghi, M. A., 218
Sadler, M. S., 335
Safford, S., 225
Saffrey, C., 419, 429, 432
Safron, A., 233
Safron, C., 409, 412, 413
Sagarin, B. J., 358, 360
Sagrestano, L. M., 301, 302, 323, 328, 330
Sahlstein, E., 277
Sahlstein, E. M., 264
Salovey, P., 358, 360, 361, 363, 365
Salt, R. E., 171
Samp, J., 317, 321, 340
Samp, J. A., 323
Samter, W., 190, 192, 360, 383
Sanchez, D. T., 429
Sanderson, C. A., 184
Santagata, R., 301 *box*
Sargent, J., 154
Sarmento, P., 210
Savin-Williams, R. C., 236
Scabini, E., 26
Scardino, T. J., 107
Schachter, S., 80
Schäfer, T., 77
Scharfe, E., 387
Scheck, S., 210
Scheflen, A. E., 240, 241, 334
Scheidt, L. A., 262
Schenck-Hamlin, W., 327, 328, 329, 330
Scherer, K. R., 179, 335
Schlenker, B. R., 26, 35, 38, 39, 42, 43, 44,
    45, 46, 48, 52, 389
Schmeeckle, M., 322
Schmidt, L., 73
Schmitt, D. P., 65
Schmookler, T., 233
Schmukle, S. C., 60
Schneider, D. J., 160
Schneider, F. W., 178

Schneider, K. T., 251
Schoenebeck, S. Y., 119
Schrodt, P., 159, 324, 415, 431
Schulz, B. E., 390, 391
Schutz, W. C., 7, 8
Schwartz, I., 164
Schwartz, P., 9, 234, 235, 243, 320, 328,
    340, 356, 408, 409, 410, 412, 414
Schwartz, R., 264 *box*
Schwarz, N., 257
Schwarzwald, J., 320
Schweinle, W. E., 309
Scissors, L. E., 299 *box*
Scobie, E. D., 393
Scobie, G. E., 393
Scott, G. G., 82 *box*
Scott, L., 175
Scott, M. D., 8, 412
Scott, 278
Scott-Sheldon, L. A. J., 253 *box*
Sears, D. O., 72
Sebby, R. A., 339
Seeley, J. R., 432
Segrin, C., 8, 257, 430, 431
Sehnder, C., 322
Seiffge-Krenke, I., 40
Seiter, J. S., 351, 352 *box*, 354
Semmelroth, J., 358
Sen, A., 409
Senchak, M., 221
Sereno, K. K., 174, 176
Screwicz, M. C. M., 11, 107, 280
Shackelford, T. K., 231, 333, 356, 357, 358,
    374, 411
Shakespeare, William, 41
Shannon, E. A., 310
Sharabany, R., 193
Sharma, V., 73
Sharp, L. K., 192
Sharpsteen, D. J., 218, 363
Shaver, P., 214, 217, 219, 220, 239
Shaver, P. R., 113, 193, 215, 218
Shaw, C., 106, 230
Shea, B. C., 259
Shechory, M., 341
Sheets, V. L., 360
Shelton, J. N., 115
Shen, L., 327
Shen, P. D., 432
Shenk, J. L., 302, 415
Shepard, C., 218
Sheppard, B. M., 81
Sheppard, V. J., 357
Sherman, M. A., 1
Sherman, R. A., 229
Sherrod, D., 267
Shimkowski, J. R., 324
Shotland, R. L., 269
Showers, C. J., 78, 79

Shrout, P. E., 188
Shuster, P. L., 161
Sias, P. M., 81, 119
Sibley, C. G., 328
Sibona, C., 423 *box*
Sicoly, F., 281
Siebold, D., 327
Sigall, H., 71
Sigert, J. R., 290
Sillars, A., 309, 431
Sillars, A. L., 289, 290, 291, 295, 296, 297,
    298, 330
Silva, S., 210
Silver, R. L., 163
Silvera, D. H., 253
Silverberg, S. B., 338
Silverman, J., 372
Silvestri, S., 64
Simmons, K. B., 175
Simon, E. P., 218, 220
Simon, P. J., 323
Simonds, C. J., 140
Simoni, J. M., 234
Simons, L. G., 238
Simons, R. L., 238
Simpson, J. A., 70, 218, 220, 238, 239, 328,
    411, 429
Singer, B. H., 2
Singh, 15, 75
Singh, D., 69
Singh, P., 211
Sleight, C., 311
Sline, R., 127
Slosnerick, M., 356
Slotter, E. B., 433
Slovic, P., 39
Slovik, L., 305
Smith, D. A., 298, 301, 306
Smith, E., 382
Smith, G., 81
Smith, G. T., 237
Smith, J. C. S., 335
Smith, K., 15 *box*
Smith, M., 43
Smith-Lovin, L., 40
Smollan, D., 36
Smutzler, N., 302, 310
Snow, D. A., 44
Snyder, M., 63, 321
Solomon, D. H., 86, 88 *box*, 100, 101, 321,
    323, 340, 347
Somera, L., 311
Sorensen, R. C., 236
Soule, K. P., 323
Spalding, L. R., 9
Spears, R., 9
Speilmann, S. S., 432
Sperling, M. B., 67
Spiegel, D., 163

Spiekermann, S., 31
Spiro, E. S., 153 *box*
Spitzberg, B. H., 14, 42, 179, 246, 293, 295, 296, 329, 345, 356, 365, 369, 370, 371, 372, 399
Sprecher, S., 65, 68, 70, 72, 146, 200, 203 *box*, 209, 210, 211, 230, 231, 235, 236, 237, 239, 242, 243, 244, 252 *box*, 282, 319, 322, 356, 358, 369, 409, 416, 425, 428, 429
Sprenkle, D. H., 382
Springer, C., 346
Springer, K. W., 257
Stafford, L., 258, 259, 262, 265, 266, 267, 275, 276, 277, 278, 280, 281, 282
Stamp, G. H., 290
Standfeld, S., 2
Stangor, C., 39
Stanley, S. M., 277, 278, 410
Staple, D. A., 323
Starcher, S. C., 150
Stark, P. B., 311
Stassen-Ferrara, H. M., 259
Steelman, L. C., 319
Steers, MLN, 34
Stefanone, M. A., 82 *box*, 145, 146
Steil, L. K., 311, 339, 340
Steinberg, L. D., 338, 339
Steinberg, M., 4
Steinbugler, A. C., 37
Steinfield, C., 15 *box*
Steinmetz, S. K., 338
Stelzner, M. A., 179
Stephan, C. W., 239
Stephan, W., 351
Stern, L. A., 102
Sternberg, D. P., 178
Sternberg, R. J., 176, 197, 198, 199, 200, 201, 202, 207, 413, 433
Steuber, K. R., 101, 158
Stevens, D. C., 395
Stier, D. S., 335
Stier, H., 339
Stiff, J. B., 311, 354
Stiles, W. B., 161
Stillman, T. F., 232 *box*
Stillwell, A. M., 43, 368
Sting, 208
Stoker, J. I., 316
Stokes, J. P., 124, 140, 142
Stokes, R., 50
Stone, E. A., 231
Stoner, M., 353
Stones, M. H., 163
Straus, M. A., 372
Strauss, G. P., 233
Street, A., 396
Street, A. E., 417, 418
Strelan, P., 340

Strong, S. R., 78
Struckman-Johnson, C., 248, 249, 250
Struckman-Johnson, D., 248, 249, 250
Strzyzewski, K. D., 354
Stuart, G. L., 302
Subrahmanyam, K., 33
Sue, S., 153 *box*
Suhr, J. A., 184
Suizzo, M. A., 323
Sullivan, C. M., 326
Sullivan, D., 89
Sulsky, L. M., 393
Sunnafrank, M., 71, 74, 95 *box*, 97, 98, 107, 118
Surra, C. A., 210, 397
Suter, E. A., 132
Sutton, P. D., 257
Suzuki, N., 281 *box*
Swan, S., 251
Swan, S. C., 250
Swann, W. B., 39, 40, 45, 253, 413
Sweeney, B. N., 233
Swift, Taylor, 368
Sylva, D., 233

Tafoya, M. A., 173, 289, 356
Tagawa, N., 204
Tai, Y. T., 33
Takhteyev, Y., 33, 35
Tangney, J. P., 37
Tanis, M., 34 *box*
Tanke, E. D., 63
Tannen, D., 269 *box*
Taraban, C. B., 204, 209
Tardy, C. H., 59 *box*, 146
Tashiro, T., 433
Taylor, D. A., 4, 113, 116, 118, 120, 140, 141, 145, 146
Taylor, M. E., 431
Taylor, P., 30, 33
Taylor, S. E., 2
Teachman, J. D., 278
Tedeschi, J. T., 45, 80
Teitelman, A. M., 326
Tejada-Vera, B., 257
Terry, D. J., 253, 254
Tesser, A., 421
Thagaard, T., 340
Theil-Stern, S., 238
Theiss, J. A., 100, 101, 243
Thelwall, M., 35
Therrien, L. F., 107
Theune, K. E., 71
Thibaut, J. W., 4, 379, 380, 381
Thieme, A., 422, 425, 426
Thomas, K. W., 293, 297
Thomas, R., 202
Thomas, S. J., 416
Thompson, L., 340

Thompson, T. L., 254
Thorton, A., 278
Thurau, D., 231
Tice, D. M., 43
Tidwell, L. C., 75, 145
Tiedens, L. Z., 322, 334
Tillman, K., 234
Tilton-Weaver, L., 158
Timmerman, L., 264, 331, 332
Tingle, L. R., 201
Ting-Toomey, S., 352 *box*
Tobin, E., 350
Todd, M. J., 198, 346
Tokunaga, R. S., 34, 35, 423 *box*
Tolhuizen, J. H., 120, 121 *box*, 210
Tolstedt, B. E., 124, 140, 142
Toma, C. L., 34, 41, 42, 143
Tong, S. T., 82 *box*, 95 *box*, 399 *box*, 424
Tooke, W., 355
Tornblom, K. Y., 380
Toro-Morn, M., 210, 211
Tracy, J. L., 335
Tracy, S. J., 42
Trail, T. E., 115
Traupmann, J., 280, 282
Treger, S., 146, 237
Trethewey, A., 42
Triandis, H. C., 352 *box*
Trost, M. R., 231, 358, 363
Troy, B. A., 28
Trussell, J., 243
Tsai, C. W., 432
Tucker, J. S., 218, 219
Turban, D. B., 250
Turner, L. H., 92
Turner, R. E., 350
Tusing, K. J., 335
Tutzauer, F., 295
Tvesky, A., 39
Twenge, J. M., 30, 229, 232, 235, 257
Twohig, M. P., 232 *box*
Tyler, W. J. C., 99

Underwood, J. D., 33
Urquiza, A. J., 222
Urrutia, I. C., 351
Utz, S., 34 *box*, 40, 42, 361

Valkenburg, P. M., 92, 145
Vallade, J. I., 347
VanDellen, M. R., 327
VandenHeuvel, A., 278
VanderDrift, L. E., 230, 410, 413, 419
Van Der Heide, B., 82 *box*
Van Dijk, E., 319
Vangelisti, A. L., 42, 72, 113, 116, 117 *figure*, 118, 122, 126, 155, 156, 163, 259, 290, 295, 302, 347, 348, 349, 418, 429
Van Hasselt, V. B., 294

Van Horn, K. R., 275, 277
Van Lange, P. A. M., 383, 384
Vanni, D., 429
Van Rosmalen-Nooijens, K. A. W. L., 234
Van Straaten, I., 231, 233
Vasilenko, S. A., 231
Vasiljevic, M., 340
Vaughn, D., 409, 419, 420, 421
Vazsonyi, A. T., 237
Vedes, A., 204, 207, 209
Veksler, A. E., 261
Veltri, N. F., 153 box
Verette, J., 379, 384
Vergeer, C. M., 234
Vermeulen, I., 34 box
Vermulst, A. A., 162
Veroff, J., 290
Verrette, J., 305
Vershure, B., 72
Vietor, N. A., 290
Vignoles, L., 26, 35, 39, 45
Villagran, M., 127
Villagran, P., 127
Vinsel, A., 159
Virchota, D. A., 91
Vitak, J., 105, 276
Vivian, D., 298
Vogel, D. L., 335, 429
Vogl-Bauer, S., 72
Vogler, C., 320, 340
Vohs, K. D., 231, 232
Vorrell, M., 273
Vrangalova, Z., 236, 239
Vrij, A., 350
Vyse, S. A., 210

Wabnik, A. I., 259
Waddoups, S. L., 412
Wade, L., 229
Waerness, K., 340
Waite, L. J., 278
Walczak, S., 423 box
Waldron, V. R., 390, 391, 392, 393, 395, 396
Walgren, K., 2
Walker, A. J., 340
Walker, L. E., 374
Wall, S., 214
Wallace, H., 372
Wallace, L. A., 262
Wallpe, K., 146
Walsh, R., 236
Walsh-Buhi, E. R., 231
Walster, E., 73, 76, 280, 281, 282, 283
Walster, E. H., 4, 70, 73
Walster, G. W., 76, 280, 281, 282, 283
Walther, J. B., 26, 42, 82 box, 95 box, 108, 145, 186 box, 264, 399 box, 424
Waltz, J., 302
Wang, C. C., 33

Wang, H., 40
Wang, L., 429, 432
Wang, S. S., 82 box
Wang, Z., 108
Wanzer, M. B., 98
Warber, K. M., 117, 118
Ward, D. E., 433
Ward, L. M., 237
Warren, C., 239
Warren, J., 27
Warshaw, P. R., 81
Waters, E., 214
Waters, L. L., 352 box
Watson, K. W., 311
Watzlawick, P., 15–16, 18, 19, 301
Webb, L., 66
Weber, G. R., 229
Weber, I., 78, 125
Weber, K. D., 381
Webster, G. D., 333
Weger, H., 218, 230, 233, 270
Wegner, D. M., 155, 160, 161, 163
Weick, M., 340
Weigel, D. J., 171, 259, 260, 266, 281
Weigold, M. F., 44, 48, 52
Weinbach, R., 356
Weinberg, M. A., 234
Weiner, J. L., 98, 176, 253, 356
Weir, T., 158
Weis, D. L., 356
Weisskirch, R. S., 43, 220
Weitzel, T., 188
Welch, S. A., 124
Weller, A., 64
Wellman, B., 33, 35
Wells, B. E., 229, 232, 235
Wentland, J. J., 229
Werking, K., 268, 270
Werking, K. J., 192
Werner, C. M., 131 figure
West, D. V., 122
West, L., 131
West, S. G., 72
West, T. V., 115
Westen, D., 358
Westerman, C. Y. K., 281 box, 283
Westerman, D., 220
Wexler, P., 282
Wheeless, L. R., 245 box
Wheeless, V. E., 245 box
Wheldon, C., 231
White, G. L., 80, 361, 363, 365
White, T. L., 160
Whiteman, S. D., 337
Whiting, J. B., 357
Whitman, R. N., 178
Whitney, G. A., 305
Whitson, J. A., 323
Whitty, M. T., 41, 42

Wiederman, M. W., 356, 358
Wiedmair, B., 230
Wiedmair, B. J., 229
Wiemann, J. M., 332
Wieselquist, J., 306
Wiggins, J. D., 357
Wiggins, R. D., 320
Wight, D., 238
Wildermuth, S. M., 72
Wildschut, T., 384
Wilkins, R., 211 box
Willetts, M. C., 230, 233, 235, 253
Williams, A., 30, 31, 32
Williams, J., 106, 230
Williams, M. J., 322, 334
Williams, S., 9, 28, 412
Williams, Serena, 29
Willitts, M., 2
Willoughby, B. J., 277, 278, 279, 397
Wilmot, W. W., 8–9, 20, 45, 89, 96, 97, 122, 155, 243, 288, 294, 296, 395, 421, 422, 425, 429, 432, 433
Wilmott, 297
Wilson, A. E., 432
Wilson, C. E., 290, 291, 296
Wilson, C. L., 238
Wilson, J., 419
Wilson, P., 249
Wilson, S. E., 412
Wineberg, H., 397
Wing, E., 2
Winke, T., 291
Winstead, B. A., 158
Winterheld, H. A., 238
Winters, L. C., 177, 178
Wirtz, D., 204
Wirtz, J. G., 192
Wiseman, J. P., 346
Wiseman, R. L., 327, 328, 329, 330
Witt, P. L., 324
Witteman, H., 340
Wittenberg, E., 127
Wittenberg, M. T., 113
Wittenberg, W., 115 box
Wittenman, 85, 81
Wittig, B. A., 214, 216
Wolf, N. R., 63
Wolfinger, N. H., 431
Wondra, D. J., 146
Wood, B., 388
Wood, J. T., 9, 12, 192, 269 box, 374
Woods, J. T., 131
Worley, T. R., 317, 340
Worthington, E. L., 389
Worthington, E. L., Jr., 396
Wortman, C. B., 164
Wotipka, C. D., 66
Wotman, S. R., 368
Wozniak, P., 338

Wrape, E. R., 429
Wright, C. N., 2, 103
Wright, E., 262
Wright, K. B., 263
Wright, P. H., 267
Wright, R. A., 73
Wyden, P., 300
Wyer, M. M., 349
Wyer, R. S., 298
Wygant, K., 350

Xu, F., 352 *box*
Xu, X., 202

Yang, J., 48
Yashida, T., 204

Yates, S. J., 264 *box*
Yelsma, P., 278
Yermolayeva, V. A., 399 *box*
Yildirim, F. B., 429, 430, 432
Yin, L., 264 *box*
Yingling, J., 337
Yodanis, C., 320
Yoshimura, S. M., 356, 363
Young, K. S., 357
Young, L. R., 66
Young, S. L., 319, 347, 368, 369, 397
Young, S. M., 60
Yovetich, N. A., 384

Zagoory-Sharon, O., 64
Zane, N., 153 *box*

Zeeman, E. C., 421
Zeifman, D., 239
Zeki, S., 64
Zelley, E., 267
Zembrodt, I. M., 306, 384, 411
Zhang, S., 108, 211
Zillman, D., 80, 307
Zimmerman, C., 425
Zimmerman, M. A., 222
Zimmerman, R. S., 252
Zimring, L., 43
Ziv, R., 341
Zuckerman, A., 188
Zuckerman, M., 354
Zurbriggen, E. L., 82 *box*, 326, 328
Zusman, M. E., 273

SUBJECT INDEX

Abstinence, 252 *box*

Abusive relationships:
physical abuse, 417–418
psychological abuse, 408
secret keeping and, 149, 151, 155–156, 161, 162, 164

Abusive communication, 417–418

Access, online support and, 186 *box*

Accidental communication, 18

"Accidental revelation," 47

Accommodation:
constructive behavior, 385–387
destructive behavior, 384–385
investment model view of, 379–383
model of, 384–387
principle of, 305–306

Accounts, 52

Accusations, 105, 348 *box*

"Acers," 47

Acknowledgement, 392

Acquiescent responses, 348–349

Active distancing, 295–296

Active jealousy, 362 *box*

Active listening, 311–312

Active strategies, for uncertainty reduction, 93–94, 95 *box*

Active verbal responses, 348–349

Activities:
joint, prosocial behavior, 260 *box*
relationship turning point, 128
sharing, 212–213, 326

Acts of devotion, 105

Acts of disregard, 105

Adolescence:
cybersex and, 238
LGBT, sex and, 234
parents, sexual attitudes and, 238–239
sexual activity and, 235
See also Family *entries*

Adornment, 13,

Adult attachment styles:
changes across lifespan, 222, 225
dismissive, 217 *figure*, 219–220
fearful, 217 *figure*, 219
preoccupied, 217 *figure*, 218–219
secure, 217 *figure*, 218

Advice:
health, 326–327
relational goals and, 17
relationship, 327

Affairs. *See* Infidelity

Affection:
constructive strategy, 387
defined, 171
exaggerated, infidelity cue and, 359 *box*
linearity and, 22
manifest intimacy and, 199

need for, 7–8
post-coital, 248
prosocial behavior, 260 *box*
tokens of, 213
withdrawal of, 424–425

Affectionate communication, 169, 171–175
affection exchange theory of, 171–173
benefits of, 7–8
cognitive valence theory (CVT) of, 179–184
gender differences in closeness and, 192–194
immediacy behavior, 176–179
index, 173 *box*
nonverbal, 174–175
pillow talk, 247–248
supportive, 183–192
verbal, 174

Affection exchange theory, 171–173

Affection-instrumentality dialectic, 135

Affinity-seeking behavior, 43

African American identity, 29

Agape love (compassionate), 204, 209

Age:
communication style and, 14
cybersex and, 232 *box*
differences, relational breakups, 412
friendship maintenance and, 267
generational identity and, 30–33
physical attraction and, 66–67
privacy rights and, 154
safe sex practices and, 252 *box*
sexual activity, first, 235
sexual coercion and, 248–250
social media use and, 15
See also Family *entries*

Agency, 316

Agentic friendships, 193

Aggressiveness, 52, 310–311

Alcohol:
relational breakups and, 412
safe sex and, 253 *box*
sexual regrets and, 247–248

Alternatives. *See* Quality of alternatives

Altruism, 72

American identity, 29

American Psychological Association, 36 *figure*

Androgynous individuals, 12, 66

Angry attacks, 147, 149

Anonymity, 186 *box*

Antagonistic communication, 330

Anthropology, 5

Antisocial acts, 245, 246

Antisocial communication, 385, 385 *figure*

Antisocial maintenance behaviors, 260–261, 262 *box*

Anxious-ambivalent attachment style, 217

Apathetic communication, 359 *box*

Apologies:
corrective facework, 52
positive-tone strategy, 427
remedial strategy, 388–390

Appearance:
adornment and, 13
deception and, 355
nonverbal position of power and, 333
See also Physical attractiveness

Appeasement, 390–391

Appreciation, 417 *box*

Approach orientations, 215

Argumentativeness, aggressiveness *vs.*, 310–311

Arguments, third parties and, 300

Arousal, sexual:
cognitive valence theory (CVT) and, 179–180
gender differences in, 231–233
sexual, 231–233, 241–242
See also Emotional arousal

Arranged marriages, 11, 201, 210–211, 410

Artifacts, 13, 336

Asking-third-party tests, 96

Assertive responses, 251

Assimilation effect, 71

Assurances, 174
as constructive strategy, 387
as prosocial behavior, 260 *box*

Asymmetrical communication, 19, 33

Attachment style, 67

Attachment theory, 197, 214–225
accommodation and, 387
across life spans, 222, 224–225
adulthood, 218–220
childhood, 215–217
changes in, 222, 225
communication differences, 221 *box*
detached, 218, 218–220
determination of,
emotional, 218–219
forming, propensity for, 214–215
internal working models and, 215
personality and, 225
physical attraction and, 67
preoccupied, 218–219
prosocial, 218
relational satisfaction and, 220–222
self-test, 223 *box*–224 *box*
stabilization factors, 222, 224

Attempted communication, 18

Attention stage, 240–241

Attentiveness, 191

Attitudes:
online communication, 148

political, 326
sexual. *See* Sexual attitudes
similarity in, 74–76
Attraction, 58–60
biological aspects of, 64–65
complementarity and, 78–79
definition of, 57
demographic factors, 65–67
Eros love style and, 204, 206
expectations and, 62–64
factors influencing, 61 *figure*
fatal, 60
"hard-to-get" phenomenon, 73
interpersonal communication skills
and, 71–73
loss-gain effect, 73
online, 82 *box*
personality and, 67–68
physical environment qualities, 79–80
proximity and, 80–81
qualities of pair in, 73–78
reward value influence on, 61–62
same-sex relationships, 232–234
self-test, 59 *box*
similarity and, 74–78
social attraction, 58
social environmental and, 81–82
subjectivity of, 81
types of, 58
Attraction mechanism, 64
Attractiveness. *See* Physical
attractiveness
Attractiveness deception, 42
Attribution hypothesis, 309
Attributions, 308–310
definition of, 308
distress-maintaining, 309
patterns in, 310 *box*
relationship-enhancing, 309
Audience identity, 46
Audiences:
context, 46
impression management and, 45–46
self-presentation to, 41, 43
sensitivity to, 44
social, 38
Authentic feedback, 40
Authoritarian parents, 337
Authoritative parents, 337–338
Authorized co-owners, 150
"Autonomous" people, 44
Autonomy, 129
Autonomy-connection tension, 134 *box*, 353
Aversive stimulation, 328
Avoidance:
antisocial maintenance and, 261, 262 *box*
conflict, 296–297
disengagement strategy, 422–424
FTA correction with, 52

ORI behavior, 372
relational maintenance with, 261, 262 *box*
remedial strategy, 392
stage of relationship, 125
See also Topic avoidance
Avoidant attachment style, 422–423
Avoidant children, 216
Avoidant individuals, 219
Avoiding stage, 288

Baby talk, 179
Backstage impression management, 45–46
Bald on-record strategy, 49
Bargaining strategy, 328
Bartholomew's four attachment styles, 217 *figure*, 218
Baxter's Dialectical Tensions, 131 *figure*
Beauty:
personal and cultural preferences, 69–70 *box*
physical attraction and, 68–71
stereotypes, 70
See also Appearance; Physical attractiveness
Behavior:
ambiguity of, 104
cognitive valence theory and, 179–180
communication types and, 18 *figure*
conflict, 23
constructive, 385–387
destructive, 384–385
face-threatening, 48
frontstage and backstage, 45–46
immediacy, 176–179
impression management in, 43–44
infidelity cues in, 357–358, 359 *box*
nonverbal, 13
relational maintenance, 259–265
rules of conduct and, 45
self-fulfilling prophecy and, 39
symmetrical, 331
unattended, 17
uncertainty increasing, 92
uncharacteristic relational, 105
verbal, 14
visual, 177–178
vocalic, 175
Behavioral control, 8
Behavioral expectations, 103
Behavioral familiarity, 354
Behavioral interdependence, 6
Beliefs:
attraction and, 67
gender and, 66
preexisting, 312
relationship, 67
similar, 74

Benefit-cost ratios, 283–284
Betrayal:
connectivity of, 346
confidences, 92
deception and, 349
hurtful events and, 108
jealous emotions and, 363
relational, 346–347, 386–387
secret revealing and, 164–165
sexual, 410
Betraying confidences, 92
Bias:
deception and, 354
in event interpretation, 101–102
safe sex and, 253
perceptual, 61–62
relationship superiority, 384
truth, 253, 354
Biological attraction, 64–65
Birth date similarity, 77–78
Black identity, 29
Blame game strategy, 424, 428
Blended families, 129
Blended relationships, 8–9
Blocking social media, breaking up and, 423 *box*
Body/facial symmetry, 69 *box*
Body language:
courtship and, 241–242
deception and, 353
immediacy behavior, 177
intention and, 16
kinesics, 178–179
nonverbal communication, 12–15
nonverbal power and, 333–335
passive aggression and, 295–296
Body movements. *See* Kinesics
Body proportionality, 69 *box*
Body synchrony, 179
"Bogus stranger" method, 74
Bonding stage, 122–123
Boomerang effect, 327
Boundary control, 150–151
Boundary insiders, 150
Boundary structures, 149
Boundary turbulence, 151
Brady Bunch, The, 129
Brains, attraction mechanism in, 64–65
Breadth, 140–141, 143–144 *box*
Breakups. *See* Divorce; Relational breakups
Breast feeding, 247
Broadcasters, 33
B.S. Factor, The: The Theory and Technique of Faking It in America (Herzog), 33
Bullying, 330, 427
Bush, George, 29
Bush, George Herbert Walker, 52
Button pushing, 308

Catastrophe theory, 420–421
Cell phones:
  attachment to, 33
  autonomy-connection tension and,
    134 *box*
  behavioral expectations and, 62, 105
  dismissive attachment style and, 220
  Millennials use of, 30
  relationship maintenance and, 262–263,
    264 *box*
  self-disclosure and, 140
  use of, 14–15
Centers for Disease Control and
    Prevention, 252, 252 *box*
Certainty 132
Change:
  attachment style, 222, 225
  essentialness of, 31
  personality, 92
  relationship advice, power and, 327
  See also Turning points
Channels of communication, 14, 145
Channel switching, 299 *box*
Child psychology, 5
Children:
  attachment theory and, 214–217
  aversive stimulation by, 328
  culture, sexual attitudes and, 237
  divorced parents, 125, 217, 290, 415
  individuation of, 338–339
  negative breakup effects, 430–432
  parental conflict and, 290
  parental love for, 198, 200
  parental power over, 336–338
  parental sexual attitudes and, 238–239
  respect, 339
  secret disclosure and, 162
  separation of, 338–339
  turning points, 129
  See also Family *entries*
Chilling effect, 297, 323–324
Chronemic behaviors, 179, 336
Chronic dissatisfaction, 413
Cialis, 232
Circumscribing stage, 124
Clinical psychology, 5
Close distancing, 175
Close relationships:
  communication and, 170–171, 193
  conflict and, 289. *See also* Conflict in
    relationships
  deception detection in, 353–354
  definition of, 5 *box,* 6
  emotional closeness, 170
  expectancy violations in, 104–105
  features of, 7
  forms of, 170–171
  hurtful events in, 108
  identity factors in, 45

  immediacy behavior in, 176–179
  need fulfillment in, 7
  nonverbal immediacy in, 177–179
  perceptions of, 192–193
  physical closeness, 170, 175
  relational closeness, 170
  same-sex *vs.* cross-sex. friendships, 193
  secrets in, 122, 155
  sex differences in, 192–193
  sexual intimacy in, 11–12
  subtypes, 8–9
  support in, 184–192
Close proxemic distancing, 191
Clutching activities, 241
Codependency, 412
Cognitive valence theory (CVT):
  arousal and, 181
  behavior, 179–181
  cognition and, 181
  culture and, 181, 182 *box*
  defined, 179
  online, 186 *box*
  outcomes, 180 *figure*
  perception and, 181
  personality, 182
  relational outcomes, 183
  relationship and, 183
  rewardingness, 182–183
  situation / setting, 183
  temporary states, 183
Cohabiting relationships, 9
  breakup consequences and, 430
  communication patterns, 278–279
  maintenance challenges of, 277–279
  relational maintenance and, 266
  relational quality, 278
  stability, 277
  types of couples, 279
Collaborating conflict style, 294–295
Collectivism, 28 *box*, 153 *box*, 352 *box*
Coloring preference, 69 *box*
Coming apart stages of relationship:
  avoidance, 125
  circumscribing, 124
  differentiating, 123–124
  stagnation, 124–125
  termination, 126–127
  See also Relational breakups
Coming together stage of relationship,
    117–123
  bonding, 122–123
  experimenting, 118–120
  initiating, 117–118
  integrating, 122
  intensifying, 120–121 *box*
Commitment:
  accommodation and, 386
  component of love, 201
  investment model and, 380

  lack of (friends-with-benefits), 274
  similarity, complementarity and, 78–79
  turning point, 128–129
  uncertainty and, 89
Common couple violence, 373–374
Communal frame of identity, 27–28
Communication:
  affectionate. *See* Affectionate
    communication
  antisocial, 385
  attachment style differences in, 221 *box*
  attraction and, 71
  channels of self-disclosure, 145
  culture and, 10 *box*
  destructive patterns of, 324
  distributive, 330
  face-to-face *vs.* computer mediated, 14
  forgiving, 393–397
  fundamental relational themes of, 20,
    21 *box*
  genetically related *vs.* nonrelated, 11
  identity development and, 26–28
  inefficacy in, 158
  integrative, 364
  interpersonal, research, 3–4
  jealousy, responses to, 364–365
  love, 212–214
  message exchange and, 12
  online, attitudes toward, 148 *box*
  prosocial, 280, 281 *box*, 385 *figure*, 386
  relational, 19–23
  relational breakups and, 415–418
  rewarding, 104
  safe sex and, 251–254
  self-disclosure, technology and,
    143–144 *box*
  sexual satisfaction and, 243–244
  symmetrical and asymmetrical, 19
  technology and, 32
  turning points-based, 127–128
  types of behavior and, 18 *figure*
  types of relationship, 2, 6 *box*
  uncertainty and, 90–93
Communication patterns:
  cohabitation and, 278–279
  relational satisfaction and, 281
Communication privacy management
    (CPM), 149, 150 *figure*
Communication skills:
  conflict management, 116
  deficit, attribution and, 310–312
  emotional support, providing, 115
  interpersonal skills test, 114–115 *box*
  negative assertion, 116
  relationship initiation, 113
  self-disclosure, 113
  similarity, 76
  stage models for, 116–117
Communication theory of identity, 27

Communicative infidelity, 356–357
Comparison levels, 380–381
Compassionate love, 204, 209
Compatibility, culture and, 10 *box*
Compensation behaviors, 390–391
Compensatory communication, 364
Compensatory restoration, 364
Competitive fighting, 291, 294–295
Competitive symmetry, 331, 332 *box*
Complaints, 303–304
Complementarity:
    opposites attract, 78
    transact, 332 *box*
Complementary utterances, 331
Compliance-gaining strategies,
        327–328, 330
Compromising conflict style, 294
Computer-mediated communication:
    attitudes toward, 143 *box*
    characterization of, 14
    false identities and, 41–42
    humor and, 40
    lure of online support, 186 *box*
    Millennials' use of, 30
    modality switches, 108–109
    power factors in, 321 *box*
    relational maintenance with, 262–264
    self-disclosure and, 143–144 *box*, 145
    social media, 15 *box*
    social networks and, 31–33
    statistics on, 15 *figure*
    uncertainty reduction in, 95 *box*
    See also Facebook; Internet; Social
        media; Social networks;
        Technology
Concealment, 350
Concession, 388–390
Conditional forgiveness, 395–396
Condoms, 252 *box*, 253
Confidences, 92
Conflict:
    avoiding with deception, 351
    destructive, 262 *box*
    managing, 116, 260 *box*, 307 *box*
    relational breakups and, 416
    turning point, 129–130
    violent. *See* Violence *entries*
Conflict behaviors, 23, 221 *box*
Conflict interaction patterns:
    attributions, 308–310
    channel switching motives, 299 *box*
    communication skills deficit, 310–312
    demand-withdraw, 301–302
    emotional flooding, 307–306
    "four horsemen of the apocalypse,"
        302–306
    negative reciprocity, 298–301
Conflict in relationships:
    common issues, 288 *box*

definition of, 288–289
effects of, 289–290
frequency, 289
Conflict styles:
    avoiding, 296–297
    collaborating, 294–295
    competitive fighting, 291, 294–295
    compromise, 294
    indirect fighting, 295–296
    interpersonal conflict style, 291 *figure*
    research on, 290–291
    self-test, 292–293 *box*
    strategies, 291
    yielding, 297–298
Confrontation, 149
Connection-autonomy tension, 132
Consciousness, 43–44
Constructive behavior, 385–387
Constructive responses, 385 *figure*
Consummate love, 198, 199 *box*
Consumption, 31
Contempt, 303–305
Content levels, 18–19
Context:
    confidentiality breeches, privacy and,
        151–152
    expectancies and, 102
    friendship dialectics, 134
    frontstage and backstage behavior
        and, 46
    secrets, 155–156
    self-disclosure and, 143, 145–146
Contraception, 253
Control:
    antisocial behavior, 262 *box*
    coded messages, 330–331
    fear of loss of, 149
    deception and, 330
    family, 201–202
Conventionality-uniqueness tension, 132
Conversational control, 316–317
Conversations:
    cell-phone, 134 *box*
    complaints, 298
    deception detection, 353–354
    long/in-depth, 120, 142
    powerful and powerful, 331–332
    repair, 417 *box*
Cooperation, 222, 224, 291
Core identity, 29, 45
Corporate romance, 81
Corrective facework, 50–54, 51 *figure*
Cost escalation, relational
        disengagement, 425
Costs, defined, 283–284
Counter-jealousy induction, 364
Courtship:
    attention stage, 240–241
    invitations stage, 241–242

positioning stage, 241
readiness stage, 241
resolution stage, 242
sexual stage, 239–240
See also Dating
CPM. *See* Communication privacy
        management (CPM) theory
Creational orientation, 236
Crisis, 129–130
Criticism, 105, 303–304
Cross-cultural friendships, 119 *box*
Cross-generational relationships, 9
Cross-sex friendships, 9, 12
    challenges in, 268–270
    closeness and, 193
    expectancy violations, 106
    maintenance behavior in, 268
    platonic safeguarding of, 271
    romantic intent in, 270–271
    self-test, 271–272 *box*
    uncertainty in, 90
Crowdsourcing opinions, 32
Cues:
    behavioral infidelity, 357–358
    chronemic, 13, 179,
    contextual, 211 *box*
    environmental, 13, 186, 187 *figure*
    eye contact, 177–178
    immediacy, 191
    infidelity, 357–358
    kinesics, 13
    misinterpretation of flirtatious, 242
    nonverbal, 13–14, 21
    power, 317, 333, 335
    sexual advance resistance, 249
    similarity in, 21 *box*
    social, 203 *box*
    verbal, 327–330
Cultural scripts, 371
Cultural differences:
    arranged marriages, 201
    beauty and, 69–70 *box*
    break ups, 409
    cognitive valence theory (CVT), 179,
        181, 182 *box*
    coping strategies for, 388 box
    deception motives, 352 *box*
    decision-making, power and, 320
    demand-withdraw conflict interaction
        and, 301 *box*
    discovery of, 119 *box*
    divorce, 410
    equity across cultures, 281 *box*
    expressions of love, 211 *box*
    falling in love and, 201–202
    friendships from other, 119 *box*
    gender equality, 341 *box*
    gender, sex and, 12
    identity and, 27, 28 *box*, 29

immediacy behavior, 176–179
love styles, 210–211
marriage expectations and, 10 *box*
personal identity and, 28 *box*
privacy boundaries, 152–153 *box*
relational breakups and, 409
secure attachment style and, 218
sexual attitudes, 237, 238 *box*
sexual scripts and, 245
stressors, 388 *box*
uncertainty, 91 *box*
voluntary *vs.* involuntary relationships,
    10–11
Cultural similarities, 119 *box*
Cultural stressors, 388 box
*Culture of Narcissism, The: American Life
    in an Age of Diminishing Expectations*
    (Lasch), 33
Cyber emigrant relationships, 263
Cybersexuality, 232 *box*, 238
Cyberstalking, 34, 423 *box*
Cyclic alternation, 133

Dating:
    arranged marriages and, 201–202
    cell phone use and, 134 *box*
    commitment in, 78–79
    early sex in
    expectancy violation in, 106–107
    interethnic, 411–412
    Internet. *See* Internet dating
    investments in, 381–382
    narcissism in, 68
    others, to disengage, 426
    rebound, 432
    secret tests in, 96–97
    sexual behavior in, 11, 89, 229–230
    uncertainty in, 86–102
Deception:
    continuing previous, 353
    cultural aspects, 352 *box*
    detecting, 353–354
    effects on relationships, 354–356
    eye behavior and, 353
    hurt feelings and, 348 *box*, 349–350
    identity and, 41–42
    infidelity and, 356–360
    maintaining relationship with, 351–353
    motives for, 350–353
    power ploy, 330
    relational closeness, 354
    sexual history and, 355–356
    types of, 350
    uncertainty and, 92
    as verbal influence strategy, 330
    See also Courtship; First dates; Internet
        dating
Decide not to engage in FTA, 50
De-escalation, 425, 427–428

Defensiveness, 303, 303 *box*, 304
Defriending, 34, 105, 423 *box*
Delayed-involvement couples, 242
Deliberateness, 43–44
Demand-withdraw pattern, 301–302, 323
Denial:
    jealousy response, 364
    remedial strategy, 391–392
Dependence power, 321–322
Depression:
    breakup and, 429, 432
    social networking and, 34
Depth of self-disclosure, 140–141
Derogating competitors, 364
Desires-romance group, 270
Destiny beliefs, 67
Destructive behavior, 384–385
Destructive communication patterns, 324
Destructive conflict, 262 *box*
Destructive responses, 385 *figure*
Detachment, 217 *figure*, 219–220
Devaluation, 346
Development patterns, 22–23
Developmental psychology, 5
Devotion, acts of, 105
Dialectical perspective:
    certainty, 132
    definition of, 130–131
    expression, 132
    in friendship, 134–135
    integration, 132
    managing tensions, 133
    relational dialectics theory, 131
Dialectics theory:
    communication and, 21–22
    uncertainty and, 89–90
Differential importance explanation, 76
Differentiating stage of relationship,
    123–124
Direct dump strategy, 425–426
Direct emotional expressions, 174
Directive message, 348 *box*
Directness tests, 96
Direct nonverbal affectionate
    communication, 174–175
Direct requests:
    reconciliation and, 399
    verbal influence strategy, 328
Direct verbal affectionate
    communication, 174
Disabling power, 322–324
Disclaimers, 50
Disclosure:
    depth of, immediacy behavior, 176–177
    reconciliation and, 398
    secret keeping and. *See* Secret keeping
    uncertainty reduction and, 92
    See also Self-disclosure
Disclosure-liking hypothesis, 144

Discursive tensions, 131
Discussion-based forgiveness, 395
Disengagement process:
    bilateral strategies, 428–429
    catastrophe theory, 420–421
    direct strategies, 425–428
    indirect strategies, 422–425,
        424 *figure*, 428
    overview of, 421–422
    relational dissolution process model,
        418–420
    unilateral strategies, 422–428,
        424 *figure*
Disillusionment, 413
Dismissive attachment style, 217 *figure*,
    219–220, 221 *box*, 387
Display rules, 42
Dispositional hope, 386
Disqualification, 133
Disregard, acts of, 105
Disrespect:
    culture and, 10 *box*
    See also Respect
Dissatisfaction:
    attributions and, 309
    relational breakups and, 413
    uncertainty and, 88–89
Distancing, 44
Distress-maintaining attributions, 309
Distributive communication, 330
Divorce:
    children and, 430–432
    communication that prevents, 417 *box*
    conflict patterns in, 302–303
    cultural consequences of, 410 *box*
    intergenerational transmission of, 431
    reasons for, 409 *box*
    See also Relational breakups
Dominance, 315
    annoying, 319
    definition of, 316
    establishment of, 333
    intimidation and, 333–334
    levels of, 335
    parental, 327
    relational communication, 21 *box*
    smiling and, 335
    testing interpersonal, 318 *box*
    perception of, 72, 335
Double-shot hypothesis, 358–360
Drama, conflict interaction and, 300
Dramaturgical perspective, 26, 44
Drugs:
    relational breakups and, 412
    safe sex and, 253 *box*
    sex-enhancing, for men, 233
Dual process model of supportive
    communication, 185–186, 187 *figure*
Dyadic effect, 146

Dyadic power theory, 317
Dyadic processes, 419

Echo boomers. *See* Millennials
Effectiveness, 17–18
Efficacy assessment, 99
Egalitarian marriage, 339–341
E-mail, 14
Embarrassment, 51–52
Emoticons, 14
Emotional arousal, 21 *box*
Emotional attachment:
    close relationships, 7
    romantic *vs.* nonromantic relationships,
        11–12
    to social media, 33
Emotional bond challenge, 268–269
Emotional closeness, 170
Emotional disengagement, 359 *box*
Emotional expression, 221 *box*
Emotional flooding, 307–306
Emotional infidelity, 356–358, 359 *box*,
    410–411. *See also* Infidelity
Emotional insensitivity, 323
Emotional intimacy, 192
Emotional labor, 42
Emotional responses, 101
Emotional style of attachment, 217 *figure*,
    218–219
Emotional support:
    communication of, 115, 184
    cross-sex friendships, 268–269
    providing, 115
Emotional transformation, 393
Emotions:
    expectancy violations and, 104
    jealous, 363
    relationship conflict and, 289. *See also*
        Conflict in relationships
    sexual desire and, 64–65
Empathetic individual, 323
Empathy, forgiveness and, 389 *figure*
Employment, sexual harassment and,
    250–251
Empty love, 199 *box*, 201
Empty threats, 308
Enabling power, 322–324
Enactment of communication frame, 27, 28
Endurance tests, 96
Engaged cohabitation couple, 279
Entertainment rules, 31
Environment:
    cues, 13, 186
    physical, attraction effects of, 79–80
    proximity, 80–81
    social, attraction effects of, 81–82
Envy, 361, 362 *figure*, 363
Equality:
    distribution of resources, 281 *box*

traditional *vs.* egalitarian marriages,
    339–341
Equity:
    benefit-cost ratios and, 283–284
    benefits of equity, 280–282
    culture and, 281 *box*
    definition of, 279
    family obligations, 413–415
    leaving relationship and, 283
    principles of, 280
    psychological equity, adjusting, 283
    reducing distress, 283
    restoring actual equity, 283
    theory, 258, 279–284
    types of, 280
Equivocation, 350
Eros love style, 203–206, 204 *figure*
Esteem support, 184
Ethnic identity, 27–29
Evaluation message, 348 *box*
Evasion, 392
"Every Breath You Take" (Sting), 208
Evolutionary hypothesis for infidelity,
    358–360
Exaggeration, 350
Excitation transfer, 80
Exclusivity, 128–129
Excuses, 391. *See also* Accounts
Exit:
    accommodation and, 384,
        385 *figure*, 387
    coping strategy, 384
    destructive behavior and, 385
Expanding identity, 36–37
Expectancy effects, 63
Expectancy violations:
    close relationships, 104–105
    first dates, 106–107
    flirtation, 106
    hurtful events, 108
    modality switches, 108–109
    sexual activity, 106
Expectancy violations theory, 86
    behavior and, 103
    defining types of, 102–103
    factors affecting, 102
    rewardinginess of partner, 103–104
Expectations:
    attraction process role of, 62–64
    attractiveness, 64–65
    behavioral, 62–64
    face needs, 48
    halo effect and, 58
    identity and, 39
    marriage, 10 *box*
    outcome, 98
    predictive, 102
    prescriptive, 102
Experimenting stage, 118–120

Explanations:
    reconciliation and, 398
    remedial strategy, 391
Explicit forgiveness, 393, 395
Explicit relational talk, 395
Exploratory affective exchange, 116
Exposure, fear of, 147
Expression:
    desired message, 348 *box*
    dialectic of, 132
    emotional and physical closeness, 245
    love, cultural differences and, 211 *box*
Expressive friendships, 193
Expressive-protective dialectic, 134–135
External competition, 128–129
External manifestations, 131
Extractive strategies, uncertainty
    reduction online, 95 *box*
Extramarital sex. *See* Infidelity
Extrinsic investments, 381–382
Extroverts, 33, 60, 78
Eye contact:
    deception and, 353
    immediacy behavior and, 177–178, 190
    power and, 334

Fabricated identities, 41–42
Fabrications, 350
Facebook:
    attraction and, 82 *box*
    adult use of, 14
    breakups on, 423
    communication via, 15 *box*
    defriending, 423 *box*
    expectancy violations, 105
    false identities and, 41–42
    friendship, maintenance, 267
    generational use of, 30
    identity surveillance, 34
    maintenance behavior, 263
    mega-friending on, 34 *box*
    mental health promotion and, 34
    popularity of, 15 *figure*
    privacy and, 31–32, 153 *box*
    reconnection/relational repair on,
        399 *box*
    relationship status and, 33–34
    self-presentation and, 25
    sex offenders use of, 35
    See also Social media *entries*
Face-repairing responses, 53–54 *box*
Face-threatening:
    behavior rules of conduct, 45
    factors of behavior, 48
    loss sequence, 51 *figure*
    politeness theory, 46
    saving face, 46
Face-threatening acts (FTAs), 47
    correction strategies, 52

options for dealing with, 49 *figure*
refusal to engage in, 50
repairing face (self-test), 53–54 *box*
See also Embarrassment
Face-to-face communication:
  computer-mediated communication
    vs., 14
  expectancy violations, 108
  identity management and, 25–26
  intentional/unintentional, 16
  online support as alternative, 186 *box*
  proxemic behaviors, 178
  self-disclosure and, 142, 143, 145
  social media as substitute for, 33
Facework, 49–54
Facial expressions:
  modality of maintenance behavior,
    261–262
  nonverbal immediacy and, 190
  nonverbal power and, 334–335
Facial maturity, 70 *box*
Facial neoteny, 70 *box*
Facial symmetry, 69 *box*
Fading away strategy, 428
Fait accompli approach, 425–426
Falling in friendship:
  characteristics of, 202
  trajectory of, 22
  turning points in, 127
Falling in love, 201–202
False identities, 41–42
Falsifications, 350
Family:
  attachment theory and, 214–215
  boundary control, 150–151
  children attachment styles, 216–217
  hurtful messages, 348
  jealousy, 362 *box*
  love and, 198
  moral identity and, 26
  nontraditional, 9
  obligations, 408, 413–415
  parental interference in relationships,
    81–82, 202
  parental sexual attitudes, 238–239
  power in. See Family, power/influence in
  proximity/distance and, 129
  related *vs.* nonrelated relationships, 11
  secret keeping and, 149, 151, 155–156,
    161–162, 164
  sex and, 12
  sibling rivalry, 361
  social inclusion and, 8
  topic avoidance in, 157
  traditional, culture marriage and,
    10 *box*
  turning points, 129
  whole-family secrets, 156
  working women and, 413–415

turning points, 127, 128
violence history, 418
Family, power/influence in:
  individuation, 338–339
  parent–child relationships, 336–338
  parenting styles, 337–338
  power assertion, 338
  power structures in, 162
  traditional *vs.* egalitarian marriages
    and, 339–341
Family studies, 5
Fatal attraction, 60
Fear:
  attachment style and, 67, 217 *figure*,
    219, 221 *box*, 387
  attraction, 80
  classic, 225
  disclosure of, 141
  exposure fear, 147
  interaction patterns of, 219
  jealousy and, 361, 363
  rejection, 147, 270
  retaliation, 147, 149
  self-disclosure, 147, 149
  uncertainty and, 90
Fearful individuals, 219, 221 *box*
Feedback:
  identity-consistent, 40
  interpretation of, 39
  looking-glass self, 38–39
  self-putdowns, 96
Fertility, 172
Fever model of self-disclosure, 161
Fidelity checks, uncertainty reduction, 96
Financial consequences, of breakups, 430
First date:
  expectations of, 106–107
  ideal, 72
  performance at, 45
  sex during, 107, 230, 242
  social attractiveness and, 68–69
  turning points, 127
Flaming, 298
Flirtation:
  antisocial behavior and, 262 *box*
  expectancy violation, 106
  sexual communication, 239–240
Flirting styles, 240
Forgiveness:
  acknowledgment of harmful conduct, 392
  communication of, 389–391
  conditional, 395–396
  conditions promoting, 396–397
  definition of, 392
  discussion, 395
  emotional transformation and, 393
  explicit, 393, 395
  extension of undeserved mercy, 393
  minimizing approach to, 395

nonverbal displays of, 395
  partner characteristics and, 396–397
  relationship renegotiation, 393
  seriousness of transgression and, 396
  sexual infidelity and, 411
Forgiveness process, 389 *figure*
Formal language, 14, 20, 21 *box*
Forms of address, 176
"Four horsemen of the apocalypse,
    302–306
Frames of identity, 27
Free agents, 316
Frequency:
  conflict, in relationships, 289
  self-disclosure, 140–142, 143–144 *box*
  sexual, satisfaction and, 243
Friending:
  necessity of, 31, 34
  social media and, 30
  See also Mega-friending
Friend jealousy, 362 *box*
Friendship:
  agentic, 193
  closeness preferences in, 193
  cross-cultural, 119 *box*
  cross-sex, 90, 105, 106, 135
  development of, 11, 22
  dialectical tensions in, 134–135
  expectancy violations, 106
  expressive, 193
  friends-with-benefits, 229–230
  gender-based, 12
  maintenance of, 258–260, 260 *box*
  maintenance in same-sex, 267–268
  partner interference in, 129
  role in attraction, 82 *box*
  similarity in, 74–78
  social capital and, 34
  Sternberg's theory of, 198, 199 *box*
  tensions in, 135
  turning points, 129
  types of, 12
  uncertainty and, 90
  workplace, 81
Friendship love, 198, 199 *box*, 204, 207
Friends-with-benefits relationships, 11, 12
  advantages/disadvantages, 274
  expectancy violations, 106
  maintenance challenges, 273–275
  seven types of, 273
  sex and, 230
  uncertainty and, 90
Frontstage impression management,
    45–46
FTAs. *See* Face-threatening Acts, 47
Fundamental relational themes, 20, 21 *box*
Futility of discussion, 158
Future interaction expectation, 63
"Fuzzy" relationships, 9

Gaining assistance, 325–326
Gambling, 44
Game-playing love (ludus), 204, 207–208
Gandhi, Mahatma, 319
Gatekeepers, 31
Gay and lesbian relationships. *See* Sexual
    orientation
Gender:
    online identity and, 42
    social/cultural construct, 12
    stereotyped roles, 66
    See also Sex (gender)
Gender differences:
    friendship maintenance, 268, 269 *box*
    gender equality, 341 *box*
    physical attraction, 65–66
    sexual harassment, 250–251
Gender politics hypothesis, 335
General equity, 280
Generational identity, 30–33
Generation Y. *See* Millennials
Generation Z, 30–33
Genetically related relationships, 11
Genetics, 26
Gestures of inclusion, 105
Ghosting, 126, 422
Gifts, 213
Goal achievement, 40
Goal interruptions, 101
Goal-linking, 371
Going off-record strategy, 50
Golden ratio of f, 69–70 *box*
Google+, 15 *figure*
Gossip, 262 *box*
Gradual-involvement couples, 242
Gradual separators, 401, 402 *box*
Grave-dressing process, 420
Groups:
    communal frame of identity, 27–28
    membership in, identity and, 27
    minority, identity and, 27
    social inclusion and, 8
Growing apart, 412–413
Growth beliefs, 67
Guilty communication, 359 *box*
Gunnysacking, 300, 307 *box*

Habitual behavior, 43–44
Halo effect, 58, 70–71
Happiness, determinates of, 257
Haptics, 13, 178, 335
Harassment, sexual, 250–251
"Hard-to-get" phenomenon, 73
Harm, FTAs and, 48
Healing, 432–433
Health:
    advice, 326–327
    affection exchange theory and, 172–173
    breakups and, 412, 432

healing after separation, 432–433
    sexual, 238
"Heart of hearts" concept, 30
Height:
    attraction and, 69, 69 *box*
    nonverbal power and, 333
Hesitant attachment style, 217
    figure, 219
Heterosexual relationships, 9
Heuristics, 30
Hierarchical structure, identity and, 38
High outcome value, 97–98
High-risk sex, avoid, 252 *box*
Hinting:
    sexual initiation, 245
    verbal influence, 329
Hispanic identity, 29
HIV/AIDS, 252, 252 *box*, 253
Homelessness, 44
Homosexuality. *See* Gay and lesbian
    relationships
Honesty:
    impression management and, 42
    safe sex and, 253 *box*
Honeymoon stage, 200, 266
Hook-ups, 229–230
Hope, 386
Hormones:
    affection exchange theory and, 173
    attraction, 64
    courtship and, 241
    power and, 323
Hot component of love, 200–201
Household chores, 415
Hugs, 191
Humanistic psychology, 5
Human nature, identity and, 26
Humor:
    corrective facework, 52
    differences and, 388 *box*
    hurtful messages and, 348 *box*
    online intimacy and, 40
    prosocial behavior, 260 *box*
Hurt feelings:
    deception and, 349–350
    infidelity and. *See* Infidelity *entries*
    jealousy and. *See* Jealousy *entries*
    messages, hurtful, 347–348
    nature of, 345–346
    obsessive relational intrusion (ORI),
        369–372
    unrequited love, 368–369
Hurtful events, 108. *See also*
    Transgressions
Hurtful messages, 347–348
    responding to, 348–349
    types of, 348 *box*
Hygienic activities, backstage behavior, 46
Hyperaccessibility, 160–161

Hyperintimacy, 370
Hyperpersonal model, 145

IARR. *See* International Association for
    Relationship Research (IARR)
Idealization, 275–277
Idealization effect, 108
Ideal-real dialectic, 135
Identity:
    communication and, 26–28
    online, 32–33
    indispensability of, 31
    creation of, 29–30
    cultural and ethnic, 29
    definition of, 26
    development of, 26–37
    expansion of, 36–37
    expectations for, 39
    feedback and, 34, 38, 39
    frames of, 27
    generational, 30–33
    goal achievement and, 40
    hierarchical structure of, 38
    human nature and, 26
    Millennials' rules, 30–31
    relationships and, 40–41
    self-evaluation and, 39–40
    social networking and, 30–34
    theoretical models of, 26–29
Identity communication:
    manipulating identity, 41–42
    self-presentation issues, 41
Identity-consistent behavior, 40
Identity gaps, 28
Identity management, 157
    communication competence,
        42–43
    definition of, 25
    deliberate, 43–44
    dramaturgical perspective, 44
    feedback interpretation and, 39
    goal achievement and, 40
    hierarchical structure and, 38
    looking-glass self and, 38–39
    personal, 26–37. *See also*
        Personal identity
    politeness theory of, 46–54
    principles of, 38–41
    relationships and, 40–41
    secret keeping and, 157
    self-evaluation, 39–40
    See also Impression management;
        Self-presentation
Identity surveillance, 34
Ideologies, love, 203–204
Idiomatic behaviors, 175
Idioms, 175
"Ignorance is bliss," 76
Illicit ingratiation, 329

Image:
  artificial, 33
  creating identity and, 29–30
  rules about, 31
Immaturity, 409
Immediacy behavior:
  chronemic behaviors, 179
  definition of, 176
  disclosure, depth of, 176–177
  forms of address, 176
  kinesics, 178–179
  nonverbal, 177
  proxemics, 178
  relationship indicators, 177
  visual/oculesic behaviors, 177–178
  vocalic communication, 179
  word choice, 176
Immediacy cues, 190
Immigrants, identity and, 29
Implicit egotism, 77, 78
Impression management, 42
  core aspects of self, behavior and, 44–45
  face-threatening acts, 47, 48
  facework strategies, 49–50
  frontstage/backstage, 45–46
  politeness theory and, 46
  positive face *vs.* negative, 46–48
  relationship performance success
    and, 45
  role, audience, context and, 46
  rules of conduct and, 45
  See also Identity management
Inaction conflict style, 296–297
Inclusion, gestures of, 105
Inclusion-of-others-in-self scale, 36 *figure*
Inclusion-seclusion tension, 132
Income, power and, 320
Incompatibility, 411–412
Increased miscellaneous touch, 191
Independent-dependent dialectics,
    134–135
Indirect fighting, 291 *figure,* 295–296
Indirect nonverbal affectionate
    communication, 175, 240
Indirect request, 329
Indirect suggestion tests, 96–97
Individual identity, culture and, 28 *box*
Individualistic cultures, 352 *box*
Individuality, 149
Individuation, separation and, 338–339
Inductive philosophy, 338
Inequity:
  distress reduction in, 280
  divorce and, 415
  occurrence of, 280
  over benefited, 282–283
  traditional *vs.* egalitarian marriages
    and, 339–341
  underbenefited, 282

Infatuation, 199 *box,* 200–201
Infidelity, 261, 262 *box*
  deception and, 351
  detecting, 357–358, 359 *box*
  discovery methods, 356
  double-shot hypothesis, 358–360
  evolutionary hypothesis for, 358–360
  gender-based reactions to, 358–360
  jealousy and, 360–361. *See also*
    Jealousy entries
  reasons for, 357
  relational breakups and, 410–411
  types of, 356–357
Influence:
  accept, 417 *box*
  mutual, 6
  power and, 317
  verbal strategies for, 327–330.
    See also Verbal influence
    strategies
Influence strategies, 327–328
Informal language, 14, 21 *box*
Information:
  disclosure, uncertainty reduction
    and, 94
  theory of motivated information
    management, 98–100
  uncertainty reduction theory and, 91
Informational familiarity, 354
Informational support, 184
Information-based secret keeping,
    157–158
Information-seeking strategy, 94, 95 *box*
Information verification, s 34
Informative statement message, 348 *box*
Ingratiation, 328–329
Initiation:
  skills, for relationship, 113, 117–118
  sexual activity, 245–246, 326
INPR. *See* International Network on
    Personal Relationships (INPR)
Insecure attachment, 387
Insincerity, 82 *box*
Instagram:
  attraction and, 82 *box*
  communication via, 15 *box*
  generational use of, 30
  popularity of, 15 *figure*
Instrumental goals, 17
Integrating stage, 122
Integration, dialectical theory of, 132
Integrative communication, 364, 386
Intellectual intimacy, 192
Intelligence differences, 412
Intensification effect, 145
Intensifying stage, 120, 121 *box*
Interaction:
  condition of, 46
  expectation of future, 63

factors influencing attraction and,
    61 *figure*
  ongoing, communication and, 20
Interaction appearance theory, 70–71
Interaction management, 186 *box*
Interactive strategies, uncertainty
    reduction, 94–95, 95 *box*
Interactors, 33
Intercultural relationships:
  challenges of, 28
  development of, 119, 119 *box*
  dynamics of, 9
  generalizations of, 387
  romance in, 11
  stressors in, 388 *box*
Intergenerational transmission of
    divorce, 431
Internal manifestations, 131
Internal working models, 215
International Association for Relationship
    Research (IARR), 5
International Network on Personal
    Relationships (INPR), 5
International Society for the Study of
    Personal Relationships (ISSPR), 5
Internet:
  communicating via, 15 *box*
  conflicts on, 299 *box*
  courtship on, 202
  cybersexuality, 232 *box*
  fake identities on, 41
  finding love on, 202, 203 *box*
  identity management on, 25
  infidelity and, 357
  online attraction, 82 *box*
  pornography on, 232, 233 *box*
  self-presentation and, 25
  sexual material on, 238
  terminating relationship via, 423 *box*
Internet dating:
  advantages/disadvantages of, 203 *box*
  deception in, 355
  websites for, 15
  See also Online dating
Internet Filter Learning Center,
    232 *box,* 233
Internet relationships, 9
Interpersonal Attraction (Berscheid &
    Walster), 4
Interpersonal communication, 2
  attraction and, 71–73
  channels of, 14
  cohabitation patterns, 278–279
  computer-mediated, 14, 15 *box*
  content *vs.* relational information, 18–19
  definition of, 6 *box,* 12
  effectiveness in, 17–18
  goals of, 16–17
  inevitability of, 15–16

information in, 18–19
patterns of development, 22–23
personal identity and, 26–28
principles of, 12–19
relational goals, 17
research on, 2–5
self-presentation in, 16–17, 42–43
shared meaning in, 17–18
style similarity in, 71–73
symmetry in, 19
verbal/nonverbal messages in, 12–15
See also Message exchange; Relational
    communication
Interpersonal communication skills,
    71–73
Interpersonal conflict style, 291 *figure*
    competitive fighting, 291–292
    indirect fighting, 291 *figure*, 295–296
Interpersonal dominance, testing, 318 *box*
Interpersonal influence:
    direct requests, 328
    goals, power and 325–327
Interpersonally sensitive, 323
Interpersonal need:
    affection, 7–8
    behavioral control, 8
    social inclusion, 8
Interpersonal relationship:
    definition of, 4, 5 *box*, 6–7
    goals of, 16
Interpersonal skills:
    attraction and, 71–73
    chronemic behavior, 179
    relationship development,
        114–115 *box*
    violent behavior and, 373
Interpersonal skills test, 114–115 *box*,
    394 *box*
Interpersonally sensitive individuals, 323
Interpersonal valence, 182–183
Interracial couples, 9, 28
Intimacy:
    attachment styles and, 221 *box*
    components of, 200–201
    emotional closeness in, 11–12
    hyperintimacy, 370
    lack of, 413, 415–417
    latent, 199
    level of, 20, 21 *box*
    love and, 198–201
    manifest, 199
    relational breakups and, 416–417
    Sternberg's theory of, 198–201
    types of, closeness and, 192
    warm component of love, 198–200
Intimacy jealousy, 362 *box*
Intimate terrorism, 374, 418
Intimate zone, 178
Intoxication, safe sex and, 253 *box*

Intrafamily secrets, 156
Intrapsychic processes, 419
Intrinsic investments, 381–382
Introverts:
    complementarity and, 78
    social networking and, 33
Intrusions, obsessional, 369–372
Investment model of relationship
    maintaining behavior:
    commitment, 380
    definition of, 379–380
    investments, 381–382
    pro-relational behaviors, 382–384
    quality of alternatives, 382
    satisfaction, 380–381
    superiority, perceiving relational,
        383–384
Invisible support phenomenon, 188
Invitations stage of courtship, 241–242
Invocation, relationship talk, 392
Involuntary relationships, 10–11
Invulnerable responses, 348–349
iPods, 30
Irreplaceability, 4, 7
Isolated common couple violence, 373
ISSPR. *See* International Society for the
    Study of Personal Relationships
    (ISSPR)

Jealousy:
    characteristics of, 360–361
    communicating responses to, 364–365,
        366 *box*–367 *box*
    destructive responses to, 364
    differences between types of, 362 *figure*
    emotions and, 363
    envy/rivalry vs., 361
    manic love and, 208
    positive aspects of, 363
    relational satisfaction and, 365
    romantic, 360, 361
    sex differences, in responses to,
        365, 367
    thoughts and, 361, 363
    types of, 362 *box*
    unrequited love and, 368
Jealousy induction, a261, 262 *box*
Jealousy tests, 96
Jihadists, 29
Joint activities:
    power and, 326
    prosocial behavior, 260 *box*
Jokes, 348 *box*
*Journal of Personality and Social
    Psychology*, 4
*Journal of Social and Personal
    Relationships*, 5, 9
Judgment-acceptance dialectic, 135
Justification, 391, 426

Kinesics:
    cues, 13
    definition of, 13, 178–179
    power of, 334–335
King, Martin Luther, Jr., 319
Kitchen sinking, 300, 307 *box*
Koinophilia, 70 *box*

Language:
    cross-cultural encounters and, 119 *box*
    gender differences, 331–332
    interpersonal communication, 14
    love, 212–214
    relationship indicator, 177
Latent intimacy, 199
Latin American identity, 29
Least interest principle, 322
Lesbian relationships. *See also* Sexual
    orientation
Less to lose principle, 321
LGBT. *See* Sexual orientation
Lies, 350
Lifestyle changes, 325
Liking:
    Facebook posts, 399 *box*
    love *vs.*, 198–200
    love triangle, 199 *box*
Liking-disclosure hypothesis, 144
Linear relationship development, 22–23
Listening skills, 311–312
Loneliness, 430
Long-distance relationships, 9
    dynamic nature of, 21–22
    expectancy violations, 108
    idealization in, 276–277
    maintenance of, 263, 275–277
    military couples, 277
    turbulence model and, 101
Looking-glass self, 38–39
Loss-gain effect, 73
Love:
    attachment theory and, 214
    communicating, 212–214
    consummate, 198
    cool component of (commitment), 201
    definition of, 198
    falling in, 201–202
    friendship, 198
    honeymoon stage, 200
    languages, 212–213
    liking *vs.*, 198–200
    loss of, relational breakups and, 413
    online, advantages / disadvantages,
        203 *box*
    styles of. *See* Love styles
    warm component of (intimacy), 198–200
"Love Competition," 64
Love languages, 212–213
Love styles, 197, 203–204

agape, 209
color wheel of, 204 *figure*
cultural differences, 210–211, 211 *box*
determination of, 205 *box*
Eros, 204–206
ludus, 207–208
mania, 208–209
pragma, 209–210
self-test for, 205 *box*–206 *box*
storge, 204, 207
Love triangle, 198, 199 *box*
Love ways, 212
Low-involvement couples, 242
Low outcome value, 97–98
Loyalty, 386, 387
accommodation response, 384,
385 *figure*
coping strategy, 395
Ludus love style, 204, 207
Lying, 350–353. *See also* Deception

Machiavellianism strategies, 425
Magazines, sexual attitudes and, 237
Maintenance behavior. *See* Relational
maintenance
Male *vs.* female, 12
Manic love, 204, 208–209
Manifest intimacy, 199
Manipulation:
relational breakups and, 424
verbal influence strategy, 329
Marriage:
arranged, 201
cohabitation and, 277, 278
conflicts in, 289–290
cultural differences in, 10 *box*
maintenance of, 259–260
power in, 331, 332 *box*, 339–341
relational maintenance, 266
same-sex, 233
traditional *vs.* egalitarian, 339–341
See also Divorce
Masculine *vs.* feminine, 12
Matching hypothesis, 76–77
Matchmakers, 201
Media, sexual attitudes and, 237–238
Mega-friending, 34 *box*
*Men Are From Mars, Women Are From
Venus* (Gray), 3 *box*
Mental health:
affection exchange theory and, 172
Facebook use and, 34
Mental maps, 312
Merchant of Venice, The (Shakespeare), 41
Mercy, 393
Message exchange:
content *vs.* relational levels of, 18–19
contextualization and, 20
effectiveness, 17–18

intentional, 16
miscommunication and, 12
misinterpretation, 18
shared meaning, 17–18
verbal/nonverbal, 12–15
Messages:
fundamental relational, 20, 21 *box*
hurtful, 347–349
modality of maintenance behavior,
261–264
one-up/one-down/one-across, 330
person-centered, 190–191
rejection, 369
transgression, 347
Metaconflict, 296
Metatalk, 392
Military, long-distance relationships and, 277
Millennials, 30–33
Minority groups, 27
Miscarriage, 409
Miscommunication, 12
Misinterpretation, 18
Modality, relationship maintenance, 259,
261–264
Modality switches, 108–109
Model of relational turbulence, 100
Moderation, 133
Money, relational breakups and, 409
Money and power, 320–321
Moral appeals, 329
Moral identity, 26, 323
Moral violations, 108
Motivation:
affection exchange theory and, 172
deception, 350–353
forgiveness, 396–397
self-disclosure privacy and, 154
supportive communication, 185
Multitasking, 32
Musical preference, 77
Mutual influence, 6
Mutual love and caring marriages, 10 *box*
Mutual romance, 270
MySpace, 30

Names, similarity in, 77–78
Narcissism:
attraction and, 68, 82 *box*
defined, 60
fatal attraction and, 60
mega-friending on Facebook and, 34 *box*
Millennials and, 30
negative behavior, 42
National Center for Health, 277
National Science Foundation, 2
Need fulfillment, 7
Needs:
affection, 7–8, 171
children's, 214–217

contradictory, 130
dialectics of, 130
face, 46–48
fulfilment in close relationships, 7–8
power, 322
social inclusion, 8
Negative affect strategy, 328
Negative altercasting, 329
Negative assertions, 116
Negative communication:
emotional infidelity, 359 *box*
jealousy response, 364
relational breakups and, 416
Negative emotions, 416, 429–430
Negative expectancy violations, 104
Negative face, 46–48
Negative identity management, 426
Negative moral appeals, 329
Negative politeness strategy, 49
Negative psychic change, 130
Negative reciprocity conflict, 298–301
Neglect:
accommodation and, 385 *figure,* 387
accommodation response, 384
coping strategy, 395
Negotiated farewell strategy, 428–429
Network opportunism, 273
Network support, 184
Neurobiology, 64
Neutralization tensions, 133
Neutral symmetry, 331, 332 *box*
New York Post, 81
Nondirected disclosure, 145
Nonlinear relationship development,
22–23
Nonromantic relationships, 11–12
Nonrelated relationships, 11
Nonverbal affectionate communication,
post-coital, 248
Nonverbal behaviors:
affectionate, 174–175
categories, 13
comforting, 190–191
forgiveness, 390
immediacy, 177, 190–191
prerogative principle and, 325
Nonverbal cues, 13, 174–175
Nonverbal displays, forgiveness and, 395
Nonverbal intimacy, attachment and,
221 *box*
Nonverbal messages, 12–15
Nonverbal positions of power:
artifacts, 336
body movements, 334–335
definition of, 332–333
eye behavior, 334
physical appearance, 333
spatial behavior, 333–334
time, 336

touch and, 335
voice, 335–336
Norms. *See* Social norms
Novelty, 89. *See also* Uncertainty

Objective power, 317
Obsessive relational intrusion (ORI):
consequences of, 372
definition of, 369–370
reasons for, 370–372
Oculesic behaviors, 177–178
Omissions, as deception, 351
On-again, off-again relationships,
400–403, 402 *box*
One-across messages, 330
One-down messages, 330–331
One-night stand, 229–230
One-up messages, 330–331
Online attraction, 82 *box*, 108–109
Online communication, attitudes, 148 *box*
Online dating:
advantages/disadvantages, 203 *box*
deception and, 355
disclosures in, 92
falling in love and, 202, 203 *box*
impression management and, 42
maintenance behavior, 263–264
uncertainty reduction and, 90–93,
95 *box*
See also Internet dating
Online identity, 32–33, 42, 45–46
Online infidelity, 357
Online sex, 233 *box*
Online support, 186 *box*
Open-and-honest approach, 425–426
Openness:
prosocial behavior, 260 *box*
relational breakups and, 416–417
Openness-closedness tension, 132
Opinions, crowdsourcing, 32
Opposites attract, complementarity, 78
Oral sex, 235, 237
Orgasm, 247
ORI. *See* Obsessive relational
intrusion (ORI)
Orientation stage of relationship, 116
Orphans, 9
OT. *See* Oxytocin
Other people's qualities:
definition of, 61
hard-to-get, 73
interpersonal communication skills,
71–73
physical attractiveness, 68–71
Outcome, 380
Outcome expectancy, 98
Outcome values, 97–98
"Out of context," 20
Overbenefited individuals, 281–283

Ownership, of privacy, 149–150
Oxytocin, 64, 241, 247

Panache, 316
Paradox of affection, 171
Paralinguistics, 335–336
Parenting styles, 337–338
Parents:
children's attachment to, 215–217
children's relationship to, 336–339
interference in child's relationships,
81–82
relationship changes, 129
sexual attitudes of, 238–239
Partner-focused deceptions, 350–351
Partner uncertainty, 86
Partner unresponsiveness, 157
Passion:
commitment and, 200
definition of, 198
events related to, 128
hot component of love, 200–201
jealousy and, 363
love triangle, 198, 199 *box*
manic lover and, 208
Sternberg's theory of, 198–199
Passionate event turning point, 128
Passionate love, 204–206
Passive aggression, 295–296,
329–330, 364
Passive responses:
relational dissatisfaction, 385 *figure*
sexual harassment, 251
Pats, 191
Peer marriage, 340
Peers, sexual attitudes and, 239
Perception:
closeness, 192–193
cognitive valence theory (CVT) and, 180
power as, 317, 319
reality and, 33
reward value, 61–62
self-esteem, identity and, 35–36
of similarity, 75–76
turbulent, 102
Perceptual changes, 130
Permissive parents, 337
Personal attacks, 311
Personal choice, 323
Personal disclosure, 92, 153 *box*, 181.
See also Self-disclosure
Personal frame of identity, 27, 28
Personal growth, 433
Personal identity development:
communication and, 26–28
cultural, 29
defining identity, 26
expanding identity, 36–37
frames of, 27

generational, 30–33
human nature and, 26
image and creation of, 29–30
perception, self-esteem and, 35
social networking and, 33–35
Personalistic self-disclosure, 145, 158
Personality:
attraction and, 60–62
cognitive valence theory (CVT), 181
"Dark Triad," 60
physical attraction and, 67–68
self-disclosure and, 152
Personal power, 323
Personal qualities:
definition of, 60–61
expectations, 62–63
perceptions of reward value, 61–62
Personal relationships:
categories of, 8–10
communication in, 1–2, 12–19
distinctions among, 7
gender differences in, 12
general types of, 6–7
genetically related vs. nonrelated, 11
humanity and, 1
identity expansion in, 37
romantic vs. nonromantic, 11–12
sexual vs. platonic, 11
voluntary vs. involuntary, 10–11
Personal Relationships (journal), 5
Person-centered messages, 190–191
Pew Research Center, 15 *figure*, 321
Physical abuse, 417–418
Physical appearance, power and, 333
Physical attraction:
age and, 66–67
attachment style, 67
biological aspects of, 64–65
defined, 58
gender differences in, 66
narcissism and, 68
personality and, 67–68
relationship beliefs, 67
self-esteem and, 67–68
sex differences in, 65–66
Physical attractiveness:
cognitive valence theory (CVT) and,
181–183
deception and, 355
face-to-face communication and,
82 *box*
qualities of others, 68–71
qualities of the pair, 73–79
self-disclosure and, 143
sexual desire and, 230–231
similarity in, 76–77
See also Appearance
Physical attributes, 13
Physical closeness, 170

Physical distance, 129
Physical environment qualities:
    attraction and, 79–80
    defined, 61
Physical fitness, 69
Physical flirting style, 240
Physical health, affection exchange theory
    and, 172–173
Physical signs of infidelity, 359 box
Physical touch, 213
Physiological self-soothing vs.
    stonewalling, 303 box, 305
Pillow talk, 247–248
Pinocchio relationships, 263
Platonic relationships, 11, 271–272 box
Playboy magazine, 237
Poise, 316
Polite flirting style, 240
Politeness theory, 26
    face-threatening behaviors, factors, 48
    positive vs. negative face, 46–48
    saving face and, 46
    self-presentation and, 43–44
Polygamy, 9
Popularity, social network displays and, 32
Pornography, 232 box
Position-centered messages, 190–191
Positioning stage, 241
Positive altercasting, 329
Positive attitudes, 71–72
Positive consequences, 45
Positive expectancy violations, 104
Positive face, 46–48
Positive feedback, 40
Positive involvement behaviors, 176
Positive model of others, 217 figure
Positive moral appeals, 329
Positive politeness strategy, 49
Positive psychic change, 130
Positive reciprocity, 298
Positive-tone strategy, 427
Positivity, 260 box, 265, 387
Possessive love, 204, 208–209
Post-coital regrets, 247–248
Power:
    assertion of, parenting and, 338
    dependency and, 321–322
    digital divide and, 321 box
    enabling/disabling, 322–324
    families and, 336–341
    FTAs and, 48
    interpersonal influence goals and,
        325–327
    nonverbal positions of, 332–333
    perception and, 317, 319
    prerogative principle, 324–325
    relational concept, 319
    resource-based, 319–321
    terms of, 316–317

testing interpersonal dominance,
    318 box
    verbal. See Verbal influence strategies;
        Verbal relational control
Powerful speech, 331–332
Power jealousy, 362 box
Powerless speech, 332
Power struggles, 315
Practical (pragmatic) love, 204, 209–210
Predictability, 89, 92
Predictability-novelty tensions, 132
Predicted outcome value theory, 86, 97–98
Predictive expectancies, 102
Pregiving, 328
Prejudice:
    Millennials and, 31
    relationships and, 10
Premarital sex, 235
Preoccupied attachment style, 217 figure,
    218–219, 221 box, 387
Prerogative principle, 324–325
Prescriptive expectancies, 102
Presentation of Self in Everyday Life, The
    (Goffman), 44
Pressure and manipulation, 245, 246
Preventive facework, 50–54, 51 figure
Primary appraisals, 361
Principle of elevation, 333
Principle of least interest, 322
Principle of negative reciprocity, 298–301
Privacy:
    boundaries and, 149
    control, 149
    culture and, 152–153 box
    Millennials and, 31
    ownership, 149–150
    self-disclosure and, 149–154
    violations of, 153–154
    See also Communication privacy
        management (CPM) theory
Privacy control, 149
Privacy maintenance, 152–153 box, 157
Privacy ownership, 149–150
Privacy turbulence, 149, 151–152
Process model of relational dissolution,
    418–420
    dyadic process phase of, 419
    grave-dressing processes phase of, 420
    intrapsychic process phase of, 419
    resurrection processes phase of, 420
    social process phase of, 419–420
Procreational orientation, 236
Promises:
    breaking, 108, 388
    dialectical tensions of, 133
    deception and, 353
    false, 330
    forgiveness and, 389
    reconciliation, 398

Promising, 328
Pronoun choice, 176
Prosocial attachment style, 217 figure, 218
Prosocial communication, 385 figure, 386
Proxemics, 13, 178, 333–334
Proximity, 129
Proximity effect, 80–81
Psuedo de-escalation, 425
Psychological abuse, 408, 417–418
Psychological equity, 283
Psychological reactance, 327
Psychology:
    disciplines in relationship studies, 5
    social, 4–5
Psychology Today, 3 box
Public displays of affection, 37
Public presentation challenge, 270–272
Public presentation tests, 96
Public-private dialectic, 135
Punctuation, 301
Punishment, 384–385, 385 figure, 387

Qualities of the other, 61
Qualities of the pair:
    attitudinal similarities, 74–76
    attraction and, 73–74
    birds of a feather, 74
    birth date similarity, 77–78
    commitment, similarity /
        complementarity and, 78–79
    communication skills, similarity, 76
    definition of, 61
    musical preferences, 77
    name similarity, 77–78
    opposites attract, 78
    physical attractiveness, 76–77
Qualities of the physical/social
    environment:
    physical, 79–80
    proximity, 80–81
    social, 81–82
Quality of alternatives:
    accommodation and, 386
    derogating alternatives, 383
    investment model of relationship
        maintenance behavior, 382
    power and, 321–322
Quasi-courtship, 242
Question, as hurtful message, 348 box
"Question-answer chain," 47
Quid pro quo strategy, 328

Racial identity, 27–30
Rape, 248–250
Rapid-involvement couples, 242
Readiness stage, 241
Reagan, Ronald, 52
Rebound effect, 161
Receiver's response, 145

Reciprocity, 145–146
Recognition stage of courtship, 241
Reconciliation, 393, 400–403
Recreational intimacy, 192
Recreational orientation, 236
Reflection enhancing, 338
Reframing tensions, 133, 388 box
Reinforcement effect, 224
Reinforcement effect model, 79
Reinforcement model, 75
Rejection, fear of, 147
Rejection messages, 369
Rejects-romance group, 270
Relational breakups:
    communication issues and, 415–418
    disengagement process, 418–420
    divorce, reasons for, 409 box
    equity, family obligations and, 413–415
    growing apart, 412–413
    incompatibility, 411–412
    infidelity and, 410–411
    loss of love and, 413
    negative outcomes, 430–433
    positive outcomes, 433
    predicting, 408
    reasons for, 410
    social media, 423 box
    strategies for, 421–429
    substance abuse and, 412
    See also Relationship termination
Relational communication, 2
    contextualization of messages, 20
    definition of, 6 box, 12
    dynamic, 21–22
    goals of, 16–17
    ongoing interactions and, 20
    See also Communication
Relational control:
    deception and, 353
    one-up/one-down messages,
        330–331
    See also Verbal relational control
Relational dialectics theory, 131
Relational dissatisfaction:
    emotional infidelity, 359 box
    responses to, 385 figure
Relational goal pursuit theory, 370
Relational goals, 17. See also Goals, of
    communication
Relational levels, 18–19
Relational maintenance:
    antisocial behaviors, 260–261, 262 box
    attachment and, 221 box
    cell phones and, 264 box
    challenges, 273–279
    cross-sex friendships, 268–273
    deception and, 351–353
    definitions of, 258
    modalities of, 261–264

prosocial behaviors for, 259, 260,
    260 box
    romantic relationships and, 265–266
    routine, 265–267
    same-sex friendships, 267–268
    strategic, 265–267
Relational orientation, 236
Relational outcomes, cognitive valence
    theory (CVT) and, 183
Relational reconciliation:
    definition of, 397
    direct requests, 399
    explanation/disclosure, 398
    promises, 398
    relationship preferences, 398
    social network reintegration of, 400
    stage-setting, 398
    strategies, 397, 399–400
    vulnerable appeals, 398–399
Relational redefinition, 403–404
Relational renegotiation, 393
Relational ruses, 424
Relational satisfaction:
    affection and, 172
    antisocial maintenance and, 261
    attachment and, 220–222
    cohabitation and, 278
    communication about, 243–244
    communication patterns, 281
    definition of, 259
    jealousy and, 365
    long-distance relationships, 275
    maintenance behaviors and, 265
Relational stressors, 409
Relational talk, 395–396
Relational threats, 308
Relational transgressions, 346–347.
        See also Transgressions
Relational turbulence theory, 86, 100–102
Relational uncertainty scale, 87–88 box
Relationship-based motivations, for
    secret keeping, 156–157
Relationship beliefs, attraction and, 67
Relationship de-escalation, 157
Relationship disillusionment, 413
Relationship disillusionment scale,
    414 box
Relationship-enhancing attribution, 309
Relationship frame of identity, 27, 28
Relationship invocation, 392
Relationship longevity, 80
Relationship management:
    accommodation model for, 384–387
    forgiveness in, 392–397
    interdependence theory of, 379–380
    investment model of, 379–384
    relational redefinition as, 403–404
    remedial strategies in, 387–392
Relationship protection, 156

Relationship references, 398
Relationship renegotiation, 393
Relationship research:
    affinity seeking behavior, 43
    critical assessment of, 3 box
    dating, 229
    disciplinary diversity in, 5
    Facebook, 33–34, 34 box
    feedback interpretation, 39
    history of, 2–5
    identity gaps, 28
    identity management, 40
    interpersonal communication-based,
        3–4
    key terms of, 5–6 box
    LGBT relationships, 9–10
    literature and organizations, 5
    self-expansion theory and, 36–37
    social networks and, 35
    social psychology-based, 4–5
Relationship status, on social media,
    423 box
Relationship success, 45
Relationship superiority, 383–384
Relationship-talk trick, 427
Relationship terminations:
    atrophy role, 413
    catastrophe theory of, 418, 420–421
    communication factors, 415–418
    cultural factors in, 409, 410 box
    disintegration process in, 408
    dissatisfaction and, 411, 413
    dyadic processes, 419
    equity issues in, 413–415
    grave-dressing process, 420
    healing after, 432–433
    incompatibility's role, 411–412
    infidelity's role in, 410–411
    intrapsychic processes, 419
    love's role, 409
    negative outcomes for, 429–432
    positive outcomes, 433
    resurrection processes, 420
    social processes, 419–420
    substance abuse role, 412
    See also Disengagement process;
        Divorce; Relational breakups
Relationship-talk trick, 424 box, 427
Relationship transitions, 159
Relationship uncertainty, 86
Relation-specific hope, 386
Relative power, 317
Religious beliefs:
    marriage and dating rules, 383
    pragmatic love and, 209
    reconciliation and, 397
    relationships and, 2
    as resource, 321
    self-disclosure of, 140

sexual values and, 236–238, 252 *box*
similarity of, 74
social identity and, 27, 29, 35, 37
social scientific knowledge and, 2
staying together and, 201
Remedial strategies:
   apologies/concessions, 388–390
   appeasement, 390–391
   avoidance/evasion, 392
   cultural stressors and, 388 *box*
   definition of, 387–388
   denials, 391–392
   explanations, 391
   forgiveness process, 389 *figure*
   relationship talk, 392
Remediation, 52
Repair strategies, 387
Repeated couple violence, 373
"Repressed bubbling," 47
Research. *See* Relationship research
Resolution stage, of courtship, 242
Resources, power struggles and,
      319–321
Respect:
   authority figures, 352 *box*
   betrayal and, 346
   children, 339
   conflict and, 303 *box*, 304–305
   contempt *vs.*, 304–305
   cultural factors, 10 *box*, 28 *box*, 352 *box*
   expectations for, 62–63
   liking and, 198
   marriage and, 10 *box*
   mutual, 328, 339, 403
   nonverbal behavior and, 334
   parental, 46, 348
   peer relationships and, 339
   politeness theory and, 48
   sexual interest and, 62–63, 245, 252 *box*
   spatial behavior and, 334
Respectfulness and gentleness
      marriages, 10 *box*
Responsiveness, 115, 188–189
Resurrection processes, 420
Retaliation, fear of, 147, 149
Retaliatory responses, 251
Revelation-concealment tension, 132
Reversal hypothesis, 116
Reward-cost ratio, 380
Rewards and costs, 379
   reconciliation and, 397
   satisfaction and, 380–381
Rewardingness:
   cognitive valence theory (CVT) and,
      181–182
   expectancy violations and, 103–104
Rewards through association, 71
Reward value, physical attraction
      and, 62

Risks:
   aversion, 271
   disengagement, 412, 415–417
   experimentation, 118
   safe sex and, 252 *box*
   self-disclosure, 146–150
Rituals for connection, 417 *box*
Rivalry, 361– 364, 362 *figure*
Role flexibility, 43
Role identity, 46
Role relationships, 4, 5 *box*, 6
Roles, stereotyped gender, 66
Romantic event transitions, 128
Romantic intent, 270–271
Romantic jealousy, 362 *box*
   definition of, 360
   experiencing, 361
   jealous thoughts, 361, 363
Romantic love, 198, 199 *box*,
      204–206
Romantic relationships:
   attachment styles in, 214, 217–222
   characteristics of, 11–12
   computer-mediated communication
      and, 120
   dialectal tensions in, 134–135
   event transitions in, 128
   initial stage of, 204, 206
   institutionalizing, 122–123
   integrating stage, 122
   jealousy in. *See* Romantic jealousy
   lasting, 292
   maintenance behaviors and,
      265–266
   maintenance of, 260 *box*, 262–267,
      262 *box*, 264 *box*
   nonromantic *vs.*, 11–12
   power imbalances in, 306, 319, 324
   prosocial behavior, 260 *box*
   research on LGBT, 9
   same-sex, 266–267
   secret keeping and, 155–157
   sex and, 230–231
   subtypes, 8–9
   terminating stage, 125–128
   terrorism in, 373–374
   topic avoidance during, 159
   topic avoidance in, 159–160
   traditional, 231
   turning points in, 126–128
"Romeo and Juliet" effect, 81–82
"Rose-colored glasses," 413
Routine maintenance behaviors, 265
RTT. *See* Relational turbulence model
Rules of conduct, behavior and, 45
Rule violations:
   FTAs and, 48
   relational breakups and, 416
Rumination, 371

Sacrifice, 130, 383
Safe sex:
   communication and, 251–254
   practices, rules, 252 *box*
   See also Sexually transmitted disease
Same-sex friendship, 12
   closeness and, 193
   maintenance behavior in, 267–268
Same-sex relationships:
   attraction, 233–234
   gay men, 234–235
   income, power and, 320
   Internet dating and, 202
   lesbian, 234
   maintenance, 266–267
   sex in, 233–234
   See also Sexual orientation
Satisfaction:
   attributions and, 309
   investment model, 380–381
   relational, 220–222, 243–244
   sexual, 243–244, 244–245 *box*
Saving face, 46
Scarcity, power and, 321
Scarcity hypothesis, 320
Scripts:
   cultural, 371
   definition of, 245
   ORIs, 371
   rejection, 369
   sexual, 245–247, 250, 255, 326
   unrequited love, 368
Secondary abstinence, 252 *box*
Secondary appraisals, 363
Secret keeping:
   children and, 162
   individual-based motivations for, 157
   information-based motivations for, 157–158
   negative consequences of, 160–163
   positive consequences of, 163
   relationship-based motivations for, 156–157
   topic avoidance and, 154–155
   types of, 155–156
Secret revealing:
   decision-making model for, 165 *figure*
   negative consequences of revealing,
      164–165
   positive consequences of revealing,
      163–164
Secrets, privacy control and, 150–151
Secret tests, 96–97
Secure attachment style, 217 *figure*, 218,
      221 *box*, 387, 432
Secure base, 214
Secure children, 216
Secure individuals, 218, 220–222, 221 *box*,
      224–225
Selection effect, 278
Selection tensions, 133

Self, theory of, 35
Self-assurance, 316
Self-disclosure, 14, 40
    aspects of, 140
    attachment style and, 221 *box*
    communication channel of, 145
    communication technologies and, 145
    cultural differences, love and, 211 *box*
    depth and breadth of, 140–141, 176–177
    direct verbal affectionate
        communication, 174
    dyadic effect, 146
    exposure and rejection fears, 147
    fever model of, 161
    frequency and duration, 141–142
    individuality, fear of losing, 148
    liking and, 144
    linearity and, 22
    loss of control, fear of, 149
    online communication, attitudes
        towards, 148 *box*
    personalistic *vs.* nondirected, 145
    privacy and, 149–154
    receiver's response, 145
    reciprocity of, 145–146
    retaliation fear, 147, 149
    risks of, 146–147
    skills in, 113
    technology and, 143–144 *box*
    timing of, 144–145
    valence/veracity and, 142–143
    See also Disclosure; Personal
        disclosure; Secret revealing
Self-esteem:
    attraction and, 67–68
    identity and, 26
    mega-friending and, 34 *box*
    vision of self and, 35
Self-evaluation, 39–40
Self-expansion theory, 36–37
Self-focused motives, for deception,
    350–351
Self-fulfilling prophecy, 39, 63
Self-inflicted threat, 47
Self-models, attachment and, 215
Self-presentation:
    audience/context, 46
    communication competence and, 42–43
    deliberateness of, 43–44
    dramaturgical perspective, 44
    goals of, 16–17
    identity and, 25
    issues in, 41
    manipulation and, 41–42
Self-promotion, 42
Self-putdowns, 96
Self-scale, inclusion of others in, 36 *figure*
Self-soothing, conflict and, 303 *box*, 305
Self-uncertainty, 86

Separation anxiety, 216
Separation and individuation, 338–339
Separation tensions, 133
Separation tests, 96
Serial monogamy, 236
776 Stupidest Things Ever Said (Petra &
    Petra), 52
Sex (gender), 12
    closeness differences in, 192–193
    cybersex and, 238
    differences. *See* Gender differences
    friendship maintenance and, 268
    gender role flexibility, 388 *box*
    hook-ups and, 229–230
    income, power and, 320
    infidelity and, 358–360, 411
    intimate terrorism and, 418
    jealous emotions, 365, 367
    love styles, 210–211
    powerful/powerless speech and,
        331–332
    power needs of, 323
    self-disclosure differences and, 154
    sexual coercion and, 248–250
    sexual initiation strategies, 245–247
    sexual satisfaction and, 243
    sexual scripts, 245. *See also*
        Sexual scripts
    virginity and, 236–237
    working women, relational equity,
        413–415
    See also Gender *entries*
Sex and the Single Girl (Gurley Brown), 237
Sex drive, 231–233
Sex offenders:
    false identities and, 41–42
    social media use and, 35
Sexting, 43, 238
Sexual abuse, 161
Sexual activity:
    biological sex difference in, 231–233
    cybersexuality, 232 *box*
    early dating, 229–230
    expectancy violation, 106
    gay men, 234–235
    high risk, 252 *box*
    initiating, power and, 326
    involvement types, 242
    lesbian, 234
    long-term, 230–231
    negotiating, 245
    refusal, 249–250
    regrets, alcohol and, 247–248
    romantic *vs.* nonromantic relationships
        and, 11–12
    same-sex, 233–234
    secrets and, 155–157
    short-term, 229–230
    uncertainty and, 92

    violence and, 374
Sexual activity, communication about:
    courtship/flirtation, 239–240
    initiation strategies, 245–246
    invitations, 246–247
    pillow talk, 247–248
    safe sex and, 251–254
    satisfaction, 243–244, 244 *box*–245 *box*
    scripts, 245
    stages of courtship, 240–243. *See also*
        Courtship
Sexual arousal. *See* Arousal, sexual
Sexual attitudes:
    culture and, 237, 238 *box*
    media and, 237–238
    parents and, 238–239
    past relationships and, 239
    peers and, 239
    purpose of sex, 236
    revolution in, 235–236
    types of, 236
Sexual attraction, 58
Sexual behavior:
    college students, 229–230
    dating and, 11, 89, 229–230
    expectancy violations in, 106–107
    gay and lesbian, 234–235
    gender differences in, 235
    safe sex and, 252 *box*
    subtypes of, 230
    uncertainty in, 89, 91 *box*, 92, 94
    See also Sexual orientation
Sexual coercion, 248–250
Sexual desire, 64–65
Sexual disinterest, 359 *box*
Sexual harassment, 250–251
Sexual history, 355–356
Sexual identity, 37
Sexual incompatibility, 412
Sexual infidelity, 356–358, 359 *box*,
    410–411. *See also* Infidelity *entries*
Sexual invitations, 246–247
Sexual jealousy, 362 *box*
Sexually transmitted disease, 89, 246,
    251–254, 252 *box*. *See also* Safe sex
Sexual orientation:
    gay relationships, 234–235
    Internet dating and, 202
    lesbian relationships, 234
    LGBT research and, 9–10
    masculine *vs.* feminine, 12
    physical attraction and, 66–67
    public displays of affection and, 37
    relational maintenance in gay/lesbian,
        267–268
    romantic *vs.* nonromantic relationships
        and, 11–12
    sexual coercion and, 248–250
    See also Sex (gender)

Sexual passion, 201
Sexual relationships, 11
Sexual satisfaction, 243–244,
    244 box–245 box
Sexual scripts:
    compliance-resisting, 246–247
    definition of, 245
    difficulty in, 245, 247
    initiation strategies, 245–246
    pillow talk, 247–248
Shared meaning, 17–18
Sharing activities, 326
Shift in motivation, 371
Short-term sex, 229–230
Siblings:
    affection for, 172
    attachment to, 214
    blended relationships, 8–9
    conflicts among, 288 box, 289
    influence over, 337
    privacy of, 152 box
    rivalry, 129, 361
    secret-keeping and, 155, 157
    violence among, 372
Sibling rivalry, 129, 361
Signs of possession, 364
Silence, as jealousy response, 364
Silent treatment, 295, 364
Similarity, 388 box
    actual, 74
    attitudinal, 74–76
    birds of a feather, 74
    birth dates, 77–78
    communication skills, 76
    communication, 21 box
    complementarity vs., 78–79
    musical preferences, 77
    names, 77–78
    perceived, 74–75
    physical attractiveness, 76–77
Simple request, 328
Sincere flirting style, 240
Singing, as backstage behavior, 46
Single-parent families, 9
Situation, in cognitive valence theory
    (CVT), 183
Sleeping With the Enemy, 374
Small talk, 118
Smartphones, 14, 30
Smiling, 334–335
Snapchat:
    attraction and, 82 box
    communication via, 15 box
    generational use of, 30
    instant/frequent contact, 32
    popularity of, 15 figure
    relational maintenance and, 267
    third parties and, 400
    See also Social media entries

Sociability, attraction and, 72
Social attraction, 58. See also Attraction
Social behavior, 45
Social capital, 34
Social comparison, 39–40
Social compensation, 33
Social composure, 20, 21 box
Social depenetration, 116
Social distance, 48, 186 box
Social environment qualities:
    attraction and, 81–82
    defined, 61
Social group identity, 26–27
Social identity theory, 26–27
Social inclusion, 8
Social influence, 317
Social intimacy, 192
Socialization, behavior, gender and, 66
Socialization effect, 290
Social lubrication effect, 106
Social meaning model of nonverbal
    communication, 174–175
Social media:
    addiction, 34
    breaking up and, 423 box
    coming apart stage and, 125
    emotional attachment to, 33
    experimenting stage of relationship, 118
    face-to-face communications vs., 33
    generational use of, 30
    ghosting, 126, 422
    jealousy trigger, 360–361
    modality of maintenance behavior, 262
    online attraction, 82 box
    popularity of, 15 box
    power, status, digital divide and,
        321 box
    privacy and. See Privacy,
        self-disclosure and
    reconnection, relational repair,
        Facebook, 399 box
    relational maintenance and, 258
    same-sex friendships, maintaining, 267
    social comparison and, 39–40
    unintended consequences of, 31
    use of, 14
    websites, 15 figure
    See also Social networks
Social networks:
    arranged marriages and, 201
    broadcasters and, 33
    changes, as turning point, 129
    disapproval, relational breakups
        and, 409
    identity and, 33–35
    negative aspects, 34–35
    popularity displays and, 32
    prosocial behavior, 260 box
    reconciliation, reintegration of and, 400

relational dissolution and, 419–420
    self-disclosure and, 146
    sex offenders and, 35
    See also Social media
Social norms:
    individualist vs. collectivist cultures,
        352 box
    sexuality and, 232, 235, 240 box
    touch and, 335
Social Penetration: The Development of
    Interpersonal Relationships (Altman &
    Taylor), 4
Social penetration theory, 140
Social penetration theory:
    definition of, 140
    principles of, 120, 122, 127
    self-disclosure and, 120, 144
    social depenetration and, 116
Social prestige, 320
Social processes, 419–420
Social psychology, 4–5
Social Psychology of Groups, The (Thibaut
    & Kelley), 4
Social skills:
    argumentativeness, 310
    attachment styles and, 221 box
Social support withdrawal, 424–425
Social violations, 108
Sociology, 5
"Sour grapes," 76
Spatial behavior, 178, 333–334
Special occasions, as turning point, 128
Specific equity, 280
Speech:
    nonverbal power and, 335–336
    powerful vs. powerless, 331–332
Spies, identity surveillance, 34
Spillover effect, 290
Split loyalty pattern, 162
Spying, 261, 262 box
Stability:
    attachment styles across lifespan, 222
    cohabitation relationships, 278
    explanations for, 222, 224
    reinforcement effect, 224
Stable exchange stage, 116
Stage model of relationship development:
    affective exchange, 116
    avoidance, 125
    bonding, 122–123
    circumscribing, 124
    coming apart, 123–126
    coming together, 117–123
    comparing, 266
    differentiating, 123–124
    experimenting, 118–120
    exploratory affective exchange, 116
    initiating, 117–118
    integrating, 122

intensifying, 120–121 *box*
models for, 116–117
ordering / timing of, 127
orientation, 116
reversal hypothesis, 116
social depenetration, 116
stable exchange, 116
stagnation, 124–125
staircase model of, 117 *figure*
termination, 126–127
turning points, 126–127. *See also*
   Turning points
Stage-setting in reconciliation, 398
Stagnation, 37
Stagnation stage, 124–125
Stalking, 261
   obsessive relational intrusions (ORI),
      369–372
   social media and, 423 *box*
   unrequited love, 369
   See also Cyberstalking
Stanford University, Center for Cognitive
   and Neurobiological Imaging, 64
Standards for openness hypothesis, 160
Status, digital divide and, 321 *box*
Stepfamilies, 9
Stereotype, 70
   eye behavior, deception and, 353
   hook-ups and, 229–230
Sternberg's triangle of love, 197
   intimacy, 198
   latent / manifest intimacy, 199
Stonewalling effect, 125, 303,
   303 *box*, 305
Storge love, 204, 207
"Stranger on the plane" phenomenon, 142
Strategic maintenance behaviors, 265
Submission, 315, 334–335
Submissive symmetry, 331, 332 *box*
Subtweets, 32
Successful communication, 17
Suggesting, 323
Suicide, 149–150
Superiority, relational, 383–384
Superwoman syndrome, 415
Supportive communication:
   dual process model of, 186, 187 *figure*
   invisible support, 188–189
   need for, distress and, 184–186
   nonverbal immediacy, 191–192
   online, 185 *box*
   person-centered messages, 190–191
   types of, 184–185
Supportiveness, prosocial behavior,
   260 *box*
Surveillance, 261, 364
Switching channels, during conflict
   interaction, 299 *box*
Symmetrical behavior, 331

Symmetrical communication, 19
Symmetry, physical attraction and,
   69 *box*

Talking *vs.* doing, 267–268
Tangible aid, 184
Targeted socializing, 119 *box*
Task attraction, 58
Task-oriented goals, 17
Task sharing, 265, 266, 267
Task-social orientation messages, 20,
   21 *box*
Technology:
   generational identity and, 30–33
   See also Computer-mediated
      communication
Telephonica Global Millennial Survey
   (2014), 30, 31
Temporary states, cognitive valence
   theory (CVT) and, 183
Tensions, dialectical, 130–135, 353. *See
   also* Dialectical perspective
Termination stage of relationship,
   126–127
Terms of power, 316–317
Terrorism, identity and, 29
Testing, sexually transmitted diseases,
   252 *box*
Testosterone, 247, 323
Text messaging, 14
Theory of motivated information
   management (TMIM), 86, 98–100
Third parties:
   in arguments, 300
   infidelity and, 410–411
   ludic individuals and, 208
   reconciliation facilitators, 400
   storgic individuals and, 207
   uncertainty reduction and, 94
Threats:
   conflict and, 308
   hurtful messages, 348 *box*
   relational disengagement and, 427
   verbal influence strategy, 330
Time:
   nonverbal power, 336
   reluctance to spend together,
      emotional infidelity, 359 *box*
   together, as language of love, 212–213
Timing, of self-disclosure, 144–145
TMIM. *See* Theory of motivated
   information management (TMIM)
Tone of voice, 335–336
Topical segmentation, 133
Topic avoidance:
   consequences of, 159–160
   definition of, 154–155
   engaging in, 158–159
   family transitions and, 159

reasons for, 156–158. *See also* Secret
   keeping
relationship transitions and, 159
romantic relationships and, 159
secrets and, 155–156
Touch:
   culture and, 182 *box*
   language of, love and, 213
   manifest intimacy and, 199
   nonverbal immediacy and, 191
   nonverbal power and, 335
   physical closeness and, 175
   prerogative principle, power and, 325
   sexual harassment and, 250–251
Traditional family-home marriages, 10
   box, 339–341
Transact utterances, 331, 332 *box*
Transgression-maximizing messages, 347
Transgression-minimizing messages, 347
Transgressions:
   deception and, 349–356
   expectancy violation, 105
   forgiveness of, 392–397
   hurtful messages, 347–349, 348 *box*
   infidelity and, 356–360
   jealousy and, 360–367
   ORIs, 369–372
   relational, 346–347
   remediation for, 387–392
   seriousness of, 396
   unrequited love, 368–372
   violence and, 372–374
Transition out, 273
Transitions:
   cohabitation and, 277–279, 428
   families and social networks, 129
   relational control move patterns, 331,
      332 *box*
   relational turbulence and, 100–101
   relationship subtypes, 230, 273–274
   romantic relationships and, 128,
      403–405
   on-again, off-again relationships,
      401–402, 402 *box*, 419, 428
   separation and individuation, 338–339
   topic avoidance during, 159
Triangle of love (Sternberg), 197
Triangle tests, 96
True friends, 273
Trust:
   communication of, 12–13
   disclosures and, 120, 141, 143–145,
      153 *box*
   erosion of, 165
   feedback, 40
   oxytocin-based, 64
   similarity and, 75
   uncertainty reduction and, 93–94
   emotional support and, 115

bonding and, 123
privacy violations and, 154
secret keeping and, 160–165
female same-sex friendships and, 192
love and, 201
storgic love, 207
sexual activity and, 241, 251, 252 *box*, 253
prosocial behavior, 259
Trust violation:
    deception and, 349–350. *See also*
        Deception *entries*
    hurtful event as, 108
Truth, 349–350
    self-disclosure, 140, 142–143
    See also Deception entries
Truth bias, safe sex and, 253
Tumblr, 15 *figure*
Turbulence model of relational
    uncertainty, 100–102
Turning point analysis, 127
Turning points:
    activities and special occasions, 128
    commitment/exclusivity events,
        128–129
    communication-based, 127–128
    crisis/conflict, 129–130
    defining relationship, 126–127
    family/social network changes, 129
    passionate/romantic events, 128
    perceptual changes, 130
    proximity/distance, 129
    sample, 127 *figure*
Twitter:
    audience for, 35
    broadcasters and, 33
    coming apart stages and, 125–125
    communication via, 15 *box*
    generational use of, 30–32
    maintenance behavior, 263
    muting function, 423
    popularity of, 15 *figure*
    subtweets, 32
    See also Social media *entries*

Unattended behavior, 17
Uncertain-avoidant cultures, 91 *box*
Uncertainty:
    commitment and, 89
    communication and, 90–93
    dissatisfaction and, 88–89
    first dates, 106–107
    flirtation/sexual activity, 106
    hurtful events, 108
    modality switches, 108–109
    motivation to reduce, 88–90
    predicted value outcome tests, 97–98
    reduction theory, 86, 88
    relational turbulence theory, 100–102
    relational uncertainty scale, 87–88 *box*

theory of motivated information
    management, 98–100
types of, 86
Uncertainty-increasing behaviors, 92
Uncertainty management theory, 89
Uncertainty reduction theory, 85–86
    active strategies, 93–94
    disclosure and, 91
    information gathering and, 91, 92
    interactive strategies, 94–95
    issues/challenges, 86, 88
    online, 95 *box*
    passive observation strategies, 93
    secret tests, 96–97
Underbenefited individuals, 281, 282
Understatement deceptions, 350
Unilateral/direct disengagement
    strategies, 426
    dating other people, 426
    de-escalation, 427–428
    direct dump, 425–426
    justification, 426
    positive tone, 427
    relationship-talk trick, 427
    threats/bullying, 427
Unilateral/indirect disengagement
    strategies:
    avoidance, 422–424
    cost escalation, 425
    pseudo de-escalation, 425
    relational ruses, 424
    withdrawal of supportiveness /
        affection, 424–425
Unique interaction patterns, 7
Unrequited love, 368–369
U.S. Census Bureau, 29

Valence:
    self-disclosure and, 140, 142–143,
        143–144 *box*
    relational outcomes, 183
    See also Cognitive valence
        theory (CVT)
Validation, 47
Value:
    predicted outcomes and, 97–98
    reward, perceptions, 61–62
    visual communication, 32
Veracity:
    self-disclosure, 140, 142–143
    See also Truth
Verbal aggressiveness
Verbal behaviors, 14
Verbal communication:
    affection, 174
    aggressiveness in, 310–311
    coding of, 330–331
    interpersonal communication,
        12–15

responses to hurtful, 349
Verbal immediacy, 176. *See also*
    Immediacy behavior
Verbal influence strategies, 332
    aversive stimulation, 328
    bargaining strategy, 328
    deception, 330
    definition of, 327–328
    direct requests, 328
    distributive communication, 330
    hinting, 329
    ingratiation, 328–329
    manipulation, 329
    moral appeal, 329
    threats, 330
    withdrawal, 329–330
Verbal relational control,
    330–331
Verbal self-handicapping,
    50–51
Viability, 172
Viagra, 232
Video games, 267
Vine (videos), 15 *figure*
Violence:
    cohabitation and, 279
    common couple, 373–374
    demand-withdrawal patterns and,
        301–302, 301 *box*
    emotional infidelity and, 411
    family history of, 418
    intimate terrorism, 374
    ORIs and, 372
    physical abuse, 417–418
    relational, 372–373
    substance abuse and, 412
    victims of, 374
Violent communication, 364
Virginity, 236–237
Virtual relationships, 263
Vision of self, 35
Visual behaviors, 177–178
Visual centrality, 334
Visual communication, 32
Visual dominance ratio, 334
Vocalics, 13, 179
Voice:
    accommodation and, 385 *figure*,
        386, 387
    accommodation response, 384
    coping strategy, 395
    nonverbal position of power and,
        335–336
Voice-to-voice communication, 14
Voluntary relationships, 10–11
Vulnerable appeals, 398–399

Waist-to-hip ratio, 69–70 *box*
Waiting, power and, 336

Warm component of love, 198–200
Weight preference, 69 *box*
WhatsApp, 267
Whole-family secrets, 156
Wings, 45
Withdrawal:
   relational breakups and, 415

support and affection, 424–425
verbal influence strategy, 329–330
   See also Demand-withdrawal *entries*
Withering away, 412
Word choice, 176. *See also* Immediacy
   behavior, affectionate communication
Work ethic, Millennials and, 30

Workplace relationships, 81
World Wide Web, 186 *box*

Yielding conflict style, 297–298
You Just Don't Understand: Women and
   Men in Conversation (Tannen), 269 box
YouTube, 30

ABOUT THE AUTHORS

Laura K. Guerrero (PhD, University of Arizona, 1994) is a professor in the Hugh Downs School of Human Communication at Arizona State University, where she teaches courses in relational communication, nonverbal communication, emotional communication, research methods, and data analysis. She has also taught at the Pennsylvania State University and San Diego State University. Her research focuses on communication in close relationships, such as those between romantic partners, friends, and family members. Her research has examined both the "bright side" of personal relationships, including nonverbal intimacy, forgiveness, relational maintenance, and communication skill, and the "dark side" of personal relationships, including jealousy, hurtful events, conflict, and anger. She recently developed a theoretical framework (hurtful events response theory) to explain patterns of communication following hurtful events in close relationships. Dr. Guerrero has published more than 100 journal articles and chapters related to these topics. In addition to *Close Encounters,* her book credits include *Nonverbal Communication in Close Relationships* (coauthored with K. Floyd), *Nonverbal Communication* (coauthored with J. Burgoon & K. Floyd), *The Handbook of Communication and Emotion* (coedited with P. Andersen), and *The Nonverbal Communication Reader* (coedited with M. Hecht). She has received several research awards, including the Early Career Achievement Award from the International Association for Relationship Research, the Dickens Research Award from the Western States Communication Association, and the Outstanding Doctoral Dissertation Award from the Interpersonal Communication Division of The International Communication Association. Dr. Guerrero serves on editorial boards for several top journals in communication and relationships. She lives in Phoenix (during the school year) and San Diego (during the summer) with her husband, Vico, and their daughters, Gabrielle and Kristiana. She enjoys reading, writing fiction (when not writing nonfiction), dancing, and taking long walks in the mountains or on the beach.

Peter A. Andersen (PhD, Florida State University, 1975) is professor emeritus in the School of Communication at San Diego State University and was a visiting professor in 2017 at Chapman University. He has also taught at the University of Washington; Ohio University; the University of Montana; Illinois State University, Florida State University, California State University, Fullerton; and California State University, Long Beach. Dr. Andersen's most recent research focuses on theories of relational communication, nonverbal communication, risk and crisis communication, health communication including skin cancer prevention, helmet safety and tobacco control, social influence, nonverbal intimacy and immediacy, and interpersonal touch. He developed cognitive valence theory to explain how people react to increases in intimacy and immediacy. Dr. Andersen has authored 160 book chapters and journal articles and has received recognition as one of the 100 most published scholars in the history of the field of communication. In addition to *Close Encounters,* he is the author of *The Handbook of Communication and Emotion* (1998, edited with L. Guerrero), *Nonverbal Communication: Forms and Functions* (2008), and *The Complete Idiot's Guide to Understanding Body Language*

(2004). He has served as the President of the Western Communication Association, director of research for the Japan-U.S. Telecommunications Research Institute, and editor of the *Western Journal of Communication*. He has served as a coinvestigator on sun safety, tobacco control, and cancer prevention grants from the National Cancer Institute and risk communication grants from the U.S. Department of Homeland Security and the county of San Diego. He cherishes the relationships he has with Janis, his wife of 44 years; his daughter Kirsten and her husband Jonathan; and his granddaughter Elise. They all live in San Diego, California. He is a fast skier, a strong swimmer, and a truly slow long distance runner.

Walid A. Afifi (PhD, University of Arizona, 1996) is a professor in the Department of Communication at the University of California at Santa Barbara. He has taught several courses including interpersonal communication, relational communication, nonverbal communication, and social marketing. Dr. Afifi previously held faculty positions at The Pennsylvania State University, the University of Delaware, and the University of Iowa. His primary research program revolves around people's experience of uncertainty and their decisions to seek or avoid information in relational contexts. He has applied these interests across several domains, including the experience of family discussions about organ donation, college students' search information about their partners' sexual health, people's negotiation of cross-sex friendships, and the experience of Palestinian refugees in Lebanon. He has also examined people's decisions to avoid disclosure and/or keep secrets. His most recent research projects approach uncertainty from a more sociological lens, examining uncertainty during or after traumatic community events (e.g., fires, war) and assessing its impact on well-being. He has published more than 70 articles and chapters and coedited the book, *Uncertainty, Information Management, and Disclosure Decisions* with T. Afifi. He serves as a member of several editorial boards, has occupied the role of associate editor for both Personal Relationships and the Journal of Social and Personal Relationships, and has chaired the Interpersonal Communication division of both the International Communication Association and the National Communication Association. He grew up in Beirut, Lebanon, where his sister and her family still reside, and where he recently spent some time as visiting professor in the Department of Health Behavior and Education at the American University of Beirut. He lives in Santa Barbara, California, with his wife Tammy (who studies stress and resilience and is a faculty member in the same department), two daughters (Leila and Rania), and two dogs (Maddie and Charlie). He is committed to social justice issues, is an avid sports fan (a highlight being that he was able to get into Game 4 of the 2016 Cubs World Series), is a political junkie, and loves outdoor activities of all kinds.